ROAD ATLAS EUROPE

Contents

Distance map and chart

ii – iii	Map symbols
iv	International road signs and travel web links
v	Key to map pages
vi – xvii	Route planning maps 1:4 654 000
2 – 181	Road maps 1:1 000 000
182 – 187	Road maps 1:750 000
188 – 191	Index to place names 1:750 000
192 – 207	City through-route maps
192	Amsterdam, Athina, Barcelona, Belfast
193	Beograd, Berlin, Bern, Birmingham
194	Bonn, Bordeaux, Bratislava, Bruxelles
195	Bucureşti, Budapest, Cardiff, Chişinau
196	Dublin, Edinburgh, Firenze, Frankfurt
197	Glasgow, Göteborg, Den Haag, Hamburg
198	Helsinki, İstanbul, København, Köln
199	Leipzig, Lisboa, Ljubljana, London
200	Lyon, Madrid, Manchester, Marseille
201	Milano, München, Napoli, Oslo
202	Palermo, Paris, Podgorica, Praha
203	Rīga, Roma, Rotterdam, Sankt Peterburg
204	Sarajevo, Sevilla, Skopje, Sofiya
205	Stockholm, Strasbourg, Tallinn, Torino
206	Toulouse, Valencia, Venezia, Vilnius
207	Warszawa, Wien, Zagreb, Zürich
208 – 211	City street plans
208	Amsterdam, Athina, Berlin, Bern,
209	Bruxelles, Dublin, Helsinki, København,
210	Lisboa, London, Madrid, Oslo
211	Paris, Roma, Stockholm, Wien
212 – 272	Index to place names 1:1 000 000
	Driving information and web links

Country identifiers

A	Austria		
AL	Albania		
AND	Andorra		
B	Belgium	Belgique	Belgien
BG	Bulgaria	Bulgarie	Bulgarien
BIH	Bosnia - Herzegovina	Bosnie Herzégovine	Bosnien-Herzegowina
BY	Belarus	Bélarus	Belarus
CH	Switzerland	Suisse	Schweiz
CY	Cyprus	Chypre	Zypern
CZ	Czech Republic	République tchèque	Tschechische Republik
D	Germany	Allemagne	Deutschland
DK	Denmark	Danemark	Dänemark
DZ	Algeria	Algérie	Algerien
E	Spain	Espagne	Spanien
EST	Estonia	Estonie	Estland
F	France	France	Frankreich
FIN	Finland	Finlande	Finnland
FL	Liechtenstein	Liechtenstein	Liechtenstein
FO	Faroe Islands	Iles Féroé	Färöer-Inseln
GB	United Kingdom GB & NI	Grande-Bretagne	Grossbritannien
GBA	Alderney	Alderney	Alderney
GBG	Guernsey	Guernsey	Guernsey
GBJ	Jersey	Jersey	Jersey
GBM	Isle of Man	île de Man	Insel Man
GBZ	Gibraltar	Gibraltar	Gibraltar
GR	Greece	Grèce	Griechenland
H	Hungary	Hongrie	Ungarn
HR	Croatia	Croatie	Kroatien
I	Italy	Italie	Italien
IRL	Ireland	Irlande	Irland
IS	Iceland	Islande	Island
L	Luxembourg	Luxembourg	Luxemburg
LT	Lithuania	Lituanie	Litauen
LV	Latvia	Lettonie	Lettland
M	Malta	Malte	Malta
MA	Morocco	Maroc	Marokko
MC	Monaco	Monaco	Monaco
MD	Moldova	Moldavie	Moldawien
MK	Macedonia (F.Y.R.O.M.)	Ancienne République yougoslave de Macédoine	Ehemalige jugoslawische Republik Mazedonien
MNE	Montenegro	Monténégro	Montenegro
N	Norway	Norvège	Norwegen
NL	Netherlands	Pays-Bas	Niederlande
P	Portugal	Portugal	Portugal
PL	Poland	Pologne	Polen
RKS	Kosovo	Kosovo	Kosovo
RO	Romania	Roumanie	Rumänien
RSM	San Marino	Saint-Marin	San Marino
RUS	Russian Federation	Russie	Russische Föderation
S	Sweden	Suède	Schweden
SK	Slovakia	République slovaque	Slowakei
SLO	Slovenia	Slovénie	Slowenien
SRB	Serbia	Sérbie	Serbien
TN	Tunisia	Tunisie	Tunisien
TR	Turkey	Turquie	Türkei
UA	Ukraine	Ukraine	Ukraine

Road Atlas Europe

Collins
An imprint of HarperCollins Publishers
Westerhill Road
Bishopbriggs
Glasgow G64 2QT

Revised edition

Printed in China by South China Printing Co.Ltd.

ISBN 978-0-00-752482-2 Imp 001

All mapping in this title is generated from Collins Bartholomew™ digital databases.
Collins Bartholomew™, the UK's leading independent geographical information supplier, can provide a digital, custom, and premium mapping service to a variety of markets.
For further information:
tel: +44 (0) 208 307 4515
e-mail: collinsbartholomew@harpercollins.co.uk
or visit our website: www.collinsbartholomew.com

We also offer a choice of books, atlases and maps that can be customised to specified requirements.
For further information:
tel: +44 (0) 208 307 4515
e-mail: collinsbartholomew@harpercollins.co.uk
omew.com
llinsmaps

Aberdeenshire

Map symbols

Road maps / Carte routière / Strassenkarten

Symbol	English	French	German
E55	Euro route number	Route européenne	Europastrasse
A13	Motorway	Autoroute	Autobahn
	Motorway – toll	Autoroute à péage	Gebührenpflichtige Autobahn
	Motorway – toll (vignette)	Autoroute à péage (vignette)	Gebührenpflichtige Autobahn (Vignette)
37	Motorway junction – full access	Echangeur d'autoroute avec accès libre	Autobahnauffahrt mit vollem Zugang
12	Motorway junction – restricted access	Echangeur d'autoroute avec accès limité	Autobahnauffahrt mit beschränktem Zugang
	Motorway services	Aire de service sur autoroute	Autobahnservicestelle
309	Main road – dual carriageway	Route principale à chaussées séparées	Hauptstrasse – Zweispurig
	Main road – single carriageway	Route principale à une seule chaussée	Hauptstrasse – Einspurig
516	Secondary road – dual carriageway	Route secondaire à chaussées séparées	Zweispurige Nebenstrasse
	Secondary road – single carriageway	Route secondaire à seule chaussée	Einspurige Nebenstrasse
	Other road	Autre route	Andere Strasse
	Motorway tunnel	Autoroute tunnel	Autobahntunnel
	Main road tunnel	Route principale tunnel	Hauptstrassetunnel
	Motorway/road under construction	Autoroute/route en construction	Autobahn/Strasse im Bau
	Road toll	Route à péage	Gebührenpflichtige Strasse
16 / 10	Distance marker / Distances in kilometres / Distances in miles (UK only)	Marquage des distances / Distances en kilomètres / Distances en miles (GB)	Distanz-Markierung / Distanzen in Kilometern / Distanzen in Meilen (GB)
	Steep hill	Colline abrupte	Steile Strasse
2587	Mountain pass (height in metres)	Col (Altitude en mètres)	Pass (Höhe in Metern)
	Scenic route	Parcours pittoresque	Landschaftlich schöne Strecke
	International airport	Aéroport international	Internationaler Flughafen
	Car transport by rail	Transport des autos par voie ferrée	Autotransport per Bahn
	Railway	Chemin de fer	Eisenbahn
	Tunnel	Tunnel	Tunnel
	Funicular railway	Funiculaire	Seilbahn
Rotterdam	Car ferry	Bac pour autos	Autofähre
2587	Summit (height in metres)	Sommet (Altitude en mètres)	Berg (Höhe in Metern)
	Volcano	Volcan	Vulkan
	Canal	Canal	Kanal
	International boundary	Frontière d'Etat	Landesgrenze
	Disputed International boundary	Frontière litigieuse	Umstrittene Staatsgrenze
GB	Country abbreviation	Abréviation du pays	Regionsgrenze
	Urban area	Zone urbaine	Stadtgebiet
28	Adjoining page indicator	Indication de la page contigüe	Randhinweis auf Folgekarte
	National Park	Parc national	Nationalpark

1:1 000 000

1 centimetre to 10 kilometres — 0 10 20 30 40 50 60 70 80 km — 1 inch to 16 miles
0 10 20 30 40 50 miles

City maps and plans / Plans de ville / Stadtpläne

★	Place of interest	Site d'intérêt	Sehenswerter Ort
	Railway station	Gare	Bahnhof
	Parkland	Espace vert	Parkland
	Woodland	Espace boisé	Waldland
	General place of interest	Site d'intérêt général	Sehenswerter Ort
	Academic/Municipal building	Établissement scolaire/installations municipales	Akademisches/Öffentliches Gebäude
	Place of worship	Lieu de culte	Andachtsstätte
	Transport location	Infrastructure de transport	Verkehrsanbindung

ii

Places of interest

🏛	Museum and Art Gallery	Musée / Gallerie d'art	Museum / Kunstgalerie
	Castle	Château	Burg / Schloss
	Historic building	Monument historique	historisches Gebäude
	Historic site	Site historique	historische Stätte
	Monument	Monument	Denkmal
	Religious site	Site religieux	religiöse Stätte
	Aquarium / Sea life centre	Aquarium / Parc Marin	Aquarium
	Arboretum	Arboretum	Arboretum, Baumschule
	Botanic garden (National)	Jardin botanique national	botanischer Garten
	Natural place of interest (other site)	Réserve naturelle	landschaftlich interessanter Ort
	Zoo / Safari park / Wildlife park	Parc Safari / Réserve sauvage / Zoo	Safaripark / Wildreservat / Zoo
	Other site	Autres sites	Touristenattraktion
	Theme park	Parc à thème	Freizeitpark
	World Heritage site	Patrimoine Mondial	Weltkulturerbe
	Athletics stadium (International)	Stade international d'athlétisme	internationales Leichtathletik Stadion
	Football stadium (Major)	Stade de football	Fußballstadion
	Golf course (International)	Parcours de golf international	internationaler Golfplatz
	Grand Prix circuit (Formula 1) / Motor racing venue / MotoGP circuit	Circuit auto-moto	Autodrom
	Rugby ground (International - Six Nations)	Stade de rugby	internationales Rugbystadion
	International sports venue	Autre manifestation sportive	internationale Sportanlage
	Tennis venue	Court de tennis	Tennis
Valcotos	Winter sports resort	Sports d'hiver	Wintersport

Be aware!

★ On the spot fines for motoring offences are common in many European countries, including France, Spain, and Italy. For each fine an official receipt should be issued.

★ Speed camera detectors are illegal in many European countries whether in use or not. You should ensure that they are removed from your vehicle. In France you are liable to a prison sentence, a fine, and confiscation of the device and your vehicle. GPS/satellite navigation systems which show speed camera locations are illegal.

★ In Austria, Bulgaria, Czech Republic, Hungary, Romania, Slovakia, Slovenia and Switzerland, all vehicles using motorways and expressways must display a motorway vignette. Failure to do so will result in a heavy on-the-spot fine. Vignettes are available at major border crossing points and major petrol stations.

★ Dipped headlights are compulsory when using road tunnels in Austria, Switzerland and Germany.

★ Penalties for speeding or drink-driving in many European countries are often more severe than in the UK, e.g. in France traffic offences are subject to on-the-spot fines, where it is also compulsory to carry a breathalyser kit, and recommended to carry two.

★ In many European countries you must drive with dipped headlights at all times. In France it is mandatory to do so in poor visibility only, but is recommended at all times.

★ In Denmark you must indicate when changing lanes on a motorway.

★ In Spain you must carry two red warning triangles to be placed in front and behind the vehicle in the event of accident or breakdown.

★ In many European countries, as in the UK and Ireland, the use of mobile phones while driving is not permitted unless 'hands-free'.

★ Fluorescent waistcoats and warning triangles should be carried inside the car and not in the boot.

★ In Austria, Bosnia-Herzegovina, Estonia, Finland, Iceland, Latvia, Lithuania, Norway, Slovenia and Sweden, cars must have winter tyres fitted between December and March.

★ Some European cities have introduced an environmental zone for vehicle emission levels. This is usually accompanied by a charge to drive into the designated central zone.

International road signs and travel web links

Informative signs

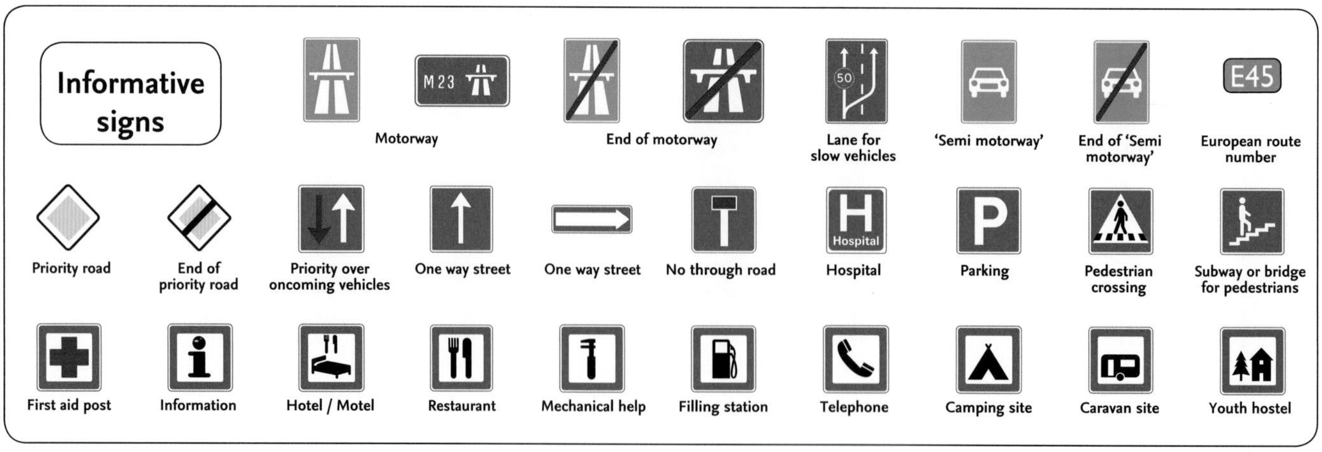
M23
Motorway
End of motorway
50
Lane for slow vehicles
'Semi motorway'
End of 'Semi motorway'
E45
European route number
Priority road
End of priority road
Priority over oncoming vehicles
One way street
One way street
No through road
Hospital
Hospital
Parking
Pedestrian crossing
Subway or bridge for pedestrians
First aid post
Information
Hotel / Motel
Restaurant
Mechanical help
Filling station
Telephone
Camping site
Caravan site
Youth hostel

Warning signs

Right bend
Left bend
Double bend
Roundabout
Intersection with non-priority road
Traffic merges from left
Traffic merges from right
Road narrows
Road narrows at left
Road narrows at right
Give way
Slippery road
Uneven road
10%
Steep hill – descent
Tunnel
Opening bridge
Road works
Loose chippings
Level crossing with barrier
Level crossing without barrier
Tram
'Count down' posts
'Danger' level crossing
Low flying aircraft
Falling rocks
Cross wind
Quayside or river bank
Two-way traffic
Traffic signals ahead
Pedestrians
Children
Animals
Wild animals
Other dangers
3,5 m
Width of carriageway
Beginning of regulation
Repetition sign
End of regulation

Regulative signs

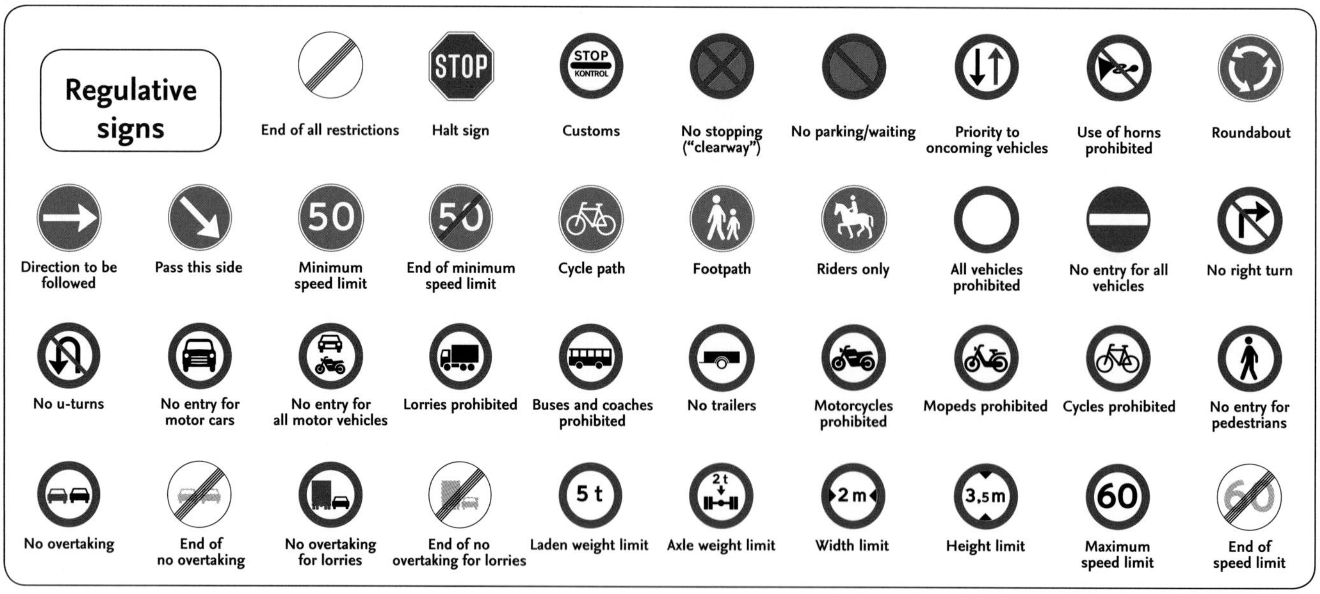
End of all restrictions
STOP
Halt sign
STOP
KONTROL
Customs
No stopping ("clearway")
No parking/waiting
Priority to oncoming vehicles
Use of horns prohibited
Roundabout
Direction to be followed
Pass this side
50
Minimum speed limit
50
End of minimum speed limit
Cycle path
Footpath
Riders only
All vehicles prohibited
No entry for all vehicles
No right turn
No u-turns
No entry for motor cars
No entry for all motor vehicles
Lorries prohibited
Buses and coaches prohibited
No trailers
Motorcycles prohibited
Mopeds prohibited
Cycles prohibited
No entry for pedestrians
No overtaking
End of no overtaking
No overtaking for lorries
End of no overtaking for lorries
5 t
Laden weight limit
2 t
Axle weight limit
2 m
Width limit
3,5 m
Height limit
60
Maximum speed limit
60
End of speed limit

Travel & route planning

Driving information	www.drive-alive.co.uk
The AA	www.theaa.com
The RAC	www.rac.co.uk
ViaMichelin	www.viamichelin.com
Bing Maps	www.bing.com/maps
Motorail information	www.railsavers.com
Ferry information	www.aferry.com
Eurotunnel information	www.eurotunnel.com

General information

UK Foreign & Commonwealth Office	https://www.gov.uk/government/organisations/foreign-commonwealth-office
Country profiles	https://www.cia.gov/library/publications/the-world-factbook/index.html
World Heritage sites	http://whc.unesco.org/en/list
World time	wwp.greenwichmeantime.com
Weather information	www.metoffice.gov.uk

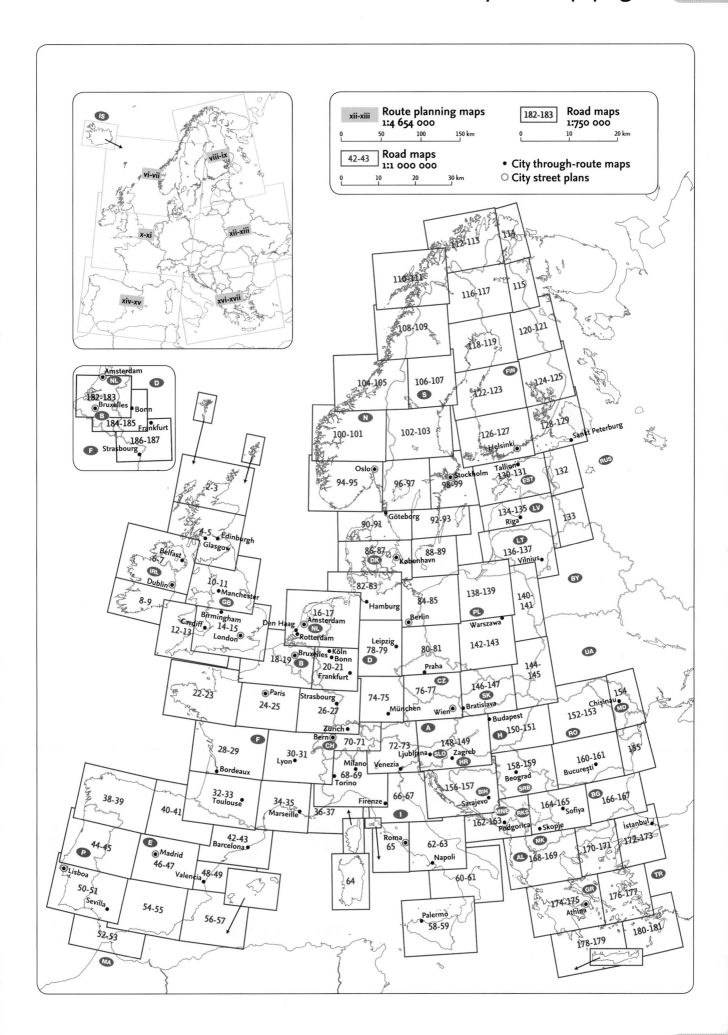

Route planning maps
1:4 654 000
0 50 100 150 km

Road maps
182-183 1:750 000
0 10 20 km

42-43 Road maps
1:1 000 000
0 10 20 30 km

• City through-route maps
○ City street plans

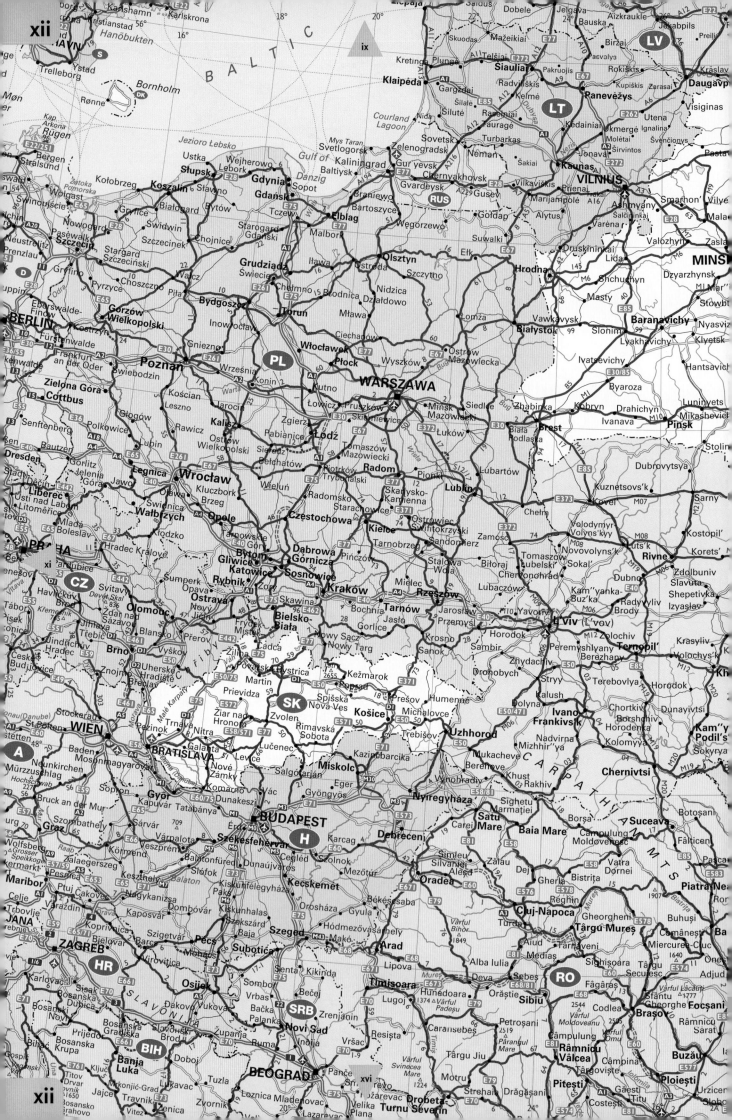

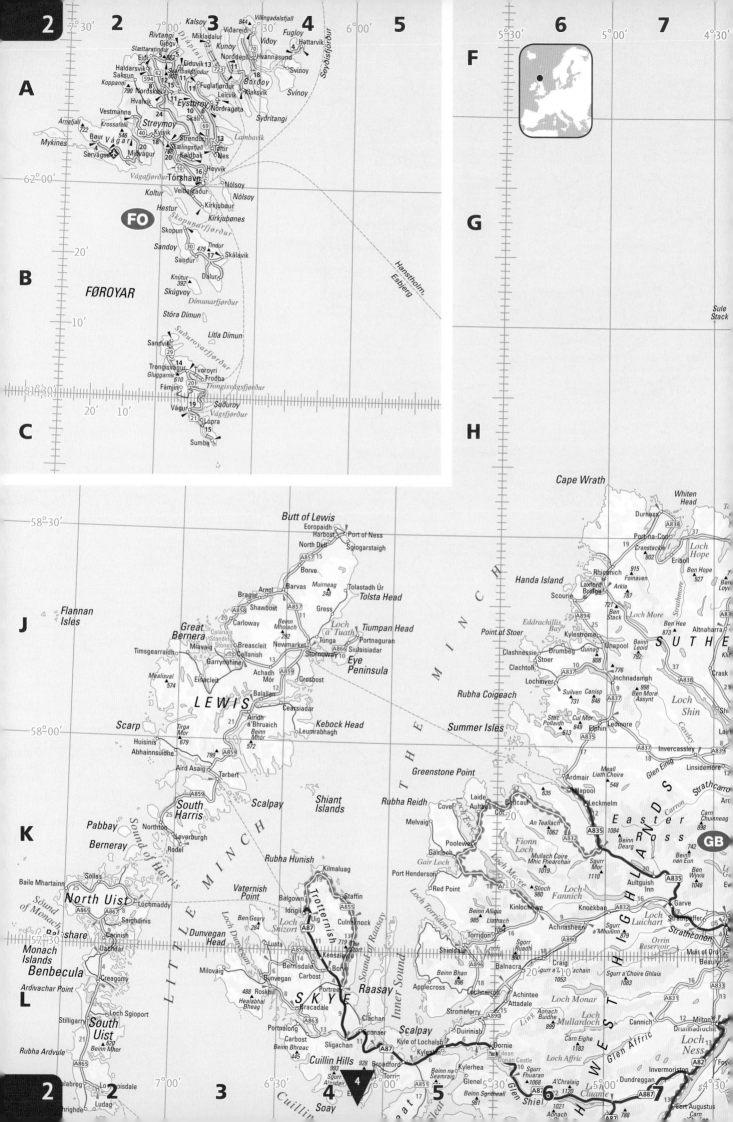

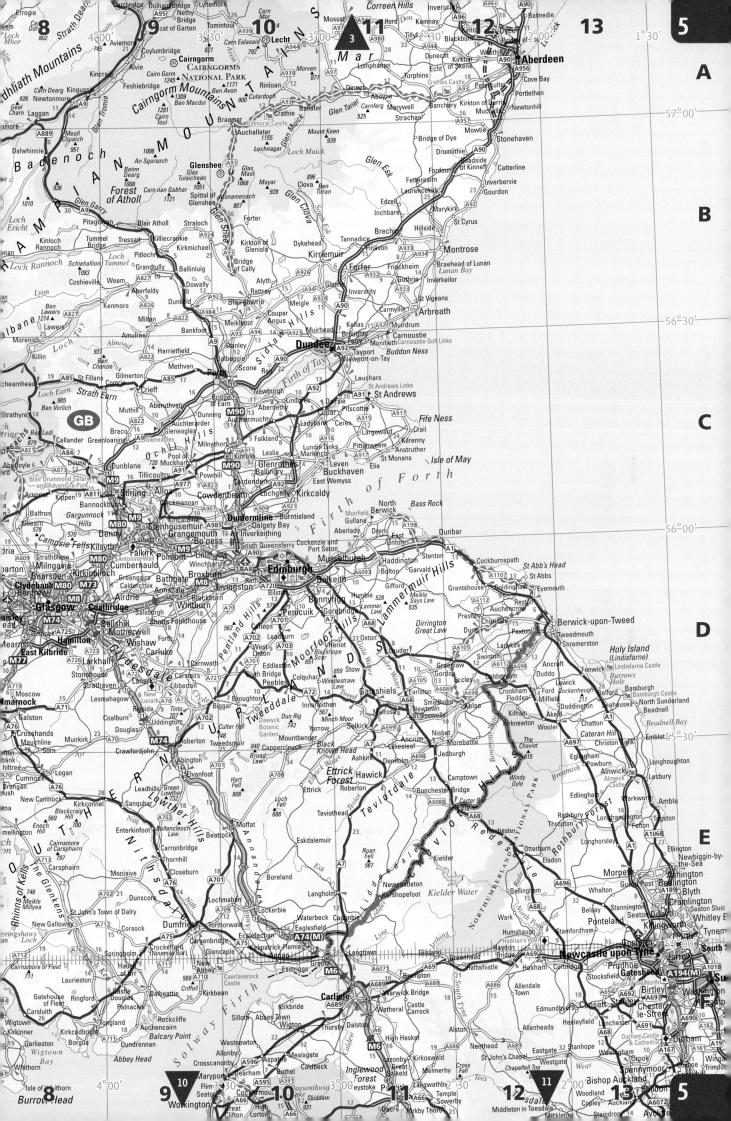

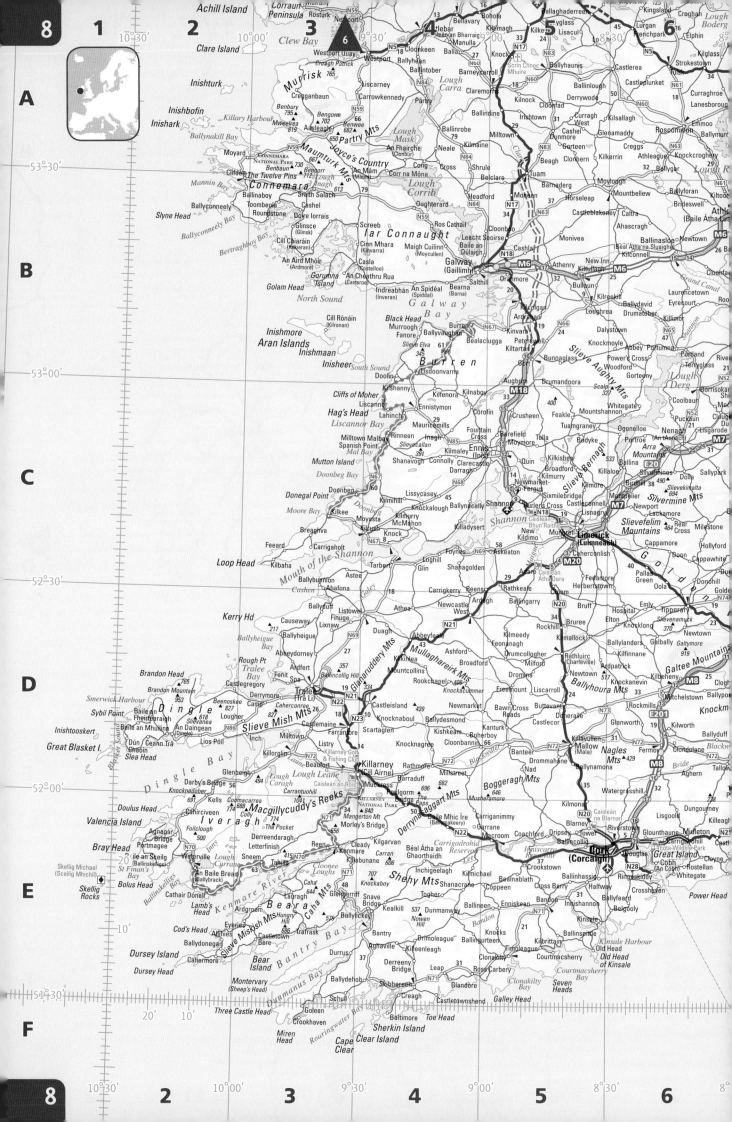

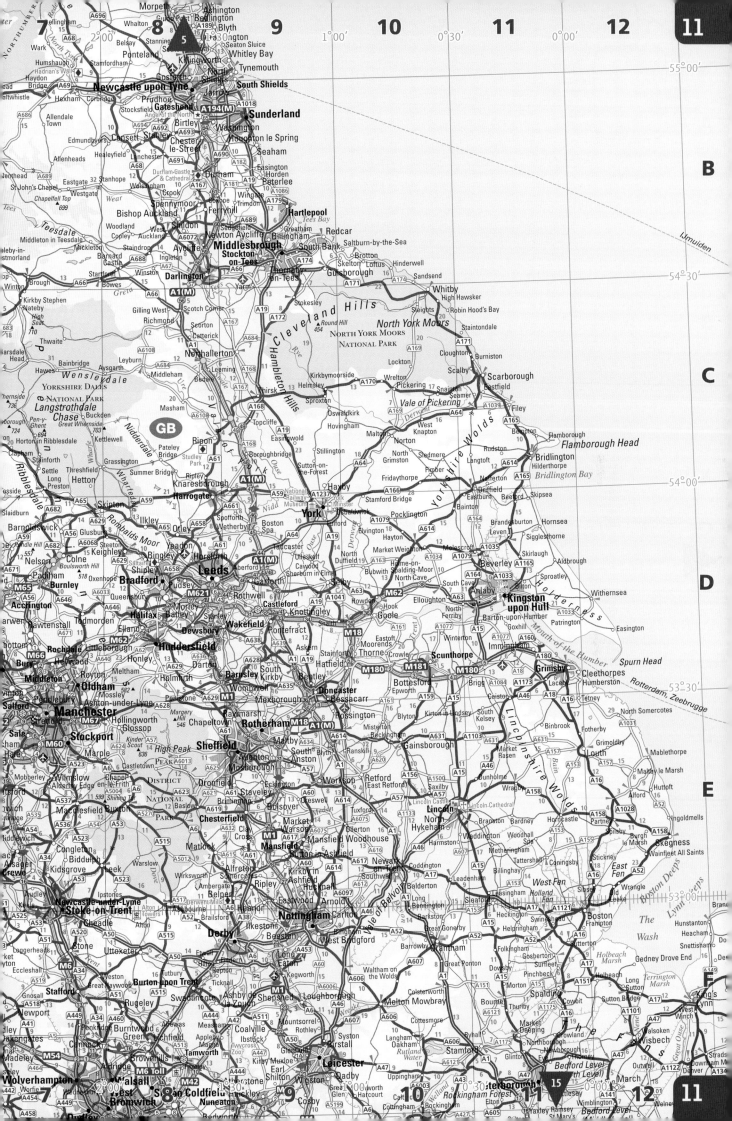

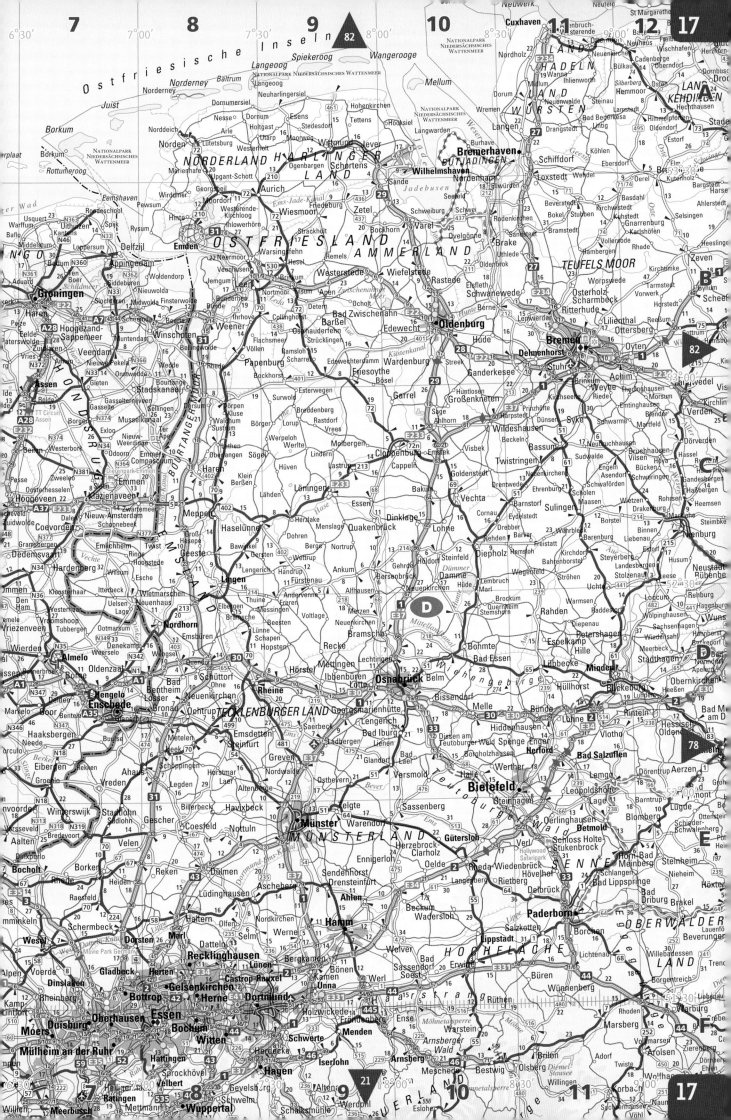

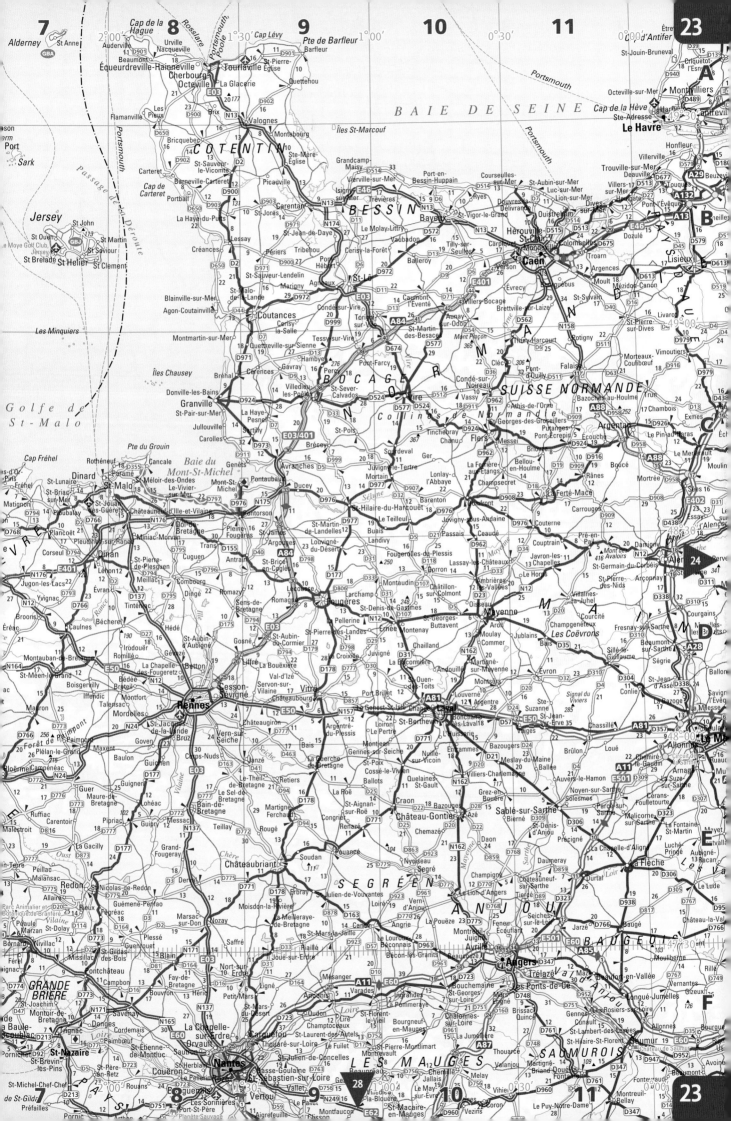

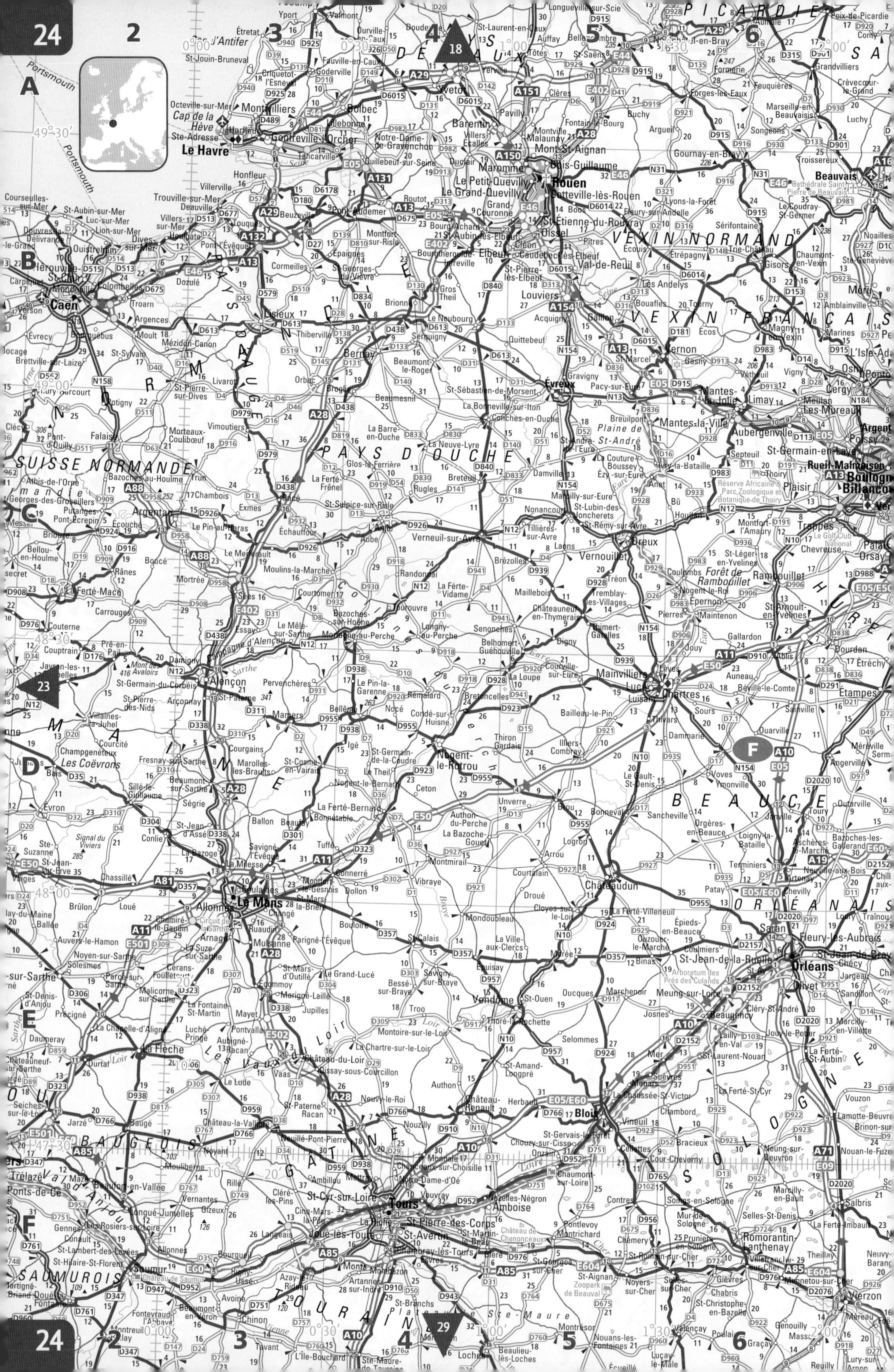

PICARDIE
PAYS DE CAUX
VEXIN NORMAND
VEXIN FRANÇAIS
PAYS D'AUGE
PAYS D'OUCHE
SUISSE NORMANDE
BEAUCE
ORLÉANAIS
SOLOGNE
BAUGEOIS
SAUMUROIS
TOURAINE
GÂTINE
Le Havre
Rouen
Caen
Lisieux
Évreux
Beauvais
Dreux
Chartres
Alençon
Le Mans
Orléans
Tours
Blois
Vendôme
Châteaudun
Saumur
Chinon
Amboise
Vierzon
Romorantin-Lanthenay
Nogent-le-Rotrou
Argentan
Falaise
Bernay
Honfleur
Deauville
Fécamp
Yvetot
Bolbec
Pont-Audemer
Louviers
Vernon
Mantes-la-Jolie
Rambouillet
Étampes
Épernon
La Flèche
Sablé-sur-Sarthe
Cergy
Portsmouth
Cap de la Hève
Forêt de Rambouillet
Plaine de St-André
Les Coëvrons
Parc Zoologique et Botanique de Thoiry
Zoopark de Beauval
Château de Chenonceaux
Circuit de la Sarthe

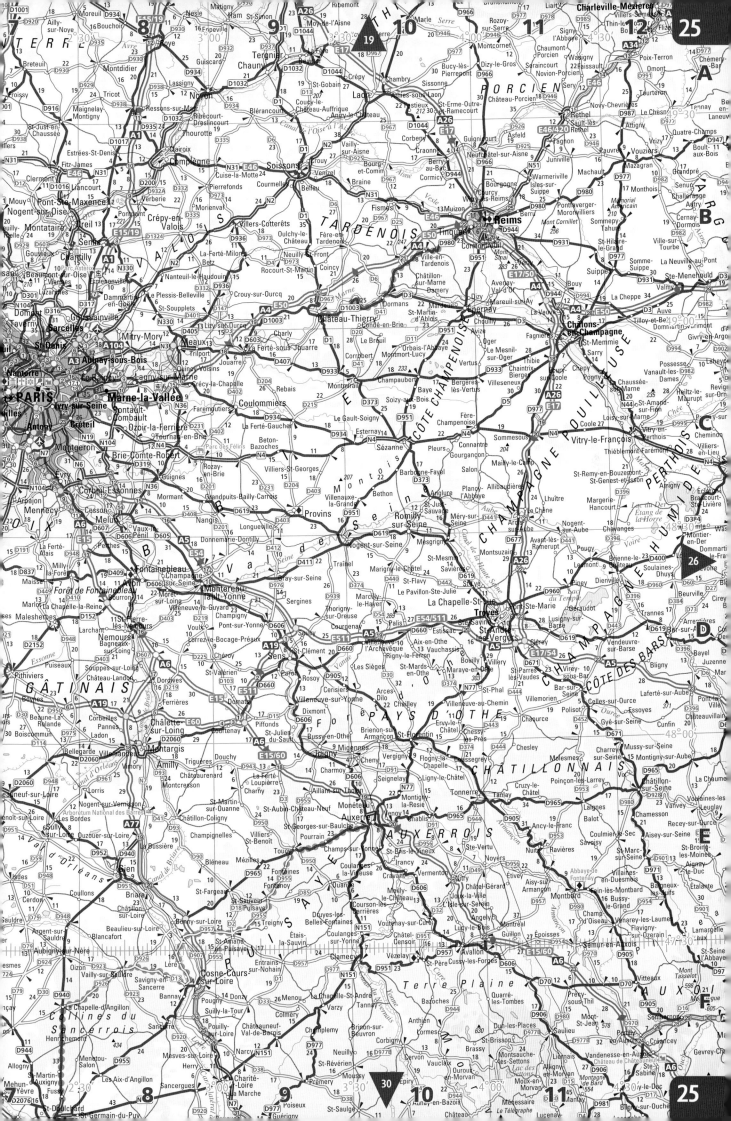

Reims
Châlons-en-Champagne
Sedan
Verdun
Metz
Nancy
LUXEMBOURG
Thionville
Bar-le-Duc
St-Dizier
Vitry-le-François
Chaumont
Langres
Épinal
Vesoul
Dijon
Besançon
Troyes
Lunéville
Toul
Pont-à-Mousson
Neufchâteau
Gray
Dole
Arlon
Longwy
Esch-sur-Alzette
Forbach
Sarrebourg
ARGONNE
GAUME
LORRAINE
Plateau Lorrain
SAULNOIS
XAINTOIS
BASSIGNY
La Vôge
Plateau de Haute-Saône
CHAMPAGNE POUILLEUSE
CHAMPAGNE HUMIDE
PERTHOIS
VALLAGE
CÔTE DES BARS
CHÂTILLONNAIS
AUXOIS
Côtes de Meuse
Plaine Lorraine
Forêt de Wœvre
Plaine de la Woëvre
Massif de la Serre
Mont des Fourches
Lac du Der Étang de la Horre
Forêt de Chiny
20
25
31
1
2
3
4
5
6
A
B
C
D
E
F

NORDPFÄLZER BERGLAND
ODENWALD
KRAICHGAU
SCHÖNBUCH
SCHWARZWALD
BAAR
HEGAU
BREISGAU
HOTZENWALD
SUNDGAU
VOSGES
PLAINE D'ALSACE
D
CH
Worms
Mannheim
Ludwigshafen am Rhein
Heidelberg
Kaiserslautern
Neustadt an der Weinstraße
Saarbrücken
Speyer
Landau in der Pfalz
Pirmasens
Zweibrücken
Karlsruhe
Pforzheim
Heilbronn
Ludwigsburg
Stuttgart
Baden-Baden
Strasbourg
Offenburg
Tübingen
Reutlingen
Freiburg im Breisgau
Colmar
Mulhouse
Basel
Belfort
Schaffhausen
Konstanz
Winterthur
Zürich
Biel
Le Bonhomme
Ventron
St-Maurice sur Moselle
Feldberg
Schonach
21
70
74
6
7
8
9
10
11
A
B
C
D
E
F

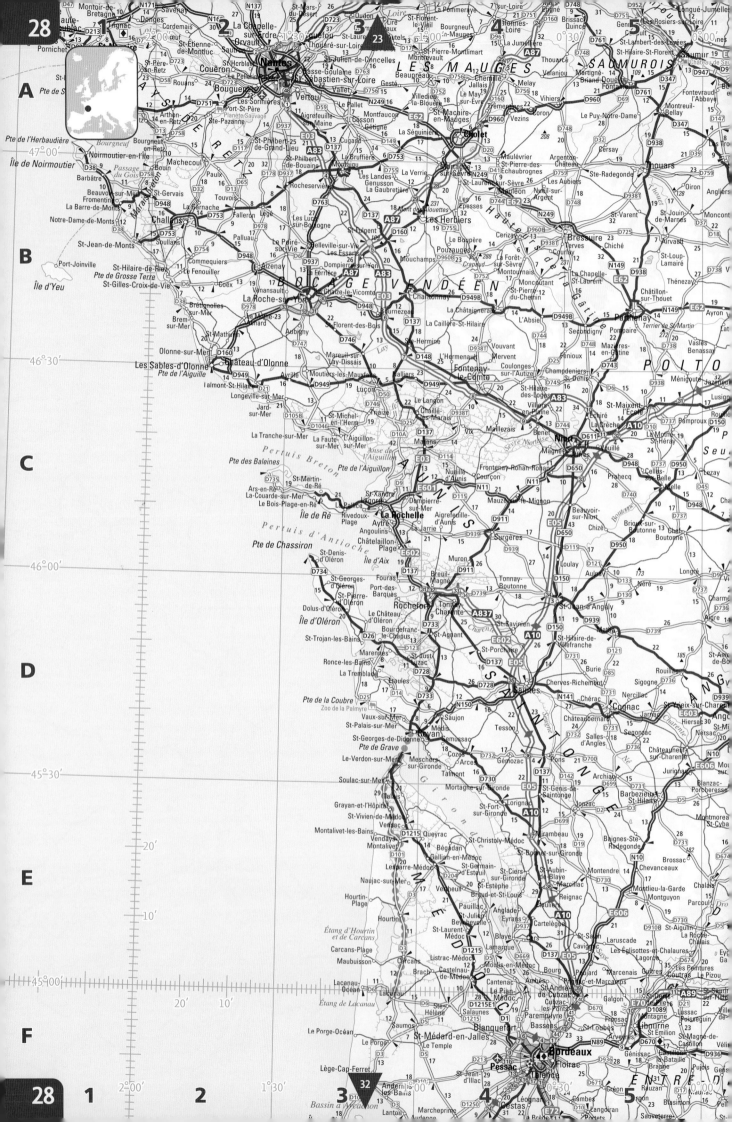

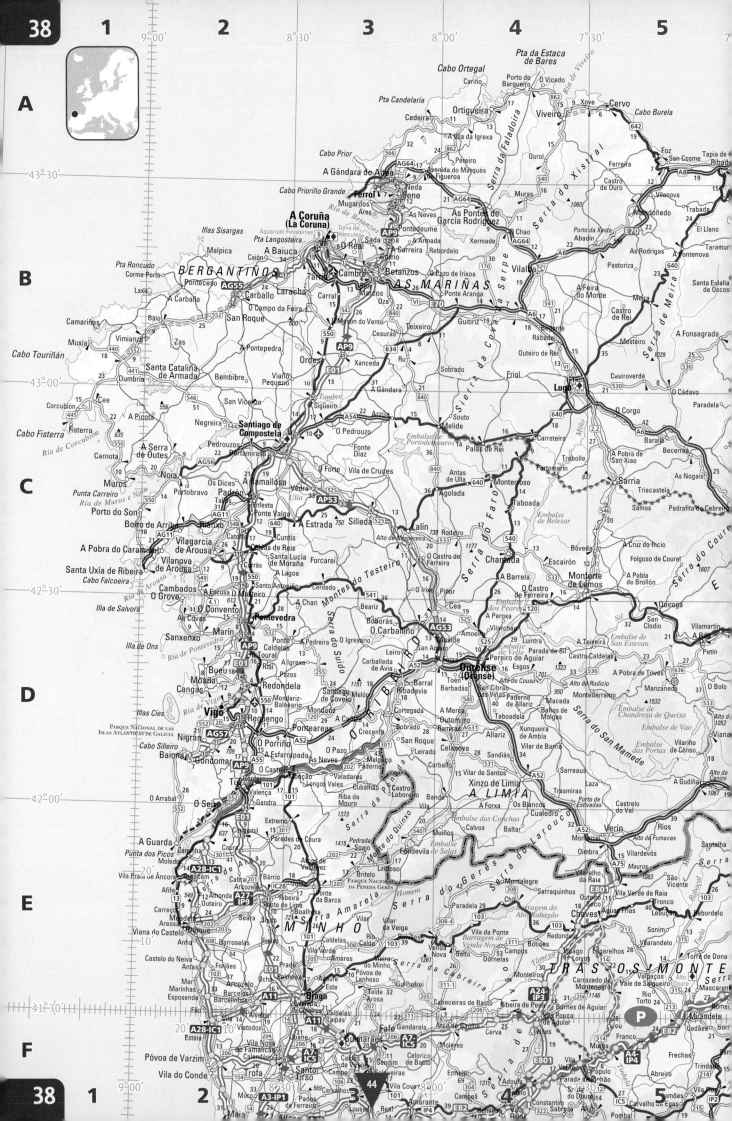

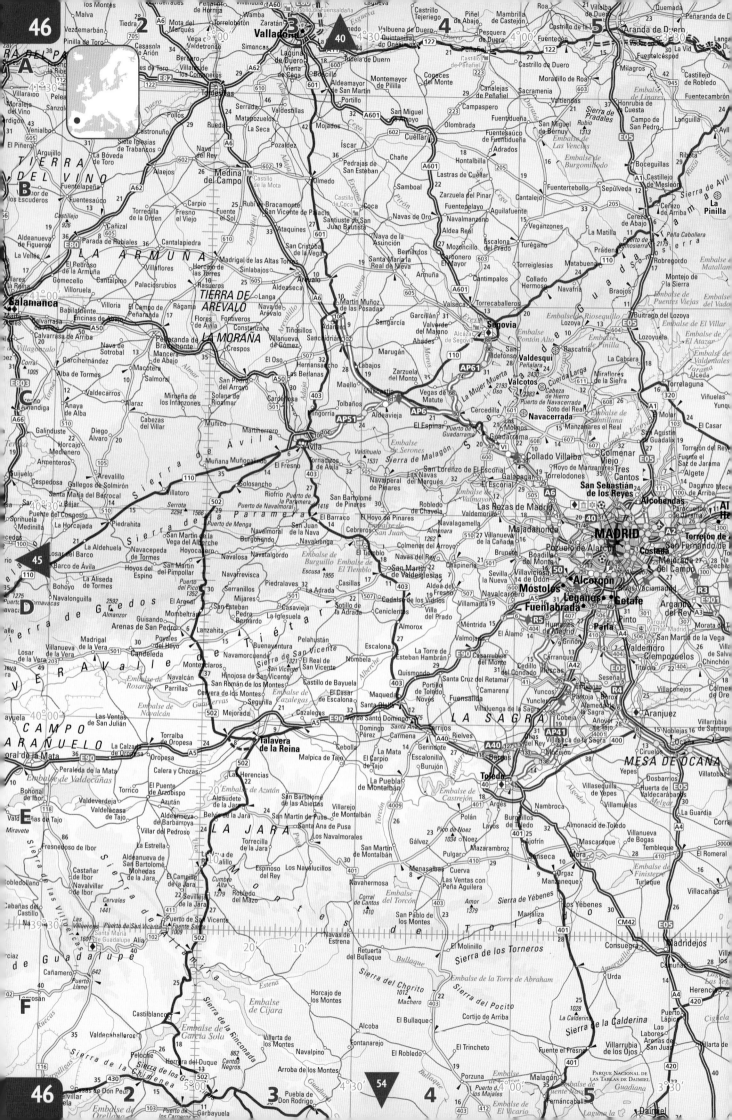

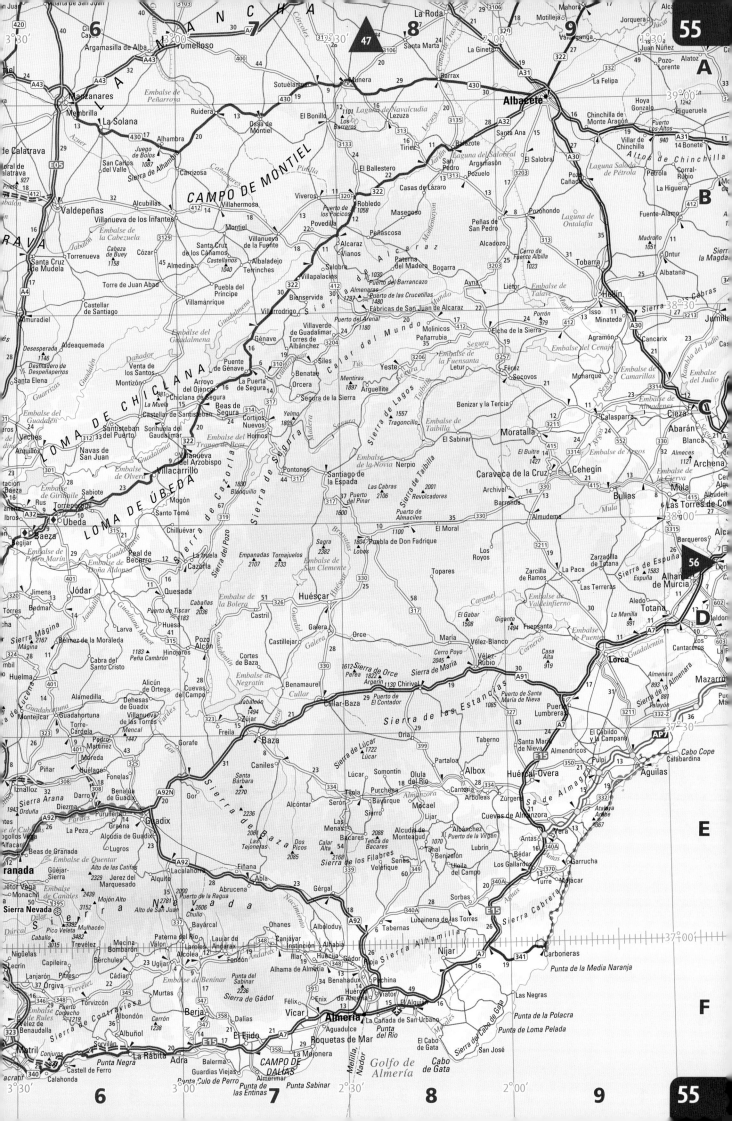

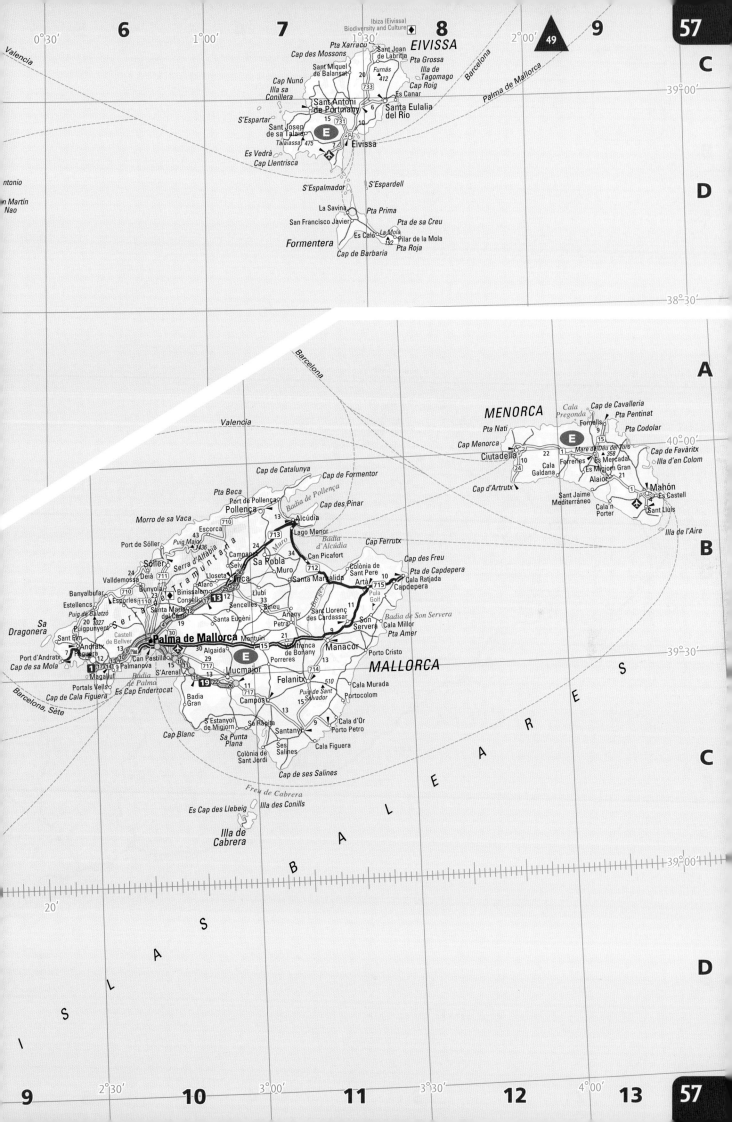

0°30'   1°00'   1°30'   2°00'

Valencia

Ibiza (Eivissa)
Biodiversity and Culture
EIVISSA

Pta Xarraco
Cap des Mossons
Sant Joan
de Labritja
Pta Grossa
Illa de
Tagomago
Cap Roig

Sant Miquel
de Balansat
Furnàs
412
Barcelona
Palma de Mallorca
39°00'

Cap Nunó
Illa sa
Conillera
733
Es Canar

Sant Antoni
de Portmany
Santa Eulalia
del Río

S'Espartar
15 731
6

Sant Josep
de sa Talaia
Talaiassa 475
E
10

Es Vedrà
Cap Llentrisca
7
Eivissa

49

C

Antonio

n Martín
Nao

S'Espalmador
S'Espardell

D

La Savina
Pta Prima

San Francisco Javier
Pta de sa Creu

Es Caló
La Mola
Pilar de la Mola
192
Pta Roja

Formentera

Cap de Barbaria

38°30'

Barcelona

A

Valencia

Cala
Pregonda
Cap de Cavalleria
MENORCA
Pta Pentinat

Pta Nati
Fornells
9
Pta Codolar

Cap de Catalunya
Cap de Formentor

Cap Menorca
E
Mare de Déu del Toro
40°00'
Cap de Favàritx
Illa d'en Colom

Pta Beca
Port de Pollença
Badia de Pollença
Cap des Pinar

Ciutadella
22
358
Ferreries
Es Mercadal
Es Migjorn Gran

Morro de sa Vaca
Pollença
13
Alcúdia

10
24
Cala
Galdana

Alaior
21
Mahón
Es Castell

Escorça
710
Lago Menor
713

Cap d'Artrutx
Sant Jaime
Mediterráneo
Cala'n
Porter
Sant Lluís

Port de Sóller
Puig Major
1436
43
Serra d'Alfàbia
24
Muro
Campanet
Badia
d'Alcúdia
Can Picafort
Cap Ferrutx

Illa de l'Aire

Sóller
711
Selva
30
Sa Pobla
34
Colònia de
Sant Pere
Cap des Freu

B

Valldemossa
Deià
Lloseta
Inca
Muro
712
Santa Margalida
Artà
Pta de Capdepera
Cala Ratjada
Capdepera

Banyalbufar
Esporles
710
Bunyola
23
Alaró
Binissalem
Consell
17
13
12
Llubí
Sencelles
Sineu
33
Pula
Golf
715
10

Estellencs
1110
Santa Maria
del Camí
19
Santa Eugèni
Anany
Petra
Sant Llorenç
des Cardassar
11

Puig de Galatzó
1027
Puigpunyent
20
Castell
de Bellver
21
Montuïri
Villafranca
de Bonany
Son
Servera
Cala Millor
Pta Amer
Badia de Son Servera

Sa
Dragonera
Sant Elm
Andratx
Peguera
13
Palma de Mallorca
30
Algaida
Porreres
15
Manacor
Porto Cristo
39°30'

Port d'Andratx
Cap de sa Mola
7
12
14
Can Pastilla
Palmanova
15
11
717
E
13
714

Magaluf
1
17
Palmanova
S'Arenal
15
Llucmajor
Felanitx
510
Cala Murada
Portocolom
MALLORCA

Barcelona, Sète
Portals Vells
Badia
de Palma
Es Cap Enderrocat
19
22
11
717
Puig de Sant
Salvador
15
Cala d'Or
Porto Petro

Cap de Cala Figuera
Badia
Gran
Campos
13

S'Estanyol
de Migjorn
Sa Ràpita
Santanyí
9
Cala Figuera

Cap Blanc
Sa Punta
Plana
Ses
Salines
Cala Figuera

Colònia de
Sant Jordi
Cap de ses Salines

C

Freu de Cabrera
Es Cap des Llebeig
Illa des Conills

B
A
L
E
A
R
E
S
39°00'

Illa de
Cabrera

20'

B

I
S
L
A
S

D

2°30'   3°00'   3°30'   4°00'

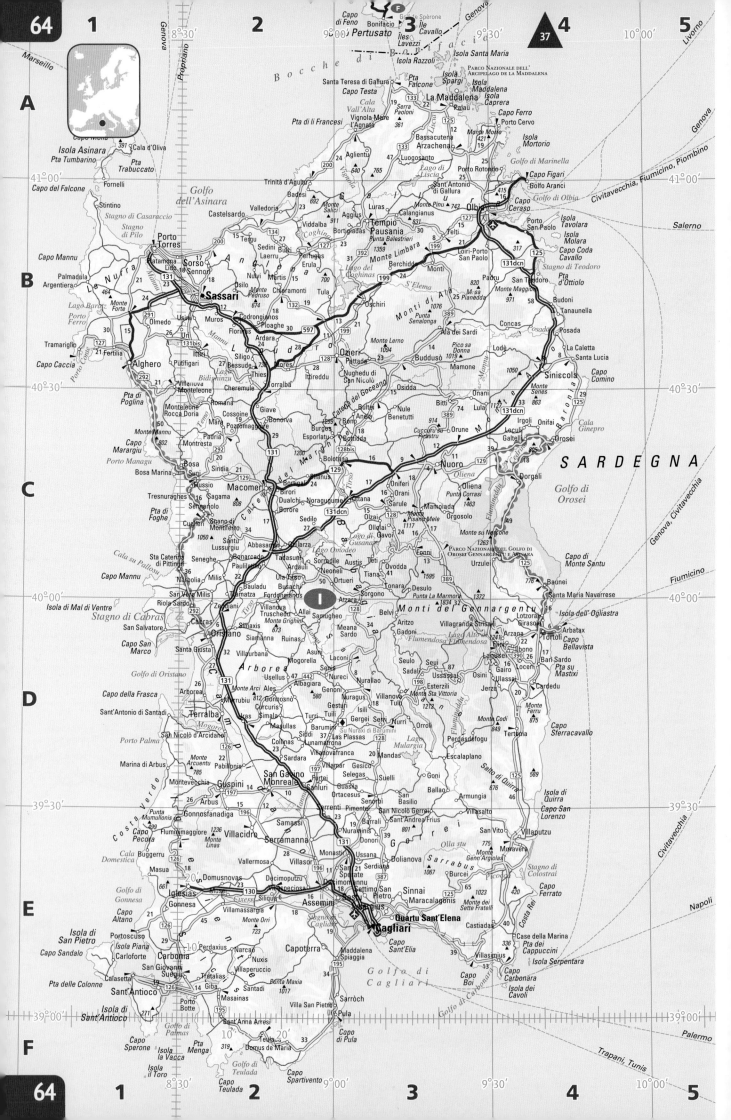

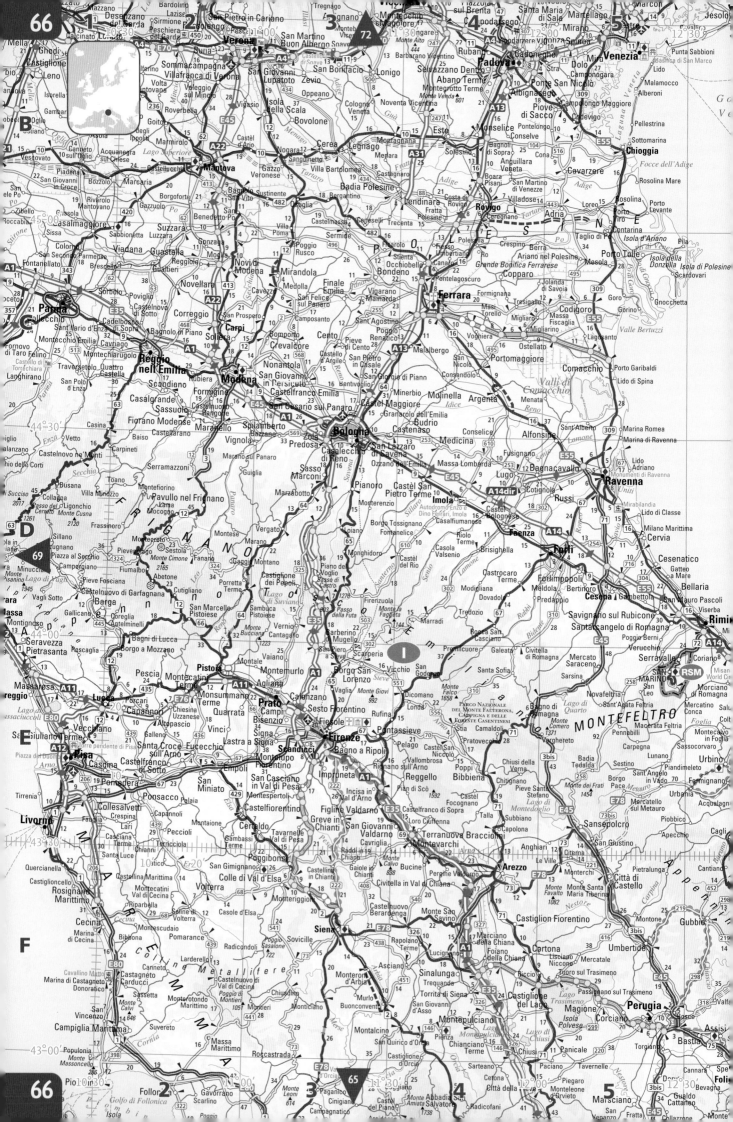

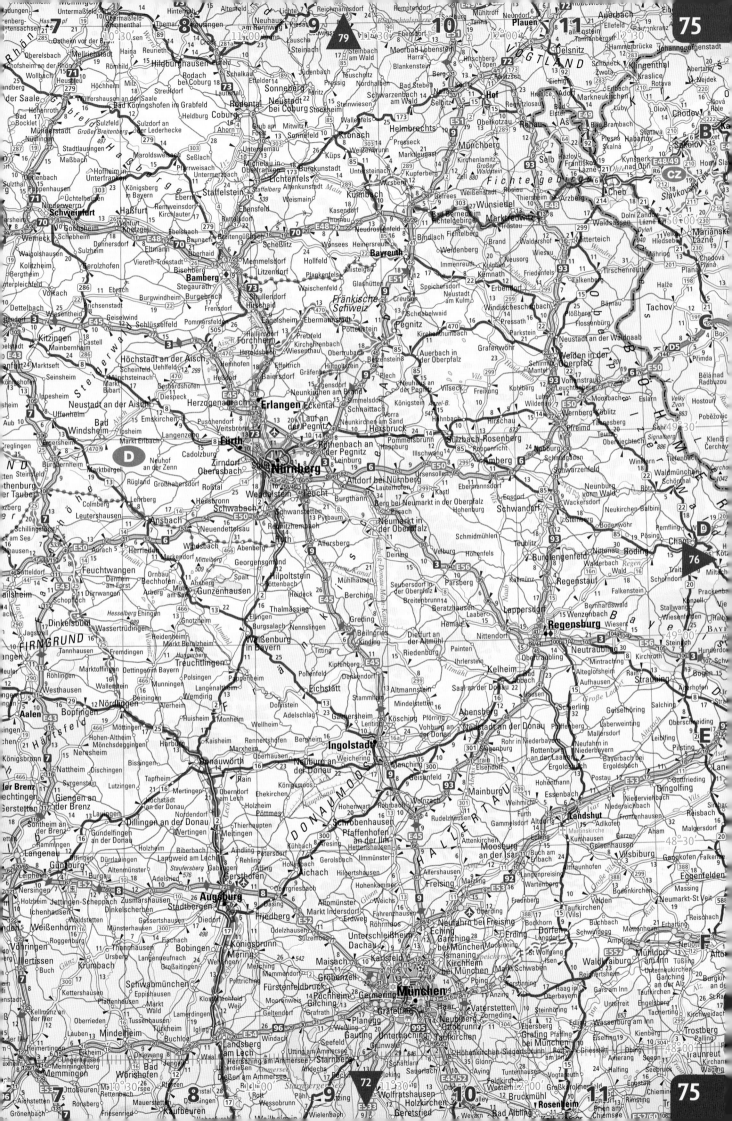

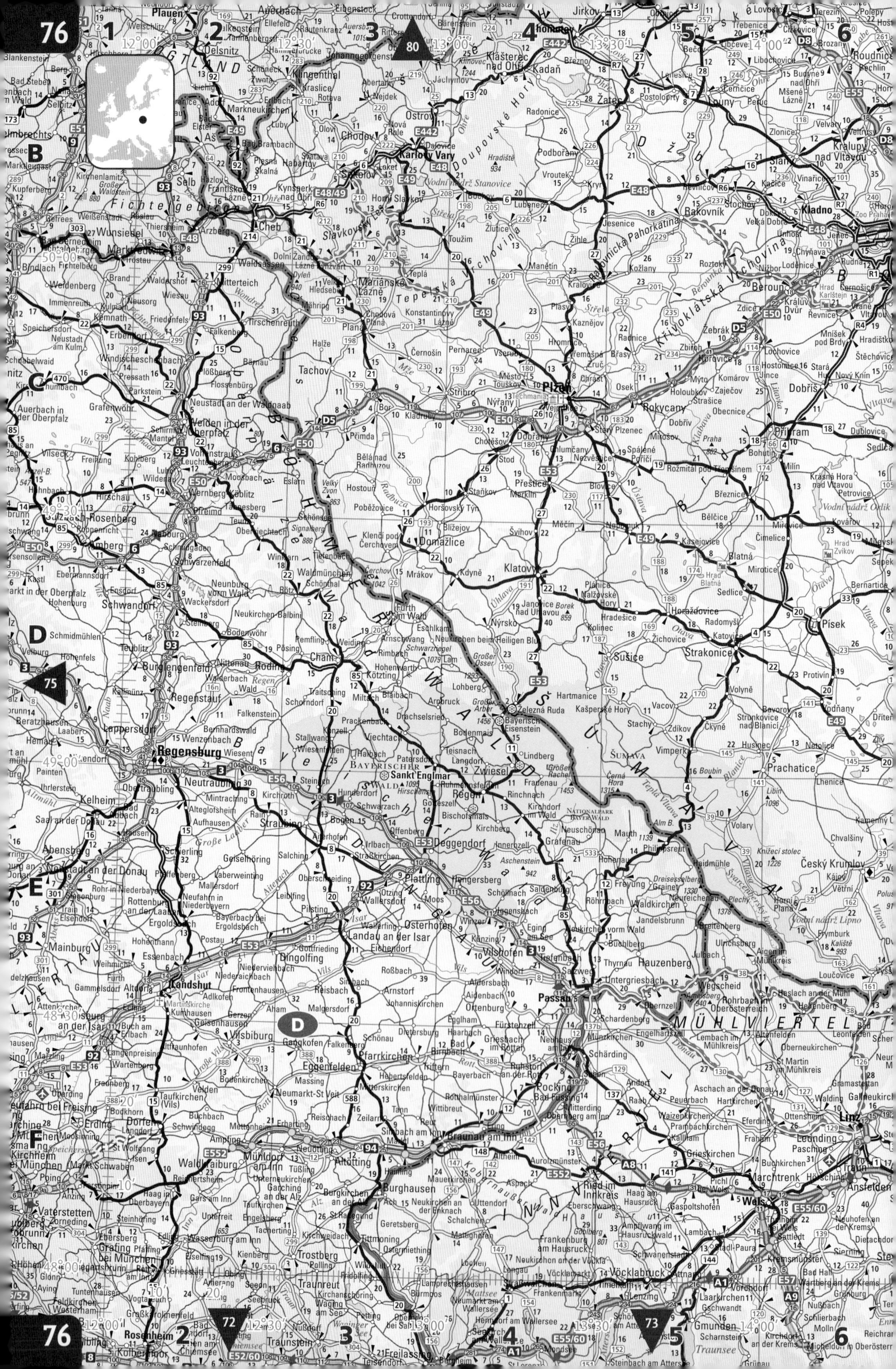

1
2
3
4
5
6
B
C
D
E
F
80
75
72
73
12°00'
12°30'
13°00'
13°30'
14°00'
49°30'
49°00'
48°30'
48°00'
Plauen
Auerbach
Oelsnitz
Klingenthal
Cheb
Karlovy Vary
Sokolov
Chomutov
Klášterec nad Ohří
Kadaň
Žatec
Louny
Roudnice
Slaný
Kralupy nad Vltavou
Kladno
Rakovník
Beroun
Praha
Plzeň
Rokycany
Příbram
Dobříš
Mariánské Lázně
Tachov
Stříbro
Domažlice
Klatovy
Sušice
Strakonice
Písek
Vimperk
Prachatice
Český Krumlov
Selb
Wunsiedel
Marktredwitz
Weiden in der Oberpfalz
Amberg
Schwandorf
Cham
Regensburg
Straubing
Deggendorf
Plattling
Landshut
Dingolfing
Passau
Pocking
Braunau am Inn
Mühldorf am Inn
Altötting
Burghausen
Ried im Innkreis
Wels
Linz
Vöcklabruck
Gmunden
Traunstein
Rosenheim
Kelheim
Mainburg
Erding
Freising
Fichtelgebirge
Oberpfälzer Wald
Bayerischer Wald
Šumava
Mühlviertel
Doupovské Hory
Křivoklátská Vrchovina
D

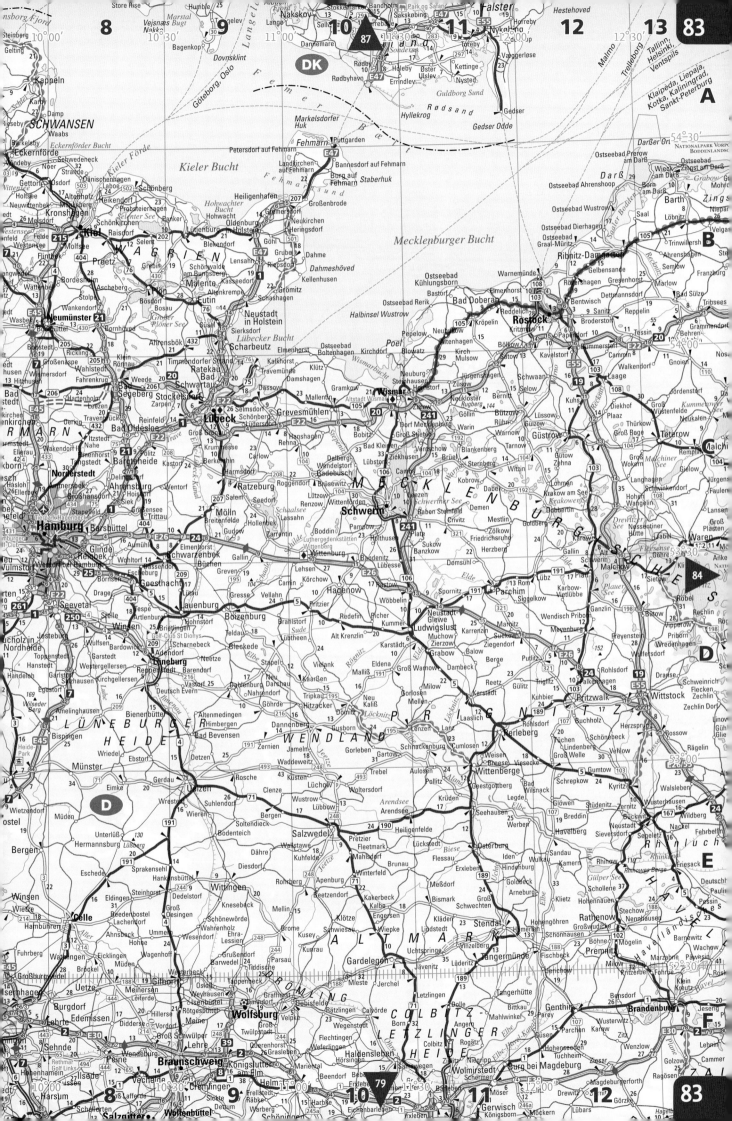

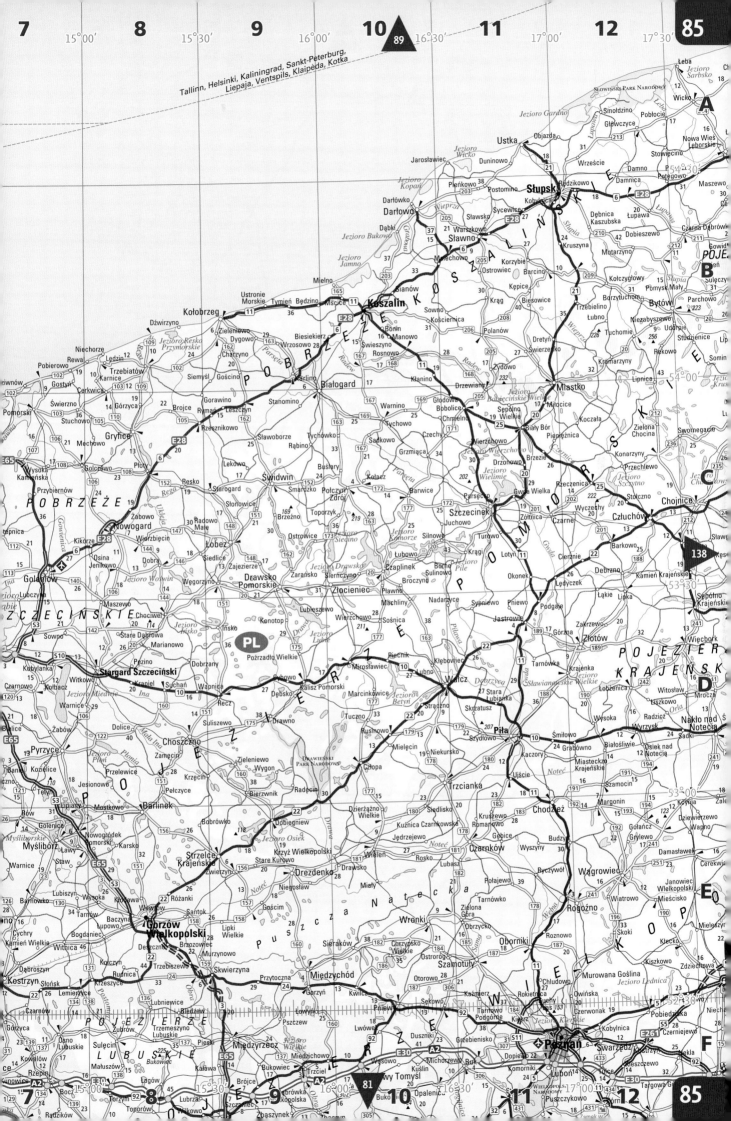

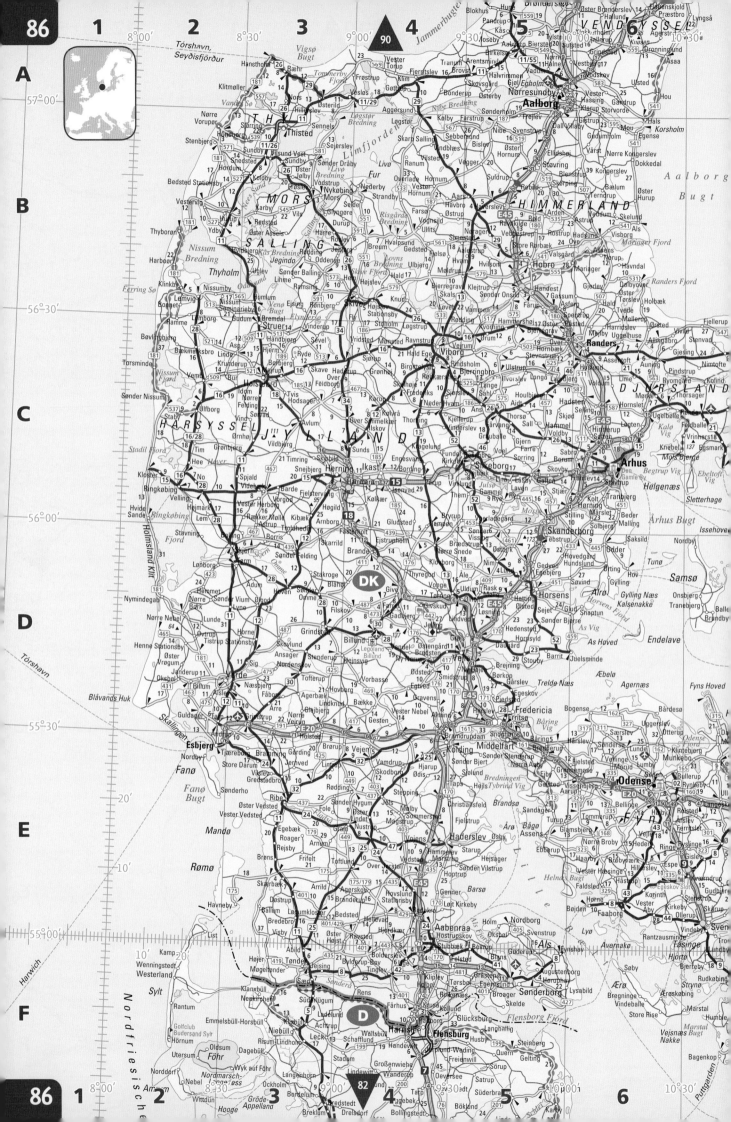

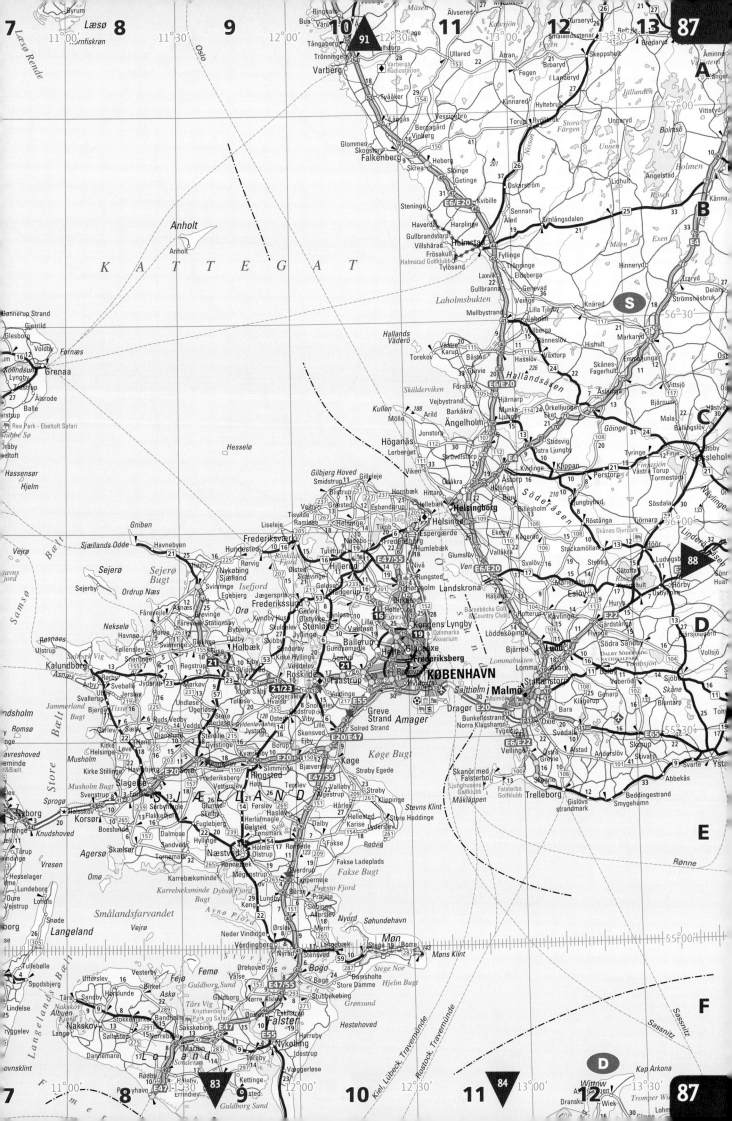

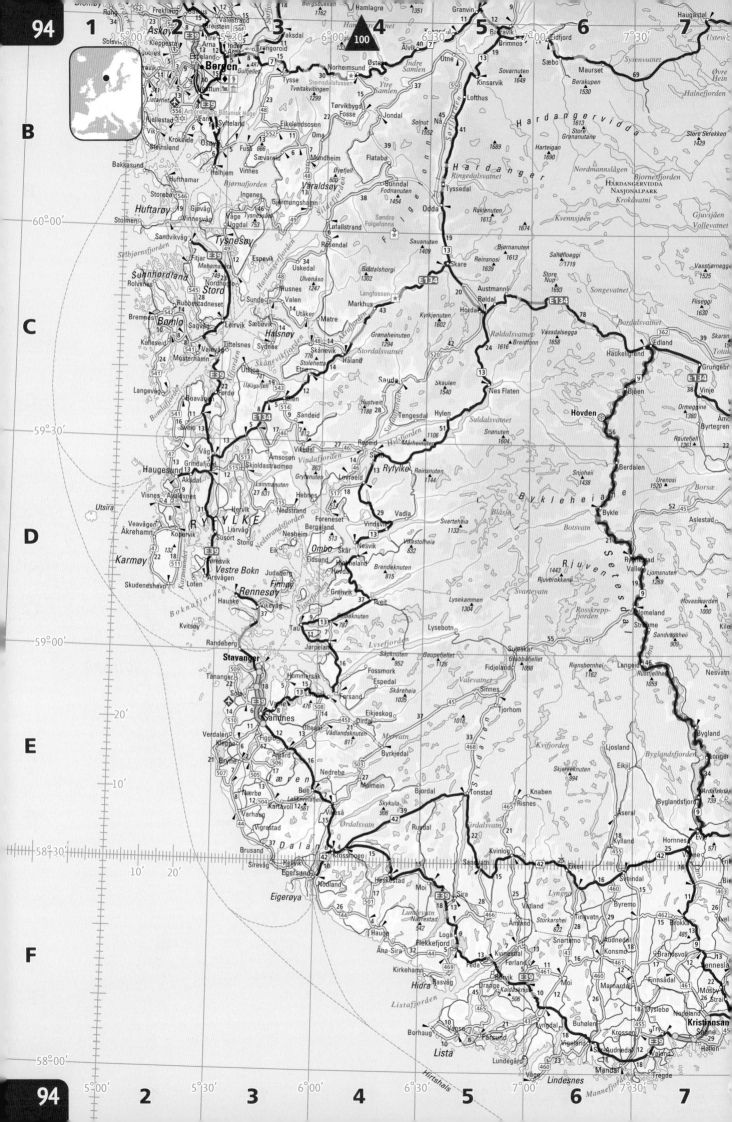

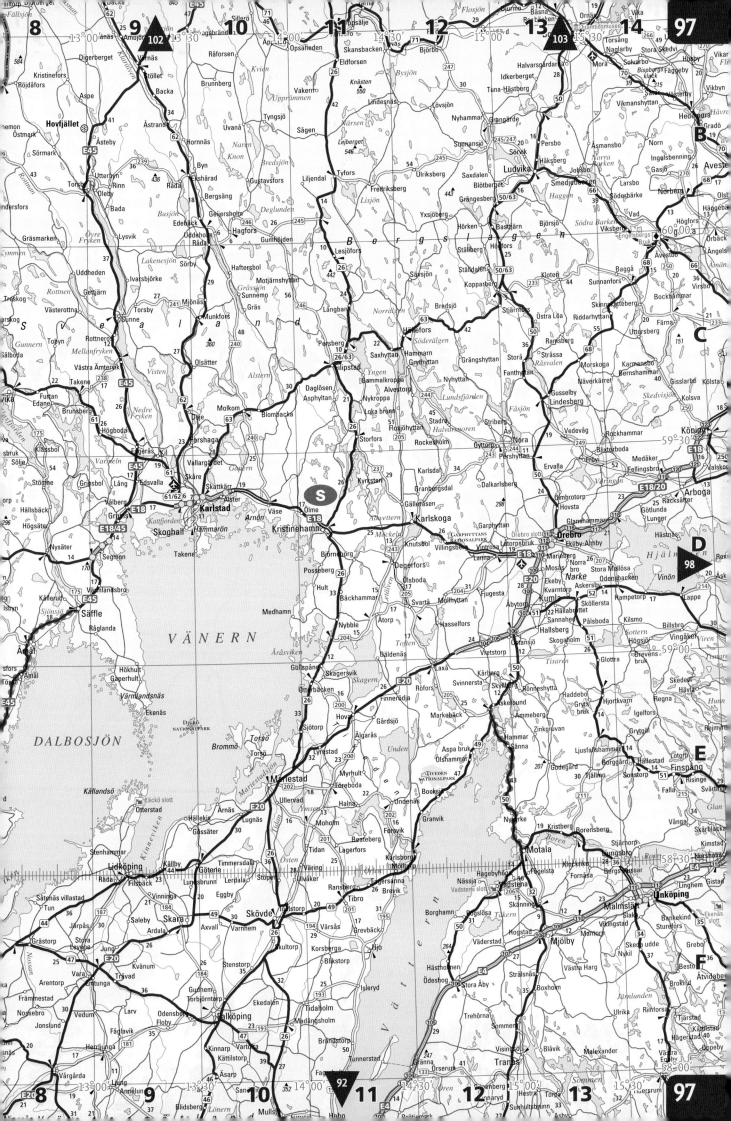

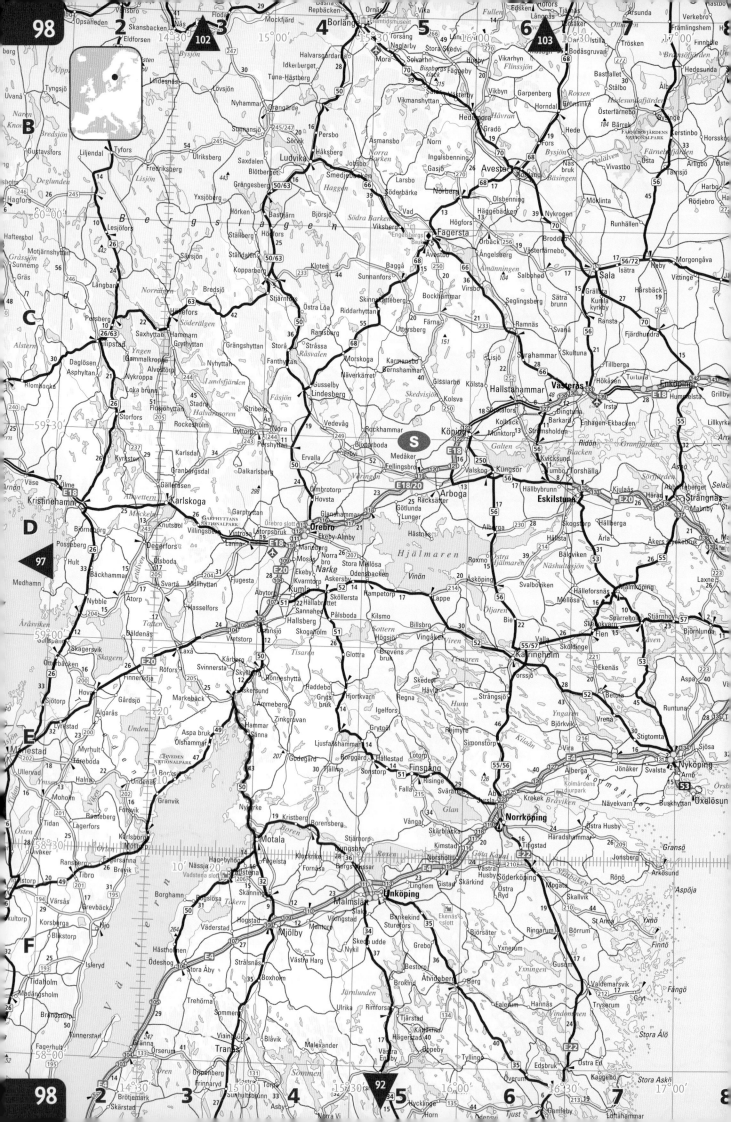

1 7°00' **2** 7°30' **3** 8°00' **4** 8°30' **5** 9°00' **6** 9°30' **7** 10°00' **8** 10

A

65°00'

B

64°30'

C

Såte
Svel
Vingsand

Brandsfjorden

Utro
Røan
Kiran   Nordskjør
Bessaker

Harbak   Kjerringheid
540

Tørrvika   Harsvik

64°00'   Ratvika   30   723   715   By
Tärnes   715
Selnes   Eide   Mørrevatnet
Vallersund   Lysøysund
Oksvoll   721   Teksdal   22   715
Tarva   Bjugn   13   Botngård   24   710
Uthaug   Opphaug   3   23
Frohavet   Brekstad   718   42   Sørelva
Austråt   Stjørnfjorden   611   Olsøy
Norddyrøy   Svellingen   Selvåg   Fevåg   14   715
Hellesvik   714   Granðefjæra   Rissa   717   Storvatnet   609   30
Frøya   Sistranda   Munken   Garten   Reinskloster   13   755   Hindrem
Tuvnes   Flatval   Hammarvika   Selva   715   7   Vannvikan
Titran   13   716   Knarrlagsund   Grønningen   Selbekken   Stadsbygd
Storhallaren   714   Hestvika   Åstan   656   Øyangen
Kjerringvåg   9   714   Kongsvoll   Flakk   715   13
Frøyfjorden   Hestnes   6   Fillan   Sandstad   Sunde   Kjøra   Botaniske
63°30'   Veidholmen   713   Straum   21   Gjengstø   Helm   34   Byneset   566   Trondh
10   Kvenvær   12   Trøndheimsleia   Helland   Skorild   Gjølme   709   Heim
Dyrnes   8   Nordvika   Forsnes   17   Vikan   722   Storodden   Omnsfjellet   714   Buvika   704
Frostadheia   28   345   Vihalsen   847   E39   13   Telhus
Smøla   669   Åmes   Arvågen   14   Orkanger   15   E6
Straumen   17   Svinvika   Kyrksæterøra   Berdal   Vormstad   708   Ler
Austsmøla   Leira   682   Todalsfjellet   Rovatnet   65   Svorkmo   Anø
20'   Rossvoll   Solskjela   Vinsternes   Almo   Søya   Hoston   Korsvegen   33   Lundamo
Kørsvoll   Aukan   680   Vinjeøra   Svøssli   17   700   Gåsbakken   Hovin
Tustna   Stabblandet   Evjik   E39   Gråfjellet   Okla   12   Løkken   Støren   12   R
Kristiansund   908   Arasvika   Todal   1040   Storås   701   Meldal   30
Sveggesundet   6   Hennset   Renndal   Drystolan   Rindal   710   Restfjellet
Reinsvik   13   929   Brattset   23   Sætra   Ilfjellet
Hasløya   Kvalvåg   Betna   Hjelmen   31   1162   1218
Hurtigruten   70   Kvisvik   65   Valsøybotn   Harang   Follsjøen   E6
Vevång   9   Karvåg   Øydegarden   Åsskard   Bøverfjord   Grindal
63°00'   16   Bruhagen   Kånestraum   Surnadalsøra   Honnstadknyken   700
Averøya   64   Heggem   Torvik   1071   Tindfjellet   Berkåk
Bud   10   Ørj   Hogset   666   Aksnes   670   1167   Gråsjøen   E6
Hostadvatnet   13   Torvikbukt   689   Roemo   689   Svinvik Arboretum   Snota   Ulsberg
Eide   Båtnfjordsøra   994   20   Aure   Rognnebba   1668   37   700
Elnesvågen   664   Reinsfjellet   Tingvoll   13   1497
NORDMØRE   21   Angvik   Kvanne   Smisetnebba   Virumkjerringa   Ilv
Gossen   979   Hjelset   Steinløysa   16   70   Ålvund   1175   1374
Aurgosen   662   10   Kleive   Eidsøra   Smisetnebba
Orten   18   Molde   E39   Tjelle   22   Eidsvåg   fjell   254   Ila
Aukra   23   Hjelstranda   660   Nause   579   Gjevil   Kamman   Nersk   254   Svardal
23°   1627   101   Enmo

100   101

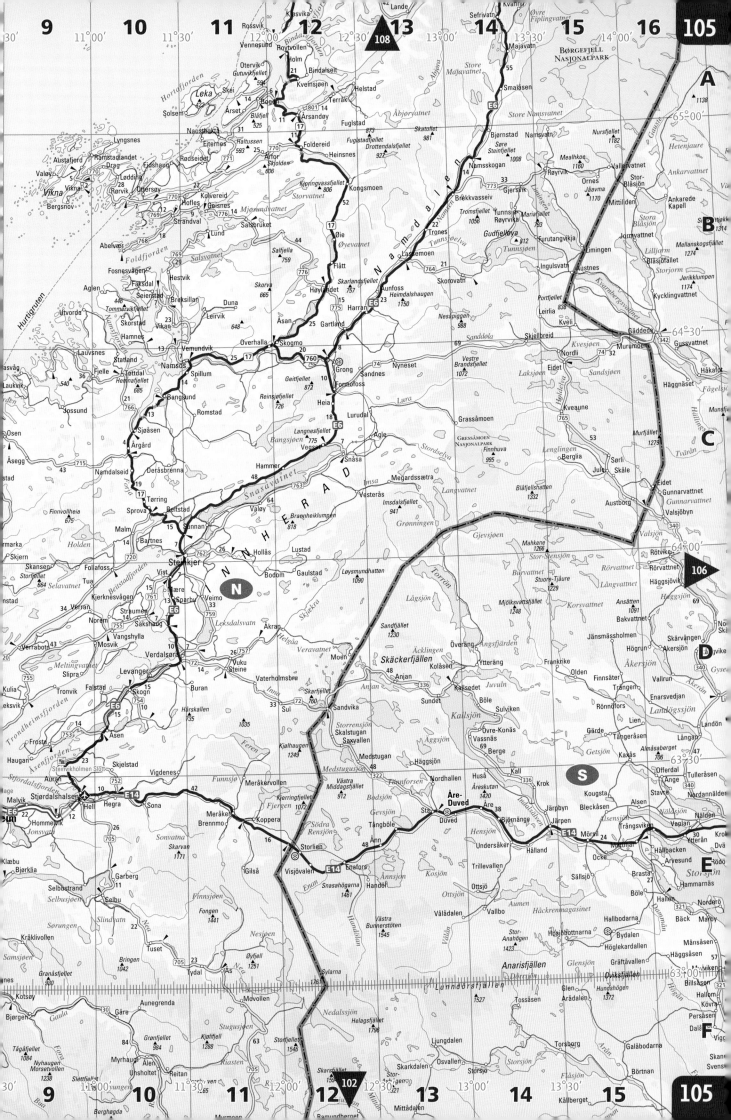

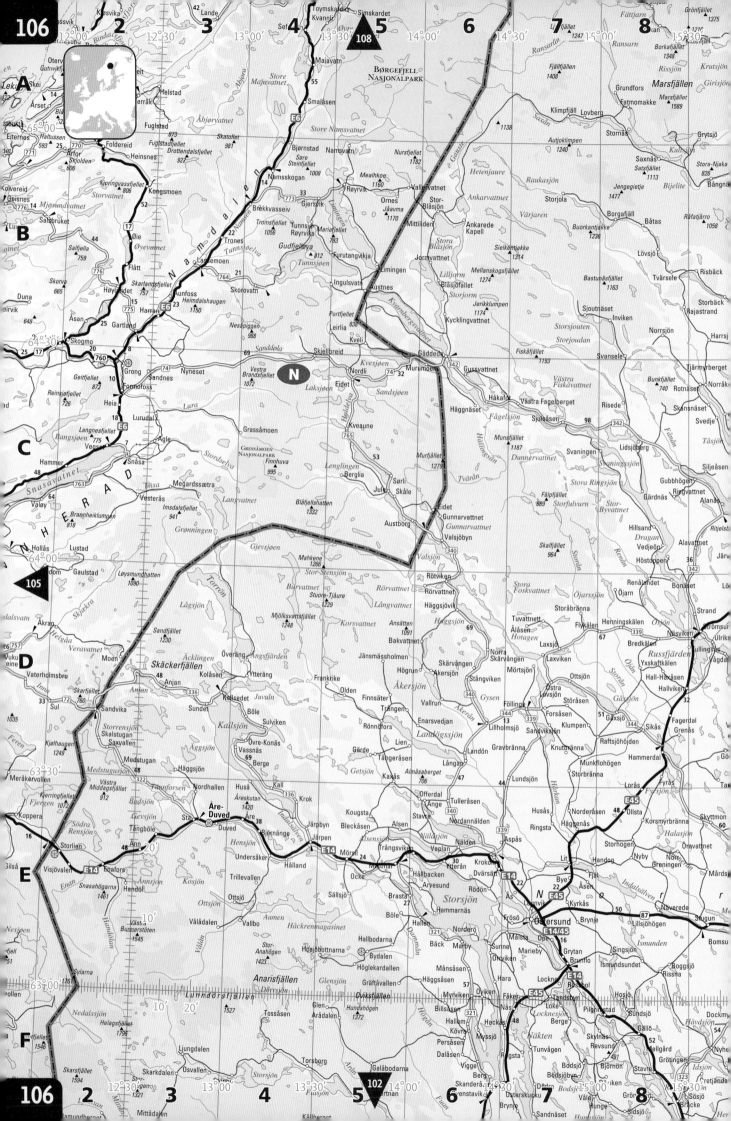

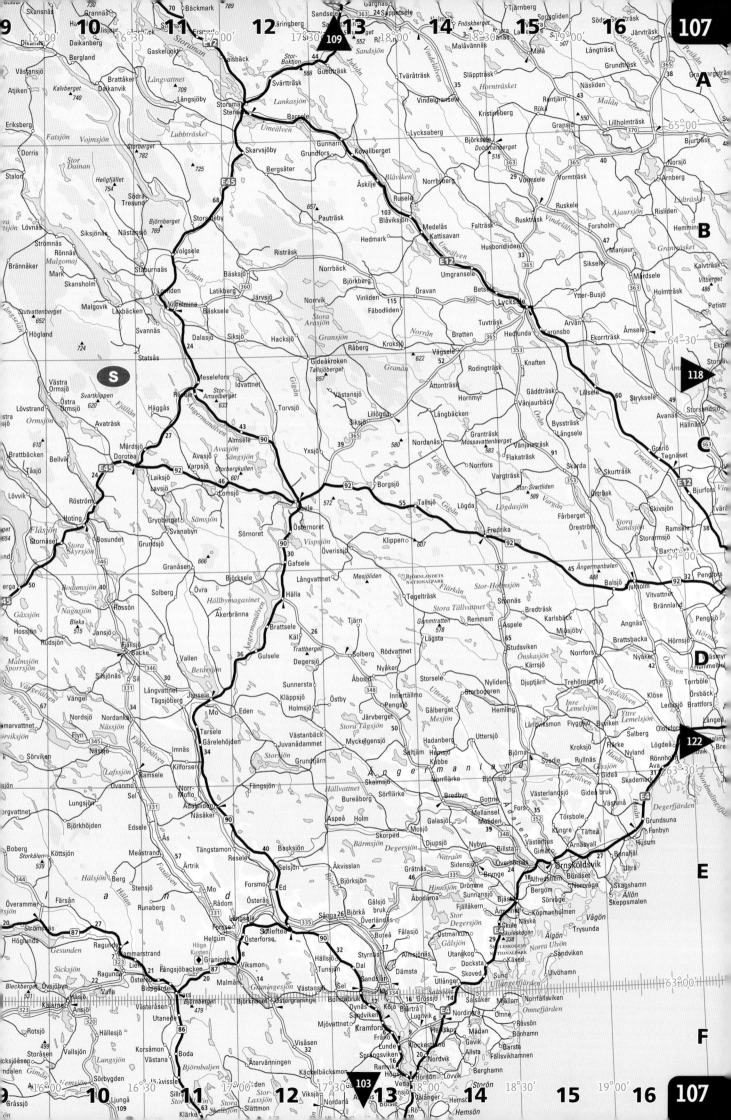

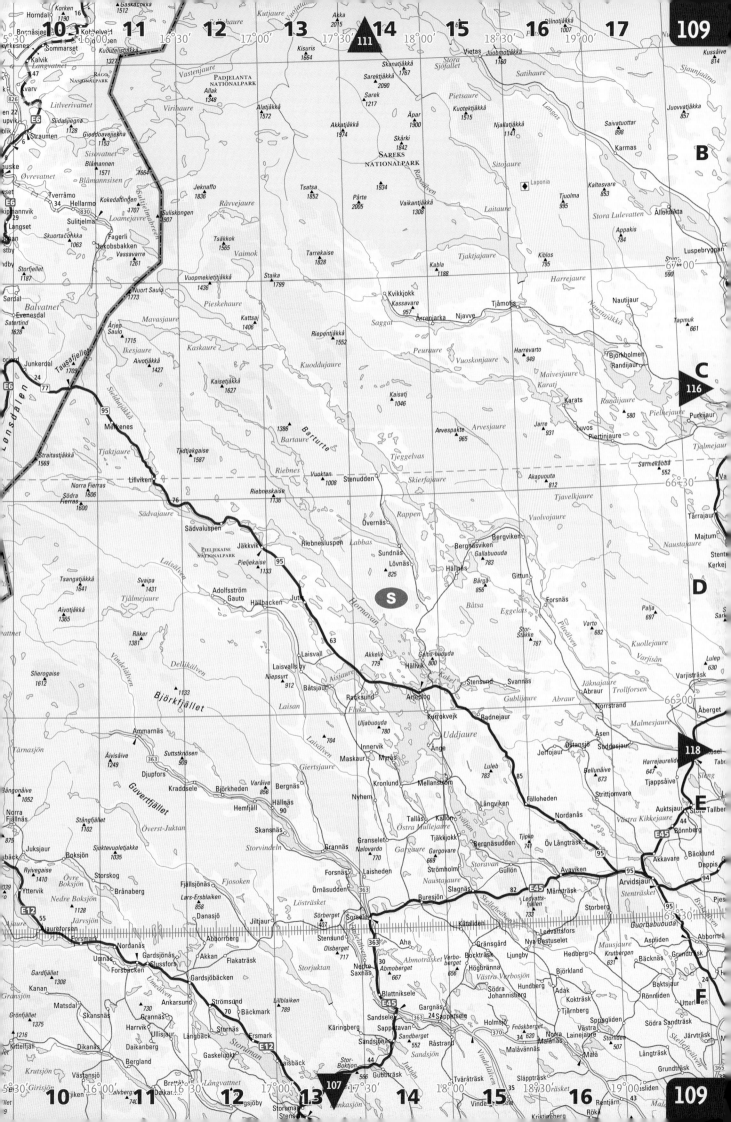

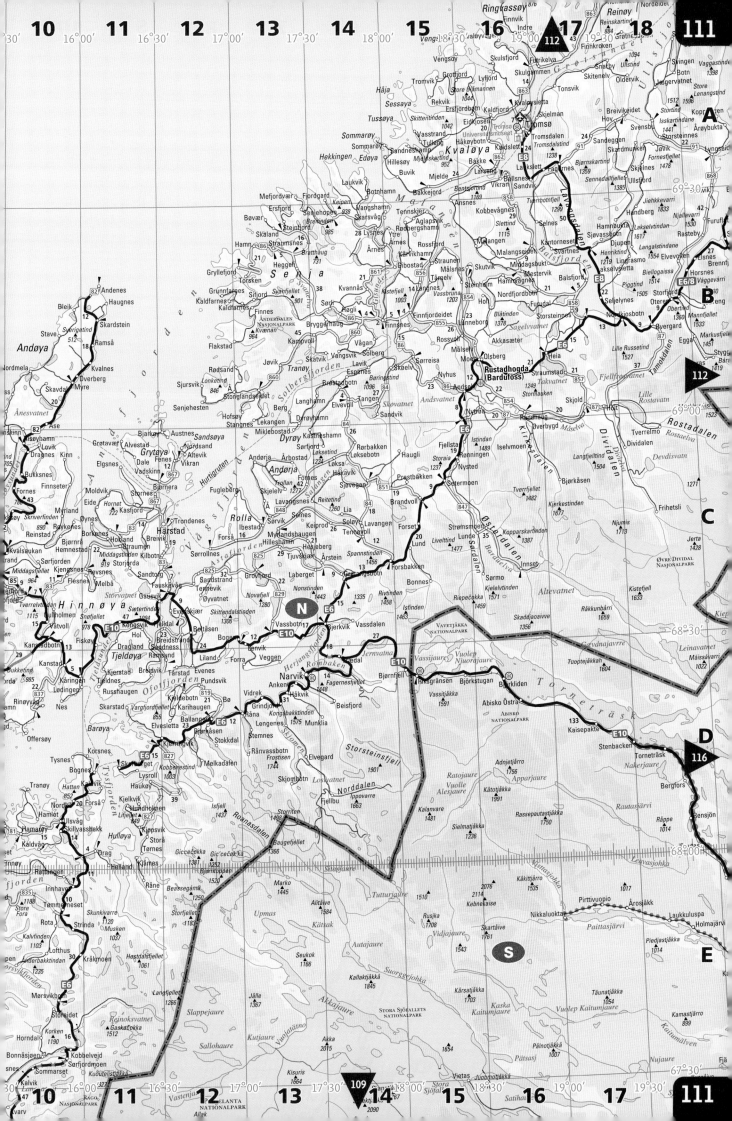

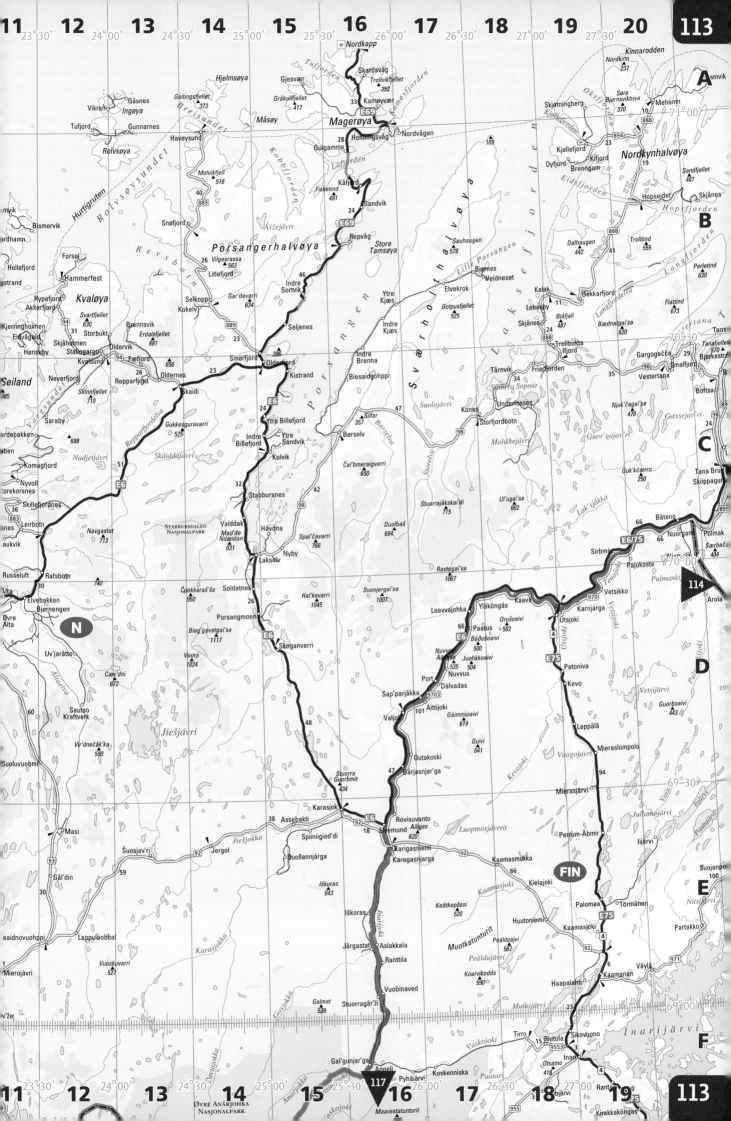

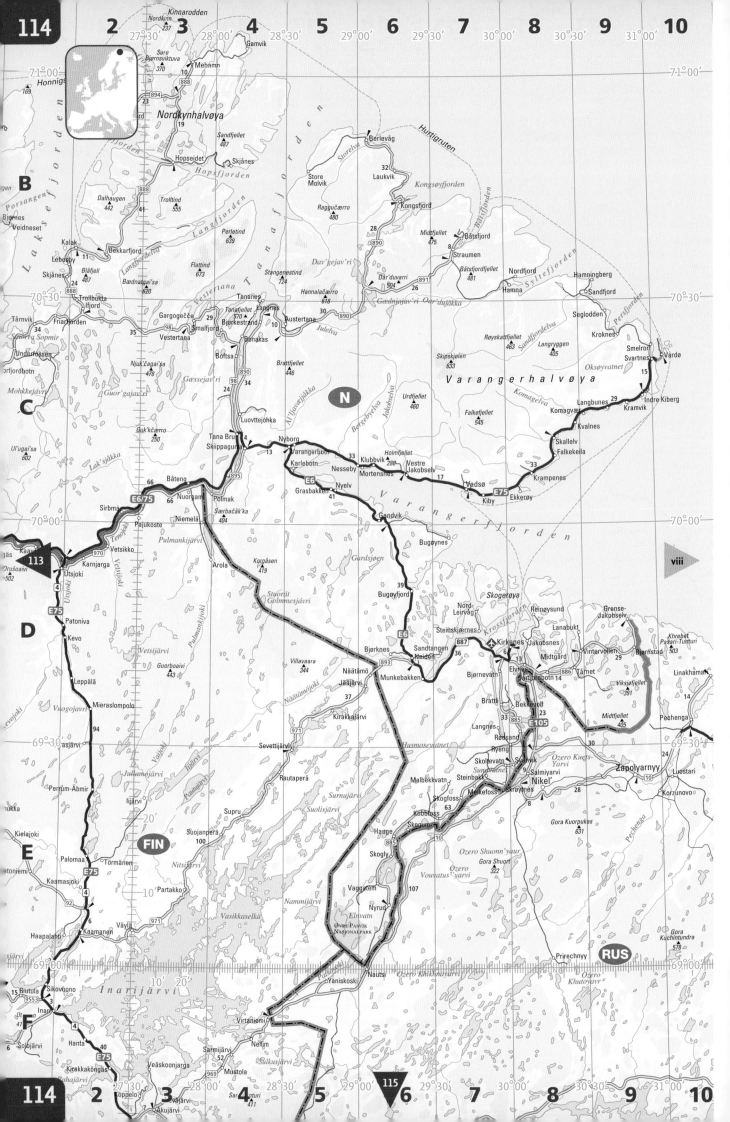

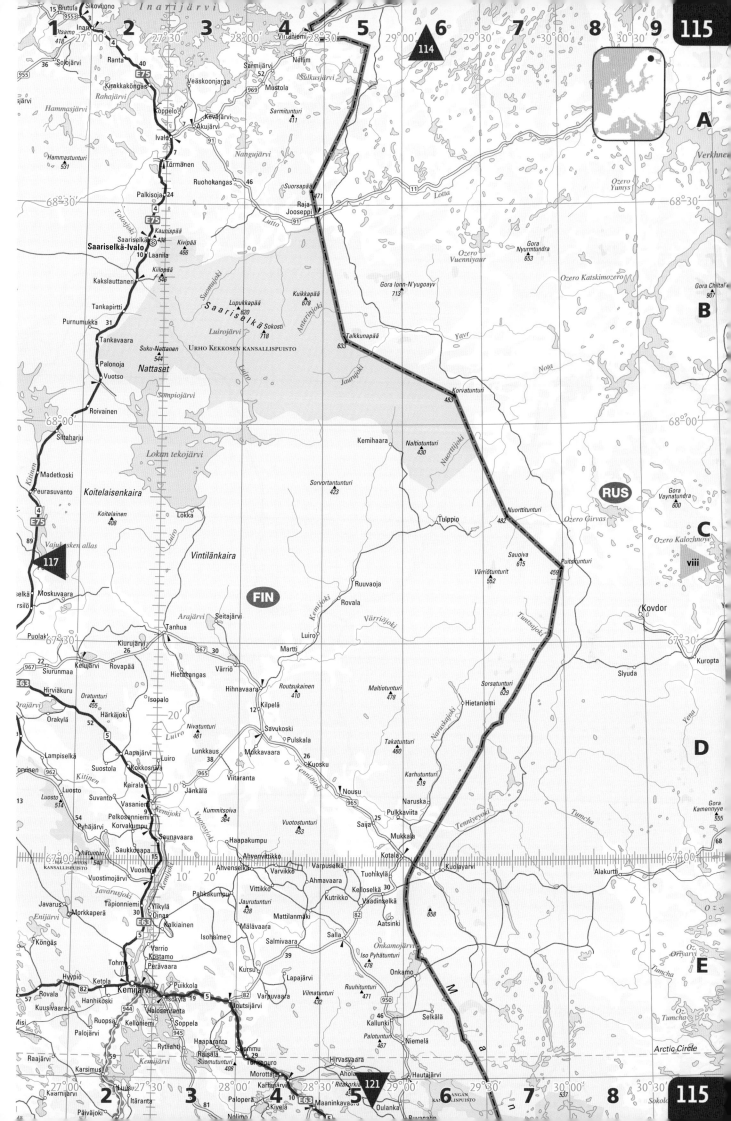

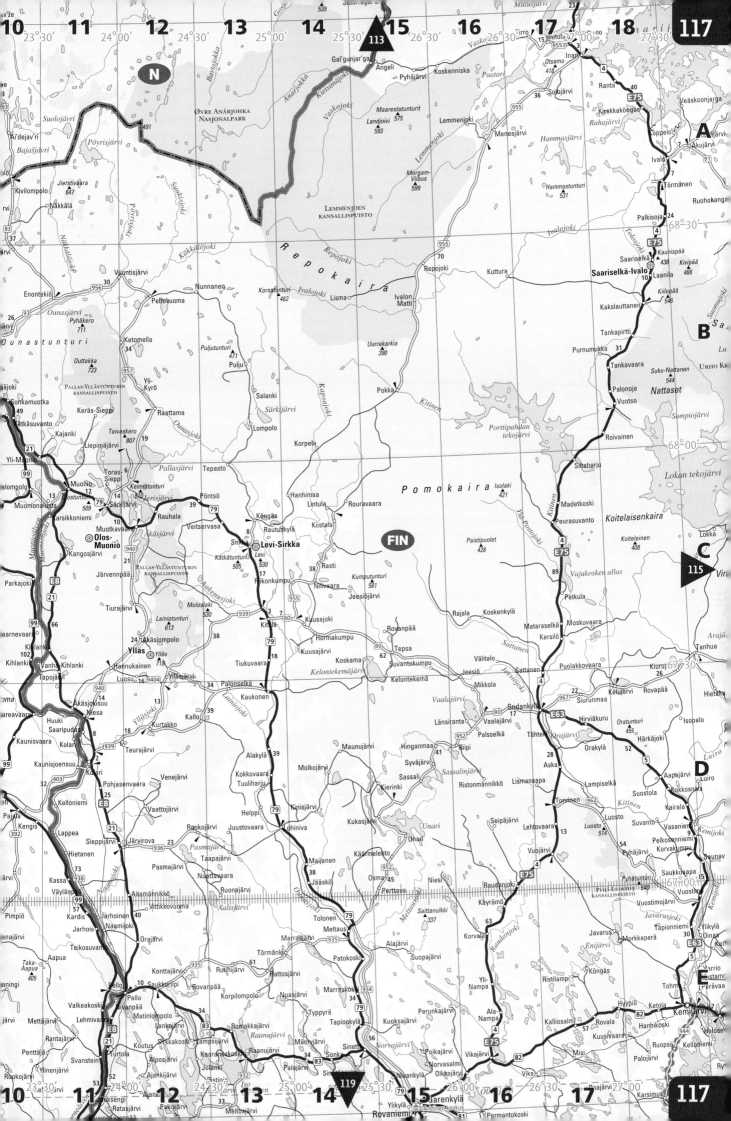

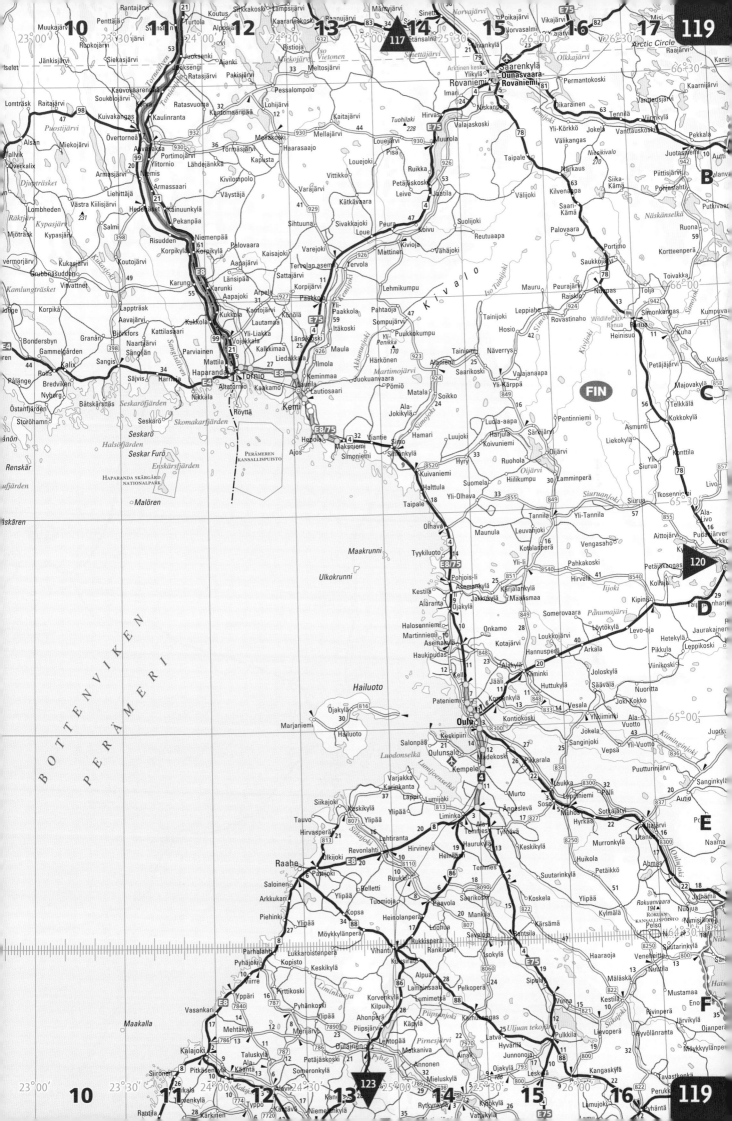

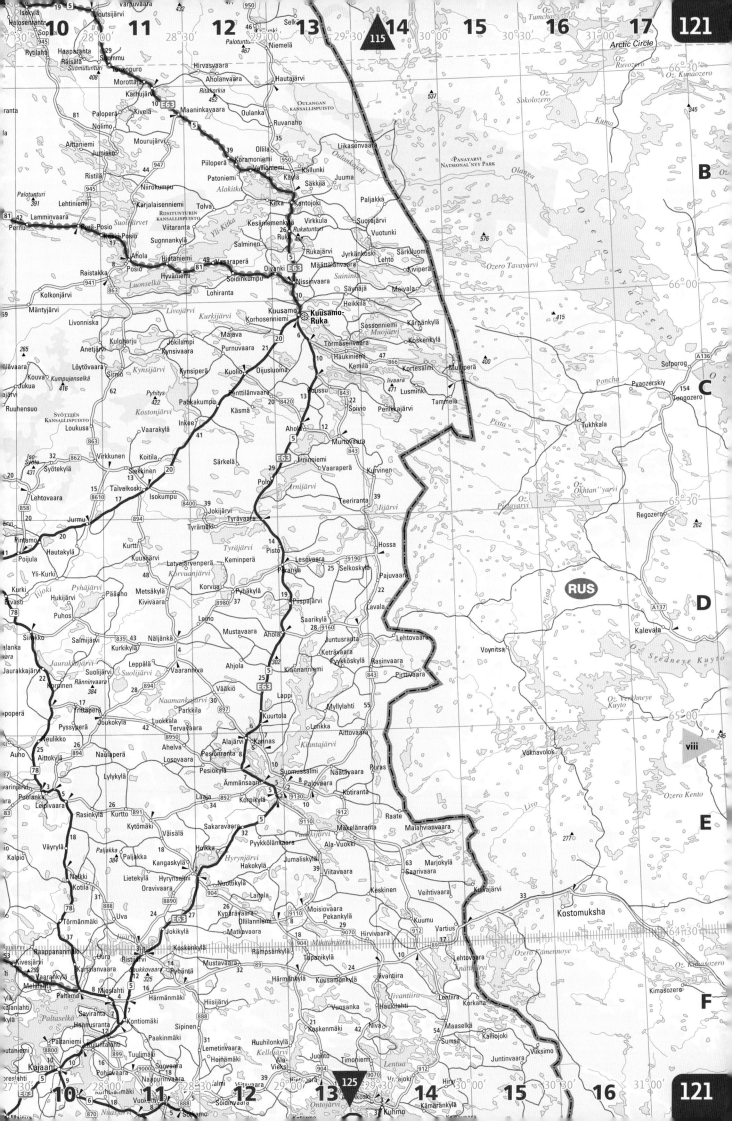

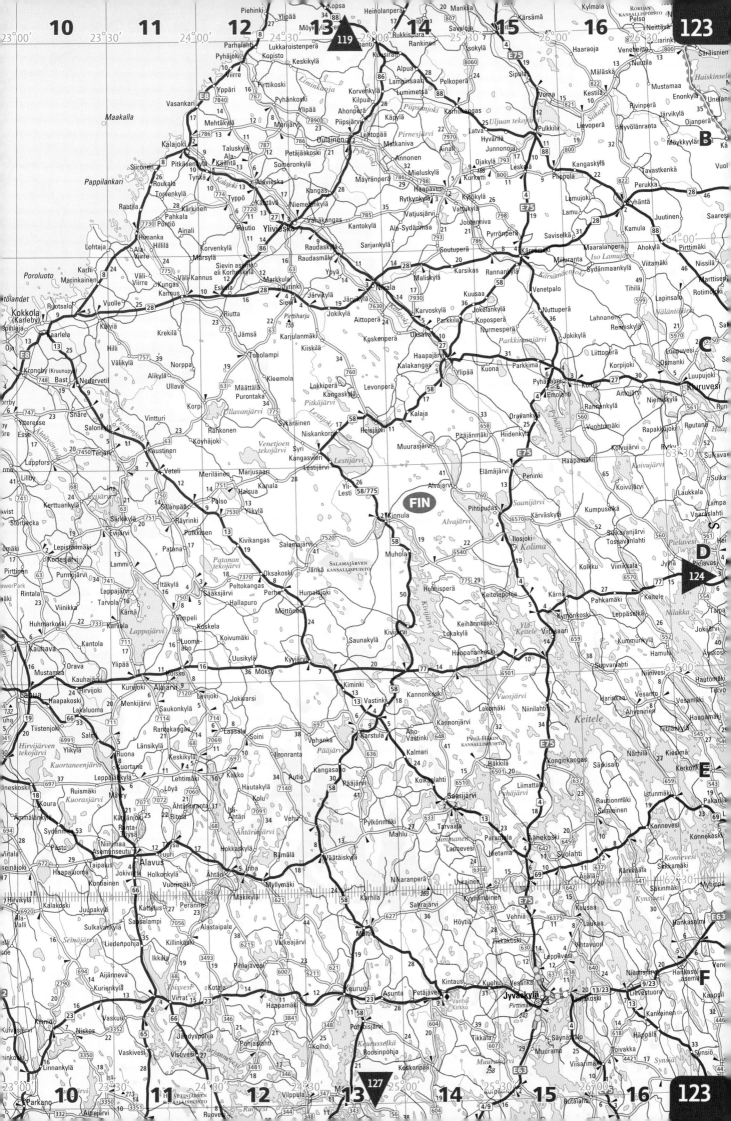

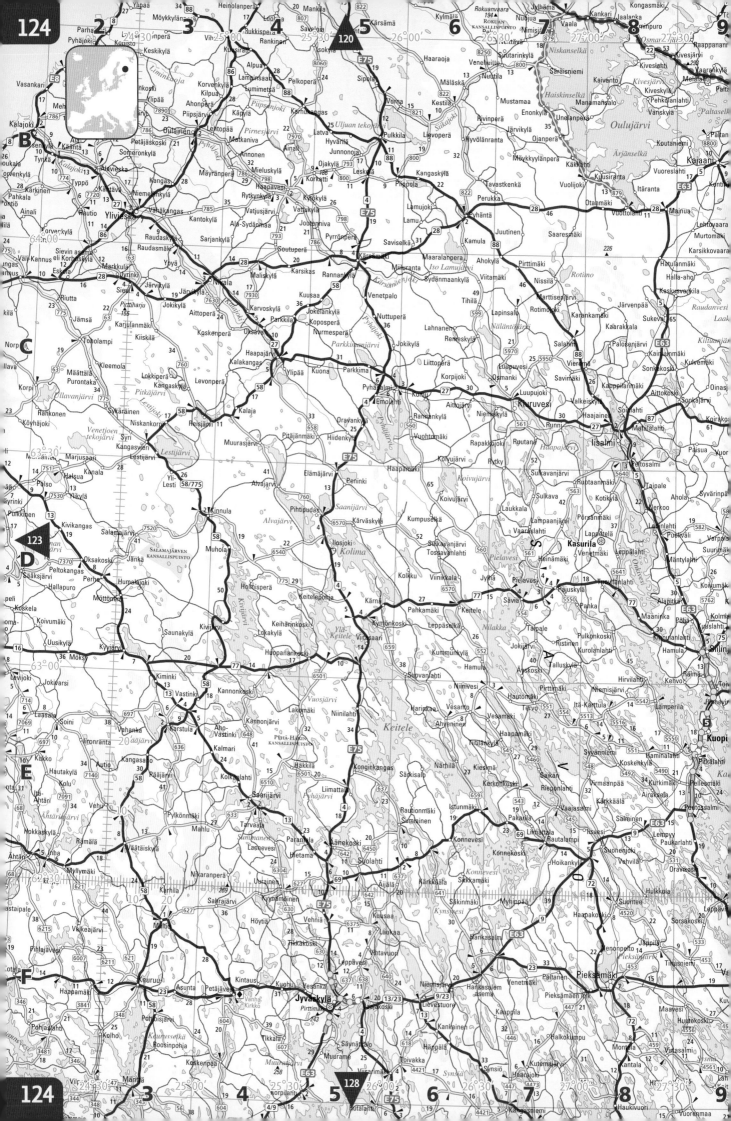

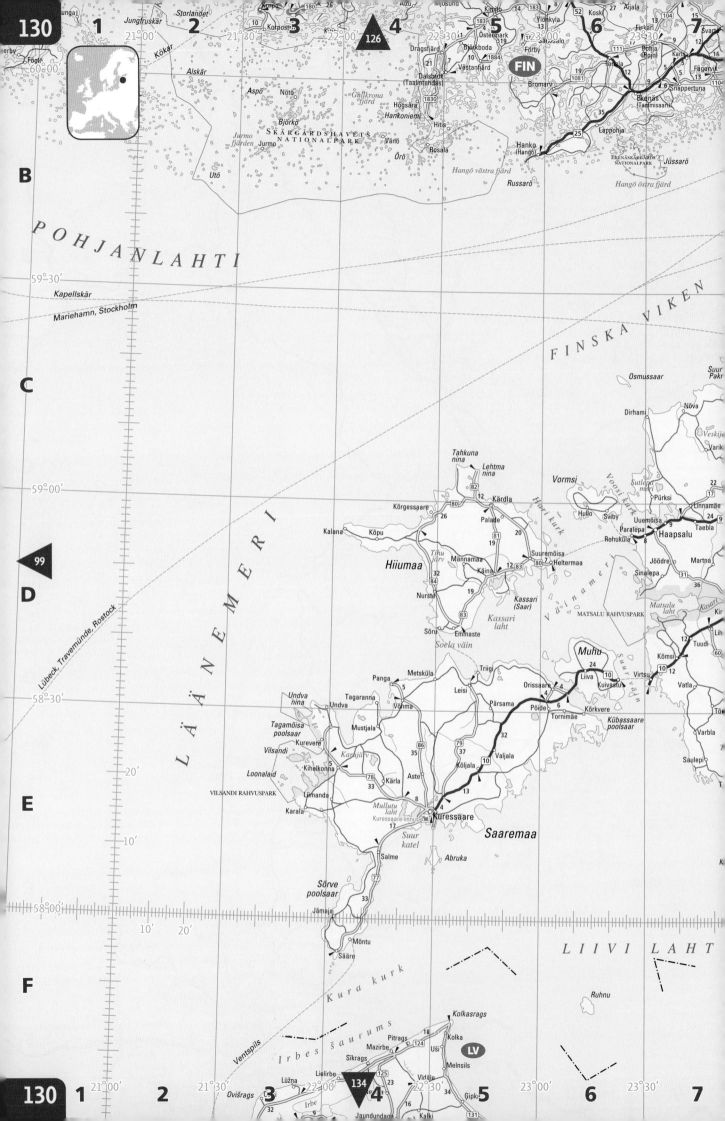

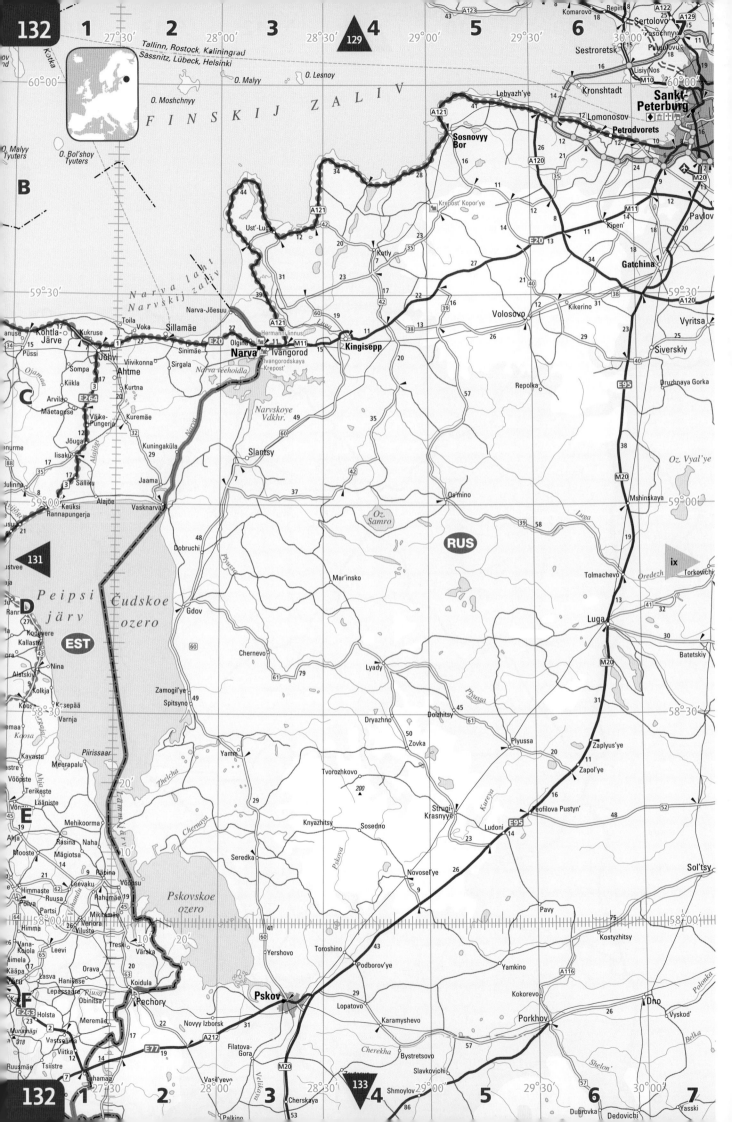

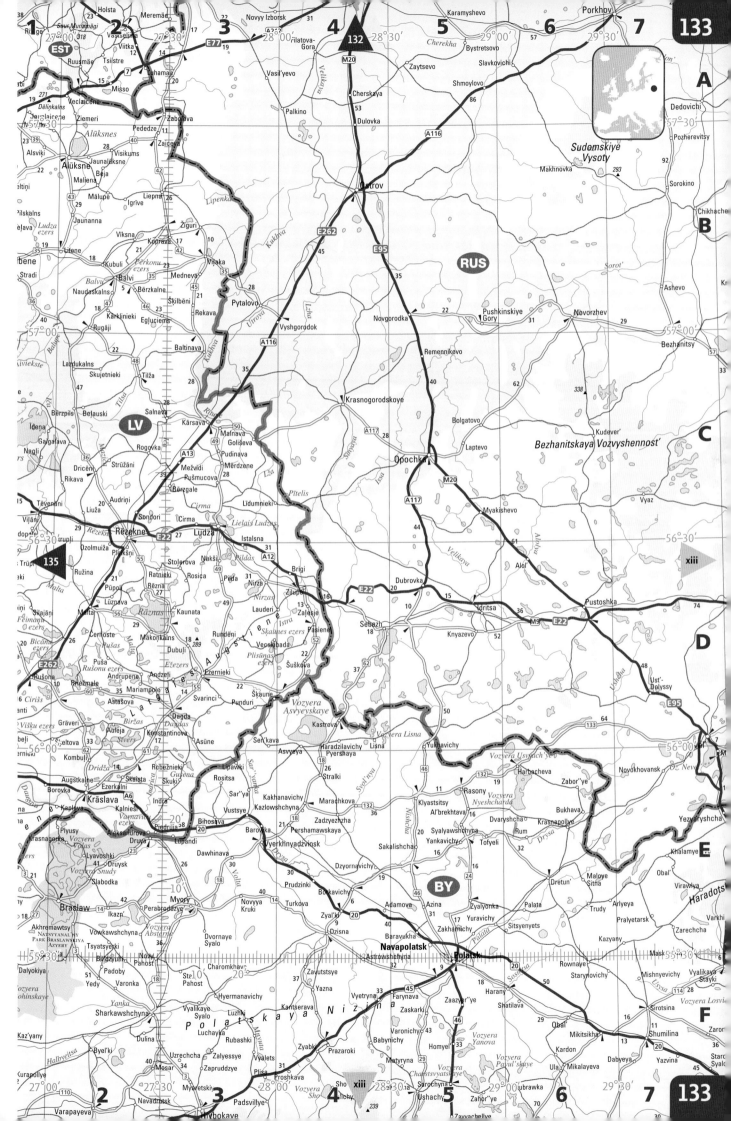

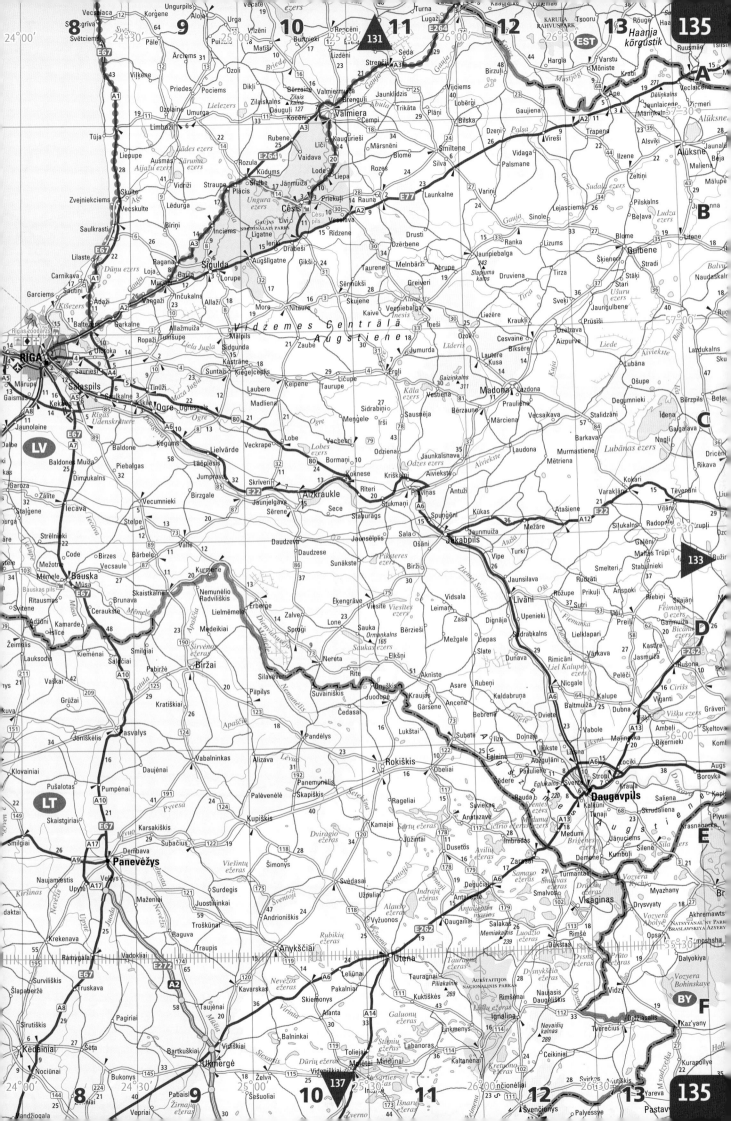

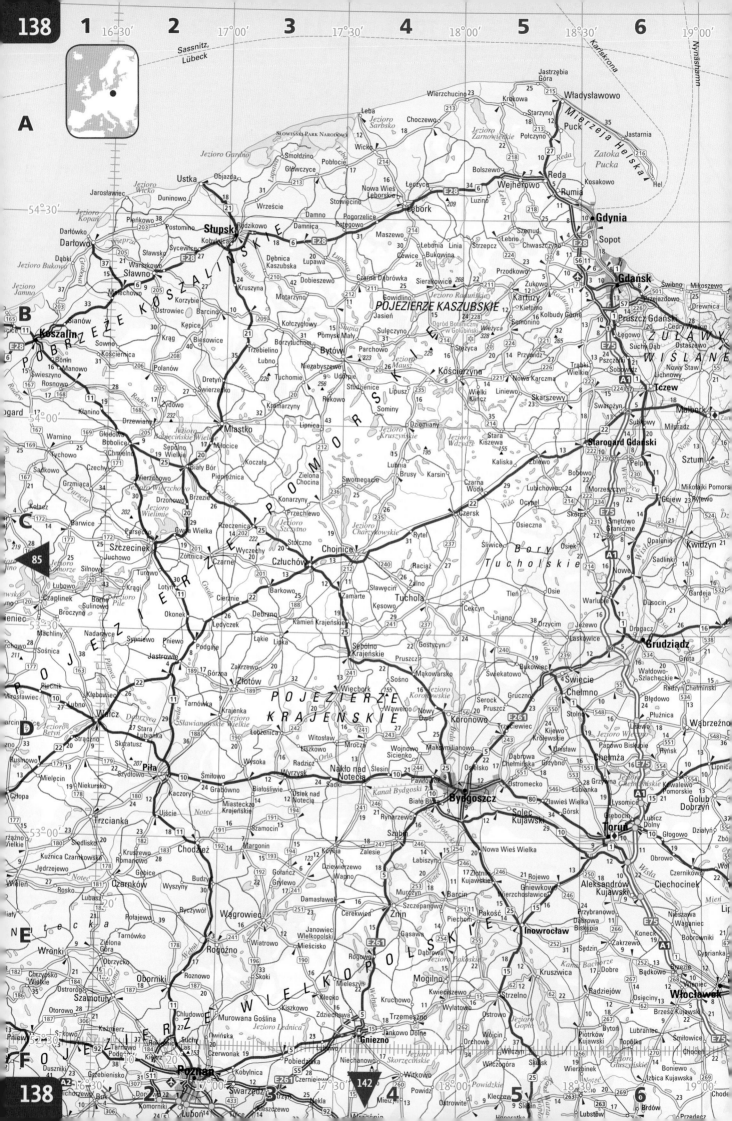

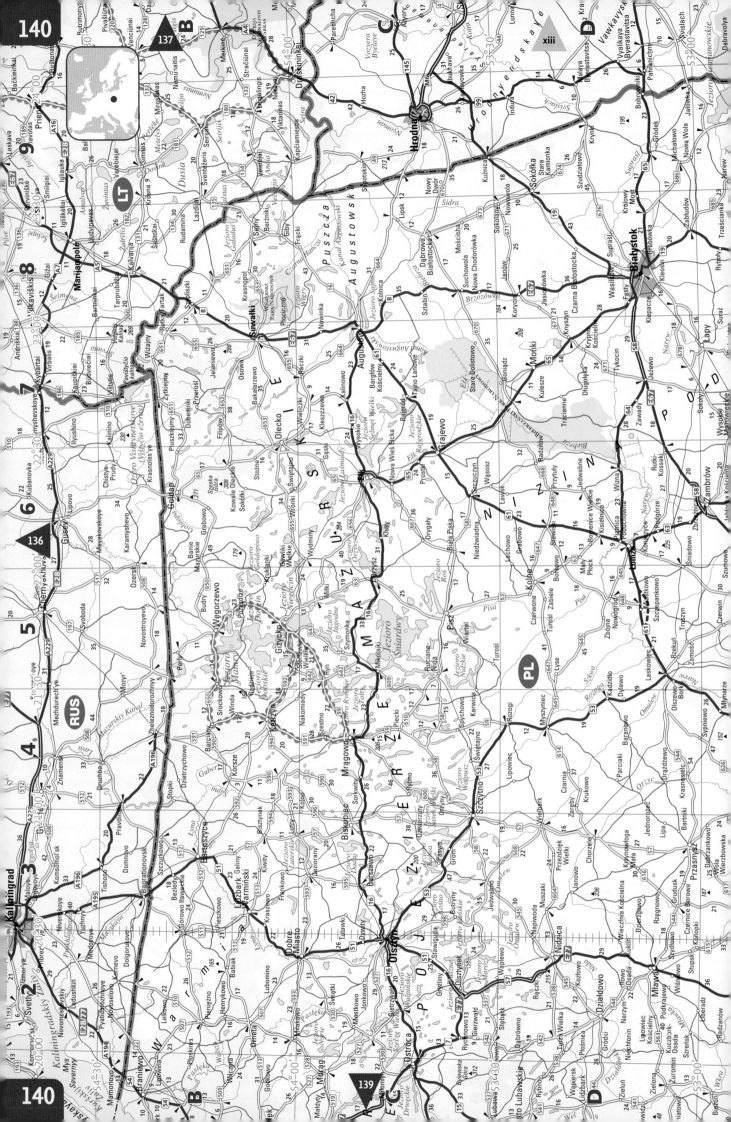

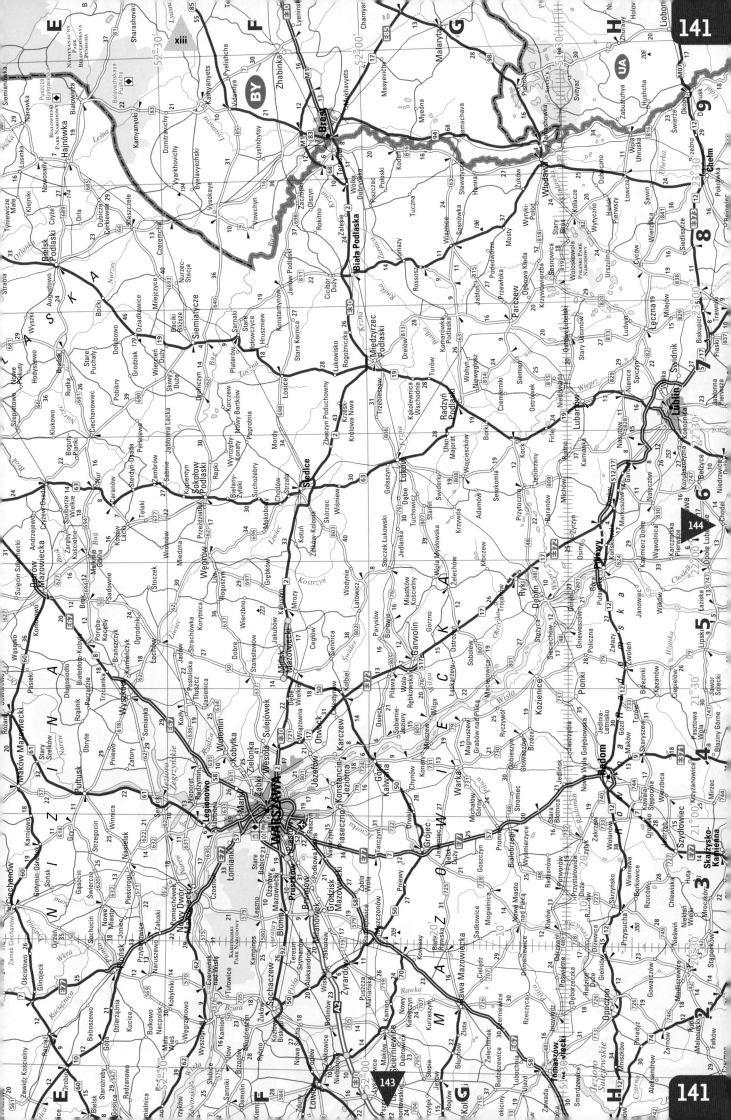

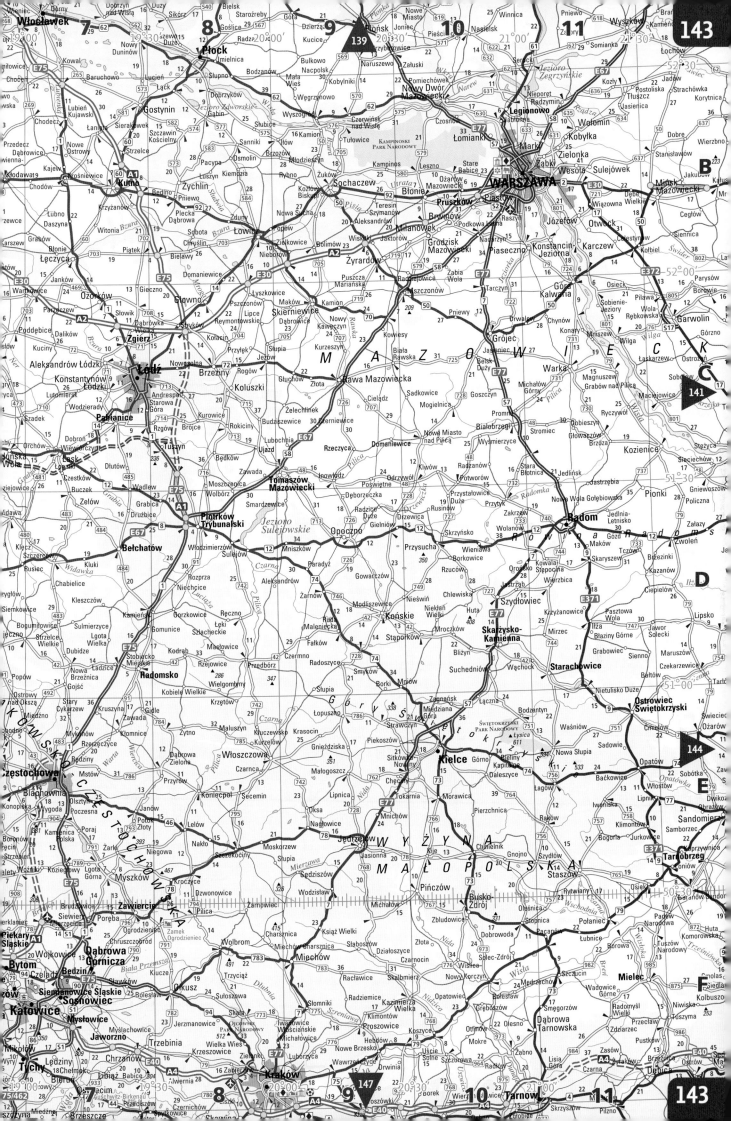

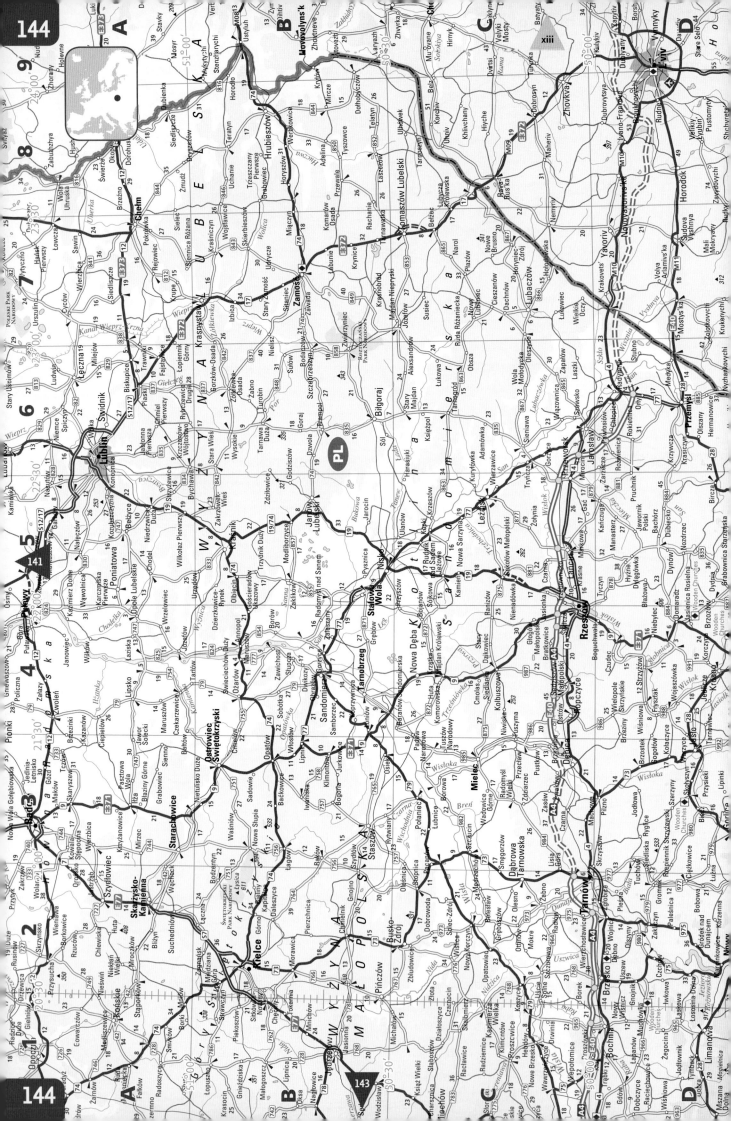

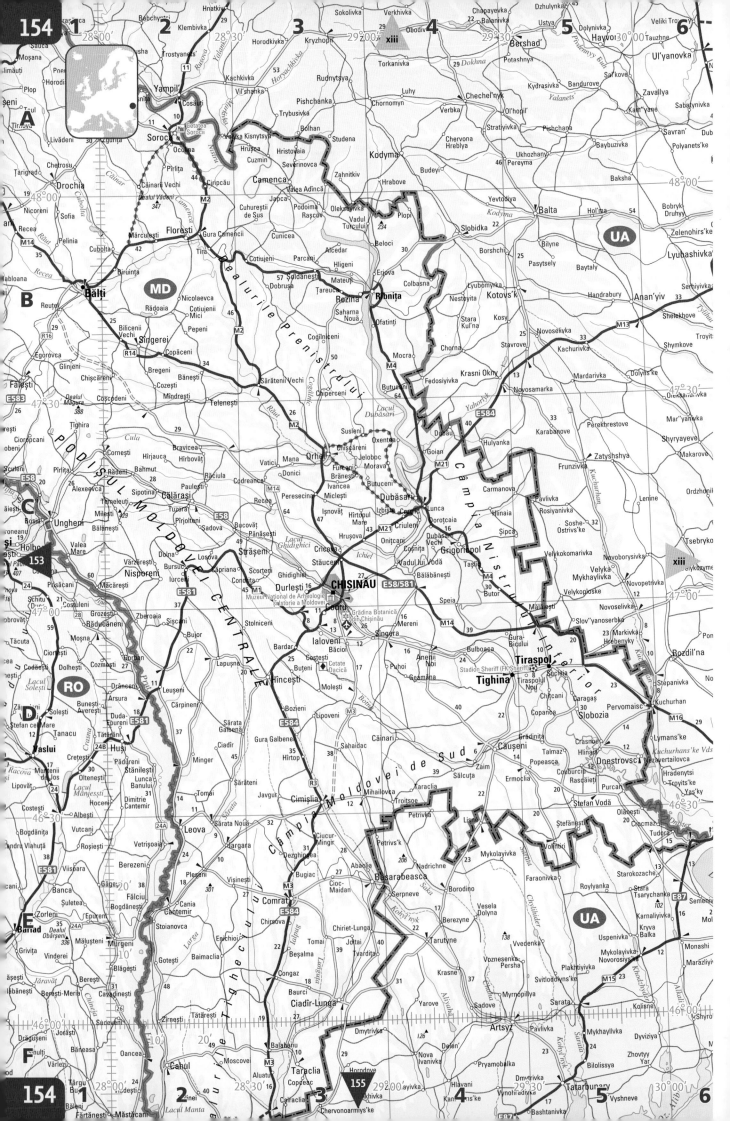

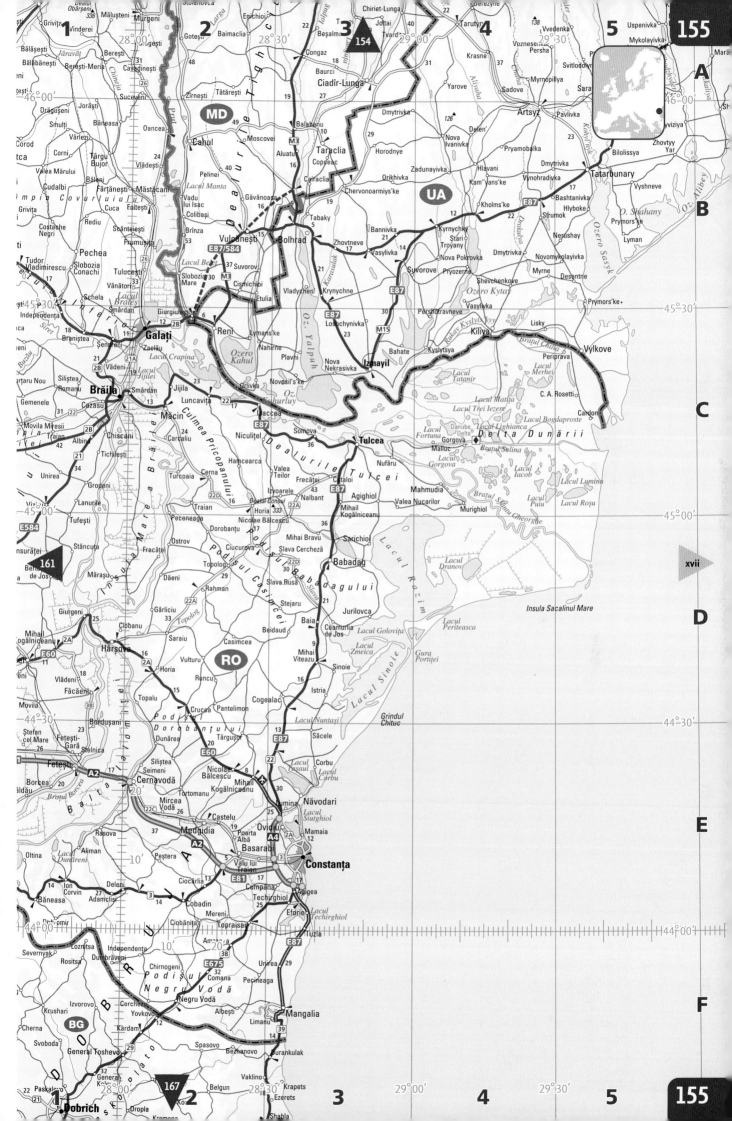

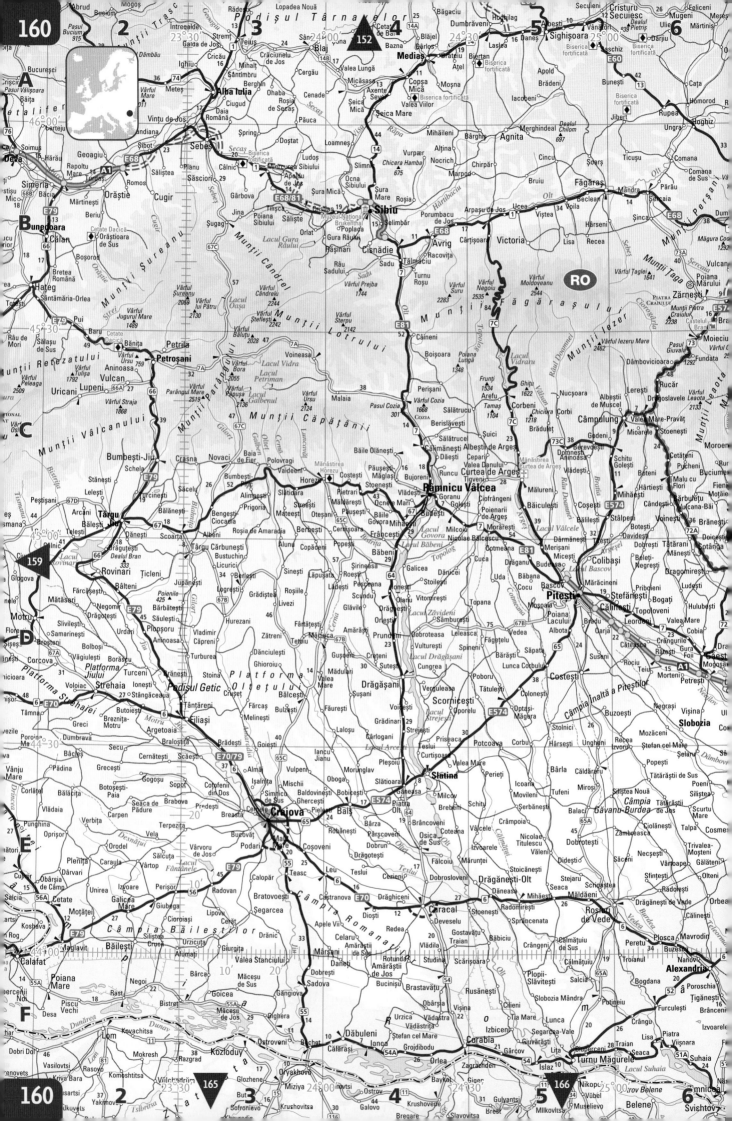

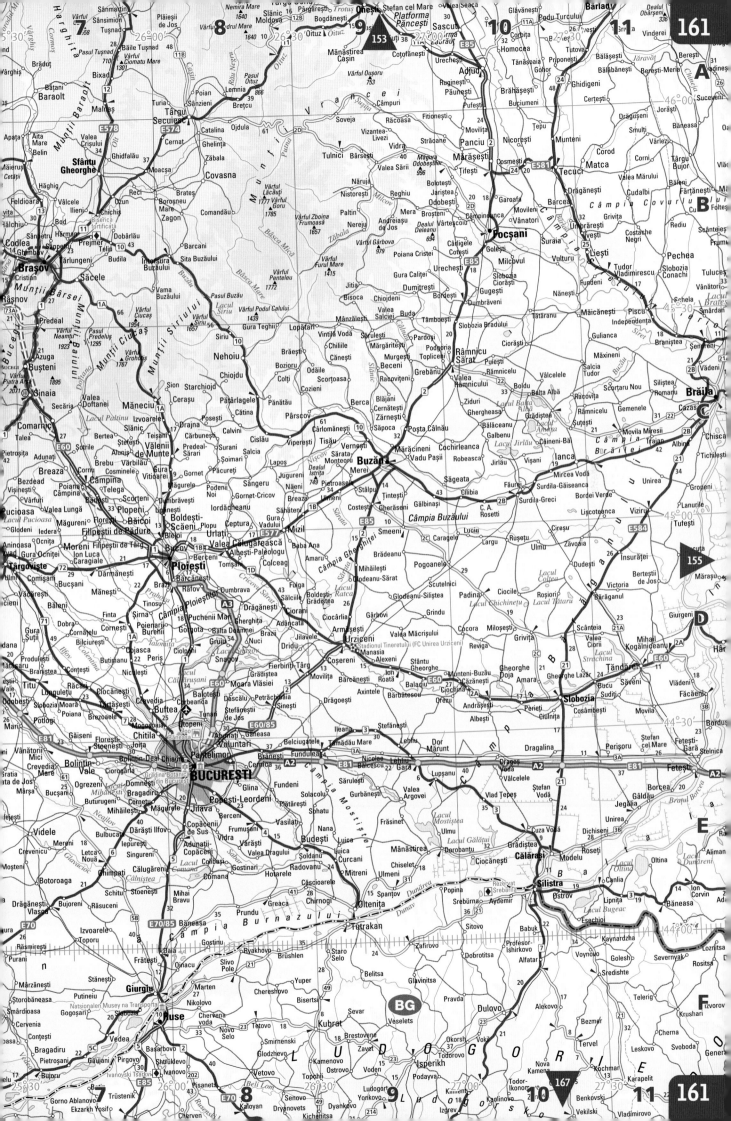

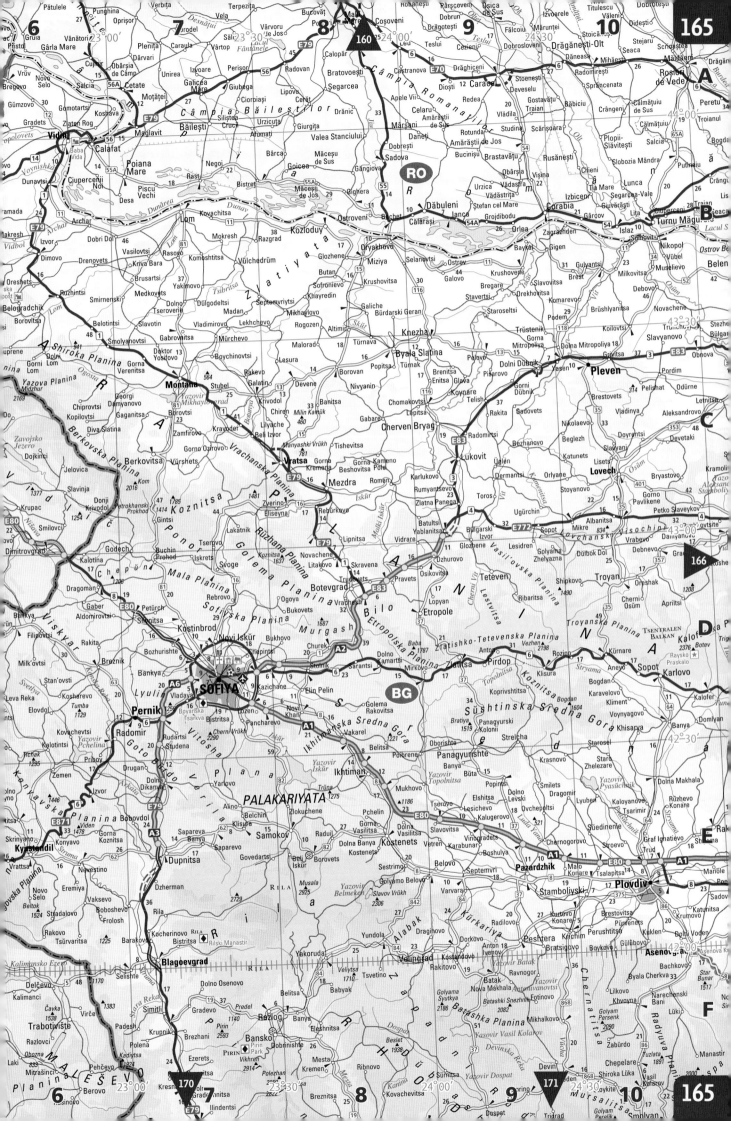

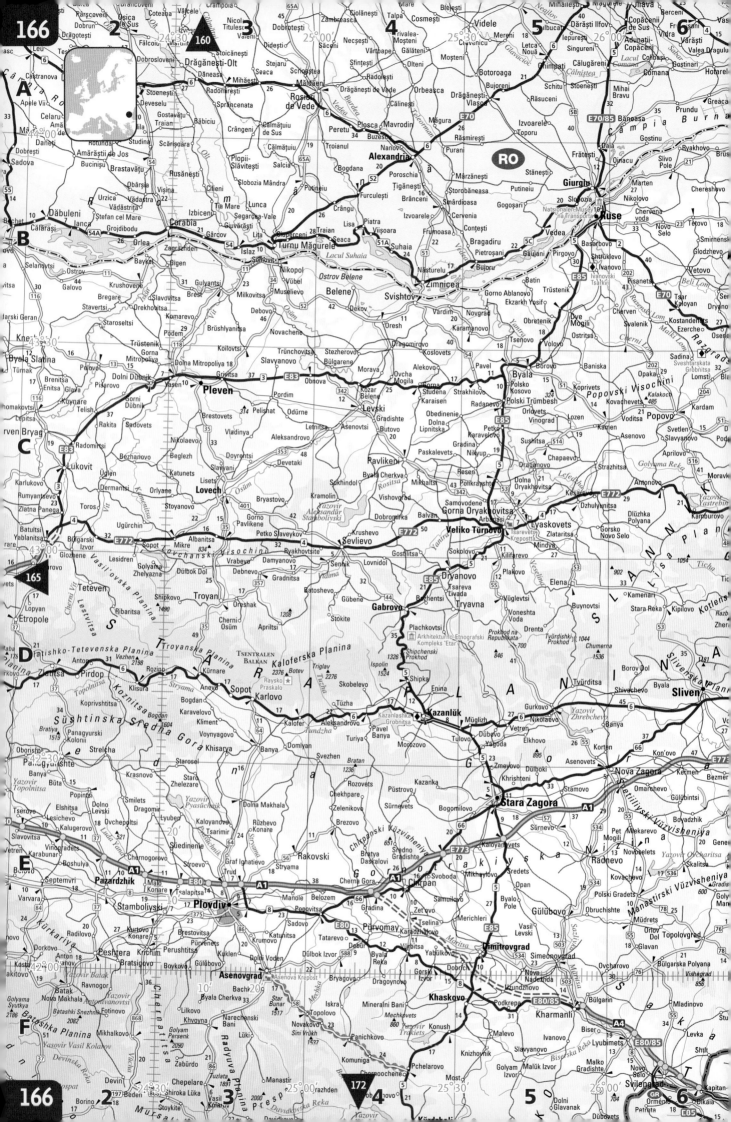

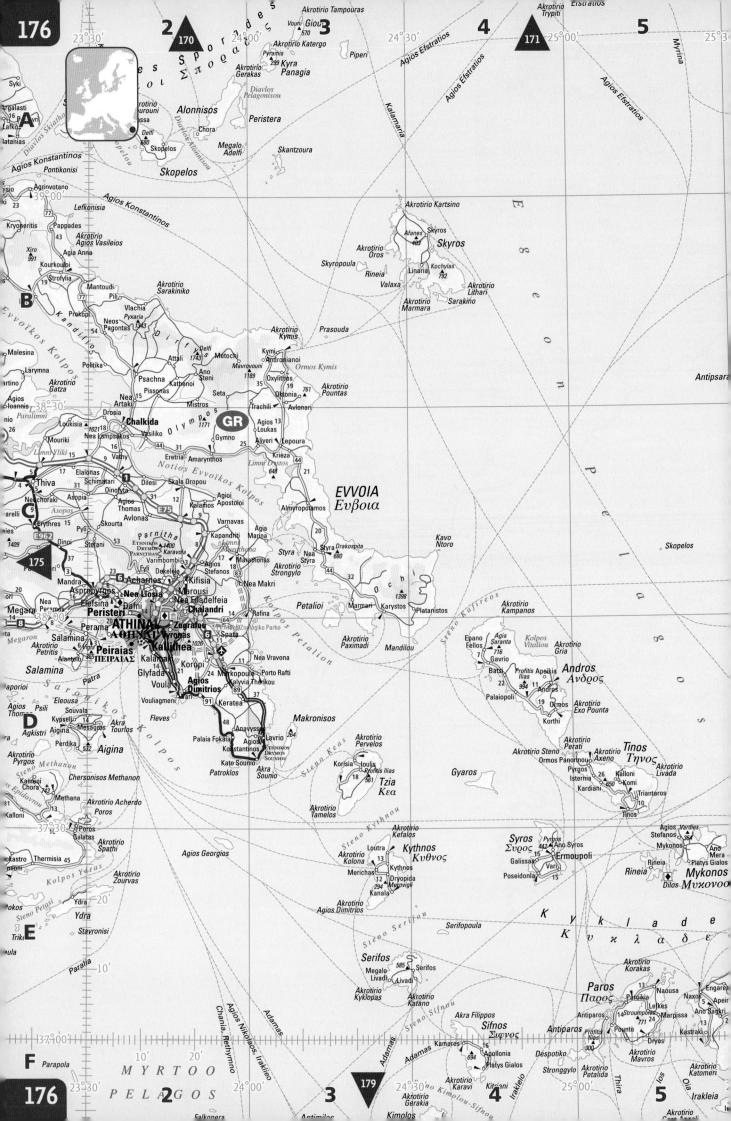

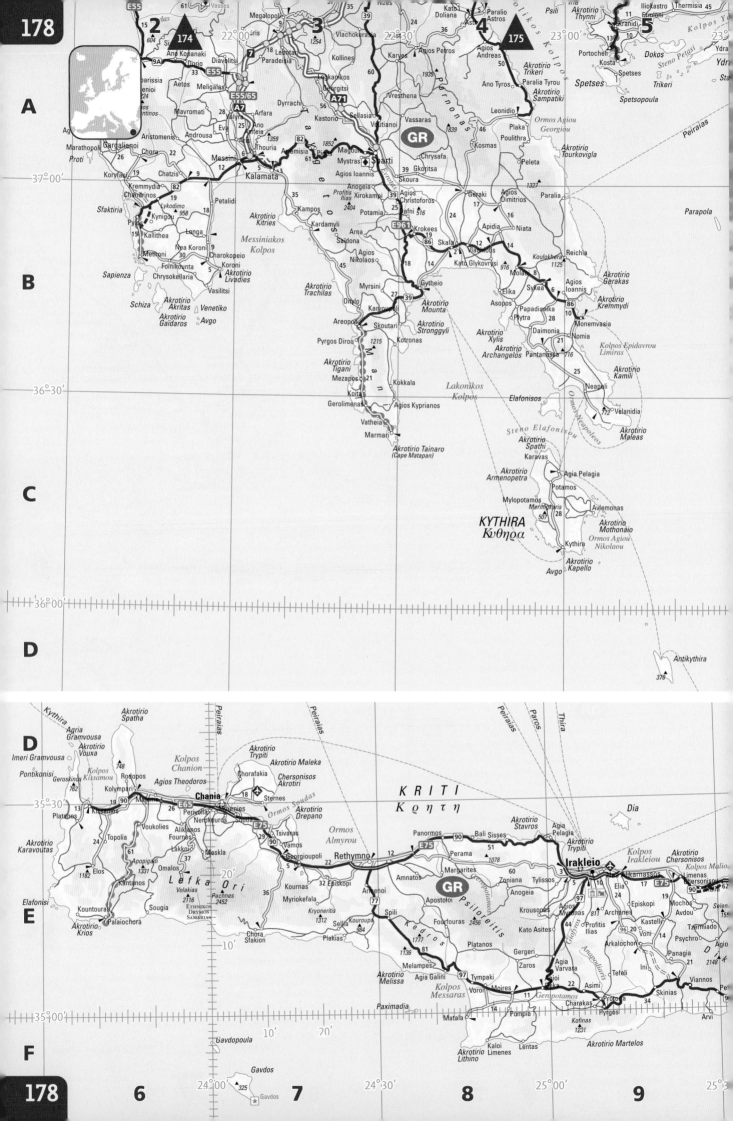

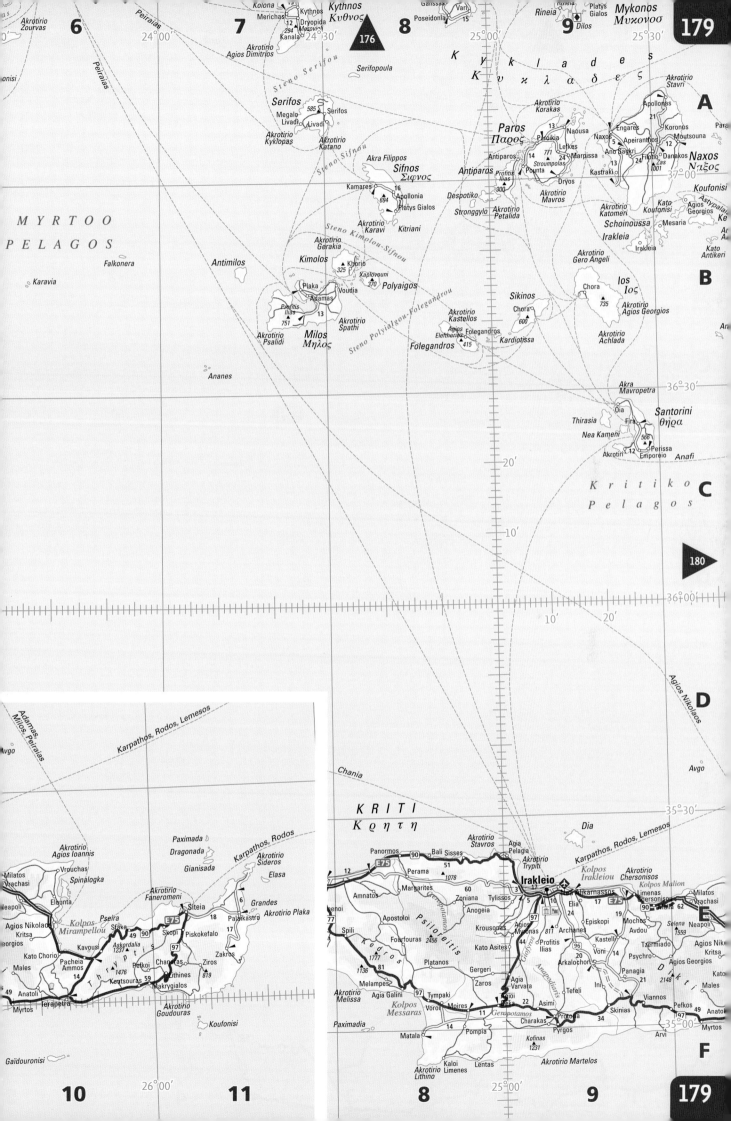

1 2 3 4 5

Istemia
Kardiani 650 Komi
Triantaros
25°00' Tinos 176 Tinos 25°30' Evdilos Raches Evdilos Fournoi Agios Samiopoula
Amalo 1037 Agios Minas
Peiraias 26°00' Ikaria Kirykos Thymaina 26°30' Megalos
Ikaria Ikaria Anthropofagos
Makronisi

Agios Vardies
Stefanos 364
Mykonos Ano Mera
Syros Platys Mykonos Tragonisi Petrokaravo Anydros Arkoi
noupoli Rineia Gialos Μυκονοσ Patmos Patmos
Rineia Dilos Patmos Patmos
Leipsoi

B

Serifopoula Akrotirio Stavri Archangelos
Akrotirio Apollonas Donousa Agia
Korakas 21 Agia Paraskevi
sfnou 13 Naousa Koronos
Paros Parikia Engares Moutsouna Kinaros Mavria Levitha
Paros Lefkes Naxos Apeiranthos 12
Antiparos Stroumpos 5 Ano Sagkri Danakos Naxos
Sifnos 14 Marpissa 13 24 Filoti 1001 Naxos Liadi
Sifnos Profitis 771 24 Zas Νάξος
Akra Filippos Ilias Pounta Kastraki Dryos
Apollonia 300 Dryos Koufonisi Akrotirio
Kamares 694 Akrotirio Akrotirio Keros Xodoto Chorafakia
Platys Gialos Mavros Katomeri Agios Keros Nikouria 821 Aigiali
Akrotirio Stronggylo Akrotirio Georgios Ano Akrotirio
Karavi Kitriani Petalida Schoinoussa Antikeri Katapola Xodoto
Kimolou-Sifnou Irakleia Kato Arkesini Amorgos
brio Akrotirio Antikeri 607 Amorgos
Xaplovouni Gero Angeli Irakleia Akrotirio
ia Polyaigos Koraxas

C Polyaigos
seno Polyiaglou-Folegandrou Sikinos Chora Ios Astypalaia
hi Chora Ios Akrotirio Akrotirio
Akrotirio 735 Flouda
Kastellos 600 Akrotirio Fokonisia Exo Vathy
Agios Agios Georgios GR Astypalaia
Eleftherios Folegandros Kardiotissa Anydros Ofidoussa Pontikoussa Vardia Astypalaia
Folegandros 415 Akrotirio 482 Koutsomytis
Achlada Kounoupoi
Akrotirio
Akra Echeili
Mavropetra Adelfoi
Thirasia Oia Santorini
Nea Kameni Fira θηρα Anafi Syrna
566 Akrotiri 484 Akrotirio
D 179 12 Perissa Anafi Kalamos Tria
Akrotiri Emporeio Nisia

K r i t i k o
P e l a g o s Pacheia Makra
Sofrana

36°00' Peiraias
Karavonisia

E 20'

Chamili
10' Divounia

Avgo

Chania 35°30' Dia 20'
10'

Akrotirio Agia KRITI
Stavros Pelagia Κρητη
normos Bali Sisses Akrotirio Akrotirio Paximada
E75 90 Trypiti Chersonisos Agios Ioannis Dragonada
Perama 51 Kolpos Akrotirio
Margarites 1078 Irakleio Irakleiou Limenas Gianisada Sideros
F 60 Irakleio Nikarnassos Chersonisos Milatos Elasa
Zoniana 3 17 Kolpos Malion Vrachasi
Psiloreitis Tylissos 5 10 Elia 17 E75 Malia 62 Vrouchas Akrotirio
Fourfouras Anogeia Agios 24 Mochos 90 Spinalonga Faneromeni
2456 Krousonas Myronas 811 Episkopi 19 Avdou Neapoli Elounta 18 Siteia
GR Kato Asites Archanes Selena Tsermiado Agius Nikolaos 49 90 Skopi
Gergeri 44 Profitis 96 Kastelli 1559 Kritsa Pseira Piskokefalo 17 Palaikastro
Platanos Ilias Voni 14 Psychro 2148 Agios Georgios Kolpos Sfaka Chamezi Akrotirio Plaka
Galini Zaros Arkalochori Dikti Kato Chorio Mirampellou Kavousi Askordalia Zakros Grandes
97 Agia Panagia 21 Males Pacheia 1237 1476 Ziros
Tympaki Varvara Tefeli Ini Viani 25°30' Ammos 819 Ziros
Moires Asimi Vianos Anatoli 97 59 Makrygialos
14 Pompia 1 11 Protoria 34 Skinias Pefkos 49 Koutsouras
Charakas Ierapetra 26°00'
Pyrgos 2

1 2 3 4 5

1 2 3 4 5

A

Aachen D 183 D8
Aalen D 187 D9
Aalsmeer NL 182 A5
Aalst B 182 D4
Aalst NL 183 B6
Aalten NL 183 B9
Aardenburg NL 182 C2
Aarle NL 183 C7
Aarschot B 182 D5
Aartrijke B 182 C2
Aartselaar B 182 C4
Abcoude NL 182 A5
Abreschviller F 186 D3
Abtsgmünd D 187 D8
Achel B 183 C6
Achern D 186 D5
Achstetten D 187 E8
Adegem B 182 C3
Adelmannsfelden D 187 D8
Adelsheim D 187 C7
Adenau D 185 D6
Aglasterhausen D 187 C6
Ahaus D 183 A10
Ahlen D 185 A8
Ahrbrück D 183 E9
Aichhalden D 187 E5
Aiglemont F 184 E2
Albergen NL 183 A9
Albertshofen D 187 B9
Albestroff F 186 D2
Albisheim (Pfrimm) D 186 B5
Alblasserdam NL 182 B5
Aldenhoven D 183 D8
Alf D 185 D7
Alfdorf D 187 D8
Alken D 183 D6
Allarmont F 186 E3
Allmendingen D 187 E8
Almelo D 183 A9
Almere NL 183 A6
Almkerk NL 182 B5
Alost B 182 D4
Alpen D 183 B9
Alpenrod D 185 C8
Alphen NL 182 C5
Alphen aan den Rijn NL 182 A5
Alpirsbach D 187 E5
Alsbach D 187 B6
Alsdorf D 183 D8
Alsenborn D 186 C4
Alsenz D 186 B4
Alsheim D 185 E9
Alsting F 186 C2
Altena D 185 B8
Altenahr D 183 D9
Altenbuch D 187 B7
Altendiez D 185 D8
Altenglan D 186 B3
Altenheim D 186 E4
Altenkirchen (Westerwald) D 185 C8
Altenstadt D 187 A6
Altensteig D 187 D6
Altheim (Alb) D 187 D9
Althengstett D 187 D6
Altleiningen D 186 B5
Altrich D 185 E6
Alzenau in Unterfranken D 187 A7
Alzey D 186 B5
Amay B 183 D6
Amberloup B 184 D4
Ameide NL 182 B5
Amel B 184 D5
Amerongen NL 183 B6
Amersfoort NL 183 A6
Ammerbuch D 187 D6
Ammerzoden NL 183 B6
Amnéville F 186 C1
Amorbach D 187 B7
Amstelveen NL 182 A5
Amsterdam NL 182 A5
Amstetten D 187 D8
Andelst NL 183 B7
Andenne B 183 E6
Anderlecht B 182 D4
Anderlues B 182 E4
Andernach D 185 D7
Andlau F 186 E3
Anhée B 184 D2
Annœullin F 182 D1
Annweiler am Trifels D 186 C4
Anröchte D 185 A9
Ans B 183 D7
Anseremme B 184 D2
Antoing B 182 D2
Antwerpen B 182 C4
Anvers B 182 C4
Anzegem B 182 D2
Apeldoorn NL 183 A7
Appenweier D 186 D4
Arcen NL 183 C8
Ardooie B 182 D2
Arendonk B 183 C6
Argenthal D 185 E8
Armentières F 182 D1
Armsheim D 185 E9
Arnemuiden NL 182 C3
Arnhem NL 183 B7
Arnsberg D 185 B9
Arnstein D 187 B8
Arracourt F 186 D2
Arry F 186 C1
Arzbach D 185 D8
Arzfeld D 185 D5
As B 183 C7
Asbach D 185 C7
Ascheberg D 185 A8
Asperen NL 183 B6
Assamstadt D 187 C8
Asse B 182 D4
Assenede B 182 C3
Asten NL 183 C7
Ath B 182 D3
Attendorn D 185 B8
Aub D 187 B9
Aubel B 183 D7
Aubenton F 184 E1
Auby F 182 E2
Aulnois-sur-Seille F 186 D1
Aura im Sinngrund D 187 A8
Auvelais B 182 E5
Auvillers-les-Forges F 184 E1
Avelgem B 182 D2
Avricourt F 186 D2

Awans B 183 D6
Axel NL 182 C3
Aywaille B 183 E7

B

Baarle-Hertog B 182 C5
Baarle-Nassau NL 182 C5
Baarn NL 183 A6
Babberich NL 183 B8
Babenhausen D 187 B6
Baccarat F 186 E2
Bacharach D 185 D8
Backnang D 187 D7
Bad Bentheim D 183 A10
Bad Bergzabern D 186 C4
Bad Berleburg D 185 B9
Bad Bertrich D 185 D7
Bad Breisig D 185 D7
Bad Camberg D 185 D9
Bad Dürkheim D 187 C5
Bad Ems D 185 D8
Baden-Baden D 186 D5
Bad Friedrichshall D 187 C7
Bad Herrenalb D 187 D6
Badhoevedorp NL 182 A5
Bad Homburg vor der Höhe D 187 A6
Bad Honnef D 185 C7
Bad Hönningen D 185 C7
Bad Kissingen D 187 A9
Bad König D 187 B7
Bad Kreuznach D 185 E8
Bad Laasphe D 185 C9
Bad Liebenzell D 187 D6
Bad Marienberg (Westerwald) D 185 C8
Bad Mergentheim D 187 C8
Bad Münstereifel D 183 D9
Bad Neuenahr-Ahrweiler D 183 D10
Badonviller F 186 E2
Bad Orb D 187 A7
Bad Peterstal D 187 E5
Bad Rappenau D 187 C7
Bad Sassendorf D 185 A9
Bad Schönborn D 187 C6
Bad Schwalbach D 185 D9
Bad Sobernheim D 185 E8
Bad Überkingen D 187 D8
Bad Urach D 187 E7
Bad Vilbel D 187 A6
Bad Wildbad im Schwarzwald D 187 D6
Bad Wimpfen D 187 C7
Baelen B 183 D7
Baesweiler D 183 D8
Baiersbronn D 187 D5
Baillonville B 184 D3
Bakel NL 183 C7
Balen B 183 C6
Balingen D 187 E7
Balve D 185 B8
Bammental D 187 C6
Barneveld NL 183 A7
Baronville F 186 D2
Barr F 186 E3
Bartenstein D 187 C8
Bartholomä D 187 D8
Barvaux B 184 D3
Basècles B 182 D3
Bassenge B 183 D7
Bastogne B 184 D4
Bathmen NL 183 A8
Battice B 183 D7
Baumholder D 186 B3
Bausendorf D 185 D6
Bavel NL 182 B5
Bayon F 186 E1
Beaumont B 184 D1
Beauraing B 184 D2
Becherbach D 186 B4
Bechhofen D 187 B5
Bechtheim D 187 B5
Beckingen D 186 C2
Beckum D 185 A9
Bedburg D 183 D9
Bedburg-Hau D 183 B8
Beek NL 183 B7
Beek NL 183 B7
Beekbergen NL 183 A7
Beerfelden D 187 B6
Beernem B 182 C2
Beers NL 183 B7
Beerse B 182 C5
Beersel B 182 D4
Beerst B 182 C1
Beesd NL 183 B6
Begijnendijk B 182 C5
Behren-lès-Forbach F 186 C2
Beilstein D 187 C7
Beimerstetten D 187 E8
Belfeld NL 183 C8
Bell D 185 D7
Bell (Hunsrück) D 185 D7
Bellenberg D 187 E9
Belles-Forêts F 186 D2
Bellheim D 187 C5
Belœil B 182 D3
Beltheim D 185 D7
Beltrum NL 183 B8
Bemmel NL 183 B7
Bendorf D 185 D8
Beneden-Leeuwen NL 183 B6
Bénestroff F 186 D2
Benfeld F 186 E4
Bennebroek NL 182 A5
Bennekom NL 183 A7
Bensheim D 187 B6
Bentelo NL 183 A9
Berchem B 182 D3
Berg D 183 D9
Berg L 184 E5
Berg NL 183 D7
Berg NL 183 D7
Berg (Pfalz) D 187 D5
Bergen op Zoom NL 182 C4
Bergeyk NL 183 C6
Bergharen NL 183 B7
Berghaupten D 186 E4
Bergheim (Erft) D 183 D9
Berghem NL 183 B7
Berghülen D 187 E8
Bergisch Gladbach D 183 D10
Bergkamen D 185 A8
Bergneustadt D 185 B8
Bergschenhoek NL 182 B5
Bergtheim D 187 B9
Beringe NL 183 C7
Beringen B 183 C6
Berkel NL 182 B4

Berkel-Enschot NL 183 B6
Berlicum NL 183 B6
Bernissart B 182 E3
Bernkastel-Kues D 185 E7
Bernstadt D 187 D9
Bertogne B 184 D4
Bertrange L 186 B1
Bertrichamps F 186 E2
Bertrix B 184 E3
Beselich-Obertiefenbach D 185 D9
Besigheim D 187 D7
Bessenbach D 187 B7
Best NL 183 B6
Bestwig D 185 B9
Betschdorf F 186 D4
Bettelainville F 186 C1
Bettembourg L 186 B1
Bettendorf L 184 E5
Bettingen D 185 E5
Betzdorf D 185 C8
Betzdorf L 186 B1
Beuningen NL 183 B7
Beuvrages F 182 E2
Beveren B 182 C4
Beverlo B 183 C6
Bexbach D 186 C3
Biberach D 186 E5
Biblis D 187 B5
Bieber D 187 A7
Biebesheim am Rhein D 187 B5
Bietigheim D 187 D5
Bietigheim-Bissingen D 187 D7
Bièvre B 184 E3
Billigheim D 187 C7
Bilthoven NL 183 A6
Bilzen B 183 D7
Binche B 182 E4
Bingen am Rhein D 185 E8
Bingerden NL 183 B8
Birkenau D 187 B6
Birkenfeld D 186 B3
Birkenfeld D 187 B8
Birkenfeld D 187 D6
Birken-Honigsessen D 185 C8
Birresborn D 185 D6
Bischbrunn D 187 B7
Bischheim F 186 D4
Bischoffsheim F 186 E3
Bischofsheim D 185 E9
Bischwiller F 186 D4
Bisingen D 187 E6
Bissen L 184 E5
Bitburg D 185 E6
Bitche F 186 C3
Bladel NL 183 C6
Blainville-sur-l'Eau F 186 D1
Blâmont F 186 D2
Blankenberge B 182 C2
Blankenheim D 183 E9
Blankenrath D 185 D7
Blaricum NL 183 A6
Blaton B 182 D3
Blaubeuren D 187 E8
Blaufelden D 187 C8
Blaustein D 187 E8
Blegny B 183 D7
Bléharies B 182 D2
Bleialf D 185 D5
Bleidenstadt D 185 D9
Bleiswijk NL 182 A5
Blerick NL 183 C8
Bleskensgraaf NL 182 B5
Blieskastel D 186 C3
Bobenheim-Roxheim D 187 B5
Böblingen D 187 D7
Bocholt B 183 C7
Bocholt D 183 B9
Bochum D 185 B7
Bockenheim an der Weinstraße D 187 B5
Bodegraven NL 182 A5
Bodelshausen D 187 E6
Bodenheim D 185 E9
Boechout B 182 C4
Boekel NL 183 C7
Boekhoute B 182 C3
Bogny-sur-Meuse F 184 E2
Böhl D 187 C5
Bolanden D 186 B5
Bolnes NL 182 B5
Bomal B 184 D4
Bondorf D 187 D6
Bondues F 182 D2
Bönen D 185 A8
Bonheiden B 182 C5
Bonn D 183 D10
Bönnigheim D 187 C7
Boom B 182 C4
Boortmeerbeek B 182 D5
Boppard D 185 D8
Borculo NL 183 A9
Borg D 186 B1
Borgloon B 183 D6
Borken NL 183 C7
Born NL 183 C7
Borne NL 183 A9
Bornem B 182 C4
Bornerbroek NL 183 A9
Bornheim D 183 D9
Bornhofen D 185 D8
Bornich D 185 D8
Borssele NL 182 C3
Boskoop NL 182 A5
Bottrop D 185 B7
Bouillon B 184 E3
Boulay-Moselle F 186 C1
Bourdonnay F 186 D2
Bourscheid L 184 E5
Bousse F 186 C1
Boussu B 182 E3
Boutersem B 182 D5
Bouxières-aux-Dames F 186 D1
Bouxwiller F 186 D3
Bouzonville F 186 C2
Bovigny B 184 D4
Boxberg D 187 C8
Boxmeer NL 183 B7
Boxtel NL 183 B6
Brachbach D 185 C8
Brackenheim D 187 C7
Braine-l'Alleud B 182 D4
Braine-le-Comte B 182 D4
Braives B 183 D6
Brakel D 187 B7
Brasschaat B 182 C4
Braubach D 185 D8
Braunlage D 185 E6
Braunsbach D 187 C8
Brecht B 182 C5
Breckerfeld D 185 B7

Breda NL 182 B5
Bredene B 182 C1
Bredevoort NL 183 B9
Bree B 183 C7
Breidenbach D 185 C9
Breitenbach D 186 C3
Breitscheid D 185 C9
Breitscheid D 185 C7
Breitscheid D 185 D7
Bremm D 185 D7
Brensbach D 187 B6
Breskens NL 182 C3
Bretten D 187 D6
Bretzenheim D 185 E8
Bretzfeld D 187 C7
Breuberg-Neustadt D 187 B7
Breugel NL 183 B7
Breukelen NL 183 A6
Briedel D 185 D7
Brielle NL 182 B4
Brin-sur-Seille F 186 D1
Broekhuizenvorst NL 183 C8
Brohl D 185 D7
Brouvelieures F 186 E2
Brouwershaven NL 182 B3
Bruchköbel D 187 A6
Bruchmühlbach D 186 C3
Bruchsal D 187 C6
Bruchweiler-Bärenbach D 186 C4
Brüggen D 186 B3
Brücken (Pfalz) D 186 C3
Brugelette B 182 D3
Bruges B 182 C2
Brugge B 182 C2
Brüggen D 183 C8
Brühl D 183 D9
Brühl D 187 C6
Bruinisse NL 182 B4
Brûly B 184 E2
Brumath F 186 D4
Brummen NL 183 A8
Brunehamel F 184 E1
Brunssum NL 183 D7
Brussel B 182 D4
Brussels B 182 D4
Bruttig-Fankel D 185 D7
Bruxelles B 182 D4
Büchel D 185 D7
Buchen (Odenwald) D 187 B7
Büchenbeuren D 185 E7
Buchholz (Westerwald) D 185 C7
Budel NL 183 C7
Budenheim D 185 D9
Büdesheim D 187 A6
Buer D 183 B10
Buggenhout B 182 C4
Bühl D 186 D5
Bühlertal D 187 D5
Bühlertann D 187 C8
Bühlerzell D 187 C8
Bullay D 185 D7
Büllingen B 184 D5
Bundenbach D 185 E7
Bunschoten-Spakenburg NL 183 A6
Burbach D 185 C9
Burdinne B 183 D6
Buren NL 183 B6
Burgbrohl D 185 D7
Burgh-Haamstede NL 182 B3
Burgsinn D 187 A8
Bürgstadt D 187 B7
Burladingen D 187 E7
Bürstadt D 187 B5
Bussum NL 183 A6
Bütgenbach B 184 D5
Büttelborn D 187 B6
Bütthard D 187 B8
Buurse NL 183 A9

C

Calw D 187 D6
Capelle aan de IJssel NL 182 B5
Carling F 186 C2
Carlsberg D 186 C5
Carvin F 182 E1
Castrop-Rauxel D 185 A7
Cattenom F 186 C1
Ceintrey F 186 E1
Celles B 182 D2
Cerfontaine B 184 D1
Chaam NL 182 C5
Chaligny F 186 E1
Champagney F 186 D1
Champigneulles F 186 D1
Chapelle-lez-Herlaimont B 182 E4
Charleroi B 182 E4
Charmes F 186 E1
Chastre B 182 D5
Château-Salins F 186 D2
Châtelet B 184 D2
Châtel-sur-Moselle F 186 E1
Châtenois F 186 E3
Chaudfontaine B 183 D7
Chavelot F 186 E1
Chièvres B 182 D3
Chimay B 184 D1
Chooz F 184 D2
Ciney B 184 D3
Cirey-sur-Vezouze F 186 D2
Clavier B 183 E6
Clervaux L 184 D5
Clinge NL 182 C4
Cochem D 185 D7
Coesfeld D 183 B10
Colijnsplaat NL 182 B3
Colroy-la-Grande F 186 E3
Comblain-au-Pont B 183 E7
Comines B 182 D1
Condé-sur-l'Escaut F 182 E3
Consdorf L 186 B1
Contwig D 186 C3
Cothen NL 183 A6
Courcelles B 182 E4
Courcelles-Chaussy F 186 C1
Courcelles-sur-Nied F 186 C1
Courrières F 182 E1
Courtrai B 182 D2
Court-St-Etienne B 182 D5
Couvin B 184 D2
Crailsheim D 187 C9
Creglingen D 187 C9
Créhange F 186 C2
Creutzwald F 186 C2
Crévéchamps F 186 E1
Cuijk NL 183 B7
Culemborg NL 183 B6
Custines F 186 D1
Cysoing F 182 D2

D

Daaden D 185 C8
Dabo F 186 D3
Dahlem D 185 D6
Dahlhausen D 183 C10
Dahn D 186 C4
Daknam B 182 C3
Daleiden D 184 D5
Dalhem B 183 D7
Dalstein F 186 C1
Damas-aux-Bois F 186 E1
Dambach-la-Ville F 186 E3
Damelevières F 186 D1
Damme B 182 C2
Darmstadt D 187 B6
Datteln D 185 A7
Daun D 185 D6
De Bilt NL 183 A6
Deerlijk B 182 D2
Deggingen D 187 D8
De Haan B 182 C2
Deidesheim D 187 C5
Deinze B 182 D3
Delden NL 183 A9
Delft NL 182 B4
Delme F 186 D1
De Meern NL 183 A6
Den Bommel NL 182 B4
Denderleeuw B 182 D4
Dendermonde B 182 C4
Den Dungen NL 183 B6
Denekamp NL 183 A10
Den Haag NL 182 A4
Denkendorf D 187 D7
Dentergem B 182 D2
Dernau D 183 D10
Dessel B 183 C6
De Steeg NL 183 A8
Destelbergen B 182 C3
Dettelbach D 187 B9
Dettenhausen D 187 D7
Dettingen an der Erms D 187 D7
Dettwiller F 186 D3
Deurne NL 183 C7
Deventer NL 183 A8
Deville F 184 E2
Dhron D 185 E6
Didam NL 183 B8
Dieblich D 185 D7
Dieburg D 187 B6
Diekirch L 184 E5
Dielheim D 187 C6
Diemen NL 182 A5
Diepenbeek B 183 D6
Diepenheim NL 183 A9
Diepenveen NL 183 A8
Dierdorf D 185 C8
Dieren NL 183 A8
Diessen NL 183 C6
Diest B 183 D6
Dietenbach D 187 A6
Dietzhölztal-Ewersbach D 185 C9
Dieuze F 186 D2
Dikkebus B 182 D1
Diksmuide B 182 C1
Dilbeek B 182 D4
Dillenburg D 185 C9
Dilsen B 183 C7
Dinant B 184 D2
Dinslaken D 183 B9
Dinteloord NL 182 B4
Dinther NL 183 B6
Dinxperlo NL 183 B8
Dirksland NL 182 B4
Dirmstein D 187 B5
Dison B 183 D7
Ditzingen D 187 D7
Dockweiler D 185 D6
Dodewaard NL 183 B7
Doesburg NL 183 A8
Doetinchem NL 183 B8
Doische B 184 D2
Dombasle-sur-Meurthe F 186 D1
Domburg NL 182 B3
Domèvre-sur-Vezouze F 186 D2
Dommershausen D 185 D7
Dongen NL 182 B5
Donk NL 183 C7
Donzdorf D 187 D8
Doorn NL 183 A6
Doornspijk NL 183 A7
Dordrecht NL 182 B5
Dorlisheim F 186 D3
Dormagen D 183 C9
Dornburg-Frickhofen D 185 C9
Dornhan D 187 E5
Dornstadt D 187 E8
Dornstetten D 187 E5
Dorsten D 183 B9
Dorstfeld D 185 A7
Dortmund D 185 A7
Dörzbach D 187 C8
Dossenheim D 187 C6
Dreieich D 187 A6
Dreis D 185 E6
Drenststeinfurt D 185 A8
Dreumel NL 183 B6
Driebergen NL 183 A6
Driedorf D 185 C9
Drolshagen D 185 B8
Drongen B 182 C3
Drulingen F 186 D3
Drusenheim F 186 D4
Druten NL 183 B7
Dudelange L 186 C1
Dudeldorf D 185 E6
Duffel B 182 C5
Duisburg D 183 C9
Dümpelfeld D 183 D9
Düngenheim D 185 D7
Durbach D 186 D5
Durbuy B 184 D3
Düren D 183 D8
Durmersheim D 187 D5
Düsseldorf D 183 C9
Dussen NL 182 B5

E

Eberbach D 187 C6
Ebersbach an der Fils D 187 D7
Ebersmunster F 186 E4
Ebhausen D 187 D6
Écaussinnes-d'Enghien B 182 D4

Erht NL 183 C7
Echternach L 185 E5
Eckbolsheim F 186 D4
Ede NL 183 A7
Edegem B 182 C4
Edenkoben D 186 C5
Edesheim D 186 C5
Ediger-Eller D 185 D7
Eefde NL 183 A8
Eerbeek NL 183 A8
Eernegem B 182 C2
Eersel NL 183 C6
Eggenstein-Leopoldshafen D 187 C5
Eghezée B 182 D5
Ehingen (Donau) D 187 E8
Ehningen D 187 D6
Ehringshausen D 185 C9
Eibelstadt D 187 B9
Eibergen NL 183 A9
Eich D 187 B5
Eichenbühl D 187 B7
Eijsden NL 183 D7
Eindhoven NL 183 C6
Einville-au-Jard F 186 D1
Eisden B 183 D7
Eisenberg (Pfalz) D 186 B5
Eislingen (Fils) D 187 D8
Eitelborn D 185 D8
Eitorf D 185 C7
Ekeren B 182 C4
Eksaarde B 182 C3
Eksel B 183 C6
Elchingen D 187 E9
Elfershausen D 187 A8
Elkenroth D 185 C8
Ellenberg D 187 C9
Ellezelles B 182 D3
Ellwangen (Jagst) D 187 D9
Elsdorf D 183 D9
Elsenborn B 183 E8
Elsenfeld D 187 B7
Elsloo NL 183 D7
Elspeet NL 183 A7
Elst D 185 E6
Elst NL 183 B7
Eltville am Rhein D 185 D9
Elz D 185 D9
Emmelshausen D 185 D8
Emmerich D 183 B8
Empel NL 183 B6
Empfingen D 187 E6
Emptinne B 184 D3
Emst NL 183 A7
Engden D 183 A10
Engelskirchen D 185 C7
Enghien B 182 D4
Engis B 183 D6
Engstingen D 187 E7
Eningen unter Achalm D 187 E7
Enkenbach D 186 C4
Ennepetal D 185 B7
Ennery F 186 C1
Enschede NL 183 A9
Ensdorf D 186 C2
Ense D 185 B9
Ensheim D 186 C3
Enter NL 183 A9
Enzklösterle D 187 D5
Epe NL 183 A7
Epfendorf D 187 E6
Eppelborn D 186 C2
Eppelheim D 187 C6
Eppenbrunn D 186 C4
Eppertshausen D 187 B6
Eppingen D 187 C6
Eppstein D 187 A5
Erbach D 187 B7
Erbach D 187 E8
Erftstadt D 183 D9
Erkelenz D 183 C8
Erlenbach am Main D 187 B7
Ermelo D 183 A7
Erndtebrück D 185 C9
Erp D 183 D9
Erpel D 185 C7
Erquelinnes B 184 D1
Erstein F 186 E4
Ertvelde B 182 C3
Erwitte D 185 A9
Erzhausen D 187 B6
Esch NL 183 B6
Eschau D 187 B7
Eschau F 186 E4
Eschborn D 187 A6
Eschburg B 185 E5
Eschburg-Eibelshausen D 185 C9
Esch-sur-Sûre L 184 E4
Eschweiler D 183 D8
Eslohe (Sauerland) D 185 B9
Esneux B 183 D7
Essen B 182 C4
Essen D 183 C10
Essingen D 187 D9
Esslingen am Neckar D 187 D7
Estaimpuis B 182 D2
Estenfeld D 187 B9
Étival-Clairefontaine F 186 E2
Ettelbruck L 184 E5
Ettenheim D 186 E4
Etten-Leur NL 182 B5
Ettlingen D 187 D5
Ettringen D 185 D7
Eubigheim D 187 B8
Euerdorf D 187 A9
Eupen B 183 D8
Euskirchen D 183 D9
Eußenheim D 187 A8
Eutingen im Gäu D 187 E6
Everdingen NL 183 B6
Evergem B 182 C3

F

Faches-Thumesnil F 182 D2
Faid D 185 D7
Faimes B 183 D6
Falck F 186 C2
Fameck F 186 C1
Farciennes B 182 E5
Farébersviller F 186 C2
Faulbach D 187 B7
Faulquemont F 186 C2
Feilbingert D 185 E8
Fell D 186 B2
Fellbach D 187 D7
Fénétrange F 186 D3
Fépin F 184 E2
Ferrières B 183 E7

Ferschweiler D 185 E5
Fichtenberg D 187 D8
Fijnaart NL 182 B4
Finnentrop D 185 B8
Fischbach D 186 B3
Fischbach bei Dahn D 186 C4
Flavigny-sur-Moselle F 186 D1
Flein D 187 C7
Flémalle B 183 D6
Fléron B 183 D7
Flers-en-Escrebieux F 182 E2
Fleurus B 182 E5
Flines-lez-Raches F 182 E2
Florange F 186 C1
Floreffe B 182 E5
Florennes B 184 D2
Flörsbach D 187 A7
Flörsheim am Main D 187 A5
Flörsheim-Dalsheim D 187 B5
Focant D 184 D3
Föhren D 185 E6
Folschviller F 186 C2
Fontaine-l'Évêque B 182 E4
Forbach D 186 D5
Forbach F 186 C2
Forchtenberg D 187 C8
Forst D 187 C6
Fosses-la-Ville B 184 D2
Fraire B 184 D2
Frameries B 182 E3
Frammersbach D 187 A7
Francorchamps B 183 E7
Frankenthal (Pfalz) D 187 B5
Frankfurt am Main D 187 A6
Frasnes-lez-Buissenal B 182 D3
Frasnes-lez-Gosselies B 182 D4
Frechen D 183 D9
Freinsheim D 187 B5
Freisen D 186 B3
Freistroff F 186 C2
Fresnes-sur-Escaut F 182 E3
Freudenberg D 185 C8
Freudenberg D 187 B7
Freudenburg D 186 B2
Freudenstadt D 187 E5
Freyming-Merlebach F 186 C2
Friedewald D 185 C8
Friedrichsdorf D 187 A6
Friesenhagen D 185 C8
Friesenheim D 186 E4
Frisange L 186 B1
Frœschwiller F 186 C4
Fromelennes F 184 D2
Fröndenberg D 185 B8
Frouard F 186 D1
Fumay F 184 E2
Fürth D 187 B6

G

Gaanderen NL 183 B8
Gaggenau D 187 D5
Gaildorf D 187 D8
Gambsheim F 186 D4
Gammertingen D 187 E7
Gand B 182 C3
Ganshoren B 182 D4
Garderen NL 183 A7
Gärtringen D 187 D6
Gau-Algesheim D 185 E9
Gaukönigshofen D 187 B8
Gau-Odernheim D 185 E9
Gavere B 182 D3
Gebhardshain D 185 C8
Gechingen D 187 D6
Gedinne B 184 D2
Geel B 183 C6
Geertruidenberg NL 182 B5
Geesteren NL 183 A9
Geetbets B 183 D6
Geffen NL 183 B6
Geilenkirchen D 183 D8
Geiselbach D 187 A7
Geisenheim D 185 E8
Geislingen D 187 E6
Geislingen an der Steige D 187 D8
Geispolsheim F 186 D4
Gelchsheim D 187 B9
Geldermalsen NL 183 B6
Geldern D 183 B8
Geldersheim D 187 A9
Geldrop NL 183 C7
Geleen NL 183 D7
Gelnhausen D 187 A7
Gelsenkirchen D 183 B10
Gembloux B 182 D5
Gemert NL 183 B7
Gemmingen D 187 C6
Gemünden D 185 E7
Gemünden am Main D 187 A8
Genappe B 182 D4
Gendringen NL 183 B8
Gendt NL 183 B7
Gengenbach D 186 E5
Genk B 183 D7
Gennep NL 183 B7
Gensingen D 185 E8
Gent B 182 C3
Geraardsbergen B 182 D3
Gerabronn D 187 C8
Gerbéviller F 186 E2
Gerbrunn D 187 B8
Gerchsheim D 187 B8
Gerlingen D 187 D7
Germersheim D 187 C5
Gernsbach D 187 D5
Gernsheim D 187 B5
Gerolstein D 185 D6
Gerpinnes B 184 D2
Gersheim D 186 C3
Gerstetten D 187 D9
Gerstheim F 186 E4
Gescher D 183 B10
Gespunsart F 184 E2
Gesves B 184 D3
Gevelsberg D 185 B7
Ghislenghien B 182 D3
Giebelstadt D 187 B8
Gierle B 182 C5
Gillenfeld D 185 D6
Gilze NL 182 B5
Gingelom B 183 D6
Gingen an der Fils D 187 D8
Ginsheim D 185 E9
Gistel B 182 C1
Givet F 184 D2
Gladbeck D 183 B9
Glanerbrug NL 183 A9
Gläshütten D 187 A5
Goch D 183 B8

Goddelau D 187 B6
Goedereede NL 182 B3
Goes NL 182 B3
Göggingen D 187 D8
Goirle NL 183 B6
Göllheim D 186 B5
Gomadingen D 187 E7
Gomaringen D 187 E7
Gondelsheim D 187 C6
Gondershausen D 185 D7
Gondorf D 185 D7
Goor NL 183 A9
Göppingen D 187 D8
Gorinchem NL 182 B5
Gorssel NL 183 A8
Gorxheimertal D 187 B6
Gouda NL 182 A5
Goudswaard NL 182 B4
Gouvy B 184 D4
Graben-Neudorf D 187 C5
Grâce-Hollogne B 183 D6
Gräfendorf D 187 A8
Grafenrheinfeld D 187 B9
Grandvillers F 186 E2
Grave NL 183 B7
Greifenstein D 185 C9
Grevenbicht NL 183 C7
Grevenbroich D 183 C9
Grevenmacher L 186 B1
Grez-Doiceau B 182 D5
Gries F 186 D4
Griesbach D 187 E5
Griesheim D 187 B6
Grimbergen B 182 D4
Grobbendonk B 182 C5
Groenlo NL 183 A9
Groesbeek NL 183 B7
Gronau (Westfalen) D 183 A10
Groß-Bieberau D 187 B6
Großbottwar D 187 D7
Grosselfingen D 187 E6
Groß-Gerau D 187 B5
Großheubach D 187 B7
Großlangheim D 187 B9
Großlittgen D 185 D6
Großmaischeid D 185 C8
Großostheim D 187 B7
Großrinderfeld D 187 B8
Groß-Rohrheim D 187 B5
Großrosseln D 186 C2
Groß-Umstadt D 187 B6
Großwallstadt D 187 B7
Groß-Zimmern D 187 B6
Grostenquin F 186 D2
Grubbenvorst NL 183 C8
Grünsfeld D 187 B8
Grünstadt D 187 B5
Gschwend D 187 D8
Guénange F 186 C1
Güglingen D 187 C6
Gulpen NL 183 D7
Gummersbach D 185 B8
Gundelsheim D 187 C7
Gundershoffen F 186 D4
Guntersblum D 185 E9
Güntersleben D 187 B8
Gusterath D 186 B2
Gutach (Schwarzwaldbahn) D 187 E5

H

Haacht B 182 D5
Haaften NL 183 B6
Haaksbergen NL 183 A9
Haaltert B 182 D4
Haaren NL 183 B6
Haarlem NL 182 A5
Haastrecht NL 182 B5
Hachenburg D 185 C8
Hackenheim D 185 E8
Hadamar D 185 D9
Haelen NL 183 C7
Hagen D 185 B7
Hagenbach D 187 C5
Hagondange F 186 C1
Haguenau F 186 D4
Hahnstätten D 185 D9
Haibach D 187 B7
Haiger D 185 C9
Haigerloch D 187 E6
Haiterbach D 187 D6
Halen B 183 D6
Halfweg NL 182 A5
Halle B 182 D4
Halle NL 183 B8
Halluin B 182 D2
Halsenbach D 185 D8
Halsteren NL 182 B4
Halstroff F 186 C1
Haltern D 183 B10
Halver D 185 B7
Hambach F 186 C3
Hambrücken D 187 C6
Hamm D 185 A8
Hamm (Sieg) D 185 C8
Hamme B 182 C4
Hammelburg D 187 A8
Hamme-Mille B 182 D5
Hamminkeln D 183 B9
Hamoir B 183 E7
Hamois B 184 D3
Hamont B 183 C7
Hampont F 186 D2
Ham-sous-Varsberg F 186 C2
Ham-sur-Heure B 184 D1
Hanau D 187 A6
Handzame B 182 C2
Hannut B 183 D6
Han-sur-Nied F 186 D1
Hapert NL 183 C6
Haps NL 183 B7
Harderwijk NL 183 A7
Hardheim D 187 B7
Hardinxveld-Giessendam NL 182 B5
Harelbeke B 182 D2
Hargesheim D 185 E8
Hargimont B 184 D3
Hargnies F 184 D2
Harmelen NL 182 A5
Harnes F 182 E1
Haroué F 186 E1
Harthausen D 187 C5
Haslach im Kinzigtal D 186 E5
Hasselt B 183 D6
Haßloch D 187 C5
Haßmersheim D 187 C7
Hastière-Lavaux B 184 D2
Hattersheim am Main D 187 A5
Hattert D 185 C8
Hattingen D 183 C10
Hatzenbühl D 187 C5
Haubourdin F 182 D1
Hauenstein D 186 C4
Hausach D 187 E5
Hausen bei Würzburg D 187 B9
Haut-Fays B 184 D3
Havelange B 184 D3
Haversin B 184 D3
Hayange F 186 C1
Haybes F 184 D2
Hayingen D 187 E7
Hazerswoude-Rijndijk NL 182 A5
Hechingen D 187 E6
Hechtel B 183 C6
Heddesheim D 187 C6
Hedel NL 183 B6
Heek D 183 A10
Heel NL 183 C7
Heemstede NL 182 A5
Heenvliet NL 182 B4
Heer B 184 D2
Heerde NL 183 A8
Heerewaarden NL 183 B6
Heerlen NL 183 D7
Heers B 183 D6
Heesch NL 183 B7
Heeswijk NL 183 B6
Heeten NL 183 A8
Heeze NL 183 C7
Heidelberg D 187 C6
Heiden D 183 B9
Heidenheim an der Brenz D 187 D9
Heigenbrücken D 187 A7
Heilbronn D 187 C7
Heiligenhaus D 183 C9
Heimbach D 186 B3
Heimbuchenthal D 187 B7
Heimsheim D 187 D6
Heinkenszand NL 182 C3
Heino NL 183 A8
Heinsberg D 183 C8
Heisingen D 183 C10
Heist-op-den-Berg B 182 C5
Hekelgem B 182 D4
Helchteren B 183 C6
Heldenbergen D 187 A6
Hellendoorn NL 183 A8
Hellenthal D 183 E8
Hellevoetsluis NL 182 B4
Helmond NL 183 C7
Helmstadt D 187 B8
Heltersberg D 186 C4
Helvoirt NL 183 B6
Hem F 182 D2
Hemer D 185 B8
Hemsbach D 187 B6
Hengelo NL 183 A8
Hengelo NL 183 A9
Hengevelde NL 183 A9
Hénin-Beaumont F 182 E1
Hennef (Sieg) D 185 C7
Hennweiler D 185 E7
Heppen B 183 C6
Heppenheim (Bergstraße) D 187 B6
Herbeumont B 184 E3
Herborn D 185 C9
Herbrechtingen D 187 D9
Herdecke D 185 B7
Herdorf D 185 C8
Herent B 182 D5
Herentals B 182 C5
Herenthout B 182 C5
Herk-de-Stad B 183 D6
Herkenbosch NL 183 C8
Herkingen NL 182 B4
Hermersberg D 186 C4
Hermeskeil D 186 B2
Herne B 182 D4
Herne D 185 A7
Héron B 183 D6
Herrenberg D 187 D6
Herrlisheim F 186 D4
Herschbach D 185 C8
Herscheid D 185 B8
Herschweiler-Pettersheim D 186 C3
Herselt B 182 C5
Herstal B 183 D7
Herten D 183 B10
Herve B 183 D7
Herwijnen NL 183 B6
Herzele B 182 D3
Herzogenrath D 183 D8
Hespérange L 186 B1
Heßheim D 187 B5
Hettange-Grande F 186 C1
Hettenleidelheim D 186 B5
Hetzerath D 185 E6
Heubach D 187 D8
Heukelum NL 183 B6
Heusden B 183 C6
Heusden NL 183 B6
Heusenstamm D 187 A6
Heusweiler D 186 C2
Heythuysen NL 183 C7
Hilchenbach D 185 C9
Hilden D 183 C9
Hillegom NL 182 A5
Hillesheim D 185 D6
Hilsenheim F 186 E4
Hilvarenbeek NL 183 C6
Hilversum NL 183 A6
Hinterweidenthal D 186 C4
Hirrlingen D 187 E6
Hirschhorn (Neckar) D 187 C6
Hochfelden F 186 D4
Hochspeyer D 186 C4
Hochstadt (Pfalz) D 187 C5
Hochstetten-Dhaun D 185 E7
Höchst im Odenwald D 187 B6
Hockenheim D 187 C6
Hoek NL 182 C3
Hoek van Holland NL 182 B4
Hoenderloo NL 183 A7
Hœnheim F 186 D4
Hoensbroek NL 183 D7
Hœrdt F 186 D4
Hoeselt B 183 D6
Hoevelaken NL 183 A6
Hoeven NL 182 B5
Hof D 185 C9
Hofheim am Taunus D 187 A5
Hohberg D 186 E4
Höhn D 185 C8
Höhr-Grenzhausen D 185 D8
Hollange B 184 E4
Holten NL 183 A8
Holzappel D 185 D8
Holzgerlingen D 187 D7
Holzhausen an der Haide D 185 D8
Holzheim D 187 E9
Holzwickede D 185 A8
Hombourg-Budange F 186 C1
Hombourg-Haut F 186 C2
Homburg D 186 C3
Hoofddorp NL 182 A5
Hoogerheide NL 182 C4
Hoog-Keppel NL 183 B8
Hoogland NL 183 A6
Hoogstraten B 182 C5
Hoogvliet NL 182 B4
Hoornaar NL 182 B5
Hoppstädten D 186 B3
Horb am Neckar D 187 E6
Hörde D 185 B7
Hornbach D 186 C3
Horst NL 183 C8
Hösbach D 187 A7
Hosingen L 184 D5
Hotton B 184 D3
Houffalize B 184 D4
Houten NL 183 A6
Houthalen B 183 C6
Houthulst B 182 D1
Houyet B 184 D3
Hückelhoven D 183 C8
Hückeswagen D 185 B7
Huijbergen NL 182 C4
Huissen NL 183 B7
Huizen NL 183 A6
Hüls D 183 C8
Hulsberg NL 183 D7
Hulst NL 182 C4
Hummelo NL 183 A8
Hundsangen D 185 D8
Hünfelden-Kirberg D 185 D9
Hunsel NL 183 C7
Hunspach F 186 D4
Hünxe D 183 B9
Hürth D 183 D9
Hütschenhausen D 186 C3
Hüttisheim D 187 E8
Hüttlingen D 187 D9
Huy B 183 D6
Hymont F 186 E1

I

Ichenheim D 186 E4
Ichtegem B 182 C2
Idar-Oberstein D 186 B3
Idstein D 185 D9
Ieper B 182 D1
Iffezheim D 187 D5
Igel D 186 B2
Igersheim D 187 C8
Iggelheim D 187 C5
Igney F 186 E1
IJsselstein NL 183 A6
IJzendijke NL 182 C3
Illingen D 186 C3
Illingen D 187 D6
Illkirch-Graffenstaden F 186 D4
Ilsfeld D 187 C7
Incourt B 182 D5
Ingelfingen D 187 C8
Ingelheim am Rhein D 185 E9
Ingelmunster B 182 D2
Ingwiller F 186 D3
Insming F 186 D2
Iphofen D 187 B9
Ippesheim D 187 B9
Irrel D 185 E5
Irsch D 186 B2
Iserlohn D 185 B8
Ispringen D 187 D6
Isselburg D 183 B8
Issum D 183 B8
Ittre B 182 D4
Ixelles B 182 D4
Izegem B 182 D2

J

Jabbeke B 182 C2
Jagsthausen D 187 C7
Jagstzell D 187 C9
Jalhay B 183 D7
Jarville-la-Malgrange F 186 D1
Jemeppe B 182 E5
Jockgrim D 187 C5
Jodoigne B 182 D5
Jouy-aux-Arches F 186 C1
Jüchen D 183 C8
Jülich D 183 D8
Jungingen D 187 E7
Junglinster L 186 B1
Jünkerath D 185 D6
Juprelle B 183 D7
Jurbise B 182 D3

K

Kaarst D 183 C9
Kaatsheuvel NL 183 B6
Kahl am Main D 187 A7
Kaisersesch D 185 D7
Kaiserslautern D 186 C4
Kalkar D 183 B8
Kall D 183 D9
Kalmthout B 182 C4
Kamen D 185 A8
Kamerik NL 182 A5
Kamp D 185 D8
Kampenhout B 182 D5
Kämpfelbach D 187 D6
Kamp-Lintfort D 183 C9
Kandel D 187 C5
Kapelle NL 182 C3
Kapellen B 182 C4
Kapelle-op-den-Bos B 182 C4
Kappel D 185 E7
Kappel-Grafenhausen D 186 E4
Kappelrodeck D 186 D5
Kaprijke B 182 C3
Karben D 187 A6
Karden D 185 D7
Karlsbad D 187 D6
Karlsdorf-Neuthard D 187 C6
Karlsruhe D 187 C5
Karlstadt D 187 B8
Kastellaun D 185 D7
Kasterlee B 182 C5
Katwijk aan Zee NL 182 A4
Katzenelnbogen D 185 D8
Katzweiler D 186 B4
Kaub D 185 D8
Kaulille B 183 C7
Kautenbach L 184 E5
Kehl D 186 D4
Kehlen L 186 B1
Kehrig D 185 D7
Kelberg D 185 D6
Kelkheim (Taunus) D 187 A5
Kell D 186 B2
Kelmis B 183 D8
Kempen D 183 C8
Kempenich D 183 E10
Kenn D 185 E6
Kerkdriel NL 183 B6
Kerken D 183 C8
Kerkrade NL 183 D8
Kerkwijk NL 183 B6
Kerpen D 183 D9
Kessel B 182 C5
Kessel NL 183 C8
Kesteren NL 183 B7
Ketsch D 187 C6
Kettwig D 183 C9
Kevelaer D 183 B8
Kieldrecht B 182 C4
Kierspe D 185 B8
Kinderbeuern D 185 D7
Kindsbach D 186 C4
Kinrooi B 183 C7
Kippenheim D 186 E4
Kirchardt D 187 C6
Kirchberg (Hunsrück) D 185 E7
Kirchberg an der Jagst D 187 C8
Kirchellen D 183 B9
Kirchen (Sieg) D 185 C8
Kirchheim D 187 B8
Kirchheim am Neckar D 187 C7
Kirchheim-Bolanden D 186 B5
Kirchheim unter Teck D 187 D7
Kirchhundem D 185 B9
Kirchzell D 187 B7
Kirkel-Neuhäusel D 186 C3
Kirn D 185 E7
Kirschweiler D 186 B3
Kist D 187 B8
Kitzingen D 187 B9
Klaaswaal NL 182 B4
Klausen D 185 E6
Kleinblittersdorf D 186 C3
Kleinheubach D 187 B7
Kleinrinderfeld D 187 B8
Kleinwallstadt D 187 B7
Kleve D 183 B8
Klingenberg am Main D 187 B7
Kloetinge NL 182 C3
Kloosterzande NL 182 C4
Klotten D 185 D7
Klundert NL 182 B5
Knesselare B 182 C2
Knittlingen D 187 C6
Knokke-Heist B 182 C2
Kobern D 185 D7
Koblenz D 185 D8
Koekelare B 182 C1
Koersel B 183 C6
Koewacht NL 182 C3
Kolitzheim D 187 B9
Köln D 183 D9
Königheim D 187 B8
Königsbronn D 187 D9
Königstein im Taunus D 187 A5
Königswinter D 185 C7
Konz D 186 B2
Kootwijkerbroek NL 183 A7
Kopstal L 186 B1
Kordel D 185 E6
Kornwestheim D 187 D7
Körperich D 185 E5
Kortemark B 182 C2
Kortenhoef NL 183 A6
Kortessem B 183 D6
Kortgene NL 182 B3
Kortrijk B 182 D2
Kottenheim D 185 D7
Koudekerke NL 182 C3
Krabbendijke NL 182 C4
Kranenburg D 183 B8
Krautheim D 187 C8
Krefeld D 183 C9
Kreuzau D 183 D8
Kreuztal D 185 C8
Kreuzwertheim D 187 B8
Krimpen aan de IJssel NL 182 B5
Kronau D 187 C6
Kronberg im Taunus D 187 A5
Kröv D 185 E7
Kruft D 185 D7
Kruibeke B 182 C4
Kruiningen NL 182 C4
Kruishoutem B 182 D3
Kuchen D 187 D8
Külsheim D 187 B8
Kunrade NL 183 D7
Künzelsau D 187 C8
Kupferzell D 187 C8
Kuppenheim D 187 D5
Kürnach D 187 B9
Kürnbach D 187 C6
Kusel D 186 B3
Kusterdingen D 187 D7
Kuurne B 182 D2
Kwaadmechelen B 183 C6
Kyllburg D 185 D6

L

Laarne B 182 C3
La Broque F 186 E3
Lachen-Speyerdorf D 187 C5
Ladenburg D 187 C6
Lafrimbolle F 186 D3
Lage Mierde NL 183 C6
Lahnstein D 185 D8
Lahr (Schwarzwald) D 186 E4
Laichingen D 187 E8
Laifour F 184 E2
Lallaing F 182 E2
La Louvière B 182 E4
Lambersart F 182 D2
Lambrecht (Pfalz) D 186 C5
Lambsheim D 187 B5
Lampertheim D 187 B5
Lanaken B 183 D7
Landau in der Pfalz D 186 C5
Landen B 183 D6
Landersheim F 186 D3
Landgraaf NL 183 D8
Landscheid D 185 E6
Landsmeer NL 182 A5
Landstuhl D 186 C4
Langemark B 182 D1
Langen D 187 B6
Langenau D 187 E9
Langenaubach D 185 C9
Langenberg D 183 C10
Langenberg D 185 A9
Langenburg D 187 C8
Langenfeld (Rheinland) D 183 C9
Langenhahn D 185 C8
Langenlonsheim D 185 E8
Langenselbold D 187 A7
Langsur D 186 B2
Lannoy F 182 D2
La Petite-Pierre F 186 D3
Laren NL 183 A6
Laren NL 183 A8
La Roche-en-Ardenne B 184 D4
Larochette L 186 B1
Lasne B 182 D4
Lattrop NL 183 A9
Laubach D 185 D7
Lauda-Königshofen D 187 B8
Lauf D 186 D5
Laufach D 187 A7
Lauffen am Neckar D 187 C7
Lautenbach D 186 D5
Lauterbourg F 187 D5
Lauterecken D 186 B4
Lauterstein D 187 D8
La Wantzenau F 186 D4
Laxou F 186 D1
Lebach D 186 C2
Le Ban-St-Martin F 186 C1
Lebbeke B 182 C4
Lede B 182 D3
Ledegem B 182 D2
Leende NL 183 C7
Leerdam NL 183 B6
Leersum NL 183 A6
Leffinge B 182 C1
Leforest F 182 E2
Legden D 183 A10
Léglise B 184 E4
Lehmen D 185 D7
Le Hohwald F 186 E3
Leichlingen (Rheinland) D 183 C10
Leiden NL 182 A5
Leiderdorp NL 182 A5
Leidschendam NL 182 A4
Leimen D 187 C6
Leimuiden NL 182 A5
Leinfelden-Echterdingen D 187 D7
Leinzell D 187 D8
Leiwen D 185 E6
Lembeke B 182 C3
Lemberg D 186 C4
Lemberg F 186 C3
Lendelede B 182 D2
Léning F 186 D2
Lennestadt D 185 B9
Lenningen D 187 D7
Lens B 182 D3
Lent NL 183 B7
Leonberg D 187 D7
Leopoldsburg B 183 C6
Les Hautes-Rivières F 184 E2
Les Mazures F 184 E2
Lessines B 182 D3
Leun D 185 C9
Leusden NL 183 A6
Leutesdorf D 185 D7
Leuven B 182 D5
Leuze-en-Hainaut B 182 D3
Leverkusen D 183 C9
L'Hôpital F 186 C2
Libin B 184 E3
Libramont B 184 E3
Lichtaart B 182 C5
Lichtenau D 186 D5
Lichtenvoorde NL 183 B9
Lichtervelde B 182 C2
Liège B 183 D7
Liempde NL 183 B6
Lienden NL 183 B7
Lier B 182 C5
Lierneux B 184 D4
Lieser D 185 E7
Lieshout NL 183 B7
Liessel NL 183 C7
Ligneuville B 184 D5
Lille B 182 C5
Lille F 182 D2
Limbach D 186 C2
Limbach D 187 C7
Limbourg B 183 D7
Limburg an der Lahn D 185 D9
Limburgerhof D 187 C5
Lincent B 183 D6
Lindenfels D 187 B6
Lindlar D 185 B7
Lingenfeld D 187 C5
Lingolsheim F 186 D4
Linnich D 183 D8
Linz am Rhein D 185 C7
Lippstadt D 185 A9
Lisse NL 182 A5
Lissendorf D 185 D6
Lith NL 183 B6
Lixing-lès-St-Avold F 186 C2
Lobith NL 183 B8
Lochem NL 183 A8
Lochristi B 182 C3
Loenen NL 183 A8
Löf D 185 D7
Lohmar D 185 C7
Löhnberg D 185 C9
Lohr am Main D 187 B8
Lokeren B 182 C4
Lomme F 182 D1
Lommel B 183 C6
Londerzeel B 182 D4
Longeville-lès-St-Avold F 186 C2
Longlier B 184 E3
Lonneker NL 183 A9
Lonny F 184 E2
Lonsee D 187 D8
Lontzen B 183 D8
Loon op Zand NL 183 B6
Loos F 182 D2
Lopik NL 182 B5
Lorch D 185 D8
Lorch D 187 D8
Lorquin F 186 D2
Lorsch D 187 B6
Losheim D 186 B2
Loßburg D 187 E5
Losser NL 183 A9
Lotenhulle B 182 C2
Lottum NL 183 C8
Louvain B 182 D5
Louveigné B 183 D7
Lovendegem B 182 C3
Löwenstein D 187 C7
Lubbeek B 182 D5
Lüdenscheid D 185 B8
Lüdinghausen D 185 A7
Ludres F 186 D1
Ludwigsburg D 187 D7
Ludwigshafen am Rhein D 187 C5
Luik B 183 D7
Lummen B 183 D6
Lünebach D 185 D5
Lünen D 185 A8
Lunéville F 186 D1
Lunteren NL 183 A7
Luppy F 186 D1
Lustadt D 187 C5
Luttenberg NL 183 A8
Lützelbach D 187 B7
Lutzerath D 185 D7
Luxembourg L 186 B1
Luyksgestel NL 183 C6

M

Maarheeze NL 183 C7
Maarn NL 183 A6
Maarssen NL 183 A6
Maarssenbroek NL 183 A6
Maasbracht NL 183 C7
Maasbree NL 183 C8
Maasdam NL 182 B5
Maaseik B 183 C7
Maasland NL 182 B4
Maasmechelen B 183 D7
Maassluis NL 182 B4
Maastricht NL 183 D7
Machelen B 182 D4
Mackenbach D 186 C4
Made NL 182 B5
Magnières F 186 E2
Mahlberg D 186 E4
Maikammer D 186 C5
Mainaschaff D 187 B7
Mainbernheim D 187 B9
Mainhardt D 187 C8
Mainz D 185 D9
Maizières-lès-Metz F 186 C1
Malborn D 186 B2
Maldegem B 182 C2
Malden NL 183 B7
Malines B 182 C4
Malmédy B 183 E8
Malsch D 187 D5
Manage B 182 E4
Mandelbachtal-Ormesheim D 186 C3
Manderscheid D 185 D6
Manhay B 184 D4
Mannheim D 187 C5
Manternach L 186 B1
Marange-Silvange F 186 C1
Marbach am Neckar D 187 D7
Marche-en-Famenne B 184 D3
Marchiennes F 182 E2
Marchin B 183 E6
Marcq-en-Barœul F 182 D2
Margraten NL 183 D7
Mariembourg B 184 D2
Marienheide D 185 B8
Markelo NL 183 A9
Markgröningen D 187 D7
Marktbreit D 187 B9
Marktheidenfeld D 187 B8
Marktseft D 187 B9
Marl D 183 B10
Marlenheim F 186 D4
Marly F 186 C1
Marmoutier F 186 D3
Marnheim D 186 B5
Marpingen D 186 C3
Marsal F 186 D2
Martelange B 184 E4
Marxzell D 187 D5
Maßbach D 187 A9
Mastershausen D 185 D7
Mattaincourt F 186 E1
Maubert-Fontaine F 184 E1
Maulbronn D 187 D6
Maurik NL 183 B6
Maxéville F 186 D1
Maxsain D 185 C8
Mayen D 185 D7
Mayschoss D 183 D10
Mechelen B 182 C4
Mechelen NL 183 D7
Mechernich D 183 D9
Meckenheim D 183 D10
Meckesheim D 187 C6
Meddersheim D 186 B4
Meddo NL 183 A9
Meer B 182 C5
Meerbusch D 183 C9
Meerhout B 183 C6
Meerkerk NL 182 B5
Meerle B 182 C5
Meerlo NL 183 B8
Meerssen NL 183 D7
Meetkerke B 182 C2
Meeuwen B 183 C7
Megen NL 183 B7
Mehren D 185 D6
Mehring D 185 E6
Mehrstetten D 187 E8
Meijel NL 183 C7
Meinerzhagen D 185 B8
Meise B 182 D4
Meisenheim D 186 B4
Meißenheim D 186 E4
Melick NL 183 C8
Meliskerke NL 182 B3
Melle B 182 C3
Menden (Sauerland) D 185 B8
Mendig D 185 D7
Menen B 182 D2
Mengerskirchen D 185 C9
Ménil-sur-Belvitte F 186 E2
Menin B 182 D2
Merbes-le-Château B 184 D1
Merchtem B 182 D4
Mere B 182 D3
Merelbeke B 182 D3
Merenberg D 185 C9
Merklingen D 187 D8
Merksplas B 182 C5
Mersch L 186 B1
Mertert L 186 B1
Mertesdorf D 186 B2
Mertloch D 185 D7
Mertzwiller F 186 D4
Merzig D 186 C2
Meschede D 185 B9
Mespelbrunn D 187 B7
Metelen D 183 A10
Mettendorf D 185 E5
Mettet B 184 D2
Mettlach D 186 C2
Mettmann D 183 C9
Metz F 186 C1
Metzervisse F 186 C1
Metzingen D 187 D7
Meudt D 185 D8
Meulebeke B 182 D2
Michelbach an der Bilz D 187 C8
Michelfeld D 187 C8
Michelstadt D 187 B7
Middelbeers NL 183 C6
Middelburg NL 182 B3
Middelharnis NL 182 B4
Middelkerke B 182 C1
Miehlen D 185 D8
Mierlo NL 183 C7
Miesau D 186 C3
Miesenbach D 186 C4
Mijdrecht NL 182 A5
Mill NL 183 B7
Millingen aan de Rijn NL 183 B8
Milmort B 183 D7
Miltenberg D 187 B7
Minderhout B 182 C5
Minfeld D 186 C5
Mirecourt F 186 E1
Mittelsinn D 187 A8
Mittersheim F 186 D2
Möckmühl D 187 C7
Modave B 183 E6
Moerbeke B 182 C3
Moergestel NL 183 B6
Moerkerke B 182 C2
Moers D 183 C9
Mögglingen D 187 D8
Möglingen D 187 D7
Mol B 183 C6
Molenbeek-St-Jean B 182 D4
Molenstede B 183 C6
Molsheim F 186 D3
Mömbris D 187 A7
Momignies B 184 D1
Moncel-sur-Seille F 186 D1
Mönchengladbach D 183 C8
Mondorf-les-Bains L 186 B1
Mons B 182 E3
Monschau D 183 D8
Monsheim D 187 B5
Mönsheim D 187 D6
Monster NL 182 A4
Montabaur D 185 D8
Montcy-Notre-Dame F 184 E2
Montfoort NL 182 A5
Montfort NL 183 C7
Monthermé F 184 E2
Montignies-le-Tilleul B 184 D1
Montigny F 186 D2
Montigny-lès-Metz F 186 C1
Montzen B 183 D7
Monzelfeld D 185 E7
Monzingen D 185 E8
Mook NL 183 B7
Moorslede B 182 D2
Morbach D 185 E7
Mörfelden D 187 B6
Morhange F 186 D2
Morlanwelz B 182 E4
Mörlenbach D 187 B6
Morsbach D 185 C8
Mortsel B 182 C4
Mosbach D 187 C7
Mössingen D 187 E7
Mouscron B 182 D2
Moussey F 186 E3
Moyenmoutier F 186 E2
Much D 185 C7
Mudau D 187 B7
Müdelheim D 183 C9
Mudersbach D 185 C8
Muggensturm D 187 D5
Mühlacker D 187 D6
Mühlhausen D 187 C6
Mulfingen D 187 C8
Mülheim an der Ruhr D 183 C9
Mülheim-Kärlich D 185 D7
Münchweiler an der Rodalb D 186 C4
Munderkingen D 187 E8
Mundolsheim F 186 D4
Munkzwalm B 182 D3
Münnerstadt D 187 A9
Münsingen D 187 E7
Münster D 187 B6
Munstergeleen NL 183 D7
Münstermaifeld D 185 D7
Murrhardt D 187 D8
Müschenbach D 185 C8
Mutterstadt D 187 C5
Mutzig F 186 D3

N

Naaldwijk NL 182 B4
Naarden NL 183 A6
Nackenheim D 185 E9
Nagold D 187 D6
Nalbach D 186 C2
Namborn D 186 B3
Namur B 182 E5
Nancy F 186 D1
Nandrin B 183 D6
Nassau D 185 D8
Nassogne B 184 D3
Nastätten D 185 D8
Nauheim D 187 B5
Nauroth D 185 C8
Neckarbischofsheim D 187 C6
Neckargemünd D 187 C6
Neckarsteinach D 187 C6
Neckarsulm D 187 C7
Neckartenzlingen D 187 D7
Nederhorst den Berg NL 183 A6
Nederlangbroek NL 183 A6
Nederweert NL 183 C7
Neede NL 183 A9
Neer NL 183 C8
Neerijnen NL 183 B6
Neeroeteren B 183 C7
Neerpelt B 183 C6
Nellingen D 187 D8
Nentershausen D 185 D8
Neroth D 185 D6
Nersingen D 187 E9
Netphen D 185 C9
Nettersheim D 183 E9

Nettetal D 183 C8
Neubrunn D 187 B8
Neubulach D 187 D6
Neuenbürg D 187 D6
Neuenkirchen-Seelscheid D 185 C7
Neuenrade D 185 B8
Neuenkirchen am Main D 187 A6
Neuenstadt am Kocher D 187 C7
Neuenstein D 187 C8
Neuerburg D 185 D5
Neufchâteau D 184 E3
Neuffen D 187 D7
Neufmanil D 184 E2
Neufra D 187 E7
Neuhausen D 187 D6
Neuhofen D 187 C5
Neu-Isenburg D 187 A6
Neuler D 187 D9
Neumagen D 185 E6
Neunkirchen D 185 C7
Neunkirchen D 186 C3
Neuss D 183 C9
Neustadt (Wied) D 185 C7
Neustadt an der Weinstraße D 186 C5
Neu-Ulm D 187 E9
Neuves-Maisons F 186 D1
Neuweiler D 187 D6
Neuwied D 185 D7
Nevele B 182 C3
Newel D 185 E6
Niederanven L 186 B1
Niederbrechen D 185 D9
Niederbreitbach D 185 C7
Niederbronn-les-Bains F 186 D4
Niederfischbach D 185 C8
Niederkassel D 183 D10
Niederkirchen D 186 B4
Niederkrüchten D 183 C8
Niederneisen D 185 D9
Niedernhall D 187 C8
Niedernhausen D 185 D9
Nieder-Olm D 185 E9
Nieder-Rodenbach D 187 A7
Niederselters D 185 D9
Niederstetten D 187 C8
Niederwerrn D 187 A9
Niederwörresbach D 186 B3
Niederzissen D 185 D7
Niefern-Öschelbronn D 187 D6
Niel B 182 C3
Nierstein D 185 E9
Nieuw-Bergen NL 183 B8
Nieuwegein NL 183 A6
Nieuwerkerk NL 182 B4
Nieuwerkerk aan de IJssel NL 182 B5
Nieuwerkerken B 183 D6
Nieuwe-Tonge NL 182 B4
Nieuw-Heeten NL 183 A8
Nieuwkoop NL 182 A5
Nieuw-Loosdrecht NL 183 A6
Nieuw-Milligen NL 183 A7
Nieuw-Namen NL 182 C4
Nieuwveen NL 182 A5
Nieuw-Vennep NL 182 A5
Nieuw-Vossemeer NL 182 B4
Nievern D 185 D8
Nijkerk NL 183 A6
Nijlen B 182 C5
Nijmegen NL 183 B7
Nijverdal NL 183 A8
Nilvange F 186 C1
Ninove B 182 D4
Nismes B 184 D2
Nispen NL 182 C4
Nistelrode NL 183 B7
Nittel D 186 B1
Nivelles B 182 D4
Nohfelden D 186 B3
Noisseville F 186 C1
Nomeny F 186 D1
Nomexy F 186 E1
Nonnenweier D 186 E4
Nonnweiler D 186 B2
Noordwijk aan Zee NL 182 A4
Noordwijk-Binnen NL 182 A4
Noordwijkerhout NL 182 A5
Nootdorp NL 182 A4
Nordheim D 187 C7
Nordkirchen D 183 A8
Nouzonville F 184 E2
Noville B 184 D4
Nüdlingen D 187 A9
Nuenen NL 183 C7
Nuland NL 183 B6
Numansdorp NL 182 B4
Nunkirchen D 186 C2
Nunspeet NL 183 A7
Nürtingen D 187 D7
Nuth NL 183 D7

O
Oberderdingen D 187 C6
Oberfell D 185 D7
Oberharmersbach D 186 E5
Oberhausen D 183 C9
Oberhausen-Rheinhausen D 187 C5
Oberhoffen-sur-Moder F 186 D4
Oberkirch D 186 D5
Oberkochen D 187 D9
Obermoschel D 186 B4
Obernai F 186 E3
Obernburg am Main D 187 B7
Oberndorf am Neckar D 187 E6
Obernheim-Kirchenarnbach D 186 C4
Ober-Olm D 185 E9
Ober-Roden D 187 B6
Oberrot D 187 C8
Obersinn D 187 A8
Obersontheim D 187 C7
Oberstenfeld D 187 C7
Oberthal D 186 B3
Oberthulba D 187 A8
Obertshausen D 187 A6
Oberwesel D 185 D8
Oberwolfach D 187 E5
Obrigheim D 187 C7
Obrigheim (Pfalz) D 187 B5
Ochsenfurt D 187 B9
Ochtrup D 183 A10
Öderheim am Glan D 186 B4
Oedelem B 182 C2
Oeffelt NL 183 B7
Oegstgeest NL 182 A5
Oene NL 183 A8

Oerlenbach D 187 A9
Oestrich-Winkel D 185 D8
Offenbach am Main D 187 A6
Offenbach an der Queich D 187 C5
Offenburg D 186 E4
Offerdingen D 187 E7
Oftersheim D 187 C6
Ogéviller F 186 D2
Ohey B 183 E6
Ohlsbach D 186 E4
Öhringen D 187 C7
Oignies F 182 E1
Oijen NL 183 B6
Oirschot NL 183 B6
Oisterwijk NL 183 B6
Oldenzaal NL 183 A9
Olen B 182 C5
Olfen D 185 A7
Olpe D 185 B8
Olst NL 183 A8
Onstmettingen D 187 E6
Ooltgensplaat NL 182 B4
Oostakker B 182 C2
Oostburg NL 182 C2
Oostende B 182 C1
Oosterbeek NL 183 B7
Oosterhout NL 182 B5
Oosterland NL 182 B4
Oosterzele B 182 D3
Oostham B 183 C6
Oostkamp B 182 C2
Oostkapelle NL 182 B3
Oostmalle B 182 C5
Oost-Souburg NL 182 C3
Oostvoorne NL 182 B4
Ootmarsum NL 183 A9
Opglabbeek B 183 C7
Opheusden NL 183 B7
Opitter B 183 C7
Oploo NL 183 B7
Opoeteren B 183 C7
Oppenau D 187 E5
Oppenheim D 185 E9
Oppenweiler D 187 D7
Opwijk B 182 D4
Orchies F 182 E2
Orenhofen D 185 E6
Oreye B 183 D6
Ortenberg D 186 E4
Osburg D 186 B2
Oss NL 183 B7
Ossendrecht NL 182 C4
Ostend B 182 C1
Osterburken D 187 C7
Ostfildern D 187 D7
Osthofen D 187 B5
Ostricourt F 182 E2
Östringen D 187 C6
Ostwald F 186 D4
Ötigheim D 187 D5
Ötisheim D 187 D6
Ottenheim D 186 E4
Ottenhöfen im Schwarzwald D 187 E5
Otterbach D 186 C4
Otterberg D 186 B4
Otterlo NL 183 A7
Ottersweier D 186 D5
Ottignies B 182 D5
Ottweiler D 186 C3
Oud-Beijerland NL 182 B4
Ouddorp NL 182 B3
Oudenaarde B 182 D3
Oudenbosch NL 182 B5
Oudenburg B 182 C2
Oude-Tonge NL 182 B4
Oudewater NL 182 A5
Oud-Gastel NL 182 B4
Oud-Turnhout B 182 C5
Oud-Vossemeer NL 182 B4
Oudzele B 182 C2
Ouffet B 183 E6
Oulder B 184 D5
Oupeye B 183 D7
Overath D 185 C7
Overdinkel NL 183 A10
Overijse B 182 D5
Overloon NL 183 B7
Overpelt B 183 C6
Ovezande NL 182 B4
Owen D 187 D7

P
Paal B 183 C6
Padoux F 186 E2
Paliseul B 184 E3
Palzem D 186 B1
Pange F 186 C1
Panningen NL 183 C7
Papendrecht NL 182 B5
Partenstein D 187 A8
Pâturages B 182 E3
Pecq B 182 D2
Peer B 183 C6
Pelm D 185 D6
Pepingen B 182 D4
Pepinster B 183 D7
Perl D 186 C1
Péruwelz B 182 D3
Perwez B 182 D5
Petite-Rosselle F 186 C2
Petitmont F 186 D2
Pexonne F 186 E2
Pfaffenhofen an der Roth D 187 E9
Pfaffenhoffen F 186 D4
Pfalzfeld D 185 D8
Pfalzgrafenweiler D 187 D6
Pfedelbach D 187 C7
Pforzheim D 187 D6
Pfronstetten D 187 E7
Pfullingen D 187 E7
Pfungstadt D 187 B5
Phalsbourg F 186 D3
Philippeville B 184 D2
Philippine NL 182 C3
Philippsburg D 187 C5
Piershil NL 182 B4
Piesport D 185 E6
Pijnacker NL 182 A4
Pirmasens D 186 C4
Pittem B 182 D2
Plaidt D 185 D7
Plettenberg D 185 B8
Pliezhausen D 187 D7
Plobsheim F 186 E4
Plochingen D 187 D7
Ploegsteert B 182 D1
Plüderhausen D 187 D8

Poederlee B 182 C5
Polch D 185 D7
Polsbroek NL 182 B5
Pompey F 186 D1
Pont-à-Celles B 182 D4
Pont-à-Marcq F 182 D2
Pont-de-Loup B 182 E5
Poppenhausen D 187 A9
Portieux F 186 E1
Posterholt NL 183 C8
Poussay F 186 E1
Pracht D 185 C8
Prinsenbeek NL 182 B5
Profondeville B 184 D2
Pronsfeld D 185 D5
Provenchères-sur-Fave F 186 E3
Prüm D 185 D5
Puderbach D 185 C8
Pulheim D 183 C9
Putte B 182 C5
Puttelange-aux-Lacs F 186 C2
Putten NL 183 A7
Püttlingen D 186 C2
Puurs B 182 C4

Q
Quaregnon B 182 E3
Queidersbach D 186 C4
Quendorf D 183 A10
Quesnoy-sur-Deûle F 182 D2
Quierschied D 186 C3
Quiévrain B 182 E3
Quiévrechain F 182 E3

R
Raalte NL 183 A8
Raamsdonksveer NL 182 B5
Radevormwald D 185 B7
Raeren B 183 D8
Raesfeld D 183 B9
Ralingen D 185 E6
Rambervillers F 186 E2
Rambrouch L 184 E4
Ramillies B 182 D5
Rammelsbach D 186 B3
Rammingen D 187 D9
Ramstein D 186 C4
Rance B 184 D1
Randersacker D 187 B8
Rangendingen D 187 E6
Ransbach-Baumbach D 185 D8
Ranst B 182 C5
Raon-l'Étape F 186 E2
Rastatt D 187 D5
Ratingen D 183 C9
Raubach D 185 C8
Ravels B 182 C5
Ravenstein NL 183 B7
Rebecq B 182 D4
Réchicourt-le-Château F 186 D2
Recht B 184 D5
Rechtenbach D 187 B8
Recklinghausen D 183 B10
Réding F 186 D3
Rees D 183 B8
Rehlingen-Siersburg D 186 C2
Reichelsheim (Odenwald) D 187 B6
Reichenbach D 187 B6
Reichenberg D 187 B8
Reicholzheim D 187 B8
Reichshoffen F 186 D4
Reichstett F 186 D4
Reil D 185 D7
Reilingen D 187 C6
Reinheim D 187 B6
Reinsfeld D 186 B2
Reken D 183 B10
Rekken NL 183 A9
Remagen D 185 C7
Remich L 186 B1
Remicourt B 183 D6
Remouchamps B 183 E7
Remscheid D 183 C10
Renchen D 186 E5
Renesse NL 182 B3
Rengsdorf D 185 C7
Renkum NL 183 B7
Rennerod D 185 C9
Renningen D 187 D6
Renswoude NL 183 A7
Renwez F 184 E2
Retie B 183 C6
Reusel NL 183 C6
Reutlingen D 187 E7
Reuver NL 183 C8
Revin F 184 E2
Rhaunen D 185 E7
Rhede D 183 B9
Rheden NL 183 A8
Rheinau D 186 D4
Rheinbach D 183 D9
Rheinberg D 183 B9
Rheinböllen D 185 E8
Rheinbreitbach D 185 C7
Rheinbrohl D 185 D7
Rheinstetten D 187 D5
Rheinzabern D 187 C5
Rhenen NL 183 B7
Rhens D 185 D8
Rhinau F 186 E4
Rhisnes B 182 D5
Rhoon NL 182 B4
Richardménil F 186 D1
Ridderkerk NL 182 B4
Riegelsberg D 186 C2
Riemst B 183 D7
Rieneck D 187 A8
Riethoven NL 183 C6
Rijen NL 182 B5
Rijkevorsel B 182 C5
Rijnsburg NL 182 A4
Rijsbergen NL 182 B5
Rijsel F 182 D2
Rijssen NL 183 A9
Rijswijk NL 182 A4
Rilland NL 182 C4
Rimbach D 187 B6
Rimogne F 184 E2
Rips NL 183 B7
Rittersdorf D 185 D5
Rixensart B 182 D5
Rochefort B 184 D3
Rochehaut B 184 E3
Rochin F 182 D2
Rockanje NL 182 B4

Rockenhausen D 186 B4
Rocroi F 184 E2
Rodalben D 186 C4
Roermond NL 183 C7
Roeselare B 182 D2
Roetgen D 183 D8
Roggel NL 183 C7
Rohrbach-lès-Bitche F 186 C3
Rombas F 186 C1
Rommerskirchen D 183 C9
Ronse B 182 D3
Roosendaal NL 182 B5
Rosée B 184 D2
Rosenfeld D 187 E6
Rosheim F 186 D3
Rosmalen NL 183 B6
Rösrath D 185 C7
Roßdorf D 187 B6
Rossum NL 183 B6
Rot am See D 187 C9
Rothenberg D 187 B6
Rothenbuch D 187 B7
Rothenburg ob der Tauber D 187 C9
Rothenfels D 187 B8
Rotheux-Rimière B 183 D6
Rotselaar B 182 D5
Rottenacker D 187 E8
Rottenburg am Neckar D 187 E6
Rottendorf D 187 B9
Rottingham D 183 A10
Röttingen D 187 B8
Roubaix F 182 D2
Roulers B 182 D2
Rouvroy F 182 E1
Rouvroy-sur-Audry F 184 E2
Rozenburg NL 182 B4
Rozendaal NL 183 A7
Ruddervoorde B 182 C2
Rudersberg D 187 D8
Rüdesheim D 185 E8
Ruiselede B 182 C2
Rülzheim D 187 C5
Rumes B 182 D2
Rumigny F 184 E1
Rumst B 182 C4
Runkel D 185 D9
Rüsselsheim D 187 A5
Rutesheim D 187 D6
Rüthen D 185 B9
Rütten-Scheid D 183 C9
Ruurlo NL 183 A8

S
Saales F 186 E3
Saarbrücken D 186 C2
Saarburg D 186 B2
Saarlouis D 186 C2
Saarwellingen D 186 C2
Sachsenheim D 187 D7
St-Amand-les-Eaux F 182 E2
St-Avold F 186 C2
St-Blaise-la-Roche F 186 E3
St-Clément F 186 D2
St-Dié F 186 E2
Ste-Marguerite F 186 E2
Ste-Marie-aux-Mines F 186 E3
St-Firmin F 186 E1
St-Ghislain B 182 E3
St-Hubert B 184 D4
St-Louis-lès-Bitche F 186 D3
St-Max F 186 D1
St-Michel F 184 E1
St-Michel-sur-Meurthe F 186 E2
St-Nicolas B 183 D7
St-Nicolas-de-Port F 186 D1
St-Oedenrode NL 183 B6
St-Quirin F 186 D3
St-Vith B 184 D5
Salmtal D 185 E6
Sandhausen D 187 C6
Sankt Augustin D 185 C7
Sankt Goar D 185 D8
Sankt Goarshausen D 185 D8
Sankt Ingbert D 186 C3
Sankt Julian D 186 B4
Sankt Katharinen D 185 C7
Sankt Wendel D 186 C3
Santpoort NL 182 A5
Sarralbe F 186 C3
Sarrebourg F 186 D3
Sarreguemines F 186 C3
Sarre-Union F 186 D3
Sart B 183 D7
Sasbach D 186 D5
Sasbachwalden D 186 D5
Sassenheim NL 182 A5
Sas Van Gent NL 182 C3
Satteldorf D 187 C9
Saulheim D 185 E9
Saverne F 186 D3
Schaafheim D 187 B7
Schaarsbergen NL 183 A7
Schaerbeek B 182 D4
Schaesberg NL 183 D8
Schaijk NL 183 B7
Schalkhaar NL 183 A8
Schalksmühle D 185 B8
Scharendijke NL 182 B3
Schebheim D 187 B9
Schenkenzell D 187 E5
Schermbeck D 183 B9
Scherpenheuvel B 182 D5
Scherpenzeel NL 183 A6
Scherwiller F 186 E3
Schiedam NL 182 B4
Schieren L 184 E5
Schifferstadt D 187 C5
Schiffweiler D 186 C3
Schijndel NL 183 B6
Schilde B 182 C5
Schillingen D 186 B2
Schiltach D 187 E5
Schiltigheim F 186 D4
Schinnen NL 183 D7
Schinveld NL 183 D7
Schipluiden NL 182 B4
Schirmeck F 186 E3
Schlangenbad D 185 D9
Schleiden D 185 D5
Schmallenberg D 185 B9
Schmelz D 186 C2
Schnelldorf D 187 C9
Schnürpflingen D 187 E8
Schoenberg B 185 D5
Schöllkrippen D 187 A7
Schömberg D 187 D6

Schönaich D 187 D7
Schondra D 187 A8
Schönecken D 185 D5
Schönenberg-Kübelberg D 186 C3
Schöntal D 187 C8
Schoondijke NL 182 C3
Schoonhoven NL 182 B5
Schorndorf D 187 D8
Schoten B 182 C4
Schriesheim D 187 C6
Schrozberg D 187 C9
Schuttertal D 186 E4
Schutterwald D 186 E4
Schüttorf D 183 A10
Schwäbisch Gmünd D 187 D8
Schwäbisch Hall D 187 C8
Schwaigern D 187 C7
Schwalbach D 186 C2
Schwegenheim D 187 C5
Schweich D 185 E6
Schweigen-Rechtenbach D 186 C4
Schweinfurt D 187 A9
Schwelm D 185 B7
Schwerte D 185 B8
Schwieberdingen D 187 D7
Seckach D 187 C7
Seclin F 182 D2
Seebach D 187 D5
Seeheim-Jugenheim D 187 B6
Seilles B 183 D6
Seinsheim D 187 B9
Sélestat F 186 E3
Seligenstadt D 187 A6
Selm D 185 A7
Selters (Westerwald) D 185 C8
Seltz F 186 D5
Senden D 187 E9
Seneffe B 182 D4
Senones F 186 E2
Seraing B 183 D7
Serooskerke NL 182 B3
Serrig D 186 B2
Sevenum NL 183 C8
's-Gravendeel NL 182 B5
's-Gravenhage NL 182 A4
's-Gravenmoer NL 182 B5
's-Gravenpolder NL 182 C3
's-Gravenvoeren B 183 D7
's-Gravenzande NL 182 A4
's-Heerenberg NL 183 B8
's-Heerenhoek NL 182 C3
's-Hertogenbosch NL 183 B6
Siebengewald NL 183 B8
Siegburg D 185 C7
Siegen D 185 C9
Sierck-les-Bains F 186 C1
Siershahn D 185 D8
Signy-le-Petit F 184 E1
Sijsele B 182 C2
Silenrieux B 184 D1
Simmerath D 183 D8
Simmern (Hunsrück) D 185 E8
Simpelveld D 183 D7
Sindelfingen D 187 D6
Singhofen D 185 D8
Sinn D 185 C9
Sinsheim D 187 C6
Sint Annaland NL 182 B4
Sint Anthonis NL 183 B7
Sint-Genesius-Rode B 182 D4
Sint-Gillis-Waas B 182 C4
Sint-Huibrechts-Lille B 183 C6
Sint Jansteen NL 182 C4
Sint-Katelijne-Waver B 182 C5
Sint-Laureins B 182 C2
Sint-Lenaarts B 182 C5
Sint Maartensdijk NL 182 B4
Sint-Margriete B 182 C3
Sint-Maria-Lierde B 182 D3
Sint-Martens-Latem B 182 C2
Sint Michielsgestel NL 183 B6
Sint-Niklaas B 182 C4
Sint Odilienberg NL 183 C8
Sint-Pauwels B 182 C4
Sint Philipsland NL 182 B4
Sint-Pieters-Leeuw B 182 D4
Sint-Truiden B 183 D6
Sinzheim D 187 D5
Sinzig D 185 C7
Sittard NL 183 D7
Sivry B 184 D1
Sleidinge B 182 C3
Sliedrecht NL 182 B5
Sluis NL 182 C2
Sluiskil NL 182 C3
Soerendonk NL 183 C7
Soest D 185 A9
Soest NL 183 A6
Soesterberg NL 183 A6
Soheit-Tinlot B 183 E6
Sohren D 185 E7
Soignies B 182 D4
Solingen D 183 C10
Sombreffe B 182 D5
Someren NL 183 C7
Somme-Leuze B 184 D3
Somzée B 184 D1
Son NL 183 B6
Souffelnheim F 186 D4
Soultz-sous-Forêts F 186 D4
Soumagne B 183 D7
Spa B 183 E7
Spabrücken D 185 E8
Spay D 185 D8
Speicher D 185 E6
Speyer D 187 C5
Spiere B 182 D2
Spiesen-Elversberg D 186 C3
Spijkenisse NL 182 B4
Spontin B 184 D3
Spraitbach D 187 D8
Sprendlingen D 185 E8
Sprimont B 183 D7
Sprockhövel D 185 B7
Staden B 182 D2
Stadtkyll D 185 D6
Stadtlohn D 183 B9
Staig D 187 E8
Standdaarbuiten NL 182 B5
Stavelot B 184 D4
Stavenisse NL 182 B4
Steenbergen NL 182 B4
Steenderen NL 183 A8
Stein NL 183 D7
Steinach D 186 E5
Steinfeld D 185 D5
Steinfeld D 187 B8
Steinheim am Albuch D 187 D9

Steinheim an der Murr D 187 D7
Steinsfeld D 187 C9
Steinwenden D 186 C4
Stekene B 182 C4
Stellendam NL 182 B4
Stevensweert NL 183 C6
Stimpfach D 187 C9
Stiring-Wendel F 186 C2
Stockstadt am Rhein D 187 B5
Stolberg (Rheinland) D 183 D8
Stoumont B 183 E7
Straelen D 183 C8
Straimont B 184 E3
Stramproy NL 183 C7
Strasbourg F 186 D4
Strassen L 186 B1
Straßenhaus D 185 C8
Strijen NL 182 B5
Stromberg D 185 E8
Sturzelbronn F 186 C4
Stuttgart D 187 D7
Sundern D 183 A10
Sulz am Neckar D 187 E6
Sulzbach an der Murr D 187 C7
Sulzbach-Laufen D 187 D8
Sulzbach/Saar D 186 C3
Sulzfeld D 187 C6
Sulzthal D 187 A9
Sundern (Sauerland) D 185 B9
Susteren NL 183 C7
Swalmen NL 183 C8

T
Taintrux F 186 E2
Talange F 186 C1
Tamm D 187 D7
Tantonville F 186 E1
Tauberbischofsheim D 187 B8
Tawern D 186 B2
Tegelen NL 183 C8
Tellin B 184 D3
Templeuve F 182 D2
Temse B 182 C4
Tenneville B 184 D4
Ter Aar NL 182 A5
Terborg-Silvolde NL 183 B8
Terheijden NL 182 B5
Terneuzen NL 182 C3
Tervuren B 182 D5
Tessenderlo B 183 C6
Testelt B 182 C5
Teteringen NL 182 B5
Thaleischweiler-Fröschen D 186 C4
Thalfang D 186 B2
Thaon-les-Vosges F 186 E1
't Harde NL 183 A7
Theux B 183 D7
Thionville F 186 C1
Tholen NL 182 B4
Tholey D 186 C3
Thommen B 184 D5
Thorn NL 183 C7
Thuin B 184 D1
Thüngen D 187 B8
Thüngersheim D 187 B8
Tiefenbronn D 187 D6
Tiel NL 183 B6
Tielen B 182 C5
Tielt B 182 D2
Tienen B 182 D5
Tilburg NL 183 B6
Tongeren B 183 D6
Tönisvorst D 183 C8
Torhout B 182 C2
Tourcoing F 182 D2
Tournai B 182 D2
Traar D 183 C9
Traben D 185 E7
Trarbach D 185 E7
Trebur D 187 B5
Treis D 185 D7
Tremelo B 182 D5
Trier D 186 B2
Trierweiler D 186 B2
Trippstadt D 186 C4
Trittenheim D 185 E6
Trochtelfingen D 187 E7
Troisdorf D 183 D10
Troisfontaines F 186 D3
Trois-Ponts B 184 D4
Troisvierges L 184 D5
Trooz B 183 D7
Truchtersheim F 186 D4
Trulben D 186 C4
Tubbergen NL 183 A9
Tübingen D 187 D7
Tubize B 182 D4
Turnhout B 182 C5
Twello NL 183 A8

U
Übach-Palenberg D 183 D8
Überherrn D 186 C2
Ubstadt-Weiher D 187 C6
Uccle B 182 D4
Üchtelhausen D 187 A9
Uckange F 186 C1
Uddel NL 183 A7
Uden NL 183 B7
Üdersdorf D 185 D6
Uettingen D 187 B8
Uffenheim D 187 B9
Uhingen D 187 D7
Uithoorn NL 182 A5
Ulft NL 183 B8
Ulicoten NL 182 C5
Ulm D 187 E8
Ulmen D 185 D6
Ulvenhout NL 182 B5
Undingen D 187 E7
Unkel D 185 C7
Unnau D 185 C9
Untermünkheim D 187 C8
Unterpleichfeld D 187 B9
Urbach D 185 C8
Urbar D 185 D8
Urberach D 187 B6
Utrecht NL 183 A6
Üxheim D 185 D6

V
Vaals NL 183 D8
Vaassen NL 183 A7
Valkenburg NL 183 D7
Valkenswaard NL 183 C6
Vallendar D 185 D8
Vandœuvre-lès-Nancy F 186 D1
Varik NL 183 B6
Varsseveld NL 183 B8
Vaux-sur-Sûre B 184 E4
Veendam NL 183 A7
Veere NL 182 B3
Veerle B 182 C5
Veghel NL 183 B7
Velbert D 183 C10
Veldegem B 182 C2
Velden NL 183 C8
Veldhoven NL 183 C6
Velen D 183 B9
Vellberg D 187 C8
Velp NL 183 B7
Vendenheim F 186 D4
Venlo NL 183 C8
Venray NL 183 B7
Vergaville F 186 D2
Verlaine B 183 D6
Verny F 186 C1
Verviers B 183 D7
Vessem NL 183 C6
Vettelschoss D 185 C7
Vianden L 184 E5
Vianen NL 183 B6
Vic-sur-Seille F 186 D2
Vielsalm B 184 D4
Vierlingsbeek NL 183 B7
Viernheim D 187 B6
Viersen D 183 C8
Vieux-Condé F 182 E3
Vigy F 186 C1
Villé F 186 E3
Villeneuve-d'Ascq F 182 D2
Villers-le-Bouillet B 183 D6
Villers-lès-Nancy F 186 D1
Villmar D 185 D9
Vilvoorde B 182 D4
Vincey F 186 E1
Vinkt B 182 C2
Vinningen D 186 C4
Vireux-Molhain F 184 E2
Vireux-Wallerand F 184 D2
Visé B 183 D7
Vlaardingen NL 182 B4
Vleuten NL 183 A6
Vlijmen NL 183 B6
Vlissingen NL 182 C3
Voerde (Niederrhein) D 183 B9
Vogelenzang NL 182 A5
Vogelweh D 186 C4
Vöhringen D 187 E6
Vöhringen D 187 E9
Volkach D 187 B9
Volkel NL 183 B7
Völklingen D 186 C2
Volmunster F 186 C3
Voorburg NL 182 A4
Voorhout NL 182 A4
Voorschoten NL 182 A4
Voorst NL 183 A8
Voorthuizen NL 183 A7
Vorden NL 183 A8
Vorst B 183 C6
Vosselaar B 182 C5
Vrasene B 182 C4
Vreden D 183 A9
Vreeland NL 183 A6
Vresse B 184 E2
Vriezenveen NL 183 A9
Vrouwenpolder NL 182 B3
Vught NL 183 B6

W
Waalre NL 183 C6
Waalwijk NL 183 B6
Waarschoot B 182 C3
Wachenheim an der Weinstraße D 187 C5
Wachtebeke B 182 C3
Wächtersbach D 187 A7
Waddinxveen NL 182 A5
Wadern D 186 B2
Wadersloh D 185 A9
Wadgassen D 186 C2
Wageningen NL 183 B7
Waghäusel D 187 C6
Waiblingen D 187 D7
Waibstadt D 187 C6
Waigolshausen D 187 B9
Waimes B 183 D8
Walcourt B 184 D1
Waldachtal D 187 E6
Waldböckelheim D 185 E8
Waldbreitbach D 185 C8
Waldbröl D 185 C8
Waldbrunn-Lahr D 185 C9
Waldbüttelbrunn D 187 B8
Waldenbuch D 187 D7
Waldenburg D 187 C8
Waldesch D 185 D8
Waldfischbach-Burgalben D 186 C4
Wald-Michelbach D 187 B6
Waldmohr D 186 C3
Waldrach D 186 B2
Waldsee D 187 C5
Waldstetten D 187 D8
Walferdange L 186 B1
Walldorf D 187 A6
Walldorf D 187 C6
Walldürn D 187 B7
Wallhausen D 185 C9
Wallhausen D 187 C9
Wamel NL 183 B6
Wandre B 183 D7
Wanne-Eikel D 183 B10
Wanroij NL 183 B7
Wanssum NL 183 B8
Wanze B 183 D6
Wapenveld NL 183 A8
Waregem B 182 D2
Waremme B 183 D6
Warmond NL 182 A5
Warnsveld NL 183 A8
Warstein D 185 B9
Wartmannsroth D 187 A8
Wäschenbeuren D 187 D8
Waspik NL 182 B5
Wasseiges B 183 D6
Wasselonne F 186 D3

Wassenaar *NL* **182** A4
Wassenberg *D* **183** C8
Wasseralfingen *D* **187** D9
Wasserbillig *D* **186** B2
Wasserliesch *D* **186** B2
Wasserlosen *D* **187** A9
Wateringen *NL* **182** A4
Waterland-Oudeman *B* **182** C3
Waterloo *B* **182** D4
Watten-Scheid *D* **183** C10
Wavre *B* **182** D5
Wavrin *F* **182** D1
Waxweiler *D* **185** D5
Waziers *F* **182** E2
Weelde *B* **182** C5
Weerselo *NL* **183** A9
Weert *NL* **183** C7
Weesp *NL* **183** A6
Weeze *D* **183** B8
Wegberg *D* **183** C8
Wehl *NL* **183** B8
Weibern *D* **183** E10
Weibersbrunn *D* **187** B7
Weidenstetten *D* **187** D8
Weidenthal *D* **186** C4
Weiersbach *D* **186** B3
Weikersheim *D* **187** C8
Weilbach *D* **187** B7
Weilburg *D* **185** D9
Weil der Stadt *D* **187** D6
Weilerbach *D* **186** C4
Weilerswist *D* **183** D9
Weilheim an der Teck *D* **187** D8
Weilmünster *D* **185** D9
Weinbach *D* **185** D9

Weingarten (Baden) *D* **187** C6
Weinheim *D* **187** B6
Weinsberg *D* **187** C7
Weinsheim *D* **185** D5
Weinsheim *D* **185** E8
Weinstadt *D* **187** D7
Weiskirchen *D* **186** B2
Weissach *D* **187** D6
Weißenhorn *D* **187** E9
Weißenthurm *D* **185** D7
Weiswampach *L* **184** D5
Weitbruch *F* **186** D4
Weitefeld *D* **185** C8
Weiterstadt *D* **187** B6
Wekerom *NL* **183** A7
Welkenraedt *B* **183** D7
Well *NL* **183** B8
Wellen *B* **183** D6
Wellin *B* **184** D3
Welling *D* **185** D7
Welschbillig *D* **185** E6
Welver *D* **185** A8
Welzheim *D* **187** D8
Wemeldinge *NL* **182** B4
Wendelsheim *D* **186** B5
Wenden *D* **185** C8
Wendlingen am Neckar *D* **187** D7
Wenduine *B* **182** C2
Wengsel (Isterberg) *D* **183** A10
Wépion *B* **182** E5
Werbach *D* **187** B8
Werbomont *B* **184** D4
Werdohl *D* **185** B8
Werkendam *NL* **182** B5

Werl *D* **185** A8
Wermelskirchen *D* **185** B7
Wernau *D* **187** D7
Werne *D* **185** A8
Werneck *D* **187** B9
Wertheim *D* **187** B8
Wervik *B* **182** D2
Wesel *D* **183** B9
Wesepe *NL* **183** A8
Wesseling *D* **183** D9
Wessem *NL* **183** C7
Westerburg *D* **185** C8
Westerheim *D* **187** D8
Westerhoven *NL* **183** C6
Westerlo *B* **182** C5
Westerstetten *D* **187** D8
Westervoort *NL* **183** B7
Westhausen *D* **187** D9
Westhofen *D* **187** B5
Westhoffen *F* **186** D3
Westkapelle *NL* **182** B2
Westmalle *B* **182** C5
Wetter (Ruhr) *D* **185** B7
Wetteren *B* **182** C3
Wevelgem *B* **182** D2
Weyerbusch *D* **185** C8
Weyersheim *F* **186** D4
Wichelen *B* **182** C3
Wickede (Ruhr) *D* **185** B8
Wiehl *D* **185** C8
Wielsbeke *B* **182** D2
Wierden *NL* **183** A9
Wiernsheim *D* **187** D6
Wiesbaden *D* **185** D9
Wiesen *D* **187** A7

Wiesensteig *D* **187** D8
Wiesloch *D* **187** C6
Wijchen *NL* **183** B7
Wijhe *NL* **183** A8
Wijk bij Duurstede *NL* **183** B6
Wijk en Aalburg *NL* **183** B6
Wildberg *D* **187** D6
Wilhelminadorp *NL* **183** C6
Willebroek *B* **182** C4
Willemstad *NL* **182** B4
Willich *D* **183** C9
Willstätt *D* **186** D4
Wilnis *NL* **182** A5
Wilnsdorf *D* **185** C9
Wilp *NL* **183** A8
Wiltingen *D* **186** B2
Wiltz *L* **184** E4
Wincheringen *D* **186** B1
Wincrange *L* **184** D4
Windesheim *D* **185** E8
Windhagen *D* **185** C7
Wingene *B* **182** C2
Wingen-sur-Moder *F* **186** D3
Winnenden *D* **187** D7
Winningen *D* **185** D8
Winnweiler *D* **186** B4
Winssen *NL* **183** B7
Winterswijk *NL* **183** B9
Wintrich *D* **185** E6
Wipperfürth *D* **185** B7
Wirges *D* **185** D8
Wissembourg *F* **186** C4
Wissen *D* **185** C8
Wissenkerke *NL* **182** B3
Witten *D* **185** B7

Wittighausen *D* **187** B8
Wittlich *D* **185** E6
Woensdrecht *NL* **182** C4
Woerden *NL* **182** A5
Wœrth *F* **186** D4
Woippy *F* **186** C1
Wolfach *D* **187** E5
Wolfstein *D* **186** B4
Wolpertshausen *D* **187** C8
Wolphaartsdijk *NL* **182** B3
Wommelgem *B* **182** C5
Wormeldange *L* **186** B1
Worms *D* **187** B5
Wörrstadt *D* **185** E9
Wortel *B* **182** C5
Wörth am Main *D* **187** B7
Wörth am Rhein *D* **187** C5
Woudenberg *NL* **183** A6
Woudrichem *NL* **182** B5
Woustviller *F* **186** C3
Wouw *NL* **182** B4
Wuppertal *D* **183** C10
Würselen *D* **183** D8
Würzburg *D* **187** B8
Wüstenrot *D* **187** C7
Wuustwezel *B* **182** C5

X

Xanten *D* **183** B8

Y

Yerseke *NL* **182** C4
Ysselsteyn *NL* **183** C7
Yutz *F* **186** C1
Yvoir *B* **184** D2

Z

Zaamslag *NL* **182** C3
Zaandam *NL* **182** A5
Zaltbommel *NL* **183** B6
Zandhoven *B* **182** C5
Zandvliet *B* **182** C4
Zandvoort *NL* **182** A5
Zarren *B* **182** C1
Zaventem *B* **182** D4
Zeddam *NL* **183** B8
Zedelgem *B* **182** C2
Zeebrugge *B* **182** C2
Zeeland *NL* **183** B7
Zeewolde *NL* **183** A7
Zeiskam *D* **187** C5
Zeist *NL* **183** A6
Zeitlofs *D* **187** A8
Zele *B* **182** C4
Zelhem *NL* **183** A8
Zell (Mosel) *D* **185** D7
Zell am Harmersbach *D* **186** E5
Zell am Main *D* **187** B8
Zellingen *D* **187** B8
Zeltingen-Rachtig *D* **185** E7

Zelzate *B* **182** C3
Zemmer *D* **185** E6
Zemst *B* **182** D4
Zerf *D* **186** B2
Zevenaar *NL* **183** B8
Zevenbergen *NL* **182** B5
Zierikzee *NL* **182** B3
Zoelen *NL* **183** B6
Zoersel *B* **182** C5
Zoetermeer *NL* **182** A4
Zolder *B* **183** C6
Zomergem *B* **182** C3
Zonhoven *B* **183** D6
Zonnebeke *B* **182** D1
Zornheim *D* **185** E9
Zottegem *B* **182** D3
Zoutleeuw *B* **183** D6
Zuid-Beijerland *NL* **182** B4
Zuidland *NL* **182** B4
Zuienkerke *B* **182** C2
Zülpich *D* **183** D9
Zulte *B* **182** D2
Zundert *NL* **182** C5
Zutendaal *B* **183** D7
Zutphen *NL* **183** A8
Zweibrücken *D* **186** C3
Zwevegem *B* **182** D2
Zwevezele *B* **182** C2
Zwiefalten *D* **187** E7
Zwijndrecht *B* **182** C4
Zwijndrecht *NL* **182** B5
Zwingenberg *D* **187** B6

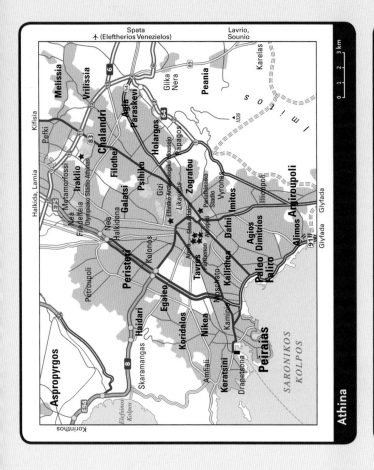

Athina

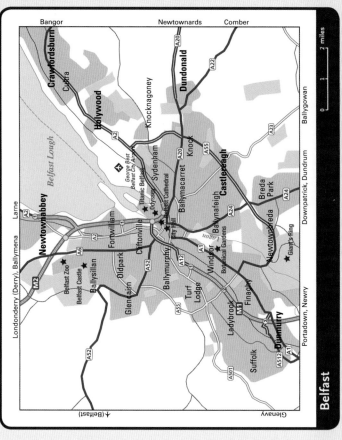

Belfast

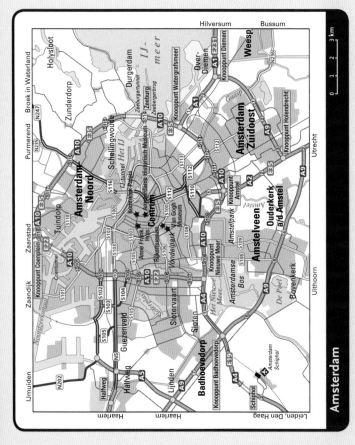

Amsterdam

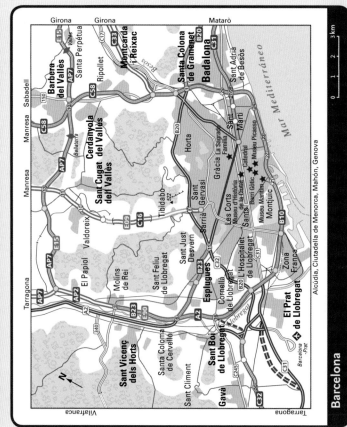

Barcelona

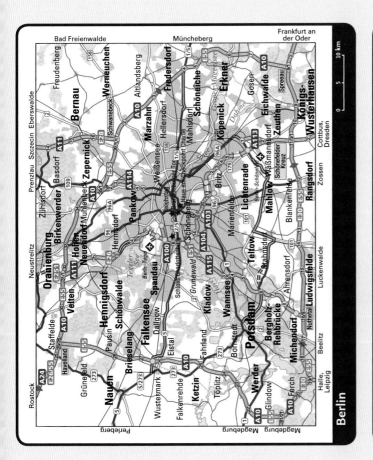

Berlin

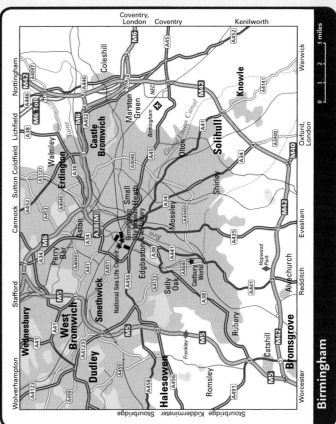

Birmingham

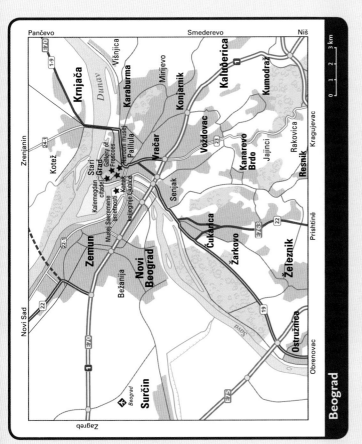

Beograd

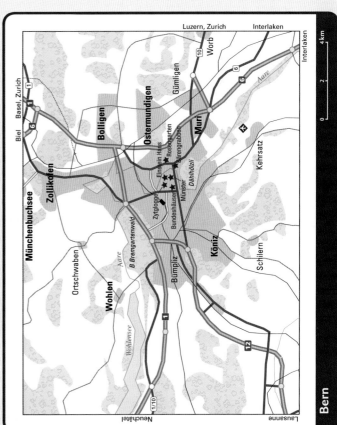

Bern

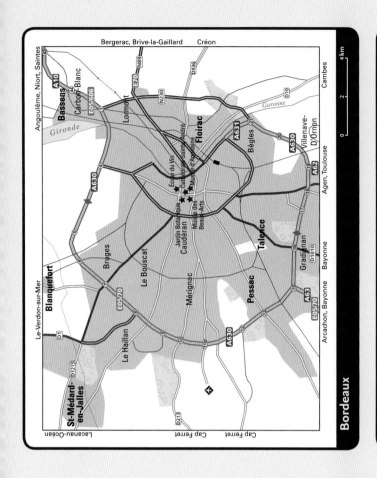

Bordeaux

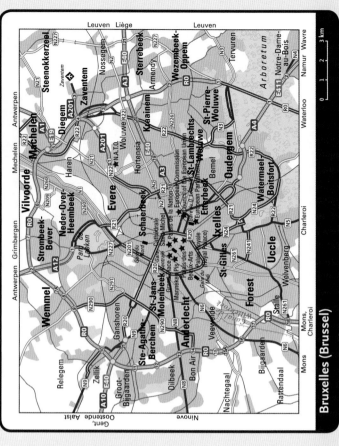

Bruxelles (Brussel)

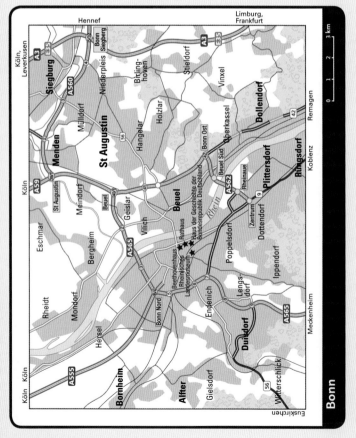

Bonn

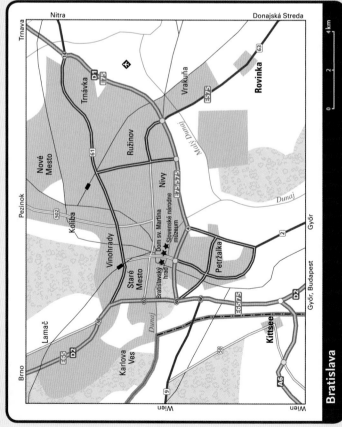

Bratislava

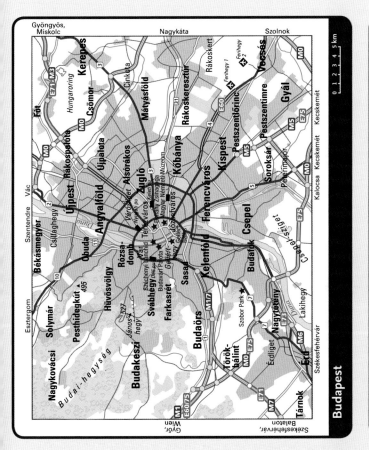

Budapest

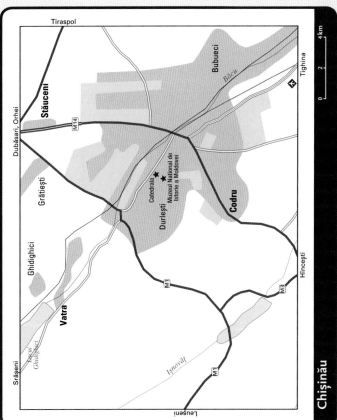

Chişinău

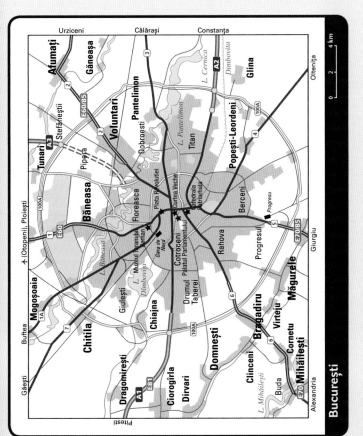

Bucureşti

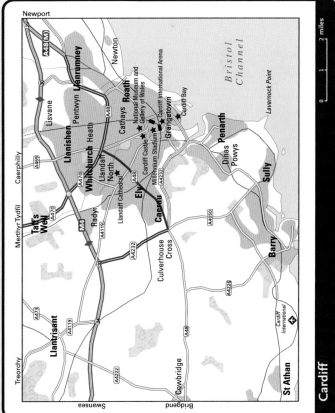

Cardiff

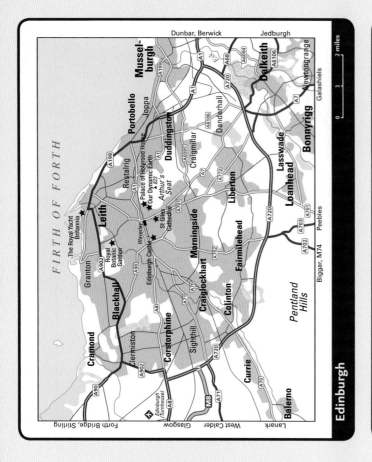

Edinburgh

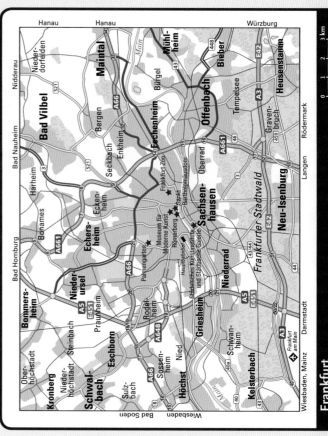

Frankfurt

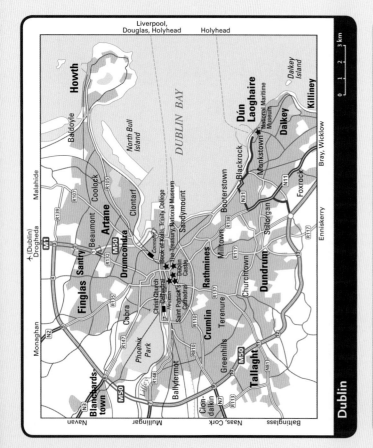

Dublin

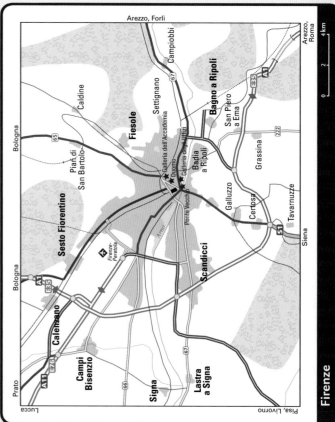

Firenze

Glasgow Göteborg Den Haag Hamburg 197

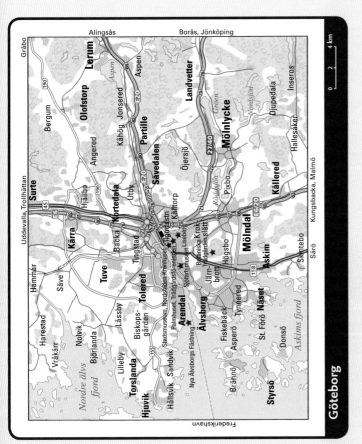

Göteborg

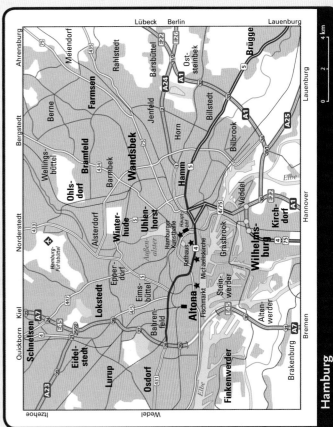

Hamburg

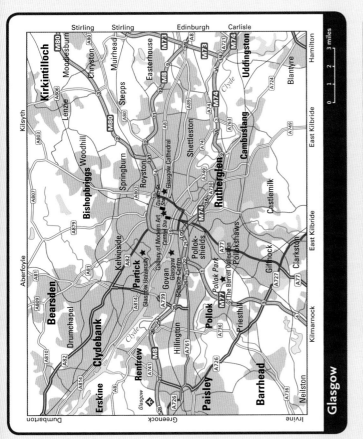

Glasgow

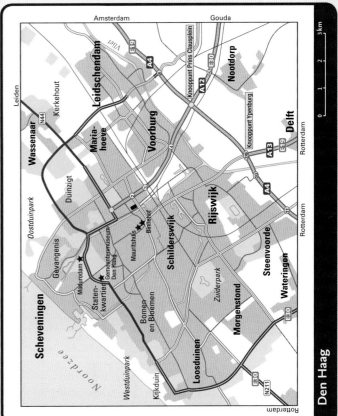

Den Haag

197

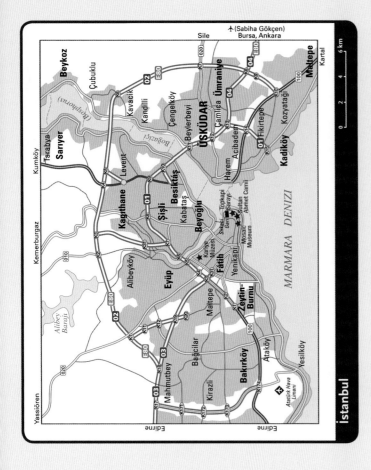

İstanbul

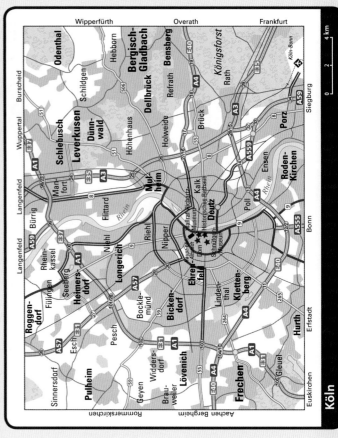

Köln

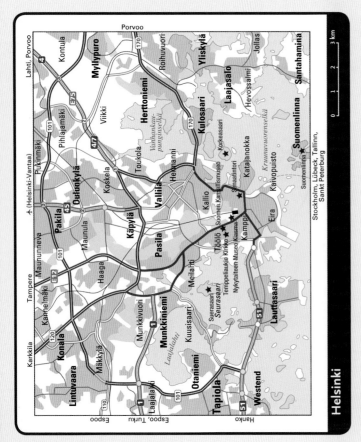

Helsinki

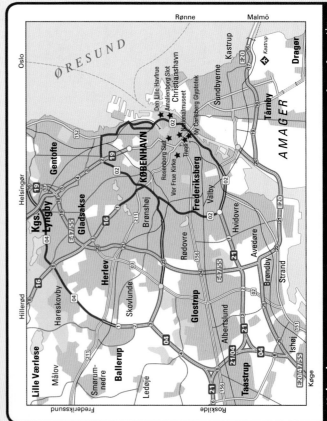

København

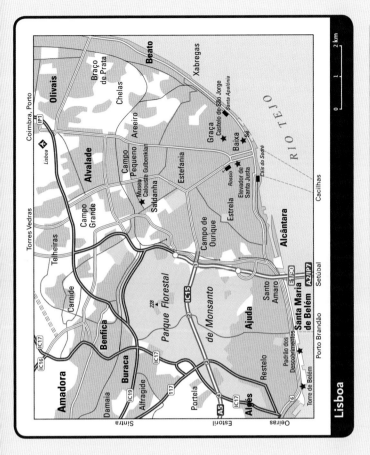

Lisboa

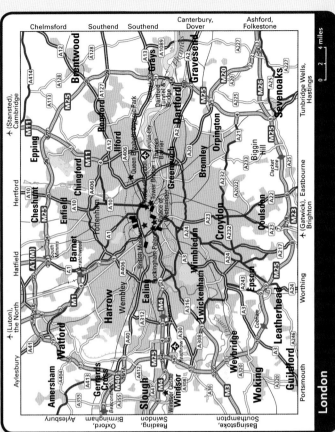

London

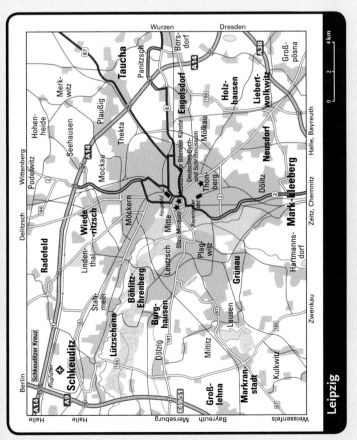

Leipzig

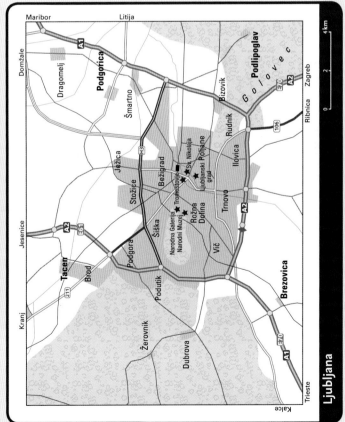

Ljubljana

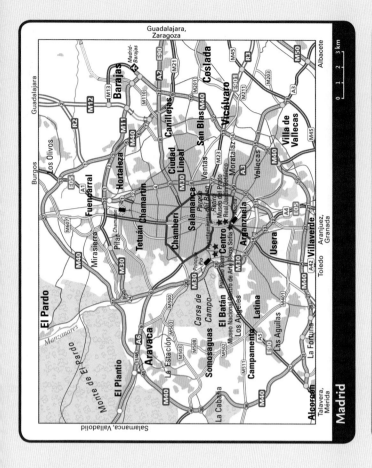

Madrid

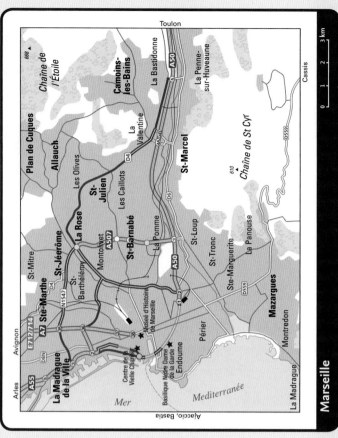

Marseille

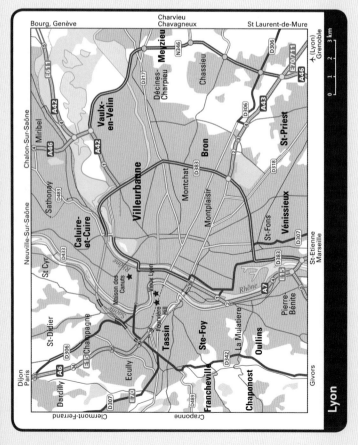

Lyon

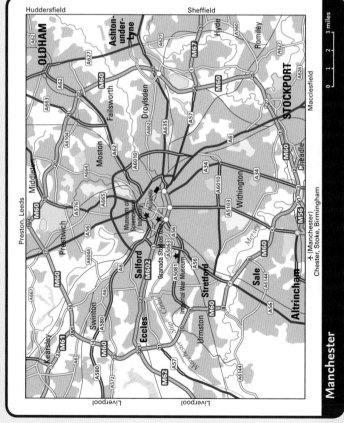

Manchester

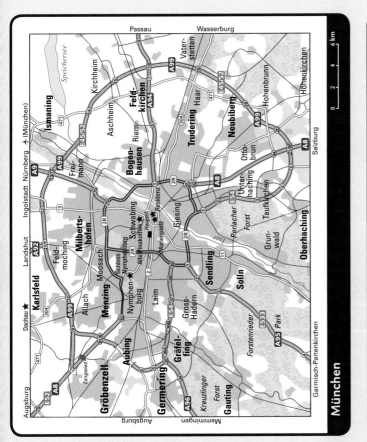

München

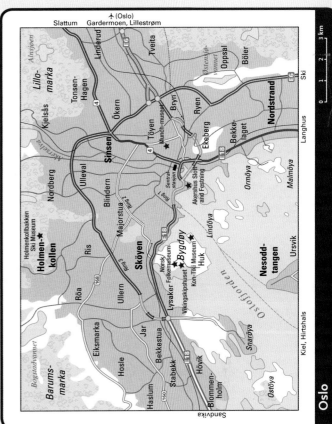

Oslo

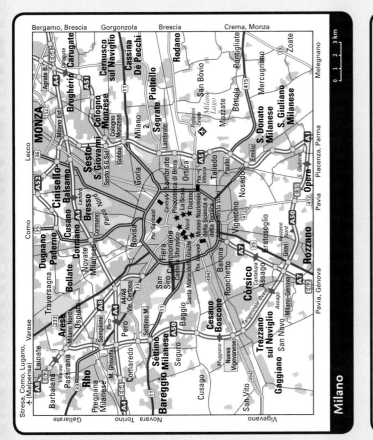

Milano

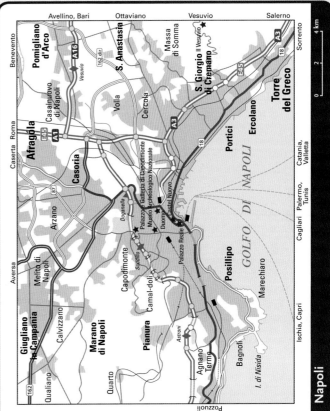

Napoli

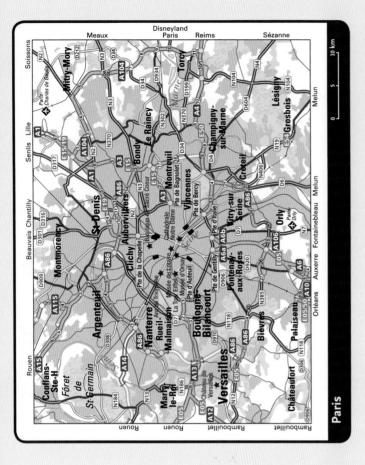

Paris

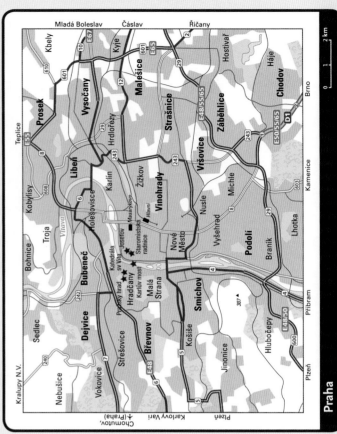

Praha

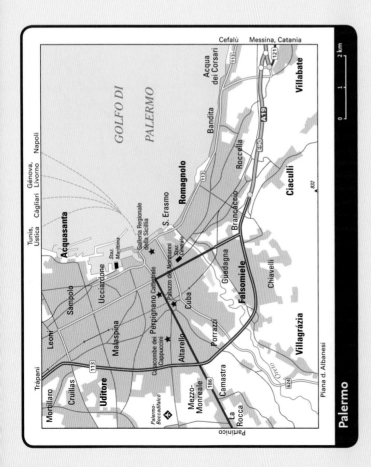

Palermo

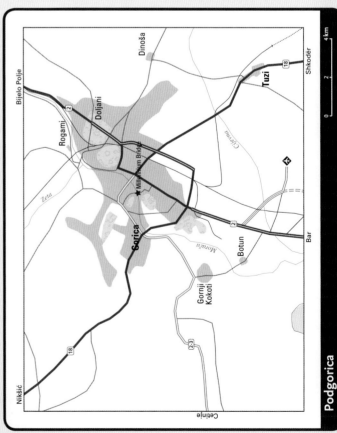

Podgorica

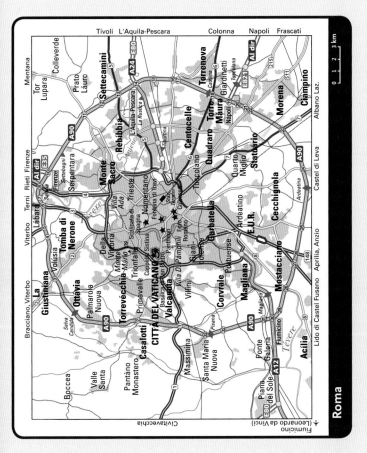

Roma

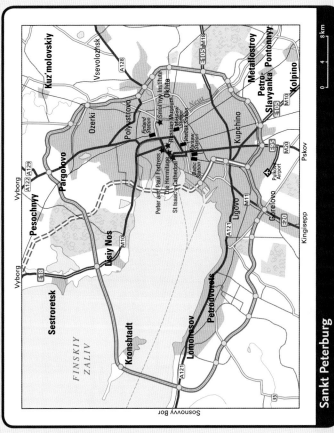

Sankt Peterburg

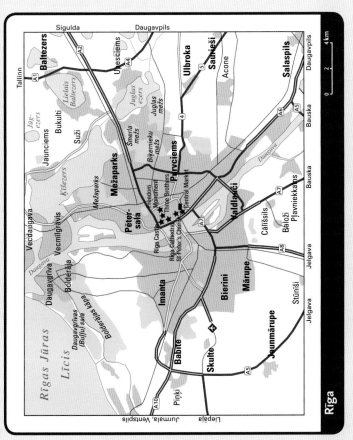

Rīga

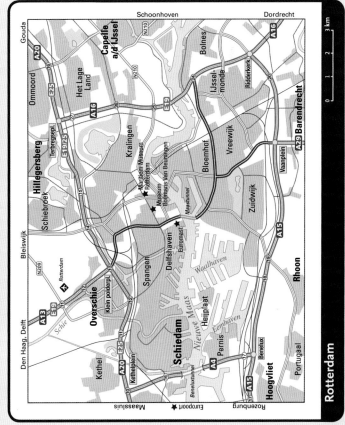

Rotterdam

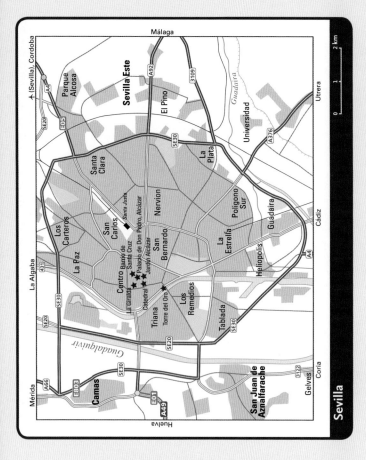

Sevilla

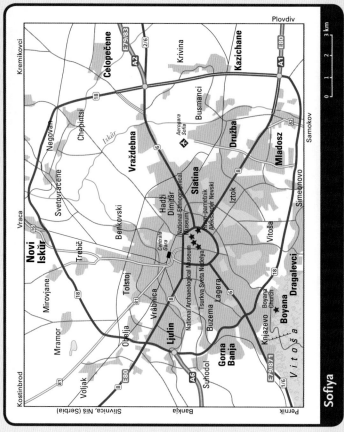

Sofiya

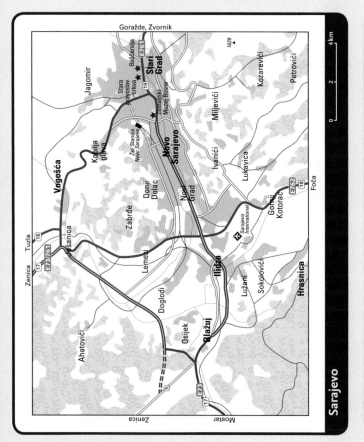

Sarajevo

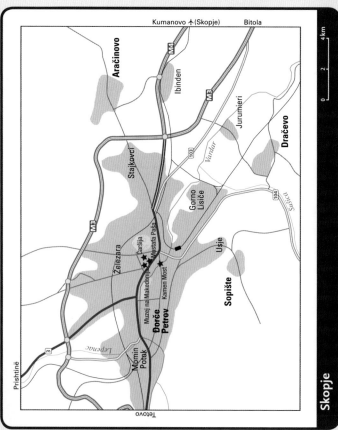

Skopje

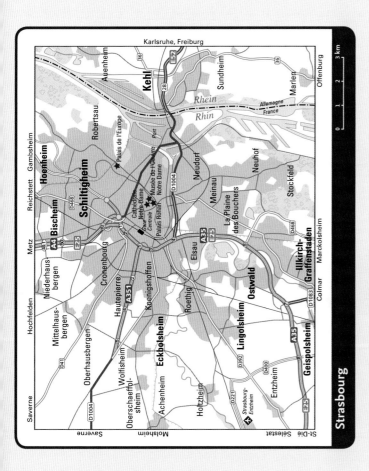

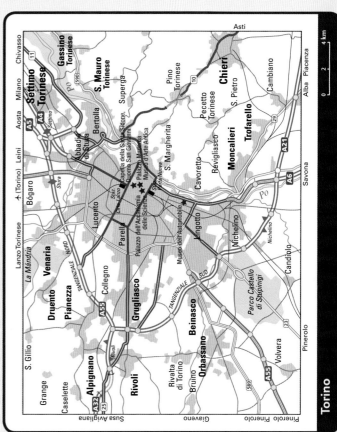

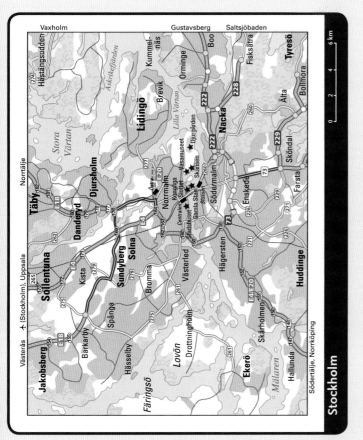

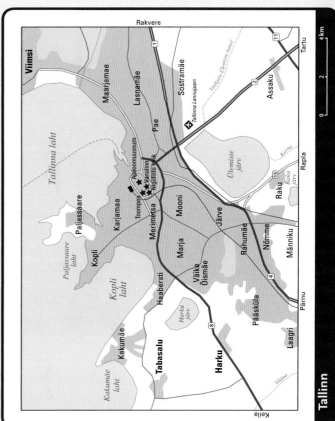

Strasbourg

Torino

Stockholm

Tallinn

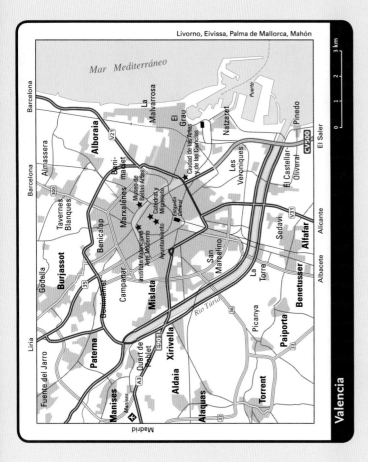

Valencia

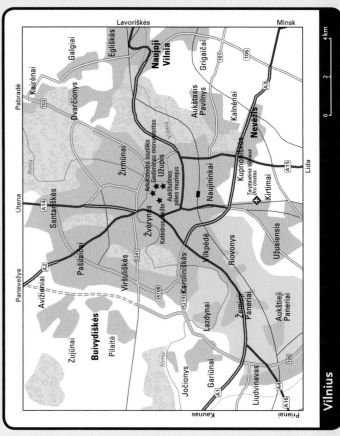

Vilnius

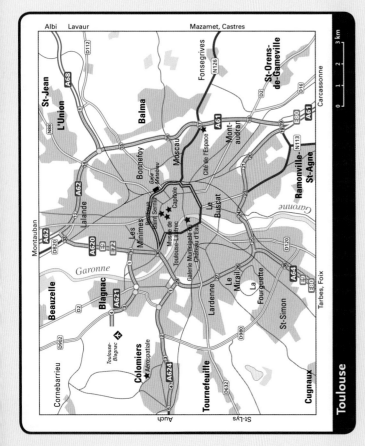

Toulouse

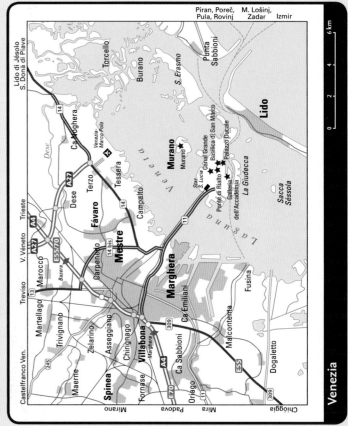

Venezia

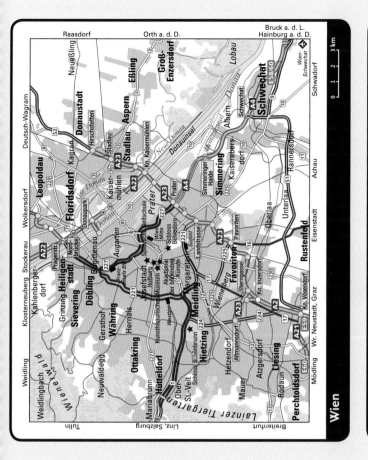

Wien

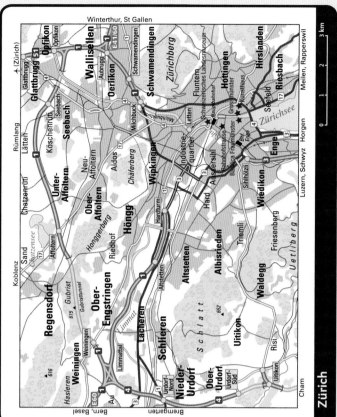

Zürich

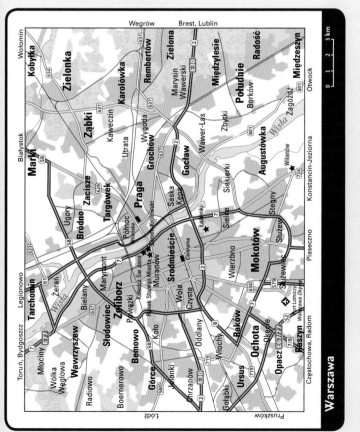

Warszawa

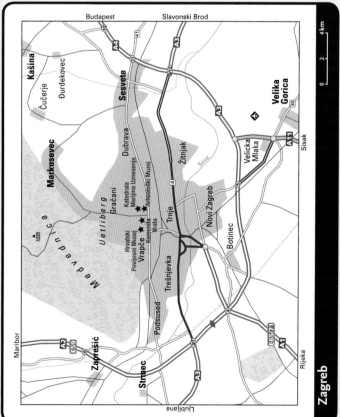

Zagreb

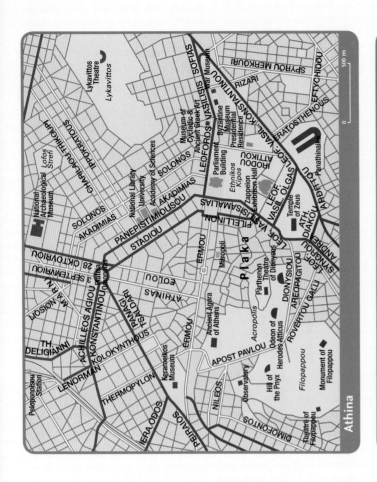

Athina

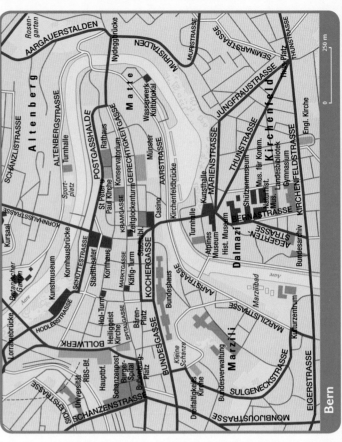

Bern

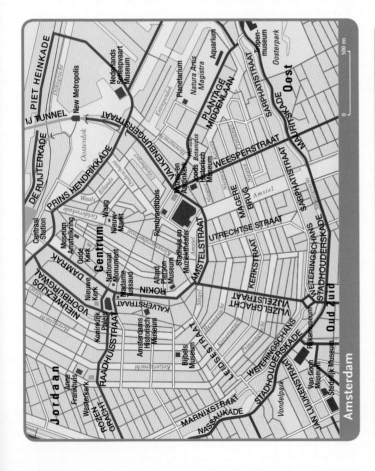

Amsterdam

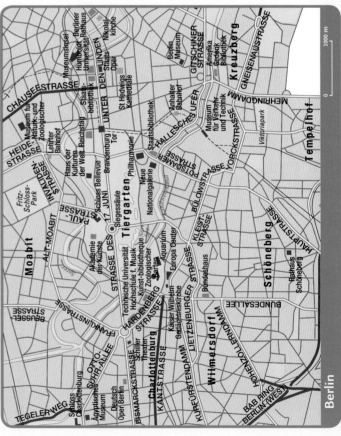

Berlin

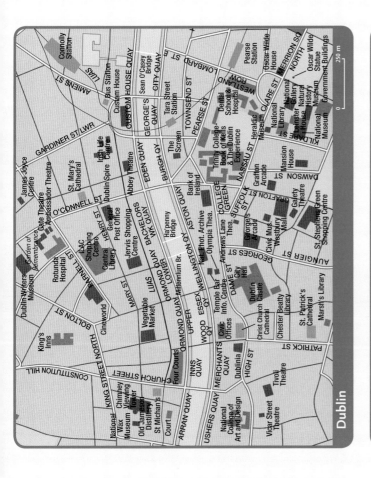

Dublin

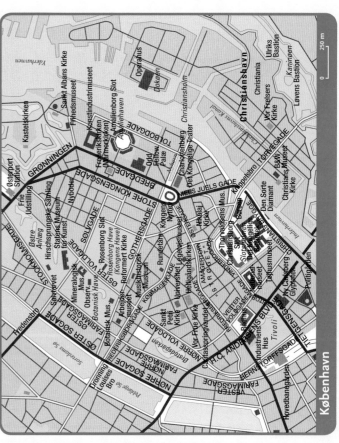

København

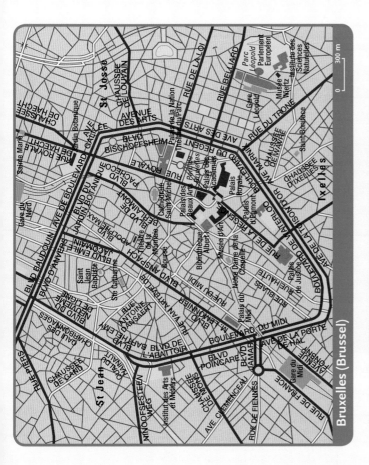

Bruxelles (Brussel)

Helsinki

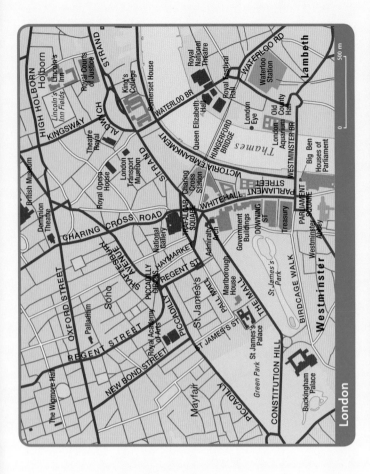

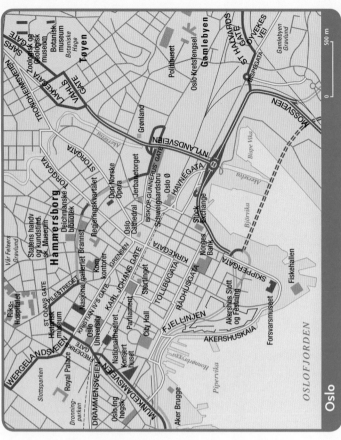

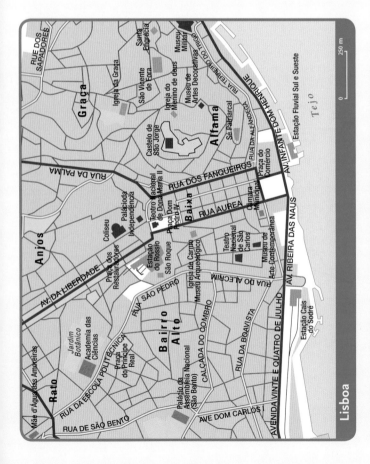

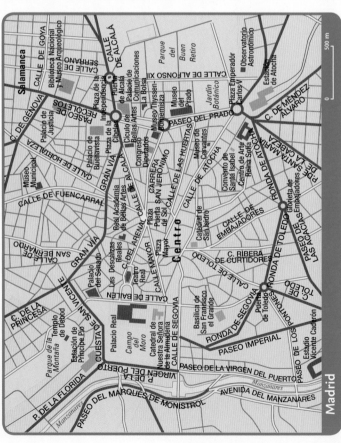

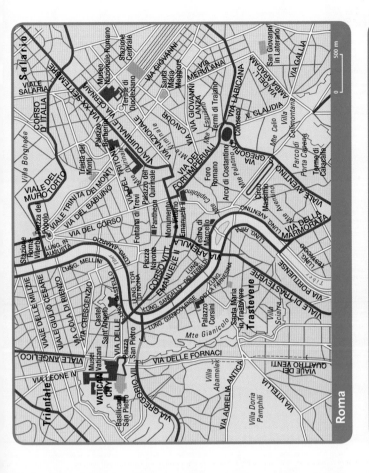

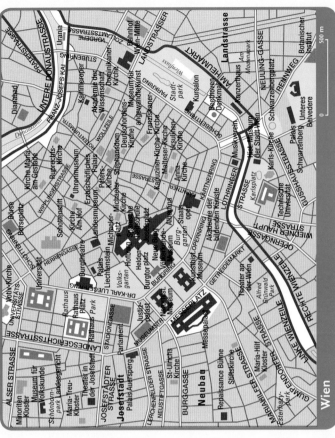

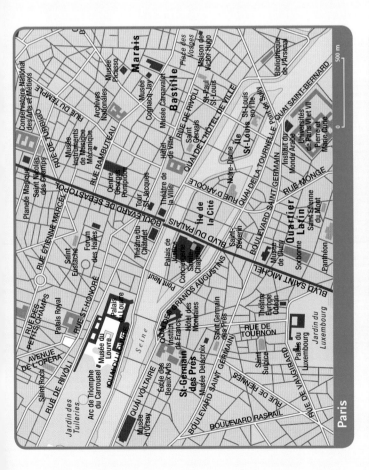

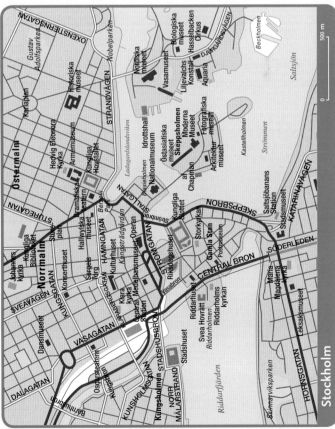

A

Å N 104 F7
Å N 110 E4
Å N 111 B12
Å N 111 C13
Aabenraa DK 86 E4
Aabybro DK 86 A5
Aachen D 20 C6
Aadorf CH 27 F10
Aakirkeby DK 89 E7
Aalborg DK 86 A5
Aalen D 75 E7
Aalestrup DK 86 B4
Aalsmeer NL 16 D3
Aalst B 19 C9
Aalst NL 183 B6
Aalten NL 17 E7
Aalter B 19 B7
Äänekoski FIN 123 E15
Aapajärvi FIN 115 D2
Aapajärvi FIN 119 B12
Aapajoki FIN 119 B12
Aapua S 117 E11
Aarau CH 27 F9
Aardenburg NL 19 B7
Aareavaara S 117 D10
Aarle NL 16 F5
A Armada E 38 B3
Aars DK 86 B5
Aarschot B 19 C10
Aartrijke B 182 C2
Aartselaar B 19 B9
Aarup DK 86 E6
Aarwangen CH 27 F8
Aasleagh IRL 6 E3
Ääsmäe EST 131 C9
Aaspere EST 131 C12
Aatsinki FIN 115 E5
Aavajärvi S 119 C11
Aavasaksa FIN 119 B11
Aba H 149 B11
Abaclia MD 154 E3
Abades E 46 C4
Abadín E 38 B5
Abadiño-Zelaieta E 41 B6
Abádszalók H 150 C6
A Baiuca E 38 B3
Abak TR 181 A7
Abánades E 47 C8
Abanilla E 56 E2
Abano Terme I 66 B4
Abarán E 55 C10
A Barrela E 38 C4
Abasár H 150 B5
Abaújszántó H 145 G3
Abbadia San Salvatore I 62 B1
Abbasanta I 64 C2
Abbekås S 87 E13
Abbeville F 18 D4
Abbey IRL 6 F6
Abbeydorney IRL 8 D3
Abbeyfeale IRL 8 D4
Abbeyleix IRL 9 C8
Abbey Town GB 5 F10
Abbiategrasso I 69 C6
Abborberget S 98 D8
Abborrträsk S 109 F17
Abbotsbury GB 13 D9
Abbots Langley GB 15 D8
Abcoude NL 16 D3
Abejar E 40 E6
Abejuela E 48 E3
Abela P 50 C2
Abelvær N 105 B10
Abenberg D 75 D8
Abenójar E 54 B4
Abensberg D 75 E10
Aberaeron GB 12 A6
Aberaman GB 13 B8
Aberchirder GB 3 K11
Aberdare GB 13 B8
Aberdaron GB 10 F2
Aberdeen GB 3 L12
Aberdovey GB 10 F3
Aberfeldy GB 5 B9
Aberffraw GB 10 E3
Aberford GB 11 D9
Aberfoyle GB 5 C8
Abergavenny GB 13 B8
Abergele GB 10 E4
Åberget S 109 E18
Abergwaun GB 12 B5
Abergynolwyn GB 10 F4
Aberlady GB 5 C11
Aberlour GB 3 L10
Abernethy GB 5 C10
Aberporth GB 12 A5
Abersoch GB 10 F2
Abertamy CZ 75 B12
Abertawe GB 13 B7
Abertillery GB 13 B8
Abertura E 45 F9
Aberuthven GB 5 C9
Aberystwyth GB 12 A6
Abetone I 66 D2
Abfaltersbach A 72 C6
Abhainnsuidhe GB 2 K2
Abia de la Obispalía E 47 D8
Abiego E 42 C3
Abild DK 86 F3
Abilly F 29 B7
Abingdon GB 13 B12
Abington GB 5 E9
Abisko Östra S 111 D16
Abja-Paluoja EST 131 E10
Abla E 55 E7
Ablis F 24 C5
Ablitas E 41 E8
Abmelaseter N 112 E6
Abo FIN 126 E7
Åbo S 103 C10
Åbodarna S 107 E14
Åbogen N 96 B7
Abondance F 31 C10
Abony H 150 C5
Åbosjö S 107 D13
Aboyne GB 5 A11
Abragão P 44 B4
Abram RO 151 C9
Abrămuț RO 151 C9
Abrantes P 44 F4
Abraur S 109 D16
Abreiro P 38 E5
Abrest F 30 C3
Abriès F 31 F10
Abrigada P 44 F2
Abriola I 60 B5
Abrucena E 55 E7

Abrud RO 151 E11
Abrupe LV 135 B11
Absam A 72 B4
Absberg D 75 D8
Absdorf A 77 F9
Abtenau A 73 A7
Abtsgmünd D 74 E6
Abukhava BY 140 C10
Åby S 89 A7
Åby S 93 B8
Åbyen DK 90 D7
Åbyggeby S 103 E13
Åbyn S 118 D6
Åbytorp S 92 A6
Acaill IRL 6 E3
A Cañiza E 38 D3
A Carballa E 38 B2
Acarlar TR 177 D10
A Carreira E 38 B3
Acâș RO 151 B10
Acate I 58 E5
Accadia I 60 A4
Acceglio I 36 C5
Accettura I 60 C6
Acciano I 62 C5
Acciaroli I 60 C4
Accous F 32 E4
Accrington GB 11 D7
Accumoli I 62 B4
Acebo E 45 D7
Acedera E 45 F9
Acedo E 32 E1
Acehuche E 45 E7
Aceituna E 45 D8
Acered E 47 B9
Acerenza I 60 B5
Acerno I 60 B4
Acerra I 60 B2
Aceuchal E 51 B7
Ach A 76 F3
Achadh Mòr GB 2 J3
A Chan E 38 D3
Acharacle GB 4 B5
Acharnes GB 175 C8
Achavanich GB 3 J10
Achel B 183 C6
Achenkirch A 72 A4
Achern D 27 D9
Acheux-en-Amiénois F 18 D6
Achicourt F 18 D6
Achill IRL 6 E3
Achillio GR 175 A6
Achim D 17 B12
Achintee GB 2 L6
Achladochori GR 169 B10
Achladokampos GR 175 D6
Achnacroish GB 4 B6
Achnasheen GB 2 K6
Achosnich GB 4 B4
Achstetten D 71 A9
Achtrup D 82 A6
Aci Castello I 59 D7
Aci Catena I 59 D7
Acireale I 59 D7
Aci Sant'Antonio I 59 D7
Aci Trezza I 59 D7
Acktjära S 103 D11
Acle GB 15 B11
A Coruña E 38 B3
Acquacalda I 59 B6
Acqualagna I 67 E6
Acquanegra sul Chiese I 66 B1
Acquapendente I 62 B1
Acquappesa I 60 E5
Acquaro I 59 B9
Acquarossa CH 71 E7
Acquasanta Terme I 62 B4
Acquasparta I 62 B3
Acquedolci I 59 C6
Acquigny F 24 B5
Acqui Terme I 37 B8
Acri I 61 E6
A Cruz do Incio E 38 C5
Ács H 149 A10
Acsa H 150 B3
Acuto I 62 D4
Ada SRB 150 F5
Adács H 150 B5
Adahuesca E 42 C3
Adak S 109 F16
Ådalsliden S 107 E11
Adamas E 179 B7
Adamclisi RO 155 E1
Adamov CZ 77 D11
Adamova BY 133 E4
Adamów PL 141 G6
Adamówka PL 144 C6
Adamstown IRL 9 D9
Ádämuș RO 152 E4
Adamuz E 53 A7
Adâncata RO 153 B8
Adâncata RO 161 D8
Adánd H 149 C10
Adanero E 46 C3
Adão P 45 D6
Adare IRL 8 C5
Adatepe TR 173 D6
Adaúfe P 38 E3
Adavere EST 131 D11
Ádázl LV 135 B8
Adderbury GB 13 A12
Addlestone GB 15 E8
Adegem B 182 C2
Adelboden CH 31 C12
Adelebsen D 78 C6
Adelfia I 61 A7
Adelina PL 144 B3
Adelmannsfelden D 187 D8
Adelschlag D 75 E9
Adelsheim D 27 B11
Adelsried D 75 F8
Ademuz E 47 D10
Adenau D 21 D7
Adendorf D 83 D8
Adendro GR 169 C8
Adenstedt D 79 B7
Adjud RO 153 E10
Adlešiči SLO 148 E4
Adliswil CH 27 F10
Adlkofen D 75 E11
Admont A 73 A9
Adolfsström S 109 D12
Adony H 149 B11
Adorf D 75 B11
Adorf (Diemelsee) D 17 F11
Adoufe P 38 F4
Adra E 55 F6
Adradas E 41 F7
Adrados E 40 F3
Adrano I 59 D6
Adria I 66 B5
Adriani GR 171 B6

Adriers F 29 C7
Aduard NL 17 B6
Adulsbruk N 101 E14
Ådum DK 86 D3
Adunați RO 161 C7
Adunații-Copăceni RO 161 E8
Adutiškis LT 135 F13
Adzaneta de Albaida E 56 D4
Adžūni LV 135 D8
Aegviidu EST 131 C11
Aerino GR 169 F8
Ærøskøbing DK 86 F6
Aerzen D 17 D12
A Escusa E 38 C2
A Esfarrapada E 38 D2
A Estrada E 38 C3
Aetos GR 169 C6
Aetos GR 174 B3
Aetos GR 174 B3
Äetsä FIN 126 C8
Afantou GR 181 D8
Åfarnes N 100 A7
A Feira do Monte E 38 B4
Affing D 75 F8
Afife P 38 E2
Afisos GR 169 F9
Åfjord N 104 D8
Aflenz Kurort A 73 A11
A Fonsagrada E 38 B5
A Forxa E 38 D4
A Forxa E 38 D4
Åfoss N 90 A6
Afragola I 60 B2
Afritz A 73 C8
Áfytos GR 169 D9
Aga D 79 E11
Ağaçli TR 173 D10
Ağaköy TR 173 D7
Agalas GR 174 D2
Agallas E 45 D8
A Gándara E 38 B3
A Gándara de Altea E 38 A3
Agapia RO 153 C8
Ağaş RO 153 D8
Agasegyháza H 150 D3
Agde F 34 D5
Ager E 42 C5
Agerbæk DK 86 D3
Agerskov DK 86 A6
Agersted DK 86 A6
Ågerup DK 87 D10
Agfalva H 149 A7
Aggersund DK 86 A4
Aggius I 64 B3
Aggsbach Markt A 77 F8
Aghaboe IRL 9 C7
Aghagallon GB 7 C10
Aghalee GB 7 C10
Aghanloo GB 4 E2
Aghaville IRL 8 E4
Aghern IRL 8 D6
Aghione F 37 G10
Aghireşu RO 151 C11
Aghleam IRL 6 D2
Aghnagar Bridge IRL 8 E2
Agia GR 169 E8
Agia Anna GR 175 B8
Agia Anna GR 175 C6
Agia Effimia GR 174 C2
Agia Efthymia GR 174 C5
Agia Galini GR 178 E8
Agia Kyriaki GR 174 E4
Agia Marina GR 175 B6
Agia Marina GR 175 C9
Agia Marina GR 177 E6
Agia Paraskevi GR 168 D4
Agia Paraskevi GR 171 A6
Agia Paraskevi GR 177 E6
Agia Pelagia GR 178 C4
Agia Pelagia GR 178 E9
Agiasma GR 171 C7
Agiasos GR 177 A7
Agia Triada GR 174 B3
Agia Triada GR 175 D6
Agia Varvara GR 169 D7
Agia Varvara GR 178 E9
Agigea RO 155 E3
Agighiol RO 155 C3
Agino Selo BIH 157 C7
Agiofyllo GR 169 E6
Agioi Anargyroi GR 169 E7
Agioi Apostoloi GR 175 C8
Agioi Deka GR 178 E8
Agioi Theodoroi GR 169 E5
Agioi Theodoroi GR 175 A6
Agioi Theodoroi GR 175 D7
Agiokampos GR 169 E8
Agiokampos GR 175 B7
Agionori GR 175 D6
Agios Andreas GR 175 E6
Agios Athanasios GR 169 C8
Agios Athanasios GR 171 B6
Agios Charalampos GR 171 C9
Agios Christoforos GR 175 F5
Agios Dimitrios GR 169 D7
Agios Dimitrios GR 175 A8
Agios Dimitrios GR 175 F6
Agios Efstratios GR 171 E7
Agios Georgios GR 169 C7
Agios Georgios GR 174 B3
Agios Georgios GR 175 C6
Agios Georgios GR 177 F6
Agios Georgios GR 178 E9
Agios Germanos GR 168 C5
Agios Ioannis GR 174 E5
Agios Ioannis GR 174 E5
Agios Ioannis GR 178 B4
Agios Kirykos GR 177 D7
Agios Konstantinos GR 174 B3
Agios Konstantinos GR 175 B6
Agios Konstantinos GR 175 D6
Agios Konstantinos GR 177 D7
Agios Kyprianos GR 178 C3
Agios Leon GR 174 D2
Agios Loukas GR 169 C7
Agios Loukas GR 175 C9
Agios Mamas GR 169 D9
Agios Matthaios GR 168 F2
Agios Myronas GR 178 E9
Agios Nikolaos GR 168 E5
Agios Nikolaos GR 168 E5
Agios Nikolaos GR 174 B2
Agios Nikolaos GR 174 B3
Agios Nikolaos GR 174 B3
Agios Nikolaos GR 174 E5
Agios Nikolaos GR 179 E10
Agios Panteleïmonas GR 169 C6
Agios Paraskevi GR 171 E10
Agios Petros GR 169 C8

Agios Petros GR 174 B2
Agios Petros GR 175 E6
Agios Spyridonas GR 169 D7
Agios Spyridonas GR 174 A2
Agios Stefanos GR 175 C8
Agios Stefanos GR 176 E5
Agios Thomas GR 175 C8
Agios Vasileios GR 169 C9
Agios Vasileios GR 175 D6
Agira I 59 D6
Agivey GB 4 E3
Agkathia GR 169 C7
Agkistro GR 169 B9
Aglansvik N 111 B15
Aglasterhausen D 187 C6
Agle CH 105 C13
Aglen N 105 B10
Agliana I 66 E3
Aglientu I 64 A3
Aglish IRL 9 D7
Agnadello I 69 C8
Agnanta GR 168 F5
Agnantero GR 169 F6
Agneaux F 23 B9
Agnita RO 152 E5
Agno CH 69 A6
Agnone I 63 D6
Agolada E 38 C3
Agoncillo E 32 F1
Agon-Coutainville F 23 B8
Agordo I 72 D5
Agost E 56 E3
Agos-Vidalos F 32 D5
Ágotnes N 94 B2
Agra GR 177 A7
Agramón E 55 C9
Agramunt E 42 D6
Agrate Brianza I 69 B7
Agreda E 41 E8
Agrés E 56 D4
Agria GR 169 F9
Agridi GR 174 D4
Agrigento I 58 E4
Agrij RO 151 C11
Agrili GR 174 E4
Agrinio GR 174 B3
Agriovotano GR 175 A7
Agrochão P 39 E5
Agropoli I 60 C4
A Gudiña E 38 D5
Agudo E 54 B3
Águeda P 44 C4
Aguessac F 34 B5
Agugliano I 67 E7
Aguiar P 50 B3
Aguiar da Beira P 44 C5
Aguilafuente E 46 B4
Aguilar de Alfambra E 42 F2
Aguilar de Campóo E 40 C3
Aguilar de la Frontera E 53 A7
Aguilar del Río Alhama E 41 E8
Águilas E 55 E9
Agullana E 34 F4
Agullent E 56 D3
Aha S 109 F17
Ahafona IRL 8 C3
Aham D 75 E11
Ahascragh IRL 6 F6
Ahaus D 17 D8
Ahelva FIN 121 E11
Ahigal E 45 D8
Ahigal de Villarino E 45 B8
Ahillones E 51 C8
Ahja EST 131 E14
Ahjola FIN 121 D12
Ahlainen FIN 126 B6
Ahlatli TR 167 E8
Ahlbeck D 84 C6
Ahlbeck, Seebad D 82 E7
Ahlden (Aller) D 82 E7
Ahlen D 17 E9
Ahlerstedt D 17 B12
Ahlhorn D 17 C10
Ahmas FIN 119 E17
Ahmavaara FIN 115 E5
Ahmetbey TR 173 B8
Ahmetbeyli TR 177 C9
Ahmetçeeli TR 172 E4
Ahmetli TR 177 C9
Ahmovaara FIN 125 D13
Ahoghill GB 4 F4
Ahokylä FIN 123 C17
Ahola FIN 121 B11
Ahola FIN 121 C13
Ahola FIN 124 D9
Aholanvaara FIN 115 E5
Ahonperä FIN 119 F13
Ahorn D 75 B8
Aho-Vastinki FIN 123 E14
Ahrbrück D 21 D7
Ahrensbök D 83 B9
Ahrensburg D 83 C8
Ahrenshagen D 83 B13
Ahrenshoop, Ostseebad D 83 B12
Ähtäri FIN 123 E12
Ähtärinranta FIN 123 E12
Ahtme EST 132 C1
Ahula EST 131 C11
Ahun F 29 C10
Åhus S 88 D6
Ahveninen FIN 123 E14
Ahvensalmi FIN 125 E10
Ahvenselkä FIN 115 E4
Ahvenvittikko FIN 117 B11
Ahvionsaari FIN 129 B10
Aiani GR 169 D6
Aianteio GR 175 D7
Aibar E 32 E3
Aibl A 73 C11
Aichach D 75 F9
Aichhalden D 27 D9
Aichstetten D 71 B10
Ai'dejav'ri N 117 A10
Aidenbach D 76 E4

Aidipsos GR 175 B7
Aidone I 58 E5
Aidonochori GR 169 C10
Aidt DK 86 C5
Aidu EST 131 D12
Aiello Calabro I 59 A9
Aielo de Malferit E 56 D3
Aieta I 60 D5
Aiffres F 28 C5
Aigeira GR 174 C5
Aigen im Ennstal A 73 A9
Aigen im Mühlkreis A 76 E5
Aigiali GR 177 F6
Aigina GR 175 D7
Aiginio GR 169 D8
Aigio GR 174 C5
Aigle CH 31 C10
Aiglemont F 184 E2
Aignan F 33 C6
Aignay-le-Duc F 25 E12
Aigre F 28 D5
Aigrefeuille-d'Aunis F 28 C4
Aigrefeuille-sur-Maine F 28 A3
A Igrexa E 38 D2
Aiguafreda E 43 D8
Aiguebelle F 31 D9
Aigueblanche F 31 D10
Aigueperse F 30 C3
Aigues-Mortes F 35 C7
Aigues-Vives F 34 C5
Aigues-Vives F 34 C7
Aiguilhe F 30 E4
Aiguilles F 31 F10
Aiguillon F 33 B6
Aigurande F 29 C9
Äijäjoki FIN 116 B10
Äijälä FIN 123 F11
Aijala FIN 127 E9
Äijänneva FIN 123 F11
Aillant-sur-Tholon F 25 E9
Aillas F 32 B5
Aillevillers-et-Lyaumont F 26 E5
Ailly-le-Haut-Clocher F 18 D4
Ailly-sur-Noye F 18 E5
Ailly-sur-Somme F 18 E5
Ailt an Chorráin IRL 6 C6
Aimargues F 35 C7
Aime F 31 D10
Ainali FIN 119 E14
Ainali FIN 123 B11
Ainay-le-Château F 29 B11
Aindling D 75 E8
Ainet A 73 C6
Ainsa E 33 F6
Ainzón E 41 E9
Airaines F 18 E4
Airasca I 31 F11
Aird Asaig GB 2 K3
Airdrie GB 5 D9
Aire-sur-l'Adour F 32 C5
Aire-sur-la-Lys F 18 C5
Airidh a'Bhruaich GB 2 J3
Airola I 60 A3
Airole I 37 D7
Airolo CH 71 D7
Airvault F 28 B5
Aisey-sur-Seine F 25 E12
Aïssey F 26 F5
Aisymi GR 171 B9
Aisy-sur-Armançon F 25 E11
Aitamännikkö FIN 117 D12
Aita Mare RO 153 F7
Aiterhofen D 75 E12
Aith GB 3 E14
Aith GB 3 G11
Aitolahti FIN 127 B10
Aitoliko GR 174 C3
Aiton RO 152 D3
Aitoo FIN 127 C11
Aitrach D 71 B10
Aitrang D 71 B11
Aittaniemi FIN 121 B10
Aittijoki FIN 113 D17
Aittojärvi FIN 123 C16
Aittokoski FIN 124 C8
Aittokylä FIN 121 E10
Aittoperä FIN 123 C13
Aittovaara FIN 121 D13
Aiud RO 152 E3
Aiviekste LV 135 C11
Aix-en-Othe F 25 D10
Aix-en-Provence F 35 C9
Aixe-sur-Vienne F 29 D8
Aix-les-Bains F 31 D8
Aizenay F 28 B2
Aizkraukle LV 135 C10
Aizpún E 32 E2
Aizpurve LV 135 C12
Aizpute LV 134 C2
Aizviķi LV 134 C3
Ajaccio F 37 H9
Ajanki FIN 117 C12
Ajankjärvi FIN 117 C12
Ajat F 29 E8
Ajaureforsen S 109 E10
Ájdovščina SLO 73 E8
Ajka H 149 B9
Ajo E 40 B4
Ajofrín E 46 E5
Ajos FIN 119 C13
Akäcijas LV 134 C6

Akmendziras LV 134 B3
Akmenė LT 134 D5
Aknīstes LV 135 D11
Aknīste LV 135 D11
Akonkoski FIN 125 F11
Akonpohja FIN 125 D10
Akpınar TR 173 B10
Akraifnio GR 175 C7
Akran N 105 D12
Akrata GR 174 C5
Åkrehamn N 94 D2
Akrini GR 169 D6
Akrolimni GR 169 C7
Akrotiri GR 179 C9
Aksakal TR 173 D9
Aksaz TR 173 D7
Aksdal N 94 D2
Aksnes N 104 F4
Akujärvi FIN 114 F3
Åkullsjön S 118 E5
Åkvisslan S 107 E13
Ala I 69 B11
Ala S 93 E13
Alacaat TR 173 E10
Alacaoğlu TR 173 B7
Alaçatı TR 177 C7
Alà dei Sardi I 64 B3
Ala di Stura I 31 E11
Alaejos E 39 F9
Alagna Valsesia I 68 B4
A Lagoa E 38 D2
Alagoa P 44 F5
Alagón E 41 E9
Alahärmä FIN 122 D9
Ala-Honkajoki FIN 126 B7
Alaigne F 33 D10
Alaior E 57 B13
Alájar E 51 D6
Alajärvi FIN 117 E15
Alajärvi FIN 121 E12
Alajärvi FIN 123 D11
Alajõe EST 132 C1
Ala-Jokikylä FIN 119 C14
Ala-Käänta FIN 119 E13
Ala-Keyritty FIN 125 D10
Alakurtti RUS 115 B9
Alakylä FIN 117 D13
Alakylä FIN 119 D15
Alakylä FIN 126 B6
Ala-Livo FIN 119 D17
Alameda E 53 B7
Alameda de Cervera E 47 F6
Alameda de la Sagra E 46 D5
Alamedilla E 55 D6
Alamillo E 54 B3
Alaminos E 47 C7
Alan HR 67 B10
Ala-Nampa FIN 117 E16
Alanäs S 106 D7
Ålandsbro S 103 A14
Ålange E 51 B7
Alaniemi FIN 119 C14
Alanís E 51 C8
Alanta LT 135 F10
Alap H 149 C11
Alapitkä FIN 124 D9
Alaquàs E 48 F4
Alaranta FIN 119 D14
Alaraz E 45 C10
Alarcón E 47 E8
Alar del Rey E 40 C3
Alaró E 49 E10
Alarup AL 168 F1
Ålåsen S 106 D7
Alaskylä FIN 127 B8
Alassio I 37 C8
Alastaipale FIN 123 F11
Alastaro FIN 126 D8
Ala-Sydänmaa FIN 123 B14
Alata F 37 H9
Ala-Temmes FIN 119 E15
Alatoz E 47 F10
Alatri I 62 D4
Alatskivi EST 131 D14
Alattyán H 150 C5
Alavere EST 131 C10
Alavieska FIN 119 F12
Ala-Vieksi FIN 121 F12
Ala-Vuokki FIN 121 E13
Ala-Viirre FIN 123 B11
Ala-Vuotto FIN 119 D16
Alavus FIN 123 E11
Alba I 37 B8
Alba Adriatica I 62 B5
Albac RO 151 E10
Albacken S 103 A11
Alba Iulia RO 152 E3
Albaladejo E 55 B7
Alba-la-Romaine F 35 A8
Albalate de Arzobispo E 42 E3
Albalate de Cinca E 42 D4
Albalate de las Nogueras E 47 D8
Albalate de Zorita E 47 D7
Albalatillo E 42 D3
Alban F 33 C10
Albánchez E 55 E8
Albanella I 60 C4
Albano di Lucania I 60 B6
Albano Laziale I 62 D3
Albano Vercellese I 68 C5
Albanyà E 43 C9
Albaredo per San Marco I 69 A8
Albaret-le-Comtal F 30 F3
Albaret-Ste-Marie F 30 F3
Albaron F 35 C7
Albarracín E 47 D10
Albatana E 55 B9
Albatàrrec E 42 D5
Albatera E 56 E3
Albbruck D 27 E9
Albelda E 42 D4
Albelda de Iregua E 41 D7
Albella E 32 F5
Albendea E 47 D8
Albendín E 53 A8
Albenga I 37 C8
Albeni RO 160 C3
Albens F 31 D8
Albentosa E 48 D3
Ålberga S 93 B9

Alberga S 98 D6
Albergaria-a-Velha P 44 C4
Albergaria dos Doze P 44 E3
Albergen NL 183 A9
Alberic E 48 F4
Alberndorf in der Riedmark A 77 F6
Albernoa P 50 D4
Albero Alto E 41 D11
Alberobello I 61 B8
Alberona I 60 A4
Alberoni I 66 B5
Aberschwende A 71 C9
Albersdorf D 82 B6
Albert F 18 D6
Albertacce F 37 G9
Alberta Ligure I 37 B10
Albertirsa H 150 C4
Albertshofen D 187 B9
Albertville F 31 D9
Alberuela de Tubo E 42 D3
Albesa E 42 D5
Albești RO 152 E5
Albești RO 153 B10
Albești RO 153 D11
Albești RO 155 F2
Albești RO 161 D10
Albeștii de Argeș RO 160 C5
Albeștii de Muscel RO 160 C6
Albești-Paleologu RO 161 D8
Albestroff F 27 C6
Albi F 33 B10
Albias F 33 B8
Albidona I 61 D6
Albignasego I 66 B4
Albina RO 155 C1
Albino I 69 B8
Albires E 39 D9
Albisheim (Pfrimm) D 21 E10
Albisola Marina I 37 C9
Albisola Superiore I 37 C9
Ablasserdam NL 16 E3
Ålbo S 98 B7
Abocàsser E 48 D5
Abloduby E 55 E7
Abolote E 53 B9
Albon F 30 E6
Abondón E 55 F6
Alboraya E 48 E4
Alborea E 47 F10
Albota RO 160 D5
Albox E 55 E8
Albrechtice nad Orlicí CZ 77 B10
Al'brekhtava BY 133 E5
Abstadt D 27 D11
Albu EST 131 C11
Albudeite E 55 C10
Albufeira P 50 E3
Albujón E 56 F2
Albuñol E 55 F6
Albuñuelas E 53 C9
Alburquerque E 45 F7
Alby S 89 C11
Alby S 103 A9
Alby-sur-Chéran F 31 D9
Alcácer E 48 F4
Alcácer do Sal P 50 C2
Alcáçovas P 50 C3
Alcadozo E 55 B9
Alcafozes P 45 E6
Alcaine E 42 F2
Alcains P 44 E6
Alcalá de Guadaira E 51 E8
Alcalá de Gurrea E 41 D10
Alcalá de Henares E 46 D6
Alcalá del Júcar E 47 F10
Alcalá de los Gazules E 52 D5
Alcalá del Río E 51 D8
Alcalá del Valle E 51 F9
Alcalà de Xivert E 48 D5
Alcalá la Real E 53 B9
Alcalalí E 56 D4
Alcamo I 58 D2
Alcampell E 42 D4
Alcanadre E 32 F1
Alcanede P 44 F3
Alcanena P 44 F3
Alcanhões P 44 F3
Alcañices E 39 E7
Alcañiz E 42 E3
Alcántara E 45 E7
Alcantarilla E 56 F2
Alcantud E 47 C8
Alcaracejos E 54 C3
Alcara li Fusi I 59 C6
Alcaraz E 55 B8
Alcarràs E 42 D5
Alcaucín E 53 C8
Alcaudete E 53 A8
Alcaudete de la Jara E 46 E3
Alçay-Alçabéhéty-Sunharette F 32 D4
Alcázar del Rey E 47 D7
Alcázar de San Juan E 47 F6
Alcedar MD 154 B3
Alcester GB 13 A11
Alçıtepe TR 171 D10
Alcoba E 46 F4
Alcobaça P 44 E3
Alcobendas E 46 C5
Alcocer E 47 D7
Alcocero de Mola E 40 D5
Alcochete P 50 B2
Alcoentre P 44 F3
Alcolea E 53 A7
Alcolea E 55 F7
Alcolea de Calatrava E 54 B4
Alcolea de Cinca E 42 D4
Alcolea del Pinar E 47 B8
Alcolea del Río E 51 D8
Alcollarín E 45 F9
Alconchel E 51 B5
Alcóntar E 55 E7
Alcorcón E 46 D5
Alcorisa E 42 F3
Alcoroches E 47 C9
Alcossebre E 48 D5
Alcoutim P 50 E5
Alcover E 42 E6
Alcoy-Alcoi E 56 D4
Alcsútdoboz H 149 B11
Alcubierre E 41 D11
Alcubilla de Avellaneda E 40 E5
Alcubillas E 55 B6
Alcublas E 48 E3
Alcúdia E 57 B11
Alcudia de Guadix E 55 E6
Alcudia de Monteagud E 55 E8
Alcuéscar E 45 F8
Aldbrough GB 11 D11
Aldeacentenera E 45 E9
Aldeadávila de la Ribera E 45 B7

Aldea del Cano E 45 F8
Aldea del Fresno E 46 D4
Aldea del Obispo E 45 C7
Aldea del Rey E 54 B5
Aldea de Trujillo E 45 E9
Aldealafuente E 41 E7
Aldealpozo E 41 E7
Aldeamayor de San Martín E 39 E10
Aldeanueva de Barbarroya E 45 E10
Aldeanueva de Ebro E 41 D8
Aldeanueva de Figueroa E 45 B9
Aldeanueva de la Vera E 45 D9
Aldeanueva del Camino E 45 D9
Aldeanueva de San Bartolomé E 45 E10
Aldeaquemada E 55 C6
Aldea Real E 46 B4
Aldearrodrigo E 45 B9
Aldeaseca E 46 B3
Aldeatejada E 45 C9
Aldeavieja E 46 C4
Aldeburgh GB 15 C12
Aldehuela de la Bóveda E 45 C8
Aldehuela de Yeltes E 45 C8
Aldeia da Mata P 44 F5
Aldeia da Ponte P 45 D7
Aldeia de João Pires P 45 D6
Aldeia do Bispo P 45 D6
Aldeia dos Elvas P 50 D3
Aldeia dos Fernandes P 50 D3
Aldeia dos Palheiros P 50 D3
Aldeia Velha P 44 F4
Aldenhoven D 20 C6
Aldeno I 69 B11
Alderbury GB 13 C11
Alderholt GB 13 D11
Alderley Edge GB 11 E7
Aldersbach D 76 E4
Aldershot GB 15 E7
Aldinac SRB 164 B5
Aldinci MK 164 F3
Aldingham GB 10 C5
Aldomirovtsi BG 165 D6
Aldover E 42 F5
Aldridge GB 11 F8
Aldudes F 32 D3
Åle DK 86 D5
Åled S 87 B11
Aledo E 55 D9
Alekovo BG 161 F10
Alekovo BG 166 C4
Aleksandriškės LT 137 D10
Aleksandrova LV 133 E2
Aleksandrovac SRB 159 E7
Aleksandrovac SRB 163 C11
Aleksandrovo BG 165 C10
Aleksandrovo BG 166 D4
Aleksandrovo BG 167 E7
Aleksandrów PL 141 F2
Aleksandrów PL 141 H1
Aleksandrów Kujawski PL 138 E6
Aleksandrów Łódzki PL 143 C7
Aleksa Šantić SRB 150 F3
Aleksinac SRB 164 B4
Ålem S 89 B10
Ålen N 101 A14
Alençon F 23 D12
Alenquer P 44 F3
Alénya F 34 E4
Alerheim D 75 E8
Aléria F 37 G11
Alerre E 41 D11
Alès F 35 B7
Ales I 64 D2
Aleşd RO 151 C9
Alesón E 41 D6
Alessandria I 37 B9
Alessandria del Carretto I 61 D6
Alessandria della Rocca I 58 D3
Alessano I 61 D10
Ålesund N 100 B4
Alet-les-Bains F 33 D10
Alexandreia GR 169 C7
Alexandria GB 4 D7
Alexandria RO 160 F6
Alexandroupoli GR 171 C9
Alexandru Vlahuţă RO 153 E11
Alexeevca MD 153 C11
Alexeni RO 161 D9
Alexsandrów PL 144 C6
Alezio I 61 C10
Alf D 21 D8
Alfacar E 53 B9
Alfafar E 48 F4
Alfaiates P 45 D7
Alfajarín E 41 E10
Alfambra E 42 F1
Alfambras P 50 E2
Alfamén E 41 F9
Alfândega da Fé P 39 F6
Alfántega E 42 D4
Alfarim P 50 C1
Alfaro E 41 D8
Alfarràs E 42 D5
Alfatar BG 161 F10
Alfdorf D 74 E6
Alfedena I 62 D6
Alfeizerão P 44 E2
Alfeld (Leine) D 78 C6
Alfena P 44 B3
Alferce P 50 E3
Alfhausen D 17 C9
Alfonsine I 66 D5
Alford GB 3 L11
Alford GB 11 E12
Alforja E 42 E5
Alfredshem S 107 E15
Alfreton GB 11 E9
Alfta S 103 D11
Alfundão P 50 C3
Algaida E 57 B10
Algajola F 37 F9
Algámitas E 53 B6
Algar E 52 C5
Algarås S 92 B4
Algård N 94 E3
Algarinejo E 53 B8
Algarrobo E 53 C8
Algatocín E 53 C6
Algeciras E 53 D6
Algemesí E 48 F4
Algered S 103 B12
Algermissen D 79 B6
Algerri E 42 D5
Algestrup DK 87 E10
Algete E 46 C6
Alghero I 64 B1
Alghult S 89 A9
Alginet E 48 F4
Algnäs S 103 D12
Algodonales E 51 F9
Algodor P 50 D4
Algora E 47 C7
Algorta E 40 B6
Algoso P 39 F6
Algoz P 50 E3
Algrange F 20 F6
Alguaire E 42 D5
Alguazas E 56 E2
Algueirão-Mem Martins P 50 B1
Algueña E 56 E3
Algutsrum S 89 B11
Alhabia E 55 F7
Alhama de Almería E 55 F7
Alhama de Aragón E 41 F8
Alhama de Granada E 53 B9
Alhama de Murcia E 55 D10
Alhambra E 55 B6
Alhamn S 118 D7
Alhaurín de la Torre E 53 C7
Alhaurín el Grande E 53 C7
Alhendín E 53 B9
Alhojärvi FIN 127 B13
Alhóndiga E 47 C7
Ålhult S 92 D7
Alía E 45 F10
Alia I 58 D4
Aliaga E 42 F2
Aliağa TR 177 B8
Aliaguilla E 47 E10
Aliano I 60 C6
Aliartos GR 175 C7
Alibunar SRB 159 C6
Alicante E 56 E4
Alicún de Ortega E 55 D6
Alife I 60 A2
Alija del Infantado E 39 D8
Alijó P 38 F5
Alikianos GR 178 E6
Alikylä FIN 123 C11
Aliman RO 155 E1
Alimena I 58 D5
Aliminusa I 58 D4
Alimpeşti RO 160 C3
Alingsås S 91 D12
Alino BG 165 E7
Alionys 1 LT 137 C11
Aliseda E 45 F7
Alistrati GR 170 B5
Ali Terme I 59 C7
Aliveri GR 175 C9
Alizava LT 135 E10
Aljaraque E 51 E5
Aljezur P 50 E2
Aljinovići SRB 163 C8
Aljubarrota P 44 E3
Aljucén E 51 A7
Aljustrel P 50 D3
Alken B 19 C11
Alkkia FIN 122 F9
Alkmaar NL 16 C3
Allai I 64 D2
Allaire F 23 E7
Allambres AL 168 C2
Allan F 35 A8
Allanche F 30 E2
Allariz E 38 D4
Allarmont F 27 D7
Allassac F 29 E8
Allaži LV 135 B9
Allažmuiža LV 135 B9
Alle CH 27 F7
Alleghe I 72 D5
Allègre F 30 E4
Alleins F 35 C9
Allemond F 31 E9
Allen IRL 7 F9
Allendale Town GB 5 F12
Allendorf (Eder) D 21 B11
Allenheads GB 5 F12
Allensbach D 27 E11
Allentsteig A 77 E8
Allenwood IRL 7 F9
Allepuz E 42 G2
Allerona I 62 B1
Allersberg D 75 D9
Allershausen D 75 F10
Allerslev DK 87 E10
Allevard F 31 E9
Allex F 30 F6
Allibaudières F 25 C11
Alligny-en-Morvan F 25 F11
Allihies IRL 8 E2
Allingåbro DK 86 C6
Allinges F 31 C9
Allinge-Sandvig DK 89 E7
Alliste I 61 D10
Allmendingen D 74 F6
Allo E 32 E1
Alloa GB 5 C9
Allogny F 25 F7
Allonluokta S 109 B17
Allonby GB 5 F10
Allonnes F 23 E12
Allonnes F 23 F12
Allons F 32 B5
Allos F 36 C5
Alloue F 29 C7
Alloza E 42 F2
Allschwil CH 27 E8
Allsta S 103 A15
Allstad N 110 D6
Allstedt D 79 D9
Allumiere I 62 C1
Alluy F 30 A4
Almacelles E 42 D4
Almáchar E 53 C8
Almada P 50 B1
Almadén E 54 B3
Almadén de la Plata E 51 D7
Almadenejos E 54 B3
Almagro E 54 B5
Almăj RO 160 E3
Almajano E 41 E7
Almalaguês P 44 D4
Almaluez E 41 F7
Almansa E 56 D2
Almansil P 50 E3
Almanza E 39 C9
Almaraz E 45 E9
Almargen E 53 B6
Almarza E 41 E7
Almaş RO 151 E9
Almásfüzitő H 149 A10
Almaşu RO 151 D11
Almaşu Mare RO 151 E11
Almazán E 41 F6
Almazora E 48 E4
Almazul E 41 E7
Almedina E 55 B7
Almedinilla E 53 B8
Almeida de Sayago E 39 F7
Almeirim P 44 F3
Almelo NL 17 D7
Almenar E 42 D5
Almenara E 48 E4
Almenar de Soria E 41 E7
Almendra E 45 B8
Almendra P 45 B6
Almendral E 51 B6
Almendralejo E 51 B7
Almendricos E 55 E9
Almendros E 47 E7
Almere NL 16 D4
Almería E 55 F8
Almerimar E 55 F7
Älmestad S 91 D13
Älmhult S 88 B6
Almind DK 86 D4
Almkerk NL 16 E3
Ålmo N 104 E4
Almodôvar P 50 D3
Almodóvar del Campo E 54 B4
Almodóvar del Pinar E 47 E9
Almodóvar del Río E 53 A6
Almofala P 44 C5
Almogía E 53 C7
Almograve P 50 D2
Almoguera E 47 D7
Almoharín E 45 F8
Almonacid de la Sierra E 41 F9
Almonacid del Marquesado E 47 E7
Almonacid del Zorita E 47 D7
Almonacid de Toledo E 46 E5
Almonaster la Real E 51 D6
Almondsbury GB 13 B9
Almonte E 51 E6
Almoradí E 56 E3
Almorchón E 51 B9
Almorox E 46 D4
Álmosd H 151 C8
Almoster P 44 E4
Almsele S 107 C12
Almsjönäs S 107 E14
Älmsta S 99 C11
Almstedt D 79 B6
Almudema E 55 C9
Almudévar E 41 D10
Almuñécar E 53 C9
Almunge S 99 C10
Almuniente E 41 E11
Almünster A 73 A8
Almuradiel E 55 B6
Almussafes E 48 F4
Almvik S 93 D9
Almyropotamos GR 175 C9
Almyros GR 175 A6
Alnes N 100 B4
Alness GB 3 K8
Alnwick GB 5 E13
Alobras E 47 D10
Alocén E 47 C7
Aloja LV 131 F9
Alol' RUS 133 D6
Alonia GR 169 D8
Álora E 53 C7
Alós d'Ensil E 33 E8
Alosno E 51 D5
Alost B 19 C9
Alost B 182 D4
Alovera E 47 C6
Alozaina E 53 C7
Alp E 33 F9
Alpalhão P 44 F5
Alpanseque E 41 F6
Alpbach A 72 B4
Alpedrinha P 44 D6
Alpedriz P 44 E3
Alpen D 17 E7
Alpenrod D 21 C9
Alpens E 43 C8
Alpera E 56 D2
Alphen NL 16 F3
Alphen aan den Rijn NL 16 D3
Alpiarça P 44 F3
Alpirsbach D 27 D9
Alpnach CH 70 D6
Alposjärvi FIN 117 E12
Alpua FIN 119 F14
Alpuente E 47 E11
Alpullu TR 173 B7
Alquería de la Condesa E 56 D4
Alquerías E 56 E2
Alqueva P 50 C4
Alquife E 55 E6
Alrance F 34 B4
Alrewas GB 11 F8
Als DK 86 B6
Alsager GB 11 E7
Alsån S 119 B9
Alsbach D 187 B6
Alsdorf D 20 C6
Alsėdžiai LT 134 D4
Alsen S 105 E15
Alsenborn D 21 F9
Alseno I 69 D8
Alsenz D 21 E9
Alsfeld D 21 C12
Alsheim D 185 E9
Alsike S 99 C9
Alsjö S 103 B11
Alsleben (Saale) D 79 C10
Alslev DK 86 D2
Alsmo N 100 D6
Alsónémedi H 150 C3
Alsópáhok H 149 C8
Alsos N 108 A8
Alsóvadász H 145 G2
Alsózsolca H 145 G2
Alsrode DK 87 C7
Ålstad N 110 E9
Alstad S 87 E12
Alstahaug N 108 E3
Alstakan S 97 C8
Alster S 97 D10
Alsterbro S 89 B9
Alstermo S 89 B9
Alsting F 186 C2
Alston GB 5 F12
Alsunga LV 134 C3
Alsvåg N 110 C9
Alsvik N 108 B7
Alsviķi LV 133 B1
Alta N 113 D11
Älta S 99 D10
Altafulla E 43 E6
Altamura I 61 B7
Altare I 37 C8
Altatornio FIN 119 C12
Altaussee A 73 A8
Altavilla Irpina I 60 B3
Altavilla Silentina I 60 B4
Altdöbern D 80 C6
Altdorf CH 71 D7
Altdorf D 75 E11
Altdorf bei Nürnberg D 75 D9
Alt Duvenstedt D 82 B7
Alte P 50 E3
Altea E 56 D4
Altefähr D 84 B4
Alteglofsheim D 75 E11
Alteidet N 112 C9
Altena D 17 F9
Altenahr D 21 C7
Altenau D 79 C7
Altenberg D 80 E5
Altenberge D 17 D8
Altenbruch-Westerende D 17 A11
Altenbuch D 74 C5
Altenburg D 79 E11
Altendiez D 21 D9
Altenfeld D 75 A8
Altenfelden A 76 F5
Altenglan D 21 E8
Altenhagen D 83 B11
Altenheim D 27 D8
Altenhof D 84 E5
Altenholz D 83 B8
Altenkirchen D 84 A4
Altenkirchen (Westerwald) D 21 C9
Altenkrempe D 83 B9
Altenkunstadt D 75 B9
Altenmarkt an der Triesting A 77 F9
Altenmarkt bei Sankt Gallen A 73 A10
Altenmarkt im Pongau A 73 B7
Altenmedingen D 83 D9
Altenmünster D 75 F8
Altenstadt D 21 D11
Altenstadt D 71 A10
Altenstadt D 71 B11
Altensteig D 27 C10
Altentreptow D 84 C4
Alter do Chão P 44 F5
Altes Lager D 80 B4
Altevik N 111 C12
Altfraunhofen D 75 F11
Altheim A 76 F4
Altheim D 27 D11
Altheim (Alb) D 187 D9
Althengstett D 187 D6
Althofen A 73 C9
Altier F 35 B6
Altimir BG 165 B8
Altîna RO 152 F4
Altındağ TR 177 C9
Altinoluk TR 172 E6
Altinova TR 177 A8
Altıntaş TR 181 A8
Altkirch F 27 E7
Alt Krenzlin D 83 D10
Altlandsberg D 80 A5
Altleiningen D 21 E10
Altmannstein D 75 E10
Altnaharra GB 2 J8
Altofonte I 58 C3
Altomonte I 60 D6
Altomünster D 75 F9
Alton GB 11 F8
Alton GB 14 E7
Altopascio I 66 E2
Altorricón E 42 D4
Altötting D 75 F12
Altrich D 185 E6
Altrincham GB 11 E7
Alt Ruppin D 84 E3
Altsasu E 32 E1
Alt Schwerin D 83 C12
Altshausen D 71 B9
Altstätten CH 71 C9
Alttajärvi S 116 C5
Altura E 48 E4
Altusried D 71 B10
Alu EST 131 C9
Aluatu MD 154 F3
Alūksne LV 133 B2
Ålund S 118 D6
Alunda S 99 B10
Aluniş RO 152 C3
Aluniş RO 152 D5
Aluniş RO 161 C7
Alunu RO 160 C3
Alustante E 47 C9
Alva S 93 E12
Alvaiázere P 44 E4
Alvajärvi FIN 123 D14
Alvalade P 50 D3
Alvaneu CH 71 D9
Älvängen S 91 D11
Alvarenga P 44 C4
Álvares P 44 D4
Álvaro P 44 E5
Alvdal N 101 B13
Älvdalen S 102 D7
Alvega P 44 F4
Alveley GB 13 A10
Alvelos P 38 E2
Alverca P 50 B1
Alverca da Beira P 45 C6
Alvesta S 88 B7
Alvestad N 111 C11
Alvestorp S 97 C12
Alvettula FIN 127 C11
Alvhem S 91 C11
Älvho S 102 D8
Alviano I 62 B2
Alvie GB 3 L9
Alvignac F 29 F9
Ålvik N 94 B4
Alvik S 102 E8
Alvik S 103 B13
Alvik S 118 C7
Alvito I 62 D5
Alvito P 50 C4
Älvkarleby S 103 E13
Älvkarleö S 99 A8
Alvnes N 108 B9
Alvnes N 110 E9
Alvoco da Serra P 44 D5
Älvros S 102 B8
Älvsbyn S 118 C6
Älvsered S 87 A11
Ålvund N 101 A9
Ålvundeid N 101 A9
Alwernia PL 143 F8
Alyki GR 174 A3
Alyth GB 5 B10
Alytus LT 137 E9
Alzenau in Unterfranken D 21 D12
Alzey D 21 E10
Alzira E 48 F4
Alzon F 34 C5
Alzonne F 33 D10
Åmådalen S 102 D8
Amadora P 50 B1
Amaiur-Maia E 32 D3
Åmål S 91 A12
Åmål S 91 B12
Amalfi I 60 B3
Amaliada GR 174 D3
Amaliapoli GR 175 A6
Amalo GR 177 D6
Amance F 26 E5
Amancey F 31 A9
Amandola I 62 B4
Amantea I 60 E6
Amara RO 161 D10
Amarante P 38 F3
Amarantos GR 168 E5
Amărăşti RO 160 D4
Amărăştii de Jos RO 160 F4
Amărăştii de Sus RO 160 F4
Amareleja P 51 C5
Amares P 38 E3
Amaroni I 59 B9
Amaru RO 161 D9
Amarynthos GR 175 C8
Amaseno I 62 E4
Amatrice I 62 B4
Amaxades GR 171 B8
Amay B 19 C11
Ambasaguas E 39 C9
Ambazac F 29 D8
Ambel E 41 E8
Ambeļi LV 135 D13
Amberg D 75 D10
Ambergate GB 11 E9
Ambérieu-en-Bugey F 31 D7
Amberloup B 19 D12
Ambert F 30 D4
Ambès F 28 E4
Ambierle F 30 C4
Ambillou F 24 F3
Ambjörby S 97 B9
Ambjörnarp S 91 E13
Ambla EST 131 C11
Amblainville F 24 B7
Amble GB 5 E13
Ambleside GB 10 C6
Ambleteuse F 15 F12
Amboise F 24 F4
Ambon F 22 E6
Ambrault F 29 B9
Ambrières-les-Vallées F 23 D10
Ambronay F 31 C7
Ambrosden GB 13 B12
Åmdals Verk N 95 D8
Ameglia I 69 E8
Ameide NL 182 B5
Ameixial P 50 E4
Amel B 20 D6
Amele LV 134 B4
Amelia I 62 B2
Amélie-les-Bains-Palalda F 34 F4
Amelinghausen D 83 D8
Amêndoa P 44 E4
Amendoeira P 50 D4
Amendolara I 61 D7
Amer E 43 C9
Amerang D 75 G11
A Merca E 38 D4
Amerongen NL 183 B6
Amersfoort NL 16 D4
Amersham GB 15 D7
Amesbury GB 13 C11
Amezketa E 32 D1
Amfikleia GR 175 B6
Amfilochia GR 174 B3
Amfipoli GR 169 C10
Amfissa GR 174 B5
Amieira P 50 C4
Amiens F 18 E5
Amilly F 25 E8
Åminne FIN 122 E7
Åminne S 87 A14
Åmland N 94 F5
Åmli N 90 A3
Åmli N 90 B3
Amlwch GB 10 E3
Ämmälänkylä FIN 123 E9
Ammanford GB 12 B7
Ämmänsaari FIN 121 E12
Ammarnäs S 109 E11
Åmmeberg S 92 B6
Ammenäs S 91 C10
Ammerbuch D 187 D6
Ammern D 79 D7
Ammersbek D 83 C8
Ammerzoden NL 183 B6
Ammochori GR 169 C5
Ammotopos GR 168 F4
Ammoudia GR 169 B9
Amnatos GR 178 E8
Amnéville F 186 C1
Amoeiro E 38 D4
Amonde P 38 E2
Amorbach D 21 E12
Amorebieta E 40 B6
Amorgos GR 177 F6
Amori GR 171 B10
Åmot N 94 C7
Åmot N 95 B11
Åmot N 95 C8
Åmot N 95 C10
Åmot S 103 E11
Åmotfors S 96 C7
Amou F 32 C4
Åmøyhamn N 108 C5
Ampelakia GR 169 E8
Ampeleia GR 169 F7
Ampelokipoi GR 169 C8
Ampelonas GR 169 E7
Ampezzo I 73 D6
Ampfing D 75 F11
Ampflwang im Hausruckwald A 76 F5
Amplepuis F 30 D5
Amposta E 42 F5
Ampthill GB 15 C8
Ampudia E 39 E10
Ampuero E 40 B5
Ampus F 36 D4
Amriswil CH 27 E11
Åmsele S 107 B16
Åmsosen N 94 D3
Amstelveen NL 16 D3
Amsterdam NL 16 D3
Amstetten A 77 F7
Amstetten D 187 D8
Amulree GB 5 B9
Amurrio E 40 B6
Amusco E 40 D3
Amvrosia GR 171 B8
Amygdaleonas GR 171 C6
Amygdalia GR 174 C5
Åmynnet S 107 E15
Amyntaio GR 169 C6
Amzacea RO 155 F2
Anacapri I 60 B2
Anadia P 44 D4
Anafi GR 180 D3
Anafonitria GR 174 D2
Anagaire IRL 6 B6
Anagni I 62 D4
An Aird Mhóir IRL 6 F3
Añana-Gesaltza E 40 C6
Anan'yiv UA 154 B5
Anarcs H 145 G5
Anargyroi GR 169 C6
Anarrachi GR 169 D6
Ånäset S 118 F6
Åna-Sira N 94 F4
Anatazavė LT 135 E11
Anatoli GR 168 E4
Anatoli GR 169 E8
Anatoli GR 179 E10
Anatoliki Fragkista GR 174 B4
Anatoliko GR 169 C6
Anatoliko GR 169 C8
Anavatos GR 177 C7
Anavra GR 174 A5
Anavra GR 175 A6
Anavyssos GR 175 D8
Anaya de Alba E 45 C10
An Baile Breac IRL 8 E2
An Baile Nua IRL 8 D5
An Bhlarna IRL 8 E5
An Bun Beag IRL 6 B6
An Cabhán IRL 7 E8
An Caiseal IRL 6 F3
An Caisleán Riabhach IRL 6 E6
An Caisléan Nua IRL 7 F10
An Caisléan Nua IRL 8 D4
An Cathair IRL 9 D7
Ance LV 134 A4
Ancelle F 36 B4
Ancene LV 135 D11
Ancenis F 23 F9
Ancerville F 26 C3
An Charraig IRL 6 C5
An Cheathru Rua IRL 6 F3
An Chill IRL 7 F9
Ancín E 32 E1
An Cionn Garbh IRL 6 C6
An Clochán IRL 7 C7
An Clochán Liath IRL 6 C6
An Cóbh IRL 8 E6
An Coimín IRL 7 C7
An Coireán IRL 8 E2
Ancona I 67 E8
Ancroft GB 5 D13
Ancrum GB 5 D11
Ancy-le-Franc F 25 E11
Anda N 100 C4
An Daingean IRL 8 D2
Andalo I 69 A11
Åndalsnes N 100 A7
Andau A 149 A8
Andavías E 39 E8
Anddalsvågen N 108 E3
Andebu N 95 D12
Andechs D 75 G9
Andeer CH 71 D8
Andelfingen CH 27 E10
Andelot-Blancheville F 26 D3
Andelst NL 16 E5
Andenes N 111 B11
Andenne B 19 D11
Anderlecht B 19 C9
Anderlues B 19 D9
Andermatt CH 71 D7
Andernach D 185 D7
Andernos-les-Bains F 28 F3
Andersbo S 99 B9
Anderslöv S 87 E12
Anderstorp S 88 A5
Andervenne D 17 C9
Andfiskå N 108 D7
Andijk NL 16 C4
Andilly-en-Bassigny F 26 E4
Andlau F 27 D7
Andoain E 32 D1
Andocs H 149 C9
Andolsheim F 27 D7
Andorf A 76 F5
Andørja N 111 C13
Andorno Micca I 68 B5
Andorra E 42 F2
Andorra la Vella AND 33 E9
Andosilla E 32 F2
Andouillé F 23 D10
Andover GB 13 C12
Andrano I 61 D10
Andrăşeşti RO 161 D10
Andratx E 49 E9
Andravida GR 174 D3
Andreas GBM 10 C3
Andreiaşu de Jos RO 153 F9
Andrespol PL 143 C8
Andrest F 33 D6
Andretta I 60 B4
Andria I 60 A6
Andrid RO 151 B9
Andrieşeni RO 153 B10
Andrijaševci HR 157 B10
Andrijevica MNE 163 D8
Andrioniškis LT 135 E10
Andriškiai LT 136 D6
Andritsaina GR 174 E4
Andronianoi GR 175 B9
Andros GR 176 D4
Androusa GR 174 E4
Andrup DK 86 D3
Andrupene LV 133 D2
Andrychów PL 147 B8
Andrzejewo PL 141 E6
Andselv N 111 B15
Andsnes N 112 C7
An Dúchoraidh IRL 6 C6
Andújar E 53 A8
Anduze F 35 B6
Andzeļi LV 133 D3
An Eachléim IRL 6 D2
Aneby N 95 B13
Aneby S 92 D5
Anela I 64 C3
Anenii Noi MD 154 D4
Ånes N 104 E4
Anet F 24 C5
Anetjärvi FIN 121 C10
Anevo BG 165 D10
Aneza GR 174 A2
An Fál Carrach IRL 6 B6
An Féar Bán IRL 7 F7
An Fhairche IRL 6 E4
Anfo I 69 B9
Ång S 92 D5
Anga S 93 E13
Ånge S 103 A10
Ånge S 105 E16
Ånge S 109 E14
An Geata Mór IRL 6 D2
Ängebo S 103 C11
Angeja P 44 C3
Ängelholm S 87 C11
Angeli FIN 113 F16
Angelniemi FIN 127 E8
Angelochori GR 169 C7
Angelokastro GR 174 B3
Angelokastro GR 175 D7
Ängelsberg S 97 C15
Angelstad S 87 B13
Angely F 25 E11
Anger D 73 A6
Angera I 68 B6
Angermünde D 84 D6
Angern D 79 B10
Angern an der March A 77 F11
Angers F 23 F10
Ångersjö S 102 C8
Ångersjö S 122 C3
Angersnes N 108 D4
Angervikko FIN 125 D10
Angerville F 24 D7
Ängesån S 116 E8
Ängeslevä FIN 119 E15
Ängesträsk S 118 B8
Anghiari I 66 E5
Anglade F 28 E4
Angle GB 9 E12
Anglès E 43 D9
Anglès F 34 C4
Anglesola E 42 D5
Anglesona E 42 D6
Angles-sur-l'Anglin F 29 B7
Anglet F 32 D2
Angliers F 29 B6
Anglure F 25 C10
Angnäs S 107 D16
Angoisse F 29 E8
Angom S 103 B13
An Gort IRL 6 F5
Angoulême F 29 D6
Angoulins F 28 C3
Angri I 60 B3
Angrie F 23 E10
Angüés E 42 C3
Anguiano E 40 D6
Anguillara Sabazia I 62 C2
Anguillara Veneta I 66 B4
Anguita E 47 B8
Angvik N 100 A8
Anha P 38 E2
Anhée B 19 D10
Anholt DK 87 B9
Aniane F 35 C6
Aniche F 19 D7
Anif A 73 A7
Anina RO 159 C8
Aninoasa RO 160 C2
Aninoasa RO 160 C5
Aninoasa RO 160 D2
Aninoasa RO 161 D6
Anizy-le-Château F 19 E7
Anjalankoski FIN 128 D6
Anjan S 105 D13
Anjum NL 16 B6
Ankaran SLO 73 E8
Ankarede Kapell S 105 B16
Ankarsrum S 93 D8
Ankarsund S 109 F12
Ankarsvik S 103 B13
Ankenes N 111 D13
Ankerlia N 112 E6
Ankershagen D 84 D3
Anklam D 84 C5
Ankum D 17 C9
Anlaby GB 11 D11
An Leadhb Gharbh IRL 6 C5
Anlezy F 30 B4
An Longfort IRL 7 E7
An Mám IRL 6 E3
An Mhala Raithní IRL 6 E3
An Móta IRL 7 F7
An Muileann gCearr IRL 7 E8
Ånn S 105 E13
Anna E 56 C3
Anna EST 131 C11
Annaberg A 77 G8
Annaberg-Buchholtz D 80 E4
Annaburg D 80 C4
Annagassan IRL 7 E10
Annagry IRL 6 B6
Annahilt GB 7 D10
Annahütte D 80 C5
Annalong GB 7 D11
Annamoe IRL 7 F10
Annan GB 5 F10
Anna Paulowna NL 16 C3
Annarode D 79 C9
An Nás IRL 7 F9
Annayalla IRL 7 D9
Annbank GB 4 E7
Anneberg S 91 D11
Anneberg S 92 D5
Annecy F 31 D9
Annecy-le-Vieux F 31 D9
Annefors S 103 D11
Annelund S 91 D13
Annemasse F 31 C9
Annen NL 17 B7
Annenieki LV 134 C6
Annestown IRL 9 D8
Anneyron F 30 E6
Annikvere EST 131 C12
Annœullin F 182 D1
Annonay F 30 E6
Annonen FIN 119 F14
Annopol PL 144 B4
Annot F 36 D5
Annweiler am Trifels D 21 F9
Ano Agios Vlasios GR 174 B4
Ano Amfeia GR 174 E5
Ano Chora GR 174 B4
Ano Diakofto GR 174 C5
Ano Drosini GR 171 B9
Anoeta E 32 D1
Anogeia GR 174 F5
Anogeia GR 178 E8
Ano Kalliniki GR 168 C5
Ano Kardamyla GR 177 B7
Ano Kavallari GR 169 C9
Ano Komi GR 169 D6
Ano Kopanaki GR 174 E4
Ano Lechonia GR 169 F9
Ano Lefkimmi GR 168 F3
Ano Mera GR 176 E5
Añón E 41 E8
Ano Poroia GR 169 B9
Anor F 19 E9
Añora E 54 C3
Ano Sagkri GR 176 E5
Ano Steni GR 175 B8

Ano Syros *GR* 176 E4
Ano Trikala *GR* 174 D5
Ano Tyros *GR* 175 E6
Anould *F* 27 D6
Añover de Tajo *E* 46 E5
Ano Vrontou *GR* 169 B10
Anquela del Ducado *E* 47 C8
Anras *A* 72 C6
An Rinn *IRL* 9 D7
Anröchte *D* 185 A9
An Ros *IRL* 7 E10
Ans *B* 19 C12
Ans *DK* 86 C5
Ansac-sur-Vienne *F* 29 D7
Ansager *DK* 86 D3
Ansbach *D* 75 D8
An Sciobairin *IRL* 8 E4
Anse *F* 30 D6
Ansedonia *I* 65 C4
Anseremme *B* 19 D10
Ansfelden *A* 76 F6
Ansião *P* 44 E4
Ansizca *TR* 177 C9
Ansjö *S* 103 A11
Ansnes *N* 111 B15
Ansó *E* 32 E4
An Spidéal *IRL* 6 F4
Anspoki *LV* 135 D13
Ansprung *D* 80 E4
Ånstad *N* 110 C8
Anstruther *GB* 5 C11
Ånsvik *N* 109 B9
Antalieptė *LT* 135 E11
Antanhol *P* 44 D4
An tAonach *IRL* 8 C6
Antas *E* 55 E9
Antas *P* 38 E2
Antas *P* 44 C6
Antas de Ulla *E* 38 C4
An Teampall Mór *IRL* 9 C7
An Tearmann *IRL* 7 B7
Antequera *E* 53 B7
Anterselva di Sopra *I* 72 C5
Anthéor *F* 36 E5
Anthien *F* 25 F10
Anthili *GR* 175 B5
Anthotopos *GR* 175 A6
Anthrakitis *GR* 168 E4
Antibes *F* 36 D6
Antigonos *GR* 169 C6
Antikyra *GR* 175 C6
Antillo *I* 59 D7
Antimacheia *GR* 177 F9
An tInbhear Mór *IRL* 9 C10
Antiparos *GR* 176 E5
Antirrio *GR* 174 C4
Antisanti *F* 37 G10
Antissa *GR* 171 F9
Antjärn *S* 103 A14
Antnäs *S* 118 C7
Antoing *B* 19 C7
Antol *SK* 147 E7
Anton *BG* 165 D9
Anton Ivanov *BG* 165 E9
Antonivka *UA* 145 F6
Antonne-et-Trigonant *F* 29 E7
Antonovo *BG* 166 C6
Antony *F* 25 C7
Antraigues-sur-Volane *F* 30 F5
Antrain *F* 23 D9
Antrim *GB* 4 F4
Antrodoco *I* 62 C4
An tSeanga Mheáin *IRL* 6 C6
Antsla *EST* 131 F13
Anttis *S* 116 D9
Anttola *FIN* 128 B8
An Tulch *IRL* 9 C9
Antully *F* 30 B5
Antunovac Tenjski *HR* 149 F11
Antuži *LV* 135 C11
Antwerpen *B* 19 B9
Antzuola *E* 32 D1
An Uaimh *IRL* 7 E9
Anvers *B* 19 B9
Anvers *B* 182 C4
Anvin *F* 18 D5
Anykščiai *LT* 135 E10
Anzano di Puglia *I* 60 A4
Anzat-le-Luguet *F* 30 E3
Anzegem *B* 19 C7
Anzère *CH* 31 C11
Anzi *I* 60 B5
Anzin *F* 19 D7
Anzing *D* 75 F10
Anzio *I* 62 E3
Aoiz *E* 32 E3
Aoradh *B* 4 D4
Aós *E* 32 E3
Aosta *I* 31 D11
Aouste-sur-Sye *F* 31 F7
Apa *RO* 151 B11
Apagy *H* 145 H4
Apahida *RO* 152 D3
Apaj *H* 150 C3
Apața *RO* 153 F7
Apateu *RO* 151 D8
Apátfalva *H* 150 E6
Apatin *SRB* 158 B2
Apatovac *HR* 149 D7
Apc *H* 150 B4
Ape *LV* 131 F13
Apecchio *I* 66 E5
A Pedreira *E* 38 D3
Apeiranthos *GR* 177 E6
Apeldoorn *NL* 16 D5
Apelern *D* 17 D12
Apele Vii *RO* 160 E4
Apen *D* 17 B9
Apenburg *D* 83 E10
Apensen *D* 82 D7
Aperi *GR* 181 E6
A Peroxa *E* 38 D4
Apgulde *LV* 134 C6
Apice *I* 60 A3
A Picota *E* 38 C2
Apidia *GR* 175 F6
Apiro *I* 67 F7
Aplared *S* 91 D13
A Pobla de Brollón *E* 38 C5
A Pobla de San Xiao *E* 38 C5
A Pobla de Trives *E* 38 D5
A Pobra do Caramiñal *E* 38 C2
Apoikia *GR* 176 D4
Apolakkia *GR* 181 D7
Apold *RO* 152 E5
Apolda *D* 79 D9
Apoldu de Jos *RO* 152 F3
Apollona *GR* 181 D7
Apollonas *GR* 177 E6
Apollonia *GR* 176 F4
A Pontenova *E* 38 B5
A Pontepedra *E* 38 B2
Áporka *H* 150 C3

Apostag *H* 149 C11
Apostoloi *GR* 178 E8
Äppelbo *S* 97 B11
Appenweier *D* 186 D4
Appenzell *CH* 27 F11
Appiano sulla Strada del Vino *I* 72 D3
Appietto *F* 37 G9
Appignano *I* 67 F7
Appingedam *NL* 17 B7
Appleby-in-Westmorland *GB* 10 B7
Appleby Magna *GB* 11 F8
Applecross *GB* 2 L5
Appledore *GB* 12 C6
Appledore *GB* 15 E10
Aprelevo *RUS* 132 E2
Apremont-la-Forêt *F* 26 C4
Aprica *I* 69 A9
Apricale *I* 37 D7
Apricena *I* 63 D8
Aprigliano *I* 61 E6
Apriki *LV* 134 C3
Aprilovo *BG* 166 C6
Apriltsi *BG* 165 D10
A Proba *E* 39 C6
Apsalos *GR* 169 C7
Apšuciems *LV* 134 B6
Apt *F* 35 C9
Aquavilla delle Fonti *I* 61 B7
Aquilonia *I* 60 B4
Aquilué *E* 32 F5
Aquino *I* 62 E5
Aracena *E* 51 D6
Arachnaio *GR* 175 D6
Arachova *GR* 175 C6
Aračinovo *MK* 164 E4
Arad *RO* 151 E7
Aradac *SRB* 158 C5
Arãdalen *S* 102 A6
Aradeo *I* 61 C10
Aragnouet *F* 33 E6
Aragona *I* 58 E4
Aragoncillo *E* 47 C8
Araia *E* 32 E1
A Ramallosa *E* 38 C2
Aramits *F* 32 D4
Aramon *F* 35 C8
Aranda de Duero *E* 40 E4
Aranda de Moncayo *E* 41 E8
Arandelovac *SRB* 158 E6
Aranhas *P* 45 D6
Aranitas *AL* 168 C2
Aranjuez *E* 46 D5
Arano *E* 32 D2
Aranzueque *E* 47 D6
Araovacik *TR* 173 C7
Arapaj *AL* 168 B2
Arapiles *E* 45 C9
Aras *E* 32 E1
Aras de Alpuente *E* 47 E10
Arasvika *N* 104 E4
Aratos *GR* 171 B9
Araules *F* 30 E5
Aravete *EST* 131 C11
Aravissos *GR* 169 C7
Arazede *P* 44 D3
Arbanasi *BG* 166 C5
Arbas *F* 33 E7
Arbatax *I* 64 D4
Arbeca *E* 42 D5
Arbecey *F* 26 E4
Arbedo *CH* 69 A7
Arbéost *F* 32 E5
Arberg *D* 75 D8
Arbesbach *A* 77 E7
Arbeteta *E* 47 C8
Arboga *S* 97 D14
Arbois *F* 31 B8
Arboleas *E* 55 E8
Arbon *CH* 27 E11
Arbore *RO* 153 B7
Arborea *I* 64 D2
Arborio *I* 68 C5
Årbostad *N* 111 C13
Arbrå *S* 103 D11
Arbroath *GB* 5 B11
Arbúcies *E* 43 D9
Arbus *I* 64 D2
Ärby *DK* 87 D8
Ärbyn *S* 118 C8
Arcachon *F* 32 A3
Arcangues *F* 32 D2
Arcani *RO* 159 C11
Arce *I* 62 E5
Arcen *NL* 16 F6
Arc-en-Barrois *F* 26 E3
Arces *F* 28 D4
Arces-Dilo *F* 25 D10
Arc-et-Senans *F* 31 A8
Arcevia *I* 67 E6
Archaia Epidavros *GR* 175 D7
Archaia Korinthos *GR* 175 D6
Archaia Olympia *GR* 174 D4
Archanes *GR* 178 E9
Archangelos *GR* 181 D8
Archar *BG* 159 F10
Archena *E* 55 C10
Archiac *F* 28 D5
Archidona *E* 53 B8
Archipoli *GR* 181 D8
Archiş *RO* 151 D9
Archivel *E* 55 C9
Arcidosso *I* 65 B5
Árciems *LV* 131 F10
Arcis-sur-Aube *F* 25 C11
Arc-lès-Gray *F* 26 F4
Arco *I* 69 B10
Arco de Baúlhe *P* 38 F4
Arcola *I* 69 E8
Arçon *F* 31 B9
Arçonnay *F* 23 D12
Arcos *E* 40 B4
Arcos *P* 50 B4
Arcos de Jalón *E* 47 B8
Arcos de la Frontera *E* 52 C5
Arcos de las Salinas *E* 47 E10
Arcos de Valdevez *P* 38 E3
Arcozelo *P* 38 E2
Arcozelo *P* 38 E2
Arc-sur-Tille *F* 26 F3
Arcusa *E* 33 F6
Arda *BG* 171 B7
Ardagger Markt *A* 77 F7
Árdal *N* 100 C4
Ardala *S* 91 C13
Ardales *E* 53 C7
Årdalstangen *N* 100 D7
Ardanaz *E* 32 E3
Ard an Rátha *IRL* 6 C6
Ardara *I* 64 B2

Ardara *IRL* 6 C6
Ardauli *I* 64 C2
Ardea *I* 62 D3
Ardee *IRL* 7 E9
Ardeluța *RO* 153 D8
Arden *DK* 86 B5
Arden *GB* 4 C7
Ardentes *F* 29 B9
Ardeoani *RO* 153 D9
Ardersier *GB* 3 K8
Ardes *F* 30 E3
Ardez *CH* 71 D10
Ardfinnan *IRL* 9 D7
Ardglass *GB* 7 D11
Ardgroom *IRL* 8 E3
Ardino *BG* 171 A7
Ardkeen *GB* 7 D11
Ardlui *GB* 4 C7
Ardlussa *GB* 4 C5
Ardmair *GB* 2 K6
Ardminish *GB* 4 D5
Ardmore *IRL* 6 F3
Ardmore *IRL* 9 E7
Ardon *CH* 31 C11
Ardooie *B* 19 C7
Ardore *I* 59 C9
Ardpatrick *IRL* 8 D5
Ardrahan *IRL* 6 F5
Ardre *S* 93 E13
Ardres *F* 18 C4
Ardrishaig *GB* 4 C6
Ardrossan *GB* 4 D7
Ardscull *IRL* 7 F9
Ardtoe *GB* 4 B5
Ardu *EST* 131 C10
Ardud *RO* 151 B10
Ardusat *RO* 151 B11
Ardvasar *GB* 4 A5
Åre *EST* 131 D7
Åre *S* 105 E14
Areatza *E* 40 B6
Arefu *RO* 160 C5
Areias *P* 44 E4
Arén *E* 42 C5
Arenas de Iguña *E* 40 B3
Arenas del Rey *E* 53 C9
Arenas de San Juan *E* 46 F5
Arenas de San Pedro *E* 45 D10
Arendal *N* 90 C4
Arendonk *B* 16 F4
Arendsee (Altmark) *D* 83 E10
Arengosse *F* 32 B4
Arenillas *E* 40 F6
Arenshausen *D* 79 D6
Arentorp *S* 91 C12
Arentsminde *DK* 86 A5
Arenys de Mar *E* 43 D9
Arenzano *I* 37 C9
Areópoli *GR* 178 B3
Areosa *P* 38 E2
Ares *E* 38 B3
Arès *F* 28 F3
Ares del Maestre *E* 48 D4
Aresing *D* 75 E9
Arespalditza *E* 40 B5
Arethousa *GR* 169 C10
Arette *F* 32 D4
Arette-Pierre-St-Martin *F* 32 E4
Aretxabaleta *E* 41 B7
Arevalillo *E* 45 C10
Arévalo *E* 46 B3
Arezzo *I* 66 F4
Arfara *GR* 174 E5
Arfons *F* 33 D10
Ärför *N* 105 B11
Argalasti *GR* 169 F9
Argallón *E* 51 C9
Arganda del Rey *E* 46 D6
Arganil *P* 44 D4
Arganza *E* 39 C6
Årgård *N* 105 C10
Argegno *I* 69 B7
Argelès-Gazost *F* 32 D5
Argelès-sur-Mer *F* 34 E5
Argeliers *F* 34 D4
Argelita *E* 48 D4
Argentan *F* 23 D12
Argens *F* 23 B11
Argenta *I* 66 C4
Argentan *F* 23 C5
Argentat *F* 29 E9
Argente *E* 47 C10
Argentera *I* 36 C5
Argenteuil *F* 25 C7
Argenthal *D* 21 E9
Argentiera *I* 64 B1
Argentière *F* 31 D10
Argentine *F* 31 E9
Argenton-Château *F* 28 B5
Argenton-sur-Creuse *F* 29 B9
Argentre *F* 23 D10
Argentré-du-Plessis *F* 23 E9
Argent-sur-Sauldre *F* 25 E7
Argés *E* 46 E4
Argetoaia *RO* 160 D2
Arginonta *GR* 177 E8
Argonay *F* 31 D9
Argos *GR* 175 D6
Argos Orestiko *GR* 168 C5
Argostoli *GR* 174 C1
Argouges *F* 23 D9
Arguedas *E* 41 D8
Argueil *F* 18 E4
Arguellite *E* 55 C8
Arguis *E* 32 F5
Arguisuelas *E* 47 E9
Argujillo *E* 39 F8
Argyrades *GR* 168 F2
Argyropouli *GR* 169 E7
Århus *DK* 86 C6
Ariano Irpino *I* 60 A4
Ariano nel Polesine *I* 66 C5
Ariany *E* 57 B11
Aribe *E* 32 E3
Ariccia *I* 62 D3
Aridaia *GR* 169 C7
Arieşeni *RO* 151 E10
Arignac *F* 33 E9
Arija *E* 40 C4
Arild *S* 87 C11
Arileod *GB* 4 B3
Arilje *SRB* 158 F5
Arinagour *GB* 4 B3
Ariniş *RO* 151 C11
Ariolos *RO* 160 E2
Ariño *E* 42 E2

Arinsal *AND* 33 E8
Arinthod *F* 31 C8
Ariogala *LT* 134 F5
Aris *GR* 174 E5
Arisaig *GB* 4 B5
Aristomenis *GR* 174 E4
Arisvi *GR* 171 B9
Aritzo *I* 64 D3
Ariz *P* 44 C5
Ariza *E* 41 F7
Arizgoiti *E* 40 B6
Arizola *E* 32 E2
Årjäng *S* 96 D7
Arjona *E* 53 A8
Arjonilla *E* 53 A8
Arkala *FIN* 119 D16
Arkalochori *GR* 178 E9
Arkasa *GR* 181 F6
Arkelstorp *S* 88 C6
Arkesini *GR* 180 C3
Arkitsa *GR* 175 B7
Arkkukari *FIN* 119 E12
Arklow *GB* 9 C10
Arkna *EST* 131 C12
Arkösund *S* 93 C9
Årla *S* 98 D7
Arlanc *F* 30 E4
Arlanzón *E* 40 D5
Arle (Großheide) *D* 17 A8
Arlena di Castro *I* 62 C1
Arles *F* 35 C8
Arleuf *F* 30 A5
Arleux *F* 19 D7
Arligbo *S* 98 B8
Arló *H* 145 G1
Arlon *B* 19 E12
Arluno *I* 69 B6
Arlyeya *BY* 133 E6
Armação de Pêra *P* 50 E2
Armadale *GB* 5 D9
Armağan *TR* 167 F8
Armagh *GB* 7 D9
Armallones *E* 47 C8
Armamar *P* 44 B5
Armãseşti *RO* 161 D9
Armasjärvi *S* 119 B11
Armassaari *FIN* 119 B11
Armen *AL* 168 C2
Armenioi *GR* 174 E4
Armeniş *RO* 159 C9
Armenistis *GR* 177 D7
Armeno *I* 68 B5
Armenochori *GR* 168 C5
Armenoi *GR* 178 E7
Armenteros *E* 45 C10
Armentières *F* 18 C6
Armento *I* 60 C5
Armilla *E* 53 B9
Armissan *F* 34 D5
Armolia *GR* 177 C7
Armoy *GB* 4 E4
Armuña *E* 46 B4
Armungia *I* 64 E3
Armunia *S* 119 C8
Armutalani *TR* 181 C8
Armutlu *TR* 173 C10
Armutlu *TR* 177 C10
Arna *GR* 175 F6
Arnac-Pompadour *F* 29 E8
Arnad *F* 23 E12
Arnaia *GR* 169 D10
Årnäs *S* 91 B14
Arnäs *S* 102 D5
Årnäs *S* 102 E5
Arnåsvall *S* 107 E15
Arnavutköy *TR* 173 B10
Arnay-le-Duc *F* 25 F11
Arnberg *S* 107 B16
Arnborg *DK* 86 C3
Arnbruck *D* 76 D3
Arneburg *D* 83 E12
Arnedillo *E* 41 D7
Arnedo *E* 41 D7
Arnéguy *F* 32 E3
Arnemark *S* 118 D6
Arnemuiden *NL* 16 F1
Arnes *E* 42 F4
Årnes *N* 95 B14
Årnes *N* 104 F5
Årnes *N* 111 B15
Arnfels *A* 148 C5
Arnhem *NL* 16 E5
Arnionys 1 *LT* 137 C12
Arnissa *GR* 169 C6
Arnö *S* 93 B10
Arnol *GB* 2 J3
Arnold *GB* 11 E9
Arnoldstein *A* 73 C8
Arnot *H* 145 G2
Arnöviken *S* 103 C13
Arnoyhamn *N* 112 C6
Arnprior *GB* 5 C8
Arnreit *D* 76 E5
Arnsberg *D* 17 F10
Arnschwang *D* 76 D3
Arnstadt *D* 79 E8
Arnstein *D* 74 C6
Arnstorf *D* 76 E3
Arnum *DK* 86 E3
Aroania *GR* 174 D5
Ároktõ *H* 151 B6
Arola *FIN* 113 C9
Arolla *CH* 31 C11
Arolsen *D* 17 F12
Aron *F* 23 D10
Arona *I* 68 B6
Aroneanu *RO* 153 C11
Aronkylä *FIN* 122 F8
Åros *N* 95 C12
Arosa *P* 38 E3
Arosa *CH* 71 D9
Årosjåkk *S* 111 E17
Arouca *P* 44 C4
Årøybukta *N* 111 A19
Årøysund *N* 90 A7
Arpajon *F* 25 C7
Arpajon-sur-Cère *F* 29 F10
Arpaşu de Jos *RO* 152 F5
Arpela *FIN* 119 B12
Arpino *I* 62 D5
Arquata del Tronto *I* 62 B4
Arquata Scrivia *I* 37 B9
Arques *F* 18 C5
Arques *F* 33 E10
Arques-la-Bataille *F* 18 E3

Arranhó *P* 50 B1
Arras *F* 18 D6
Arrasate *E* 41 B7
Årre *DK* 86 D3
Arreau *F* 33 E6
Arredondo *E* 40 B4
Arrén *AL* 168 D3
Arrentières *F* 25 D12
Arrianà *GR* 171 B9
Arriach *A* 73 C8
Arriana *GR* 171 B9
Arriate *E* 53 C6
Arrifana *P* 45 C6
Arrigny *F* 25 C12
Arrigorriaga *E* 40 B6
Arrild *DK* 86 E3
Arriondas *E* 39 B9
Arroba de los Montes *E* 46 F3
Arrochar *GB* 4 C7
Arronches *P* 45 F6
Arrone *I* 62 B3
Arroniz *E* 32 E1
Arrou *F* 24 D5
Arroyal *E* 40 C3
Arroyo de la Luz *E* 45 E7
Arroyo del Ojanco *E* 55 C7
Arroyo de San Serván *E* 51 B7
Arroyomolinos de León *E* 51 C7
Arruda dos Vinhos *P* 50 B1
Arry *F* 186 C1
Årsandøy *N* 105 A12
Årsdale *DK* 89 E8
Arseni *GR* 169 C7
Arses-Formans *F* 30 E6
Ars-sur-Moselle *F* 26 B5
Årstein *N* 111 C14
Årsunda *S* 98 A7
Arsura *RO* 153 D12
Arsvågen *N* 94 D2
Artà *E* 57 B11
Arta *GR* 174 A2
Artajona *E* 32 E2
Artana *E* 48 E4
Artannes-sur-Indre *F* 24 F4
Artemisia *GR* 174 E5
Artemisio *GR* 174 D5
Artemisio *GR* 175 A7
Artèn *I* 72 D4
Artena *I* 62 D3
Artenay *F* 24 D6
Artern (Unstrut) *D* 79 D9
Artés *E* 43 D7
Artesa de Segre *E* 42 D6
Artesiano *GR* 169 F6
Arth *CH* 71 C7
Arthez-d'Asson *F* 32 D5
Arthez-de-Béarn *F* 32 D4
Arthon *F* 29 B9
Arthon-en-Retz *F* 23 F8
Artieda *E* 32 E4
Artigat *F* 33 D8
Artix *F* 32 D4
Artjärvi *FIN* 127 D15
Årtled *S* 103 E9
Artlenburg *D* 83 D8
Artogne *I* 69 B9
Årtrik *S* 107 E11
Artsyz *UA* 154 F4
Artziniega *E* 40 B5
A Rúa *E* 38 D5
Arudy *F* 32 D5
Aruküla *EST* 131 C10
Aruküla *EST* 131 C12
Arundel *GB* 15 F7
Arvagh *IRL* 7 E7
Arvån *S* 107 B16
Arvesund *S* 105 E13
Arveyres *F* 28 F5
Arvi *GR* 178 F9
Arvidsjaur *S* 109 E17
Arvidsträsk *S* 118 C5
Arvieu *F* 34 B4
Arvieux *F* 31 F10
Årvik *N* 100 B3
Årviksand *N* 112 C6
Arvila *EST* 131 C14
Åryd *S* 89 B7
Åryd *S* 89 B9
Arzachena *I* 64 A3
Arzacq-Arraziguet *F* 32 C5
Arzana *I* 64 D4
Arżano *HR* 157 E7
Arzbach *D* 21 D9
Arzberg *D* 80 C4
Arzfeld *D* 20 D6
Arzignano *I* 66 A3
Arzl im Pitztal *A* 71 C11
Arzúa *E* 38 C3
Aš *B* 19 B12
Aš *CZ* 75 B11
Ås *N* 95 C13
Ås *N* 105 E11
Ås *S* 96 C7
Ås *S* 97 C12
Ås *S* 106 E7
Ås *S* 107 E11
Ås *N* 95 B12
Åsa *FIN* 126 E7
Asa *S* 89 A8
Asaa *DK* 86 A6
Aşağiçobanisa *TR* 177 B10
Aşağişevindikli *TR* 173 B8
Åsan *N* 105 B12
Åsanja *SRB* 158 D5
Asare *LV* 135 D11
Åsarna *S* 102 A7
Åsarp *S* 91 D14
Åsa-Arros *F* 32 C4
Asarna *F* 32 C3
Asasp-Arros *F* 32 C4
Asbach *D* 21 C9
Åsbacka *S* 103 D11
Asby *S* 92 D6
Ascain *F* 32 D2
Ascea *I* 60 C4
Ascha *D* 76 E3
Aschach an der Donau *A* 76 F6
Aschaffenburg *D* 21 E12
Ascharia *D* 17 F10
Ascheberg (Holstein) *D* 83 B8
Ascheberg *D* 17 E9
Aschères-le-Marché *F* 24 D7
Aschersleben *D* 79 C9
Aschhelm *D* 17 C8
Aschheim *D* 75 F9
Asciano *I* 66 F4
Ascó *E* 42 E5

Asco *F* 37 G10
Ascoli Piceno *I* 62 B5
Ascoli Satriano *I* 60 A5
Ascona *CH* 68 A6
Ascou *F* 33 E9
Åse *N* 111 B10
Åsebyn *S* 96 D7
Åseda *S* 89 A8
Åsegg *N* 105 C9
Åsele *S* 107 C12
Åselet *S* 118 C6
Asemakylä *FIN* 119 D14
Asemankylä *FIN* 119 D14
Asemanseutu *FIN* 123 E11
Åsen *N* 105 D10
Åsen *S* 102 C7
Åsen *S* 102 D6
Åsen *S* 106 E7
Åsen *S* 109 E16
Åsenbruk *S* 91 B11
Åsendorf *D* 17 C12
Asenovets *BG* 166 D5
Asenovgrad *BG* 165 E10
Asenovo *BG* 166 C6
Asenovo *BG* 165 C11
A Serra de Outes *E* 38 C2
Asfaka *GR* 168 E4
Asfeld *F* 19 F9
Asfendiou *GR* 177 F9
Asferg *DK* 86 B5
Asgårdstrand *N* 90 D12
Åsgeir *N* 90 A7
Aseral *N* 90 B7
Aseri *EST* 131 C13
Asfjorden *N* 94 D2
Asha *GR* 174 C2
Åsheim *N* 101 E11
Ashammar *S* 103 E12
Ashbourne *GB* 11 E8
Ashbourne *IRL* 7 E10
Ashburton *GB* 13 D7
Ashbury *GB* 13 C9
Ashby de la Zouch *GB* 11 F9
Ashcott *GB* 13 C9
Ashevo *RUS* 133 B7
Ashford *GB* 15 E10
Ashford *GB* 15 C9
Ashford *IRL* 8 D4
Ashill *GB* 11 G12
Ashington *GB* 5 E13
Ashkirk *GB* 5 E11
Ashley *GB* 15 C9
Ashmyany *BY* 137 D13
Ashmyany *BY* 137 E12
Ashton-under-Lyne *GB* 11 E7
Ashurst *GB* 13 D11
Ashwick *GB* 13 C9
Asiago *I* 72 E4
Asikkala *FIN* 127 C14
Asila *MA* 163 E10
Asilah *MA* 163 F9
Asimi *GR* 178 E9
Asín *E* 32 F3
Asiros *GR* 169 C9
Askvoll *N* 100 D2
Ask *N* 95 B14
Aska *FIN* 117 C13
Askainen *FIN* 126 D6
Askeaton *IRL* 8 C5
Asker *N* 95 C12
Askern *GB* 11 D9
Askersby *S* 92 A6
Askersund *S* 92 B5
Askije *S* 107 B13
Askim *N* 95 C14
Asklipieio *GR* 175 D7
Asklipieio *GR* 181 D7
Askogen *S* 118 C7
Askola *FIN* 127 E14
Åsköping *S* 92 A8
Askos *GR* 169 C9
Askvoll *N* 100 D2
Asli *N* 101 E11
Åsljunga *S* 87 C12
Asmali *TR* 173 C8
Asmansbo *S* 97 B13
Åsmarka *N* 101 D13
Asmunti *FIN* 119 C17
Asnæs *DK* 87 D8
As Neves *E* 38 B3
As Neves *E* 38 D3
As Nogais *E* 38 C5
Asola *I* 66 B1
Asolo *I* 72 E4
Asopia *GR* 175 C8
Asopos *GR* 178 B4
Asos *GR* 174 C2
Asótthalom *H* 150 E4
Asp *DK* 86 C3
Aspa *S* 93 B10
Aspach *A* 76 F4
Aspan *S* 102 B8
Aspang-Markt *A* 148 A6
Asparn an der Zaya *A* 77 E10
Asparukhovo *BG* 167 D8
Aspås *S* 106 E7
Aspatria *GB* 5 F10
Aspe *E* 56 E5
Aspe *S* 97 B8
Aspeå *S* 107 E12
Aspele *S* 107 C14
Asperen *NL* 183 B6
Asperg *D* 27 C11
Aspet *F* 33 D7
Asphyltan *S* 97 C11
Aspliden *S* 109 F17
Aspliden *S* 118 B7
Aspnäs *S* 103 A14
Aspö *S* 93 B12
Åsa *N* 95 B11
Åsa *N* 93 E11
Asptranda *FIN* 126 E7
As Pontes de García Rodríguez *E* 38 A4
Aspremont *F* 35 A10
Aspres-sur-Buëch *F* 35 A10
Aspropyrgos *GR* 175 C8
Asprovalta *GR* 169 C10
Aspudden *S* 116 E3
As Rodrigas *E* 38 B5
Assamstadt *D* 74 D6
Asse *B* 19 C9
Assebakti *S* 113 E15
Asseiceira *P* 44 E4
Assemini *I* 64 E3
Assen *NL* 17 C7
Assendelft *NL* 16 D3
Assens *DK* 86 B6
Assens *DK* 86 E5
Assenthft *DK* 86 C6
Assérac *F* 23 F8
Assergi *I* 62 C5
Assesse *B* 19 D11
Assier *F* 33 A9
Assisi *I* 62 A3
Assos *GR* 174 C2
Åssjö *S* 103 B12

Åsskard *N* 104 E5
Aßlar *D* 21 C10
Assling *A* 73 C6
Asso *I* 69 B7
Asson *F* 32 D5
Assoro *I* 58 D5
Assos *GR* 168 F1
Assumar *P* 44 F6
Åsta *N* 101 D14
Astaffort *F* 33 B7
Astakos *GR* 174 B3
Åstan *N* 104 E7
Astašova *LV* 133 D2
Aste *EST* 130 E4
Åsteby *S* 97 B9
Astee *IRL* 8 C4
Asten *A* 76 F6
Asten *NL* 16 F5
Asti *I* 37 B8
Astikkala *FIN* 129 B12
Aştileu *RO* 151 C9
Astomilitsa *GR* 168 D4
Aston Clinton *GB* 15 D7
Astorga *E* 39 D7
Åstorp *S* 87 C11
Åstrand *S* 97 B9
Astravyets *BY* 137 D12
Astrazup *KS* 163 E10
Astros *GR* 175 E6
Astrowna *BY* 133 E7
Astrowshchyna *BY* 133 F4
Astrup *DK* 86 A5
Astrup *DK* 86 B3
Astrup *DK* 86 C3
Astrup *DK* 90 E7
Astudillo *E* 40 D3
Astypalaia *GR* 180 C4
Asuaju de Sus *RO* 151 B11
Asüne *LV* 133 D3
Asuni *I* 64 D2
Asunta *FIN* 123 F13
Ásványráró *H* 146 F5
Asvestopetra *GR* 169 D6
Asvyeya *BY* 133 D4
Aszaló *H* 145 G2
Aszód *H* 150 B3
Atalaia *P* 44 F4
Atalaia *P* 44 F5
Atalanti *GR* 175 B7
Atalaya del Cañavate *E* 47 E8
Ataquines *E* 46 B3
Atarfe *E* 53 B9
Atašiene *LV* 135 C12
Atea *E* 47 B9
Ateca *E* 41 F8
A Teixeira *E* 38 D5
Atel *RO* 152 E4
Ateleta *I* 63 D6
Atella *I* 60 B5
Atena Lucana *I* 60 C5
Återvänningen *S* 103 A13
Atessa *I* 63 C7
Ath *B* 19 C8
Athani *GR* 174 B2
Áth an Sceire *IRL* 7 F10
Athboy *IRL* 7 E9
Athea *IRL* 8 C4
Athenry *IRL* 6 F5
Athenstedt *D* 79 C8
Atheras *GR* 174 C1
Atherington *GB* 12 C6
Atherstone *GB* 11 F8
Athies *F* 18 E6
Athies-sous-Laon *F* 19 E8
Athikia *GR* 175 D6
Athina *GR* 175 D8
Athis-de-l'Orne *F* 23 C11
Athleague *IRL* 6 E6
Athlone *IRL* 7 F7
Áth Trasna *IRL* 8 D4
Athy *IRL* 7 G9
Athyra *GR* 169 C8
Atid *RO* 152 E6
Atienza *E* 47 B7
Atina *I* 62 D5
Ațintiş *RO* 152 E4
Atjiken *S* 107 A9
Atkár *H* 150 B4
Atna *N* 101 C13
Åtorp *S* 92 A4
Atouguia da Baleia *P* 44 F2
Åtran *S* 87 A11
Åträsk *S* 118 C5
Åträsk *S* 118 D5
Atri *I* 62 B5
Atripalda *I* 60 B3
Atsiki *GR* 171 E8
Attadale *GB* 2 L6
Attala *H* 149 C8
Attali *GR* 175 B8
Attanagh *IRL* 9 C8
Attavalley *IRL* 6 D3
Attendorn *D* 21 B9
Attenkirchen *D* 75 E10
Attersee *A* 73 A8
Attert *B* 19 E12
Attica *GB* 7 D10
Attigliano *I* 62 B2
Attignat *F* 31 C7
Attigny *F* 19 F10
Attleborough *GB* 15 B11
Attnang *A* 76 F5
Åttonträsk *S* 107 C14
Attu *FIN* 126 E7
Atur *F* 29 E7
Åtvidaberg *S* 92 C7
Atzara *I* 64 D3
Atzenbrugg *A* 77 F9
Atzendorf *D* 79 C10
Atzeneta del Maestrat *E* 48 D4
Au *A* 71 C9
Au *CH* 71 C9
Aub *D* 75 C7
Aubagne *F* 35 D10
Aubange *B* 19 E12
Aube *F* 24 C1
Aubenas *F* 35 A8
Aubenas *F* 35 E9
Aubergenville *F* 24 C6
Auberive *F* 26 E3
Aubeterre-sur-Dronne *F* 29 E6
Aubiet *F* 33 C7
Aubignan *F* 35 B9
Aubigné-Racan *F* 23 E12
Aubignosc *F* 35 B10
Aubigny *F* 28 B3
Aubigny-en-Artois *F* 18 D6
Aubigny-sur-Nère *F* 25 F7
Aubin *F* 33 A10
Aubonne *CH* 31 B9
Auboué *F* 20 F5
Aubord *F* 35 C7
Aubusson *F* 29 D10

Auby F 19 D7
Aucamville F 33 C8
Auce LV 134 D5
Auch F 33 C7
Auchallater GB 5 B10
Auchenbreck GB 4 D6
Auchencairn GB 5 F9
Auchencrow GB 5 D12
Auchnagatt GB 3 L12
Auchterarder GB 5 C9
Auchtermuchty GB 5 C10
Auchy-au-Bois F 18 C5
Aucun F 32 E5
Audenge F 32 A3
Auderville F 23 A8
Audeux F 26 F4
Audevälja EST 131 C8
Audierne F 22 D2
Audincourt F 27 F6
Audlem GB 10 F6
Audley GB 11 E7
Audnedal N 90 C1
Audon F 32 C4
Audresselles F 15 F12
Audriņi LV 133 C2
Audru EST 131 E8
Audruicq F 18 C5
Audun-le-Roman F 20 F5
Aue D 79 E12
Auerbach D 75 A11
Auerbach in der Oberpfalz D 75 C10
Auersthal A 77 F11
Auffay F 18 E3
Aufhausen D 75 E11
Augbrim IRL 6 F5
Auggen D 27 E8
Augher GB 7 D8
Aughnacloy GB 7 D9
Aughrim IRL 6 F5
Aughrim IRL 9 C10
Aughton GB 11 E9
Augignac F 29 D7
Augsburg D 75 F8
Augšlīgatne LV 135 B10
Augstkalne LV 133 E2
Augstkalne LV 134 D6
Augusta I 59 E7
Auguste LV 134 D3
Augustenborg DK 86 F5
Augustów PL 136 F6
Augustowo PL 141 E8
Augustusburg D 80 E4
Auho FIN 121 E10
Aukan N 104 E4
Aukra N 100 A5
Aukrug D 82 B7
Aukštadvaris LT 137 D10
Aukštelkai LT 134 E7
Aukštelkė LT 134 E6
Auktsjaur S 109 E17
Auleja LV 133 D2
Aulendorf D 71 B9
Auletta I 60 B4
Aulla I 69 E8
Aullène F 37 H10
Aulnat F 30 D3
Aulnay F 28 C5
Aulnay-sous-Bois F 25 C8
Aulnois sur-Seille F 26 C5
Aulnoye-Aymeries F 19 D8
Aulon F 33 D7
Aulosen D 83 E11
Ault F 18 D3
Aultbea GB 2 K5
Aultguish Inn GB 2 K7
Aulus-les-Bains F 33 E8
Auma D 79 E10
Aumale F 18 E4
Aumetz F 20 F5
Aumont F 31 B8
Aumont-Aubrac F 30 F3
Aumühle D 83 C8
Aunay-en-Bazois F 25 F10
Aunay-sur-Odon F 23 B10
Auneau F 24 D6
Aunegrenda N 105 F10
Aunfoss N 105 B13
Auning DK 86 C6
Auñón E 47 C7
Aups F 36 D4
Aura FIN 126 D8
Aurach D 75 D7
Aurach bei Kitzbühel A 72 B5
Aura im Sinngrund D 74 B6
Auran N 105 E9
Auray F 22 E6
Aurdal N 101 E10
Aure N 104 E5
Aurec-sur-Loire F 30 E5
Aureilhan F 33 D6
Aureille F 35 C8
Aurejärvi FIN 123 G10
Aurel F 35 A9
Aurel F 35 B9
Aurensan F 32 C5
Aureosen N 100 A6
Auri LV 134 C6
Aurich D 17 B8
Aurignac F 33 D7
Aurillac F 29 F10
Auriol F 35 D10
Aurisina I 73 E8
Auritz E 32 E3
Aurland N 100 E6
Aurolzmünster A 76 F4
Auron F 36 C5
Auronzo di Cadore I 72 C5
Auros F 32 A5
Auroux F 30 F4
Aurskog N 95 C14
Ausa-Corno I 73 E7
Ausejo E 32 F1
Auşeu RO 151 C10
Ausleben D 79 B9
Ausmas LV 135 B9
Ausonia I 62 E5
Außervillgraten A 72 C5
Aussillon F 33 C10
Aussonne F 33 C8
Austafjord N 105 B9
Austbø N 95 C8
Austborg N 105 C15
Austertana N 114 C5
Austis I 64 C3
Austmannli N 94 C5
Austnes N 100 A4
Austnes N 105 B15
Austnes N 111 C12
Austrått N 104 D7
Austsmøla N 104 E4
Auterive F 33 D8
Authon F 24 E4
Authon F 36 C4
Authon-du-Perche F 24 D4
Autio FIN 119 E17
Autio FIN 123 E13
Autol E 41 D7
Autrans F 31 E8
Autreville F 26 D4
Autrey-lès-Gray F 26 F3
Autry F 19 F10
Autti FIN 119 B18
Auttoinen FIN 127 C13
Autun F 30 B5
Auve F 25 B12
Auvelais B 19 D10
Auvers-le-Hamon F 23 E11
Auvillar F 33 B7
Auvillers-les-Forges F 184 E1
Auxerre F 25 E10
Auxi-le-Château F 18 D5
Auxonne F 26 F3
Auxy F 30 B5
Auzances F 29 C10
Auzat F 33 E8
Auzat-sur-Allier F 30 E3
Aužgulāni LV 135 E12
Auzon F 30 E3
Åva FIN 126 E5
Ava S 107 D16
Avafors S 118 B8
Availles-Limouzine F 29 C7
Avaldsnes N 94 D2
Avallon F 25 E10
Avan S 118 C7
Avanäs S 107 C17
Avanca P 44 C3
Avançon F 36 B4
Avantas GR 171 C9
Avant-lès-Ramerupt F 25 D11
Avasjö S 107 C11
Avato GR 171 C7
Avaträsk S 107 C10
Avaviken S 109 E16
Avdira GR 171 C7
Avdou GR 178 E9
A Veiga E 39 D6
Aveiras de Cima P 44 F3
Aveiro P 44 C3
Avelar P 44 E4
Avelãs de Caminho P 44 D4
Aveleda P 38 E3
Aveleda P 39 E6
Avelgem B 19 C7
Avella I 60 B3
Avellino I 60 B3
Avenay-Val-d'Or F 25 B11
Avenches CH 31 B11
Avenhorn NL 16 C3
Avenida do Marquês de Figueroa E 38 A3
Avermes F 30 B3
Avers CH 71 E9
Aversa I 60 B2
Avesnes-le-Comte F 18 D6
Avesnes-sur-Helpe F 19 D8
Avesta S 98 B6
Åvestbo S 97 C14
Avetrano I 61 C9
Avezzano I 62 C4
Avgerinos GR 168 D5
Avià E 43 C7
Aviano I 73 D6
Aviemore GB 3 L9
Avigliana I 31 E11
Avigliano I 60 B5
Avigliano Umbro I 62 B2
Avignon F 35 C8
Ávila E 46 C3
A Vila da Igrexa E 38 A4
Avilés E 39 A8
Avilley F 26 F5
Avintes P 44 B3
Avinurme EST 131 D13
Avinyó E 43 D7
Avio I 69 B10
Avion F 18 D6
Avioth F 19 E11
Avis P 44 F5
Avispea EST 131 C12
Åvist FIN 122 D9
Avize F 25 C11
Avižieniai LT 137 D11
Avlakia GR 177 D8
Avlemonas GR 178 C5
Avliotes GR 168 E2
Avlonari GR 175 B9
Avlonas GR 175 C8
Avlum DK 86 C3
Avoca IRL 9 C10
Avoine F 23 F12
Avola I 59 F7
Avon F 25 D8
Avonmouth GB 13 B9
Avord F 29 A11
Avoriaz F 31 C10
Avoudrey F 26 F5
Avrămeni RO 153 A9
Avrămeşti RO 152 E6
Avram Iancu RO 151 D8
Avram Iancu RO 151 E10
Avranches F 23 C9
Avren BG 171 B9
Avricourt F 186 D2
Avrig RO 152 F4
Avril F 20 F5
Avrillé F 23 E10
Avrillé F 28 C3
Avtovac BIH 157 F10
Av'že N 112 E10
Awans B 183 D6
Axams A 72 B3
Axat F 33 E10
Axel NL 16 F1
Axente Sever RO 152 E4
Axintele RO 161 D9
Axioupoli GR 169 C8
Ax-les-Thermes F 33 E9
Axmar S 103 D13
Axmarsbruk S 103 D13
Axminster GB 13 D9
Axos GR 169 C7
Axvall S 91 C14
Ayamonte E 50 E5
Aycliffe GB 5 F13
Aydat F 30 D2
Aydemir BG 161 E10
Ayen F 29 E8
Ayerbe E 32 F4
Aying D 72 A4
Aylesbury GB 15 D7
Ayllón E 40 F5
Aylsham GB 15 B11
Aymavilles I 31 D11
Ayna E 55 B8
Aynac F 29 F9
Ayoo de Vidriales E 39 D7
Ayora E 47 F10
Ayr GB 4 E7
Ayrancılar TR 177 C9
Ayron F 28 B6
Ayşebaci TR 173 E8
Aysgarth GB 11 C8
Äyskoski FIN 123 D17
Äystö FIN 122 F7
Aytos BG 167 D8
Aytré F 28 C3
Ayvacık TR 171 E10
Ayvalık TR 172 F6
Aywaille B 19 D12
Azagra E 32 F2
Azaila E 41 F11
Azambuja P 44 F3
Azanja SRB 159 E6
Azanúy E 42 D4
Azaruja P 50 B4
Azatlı TR 172 B6
Azay-le-Ferron F 29 B8
Azay-le-Rideau F 24 F3
Azé F 23 E10
Azerables F 29 C8
Azina BY 133 E5
Azinhaga P 44 F3
Azinhal P 50 E5
Azinheira dos Barros P 50 C3
Azinhoso P 39 F6
Azkoitia E 32 D1
Aznalcázar E 51 E7
Aznalcóllar E 51 D7
Azóia P 50 C1
Azpeitia E 32 D1
Azuaga E 51 C8
Azuara E 41 F10
Azuel E 54 C4
Azuelo E 32 E1
Azuga RO 161 C7
Azuqueca de Henares E 47 C6
Azur F 32 C3
Azután E 45 E10
Azy-le-Vif F 30 B3
Azyory BY 140 C10
Azzano Decimo I 73 E6
Azzone I 69 B9

B

Baalberge D 79 C10
Baâlon F 19 F11
Baar CH 27 F10
Baarle-Hertog B 16 F3
Baarle-Nassau NL 16 F3
Baarn NL 16 D4
Baba Ana RO 161 D8
Babadag RO 155 D3
Babaeski TR 173 B7
Babaköy TR 173 E9
Baban AL 168 C4
Băbana RO 160 D5
Babberich NL 183 B8
Babchyntsi UA 154 A2
Babenhausen D 21 E11
Băbeni RO 151 C11
Băbeni RO 160 D4
Babiak PL 136 E1
Babiak PL 138 F6
Babice CZ 146 C4
Babice PL 143 F7
Babice nad Svitavou CZ 77 D11
Babići BIH 157 D7
Băbiciu RO 160 E5
Babilafuente E 45 C10
Babimost PL 81 B9
Babín SK 147 C8
Babina SRB 164 D5
Babina Greda HR 157 B10
Babino Polje HR 162 D4
Babīte LV 135 C7
Babno Polje SLO 73 E10
Babócsa H 149 D8
Bábolna H 149 A9
Baborów PL 142 F4
Baboszewo PL 139 E9
Babót H 149 A8
Babrrujë AL 168 B2
Babtai LT 137 C8
Babuk BG 161 E10
Babušnica SRB 164 C5
Babyak BG 165 F8
Babynichy BY 133 F4
Bač MNE 163 D9
Bač SRB 158 C3
Băcani RO 153 E11
Bacares E 55 E8
Bacău RO 153 D9
Baccarat F 27 D6
Baceno I 68 A5
Băceşti RO 153 D10
Bach A 71 C10
Bacharach D 21 D9
Bachkovo BG 165 F10
Bachórz PL 144 D5
Băcia RO 151 F11
Baciki Bliższe PL 141 F7
Băcioi MD 154 D3
Baciu RO 152 D3
Bäck S 105 E16
Backa S 91 E10
Backa S 97 A9
Backa S 97 B9
Backaland GB 3 G11
Bačka Palanka SRB 158 C3
Backaryd S 89 C8
Bačka Topola SRB 150 F4
Backberg S 103 E12
Backe S 107 D10
Bäckebo S 89 B10
Bäckefors S 91 B11
Bäckhammar S 91 A15
Bački Breg SRB 150 F2
Bački Brestovac SRB 158 B3
Bački Jarak SRB 158 C4
Bački Monoštor SRB 150 F2
Bačkininkai LT 137 D8
Bački Petrovac SRB 158 C4
Bäcklund S 109 E17
Bäckmark S 107 A11
Backnang D 27 C11
Bäcknäs S 109 F17
Bačko Dobro Polje SRB 158 B4
Bačko Gradište SRB 158 B5
Bačko Novo Selo SRB 157 B11
Bačko Petrovo Selo SRB 158 B5
Baćkowice PL 143 E11
Backträsk S 118 C6
Bäckvallen S 102 B8
Băcleş RO 159 E11
Bacoli I 60 B2
Bacqueville-en-Caux F 18 E2
Bácsalmás H 150 E3
Bácsbokod H 150 E3
Bácsborsód H 150 E3
Bacúch SK 147 D9
Baczyna PL 85 E8
Bada S 97 B9
Bad Abbach D 75 E11
Bad Aibling D 72 A5
Badajoz E 51 B6
Badalona E 43 E8
Badalucco I 37 D7
Bádames E 40 B5
Badarán E 40 D6
Bad Aussee A 73 A8
Bad Bederkesa D 17 A11
Bad Bentheim D 17 D8
Bad Bergzabern D 27 B8
Bad Berka D 79 E9
Bad Berleburg D 21 B10
Bad Berneck im Fichtelgebirge D 75 B10
Bad Bertrich D 21 D8
Bad Bevensen D 83 D9
Bad Bibra D 79 D10
Bad Birnbach D 76 F4
Bad Blankenburg D 79 E9
Bad Bocklet D 75 B7
Bad Brambach D 75 B11
Bad Bramstedt D 83 C7
Bad Breisig D 185 D7
Bad Brückenau D 74 B6
Bad Buchau D 71 A9
Bad Camberg D 21 D10
Badcaul GB 2 K6
Badderen N 112 D9
Bad Doberan D 83 B11
Bad Driburg D 17 E12
Bad Düben D 79 C12
Bad Dürkheim D 21 F10
Bad Dürrenberg D 79 D11
Bad Dürrheim D 27 D10
Badeborn D 79 C9
Badefols-d'Ans F 29 E8
Bad Elster D 75 B11
Bademler TR 177 C8
Bademli TR 171 F10
Bademli TR 173 D10
Bademli TR 177 B8
Bad Ems D 21 D9
Baden A 77 F10
Baden CH 27 F9
Baden F 22 E6
Bádenas E 47 B10
Baden-Baden D 27 C9
Bad Endorf D 72 A5
Badenscoth GB 3 L12
Badenweiler D 27 E8
Baderna HR 67 B8
Badersleben D 79 C8
Badesi I 64 B2
Bad Essen D 17 D10
Bădeuţi RO 153 B7
Bad Feilnbach D 72 A5
Bad Frankenhausen (Kyffhäuser) D 79 D9
Bad Freienwalde D 84 E6
Bad Friedrichshall D 21 F12
Bad Füssing D 76 F4
Bad Gams A 73 C11
Bad Gandersheim D 79 C7
Badgastein A 73 B7
Bad Gleichenberg A 148 C5
Bad Goisern A 73 A8
Bad Großpertholz A 77 E7
Bad Grund (Harz) D 79 C7
Bad Hall A 76 F6
Bad Harzburg D 79 C8
Bad Herrenalb D 27 C9
Bad Hersfeld D 78 E6
Badhoevedorp NL 182 A5
Bad Hofgastein A 73 B7
Bad Homburg vor der Höhe D 21 D11
Bad Honnef D 21 C8
Bad Hönningen D 185 C7
Badia I 72 C4
Badia Calavena I 69 B11
Badia Gran E 49 F10
Badia Polesine I 66 B3
Badia Tedalda I 66 E5
Bad Iburg D 17 D10
Bădiceni MD 153 A12
Badín SK 147 D8
Bad Ischl A 73 A8
Bad Karlshafen D 78 C5
Bad Kissingen D 75 B7
Bad Kleinen D 83 C10
Bad Kleinkirchheim A 73 C8
Bad König D 21 E12
Bad Königshofen im Grabfeld D 75 B7
Bad Kösen D 79 D10
Bad Köstritz D 79 E11
Bądkowo PL 138 E6
Bad Kreuzen A 77 F7
Bad Kreuznach D 21 E9
Bad Krozingen D 27 E8
Bad Laasphe D 21 C10
Bad Laer D 17 D10
Bad Langensalza D 79 D8
Bad Lauchstädt D 79 D10
Bad Lausick D 79 D12
Bad Lauterberg im Harz D 79 C7
Bad Leonfelden A 76 E6
Bad Liebenstein D 79 E7
Bad Liebenwerda D 80 C4
Bad Liebenzell D 27 C10
Bad Lippspringe D 17 E11
Badljevina HR 149 E8
Bad Marienberg (Westerwald) D 21 C9
Bad Mergentheim D 74 D6
Bad Mitterndorf A 73 A8
Bad Münder am Deister D 78 B5
Bad Münstereifel D 21 C7
Bad Muskau D 81 C7
Bad Nauheim D 21 D11
Bad Nenndorf D 17 D12
Bad Neuenahr-Ahrweiler D 21 C8
Bad Neustadt an der Saale D 75 B7
Badolato I 59 B10
Badolatosa E 53 B7
Bad Oldesloe D 83 C8
Badonviller F 27 C6
Bad Orb D 21 D12
Badovinci SRB 158 D3
Bad Peterstal D 27 D9
Bad Pirawarth A 77 F11
Bad Pyrmont D 17 E12
Bad Radkersburg A 148 C5
Bad Ragaz CH 71 C9
Bad Rappenau D 187 C7
Bad Reichenhall D 73 A6
Bad Saarow-Pieskow D 80 B6
Bad Sachsa D 79 C8
Bad Säckingen D 27 E8
Bad Salzdetfurth D 79 B7
Bad Salzuflen D 17 D11
Bad Salzungen D 79 E7
Bad Sankt Leonhard im Lavanttal A 73 C10
Bad Sassendorf D 17 E10
Bad Schandau D 80 E6
Bad Schmiedeberg D 79 C12
Bad Schönborn D 187 C6
Bad Schussenried D 71 A9
Bad Schwalbach D 21 D10
Bad Schwartau D 83 C9
Bad Segeberg D 83 C8
Bad Sobernheim D 185 E8
Bad Soden-Salmünster D 74 B5
Bad Sooden-Allendorf D 79 D6
Bad Steben D 75 B10
Bad Sulza D 79 D10
Bad Sülze D 83 B13
Bad Tennstedt D 79 D8
Bad Tölz D 72 A4
Bad Überkingen D 187 D8
Badules E 47 B10
Bad Urach D 27 D11
Bad Vilbel D 21 D11
Bad Vöslau A 77 G10
Bad Waldsee D 71 B9
Bad Waltersdorf A 148 B6
Bad Wildbad im Schwarzwald D 187 D6
Bad Wildungen D 21 B12
Bad Wilsnack D 83 E11
Bad Wimpfen D 21 F12
Bad Windsheim D 75 C7
Bad Wörishofen D 71 B11
Bad Wurzach D 71 B9
Bad Zell A 77 F7
Bad Zwesten D 21 B12
Bad Zwischenahn D 17 B10
Bække DK 86 D4
Bækmarksbro DK 86 C2
Baelen B 183 D7
Bælum DK 86 B6
Baena E 53 A8
Bærums Verk N 95 C12
Baesweiler D 20 C6
Baeza E 53 A10
Baflo NL 17 B7
Bagà E 43 C7
Băgaciu RO 152 E4
Bagaladi I 59 C8
Bagamér H 151 C8
Bağarasi TR 177 B8
Bağarasi TR 177 D10
Bagard F 35 B7
Bağcılar TR 181 B8
Bâgé-le-Châtel F 30 C6
Bagenalstown IRL 9 C9
Bagenkop DK 83 A9
Bages F 34 E4
Baggå S 97 C14
Bagheria I 58 C4
Bagn N 101 E11
Bagnacavallo I 66 D4
Bagnac-sur-Célé F 33 A10
Bagnara Calabra I 59 C8
Bagnaria I 37 B10
Bagnaria Arsa I 73 E7
Bagnasco I 37 C8
Bagneaux-sur-Loing F 25 D8
Bagnères-de-Bigorre F 33 D6
Bagnères-de-Luchon F 33 E7
Bagni di Lucca I 66 D2
Bagni di Masino I 69 A8
Bagni di Rabbi I 71 E11
Bagno a Ripoli I 66 E3
Bagno di Romagna I 66 E4
Bagnoli del Trigno I 63 D6
Bagnoli di Sopra I 66 B4
Bagnoli Irpino I 60 B4
Bagnolo in Piano I 66 C2
Bagnolo Mella I 66 B1
Bagnolo Piemonte I 31 F11
Bagnolo San Vito I 66 B2
Bagnols-les-Bains F 35 A6
Bagnols-sur-Cèze F 35 B8
Bagnoregio I 62 B2
Bagod H 149 C7
Bagolino I 69 B9
Bagrationovsk RUS 136 E2
Bagrdan SRB 159 E7
Bagshot GB 15 E7
Báguena E 47 B10
Bágyogszovát H 149 A8
Bağyurdu TR 177 C10
Bağyüzü TR 173 F6
Bahabón de Esgueva E 40 E4
Bahate UA 155 C3
Bahçeburun TR 181 B7
Bahçeköy TR 173 B10
Bahçeli TR 171 E10
Bahíllo E 39 D10
Bahmut MD 153 C12
Bahna RO 153 D9
Bahnea RO 152 E4
Báhoň SK 146 E4
Bahrenborstel D 17 C11
Bahrendorf D 79 C10
Baia RO 153 C8
Baia RO 155 D3
Baia de Aramă RO 159 D10
Baia de Arieş RO 151 E11
Baia de Criş RO 151 E10
Baia de Fier RO 160 C3
Baia della Zagare I 63 D10
Baia Mare RO 152 B3
Baiano I 60 B3
Baiardo I 37 D7
Baia Sprie RO 152 B3
Băicoi RO 161 C7
Băiculeşti RO 160 C5
Baiersbronn D 27 C9
Baiersdorf D 75 C9
Baignes-Ste-Radegonde F 28 E5
Baigneux-les-Juifs F 25 E12
Baile an Bhiataigh IRL 7 E10
Baile an Bhuinneánaigh IRL 8 C3
Baile an Chinnéidigh IRL 7 F10
Baile an Dúlaigh IRL 6 F4
Baile an Fheirtéaraigh IRL 8 D2
Baile an Mhóta IRL 6 D5
Baile an Mhuilinn IRL 8 D2
Baile an Róba IRL 6 E4
Baile an Sceilg IRL 8 E2
Baile Átha an Rí IRL 6 F5
Baile Átha Buí IRL 7 E9
Baile Átha Cliath IRL 7 F10
Baile Átha Fhirdhia IRL 7 E9
Baile Átha Í IRL 7 G9
Baile Átha Luain IRL 7 F7
Baile Átha Troim IRL 7 E9
Baile Brigin IRL 7 E10
Baile Coimin IRL 7 F9
Băile Govora RO 160 C4
Băile Herculane RO 159 D9
Baile Loch Riach IRL 6 F5
Baile Mhartainn GB 2 K2
Baile Mhic Andáin IRL 9 C8
Baile Mhic Íre IRL 8 E4
Baile Mhistéala IRL 8 D6
Bailén E 54 C5
Baile na Finne IRL 6 C6
Baile na Lorgan IRL 7 D9
Băile Olăneşti RO 160 C4
Baile Órthaí IRL 7 E9
Băileşti RO 160 E2
Băile Tuşnad RO 153 E7
Baile Uilcín IRL 7 E9
Bailieborough IRL 7 E9
Baillargues F 35 C7
Bailleau-le-Pin F 24 D5
Bailleul F 18 C6
Baillonville B 19 D11
Bailo E 32 E4
Baimaclia MD 154 E2
Bainbridge GB 11 C7
Bain-de-Bretagne F 23 E8
Baindt D 71 B9
Bains F 30 E4
Bains-les-Bains F 26 D5
Bainton GB 11 D10
Baio E 38 B2
Baiona E 38 D2
Bais F 23 D9
Bais F 23 D11
Baiso I 66 D2
Băişoara RO 151 D11
Baisogala LT 134 E7
Băiţa RO 151 E10
Băiţa de sub Codru RO 151 B11
Baix F 35 A8
Baixa da Banheira P 50 B1
Baixas F 34 E4
Baj H 149 A10
Baja H 150 E2
Bajč SK 146 F6
Bajgorë KS 164 D3
Bajina Bašta SRB 158 F4
Bajmok SRB 150 F3
Bajna H 149 A11
Bajót H 149 A11
Bajovo Polje MNE 157 F10
Bajram Curri AL 163 E9
Bajša SRB 150 F4
Bak H 149 C7
Baka SK 146 F5
Bakacak TR 173 D7
Bakałarzewo PL 136 E6
Bakar HR 67 B10
Bakel NL 16 F5
Bakir TR 177 A10
Bakırköy TR 173 C10
Bakkasund N 94 B2
Bakke N 111 A16
Bakkeby N 112 D6
Bakkejord N 111 A15
Bakken N 101 E15
Bakko N 95 C9
Bakonszeg H 151 C7
Bakonybél H 149 B9
Bakonycsernye H 149 B10
Bakonysárkány H 149 B10
Bakonyszentkirály H 149 B9
Bakonyszentlászló H 149 B9
Bakonyszombathely H 149 B9
Bakov nad Jizerou CZ 77 B7
Baks H 150 D5
Baksa H 149 E10
Baksha UA 154 A5
Baktalórántháza H 145 H5
Baktsjaur S 109 F17
Bakum D 17 C10
Bakvattnet S 105 D16
Bål S 93 D13
Bala GB 10 F4
Bala RO 159 D10
Balabancık TR 173 C6
Bălăbăneşti MD 154 C4
Bălăbăneşti RO 153 E11
Balabanu MD 154 F3
Bălăceanu RO 161 C10
Balaci RO 160 E5
Bălăciţa RO 159 E11
Balaciu RO 161 D9
Balaguer E 42 D5
Balallan GB 2 J3
Balan F 19 E10
Balan F 31 D7
Bălan RO 151 C11
Bălan RO 153 D7
Bălăneşti MD 153 C12
Bălăneşti RO 160 C2
Balanivka UA 154 A4
Balaruc-les-Bains F 35 D6
Bălăşeşti RO 153 E11
Bălăsineşti MD 153 A9
Balassagyarmat H 147 E8
Balástya H 150 E5
Balat TR 177 D9
Balaton H 145 G1
Balatonalmádi H 149 B10
Balatonberény H 149 C8
Balatonboglár H 149 C9
Balatonfőkajár H 149 B10
Balatonföldvár H 149 C9
Balatonfüred H 149 C9
Balatonfőzfő H 149 B10
Balatonkenese H 149 B10
Balatonlelle H 149 C9
Balatonszabadi H 149 C10
Balatonszárszó H 149 C9
Balatonvilágos H 149 C10
Bălăuşeri RO 152 E5
Balazote E 55 B8
Balbeggie GB 5 C10
Balbieriškis LT 137 D8
Balbigny F 30 D5
Balbriggan IRL 7 E10
Balcani RO 153 D9
Bălceşti RO 160 D3
Balchik BG 167 C10
Balcılar TR 173 D6
Balçova TR 177 C9
Balderton GB 11 E10
Baldock GB 15 D8
Baldone LV 135 C8
Baldones Muiža LV 135 C8
Baldovineşti RO 160 E4
Bale HR 67 B8
Baleizão P 50 C4
Balemartine GB 4 C3
Balen B 19 B11
Băleni RO 153 F11
Băleni RO 161 D7
Balephuil GB 4 C3
Balerma E 55 F7
Băleşti RO 159 C11
Balestrand N 100 D5
Balestrate I 58 C3
Balfour GB 3 G11
Balfron GB 5 C8
Balgale LV 134 B5
Balgown GB 2 K4
Bälgviken S 98 D6
Bali GR 178 E8
Baligród PL 145 E5
Balikesir TR 173 E8
Balıklıçeşme TR 173 D7
Balıkliova TR 177 C8
Bălileşti RO 160 C5
Bälinge S 99 C9
Bälinge S 118 C7
Balingen D 27 D10
Balinka H 149 B10
Balinţ RO 151 F8
Balintore GB 3 K9
Balje D 17 A12
Baljevac BIH 156 C4
Baljevac SRB 163 C10
Baljvine BIH 157 D7
Balk NL 16 C5
Balkány H 151 B8
Balkbrug NL 16 C6
Balla IRL 6 E4
Ballaban AL 168 D3
Ballabio I 69 B7
Ballachulish GB 4 B6
Ballaghaderreen IRL 6 E5
Ballaghkeen IRL 9 D10
Ballangen N 111 D12
Ballantrae GB 4 E6
Ballao I 64 D3
Ballasalla GBM 10 C2
Ballater GB 5 A10
Ballaugh GBM 10 C2
Balle DK 87 C7
Ballée F 23 E11
Ballee GB 7 D11
Ballen DK 86 D7
Ballenstedt D 79 C9
Balleroy F 23 B10
Ballerup DK 87 D10
Ballesteros de Calatrava E 54 B5
Balli TR 173 C7
Ballina IRL 6 D4
Ballina IRL 8 C6
Ballinaboy IRL 6 F2
Ballinafad IRL 6 D6
Ballinagar IRL 7 F8
Ballinagh IRL 7 E8
Ballinakill IRL 9 C8
Ballinalack IRL 7 E8
Ballinalee IRL 7 E7
Ballinamallard GB 7 D7
Ballinamore IRL 7 D7
Ballinamult IRL 9 D7
Ballinasloe IRL 6 F6
Ballincollig IRL 8 E5
Ballindine IRL 6 E5
Ballindooly IRL 6 F4
Ballineen IRL 8 E5
Ballingarry IRL 8 D5
Ballingarry IRL 9 C7
Ballingeary IRL 8 E4
Ballingry GB 5 C10
Ballingslöv S 87 C13
Ballingurteen IRL 8 E4
Ballinhassig IRL 8 E5
Ballinlough IRL 6 E5
Ballinluig GB 5 B9
Ballinrobe IRL 6 E4
Ballinskelligs IRL 8 E2
Ballinspittle IRL 8 E5
Ballintober IRL 6 E4
Ballintoy GB 4 E4
Ballintra IRL 6 C6
Ballintubber IRL 6 E4
Ballinure IRL 9 C7
Ballivor IRL 7 E9
Ballobar E 42 D4
Ballon F 23 D12
Ballon IRL 9 C9
Ballószög H 150 D4
Ballots F 23 E9
Ballsh AL 168 C2
Ballsnes N 111 A16
Ballstad N 110 D6
Ballstädt D 79 D8
Ballum DK 86 E3
Ballum NL 16 B5
Ballure IRL 6 C6
Ballybay IRL 7 D9
Ballybofey IRL 7 C7
Ballybrack IRL 7 F10
Ballybrack IRL 8 E2
Ballybrittas IRL 7 F8
Ballybunion IRL 8 C3
Ballybunnion IRL 8 C3
Ballycahill IRL 9 C7
Ballycanew IRL 9 C10
Ballycarry GB 4 F5
Ballycastle GB 4 E4
Ballycastle IRL 6 D4
Ballyclare GB 4 F5
Ballycolla IRL 9 C8
Ballyconneely IRL 6 F2
Ballyconnell IRL 7 D7
Ballycotton IRL 8 E6
Ballycroy IRL 6 D3
Ballydavid IRL 6 F6
Ballydehob IRL 8 E4
Ballydesmond IRL 8 D4
Ballydonegan IRL 8 E2
Ballyduff IRL 8 D3
Ballyduff IRL 8 D6
Ballyfarnan IRL 6 D6
Ballyfarnon IRL 6 D6
Ballyfeard IRL 8 E6
Ballyferriter IRL 8 D2
Ballyforan IRL 6 F6
Ballygar IRL 6 E6
Ballygarrett IRL 9 C10
Ballygawley GB 7 D8
Ballygeary IRL 9 D10
Ballyglass IRL 6 E5
Ballygorman IRL 4 E2
Ballygowan GB 7 C11
Ballyhaise IRL 7 D8
Ballyhalbert GB 7 D12
Ballyhale IRL 9 D8
Ballyhaunis IRL 6 E5

Ballyhean IRL 6 E4
Ballyheigue IRL 8 D3
Ballyjamesduff IRL 7 E8
Ballykeeran IRL 7 F7
Ballykelly GB 4 E2
Ballykilleen IRL 7 F8
Ballylanders IRL 8 D6
Ballylickey IRL 8 E4
Ballyliffen IRL 4 E2
Ballyliffin IRL 4 E2
Ballylynan IRL 9 C8
Ballymacarberry IRL 9 D7
Ballymacmague IRL 9 D7
Ballymadog IRL 9 E7
Ballymagorry GB 4 F2
Ballymahon IRL 7 F7
Ballymakeery IRL 8 E4
Ballymartin GB 7 D11
Ballymoney GB 4 E3
Ballymore IRL 7 F7
Ballymote IRL 6 D5
Ballymurphy IRL 9 C9
Ballymurry IRL 6 E6
Ballynacally IRL 8 C4
Ballynafid IRL 7 E8
Ballynahinch GB 7 D11
Ballynahowen IRL 7 F7
Ballynakill IRL 7 F7
Ballynamona IRL 8 D5
Ballyneaner GB 4 F2
Ballynunty IRL 9 C7
Ballynure GB 4 F5
Ballyporeen IRL 8 D6
Ballyragget IRL 9 C8
Ballyroan IRL 9 C8
Ballyronan GB 4 F3
Ballyshannon IRL 6 C6
Ballyvaldon IRL 9 D10
Ballyvaughan IRL 6 F4
Ballyvoy GB 4 E4
Ballyvoyle IRL 9 D7
Ballywalter GB 7 C12
Ballyward GB 7 D10
Balma F 33 C9
Balmaha GB 4 C7
Balmaseda E 40 B5
Balmazújváros H 151 B7
Balme I 31 E11
Balmedie GB 3 L12
Balmuccia I 68 B5
Balnacra GB 2 L6
Balnapaling GB 3 K8
Balneario de Panticosa Huesca E 32 E5
Balninkai LT 135 F10
Balocco I 68 C5
Balogunyom H 149 B7
Balot F 25 E11
Balotaszállás H 150 E4
Baloteşti RO 161 D8
Balow D 83 D11
Balrath IRL 7 E10
Balş RO 160 E4
Balşa RO 151 E11
Balsa de Ves E 47 F10
Balsa Pintada E 56 F2
Balsareny E 43 D7
Balsfjord N 111 B17
Balsicas E 56 F3
Balsjö S 107 D16
Balsorano I 62 D5
Bålsta S 99 C9
Balsthal CH 27 F8
Balta RO 159 D10
Balta UA 154 B5
Balta Albă RO 161 C10
Balta Berilovac SRB 164 C5
Balta Doamnei RO 161 D8
Baltanás E 40 E3
Baltar E 38 E4
Baltasound GB 3 D15
Bălţăteşti RO 153 C8
Bălţaţi RO 153 C10
Bălţeni RO 153 D11
Bălţeni RO 159 D11
Baltezers LV 135 B8
Bălţi MD 153 B11
Baltimore IRL 8 F4
Baltinava LV 133 C3
Baltinglass IRL 9 C9
Baltiysk RUS 139 A8
Baltmuiža LV 135 D13
Baltoji Vokė LT 137 E11
Baltora S 99 C11
Bałtów PL 143 D12
Baltray IRL 7 E10
Băluşeni RO 153 B9
Balvan BG 166 C4
Bălvăneşti RO 159 D10
Balvano I 60 B5
Balve D 17 F9
Balvi LV 133 B2
Balvicar GB 4 C5
Balya TR 173 E8
Balzers FL 71 C9
Bamberg D 75 C8
Bamburgh GB 5 D13
Bampini GR 174 B3
Bampton GB 13 B11
Bampton GB 13 D8
Bana H 149 A9
Banafjäl S 107 E16
Banagher IRL 7 F7
Banarli TR 173 B7
Banassac F 34 B5
Banatski Brestovac SRB 159 D6
Banatski Dvor SRB 158 B6
Banatski Karlovac SRB 159 C7
Banatsko Aranđelovo SRB 150 E5
Banatsko Karađorđevo SRB 158 B6
Banatsko Novo Selo SRB 159 D6
Banatsko Veliko Selo SRB 150 F6
Banbridge GB 7 D10
Banbury GB 13 A12
Banchory GB 5 A12
Band RO 152 D4
Bandenitz D 83 D10
Bandholm DK 83 A10
Bandirma TR 173 D8
Bandol F 35 D10
Bandon IRL 8 E5
Dandurove UA 154 A5
Băneasa RO 153 F11
Băneasa RO 155 E1
Băneasa RO 161 E8
Băneşti MD 154 B2

Bănești RO 161 C7
Banevo BG 167 D8
Banff GB 3 K11
Bångnäs S 106 B9
Bangor GB 4 F5
Bangor GB 10 E3
Bangor IRL 6 D3
Bangor Erris IRL 6 D3
Bangsund N 105 C10
Banham GB 15 C11
Bánhorváti H 145 G2
Bánia RO 159 D9
Banie PL 85 D7
Banie Mazurskie PL 136 E5
Baniska BG 166 C5
Bănişor RO 151 C10
Băniţa RO 159 C11
Banite BG 171 A8
Banja BG 165 D10
Banja SRB 163 B8
Banja Lučica BIH 157 D10
Banja Luka BIH 157 C7
Banja Vrućia BIH 157 C8
Bankekind S 92 C7
Bankeryd S 92 D4
Bankfoot GB 5 B9
Bankya BG 165 D6
Bankya BG 165 D7
Banloc RO 159 C7
Bannalec F 22 E4
Bannay F 25 F8
Bannesdorf auf Fehmarn D 83 B10
Bannewitz D 80 E5
Bannivka UA 155 B3
Bannockburn GB 5 C9
Bañobárez E 45 C7
Bañón E 47 C10
Banon F 35 B10
Baños de la Encina E 54 C5
Baños de Molgas E 38 D4
Baños de Montemayor E 45 D9
Baños de Río Tobía E 40 D6
Baños de Valdearados E 40 E4
Bánov CZ 146 D5
Bánov SK 146 E6
Banova Jaruga HR 149 F7
Bánovce nad Bebravou SK 146 D6
Banovići BIH 157 D10
Bánréve H 145 G1
Bansin, Seebad D 84 C6
Banská Belá SK 147 E7
Banská Bystrica SK 147 D8
Banská Štiavnica SK 147 E7
Banské SK 145 F4
Bansko BG 165 F7
Bant NL 16 C5
Banteer IRL 8 D5
Banteln D 78 B6
Bantheville F 19 F11
Bantry IRL 8 E4
Banya BG 165 D10
Banya BG 165 E9
Banya BG 165 E8
Banya BG 165 E6
Banya BG 167 D9
Banyalbufar E 49 E10
Banyeres de Mariola E 56 D3
Banyuls IRL 9 C8
Banyliv UA 152 A6
Banyliv-Pidhirnyy UA 152 A7
Banyoles E 43 C9
Banyuls-sur-Mer F 34 F5
Banzi I 60 B6
Banzkow D 83 C11
Bapaume F 18 D6
Bar MNE 163 E7
Bara RO 151 F8
Bâra RO 153 C10
Bara S 87 D12
Barabás H 145 G5
Baracska H 149 B11
Bărăganul RO 161 D11
Barahona E 41 F6
Barajas de Melo E 47 D7
Barajevo SRB 158 D5
Barakaldo E 40 B6
Barakovo BG 165 E7
Baralla E 38 C5
Barañain E 32 E2
Baranbio E 40 B6
Báránd H 151 C7
Baranello I 63 D7
Baranjsko Petrovo Selo HR 149 E10
Barano d'Ischia I 62 F5
Baranów PL 141 G6
Baranów PL 142 D5
Baranowo PL 139 D11
Baranów Sandomierska PL 143 F12
Barão de São João P 50 E2
Baraolt RO 153 E7
Baraqueville F 33 B10
Barásoain E 32 E2
Barassie GB 4 D7
Bărăşti RO 160 D5
Baravukha BY 133 E5
Barbacena P 51 B5
Barbadás E 38 D4
Barbadillo de Herreros E 40 D5
Barbadillo del Mercado E 40 D5
Barbadillo del Pez E 40 D5
Barban HR 67 B9
Barbaraville GB 3 K8
Barbaros TR 173 C7
Barbastro E 42 C4
Barbat HR 67 D10
Bărbăteşti RO 160 D3
Bărbătescu RO 160 D3
Bărbătovac SRB 164 C3
Barbâtre F 28 B1
Bārbele LV 135 D9
Barbentane F 35 C8
Barberá del Vallès E 43 D8
Barberaz F 31 D8
Barberino di Mugello I 66 D3
Barbezieux-St-Hilaire F 28 C5
Barbonne-Fayel F 25 C10
Bărbuleţu RO 160 C6
Barbullush AL 163 F8
Barby (Elbe) D 79 C10
Barç AL 168 C4
Barca F 27 D7
Barca E 41 F6
Bârca RO 160 F3
Barcabo E 42 C4
Barcada BIH 157 D10

Barca de Alva P 45 B7
Bărcănești RO 161 D8
Bărcănești RO 161 D9
Barcani RO 161 B8
Barcarrota E 51 B6
Barcea RO 153 F10
Barcelinhos P 38 E2
Barcellona Pozzo di Gotto I 59 C7
Barcelona E 43 E8
Barcelonne-du-Gers F 32 C5
Barcelonnette F 36 C5
Bárcena del Monasterio E 39 B6
Bárcena de Pie de Concha E 40 B3
Barcenillas de Cerezos E 40 B4
Barchfeld D 79 E7
Barciany PL 136 E3
Barcillonnette F 35 B10
Barcino PL 85 B11
Barcis I 72 D6
Barcones E 40 F6
Barcos P 44 B5
Barcs H 149 E8
Barcus F 32 D4
Barczewo PL 136 F2
Bardal N 108 D5
Bardar MD 154 D3
Barde DK 86 C3
Bardejov SK 145 E3
Bárdena E 41 D9
Bardenitz D 80 B3
Bârdeşde RO 160 D4
Bardi I 69 D8
Bardineto I 37 C8
Bardney GB 11 E11
Bardo PL 77 B11
Bardolino I 66 A2
Bardonecchia I 31 E10
Bardos F 32 D3
Bardowick D 83 D8
Bardsea GB 10 C5
Bârdudvarnok H 149 D10
Bare BIH 157 E10
Bare SRB 158 E6
Bare SRB 163 C8
Barèges F 33 E6
Barenburg D 17 C11
Barendorf D 83 D9
Bärenklau D 81 C7
Bärenstein D 76 D3
Bärenstein D 80 E5
Barentin F 18 E2
Barenton F 23 C10
Barevo BIH 157 C11
Barfleur F 23 A9
Barga I 66 D1
Bargagli I 37 C10
Bargas E 46 E4
Bârgăuani RO 153 D9
Barge I 31 E11
Bargemon F 36 D5
Bargen CH 27 E10
Bargenstedt D 82 B6
Barghe I 69 B9
Bârghiş RO 152 F5
Bargischow D 84 C5
Bargłów Kościelny PL 140 C7
Bargoed GB 13 B8
Bargrennan GB 4 E7
Bargstedt D 17 B12
Bargteheide D 83 C8
Bargullas AL 168 E5
Barham GB 15 E11
Bar Hill GB 15 C9
Bari I 61 A7
Barić Draga HR 156 D3
Barile I 60 B5
Barilović HR 148 F5
Barinas E 56 E2
Bâring DK 86 E5
Bari Sardo I 64 E4
Barisciano I 62 C5
Barjac F 35 B7
Bârjasnjar'ga N 113 D15
Barjols F 35 C10
Barkåkra N 95 D12
Barkåkra S 87 D12
Barkald N 101 C13
Barkarö S 98 D7
Barkava LV 135 C13
Barkelsby D 83 A7
Barkhyttan S 103 E11
Barkston GB 11 F10
Barkway GB 15 D9
Barla I 65 C11
Barlad RO 153 E11
Bârlad RO 153 E11
Barleben D 79 B10
Bar-le-Duc F 26 C3
Bârla RO 160 E5
Barletta I 60 A6
Barley GB 15 C9
Barlinek PL 85 E8
Barlingbo S 93 D12
Barmouth GB 10 F3
Barmstedt D 82 C7
Bárna H 147 E9
Barna IRL 6 F4
Bârna RO 159 B9
Barnadery IRL 9 C7
Barnard Castle GB 11 B8
Barnarp S 92 D4
Barnatra IRL 6 D3
Bârnau D 75 C11
Barnbach A 73 B11
Barneberg D 79 B9
Barneveld NL 16 D5
Barneville-Carteret F 23 B8
Barnewitz D 79 A12
Barneycarroll IRL 6 E5
Barnoldswick GB 11 D7
Bârnova RO 153 C11
Barnowko PL 85 E7
Barnowo PL 85 E7
Barnstaple GB 12 C6
Barnstädt D 79 D10
Barnstorf D 17 C11
Barntrup D 17 E12
Baronissi I 60 B3
Baronville F 26 C6
Barošević SRB 158 E5
Barovo MK 169 B7
Barowka BY 133 E3
Barqueros E 55 D10
Barquinha P 44 F4
Barr F 27 D7
Barr GB 4 E7
Barracas E 48 D3
Barrachina E 47 C10
Barraduff IRL 8 D4

Barrafranca I 58 E5
Barral E 38 D3
Barrali I 64 E3
Barranco do Velho P 50 E4
Barrancos P 51 C6
Barranda E 55 C9
Barrapoll GB 4 C3
Barrax E 55 A8
Barre-des-Cévennes F 35 B6
Barreiro P 50 B1
Bárrek S 98 B7
Barrême F 36 D4
Barrhead GB 4 D8
Barrhill GB 4 E7
Barriada Nueva E 43 D8
Bárrio P 38 E2
Barrio del Peral E 56 F3
Barrio Mar E 48 E4
Barrit DK 86 D5
Barr na Trá IRL 6 D3
Barroca P 44 D5
Barroselas P 38 E2
Barrowby GB 11 F10
Barrow-in-Furness GB 10 C5
Barrow-upon-Humber GB 11 D11
Barry GB 13 C8
Barry IRL 7 E7
Bârsa RO 151 E9
Barsac F 32 A5
Bârsana RO 145 H9
Bârsău RO 151 B11
Barsbüttel D 83 C8
Bârse DK 87 E9
Barsele S 107 A12
Bârseşti RO 153 E9
Barsinghausen D 78 B5
Barßel D 17 B9
Barsta S 103 A15
Barstyčiai LT 134 D3
Bar-sur-Aube F 25 D12
Bar-sur-Seine F 25 D11
Bârta LV 134 D2
Bartenheim F 27 E8
Bartenstein D 74 D6
Barth D 83 B13
Bartholomä D 74 E6
Bartholomäberg A 71 C9
Bartkuškiai LT 135 F9
Bartkuškis LT 137 D9
Bartnes N 105 C10
Bartniki PL 139 D10
Bartninkai LT 136 E7
Barton GB 10 D6
Barton-upon-Humber GB 11 D11
Bartoszyce PL 136 E2
Baru RO 159 C11
Baruchowo PL 139 E7
Barulho P 45 F6
Barumini I 64 D3
Baruth D 80 B5
Barvas GB 2 J3
Barvaux B 19 D11
Barver D 17 C11
Barwedel D 79 A8
Barwice PL 85 C10
Barxeta E 56 C4
Bârza RO 160 E4
Bârzana S 93 B8
Barzio I 69 A7
Bârzava RO 151 E9
Bârzava RO 160 E4
Bašaid SRB 158 B5
Basarabeasca MD 154 E3
Basarabi RO 155 E2
Basarbovo BG 161 F7
Bàscara E 43 C9
Baschi I 62 B2
Baschurch GB 10 F6
Basciano I 62 B5
Basconcillos del Tozo E 40 C4
Bascons F 32 C5
Bascous F 33 C6
Bascov RO 160 D5
Basdahl D 17 B12
Basdorf D 84 E4
Basécles B 19 D7
Basel CH 27 E8
Baselga di Pinè I 69 A11
Baselice I 60 A3
Bas-en-Basset F 30 E5
Bâsești RO 151 C11
Basford GB 11 E8
Bashtanivka UA 154 F4
Basigo E 40 B6
Basildon GB 15 D9
Basiliano I 73 D7
Basingstoke GB 13 C12
Baška CZ 146 B6
Baška HR 67 C10
Baška Voda HR 157 F6
Baskemölla S 88 D6
Bäsksele S 107 B11
Bäsksjö S 107 B12
Baslow GB 11 E8
Bāsna S 97 A13
Bassacutena I 64 A3
Bassano del Grappa I 72 E4
Bassano Romano I 62 C2
Bassecourt CH 27 F7
Basse-Goulaine F 23 F9
Bassenge B 19 C12
Bassens F 28 F4
Bassiano I 62 E4
Bassoues F 33 C6
Bassum D 17 C11
Bassy F 31 D8
Bast FIN 123 C10
Båstad S 87 C11
Bastardo I 62 B3
Bastasi BIH 156 D5
Bastasi BIH 157 E8
Bastelica F 37 G10
Bastelicaccia F 37 H9
Bastennes F 32 C4
Bastfallet S 98 B7
Bastia F 37 F10
Bastia I 62 A3
Bastogne B 19 D12
Bastorf D 83 B11
Bastuträsk by S 118 E3
Bastuträsk S 107 C16
Báta H 149 D11
Bata RO 151 E9
Batajnica SRB 158 D5
Batak BG 165 F9
Batalha P 44 E3
Bățani RO 153 E7
Batăr RO 151 D8
Bătarci RO 145 G7

Bâtas S 106 B8
Bátaszék H 149 D11
Batelov CZ 77 D8
Bâteng N 113 C20
Baterno E 54 B3
Batetskiy RUS 132 D7
Bath GB 13 C10
Bathford GB 13 C10
Bathgate GB 5 D9
Bathmen NL 16 D6
Batin BG 161 F7
Batina HR 149 E11
Batizovce SK 145 E1
Batković BIH 158 D3
Batley GB 11 D8
Batllavë KS 164 D3
Bátmonostor H 150 E2
Bâtnfjordsøra N 100 A7
Batočina SRB 159 E7
Bátonyterenye H 147 F9
Bátorove Kosihy SK 146 F6
Batoş RO 152 D5
Batoshevo BG 166 D4
Bátovce SK 147 E7
Batovo BG 167 C9
Batrina HR 157 B8
Bâtsfjord N 114 B7
Batsi GR 176 D4
Bâtsjaur S 109 D13
Bâtskärsnäs S 119 C10
Battenberg (Eder) D 21 B11
Battenberg D 187 E8
Battice B 183 D7
Battipaglia I 60 B3
Battle GB 15 F9
Battonya H 151 E7
Batulti BG 165 C9
Bátya H 150 D2
Batyatychi UA 144 C9
Batz-sur-Mer F 22 F7
Baucina I 58 D4
Baud F 22 E5
Bauduen F 36 D4
Bauen CH 71 D7
Baugé F 23 F11
Baugy F 25 F8
Bauladu I 64 C2
Baulon F 23 D8
Baume-les-Dames F 26 F5
Baumgarten D 83 C11
Baumholder D 186 B3
Baunach D 75 C8
Baunei I 64 C4
Baurci MD 154 F3
Bausendorf D 21 D7
Bauska LV 135 D8
Băuţar RO 159 B10
Bautzen D 80 D6
Bavanište SRB 159 D6
Bavay F 19 D8
Bavel NL 182 B5
Baveno I 68 B6
Bavilliers F 27 E6
Bavorov CZ 76 D6
Bawdeswell GB 15 B11
Bawdsey GB 15 C11
Bawinkel D 17 C8
Bawn Cross Roads IRL 8 D5
Bayárcal E 55 E7
Bayarque E 55 E8
Baye F 25 C10
Baybuzivka UA 154 A5
Bayel F 25 D12
Bayerbach D 21 D7
Bayerbach bei Ergoldsbach D 75 E11
Bayerisch Eisenstein D 76 D4
Bayersoien D 71 B12
Bayeux F 23 B10
Bayindir TR 177 C10
Bayir TR 181 B8
Bayirköy TR 172 D6
Baykal BG 160 F5
Bayon F 26 D5
Bayonne F 32 D3
Bayramiç TR 173 C6
Bayramiç TR 172 E6
Bayramli TR 173 B6
Bayreuth D 75 C10
Bayrischzell D 72 A5
Bayston Hill GB 10 F6
Baytaly UA 154 B5
Bayubas de Abajo E 40 E6
Baza E 55 D7
Bázakerettye H 149 C7
Bazar'yanka UA 154 F6
Bazas F 32 B5
Bazet F 33 D6
Bazièges F 33 D9
Bazizac F 33 D6
Bazna RO 152 E4
Bazoches F 25 F10
Bazoches-au-Houlme F 23 C11
Bazoches-les-Gallerandes F 24 D7
Bazoches-sur-Hoëne F 24 C3
Bazouges F 23 E10
Bazzano I 66 D3
Beaconsfield F 15 D7
Beadnell GB 5 D13
Beagh IRL 7 E7
Bealach A Doirín IRL 6 E5
Bealach Conglais IRL 9 C9
Bealach Feich IRL 7 C7
Bealaclugga IRL 6 F4
Béal an Átha IRL 6 D4
Béal an Mhuirthead IRL 6 D3
Béal Átha an Ghaorthaidh IRL 8 E4
Béal Átha Beithe IRL 7 D9
Béal Átha Liag IRL 7 F7
Béal Átha na Muice IRL 6 E5
Béal Átha na Sluaighe IRL 6 F6
Béal Átha Seanaidh IRL 6 C6
Béal Deirg IRL 6 D3
Béal Easa IRL 6 E4
Bealnablath IRL 8 E5
Beaminster GB 13 D9
Beamud E 47 D9
Beannchar IRL 7 F7
Beantraí IRL 8 E4
Beariz E 38 D3
Bearna IRL 6 F4
Bearsden GB 5 D8
Beas E 51 E6
Beasain E 32 D1
Beas de Granada E 53 B10
Beas de Segura E 55 C7
Beateberg S 92 B4
Beattock GB 5 E10
Beaucaire F 35 C8

Beaucamps-le-Vieux F 18 E4
Beauchastel F 30 F6
Beaucouzé F 23 F10
Beaufay F 24 D3
Beaufort F 31 B7
Beaufort F 31 D10
Beaufort IRL 8 D3
Beaufort-en-Vallée F 23 F11
Beaugency F 24 E6
Beaujeu F 30 C6
Beaujeu F 36 C4
Beaujeu-St-Vallier-Pierrejux-et-Quitteur F 26 F4
Beaulieu F 35 C7
Beaulieu-lès-Loches F 24 F5
Beaulieu-sur-Dordogne F 29 F9
Beaulieu-sur-Loire F 25 E8
Beaulon F 30 B4
Beauly GB 2 L8
Beaumarchés F 33 C6
Beaumaris GB 10 E3
Beaumesnil F 24 B4
Beaumetz-lès-Loges F 18 D6
Beaumont B 19 D9
Beaumont F 23 A8
Beaumont F 29 B6
Beaumont F 29 F7
Beaumont-de-Lomagne F 33 C7
Beaumont-de-Pertuis F 35 C10
Beaumont-en-Argonne F 19 E11
Beaumont-en-Véron F 23 F12
Beaumont-le-Roger F 24 B4
Beaumont-lès-Valence F 30 F6
Beaumont-sur-Oise F 25 B7
Beaumont-sur-Sarthe F 23 D12
Beaune F 30 A6
Beaune-La Rolande F 25 D7
Beaupréau F 23 F10
Beauquesne F 18 D5
Beauraing B 19 D10
Beaurepaire F 31 E7
Beaurepaire-en-Bresse F 31 B7
Beaurières F 35 A10
Beausite F 26 C3
Beausoleil F 37 D6
Beautor F 19 E7
Beauvais F 18 F5
Beauval F 18 D5
Beauvezer F 36 C5
Beauville F 33 B7
Beauvoir-sur-Mer F 28 B1
Beauvoir-sur-Niort F 28 C5
Beauzac F 30 E5
Beauzelle F 33 C8
Beba Veche RO 150 E5
Bebertal D 79 B9
Bebra D 78 E6
Bebrina HR 157 B8
Beccles GB 15 C12
Becedas E 45 D9
Beceite E 42 F4
Bečej SRB 158 B5
Beceni RO 161 C9
Becerreá E 38 C5
Becerril de Campos E 39 D10
Becherbach D 186 B4
Bécherel F 23 D8
Bechet RO 160 F3
Bechhofen D 21 F8
Bechhofen D 75 D8
Bechlín CZ 76 B6
Bechyně CZ 77 D6
Bečići MNE 163 E6
Becilla de Valderaduey E 39 D9
Beçin TR 181 B7
Beckdorf D 82 D7
Beckedorf D 17 D12
Beckeln D 17 C11
Beckingen D 21 F7
Beckingham GB 11 E10
Beckov SK 146 D5
Beckum D 17 E10
Beclean RO 152 C4
Beclean RO 152 F5
Bécon-les-Granits F 23 F10
Bečov CZ 76 B3
Becsehely H 149 D7
Becsvölgye H 149 C7
Bečváry CZ 77 C8
Bedale GB 11 C8
Bédar E 55 E9
Bédarieux F 34 C5
Bédarrides F 35 B8
Bedburg D 21 C7
Bedburg-Hau D 183 B8
Beddgelert GB 10 E3
Beddingestrand S 87 E12
Bédée F 23 D8
Bedekovčina HR 148 D5
Beden BG 165 F9
Beder DK 86 C6
Bedford GB 15 C8
Bedirhoşt CZ 77 D12
Bjdków PL 143 C8
Bedlington GB 5 E13
Bedlno PL 143 B8
Bedmar E 53 A10
Bednja HR 148 D5
Bedonia I 37 B11
Bedous F 32 D4
Bedsted Stationsby DK 86 B2
Bedum NL 17 B7
Bedwas GB 13 C8
Bedworth GB 13 A12
Będzin PL 143 F7
Bjdzino PL 85 B9
Beeford GB 11 D11
Beek NL 16 E5
Beek NL 183 D7
Beekbergen NL 183 A7
Beelen D 17 E10
Beelitz D 79 B12
Beendorf D 79 B9
Beerfelden D 21 E11
Beernem B 19 B7
Beers NL 16 E5
Beerse B 16 F3
Beerst B 19 C9
Beersel B 182 D4
Beesd NL 183 B6
Beesenstedt D 79 C10

Beesten D 17 D9
Beeston GB 11 F9
Beetsterzwaag NL 16 B6
Beetzendorf D 83 E10
Bégaar F 32 C4
Bégadan F 28 E4
Begaljica SRB 158 D6
Bégard F 22 C5
Begeçi SRB 158 C4
Beğendik TR 172 C6
Begíjar E 53 A9
Begijnendijk B 19 B10
Beglezh BG 165 C10
Begnište MK 169 B6
Begonte E 38 B4
Begur E 43 D10
Behramkale TR 171 F10
Behren-lès-Forbach F 27 B6
Behren-Lübchin D 83 B13
Behringen D 79 D8
Beica de Jos RO 152 D5
Beidaud RO 155 D3
Beierfeld D 79 E12
Beierstedt D 79 B8
Beilen NL 17 C7
Beilngries D 75 D9
Beilstein D 187 B11
Beimerstetten D 187 E8
Beinasco I 37 A7
Beinette I 37 C7
Beinwil CH 27 F9
Beira P 44 E5
Beisfjord N 111 D14
Beisland N 90 C3
Beith GB 4 D7
Beitostølen N 101 D9
Beitstad N 105 C10
Beius RO 151 D9
Beja LV 133 B2
Beja P 50 C4
Bejar AL 168 D2
Béjar E 45 D9
Bejís F 48 E3
Bekecs H 145 G3
Békés H 151 D7
Békéscsaba H 151 D7
Békéssámson H 150 E6
Békésszentandrás H 150 D6
Bekkarfjord N 113 B19
Bekken N 101 C15
Bekkevoll N 114 D8
Belá SK 147 C7
Bélâbre F 29 B8
Bela Crkva SRB 159 D7
Beladice SK 146 E6
Belá-Dulice SK 147 C7
Belalcázar E 51 B9
Belá nad Cirochou SK 145 F5
Belá nad Radbuzou CZ 75 C12
Bellanicë KS 163 E10
Belanovce MK 164 E4
Belanovica SRB 158 E5
Bela Palanka SRB 164 C5
Bélapátfalva H 145 G2
Bělá pod Bezdězem CZ 77 A7
Bělá pod Pradědem CZ 77 B12
Belascoáin E 32 E2
Belauski LV 133 C2
Belava LV 135 B13
Belazaima do Chão P 44 C4
Belcaire F 33 E9
Belcastel F 33 B10
Belcești RO 153 C10
Belchatów PL 143 D7
Belchin BG 165 E7
Belchite E 41 F10
Bělčice CZ 76 C5
Bělčovice RO 161 E8
Belclare IRL 6 F5
Belcoo GB 7 D7
Belderg IRL 6 D5
Beldibi TR 181 C8
Beled H 149 B8
Belegiš SRB 158 C5
Belej HR 67 C9
Belene BG 160 F6
Belești RO 152 F5
Beleti-Negrești RO 160 D5
Belevi TR 177 C9
Beleznna H 149 D7
Belfast GB 7 C11
Belfeld NL 16 F6
Belford GB 5 D13
Belfort F 27 E6
Belfort-du-Quercy F 33 B9
Belforte del Chienti I 67 F7
Belgern D 80 D4
Belgershain D 79 D12
Belgioioso I 69 C7
Belgodère F 37 F9
Belgooly IRL 8 E6
Belgun BG 155 F2
Belhomert-Guéhouville F 24 C5
Beli HR 67 B9
Belianes E 42 D6
Belica HR 149 C6
Beli Iskăr BG 165 E8
Beli Izvor BG 165 C7
Beli Manastir HR 149 E11
Belin RO 153 F7
Belin-Béliet F 32 B4
Belinchón E 47 D6
Beliņt RO 151 F8
Beli Potok SRB 164 B5
Belis RO 151 D11
Belišće HR 149 E10
Belitsa BG 165 D8
Belitsa BG 165 F8
Beliu RO 151 E9
Bělkovice-Lašťany CZ 146 B4
Bell D 21 D8
Bell (Hunsrück) D 185 D7
Bella I 60 B5
Bellac F 29 C8
Bellacorick IRL 6 D4
Bellaghy GB 4 F3
Bellagio I 69 B7
Bellahy IRL 6 E5
Bellano I 69 A7
Bellante I 62 B5
Bellaria I 66 D5
Bellavary IRL 6 E4
Bellavista E 51 E8
Bellcaire d'Urgell E 42 D5
Belleek GB 7 D10
Bellegarde F 25 E8
Bellegarde F 35 C8
Bellegarde-en-Marche F 29 D10
Bellegarde-sur-Valserine F 31 C8
Belle-Isle-en-Terre F 22 C5

Bellême F 24 D4
Bellenaves F 30 C3
Bellenberg D 71 A10
Bellencombre F 18 E3
Bellerive-sur-Allier F 30 C3
Belles-Forêts F 27 C6
Belleu F 19 F7
Bellevaux F 31 C10
Belleville F 30 C6
Belleville-sur-Meuse F 26 B3
Belleville-sur-Vie F 28 B3
Belley F 31 D8
Bellheim D 21 F10
Bellherbe F 26 F6
Bellignat F 31 C8
Bellinge D 86 E6
Bellingham GB 5 E12
Bellingwolde NL 17 B8
Bellinzago Novarese I 68 B6
Bellinzona CH 69 A7
Bellizzi I 60 B3
Bell-Lloc d'Urgell E 42 D5
Bello E 47 C10
Bellobradě KS 163 C10
Bellou-en-Houlme F 23 C11
Bellpuig E 42 D6
Bellreguard E 56 D4
Bellshill GB 5 D8
Belluno I 72 D5
Bellver de Cerdanya E 33 F9
Bellvik S 107 C10
Belm D 17 D10
Bélmegyer H 151 D7
Bélmez F 51 C9
Bélmez de la Moraleda E 53 A10
Belmont GB 3 D15
Belmont-de-la-Loire F 30 C5
Belmonte E 39 B7
Belmonte E 47 E7
Belmonte P 45 D6
Belmonte Calabro I 60 E6
Belmonte del Sannio I 63 D6
Belmonte in Sabina I 62 C3
Belmontejo E 47 E8
Belmont-sur-Rance F 34 C4
Belmullet IRL 6 D3
Belo Brdo KS 163 C10
Beloci MD 154 B4
Belœil B 19 C8
Belogradchik BG 159 F10
Beloiannisz H 149 B11
Belojin SRB 164 C3
Belorado E 40 D5
Beloslav BG 167 C9
Bělotín CZ 146 B5
Belotintsi BG 165 B6
Belozem BG 166 E4
Belp CH 31 B11
Belpasso I 59 D6
Belpech F 33 D9
Belper GB 11 E9
Belsay GB 5 E13
Belsh AL 168 C2
Belsk Duży PL 141 G3
Beltheim D 21 D8
Beltinci SLO 148 C6
Beltiug RO 151 B10
Beltra IRL 6 D5
Beltra IRL 6 E4
Beltrum NL 183 A9
Belturbet IRL 7 D8
Beluša SK 146 C6
Belušić SRB 159 F7
Belvédère-Campomoro F 37 H9
Belvedere Marittimo I 60 D5
Belvedere Ostrense I 67 E7
Belver de Cinca E 42 D4
Belver de los Montes E 39 E9
Belvès F 29 F8
Belvèze-du-Razès F 33 D10
Belvi I 64 D3
Belville IRL 6 D4
Belvís de la Jara E 46 E3
Belz F 22 E5
Belz UA 144 C9
Belżec D 79 B12
Belżyce PL 141 H6
Bembibre E 38 B2
Bembibre E 39 C7
Bemmel NL 16 E5
Bemposta P 39 F7
Bemposta P 44 F4
Bempton GB 11 C11
Benabarre E 42 C4
Benacazón E 51 E7
Benahadux E 55 F8
Benahavís E 53 D6
Benalmádena E 53 C7
Benalúa de Guadix E 55 E6
Benalúa de las Villas E 53 B9
Benalup de Sidonia E 52 D5
Benamargosa E 53 C8
Benamaurel E 55 D7
Benameji E 53 B7
Benamocarra E 53 C8
Benaocaz E 53 C6
Benaoján E 53 C6
Benasal E 48 D4
Benasau E 56 D4
Benasque E 33 E7
Benassay F 28 B6
Benatae E 55 C7
Benátky nad Jizerou CZ 77 B7
Benavente E 39 D8
Benavente P 50 B2
Benavides de Orbigo E 39 D8
Benavila P 44 F5
Benburb GB 7 D9
Bencatel P 50 B5
Bendorf D 21 D9
Bēne LV 134 D6
Benecko CZ 81 E9
Beneden-Leeuwen NL 16 E4
Benedikt SLO 148 C6
Benedita P 44 F3
Benegiles E 39 E8
Bénéjacq F 32 D5
Benejúzar E 56 E3
Benesat RO 151 C11
Benešov CZ 77 C7
Benešov nad Černou CZ 77 E7
Benešov nad Ploučnicí CZ 80 E6
Bénesse-Maremne F 32 C3
Benestare I 59 D9
Bénestroff F 27 C6
Benet F 28 C4
Benetutti I 64 C3
Bene Vagienna I 37 B7

Bénévent-l'Abbaye F 29 C9
Benevento I 60 A3
Benfeld F 27 D8
Benfica do Ribatejo P 44 F3
Bengeşti-Ciocadia RO 160 C3
Bengtsfors S 91 A11
Bengtsheden S 103 E10
Benia de Onís E 39 B10
Beniarbeig E 56 D5
Beniarrés E 56 D4
Beničanci HR 149 E11
Benicarló E 48 D5
Benicasim E 48 D5
Benidorm E 56 D4
Beniel E 56 E3
Benifaió E 48 F4
Benifallet E 42 F5
Benifallim E 56 D4
Benigánim E 56 D4
Benilloba E 56 D4
Benissa E 56 D5
Benissanet E 42 E5
Benitachell E 56 D5
Benitses GR 168 E2
Benizalón E 55 E8
Benken CH 27 F11
Benkovac HR 156 D4
Benkovski BG 161 F10
Benkovski BG 171 B8
Benllech GB 10 E3
Benlloch E 48 D5
Bennebroek NL 182 A5
Bennekom NL 183 A7
Bennewitz D 79 D12
Bennungen D 79 D9
Bénodet F 22 E3
Benquerença P 45 D6
Benquerenças P 44 E5
Benquerencia de la Serena E
51 B9
Benquet F 32 C4
Bensafrim P 50 E2
Bensbyn S 118 C8
Bensdorf D 79 B11
Benshausen D 79 E8
Bensheim D 21 E11
Bensjö S 103 A9
Bentelo NL 17 D7
Benson GB 13 B12
Bentley GB 11 D9
Bentwisch D 83 B12
Bentzin D 84 C4
Beňuš SK 147 D9
Benzingerode D 79 C8
Beočin SRB 158 C4
Beograd SRB 158 D5
Bera de Bidasoa E 32 D2
Beragh GB 7 C8
Berane MNE 163 C8
Beranga E 40 B4
Berango E 40 B6
Berantevilla E 40 C6
Berat AL 168 C2
Bérat F 33 D8
Beratzhausen D 75 D10
Berbegal E 42 D3
Berbešti RO 160 C3
Berca RO 161 C9
Bercedo E 40 B5
Bercel H 147 F8
Berceni RO 161 D8
Berceni RO 161 E8
Bercero E 39 E9
Berceşti RO 160 D3
Berchem B 19 C8
Berchidda I 64 B3
Berching D 75 D9
Berchtesgaden D 73 A7
Bérchules E 55 F6
Bercianos del Páramo E 39 D8
Berck F 15 G12
Bercu RO 145 H6
Berdal N 104 E6
Berdalen N 94 D6
Berdún E 32 D4
Bere Alston GB 12 E6
Beregdaróc H 145 G6
Bereguardo I 69 C7
Berehomet UA 152 A6
Berehove UA 145 G6
Berek HR 149 E7
Berekböszörmény H 151 C8
Berekfürdő H 150 C6
Beremend H 149 E10
Bereşti RO 153 E11
Bereşti-Meria RO 153 E11
Bereşti-Tazlău RO 153 E9
Berettyóújfalu H 151 C8
Berevoeşti RO 160 C5
Berezeni RO 154 D2
Berezyne UA 154 E4
Berg D 71 B9
Berg D 75 B10
Berg D 183 D9
Berg L 20 E6
Berg N 96 B7
Berg N 108 F3
Berg N 111 B13
Berg NL 19 C12
Berg NL 183 D7
Berg S 92 C8
Berg S 92 C7
Berg S 107 E10
Berg (Pfalz) D 27 C9
Berga D 79 D9
Berga D 79 D9
Berga E 43 C7
Berga S 89 A10
Bergagård S 87 B11
Bergaland N 94 D4
Bergama TR 177 A9
Bergamo I 69 B8
Bergantino I 66 B3
Bergara E 32 D1
Bergasa E 32 F1
Bergatreute D 71 B9
Berg bei Neumarkt in der
Oberpfalz D 75 D9
Bergby S 103 E13
Berge D 17 C9
Berge D 83 D11
Berge N 90 A8
Berge N 94 D7
Bergeforsen S 103 A13
Bergeggi I 37 C8
Bergen D 73 A6
Bergen D 79 D9
Bergen D 84 B4
Bergen N 94 B2

Bergen NL 16 C3
Bergen (Dumme) D 83 E9
Bergen op Zoom NL 16 F2
Berger N 95 C12
Bergerac F 29 F6
Bergères-lès-Vertus F 25 C11
Bergesserin F 30 C6
Bergeyk NL 16 F4
Berghamn S 103 A15
Berghamn N 111 B13
Bergharen NL 183 B7
Bergheim A 73 A7
Bergheim D 75 E9
Bergheim (Edertal) D 21 B12
Bergheim (Erft) D 21 C7
Berghem NL 16 E5
Berghem S 91 E12
Berghin RO 152 E3
Berghülen D 74 F6
Berg im Drautal A 73 C7
Bergisch Gladbach D 21 C8
Bergkamen D 17 E9
Bergkarlås S 102 D8
Bergkvara S 89 C10
Bergland S 107 A10
Berglia N 105 C15
Bergmo N 112 D7
Bergnäs S 109 E13
Bergnäset S 118 C8
Bergnäsviken S 109 D15
Bergneustadt D 185 B8
Bergö FIN 99 B13
Bergö FIN 122 E6
Bergom S 107 E15
Bergsåker S 103 B13
Bergsäng S 97 B10
Bergsäter S 107 B12
Bergsbyn S 118 E6
Bergschenhoek NL 182 B5
Bergsgården S 103 E10
Bergshamra S 99 C11
Bergsjö S 103 C13
Bergsnov N 105 B9
Bergs slussar S 92 C7
Bergstod N 95 D9
Bergström N 96 D6
Bergsviken S 118 D6
Bergtheim D 75 C7
Bergues F 18 C5
Bergün CH 71 D9
Bergvik S 103 D12
Bergviken S 109 D16
Bergwitz D 79 C12
Berhida H 149 B10
Beringe NL 183 C7
Beringel P 50 C4
Beringen B 19 B11
Berislăveşti RO 160 C4
Beriu RO 151 F11
Berja E 55 F7
Berka F 29 E7
Berkåk N 101 A12
Berkel NL 16 D4
Berkel-Enschot NL 16 E4
Berkeley GB 13 B10
Berkenthin D 83 C9
Berkheim D 71 A10
Berkhout NL 16 C4
Berkovići BIH 157 F9
Berkovitsa BG 165 C7
Berlanga E 51 C8
Berlanga de Duero E 40 F6
Berleşti RO 160 D3
Berlevåg N 114 B6
Berlicum NL 183 B6
Berlin D 80 A4
Berlingerode D 79 D7
Berliste RO 159 D7
Berlstedt D 79 D9
Bermatingen D 27 E11
Bermeo E 40 B6
Bermillo de Sayago E 39 F7
Bern CH 31 B10
Bernac-Dessus F 33 D6
Bernalda I 61 C7
Bernardos E 46 B4
Bernartice CZ 76 D6
Bernartice CZ 81 E9
Bernăţi LV 134 D1
Bernau D 27 E9
Bernau am Chiemsee D 72 A5
Bernaville F 18 D5
Bernay F 24 B4
Bernbeuren D 71 B11
Bernburg (Saale) D 79 C10
Berndorf A 77 G10
Berne D 17 B10
Bernecebaráti H 147 E7
Bernedo E 41 C7
Bernhardsthal A 77 E11
Bernhardswald D 75 D11
Bernin F 31 E8
Bernis F 35 C7
Bernisdale GB 2 L4
Bernissart B 19 D8
Bernitt D 83 C11
Bernkastel-Kues D 21 E8
Bernolákovo SK 146 E4
Bernsdorf D 80 D6
Bernshammar S 97 C14
Bernstadt D 81 D7
Bernstein A 148 B6
Beromünster CH 27 F9
Beronovo BG 167 D7
Beroun CZ 76 C6
Berovo MK 165 F6
Berra I 66 C4
Berre-l'Étang F 35 D9
Berriedale GB 3 J9
Berrien F 22 D4
Berriozar E 32 E2
Berru F 19 F9
Berry-au-Bac F 19 F8
Bersenbrück D 17 C9
Bershad' UA 154 A5
Beršići BIH 158 C6
Bersone I 69 B10
Bërstele LV 135 D7
Bertamirans E 38 C2
Bertea RO 161 C7
Berteştii de Jos RO 155 D1
Bertinoro I 66 D5
Bertnes N 108 B8
Bertogne B 19 D12
Bertrange L 186 B1
Bertrichamps F 27 D6
Bertrix B 19 E11
Běrunice CZ 77 B8

Berveni RO 151 B9
Bërvircava LV 134 D7
Berwick-upon-Tweed GB 5 D12
Bërzaine LV 131 F10
Berzasca RO 159 D8
Bërzciems LV 134 B6
Bërzgale LV 133 C3
Bërzkalne LV 133 B2
Berzovia RO 159 C8
Bërzpils LV 133 C2
Berzunţi RO 153 E9
Besalú E 43 C9
Besançon F 26 F5
Besande E 39 C10
Bescanó E 43 D9
Beselich-Obertiefenbach D
21 D10
Bešeňov SK 146 E6
Besenyőtelek H 150 B5
Besenyszög H 150 C5
Besigheim D 27 C11
Beşiktaş TR 173 B11
Beška SRB 158 C5
Besko PL 145 D4
Besni Fok SRB 158 D5
Besnyő H 149 B11
Besozzo I 68 B6
Bessacarr GB 11 D9
Bessaker N 104 C8
Bessan F 34 D5
Bessay-sur-Allier F 30 C3
Bessbrook GB 7 D10
Besse F 31 E9
Besse-et-St-Anastaise F 30 D2
Bessèges F 35 B7
Bessenbach D 187 B7
Bessé-sur-Braye F 24 E4
Besse-sur-Issole F 36 E4
Bessières F 33 C9
Bessines-sur-Gartempe F 29 C8
Bessude I 64 B2
Best NL 16 E4
Bestensee D 80 B5
Bestorp S 92 C7
Bestwig D 17 F10
Bestwina PL 147 B8
Beszterec H 145 G4
Betanzos E 38 B3
Betelu E 32 D2
Bétera E 48 E4
Beteta E 47 C8
Bethausen RO 151 F8
Bethon F 25 C10
Béthune F 18 C6
Betna N 104 E4
Beton-Bazoches F 25 C9
Betschdorf F 186 D4
Betsele S 107 B15
Bettainville F 186 C1
Bettembourg L 20 E6
Bettendorf L 20 E6
Bettingen D 20 D6
Bettna S 93 B9
Bettola I 37 B10
Betton F 23 D8
Bettyhill GB 3 H8
Bettystown IRL 7 E10
Betws-y-coed GB 10 E4
Betygala LT 134 F6
Betz F 25 B8
Betzdorf D 21 C9
Betzdorf L 186 B1
Betzenstein D 75 C9
Betzigau D 71 B10
Beucha D 79 D12
Beuil F 36 C5
Beuningen NL 16 E6
Beuren D 79 D7
Beuron D 27 D10
Beurville F 25 D12
Beuvrages F 182 E2
Beuzeville F 23 B12
Bevagna I 62 B3
Bevaix CH 31 B10
Beveren B 19 B9
Beverley GB 11 D11
Beverlo B 183 C6
Bevern D 78 C5
Beverstedt D 17 B11
Beverungen D 21 A12
Beverwijk NL 16 D3
Bewcastle GB 5 F11
Bewdley GB 13 A10
Bex CH 31 C11
Bexbach D 21 F8
Bexhill GB 15 F9
Beyağaç TR 181 B9
Beyazköy TR 173 B8
Beyçayiri TR 173 D6
Beyel TR 173 E10
Beyendorf D 79 B10
Beykoz TR 173 B11
Beynat F 29 E9
Beynost F 31 D7
Beyoba TR 177 B10
Beyobasi TR 181 C9
Bezas E 47 D10
Bezau A 71 C9
Bezdan SRB 150 F2
Bezdead RO 161 C6
Bezdonys LT 137 D12
Bèze F 26 F3
Bezenye H 146 F4
Bezhanitsy RUS 133 C7
Bezhanovo BG 165 C9
Béziers F 34 D5
Bezledy PL 136 E2
Bezmer BG 161 F10
Bezmer BG 166 E6
Bezouce F 35 C8
Bežovce SK 145 F5
Biadki PL 142 C4
Biała PL 142 E4
Biała-Parcela Pierwsza PL
142 D5
Biała Piska PL 139 C13
Biała Podlaska PL 141 F8
Biała Rawska PL 141 G2
Białe Błota PL 138 D4
Białebłoto-Kobyla PL 139 E12
Białka PL 145 E1

Białobrzegi PL 141 G3
Białogard PL 85 C9
Białośliwie PL 85 D12
Białowieża PL 141 E9
Biały Bór PL 85 C11
Biały Dunajec PL 147 C10
Białystok PL 140 D8
Biancavilla I 59 D6
Bianco I 59 D9
Biandrate I 68 C5
Bians-les-Usiers F 31 B9
Bianzè I 68 C5
Biar E 56 D3
Biarritz E 32 D2
Biarrotte F 32 C3
Biars-sur-Cère F 29 F9
Bias F 32 B3
Bias F 33 B7
Biasca CH 71 E7
Biatorbágy H 149 B11
Bibbiena I 66 E4
Bibbona I 66 F2
Biberach D 27 D9
Biberach an der Riß D 71 A9
Biberbach D 75 E8
Biberist CH 27 F8
Bibinje HR 156 D3
Bibione I 73 E7
Biblis D 21 E11
Bibury GB 13 B11
Bicaj AL 163 E9
Bicaz RO 153 D8
Bicaz RO 151 C10
Bicaz-Chei RO 153 D7
Bicazu Ardelean RO 153 D7
Biccari I 60 A4
Bicester GB 13 B12
Bichiş RO 152 E4
Bichl D 72 A3
Bichlbach A 71 C11
Bickleigh GB 13 D7
Bicorp E 48 F3
Bicos P 50 D3
Bicske H 149 A11
Bicton GB 10 F6
Bidache F 32 D3
Bidart F 32 D2
Biddenden GB 15 E10
Biddinghuizen NL 16 D5
Biddulph GB 11 E7
Bideford GB 12 C6
Bidjovagge N 112 E10
Bidos F 32 D4
Bidovce SK 145 F3
Bie S 93 A8
Bieber D 21 D12
Biebesheim am Rhein D 21 E10
Biecz PL 144 D3
Biedenkopf D 21 C11
Biel CH 27 F7
Biel E 32 F3
Bielany-Żyłaki PL 141 F6
Bielawa PL 81 E11
Bielawy PL 143 B8
Bielefeld D 17 D11
Bielice PL 85 D7
Bieliny Kapitulne PL 143 E10
Biella I 68 B5
Bielle F 32 D5
Bielsa E 33 E6
Bielsk PL 139 E8
Bielsko-Biała PL 147 B8
Bielsk Podlaski PL 141 E8
Bienenbüttel D 83 D8
Bieniów PL 81 C8
Bienno I 69 B9
Bienservida E 55 B7
Bienvenida E 51 C7
Bierawa PL 142 F5
Bierdzany PL 142 E5
Bière CH 31 B9
Bierge E 42 C3
Bierné F 23 E10
Biersted DK 86 A5
Biert F 33 E8
Biertan RO 152 E5
Bieruń PL 143 F7
Bierutów PL 142 D4
Bierzwienna-Długa PL 142 B6
Bierzwnik PL 85 D9
Biesiadgohppi N 113 C16
Biescas E 32 E5
Biesenthal D 84 E5
Biesiekierz PL 85 B10
Biesles F 26 D3
Biesowice PL 85 B11
Biessenhofen D 71 B11
Bietigheim D 27 C9
Bietigheim-Bissingen D 27 C11
Bietikow D 84 D5
Bièvre B 19 E11
Biga TR 173 D7
Bigadiç TR 173 F9
Biganos F 32 A4
Bigastro E 56 E3
Bigauņciems LV 134 C7
Bigbury-on-Sea GB 13 E7
Biggar GB 5 D9
Biggleswade GB 15 C8
Bignan F 22 E6
Bignasco CH 71 E7
Bigor MNE 163 E7
Bigüézal E 32 E3
Biguglia F 37 F10
Biharia RO 151 C8
Biharkeresztes H 151 C8
Biharnagybajom H 151 C7
Bihartorda H 151 C7
Biharugra H 151 D8
Bihosava BY 133 E3
Bijela MNE 163 E6
Bijela Poljane MNE 163 D6
Bijeljani BIH 157 F9
Bijeljina BIH 158 D3
Bijelo Brdo HR 149 E11
Bijelo Bučje BIH 157 D8
Bijelo Polje MNE 163 C8
Bilač HR 156 E4
Bilbao E 40 B6
Bilbor RO 153 C7
Bilca RO 153 B7
Bilciureşti RO 161 D7
Bil'dzyuhi BY 133 F2
Bileća BIH 162 D5
Bilecik TR 173 D10
Bilfgoraj PL 144 B6
Bilicenii Vechi MD 153 B12

Bílina CZ 80 E5
Bilisht AL 168 C4
Biljača SRB 164 E4
Bilje HR 149 E11
Bilky UA 145 G7
Billdal S 91 D10
Billerbeck D 17 E8
Billère F 32 D5
Billericay GB 15 D9
Billesholm S 87 C11
Billigheim D 21 F12
Billingham GB 5 F14
Billinghay GB 11 E11
Billingsfors S 91 B11
Billingshurst GB 15 E8
Billom F 30 D3
Billsåsen S 105 F16
Billsbro S 92 A7
Billsta S 107 E15
Bilstagno I 37 B8
Bilstein D 17 D10
Bilten CH 27 F11
Biltoven NL 16 D4
Bilto N 112 E7
Bilton GB 11 D11
Bilyaivka UA 154 E6
Bilychi UA 145 E6
Bilyne UA 154 B5
Bilzen B 19 C12
Bimbister GB 3 G10
Biňa SK 147 F7
Binaced E 42 D4
Binas F 24 E5
Binasco I 69 C7
Binbrook GB 11 E11
Binche B 19 D9
Bindalseit N 105 A12
Bindlach D 75 C10
Bindslev DK 90 D7
Binefar E 42 D4
Bingen D 27 D11
Bingen am Rhein D 21 E9
Bingerden NL 183 B8
Bingham GB 11 F10
Binghamstown IRL 6 D2
Bingley GB 11 D8
Bingsjö S 103 D10
Binic F 22 C6
Biniés E 32 E4
Binissalem E 49 E10
Binnen D 17 C12
Binz, Ostseebad D 84 B5
Binzen D 27 E8
Biograd na Moru HR 156 E3
Biokovina BIH 157 D7
Biol F 31 E7
Bionaz I 31 D11
Biorra IRL 7 F7
Biosca E 43 D6
Biot F 36 D6
Biota E 41 D9
Birchington GB 15 E11
Birchiş RO 151 F9
Bircza PL 144 D5
Birdhill IRL 8 C6
Birgittelyst DK 86 C4
Biri N 101 E13
Biri N 101 E13
Biřini LV 135 B9
Birkeland N 90 C3
Birkeland N 90 C3
Birkelse DK 86 A6
Birkenau D 187 B6
Birkenfeld D 21 E8
Birkenfeld D 27 C10
Birkenfeld D 74 C6
Birkenhead GB 10 E5
Birken-Honigsessen D 185 C8
Birkenwerder Berlin D 84 E4
Birkerød DK 87 D10
Birket DK 87 F9
Birketveit N 90 C2
Birkfeld A 148 B5
Birkungen D 79 D7
Birmingham GB 13 A11
Birnbaum A 73 C6
Biron F 33 A7
Birori I 64 C2
Birr IRL 7 F7
Birresborn D 21 D7
Birsay GB 3 G10
Birstall GB 11 F9
Birstein D 21 D12
Birštonas LT 137 D9
Birtavarre N 112 D6
Birtley GB 5 F13
Biruintsa MD 153 B12
Biržai LT 135 D9
Birzes LV 135 D8
Birzgale LV 135 C9
Birži LV 135 D11
Birzuli LV 131 F11
Biš SLO 148 C5
Bisaccia I 60 A4
Bisacquino I 58 D3
Biscarrosse F 32 B3
Biscarrosse-Plage F 32 B3
Bisceglie I 61 A7
Bischberg D 75 C8
Bischbrunn D 187 B7
Bischhausen (Waldkappel) D
78 D6
Bischheim F 27 C8
Bischoffen D 21 C10
Bischofferode D 79 D7
Bischofswerda D 80 D6
Bischofswiesen D 73 A6
Bischofszell CH 27 E11
Bischwiller F 27 C8
Bisenti I 62 B5
Biser BG 166 F5
Bisertsi BG 161 F9
Bishop Auckland GB 5 F13
Bishop's Castle GB 10 G6
Bishop's Cleeve GB 13 B10
Bishop's Lydeard GB 13 C8
Bishop's Stortford GB 15 D9
Bishop's Waltham GB 13 D12
Bishqem AL 168 B2
Bishtazhin KS 163 E10

Bisignano I 60 D6
Bisingen D 27 D10
Biskupice PL 141 H7
Biskupice PL 142 D5
Biskupice SK 147 E9
Biskupiec PL 136 F2
Biskupiec PL 139 C7
Bislev DK 86 B5
Bismark (Altmark) D 83 E11
Bismervik N 113 B11
Bismo N 101 C11
Bisoca RO 161 B9
Bispgården S 107 E11
Bispingen D 83 D8
Bissen L 20 E6
Bissendorf D 17 D10
Bissendorf (Wedemark) D 78 A6
Bissingen D 75 E8
Bistagno I 37 B8
Bistarac BIH 157 D9
Bistra RO 151 C9
Bistra RO 152 B4
Bistreţ RO 160 F3
Bistrets BG 167 E8
Bistrica BIH 157 B7
Bistrica BIH 157 D8
Bistrica BIH 157 E8
Bistrica BIH 157 E10
Bistrica SLO 73 D9
Bistrica SLO 148 C6
Bistričak BIH 157 D8
Bistrita RO 152 C5
Bistrita Bârgăului RO 152 C5
Bistrita BG 165 E7
Bistritsa BG 165 E7
Bisztynek PL 136 E2
Bitburg D 21 E7
Bitche F 27 B7
Bitetto I 61 A7
Bitincë AL 168 C4
Bitola MK 168 B5
Bitonto I 61 A7
Bitritto I 61 A7
Bitschwiller-lès-Thann F 27 E7
Bitterfeld D 79 C12
Bitterstad N 110 C9
Bitti I 64 C3
Bittkau D 79 B10
Bitton GB 13 C10
Bitz D 27 D11
Biurrun E 32 E2
Bivio CH 71 D9
Bivolari RO 153 B10
Bivona I 58 D3
Bixad RO 145 H7
Bixad RO 153 E7
Bixter GB 3 E14
Biyikali TR 173 B7
Biyikli TR 177 D10
Bizanet F 34 D4
Bizanos F 32 D5
Bizovac HR 149 E10
Bjåen N 94 C6
Bjærangen N 108 C6
Bjæverskov DK 87 E10
Bjännberg S 122 C3
Bjärkøy N 111 C12
Bjärnum S 87 C13
Bjärred S 87 D11
Bjärsjölagård S 87 D13
Bjärtrå S 107 F13
Bjåsta S 107 E15
Bjela BIH 157 F10
Bjelajci BIH 157 D6
Bjelovar HR 149 E7
Bjerby DK 90 D7
Bjerge DK 87 D8
Bjerka N 108 D6
Bjerkvik N 111 C14
Bjerreby DK 86 F7
Bjerregrav DK 86 B5
Bjerringbro DK 86 C5
Bjøllånes N 108 C8
Bjoneroa N 95 A12
Bjønnes N 108 D7
Bjørbo S 97 B12
Björboholm S 91 D11
Bjordal N 94 E4
Bjørgen N 105 F9
Bjørgo N 101 D11
Bjørkåsen N 111 C17
Bjørkåsen N 111 D12
Björkberg S 103 C9
Björkberg S 107 B13
Björkberg S 118 C5
Björkboda FIN 126 E8
Björke S 93 C12
Björkeflåta N 95 B9
Bjørkelangen N 95 C15
Björkeset N 95 C15
Bjørkestrand N 114 C4
Björketorp S 91 E12
Björkfors S 119 C10
Björkheden S 109 E12
Björkhöjden S 107 E10
Björkholmen S 109 C17
Björkland S 109 F16
Björklia S 105 E9
Björklden S 111 D16
Björklinge S 99 B9
Björknäset S 107 F12
Björknäset S 107 F12
Björkö FIN 126 E4
Björköby FIN 122 D6
Björköby S 92 D5
Björkön S 103 B14
Björksele S 107 B15
Björksele S 107 B12
Björksjön S 107 E12
Björkstugan S 111 D13
Björkvik S 93 B9
Bjorli N 100 B8
Bjorn N 108 D4
Björna S 107 D15
Bjørnar N 111 C15
Bjørnbæt N 104 D7
Bjørnbo N 113 D11
Björnänge N 105 E14
Björnänge N 105 E14
Bjørnestad N 94 F5
Bjørneryd N 111 D19
Bjørnevatn N 114 D7
Bjørnfjell N 111 C15
Bishop's Castle GB 10 G6
Björnhult S 89 A10
Björnliden S 102 B3
Björnlunda S 93 A10
Björnrike S 102 B6
Björnsjö S 107 D14

Bjørnskinn N 111 B10
Bjørnstad N 105 B14
Bjørnstad N 114 D9
Björsarv S 103 B11
Björsäter S 92 C8
Björsbo S 103 C12
Björsjö S 97 B13
Bjugn N 104 D7
Bjurå S 118 B8
Bjuråker S 103 C12
Bjurberget S 97 A8
Bjurfors S 107 C17
Bjurfors S 118 E5
Bjurholm S 107 D16
Bjursås S 103 E9
Bjurselet S 118 E6
Bjurträsk S 107 B17
Bjuv S 87 C11
Blace MK 164 E3
Blace SRB 164 C3
Blachownia PL 143 E6
Black Bourton GB 13 B11
Black Bull IRL 7 F10
Blackburn GB 3 L12
Blackburn GB 5 D9
Blackburn GB 10 D7
Blackmoor Gate GB 13 C7
Blackpool GB 10 D5
Blackrock IRL 7 E10
Blackstad S 93 D8
Blacktown GB 7 C7
Blackwater IRL 9 D10
Blackwaterfoot GB 4 D6
Blackwood GB 13 B8
Bladel NL 16 F4
Blaenau Ffestiniog GB 10 F4
Blaenavon GB 13 B8
Blagaj BIH 157 F8
Blagaj Japra BIH 156 B5
Blagdon GB 13 C9
Blăgești RO 153 D9
Blăgești RO 153 E12
Blagnac F 33 C8
Blagoevgrad BG 165 E7
Blagoevo BG 166 C6
Blåhøj DK 86 D4
Blaibach D 75 D12
Blain F 23 F8
Blainville-sur-l'Eau F 186 D1
Blainville-sur-Mer F 23 B8
Blair Atholl GB 5 B9
Blairgowrie GB 5 B10
Blaiserives F 25 D12
Blaj RO 152 E3
Blajan F 33 D7
Blăjani RO 161 C9
Blăjel RO 152 E4
Blăjeni RO 151 E10
Blakeney GB 13 B10
Blakeney GB 15 B11
Blakstad N 90 C4
Blâmont F 27 C6
Blan F 33 C10
Blanca E 55 C10
Blancafort F 25 E8
Blancas E 47 C10
Blandford Forum GB 13 D10
Blandiana RO 151 F11
Blanes E 43 D9
Blaney GB 7 D7
Blangy-sur-Bresle F 18 E4
Blankaholm S 93 D9
Blankenberg D 83 C11
Blankenberge B 19 B7
Blankenburg (Harz) D 79 C8
Blankenfelde D 80 B4
Blankenhain D 79 E9
Blankenhain D 79 E11
Blankenheim D 21 D7
Blankenrath D 21 D8
Blankensee D 84 D4
Blankenstein D 75 B10
Blanquefort F 28 F4
Blans DK 86 F5
Blansko CZ 77 D11
Blanzac-Porcheresse F 28 E6
Blanzay F 29 C6
Blanzy F 30 B5
Blaricum NL 183 A6
Blarney IRL 8 E5
Blasimon F 28 F5
Blåsjöfallet S 105 B16
Blåsmark S 118 D6
Błaszki PL 142 C5
Blatec MK 164 F6
Blatets BG 167 D7
Blatna BIH 156 C5
Blatná CZ 76 D5
Blatné SK 146 E4
Blatnica BIH 157 D8
Blato HR 162 D2
Blaton B 182 D3
Blattniksele S 109 F14
Blaubeuren D 74 F6
Blaufelden D 74 D6
Blausasc F 37 D6
Blaustein D 187 E8
Blåvik S 92 C6
Blåviksjön S 107 B14
Blavozy F 30 E4
Blaye F 28 E4
Blaževo SRB 163 C10
Błażiny Górne PL 141 H4
Blāzma LV 134 B4
Blažovice CZ 77 D11
Błażowa PL 144 D5
Blázquez E 51 C9
Blažuj BIH 157 E9
Bleckåsen S 105 E15
Bleckede D 83 D9
Blecua E 42 C3
Bled SLO 73 D9
Błędowo PL 138 D6
Bledzew PL 81 A8
Blegny B 19 C12
Bléharies B 19 C7
Bleialf D 20 D6
Bleiburg A 73 C10
Bleicherode D 79 D8
Bleidenstadt D 185 D9
Bleik N 111 B10
Bleikvassli N 108 E6
Bleiswijk NL 182 A5
Blejești RO 161 E6
Blejoi RO 161 D8
Blekendorf D 83 B9
Bleket S 91 D10
Blender D 17 C12
Bléneau F 25 E8
Blénod-lès-Toul F 26 C4
Blenstrup DK 86 B6
Blentarp S 87 D13
Blera I 62 C2
Blérancourt F 19 E7
Bléré F 24 F4
Blerick NL 16 F6
Blesa E 42 E2
Bleskensgraaf NL 182 B5
Blesle F 30 E3
Blessington IRL 7 F9
Blet F 29 B11
Bletchley GB 15 D7
Blīdene LV 134 C5
Blidsberg S 91 D14
Blieskastel D 21 F8
Bligny F 25 D12
Bligny-sur-Ouche F 25 F12
Blikstorp S 91 C15
Bliksund N 90 C3
Blimea E 39 B8
Blindow D 84 D5
Blinja HR 149 F6
Blistrup DK 87 C10
Blixterboda S 97 D13
Blizanów PL 142 C5
Blížejov CZ 76 D3
Blížkovice CZ 77 E9
Bliznatsi BG 167 C9
Bliżyn PL 141 H3
Bllacë KS 163 E10
Blois F 24 E5
Blokhus DK 86 A5
Blokzijl NL 16 C5
Blombacka S 97 C10
Blomberg D 17 E12
Blome LV 135 B11
Blome LV 135 B13
Blomsøy N 108 E3
Blomstermåla S 89 B10
Błonie PL 141 F3
Błonie PL 143 B7
Blönsdorf D 79 C12
Blötberget S 97 B13
Blousson-Sérian F 33 D6
Blovice CZ 76 C5
Blowatz D 83 C11
Bloxham GB 13 A12
Bludenz A 71 C9
Bludov CZ 77 C11
Blue Ball IRL 7 F7
Blumau in Steiermark A 148 B6
Blumberg D 27 E10
Blumberg D 80 A5
Blumenhagen D 84 C5
Blumenholz D 84 D4
Blŭskovo BG 167 C8
Blyberg S 102 D7
Blyth GB 5 E13
Blyth GB 11 E9
Blyth Bridge GB 5 D10
Blyton GB 11 E10
Bø N 95 D10
Bø N 110 C8
Bo N 111 B10
Bø N 111 D12
Boada E 45 C8
Boadilla del Monte E 46 D5
Boadilla de Rioseco E 39 D10
Boal E 39 B6
Boalhosa P 38 E3
Boan MNE 163 D7
Boara Pisani I 66 B4
Boat of Garten GB 3 L9
Boa Vista P 44 E3
Boavista P 44 F2
Bobadilla E 53 B7
Bobâlna RO 152 C3
Bobbio I 37 B10
Bobbio Pellice I 31 F11
Bobenheim-Roxheim D 187 B5
Boberg S 107 E9
Boberka UA 145 E6
Bobicești RO 160 E4
Böbing D 71 B12
Bobingen D 71 A11
Bobitz D 83 C10
Bobivtsi UA 153 A7
Böblingen D 27 C11
Bobolice PL 85 C11
Boborás E 38 D3
Boboshevo BG 165 E7
Bobota HR 149 F11
Bobota RO 151 C10
Bobovdol BG 165 E7
Bobove UA 145 G6
Bobowa PL 144 D2
Bobowo PL 138 C6
Bobrov SK 147 C9
Bobrovec SK 147 C9
Bobrowice PL 81 C8
Bobrówko PL 85 E8
Bobrowniki PL 138 E6
Bobrowniki PL 140 D9
Bobryk-Druhyy UA 154 B6
Bocacara E 45 C8
Bocairent E 56 D3
Bočar SRB 150 F5
Bocchigliero I 61 E7
Boceguillas E 40 F4
Bocfölde H 149 C7
Bochnia PL 144 D1
Bocholt B 19 B12
Bocholt D 17 E7
Bochov CZ 76 B4
Bochum D 17 F8
Bockara S 89 A10
Bockenem D 79 B7
Bockenheim an der Weinstraße D 187 B5
Bockhammar S 97 C14
Bockhorn D 17 B10
Bockhorn D 75 F10
Bockhorst D 17 B9
Boćki PL 141 E8
Bocksjö S 92 B5
Bockträsk S 109 F15
Bocognano F 37 G10
Boconád H 150 B5
Bőcs H 145 G2
Bócsa H 150 D3
Bocșa RO 151 C10
Bocșa RO 159 C8
Bocsig RO 151 E8
Boczów PL 81 B7
Bod RO 153 F7
Böda S 89 A12
Boda S 103 A12
Boda S 103 D9
Boda bruk S 103 C12
Bodaczów PL 144 B7
Bodafors S 92 D5
Boda glasbruk S 89 B9
Bodajk H 149 B10
Bodåsgruvan S 98 B6
Bodbacka FIN 122 E6
Bodbyn S 122 B4
Boddam GB 3 F14
Boddam GB 3 L13
Boddin D 83 C10
Bodegraven NL 182 A5
Bodelshausen D 187 E6
Boden S 118 C7
Bodenfelde D 78 C6
Bodenham GB 13 A9
Bodenheim D 21 E10
Bodenkirchen D 75 F11
Bodenmais D 76 D4
Bodenteich D 83 E9
Bodenwerder D 78 C6
Bodenwöhr D 75 D11
Bodești RO 153 C8
Bodman D 27 E11
Bodmin GB 12 E5
Bodnegg D 71 B9
Bodø N 108 B7
Bodom N 105 D11
Bodonal de la Sierra E 51 C6
Bodoney GB 7 C8
Bodony H 147 F10
Bodroghalom H 145 G4
Bodrogkisfalud H 145 G3
Bodrum TR 177 E9
Bodsjö S 102 A8
Bodsjöbyn S 102 A8
Bodträskfors S 118 B5
Bódvaszilas H 145 F2
Bodyke IRL 8 C5
Bodzanów PL 139 E9
Bodzanów PL 142 F3
Bodzentyn PL 143 E10
Boé F 33 B7
Boechout B 19 B9
Boecillo E 39 E10
Boekel NL 16 E5
Boekhoute B 182 C3
Boën F 30 D5
Boeslunde DK 87 E8
Boeza E 39 C7
Boffres F 30 F6
Boffzen D 21 A12
Boftsa N 113 C21
Bogács H 145 H2
Bogajo E 45 C7
Bogarra E 55 B8
Bogați RO 160 D6
Bogatić SRB 158 D4
Bogatići BIH 157 E9
Bogatynia PL 81 E7
Boğaziçi TR 177 C10
Bogda RO 151 F8
Bogdan BG 165 D10
Bogdana RO 153 D11
Bogdana RO 160 F6
Bogdanci MK 169 B8
Bogdand RO 151 C10
Bogdănești RO 153 E9
Bogdănești RO 154 E2
Bogdaniec PL 85 E8
Bogdănița RO 153 E11
Bogdan Vodă RO 152 B4
Boge S 93 D13
Bogen D 75 E12
Bogen N 105 A11
Bogen N 111 C12
Bogense DK 86 D6
Boggsjö S 106 E8
Boghești RO 153 E10
Bogilice BIH 158 F3
Bogliasco I 37 C10
Bognanco I 68 A5
Bognelv N 112 C9
Bognes N 111 D11
Bogniebrae GB 3 L11
Bognor Regis GB 15 F7
Bogny-sur-Meuse F 184 E2
Bogø DK 87 F10
Bogodol BIH 157 F8
Bogojevo SRB 157 A11
Bogomilovo BG 166 E5
Bogoria PL 143 E11
Bogorojca MK 169 B8
Bogovina SRB 159 F8
Bogovinje MK 163 F10
Bogovy N 110 E9
Bograngen S 102 E4
Boguchwała PL 144 D4
Bogumiłowice PL 143 D7
Boguszów-Gorce PL 81 E10
Boguty-Pianki PL 141 E6
Bogyiszló H 149 D11
Bohain-en-Vermandois F 19 E7
Bohars F 22 D3
Bohdalov CZ 77 D9
Bohdan UA 152 A4
Bohdíkov CZ 77 B11
Boherboy IRL 8 D4
Boherbue IRL 8 D4
Bohinjska Bistrica SLO 73 D8
Böhl D 187 C5
Böhlen D 79 D11
Böhme D 82 E6
Bohmte D 17 D10
Böhne D 79 A11
Bohola IRL 6 E4
Bohonal de Ibor E 45 E10
Böhönye H 149 D8
Bohoyo E 45 D10
Bohumín CZ 146 B6
Bohuňovice CZ 146 B4
Bohuslavice CZ 146 B6
Bohutín CZ 76 C5
Boianu Mare RO 151 C10
Boiro de Arriba E 38 C2
Boiscommun F 25 D7
Bois-d'Amont F 31 B9
Boisgervilly F 23 D7
Bois-Guillaume F 18 F3
Boișoara RO 160 C4
Boisset-et-Gaujac F 35 B7
Boissezon F 33 C10
Boitzenburg D 84 D5
Boiu Mare RO 152 C3
Boizenburg D 83 D9
Bojadła PL 81 C9
Bojano I 63 E6
Bojanów PL 144 C4
Bojanowo PL 81 C11
Bøjden DK 86 E6
Bojkovice CZ 146 C5
Bojná SK 146 D6
Bojnice SK 147 D7
Bojničky SK 146 E5
Bojnik SRB 164 C4
Bojszów PL 142 F5
Bojszowy PL 143 F7
Boka SRB 159 C6
Bokel D 17 B11
Böklund D 82 A7
Bokod H 149 A10
Bököny H 151 B8
Bokšić HR 149 E10
Boksjön S 109 E10
Bol HR 156 F6
Bölan S 103 D12
Bolanden D 186 B5
Bolandoz F 31 A9
Bolaños de Calatrava E 54 B5
Bolătău RO 153 D8
Bolayir TR 173 C6
Bolbaite E 56 C3
Bolbec F 18 E1
Bolboși RO 159 D11
Bölcske H 150 D2
Boldekow D 84 C5
Bolderslev DK 86 F4
Boldești-Grădiștea RO 161 D9
Boldești-Scăeni RO 161 C8
Boldog H 150 B4
Boldogkőváralja H 145 G3
Boldre GB 13 D11
Boldu RO 161 C10
Boldur RO 159 B8
Boldva H 145 G2
Böle S 99 B9
Böle S 102 B7
Böle S 105 D14
Böle S 105 E15
Böle S 118 C8
Böle S 118 D6
Bolea E 41 D10
Bolekhiv UA 145 E8
Boleráz SK 146 E5
Bolesław PL 143 F7
Bolesław PL 143 F10
Bolesławiec PL 81 D9
Bolesławiec PL 142 D5
Boleszkowice PL 84 E7
Bolga N 108 C5
Bolgatovo RUS 133 C5
Bolhan UA 154 A3
Bolhrad UA 155 B3
Boliden S 118 E4
Bolimów PL 141 F2
Bolintin-Deal RO 161 E7
Bolintin-Vale RO 161 E7
Boliqueime P 50 E3
Boljanić BIH 157 C9
Boljanići MNE 163 C7
Boljevac SRB 159 F8
Boljevci SRB 158 D5
Bölkow D 83 B11
Bolków PL 81 E10
Boll D 74 E6
Bollebygd S 91 D12
Bollène F 35 B8
Bollengo I 68 C4
Bollermoen N 108 D6
Bolligen CH 31 B11
Bolling DK 86 D3
Bollingstedt D 82 A6
Bollnäs S 103 D11
Bollsbyn S 91 A12
Bollstabruk S 107 E13
Bollullos Par del Condado E 51 E6
Bolnes NL 182 B5
Bolnhurst GB 15 C8
Bologna I 66 D3
Bologne F 26 D3
Bolognetta I 58 D3
Bolognola I 62 B4
Bolotana I 64 C2
Bolotești RO 153 F10
Bolsena I 62 B1
Bol'shakovo RUS 136 D4
Bolsover GB 11 E9
Bolsward NL 16 B5
Bolszewo PL 138 A5
Boltaña E 33 F6
Boltåsen N 111 C12
Boltenhagen, Ostseebad D 83 C10
Boltigen CH 31 B11
Bolton GB 5 D11
Bolton GB 11 D7
Bölüntü TR 181 A7
Bolvașnița RO 159 C9
Bolventor GB 12 D5
Bóly H 149 E11
Bolyarovo BG 167 E7
Bolzano I 72 D3
Bomal B 19 D12
Bomba I 63 C6
Bombarral P 44 F2
Bomlitz D 82 E7
Bompas F 34 E4
Bompensiere I 58 E4
Bompietro I 58 D5
Bomporto I 66 C3
Bomsund S 107 E9
Bona F 30 A3
Bonaduz CH 71 D8
Bonakas N 113 C21
Bönan S 103 E13
Bonanza E 52 C4
Boñar E 39 C9
Bonar Bridge GB 3 K8
Bonarcado I 64 C2
Bonares E 51 E6
Bonäs S 102 D7
Bonäset S 106 D8
Bönäset S 107 E15
Bonassola I 37 C11
Bonawe GB 4 C6
Bonboillon F 26 F4
Bonchamp-lès-Laval F 23 D10
Bonchester Bridge GB 5 E11
Boncourt CH 27 F7
Bondeno I 66 C3
Bondersbyn S 119 C9
Bonderup DK 86 A4
Bondorf D 187 D6
Bondsjö S 103 A14
Bondues F 182 D2
Bönebüttel D 83 B8
Bonefro I 63 D7
Bönen D 17 E9
Bo'ness GB 5 C9
Bonete E 55 B10
Bönhamn S 103 A15
Bonheiden B 19 B10
Boniches E 47 E9
Boniewo PL 138 F6
Bonifacio F 37 J10
Bonifati I 60 D5
Bönigen CH 70 D5
Bonin PL 85 B10
Bonn D 21 C8
Bonnåsjøen N 109 A10
Bonnat F 29 C9
Bonndorf im Schwarzwald D 27 E9
Bønnerup Strand DK 87 B7
Bonnes N 111 C15
Bonnet DK 86 B2
Bonnétable F 24 D3
Bonneuil-Matours F 29 B7
Bonneval F 24 D5
Bonneval F 31 D10
Bonneval-sur-Arc F 31 E11
Bonnevaux F 31 B9
Bonneville F 31 C9
Bonnieux F 35 C9
Bönnigheim D 27 B11
Bonnyrigg GB 5 D10
Bonny-sur-Loire F 25 E8
Bono F 22 E6
Bono I 64 C3
Bonorva I 64 C2
Bons-en-Chablais F 31 C9
Bonson F 30 D5
Bonțida RO 152 D3
Bőny H 149 A9
Bonyhád H 149 D11
Boo S 99 D10
Boock D 84 D6
Boom B 19 B9
Boortmeerbeek B 19 C10
Boos F 18 F3
Boostedt D 83 B8
Bootle GB 10 E6
Bopfingen D 75 E7
Boppard D 21 D9
Bor CZ 75 C12
Bor S 88 A6
Bor SRB 159 E9
Borač SRB 158 F6
Borås S 91 D12
Borăscu RO 160 D2
Borba P 50 B5
Borbjerg DK 86 C3
Borca RO 153 C7
Borča SRB 158 D5
Borcea RO 155 E1
Borchen D 17 E11
Borci BIH 157 C7
Borci BIH 157 E9
Börcs H 149 A9
Borculo NL 17 D7
Bordalba E 41 F7
Bordány H 150 E4
Bordeaux F 28 F4
Bordeira P 50 E2
Bordei Verde RO 161 C11
Bordelum D 82 A5
Bordères-Louron F 33 E6
Bordères-sur-l'Échez F 33 D6
Bordes F 32 D5
Bordes F 33 D6
Bordesholm D 83 B8
Bordești RO 161 B10
Bordighera I 37 D7
Bordils E 43 C9
Bording DK 86 C4
Bordón E 42 F3
Bordușani RO 155 E1
Bore I 69 D8
Boreham GB 15 D10
Borehamwood GB 15 D8
Borek PL 143 F10
Borek Strzeliński PL 81 E12
Borek Wielkopolski PL 81 C12
Boreland GB 5 E10
Børelva N 108 B8
Borensberg S 92 B6
Borg D 20 E6
Borgå FIN 127 E14
Borgafjäll S 106 B8
Borgentreich D 17 E12
Börger D 17 C9
Borger NL 17 C7
Borggård S 92 B7
Borghamn S 92 C5
Borgheim N 90 A7
Borghetto d'Arroscia I 37 C7
Borghetto di Borbera I 37 B9
Borghetto di Vara I 69 E8
Borghetto Santo Spirito I 37 C8
Borgholm S 89 B11
Borgholzhausen D 17 D10
Borgia I 59 B10
Borgloon B 19 C11
Børglum DK 90 E6
Borgo F 37 F10
Borgo a Mozzano I 66 E2
Borgo d'Ale I 68 C5
Borgoforte I 66 B2
Borgofranco d'Ivrea I 68 B4
Borgo Grappa I 61 C10
Borgo-lavezzaro I 68 C6
Borgomanero I 68 B5
Borgomaro I 37 D7
Borgone Susa I 31 E11
Borgonovo Val Tidone I 69 C7
Borgo Pace I 66 E5
Borgorose I 62 C4
Borgo San Dalmazzo I 37 C6
Borgo San Lorenzo I 66 E3
Borgo San Martino I 68 C6
Borgosesia I 68 B5
Borgo Tossignano I 66 D4
Borgo Val di Taro I 69 E8
Borgo Valsugana I 72 D3
Borgo Velino I 62 C4
Borgo Vercelli I 68 C5
Borgsjö S 103 A10
Borgsjö S 107 C13
Borgstedt D 82 B7
Borgstena S 91 D13
Borgue GB 5 F8
Borgvattnet S 107 E9
Borhaug N 94 F5
Boriaeva BG 171 B7
Borike BIH 157 E11
Borino BG 165 F9
Bořitov CZ 77 D11
Borja E 41 E8
Borjabad E 41 E7
Borjana SLO 73 D7
Borjelslandet S 118 C8
Borkan S 106 A8
Borkavichy BY 133 E4
Borken D 17 E7
Borken (Hessen) D 21 B12
Borkenes N 111 C11
Borki PL 141 G7
Borki PL 143 D9
Børkop DK 86 D5
Borkowice PL 141 H3
Borkowo PL 139 D12
Borkum D 17 A7
Borlänge S 97 B13
Borlești RO 153 D9
Bormani LV 135 C10
Børmarka N 104 C8
Bormio I 71 E10
Born D 79 B9
Born NL 183 C7
Borna D 79 D12
Borna D 80 D4
Born am Darß D 83 B13
Borne NL 17 D7
Bornem B 19 B9
Bornerbroek NL 17 D7
Bornes P 39 F6
Bornes de Aguiar P 38 E4
Borne Sulinowo PL 85 C11
Bornheim D 21 C7
Bornhofen D 21 D9
Bornhöved D 83 B8
Bornich D 185 D8
Bornos E 51 F8
Bornova TR 177 C9
Börnsen D 83 D8
Boroaia RO 153 C8
Borobia E 41 E8
Borod RO 151 D10
Borodino UA 154 E4
Borodinskoye RUS 129 C11
Borohrádek CZ 77 B10
Borojevići BIH 157 F8
Boronów PL 143 E6
Borore I 64 C2
Boroșneu Mare RO 153 F8
Boroszów PL 142 E5
Borota H 150 E3
Boroughbridge GB 11 C9
Borovan BG 165 C8
Borovany CZ 77 E7
Borov Dol BG 166 D6
Borovets BG 165 E8
Borovik HR 149 F10
Borovitsa BG 165 B6
Borovka LV 133 E1
Borovnica BIH 157 D9
Borovnica SLO 73 E9
Borovo BG 166 C5
Borovo Selo HR 157 B10
Borovtsi BG 165 C7
Borów PL 81 E11
Borów PL 144 B4
Borowa PL 143 F11
Borowie PL 141 G5
Borox E 46 D5
Borrby S 88 E6
Borre DK 87 F10
Borre N 95 D12
Borrentin D 84 C3
Borrèze F 29 F8
Borriol E 48 D4
Borris DK 86 D3
Borris IRL 9 C9
Borris-in-Ossory IRL 9 C7
Borrisokane IRL 6 G6
Borrisoleigh IRL 9 C7
Borrowdale GB 10 B5
Børrud N 96 B7
Börrum S 93 C9
Borș RO 151 C8
Børsa N 104 E8
Borșa RO 152 B5
Borșa RO 152 D3
Borša SK 145 G4
Borsbeek B 19 B10
Borsec RO 153 D7
Børselv N 113 C16
Borsh AL 168 D2
Borshchi UA 154 B5
Borshchovychi UA 144 D9
Boršice u Buchlovic CZ 146 C4
Borsio GR 174 D3
Borský Svätý Jur SK 77 E12
Borsodbóta H 145 G1
Borsodnádasd H 145 G1
Borsodszentgyörgy H 145 G1
Borsodszirák H 145 G2
Borsosberény H 147 F8
Borssele NL 182 C3
Borstel D 17 C11
Borth GB 10 G3
Bortigali I 64 C2
Bortigiadas I 64 B3
Bort-les-Orgues F 29 E10
Börtnan S 102 A6
Bortnen N 100 C2
Borum DK 86 C6
Borup DK 87 E9
Borve GB 2 L4
Borynya UA 145 E6
Boryslav UA 145 E7
Borzęciczki PL 81 C12
Borzonasca I 37 C10
Borzytuchom PL 85 B12
Bosa I 64 C2
Bošáca SK 146 D5
Bosa Marina I 64 C1
Bosanci RO 153 B8
Bosanska Rača BIH 158 D3
Bosanska Dubica BIH 157 B6
Bosanska Gradiška BIH 157 B7
Bosanska Kostajnica BIH 156 B6
Bosanska Krupa BIH 156 C5
Bosanski Brod BIH 157 B9
Bosanski Kobas BIH 157 B8
Bosanski Novi BIH 156 B5
Bosanski Petrovac BIH 156 C5
Bosanski Šamac BIH 157 B9
Bosansko Grahovo BIH 156 D5
Bošany SK 146 D6
Bősárkány H 149 A8
Bosau D 83 B8
Boscastle GB 12 D5
Bosco I 66 F5
Bosco Chiesanuova I 69 B11
Bosco Marengo I 37 B9
Boscotrecase I 60 B2
Bösdorf D 83 B8
Bösebo S 89 A9
Bösel D 17 B9
Boshulya BG 165 E9
Bosia RO 153 C11
Bosilegrad SRB 164 E5
Bosiljevo HR 148 F4
Boskoop NL 16 D3
Boskovice CZ 77 D11
Bošnjace SRB 164 D4
Bošnjaci HR 157 B10
Bošnjane SRB 159 F7
Bošnjane SRB 159 F7
Boșorod RO 159 B11
Bössbod S 102 D7
Bosset F 29 F6
Bossolasco I 37 B8
Bòssost E 33 E7
Bostad N 110 D6
Bostan BIH 157 F7
Bøstølen N 100 B6
Boston GB 11 F11
Boston Spa GB 11 D9
Bostrak N 90 A4
Bosundet S 107 C10
Botão P 44 D4
Boteå S 107 E13
Boteni RO 160 C6
Botesdale GB 15 C11
Botești RO 153 C9
Botești RO 160 C6
Botevgrad BG 165 D8
Botevo BG 167 C9
Bothel GB 5 F10
Boticas P 38 E4
Botiz RO 151 B10
Botiza RO 152 B4
Botn N 110 E9
Botn N 111 A18
Botn N 112 D4
Botngård N 104 D7
Botnhamn N 111 A14
Botoroaga RO 161 E7
Botorrita E 41 E9
Botoš SRB 158 C6
Botoșana RO 153 B7
Botoșani RO 153 B9
Botoșești-Paia RO 159 E11
Botricello I 61 F7
Bötsle S 103 A14
Botsmark S 118 F4
Bottendorf (Burgwald) D 21 B11
Bottesford GB 11 D10
Bottidda I 64 C3
Bottnaryd S 91 D14
Bottrop D 17 E7
Botun MK 168 B4
Bötzingen D 27 D8
Bouafles F 24 B5
Boucau F 32 C3
Bouc-Bel-Air F 35 D9
Boucé F 23 C11
Bouchain F 19 D7
Bouchemaine F 23 F10
Bouchoir F 18 E6
Boudry CH 31 B10
Boué F 19 D8
Bouglon F 33 B6
Bouguenais F 23 F8
Bouillargues F 35 C7
Bouillon B 19 E11
Bouilly F 25 D10
Bouin F 28 B1
Boujailles F 31 B9
Boujan-sur-Libron F 34 D5
Boulay-Moselle F 26 B5
Boulazac F 29 E7
Boulbon F 35 C8
Bouligny F 19 F12
Bouloc F 33 C8
Boulogne-Billancourt F 25 C7
Boulogne-sur-Gesse F 33 D7
Boulogne-sur-Mer F 15 F12
Bouloire F 24 E4
Boulouris F 36 E5
Boult-aux-Bois F 19 F10
Boulzicourt F 19 E10
Bouniagues F 29 F7
Bøur FO 2 A2
Bourbon-Lancy F 30 B4
Bourbon-l'Archambault F 30 B3
Bourbonne-les-Bains F 26 E4
Bourbourg F 18 C5
Bourbriac F 22 D5
Bourcefranc-le-Chapus F 28 D3
Bourdeaux F 35 A9
Bourdeilles F 29 E7
Bourdonnay F 27 C6
Bouresse F 29 C7
Bourg F 28 E4
Bourg-Achard F 18 F2
Bourganeuf F 29 D9
Bourg-Argental F 30 E6
Bourg-de-Péage F 31 E7
Bourg-de-Thizy F 30 C5
Bourg-de-Visa F 33 B7
Bourg-Dun F 18 E2
Bourg-en-Bresse F 31 C7
Bourges F 29 A10
Bourg-et-Comin F 19 F8
Bourg-Lastic F 29 D11
Bourg-lès-Valence F 30 F6
Bourgneuf-en-Mauges F 23 F10
Bourgneuf-en-Retz F 28 A2
Bourgogne F 19 F9
Bourgoin-Jallieu F 31 D7
Bourg-St-Andéol F 35 B8
Bourg-St-Bernard F 33 C9
Bourg-St-Maurice F 31 D10
Bourgtheroulde-Infreville F 18 F2
Bourguébus F 23 B11
Bourgueil F 23 F12
Bourmont F 26 D4
Bourne GB 11 F11
Bournemouth GB 13 D11
Bournezeau F 28 B3
Bourran F 33 B6
Bourriot-Bergonce F 32 B5
Bourron-Marlotte F 25 D8
Bourscheid L 184 E5
Bourtange NL 17 B8
Bourton GB 13 C10
Boussac F 29 C10
Bousse F 186 C1
Boussens F 33 D7
Boussières F 26 F4
Boussois F 19 D9
Boussu B 19 D8
Boutersem B 19 C10
Bouveret CH 31 C10
Bouvières F 35 A9
Bouvron F 23 F8
Bouxières-aux-Dames F 26 C5
Bouxwiller F 27 C7
Bouy F 25 B11
Bouzonville F 21 F7
Bouzov CZ 77 C11
Bova I 59 C8
Bøvær N 111 B13
Bovalino I 59 C9
Bovallstrand S 91 C9
Bova Marina I 59 D8
Bovan SRB 159 F8
Bovec SLO 73 D8
Bóveda E 38 C5
Boveda E 40 C5
Bovegno I 69 B9
Bovenden D 78 C6
Bøverfjord N 104 E5
Boves F 18 E5
Boves I 37 C7
Bovigny B 20 D5
Boviken S 118 E6

Boville Ernica I 62 D4
Bovino I 60 A4
Bøvlingbjerg DK 86 C2
Bovolone I 66 B3
Bovrup DK 86 F5
Bow GB 3 H10
Bowes GB 11 B7
Bowmore GB 4 D4
Box FIN 127 E13
Boxberg D 81 D7
Boxberg D 187 C8
Boxdorf D 80 D5
Boxholm S 92 C6
Boxmeer NL 16 E5
Boxtel NL 16 E4
Boyadzhik BG 166 E6
Boyanovo BG 167 E7
Boychinovtsi BG 165 C7
Boykovo BG 165 E10
Boyle IRL 6 E6
Bøylefoss N 90 B4
Boynes F 25 D7
Boynitsa BG 159 F10
Bøyum N 100 D5
Božava HR 67 D10
Bozburun TR 181 C8
Bozeat GB 15 C7
Bozel F 31 E10
Boževac SRB 159 D7
Bożewo PL 139 E8
Bozhentsi BG 166 D4
Bozhurishte BG 165 D7
Božica SRB 164 D5
Božíce CZ 77 E10
Bozieni MD 154 D3
Bozieni RO 153 D10
Bozioru RO 161 C8
Božjakovina HR 148 E6
Bozlar TR 173 D7
Bozouls F 34 B4
Bozovici RO 159 D9
Bozveliysko BG 167 C8
Bozzolo I 66 B1
Bra I 37 B7
Braås S 89 A8
Bråbo S 89 A10
Brabova RO 160 E2
Bracadale GB 2 L4
Bracciano I 62 C2
Brach F 28 E4
Brachbach D 185 C8
Bracieux F 24 E6
Bräcke S 103 A9
Brackenheim D 27 B11
Brackley GB 13 A12
Bracknagh IRL 7 F8
Bracknell GB 15 E7
Braco GB 5 C9
Brad RO 151 E10
Bradashesh AL 168 B3
Brădeanu RO 161 D9
Brădeni RO 152 E5
Brădești RO 152 E6
Brădești RO 160 E3
Bradford GB 11 D8
Bradford-on-Avon GB 13 C10
Bradpole GB 13 D9
Bradu RO 160 D5
Brădulеț RO 160 C5
Brăduț RO 153 E7
Bradwell GB 15 B12
Bradwell Waterside GB 15 D10
Brae GB 3 E14
Brædstrup DK 86 D5
Braehead of Lunan GB 5 B11
Braemar GB 5 A10
Brăești RO 153 B8
Brăești RO 153 C10
Brăești RO 161 C9
Bràfim E 43 E6
Braga P 38 E3
Bragadiru RO 161 E7
Bragadiru RO 161 F7
Bragança P 39 E6
Bragar GB 2 J3
Brăhășești RO 153 E10
Brahlstorf D 83 D9
Brăila RO 155 C1
Brailsford GB 11 F8
Braine F 19 F8
Braine-l'Alleud B 19 C9
Braine-le-Comte B 19 C9
Braintree GB 15 D10
Braives B 19 C11
Brajkoviči BIH 157 D8
Brake (Unterweser) D 17 B10
Brakel B 19 C8
Brakel D 17 E12
Bräkne-Hoby S 89 C8
Brålanda S 91 B11
Bralin PL 142 D4
Brallo di Pregola I 37 B10
Bralos GR 174 B5
Braloștița RO 160 D3
Bram F 33 D10
Bramans F 31 E10
Bramberg am Wildkogel A 72 B5
Bramdrupdam DK 86 D4
Bramming DK 86 E3
Brampton GB 5 F11
Brampton GB 15 C12
Bramsche D 17 D8
Bramsche D 17 D10
Bramstedt D 17 B11
Bran RO 160 B6
Brånaberg S 109 E11
Branäs S 102 E4
Brancaleone I 59 D9
Brancaster GB 15 B10
Brânceni RO 160 F6
Brâncovenești RO 152 D5
Brâncoveni RO 160 E4
Brand A 71 C9
Brand D 75 C10
Brandal N 100 B4
Brändåsen S 102 B4
Brändbo S 103 B11
Brandbu N 95 B13
Brande DK 86 D4
Brande-Hörnerkirchen D 82 C7
Brandenberg A 72 B4
Brandenburg D 79 B12
Brand-Erbisdorf D 80 E4
Branderup DK 86 E4
Brandesburton GB 11 D11
Brandis D 80 C4
Brand-Nagelberg A 77 E8
Brando F 37 F10
Brändö FIN 126 E5
Brandon GB 15 C10
Brändön S 118 C8
Brändövik FIN 122 D6
Brandshagen D 84 B4
Brandstorp S 92 C4
Brandsvoll N 90 C2
Brandval N 96 B7
Brandvoll N 111 C15
Brandýs nad Labem-Stará Boleslav CZ 77 B7
Brandýs nad Orlicí CZ 77 B10
Branes N 96 A6
Brănești MD 154 C3
Brănești RO 160 C6
Brănești RO 160 D2
Brănești RO 161 E8
Branice PL 142 F4
Braniewo PL 139 B8
Branik SLO 73 E8
Brănișca RO 151 F10
Braniștea RO 152 C4
Braniștea RO 155 C1
Braniștea RO 161 D7
Brankas LV 134 C7
Bränna S 91 B11
Brännåker S 107 B9
Brännås S 103 B11
Brännberg S 118 C6
Branne F 28 F5
Brännland S 107 D16
Brännland S 122 C4
Brañosera E 40 C3
Brańsk PL 141 E7
Branston GB 11 E11
Brańszczyk PL 139 E12
Brantevik S 88 D6
Brantice CZ 142 F4
Brantôme F 29 E7
Branzi I 69 A8
Braojos E 46 B5
Braone I 69 B9
Braskereidfoss N 101 E15
Braslaw BY 133 E2
Brașov RO 161 B7
Brassac F 33 C10
Brasschaat B 16 F2
Brassy F 25 F10
Brasta S 105 E16
Brastad S 91 C10
Brastavățu RO 160 F4
Břasy CZ 76 C5
Brataj AL 168 D2
Bratca RO 151 D10
Bråte N 95 C14
Brateiu RO 152 E4
Brateljevici BIH 157 D10
Brateș RO 153 F8
Bratislava SK 77 F12
Bratkowice PL 144 C4
Bratovoești RO 160 E3
Bratsigovo BG 165 E9
Brattåker S 107 A11
Brattbäcken S 107 C9
Bratten S 107 B14
Brattfors S 103 E12
Brattfors S 107 D17
Brattli N 114 D7
Brattmon S 102 E4
Bratton GB 13 C10
Brattsbacka S 107 D16
Brattsele S 107 D12
Brattset N 104 E5
Brattvåg N 100 A4
Bratunac BIH 158 E3
Brătușeni MD 153 A10
Bratya Daskalovi BG 166 E4
Braubach D 21 D9
Braud-et-St-Louis F 28 E4
Braunau am Inn A 76 F4
Brauneberg D 185 E6
Braunfels D 21 C10
Braunlage D 79 C8
Bräunlingen D 27 E9
Braunsbach D 187 C8
Braunsbedra D 79 D10
Braunschweig D 79 B8
Braunton GB 12 C6
Bravicea MD 154 C2
Bravnica BIH 157 D7
Bray IRL 7 F10
Bray-sur-Seine F 25 D9
Bray-sur-Somme F 18 E6
Brazatortas E 54 B4
Brazey-en-Plaine F 26 F3
Brazi RO 161 D8
Brazii RO 151 E9
Brazii RO 161 D8
Brbinj HR 67 D11
Brčigovo BIH 157 E11
Brčko BIH 157 C10
Brdów PL 138 F6
Bré IRL 7 F10
Brea E 41 E8
Brea de Tajo E 47 D6
Breaghva IRL 8 C3
Breascleit GB 2 J3
Breasta RO 160 E3
Breaza RO 152 B6
Breaza RO 152 D5
Breaza RO 161 C7
Breaza RO 161 C9
Brebeni RO 160 E4
Brebu RO 159 C8
Brebu RO 161 C7
Brebu Nou RO 159 C9
Brécey F 23 C9
Brech F 22 E6
Brechfa GB 12 B6
Brechin GB 5 B11
Brecht B 16 F3
Breckerfeld D 185 B7
Břeclav CZ 77 E11
Brecon GB 13 B8
Breda E 43 D9
Breda NL 16 E3
Bredared S 91 D12
Bredaryd S 87 A13
Bredbyn S 107 E14
Breddenberg D 17 C9
Breddin D 83 E12
Bredebro DK 86 E3
Bredene B 18 B6
Bredereiche D 84 D4
Bredevoort NL 17 E7
Bredkälen S 106 D8
Bredsätra S 89 B11
Bredsel S 118 C4
Bredsjö S 97 C12
Bredsjön S 103 A13
Bredstedt D 82 A5
Bredsten DK 86 D4
Bredträsk S 107 D15
Bredvik S 107 D17
Bredviken S 108 D8
Bredviken S 119 C10
Bree B 19 B12
Breese D 83 D11
Bregana HR 148 E5
Breganze I 72 E4
Bregare BG 165 B9
Bregeni MD 153 B12
Bregenz A 71 B9
Breg-Lum AL 163 E9
Breg-Lum AL 168 B2
Bregninge DK 86 F6
Bregovo BG 159 E10
Breguzzo I 69 B10
Bréhal F 23 C8
Bréhan F 22 D6
Brehna D 79 C11
Breidenbach D 21 C10
Breidenbach F 27 B7
Breidstrand N 111 C12
Breidvik N 108 B9
Breidvik N 110 C8
Breidvik N 110 E9
Breidvik N 111 D11
Breiholz D 82 B7
Breil CH 71 D8
Breil-sur-Roya F 37 D7
Breisach am Rhein D 27 D8
Breistein N 94 B2
Breitenbach CH 27 F8
Breitenbach D 21 F8
Breitenbach (Schauenburg) D 17 F12
Breitenbach am Herzberg D 78 E6
Breitenbach am Inn A 72 B4
Breitenberg D 76 E5
Breitenbrunn D 75 D10
Breitenburg D 82 C7
Breitenfelde D 83 C9
Breitengüßbach D 75 C8
Breitenhagen D 79 C10
Breitnau D 27 E9
Breitscheid D 183 C9
Breitscheid D 185 C7
Breitscheid D 185 C9
Breitungen D 79 E7
Breivik N 111 C12
Breivik N 112 B9
Breivikbotn N 112 B9
Breivikeidet N 111 A18
Brejning DK 86 D5
Brekka N 108 B9
Brekken N 101 A15
Brekken N 108 E5
Brekkestø N 90 C3
Brekkhus N 100 E4
Brekkvasseiv N 105 B14
Breklum D 82 A5
Brekovo SRB 158 F5
Breksillan N 105 B10
Brekstad N 104 D7
Brélès F 22 D2
Brelingen (Wedemark) D 78 A6
Bremdal DK 86 B3
Bremen D 17 B11
Bremerhaven D 17 A11
Bremervörde D 17 B12
Bremgarten CH 27 F9
Bremm D 21 D8
Bremnes N 94 C2
Bremnes N 110 C9
Brem-sur-Mer F 28 B2
Brenderup DK 86 E5
Brenes E 51 D8
Brenguļi LV 131 F11
Brenitsa BG 165 C9
Brenna N 108 F5
Brenna N 110 D7
Brenna PL 147 B7
Brennero I 72 C4
Brennes N 112 D5
Brennfjell N 112 E5
Brenngam N 113 B19
Brennhaug N 101 C10
Brennmo N 105 E11
Brennsvik N 113 B13
Breno I 69 B9
Brénod F 31 C8
Brens F 33 C9
Brensbach D 187 B6
Brent Knoll GB 13 C9
Brentwood GB 15 D9
Brenzone I 69 B10
Bresalc KS 164 E3
Brescello I 66 C2
Brescia I 66 A1
Breskens NL 16 F1
Bresnica SRB 158 F6
Bressana Bottarone I 69 C7
Bressanone I 72 C4
Bressols F 33 C8
Bressuire F 28 B5
Brest BG 160 F5
Brest BY 141 F9
Brest F 22 D3
Brestak BG 167 C9
Brestanica SLO 148 E4
Bresternica SLO 148 C5
Brestova HR 67 B9
Brestovac SRB 159 E9
Brestovac SRB 164 C4
Brestovac Požeški HR 149 F9
Brestovăț RO 151 F8
Brestovene BG 161 F9
Brestovets BG 165 C10
Brestovitsa BG 165 E10
Bretagne-d'Armagnac F 33 C6
Brețcu RO 153 E8
Bretea Română RO 159 B11
Breteil F 23 D8
Bretenoux F 29 F9
Breteuil F 18 E5
Breteuil F 24 C4
Brétignolles-sur-Mer F 28 B2
Bretnig D 80 D6
Bretocino E 39 E8
Bretoncelles F 24 D4
Bretten D 27 B10
Bretton GB 10 E6
Brettville-sur-Laize F 23 B11
Bretzenheim D 185 E8
Bretzfeld D 187 C7
Breuberg-Neustadt D 21 E12
Breuches F 26 E5
Breugel NL 183 B7
Breuil-Cervinia I 68 B4
Breuil-Magné F 28 D4
Breuilpont F 24 C5
Breukelen NL 16 D4
Breum DK 86 B4
Breuna D 17 F12
Breuvannes-en-Bassigny F 26 D4
Brevens bruk S 92 A7
Brevik N 90 A6
Brevik S 92 C4
Brevik S 93 A12
Brevik S 99 D10
Breviken S 96 D7
Brevörde D 78 C5
Breza BIH 157 D9
Breza SK 147 C8
Brežđe SRB 158 E5
Breze SLO 148 D4
Brezhani BG 165 F7
Březí CZ 77 E11
Brezičani BIH 157 B6
Brežice SLO 148 E5
Brezna SRB 163 B10
Breznica HR 148 D6
Breznica SK 145 E4
Březnice CZ 76 C5
Breznik BG 165 D6
Breznița-Motru RO 159 D11
Breznița-Ocol RO 159 D10
Breznitsa BG 165 F8
Březno CZ 76 B4
Brezno SK 147 D9
Brezoaele RO 161 D7
Brézolles F 24 C5
Březolupy CZ 146 C5
Březová CZ 146 D5
Březová nad Svitavou CZ 77 C11
Brezová pod Bradlom SK 146 D5
Brezovica SK 145 E2
Brezovica SK 147 C9
Brezovica SLO 73 D9
Brezovo BG 166 E4
Brezovo Polje BIH 157 C10
Brezovo Polje HR 156 B5
Briançon F 31 F10
Briare F 25 E8
Briatexte F 33 C9
Briceni MD 153 A10
Bricherasio I 31 F11
Bricon F 26 D2
Bricquebec F 23 B8
Brides-les-Bains F 31 E10
Brideswell IRL 6 F6
Bridgeland IRL 9 C9
Bridgend GB 4 C6
Bridgend GB 4 D4
Bridgend GB 13 B7
Bridge of Cally GB 5 B10
Bridge of Don GB 3 L12
Bridge of Dye GB 5 B11
Bridge of Earn GB 5 C10
Bridge of Orchy GB 4 B7
Bridge of Weir GB 4 D7
Bridgetown IRL 9 D9
Bridgnorth GB 11 F7
Bridgwater GB 13 C8
Břidličná CZ 146 B4
Bridlington GB 11 C11
Bridport GB 13 D9
Brie F 29 D6
Briec F 22 D4
Brie-Comte-Robert F 25 C8
Briedel D 185 D7
Brielle NL 16 E2
Brienne-le-Château F 25 D12
Briennon F 30 C5
Brienon-sur-Armançon F 25 D10
Brienz CH 70 D6
Brienza I 60 C5
Briesen D 80 B6
Brieske D 80 D5
Brieskow-Finkenheerd D 81 B7
Briesnig D 81 C7
Brietlingen D 83 D8
Briey F 20 F5
Brig CH 68 A4
Brigg GB 11 D11
Brighstone GB 13 D12
Brightlingsea GB 15 D11
Brighton GB 15 F8
Brigi LV 133 D4
Brignais F 30 D6
Brignogan-Plage F 22 C3
Brignoles F 36 E4
Brigstock GB 15 C7
Brihuega E 47 C7
Brijesta HR 162 D4
Brillon-en-Barrois F 26 C3
Brilon D 17 F11
Brimington GB 11 E9
Brimnes N 94 B5
Brinches P 50 C4
Brincones E 45 B8
Brindisi I 61 B9
Brindisi Montagna I 60 B5
Bringsinghaug N 100 B2
Bringsli N 108 B9
Brinian GB 3 G11
Brinje HR 67 B11
Brinkum D 17 B9
Brinkum D 17 B11
Brinlack IRL 6 B6
Brinon-sur-Beuvron F 25 F9
Brinon-sur-Sauldre F 25 E7
Brin-sur-Seille F 26 C5
Brînza MD 155 B2
Brînzeni MD 153 A10
Brion F 30 F3
Briones E 40 C6
Brionne F 24 B4
Brioude F 30 E3
Brioux-sur-Boutonne F 28 C5
Briouze F 23 C11
Briscous F 32 D3
Brisighella I 66 D4
Brissac-Quincé F 23 F11
Bristol GB 13 C9
Briston GB 15 B11
Britelo P 38 E3
Britof SLO 73 D9
Briton Ferry GB 13 B7
Brittas IRL 7 F10
Brittas Bay IRL 9 C10
Britvica BIH 157 F8
Britz D 84 E5
Brive-la-Gaillarde F 29 E9
Briviesca E 40 C5
Brix F 23 A8
Brixen im Thale A 72 B5
Brixham GB 13 E7
Brixworth GB 15 C7
Brka BIH 157 C10
Brložnik BIH 157 D11
Brna HR 162 D2
Brnaze HR 157 E6
Brněnec CZ 77 C11
Brniště CZ 81 E7
Brnjica SRB 159 D8
Brnjica SRB 163 C9
Brno CZ 77 D11
Bro S 93 D12
Bro S 99 C9
Broadford GB 2 L5
Broadford IRL 8 C5
Broadford IRL 8 D5
Broad Haven GB 9 E12
Broadheath GB 13 A10
Broadstairs GB 15 E11
Broadway GB 13 A11
Broadwey GB 13 D10
Broadwindsor GB 13 D9
Broager DK 86 F5
Broaryd S 87 A12
Broby S 88 C6
Broby S 99 C11
Brobyværk DK 86 E6
Broc CH 31 B11
Broćanac BIH 157 F7
Brocas F 32 B4
Brocēni LV 134 C5
Bröckel D 79 A7
Brockum D 17 D10
Brockworth GB 13 B10
Broczyno PL 85 C10
Brod BIH 157 F10
Brod MK 168 A5
Brod MK 169 C6
Brod SRB 163 F10
Brod SRB 164 E3
Brodalen S 91 C10
Brodarevo SRB 163 C8
Broddbo S 98 C6
Brodek u Prostějova CZ 77 D12
Broderstorf D 83 B12
Brodica SRB 159 E8
Brodick GB 4 D6
Brodilovo BG 167 E9
Brodina RO 152 B6
Brodnica PL 81 B11
Brodnica PL 139 D7
Brodosanë KS 163 E10
Brodské SK 77 E12
Brodski Stubnik HR 157 B8
Brody PL 81 B8
Brody PL 81 C7
Broekhuizenvorst NL 183 C8
Broglie F 24 B4
Brohl D 185 D7
Brohm D 84 C5
Broin F 26 F3
Brójce PL 81 B9
Brojce PL 85 C8
Brójce PL 143 C8
Brok PL 139 E12
Brokdorf D 17 A12
Brokind S 92 C7
Brokka N 90 C2
Brokstedt D 83 C7
Brolo I 59 C6
Bromarv FIN 127 F9
Brome D 79 A8
Bromma N 95 B10
Bromnes N 112 C2
Bromölla S 88 C6
Brömsebro S 89 C10
Bromsgrove GB 13 A10
Bromyard GB 13 A9
Bron F 30 D6
Bronchales E 47 C9
Brønderslev DK 86 A5
Broni I 69 C7
Bronice PL 81 C7
Brønnøysund N 108 F3
Bronnytsya UA 154 A1
Brøns DK 86 E3
Bronte I 59 D6
Bronzani Majdan BIH 157 C6
Brooke GB 15 B11
Brookeborough GB 7 D8
Broons F 23 D7
Broquiès F 34 B4
Brora GB 3 J9
Brørup DK 86 E4
Brösarp S 88 D6
Broscăuți RO 153 B8
Broseley GB 10 F7
Broshniv Osada UA 145 F9
Brossac F 28 E5
Brøstadbotn N 111 B14
Broșteni RO 153 C7
Broșteni RO 153 F10
Broșteni RO 159 D10
Brotas P 50 B3
Brötjemark S 92 D4
Broto E 32 E5
Brottby S 99 C10
Brottes F 26 D3
Brotton GB 11 B10
Brøttum N 101 D13
Brou F 24 D5
Brough GB 3 H10
Brough GB 11 B7
Broughshane GB 4 F4
Broughton GB 5 D10
Broughton GB 10 E6
Broughton in Furness GB 10 C5
Broughtown GB 3 G11
Broughty Ferry GB 5 C11
Broumov CZ 81 E10
Brousseval F 26 D2
Broutzaiika GR 175 D6
Brouvelieures F 26 D6
Brouwershaven NL 16 E1
Brovst DK 86 A5
Brownhills GB 11 F8
Broxburn GB 5 D10
Brozany CZ 76 B6
Brozas E 45 E7
Brožiai LT 134 E3
Brozzo I 69 B9
Brštanovo HR 156 E5
Brtnice CZ 77 D9
Bruay-la-Bussière F 18 D6
Bruchhausen-Vilsen D 17 C12
Bruchköbel D 187 A6
Bruchmühlbach D 21 F8
Bruchsal D 27 B10
Bruchweiler-Bärenbach D 186 C4
Brück D 79 B12
Bruck an der Großglocknerstraße A 73 B6
Bruck an der Leitha A 77 F11
Bruck an der Mur A 73 B11
Brücken D 21 E8
Brücken (Helme) D 79 D9
Brücken (Pfalz) D 21 F8
Brückl A 73 C10
Bruckmühl D 72 A4
Brudzeń Duży PL 139 E8
Brudzew PL 142 B6
Brudzowice PL 143 E7
Brue-Auriac F 35 C10
Brüel D 83 C11
Bruère-Allichamps F 29 B10
Bruff IRL 8 D5
Brugelette B 182 D3
Bruges B 19 B7
Bruges B 182 C2
Brugg CH 27 F9
Brugge B 19 B7
Brüggen D 16 F6
Brüggen D 78 B6
Brugnato I 69 E8
Brugnera I 72 E6
Bruguières F 33 C8
Bruhagen N 104 E3
Brühl D 21 C7
Brühl D 187 C6
Bruinisse NL 16 E2
Bruiu RO 152 F5
Bruksvallarna S 102 A3
Brûlon F 23 E11
Brûly B 19 E10
Brumath F 27 C8
Brummen NL 183 A8
Brumov-Bylnice CZ 146 C6
Brumunddal N 101 E13
Brumundsag N 101 E13
Brunau D 83 E10
Brunava LV 135 D8
Brundby DK 86 D7
Brundish GB 15 C11
Brunehamel F 19 E9
Brunete E 46 D5
Brunflo S 106 E7
Brunico I 72 C4
Bruniquel F 33 B9
Brunkeberg N 95 D8
Brunn D 84 C4
Brunna S 99 C8
Brunna S 99 C9
Brunn am Gebirge A 77 F10
Brunnberg S 97 B10
Brunne S 103 A14
Brunnen CH 71 C7
Brunnsberg S 102 D6
Brunsberg S 97 C8
Brunsbüttel D 17 A12
Brunssum NL 20 C5
Bruntál CZ 142 G3
Bruravik N 94 B5
Bruree IRL 8 D5
Brus SRB 163 C11
Brusago I 69 A11
Brusand N 94 E3
Brušane HR 156 C3
Brusartsi BG 159 F11
Brüsewitz D 83 C10
Brŭshlen BG 161 F8
Brŭshlyanitsa BG 165 B10
Brusio CH 69 A9
Brusnik SRB 159 E9
Brusnika Velika BIH 157 B9
Brusno SK 147 D8
Brusque F 34 C4
Brussel B 19 C9
Brussel B 182 D4
Brusson I 68 B4
Brüssow D 84 D6
Brusturi RO 151 C9
Brusturi-Drăgănești RO 153 C8
Brusturiv UA 152 A5
Brusturoasa RO 153 D8
Brusy PL 138 C4
Bruton GB 13 C10
Bruttig-Fankel D 21 D8
Bruvno HR 156 D4
Bruxelles B 19 C9
Bruyères F 26 D6
Bruz F 23 D8
Bruzaholm S 92 D6
Brvnište SK 146 C6
Brwinów PL 141 F3
Bryagovo BG 166 F4
Bryastovo BG 165 C10
Bryggerhaug N 111 B14
Brymbo GB 10 E5
Brynamman GB 13 B7
Bryne N 94 E3
Brynford GB 10 E5
Brynge S 107 E14
Bryngelhögen S 102 B7
Brynje S 102 A8
Brynje S 106 E7
Brynmawr GB 13 B8
Bryrup DK 86 C5
Bryukhovychi UA 144 D8
Brzan SRB 159 E7
Brza Palanka SRB 159 E9
Brzeće SRB 163 C10
Brzeg PL 142 E3
Brzeg Dolny PL 81 D11
Brześć Kujawski PL 138 E6
Brzesko PL 143 G10
Brzeszcze PL 143 G7
Brzezie PL 85 C11
Brzezie PL 138 E6
Brzezinki PL 141 H5
Brzeziny PL 142 C5
Brzeziny PL 143 C8
Brzeziny PL 144 D4
Brzeźnica PL 81 C8
Brzeźnica PL 143 F11
Brzeźnica PL 147 B9
Brzeźno PL 85 C9
Brzeźno PL 141 H9
Brzeźno PL 142 B5
Brzostek PL 144 D3
Brzotín SK 145 F1
Brzóza PL 141 G4
Brzozów PL 141 F2
Brzozów PL 144 D5
Brzozowiec PL 81 A8
Brzuze PL 139 D7
Bû F 24 C6
Bua S 87 A10
Buais F 23 C10
Buarcos P 44 D3
Buavågen N 94 C2
Bubbio I 37 B8
Bubiai LT 134 E6
Bubry F 22 E5
Bubwith GB 11 D10
Búč SK 149 A10
Buca TR 177 C9
Bučany SK 146 E5
Buccheri I 59 E6
Bucchianico I 63 C6
Buccinasco I 69 C7
Buccino I 60 B4
Bucecea RO 153 B8
Bucelas P 50 B1
Buceș RO 151 E10
Bucey-lès-Gy F 26 F4
Buch D 71 A10
Buch am Erlbach D 75 F11
Buchbach D 75 F11
Buch bei Jenbach A 72 B4
Buchboden A 71 C9
Büchel D 21 D8
Büchen D 83 D9
Buchen (Odenwald) D 27 A11
Büchenbeuren D 185 E7
Buchholz D 83 D12
Buchholz (Aller) D 82 E7
Buchholz (Westerwald) D 21 C8
Buchin RO 159 C9
Buchin Prohod BG 165 D7
Buchkirchen A 76 F6
Büchlberg D 76 E5
Buchloe D 71 A11
Buchlovice CZ 146 C4
Bucholz in der Nordheide D 83 D7
Buchs CH 71 C8
Buchy F 18 E3
Bučim MK 164 F5
Buçimas AL 168 C4
Bučin MK 168 B5
Bucine I 66 F4
Bucinișu RO 160 F4
Bučište MK 164 F5
Bucium RO 151 E11
Buciumeni RO 153 F10
Buciumeni RO 161 C6
Buciumi RO 151 C11
Bučje SRB 159 F9
Bučje SRB 163 C7
Buckden GB 11 C7
Bückeburg D 17 D12
Bücken D 17 C12
Buckfastleigh GB 13 E7
Buckhaven GB 5 C10
Buckie GB 3 K11
Buckingham GB 14 D7
Buckley GB 10 E5
Buckode IRL 6 D6
Buckow Märkische Schweiz D 80 A6
Bückwitz D 83 E12
Bucoșnița RO 159 C9
Bucov RO 161 D8
Bucovăț MD 154 C2
Bucovăț RO 160 E3
Bucovica BIH 157 E7
Bučovice CZ 77 D12
Bucsa H 151 C7
Bucșani RO 161 D7
Bucșani RO 161 E7
Bucu RO 161 D11
Bucureșci RO 151 E10
București RO 161 E8
Bucy-lès-Pierrepont F 19 E8
Bucz PL 81 B10
Buczek PL 143 D7
Bud N 100 A5
Buda RO 161 B9
Budacu de Jos RO 152 C5
Budakalász H 150 B3
Budakeszi H 149 A11
Budakovo MK 168 B5
Budaörs H 149 B11
Budapest H 150 C3
Budča SK 147 D8
Buddusò I 64 B3
Bude GB 12 D5
Budeasa RO 160 D5
Budel NL 16 F5
Büdelsdorf D 82 B7
Budenets' UA 153 A7
Budenheim D 21 D10
Budens P 50 E2
Büdesheim D 21 D11
Budești RO 152 B3
Budești RO 152 D4
Budești RO 160 C4
Budești RO 161 E8
Budeyi UA 154 A4
Budia E 47 C7
Budila RO 161 B7
Budimci HR 149 F10
Budimlič Japra BIH 156 C5
Budiná SK 147 E8
Büdingen D 21 D12
Budinšćina HR 148 D6
Budišov CZ 77 D9
Budišov nad Budišovkou CZ 146 B5
Budkovce SK 145 F4
Budleigh Salterton GB 13 D8
Budmerice SK 146 E4
Budoia I 72 D6
Budoni I 64 B4
Budrio I 66 C4
Budry PL 136 E4
Budureasa RO 151 D10
Buduslău RO 151 C9
Budva MNE 163 E6
Būdviečiai LT 136 D6
Budyně nad Ohří CZ 76 B6
Budziszewice PL 141 G1
Budzów PL 147 B9
Budzyń PL 85 E11
Bue N 94 E3
Bueña E 47 C10
Buenache de Alarcón E 47 E8
Buenache de la Sierra E 47 D8
Buenaventura E 46 D3
Buenavista de Valdavia E 39 C10
Buendía E 47 D7
Buer D 183 B10
Buer N 96 D6
Bueu E 38 D2
Bufleben D 79 D8
Buftea RO 161 D7
Bugac H 150 D4
Bugarra E 48 E3
Buğdayli TR 173 D8
Bugeat F 29 D9
Buggenhout B 182 C4
Buggerru I 64 E1
Buggingen D 27 E8
Bugiac MD 154 E3
Bugnara I 62 C5
Bugnein F 32 D4
Bugojno BIH 157 D7
Bugøyfjord N 114 D6
Bugøynes N 114 D7
Bugyi H 150 C3
Bühl D 27 C9
Bühlertal D 27 C9
Bühlertann D 74 D6
Bühlerzell D 74 D6
Buhoci RO 153 D10
Buhølen N 90 C1
Buhuși RO 153 D9
Buia I 73 D7
Builth Wells GB 13 A8
Buis-les-Baronnies F 35 B9
Buitenpost NL 16 B6

Buitrago del Lozoya E 46 C5
Buivydiškės LT 137 D11
Buivydžiai LT 137 D12
Buják H 147 F9
Bujalance E 53 A8
Bujan AL 163 E9
Bujanovac SRB 164 E4
Bujaraloz E 42 E3
Buje HR 67 B8
Bujor MD 154 D2
Bujoreni RO 160 C4
Bujoreni RO 161 E7
Bujoru RO 161 F7
Bük H 149 B7
Buk PL 81 B11
Bukaiši LV 134 D6
Bukhava BY 133 E6
Bukhovo BG 165 D8
Bukhovtsi BG 167 C7
Bükkábrány H 145 H2
Bükkösd H 149 D9
Bukksnes N 111 C10
Bükkszék H 145 H1
Bükkszentkereszt H 145 G2
Bükkzsérc H 145 H2
Buko D 79 C11
Bukonys LT 135 F8
Bukova Gora BIH 157 E7
Bukovče SRB 159 E10
Bukovec CZ 147 B7
Bukovets BG 165 D8
Bukovje SLO 73 E9
Bukovo MK 168 C5
Buków PL 81 B9
Bukowe PL 142 B4
Bukowice PL 81 D12
Bukowiec PL 81 B9
Bukowiec PL 81 B10
Bukowiec PL 138 D5
Bukowina PL 138 B4
Bukowina Tatrzańska PL 145 E1
Bukownica PL 142 D5
Bukowsko PL 145 E5
Bülach CH 27 E10
Bulboaca MD 154 D4
Bulbucata RO 161 E7
Bulçar AL 168 C3
Buldoo GB 3 H9
Bulford GB 13 C11
Bŭlgarene BG 165 C11
Bŭlgarevo BG 167 C10
Bŭlgari BG 167 E9
Bŭlgarin BG 166 F5
Bŭlgarovo BG 167 D8
Bŭlgarska Polyana BG 166 E6
Bŭlgarski Izvor BG 165 C9
Bulgnéville F 26 D4
Bülkau D 17 A11
Bulkington GB 13 A12
Bulkowo PL 139 E9
Bullas E 55 C9
Bullaun IRL 6 F5
Bullay D 21 D8
Bulle CH 31 B11
Bullerup DK 86 E6
Büllingen B 20 D6
Bullmark S 122 B4
Bully-les-Mines F 18 D6
Bulqizë AL 168 A3
Bultei I 64 C3
Bulz RO 151 D10
Bulzești RO 160 D3
Bulzeștii de Sus RO 151 E10
Bulzi I 64 B2
Bumbești-Jiu RO 160 C2
Bumbești-Pițic RO 160 C3
Buna BIH 157 F8
Bunacurry IRL 6 E3
Bunalty IRL 6 D3
Bun an Churraigh IRL 6 E3
Bun an Phobail IRL 4 E2
Bun an Tábhairne IRL 8 E6
Bunbeg IRL 6 B6
Bunclody IRL 9 C9
Bun Clóidí IRL 9 C9
Buncrana IRL 4 E2
Bun Cranncha IRL 4 E2
Bunde D 17 B8
Bünde D 17 D11
Bundenbach D 21 E8
Bunderhee D 17 B8
Bun Dobhrain IRL 6 D6
Bundoran IRL 6 D6
Bunessan GB 4 C4
Bunești RO 152 E6
Bunești RO 153 B8
Bunești-Averești RO 153 D11
Bungay GB 15 C11
Bunge S 93 D14
Bunić HR 156 C4
Buniel E 40 D4
Bunila RO 159 B10
Bunka LV 134 D3
Bunkeflostrand S 87 D11
Bunkris S 102 D5
Bunmahon IRL 9 D8
Bunnaglass IRL 6 F5
Bun na hAbhna IRL 6 D3
Bunnahowen IRL 6 D3
Bun na Leaca IRL 6 B6
Bunnanaddan IRL 6 D5
Bunnanadden IRL 6 D5
Buñol E 48 F3
Bunschoten-Spakenburg NL 16 D4
Buntești RO 151 D10
Buntingford GB 15 D8
Bunyola E 49 E10
Buoač BIH 157 C7
Buochs CH 71 D6
Buollannjárga N 113 E15
Buonabitacolo I 60 C5
Buonalbergo I 60 A3
Buonconvento I 66 F3
Buonvicino I 60 D5
Bur DK 86 C2
Buran N 105 D11
Burbach D 21 C10
Burbage GB 13 C11
Burbáguena E 47 B10
Burcei I 64 E3
Bŭrdarski Geran BG 165 B8
Burdinne B 19 C11
Bureå S 118 E6
Bureåborg S 107 E13
Büren D 17 E11
Buren NL 183 B6
Büren an der Aare CH 27 F7
Bures GB 15 D10
Buresjön S 109 E14
Burfjord N 112 D9
Burford GB 13 B11
Burg D 80 C6
Burg (Dithmarschen) D 82 C6
Burganes de Valverde E 39 E8
Burgas BG 167 E8
Burgau A 148 B6
Burgau D 75 F7
Burgau P 50 E2
Burg auf Fehmarn D 83 B10
Burg bei Magdeburg D 79 B10
Burgberg im Allgäu D 71 B10
Burgbernheim D 75 D7
Burgbrohl D 185 D7
Burgdorf CH 70 C5
Burgdorf D 79 B7
Burgdorf D 79 B7
Burgebrach D 75 C8
Bürgel D 79 E10
Burgess Hill GB 15 F8
Burghausen D 76 F3
Burghclere GB 13 C12
Burghead GB 3 K10
Burgh-Haamstede NL 16 E1
Burgh le Marsh GB 11 E12
Burgio I 58 D3
Burgkirchen an der Alz D 75 F12
Burgkunstadt D 75 B9
Bürglen CH 27 E11
Bürglen CH 71 D7
Burglengenfeld D 75 D11
Burgohondo E 46 D3
Burgos E 40 D4
Burgos I 64 C2
Burgsalach D 75 D9
Burgsinn D 74 B6
Bürgstadt D 21 E12
Burgstädt D 79 E12
Burg Stargard D 84 D4
Burgsvik S 93 E12
Burgthann D 75 D9
Burgtonna D 79 D8
Burgui E 32 E3
Burguillos E 51 D8
Burguillos del Cerro E 51 C6
Burguillos de Toledo E 46 E5
Burgum NL 16 B6
Burgwindheim D 75 C8
Burhaniye TR 173 F6
Burhave (Butjadingen) D 17 A10
Buriasco I 31 F11
Burie F 28 D5
Burila Mare RO 159 E10
Burizanë AL 168 A2
Burjassot E 48 E4
Burjuc RO 151 F10
Burkardroth D 74 B6
Burkhardtsdorf D 80 E3
Burlada E 32 E2
Burladingen D 27 D11
Burlats F 33 C10
Bürmoos A 76 G3
Burnchurch IRL 9 C8
Burness GB 3 G11
Burnfoot GB 4 F3
Burnfoot IRL 4 E2
Burnham GB 15 D7
Burnham Market GB 15 B10
Burnham-on-Crouch GB 15 D10
Burnham-on-Sea GB 13 C9
Burniston GB 11 C11
Burnley GB 11 D7
Burntisland GB 5 C10
Burntwood Green GB 11 F8
Burón E 39 B9
Buronzo I 68 C5
Buros F 32 D5
Burovac SRB 159 E7
Burow D 84 C4
Burøysund N 112 C4
Burravoe GB 3 E14
Burrel AL 168 A3
Burren GB 7 D10
Burren IRL 6 F4
Burriana E 48 E4
Burry Port GB 12 B6
Bürs A 71 C9
Burs S 93 D13
Bursa TR 173 D11
Burscough Bridge GB 10 D6
Burseryd S 87 A12
Bursfelde D 78 C6
Bürstadt D 21 E10
Burstow GB 15 E8
Bursuc MD 154 C2
Burtnieki LV 131 F10
Burton-in-Kendal GB 10 C6
Burton Latimer GB 15 C7
Burtonport IRL 6 C6
Burton upon Trent GB 11 F8
Burträsk S 118 E5
Buru RO 152 D3
Burujón E 46 E4
Burwarton GB 13 A9
Burwash GB 15 F9
Burwell GB 15 C9
Burwick GB 3 H11
Bury GB 11 D7
Bury St Edmunds GB 15 C10
Burzenin PL 142 D6
Busachi I 64 C2
Busalla I 37 B9
Busana I 66 D1
Busanski Dubočac BIH 157 B8
Busca I 37 B6
Buscemi I 59 E6
Busdorf D 82 B7
Buseto Palizzolo I 58 C2
Buševec HR 148 E6
Busha UA 153 A12
Bushmills GB 4 E3
Bushtricë AL 163 F9
Bushtyna UA 145 G7
Busigny F 19 D7
Busilovac SRB 159 F7
Bušince SK 147 E9
Buskhyttan S 93 B9
Busko-Zdrój PL 143 F10
Bušlary PL 85 C10
Bušletić BIH 157 C9
Busnes N 108 D6
Busot E 56 E4
Busovača BIH 157 D8
Bussang F 27 E6
Busseto I 69 C9
Bussière-Badil F 29 D7
Bussière-Galant F 29 D8
Bussière-Poitevine F 29 C7
Bussigny CH 31 B10
Bussi sul Tirino I 62 C5
Büßleben D 79 E9
Bussolengo I 66 B2
Bussoleno I 31 E11
Bussum NL 16 D4
Bussy-en-Othe F 25 D10
Bussy-le-Grand F 25 E12
Bușteni RO 161 C7
Bustillo del Páramo E 39 D8
Busto Arsizio I 69 B6
Bustuchin RO 160 D3
Busturi-Axpe E 41 B6
Büsum D 82 B5
Būta BG 165 E9
Butan BG 160 F3
Buțeni MD 154 D3
Buteni RO 151 E9
Butera I 58 E5
Butești MD 153 B10
Bütgenbach B 20 D6
Butimanu RO 161 D7
Būtingė LT 134 D2
Butlers Bridge IRL 7 D8
Butoiești RO 160 D2
Butor MD 154 C4
Butovo BG 166 C4
Bütow D 83 D12
Butrimonys LT 137 D9
Butrimonys LT 137 E11
Butryny PL 139 C10
Bütschwil CH 27 F11
Büttelborn D 187 B6
Buttelstedt D 79 D9
Buttermere GB 10 B5
Buttevant IRL 8 D5
Bütthard D 187 B8
Buttigliera d'Asti I 37 A7
Buttle S 93 E13
Buttstädt D 79 D9
Büttstedt D 79 D7
Butuceni MD 154 B4
Butuceni MD 154 C3
Buturugeni RO 161 E7
Butzbach D 21 D11
Bützow D 83 C11
Buurse NL 17 D7
Buvåg N 110 D9
Buvik N 111 A15
Buvika N 104 E8
Buxerolles F 29 B6
Buxheim D 71 B10
Buxières-les-Mines F 30 C2
Buxted GB 15 F9
Buxtehude D 82 D7
Buxton GB 11 E8
Buxy F 30 B6
Buynovtsi BG 166 D5
Büyükada TR 173 C11
Büyükaltıağaç TR 171 B10
Büyükanafarta TR 171 D10
Büyükbelen TR 173 B7
Büyükçavuşlu TR 173 B9
Büyükçekmece TR 173 B10
Büyükçiğli TR 177 C9
Büyükdöllük TR 167 F7
Büyük Evren TR 171 C10
Büyükgerdelli TR 167 F7
Büyükkarakarli TR 173 B7
Büyükkariştiran TR 173 B8
Büyükkiliçli TR 173 B9
Büyükorhan TR 173 E10
Büyükyenice TR 173 F7
Büyükyoncali TR 173 B8
Buza RO 152 D4
Buzançais F 29 B8
Buzancy F 19 F10
Buzău RO 161 C9
Buzescu RO 160 E6
Buzet HR 67 B8
Buzet-sur-Baïse F 33 B6
Buzet-sur-Tarn F 33 C9
Buziaș RO 159 B8
Buzica SK 145 F3
Bužim BIH 156 B5
Buzoești RO 160 D5
Buzsák H 149 C9
By N 104 D8
Byala BG 166 C5
Byala BG 166 D6
Byala BG 167 D9
Byala Cherkva BG 165 F10
Byala Cherkva BG 166 C4
Byala Reka BG 166 E4
Byala Reka BG 167 D7
Byala Slatina BG 165 C8
Byal Izvor BG 171 A8
Byalo Pole BG 166 E5
Byberget S 103 A9
Bybjerg DK 87 D9
Bychawa PL 144 A6
Bycina PL 142 F6
Byczyna PL 142 D5
Bydalen S 105 E15
Bydgoszcz PL 138 D5
Bye S 106 E7
Byelavyezhski BY 141 F8
Byel'ki BY 133 F2
Byenyakoni BY 137 E11
Byershty BY 137 F9
Byfield GB 13 A12
Bygdeå S 122 B5
Bygdeträsk S 118 F5
Bygdsiljum S 118 F5
Bygland N 90 B2
Byglandsfjord N 90 B2
Bygstad N 100 D3
Byhleguhre D 80 C6
Bykle N 94 D6
Bylchau GB 10 E4
Bylderup-Bov DK 86 F4
Byn S 97 B10
Byneset N 104 E8
Byremo N 90 C1
Byrkjedal N 94 E4
Byrkjelo N 100 C5
Byrknes N 100 E1
Byrtegrend N 94 C7
Byrum DK 87 A7
Byšice CZ 77 B7
Byske S 118 E6
Bysstråsk S 107 C15
Bystřany CZ 80 E5
Bystré CZ 77 C10
Bystré SK 145 E4
Bystřec CZ 77 B11
Bystretsovo RUS 132 F4
Bystričany SK 147 D7
Bystřice CZ 77 C7
Bystřice CZ 147 B7
Bystřice nad Pernštejnem CZ 77 C10
Bystřice pod Hostýnem CZ 146 C5
Bystrička SK 147 C7
Bystrzyca PL 142 E3
Bystrzyca Kłodzka PL 77 B11
Bytča SK 147 C7
Bytnica PL 81 B8
Bytom PL 143 F6
Bytom Odrzański PL 81 C9
Bytoń PL 138 E6
Bytów PL 85 B12
Byvallen S 102 B7
Byviken S 107 D16
Byxelkrok S 89 A12
Bzenec CZ 146 D4
Bzince pod Javorinou SK 146 D5

C

Cabacés E 42 E5
Cabaj-Čápor SK 146 E6
Cabanac-et-Villagrains F 32 A4
Cabañaquinta E 39 B8
Cabañas del Castillo E 45 E9
Cabanas de Viriato P 44 D5
Cabañas Raras E 39 C6
Cabanes E 48 D5
Cabanillas E 41 D8
Cabannes F 35 C8
Čabar HR 73 E10
Cabasse F 36 E4
Cabeça Gorda P 50 D4
Cabeção P 50 B3
Cabeceiras de Basto P 38 E4
Cabeço de Vide P 44 F5
Cabella Ligure I 37 B10
Căbești RO 151 D9
Cabeza de Framontanos E 45 B8
Cabeza del Buey E 51 B9
Cabeza del Caballo E 45 B7
Cabeza la Vaca E 51 C7
Cabezamesada E 47 E6
Cabezarados E 54 B4
Cabezarrubias del Puerto E 54 B4
Cabezas del Villar E 45 C10
Cabezas Rubias E 51 D5
Cabezón de Cameros E 41 D6
Cabezón de la Sal E 40 B3
Cabezón de Liébana E 39 B10
Cabezuela del Valle E 45 D9
Čabiny SK 145 E4
Cabo de Palos E 56 F3
Cabolafuente E 47 B8
Cabra E 53 B8
Cabração P 38 E2
Cabra del Camp E 42 E6
Cabra del Santo Cristo E 55 D6
Cabra de Mora E 48 D3
Cabras I 64 D2
Cabrejas del Pinar E 40 E6
Cabrela P 50 B3
Cabrerets F 33 A9
Cabrières-d'Aigues F 35 C10
Cabril P 44 D5
Cabrillanes E 39 C7
Cabrillas E 45 C8
Cabuna HR 149 E9
Cacabelos E 39 C6
Čačak SRB 158 F5
Caçarelhos P 39 E7
Caccamo I 58 D4
Caccuri I 61 E7
Cacém P 50 B1
Cáceres E 45 F8
Cachopo P 50 E4
Čachtice SK 146 D5
Cacica RO 153 B7
Čačin E 53 B9
Čačinci HR 149 E9
Cadalso de los Vidrios E 46 D4
Cadamstown IRL 7 F7
Cadaqués E 43 C10
Cadaval P 44 F2
Čađavica BIH 157 D6
Čađavica HR 149 E9
Čađavica Gornja BIH 157 C11
Čadca SK 147 C7
Cadelbosco di Sopra I 66 C2
Cadenazzo CH 69 A6
Cadenberge D 17 A12
Cadenet F 35 C9
Cadeo I 69 D8
Cádiar E 55 F6
Cadillac F 32 A5
Cádiz E 52 C4
Cadolzburg D 75 D8
Cadoneghe I 66 B4
Cadours F 33 C8
Cadreita E 41 D8
Cadrete E 41 E10
Caen F 23 B11
Caerau GB 13 C8
Caerdydd GB 13 C8
Caerfyrddin GB 12 B6
Caergybi GB 10 E2
Caerhun GB 10 E4
Caerleon GB 13 B9
Caernarfon GB 10 E3
Caerphilly GB 13 B8
Cafasse I 31 E12
Caggiano I 60 B5
Çağış TR 173 E8
Cagli I 66 E6
Cagliari I 64 E3
Čaglin HR 149 F9
Cagnac-les-Mines F 33 C10
Cagnano Varano I 63 D9
Cagnes-sur-Mer F 36 D6
Caherconlish IRL 8 C6
Cahermore IRL 8 E2
Cahir IRL 9 D7
Cahirciveen IRL 8 E2
Cahors F 33 B8
Cahul MD 154 F2
Cahuzac-sur-Vère F 33 C9
Căianu RO 152 D3
Căianu Mic RO 152 C4
Caiazzo I 60 A2
Căinari MD 154 D4
Căinarii Vechi MD 153 A12
Căineni RO 160 C4
Căineni-Băi RO 161 C10
Caión E 38 B2
Cairaclia MD 154 F3
Cairanne F 35 B8
Cairnbaan GB 4 C6
Cairnryan GB 4 F6
Cairo Montenotte I 37 C8
Caiseal IRL 9 C7
Caisleán an Bharraigh IRL 6 E4
Caisleán an Chomair IRL 9 C8
Caisleán Uí Chonaill IRL 8 C5
Caissargues F 35 C7
Caister-on-Sea GB 15 B12
Caistor GB 11 E11
Căiuți RO 153 E9
Caivano I 60 B2
Cajarc F 33 B9
Čajetina SRB 158 F4
Čajić BIH 157 E6
Čajkov SK 147 E7
Čajniče BIH 157 E11
Cajvana RO 153 B7
Čaka SK 146 E6
Čakajovce SK 146 E6
Çakılköy TR 173 D9
Çakilli TR 173 A8
Çakir TR 173 E7
Çakirli TR 173 D7
Çakmakköy TR 172 B6
Čakovec HR 149 D6
Cala E 51 D7
Calabardina E 55 E9
Calabritto I 60 B4
Calaceite E 42 E4
Calacuccia F 37 G10
Cala d'Oliva I 64 A1
Cala d'Or E 57 C11
Calaf E 43 D7
Calafat RO 159 F10
Calafell E 43 E7
Cala Figuera E 57 C11
Calafindești RO 153 B8
Cala Galdana E 57 B12
Calahonda E 53 C10
Calahorra E 32 F2
Calais F 15 F12
Calalzo di Cadore I 72 D5
Calamandrana I 37 B8
Cala Millor E 57 B11
Calamocha E 47 C10
Calamonaci I 58 D3
Calamonte E 51 B7
Cala Murada E 57 C11
Călan RO 151 F11
Calañas E 51 D6
Calanda E 42 F3
Calangianus I 64 B3
Calanna I 59 C8
Cala'n Porter E 57 B13
Calarașăuca MD 154 A1
Călărași MD 154 C2
Călărași RO 152 E3
Călărași RO 153 B10
Călărași RO 160 F4
Călărași RO 161 E10
Cala Ratjada E 57 B11
Calascibetta I 58 D5
Calasetta I 64 E1
Calasparra E 55 C9
Calatafimi I 58 D2
Calatayud E 41 F8
Călățele RO 151 D11
Calatorao E 41 E9
Calau D 80 C5
Calbe (Saale) D 79 C10
Calcatoggio F 37 G9
Calcinato I 66 B1
Calcio I 69 B8
Căldăraru RO 160 E5
Caldarola I 67 F7
Caldaro sulla Strada del Vino I 72 D3
Caldas da Rainha P 44 F2
Caldas de Reis E 38 C2
Caldas de Vizela P 38 F3
Caldbeck GB 5 F10
Caldearenas E 32 F4
Caldecott GB 11 F10
Caldelas P 38 E3
Caldelas Taipas P 38 F3
Calden D 21 B12
Caldercruix GB 5 D9
Caldes de Malavella E 43 D9
Caldes de Montbui E 43 D8
Caldes d'Estrac E 43 D9
Caldicot GB 13 B9
Caldogno I 72 E4
Caldonazzo I 69 A11
Calella E 43 D9
Calendário P 38 F2
Calenzana F 37 F9
Calenzano I 66 E3
Calera de León E 51 C7
Calera y Chozas E 45 E10
Caleruega E 40 E5
Calfsound GB 3 G11
Calgary GB 4 B4
Çali TR 173 D10
Calig E 42 G4
Călimănești RO 160 C4
Calimera I 61 C10
Călinești MD 153 B10
Călinești RO 152 B3
Călinești RO 160 D6
Călinești RO 160 E6
Călinești-Oaș RO 145 H7
Calitri I 60 B4
Calizzano I 37 C8
Çalköy TR 173 E7
Callac F 22 D5
Callain IRL 9 C8
Callan IRL 9 C8
Callander GB 5 C8
Callanish GB 2 J3
Callantsoog NL 16 C3
Callas F 36 D5
Callen F 32 B5
Callian F 36 D5
Calliano I 37 A8
Callington GB 12 D6
Callosa d'En Sarrià E 56 D4
Callosa de Segura E 56 E3
Čalma SRB 158 C4
Călmățuiu RO 160 F5
Călmățuiu de Sus RO 160 E5
Calmont F 33 B11
Calmont F 33 D9
Calne GB 13 C10
Călnic RO 152 F3
Călnic RO 159 D11
Calolziocorte I 69 B7
Calomarde E 47 D9
Calonge E 43 D10
Călopăr RO 160 E3
Čalovec SK 146 F5
Calpe E 56 D5
Caltabellotta I 58 D3
Caltagirone I 59 E6
Caltanissetta I 58 E5
Caltavuturo I 58 D4
Caltignaga I 68 B6
Çaltılıbük TR 173 E10
Caltojar E 40 F6
Caltra IRL 6 F6
Călugăreni RO 161 E7
Caluso I 68 C4
Calvão P 44 D3
Calvarrasa de Abajo E 45 C9
Calvarrasa de Arriba E 45 C9
Calvello I 60 C5
Calverstown IRL 7 F9
Calvi F 37 F9
Calvi dell'Umbria I 62 C3
Calvignac F 33 B9
Calvinet F 29 F10
Calvini RO 161 C8
Calvi Risorta I 60 A2
Calvisson F 35 C7
Calvörde D 79 B9
Calvos E 38 E4
Calw D 27 C10
Calzada de Calatrava E 54 B5
Calzada de Valdunciel E 45 B9
Calzadilla E 45 D7
Calzadilla de los Barros E 51 C7
Camaldoli I 66 E4
Camaleño E 39 B10
Camallera E 43 C9
Camañas E 47 C10
Camăr RO 151 C10
Camarasa E 42 D5
Cămărașu RO 152 D4
Camarena E 46 D4
Camarena de la Sierra E 47 D10
Camarès F 34 C4
Camaret-sur-Aigues F 35 B8
Camaret-sur-Mer F 22 D2
Camarillas E 42 F2
Camariñas E 38 B1
Cămărzana RO 145 H7
Camarzana de Tera E 39 D7
Camas E 51 E7
Camastra I 58 E4
Cambados E 38 C2
Camberley GB 15 E7
Cambes F 28 F5
Cambil E 53 A9
Cambo-les-Bains F 32 D3
Camborne GB 12 E4
Cambra de Baixo P 44 C4
Cambrai F 19 D7
Cambre E 38 B3
Cambridge GB 15 C9
Cambrils E 42 E6
Cambron F 18 D4
Cambs D 83 C11
Camburg D 79 D10
Camelford GB 12 D5
Camenca MD 154 A3
Camerano I 67 E8
Cameri I 68 B6
Camerino I 67 F7
Camerles E 42 F5
Camerota I 60 C4
Çamiçi TR 177 E10
Camigliatello Silano I 61 E6
Camin D 83 D9
Caminha P 38 E2
Caminomorisco E 45 D8
Caminreal E 47 C10
Çamlica TR 172 C6
Çamlik TR 177 D9
Cammarata I 58 D4
Cammer D 79 B12
Cammin D 83 C12
Camogli I 37 C10
Camolin IRL 9 C10
Camon F 18 E5
Camors F 22 E6
Camp IRL 8 D3
Campagna I 60 B4
Campagnano di Roma I 62 C2
Campagnatico I 65 B4
Campagne F 29 F7
Campagne-lès-Hesdin F 15 G12
Campan F 33 D6
Campana I 61 E7
Campanario E 51 B8
Campanet E 57 B10
Câmpani RO 151 D10
Campano E 52 D4
Campaspero E 40 F3
Campbeltown GB 4 E5
Campbon F 23 F8
Campdevànol E 43 C8
Campeã P 38 F4
Campello E 56 E4
Campello sul Clitunne I 62 B3
Campelo P 44 E4
Campelos P 44 F2
Campénéac F 23 E7
Câmpeni RO 151 E11
Campertogno I 68 B5
Câmpia Turzii RO 152 D3
Campi Bisenzio I 66 E3
Campiglia Marittima I 65 A3
Campiglia Soana I 31 D12
Campillo de Alto Buey E 47 E9
Campillo de Arenas E 53 A9
Campillo de Dueñas E 47 C9
Campillo de Llerena E 51 B8
Campillos E 53 B7
Campillos-Paravientos E 47 E9
Câmpina RO 161 C7
Câmpineanca RO 153 F10
Campinho P 50 C5
Campisábalos E 40 F5
Campi Salentina I 61 C10
Campli I 62 B5
Campo E 33 F6
Campo P 38 F3
Campobasso I 63 D7
Campobello di Licata I 58 E4
Campobello di Mazara I 58 D2
Campodarsego I 66 A4
Campo de Caso E 39 B9
Campo de Criptana E 47 F6
Campo de San Pedro E 40 F4
Campodimele I 62 E5
Campo di Trens I 72 C3
Campodolcino I 71 E8
Campofelice di Roccella I 58 D4
Campofiorito I 58 D3
Campoformido I 73 D7
Campofranco I 58 D4
Campofrío E 51 D6
Campoli Appennino I 62 D5
Campo Ligure I 37 B9
Campolongo Maggiore I 66 B5
Campo Lugar E 45 F9
Campo Maior P 51 A5
Campomarino I 61 C9
Campomarino I 63 D8
Campomorone I 37 B9
Componaraya E 39 C6
Camponogara I 66 B5
Campora San Giovanni I 59 A9
Camporeale I 58 D3
Campo Redondo P 50 D2
Camporgiano I 66 D1
Čamporosso I 37 D7
Camporrells E 42 D5
Camporrobles E 47 E10
Campos E 57 C11
Campos P 38 E4
Camposampiero I 66 A4
Camposanto I 66 C3
Campotéjar E 53 B9
Campotosto I 62 B4
Campo Tures I 72 C4
Camprodon E 33 F10
Camptown GB 5 E11
Câmpulung RO 160 C6
Câmpulung la Tisa RO 145 H8
Câmpulung Moldovenesc RO 153 B7
Câmpuri RO 153 E9
Camrose GB 12 B4
Camuñas E 46 F6
Çamyayla TR 181 B8
Çan TR 173 D7
Čaňa SK 145 F3
Cañada E 56 D3
Cañada de Benatanduz E 42 F2
Cañada del Hoyo E 47 E9
Cañada Vellida E 42 F2
Čanak HR 156 C3
Çanakçi TR 173 F10
Çanakkale TR 171 D10
Canale I 37 B7
Canale-di-Verde F 37 G10
Canalejas del Arroyo E 47 D8
Canalejas de Peñafiel E 40 E3
Canals E 56 D3
Canals F 33 C8
Canàl San Bovo I 72 D4
Cañamares E 47 D8
Cañamero E 45 F10
Canaples F 18 D5
Canari F 37 F10
Canaro I 66 C4
Cañaveral E 45 E8
Cañaveral de León E 51 C6
Cañaveras E 47 D8
Cañaveruelas E 47 D7
Canazei I 72 D4
Cancale F 23 C8
Cancarix E 55 C9
Cancellara I 60 B5
Cancello ed Arnone I 60 A2
Cancon F 33 A7
Candanchú E 32 E4
Çandarli TR 177 B8
Candás E 39 A8
Candasnos E 42 D4
Candé F 23 E9
Candela I 60 A5
Candelario E 45 D9
Candeleda E 45 D10
Candelo I 68 B5
Candemil P 38 E2
Cândești RO 153 D9
Cândești RO 160 C6
Candia Lomellina I 68 C6
Candilichera E 41 E7
Candín E 39 C6
Canedo P 44 B4
Canelli I 37 B8
Canena E 55 C6
Canepina I 62 C2
Canero E 39 A7
Cănești RO 161 C9
Canet F 34 C5
Canet F 34 D4
Canet de Mar E 43 D9
Cañete E 47 D9
Cañete de las Torres E 53 A8
Cañete la Real E 53 C6
Canet-en-Roussillon F 34 E5
Canet lo Roig E 42 F4
Canet-Plage F 34 E5
Cangas E 38 D2
Cangas del Narcea E 39 B6
Cangas de Onís E 39 B9
Cangonj AL 168 C4
Canha P 50 B2
Canhestros P 50 C3
Cania MD 154 E2
Canicattì I 58 E4
Canicattini Bagni I 59 E7
Canicosa de la Sierra E 40 E5
Caniles E 55 E7
Canillas de Aceituno E 53 C8
Canino I 62 C1
Cañizal E 45 B10
Cañizares E 47 C8
Cañizo E 39 E9
Canjáyar E 55 E7
Canlia RO 161 E11
Canna I 61 C7
Cannara I 62 B3
Cannero Riviera I 68 A6
Cannes F 36 D6
Canneto I 59 C6
Canneto I 66 F2
Canneto sull'Oglio I 66 B1
Cannich GB 2 L7
Canningstown IRL 7 E8
Cannington GB 13 C8
Cannobio I 68 A6
Cannock GB 11 F7
Cano P 50 B4
Canolo I 59 C9
Canonbie GB 5 E11
Canosa di Puglia I 60 A6
Cánovas E 56 F2
Can Pastilla E 49 E10
Can Picafort E 57 B11
Canredondo E 47 C8
Cansano I 62 D6
Cantagallo I 66 D3
Cantalapiedra E 45 B10
Cantalejo E 40 F4
Cantalice I 62 C3
Cantalpino E 45 B10
Cantanhede P 44 D3
Cantavieja E 42 F3
Čantavir SRB 150 F4
Cantemir MD 154 E2
Cantenac F 28 E4
Canteras E 56 F2
Canterbury GB 15 E11
Cantiano I 66 F6
Cantillana E 51 D8
Cantimpalos E 46 B4
Cantoira I 31 E11
Cantoria E 55 E8
Cantù I 69 B7
Canvey Island GB 15 D10
Cany-Barville F 18 E2
Canyelles E 43 E7
Caolas GB 4 B3
Caorle I 72 E6
Capaccio I 60 C4
Capaci I 58 C3
Capafonts E 42 E6
Capalbio I 65 C4
Căpâlna RO 151 D9
Căpâlnița RO 153 E6

Capannoli I 66 E2
Capannori I 66 E2
Caparde BIH 157 D10
Capari MK 168 B5
Caparica P 50 B1
Caparrosa P 44 C4
Caparroso E 32 F2
Cap-Blanc E 48 F4
Capbreton F 32 C3
Cap d'Agde F 34 D6
Capdenac F 33 A10
Capdenac-Gare F 33 A10
Capdepera E 57 B11
Capel Curig GB 10 E4
Capelins P 51 B5
Capelle aan de IJssel NL 16 E3
Capellen L 20 E6
Capel St Mary GB 15 C11
Capendu F 34 D4
Capestang F 34 D5
Capestrano I 62 C5
Cap Ferret F 32 A3
Capileira E 55 F6
Capilla E 54 B2
Capinha P 44 D6
Capistrello I 62 D4
Capizzi I 58 D5
Căpleni RO 151 B10
Čapljе BIH 157 C6
Čapljina BIH 157 F8
Capodimonte I 62 B1
Capo di Ponte I 69 A9
Capo d'Orlando I 59 C6
Capoliveri I 65 B2
Capolona I 66 E4
Caposele I 60 B4
Capoterra I 64 E2
Cappadocia I 62 C4
Cappagh White IRL 8 C6
Cappamore IRL 8 C6
Cappawhite IRL 8 C6
Cappeen IRL 8 E5
Cappelle sul Tavo I 62 C6
Cappeln (Oldenburg) D 17 C10
Capperclеuch GB 5 E10
Cappoquin IRL 9 D7
Capracotta I 63 D6
Capraia Isola I 65 A1
Capranica I 62 C2
Caprarola I 62 C2
Căpreni RO 160 D3
Capri I 60 B2
Căpriana MD 154 C2
Capriati a Volturno I 63 E6
Capri Leone I 59 C6
Caprino Bergamasco I 69 B7
Caprino Veronese I 69 B10
Captieux F 32 B5
Capua I 60 A2
Capurso I 61 A7
Căpuşu Mare RO 151 D11
Capvern-les-Bains F 33 D6
Carabaña E 47 D6
Caracal RO 160 E4
Caracuel de Calatrava E 54 B4
Caragaş MD 154 D5
Caragele RO 161 D10
Caraglio I 37 C6
Caraman F 33 C9
Caramanico Terme I 62 C6
Caramulo P 44 C4
Cărand RO 151 E9
Caranga E 39 B7
Caranguejeira P 44 E3
Caransebeş RO 159 C9
Carantec F 22 C4
Carapelle I 60 A5
Carapinheira P 44 D3
Carasco I 37 C10
Caraşova RO 159 C8
Caraula RO 159 E11
Caravaca de la Cruz E 55 C9
Caravaggio I 69 C8
Carbajales de Alba E 39 E8
Carballeda de Avia E 38 D3
Carballo E 38 B2
Carballo E 38 D4
Carbellino E 45 B8
Carbonera de Frentes E 41 E6
Carboneras E 55 F9
Carboneras de Guadazaón E 47 E9
Carbonero El Mayor E 46 B4
Carboneros E 54 C5
Carbonia I 64 E2
Carbonìn I 72 C5
Carbonne F 33 D8
Carbost GB 2 L4
Carbost GB 2 L4
Cărbunari RO 159 D8
Cărbuneşti RO 161 C8
Carbury IRL 7 F9
Carcaboso E 45 D8
Carcabuey E 53 B8
Carcaixent E 48 F4
Carcaliu RO 155 C2
Carcans F 28 E3
Carcans-Plage F 28 E3
Carção P 39 E6
Carcar E 32 F2
Carcare I 37 C8
Carcassonne F 33 D10
Carcastillo E 32 F3
Carcelén E 47 F10
Carcès F 36 E4
Carchelejo E 53 A9
Carcoforo I 68 B5
Cardaillac F 29 F9
Çardak TR 172 D6
Cardedeu E 43 D8
Cardedu I 64 D4
Cardeña E 54 C4
Cardeñadijo E 40 D4
Cardenden GB 5 C10
Cardenete E 47 E9
Cardeñosa E 46 C3
Cardeto I 59 C8
Cardiff GB 13 C8
Cardigan GB 12 A5
Cardigos P 44 E4
Cardinale I 59 B9
Cardito I 62 D5
Cardon RO 155 C5
Cardona E 43 D7
Cardosas P 50 E2
Carei RO 151 B9
Carenas E 41 F8
Carentan F 23 B9
Carentoir F 23 E7
Carevdar HR 149 D7
Carev Dvor MK 168 B5
Cargenbridge GB 5 E9
Cargèse F 37 G9
Carhaix-Plouguer F 22 D4
Caria P 44 D6
Cariati I 61 E7
Caridade P 50 C4
Carife I 60 A4
Carignan F 19 E11
Carignano I 37 B7
Cariñena E 41 F9
Carini I 58 C3
Carinish GB 2 K2
Cariño E 38 A4
Carinola I 60 A1
Carisio I 68 C5
Carisolo I 69 A10
Cârjiţi RO 151 F10
Carland GB 7 C9
Carlanstown IRL 7 E9
Carlantino I 63 D7
Carlat F 29 F11
Carlentini I 59 E7
Carlet E 48 F3
Cârlibaba RO 152 B6
Cârligele RO 153 F10
Carling F 186 C2
Carlingford IRL 7 D10
Carlisle GB 5 F11
Carloforte I 64 E1
Cârlogani RO 160 D4
Cârlomăneşti RO 161 C9
Carlopoli I 59 A9
Carlops GB 5 D10
Carlow D 83 C9
Carlow IRL 9 C9
Carloway GB 2 J3
Carlsberg D 186 C5
Carlton GB 11 F9
Carlton Colville GB 15 C12
Carluke GB 5 D9
Carlux F 29 F8
Carmagnola I 37 B7
Carmanova MD 154 C5
Carmarthen GB 12 B6
Carmaux F 33 B10
Carmena E 46 E4
Cármenes E 39 C8
Carmiano I 61 C10
Carmona E 51 E8
Carmonita E 45 F8
Carmyllie GB 5 B11
Carnac F 22 E5
Carnagh GB 7 D9
Carndonagh IRL 4 E2
Carnew IRL 9 C10
Carnforth GB 10 C6
Carnières F 19 D7
Carnikava LV 135 B8
Carnlough GB 4 F5
Carno GB 10 F4
Carnota E 38 C1
Carnoules F 36 E4
Carnoustie GB 5 B11
Carnoux-en-Provence F 35 D10
Carnteel GB 7 D9
Carnwath GB 5 D9
Carolei I 60 E6
Carolles F 23 C8
Carona I 69 A8
Caronia I 58 C5
C. A. Rosetti RO 155 C5
C. A. Rosetti RO 161 C10
Carosino I 61 C8
Carovigno I 61 B9
Carovilli I 63 D6
Carpaneto Piacentino I 69 D8
Carpegna I 66 E5
Carpen RO 159 E11
Carpenedolo I 66 B1
Carpentras F 35 B9
Carpi I 66 C2
Carpignano Salentino I 61 C10
Carpignano Sesia I 68 B5
Cărpineni MD 154 D2
Cărpinet RO 151 E10
Carpineti I 66 D1
Carpineto Romano I 62 D4
Cărpiniş RO 151 F6
Carpino I 63 D9
Carpinone I 63 D6
Carpio E 40 F1
Carpiquet F 23 B11
Carquefou F 23 F9
Carqueiranne F 36 E4
Carracastle IRL 6 E5
Carracedelo E 39 C6
Carradale East GB 4 D6
Carragh IRL 7 F9
Carraig Airt IRL 7 B7
Carraig na Siuire IRL 9 D8
Carraig Thuathail IRL 8 E6
Carral E 38 B3
Carralevë KS 163 E10
Carranque E 46 D5
Carrapateira P 50 E2
Carrapichana P 44 C6
Carrara I 69 E9
Carraroe IRL 6 F3
Carrascal del Obispo E 45 C9
Carrascosa E 47 C8
Carrascosa del Campo E 47 D7
Carratraca E 53 C7
Carrazeda de Ansiães P 45 B6
Carrazedo de Montenegro P 38 E5
Carrbridge GB 3 L9
Carreço P 38 E2
Carregado P 50 A2
Carregal do Sal P 44 D5
Carregueiros P 44 E4
Carreira P 44 E3
Carreña E 39 B10
Carreteira E 38 C4
Carriazo E 40 B4
Carrick IRL 6 C5
Carrick IRL 9 D9
Carrickart IRL 7 B7
Carrickfergus GB 4 F5
Carrickmacross IRL 7 E9
Carrickmore GB 4 F2
Carrick-on-Shannon IRL 6 E6
Carrick-on-Suir IRL 9 D8
Carriço P 44 E3
Carrigaholt IRL 8 C3
Carrigallen IRL 7 E7
Carriganima IRL 8 E4
Carriganimmy IRL 8 E4
Carrigart IRL 7 B7
Carrigkerry IRL 8 D4
Carrig Mhachaire IRL 7 E9
Carrigtohill IRL 8 E6
Carrigtwohill IRL 8 E6
Carrio E 38 B3
Carrión de Calatrava E 54 A5
Carrión de los Céspedes E 51 E7
Carrión de los Condes E 39 D10
Carrizo de la Ribera E 39 C8
Carrizosa E 55 B7
Carronbridge GB 5 E9
Carros F 37 D6
Carrouges F 23 C11
Carrowkeel IRL 4 E2
Carrowkeel IRL 7 B7
Carrowkennedy IRL 6 E3
Carrù I 37 C7
Carryduff GB 7 C11
Carry-le-Rouet F 35 D9
Cars F 28 E4
Carsac-Aillac F 29 F8
Carsluith GB 5 F8
Carsoli I 62 C4
Carspach F 27 E7
Carsphairn GB 5 E8
Carstairs GB 5 D9
Cartagena E 56 F3
Cártama E 53 C7
Cartaxo P 44 F3
Cartaya E 51 E5
Cartelègue F 28 E4
Carteret F 23 B8
Carterton GB 13 B11
Cartes E 40 B3
Cârţişoara RO 152 F5
Cartoceto I 67 E6
Carucedo E 39 D6
Carunchio I 63 D7
Carvalhal P 44 E4
Carvalhal P 50 C2
Carvalho de Egas P 38 F5
Carvalhosa P 38 F3
Carviçais P 45 B7
Carvin F 18 D6
Carvoeira P 44 F2
Carvoeiro P 50 E3
Čáry SK 77 E12
Casabermeja E 53 C8
Casabona I 61 E7
Casa Branca P 50 B3
Casa Branca P 50 B4
Casacalenda I 63 D7
Casagiove I 60 A2
Casaglione F 37 G9
Casa l'Abate I 61 C10
Casalanguida I 63 C6
Casalarreina E 40 C6
Casalbordino I 63 C7
Casalbore I 60 A4
Casalborgone I 68 C4
Casalbuono I 60 C5
Casalbuttano ed Uniti I 69 C8
Casàl Cermelli I 37 B9
Casàl di Principe I 60 A2
Casalecchio di Reno I 66 D3
Casale Monferrato I 68 C5
Casaletto Spartano I 60 C5
Casalfiumanese I 66 D4
Casalgrande I 66 C2
Casalgrasso I 37 B7
Casalmaggiore I 66 C1
Casalnuovo Monterotaro I 63 D8
Casalpusterlengo I 69 C8
Casalvecchio di Puglia I 63 D8
Casàl Velino I 60 C4
Casamassima I 61 B7
Casamozza F 37 F10
Casarabonela E 53 C7
Casarano I 61 C10
Casar de Cáceres E 45 E8
Casar de Palomero E 45 D8
Casarejos E 40 E5
Casares E 39 B7
Casares E 53 D6
Casares de las Hurdes E 45 D8
Casariche E 53 B7
Casarrubios del Monte E 46 D4
Casarsa della Delizia I 73 E6
Casarza Ligure I 37 C10
Casas Altas E 47 D10
Casas Bajas E 47 D10
Casas de Benítez E 47 F8
Casas de Don Pedro E 45 F10
Casas de Fernando Alonso E 47 F8
Casas de Haro E 47 F8
Casas de Juan Gil E 47 F10
Casas de Juan Núñez E 47 F9
Casas de Lázaro E 55 B8
Casas del Monte E 45 D9
Casas de los Pinos E 47 F8
Casas del Puerto E 56 E2
Casas de Millán E 45 E8
Casas de Reina E 51 C8
Casas de Ves E 47 F10
Casas-Ibáñez E 47 F10
Casasimarro E 47 F8
Casas Novas de Mares P 50 B5
Casasola de Arión E 39 E9
Casatejada E 45 E9
Casatenovo I 69 B7
Casavieja E 46 D3
Cascais P 50 B1
Cascante E 41 D8
Cascante del Río E 47 D10
Cascia I 62 B4
Casciana Terme I 66 E2
Cascina I 66 E2
Căscioarele RO 161 E8
Casebres P 50 B2
Caseda E 32 E3
Case della Marina I 64 E4
Casei Gerola I 37 A9
Căşeiu RO 152 C3
Casekow D 84 D6
Casella I 37 B9
Caselle in Pittari I 60 C5
Caselle Torinese I 68 C4
Case Perrone I 61 B7
Caseras E 42 E4
Caserta I 60 A2
Casével P 50 D3
Cashel IRL 6 E5
Cashel IRL 6 F3
Cashel IRL 7 B7
Cashel IRL 9 C7
Cashla IRL 6 F5
Casillas E 46 D3
Casillas de Flores E 45 D7
Casimcea RO 155 D2
Caşin RO 153 E9
Casina I 66 C1
Casinos E 48 E3
Casla IRL 6 F3
Čáslav CZ 77 C8
Casnewydd GB 13 B9
Casola in Lunigiana I 66 D1
Casola Valsenio I 66 D4
Casole d'Elsa I 66 F3
Casoli I 63 C6
Casoria I 60 B2
Caspe E 42 E3
Casperia I 62 C3
Cassà de la Selva E 43 D9
Cassagnes-Bégonhès F 33 B11
Cassaniouze F 29 F10
Cassano allo Ionio I 61 D6
Cassano delle Murge I 61 B7
Cassano Magnano I 69 B6
Cassano Spinola I 37 B9
Cassaro I 59 E6
Cassel F 18 C5
Casseneuil F 33 B7
Casserres E 43 C7
Cassibile I 59 F7
Cassine I 37 B9
Cassino I 62 E5
Cassis F 35 D10
Cassola I 72 E4
Cassuéjouls F 30 F2
Častá SK 146 E4
Castagliona Olona I 69 B6
Castagnaro I 66 B3
Castagneto Carducci I 66 F2
Castagnole delle Lanze I 37 B8
Castagnole Monferrato I 37 B8
Castalla E 56 D3
Castañar de Ibor E 45 E10
Castañares de Rioja E 40 C6
Castanet-Tolosan F 33 C9
Castanheira P 44 C6
Castanheira de Pêra P 44 D4
Castano Primo I 68 B6
Castasegna CH 69 A8
Casteggio I 37 A10
Castejón E 41 D8
Castejón del Puente E 42 D4
Castejón de Monegros E 42 D3
Castejón de Sos E 33 E6
Castejón de Valdejasa E 41 E10
Castelbellino I 67 F7
Castèl Bolognese I 66 D4
Castelbuono I 58 D5
Castelcivita I 60 C4
Castel d'Ario I 66 B2
Castel de Cabra E 42 F2
Casteldelfino I 36 B6
Castèl del Monte I 62 C5
Castèl del Piano I 65 B5
Castèl del Rio I 66 D4
Castèl di Iudica I 59 E6
Castèl di Lama I 62 B5
Castèl di Lucio I 58 D5
Castèl di Sangro I 62 D6
Casteleiro P 45 D6
Castelfidardo I 67 F8
Castelfiorentino I 66 E2
Castelflorite E 42 D3
Castèl Focognano I 66 E4
Castelforte I 62 E5
Castelfranci I 60 B4
Castelfranco di Sopra I 66 E4
Castelfranco di Sotto I 66 E2
Castelfranco Emilia I 66 C3
Castelfranco in Miscano I 60 A4
Castelfranco Veneto I 72 E4
Castèl Frentano I 63 C6
Castèl Gandolfo I 62 D3
Castelginest F 33 C8
Castèl Giorgio I 62 B1
Castèl Goffredo I 66 B1
Castelgrande I 60 B4
Casteljaloux F 33 B6
Castell D 75 C7
Castellabate I 60 C3
Castell'Alfero I 37 B8
Castellalto I 62 B5
Castellammare del Golfo I 58 C2
Castellammare di Stabia I 60 B2
Castellamonte I 68 C4
Castellana Grotte I 61 B8
Castellane F 36 D5
Castellaneta I 61 B7
Castellanos de Castro E 40 D3
Castellarano I 66 C2
Castellar de la Frontera E 53 D6
Castellar de la Muela E 47 C9
Castellar de la Ribera E 43 C6
Castellar de Santiago E 55 B6
Castellar de Santisteban E 55 C6
Castell'Arquato I 69 D8
Castell'Azzara I 62 B1
Castellazzo Bormida I 37 B9
Castelldans E 42 E5
Castell de Cabres E 42 F4
Castell de Castells E 56 D4
Castelldefels E 43 E7
Castell de Ferro E 55 F6
Castelleone I 69 C8
Castelletto sopra Ticino I 68 B6
Castellfort E 42 F3
Castellina in Chianti I 66 F3
Castellina Marittima I 66 F2
Castelliri I 62 D5
Castellnou de Bassella E 43 C6
Castellnovo E 48 E4
Castelló d'Argile I 66 C3
Castelló de Farfanya E 42 D5
Castelló d'Empúries E 43 C10
Castelló de Rugat E 56 D4
Castello di Annone I 37 B8
Castellón de la Plana E 48 E4
Castellote E 42 F3
Castello Tesino I 72 D4
Castellserá E 42 D5
Castellterçol E 43 D8
Castellucchio I 66 B2
Castelluccio dei Sauri I 60 A4
Castelluccio Inferiore I 60 C5
Castellucio Valmaggiore I 60 A4
Castell'Umberto I 59 C6
Castelluzzo I 58 C2
Castell-y-Nedd GB 13 B7
Castèl Madama I 62 D3
Castèl Maggiore I 66 C3
Castelmagno I 37 C6
Castelmassa I 66 B3
Castelmauro I 63 D7
Castelmoron-sur-Lot F 33 B6
Castelnau-Barbarens F 33 C7
Castelnaudary F 33 D9
Castelnau-d'Auzan F 33 C6
Castelnau-de-Médoc F 28 E4
Castelnau-de-Montmiral F 33 C9
Castelnau d'Estréfonds F 33 C8
Castelnau-le-Lez F 35 C6
Castelnau-Magnoac F 33 D7
Castelnau-Montratier F 33 B8
Castelnau-Rivière-Basse F 32 C5
Castelnovo di Sotto I 66 C2
Castelnovo ne'Monti I 66 D1
Castelnuovo Berardenga I 66 F4
Castelnuovo della Daunia I 63 D8
Castelnuovo di Garfagnana I 66 D1
Castelnuovo di Porto I 62 C3
Castelnuovo di Val di Cecina I 66 F2
Castelnuovo Don Bosco I 68 C4
Castelnuovo Rangone I 66 C2
Castelnuovo Scrivia I 37 B9
Castelo Bom P 45 C7
Castelo Branco P 39 F6
Castelo Branco P 44 E6
Castelo de Paiva P 44 B4
Castelo de Vide P 44 F6
Castelo do Neiva P 38 E2
Castelões P 44 B4
Castelplanio I 67 F7
Castelraimondo I 67 F7
Castèl Ritaldi I 62 B3
Castelrotto I 72 C4
Castelsagrat F 33 B7
Castèl San Giovanni I 69 C7
Castèl San Lorenzo I 60 C4
Castèl San Niccolò I 66 E4
Castèl San Pietro Terme I 66 D4
Castèl Sant'Angelo I 62 C4
Castelsantangelo sul Nera I 62 B4
Castelsaraceno I 60 C5
Castelsardo I 64 B2
Castelsarrasin F 33 B8
Castelseras E 42 F3
Casteltermini I 58 D4
Castelu RO 155 E2
Castelverde I 69 C8
Castelvetere in Val Fortore I 60 A3
Castelvetrano I 58 D2
Castelvetro Placentino I 69 C8
Castèl Viscardo I 62 B2
Castèl Volturno I 60 A1
Castenaso I 66 C3
Castéra-Verduzan F 33 C6
Castetnau-Camblong F 32 D4
Castets F 32 C3
Castiadas I 64 E4
Castielfabib E 47 D10
Castiello de Jaca E 32 E4
Castiglioncello I 66 F1
Castiglione dei Pepoli I 66 D3
Castiglione del Lago I 66 F5
Castiglione della Pescaia I 65 B3
Castiglione della Stiviere I 66 B1
Castiglione di Sicilia I 59 D7
Castiglione d'Orcia I 65 A5
Castiglione in Teverina I 62 B2
Castiglione Messer Marino I 63 D6
Castiglion Fiorentino I 66 F4
Castignano I 62 B5
Castilblanco E 45 F10
Castilblanco de los Arroyos E 51 D8
Castiliscar E 32 F3
Castilleja de la Cuesta E 51 E7
Castillejar E 55 D7
Castillejo de Martin Viejo E 45 C7
Castillejo de Mesleón E 40 F4
Castillejo de Robledo E 40 E5
Castillo de Bayuela E 46 D3
Castillo de Garcimuñoz E 47 E8
Castillo de Locubín E 53 A9
Castillon-en-Couserans F 33 E8
Castillon-la-Bataille F 28 F5
Castillonnès F 33 A7
Castillo-Nuevo E 32 E3
Castilruiz E 41 E7
Castione della Presolana I 69 B9
Castiòns di Strada I 73 E7
Castlebar IRL 6 E4
Castlebay GB 4 B2
Castlebellingham IRL 7 E10
Castleblakeney IRL 6 F6
Castleblayney IRL 7 D9
Castlebridge IRL 9 D10
Castle Carrock GB 5 F11
Castle Cary GB 13 C9
Castlecomer IRL 9 C8
Castleconnell IRL 8 C5
Castlecor IRL 8 D5
Castledawson GB 4 F3
Castlederg GB 4 F1
Castledermot IRL 9 C9
Castle Douglas GB 5 F9
Castleellis IRL 9 D10
Castlefinn IRL 4 F1
Castleford GB 11 D9
Castlegal IRL 6 D6
Castlegregory IRL 8 D2
Castlehill IRL 6 D4
Castleisland IRL 8 D4
Castle Kennedy GB 4 F7
Castlellis IRL 9 D10
Castlemaine IRL 8 D3
Castlemartin GB 12 B4
Castlemartyr IRL 8 E6
Castleplunket IRL 6 E6
Castlepollard IRL 7 E8
Castlerea IRL 6 E6
Castlereagh GB 7 C11
Castlerock GB 4 E3
Castletown GB 3 H10
Castletown GB 11 F7
Castletown GBM 10 C2
Castletown IRL 7 G8
Castletown Bere IRL 8 E3
Castletownshend IRL 8 E4
Castlewellan GB 7 D11
Castranova RO 160 E4
Castrejón de la Peña E 39 C10
Castrelo do Val E 38 E5
Castres F 33 C10
Castricum NL 16 C3
Castries F 35 C6
Castrignano del Capo I 61 D10
Castril E 55 D7
Castrillo de Don Juan E 40 E3
Castrillo de Duero E 40 E3
Castrillo de la Reina E 40 E5
Castrillo de la Vega E 40 E4
Castrillo Tejeriego E 40 E3
Castro I 61 C10
Castrobarto E 40 B5
Castrocalbón E 39 D8
Castro Caldelas E 38 D5
Castrocaro Terme I 66 D4
Castrocontrigo E 39 D7
Castro Daire P 44 C5
Castro dei Volsci I 62 D5
Castro del Río E 53 A8
Castro de Ouro E 38 A5
Castro de Rei E 38 B5
Castrofilippo I 58 E4
Castrogonzalo E 39 E8
Castrojeriz E 40 D3
Castro Laboreiro P 38 D3
Castro Marim P 50 E5
Castromocho E 39 D10
Castromonte E 39 E9
Castronuevo E 39 E8
Castronuño E 39 F9
Castronuovo di Sant'Andrea I 60 C6
Castronuovo di Sicilia I 58 D4
Castropignano I 63 D7
Castropodame E 39 C7
Castropol E 39 A5
Castrop-Rauxel D 17 E8
Castroreale I 59 C7
Castro-Urdiales E 40 B5
Castroverde E 38 B5
Castro Verde P 50 D3
Castroverde de Campos E 39 E9
Castrovillari I 60 D6
Castuera E 51 B8
Çata RO 152 E6
Çatalca TR 173 B9
Catalina RO 153 F8
Cataloi RO 155 C3
Catania I 59 E7
Catanzaro I 59 B10
Catanzaro Marina I 59 B10
Catarroja E 48 F4
Cătcău RO 152 C3
Căteasca RO 160 D6
Catenanuova I 59 D6
Caterham GB 15 E8
Cateri F 37 F9
Cathair Dónall IRL 8 E2
Cathair na Mart IRL 6 E3
Cathair Saidhbhín IRL 8 E2
Catherdaniel IRL 8 E2
Catí E 42 G4
Čatići BIH 157 D9
Catignano I 62 C5
Cătina RO 152 D4
Cătina RO 161 C8
Catívelos P 44 C5
Catoira E 38 C2
Caton GB 10 C6
Catral E 56 E3
Cattenom F 20 F6
Catterfeld D 79 E8
Catterick GB 11 C8
Catterline GB 5 B12
Cattolica I 67 E6
Cattolica Eraclea I 58 E3
Cătunele RO 159 D10
Catus F 33 A8
Căuaş RO 151 B10
Caudan F 22 E5
Caudebec-lès-Elbeuf F 18 F3
Caudecoste F 33 B7
Caudete E 56 D3
Caudete de las Fuentes E 47 E10
Caudiel E 48 E3
Caudiès-de-Fenouillèdes F 33 E10
Caudry F 19 D7
Caujac F 33 D8
Caulnes F 23 D7
Caulonia I 59 C9
Caumont F 33 B8
Caumont F 33 D8
Caumont-l'Éventé F 23 B10
Caumont-sur-Durance F 35 C8
Caunes-Minervois F 34 D4
Cauro F 37 H9
Căuşeni MD 154 D4
Causeway IRL 8 D3
Causeway Head GB 4 E3
Caussade F 33 B9
Cautano I 60 A3
Cauterets F 32 E5
Cava de'Tirreni I 60 B3
Cavadineşti RO 153 E12
Cavaglià I 68 C5
Cavaillon F 35 C9
Cavalaire-sur-Mer F 36 E5
Cavaleiro P 50 D2
Cavalese I 72 D3
Cavallermaggiore I 37 B7
Cavallino I 66 B6
Cava Manara I 69 C7
Cavan IRL 7 E8
Cavanagarven IRL 7 D9
Cavargna I 69 A7
Cavarzere I 66 B5
Cavazzo Carnico I 73 D7
Cave I 62 D3
Cave del Predil I 73 D8
Caveirac F 35 C7
Cavezzo I 66 C3
Cavignac F 28 E5
Čavle HR 67 B9
Cavnic RO 152 B3
Cavour I 68 D3
Cavriago I 66 C2
Cavriglia I 66 E3
Cavtat HR 162 D5
Çavuşköy TR 171 C10
Cawdor GB 3 K9
Cawood GB 11 D9
Cawston GB 15 B11
Caxarias P 44 E3
Çaybaşi TR 177 C9
Çayboyu TR 181 B8
Cayeux-sur-Mer F 18 D4
Çayirdere TR 173 B9
Caylus F 33 B9
Cazalegas E 46 D3
Cazalilla E 53 A9
Cazalla de la Sierra E 51 D8
Cazals F 33 A8
Cazals F 33 B9
Căzăneşti RO 159 D10
Căzăneşti RO 161 D10
Cazasu RO 155 C1
Cazaubon F 32 C5
Cazères F 33 D8
Cazes-Mondenard F 33 B8
Cazilhac F 33 D10
Cazin BIH 156 C4
Cazis CH 71 D8
Čažma HR 149 E7
Cazorla E 55 D7
Cazoulès F 29 F8
Cea E 38 D4
Cea E 39 D10
Ceahlău RO 153 C7
Ceamurlia de Jos RO 155 D3
Ceanannus Mór IRL 7 E9
Ceann Toirc IRL 8 D5
Ceann Trá IRL 8 D2
Ceanu Mare RO 152 D3
Cearsiadar GB 2 J3
Ceatharlach IRL 9 C9
Ceaucé F 23 D10
Ceauşu de Câmpie RO 152 D5
Céaux-d'Allègre F 30 E4
Cébazat F 30 D3
Čebín CZ 77 D10
Cebolla E 46 E3
Čebovce SK 147 E8
Cebreros E 46 D4
Ceccano I 62 D4
Cece H 149 C11
Čečejovce SK 145 F3
Čechtice CZ 77 C8
Čechynce SK 146 E6
Cecina I 66 F2
Ceclavín E 45 E7
Cecuni MNE 163 D8
Cedães P 38 F5
Čedasai LT 135 D10
Cedegolo I 69 A9
Cedeira E 38 A3
Cedillo E 44 E6
Cedillo del Condado E 46 D5
Cedrillas E 48 D3
Cedry Wielkie PL 138 B6
Cedynia PL 84 E6
Cee E 38 C1
Cefa RO 151 D8
Cefalù I 58 C5
Cefn-mawr GB 10 F5
Ceggia I 73 E6
Cegléd H 150 C4
Ceglédbercel H 150 C4
Ceglie Messapica I 61 B9
Cegłów PL 141 F5
Čegrane MK 163 F10
Cehal RO 151 C10
Cehegín E 55 C9
Cehu Silvaniei RO 151 C11
Ceica RO 151 D9
Ceikiniai LT 135 F12
Ceilhes-et-Rocozels F 34 C5
Ceinos de Campos E 39 D9
Ceintrey F 26 C5
Ceira P 44 D4
Čejč CZ 77 E11
Cejkov SK 145 G4
Cekcyn PL 138 C5
Çekirdekli TR 173 F9
Čekiškė LT 134 F7
Ceków-Kolonia PL 142 C5
Celadas E 47 D10
Čeladná CZ 146 B6
Čelákovice CZ 77 B7
Celaliye TR 173 A7
Celano I 62 C5
Celanova E 38 D4
Čelarevo SRB 158 C4
Celaru RO 160 E4
Celbridge IRL 7 F9
Čelebić BIH 157 E6
Čelebići BIH 157 F10
Celeiros P 38 E3
Celenza Valfortore I 63 D7
Celestynów PL 141 F4
Čelić BIH 157 C10
Celico I 61 E6
Čelinac Donji BIH 157 C7
Celje SLO 148 D4
Cella E 47 D10
Celldömölk H 149 B8
Celle D 79 A7
Celle Ligure I 37 C9
Cellere I 62 C1
Celles B 19 C7
Celles-sur-Belle F 28 C5
Celles-sur-Ource F 25 D11
Cellettes F 24 E5
Cellino Attanasio I 62 B5
Cellole I 62 E5
Čelopeci MK 168 B5
Čelopek MK 164 F3
Celorico da Beira P 44 C6
Celorico de Basto P 38 F4
Celrà E 43 C9
Çeltikçi TR 173 D9
Çembra I 69 A11
Čemerno BIH 157 F10
Cempi LV 135 A11
Cénac-et-St-Julien F 29 F8
Cenad RO 150 E6
Cenade RO 152 E4
Cenas LV 134 C7
Cencenighe Agordino I 72 D4
Cendras F 35 B7
Cendrieux F 29 F7
Cenei RO 159 B6
Ceneselli I 66 B3
Cengio I 37 C8
Cenicero E 41 D6
Ceniclentos E 46 D4
Čenta SRB 158 C5
Centallo I 37 B7
Centelles E 43 D8
Cento I 66 C3
Centola I 60 C4
Centuri F 37 F10
Centuripe I 59 D6
Cepagatti I 62 C6
Cepari RO 160 C5
Čepin HR 149 E11
Cepleniţa RO 153 C9
Čepovan SLO 73 D8
Ceppaloni I 60 A3
Ceppo Morelli I 68 B5
Ceprano I 62 D5
Ceptura RO 161 C8
Ceralije HR 149 E9
Cerami I 59 D6
Cerani BIH 157 C8
Cerano I 68 C6
Ceranów PL 141 E6
Cérans-Foulletourte F 23 E12
Cerasi I 59 C8
Ceraso I 60 C4
Ceraşu RO 161 C8
Cerăt RO 160 E3
Ceraukste LV 135 D8
Čeravë AL 168 C4
Cerbăl RO 151 F10
Cerbère F 34 F5
Cercal P 44 F3
Cercal P 50 D2
Čerčany CZ 77 C7
Cercedilla E 46 C4
Cercemaggiore I 63 E7
Cerchezu RO 155 F2
Cerchiara di Calabria I 61 D6

Cerchio I 62 C5
Cercy-la-Tour F 30 B4
Cerda I 58 U4
Cerdanyola del Vallès E 43 E8
Cerdedo E 38 C3
Cerdeira P 44 D5
Cerdon F 25 E7
Cere LV 134 B5
Cerea I 66 B3
Cered H 147 E9
Ceregnano I 66 B4
Cerekwica PL 85 E13
Cérences F 23 C9
Ceres GB 5 C11
Ceres I 31 E11
Ceresole Reale I 31 E11
Céreste F 35 C10
Céret F 34 F4
Čerević SRB 158 C4
Cerezo de Abajo E 46 B5
Cerezo de Arriba E 40 F4
Cerezo de Ríotirón E 40 C5
Cerfontaine B 184 D1
Cergău RO 152 E3
Cergy F 24 B7
Cerhenice CZ 77 B8
Ceriale I 37 C8
Ceriana I 37 D7
Cerignola I 60 A5
Cérilly F 30 B2
Čerín BIH 157 F8
Cerisano I 60 E6
Cerisiers F 25 D9
Cerisy-la-Forêt F 23 B10
Cerisy-la-Salle F 23 B9
Cerizay F 28 B4
Çerkezköy TR 173 B9
Çerkezmüsellim TR 173 B7
Cerklje SLO 73 D9
Cerklje SLO 148 E5
Cerkno SLO 73 D8
Cerkwica PL 85 B8
Cermei RO 151 D8
Çermé-Proshkë AL 168 B2
Cermignano I 62 B5
Cërmjan KS 163 E9
Cerna HR 157 B10
Cerna RO 155 C2
Cernache do Bonjardim P 44 E4
Černá Hora CZ 77 D11
Cernat RO 153 F8
Cernătești RO 160 E2
Cernătești RO 161 C9
Cernavodă RO 155 E2
Cernay F 27 E7
Cernay-en-Dormois F 19 F10
Černčice CZ 76 B5
Cernégula E 40 C4
Cernele RO 160 E3
Cernești RO 152 C3
Cernica RO 161 E8
Cernier CH 31 A10
Černík HR 157 B7
Černík SK 146 E6
Černilov CZ 77 B9
Cernişoara RO 160 C4
Cernobbio I 69 B7
Černoleuca MD 153 A11
Černošice CZ 76 C6
Černošín CZ 76 C3
Černilov LV 133 D2
Černovice CZ 77 D7
Černožice CZ 77 B9
Cerová SK 146 D4
Cerovac SRB 159 E6
Cerovak Tušilovički HR 148 F5
Ceroviljani BIH 157 B7
Cerovlje HR 67 B9
Cerovo SK 147 E8
Cerralbo E 45 C7
Cerreto d'Esi I 67 F6
Cerreto di Spoleto I 62 B3
Cerreto Sannita I 60 A3
Cerrigydrudion GB 10 E4
Cërrik AL 168 B2
Cerro al Volturno I 62 D6
Cersay F 28 A5
Cersosimo I 61 C6
Certaldo I 66 E3
Certeju de Sus RO 151 F10
Certești RO 153 E11
Certeze RO 145 H7
Certosa di Pavia I 69 C7
Certosa di Pesio I 37 C7
Ceru-Băcăinţi RO 151 F11
Cerujë AL 168 C3
Cerva P 38 F4
Cervaro I 62 D5
Cervatos de la Cueza E 39 D10
Červená Voda CZ 77 B11
Cervenia RO 161 F6
Červená Voda CZ 77 C12
Cervera I 42 D6
Cervera de la Cañada E 41 F8
Cervera del Llano E 47 E8
Cervera del Maestre E 48 D5
Cervera de los Montes E 46 D3
Cervera del Río Alhama E 41 D8
Cervera de Pisuerga E 40 C3
Cerveteri I 62 D2
Cervia I 66 D5
Cervignano del Friuli I 73 E7
Cervinara I 60 A3
Červiná Řečice CZ 77 C8
Cervione F 37 G10
Cervo E 38 A5
Cervo I 37 D8
Cervon F 25 F10
Cerzeto I 60 E6
Cesano Boscone I 69 C7
Cesano Maderno I 69 B7
Cesarò I 59 D6
Cesena I 66 D5
Cesenatico I 66 D5
Cesio I 37 C7
Cēsis LV 135 B10
Česká Kamenice CZ 80 E6
Česká Lípa CZ 81 E7
Česká Skalice CZ 77 B10
Česká Ves CZ 77 B12
České Brezovo SK 147 E9
České Budějovice CZ 77 E6
České Mezeříčí CZ 77 B10
Český Brod CZ 77 B7
Český Dub CZ 81 E7
Český Krumlov CZ 76 E6
Čsaký Těšín CZ 147 B7
Česljeva Bara SRB 159 D7
Çeşme TR 177 C7
Cespedosa E 45 C9
Cessalto I 73 E6

Cessenon-sur-Orb F 34 D5
Cessole I 37 B8
Lesson I 25 C8
Cesson-Sévigné F 23 D8
Cestas F 28 F4
Čestobrodica SRB 158 F5
Cesuras E 38 B3
Cesvaine LV 135 C12
Cetariu RO 151 C9
Cetate RO 152 C5
Cetate RO 159 E11
Cetatea de Baltă RO 152 E4
Cetăţeni RO 160 C6
Cetina E 41 F8
Cetingrad HR 156 B4
Cetinje MNE 163 E6
Ceto I 69 A9
Ceton F 24 D4
Cetona I 62 B1
Cetraro I 60 D5
Ceuta WHAT 53 E6
Ceutí E 56 E2
Ceva I 37 C8
Cevico de la Torre E 40 E3
Cevico Navero E 40 E3
Cevins F 31 D9
Cevio CH 68 A6
Cevizköy TR 173 A8
Čevo MNE 163 D6
Cewice PL 85 B13
Ceyreste F 35 D10
Ceyzériat F 31 C7
Cezieni RO 160 E4
Chã P 38 E4
Chaam NL 16 F3
Chabanais F 29 D7
Chabeuil F 31 F7
Chabielice PL 143 D7
Chablis F 25 E10
Chabówka PL 147 B9
Chabreloche F 30 D4
Chabris F 24 F6
Chacim P 39 F6
Chagford GB 13 D7
Chagny F 30 B6
Chaïkali GR 174 C4
Chaillac F 29 C8
Chailland F 23 D10
Chaillé-les-Marais F 28 C.3
Chailley F 25 D10
Chaintrix-Bierges F 25 C11
Chaironeia GR 175 C6
Chalabre F 33 E10
Chalais CH 31 C12
Chalais F 28 E6
Chalamera E 42 D4
Chalamont F 31 C7
Chalampé F 27 E8
Chalandri GR 175 C8
Chalandritsa GR 174 C4
Chalastra GR 169 C8
Chale GB 13 D12
Chaleix F 29 D7
Châlette-sur-Loing F 25 D8
Chalford GB 13 B10
Chalgrove GB 13 B12
Chaligny F 26 C5
Chalin PL 139 E7
Chalindrey F 26 E3
Chalivoy-Milon F 29 B11
Chalki GR 169 E8
Chalki GR 181 D7
Chalkiades GR 169 F7
Chalkiades GR 174 A2
Chalkida GR 175 C8
Chalkidona GR 169 C7
Chalkio GR 175 D6
Challans F 28 B2
Challerange F 19 F10
Challes-les-Eaux F 31 D8
Chalmoux F 30 B4
Chalonnes-sur-Loire F 23 F10
Châlons-en-Champagne F 25 C11
Chalon-sur-Saône F 30 B6
Châlus F 29 D7
Cham CH 27 F9
Cham D 75 D12
Chamalières F 30 D3
Chamaloc F 31 F7
Chamberet F 29 D9
Chambéria F 31 C8
Chambéry F 31 D8
Chambley-Bussières F 26 B4
Chambois F 23 C12
Chambon-la-Forêt F 29 D9
Chambon-sur-Voueize F 29 C10
Chambord F 24 E6
Chamboulive F 29 E9
Chambray-lès-Tours F 24 F4
Chamerolles F 25 D9
Chamesson F 25 E12
Chamonix-Mont-Blanc F 31 D10
Chamoux-sur-Gelon F 31 D9
Champagnac F 29 E10
Champagnac-de-Belair P 29 E7
Champagnac-le-Vieux F 30 E4
Champagne-Mouton F 29 D6
Champagne-sur-Seine F 25 D8
Champagney F 26 E6
Champagnole F 31 B8
Champaubert F 25 C10
Champdeniers-St-Denis F 28 C5
Champ-d'Oiseau F 25 E11
Champeix F 30 D3
Champéry CH 31 C10
Champex CH 31 C11
Champforgeuil F 30 B6
Champgenéteux F 23 D11
Champier F 31 E7
Champigné F 23 E10
Champignelles F 25 E9
Champigneulles F 186 D3
Champigny F 25 D9
Champlemy F 25 F9
Champlitte F 26 E4
Champniers F 29 D6
Champoléon F 31 F9
Champoluc I 68 B4
Champsecret F 23 C10
Champs-sur-Tarentaine-Marchal F 29 E11
Champs-sur-Yonne F 25 E10
Champ-sur-Drac F 31 E8
Champtoceaux F 23 E9
Chamrousse F 31 E8
Chamusca P 44 F4
Chanac F 34 B5
Chanas F 30 E6
Chançay P 44 F5
Chanceaux F 25 E12
Chanceaux-sur-Choisille F 24 F4
Chancelade F 29 E7
Chancelaria P 44 E3

Chandras GR 179 E11
Chandrinos GR 174 F4
Chañe E 40 F3
Changé F 23 D10
Changé F 23 E12
Changy F 30 C5
Chania GR 178 E7
Chaniotis GR 169 D10
Chantada E 38 C4
Chantelle F 30 C3
Chantilly F 25 B7
Chantonnay F 28 B3
Chanu F 23 C10
Chaource F 25 D11
Chapaevo BG 166 C5
Chapayevka UA 154 A5
Chapel-en-le-Frith GB 11 E8
Chapelle-lez-Herlaimont B 182 E4
Chapeltown GB 11 E9
Chapinería E 46 D4
Charakas GR 178 E9
Charavgi GR 169 D6
Charbonnat F 30 B5
Charcenne F 26 F4
Charchilla F 31 C8
Chard GB 13 D9
Chardstock GB 13 D9
Charenton-du-Cher F 29 B11
Charfield GB 13 B10
Chargey-lès-Gray F 26 F4
Charlbury GB 13 B12
Charleroi B 19 D9
Charlestown IRL 6 E5
Charleville IRL 8 D5
Charleville-Mézières F 19 E10
Charlieu F 30 C5
Charlottenberg S 96 C7
Charlton GB 13 C12
Charlton Kings GB 13 B10
Charly F 25 C9
Charmé F 29 D6
Charmes F 26 D5
Charmes-sur-Rhône F 30 F6
Charmey CH 31 B11
Charmouth GB 13 D9
Charmoy F 25 E9
Charny F 25 E9
Charokopeio GR 178 B2
Charolles F 30 C5
Charomkhava BY 133 F3
Charopo GR 169 B9
Chârost F 29 B10
Charquemont F 27 F6
Charrey-sur-Seine F 25 E12
Charrin F 30 B4
Charroux F 29 C6
Charsznica PL 143 F8
Chartres F 24 D5
Charvensod I 31 D11
Charvieu-Chavagneux F 31 D7
Charzyno PL 85 B9
Chassagne-Montrachet F 30 B6
Chasseneuil-sur-Bonnieure F 29 D6
Chasseradès F 35 A6
Chasse-sur-Rhône F 30 D6
Chassigny-Aisey F 26 E3
Chassillé F 23 D11
Chastre B 19 C10
Château-Arnoux F 35 B10
Châteaubernard F 28 D5
Châteaubourg F 23 D9
Châteaubriant F 23 E9
Château-Chinon F 30 A4
Château-d'Oex CH 31 C11
Château-d'Olonne F 28 B2
Château-du-Loir F 24 E3
Châteaudun F 24 D5
Châteaugiron F 23 D8
Château-Gontier F 23 E10
Château-Landon F 25 D8
Château-la-Vallière F 24 E3
Châteaulin F 22 D3
Châteaumeillant F 29 B10
Châteauneuf-de-Galaure F 31 E6
Châteauneuf-de-Randon F 35 A6
Châteauneuf-d'Ille-et-Vilaine F 23 C8
Châteauneuf-du-Faou F 22 D4
Châteauneuf-en-Thymerais F 24 C5
Châteauneuf-la-Forêt F 29 D9
Châteauneuf-les-Martigues F 35 D9
Châteauneuf-sur-Charente F 28 D5
Châteauneuf-sur-Cher F 29 B10
Châteauneuf-sur-Loire F 25 E7
Châteauneuf-sur-Sarthe F 23 E11
Châteauneuf-Val-de-Bargis F 25 F9
Châteauponsac F 29 C8
Château-Porcien F 19 E9
Châteauredon F 36 C4
Châteaurenard F 23 E8
Châteaurenard F 35 B7
Château-Renault F 24 E4
Châteauroux F 29 B9
Châteauroux F 36 B5
Château-Salins F 26 C6
Château-Thierry F 25 C9
Châteauvillain F 25 D12
Châtel F 31 C10
Châtelaillon-Plage F 28 C3
Châtelaudren F 22 C6
Châtel-Censoir F 25 E10
Châteldon F 30 C4
Châtelet B 19 D10
Châtel-Gérard F 25 E11
Châtelguyon F 30 D3
Châtellerault F 29 B7
Châtel-Montagne F 30 C4
Châtel-St-Denis CH 31 B10
Châtel-sur-Moselle F 26 D5
Châtelus-Malvaleix F 29 C10
Châtenois F 26 D4
Châtenois F 27 D7
Châtenois-les-Forges F 27 E6
Châtenoy-le-Royal F 30 B6
Chatham GB 15 E10
Châtillon B 19 E12
Châtillon I 68 B4
Châtillon-Coligny F 25 E8
Châtillon-en-Bazois F 30 A4
Châtillon-en-Diois F 35 A9

Châtillon-en-Michaille F 31 C8
Châtillon-la-Palud F 31 D7
Châtillon-sur-Chalaronne F 31 C6
Châtillon-sur-Colmont F 23 D10
Châtillon-sur-Indre F 29 B8
Châtillon-sur-Marne F 25 B10
Châtillon-sur-Seine F 25 E12
Châtillon-sur-Thouet F 28 B5
Chatte F 31 E7
Chatteris GB 15 C9
Chatton GB 5 D13
Chatuzange-le-Goubet F 31 F7
Chatzis GR 174 E4
Chauchina E 53 B9
Chaudenay F 26 E4
Chaudes-Aigues F 30 F3
Chaudeyrac F 35 A6
Chaudfontaine B 19 C12
Chauffailles F 30 C5
Chauffayer F 31 F9
Chaulnes F 18 E6
Chaumergy F 31 B7
Chaumont F 26 D3
Chaumont-en-Vexin F 18 F4
Chaumont-Porcien F 19 E9
Chaumont-sur-Aire F 26 C3
Chaumont-sur-Loire F 24 F5
Chaunay F 29 C6
Chauny F 19 E7
Chaussin F 31 B7
Chauvigny F 29 B7
Chavanay F 30 E6
Chavanges F 25 C12
Chavanoz F 31 D7
Chavari GR 174 D3
Chavelot F 26 D5
Chaves P 38 E5
Chazelles-sur-Lyon F 30 D5
Cheadle GB 11 F8
Cheb CZ 75 B11
Checa E 47 C9
Chechel'nyk UA 154 A4
Chęciny PL 143 E9
Chécy F 24 E7
Chedburgh GB 15 C10
Cheddar GB 13 C9
Chef-Boutonne F 28 C5
Chekhpare BG 166 E4
Cheles E 51 B5
Chella E 56 C3
Chełm PL 141 H8
Chełmek PL 143 F7
Chełmiec PL 145 D2
Chełmno PL 138 D6
Chełmno PL 142 B6
Chełmsford GB 15 D9
Chełmża PL 138 D6
Cheltenham GB 13 B10
Chelva E 47 E11
Chemazé F 23 E10
Chémery F 24 F5
Chémery-sur-Bar F 19 E10
Chemillé F 23 F10
Cheminon F 25 C12
Chemiré-le-Gaudin F 23 E11
Chemnitz D 80 E3
Chenecey-Buillon F 26 F4
Chénérailles F 29 C10
Cheniménil F 26 D6
Chenôve F 26 F3
Cheny F 25 E10
Chepelare BG 165 F10
Chepintsi BG 165 D7
Chepstow GB 13 B9
Chepy F 25 C11
Chera E 47 E10
Chérac F 28 D5
Chéraute F 32 D4
Cherbourg-Octeville F 23 A8
Cheremule I 64 B2
Cherepkivtsi UA 153 A7
Chereshovo BG 161 F8
Cherlenivka UA 153 A8
Cherna BG 155 F1
Cherna Gora BG 166 E4
Chernevo RUS 132 C3
Cherni Osŭm BG 165 D10
Cherni Vrŭkh BG 167 E8
Chernivtsi UA 153 A7
Chernogorovo BG 165 E9
Cherno More BG 167 D8
Chernoochene BG 166 F4
Chernyakhovsk RUS 136 D4
Chernyshevskoye RUS 136 D6
Chéroy F 25 D9
Cherskaya RUS 132 F3
Cherso GR 169 B8
Chert E 42 F4
Cherveix-Cubas F 29 E8
Cherven BG 161 F8
Cherven Bryag BG 165 C9
Cherventsi BG 167 B8
Cherves-Richemont F 28 D5
Chervona Hreblya UA 154 F3
Chervonoarmiys'ke UA 154 F3
Chervonohrad UA 144 C9
Chesham GB 15 D7
Cheshunt GB 15 D8
Chesley F 25 E11
Chessy-les-Prés F 25 D10
Cheste E 48 E3
Chester GB 10 E6
Chesterfield GB 11 E9
Chester-le-Street GB 5 F13
Chetani RO 152 E4
Chetrosu MD 153 A11
Chevagnes F 30 B4
Chevanceaux F 28 E5
Chevereşu Mare RO 159 B7
Chevillon F 26 C3
Chevilly F 24 D6
Chevreuse F 24 C7
Chew Magna GB 13 C9
Cheylade F 30 E2
Chezal-Benoît F 29 B10
Chèze F 32 E5
Chiajna RO 161 E8
Chiampo I 66 A3
Chianciano Terme I 62 A1
Chianni I 66 E2
Chiaramonte Gulfi I 59 E6
Chiaramonti I 64 B2
Chiaravalle I 67 E7
Chiaravalle Centrale I 59 B9
Chiari I 69 B8
Chiaromonte I 60 C6
Chiasso I 69 B7

Chiavari I 37 C10
Chiavenno I 69 A7
Chiché I 28 B5
Chichester GB 15 F7
Chichiş RO 153 F7
Chiclana de la Frontera E 52 D4
Chiclana de Segura E 55 C6
Chieming D 72 A6
Chienes I 72 C4
Chieri I 37 A7
Chiesa in Valmalenco I 69 A8
Chieşd RO 151 C10
Chiesina Uzzanese I 66 E2
Chieti I 63 C6
Chieuti I 63 D8
Chieveley GB 13 C12
Chièvres B 19 C8
Chigwell GB 15 D9
Chiheru de Jos RO 152 D5
Chikhachevo RUS 133 B7
Chilches E 48 E4
Chilcompton GB 13 C9
Chilham GB 15 E11
Chiliie RO 161 C8
Chiliomodi GR 175 D6
Chilleurs-aux-Bois F 24 D7
Chillón E 54 B3
Chilluévar E 55 C6
Chiloeches E 47 C6
Chimay B 19 D9
Chimeneas E 53 B9
Chinanale I 36 B6
Chinchilla de Monte Aragón E 55 B9
Chinchón E 46 D6
Chindrieux F 31 D8
Chinon F 23 F12
Chinteni RO 152 D3
Chiochiş RO 152 D4
Chioggia I 66 B5
Chiojdeni RO 161 B9
Chiojdu RO 161 C8
Chiomonte I 31 E10
Chiona GR 174 C2
Chionata GR 174 C2
Chios GR 177 C7
Chipiona E 52 C4
Chiperceni MD 154 B3
Chippenham GB 13 C10
Chipping Campden GB 13 A11
Chipping Norton GB 13 B11
Chipping Ongar GB 15 D9
Chipping Sodbury GB 13 B10
Chippis CH 31 C12
Chiprana E 42 E3
Chiprovtsi BG 165 C6
Chirbury GB 10 F5
Chiren BG 165 C8
Chiriet-Lunga MD 154 E3
Chirivel E 55 D8
Chirk GB 10 F5
Chirnogeni RO 155 F2
Chirnogi RO 161 E9
Chirnside GB 5 D12
Chiroubles F 30 C6
Chirpan BG 166 E4
Chirpăr RO 152 F5
Chirsova MD 154 E3
Chiscani RO 155 C1
Chişcareni MD 153 B12
Chişcăreni MD 154 C3
Chiselet RO 161 E9
Chişinău MD 154 C3
Chisindia RO 151 E9
Chişineu-Criş RO 151 D8
Chistye-Prudy RUS 136 E5
Chiţcani MD 154 D3
Chitignano I 66 E4
Chitila RO 161 D7
Chiuiești RO 152 C3
Chiuro I 69 A8
Chiusa I 72 C4
Chiusa di Pesio I 37 C7
Chiusaforte I 73 D7
Chiusa Sclafani I 58 D3
Chiusavecchia I 37 D7
Chiusdino I 66 F3
Chiusi I 62 A1
Chiusi della Verna I 66 E4
Chiuza RO 152 C4
Chiva E 48 F3
Chivasso I 68 C4
Chizé F 28 C5
Chlebičov CZ 146 B5
Chlebnice SK 147 C9
Chlebowo PL 81 B7
Chlewiska PL 141 H3
Chłopice PL 144 D6
Chludowo PL 81 A11
Chlumčany CZ 76 C4
Chlumec CZ 80 E5
Chlumec nad Cidlinou CZ 77 B8
Chlum u Třeboně CZ 77 E7
Chmielnik PL 143 E10
Chmielno PL 161 F8
Chmiel Pierwszy PL 144 A6
Chminianske Jakubovany SK 145 F3
Chobienia PL 81 C10
Chobienice PL 81 B9
Choceň CZ 77 B10
Choceń PL 138 E7
Chocholná-Velčice SK 146 D5
Chocianów PL 81 D9
Chocicza PL 81 B12
Chociwel PL 85 D8
Chocz PL 142 C4
Choczewo PL 138 A4
Chodecz PL 138 F7
Chodel PL 141 H6
Chodov CZ 75 B11
Chodová Planá CZ 75 C12
Chodów PL 141 H5
Chodów PL 143 B7
Chodzież PL 85 E11
Chojna PL 84 E6
Chojnice PL 85 C13
Chojno PL 81 A12
Chojnów PL 81 D9

Chora Sfakion GR 178 E7
Chorefto GR 169 F9
Chorges F 36 B4
Chorio GR 177 F8
Choristi GR 171 B6
Chorkówka PL 145 D4
Chorley GB 10 D6
Chorna UA 154 B4
Chorna Tysa UA 152 A4
Chornomyn UA 154 A4
Chorzele PL 139 D10
Chorzów PL 143 F6
Chorzyna PL 142 D6
Choszczno PL 85 D8
Chotča SK 145 E4
Chotěboř CZ 77 C9
Chotěšov CZ 76 C4
Chotín SK 149 A10
Chotilsko CZ 76 C6
Chouni GR 174 B4
Chouto P 44 F4
Chouzy-sur-Cisse F 24 E5
Chovar E 48 E3
Choye F 26 F4
Chozas de Abajo E 39 C8
Chrást CZ 76 C4
Chrast CZ 77 C9
Chrastava CZ 81 E7
Chřibská CZ 81 E6
Christchurch GB 13 D11
Christiansfeld DK 86 E4
Christon Bank GB 5 E13
Chropyně CZ 146 C4
Chróścina PL 142 E3
Chrostkowo PL 139 E7
Chrudim CZ 77 C9
Chruślin PL 143 B8
Chruszczobród PL 143 F7
Chrysa GR 171 B7
Chrysafa GR 175 E6
Chryso GR 169 B10
Chrysochorafa GR 169 B9
Chrysokellaria GR 178 B2
Chrysochori GR 171 C7
Chrysoupoli GR 171 C7
Chrzanów PL 143 F7
Chrząstowa Wielka PL 81 D12
Chrząstowice CZ 142 E5
Chrzypsko Wielkie PL 81 A10
Chtelnica SK 146 D5
Chuchelná CZ 142 C5
Chudleigh GB 13 D7
Chudoba PL 142 E5
Chulilla E 48 E3
Chulmleigh GB 13 D7
Chuprene BG 165 B6
Chur CH 71 D9
Churchdown GB 13 B10
Church Hill IRL 7 C7
Church Stretton GB 10 F6
Churek BG 165 D8
Churwalden CH 71 D9
Chuzelles F 30 D6
Cl.valčov CZ 146 C5
Chvaletice CZ 77 B8
Chvalšiny CZ 76 E6
Chwaszczyno PL 138 B5
Chynadiyeve UA 145 F6
Chyňava CZ 76 B6
Chýnov CZ 77 D7
Chynów PL 141 G4
Chyšky CZ 77 D6
Ciacova RO 159 B7
Ciadîr MD 154 D2
Ciadîr-Lunga MD 154 E3
Ciadoux F 33 D7
Ciampino I 62 D3
Cianciana I 58 D3
Ciasna PL 142 E5
Ciążeń PL 142 B4
Cibakháza H 150 D5
Ciborro P 50 B3
Ciboure F 32 D2
Cicagna I 37 C10
Cicârlău RO 151 B11
Cicciano I 60 B3
Cicârlău RO 151 B11
Ciceu-Giurgești RO 152 C4
Čičevac SRB 159 F7
Cicibór Duży PL 141 F8
Ciclova Română RO 159 C8
Čičov SK 146 F5
Çidhën AL 163 F9
Cidones E 41 E6
Ciechanów PL 139 E10
Ciechanowiec PL 141 E7
Ciechocinek PL 138 E6
Cielądz PL 141 G2
Ciempozuelos E 46 D5
Ciepielów PL 141 H5
Cierna nad Tisou SK 145 G5
Cierny Balog SK 147 D9
Cierp-Gaud F 33 E7
Cierznie PL 85 C12
Cieszanów PL 144 C7
Cieszków PL 81 C12
Cieszyn PL 142 D4
Cieszyn PL 147 B7
Cieutat F 33 D6
Cieux F 29 D7
Cieza E 55 C10
Cifer SK 146 E5
Cifliq AL 168 E3
Çiftlikköy TR 173 B7
Çiftlikköy TR 173 B9
Cifuentes E 47 C7
Cigales E 39 E10
Cigánd H 145 G4
Cigliano I 68 C5
Cikó H 149 D11
Cilibia RO 161 C10
Cilieni RO 160 F5
Cílipi HR 162 D5
Cill Airne IRL 8 D4

Cilleros E 45 D7
Cill Mhantáin IRL 7 G10
Cill Mocheallóg IRL 8 D5
Cill na Mallach IRL 8 D5
Cill Orglan IRL 8 D3
Cill Rois IRL 8 C4
Cill Rónáin IRL 6 F3
Cilybebyll GB 13 B7
Cimanes del Tejar E 39 C8
Cimballa E 47 B9
Čimdenieki LV 134 C6
Čimelice CZ 76 D6
Ciminna I 58 D4
Cimişlia MD 154 D3
Cimolais I 72 D5
Çınarcık TR 173 C11
Cinco Casas E 47 F6
Cinctorres E 42 F3
Cincu RO 152 F5
Cinderford GB 13 B10
Çine TR 181 A8
Ciñera E 39 C8
Ciney B 19 D11
Cinfães P 44 B4
Cinge TR 177 A9
Cingoli I 67 F7
Cinigiano I 65 B4
Cinisello Balsamo I 69 B7
Cinn Mhara IRL 6 F3
Cinobaňa SK 147 E9
Cinq-Mars-la-Pile F 24 F3
Cinquefrondi I 59 C9
Cintegabelle F 33 D9
Cintrey F 26 E4
Cintruénigo E 41 D8
Ciobăniţa RO 155 E2
Ciobanu RO 155 D1
Ciobîškis LT 137 D10
Cioc-Maidan MD 154 E3
Ciofrângeni RO 160 C5
Cióirtheach IRL 7 F7
Ciolănești RO 160 E6
Ciolpani RO 161 D8
Cionn tSáile IRL 8 E5
Ciorani RO 161 D9
Ciorăşti RO 161 C10
Ciorogârla RO 161 E7
Cioroiaşi RO 160 E2
Cioropcani MD 153 C11
Ciorteşti RO 153 D11
Ciprian Porumbescu RO 153 B8
Cirat E 48 D3
Cirauqui E 32 E2
Cîrava UA 154 C2
Circello I 60 A3
Cirencester GB 13 B11
Cireşu RO 159 D10
Cireşu RO 161 C10
Ciria E 41 E8
Ciriè I 68 C4
Cirigliano I 60 C6
Cirpăčau MD 154 A2
Cirkale LV 134 B4
Cirma LV 133 C3
Cirò I 61 E8
Cirò Marina I 61 E8
Çırpı TR 177 C10
Ciruelos E 46 E5
Ciruelos del Pinar E 47 B8
Čtrulj LV 134 B4
Ciry-le-Noble F 30 B5
Cisano sul Neva I 37 C8
Cisek PL 142 F5
Cislău RO 161 C8
Cismichioi MD 155 B2
Cisna PL 145 E5
Cisnădie RO 160 B4
Cisneros E 39 D10
Cisòn di Valmarino I 72 E5
Cissé F 29 B6
Cista Provo HR 157 E6
Cisterna di Latina I 62 D3
Cisternino I 61 B8
Cisterna E 39 C9
Cisterna I 66 F1
Čitluk BIH 157 B6
Čitluk BIH 157 F8
Cittadella I 72 E4
Città della Pieve I 62 B2
Città di Castello I 66 F5
Cittanova I 59 C9
Cittareale I 62 B4
Città Sant'Angelo I 62 B6
Cittiglio I 68 B6
Ciucea RO 151 D10
Ciuchici RO 159 D8
Ciuciulea MD 153 B10
Ciucsângeorgiu RO 153 D8
Ciucur-Mingir MD 154 E3
Ciucurova RO 155 D2
Ciudad Real E 54 B5
Ciudad Rodrigo E 45 C7
Ciudanovita RO 159 C8
Ciugud RO 152 D3
Ciuhoi RO 151 C9
Ciulniţa RO 161 D10
Ciumani RO 153 D7
Ciumeghiu RO 151 D8
Ciuperceni RO 159 F10
Ciuperceni RO 160 F5
Ciuperceni Noi RO 159 F10
Ciurila RO 152 D3
Ciuruleasa RO 151 E11
Ciutadella E 57 A12
Civaux F 29 C7
Cividale del Friuli I 73 D7
Civita I 60 D6
Civita Castellana I 62 C2
Civita d'Antino I 62 D4
Civitanova del Sannio I 63 D6
Civitanova Marche I 67 F8
Civitaquana I 62 C5
Civitavecchia I 62 C1
Civitella Casanova I 62 C5
Civitella del Tronto I 62 B5
Civitella di Romagna I 66 D4
Civitella in Val di Chiana I 66 F4
Civitella Roveto I 62 D4
Civray F 29 C6
Civray F 29 C6
Cizer RO 151 C10
Čížkovice CZ 76 B6
Čkyně CZ 76 D5
Clabhach GB 4 B3
Clachan GB 2 L4

Clachan GB 4 C7
Clachan of Glendaruel GB 4 C6
Clachtoll GB 2 J6
Clacton-on-Sea GB 15 D11
Cladich GB 4 C6
Clady GB 4 F1
Clady GB 4 F3
Claggan GB 4 B5
Clairac F 33 B6
Clairoix F 18 F6
Clairvaux-les-Lacs F 31 B8
Claix F 31 E8
Clamecy F 25 F10
Clane IRL 7 F9
Clans F 36 C6
Claonadh IRL 7 F9
Claonaig GB 4 D6
Clapham GB 11 C7
Clapham GB 15 C8
Clara IRL 7 F7
Clár Chlainne Mhuiris IRL 6 E5
Clarecastle IRL 8 C5
Claremorris IRL 6 E5
Claret F 35 B10
Claro CH 69 A7
Clary F 19 D7
Clashmore IRL 9 D7
Clashnessie GB 2 J6
Claudy GB 4 F2
Clausnitz D 80 E4
Claußnitz D 80 E3
Clausthal-Zellerfeld F 79 C7
Claut I 72 D6
Clauzetto I 73 D6
Clavering GB 15 D9
Clavier B 19 D11
Clay Cross GB 11 E9
Claydon GB 15 C11
Clayton GB 15 F8
Cleady IRL 8 E3
Cleat GB 3 H11
Cleator Moor GB 10 B4
Clécy F 23 C11
Cléder F 22 C3
Cleethorpes GB 11 D11
Clefmont F 26 D4
Cléguérec F 22 D5
Cleja RO 153 E9
Clelles F 31 E8
Clémency L 20 E5
Clenze D 83 B2
Cleobury Mortimer GB 13 A10
Cléon F 18 F3
Cléon-d'Andran F 35 A8
Cléré-les-Pins F 24 F3
Clères F 18 E3
Clérey F 25 D11
Clermain F 30 C6
Clermont F 18 F5
Clermont F 33 D8
Clermont-en-Argonne F 26 B3
Clermont-Ferrand F 30 D3
Clermont-l'Hérault F 34 C5
Clerval F 26 F6
Clervaux L 20 D6
Cléry-St-André F 24 E6
Cles I 72 D3
Clevedon GB 13 C9
Cleveleys GB 10 D5
Clifden IRL 6 F2
Cliffe GB 15 E9
Cliffoney IRL 6 D6
Climauți MD 153 A11
Clinge NL 16 F2
Clingen D 79 D8
Clion F 29 B8
Clisson F 28 A3
Clitheroe GB 11 D7
Cloch na Rón IRL 6 F3
Clogh GB 4 F4
Clogh IRL 9 C7
Clogh IRL 9 C8
Clogh IRL 9 C10
Cloghan IRL 7 C7
Cloghan IRL 7 F7
Clogheen IRL 8 D7
Clogher GB 7 D8
Clogherhead IRL 7 E10
Cloghy GB 7 D12
Clohars-Carnoët F 22 E4
Clohernagh IRL 9 D8
Cloich na Coillte IRL 8 E5
Clonakilty IRL 8 E5
Clonaslee IRL 7 F7
Clonbern IRL 6 E5
Clonbulloge IRL 7 F8
Clonbur IRL 6 E4
Clondrohid IRL 8 E4
Clondulane IRL 8 D6
Clonea IRL 9 D8
Clonee IRL 7 F10
Cloneen IRL 9 D7
Clones IRL 7 D8
Clonmel IRL 9 D7
Clonmellon IRL 7 E8
Clonoulty IRL 9 C7
Clonroche IRL 9 D9
Clontibret IRL 7 D9
Clonygowan IRL 7 F8
Cloonbannin IRL 8 D4
Cloonboo IRL 6 F4
Cloonfad IRL 6 E5
Cloonfad IRL 6 F6
Cloonkeen IRL 6 E4
Cloppenburg D 17 C10
Closeburn GB 5 E9
Clough GB 7 D11
Cloughjordan IRL 8 C6
Cloughmills GB 4 E4
Cloughton GB 11 C11
Clova GB 5 B10
Clovelly GB 12 D6
Clovullin GB 4 B6
Cloyes-sur-le-Loir F 24 E5
Cloyne IRL 8 E6
Cluain Bú IRL 6 F4
Cluain Eois IRL 7 D8
Cluainín IRL 6 D6
Cluain Meala IRL 9 D7
Cluis F 29 B9
Cluj-Napoca RO 152 D3
Clumanc F 36 C4
Clun GB 13 A8
Cluny F 30 C6
Cluses F 31 C10
Clusone I 69 B8
Clydach GB 13 B7
Clydebank GB 5 D8
Clynderwen GB 12 B5
Clyro GB 13 A8
Ćmielów PL 143 E12
Cmolas PL 143 F12

Coachford IRL 8 E5
Coagh GB 4 F3
Coalburn GB 5 D9
Coalisland GB 7 C9
Coalville GB 11 F9
Coaña E 39 A6
Coarnele Caprei RO 153 C10
Coarraze F 32 D5
Coast GB 2 K5
Coatbridge GB 5 D8
Cobadin RO 155 E2
Cobani MD 153 B10
Cobeja E 46 D5
Cobeta E 47 C8
Cobh IRL 8 E6
Cobia RO 160 D6
Coburg D 75 B8
Coca E 46 B3
Cocentaina E 56 D4
Cochem D 21 D8
Cochirleanca RO 161 C10
Cociuba Mare RO 151 D9
Cockburnspath GB 5 D11
Cockenzie and Port Seton GB 5 D11
Cockerham GB 10 D6
Cockermouth GB 5 F10
Cockett GB 12 B7
Cocora RO 161 D10
Cocu RO 160 D5
Cocumont F 32 B6
Codăești RO 153 D11
Coddington GB 11 E10
Code LV 135 D8
Codevigo I 66 B5
Codigoro I 66 C5
Codlea RO 161 B6
Codognò I 69 C8
Codos E 41 F9
Codreanca MD 154 C3
Codroipo I 73 E6
Codru MD 154 D3
Coesfeld D 17 E8
Coevorden NL 17 C7
Coëx F 28 B2
Cofrentes E 47 F10
Cogealac RO 155 D3
Cogeces del Monte E 40 E3
Coggeshall GB 15 D10
Coggia I 37 G9
Coggiola I 68 B5
Cogliniceni MD 154 B3
Çöğmen TR 181 C10
Cognac F 28 D5
Cognac-la-Forêt F 29 D8
Cogne I 31 D11
Cognin F 31 D8
Cogolin F 36 E5
Cogollos E 40 D4
Cogollos Vega E 53 B9
Cogolludo E 47 C6
Cogula E 45 C10
Coillan Chollaigh IRL 7 E9
Coimbra P 44 D4
Coimbrão P 44 E3
Coín E 53 C7
Coincy F 25 B9
Coja P 44 D4
Cojasca RO 161 D7
Cojocna RO 152 D3
Čoka SRB 150 F5
Colares P 50 B1
Colayrac-St-Cirq F 33 B7
Colbasna MD 154 B4
Cölbe D 21 C11
Colbitz D 79 B10
Colbordolo I 67 E6
Colceag RO 161 D8
Colchester GB 15 D10
Coldingham GB 5 D12
Colditz D 79 D12
Coldstream GB 5 D12
Coleford GB 13 B9
Coleraine GB 4 E3
Colibași RO 161 E8
Colibași RO 161 E8
Colibași RO 161 E8
Colibița RO 152 C5
Colico I 69 A7
Coligny F 31 C7
Colindres E 40 B5
Colintraive GB 4 D6
Collado Hermoso E 46 B5
Collado Villalba E 46 C5
Collagna I 66 D1
Collanzo E 39 B8
Collarmele I 62 C5
Collazzone I 62 B2
Collecchio I 66 C1
Collecorvino I 62 B5
Colledara I 62 B5
Colle di Val d'Elsa I 66 F3
Colleferro I 62 D4
Collegno I 68 C4
Colle Isarco I 72 C3
Collelongo I 62 D5
Collepardo I 62 D4
Collepasso I 61 C10
Collesalvetti I 66 E1
Colle Sannita I 60 A3
Collesano I 58 D4
Colletorto I 63 D7
Colliano I 60 B4
Colli a Volturno I 62 D6
Collieston GB 3 L13
Collinas I 64 E2
Collinée F 22 D6
Collinghorst (Rhauderfehn) D 17 B9
Collio I 69 B9
Collioure F 34 F5
Collobrières F 36 E4
Collon IRL 7 E10
Collonges I 31 C8
Collonges-la-Rouge F 29 E9
Collooney IRL 6 D6
Colmar F 27 D8
Colmars F 36 C5
Colmberg D 75 D7
Colmeal P 44 D5
Colmenar E 53 C8
Colmenar del Arroyo E 46 D4
Colmenar de Montemayor E 45 D9
Colmenar de Oreja E 46 D6
Colmenar Viejo E 46 C5
Colméry F 25 F9
Colmonell GB 4 E7
Colne GB 11 D7

Colobraro I 61 C6
Cologna Veneta I 66 B3
Cologne F 33 C7
Cologno al Serio I 69 B8
Colombelles F 23 B11
Colombey-les-Belles F 26 C4
Colombey-les-Deux-Églises F 25 D12
Colombier CH 31 B10
Colombiès F 33 B10
Colombres E 39 B10
Colomers E 43 C9
Colomiers F 33 C8
Colonești RO 153 D10
Colonești RO 160 D5
Colònia de Sant Jordi E 57 C11
Colònia de Sant Pere E 57 B11
Colonnella I 62 B5
Colorno I 66 C1
Colos P 50 D3
Côlpin D 84 C4
Colquhar GB 5 D10
Colroy-la-Grande F 27 D7
Colsterworth GB 11 F10
Colți RO 161 C8
Coltishall GB 15 B11
Colunga E 39 B9
Colwyn Bay GB 10 E4
Coly F 29 E8
Colyford GB 13 D8
Comacchio I 66 C5
Comana RO 152 F6
Comana RO 155 F2
Comana RO 161 E8
Comana de Sus RO 152 F6
Comandău RO 153 F8
Comănești RO 153 E8
Comares E 53 C8
Comarna RO 153 C11
Comarnic RO 161 D7
Combeaufontaine F 26 E4
Combe Martin GB 12 C6
Comber GB 7 C11
Comberton GB 15 C9
Comblain-au-Pont B 19 D12
Comblanchien F 25 F12
Combles F 18 D6
Combloux F 31 D10
Combourg F 23 D8
Combronde F 30 D3
Comeglians I 73 C6
Comélico Superiore I 72 C6
Comillas E 40 B3
Comines B 18 C5
Comines F 18 C5
Comișani RO 161 D7
Comiso I 59 F6
Comitini I 58 E4
Comloșu Mare RO 150 F6
Commeen IRL 7 C7
Commenailles F 31 B7
Commensacq F 32 B4
Commentry F 30 C2
Commequiers F 28 B2
Commer F 23 D10
Commercy F 26 C4
Como I 69 B7
Cómpeta E 53 C9
Compiano I 37 B11
Compiègne F 18 F6
Compolibat F 33 B10
Comporta P 50 C2
Comprégnac F 34 B4
Comps-sur-Artuby F 36 D5
Comrat MD 154 E3
Comrie GB 5 C9
Comunanza I 62 B4
Cona I 66 B5
Conca F 37 H10
Concarneau F 22 E4
Concas I 64 B4
Conceição P 50 E4
Concesio I 69 B9
Concha E 40 B5
Conches-en-Ouche F 24 C4
Concordia Sagittaria I 73 E6
Concorès F 33 A8
Concots F 33 B9
Condat F 30 E2
Condé-en-Brie F 25 B10
Condeixa-a-Nova P 44 D4
Condé-sur-Huisne F 24 D4
Condé-sur-l'Escaut F 182 E3
Condé-sur-Noireau F 23 C10
Condé-sur-Vire F 23 B9
Condino I 69 B10
Condofuri I 59 C8
Condom F 33 C6
Condove I 31 E11
Condrieu F 30 E6
Condrița MD 154 C3
Conegliano I 72 E5
Conflans-en-Jarnisy F 26 B4
Conflans-sur-Lanterne F 26 E5
Conflenti I 59 A9
Confolens F 29 C7
Cong IRL 6 E4
Congaz MD 154 E3
Congdon's Shop GB 12 D6
Congleton GB 11 E7
Congosto E 39 C7
Congosto de Valdavia E 39 C10
Congrier F 23 E9
Conil de la Frontera E 52 D4
Coningsby GB 11 E11
Coniston GB 10 C5
Conlie F 23 D11
Conliège F 31 B8
Conlig GB 4 F5
Connah's Quay GB 10 E5
Connantre F 25 C10
Connaux F 35 B8
Connel GB 4 C6
Connerré F 24 D3
Connolly IRL 8 C4
Connor GB 4 F4
Conon Bridge GB 2 K8
Çonop RO 151 E8
Conow D 84 D4
Conques F 33 A10
Conques-sur-Orbiel F 33 D10
Conquista E 54 C3
Consandolo I 66 C4
Consdorf L 186 B1
Conselice I 66 C4
Consell E 49 E10
Conselve I 66 B4
Consett GB 5 F13
Constância P 44 F4
Constanța RO 155 E3
Constantí E 42 E6
Constantim P 38 F4
Constantim P 39 E7

Constantina E 51 D8
Constantin Daicoviciu RO 159 B9
Constanzana E 46 C3
Consuegra E 46 F5
Contarina I 66 B5
Contes F 37 D6
Contessa Entellina I 58 D3
Contești RO 161 D7
Contești RO 161 F6
Conthey CH 31 C11
Contigliano I 62 C3
Contis-Plage F 32 B3
Contres F 24 F5
Contrexéville F 26 D4
Controne I 60 B4
Contursi Terme I 60 B4
Contwig D 21 F8
Conty F 18 E5
Conversano I 61 B8
Convoy IRL 7 C7
Conwy GB 10 E4
Conza della Campania I 60 B4
Cookstown GB 4 F3
Coola IRL 6 D6
Coolbaun IRL 6 G6
Coole F 25 C11
Coole IRL 7 E8
Coolmore IRL 6 C6
Coombe Bissett GB 13 C11
Cootehill IRL 7 D8
Copăcel RO 151 D9
Copăceni RO 152 F6
Copăceni MD 154 B2
Copăceni RO 160 D3
Copăcenii de Sus RO 161 E8
Copalnic-Mănăștur RO 152 C3
Copanca MD 154 D4
Copanello I 59 B10
Copceac MD 154 F3
Copertino I 61 C10
Çöpköy TR 173 B6
Copley GB 5 F13
Copons E 43 D7
Copparo I 66 C4
Coppeen IRL 8 E5
Copplestone GB 13 D7
Coppull GB 10 D6
Copșa Mică RO 152 E4
Copythorne GB 13 D11
Corabia RO 160 F5
Cora Chaitlín IRL 8 C5
Cora Droma Rúisc IRL 6 E6
Čoralići BIH 156 C4
Corato I 61 A6
Coray F 22 D4
Corbalán E 47 D11
Corbarasca RO 153 E10
Corbasca RO 153 E10
Corbeanca RO 161 D8
Corbeil-Essonnes F 25 C7
Corbeilles F 25 D8
Corbeni RO 160 C5
Corbeny F 19 F8
Corbera E 48 F4
Corbera d'Ebre E 42 E4
Corbi RO 160 C5
Corbie F 18 E6
Corbières CH 31 B11
Corbières F 35 C10
Corbii Mari RO 161 D6
Corbița RO 153 E10
Corbridge GB 5 F13
Corbu RO 153 D7
Corbu RO 155 E3
Corbu RO 160 D5
Corby GB 11 G10
Corçà E 43 D10
Corcaigh IRL 8 E6
Corcelles-lès-Cîteaux F 26 F3
Corchiano I 62 C2
Corciano I 66 F5
Corcieux F 27 D6
Corcova RO 159 D11
Corcubión E 38 C1
Cordăreni RO 153 B9
Cordemais F 23 F8
Cordenòns I 73 E6
Cordes F 33 B9
Córdoba E 53 A7
Cordobilla de Lácara E 45 F8
Corduente E 47 C9
Cordun RO 153 D9
Coreglia Antelminelli I 66 D2
Corella E 41 D8
Coreses E 39 E8
Corestăuți RO 153 A10
Corfe Castle GB 13 D10
Corfinio I 62 C5
Cori I 62 D3
Coria E 45 E7
Coria del Río E 51 E7
Coriano I 66 E6
Corigliano Calabro I 61 D7
Corinaldo I 67 E7
Corinth RO 160 C6
Çorlu TR 173 B8
Cornamona IRL 6 E4
Cornago E 41 D7
Cornaredo I 69 B7
Cornas F 30 F6
Cornățelu RO 161 D7
Cornea RO 159 C9
Cornedo all'Isarco I 72 D3
Cornedo Vicentino I 69 B11
Cornella-del-Vercol F 34 E4
Cornellà de Llobregat E 43 E8
Cornellà de Terri E 43 C9
Cornellana E 39 B7
Cornereva RO 159 C9
Cornești MD 153 C12
Cornești RO 152 D3
Cornești RO 161 D7
Cornetu RO 161 E7
Corni RO 153 B9
Corni RO 153 F11

Corniglio I 69 E9
Cornimont F 27 E6
Cornu RO 161 D7
Cornuda I 72 E5
Cornudella de Montsant E 42 E5
Cornudilla E 40 C5
Cornu Luncii RO 153 C8
Cornus F 34 C5
Corod RO 153 F11
Corofin IRL 8 C4
Coroieni RO 152 C3
Coron F 23 F10
Corovodë AL 168 C3
Corps F 31 F8
Corps-Nuds F 23 E8
Corral de Almaguer E 47 E6
Corral de Calatrava E 54 B4
Corrales E 39 F8
Corral-Rubio E 55 B10
Corre F 26 E5
Correggio I 66 C2
Corrèze F 29 E9
Corridonia I 67 F8
Corrie GB 4 D6
Corris GB 10 F4
Corr na Móna IRL 6 E4
Corrobert F 25 C10
Corry IRL 6 D6
Corsano I 61 D10
Corseul F 23 D7
Corsham GB 13 C10
Corsico I 69 C7
Corsock GB 5 E9
Corte I 37 G10
Corte F 37 G10
Corteconcepción E 51 D7
Cortegada E 38 D3
Cortegana E 51 D6
Cortemilia I 37 B8
Corteno Golgi I 69 A9
Corteolona I 69 C7
Cortes de Aragón E 42 F2
Cortes de Arenoso E 48 D3
Cortes de Baza E 55 D7
Cortes de la Frontera E 53 C6
Cortes de Pallás E 48 F3
Cortiçadas do Lavre P 50 B3
Cortijo de Arriba E 46 F4
Cortijos Nuevos E 55 C7
Cortina d'Ampezzo I 72 C5
Corton GB 15 B12
Cortona I 66 F4
Coruche P 50 B3
Corullón E 39 C6
Corund RO 152 E6
Corvara in Badia I 72 C4
Corvera E 56 F2
Corwen GB 10 F5
Coryton GB 15 D10
Cosa E 47 C10
Cosâmbești RO 161 D10
Cosbuc RO 152 C5
Cosby GB 11 F9
Coșcodeni MD 153 B12
Coscurita E 41 F7
Coșeiu RO 151 C11
Coseley GB 11 F7
Coşereni RO 161 D9
Coșești RO 160 C5
Cosham GB 13 D12
Coshieville GB 5 B9
Čoșiči BIH 157 D8
Cosio di Arroscia I 37 C7
Coslada E 46 D5
Cosmești RO 161 D10
Cosmești RO 160 E6
Cosmești MD 154 D3
Coșna RO 152 C6
Cosne-Cours-sur-Loire F 25 F8
Cosne-d'Allier F 30 C2
Coșnița MD 154 C4
Cosoleto I 59 C8
Coșoveni RO 160 E3
Cossato I 68 B5
Cossé-le-Vivien F 23 E10
Cossonine I 64 C2
Cossonay CH 31 B10
Costacciaro I 67 F6
Costache Negri RO 153 F11
Costa da Caparica P 50 B1
Costa di Rovigo I 66 B4
Costa Volpino I 69 B9
Coșteiu RO 151 F8
Costelloe IRL 6 F3
Costești MD 153 B10
Costești RO 160 D4
Costești RO 160 E5
Costești RO 161 C9
Costeștii din Vale RO 161 D6
Costișa RO 153 D9
Costuleni RO 153 C11
Coșuenda E 41 F9
Costuleni RO 153 C11
Coswig D 79 C11
Coswig D 80 D5
Coteana RO 160 E4
Cotești RO 161 B10
Cothen NL 16 D4
Coti-Chiavari F 37 H9
Cotignac F 36 D4
Cotignola I 66 D5
Cotmeana RO 160 D5
Cotnari RO 153 C9
Cotofănești RO 153 E9
Cotofenii din Dos RO 160 E3
Cotronei I 59 B10
Cottbus D 80 C6
Cottenham GB 15 C9
Cottesmore GB 11 F10
Cottingham GB 11 D10
Cottingham GB 15 F10
Cotușca RO 153 A9

Coulaures F 29 E7
Couleuvre F 30 B2
Coullons F 25 E7
Coulmier-le-Sec F 25 E11
Coulommes F 24 C6
Coulombiers F 29 C6
Coulombs F 24 C6
Coulommiers F 25 C9
Coulonges-sur-l'Autize F 28 C4
Coulounieix-Chamiers F 29 E7
Coulport GB 4 C7
Coupar Angus GB 5 B10
Couptrain F 23 D11
Coura P 38 E2
Courcelles B 182 E4
Courcelles-Chaussy F 26 B5
Courcelles-sur-Nied F 186 C1
Courchaton F 26 E5
Courchevel F 31 E10
Cour-Cheverny F 24 E5
Courçon F 28 C4
Courcy F 19 F9
Courgains F 23 D12
Courgenay CH 27 F7
Courgenay F 25 D10
Courlay F 28 B4
Courmayeur I 31 D10
Courmelles F 19 F7
Courpière F 30 D4
Courrendlin CH 27 F7
Courrensan F 33 C6
Courrières F 182 E1
Coursac F 29 E7
Coursan F 34 D5
Coursegoules F 36 D6
Courseulles-sur-Mer F 23 B11
Cours-la-Ville F 30 C5
Courson-les-Carrières F 25 E9
Court CH 27 F7
Courtalain F 24 D5
Courtelary CH 27 F7
Courtenay F 25 D9
Courthézon F 35 B8
Courtmacsherry IRL 8 E5
Courtomer F 24 C3
Courtown IRL 9 C10
Courtrai B 19 C7
Courtrai B 182 D2
Court-St-Étienne B 19 C10
Courville-sur-Eure F 24 D5
Cousance F 31 B7
Cousances-les-Forges F 26 C3
Coussac-Bonneval F 29 E8
Coussay-les-Bois F 29 B7
Coussegrey F 25 E11
Coussey F 26 D4
Coustouges F 34 F4
Coutances F 23 B9
Couterne F 23 D11
Couto de Cima P 44 C5
Coutras F 28 E5
Couvet CH 31 B10
Couvin B 19 D10
Couze-et-St-Front F 29 F7
Couzeix F 29 D8
Covaleda E 40 E6
Covarrubias E 40 D5
Covăsinț RO 151 E8
Covasna RO 153 F8
Cove GB 2 K5
Cove Bay GB 3 L13
Coventry GB 13 A11
Covilhã P 44 D6
Cowbit GB 11 F11
Cowbridge GB 13 C8
Cowdenbeath GB 5 C10
Cowes GB 13 D12
Cox F 56 E3
Cox F 33 C8
Coxheath GB 15 E9
Coxhoe GB 5 F13
Coylumbridge GB 3 L9
Cózar E 55 B6
Cozes F 28 D4
Cozești RO 161 C9
Cozieni RO 161 C9
Cozmești RO 153 D11
Cozzano F 37 H10

Craanford IRL 9 C10
Crăcăoani RO 153 C8
Crăciunelu de Jos RO 152 E4
Crăciunești RO 152 E5
Craco I 61 C6
Craidorolț RO 151 B10
Craig GB 2 L6
Craigavad GB 4 F5
Craigavon GB 7 D10
Craigellachie GB 3 L10
Craignure GB 4 C5
Crail GB 5 C11
Crailsheim D 75 D7
Craiova RO 160 E3
Craiva RO 151 D8
Cramlington GB 5 E13
Crâmpoia RO 160 E5
Cranage GB 11 E7
Cranagh GB 4 F2
Cranford IRL 7 B7
Crângeni RO 160 E5
Crângu RO 160 F6
Crângurile RO 160 D6
Cranleigh GB 15 E8
Crans-sur-Sierre CH 31 C11
Craon F 23 E10
Craonne F 19 F8
Craponne-sur-Arzon F 30 E4
Crask Inn GB 2 J7
Crasna RO 151 C11
Crasna RO 160 C3
Crasnoe MD 154 D5
Crathie GB 5 A10
Crato P 44 F5
Cravagliana I 68 B5
Cravant F 25 E10
Craven Arms GB 13 A9
Crawfordjohn GB 5 D9
Crawfordsburn GB 4 F5
Crawley GB 15 E8
Creaca RO 151 C11
Creagh IRL 8 E4
Creagorry GB 2 L2
Creamhghort IRL 7 B7
Créances F 23 B8
Créancey F 25 F12
Crecente E 38 D3
Crèches-sur-Saône F 30 C6
Crécy-en-Ponthieu F 18 D4
Crécy-la-Chapelle F 25 C8

Crécy-sur-Serre F 19 E8
Credenhill GB 13 A9
Crediton GB 13 D8
Creeslough IRL 7 B7
Creevagh IRL 6 D4
Creggan GB 4 F2
Creggan GB 7 D9
Cregganbaun IRL 6 E3
Creggs IRL 6 E6
Creglingen D 75 D7
Cregneash GBM 10 C2
Créhange F 186 C1
Creil F 18 F5
Creil NL 16 C4
Creissels F 34 B5
Crema I 69 C8
Cremeaux F 30 D4
Crémenes E 39 C9
Crémieu F 31 D7
Cremlingen D 79 B8
Cremona I 69 C9
Črenšovci SLO 148 C6
Créon F 28 F5
Crepaja SRB 158 C6
Crépey F 26 D4
Crépy F 19 E8
Crépy-en-Valois F 18 F6
Cres HR 67 C9
Crescentino I 68 C5
Crespina I 66 E2
Crespino I 66 C4
Crespos E 46 C3
Cressensac F 29 E9
Crest F 31 F7
Creswell GB 11 E9
Cretas E 42 F4
Créteil F 25 C7
Crețeni RO 160 D4
Crețești RO 153 D11
Creußen D 75 C10
Creutzwald F 21 F7
Creuzburg D 79 D7
Crevalcore I 66 C3
Crevant F 29 C9
Crévéchamps F 26 C5
Crèvecœur-le-Grand F 18 E5
Crevedia RO 161 D7
Crevedia Mare RO 161 E7
Crevenicu RO 161 E7
Crevillente E 56 E3
Crevoladossola I 68 A5
Crewe GB 10 E7
Crewkerne GB 13 D9
Crianlarich GB 4 C7
Cricău RO 152 E3
Criccieth GB 10 F3
Criciova RO 159 B9
Crickhowell GB 13 B8
Cricklade GB 13 B11
Cricova MD 154 C3
Crieff GB 5 C9
Criel-sur-Mer F 18 D3
Crikvenica HR 67 B10
Crimmitschau D 79 E11
Crimond GB 3 K13
Crinan GB 4 C5
Cringleford GB 15 B11
Crinitz D 80 C5
Cripán E 41 C7
Cripp's Corner GB 15 F10
Criquetot-l'Esneval F 18 E1
Crișcior RO 151 E10
Crișeni RO 151 C11
Crispiano I 61 B8
Crissolo I 31 F11
Cristești RO 152 D4
Cristești RO 153 B9
Cristești RO 153 D12
Cristian RO 152 F4
Cristian RO 161 B6
Cristinești RO 153 A8
Criștioru de Jos RO 151 E10
Cristóbal E 45 D9
Cristolț RO 151 C11
Cristuru Secuiesc RO 152 E5
Criuleni MD 154 C4
Criva MD 153 A9
Crivitz D 83 C11
Crkvice BIH 157 D8
Crkvice HR 162 D3
Crkvice MNE 163 C9
Crkvina BIH 157 B9
Crkvine GB 163 C9
Crljivica BIH 156 D5
Črmošnjice SLO 73 E11
Črna SLO 73 D9
Crna Bara SRB 150 F5
Crna Bara SRB 158 C5
Crnac HR 149 E9
Crnajka SRB 159 E9
Crna Trava SRB 164 D5
Crnča SRB 158 D4
Crni Lug BIH 156 D5
Crni Lug HR 67 B10
Crnjelovo BIH 157 C11
Crnkovci HR 149 E10
Crnoklište SRB 164 C5
Črnomelj SLO 148 E4
Crock D 75 B8
Crocketford GB 5 E9
Crockets Town IRL 6 D4
Crockmore GB 11 E7
Crocmaz MD 154 E5
Crocq F 29 D10
Crodo I 68 A5
Crofty GB 12 B6
Croghan IRL 6 E6
Croisilles F 18 D6
Croithlí IRL 6 B6
Crolles F 31 E8
Crolly IRL 6 B6
Cromadh IRL 8 C5
Cromarty GB 3 K8
Cromer GB 15 B11
Cromhall GB 13 B11
Cronat F 30 B4
Crook GB 5 F13
Crookham GB 5 D12
Crookhaven IRL 8 F3
Crookstown IRL 8 E5
Croom IRL 8 C5
Cropalati I 61 D7
Cropani I 59 B10
Crosbost GB 2 J4
Crosia I 61 D7
Cross IRL 6 E4
Crossaig GB 4 D6
Crossakeel IRL 7 E8
Cross Barry IRL 8 E5
Crosscanonby GB 5 F10
Crossdoney IRL 7 E8

Crossgar GB 7 D11
Crossgare GB 4 E3
Crossgates GB 13 A8
Crosshands GB 5 D8
Crosshaven IRL 8 E6
Crosshill GB 4 E7
Cross Inn GB 12 A6
Cross Keys IRL 7 E9
Crossmaglen GB 7 D9
Crotone I 61 E8
Crots F 36 B4
Crottendorf D 76 B3
Croughton GB 13 B12
Croutelle F 29 B6
Crouy F 19 F7
Crouy-sur-Ourcq F 25 B9
Crowborough GB 15 E9
Crowland GB 11 F11
Crowle GB 11 D10
Crowthorne GB 15 E7
Croy GB 3 K8
Croyde GB 12 C6
Crozant F 29 C9
Crozes-Hermitage F 30 E6
Crozon F 22 D3
Cruas F 35 A8
Crucea RO 153 C7
Crucea RO 155 D2
Crucişor RO 151 B11
Crucoli I 61 E7
Cruden Bay GB 3 L13
Cruglic MD 154 C4
Crumlin GB 4 F4
Cruseilles F 31 C9
Cruşeţ RO 160 D3
Crusheen IRL 8 C5
Crusnes F 20 F5
Cruzy F 34 D4
Cruzy-le-Châtel F 25 E11
Crvenka SRB 158 B3
Crymych GB 12 B5
Csabacsüd H 150 D6
Csabrendek H 149 B8
Csákánydoroszló H 149 C7
Csákvár H 149 B10
Csanádapáca H 151 D6
Csanádpalota H 150 E6
Csány H 150 B4
Csanytelek H 150 D5
Császár H 149 A10
Császártöltés H 150 E3
Csátalja H 150 E2
Csávoly H 150 E3
Csécse H 147 F9
Csemő H 150 C4
Csengele H 150 D4
Csenger H 151 C10
Csengőd H 150 D3
Csépa H 150 D5
Csepreg H 149 B7
Cserépfalu H 145 H2
Cserhátsurány H 147 F8
Cserkeszőlő H 150 D5
Csernely H 145 G1
Csesztreg H 149 C7
Csetény H 149 B9
Csévharaszt H 150 C3
Csikéria H 150 E3
Csókakő H 149 B10
Csökmő H 151 C7
Csököly H 149 D9
Csokonyavisonta H 149 D8
Csokvaomány H 145 G1
Csolnok H 149 A11
Csólyospálos H 150 E4
Csongrád H 150 D5
Csopak H 149 C9
Csór H 149 B10
Csorna H 149 A8
Csörnyeföld H 149 D7
Csorvás H 150 D6
Csősz H 149 B10
Csót H 149 B9
Csurgó H 149 D8

Culdrain GB 3 L11
Culemborg NL 16 E4
Culjković SRB 158 D4
Culla E 48 D4
Cullahill IRL 9 C8
Cúllar-Baza E 55 D7
Cullen GB 3 K11
Cullera E 48 F4
Cullivoe GB 3 D14
Cullompton GB 13 D8
Cully CH 31 C10
Cullybackey GB 4 F4
Cullyhanna GB 7 D9
Culmstock GB 13 D8
Culnaknock GB 2 K4
Culoz F 31 D8
Culswick GB 3 E13
Cumbernauld GB 5 D9
Cumbres de San Bartolomé E 51 C6
Cumbres Mayores E 51 C6
Cumeada P 50 E3
Cumiana I 31 F11
Cumieira P 38 F4
Cuminestown GB 3 K12
Cumlosen D 83 D11
Cumpăna RO 155 E3
Cunault F 23 F11
Cuneghes P 29 F6
Cuneo I 37 C7
Cunewalde D 81 D7
Cunfin F 25 D12
Cungrea RO 160 D4
Cunha P 44 C6
Cunicea MD 154 B3
Cunit E 43 E7
Cunningsburgh GB 3 E14
Cuntis E 38 C2
Cuorgnè I 68 C4
Cupar GB 5 C10
Cupcina MD 153 A10
Cupello I 63 C7
Cupra Marittima I 62 A5
Cupramontana I 67 F7
Ćuprija SRB 159 F7
Cupşeni RO 152 B3
Cuq-Toulza F 33 C9
Curăţele RO 151 D9
Curcani RO 161 E9
Curcuris I 64 D2
Cureggio I 68 B5
Cureşniţa MD 153 A12
Curgy F 30 B5
Curinga I 59 B9
Curon Venosta I 71 D11
Curraclee IRL 9 D10
Curraghoe IRL 6 E6
Curragh West IRL 6 E5
Currás E 38 C2
Curry IRL 6 E5
Curry Rivel GB 13 C9
Cursi I 61 C10
Curtea RO 151 F9
Curtea de Argeş RO 160 C5
Curtici RO 151 E7
Curtişoara RO 160 D4
Curtuişeni RO 151 B9
Čurug SRB 158 C5
Cusano Mutri I 60 A3
Cushendall GB 4 E4
Cushendun GB 4 E4
Cushina IRL 7 F8
Cussac F 29 D7
Cusset F 30 C3
Cussy-les-Forges F 25 F11
Custines F 26 C5
Custonaci I 58 C2
Cutigliano I 66 D2
Cutro I 61 E7
Cutrofiano I 61 C10
Cuxac-Cabardès F 33 D10
Cuxac-d'Aude F 34 D4
Cuxhaven D 17 A11
Cuzăplac RO 151 D11
Cuza Vodă RO 161 E10
Cuzmin MD 154 A3
Cuzorn F 33 A7
Čvikov CZ 81 E7
Cwmafan GB 13 B7
Cwmbrân GB 13 B8
Cybinka PL 81 B7
Cybowo PL 85 D9
Cychry PL 85 E7
Cyców PL 141 H8
Cydweli GB 12 B6
Cynghordy GB 13 A7
Cynwyl Elfed GB 12 B6
Cysoing F 182 D2
Czacz PL 81 B11
Czajków PL 142 C5
Czaplinek PL 85 C10
Czarna PL 143 F11
Czarna PL 144 C5
Czarna Białostocka PL 140 C8
Czarna Dąbrówka PL 85 B13
Czarna Górna PL 145 E6
Czarna Woda PL 138 C5
Czarncza PL 143 E8
Czarne PL 85 C11
Czarnia PL 139 D11
Czarnków PL 85 E11
Czarnocin PL 143 F10
Czarnów PL 81 A7
Czarnowąsy PL 142 E4
Czarnożyły PL 142 D6
Czarny Bór PL 81 E10
Czarny Dunajec PL 147 C9
Czastary PL 142 D5
Czaszyn PL 145 E5
Czchów PL 144 D2
Czechowice-Dziedzice PL 147 B8
Czechy PL 85 E11
Czechy PL 143 C6
Czekarzewice PL 143 D12
Czeladź PL 143 F7
Czemierniki PL 141 G7
Czeremcha PL 141 E8
Czermno PL 141 H2
Czernica PL 81 D11
Czernice Borowe PL 139 D10
Czernichów PL 143 G8
Czernichów PL 147 B8
Czernina PL 81 C11
Czersk PL 138 C4
Czerwieńsk PL 81 B8

Czerwin PL 139 E12
Czerwińsk nad Wisłą PL 139 F9
Czerwionka-Leszczyny PL 142 F6
Czerwonak PL 81 B11
Czerwone PL 139 D12
Czestków PL 143 C7
Czeszów PL 81 D12
Człopa PL 85 D10
Człuchów PL 85 C12
Czmoń PL 81 B12
Czorsztyn PL 145 E1
Czosnów PL 139 F10
Czudec PL 144 D4
Czyże PL 141 E8
Czyżew-Osada PL 141 E6

D

Daaden D 185 C8
Dăbâca RO 152 D3
Dabar HR 156 C3
Dabar HR 156 C4
Dabel D 83 C11
Dąbie PL 81 B8
Dąbie PL 141 G6
Dąbie PL 142 B6
Dąbki PL 85 B10
Dabo F 27 C7
Daborgrad BIH 157 D8
Dabrac BIH 157 D7
Dabravolya BY 140 D10
Dabrica BIH 157 F9
Dąbroszyn PL 81 A7
Dąbroszyn PL 142 B5
Dąbrowa PL 138 E4
Dąbrowa PL 142 A4
Dąbrowa PL 142 E4
Dąbrowa Białostocka PL 140 C8
Dąbrowa Biskupia PL 138 E6
Dąbrowa Chełmińska PL 138 D5
Dąbrowa Górnicza PL 143 F7
Dąbrowa Tarnowska PL 143 F10
Dąbrowa Zielona PL 143 E8
Dąbrowice PL 141 G2
Dąbrowice PL 143 B7
Dąbrówka Wielka PL 143 C7
Dąbrówka Wielkopolska PL 81 B9
Dąbrówno PL 139 D9
Dąbuleni RO 160 F4
Dabyeya BY 133 F7
Dachau D 75 F9
Dachnów PL 144 C7
Dachrieden D 79 D7
Dachwig D 79 D8
Dačice CZ 77 E8
Dacre GB 5 F11
Dad H 149 A10
Dadia GR 171 B10
Dădran S 103 C10
Dăeşti RO 160 C4
Dăeşti RO 153 D7
Dǻfjord N 112 D3
Dafnes GR 174 C4
Dafni GR 171 D6
Dafni GR 174 D5
Dafni GR 175 C8
Dafni GR 175 D7
Dág H 149 A11
Daganzo de Arriba E 46 C6
Dağardı TR 173 F11
Dağâta RO 153 D10
Dagda LV 133 D3
Dagebüll D 82 A5
Dağkızılca TR 177 C9
Daglan F 29 F8
Daglösen S 97 C11
Dagmarsellen CH 27 F8
Dağpınar TR 181 B8
Dagsmark FIN 122 F7
Dahlem D 21 D7
Dahlen D 80 D4
Dahlenburg D 83 D9
Dahlhausen D 183 C10
Dahme D 80 C4
Dahme D 83 B10
Dahn D 27 B8
Dähre D 83 E9
Daia TR 161 F7
Daia Română RO 152 E3
Daikanberg S 107 A10
Daikanvik S 107 A10
Dailly GB 4 E7
Daimiel E 46 F5
Daimonia GR 178 B4
Daingean IRL 7 F8
Dainville F 18 D6
Dainville-Berthelléville F 26 D4
Dairsie GB 5 C11
Daknam B 182 C3
Đakovo HR 149 F11
Dal N 95 B14
Dal S 107 E13
Đala SRB 150 E5
Dalaas A 71 C10
Dalabrog GB 2 L2
Dalaman TR 181 C8
Dalarö S 93 A12
Dala-Rostock S 91 B11
Dalåsen S 102 A7
Dalasjö S 107 C10
Dalbe LV 135 C7
Dalbeattie GB 5 F9
Dalberg-Wendelstorf D 83 C10
Dalboşeţ RO 159 D8
Dalby DK 86 D7
Dalby DK 87 E8
Dalby GBM 10 C2
Dalby S 87 D12
Dalbyn S 103 D9
Dalbyover DK 86 B6
Dåldenäs S 92 A4
Dale GB 9 E12
Dale N 90 B3
Dale N 100 D2
Dale N 100 E3
Dale N 111 C12
Daleiden D 20 D6
Dalen N 90 A4
Dalen N 94 D7
Dalen NL 17 C7
Daleszyce PL 143 E10
Dalfors S 103 D9
Dalfsen NL 16 C6
Dalgety Bay GB 5 C10
Dalham GB 15 C10
Dalholen N 101 B11
Dalías E 55 F7

Dalj HR 157 B10
Dalkarlsberg S 97 D12
Dalkeith GB 5 D10
Dalkey IRL 7 F10
Dallas GB 3 K10
Dallgow D 80 A4
Dall Villaby DK 86 B5
Dallmin D 83 D11
Dalmally GB 4 C7
Dalmand H 149 D10
Dalmellington GB 5 E8
Dalmine I 69 B8
Dalmose DK 87 E8
Dalry GB 4 D7
Dalrymple GB 4 E7
Dalsbruk FIN 126 E8
Dalsbygda N 101 A14
Dalselv N 108 D6
Dalsjöfors S 91 D13
Dalstein F 20 F6
Dalston GB 5 F11
Dalstorp S 91 D14
Dalstuga S 103 D10
Daluis F 36 C5
Dalum S 91 D13
Dalur FO 2 B3
Dàlvadas FIN 113 D17
Dalwhinnie GB 5 B8
Dalyan TR 181 C8
Dalyokiya BY 135 F13
Dalyston IRL 6 F6
Damachava BY 141 G9
Damas-aux-Bois F 26 D5
Damasi GR 169 E7
Damaskinia GR 168 D5
Damasławek PL 85 E13
Damazan F 33 B6
Dambach-la-Ville F 186 E3
Dâmbaslar TR 173 B7
Dambeck D 83 D11
Dâmbovicioara RO 160 C6
Damelevières F 26 C5
Damerstown IRL 9 C8
Damery F 25 B10
Damès AL 168 C2
Dângan F 22 E6
Damhead GB 4 E3
Damhliag IRL 7 E10
Dămienești RO 153 D9
Damigny F 23 D12
Damjan KS 163 E10
Dammarie F 24 D6
Dammartin-en-Goële F 25 B8
Damme B 19 B7
Damme D 17 C10
Damnica PL 85 B12
Damno PL 85 A12
Damp D 83 A7
Dampierre F 26 F4
Dampierre-sur-Linotte F 26 E5
Dampierre-sur-Salon F 26 E4
Damprichard F 27 F6
Damshagen D 83 C10
Damsholte DK 87 F10
Dâmsta S 107 E13
Dămuc RO 153 D7
Damüls A 71 C9
Damvant CH 27 F6
Damville F 24 C5
Damvillers F 19 F11
Damwoude NL 16 B6
Damyanovo BG 165 D10
Danaçalı TR 173 E10
Danakos GR 177 E6
Danamandira TR 173 B9
Danasjö S 109 E12
Dănciuleşti RO 160 D3
Dăneasa RO 160 E5
Daneş RO 152 E5
Danesfort IRL 9 C8
Dăneşti RO 153 D7
Dăneşti RO 153 D11
Dăneşti RO 160 D3
Dăneţi RO 160 F4
Dângebo S 89 B8
Dângeni RO 153 B9
Dangé-St-Romain F 29 B7
Danholn S 103 D7
Dănicei RO 160 D4
Daniec PL 142 E5
Danilovgrad MNE 163 D7
Dănişment TR 173 E7
Danjoutin F 27 E6
Dankerode D 79 C9
Danndorf D 79 B8
Dannemarie F 27 E7
Dannemora S 99 B9
Dannenberg (Elbe) D 83 D10
Dannenwalde D 84 D4
Dány H 150 B4
Daon F 23 E10
Daoulas F 22 D3
Darabani RO 153 A9
Dărăşti Ilfov RO 161 E8
Darbénai LT 134 D2
Dar Ben Karricha el Behri MA 53 E6
Darby's Bridge IRL 8 D2
Dar Chaoui MA 52 E5
Darda HR 149 E11
Dardesheim D 79 C8
Dardhas AL 168 C4
Darfo Boario Terme I 69 B9
Dargun D 83 C13
Darica TR 173 B10
Darıcı TR 173 F10
Dârjiu RO 152 E6
Darkley GB 7 D9
Darlington GB 11 B8
Dârlos RO 152 E4
Darłowo PL 85 B10
Dărmănești RO 153 B8
Dărmănești RO 153 D9
Dărmănești RO 160 C5
Dărmănești RO 161 D7
Darmstadt D 21 E11
Darney F 26 D4
Darnieulles F 26 D5
Dárnózseli H 146 F4
Daroca E 47 B10
Darova RO 159 B8
Darque P 38 E2
Darragh IRL 8 C4
Darro E 55 E6
Dartford GB 15 E9
Dartmeet GB 13 D7

Dartmouth GB 13 E7
Darton GB 11 D8
Dartsel S 118 C4
Daruvar HR 149 E8
Dârvari RO 159 E11
Darwen GB 10 D7
Dascălu RO 161 D8
Dascălu RO 161 D8
Dašice CZ 77 B9
Dasing D 75 F9
Dasochori GR 169 B9
Dasochori GR 171 C7
Dassel D 78 C6
Dassendorf D 83 D8
Dassow D 83 C9
Daszyna PL 143 B7
Datça TR 181 C7
Datteln D 17 E8
Datterode (Ringgau) D 79 D7
Daudzese LV 135 D10
Daudzeva LV 135 C10
Daugai LT 137 E9
Daugailiai LT 135 E13
Daugavpils LV 135 E13
Daugėlaičiai LT 134 E7
Daugųli LV 135 A10
Daugъnai LT 135 E9
Daujėnai LT 135 E9
Daumazan-sur-Arize F 33 D8
Daumeray F 23 E11
Daun D 21 D7
Dauphin F 35 C10
Dava GB 3 L9
Daventry GB 13 A12
Davézieux F 30 E6
Davideşti RO 160 C6
Davidkovo BG 165 F10
Daviot GB 3 L8
Davle CZ 76 C6
Davlela GR 175 B6
Dávod H 150 E2
Davor HR 157 B8
Davos CH 71 D9
Davutlar TR 177 D9
Davydiv UA 144 D9
Dawlish GB 13 E8
Dax F 32 C3
Deal GB 15 E11
Dealu RO 152 E6
Dealu Morii RO 153 E10
Dearham GB 5 F10
Deauville F 23 B12
Deba E 32 D1
Debar MK 168 A4
Debeli Lug SRB 159 E8
Debeljača SRB 158 C6
Debenham GB 15 C11
Dębica PL 143 F11
De Bilt NL 16 D4
Debnevo BG 165 D10
Dęblin PL 141 G5
Denham GB 15 D8
Den Ham NL 17 D7
Dębno PL 85 E7
Dębno PL 143 G10
Dębobserv BG 165 B10
Debrc SRB 158 D4
Debrecen H 151 B8
Debrešte MK 168 B5
Debrzno PL 85 C12
Debür BG 165 F11
Dečan KS 163 E10
Decazeville F 33 A10
Dechtice SK 146 E5
Decimomannu I 64 E2
Decimoputzu I 64 E2
Děčín CZ 80 E6
Decize F 30 B3
De Cocksdorp NL 16 B3
Decollatura I 59 A9
Decs H 149 D11
Deda RO 152 D5
Deddington GB 13 B12
Dedeleben D 79 B8
Dedeler TR 173 F9
Dedelow D 84 D5
Dedelstorf D 83 E8
Dedemsvaart NL 17 C6
Dedham GB 15 D10
Dedovichi RUS 132 F6
Deensen D 78 C6
Deerlijk B 19 C7
Dég H 149 C10
Degaña E 39 C6
Degeberga S 88 D6
Degerbäcken S 118 C4
Degerby FIN 126 E8
Degerby FIN 127 E11
Degerfors S 92 A4
Degerhamn S 89 C10
Degersjö S 107 D12
Degerträsk S 118 C4
Deggendorf D 76 E3
Deggingen D 74 E6
Değirmen TR 173 E9
Değirmendere TR 177 D9
Değirmendüzü TR 171 D10
Değirmenyeni TR 167 C8
Dego I 37 C8
Degučiai LT 135 E12
Degummieki LV 135 C13
De Haan B 19 B7
Dehesa de Campoamor E 56 F3
Dehesas de Guadix E 55 D6
Deià E 49 E10
Deidesheim D 21 F10
Deifontes E 53 B9
Deilão P 39 E6
Deining D 75 D9
Deiningen D 75 E8
Deinste D 17 A12
Deiva Marina I 37 C10
Dej RO 152 C3
Deje S 97 C9
Dejtár H 147 E8
Dekani SLO 67 A8
Dekeleia GR 175 C8
De Koog NL 16 B3
Dekov BG 165 C11
Delabole GB 12 D5
Delary S 87 B13
Delbrück D 17 E11
Delčevo MK 165 F6

Delden NL 17 D7
Délegyháza H 150 C3
Deleitosa E 45 E9
Đelekovec HR 149 D7
Delémont CH 27 F7
Delen' UA 154 F4
Deleni RO 153 C7
Deleni RO 155 E2
Deleria GR 169 E7
Deleşti RO 153 D11
Delfoi GR 175 C6
Delft NL 16 D2
Delfzijl NL 17 B7
Delia I 58 E4
Delianuova I 59 C8
Deliblato SRB 159 D7
Deliceto I 60 A4
Deligrad SRB 159 F8
Deliktaş TR 177 B8
Delingsdorf D 83 C8
Delitzsch D 79 C11
Delle F 27 E7
Delligsen D 78 C6
Dello I 66 B1
Delme F 26 C5
Delmenhorst D 17 B11
Delnice HR 67 B10
Delsbo S 103 C12
Deltebre E 42 F5
Delvin IRL 7 E8
Delvinaki GR 168 E3
Delvinë AL 168 E3
Demandice SK 147 E7
Demange-aux-Eaux F 26 C3
Dembava LT 135 E8
Demecser H 145 G4
De Meern NL 183 A6
Demen D 83 C11
Demene LV 135 E13
Demigny F 30 B6
Demiraj AL 163 E7
Demircihalil TR 167 F8
Demirdere TR 173 D9
Demirhanli TR 167 F7
Demir Hisar MK 168 B5
Demir Kapija MK 169 B7
Demirköy TR 167 F8
Demirli TR 181 C9
Demirtaş TR 173 D11
Demmin D 84 C4
Demonte I 37 C6
Dému F 33 C6
Denain F 19 D7
Denbigh GB 10 E5
Den Bommel NL 182 B4
Den Burg NL 16 B3
Denderleeuw B 182 D4
Dendermonde B 19 B9
Den Dungen NL 16 E4
Denekamp NL 17 D8
Denguin F 32 C5
Den Haag NL 16 D2
Den Haag NL 182 A4
Denham GB 15 D8
Den Ham NL 17 D7
Den Helder NL 16 C3
Denholm GB 5 E11
Denia E 56 D5
Denkendorf D 27 C11
Denkendorf D 75 E9
Denkingen D 27 D10
Denkingen D 27 E11
Denklingen D 71 B11
Dennewitz D 80 C4
Dennhausen (Fuldabrück) D 78 D5
Denny GB 5 C9
Den Oever NL 16 C4
Densow D 84 D4
Densuş RO 159 C9
Denta RO 159 C7
Dentergem B 19 C7
Dentlein am Forst D 75 D7
Denver GB 11 F12
Denzlingen D 27 D8
Déols F 29 B9
De Panne B 18 B6
Deppis S 109 E18
Deràsbrenna N 105 C10
Derby GB 11 F9
Derecske H 151 C8
Dereham GB 15 B10
Derekegyház H 150 D5
Dereköy TR 167 F8
Dereköy TR 173 F7
Derenburg D 79 C8
Derenti TR 173 E7
De Rijp NL 16 C3
Dermantsi BG 165 C9
Dermbach D 79 E7
Dermenas AL 168 C2
Derna RO 151 C9
Dernau D 21 C8
Derreen IRL 6 D4
Derreendarragh IRL 8 E3
Derreeny Bridge IRL 8 E4
Derry GB 4 F2
Derrygonnelly GB 7 D7
Derrylin GB 7 D7
Derrymore IRL 8 D3
Derrynawilt GB 7 D8
Derryrush IRL 6 F3
Derrywode IRL 6 E5
Dersca RO 153 B8
Dersingham GB 11 F13
Dersum D 17 C8
Deruta I 62 B2
Dervaig GB 4 B4
Derval F 23 E8
Dervenakia GR 175 D6
Derveni GR 174 C5
Derventa BIH 157 C8
Derviçan AL 168 E3
Dervio I 69 A7
Derviziana GR 168 F3
Dervock GB 4 E4
Desa RO 159 F10
Desana I 68 C5
Descargamaría E 45 D8
Descartes F 29 B7
Deseşti RO 152 B3
Desfina GR 175 C6
Desertines F 29 C11
Desenzano del Garda I 66 B2
Desertines F 23 D10
Desertmartin GB 4 F3
Desford GB 11 F9
Desio I 69 B7
Deskati GR 169 E6
Deskle SLO 73 D8
Despotovac SRB 159 E7
Despotovo SRB 158 C4
Dessau D 79 C11
Dessel B 16 F4
De Steeg NL 16 D6
Destelbergen B 19 B8

Deštná CZ 77 D7
Destriana E 39 D7
Desulo I 64 C3
Desvres F 15 F12
Deszczno PL 85 E8
Deszk H 150 E5
Deta RO 159 C7
Detern D 17 B9
Detk H 150 B5
Detkovac HR 149 E9
Dětmarovice CZ 146 B6
Detmold D 17 E11
Dettelbach D 75 C7
Dettenhausen D 187 D7
Dettingen an der Erms D 187 D7
Dettmannsdorf D 83 B13
Dettum D 79 B8
Dettwiller F 186 D3
Detva SK 147 E9
Deurne NL 16 F5
Deutsch Evern D 83 D8
Deutschfeistritz A 148 B4
Deutschhof D 84 E3
Deutschkreutz A 149 A7
Deutschlandsberg A 73 C11
Deutschneudorf D 80 E4
Deutsch-Wagram A 77 F11
Deutzen D 79 D11
Deva RO 151 F10
Dévaványa H 151 C6
Devecikonaği TR 173 E10
Devecser H 149 B8
Devene BG 165 C8
Deventer NL 16 D6
Devesel RO 159 E10
Deveselu RO 160 E4
Devetaki BG 165 C10
Deville F 184 E2
Devil's Bridge GB 13 A7
Devin BG 165 F9
Devizes GB 13 C11
Devletliağaç TR 167 F8
Devnya BG 167 C8
Ðevrske HR 156 E4
De Wijk NL 16 C6
Dewsbury GB 11 D8
Deza E 41 F7
Dežanovac HR 149 E8
Dezghingea MD 154 E3
Dezna RO 151 E9
Dhërmi AL 168 D2
Dhron D 185 D6
Diafani GR 181 E6
Diakofto GR 174 C5
Dialampi GR 171 B8
Diamante I 60 D5
Dianalund DK 87 D8
Diano d'Alba I 37 B8
Diano Marina I 37 D8
Diavata GR 169 C8
Diavolitsi GR 174 E4
Dichiseni RO 161 E11
Dicomano I 66 E4
Didam NL 16 E6
Didcot GB 13 B12
Didderse D 79 B7
Dideşti RO 160 E5
Didyma GR 175 E7
Didymoteicho GR 171 B10
Didžiasalis LT 135 F13
Die F 31 F7
Dieblich D 21 D8
Dieburg D 21 E11
Dieci RO 151 E9
Diedorf D 75 F8
Diego Álvaro E 45 C10
Diekhof D 83 C12
Diekholzen D 78 B6
Diekirch L 20 E6
Dielheim D 21 F11
Dielmissen D 78 C6
Dielsdorf CH 27 F9
Diemen NL 16 D3
Diémoz F 31 D7
Dienheim D 185 E9
Dienne F 30 E2
Dienville F 25 D12
Diepenau D 17 D11
Diepenbeek B 19 C11
Diepenheim NL 183 A9
Diepenveen NL 183 A8
Diepholz D 17 C10
Dieppe F 18 E3
Dierdorf D 21 C9
Dieren NL 16 D6
Dierhagen, Ostseebad D 83 B13
Diesdorf D 83 E9
Dieskau D 79 D11
Diespeck D 75 C8
Diessen NL 16 F4
Dießen am Ammersee D 72 A3
Diessenhofen CH 27 E10
Diest B 19 C11
Dietachdorf A 77 F6
Dietenheim D 71 A10
Dietersburg D 76 E4
Dietfurt an der Altmühl D 75 D10
Dietikon CH 27 F9
Dietingen D 27 D10
Dietmanns A 77 E7
Dietmanns A 77 E8
Dietmannsried D 71 B10
Dietzenbach D 21 D11
Dietzhölztal-Ewersbach D 185 C9
Dieue-sur-Meuse F 26 B3
Dieulefit F 35 A9
Dieulouard F 26 C5
Dieuze F 26 C6
Dieveniškės LT 137 E12
Diever NL 16 C6
Diex A 73 C10
Diezma E 55 E6
Differdange L 20 E5
Digerberget S 97 B9
Digerberget S 102 A8
Digermulen N 110 D8
Dignac F 29 D6
Dignája LV 135 D12
Dignano I 73 D6
Digne-les-Bains F 36 C4
Digny F 24 C5
Digoin F 30 C4
Dihtiv UA 144 B9
Dijon F 26 F3
Dikaia GR 166 F6
Dikance KS 163 E10
Dikili TR 177 A8
Dikkebus B 18 C6

Dikli LV 131 F10
Diksmuide B 18 B6
Dilar E 53 B9
Dilbeek B 182 D4
Dilesi GR 175 C8
Dilinata GR 174 C2
Dillenburg D 21 C10
Dilling N 95 D13
Dillingen (Saar) D 21 F7
Dillingen an der Donau D 75 E7
Dilove UA 145 H9
Dilsen B 19 B12
Dimaro I 71 E11
Diminio GR 169 F8
Dimitrie Cantemir RO 153 D12
Dimitritsi GR 169 C9
Dimitrovgrad BG 166 E5
Dimitrovgrad SRB 165 C6
Dimitsana GR 174 D5
Dimovo BG 159 F10
Dimzukalns LV 135 C8
Dinami I 59 B9
Dinan F 23 D7
Dinant B 19 D10
Dinard F 23 C7
Dingé F 23 D8
Dingelstädt D 79 D7
Dingelstedt am Huy D 79 C8
Dingle IRL 8 D2
Dingle S 91 B10
Dingolfing D 75 E12
Dingtuna S 98 C6
Dingwall GB 2 K8
Dinjiška HR 67 D11
Dinkelsbühl D 75 D7
Dinkelscherben D 75 F8
Dinklage D 17 C10
Dinnet GB 5 A11
Dinslaken D 17 E7
Dinteloord NL 16 E2
Dinther NL 183 B6
Dinxperlo NL 17 E6
Diö S 88 B6
Dion GR 169 D7
Diósd H 149 B11
Diosig RO 151 C9
Diósjenő H 147 F8
Dioști RO 160 E4
Diou F 30 B4
Dipignano I 60 E6
Dipotama GR 171 B7
Dipotamia GR 168 D4
Dippach L 20 E6
Dippoldiswalde D 80 E5
Dirdal N 94 E4
Dirhami EST 130 C7
Dirivaara S 116 E8
Dirkshorn NL 16 C3
Dirksland NL 16 E2
Dirlewang D 71 A11
Dirmstein D 187 B5
Dirvonėnai LT 134 E5
Dischingen D 75 E7
Disentis Muster CH 71 D7
Diseröd S 91 D11
Dison B 19 C12
Diss GB 15 C11
Dissay F 29 B6
Dissay-sous-Courcillon F 24 E3
Dissen am Teutoburger Wald D 17 D10
Distington GB 10 B4
Distomo GR 175 C6
Distrato GR 168 D5
Ditfurt D 79 C9
Ditrău RO 153 D7
Ditton GB 15 E9
Ditzingen D 27 C11
Divača SLO 73 E8
Divarata GR 174 C2
Diva Slatina BG 165 C6
Divci SRB 158 E5
Divčibare SRB 158 E5
Dives-sur-Mer F 23 B11
Dividalen N 111 C18
Divieto I 59 C7
Divín SK 147 E9
Divina SK 147 C7
Divion F 18 D6
Divišov CZ 77 C7
Divjakë AL 168 C2
Divonne-les-Bains F 31 C9
Divuša HR 156 B5
Dixmont F 25 D9
Dizy F 25 B10
Dizy-le-Gros F 19 E9
Djäkneboda S 122 B5
Djäkneböle S 122 C4
Djupen N 111 B18
Djupfjord N 110 C9
Djupfors S 109 E11
Djupsjö S 107 E14
Djuptjärn S 107 D15
Djupvik N 109 B10
Djupvik N 112 D5
Djupvik S 89 A11
Djura S 103 E8
Djurås S 97 A13
Djurmo S 97 A13
Djurö S 99 D11
Dlhá nad Oravou SK 147 C8
Dlouhá Loučka CZ 77 C12
Dlouhá Třebová CZ 77 C10
Długofjka PL 81 D12
Długofjka PL 140 D7
Długosiodło PL 139 E12
Dłutów PL 143 C7
Dlŭzhka Polyana BG 166 C6
Dmytrivka UA 154 F3
Dmytrivka UA 154 F4
Dmytrivka UA 155 B4
Dnestrovsc MD 154 D5
Dno RUS 132 F6
Doagh GB 4 F4
Doba RO 151 B10
Dobanovci SRB 158 D5
Dobârceni RO 153 B10
Dobârlău RO 153 F7
Dobbertin D 83 C12
Dobbiaco I 72 C5
Dobczyce PL 144 D1
Dobele LV 134 C6
Döbeln D 80 D4
Doberçan KS 164 E4
Doberlug-Kirchhain D 80 C5
Döbern D 81 C7
Dobersberg A 77 E8
Doberschütz D 79 D12
Dobiegniew PL 85 E9
Dobieszewo PL 85 B12
Dobieszyn PL 141 G4
Doboj BIH 157 C9
Dobova SLO 148 E5
Doboz H 151 D7
Dobrá CZ 146 B6
Dobra PL 85 C8
Dobra PL 142 C6
Dobra PL 144 D1
Dobra RO 151 F10
Dobra RO 161 D7
Dobra SRB 159 D8
Dobrá Niva SK 147 E8
Dobřany CZ 76 C4
Dobre PL 138 E6
Dobre PL 139 F12
Dobre Miasto PL 136 F1
Dobreni RO 153 D8
Dobrešinci MK 169 A8
Dobrești RO 151 D9
Dobrești RO 160 D6
Dobrești RO 160 F3
Dobrevo MK 164 E5
Dobrica SRB 159 C6
Dobričevo SRB 159 D7
Dobrich BG 155 F1
Dobrich BG 166 E5
Dobri Do SRB 164 D3
Dobri Dol BG 159 F11
Dobrin RO 151 C11
Dobrinishte BG 165 F8
Dobříš CZ 76 C6
Dobritz D 79 B11
Dobřív CZ 76 C5
Dobrljin BIH 156 B5
Dobrna SLO 73 D11
Dobrnič SLO 73 E10
Dobrnja BIH 157 C7
Dobrnja BIH 157 C10
Dobrnje SRB 159 E7
Dobro E 40 C4
Dobrodzień PL 142 E5
Döbrököz H 149 D10
Dobromierz PL 81 E10
Dobromir RO 155 E1
Dobromirka BG 166 C4
Dobromirtsi BG 171 B8
Dobromyl' UA 145 D6
Dobroń PL 143 C7
Dobron' UA 145 G5
Dobronín CZ 77 D9
Dobro Polje BIH 157 E10
Dobro Polje SRB 159 F9
Dobrošane MK 164 E4
Dobrosloveni RO 160 E4
Dobrosyn UA 144 C8
Dobroszyce PL 81 D12
Doboteasa RO 160 D4
Dobrotești RO 160 E5
Dobrotić SRB 164 C4
Dobrotich BG 167 C8
Dobrotino MK 169 B6
Dobrotitsa BG 161 F9
Dobrovăț RO 153 D11
Dobrovci BIH 157 C9
Dobrovice CZ 77 B7
Dobrovnik SLO 149 C6
Dobrovol'sk RUS 136 D5
Dobrowoda PL 143 F10
Dobruchi RUS 132 D2
Dobrun BIH 158 F3
Dobrun RO 160 E4
Dobrușa MD 154 B3
Dobruševo MK 169 B5
Dobruška CZ 77 B10
Dobrzankowo PL 139 E10
Dobrzany PL 85 D8
Dobrzeń Wielki PL 142 E4
Dobrzyca PL 142 C4
Dobrzyków PL 139 F8
Dobrzyń nad Wisłą PL 139 E7
Dobšiná SK 145 F1
Dóc H 150 E5
Docking GB 15 B10
Dockmyr S 103 A10
Docksta S 107 E14
Dockweiler D 21 D7
Doclin RO 159 C8
Doddington GB 5 D12
Dodewaard NL 183 B7
Dodonoupoli GR 168 E4
Dödre S 102 A8
Doesburg NL 16 D6
Doetinchem NL 16 E6
Dofteana RO 153 E9
Doğanbey TR 177 C8
Doğanbey TR 177 D9
Doğanci TR 173 D10
Doğanköy TR 173 D10
Döge H 145 G5
Dogliani I 37 B7
Dognecea RO 159 C8
Döğüşbelen TR 181 C9
Dohna D 80 E5
Dohňany SK 146 C6
Dohren D 17 C9
Doicești RO 160 D6
Doïrani GR 169 B8
Doire Iorrais IRL 6 F3
Doische B 19 D10
Dojč SK 146 D4
Dojkinci SRB 165 C6
Dokka N 101 E12
Dokkas S 116 D6
Dokkedal DK 86 B6
Dokkum NL 16 B5
Doksy CZ 76 B6
Doksy CZ 81 E7
Doktor Yosifovo BG 165 C7
Dokupe LV 134 B3
Dolanog GB 10 F5
Dolbenmaen GB 10 F3
Dolceacqua I 37 D7
Dol-de-Bretagne F 23 C8
Dole BIH 157 D10
Dole F 26 F3
Dølemo N 90 B3
Dolenci MK 168 B5
Dolenja Vas SLO 73 E10
Dolenjske Toplice SLO 73 E11
Dolgarrog GB 10 E4
Dolgellau GB 10 F4
Dolgen D 84 D4
Dolgorukovo RUS 136 E2
Dolhan TR 167 F8
Dolhasca RO 153 C9
Dolhești RO 153 C9
Dolhești RO 153 D11
Dołhobyczów PL 144 B9
Dolianova I 64 E3
Dolice PL 85 D8
Dolichi GR 169 D7
Doljani BIH 157 E8
Doljani HR 156 D5
Doljevac SRB 164 C4
Dolla IRL 8 C6
Dolle D 79 B10
Dollern D 82 C7
Döllnitz D 79 D11
Dollnstein D 75 E9
Dollon F 24 D4
Dolna MD 154 C2
Dolna Banya BG 165 E8
Dolna Dikanya BG 165 E7
Dolna Gradeshnitsa BG 165 F7
Dolnaja LV 135 D12
Dolná Krupá SK 146 E5
Dolna Lipnitska BG 166 C4
Dolna Makhala BG 165 E10
Dolna Melna BG 164 D6
Dolna Mitropoliya BG 165 C10
Dolna Oryakhovitsa BG 166 C5
Dolná Strehová SK 147 E8
Dolná Súča SK 146 D6
Dolná Tižina SK 147 C7
Dolna Vasilitsa BG 165 E8
Dolné Orešany SK 146 E4
Dolné Vestenice SK 146 D6
Dolni Bousov CZ 77 B8
Dolni Bukovsko CZ 77 D7
Dolní Čermná CZ 77 C11
Dolni Chiflik BG 167 D9
Dolni Dobrouč CZ 77 C11
Dolni Dŭbnik BG 165 C9
Dolní Dvořiště CZ 77 E6
Dolni Glavanak BG 166 F5
Dolní Kounice CZ 77 D10
Dolni Lom BG 165 C6
Dolní Loučky CZ 77 D10
Dolní Němčí CZ 146 D5
Dolní Podluží CZ 81 E7
Dolní Újezd CZ 77 C10
Dolní Újezd CZ 146 B5
Dolni Voden BG 165 E10
Dolní Žandov CZ 75 B12
Dolno Dupeni MK 168 C5
Dolno Ezerovo BG 167 D8
Dolno Kamartsi BG 165 D8
Dolno Konjare MK 164 F4
Dolno Levski BG 165 E9
Dolno Osenovo BG 165 F7
Dolno Selo BG 164 E5
Dolno Tserovene BG 159 F11
Dolno Uyno BG 164 E6
Dolný Hričov SK 147 C7
Dolný Kubín SK 147 C8
Dolný Pial SK 146 E6
Dolný Štál SK 146 F5
Dolo I 66 B5
Dolomieu F 31 D8
Dolores E 56 E3
Dolovo SRB 159 D6
Dölsach A 73 C6
Dolsk PL 81 C12
Dołubowo PL 141 E7
Dolus-d'Oléron F 28 D3
Dolyna UA 145 F8
Dolynivka UA 154 A5
Dolyns'ke UA 154 B5
Dolzhitsy RUS 132 D5
Domaháza H 147 E10
Domaniewice PL 141 G2
Domaniewice PL 143 B8
Domanín CZ 146 C4
Domaradz PL 144 D4
Domart-en-Ponthieu F 18 D5
Domaševo BIH 162 D5
Domašinec HR 149 D7
Domașnea RO 159 C9
Domaszek H 150 E5
Domaszków PL 77 B11
Domaszowice PL 142 D4
Domat Ems CH 71 D8
Domats F 25 D9
Domažlice CZ 76 D3
Dombås N 101 B10
Dombasle-en-Xaintois F 26 D4
Dombasle-sur-Meurthe F 186 D1
Dombegyház H 151 E7
Dombóvár H 149 D10
Dombrád H 145 G4
Dombresson CH 31 A10
Domburg NL 16 E1
Domegge di Cadore I 72 D5
Domeikava LT 137 D8
Domène F 31 E8
Domeniko GR 169 E7
Domérat F 29 C11
Domèvre-en-Haye F 26 C4
Domèvre-sur-Vezouze F 27 C6
Domfront F 23 C10
Domgermain F 26 C4
Domínce HR 162 D3
Domingo Pérez E 46 E4
Dömitz D 83 D10
Domlyan BG 165 D10
Dommartin-le-Franc F 26 D2
Dommartin-Varimont F 25 C12
Domme F 29 F8
Dommershausen D 21 D8
Dommitzsch D 80 C3
Domnești RO 160 C5
Domnești RO 161 E7
Domnitsa GR 174 B4
Domnovo RUS 136 E2
Domodossola I 68 A5
Domokos GR 174 A5
Domont F 25 B7
Domoroc KS 164 D4
Dömös H 149 A11
Domoszló H 147 F10
Dompcevrin F 26 C3
Dompierre-les-Ormes F 30 C5
Dompierre-sur-Besbre F 30 B4
Dompierre-sur-Mer F 28 C3
Dompierre-sur-Yon F 28 B3
Domrémy-la-Pucelle F 26 D4
Dömsöd H 150 C3
Domsühl D 83 D11
Domus de Maria I 64 F2
Domusnovas I 64 E2
Domvaina GR 175 C6
Domžale SLO 73 D10
Donagh GB 7 D8
Donaghadee GB 4 F5
Donaghmore GB 7 C9
Donaghmore IRL 7 F10
Don Álvaro E 51 B7
Doña Mencía E 53 A8
Donard IRL 7 F9
Donaueschingen D 27 E9
Donauwörth D 75 E8
Don Benito E 51 B8
Doncaster GB 11 D9
Donchery F 19 E10
Donduşeni MD 153 A11
Donegal IRL 6 C6
Doneraile IRL 8 D5
Doneztebe E 32 D2
Dønfoss N 100 C8
Dongen NL 16 E3
Donges F 23 F7
Dongo I 69 A7
Donici MD 154 C3
Doñinos de Salamanca E 45 C9
Donja Bela Reka SRB 159 E9
Donja Brela HR 157 F6
Donja Bukovica MNE 163 C7
Donja Dubrava HR 149 D7
Donja Kupčina HR 148 E5
Donja Lepenica BIH 157 B8
Donja Mahala BIH 157 B10
Donja Motičina HR 149 F10
Donja Šatornja SRB 158 E6
Donja Stubica HR 148 E5
Donja Višnjica HR 148 D6
Donja Vrijeska HR 149 E8
Donja Zelina HR 148 E6
Donje Pazarište HR 67 C11
Donjeux F 26 D3
Donji Andrijevci HR 157 B9
Donji Čaglić HR 149 F8
Donji Dubovnik BIH 156 C5
Donji Dušnik SRB 164 C5
Donji Kosinj HR 156 C3
Donji Krčin SRB 159 F7
Donji Krivodol SRB 165 C6
Donji Lapac HR 156 C4
Donji Miholjac HR 149 E10
Donji Milanovac SRB 159 E9
Donji Proložac HR 157 F7
Donji Rujani BIH 157 E6
Donji Seget HR 156 E5
Donji Srb HR 156 D5
Donji Striževac SRB 164 C5
Donji Svilaj BIH 157 B9
Donji Vakuf BIH 157 D7
Donji Vijačani BIH 157 C8
Donji Zemunik HR 156 D3
Donji Širovac HR 156 B5
Donk NL 183 B7
Donkerbroek NL 16 B6
Donnalucata I 59 F6
Donnas I 68 B4
Donnemarie-Dontilly F 25 D9
Donnersbach A 73 B9
Donnersdorf D 75 C7
Donohill IRL 8 C6
Donori I 64 E3
Donostia-San Sebastián E 32 D2
Donskoye RUS 139 A8
Donville-les-Bains F 23 C8
Donzdorf D 74 E6
Donzenac F 29 E9
Donzère F 35 B8
Donzy F 25 F9
Dooagh IRL 6 E2
Doochary IRL 6 C6
Dooish GB 4 F2
Doolin IRL 6 F4
Doon IRL 8 C6
Doonbeg IRL 8 C3
Doorn NL 16 D4
Doornspijk NL 183 A7
Dopiewo PL 81 B11
Dorče Petrov MK 164 E3
Dorchester GB 13 D10
Dørdal N 90 B5
Dordives F 25 D8
Dordrecht NL 16 E3
Dore-l'Église F 30 E4
Dörentrup D 17 D12
Dores GB 3 L8
Dorfen D 75 F11
Dorfgastein A 73 B7
Dorfmark D 82 E7
Dorf Mecklenburg D 83 C10
Dorgali I 64 C4
Dorgoș RO 151 E8
Dorio GR 174 E4
Dorking GB 15 E8
Dorkovo BG 165 E9
Dorlisheim F 186 D3
Dormagen D 21 B7
Dormánd H 150 B5
Dormans F 25 B10
Dor Mărunt RO 161 E9
Dorna-Arini RO 152 C6
Dorna Candrenilor RO 152 C6
Dornava SLO 148 D5
Dörnberg (Habichtswald) D 17 F12
Dornbirn A 71 C9
Dornburg (Saale) D 79 D10
Dornburg-Frickhofen D 185 C9
Dornbusch D 17 A12
Dorndorf D 79 E7
Dorndorf-Steudnitz D 79 D10
Dornelas P 38 E4
Dornes F 30 B3
Dornești RO 153 B8
Dornhan D 187 E6
Dornie GB 2 L5
Dornișoara RO 152 C6
Dornitz D 79 B11
Dorno I 69 C6
Dornoch GB 3 K8
Dornstadt D 74 F6
Dornstetten D 27 D9
Dornum D 17 A8
Dornumersiel D 17 A8
Dorobanțu RO 155 D2
Dorobanțu RO 161 E9
Dorog H 149 A11
Dorogháza H 147 F9
Dorohoi RO 153 B8
Dorohusk PL 141 H9
Dorolț RO 151 B10
Dorotcaia MD 154 C4
Dorotea S 107 C10
Dörpen D 17 C8
Dorras N 112 D8
Dorris S 107 B9
Dorstadt D 79 B8
Dorsten D 17 E7
Dorstfeld D 185 A7
Dortan F 31 C8
Dortmund D 17 E8
Dörttepe TR 177 E10
Doruchów PL 142 D5
Dorum D 17 A11
Dorupe LV 134 C7
Dörverden D 17 C12
Dörzbach D 74 D6
Dos Aguas E 48 F3
Dosbarrios E 46 E6
Dos Hermanas E 51 E8
Dospat BG 165 F9
Dossenheim D 21 F11
Doștat RO 152 F3
Dos Torres E 54 C3
Døstrup DK 86 E3
Dotnuva LT 134 F7
Dotternhausen D 27 D10
Döttingen CH 27 E9
Douai F 19 D7
Douarnenez F 22 D3
Doubrava CZ 147 B7
Doubravice nad Svitavou CZ 77 D11
Doubs F 31 B9
Douchy F 25 E9
Douchy-les-Mines F 19 D7
Doucier F 31 B8
Doudeville F 18 E2
Doudleby nad Orlicí CZ 77 B10
Doué-la-Fontaine F 23 F11
Douglas GB 5 D9
Douglas GBM 10 C3
Douglas IRL 8 E6
Douglas Bridge GB 4 F2
Doulaincourt-Saucourt F 26 D3
Doullens F 18 D5
Dounaiika GR 174 D3
Doune GB 5 C8
Dounreay GB 3 H9
Dour B 19 D8
Dourdan F 24 C7
Dourgne F 33 D10
Douriez F 18 D4
Doussard F 31 D9
Douvaine F 31 C9
Douvres-la-Délivrande F 23 B11
Douzy F 19 E11
Dovadola I 66 D4
Dover GB 15 E11
Dovhe UA 145 G7
Döviken S 103 A9
Dovilai LT 134 E2
Dovre N 101 C10
Dowally GB 5 B9
Downham Market GB 11 F12
Downpatrick GB 7 D11
Downton GB 13 D11
Dowra IRL 6 D6
Dowsby GB 11 F11
Doxato GR 171 B6
Doyet F 30 C2
Doyrentsi BG 165 C10
Dozulé F 23 B11
Drabeši LV 135 B10
Dråby DK 86 C7
Dračevo BIH 162 D5
Dračevo MK 164 F4
Drachhausen D 80 C6
Drachselsried D 76 D4
Drachten NL 16 B6
Drag N 105 B10
Drag N 111 D11
Dragacz PL 138 C6
Dragalijevac BIH 157 C11
Dragalina RO 161 E10
Dragalovci BIH 157 C8
Drăgănești RO 151 D9
Drăgănești RO 153 F10
Drăgănești RO 161 D8
Drăgănești de Vede RO 160 E6
Drăgănești-Olt RO 160 E5
Drăgănești-Vlașca RO 161 E7
Draganići HR 148 E5
Draganovo BG 166 C5
Drăganu RO 160 D5
Drăgășani RO 160 D4
Dragash KS 163 E10
Dragatuš SLO 67 A11
Drage D 83 D8
Drage HR 156 E4
Drăgești RO 151 D9
Drăghiceni RO 160 E4
Draginac SRB 158 D3
Draginje SRB 158 D4
Draginovo BG 165 E8
Dragland N 111 C11
Dragnes N 111 C10
Dragnić BIH 157 D7
Dragobi AL 163 E8
Dragočaj BIH 157 C7
Dragocvet SRB 159 F7
Dragodana RO 160 D6
Drăgoești RO 160 D4
Drăgoești RO 161 D9
Dragoevo BG 167 C7
Dragoevo MK 164 F5
Drăgoiești RO 153 B8
Dragoman BG 165 D6
Dragomance MK 164 E4
Dragomir BG 165 E9
Dragomirești RO 152 B4
Dragomirești RO 153 C9
Dragomirești RO 153 D10
Dragomirești RO 160 D6
Dragomirovo BG 166 B4
Dragoni I 60 A2
Dragør DK 87 D11
Dragoš MK 168 C5
Dragoslavele RO 160 C6
Dragoș Vodă RO 161 E10
Drăgotești RO 159 D11
Drăgotești RO 160 E4
Dragotina HR 156 B5
Dragović HR 149 F8
Dragovishtitsa BG 165 E6
Dragoychintsi BG 164 D5
Dragoynovo BG 166 F4
Dragsfjärd FIN 126 E7
Draguignan F 36 D4
Drăgușeni RO 153 A9
Drăgușeni RO 153 C8
Drăgușeni RO 153 F11
Drăguțești RO 159 D11
Drahnsdorf D 80 C5
Drahovce SK 146 D5
Drahove UA 145 G8
Drahovica Donja BIH 157 C9
Drajna RO 161 C8
Draka BG 167 E8
Drakenburg D 17 C12
Draksenić BIH 157 B6
Dralfa BG 167 C6
Drama GR 170 B6
Drammen N 95 C12
Drânceni RO 153 D12
Drange N 94 F5
Drangedal N 90 A5
Drangstedt D 17 A11
Dränic RO 160 E3
Dranse D 83 D13
Dransfeld D 78 D6
Dranske D 84 A4
Draperstown GB 4 F3
Drasenhofen A 77 E11
Draßmarkt A 149 A6
Drávafok H 149 E9
Dravagen S 102 B6
Draviskos GR 170 C5
Dravograd SLO 73 C11
Drawno PL 85 D9
Drawsko PL 85 E10
Drawsko Pomorskie PL 85 C9
Drayton GB 15 B11
Drążdżewo PL 139 D11
Dražen Vrh SLO 148 C5
Draževac SRB 158 D5
Dražgoše SLO 73 D9
Drebber D 17 C10
Drebkau D 80 C6
Drégelypalánk H 147 E8
Dreieich D 21 D11
Dreileben D 79 B9
Dreis D 21 E7
Drelów PL 141 G7
Drelsdorf D 82 A6
Drem GB 5 C11
Drenchia I 73 D8
Drenovac SRB 159 F7
Drenovci HR 157 C10
Drenovë AL 168 C4
Drenovets BG 159 F10
Drenovicë AL 168 C2
Drenovo MK 164 F4
Drenovo MK 169 B6
Drense D 84 D5
Drensteinfurt D 17 E9
Drenta BG 166 D5
Drentwede D 17 C11
Drepano GR 169 D6
Drepano GR 175 D6
Dresden D 80 D5
Dretun' BY 133 E6
Dretyń PL 85 B11
Dreumel NL 183 B6
Dreux F 24 C5
Dreverna LT 134 E2
Drevja N 108 E5
Drevjesætra N 102 D4
Dřevohostice CZ 146 C5
Drevsjø N 102 C3
Drevvatn N 108 D5
Drewitz D 79 B11
Drewnica PL 138 B6
Drezdenko PL 85 E9
Drežnica BIH 157 E8
Drežnik SRB 158 F4
Driceni LV 133 C2
Dridu RO 161 D8
Driebergen NL 16 D4
Driebes E 47 D6
Driedorf D 185 C9
Drienov SK 145 F3
Drietoma SK 146 D5
Driffield GB 11 C11
Drimmo IRL 7 F7
Drimnin GB 4 B5
Drimoleague IRL 8 E4
Drinić BIH 156 C5
Drinjača BIH 157 D11
Drinovci BIH 157 F7
Dripsey IRL 8 E5
Drisht AL 163 E8
Dřiteň CZ 76 D6
Drithas AL 168 C4
Driva N 101 A11
Drivstua N 101 B11
Drmno SRB 159 D7
Drnholec CZ 77 E11
Drniš HR 156 E5
Drnje HR 149 D7
Drnovice CZ 77 D11
Drnovice CZ 77 D11
Dro I 69 B10
Drøbak N 95 C13
Drobeta-Turnu Severin RO 159 D10
Drobin PL 139 E8
Drochia MD 153 A11
Drochtersen D 17 A12
Drogheda IRL 7 E10
Drohiczyn PL 141 F7
Drohobych UA 145 E8
Droichead Abhann IRL 8 C5
Droichead Átha IRL 7 E10
Droichead na Bandan IRL 8 E5
Droichead Nua IRL 7 F9
Droitwich Spa GB 13 A10
Drolshagen D 185 B8
Drolsum N 95 B12
Dromara GB 7 D10
Dromina IRL 8 D5
Drommahane IRL 8 D5
Drömme S 107 E14
Dromod IRL 7 E7
Dromore GB 7 C8
Dromore GB 7 D10
Dromore West IRL 6 D5
Dronero I 37 C6
Dronfield GB 11 E9
Drongan GB 5 E8
Drongen B 182 C3
Dronninglund DK 86 A6
Dronrijp NL 16 B5
Dronten NL 16 C5
Dropla BG 155 F2
Drosato GR 169 B8
Drosbacken S 102 C3
Drosendorf A 77 E9
Drosia GR 175 C8
Drösing A 77 E11
Drosopigi GR 168 C5
Droué F 24 D5
Droyßig D 79 D11
Drugan BG 165 E7
Drugovo MK 168 B4
Druid GB 10 F5
Druimdrishaig GB 4 D5
Drulingen F 27 C7
Drumandoora IRL 6 G5
Drumanespick IRL 7 E8
Drumatober IRL 6 F6
Drumbeg GB 2 J6
Drumbilla IRL 7 D10
Drumcard GB 7 D7
Drumcollogher IRL 8 D5
Drumcondra IRL 7 E9
Drumconrath IRL 7 E9
Drumcree IRL 7 E8
Drumettaz-Clarafond F 31 D8
Drumevo BG 167 C8
Drumfree IRL 4 E2
Drumkeeran IRL 6 D6
Drumlea IRL 7 D7
Drumlish IRL 7 E7
Drumlithie GB 5 B12
Drummin IRL 9 D9
Drummore GB 4 F7
Drumnadrochit GB 2 L8
Drumquin GB 4 F2
Drumshanbo IRL 6 D6
Drung IRL 7 D8
Drusenheim F 27 C8
Druskininkai LT 137 F9
Drusti LV 135 B11
Druten NL 183 B7
Druviena LV 135 B12
Druya BY 133 E2
Druyes-les-Belles-Fontaines F 25 E9
Druysk BY 133 E2
Družbice PL 143 D7
Druzhba RUS 136 E3
Druzhnaya Gorka RUS 132 C7
Družstevná pri Hornáde SK 145 F3
Drvenik HR 157 F7
Drwalew PL 141 G4
Drwinia PL 143 F9
Dryanovets BG 161 F8
Dryanovo BG 166 D4
Dryazhno RUS 132 E4
Drygały PL 139 C13
Drymaia GR 175 B6
Drymen GB 5 C8
Drymos GR 169 C8
Dryna N 100 A5
Dryopida GR 175 E9
Dryos GR 176 E5
Drysvyaty BY 135 E13
Dryszczów PL 144 A8
Drzewce PL 142 B6
Drzewiany PL 85 C11
Drzewica PL 141 H2
Drzonowo PL 85 C11
Drzycim PL 138 C5
Duagh IRL 8 D4
Dualchi I 64 C2
Dually IRL 9 C7
Duas Igrejas P 39 F7
Dub SRB 158 F4
Dubá CZ 77 A7
Dubăsari MD 154 C4
Dubăsarii Vechi MD 154 C4
Duba Stonska HR 162 D4
Dubău MD 154 C4
Dubeczno PL 141 H8
Düben D 79 C11
Duben D 80 C5
Dübendorf CH 27 F10
Dubeni LV 134 C4
Dubeninki PL 136 E6
Dubí CZ 80 E5
Dubičiai LT 137 E10
Dubicko CZ 77 C11
Dubicze Cerkiewne PL 141 E8
Dubidze PL 143 D7
Dubiecko PL 144 D5
Dubienka PL 144 A8
Dubingiai LT 137 C11
Dubino I 69 A7
Dubivka UA 153 A8
Dublin IRL 7 F10
Dublje SRB 158 D4
Dublovice CZ 76 C6
Dublyany UA 144 D9
Dublyany UA 145 E7
Dubna LV 135 D13
Dub nad Moravou CZ 146 C4
Dubňany CZ 77 E12
Dubnica nad Váhom SK 146 D6
Dubník SK 146 F6
Dubošbica BIH 157 D9
Dubova RO 159 D9
Dubovac SRB 159 D7
Dubove UA 145 G8
Dŭbovets BG 166 F5
Dubovica SK 145 E2
Dŭbovo BG 166 D5
Dubovo SRB 164 C4
Dubovsko BIH 156 C5
Dubrava BIH 157 C8
Dubrava HR 149 E7
Dubrave BIH 157 C10
Dubrave BIH 157 D6
Dubrave BIH 157 D10
Dubravica BIH 157 D8
Dubravica HR 148 E5
Dubravica SRB 159 D7
Dúbravy SK 147 D8
Dubrawka BY 133 F6
Dubrovka RUS 129 F14
Dubrovka RUS 132 F6
Dubrovka RUS 133 D5
Dubrovnik HR 162 D5
Dubrovytsya UA 144 D8
Dubuļi LV 133 D3
Dubynove UA 154 A6
Ducey F 23 C9
Ducherow D 84 C5
Duchov CZ 80 E5
Duck End GB 15 D9
Duclair F 18 F2
Duda-Epureni RO 153 D12
Dudar H 149 B9
Duddo GB 5 D12
Dudelange L 20 F6
Dudeldorf D 21 E7
Duderstadt D 79 C7
Dudești RO 161 D10
Dudestii Vechi RO 150 E5
Dudince SK 147 E7
Düdingen CH 31 B11
Dudley GB 11 F7
Dudovica SRB 158 E5
Dueñas E 40 E2
Duesund N 100 E2
Dueville I 72 E4
Duffel B 19 B10
Dufftown GB 3 L10
Duga Poljana SRB 163 C9
Duga Resa HR 148 F5
Dugi Rat HR 156 F6
Dugny-sur-Meuse F 26 B3
Dugopolje HR 156 E6
Dugo Selo HR 148 E6
Düğüncübaşı TR 173 B7
Duhort-Bachen F 32 C5
Duino I 73 E8
Duirinish GB 2 L5
Duisburg D 17 F7
Dukas AL 168 C2
Dukat AL 168 D2
Dukat i Ri AL 168 D1
Dukla PL 145 D4
Dūkštas LT 135 E12
Dŭlbok Dol BG 165 D10
Dŭlboki BG 166 E5
Dŭlbok Izvor BG 166 E4
Dulcești RO 153 D9
Duleek IRL 7 E10
Dŭlgodeltsi BG 160 F2
Dŭlgopol BG 167 C8
Dulina BY 133 F2
Duljci BIH 157 D7

Dullingham GB 15 C9
Dülmen D 17 E8
Dulnain Bridge GB 3 L9
Dulovce SK 146 F6
Dulovka RUS 133 A4
Dulovo BG 161 F10
Dulverton GB 13 C7
Dumbarton GB 4 D7
Dumbrava RO 151 F9
Dumbrava RO 159 D11
Dumbrava RO 161 D8
Dumbrava Roșie RO 153 D8
Dumbrăveni RO 152 E5
Dumbrăveni RO 153 B8
Dumbrăveni RO 155 F1
Dumbrăveni RO 161 B10
Dumbrăvești RO 161 C7
Dumbrăvița RO 151 F7
Dumbrăvița RO 152 B3
Dumbrăvița RO 153 F6
Dumbría E 38 B1
Dumești RO 153 C10
Dumești RO 153 D10
Dumfries GB 5 E9
Dumitra RO 152 C4
Dumitrești RO 161 B9
Dummerstorf D 83 C12
Dumnicë KS 164 D3
Dümpelfeld D 21 D7
Dun F 33 D9
Duna N 105 B11
Dunaegyháza H 149 C11
Dunaföldvár H 149 C11
Dunaharaszti H 150 C3
Dunajská Lužná SK 146 E4
Dunajská Streda SK 146 F5
Dunakeszi H 150 B3
Dunalka LV 134 C2
Dún an Rí IRL 7 E9
Dunapataj H 150 D3
Dunărea RO 155 E2
Dunaszeg H 149 A9
Dunaszekcső H 149 D11
Dunaszentbenedek H 149 C11
Dunaszentgyörgy H 149 C11
Dunasziget H 146 F4
Dunatetétlen H 150 D3
Dunaújváros H 149 C11
Dunava LV 135 D12
Dunavarsány H 150 C3
Dunavecse H 150 D2
Dunavtsi BG 159 F10
Dunbar GB 5 C11
Dunbeath GB 3 J10
Dunblane GB 5 C9
Dunboyne IRL 7 F10
Dún Búinne IRL 7 F10
Duncannon IRL 9 D9
Dún Chaoin IRL 8 D2
Dunchurch GB 13 A12
Duncormick IRL 9 D9
Dundaga LV 134 A4
Dundalk IRL 7 D10
Dún Dealgan IRL 7 D10
Dun Dealgan IRL 7 D10
Dundee GB 5 C11
Dunderland N 108 D8
Dundonald GB 7 C11
Dundreggan GB 2 L7
Dundrennan GB 5 F9
Dundrum GB 7 D11
Dundrum IRL 8 C6
Dunecht GB 3 L12
Dunes F 33 B7
Dunfanaghy IRL 7 B7
Dunfermline GB 5 C10
Dungannon GB 7 C9
Dún Garbhán IRL 9 D7
Dungarvan IRL 9 C8
Dungarvan IRL 9 D7
Düngenheim D 185 D7
Dungiven GB 4 F3
Dungloe IRL 6 C6
Dungourney IRL 8 E6
Dunholme GB 11 E11
Dunicë AL 168 C4
Dunières F 30 E5
Duninowo PL 85 A11
Dunje MK 169 B6
Dunkeld GB 5 B9
Dunkerque F 18 B5
Dunkerrin IRL 9 C7
Dunkitt IRL 9 D8
Dún Laoghaire IRL 7 F10
Dunlavin IRL 7 F9
Dunleer IRL 7 E10
Dún Léire IRL 7 E10
Dun-le-Palestel F 29 C9
Dun-les-Places F 25 F11
Dunlop GB 4 D7
Dunloy GB 4 E4
Dún Mánmhaí IRL 8 E4
Dunmanway IRL 8 E4
Dún Mór IRL 9 D9
Dunmore IRL 6 E5
Dunmore East IRL 9 D9
Dunmurry GB 7 C11
Dunnamanagh GB 4 F2
Dún na nGall IRL 6 C6
Dunning GB 5 C9
Dunoon GB 4 D7
Dunquin IRL 8 D2
Duns GB 5 D12
Dunscore GB 5 E9
Dünsen D 17 C11
Dunshaughlin IRL 7 E9
Dunstable GB 15 D7
Dunster GB 13 C8
Dun-sur-Auron F 29 B11
Dun-sur-Meuse F 19 F11
Dunure GB 4 E7
Dunvant GB 12 B6
Dunvegan GB 2 L3
Duplica SLO 73 D10
Dupnitsa BG 165 E7
Durach D 71 B10
Durak TR 173 E9
Durana E 41 C6
Durance F 33 B6
Durango E 41 B6
Durankulak BG 155 F3
Duras F 33 A6
Durbach D 27 C9
Durban-Corbières F 34 E4
Durbe LV 134 C2
Durbuy B 184 D3
Dúrcal E 53 C9
Durdat-Larequille F 29 C11
Đurđenovac HR 149 E10
Đurđevac HR 149 D8
Đurđevića Tara MNE 163 C7
Đurđevik BIH 157 D10
Đurđevo SRB 158 C5
Đurđevo SRB 159 E6
Düren D 20 C6
Durfort F 35 C6
Durham GB 5 F13
Ďurkov SK 145 F3
Durlas IRL 9 C7
Durlești MD 154 C3
Durmanec HR 148 D5
Dürmentingen D 71 A9
Durmersheim D 27 C9
Durness GB 2 H7
Durnești RO 153 B10
Dürnkrut A 77 F11
Durrës AL 168 B1
Durrington GB 13 C11
Dürrlauingen D 75 F7
Durrow IRL 9 C8
Durrus IRL 8 E3
Dürrwangen D 75 D7
Dursley GB 13 B10
Dursunbey TR 173 E10
Durtal F 23 E11
Duruelo de la Sierra E 40 E6
Duruitoarea MD 153 B10
Durup DK 86 B3
Durusu TR 173 B10
Dusetos LT 135 E11
Dushk i Madh AL 168 C2
Dusina BIH 157 E8
Düskotna BG 167 D8
Duškovci SRB 158 F5
Dusmenys LT 137 E9
Dusnok H 150 E2
Dusocin PL 138 C6
Düsseldorf D 21 B7
Dussen NL 16 E3
Dußlingen D 187 E7
Düßnitz D 79 C12
Duszniki PL 81 B10
Dutluca TR 173 E11
Dutovlje SLO 73 E8
Duvberg S 102 B7
Duved S 105 E13
Düvertepe TR 173 F9
Duži BIH 162 D5
Dvärsätt S 106 E6
Dvaryshcha BY 133 E6
Dve Mogili BG 161 F7
Dverberg N 111 B10
Dviete LV 135 D12
Dvirtsi UA 144 C9
Dvor HR 156 B5
Dvorce CZ 146 B5
Dvornaye Syalo BY 133 E3
Dvorníky SK 146 E5
Dvory nad Žitavou SK 146 F6
Dvůr Králové CZ 77 B9
Dwikozy PL 144 B4
Dwingeloo NL 16 C6
Dyan GB 7 D9
Dyankovo BG 161 F9
Dybvad DK 90 E7
Dyce GB 3 L12
Dychów PL 81 C8
Dydnia PL 144 D5
Dyfjord N 113 B19
Dygowo PL 85 B9
Dyke GB 3 K9
Dykehead GB 5 B11
Dykhtynets' UA 152 A6
Dylągówka PL 144 D5
Dylaki PL 142 E5
Dylewo PL 139 D11
Dymchurch GB 15 E10
Dymock GB 13 B10
Dynäs S 107 F13
Dynivtsi UA 153 A8
Dynów PL 144 D5
Dyo F 30 C5
Dyping N 110 E9
Dyrnes N 104 E3
Dyrøyhamn N 111 B13
Dyrrachi GR 174 E5
Dyulevo BG 167 E8
Dyulino BG 167 D9
Dyviziya UA 154 F5
Dywity PL 136 F1
Dzeguzēni LV 134 D6
Dzelzava LV 135 C12
Dzeņi LV 135 B12
Dzērbene LV 135 B11
Dzhebel BG 171 A8
Dzherman BG 165 E7
Dzhulynka UA 154 A5
Dzhulyunitsa BG 166 C5
Dzhuriv UA 152 A6
Dzhurovo BG 165 D9
Dziadkowice PL 141 E7
Dziadowa Kłoda PL 142 D4
Działdowo PL 139 D9
Działoszyce PL 143 F9
Działoszyn PL 142 D6
Działyń PL 138 D7
Dziemiany PL 138 B4
Dziergowice PL 142 F5
Dzierzążnia PL 139 E9
Dzierżążno Wielkie PL 85 E10
Dzierzgoń PL 139 C7
Dzierzgowo PL 139 D10
Dzierzkowice-Rynek PL 144 B5
Dzierżoniów PL 81 E11
Dzietrzniki PL 142 D6
Dzietrzychowo PL 136 E3
Dziewierzewo PL 85 E13
Džigolj SRB 164 C4
Dzirnavas LV 134 B4
Dzisna BY 133 E4
Dziwnów PL 85 B7
Dzmitravichy BY 141 F9
Džūkste LV 134 C6
Džumajlija MK 164 F4
Dźwierzuty PL 139 C10
Dźwirzyno PL 85 B8
Dzwola PL 144 B6
Dzwonowice PL 143 E8
Dzyornavichy BY 133 E4

E

Éadan Doire IRL 7 F8
Eaglesfield GB 5 E10
Eardisley GB 13 A8
Earith GB 15 C9
Earl Shilton GB 11 F9
Earlston GB 5 D11
Earl Stonham GB 15 C11
Earsairidh GB 4 B2
Easdale GB 4 C5
Easington GB 5 F14
Easington GB 11 D12
Easingwold GB 11 C9
Easky IRL 6 D5
Eastbourne GB 15 F9
Eastburn GB 11 D11
Eastfield GB 11 C11
Eastgate GB 5 F12
East Grinstead GB 15 E8
East Harling GB 15 C10
East Kilbride GB 5 D8
Eastleigh GB 13 D12
East Linton GB 5 D11
East Looe GB 12 E6
Eastoft GB 11 D10
Easton GB 13 D10
East Retford GB 11 E10
Eastriggs GB 5 F10
Eastry GB 15 E11
East Wemyss GB 5 C10
East Wittering GB 15 F7
Eastwood GB 11 E9
Eaton Socon GB 15 C8
Eaunes F 33 D8
Eauze F 33 C6
Ebberup DK 86 E5
Ebbs A 72 A5
Ebbw Vale GB 13 B8
Ebecik TR 181 A9
Ebeleben D 79 D8
Ebelsbach D 75 C8
Ebeltoft DK 86 C7
Ebene Reichenau A 73 C8
Ebenfurth A 77 G10
Eben im Pongau A 73 B7
Ebensee A 73 A8
Ebensfeld D 75 B8
Ebenthal A 73 C9
Ebenweiler D 71 B9
Eberau A 149 B6
Eberbach D 21 F11
Ebergötzen D 79 C7
Ebermannsdorf D 75 D10
Ebermannstadt D 75 C9
Ebern D 75 B8
Eberndorf A 73 C10
Ebersbach D 80 D5
Ebersbach D 81 D7
Ebersbach an der Fils D 74 E6
Ebersberg D 75 F10
Eberschwang A 76 F5
Ebersdorf A 148 B5
Ebersdorf D 17 A12
Ebersdorf D 75 B10
Ebersmunster F 186 E4
Eberstein A 73 C10
Eberswalde-Finow D 84 E5
Ebes H 151 C8
Ebhausen D 27 C10
Ebikon CH 27 F9
Ebnat-Kappel CH 27 F11
Eboli I 60 B4
Ebrach D 75 C7
Ebreichsdorf A 77 G10
Ébreuil F 30 C3
Ebsdorfergrund-Dreihausen D 21 C11
Ebstorf D 83 D8
Écaussinnes-d'Enghien B 182 D4
Ecclefechan GB 5 E10
Eccles GB 5 D12
Eccleshall GB 11 F7
Eceabat TR 171 D10
Echallens CH 31 B10
Echarri E 32 E2
Échauffour F 24 C3
Échenoz-la-Méline F 26 E5
Eching D 75 E11
Eching D 75 F10
Echinos GR 171 B7
Échiré F 28 C5
Échirolles F 31 E8
Échourgnac F 29 E6
Echsenbach A 77 E8
Echt GB 3 L12
Echt NL 19 B12
Echte D 79 C7
Echternach L 20 E6
Écija E 53 A6
Ečka SRB 158 C5
Eckartsberga D 79 D10
Eckbolsheim F 186 D4
Eckental D 75 C9
Eckernförde D 83 B7
Eckerö FIN 99 B13
Eckington GB 11 E9
Eckington GB 13 A10
Éclaron-Braucourt-Ste-Livière F 25 C12
Écommoy F 23 E12
Écos F 24 B6
Écouché F 23 C11
Écouflant F 23 E10
Écouis F 18 F3
Écrouves F 26 C4
Écs H 149 A9
Écséd H 150 B4
Écseg H 147 F9
Écsegfalva H 151 C6
Écser H 150 C3
Écueillé F 29 A8
Écuisses F 30 B6
Écury-sur-Coole F 25 C11
Ed S 91 B10
Ed S 107 E12
Eda glasbruk S 96 C7
Edam NL 16 C4
Edane S 97 C8
Ēdas LV 134 C4
Eddelak D 82 C6
Edderton GB 3 K8
Eddleston GB 5 D10
Ede NL 16 D5
Ede S 103 B12
Edebäck S 97 B10
Edefors S 118 B5
Edegem B 19 B9
Edelény H 145 G2
Edelschrott A 73 B11
Edemissen D 79 B7
Eden GB 4 F5
Eden S 107 D12
Edenderry IRL 7 F8
Edenkoben D 21 F10
Edermünde D 78 D5
Ederny GB 7 C7
Edesheim D 21 F10
Edessa GR 169 C7
Edewecht D 17 B9
Edewechterdamm D 17 B9
Edgeworthstown IRL 7 E7
Edgmond GB 11 F7
Ediger-Eller D 21 D8
Edinburgh GB 5 D10
Edincik TR 173 D8
Edineț MD 153 A10
Edirne TR 171 A11
Edland N 94 C7
Edling D 75 F11
Edlingham GB 5 E13
Edlitz A 148 A6
Edmondstown IRL 6 E5
Edmundbyers GB 5 F13
Ēdole LV 134 B3
Edolo I 69 A9
Edremit TR 173 E7
Edrosa P 39 E6
Edroso P 39 E6
Edsbro S 99 C10
Edsbruk S 93 C8
Edsbyn S 103 D10
Edsele S 107 E11
Edsken S 98 A6
Edsvalla S 97 D9
Edzell GB 5 B11
Eefde NL 183 A8
Eeklo B 19 B8
Eelde-Paterswolde NL 17 B7
Eerbeek NL 16 D6
Eernegem B 182 C2
Eersel NL 16 F4
Eferding A 76 F6
Effelder D 75 B9
Effeltrich D 75 C9
Effretikon CH 27 F10
Efkarpia GR 169 B8
Efkarpia GR 169 C10
Eforie RO 155 E3
Efpalio GR 174 C4
Efringen-Kirchen D 27 E8
Eftimie Murgu RO 159 D9
Efxeinoupoli GR 175 A6
Egby S 89 B11
Egebæk DK 86 E3
Egebjerg DK 86 D5
Egebjerg DK 87 D9
Egeln D 79 C9
Egense DK 86 B6
Eger H 145 H1
Egerbakta H 145 H1
Egernsund DK 86 F5
Egersund N 94 F4
Egerszalók H 145 H1
Egervár H 149 C7
Egeskov DK 86 D5
Egestorf D 83 D8
Egga N 111 B19
Eggby S 91 C14
Eggebek D 82 A6
Eggenburg A 77 E9
Eggenfelden D 75 F12
Eggenstein-Leopoldshafen D 27 B9
Eggersdorf D 79 C10
Eggersdorf bei Graz A 148 B5
Eggesbønes N 100 B3
Eggesin D 84 C6
Eggingen D 27 E9
Eggiwil CH 70 D5
Egglham D 76 E4
Eggolsheim D 75 C9
Eggstätt D 72 A5
Eggum N 110 D6
Eghezée B 19 C10
Eging am See D 76 E4
Églaine LV 135 E12
Égletons F 29 E10
Egling D 72 A4
Eglingham GB 5 E13
Eglinton GB 4 E2
Eglisau CH 27 E10
Eglish GB 7 D9
Egļuciems LV 133 B2
Eglwys Fach GB 10 F4
Eglwyswrw GB 12 A5
Egmond aan Zee NL 16 C3
Egna I 69 A11
Egorovca MD 153 B11
Egremont GB 10 C4
Egsmark DK 86 C7
Egtved DK 86 D4
Éguilles F 35 C9
Eguisheim F 27 D7
Éguzon-Chantôme F 29 C9
Egyek H 151 B6
Egyházaskozár H 149 D10
Ehekirchen D 75 E9
Ehingen D 75 D8
Ehingen (Donau) D 71 A9
Ehlen (Habichtswald) D 17 F12
Ehningen D 187 D6
Ehra-Lessien D 79 A8
Ehrenberg-Wüstensachsen D 74 B7
Ehrenburg D 17 C11
Ehrenfriedersdorf D 80 E3
Ehrenhausen A 148 C5
Ehringshausen D 21 C10
Eibar E 41 B7
Eibelstadt D 74 C7
Eibenstock D 75 B12
Eibergen NL 17 D7
Eibiswald A 148 C4
Eich D 21 E10
Eichenbarleben D 79 B9
Eichenbühl D 27 A11
Eichendorf D 76 E3
Eichenzell D 74 B6
Eichgraben A 77 F9
Eichigt D 75 B11
Eichstätt D 75 E9
Eichwalde D 80 B5
Eickendorf D 79 C10
Eicklingen D 79 A7
Eidapere EST 131 D9
Eide N 100 A6
Eide N 104 D8
Eide N 111 C11
Eidem N 108 E2
Eidet N 105 C15
Eidet N 105 C16
Eidet N 108 A9
Eidet N 110 D8
Eidfjord N 94 B6
Eiði FO 2 A2
Eidkjosen N 111 A16
Eidsbugarden N 101 D8
Eidsdal N 100 B6
Eidsfjord N 110 C8
Eidsfoss N 95 C12
Eidshaug N 105 B10
Eidsnes N 112 C10
Eidsøra N 100 A8
Eidstranda N 111 A19
Eidsund N 94 D3
Eidsvåg N 100 A8
Eidsvoll N 95 B14
Eidsvoll Verk N 95 B14
Eidvågeid N 113 B12
Eigeltingen D 27 E10
Eigenrieden D 79 D7
Eijsden NL 183 D7
Eik N 94 D3
Eikelandsosen N 94 B3
Eiken N 94 F6
Eikesdal N 100 B8
Eikjaberg N 100 D6
Eikjeskog N 94 E4
Eikjil N 90 B1
Eiksund N 100 B3
Eilenburg D 79 D12
Eilenstedt D 79 C9
Eilsleben D 79 B9
Eime D 78 B6
Eimen D 78 C6
Eimke D 83 E8
Eina N 101 E13
Einacleit GB 2 J3
Einbeck D 78 C6
Eindhoven NL 16 F4
Einsiedeln CH 27 F10
Einville-au-Jard F 26 C5
Einvollen N 108 F3
Eisden B 183 D7
Eiselfing D 75 F11
Eisenach D 79 E7
Eisenberg D 79 E10
Eisenberg (Pfalz) D 21 E10
Eisenerz A 73 A10
Eisenhüttenstadt D 81 B7
Eisenkappel A 73 D10
Eisenstadt A 77 G11
Eisfeld D 75 B8
Eišiškės LT 137 E10
Eislandet N 100 E3
Eisleben Lutherstadt D 79 C10
Eislingen (Fils) D 74 E6
Eisma EST 131 B12
Eitelborn D 21 D9
Eiterfeld D 78 E6
Eiternes N 105 B11
Eiterstraum N 108 E5
Eitorf D 21 C8
Eivinvik N 100 E2
Eivissa E 57 D7
Eja P 44 B4
Ejby DK 86 E5
Ejby DK 87 D9
Ejby DK 87 E10
Ejea de los Caballeros E 41 D9
Ejsing DK 86 B3
Ejstrupholm DK 86 D4
Ejulve E 42 F2
Ekeby S 87 C11
Ekeby S 92 A6
Ekeby S 99 D9
Ekeby-Almby S 97 D13
Ekedalen S 91 C14
Ekenäs FIN 127 F9
Ekenäs S 91 B13
Ekenäs S 93 B9
Ekenässjön S 92 E6
Ēkengrāve LV 135 D11
Ekeren B 182 C4
Ekerö S 99 D9
Eket S 87 C12
Ekkerøy N 114 C8
Ekmekçi TR 173 D9
Ekola FIN 122 D9
Ekorrträsk S 107 B16
Eksaarde B 182 C3
Eksel B 183 C6
Ekshärad S 97 B9
Eksjö S 92 D5
Eksta S 93 E12
Ekträsk S 118 F3
Ekzarkh-Antimovo BG 167 D7
Ekzarkh Yosif BG 161 F7
Elafos GR 169 D7
Elafotopos GR 168 E4
Elaiochori GR 171 C6
Elaionas GR 169 B10
Elaionas GR 174 B5
Elaionas GR 175 C7
El Álamo E 46 D5
El Algar E 56 F3
El Almendro E 51 D5
El Alquián E 55 F8
Elämäjärvi FIN 123 D15
El Arahal E 51 E8
El Arenal E 45 D10
Elassona GR 169 E7
El Astillero E 40 B4
Elateia GR 175 B6
Elati GR 169 D6
Elati GR 169 E6
Elatochori GR 169 D7
Elatou GR 174 B4
El Ballestero E 55 B8
El Barco de Ávila E 45 D9
El Barraco E 46 D3
Elbasan AL 168 B3
Elbergen D 17 D8
Elbeuf F 18 F3
Elbigenalp A 71 C10
Elbingerode (Harz) D 79 C8
Elbląg PL 139 B7
El Bodón E 45 D7
El Bonillo E 55 B7
El Bosque E 53 C6
El Bullaque E 46 F4
El Burgo E 53 C7
El Burgo de Ebro E 41 E10
El Burgo de Osma E 40 E5
El Burgo Ranero E 39 D9
El Buste E 41 E8
El Cabaco E 45 C8
El Cabildo y la Campana E 55 E9
El Cabo de Gata E 55 F8
El Campillo E 51 D6
El Campillo de la Jara E 45 E10
El Campo de Peñaranda E 45 C10
El Cañavate E 47 E8
El Carpio E 53 A8
El Carpio de Tajo E 46 E4
El Casar E 46 C6
El Casar de Escalona E 46 D3
El Castellar E 48 D3
El Castillo de las Guardas E 51 D7
El Catllar de Gaià E 43 E6
El Centenillo E 54 C5
El Cerro de Andévalo E 51 D6
Elche de la Sierra E 55 C8
Elche-Elx E 56 E3
Elchingen D 187 E9
Elciego E 41 C6
Elçili TR 172 B6
El Coronil E 51 E8
El Cubo de Don Sancho E 45 C8
El Cubo de Tierra del Vino E 39 F8
El Cuervo E 47 D10
El Cuervo E 51 F7
Elda E 56 E3
Eldalsosen N 100 D4
Eldena D 83 D10
Eldforsen S 97 B11
Eldingen D 83 E8
Eldsberga S 87 B12
Elduvík FO 2 A3
Elefsina GR 175 C8
Eleftheres GR 171 C6
Elefthero GR 168 D4
Eleftheroupoli GR 171 C6
Eleja LV 134 D7
El Ejido E 55 F7
Elek H 151 D7
Elektrėnai LT 137 D10
Elemir SRB 158 C5
Elena BG 166 D5
Elend D 79 C8
Eleousa GR 168 E4
El Escorial E 46 C4
Eleshnitsa BG 165 F8
El Espinar E 46 C4
El Estrecho E 56 F3
Elexalde E 40 B6
El Fendek MA 53 E5
Elfershausen D 187 A8
El Fresno E 46 C3
Elgå N 101 B15
El Garrobo E 51 D7
Elgershausen (Schauenburg) D 21 B12
Elgeta E 41 B7
Elgin GB 3 K10
Elgoibar E 32 D1
Elgol GB 2 L4
El Grado E 42 C4
El Granado E 50 D5
El Grau de Borriana E 48 E4
Elgsnes N 111 C11
El Herrumblar E 47 F9
El Hito E 47 E7
El Hoyo de Pinares E 46 C4
Elia GR 178 E9
Elice I 62 B5
Elie GB 5 C11
Elika GR 178 B4
Elimäki FIN 127 D15
Eling GB 13 D12
Elini I 64 D4
Elin Pelin BG 165 D8
Elisenvaara RUS 129 C12
Eliseyna BG 165 C8
Elizondo E 32 D2
Eljas E 45 D7
Ełk PL 136 F5
Elkenroth D 185 C8
Elkhovo BG 166 D5
Elkhovo BG 167 E7
Elkšņi LV 135 D11
Ellan S 99 B11
Elland GB 11 D8
Ellefeld D 75 B11
Ellenberg D 187 C9
Ellerau D 83 C7
Ellerbek D 83 C7
Ellesmere GB 10 F6
Ellesmere Port GB 10 E6
Ellezelles B 19 C8
Ellidshøj DK 86 B5
Elling DK 90 E7
Ellingen D 75 D8
Ellington GB 5 E13
El Llano E 38 B5
Ellmau A 72 A5
Ellon GB 3 L12
Ellös S 91 C9
El Losar del Barco E 45 D9
Elloughton GB 11 D10
Ellrich D 79 C8
Ellwangen (Jagst) D 75 E7
Ellwürden D 17 B10
Elm CH 71 D8
Elm D 17 A12
Elmacık TR 167 F8
El Masroig E 42 E5
Elmen A 71 C11
Elmenhorst D 83 B12
Elmenhorst D 83 C8
Elmenhorst D 83 C9
Elmenhorst D 83 C10
El Molar E 46 C5
El Molinillo E 46 F4
El Moral E 55 D8
El Morell E 42 E6
Elmshorn D 82 C7
Elne F 34 E4
Elnesvågen N 100 A6
Elorrio E 41 B6
Elorz E 32 E2
Elos GR 178 E6
El Oso E 46 C3
Előszállás H 149 C11
Elounta GR 179 E10
Elovdol BG 165 D6
Éloyes F 26 D6
El Palmar E 56 F2
El Palo E 53 C8
El Payo E 45 D7
El Pedernoso E 47 F7
El Pedroso E 51 D8
El Pedroso de la Armuña E 45 B10
El Peral E 47 E9
El Perdigón E 39 F8
El Perelló E 42 F5
El Perelló E 48 F4
Elpersbüttel D 82 B6
Elphin GB 2 J6
Elphin IRL 6 E6
El Picazo E 47 F8
El Pinell de Bray E 42 E5
El Piñero E 39 F8
El Pla de Santa Maria E 43 E6
El Pobo E 42 F2
El Pobo de Dueñas E 47 C9
El Pont d'Armentera E 43 E6
El Port E 48 E4
El Port de la Selva E 34 F5
El Prat de Llobregat E 43 E8
El Provencio E 47 F7
El Puente E 40 B5
El Puente de Arzobispo E 45 E10
El Puerto de Santa María E 52 C4
El Real de la Jara E 51 D7
El Real de San Vicente E 46 D3
El Recuenco E 47 C8
El Robledo E 46 F4
El Rocío E 51 E7
El Romeral E 46 E6
El Rompido E 51 E5
El Ronquillo E 51 D7
El Royo E 41 E6
El Rubio E 53 B7
El Sabinar E 41 D9
El Sabinar E 55 C8
El Saler E 48 F4
El Salobral E 55 B9
Els Arcs E 42 D5
El Saucejo E 53 B6
El Saugo E 45 D7
Elsdon GB 5 E12
Elsdorf D 21 C7
Elsenborn B 20 D6
Elsendorf D 75 E10
Elsenfeld D 21 E12
El Serrat AND 33 E9
Elsfjord N 108 D6
Elsfleth D 17 B10
Elshitsa BG 165 E9
Elsloo NL 183 D7
Elsnes N 111 B19
Elsnig D 80 C3
Elsnigk D 79 C11
El Soleràs E 42 E5
Elspeet NL 16 D5
Els Prats de Rei E 43 D7
Elst NL 16 E5
Elst NL 183 B6
Elster D 79 C12
Elsterberg D 79 E11
Elsterwerda D 80 D5
Elstra D 80 D6
El Tiemblo E 46 D4
Eltmann D 75 C8
El Toboso E 47 E7
Elton GB 11 F11
Elton IRL 8 D6
El Torno E 45 D9
El Trincheto E 46 F4
El Tumbalejo E 51 E6
Eltville am Rhein D 21 D10
Elva EST 131 E12
Elvål N 101 C14
Elvanfoot GB 5 E9
Elvas P 51 B5
Elvebakken N 113 D11
Elvegard N 111 D13
Elvekrok N 113 B17
Elvelund N 112 E6
Elvemund N 113 E16
Elven F 22 E6
El Vendrell E 43 E7
El Verger E 56 D5
Elverum N 101 E15
Elvesletta N 111 D12
Elvevoll N 111 B14
Elvevollen N 111 B18
El Villar de Arnedo E 32 F1
Elvington GB 11 D10
El Viso E 54 C3
El Viso del Alcor E 51 E8
Elvnes N 114 D8
Elxleben D 79 D8
Ely GB 13 C8
Ely GB 15 C9
Elz D 185 D9
Elzach D 27 D9
Elze D 78 B6
Elze (Wedemark) D 78 A6
Embid E 47 C9
Embid de Ariza E 41 F8
Embleton GB 5 E13
Embrun F 36 B4
Emburga LV 135 C7
Embūte LV 134 C3
Emden D 17 B8
Emecik TR 181 C7
Emiralem TR 177 B9
Emirali TR 173 B8
Emlichheim D 17 C7
Emly IRL 8 D6
Emmaboda S 89 B9
Emmaljunga S 87 C13
Emmanouil Pappas GR 169 B10
Emmaste EST 130 D5
Emmeloord NL 16 C5
Emmelsbüll-Horsbüll D 82 A5
Emmelshausen D 21 D9
Emmen CH 27 F9
Emmen NL 17 C7
Emmendingen D 27 D8
Emmer-Compascuum NL 17 C8
Emmerich D 16 E6
Emmoo IRL 6 E6
Emőd H 145 H2
Emolahti FIN 123 C15
Empel NL 16 E4
Empesos GR 174 A3
Empfingen D 187 E6
Empoli I 66 E2
Emponas GR 181 D7
Emporeio GR 179 C9
Emporeios GR 177 C7
Emptinne B 19 D11
Emsbüren D 17 D8
Emsdetten D 17 D9
Emsfors S 89 A10
Emskirchen D 75 C8
Emst NL 16 D5
Emstek D 17 C10
Emsworth GB 15 F7
Emtinghausen D 17 C11
Emtunga S 91 C12
Emyvale IRL 7 D9
Enafors S 105 E12
Enäjärvi FIN 128 D7
Enånger S 103 C13
Enarsvedjan S 105 D16
Encamp AND 33 E9
Encinas de Abajo E 45 C10
Encinasola E 51 C6
Encinas Reales E 53 B8
Encinedo E 39 D6
Enciso E 41 D7
Encs H 145 G3
Encsencs H 151 B9
Endingen D 27 D8
Endre S 93 D12
Endrefalva H 147 E9
Endriejavas LT 134 E3
Endrinal E 45 C9
Endzele LV 131 F10
Enebakk N 95 C14
Enego I 72 E4
Eneryda S 88 B6
Enese H 149 A8
Enez TR 171 C10
Enfesta E 38 C2
Enfield IRL 7 F9
Engan N 101 B11
Engan N 104 E4
Engan N 108 D3
Engares GR 176 E5

Engavågen N 108 C6
Engden D 183 A10
Engelberg CH 71 D6
Engelhartstetten A 77 F11
Engelhartszell A 76 E5
Engeln D 17 C11
Engelsberg D 75 F12
Engelskirchen D 21 C8
Engen D 27 E10
Enger D 17 D11
Engerdal N 101 C15
Engerdalssetra N 101 C15
Engerneset N 102 C3
Engersen D 79 A9
Engesland N 90 B3
Engesvang DK 86 C4
Enghien B 19 C9
Engis B 19 C11
Englefontaine F 19 D8
Engomer F 33 E8
Engstingen D 27 D11
Enguera E 56 D3
Enguidanos E 47 E9
Engure LV 134 B6
Engvik N 112 C2
Enhagen-Ekbacken S 98 C7
Enichioi MD 154 E2
Enina BG 166 D4
Eningen unter Achalm D 187 E7
Enitsa BG 165 C9
Enix E 55 F7
Enkenbach D 186 C4
Enkhuizen NL 16 C4
Enkirch D 21 E8
Enklinge FIN 99 B15
Enköping S 98 C8
Enmo N 101 A12
Enna I 58 D5
Ennepetal D 185 B7
Ennery F 186 C1
Ennezat F 30 D3
Ennigerloh D 17 E10
Ennis IRL 8 C5
Enniscorthy IRL 9 C9
Enniscrone IRL 6 D4
Enniskean IRL 8 E5
Enniskerry IRL 7 F10
Enniskillen GB 7 D7
Ennistymon IRL 8 C4
Enns A 77 F6
Eno FIN 125 E14
Enonkoski FIN 125 F11
Enonkylä FIN 119 F17
Enontekiö FIN 117 B11
Ens NL 16 C5
Enschede NL 17 D7
Ensdorf D 75 D10
Ensdorf D 186 C2
Ense D 17 F10
Ensheim D 21 F8
Ensisheim F 27 E7
Enskogen S 103 C9
Ensuès-la-Redonne F 35 D9
Enter NL 183 A9
Enterkinfoot GB 5 E9
Entlebuch CH 70 D6
Entracque I 37 C6
Entradas P 50 D3
Entraigues-sur-la-Sorgue F 35 B8
Entrains-sur-Nohain F 25 F9
Entrammes F 23 E10
Entraunes F 36 C5
Entraygues-sur-Truyère F 33 A11
Entrena E 41 D6
Entrevaux F 36 D5
Entroncamento P 44 F4
Envendos P 44 E5
Envermeu F 18 E3
Enviken S 103 E10
Enying H 149 C10
Enzklösterle D 27 C9
Eochaill IRL 9 E7
Eoropaidh GB 2 H4
Épaignes F 18 F1
Epalignes CH 31 B10
Epano Fellos GR 176 D4
Epanomi GR 169 D8
Epe NL 16 D5
Eperjes H 150 D6
Eperjeske H 145 G5
Épernay F 25 B10
Épernon F 24 C6
Epfendorf D 27 D10
Épieds-en-Beauce F 24 E6
Épierre F 31 E9
Épila E 41 E9
Épinac F 30 B6
Épinal F 26 D5
Epiry F 25 F10
Episcopia I 60 C6
Episkopi GR 169 C7
Episkopi GR 178 E7
Episkopi GR 178 E9
Epitalio GR 174 D3
Époisses F 25 E11
Epoo FIN 127 E14
Eppelborn D 21 F7
Eppelheim D 21 F11
Eppenbrunn D 186 C4
Eppertshausen D 21 E11
Eppeville F 19 E7
Epping GB 15 D9
Eppingen D 27 B10
Eppishausen D 71 A11
Eppstein D 21 D10
Epsom GB 15 E8
Eptachori GR 168 D5
Épuisay F 24 E4
Epureni RO 153 E11
Epworth GB 11 D10
Équeurdreville-Hainneville F 23 A8
Eraclea I 73 E6
Eraclea Mare I 67 A6
Eräjärvi FIN 127 B12
Eräjärvi FIN 129 C10
Erastvere EST 131 F13
Erateini GR 174 C5
Eratyra GR 169 D6
Erba I 69 B7
Erbach D 21 E12
Erbach D 74 F6
Erbendorf D 75 C11
Ērberģe LV 135 D10
Erbiceni RO 153 C10
Erbray F 23 E9
Erchie I 61 C9
Ercsi H 149 B11
Érd H 149 B11
Erdeborn D 79 D10
Erdek TR 173 D8
Erdelli TR 177 B10
Erdeven F 22 E5
Erdevik SRB 158 C3
Erding D 75 F10
Erdőkertes H 150 B3
Erdut HR 157 A11
Erdweg D 75 F9
Erdželija MK 164 F5
Éréac F 23 D7
Eremitu RO 152 D5
Eremiya BG 165 E6
Erenler TR 173 D10
Eresos GR 177 A6
Eretreia GR 169 F8
Eretria GR 175 C8
Erfde D 82 B6
Erftstadt D 21 C7
Erfurt D 79 E9
Ērģeme LV 131 F11
Ergersheim D 75 C7
Ergili TR 173 D9
Ērgļi LV 135 C11
Ergoldsbach D 75 E11
Ergué-Gabéric F 22 D3
Erharting D 75 F12
Eriboll GB 2 J7
Erice E 32 E2
Erice I 58 C2
Ericeira P 50 B1
Eriklice TR 173 C7
Eriksberg S 107 A9
Erikslund S 103 A10
Eriksmåla S 89 B8
Erikssund S 99 C9
Eringsboda S 89 C8
Eriswil CH 70 C5
Erjova MD 154 B4
Erkelenz D 20 B6
Erkheim D 71 A10
Erkner D 80 B5
Erla E 41 D10
Erlach CH 31 A11
Erlangen D 75 C9
Erlauf A 77 F8
Erlbach D 75 B11
Erlenbach am Main D 187 B7
Erli I 37 C8
Ermelo NL 16 D5
Ermelo P 38 F4
Ermenonville F 25 B8
Ermesinde P 44 B3
Ermidas do Sado P 50 C3
Ermioni GR 175 E7
Ermoclia MD 154 D5
Ermoupoli GR 176 E4
Ermsleben D 79 C9
Ermua E 41 B6
Erndtebrück D 21 C10
Ernée F 23 D10
Ernei RO 152 D5
Ernestinovo HR 149 F11
Ernstbrunn A 77 E10
Erp NL 16 E5
Érpatak H 151 B8
Erpel D 21 C8
Erquelinnes B 184 D1
Erquy F 22 C7
Erra P 50 A3
Errenteria E 32 D2
Errezil E 32 D1
Erribera E 41 B7
Errill IRL 9 C7
Errindlev DK 83 A11
Errsø DK 86 D5
Errogie GB 3 L8
Érsekcsanád H 150 E2
Ersekë AL 168 D4
Érsekvadkert H 147 E8
Ersfjord N 111 B13
Ersfjordbotn N 111 A16
Ersmark S 107 A11
Ersmark S 118 E5
Ersmark S 122 C4
Ersnäs S 118 C7
Erstein F 27 D8
Erstfeld CH 71 D7
Ersvik N 108 B7
Ertenvåg N 108 B7
Ertingen D 71 A8
Erto I 72 D5
Ertsjärv S 116 E8
Ertuğrul TR 173 E8
Ertvelde B 182 C3
Erula I 64 B2
Ervalla S 97 D13
Ervasti FIN 121 D9
Ervedosa do Douro P 44 B6
Ervenik HR 156 D4
Ervidel P 50 D3
Ervik N 104 E5
Ervillers F 18 D6
Ervy-le-Châtel F 25 D10
Erwitte D 17 E10
Erxleben D 79 B9
Erxleben D 83 E11
Erythres GR 175 C7
Erzhausen D 21 E11
Eržvilkas LT 134 F5
Esanatoglia I 67 F6
Esbjerg DK 86 E2
Esbo FIN 127 E12
Esbønderup DK 87 C10
Escairón E 38 C4
Escalante E 40 B5
Escalaplano I 64 D3
Escalhão P 45 C7
Escaló E 33 E8
Es Caló E 57 D8
Escalona E 46 D4
Escalona del Prado E 46 B4
Escalonilla E 46 E4
Escalos de Baixo P 44 E6
Escalos de Cima P 44 E6
Escamilla E 47 C7
Es Canar E 57 C8
Escañuela E 53 A8
Escariche E 47 D6
Escarigo P 45 D6
Escároz E 32 E3
Es Castell E 57 B13
Escatrón E 42 E3
Esch NL 183 B6
Eschau D 187 B7
Eschau F 186 E4
Eschborn D 187 A6
Esche D 17 C7
Escheburg D 83 D8
Eschede D 83 E8
Eschenbach CH 27 F9
Eschenburg-Eibelshausen D 21 C10
Eschenstruth (Helsa) D 78 D6
Eschershausen D 78 C6
Eschlkam D 76 D3
Escholzmatt CH 70 D5
Esch-sur-Alzette L 20 F5
Esch-sur-Sûre L 20 E5
Eschwege D 79 D7
Eschweiler D 20 C6
Escombreras E 56 F3
Escorca E 49 E10
Escorihuela E 42 F2
Escos F 32 D3
Escouloubre F 33 E10
Escource F 32 B3
Escout F 32 D4
Escragnolles F 36 D5
Escucha E 42 F2
Escurial E 45 F9
Escúzar E 53 B9
Esechioi RO 161 E10
Esence TR 173 D10
Esenköy TR 173 C10
Esenler TR 173 B8
Esens D 17 A9
Esenyurt TR 173 B10
Esgos E 38 D4
Esgueira P 44 C3
Esguevillas de Esgueva E 40 E3
Eskdalemuir GB 5 E10
Eskelhem S 93 E12
Eskiçine TR 181 A8
Eskilstrup DK 84 A1
Eskilstuna S 98 D7
Eskioba TR 177 C10
Eskisigirçi TR 173 D9
Eskogen S 99 C10
Eskola FIN 123 C12
Eskoriatza E 41 B6
Esku EST 131 D11
Eslarn D 75 C12
Eslava E 32 E3
Eslohe (Sauerland) D 17 F10
Eslöv S 87 D12
Es Mercadal E 57 B13
Es Migjorn Gran E 57 B13
Esnes F 19 D7
Esneux B 19 C12
Espa N 101 E14
Espadañedo E 39 D7
Espalion F 34 A4
Espaly-St-Marcel F 30 E4
Esparragalejo E 51 B7
Esparragosa E 51 B9
Esparragosa de la Serena E 51 B8
Esparreguera E 43 D7
Esparron F 35 C10
Esparza de Salazar E 32 E3
Espe DK 86 E6
Espedal N 94 E4
Espeja E 45 C7
Espeja de San Marcelino E 40 E5
Espejo E 53 A7
Espejón E 40 E5
Espel NL 16 C5
Espeland N 94 B2
Espelette F 32 D3
Espelkamp D 17 D11
Espenau D 78 D5
Espenes N 111 B14
Espera E 51 F8
Esperança P 45 F6
Espéraza F 33 E10
Espergærde DK 87 D11
Esperia I 62 E5
Espevik N 94 C3
Espezel F 33 E10
Espiel E 54 C3
Espinama E 39 B10
Espinasses F 36 C4
Espinhal P 44 D4
Espinho P 44 B3
Espinilla E 40 B3
Espinosa de Cerrato E 40 E4
Espinosa de Henares E 47 C6
Espinosa de los Monteros E 40 B4
Espinoso del Rey E 46 E3
Espira-de-l'Agly F 34 E4
Espírito Santo P 50 D4
Espite P 44 E3
Esplegares E 47 C8
Esplugues de Llobregat E 43 E8
Esplús E 42 D4
Espolla E 34 F5
Espondeilham F 34 D5
Esponellà E 43 C9
Espoo FIN 127 E12
Espoonlahti FIN 127 E12
Esporlatu I 64 C2
Esporles E 49 E10
Esposende P 38 E2
Espot E 33 E8
Esprels F 26 E5
Esquivias E 46 D5
Esrange S 116 C6
Essay F 23 C12
Esse FIN 123 C10
Essel D 82 E7
Essen B 16 F2
Essen D 17 F8
Essen (Oldenburg) D 17 C9
Essenbach D 75 E11
Essert F 27 E6
Essingen D 74 E7
Esslingen am Neckar D 27 C11
Essoyes F 25 D12
Essu EST 131 C12
Essvik S 103 B13
Estación de Baeza E 54 C5
Estadilla E 42 C4
Estagel F 34 E4
Estaimpuis B 19 C7
Estaing F 34 A4
Estaires F 18 C6
Estang F 32 C5
Estarreja P 44 C3
Estavayer-le-Lac CH 31 B10
Este I 66 B4
Este P 38 E3
Estela P 38 F2
Estella E 32 E1
Estellencs E 49 E10
Estenfeld D 187 B9
Estepa E 53 B7
Estepar E 40 D4
Estepona E 53 D6
Esteras de Medinaceli E 47 B8
Estercuel E 42 F2
Esternay F 25 C10
Esterri d'Aneu E 33 E8
Esterwegen D 17 C9
Esterzili I 64 D3
Estiavreilles F 30 E5
Estissac F 25 D10
Estivareilles F 29 C11
Estói P 50 E4
Estômbar P 50 E3
Estorf D 17 A12
Estorf D 17 C12
Estoril P 50 B1
Estoublon F 36 D4
Estrablin F 31 D6
Estrées-St-Denis F 18 F6
Estreito P 44 E5
Estrela P 51 C5
Estremera E 47 D6
Estremoz P 50 B4
Estriégala E 47 B7
Esvres F 24 F4
Esztár H 151 C8
Esztergom H 149 A11
Étables-sur-Mer F 22 C6
Étagnac F 29 D7
Étain F 19 F12
Étais-la-Sauvin F 25 E9
Étalante F 25 E12
Étalle B 19 E12
Étampes F 24 D7
Étang-sur-Arroux F 30 B5
Étaples F 15 F12
Étaules F 28 D3
Étauliers F 28 E4
Eteläinen FIN 127 C12
Etelä-Vartsala FIN 126 D5
Etelhem S 93 E13
Éternoz F 31 A9
Etes H 147 E9
Ethe B 19 E12
Etholmen N 91 A9
Etili TR 173 E6
Étival F 31 B8
Étival-Clairefontaine F 27 D6
Étivey F 25 E11
Etna N 101 E11
Etne N 94 C3
Étréchy F 24 D7
Étrépagny F 18 F4
Étretat F 23 A12
Étreux F 19 E8
Etrín Bajo E 51 B6
Etropole BG 165 D9
Etroubles I 31 D11
Ettelbruck L 20 E6
Ettenheim D 27 D8
Etten-Leur NL 16 E3
Ettington GB 13 A11
Ettlingen D 27 C9
Ettrick GB 5 E10
Ettringen D 21 D8
Etulia MD 155 B2
Étupes F 27 E6
Étuz F 26 F4
Etwall GB 11 F8
Etxalar E 32 D2
Etxarri-Aranatz E 32 E1
Etyek H 149 B11
Eu F 18 D3
Eubigheim D 74 C6
Euerdorf D 74 B7
Eugénie-les-Bains F 32 C5
Eugmo FIN 122 C9
Eulate E 32 E1
Eupen B 20 C6
Euper D 79 C12
Eura FIN 126 C7
Eurajoki FIN 126 C6
Eurasburg D 72 A3
Eurville-Bienville F 26 C3
Euskirchen D 21 C7
Eußenheim D 74 B6
Eutin D 83 B9
Eutingen im Gäu D 187 E6
Eutzsch D 79 C12
Euville F 26 C4
Eva GR 174 E4
Evanger N 100 E4
Evanton GB 3 K8
Évaux-les-Bains F 29 C10
Evciler TR 173 E6
Evciler TR 173 E7
Evdilos GR 177 D7
Evele LV 131 F11
Evenes N 111 D12
Evenesdal N 109 C10
Evenset N 108 B8
Evenskjær N 111 C12
Evenstad N 101 D14
Everdingen NL 183 B6
Everdrup DK 87 E9
Evergem B 19 B8
Everöd S 88 D6
Evertsberg S 102 D6
Evesham GB 13 A11
Évian-les-Bains F 31 C10
Evijärvi FIN 123 D10
Evisa F 37 G9
Evitskog FIN 127 E11
Evje N 90 B2
Evlalo GR 171 C7
Evolène CH 31 C12
Évora P 50 B4
Évora-Monte P 50 B4
Evosmos GR 169 C8
Évran F 23 D8
Évrecy F 23 B10
Evrencik TR 173 A8
Evrenli TR 173 A8
Evrensekiz TR 173 B7
Évreux F 24 B5
Évron F 23 D11
Evropos GR 169 C8
Evrostina GR 174 C5
Évry F 25 C7
Evzonoi GR 169 B8
Ewhurst GB 15 E8
Examilia GR 175 D6
Exaplatanos GR 169 C7
Exarchos GR 175 B6
Excideuil F 29 E8
Exebridge GB 13 C7
Exeter GB 13 D7
Exilles I 31 E10
Exloo NL 17 C7
Exmes F 23 C12
Exminster GB 13 D8
Exmouth GB 13 D8
Exochi GR 169 B10
Exochi GR 169 D7
Exo Chora GR 174 D2
Exo Vathy GR 180 C4
Extremo P 38 E3
Eydehavn N 90 B4
Eydelstedt D 17 C11
Eye GB 11 F11
Eye GB 15 C11
Eyemouth GB 5 D12
Eyeries IRL 8 E3
Eyguians F 35 B10
Eyguières F 35 C9
Eygurande-et-Gardedeuil F 29 E6
Eymet F 33 A6
Eymoutiers F 29 D9
Eynsham GB 13 B12
Eyragues F 35 C8
Eyrans F 28 E4
Eyrecourt IRL 6 F6
Eyrein F 29 E9
Eyzin-Pinet F 31 E6
Ezcaray E 40 D6
Ezerche BG 166 B6
Ezere LV 134 D4
Ežerėlis LT 137 D8
Ezerets BG 155 F3
Ezerets BG 165 F7
Ezeriș RO 159 C8
Ezerkalne LV 134 B5
Ezerkalni LV 133 E2
Ezernieki LV 133 D3
Ezine TR 171 E10
Ezkurra E 32 D2
Ézy-sur-Eure F 24 C5

F

Faaborg DK 86 E6
Fabara E 42 E4
Fabas F 33 D8
Fåberg N 100 C6
Fåberg N 101 D12
Fabero E 39 C6
Fábiánháza H 145 H5
Fabianki PL 138 E7
Fábiánsebestyén H 150 D5
Fåbodliden S 107 B13
Fåborg DK 86 D3
Fabrègues F 35 C6
Fabrezan F 34 D4
Fabriano I 67 F6
Fabrica di Roma I 62 C2
Fábricas de San Juan de Alcaraz E 55 B8
Fabrizia I 59 C9
Fabro I 62 B2
Făcăeni RO 155 D1
Faches-Thumesnil F 182 D2
Facinas E 52 D5
Fadd H 149 D11
Faedis I 73 D7
Fæfjord N 113 C13
Faenza I 66 D4
Faeto I 60 A4
Fafe P 38 F3
Fagagna I 73 D7
Făgăraș RO 152 F5
Fågelfors S 89 A9
Fågelmara S 89 C9
Fågelsjö S 102 C8
Fågelsta S 92 C6
Fågelsundet S 103 E14
Fagerås S 97 C9
Fagerdal S 106 D8
Fagerhaug N 101 A11
Fagerhult S 89 A9
Fagerhult S 91 C11
Fagerhult S 92 C4
Fagerli N 109 B11
Fagernes N 101 E10
Fagernes N 111 A17
Fagersanna S 92 C4
Fagersta S 97 C14
Fagervik FIN 127 E10
Fagervika N 108 D4
Fagerviken S 99 A9
Făget RO 151 F9
Făgețelu RO 160 D5
Fåggeby S 97 B14
Fåglavik S 91 C13
Fagnano Castello I 60 D6
Fagnières F 25 C11
Fahan IRL 4 E2
Fahrdorf D 82 A7
Fahrenkrug D 83 C8
Fahrenzhausen D 75 F10
Fahrland D 80 B4
Faicchio I 60 A2
Faid D 21 D8
Faido CH 71 E7
Failde P 39 E6
Faimes B 19 C11
Fain-lès-Montbard F 25 E11
Fains-Véel F 26 C3
Fairlie GB 4 D7
Fair Oak GB 13 D12
Faissault F 19 E10
Fajão P 44 D5
Fajarda P 50 B2
Fajsławice PL 144 A6
Fajsz H 149 D11
Fakenham GB 15 B10
Fåker S 106 F7
Fakiya BG 167 E8
Fakovići BIH 158 E4
Faksdal N 105 B10
Fakse DK 87 E10
Fakse Ladeplads DK 87 E10
Falaise F 23 C11
Falani GR 169 E7
Fålasjö S 107 E13
Falcade I 72 D4
Falcarragh IRL 6 B6
Falces E 32 F2
Fălciu RO 154 E2
Falck F 186 C2
Fălcoiu RO 160 E4
Falconara I 58 E5
Falconara Albanese I 60 E6
Falconara Marittima I 67 E7
Falcone I 59 C7
Faldsled DK 86 E6
Fale N 101 A9
Faleria I 62 C2
Falerna I 59 A9
Falerone I 62 A4
Falerum S 93 C8
Fălești MD 153 B11
Falkekeila N 114 C8
Falkenberg D 75 C11
Falkenberg D 75 F12
Falkenberg D 80 C4
Falkenberg S 87 B11
Falkenhagen D 83 D12
Falkenhain D 79 D12
Falkensee D 80 A4
Falkenstein D 75 B11
Falkenstein D 75 D11
Falkirk GB 5 D9
Falkland GB 5 C10
Falköping S 91 C14
Fałków PL 141 H2
Fall N 97 A8
Falla S 92 B7
Falleron F 28 B2
Fällfors S 118 D5
Fallingbostel D 82 E7
Fälloheden S 109 E15
Fällsvikhamnen S 103 A15
Falltorp S 97 A8
Falmenta I 68 A6
Falmouth GB 12 E4
Falset E 42 E5
Falstad N 105 D10
Fălticeni RO 153 C8
Falträsk S 107 B15
Falun S 103 E10
Famalicão P 44 D6
Fambach D 79 E7
Fameck F 20 F6
Fámjin FO 2 B3
Fana N 94 B2
Fanano I 66 D2
Fanari GR 171 C8
Fanbyn S 107 E16
Fångsjöbacken S 107 E11
Fångsjön S 107 E12
Fanjeaux F 33 D10
Fanlo E 32 E5
Fannrem N 104 E7
Fano I 67 E7
Fanore IRL 6 F4
Fanos GR 169 B7
Fântânele RO 151 E7
Fântânele RO 152 E5
Fântânele RO 153 B9
Fanthyttan S 97 C13
Fão P 38 E2
Fara Filiorum Petri I 63 C6
Fărăgău RO 152 D5
Fara in Sabina I 62 C3
Faraoani RO 153 E9
Faraonivka UA 154 E5
Fara San Martino I 63 C6
Farasdues E 41 D9
Fărău RO 152 E4
Fårberget S 107 C15
Fårbo S 93 E8
Fărcaș RO 160 D3
Fărcașa RO 151 B11
Fărcașa RO 153 C7
Fărcășești RO 159 D11
Farchant D 72 A3
Farciennes B 19 D10
Fardal N 90 A3
Fârdea RO 151 F9
Fardella I 60 C6
Fardhem S 93 E12
Fardrum IRL 7 F7
Farébersviller F 186 C2
Fareham GB 13 D12
Faremoutiers F 25 C9
Fårevejle DK 87 D8
Fårevejle Stationsby DK 87 D8
Färgelanda S 91 B11
Fargues-St-Hilaire F 32 A5
Fårholmen S 118 C8
Fårhus DK 86 F4
Färila S 103 C10
Faringdon GB 13 B11
Farini I 37 B11
Fariza de Sayago E 39 F7
Färjestaden S 89 B10
Farkadona GR 169 E7
Farlete E 41 E10
Fârliug RO 159 B8
Färlöv S 88 C6
Färna S 97 C14
Färnäs S 102 D8
Farnborough GB 15 E7
Farndon GB 10 E6
Farnese I 62 B1
Farnham GB 15 E7
Farnstädt D 79 D10
Faro P 50 E4
Fårö S 93 D14
Faro do Alentejo P 50 C4
Fårösund S 93 D14
Farr GB 3 L8
Farra d'Alpago I 72 D5
Farranfore IRL 8 D3
Farre DK 86 C5
Farre DK 86 D4
Farsala GR 169 F7
Färsån S 107 E10
Farsø DK 86 B4
Farstrup DK 86 B4
Farsund N 94 F5
Fărțănești RO 153 F11
Fărtățești RO 160 D3
Fårup DK 86 B5
Fårvang DK 86 C5
Farynava BY 133 F5
Fasano I 61 B8
Fåset N 101 B13
Fåssjodal S 103 B9
Fasterholt DK 86 C4
Fasty PL 140 D8
Fatela P 44 D6
Fatih TR 173 B10
Fátima P 44 E3
Fatjas S 116 E4
Fatmomakke S 106 A8
Fatnica BIH 157 F9
Fättjaur S 106 A8
Faucogney-et-la-Mer F 26 E6
Faugères F 34 C5
Fauglia I 66 E2
Fauguerolles F 33 B6
Faulbach D 187 B7
Fauldhouse GB 5 D9
Faulenrost D 83 C13
Faulquemont F 26 B6
Fauquembergues F 18 C5
Faura E 48 E4
Făurei RO 153 D9
Făurei RO 161 C10
Făurești RO 160 D3
Fauske N 108 B9
Fauskevåg N 111 C12
Fauville-en-Caux F 18 E2
Faux F 29 F7
Faux-la-Montagne F 29 D9
Favaios P 38 F5
Favale di Malvaro I 37 C10
Fåvang N 101 D12
Favara E 48 F4
Favara I 58 E4
Faverges F 31 D9
Faverney F 26 E5
Faverolles F 30 F3
Faversham GB 15 E10
Favignana I 58 D1
Fawley GB 13 D12
Fay-de-Bretagne F 23 F8
Fayence F 36 D5
Fayl-la-Forêt F 26 E4
Fayón E 42 E4
Fay-sur-Lignon F 30 F5
Fažana HR 67 C8
Fazeley GB 11 F8
Feakle IRL 8 C5
Fécamp F 18 E1
Feda N 94 F5
Fedamore IRL 8 C5
Fedje N 100 E1
Fedosiyivka UA 154 B4
Feeard IRL 8 C3
Feeny GB 4 F2
Fegen S 87 A12
Fégréac F 23 E7
Fegyvernek H 150 C6
Fehérgyarmat H 145 H6
Fehrbellin D 83 E13
Fehring A 148 C6
Feijó P 50 B1
Feilbingert D 21 E9
Feilitzsch D 75 B10
Feillens F 30 C6
Feissons-sur-Isère F 31 D9
Feistritz im Rosental A 73 C9
Feistritz ob Bleiburg A 73 C10
Feiteira P 50 E4
Feketić SRB 158 B4
Felanitx E 57 C11
Felchow D 84 D6
Felcsút H 149 B11
Feld am See A 73 C8
Feldbach A 148 C5
Feldballe DK 86 C7
Feldberg D 84 D4
Felde D 83 B7
Feldebrő H 147 F10
Feldioara RO 153 F7
Feldkirch A 71 C9
Feldkirchen in Kärnten A 73 C9
Feldkirchen-Westerham D 72 A4
Feldru RO 152 C5
Feleacu RO 152 D3
Felgar P 45 B7
Felgueiras P 38 F3
Felgyő H 150 D5
Feliceni RO 152 E6
Felindre GB 13 A8
Félines F 30 E4
Felino I 66 C1
Felitto I 60 C4
Félix E 55 F7
Felixdorf A 77 G10
Felixstowe GB 15 D11
Felizzano I 37 B8
Fell D 21 E7
Fellbach D 27 C11
Felletin F 29 D10
Fellingsbro S 97 D14
Felnac RO 151 E7
Felsberg D 21 B12
Felsődobsza H 145 G3
Felsőlajos H 150 C4
Felsőnyék H 149 C10
Felsőpakony H 150 C3
Felsőszentiván H 150 E3
Felsőszentmárton H 149 E9
Felsőtárkány H 145 H1
Felsőzsolca H 145 G2
Felsted DK 86 F4
Felton GB 5 E13
Feltre I 72 D4
Feltwell GB 11 G13
Femundsenden N 101 C15
Femundsundet N 101 C15
Fénay F 26 F3
Fendeille F 33 D9
Fene E 38 B3
Fenerköy TR 173 B9
Fenes N 111 C12
Fenestrelle I 31 E11
Fénétrange F 27 C7
Feneu F 23 E10
Fengersfors S 91 B11
Fenioux F 28 B5
Fenis I 31 D11
Fenit IRL 8 D3
Feniton GB 13 D8
Fensmark DK 87 E9
Fenstanton GB 15 C8
Fenwick GB 5 D13
Fényeslitke H 145 G5
Feofilova Pustyn' RUS 132 E5
Feolin Ferry GB 4 D4
Feonanagh IRL 8 D5
Fépin F 19 D10
Ferbane IRL 7 F7
Ferdinandea I 59 B9
Ferdinandovac HR 149 D8
Ferdinandshof D 84 C5
Fère-Champenoise F 25 C10
Fère-en-Tardenois F 25 B10
Férel F 23 F7
Ferentillo I 62 B3
Ferentino I 62 D4
Feres GR 171 C10
Férez E 55 C9
Feria E 51 B6
Feričanci HR 149 E9
Ferizaj KS 164 E3
Ferlach A 73 C9
Fermignano I 66 E6
Fermo I 67 F8
Fermoselle E 39 F7
Fermoy IRL 8 D6
Fernáncaballero E 46 F5
Fernán Núñez E 53 A7
Ferndown GB 13 D11
Ferness GB 3 L9
Ferney-Voltaire F 31 C9
Fernitz A 148 C5
Ferns IRL 9 C9
Feroleto Antico I 59 B9
Ferrals-les-Corbières F 34 D4
Ferrandina I 61 C6
Ferrara I 66 C4
Ferrazzano I 63 D7
Ferreira E 38 A5
Ferreira do Alentejo P 50 C3
Ferreira do Zêzere P 44 E4
Ferrel P 44 F2
Ferreras de Abajo E 39 E7
Ferreras de Arriba E 39 E7
Ferrere I 37 B7
Ferreries E 57 B13
Ferreruela de Huerva E 47 B10
Ferreruela de Tábara E 39 E7
Ferrette F 27 E7
Ferriere I 37 B11
Ferrières B 19 D12
Ferrières F 25 D8

Ferritslet DK 86 E7
Ferrol E 38 B3
Ferrybank IRL 9 C10
Ferryhill GB 5 F13
Ferschweiler D 185 E5
Fertilia I 64 B1
Fertőd H 149 A7
Fertőrákos H 149 A7
Fertőszentmiklós H 149 A7
Ferwert NL 16 B5
Feshiebridge GB 3 L9
Fessenheim F 27 E8
Festieux F 19 E8
Festvåg N 108 B8
Feteşti MD 153 A10
Feteşti RO 155 E1
Feteşti-Gară RO 155 E1
Fethard IRL 9 D7
Fethard IRL 9 D9
Fetsund N 95 C14
Fettercairn GB 5 B11
Feucht D 75 D9
Feuchtwangen D 75 D7
Feugarolles F 33 B6
Feuquières F 18 E4
Feuquières-en-Vimeu F 18 D4
Feurs F 30 D5
Fevåg N 104 D7
Fevik N 90 C4
Feytiat F 29 D8
Ffestiniog GB 10 F4
Ffostrasol GB 12 A6
Fiac F 33 C9
Fiamignano I 62 C4
Fiano I 31 E12
Fiano Romano I 62 C3
Fiavè I 69 B10
Ficarazzi I 58 C3
Ficarolo I 66 C3
Fichtelberg D 75 C10
Fichtenberg D 74 E6
Fichti GR 175 D6
Ficulle I 62 B2
Fiddown IRL 9 D8
Fide S 93 E12
Fidenza I 69 D9
Fidjeland N 94 E5
Fiè allo Sciliar I 72 C4
Fieberbrunn A 72 B6
Fieni RO 160 C6
Fier AL 168 C2
Fiera di Primiero I 72 D4
Fierbinţi-Târg RO 161 D8
Fierzë AL 163 E9
Fiesch CH 70 E6
Fiesole I 66 E3
Fiesso Umbertiano I 66 C4
Figaniéres F 36 D4
Figari F 37 J10
Figeac F 33 A10
Figeholm S 93 E9
Figgio N 94 E3
Figline Valdarno I 66 E3
Figueira da Foz P 44 D3
Figueira de Castelo Rodrigo P 45 C7
Figueira e Barros P 44 F5
Figueiredo de Alva P 44 C4
Figueiró da Granja P 44 C6
Figueiró dos Vinhos P 44 E4
Figueres E 43 C9
Figueroles E 48 D4
Figueruela de Arriba E 39 E7
Fijnaart NL 182 B4
Filadelfia I 59 B9
Filakio GR 171 A10
Fiľakovo SK 147 E9
Filatova-Gora RUS 132 F3
Filattiera I 69 E8
Fildu de Jos RO 151 D11
Filettino I 62 D4
Filey GB 11 C11
Filiano I 60 B5
Filiaşi RO 160 D3
Filiates GR 168 E3
Filiatra GR 174 E4
Filicudi Porto I 59 B6
Filipeni RO 153 D10
Filipeşti RO 153 D9
Filipeştii de Pădure RO 161 D7
Filipeştii de Târg RO 161 D7
Filipjakov HR 156 E3
Filipovtsi BG 165 D6
Filipów PL 136 E6
Filippiada GR 174 A2
Filipstad S 97 C11
Filisur CH 71 D9
Fillan N 104 D5
Fillinges F 31 C9
Fillyra GR 171 B9
Filotas GR 169 C6
Filotio GR 177 E6
Filottrano I 67 F7
Filsbäck S 91 C13
Filskov DK 86 D4
Filsum D 17 B9
Filton GB 13 B9
Filzmoos A 73 B8
Fimber GB 11 C10
Finale I 58 C5
Finale Emilia I 66 C3
Finale Ligure I 37 C8
Fiñana E 55 E7
Finavon GB 5 B11
Finby FIN 99 B14
Finby FIN 127 E14
Findern GB 11 F8
Findhorn GB 3 K9
Findikli TR 173 E7
Findikli TR 173 E8
Findochty GB 3 K11
Findon GB 15 F8
Finestrat E 56 D4
Finhan F 33 C8
Finiq AL 168 E3
Finiş RO 151 D9
Finja S 87 C13
Finkenstein A 73 C8
Finnbacka S 103 D10
Finnbodarna S 102 E7
Finnböle S 98 B8
Finnbyen N 110 D5
Finnea IRL 7 E8
Finneby S 103 B9
Finnentrop D 21 B9
Finnerödja S 92 B4
Finnes N 108 C6
Finnes N 111 B13
Finnfjordeidet N 111 B15
Finnfors S 118 E4
Finngruvan S 102 E7
Finnholt N 96 B6
Finningham GB 15 C11

Finnkroken N 111 A17
Finnøy N 111 D9
Finnsådal N 90 C2
Finnsäter S 105 D15
Finnset N 101 B8
Finnset N 104 E5
Finnset N 111 D9
Finnseter N 111 C10
Finnshögst S 103 D9
Finnskog N 102 E3
Finnsnes N 111 B14
Finntorp S 96 D7
Finnträsk S 118 D6
Finnvik N 111 A16
Finnvika N 108 D4
Finnygaud GB 3 K11
Fino Mornasco I 69 B7
Finowfurt D 84 E5
Finse N 100 E7
Finsjö S 89 A10
Finspång S 92 B7
Finsterwalde D 80 C5
Finsterwolde NL 17 B8
Finström FIN 99 B13
Finta RO 161 D7
Fintel D 82 D7
Fintice SK 145 E3
Fintona GB 7 D8
Fintown IRL 6 C6
Finuge IRL 8 D3
Finvoy GB 4 E4
Fiodh Ard IRL 9 D7
Fionnphort GB 4 C4
Fiorano Modense I 66 C2
Fiorenzuola d'Arda I 69 D8
Fiplingkroken N 108 F6
Fira GR 179 C9
Firenze I 66 E3
Firenzuola I 66 D3
Firlej PL 141 G7
Firmi F 33 A10
Firminy F 30 E5
Firmo I 60 D6
Fiscal E 32 E5
Fischach D 75 F8
Fischbach A 148 B5
Fischbach D 21 E8
Fischbachau D 72 A4
Fischbach bei Dahn D 27 B8
Fischbeck D 79 A11
Fischen im Allgäu D 71 C10
Fishguard GB 12 B5
Fiskå N 100 B3
Fiskardo GR 174 C2
Fiskarheden S 102 D5
Fiskari FIN 127 E10
Fiskebäckskil S 91 C9
Fiskebøl N 110 D8
Fiskefjord N 110 C9
Fiskö FIN 126 E4
Fiskøy N 111 C11
Fisksätra S 99 D10
Fismes F 19 F8
Fisterra E 38 C1
Fitero E 41 D8
Fitioneşti RO 153 F10
Fitjar N 94 C2
Fitou F 34 E4
Fitz-James F 18 F5
Fiuggi I 62 D4
Fiumalbo I 66 D2
Fiumefreddo Bruzio I 60 E6
Fiumefreddo di Sicilia I 59 D7
Fiumicino I 62 D2
Fiunary GB 4 B5
Fivemiletown GB 7 D8
Fivizzano I 66 D1
Fix-St-Geneys F 30 E4
Fizeşu Gherlii RO 152 C3
Fjær N 108 B8
Fjäl S 106 E7
Fjälkinge S 88 C6
Fjäll S 96 C7
Fjällåkern S 107 E14
Fjällåsen S 116 C4
Fjällbacka S 91 B9
Fjällnäs S 102 A3
Fjällsjö S 107 D10
Fjällsjönäs S 109 D12
Fjärås Kyrkby S 91 E11
Fjärdhundra S 98 C7
Fjätervålen S 102 C5
Fjell N 94 B2
Fjellbu N 111 D14
Fjelldal N 111 C12
Fjelle N 105 C10
Fjellerup DK 86 B7
Fjellnes N 108 B8
Fjellstad N 111 C15
Fjelsø DK 86 B4
Fjelsted DK 86 E6
Fjelstervang DK 86 C3
Fjelstrup DK 86 E5
Fjenneslev DK 87 E9
Fjerritslev DK 86 A4
Fjone N 90 A3
Fjordgard N 111 A14
Fjørvikan N 104 E4
Fjugesta S 92 A5
Flå N 95 B10
Flachau A 73 B7
Flachsmeer D 17 B8
Fladungen D 75 A7
Flagnac F 33 A10
Flaine F 31 C10
Flaka FIN 99 B14
Flakaberg S 116 E7
Flakaträsk S 107 C15
Flakaträsk S 109 F12
Flakk N 104 E8
Flakkebjerg DK 87 E8
Flakstad N 111 B13
Flåm N 100 E6
Flamanville F 23 A8
Flămânzi RO 153 B9
Flamborough GB 11 C11
Flamouria GR 169 C7
Flampouro GR 169 C9
Flärke S 107 D16
Flarken S 118 F5
Flästa S 103 D11
Flatabø N 94 B4
Flåten N 112 D6
Flattach A 73 C7
Flattnitz A 73 C9
Flatval N 104 D5
Flauenskjold DK 86 A6
Flavigny-sur-Moselle F 26 C5
Flavigny-sur-Ozerain F 25 E12
Flavin F 34 B4

Flawil CH 27 F11
Flayosc F 36 D4
Flechtingen D 79 B9
Flecken Zechlin D 83 D13
Fleet GB 15 E7
Fleetmark D 83 E10
Fleetwood GB 10 D5
Flein D 27 B11
Flekkefjord N 94 F5
Flémalle B 19 C11
Flen S 93 A9
Flensburg D 82 A6
Flerohopp S 89 B9
Flermoen N 102 D4
Flerohopp S 89 B9
Flero I 69 C9
Flesberg N 95 C11
Flesnes N 111 C10
Flessau D 83 E11
Flesvik N 104 E6
Fleurance F 33 C7
Fleuré F 29 C7
Fleurie F 30 C6
Fleurier CH 31 B10
Fleurus B 19 D10
Fleury F 34 D5
Fleury-les-Aubrais F 24 E6
Fleury-sur-Andelle F 18 F3
Fléville-Lixières F 19 F12
Flieden D 74 B6
Fließ A 71 C11
Flimby GB 5 F9
Flims CH 71 D8
Flines-lez-Raches F 182 E2
Flint GB 10 E5
Flintbek D 83 B8
Flirey F 26 C4
Flisa N 102 E3
Flisby S 92 D5
Fliseryd S 89 A10
Flix E 42 E5
Flixecourt F 18 D5
Flize F 19 E10
Floby S 91 C13
Floda S 91 D11
Floda S 97 A12
Flogned S 96 C7
Flogny-la-Chapelle F 25 E10
Floh D 79 E7
Floing F 19 E10
Floirac F 28 F4
Flokenes N 100 D2
Floq AL 168 C4
Flor S 103 B9
Florac F 35 B6
Florange F 20 F6
Floreffe B 19 D10
Florenville B 19 E11
Flores de Ávila E 45 C10
Floresta I 59 D6
Floresta I 59 D6
Floreşti MD 154 B2
Floreşti RO 152 D3
Floreşti RO 159 D10
Floreşti RO 161 C7
Floreşti-Stoeneşti RO 161 E7
Floriada GR 174 A3
Floridia I 59 E7
Florina GR 168 C5
Florinas I 64 B2
Florø N 100 C2
Flörsbach D 74 B5
Flörsheim am Main D 187 A5
Flörsheim-Dalsheim D 187 B5
Flosjöhyttan S 97 C13
Flossenbürg D 75 C11
Flöthe D 79 B7
Flötningen S 102 C3
Flötuträsk S 118 D5
Floure F 33 D10
Flovika N 110 D9
Fluberg N 101 E12
Flüelen CH 71 D7
Flühli CH 70 D6
Flumeri I 60 A4
Flumet F 31 D10
Fluminimaggiore I 64 E2
Flums CH 27 F11
Fluren S 103 C11
Flurkmark S 122 C4
Flussio I 64 C2
Flörø N 100 C2
Fly DK 86 C4
Flyggsjö S 107 D15
Flyinge S 87 D12
Flykälen S 106 D7
Flyn S 107 D10
Fobello I 68 B5
Foča BIH 157 E10
Foça TR 177 B8
Focant B 19 D11
Fochabers GB 3 K10
Focşani RO 153 F10
Focuri RO 153 C10
Foêcy F 24 F7
Foeni RO 159 B6
Foggia I 63 E9
Foglianise I 60 A3
Föglö FIN 99 B14
Fohnsdorf A 73 B10
Fohrde D 79 B11
Föhren D 21 E7
Foiano della Chiana I 66 F4
Foieni RO 151 B9
Foinikounta GR 178 B2
Foix F 33 E9
Fojnica BIH 157 E8
Fokstø F 149 C11
Földeák H 150 E6
Földes H 151 C7
Fole DK 86 E3
Folegandros GR 179 B8
Folgaria I 69 B11
Folgosinho P 44 C5
Folgoso de Courel E 38 C5
Folgoso de la Ribera E 39 C7
Folia GR 170 C6
Folignano I 62 B5
Foligno I 62 B3
Folkestad N 100 B4
Folkestone GB 15 E11
Folkingham GB 11 F11
Follafoss N 105 D10
Folldal N 101 B12
Follebu N 101 D12
Føllenslev DK 87 D8
Follina I 72 E5

Follingbo S 93 D12
Föllinge S 106 D7
Follonica I 65 B3
Folly Gate GB 12 D6
Fölsbyn S 96 D7
Folschviller F 26 B6
Fonaîtika GR 174 D3
Fondevila E 38 E3
Fondi I 62 E4
Fondón E 55 E7
Fône S 103 C10
Fönebo S 103 C12
Fonelas E 55 E6
Fonfría E 39 E7
Fonfría E 42 E1
Fønhus N 101 E11
Fonn N 100 C5
Fonni I 64 C3
Fonroque F 29 F6
Fonsorbes F 33 C8
Fontaine F 27 E6
Fontaine F 31 E8
Fontainebleau F 25 D8
Fontaine-Française F 26 E3
Fontaine-le-Bourg F 18 E3
Fontaine-le-Dun F 18 E2
Fontaine-lès-Dijon F 26 F3
Fontaine-lès-Luxeuil F 26 E5
Fontaine-l'Évêque B 19 D9
Fontainemore I 68 B4
Fontaines F 25 E9
Fontaines F 30 B6
Fontan F 37 C7
Fontanar E 47 C6
Fontanarejo E 46 F3
Fontane I 37 C7
Fontanelice I 66 D4
Fontanellato I 66 C1
Fontanès F 35 C7
Fontanigorda I 37 B10
Fontanosas E 54 B3
Fontecchio I 62 C5
Fonte Díaz E 38 B3
Fontellas E 41 D8
Fontenay-le-Comte F 28 C4
Fontenilles F 33 C8
Fontenoy F 25 E9
Fontenoy-le-Château F 26 E5
Fontes P 44 B4
Fontevraud-l'Abbaye F 23 F12
Fontiveros E 46 C3
Font-Romeu-Odeillo-Via F 33 E10
Fontstown IRL 7 F9
Fontvieille F 35 C8
Fonyód H 149 C8
Fonz E 42 C4
Fonzaso I 72 D4
Foppolo I 69 A8
Forano I 62 C3
Foraşti RO 153 C8
Forbach D 27 C9
Forbach F 27 B6
Förby FIN 126 E8
Forcall E 42 F3
Forcalquier F 35 C10
Forcarei E 38 C3
Force I 62 B4
Forchheim D 75 C9
Forchtenberg D 187 C8
Forchtenstein A 149 A6
Ford GB 4 C6
Ford GB 5 D12
Ford IRL 9 C10
Førde N 94 D2
Førde N 100 D3
Fordersted D 79 C10
Fordham GB 15 C9
Fordingbridge GB 13 D11
Fordon PL 138 D6
Fordoun GB 5 B12
Fore N 110 C7
Foreneset N 94 D2
Forenza I 60 B5
Føresvik N 94 D2
Forfar GB 5 B11
Forges-les-Eaux F 18 E4
Forgie GB 3 K10
Forino I 60 B3
Forio I 62 F5
Föritz D 75 B9
Forjães P 38 E2
Forkhill GB 7 D10
Førland N 94 F6
Forlev DK 87 E8
Forlì I 66 D5
Forlimpopoli I 66 D5
Formazza I 71 A6
Formby GB 10 D5
Formello I 62 C2
Formerie F 18 E4
Formia I 62 E5
Formiche Alto I 48 D3
Formicola I 60 A2
Formigliana I 68 C5
Formignana I 66 C4
Formiguères F 33 E10
Formofoss N 105 C12
Fornåsa S 92 C6
Fornelli I 64 A1
Fornells I 57 A13
Fornells de la Selva E 43 D9
Fornes N 111 C10
Fornes N 111 C13
Forni Avoltri I 73 C6
Forni di Sopra I 72 D6
Forni di Sotto I 73 D6
Forno Alpi Graie I 31 E11
Forno di Zoldo I 72 D5
Fornos P 45 B7
Fornos de Algodres P 44 C5
Fornovo di Taro I 66 C1
Foros de Vale Figueira P 50 B3
Foros do Arrão P 44 F4
Forotic RO 159 C8
Forøy N 108 C6
Forra N 111 D13
Forråskult H 150 F4
Forres GB 3 K9
Forró H 145 G3
Fors S 98 B6
Fors S 107 E11
Fors S 107 E15
Forså N 111 C13
Forså N 111 D12
Forsand N 94 E4
Forsåsen S 106 D7
Forsbäck S 109 E9
Forsbacka I 103 D12
Forsbacken S 109 F11
Forsbakken N 111 C14

Forsby FIN 122 C9
Forsby FIN 127 E14
Forserum S 92 D4
Forshaga S 97 C9
Forshed S 118 B8
Forsheda S 87 A13
Forsholm S 107 B16
Forsinard GB 3 J9
Forsland N 108 D4
Førslev DK 87 E10
Förslöv S 87 C11
Forsmark S 99 B10
Forsmark S 109 F10
Forsmo S 107 E12
Forsnäs S 109 D16
Forsnäs S 109 D16
Forsnäs S 118 B5
Forsnes N 104 D4
Forsøl N 113 B12
Forssa FIN 127 D10
Forsse S 107 E11
Forssjö S 93 B8
Forst D 27 B10
Forst D 81 C7
Forstinning D 75 F10
Forsträskhed S 118 B8
Forsvik S 92 B4
Fortanete E 42 F3
Forte GB 3 K12
Fortezza I 72 C4
Forth GB 5 D9
Fortios P 44 F6
Fort-Mahon-Plage F 18 D4
Fortrose GB 3 K8
Fortuna E 56 E2
Fortuneswell GB 13 D10
Fort William GB 4 B6
Forvik N 108 E3
Fos F 33 E7
Fosdinovo I 69 E9
Foskros S 102 B4
Foskvallen S 102 C4
Fosnavåg N 100 B3
Fosnesvågen N 105 B10
Fossacesia I 63 C6
Fossalta di Portogruaro I 73 E6
Fossano I 37 B7
Fossato di Vico I 67 F6
Fossby N 91 A10
Fosse N 94 B4
Fosser N 95 C14
Fosses-la-Ville B 19 D10
Fossheim N 112 D5
Fossiat F 31 C7
Fossing N 90 B5
Fossmork N 94 E4
Fossombrone I 67 E6
Fos-sur-Mer F 35 D8
Fot H 150 B3
Foteina GR 169 D7
Fotherby GB 11 E11
Fotinovo BG 165 F9
Fotolivos GR 170 B6
Foucarmont F 18 E4
Fouesnant F 22 E3
Foug F 26 C4
Fougères F 23 D9
Fougerolles F 26 E5
Fougerolles-du-Plessis F 23 D10
Fouilloy F 18 E6
Foulain F 26 D3
Foulayronnes F 33 B7
Fountain Cross IRL 8 C4
Fouras F 28 D3
Fourchambault F 30 A3
Four Elms GB 15 E9
Fourfouras GR 178 E8
Fourmies F 19 D9
Fourna GR 174 A4
Fournels F 30 F3
Fournes GB 178 E6
Fournoi GR 177 D7
Fourques F 34 E4
Fourques F 35 C8
Fours F 30 B4
Foustani GR 169 B7
Fownhope GB 13 A9
Foxdale GBM 10 C2
Foxford IRL 6 E4
Foyers GB 2 L8
Foygh IRL 7 E7
Foynes IRL 8 C4
Foz E 38 A5
Foz P 44 F4
Foz do Arelho P 44 F2
Foz Giraldo P 44 E5
Frabosa Soprana I 37 C7
Fraccisco Beira E 43 D9
Fraga E 42 E4
Fragagnano I 61 C8
Fraham A 76 F6
Frailes E 53 A9
Fraire B 19 D10
Fraize F 27 D7
Framdrés B 19 B8
Framlev DK 86 C6
Framlingham GB 15 C11
Framlingsham S 98 A7
Frammersbach D 187 A7
Frammestad S 91 C12
Framsik N 100 D5
Frampton GB 11 F11
Francavilla al Mare I 63 C6
Francavilla di Sicilia I 59 D7
Francavilla Fontana I 61 B9
Francavilla in Sinni I 60 C6
Francescas F 33 B6
Frâncești RO 160 C4
Franco P 38 F5
Francofonte I 59 E6
Francorchamps B 20 D5
Francoulès F 33 A8
Francova Lhota CZ 146 C6
Frändefors S 91 C11
Frangy F 31 C8
Frankenau D 21 B11
Frankenberg D 80 E4
Frankenberg (Eder) D 21 B11
Frankenburg am Hausruck A 76 F4
Frankenfels A 77 G3
Frankenheim D 75 A7
Frankenmarkt A 76 G4
Frankenthal (Pfalz) D 21 E10
Frankfurt am Main D 21 D11
Frankfurt an der Oder D 81 B7
Frankowo PL 136 E2

Frankrike S 105 D15
Frånö S 103 A14
Franois F 26 F4
Fränsta S 103 A11
Františkovy Lázně CZ 75 B11
Franzburg D 83 B13
Frascati I 62 D3
Frascineto I 60 D6
Fraserburgh GB 3 K12
Frasin MD 153 A11
Frasin RO 153 B7
Frasne F 31 B9
Frasnes-lez-Buissenal B 19 C8
Frasnes-lez-Gosselies B 19 C9
Frassinoro I 66 D2
Frasso Telesino I 60 A3
Frata RO 152 D4
Frătăuţii Noi RO 153 B7
Frătăuţii Vechi RO 153 B7
Fratel P 44 E5
Frăteşti RO 161 F7
Fratta Polesine I 66 B4
Fratta Todina I 62 B2
Fraubrunnen CH 31 A12
Frauenau D 76 E4
Frauenfeld CH 27 E10
Frauenkirchen A 77 G11
Frauental an der Laßnitz A 148 C4
Frauenwald D 79 E8
Fraunberg D 75 F10
Frayssinet-le-Gélat F 33 A8
Frechen D 21 C7
Frechilla E 39 D10
Freckleton GB 10 D6
Fredensborg DK 87 D11
Fredericia DK 86 E5
Frederiks DK 86 C4
Frederiksberg DK 87 E9
Frederiksberg DK 87 D11
Frederikshavn DK 90 E7
Frederikssund DK 87 D10
Frederiksværk DK 87 D10
Fredersdorf D 80 A5
Fredrika S 107 C14
Fredriksberg S 97 C13
Fredriksdal S 92 D5
Fredrikstad N 91 A8
Freemount IRL 8 D5
Fregenal de la Sierra E 51 C6
Fregene I 62 D2
Freginals E 42 F5
Fréhel F 23 C7
Freiberg D 80 E4
Freiburg (Elbe) D 17 A12
Freiburg im Breisgau D 27 D8
Freienstein D 71 C10
Freienwill D 82 A6
Freihung D 75 C10
Freila E 55 D7
Freilassing D 73 A6
Freinsheim D 187 B5
Freisen D 21 E8
Freising D 75 F10
Freißnitz A 77 F10
Freistadt A 77 E7
Freistatt D 17 C11
Freistroff F 20 F6
Freital D 80 E5
Freixedas P 45 C6
Freixianda F 44 E4
Freixiosa P 44 C5
Freixo P 38 E3
Freixo de Espada à Cinta P 45 B7
Fréjairolles F 33 C10
Frejlev DK 86 B5
Fréjus F 36 E5
Frekhaug N 94 B2
Frellstedt D 79 B8
Freluga S 103 D11
Fremdingen D 75 E7
Fremington GB 12 C6
Frencq F 15 F12
Frenchpark IRL 6 E6
Frensdorf D 75 C8
Frenštát pod Radhoštěm CZ 146 B6
Freren D 17 D9
Fresach A 73 C8
Fresagrandinaria I 63 D7
Freshford IRL 9 C8
Freshwater GB 13 D11
Fresnay-sur-Sarthe F 23 D12
Fresneda de la Sierra E 47 D8
Fresnedoso de Ibor E 45 E9
Fresnes-en-Woëvre F 26 B4
Fresnes-sur-Apance F 26 E4
Fresne-St-Mamès F 26 E4
Fresno Alhándiga E 45 C9
Fresno de la Ribera E 39 E8
Fresno de Sayago E 39 F8
Fresno el Viejo E 45 B10
Fresnoy-Folny F 18 E3
Fresnoy-le-Grand F 19 E7
Fresse-sur-Moselle F 27 E6
Fressingfield GB 15 C11
Fresvik N 100 D5
Fretigney-et-Velloreille F 26 F4
Freudenberg D 21 C9
Freudenberg D 187 B7
Freudenburg D 186 B2
Freudenstadt D 27 D9
Frévent F 18 D5
Freyburg (Unstrut) D 79 D10
Freyenstein D 83 D12
Freyming-Merlebach F 27 B6
Freyung D 76 E5
Friarfjorden N 113 C18
Frías E 40 C5
Fribourg CH 31 B11
Frick CH 27 F8
Fridafors S 88 C7
Fridaythorpe GB 11 C10
Fridingen an der Donau D 27 D10
Fridlevstad S 89 C9
Fridolfing D 76 G3
Frieda (Meinhard) D 79 D7
Friedberg A 148 B6
Friedberg (Hessen) D 21 D11
Friedberg D 71 B9
Friedeburg (Saale) D 79 C10

Friedenfels D 75 C11
Friedersdorf D 79 C11
Friedersdorf D 80 B5
Friedewald D 78 E6
Friedewald D 185 C8
Friedland D 78 E6
Friedland D 80 B6
Friedland D 84 C5
Friedrichroda D 79 E8
Friedrichsbrunn D 79 C9
Friedrichsdorf D 187 A6
Friedrichshafen D 71 B9
Friedrichsruhe D 83 C11
Friedrichstadt D 82 B6
Friedrichswalde D 84 D5
Frielendorf D 21 C12
Friemar D 79 E8
Friesach A 73 C9
Friesack D 83 E13
Friesenhagen D 185 C8
Friesenheim D 27 D8
Friesenried D 71 B11
Friesoythe D 17 B9
Frifelt DK 86 E3
Frigento I 60 A4
Friggesund S 103 C12
Frigiliana E 53 C9
Frihetsli N 111 C18
Friitala FIN 126 C6
Frikes GR 174 C2
Frikstad N 90 B2
Frillesås S 91 E11
Frinnaryd S 92 D5
Frinton-on-Sea GB 15 D11
Friockheim GB 5 B11
Friol E 38 B4
Frisange L 20 E6
Fristad S 91 D13
Fritsla S 91 D12
Fritzens A 72 B4
Fritzlar D 21 B12
Friville-Escarbotin F 18 D4
Frizington GB 10 B5
FroŠba FO 2 B3
Frödinge S 92 D8
Frodsham GB 10 E6
Frœschwiller F 186 D4
Froges F 31 E8
Frogmore GB 15 E7
Frohburg D 79 D12
Frohnleiten A 148 B4
Froideconche F 26 E5
Froissy F 18 E5
Fröjel S 93 E12
Froland N 90 B4
Frolosh BG 165 E6
Frombork PL 139 B8
Frome GB 13 C10
Fromelennes F 184 D2
Fromentine F 28 B1
Frómista E 40 D3
Fröndenberg D 17 F9
Fronhausen D 21 C11
Fronsac F 28 F5
Fronsac F 33 E7
Fronteira P 44 F5
Frontenard F 31 B7
Frontenay-Rohan-Rohan F 28 C4
Frontenhausen D 75 E12
Frontignan F 35 D6
Fronton F 33 C8
Frösakull S 87 B11
Frose D 79 C9
Fröseke S 89 B9
Frosinone I 62 D4
Frøskeland N 110 C9
Frøslev DK 86 D3
Fröso S 106 E7
Frosolone I 63 D6
Frosta N 105 D9
Frostadheia N 104 E4
Frøstrup DK 86 A3
Frouard F 26 C5
Frövi S 97 C13
Frufällan S 91 D12
Fruges F 18 C5
Frumoasa RO 153 E7
Frumoasa RO 161 F6
Frumosu RO 153 B7
Frumuşani RO 161 E8
Frumuşica RO 153 B9
Frumuşiţa RO 155 B2
Frunzivka UA 154 C5
Frutigen CH 70 D5
Fry GB 187 F5
Frýdek-Místek CZ 146 B6
Frýdlant CZ 81 E8
Frýdlant nad Ostravicí CZ 146 B6
Frygnowo PL 139 C9
Fryksås S 102 D8
Frymburk D 76 E6
Fryšták CZ 146 C5
Frysztak PL 144 D4
Fubine I 37 B8
Fucecchio I 66 E2
Fuchstal D 71 B11
Fuencaliente E 54 C4
Fuendejalón E 41 E9
Fuengirola E 53 C7
Fuenlabrada E 46 D5
Fuenmayor E 41 D6
Fuensalida E 46 D4
Fuensanta E 55 E8
Fuensanta E 55 D9
Fuensanta de Martos E 53 A9
Fuente-Álamo E 55 B10
Fuente-Álamo E 56 F2
Fuentealbilla E 47 F9
Fuentecambrón E 40 E5
Fuentecén E 40 E4
Fuente de Cantos E 51 C7
Fuente del Arco E 51 C8
Fuente del Maestre E 51 B7
Fuente de Pedro Naharro E 47 E6
Fuente de Piedra E 53 B7
Fuente el Fresno E 46 F5
Fuente el Saz de Jarama E 46 C6
Fuente el Sol E 46 B3
Fuenteguinaldo E 45 D7
Fuentelapeña E 39 F9
Fuentelcésped E 40 E4
Fuentelespino de Haro E 47 E7
Fuentelespino de Moya E 47 E10
Fuentelmonge E 41 F7
Fuentenovilla E 47 D6
Fuente Obejuna E 51 C9
Fuente Palmera E 53 A6
Fuentepelayo E 46 B4
Fuentepinilla E 40 E6

Fuenterodos E 41 F10
Fuenterrebollo E 40 F4
Fuenterroble de Salvatierra E 45 C9
Fuentesaúco E 45 B10
Fuentesaúco de Fuentidueña E 40 F3
Fuentes-Claras E 47 C10
Fuentes de Andalucía E 51 E9
Fuentes de Ebro E 41 E10
Fuentes de Jiloca E 47 C9
Fuentes de León E 51 C6
Fuentes de Nava E 39 D10
Fuentes de Oñoro E 45 C7
Fuentes de Ropel E 39 E8
Fuentespalda E 42 F4
Fuente-Tójar E 53 A8
Fuente Vaqueros E 53 B9
Fuentidueña E 40 F4
Fuerte del Rey E 53 A9
Fuertescusa E 47 D8
Fügen A 72 B4
Fuglafjørður FO 2 A3
Fugleberg N 111 C12
Fuglebjerg DK 87 E9
Fuglstad N 105 A13
Fuhrberg (Burgwedel) D 78 A6
Fulda D 74 A6
Fulford GB 11 D9
Fulga RO 161 D8
Fulham GB 15 E8
Fullbro S 93 A11
Fulnek CZ 146 B5
Fülöp H 151 B9
Fülöpháza H 150 D3
Fülöpszállás H 150 D3
Fulunäs S 102 D5
Fumay F 19 E10
Fumel F 33 B7
Fumone I 62 D4
Funäsdalen S 102 A4
Fundada P 44 E4
Fundão P 44 D5
Fundata RO 160 C6
Fundeni RO 161 B11
Fundeni RO 161 E8
Funder Kirkeby DK 86 C4
Fundulea RO 161 E9
Fundu Moldovei RO 152 B6
Funes I 32 F2
Funes I 72 C4
Funzie GB 3 D15
Furadouro P 44 C3
Furceni MD 154 C3
Furci I 63 C7
Furci Siculo I 59 D7
Furculești RO 160 F6
Furiani F 37 F10
Furnace GB 4 C6
Furnari I 59 C7
Furraleigh IRL 9 D8
Fürstenau D 17 C9
Fürstenberg D 21 A12
Fürstenberg D 84 D4
Fürstenberg (Lichtenfels) D 21 B11
Fürstenfeld A 148 B6
Fürstenfeldbruck D 75 F9
Fürstenwalde D 80 B6
Fürstenwerder D 84 D5
Fürstenzell D 76 E4
Furta H 151 C7
Furtan S 97 C8
Furtei I 64 D3
Furth D 21 E11
Fürth D 75 D8
Furth D 75 E11
Furth bei Göttweig A 77 F9
Furth im Wald D 76 D3
Furtwangen im Schwarzwald D 27 D9
Furuberg S 103 B12
Furuby S 89 B8
Furudal N 111 D9
Furudal S 103 D9
Furudals bruk S 103 D9
Furuflaten N 111 B19
Furuögrund S 118 E6
Furusjö S 91 D14
Furusund S 99 C11
Furutangvikja N 105 B14
Furuvik S 103 E13
Fusa N 94 B3
Fuscaldo I 60 E6
Fushë-Arrëz AL 163 E9
Fushë-Bardhe AL 168 D3
Fushë Kosovë KS 164 D3
Fushë-Krujë AL 168 B2
Fushë-Kuqe AL 168 A2
Fusignano I 66 D4
Fußach A 71 C9
Füssen D 71 B11
Fussy F 25 F7
Fustiñana E 41 D9
Futeau F 26 B3
Futog SRB 158 C4
Futrikelva N 111 A17
Füzesabony H 150 B5
Füzesgyarmat H 151 C7
Fužine HR 67 B10
Fyfield GB 15 D9
Fylaki GR 169 F8
Fyli GR 175 C8
Fyllinge S 87 B11
Fyllo GR 169 F7
Fynshav DK 86 F5
Fyrås S 106 D8
Fyrde N 100 B4
Fyresdal N 90 A3
Fyteies GR 174 A3
Fyvie GB 3 L12

Gać PL 144 C5
Gacé F 23 C12
Gacko BIH 157 F10
Gåda S 103 B10
Gadbjerg DK 86 D4
Gäddede S 105 B16
Gäddträsk S 107 C15
Gadmen CH 70 D6
Gadoni I 64 D3
Gádor E 55 F8
Gádoros H 150 D6
Gadstrup DK 87 D10
Gadžin Han SRB 164 C5
Gæirara P 44 F2
Gæsti RO 160 D6
Gæta I 62 E5
Gafanha da Boa Hora P 44 C3
Gafanha da Nazaré P 44 C3
Gafanha do Carmo P 44 C3
Gafanhoeira P 50 B3
Gáfete P 44 F5
Gafsele S 107 C12
Gaganitsa BG 165 C7
Găgești RO 153 E9
Gaggenau D 27 C9
Gaggi I 59 D7
Gaggio Montano I 66 D2
Gaglianico I 68 B5
Gagliano Castelferrato I 59 D6
Gagliano del Capo I 61 D10
Gagnef S 103 E9
Gagnières F 35 B7
Gagsmark S 118 D6
Găiceana RO 153 E10
Gaigalava LV 133 C2
Gaildorf D 74 E6
Gaillac F 33 C9
Gaillac-d'Aveyron F 34 B4
Gaillard F 31 C9
Gaillimh IRL 6 F4
Gaillon F 24 B5
Gaimersheim D 75 E9
Gainsborough GB 11 E10
Gaiole in Chianti I 66 F3
Gaios GR 174 A1
Gairlоch GB 2 K5
Gairo I 64 D4
Gais CH 71 C8
Gais I 72 C4
Găiseni RO 161 D7
Gaishorn A 73 A10
Gaismas LV 135 C8
Gaj SRB 159 D7
Gajanejos E 47 C7
Gajary SK 77 F11
Gakovo SRB 150 F3
Galåbodarna S 102 A6
Galambok H 149 C8
Galan F 33 D6
Gălănești RO 153 B7
Gálaniitu N 112 F10
Galanta SK 146 E5
Galapagar E 46 C5
Galaroza E 51 D6
Galåsen S 102 E4
Galashiels GB 5 D11
Galasjö S 107 E14
Galata BG 167 C9
Galatades GR 169 C7
Galatas GR 175 D7
Galatas GR 175 E7
Gălăteni RO 160 E6
Galați RO 155 C2
Galați Bistriței RO 152 D4
Galati Mamertino I 59 C6
Galatin BG 165 C8
Galatina I 61 C10
Galatini GR 169 D6
Galatista SRB 159 D9
Galatone I 61 C10
Gălăuțaș RO 152 D6
Galaxidi GR 174 C5
Galbally IRL 8 D6
Galbarra E 32 E1
Galbenu RO 161 C10
Gålberget S 107 D14
Gålbinași RO 161 C9
Galda de Jos RO 152 E3
Gâldău RO 161 E11
Galeata I 66 E4
Galende E 39 D6
Galēni LV 135 D13
Galera E 55 D8
Galera E 61 C10
Galéria F 37 G9
Gălești RO 152 E5
Galewice PL 142 D5
Galgagyörk H 150 B4
Galgahévíz H 150 B4
Gălgău RO 152 C3
Galgon F 28 F5
Gal'gunjar'ga N 113 F16
Galicea RO 160 D4
Galicea Mare RO 160 E2
Galiche BG 165 B8
Galinduste E 45 C9
Galiny PL 136 E2
Galissas GR 176 E4
Galisteo E 45 E8
Gallarate I 68 B6
Gallardon F 24 C6
Gallargues-le-Montueux F 35 C7
Galleberg N 95 C12
Gallegos de Argañan E 45 C7
Gallegos de Solmirón E 45 C10
Galleno I 66 E1
Gälleråsen S 97 D11
Gallese I 62 C2
Gallian-en-Médoc F 28 E4
Galliate I 66 D1
Gallicano I 66 D1
Gallicano nel Lazio I 62 D3
Gallin D 83 C9
Gallin D 83 C10
Gallio I 72 E4
Gallipoli I 61 C9
Gällivare S 116 D5
Gallizien A 73 C10
Gällö S 103 A9
Gallspach A 76 F5
Gallur E 41 E9
Galovo BG 160 F2
Galros IRL 7 F7
Gålsjö bruk S 107 E13
Galston GB 5 D8
Galteli I 64 C4
Galten DK 86 C5
Galterud N 96 B6

Gåltjärn S 103 A13
Gåltjärn S 103 A14
Galtström S 103 B13
Galtür A 71 D10
Galve E 42 F2
Galve de Sorbe E 47 B6
Galveias P 44 F5
Galven S 103 D11
Gálvez E 46 E4
Galway IRL 6 F4
Gama E 40 B5
Gamaches F 18 E4
Gamarde-les-Bains F 32 C4
Gamás H 149 C9
Gambara I 66 B1
Gambarie I 59 C8
Gambassi Terme I 66 E2
Gambatesa I 63 D7
Gambettola I 66 D5
Gambolò I 69 C6
Gambsheim F 27 C8
Gaming A 77 G8
Gamleby S 93 E9
Gamlingay GB 15 C8
Gamlitz A 148 C5
Gammalkroppa S 97 C11
Gammelbønning S 103 E11
Gammelgården S 119 C10
Gammel Rye DK 86 C5
Gammelsdorf D 75 E10
Gammelstaden S 118 C8
Gammelstilla S 98 B7
Gammertingen D 27 D11
Gams CH 71 C8
Gamvik N 112 C9
Gamvik N 113 A21
Gamvik N 113 B11
Gan F 32 D5
Ganagobie F 35 B10
Gand B 19 B8
Gand B 182 C3
Gandarela P 38 F3
Gandellino I 69 A8
Ganderkesee D 17 B12
Gandesa E 42 E4
Gandesbergen D 17 C12
Gandía E 56 D4
Gandino I 69 B8
Gandra P 38 D2
Gandrup DK 86 A6
Gandvik N 114 C6
Gânești RO 160 E4
Găneasa RO 161 D8
Gănești RO 152 E4
Ganfei P 38 D2
Ganges F 35 C6
Gånghester S 91 D13
Gangi I 58 D5
Gângiova RO 160 F3
Gangkofen D 75 F12
Ganløse DK 87 D10
Gannat F 30 C3
Gänserndorf A 77 F11
Ganshoren B 19 C9
Gânsvik S 103 A15
Ganzlin D 83 D12
Gaoth Dobhair IRL 6 B6
Gap F 36 B4
Gaperhult S 91 B13
Gara H 150 E3
Garaballa E 47 E10
Garagarza E 32 D1
Garaguso I 60 B6
Gara Khitrino BG 167 C7
Gara Oreshets BG 159 F10
Gârbăŭ RO 151 D10
Garbayuela E 46 F2
Garberg N 105 E10
Gârbou RO 151 C10
Gârbova RO 152 F3
Gârbovi RO 161 D9
Garbów PL 141 H6
Garbsen D 78 B6
Garching an der Alz D 75 F12
Garching bei München D 75 F10
Garchizy F 30 A3
Garcia E 42 E5
Garciaz E 45 F9
Garciems LV 135 B8
Garcihernández E 45 C10
Garcillán E 46 C4
Gârcin HR 157 B9
Gârcina RO 153 D8
Garcinarro E 47 D7
Gârcov RO 160 F5
Garda I 69 B10
Gârda de Sus RO 151 E10
Gardanne F 35 D9
Gårdås S 102 E6
Gårdby S 89 B11
Garde S 93 E13
Gärde S 105 D15
Gardeja PL 138 C6
Gardelegen D 79 A9
Gardenstown GB 3 K12
Garderen NL 183 A7
Garderhouse GB 3 E14
Gardermoen N 95 B14
Gardiki GR 174 B4
Garding D 82 B5
Gârdnäs S 106 D8
Gardone Riviera I 69 B10
Gardone Val Trompia I 69 B9
Gardonne F 29 F6
Gárdony H 149 B11
Gardouch F 33 D9
Gârdsjö S 92 B4
Gardsjöbäcken S 109 E12
Gårdsjönäs S 109 F11
Gârdskär S 103 E14
Gärds Köpinge S 88 D6
Gårdstånga S 87 D12
Gâre N 102 A1
Garein F 32 B4
Gârelehöjden S 107 D11
Garelochhead GB 4 C7
Garéoult F 36 E4
Gareșnica HR 149 E7
Garessio I 37 C8
Garforth GB 11 D9
Gargaliani GR 174 E4
Gargáligas E 45 F9
Gargallo E 42 F2
Garganta la Olla E 45 D9
Gargazzone I 72 C3
Gargilesse-Dampierre F 29 B9
Gargnano I 69 B10
Gargnäs S 107 A13
Gargogeče N 113 C20
Gargždai LT 134 E2

Garijp NL 16 B5
Garkalne LV 135 B8
Gârla Mare RO 159 E10
Garlasco I 69 C6
Gârleni RO 153 D9
Garlenz A 73 A10
Garliava LT 137 D8
Garlieston GB 5 F8
Garlin F 32 C5
Garlitos E 54 B2
Garlstorf D 83 D8
Garmisch-Partenkirchen D 72 B3
Garnes N 100 B3
Gârnic RO 159 D8
Garoafa RO 153 F10
Garons F 35 C7
Garoza LV 135 C7
Garpenberg S 98 B6
Garphyttan S 97 D12
Garrafe de Torío E 39 C8
Garralda E 32 E3
Garrane IRL 8 E4
Garray E 41 E7
Garrel D 17 C10
Garrison GB 6 D6
Garristown IRL 7 E10
Garrovillas E 45 E7
Garrucha E 55 E9
Garrynahine GB 2 J3
Garryvoe IRL 8 E6
Gars am Inn D 75 F11
Gars am Kamp A 77 E9
Garsås S 102 E8
Garsdale Head GB 11 C7
Gârsene LV 135 D11
Gârslev DK 86 D5
Gârsnäs S 88 D6
Garstang GB 10 D6
Garstedt D 83 D8
Garten N 104 D7
Garth GB 13 A7
Garthmyl GB 10 F5
Gartland N 105 B12
Gartow D 83 D10
Gärtringen D 27 C10
Gartz D 84 D6
Garvagh GB 4 F3
Garvagh IRL 7 E7
Garvaghy GB 7 D8
Garvald GB 5 D11
Garvamore GB 5 A8
Garvão P 50 D3
Garvard GB 4 C4
Garvary GB 7 D7
Garve GB 2 K7
Garwolin PL 141 G5
Garz D 84 B4
Gaşawa PL 138 E4
Gâsbakken N 104 E7
Gaschurn A 71 D10
Gâsholma S 103 D12
Gasjö S 97 B14
Gaskeluokt S 107 A11
Gäsnes N 113 A13
Gasny F 24 B6
Gâsocin PL 139 E10
Gasperina I 59 B10
Gaspoltshofen A 76 F5
Gasselte NL 17 C7
Gasselternijveen NL 17 C7
Gassino Torinese I 68 C4
Gassjö S 103 B9
Gassum DK 86 B6
Gastellovo RUS 136 C4
Gastes F 32 B3
Gastouni GR 174 D3
Gastouri GR 168 E2
Gata E 45 D7
Gata de Gorgos E 56 D5
Gătaia RO 159 C7
Gatchina RUS 132 B7
Gátér H 150 D4
Gateshead GB 5 F13
Gátova E 48 E3
Gattendorf A 77 F11
Gatteo a Mare I 66 D5
Gattières F 37 D6
Gattinara I 68 B5
Gau-Algesheim D 185 E8
Gauchy F 19 E7
Gaucín E 53 C6
Gauja LV 135 B9
Găujani RO 161 F7
Gaujiena LV 131 F12
Gaukönigshofen D 74 C6
Gaulstad N 105 D12
Gau-Odernheim D 185 E9
Gaupne N 100 D6
Gauré LT 134 F4
Gausvik N 111 C11
Gautestad N 90 B2
Gauting D 75 F9
Gauto S 109 D12
Gavà E 43 E8
Gavalou GR 174 B4
Gâvánoasa MD 155 B2
Gavardo I 69 B10
Gavarnie F 32 E5
Gávavencsellő H 145 G4
Gavere B 19 C8
Gavi I 37 B9
Gavião P 44 F5
Gavieze LV 134 C2
Gavik S 103 A15
Gavirate I 68 B6
Gavoi I 64 C3
Gavojdia RO 159 B9
Gavorrano I 65 B3
Gavray F 23 C9
Gavrio GR 176 D4
Gavrolimni GR 174 C4
Gâvsta S 99 C9
Gaweinstal A 77 F11
Gawliki Wielkie PL 136 E5
Gaworzyce PL 81 C9
Gãxsjö S 106 D8
Gaytaninovo BG 169 B10
Gayton GB 11 F13
Gaziemir TR 177 C10
Gazikoy TR 173 C7
Gazioğlu TR 173 B8
Gaziosmanpaşa TR 173 B10
Gazolaz E 32 E2
Gazoldo degli Ippoliti I 66 B2
Gazoros GR 169 C9
Gazzo Veronese I 66 B3

Gazzuolo I 66 B2
Gbelce SK 147 F7
Gbely SK 77 E12
Gdańsk PL 138 B6
Gdinj HR 157 F6
Gdov RUS 132 D2
Gdów PL 144 D1
Gdynia PL 138 A6
Geaca RO 152 D4
Gea de Albarracín E 47 D10
Geaidnovuohppi N 113 E12
Geamăna MD 154 D4
Geashill IRL 7 F8
Gebesee D 79 D8
Gebhardshain D 21 C9
Gebze TR 173 B9
Gechingen D 187 D6
Geçkinli TR 167 F7
Geddington GB 15 C7
Gédelak H 149 C11
Gedern D 21 D12
Gedinne B 19 E10
Gedney Drove End GB 11 F12
Gèdre F 32 E6
Gedser DK 83 A11
Gedsted DK 86 B4
Gedved DK 86 D5
Geel B 19 B10
Geertruidenberg NL 16 E3
Geeste D 17 C8
Geesteren NL 183 A9
Geesthacht D 83 D8
Geetbets B 19 C11
Geffen NL 183 B6
Gefrees D 75 B10
Gefyra GR 169 C8
Gefyria GR 169 F7
Gegai AL 168 C2
Gegužinė LT 137 D9
Gehrde D 17 C10
Gehren D 78 B6
Gehren D 79 E9
Geijersholm S 97 B10
Geilenkirchen D 20 C6
Geilo N 95 B8
Geiranger N 100 B6
Geisa D 78 E6
Geiselbach D 187 A7
Geiselhöring D 75 E11
Geiselwind D 75 C7
Geisenfeld D 75 E10
Geisenhausen D 75 F11
Geisenheim D 21 E9
Geising D 80 E5
Geisingen D 27 E10
Geislingen D 187 E6
Geislingen an der Steige D 74 E6
Geismar D 79 D7
Geisnes N 105 B11
Geispolsheim F 27 C8
Geisttthal A 73 B11
Geithain D 79 D12
Geithus N 95 C11
Geitvågen N 108 B8
Gela I 58 E5
Gelbensande D 83 B12
Gelchsheim D 74 C7
Geldermalsen NL 16 E4
Geldern D 16 E6
Geldersheim D 75 B7
Geldrop NL 16 F5
Geleen NL 19 C12
Gelgaudiškis LT 136 C6
Gelibolu TR 172 D6
Gellénháza H 149 C7
Gelligaer GB 13 B8
Gelnhausen D 21 D12
Gelnica SK 145 F2
Gelos F 32 D5
Gelsa E 41 F11
Gelse H 149 C7
Gelsenkirchen D 17 E8
Gelsted DK 86 E5
Gelsted DK 87 E9
Geltendorf D 71 A12
Gelting D 83 A7
Geltow D 80 B3
Gelvonai LT 137 C10
Gembloux B 19 C10
Gemeaux F 26 E3
Gemenele RO 155 C1
Gesunda S 102 E8
Gesves B 19 D11
Geszt H 151 D8
Gesztely H 145 G2
Geszteréd H 151 B8
Geta FIN 99 B13
Getafe E 46 D5
Getaria E 32 D1
Gétigné F 28 A3
Getinge S 87 B11
Getryggen S 103 D10
Getterum S 93 D8
Gettjärn S 97 C8
Gettorf D 83 B7
Gevelsberg D 17 F8
Gévezé F 23 D8
Gevgelija MK 169 B7
Gevrey-Chambertin F 26 F2
Gex F 31 C9
Geyer D 80 E3
Geyikli TR 171 E10
Gezavesh AL 168 D3
Gföhl A 77 E8
Ghedi I 66 B1
Ghelari RO 159 B10
Ghelinţa RO 153 E8
Ghemme I 68 B5
Gheorghe Doja RO 161 D10
Gheorghe Lazăr RO 161 D10
Gheorgheni RO 153 D7
Gherăești RO 153 C9
Ghercești RO 160 E3
Gherghesca RO 161 C10
Gherghiţa RO 161 D8
Gherla RO 152 C3
Gherta Mică RO 145 H7
Ghidfalău RO 153 E10
Ghidighici MD 154 C3
Ghiffa I 68 B6
Ghilarza I 64 C2
Ghimbav RO 161 B7
Ghimeş-Făget RO 153 D8
Ghimpaţi RO 161 E7
Ghindari RO 152 E6
Ghioroc RO 151 E8
Ghioroiu RO 160 D3
Ghiroda RO 151 F7
Ghislenghien B 19 C8

Genova I 37 C9
Genovés E 56 D4
Gensac F 28 F5
Gensingen D 185 E8
Gent B 19 B8
Genthin D 79 B11
Gentioux-Pigerolles F 29 D9
Genzano di Lucania I 60 B6
Genzano di Roma I 62 D3
Geoagiu RO 151 F11
George Enescu RO 153 A9
Georgensgmünd D 75 D9
Georgianoi GR 169 D7
Georgianoi GR 170 C6
Georgi Damyanovo BG 165 C7
Georgioupoli GR 178 E7
Georgitsi GR 174 E5
Georgsheil D 17 B8
Georgsmarienhütte D 17 D10
Ger E 33 F9
Ger F 23 C10
Ger F 32 D5
Gera D 79 E11
Geraardsbergen B 19 C8
Gerabronn D 74 D6
Gerace I 59 C9
Geraci Siculo I 58 D5
Gerakarou GR 169 C9
Geraki GR 175 F6
Gerakini GR 169 D9
Gérardmer F 27 D6
Geras A 77 E9
Gerasdorf bei Wien A 77 F10
Géraudot F 25 D11
Gerbéviller F 186 E2
Gerbrunn D 187 B8
Gerbstedt D 79 C10
Gérce H 149 B8
Gerchsheim D 74 C6
Gerdau D 83 E8
Gerendás H 151 D6
Geresdlak H 149 D11
Geretsberg A 76 F3
Geretsried D 72 A3
Gérgal E 55 E7
Gergei I 64 D3
Gergeri GR 178 E8
Gerhardshofen D 75 C8
Gerindote E 46 E4
Geringswalde D 80 D3
Gerjen H 149 C11
Gerlev DK 87 D10
Gerlingen D 27 C11
Gerlos A 72 B5
Germas GR 168 D5
Germay F 26 D3
Germencik TR 177 D10
Germering D 75 F9
Germersheim D 21 F10
Gernrode D 79 C9
Gernsbach D 27 C9
Gernsheim D 187 B5
Gerola Alta I 69 A8
Gerolimenas GR 178 C3
Gerolsbach D 75 F9
Gerolstein D 21 D7
Gerolzhofen D 75 C7
Gerovo HR 67 A10
Gerpinnes B 19 D10
Gersau CH 71 D7
Gersfeld (Rhön) D 74 B6
Gersheim D 27 B7
Gersten D 17 C9
Gerstetten D 74 E7
Gersthofen D 75 F8
Gerstungen D 79 E7
Gerswalde D 84 D5
Gerwisch D 79 B10
Gerzat F 30 D3
Gerzen D 75 E11
Gesäter S 91 B11
Gescher D 17 E8
Gesico I 64 D3
Gespunsart F 19 E10
Gessertshausen D 75 F8
Gestalgar E 48 E3
Gesté F 23 F9
Gesten DK 86 D4
Gesturi I 64 D3

Ghisonaccia F 37 G10
Ghisoni F 37 G10
Ghizela RO 151 F8
Ghyvelde F 18 B6
Gialtra GR 175 B6
Giannades GR 168 E2
Giannitsa GR 169 C7
Giannouli GR 169 F7
Giano dell'Umbria I 62 B3
Giardinello I 58 C3
Giardini-Naxos I 59 D7
Giarmata RO 151 F7
Giarratana I 59 E6
Giarre I 59 D7
Giat F 29 D10
Giave I 64 C2
Giaveno I 31 E11
Giba I 64 E2
Gibellina Nuova I 58 D2
Gibostad N 111 B15
Gibraléon E 51 E6
Gibraltar GBZ 53 D6
Giby PL 136 E7
Gibzde LV 134 B6
Gideå S 107 E15
Gideå bruk S 107 E16
Gideåkroken S 107 C12
Gidle PL 143 E7
Giebelstadt D 74 C6
Giebolhausen D 79 C7
Gieczno PL 143 C7
Giedraičiai LT 137 C11
Gielniów PL 141 H2
Gielow D 83 C13
Gien F 25 E8
Giengen an der Brenz D 75 E7
Giera RO 159 C6
Gierle B 182 C5
Giersleben D 79 C10
Gierstädt D 79 D8
Gierzwald PL 139 C9
Gießen D 21 C11
Gieten NL 17 B7
Gietrzwałd PL 139 C9
Gièvres F 24 F6
Giffnock GB 5 D8
Gifford GB 5 D11
Gifhorn D 79 B8
Gigean F 35 C6
Gigen BG 160 F4
Gighera RO 160 F3
Giglio Castello I 65 C3
Gignac F 35 C6
Gignac F 35 C10
Gignod I 31 D11
Gijón-Xixón E 39 A8
Gikši LV 135 B10
Gilău RO 151 D11
Gilching D 75 F9
Gilena E 53 B7
Gilette F 37 D6
Gilford GB 7 D10
Gilleleje DK 87 C10
Gillenfeld D 21 D7
Gillhov S 102 A8
Gillingham GB 13 C10
Gillingham GB 13 C16
Gilling West GB 11 C8
Gilly-sur-Isère F 31 D10
Gilly-sur-Loire F 30 B4
Gilmerton GB 5 C9
Gilså N 105 E11
Gilserberg D 21 C12
Gilsland GB 5 F11
Gilten D 82 E7
Gilwern GB 13 B8
Gimåt S 107 E15
Gimdalen S 103 A10
Gimigliano I 59 B10
Gimo S 99 B10
Gimont F 33 C7
Gimouille F 30 B3
Gimsøy N 110 D7
Ginasservis F 35 C10
Ginestas F 34 D4
Gingelom B 19 C11
Gingen an der Fils D 187 D8
Gingst D 84 B4
Ginkūnai LT 134 E6
Ginoles F 33 E10
Ginosa I 61 B7
Ginostra I 59 B7
Ginsheim D 185 E9
Gintsi BG 165 C7
Giões P 50 E4
Gioi I 60 C4
Gioia dei Marsi I 62 D5
Gioia del Colle I 61 B8
Gioia Sannitica I 60 A2
Gioia Tauro I 59 C8
Gioiosa Ionica I 59 C9
Gioiosa Marea I 59 C6
Giornico CH 71 E7
Giovinazzo I 61 A7
Gipka LV 130 F5
Giraltovce SK 145 E4
Girancourt F 26 D5
Girasole I 64 D4
Girifalco I 59 B9
Girişu de Criş RO 151 C8
Girkalnis LT 134 E6
Giroc RO 159 B7
Giromagny F 27 E6
Girona E 43 D9
Gironde-sur-Dropt F 32 A5
Gironella E 43 C7
Giroussens F 33 C9
Girov RO 153 D9
Girvan GB 4 E7
Gislaved S 88 A5
Gislev DK 86 E7
Gislinge DK 87 D9
Gislövs strandmark S 87 E12
Gisloy N 110 C9
Gisors F 18 F4
Gissi I 63 C7
Gisslarbo S 97 C14
Gistad S 92 C7
Gistel B 18 B6
Gistrup DK 86 B5
Giswil CH 70 D6
Gittelde D 79 C7
Gittun S 109 D16
Giubega RO 160 E2
Giubiasco CH 69 A6
Giugliano in Campania I 60 B2
Giulești RO 152 B3
Giuliano di Roma I 62 D4
Giulianova I 62 B5
Giulvăz RO 159 B6
Giuncugnano I 66 D1
Giurgeni RO 155 D1
Giurgița RO 160 E3

Giurgiu RO 161 F7
Giurgiulești MD 155 C2
Giuvărăști RO 160 F5
Give DK 86 D4
Givet F 19 D10
Givors F 30 D6
Givry B 19 D9
Givry F 30 B6
Givry-en-Argonne F 25 C12
Givskud DK 86 D4
Gižai LT 136 D7
Gizałki PL 142 B4
Gizeux F 23 F12
Giżycko PL 136 E4
Gizzeria I 59 B9
Gjakovë KS 163 E9
Gjærnes N 90 B5
Gjegjan AL 163 E9
Gjegjan AL 163 F9
Gjengstø N 104 E6
Gjerde N 100 C6
Gjerdebakken N 113 C11
Gjerdrum N 95 B14
Gjerlev DK 86 B6
Gjermundshamn N 94 B3
Gjern DK 86 C5
Gjerrild DK 87 C7
Gjerstad N 90 B5
Gjersvik N 105 B14
Gjesing DK 86 C6
Gjesvær N 113 A15
Gjevaldshaugen N 101 D15
Gjilan KS 164 E3
Gjirokastër AL 168 D3
Gjógv FO 2 A3
Gjøl DK 86 A5
Gjøljelia N 104 D7
Gjølme N 104 E7
Gjonaj KS 163 E10
Gjonëm AL 168 A2
Gjøra N 101 A10
Gjorm AL 168 D2
Gjøvåg N 94 B2
Gjøvik N 101 E13
Gjurakoc KS 163 D9
Gjuvberget N 102 E3
Gkoritsa GR 175 E6
Gladbeck D 17 E7
Gladenbach D 21 C11
Gladsaxe DK 87 D10
Gladstad N 108 E2
Glainans F 26 F6
Glamis GB 5 B11
Glamoč BIH 157 D6
Glåmos N 101 A14
Glamsbjerg DK 86 E6
Glandage F 35 A10
Glandon F 29 E8
Glandore IRL 8 E4
Glandorf D 17 D10
Glanegg A 73 C9
Glanerbrug NL 17 D7
Glanshammar S 97 D13
Glanworth IRL 8 D6
Glarryford GB 4 F4
Glarus CH 71 C8
Glasbury GB 13 A8
Glasgow GB 5 D8
Gläshütten D 21 D10
Glashütten D 75 C10
Glaslough IRL 7 D9
Glassan IRL 7 F7
Glastonbury GB 13 C9
Glaubitz D 80 D4
Glauchau D 79 E12
Glava S 97 C8
Glava glasbruk S 96 C7
Glavan BG 166 E6
Glăvăneşti RO 153 E10
Glavanovtsi BG 164 D6
Glavatičevo BIH 157 F9
Glavice HR 157 E6
Glavičice BIH 157 C11
Glăvile RO 160 D3
Glavinitsa BG 161 F9
Glavki GR 171 B7
Gleann Cholm Cille IRL 6 C5
Gleann Doimhin IRL 7 C7
Gleann na Muaidhe IRL 6 D3
Gleđica SRB 163 C9
Glein N 108 D4
Gleina D 79 D10
Gleisdorf A 148 B5
Gleizé F 30 D6
Glejbjerg DK 86 D3
Glemsford GB 15 C10
Glen S 102 A6
Glenade IRL 6 D6
Glenamaddy IRL 6 E5
Glenamoy IRL 6 D3
Glenariff GB 4 E4
Glenarm GB 4 F5
Glenavy GB 7 C10
Glenbarr GB 4 D5
Glenbeg GB 4 B5
Glenbeigh IRL 8 D3
Glencaple GB 5 E9
Glencar IRL 6 D6
Glencoe GB 4 B6
Glencolumbkille IRL 6 C5
Glendowan IRL 7 C7
Gleneagles GB 5 C9
Glenealy IRL 7 G10
Gleneely IRL 4 E2
Glenelg S 2 L5
Glenfield GB 11 F9
Glenfinnan GB 4 B6
Glengarriff IRL 8 E3
Glengavlen IRL 7 D7
Glenhead GB 4 E2
Glenluce GB 4 F6
Glenmore IRL 9 D8
Glenoe GB 4 F5
Glenrothes GB 5 C10
Glenties IRL 6 C6
Glère F 27 F6
Glesborg DK 87 C7
Gletsch CH 71 D6
Glewitz D 84 B3
Glibaći MNE 163 C7
Glimåkra S 88 C6
Glimboca RO 159 C9
Glin IRL 8 C4
Glina HR 148 F6
Glina RO 161 E8
Glinde D 83 C8
Glindow D 79 B12
Glinjeni MD 153 B11
Glinojeck PL 139 E9
Glinsce IRL 6 F3
Glinsk IRL 6 F3

Glinton GB 11 F11
Glissjöberg S 102 B7
Gliwice PL 142 F6
Glamnik KS 164 D3
Globočiče KS 164 E3
Glogoc KS 163 E9
Glodeanu-Sărat RO 161 D9
Glodeanu-Siliştea RO 161 D9
Glodeni MD 153 B11
Glodeni RO 152 D5
Glodeni RO 161 C6
Glödnitz A 73 C9
Głodowa PL 85 C11
Glodzhevo BG 161 F8
Gloggnitz A 148 A5
Glogova RO 159 D10
Glogovac SRB 159 E7
Głogów PL 81 C10
Głogówek PL 142 F4
Głogowo PL 138 D6
Glomfjord N 108 C6
Glommen S 87 B11
Glommersträsk S 107 A17
Glonn D 75 G10
Glória P 50 B4
Glória do Ribatejo P 44 F3
Glos-la-Ferrière F 24 C4
Glossa GR 175 A8
Glössbo S 103 D12
Glossop GB 11 E7
Glöte S 102 B5
Glöthe D 79 C10
Glottra S 92 B6
Gloucester GB 13 B10
Glounthaune IRL 8 E6
Głowaczów PL 141 G4
Główczyce PL 85 A12
Glowe D 84 A4
Glöwen D 83 E12
Głowno PL 143 C8
Głożan SRB 158 C4
Glozhene BG 160 F3
Glozhene BG 165 C9
Głubczyce PL 142 F4
Głuchołazy PL 142 F3
Głuchów PL 141 G2
Glücksburg (Ostsee) D 82 A7
Glückstadt D 17 A12
Glud DK 86 D5
Gludsted DK 86 C4
Gluggvasshaugen N 108 E5
Glumslöv S 87 D11
Glumsø DK 87 E9
Glusburn GB 11 D8
Glušci SRB 158 D4
Głuszyca PL 81 E10
Glyfa GR 175 B6
Glyfada GR 175 D8
Glyki GR 168 F4
Glyn Ceiriog GB 10 F5
Glyngøre DK 86 B3
Glynn GB 4 F5
Glynn IRL 9 D9
Glynneath GB 13 B7
Gmünd A 73 C9
Gmünd A 77 E7
Gmund am Tegernsee D 72 A4
Gmunden A 73 A8
Gnarp S 103 B13
Gnarrenburg D 17 B12
Gneisenaustadt Schildau D 80 D3
Gnesta S 93 A10
Gniebing A 148 C5
Gniew PL 138 C6
Gniewkowo PL 138 E5
Gniewoszów PL 141 H5
Gnieżdżiska PL 143 E9
Gniezno PL 85 E13
Gnisvärd S 93 D12
Gnocchetta I 66 C5
Gnoien D 83 C13
Gnojna PL 81 E12
Gnojnice BIH 157 F8
Gnojnik PL 144 D2
Gnojno PL 143 E10
Gnosall GB 11 F7
Gnosjö S 91 E14
Gnotzheim D 75 D8
Gnutz D 83 B7
Göbel TR 173 D9
Gobowen GB 10 F5
Göçbeyli TR 177 A9
Göcek TR 181 C9
Goch D 16 E6
Gochsheim D 75 C8
Goczałkowice-Zdrój PL 147 B7
Göd H 150 B3
Godačica SRB 159 F6
Godal N 95 D11
Godalming GB 15 E7
Godby FIN 99 B13
Goddelau D 187 B6
Goddelsheim (Lichtenfels) D 21 B11
Godeanu RO 159 D10
Godech BG 165 C7
Godega di Sant'Urbano I 72 E5
Godegård S 92 B6
Godelleta E 48 F3
Godeni RO 160 C5
Goderville F 18 E1
Godiasco I 37 B10
Godimilje BIH 157 E11
Godineşti RO 159 C10
Godinje MNE 163 E7
Godkowo PL 139 B8
Godmanchester GB 15 C8
Gödöllő H 150 B4
Godovič SLO 73 E9
Gödre H 149 D9
Godstone GB 15 E8
Goduš BIH 157 C11
Godzieszo Wielkie PL 142 C5
Godziszów PL 144 B5
Goedereede NL 16 E1
Goes NL 16 E1
Göfritz an der Wild A 77 E8
Göggingen D 187 D8
Gogolin PL 142 F5
Gogołów PL 144 D4
Gogoşari RO 161 F7
Gogoşu RO 159 E10
Gogoşu RO 160 E2
Göhl D 83 B9
Gohor RO 153 E10
Gohrau D 79 C12
Göhrde D 83 D9
Göhren, Ostseebad D 84 B5
Göhren-Lebbin D 83 D13

Goicea RO 160 F3
Goieşti RO 160 F3
Goirle NL 16 E4
Góis P 44 D4
Goito I 66 B2
Goizueta E 32 D2
Gojść PL 143 D7
Gökçealan TR 177 D9
Gökçebayir TR 171 E10
Gökçedağ TR 173 E10
Gökçeören TR 181 B9
Gökçeyazi TR 173 E8
Gokels D 82 B6
Gökova TR 181 C7
Göktepe TR 181 B9
Göktürk TR 173 B10
Gol N 101 E9
Gola HR 149 D8
Gołąb PL 141 H5
Golac SLO 67 A9
Golăieşti RO 153 C11
Golaj AL 163 E9
Gołańcz PL 85 E12
Golbey F 26 D5
Gölby FIN 99 B13
Gölcük TR 173 F8
Golčův Jeníkov CZ 77 C8
Golczewo PL 85 C7
Gołdap PL 136 E5
Goldach CH 71 C9
Goldbeck D 83 E11
Goldberg D 83 C12
Goldegg A 73 B7
Goldelund D 82 A6
Golden IRL 9 D7
Golden Pot GB 14 E7
Goldenstedt D 17 C10
Goleen IRL 8 F3
Golegã P 44 F4
Golemanovo BG 159 F10
Golema Rakovitsa BG 165 D8
Golema Rečica MK 163 F10
Golenice PL 85 E7
Goleniów PL 85 C7
Golesh BG 161 F11
Goleşti RO 153 F10
Goleşti RO 160 C4
Golfo Aranci I 64 B4
Golina PL 142 B5
Golinhac F 33 A11
Gölişeva LV 133 C3
Gölköy TR 177 E9
Gölle H 149 D10
Göllersdorf A 77 F10
Göllheim D 186 B5
Gollin D 83 C11
Gollin D 84 D5
Golling an der Salzach A 73 A7
Göllingen D 79 D9
Gollmitz D 84 D5
Golmes F 42 D6
Golnik SLO 73 D9
Gøløse DK 87 D10
Golovkino RUS 136 D3
Golpejas E 45 B9
Golubac SRB 159 D8
Golub-Dobrzyń PL 138 D7
Golubić HR 156 D5
Golubinje SRB 159 D9
Gołymin-Ośrodek PL 139 E10
Golzow D 79 B12
Gomadingen D 27 D11
Gómara E 41 E7
Gomaringen D 187 E7
Gomati GR 169 D10
Gomba H 150 C4
Gömeç TR 173 F6
Gomecello E 45 B9
Gomes Aires P 50 D3
Gomirje HR 67 B11
Gommern D 79 B10
Gomotartsi BG 159 E10
Gomunice PL 143 D7
Gönc H 145 G3
Gonçalo P 44 D6
Goncelin F 31 E8
Gondelsheim D 187 C6
Gondershausen D 185 D7
Gondomar E 38 D2
Gondomar P 44 B3
Gondorf D 21 D8
Gondrecourt-le-Château F 26 C4
Gondreville F 26 C4
Gondrin F 33 C6
Gönen TR 173 D8
Gonfaron F 36 E4
Gonfreville-l'Orcher F 18 E1
Goni I 64 D3
Goniądz PL 140 D7
Gonnesa I 64 E1
Gonnoi GR 169 E7
Gonnosfanadiga I 64 E2
Gonnosnò I 64 D2
Gonsans F 26 F5
Gönyő H 149 A9
Gonzaga I 66 C2
Goodwick GB 12 A5
Goole GB 11 D10
Goonhavern GB 12 E4
Goor NL 17 D7
Gopegi E 40 C6
Göppingen D 74 E6
Gor E 55 E7
Góra PL 81 C11
Góra PL 139 E9
Gorafe E 55 E6
Goraj PL 144 B6
Góra Kalwaria PL 141 G4
Goranu RO 160 D4
Góra Puławska PL 141 H5
Gorawino PL 85 C8
Goražde BIH 157 E10
Gorban RO 153 D12
Gòrbea E 40 C6
Görbeháza H 151 B7
Görcsöny H 149 E9
Gördalen S 102 C3
Gordaliza del Pino E 39 D9
Gordes F 35 C9
Gordineşti MD 153 A10
Gørding DK 86 E3
Gordola CH 69 A6
Gordon GB 5 D11
Gordona I 69 A7

Gorebridge GB 5 D10
Göreçe TR 177 C9
Gorenja Straža SLO 73 E11
Gorenja vas SLO 73 D9
Gorey IRL 9 C10
Gorgoglione I 60 C6
Gorgonzola I 69 B7
Gorgota RO 161 D8
Gorgova RO 155 C4
Gorica BIH 157 D7
Gorica BIH 157 F7
Gorica MNE 163 E7
Goričan HR 149 C7
Gorinchem NL 16 E3
Gorino I 66 C5
Gorishovë AL 168 C2
Goritsa BG 167 D9
Göritz D 84 D5
Gorizia I 73 E8
Gorleben D 83 D10
Gorlice PL 144 D3
Görlitz D 81 D7
Gorlosen D 83 D11
Gormanston IRL 7 E10
Gormanstown IRL 7 E10
Gormaz E 40 E6
Görmin D 84 C4
Gorna Belica MK 164 F3
Gorna Beshovitsa BG 165 C8
Gorna Breznitsa BG 165 F7
Gorna Koznitsa BG 165 E6
Gorna Kremena BG 165 C8
Gorna Mitropoliya BG 165 C9
Gorna Oryakhovitsa BG 166 C5
Gorna Studena BG 166 C5
Gornau D 80 E4
Gornet RO 161 C8
Gornet-Cricov RO 161 C8
Gorni Dŭbnik BG 165 C9
Gorni Lom BG 165 C6
Gornja Golubinja BIH 157 D8
Gornja Grabovica BIH 157 F8
Gornja Gračenica HR 149 E7
Gornja Ljubata SRB 164 D5
Gornja Ljuta BIH 157 E9
Gornja Ploča HR 156 D4
Gornja Radgona SLO 148 C5
Gornja Sanica BIH 157 C6
Gornja Slatina BIH 157 C9
Gornja Toponica SRB 164 C4
Gornja Trnava SRB 159 F7
Gornja Tuzla BIH 157 C10
Gornje Jelenje HR 67 B10
Gornje Peulje BIH 156 D6
Gornje Ratkovo BIH 157 C6
Gornje Vratno HR 148 D6
Gornji Agići BIH 157 C6
Gornji Babin Potok HR 156 C4
Gornji Breg SRB 150 F5
Gornji Dolac HR 157 E6
Gornji Grad SLO 73 D10
Gornji Humac HR 157 F6
Gornji Kosinj HR 156 C3
Gornji Lapac HR 156 C5
Gornji Lukavac BIH 157 D9
Gornji Majkovi HR 162 D4
Gornji Malovan BIH 157 E7
Gornji Matejevac SRB 164 C4
Gornji Milanovac SRB 158 E5
Gornji Očćauš BIH 157 D8
Gornji Podgradci BIH 157 B7
Gornji Rajić HR 157 B7
Gornji Ribnik BIH 157 D6
Gornji Tkalec HR 149 E6
Gornji Vakuf BIH 157 E8
Górno PL 143 E10
Gorno Ablanovo BG 161 F7
Gorno Aleksandrovo BG 167 D8
Gorno Orizari MK 164 F4
Gorno Ozirovo BG 165 C8
Gorno Pavlikene BG 165 C10
Goro I 66 C5
Gorobinci MK 164 F4
Górowo Iławeckie PL 136 E2
Gorredijk NL 16 B6
Gorreto I 37 B10
Gorron F 23 D10
Görsbach D 79 D8
Gorseinon GB 12 B6
Gorska Polyana BG 167 E7
Gorski Izvor BG 166 E4
Gorsko Novo Selo BG 166 C5
Gorssel NL 16 D6
Gort IRL 6 F5
Gortahork IRL 6 B6
Gort an Choirce IRL 6 B6
Gortavoy Bridge GB 7 C9
Gorteen IRL 6 E5
Gorteen IRL 6 E6
Gorteeny IRL 6 F6
Gortin GB 4 F2
Gorouia RO 159 C9
Görükle TR 173 D10
Gorun BG 167 B10
Görvik S 106 D9
Görwihl D 27 E9
Gorxheimertal D 21 E11
Gorzanów PL 77 B11
Gorze F 26 B5
Görzig D 79 C10
Görzke D 79 B11
Gorzkowice PL 143 D8
Gorzków-Osada PL 144 B7
Górzna PL 85 D11
Górzno PL 139 D8
Górzno PL 141 G5
Gorzów Śląski PL 142 D5
Gorzów Wielkopolski PL 85 E8
Górzyca PL 85 D7
Górzyca PL 85 C8
Gorzyce PL 144 B4
Gorzyce PL 144 C5
Gorzyń PL 81 A9
Gorzyn PL 81 C7
Gosaldo I 72 D5
Gosau A 73 A8
Gosberton GB 11 F11
Gościeradów Ukazowy PL 144 B4
Gościm PL 85 E9
Gościno PL 85 B9
Gościszów PL 81 D8

Gosdorf A 148 C5
Goše AL 168 B2
Gosfield GB 15 D10
Gosforth GB 5 E13
Gosforth GB 10 C5
Goslar D 79 C7
Göslice PL 139 E8
Gosné F 23 D9
Gospić HR 156 D3
Gosport GB 13 D12
Gössäter S 91 B13
Gossau CH 27 F11
Gossau CH 55 E6
Gössendorf A 148 C5
Gößl A 73 A8
Gostavățu RO 160 E5
Gostil RO 161 E8
Gostilitsa BG 166 D5
Gostinari BG 165 E10
Gostinu RO 161 E8
Gostivar MK 163 F10
Göstling an der Ybbs A 73 A10
Gostovići BIH 157 D9
Gostycyn PL 138 D4
Gostyń PL 81 C12
Gostyń PL 85 B7
Gostynin PL 139 F7
Goszcz PL 142 D3
Goszczanów PL 142 C6
Goszczyn PL 141 G3
Göta S 91 C11
Göteborg S 91 D10
Götene S 91 B13
Goteşti MD 154 E2
Gotha D 79 E8
Gothem S 93 D13
Götlunda S 97 D14
Gotse Delchev BG 169 A10
Gottböle FIN 122 F6
Gotteszell D 76 E4
Gottfrieding D 75 E11
Göttingen D 78 D6
Gottmadingen D 27 E10
Gottne S 107 E14
Götzis A 71 C9
Gouarec F 22 D5
Gouda NL 16 D3
Goudswaard NL 182 B4
Gouesnou F 22 D3
Gouhenans F 26 E5
Goult F 35 C9
Goumenissa GR 169 C7
Goumois F 27 F6
Gourdon F 29 F8
Gourdon GB 5 B12
Gourette F 32 E5
Gourgançon F 25 C11
Gouria GR 174 C3
Gourin F 22 D4
Gournay-en-Bray F 18 F4
Goussainville F 25 B7
Gout-Rossignol F 29 E6
Gouveia P 44 D5
Gouvia GR 168 E2
Gouvieux F 25 B7
Gouvy B 20 D5
Gouzon F 29 C10
Gove P 44 B6
Govedari HR 162 D3
Govedartsi BG 165 E7
Goven F 23 D8
Gowarczów PL 141 H2
Gowidlino PL 138 B4
Goworowo PL 139 E12
Gowran IRL 9 C8
Goxhill GB 11 D11
Göynükbelen TR 173 E11
Gózd PL 141 H4
Gozdnica PL 81 C8
Gozdowice PL 84 E6
Gozdowo PL 139 E8
Gozée B 19 D9
Gözler TR 173 D10
Gözsüz TR 173 C6
Gozzano I 68 B5
Graal-Müritz, Ostseebad D 83 B12
Grab BIH 157 F10
Grab BIH 162 D5
Graben-Neudorf D 187 C5
Grabica PL 143 D8
Grabjan AL 168 C2
Grabovac HR 157 F7
Grabovci SRB 158 D4
Grabovica SRB 159 E10
Grabow D 83 D11
Grabowiec PL 143 D7
Grabowiec PL 144 B8
Grabówka PL 140 D8
Grabów nad Pilicą PL 141 G4
Grabów nad Prosną PL 142 C5
Grabownica Starzeńska PL 144 D5
Grabowno Wielkie PL 142 D3
Grabowo PL 139 D13
Grabs CH 71 C8
Gračac HR 156 D4
Gračanica BIH 157 C9
Gračanica BIH 157 D10
Gračanica SRB 163 D9
Graçay F 24 F6
Gračec HR 149 E6
Graddö S 99 B11
Graddö S 99 B11
Gradac BIH 162 D5
Gradac HR 157 F7
Gradac SLO 148 E4
Gradačac BIH 157 C9
Gradara I 67 E6
Grădăşti S 109 F15
Gradec HR 149 E6
Gradec BG 166 C5
Gradec MK 169 B7
Gradefes E 39 C9
Gradets BG 167 D7
Gradevo BG 165 F7
Gradina BG 166 C5
Gradina HR 149 E8
Gradina BIH 157 F9
Gradina SRB 163 C9
Grădinari RO 159 D8
Grădinari RO 160 D4
Grădiştea RO 161 D7
Grădiştea RO 160 D3

Grădiştea RO 161 C10
Grădiştea RO 161 D8
Grădiştea RO 161 F9
Gradnitsa BG 165 D10
Grado E 39 B7
Grado I 73 E7
Gradö S 97 B15
Gradojević SRB 158 D4
Gradoli I 62 B1
Gradsko MK 169 A6
Gradskovo SRB 159 E9
Graena E 55 E6
Græsted DK 87 C10
Gräfelfing D 75 F9
Grafenau D 76 E4
Gräfenberg D 75 C9
Gräfendorf D 74 B6
Grafendorf bei Hartberg A 148 B5
Gräfenhainichen D 79 C11
Grafenhausen D 27 E9
Grafenrheinfeld D 187 B9
Gräfenroda D 79 E8
Grafenstein A 73 C9
Grafenwöhr D 75 C10
Grafenworth A 77 F9
Graffignano I 62 B2
Grafhorst D 79 B8
Graf Ignatievo BG 165 E10
Gräfinau-Angstedt D 79 E9
Grafing bei München D 75 F10
Grafrath D 75 F9
Gräfsnäs S 91 C11
Gräftåvallen S 105 E15
Gragnano I 60 B3
Grahovac MNE 163 D6
Grahovo SLO 73 D8
Gráig na Manach IRL 9 C9
Graigue IRL 9 C7
Graiguenamanagh IRL 9 C9
Grain GB 15 E10
Grainau D 71 C12
Grainet D 76 E5
Graissac F 30 F2
Graissessac F 34 C5
Graja de Iniesta E 47 E9
Grajal de Campos E 39 D9
Grajduri RO 153 D11
Grajewo PL 140 C6
Grålum N 95 D14
Gram D 86 E4
Gramada BG 159 F10
Gramastetten A 76 F6
Gramat F 29 F9
Gramatikovo BG 167 E9
Grambow D 84 D6
Grammendorf D 83 B13
Grammenitsa GR 174 A2
Grammeno GR 168 E4
Gramsh AL 168 C3
Gramzda LV 134 D3
Gramzow D 84 D6
Gran N 95 B13
Granabeg IRL 7 F10
Granada E 53 B9
Grañán S 119 C10
Granard IRL 7 E8
Granåsen S 107 C11
Granátula de Calatrava E 54 B5
Granberg S 118 D3
Granberget N 102 D3
Granbergsdal S 97 D12
Granbergsträsk S 107 A17
Grančarevo BIH 162 D5
Grancey-le-Château-Neuvelle F 26 E3
Grandas E 38 B6
Grandcamp-Maisy F 23 B9
Grand-Champ F 22 E6
Grand-Couronne F 18 F3
Grande-Synthe F 18 B5
Grande-Vabre F 33 A10
Grand-Fort-Philippe F 18 B5
Grand-Fougeray F 23 E8
Grândola P 50 C2
Grandpré F 19 F10
Grandpuits-Bailly-Carrois F 25 C8
Grandrieu F 30 F4
Grandris F 30 D5
Grandson CH 31 B10
Grandtully GB 5 B9
Grandvelle-et-le-Perrenot F 26 E5
Grandvillars F 27 E6
Grandvillers F 26 D6
Grandvilliers F 18 E4
Grañén E 41 E11
Grängärde S 97 B12
Grange IRL 9 E7
Grange-over-Sands GB 10 C6
Grängesberg S 97 C12
Granges-sur-Vologne F 27 D6
Grängshyttan S 97 C12
Grängsjö S 103 C12
Granhult S 116 D7
Granica BIH 162 D5
Grănicer RO 151 D7
Grănicești RO 153 B8
Graninge S 107 E12
Granitola-Torretta I 58 D2
Granitsa GR 174 A4
Granja P 51 C5
Granja de Moreruela E 39 E8
Granja de Torrehermosa E 51 C8
Granja do Ulmeiro P 44 D3
Gränna S 92 D5
Grannäs S 107 A10
Grannäs S 109 E13
Granneset N 108 E6
Granö S 107 C16
Granollers E 43 D8
Granön S 103 D13
Granowiec PL 142 D3
Granowo PL 81 B11
Gransee D 84 D4
Gransherad N 95 D10
Gränsgård S 109 F15
Granschütz D 79 D11
Gransjön S 103 B11
Gränssjö S 108 F8

Grantham GB 11 F10
Grantown-on-Spey GB 3 L9
Granträsk S 107 C14
Granträskmark S 118 D6
Grantshouse GB 5 D12
Gränum S 88 C7
Granvik S 92 B5
Granville F 23 C8
Granvin N 94 A5
Grapska BIH 157 C8
Gräs S 97 C10
Gräsbakken N 114 C5
Gräsgård S 89 C11
Grasleben D 79 B9
Gräsmarken S 97 B8
Grasmere GB 10 C5
Gräsmyr S 107 D17
Grassåmoen N 105 C14
Grassano I 60 B6
Grassau D 72 A5
Grasse F 36 D5
Grassington GB 11 C8
Gråssjö S 103 C10
Grästen DK 86 F5
Gröstorp S 91 C12
Gratallops E 42 E5
Gratangsbotn N 111 C14
Gratens F 33 D8
Gratia RO 161 E6
Gratini GR 171 B9
Gratkorn A 148 B4
Grätnäs S 107 D17
Gråträsk S 118 D3
Gratteri I 58 D5
Gratwein A 148 B4
Graubälle DK 86 C5
Graulhet F 33 C9
Graupa D 80 D5
Graus E 42 C4
Grávalos E 41 D8
Gravberget N 102 E3
Gravbränna S 106 D7
Gravdal N 110 D6
Grave NL 16 E5
Gravedona I 69 A7
Gravelines F 18 B5
Gravellona Toce I 68 B5
Gravelotte F 26 B5
Gravens DK 86 D4
Grävenwiesbach D 21 D10
Gräveri LV 133 D2
Gravesend GB 15 E9
Gravia GR 174 B5
Gravigny F 24 B5
Gråvika N 100 C1
Gravina di Catania I 59 D7
Gravina in Puglia I 61 B7
Gravmark S 118 F4
Gray F 26 F4
Grayan-et-l'Hôpital F 28 E3
Grays GB 15 E9
Graz A 148 B4
Grazalema E 53 C6
Grazzanise I 60 A2
Grčak SRB 163 C8
Grdelica SRB 164 D5
Greaca RO 161 E8
Greåker N 95 D14
Great Baddow GB 15 D10
Great Bircham GB 15 B10
Great Clifton GB 5 F10
Great Cornard GB 15 C10
Great Dunmow GB 15 D9
Great Glen GB 11 F9
Great Gonerby GB 11 F10
Greatham GB 11 B9
Great Harwood GB 11 D7
Great Haywood GB 11 F8
Great Linford GB 15 C7
Great Malvern GB 13 A10
Great Ponton GB 11 F10
Great Salkeld GB 5 F11
Great Shelford GB 15 C9
Great Torrington GB 12 D6
Great Wakering GB 15 D10
Great Yarmouth GB 15 B12
Grebănu RO 161 C9
Grebaštica HR 156 E4
Grebbestad S 91 B8
Grebci BIH 162 D5
Grebenac SRB 159 D7
Grebendorf (Meinhard) D 79 D7
Grebenhain D 21 D12
Grebenişu de Câmpie RO 152 D4
Grebenstein D 21 B12
Grebin D 83 B8
Grębków PL 141 F5
Grebo S 92 C7
Grębocin PL 138 D6
Grębów PL 143 F12
Greccio I 62 C3
Grecești RO 160 E2
Greci I 60 A4
Greci RO 159 D11
Gredelj BIH 157 F10
Greding D 75 D9
Gredstedbro DK 86 E3
Greencastle GB 4 F2
Greencastle GB 7 D10
Greencastle IRL 4 E3
Greene D 78 C6
Greengairs GB 5 D9
Greenhead GB 5 F11
Greenigo GB 3 H10
Greenisland GB 4 F5
Greenlaw GB 5 D12
Greenloaning GB 5 C9
Greenock GB 4 D7
Greenodd GB 10 C6
Greenore IRL 7 D10
Greenway GB 12 B5
Greggio I 68 C5
Greifenburg A 73 C7
Greifenstein D 21 C10
Greiffenberg D 84 D5
Greifswald D 84 B4
Grein A 77 F7
Greiveri LV 135 B11
Greiz D 79 E11
Grejs DK 86 D5
Gremersdorf D 83 B9
Grenaa DK 87 C7
Grenade F 33 C8
Grenade-sur-l'Adour F 32 C5
Grenant F 26 E4
Grenås S 106 D8
Grenchen CH 27 F7
Grenči LV 134 C5

Grenoble F 31 E8
Grense-Jakobselv N 114 D9
Gréoux-les-Bains F 35 C10
Gresenhorst D 83 B12
Gress GB 2 J4
Gressan I 31 D11
Gresse D 83 B10
Gressoney-la-Trinite I 68 B4
Gressvik N 91 A8
Gresten A 77 G8
Grésy-sur-Aix F 31 D8
Grésy-sur-Isère F 31 D9
Gretna GB 5 F10
Greußen D 79 D8
Greux F 26 D4
Grevbäck S 92 C4
Greve in Chianti I 66 E3
Greven D 17 D9
Greven D 83 D9
Grevena GR 168 D5
Grevenbicht NL 183 C7
Grevenbroich D 21 B7
Greveniti GR 168 E5
Grevenmacher L 20 E6
Grevesmühlen D 83 C10
Greve Strand DK 87 D10
Grevie S 87 C11
Grevinge DK 87 D9
Greyabbey GB 7 C11
Greystoke GB 5 F11
Greystones IRL 7 F10
Grez-Doiceau B 19 C10
Grez-en-Bouère F 23 E10
Grgar SLO 73 D8
Grgurevci SRB 158 C4
Griegos E 47 D9
Gries F 27 C8
Gries am Brenner A 72 B3
Griesbach D 27 D9
Griesbach im Rottal D 76 F4
Griesheim D 21 E11
Grieskirchen A 76 F5
Grießen D 81 C7
Griesstätt D 75 G11
Griffen A 73 C10
Grigiškės LT 137 D11
Grignan F 35 B8
Grigno I 72 D4
Grignols F 32 B5
Grigny F 30 D6
Grigoriopol MD 154 C4
Grijota E 40 D2
Grijpskerk NL 16 B6
Grillby S 98 C4
Grillon F 35 B8
Grimaldi I 60 E6
Grimaud F 36 E5
Grimbergen B 19 C9
Grimma D 79 D12
Grimmen D 84 B4
Grimoldby GB 11 E12
Grimsås S 91 E14
Grimsby GB 11 D11
Grimslöv S 88 B7
Grimstad N 90 C4
Grimston GB 11 F13
Grimstorp S 92 D5
Grindafjord N 94 D2
Grindaheim N 101 D11
Grindal N 101 A11
Grindelwald CH 70 D6
Grinder N 96 B7
Grindjord N 111 D13
Grindsted DK 86 D4
Grindsted DK 86 D3
Grindu RO 161 D9
Grinkiškis LT 134 E7
Griñón E 46 D5
Grins A 71 C11
Grinsbol S 97 C8
Grințieș RO 153 C7
Gripenberg S 92 D5
Grisén E 41 E9
Griškabūdis LT 136 D7
Grisolia I 60 D5
Grisolles F 33 C8
Grisslehamn S 99 B11
Gritley GB 3 H11
Grivița RO 153 E11
Grivița RO 153 F11
Grivița RO 161 D10
Grivitsa BG 165 C10
Grkinja SRB 164 C4
Grljan SRB 159 F9
Grnčari MK 168 B5
Grobbendonk B 19 B10
Gröbenzell D 75 F9
Grobiņa LV 134 C2
Gröbming A 73 B8
Gröbzig D 79 C10
Grocka SRB 158 D6
Gródby S 93 A11
Gródek PL 140 D9
Gródek nad Dunajcem PL
144 D2
Gröden D 80 D5
Grödig A 73 A7
Gröditz D 80 D4
Gródki PL 139 D10
Grodków PL 142 E3
Grodziczno PL 139 D8
Grodziec PL 142 B5
Grodzisk PL 141 E7
Grodzisk Mazowiecki PL 141 F3
Grodzisk Wielkopolski PL 81 B10
Groenlo NL 17 D7
Groesbeek NL 183 B7
Grohnde (Emmerthal) D 78 B5
Groitzsch D 79 D11
Groix F 22 E5
Grojdibodu RO 160 F4
Grójec PL 141 G3
Grom PL 139 C10
Gromadka PL 81 D9
Grömitz D 83 B9
Gromnik PL 144 D2
Gromo I 69 B8
Gronau (Westfalen) D 17 D8
Grønbjerg DK 86 C3
Grönbo S 118 C5
Gröndal S 118 C5
Grönenbach D 71 B10
Grong N 105 C12
Grönhögen S 89 C10
Grønhøj DK 86 C4
Gröningen D 79 C9
Groningen NL 17 B7
Grønnemose DK 86 E6
Grønnes N 100 A6
Grønning N 110 E9
Grønningen N 104 D7

Gronowo PL 139 B7
Grönsinka S 98 B7
Grönskåra S 89 A9
Grönsta S 103 A11
Grønvik N 94 D4
Grönviken S 103 A9
Grönviken S 103 D12
Groomsport GB 4 F5
Grootegast NL 16 B6
Gropello Cairoli I 69 C6
Gropeni RO 155 C1
Gropnița RO 153 C9
Grorud N 95 C13
Groscavallo I 31 E11
Grosi RO 152 B3
Grošnica SRB 159 F6
Grosotto I 69 A9
Großaitingen D 71 A11
Großarl A 73 B7
Groß Ammensleben D 79 B10
Groß-Bieberau D 21 E11
Groß Börnecke D 79 C9
Großbothen D 79 D12
Großbottwar D 27 C11
Großbreitenbach D 79 E9
Großburgwedel (Burgwedel) D
78 B6
Groß Dölln D 84 E5
Grosselfingen D 27 D10
Großenaspe D 83 C8
Großenbrode D 83 B10
Großenehrich D 79 D8
Groß Engersdorf A 77 F11
Großengottern D 79 D8
Großenhain D 80 D5
Großenkneten D 17 C10
Großenlüder D 78 E6
Großensee D 83 C8
Großenstein D 79 E11
Großenwiehe D 82 A6
Groß-Enzersdorf A 77 F11
Grosseto I 65 B4
Grosseto-Prugna F 37 H9
Groß Fredenwalde D 84 D5
Großfurra D 79 D8
Groß-Gerau D 21 E10
Groß-Gerungs A 77 E7
Groß Glienicke D 80 B4
Großgmain D 73 A6
Groß Grönau D 83 C9
Großhabersdorf D 75 D8
Großhansdorf D 83 C8
Großharras A 77 E11
Groß Heere (Heere) D 79 B7
Großhennersdorf D 81 E7
Groß-Hesepe D 17 C8
Großheubach D 187 B7
Grössjö S 107 F14
Großkarolinenfeld D 72 A5
Groß Kiesow D 84 B4
Großklein A 148 C4
Groß Köris D 80 B5
Groß Kreutz D 79 B12
Großkrut A 77 E11
Groß Lafferde (Lahstedt) D
79 B7
Großlangheim D 187 B9
Groß Leine D 80 B6
Groß Leuthen D 80 B6
Großlittgen D 21 D7
Großlohra D 79 D8
Großmaischeid D 185 C8
Großmehlen D 80 D5
Groß Miltzow D 84 C5
Groß Mohrdorf D 84 B3
Großmonra D 79 D9
Groß Naundorf D 80 C3
Großnaundorf D 80 D5
Groß Nemerow D 84 D4
Groß Oesingen D 79 A7
Großolbersdorf D 80 E4
Groß Oßnig D 80 C6
Großostheim D 21 E12
Großpetersdorf A 149 B6
Groß Plasten D 83 C13
Großraming A 73 A10
Großräschen D 80 C6
Großrinderfeld D 74 C6
Groß Roge D 83 C12
Groß-Rohrheim D 21 E10
Großröhrsdorf D 80 D6
Großrosseln D 186 C2
Großrudestedt D 79 D9
Großrußbach A 77 F11
Groß-Siegharts A 77 E8
Groß Stieten D 83 C10
Großthiemig D 80 D5
Groß Twülpstedt D 79 B8
Groß-Umstadt D 187 B6
Großwallstadt D 187 B7
Groß Warnow D 83 D11
Groß Welle D 83 D12
Groß weikersdorf A 77 F9
Groß Wittensee D 82 B7
Groß Wokern D 83 C12
Groß Wüstenfelde D 83 C13
Groß Ziethen D 84 E5
Groß-Zimmern D 187 B6
Grostenquin F 27 C6
Grosuplje SLO 73 E10
Grøtavær N 111 C11
Grotfjord N 111 A16
Grötholen S 102 A7
Grötingen S 103 A9
Grotli N 100 B7
Grotnesdalen N 111 A18
Grottaferrata I 62 D3
Grottaglie I 61 C9
Grottaminarda I 60 A4
Grottammare I 62 A5
Grottazzolina I 62 A5
Grotte I 58 E4
Grotte di Castro I 62 B1
Grotteria I 59 C9
Grottole I 61 B6
Grou NL 16 B5
Grove GB 13 B12
Grövelsjön S 102 B3
Gudhem S 91 C14

Grozd'ovo BG 167 C9
Grozești RO 153 D12
Grub am Forst D 75 B9
Grubbenvorst NL 183 C8
Grubbnäsudden S 119 B10
Grube D 83 B10
Grubišno Polje HR 149 E8
Gruczno PL 138 D5
Gruda BIH 157 F7
Grude BIH 157 F7
Grudusk PL 139 D10
Grudziądz PL 138 D6
Gruey-lès-Surance F 26 D5
Grugliasco I 68 C4
Gruia RO 159 E10
Gruissan F 34 D5
Gruiu RO 161 D8
Grullos E 39 B7
Grumăzești RO 153 C8
Grumbach D 80 D5
Grumo Appula I 61 A7
Grünau D 73 A8
Grünau A 77 F9
Grünberg D 21 C11
Grünburg A 76 G6
Grundagssätern S 102 B4
Grundfors S 106 A8
Grundfors S 107 B13
Grundforsen S 102 D4
Grundsel S 118 C4
Grundsjö S 107 C11
Grundsuna S 107 E16
Grundsund S 91 C9
Grundtjärn S 107 D12
Grundträsk S 107 A17
Grundträsk S 109 F17
Grundträsk S 118 B7
Grundvattnet S 118 C4
Grünendeich D 82 C7
Grünewald D 80 D5
Grünewalde D 80 C5
Grungebru N 94 C7
Grünheide D 80 B5
Grünkraut D 71 B9
Grunnfarnes N 111 B12
Grunnfjord N 112 C4
Grunnförsfjord N 110 D8
Grunow D 80 B6
Grünsfeld D 74 C6
Grünstadt D 21 E10
Grünwald D 75 F10
Grupčin MK 164 F3
Grury F 30 B4
Grüšlaukė LT 134 D2
Grußendorf (Sassenburg) D
79 A8
Gruta PL 138 D6
Gruvberget S 103 D13
Gruyères CH 31 B11
Gruža SRB 159 F6
Grūžai LT 135 D8
Grybów PL 145 D2
Gryckebo S 103 E9
Gryfice PL 85 C8
Gryfino D 84 D6
Gryfów Śląski PL 81 D8
Grygov CZ 146 B4
Grylewo PL 85 E12
Gryllefjord N 111 B12
Grynberget S 107 C11
Gryt S 93 C9
Grytan S 106 E7
Grytgöl S 92 B7
Grythyttan S 97 C12
Gryts bruk S 92 B6
Grytsjö S 106 A9
Gryttjom S 99 B8
Gryžliny PL 139 C9
Grzebienisko PL 81 B11
Grzmiąca PL 85 C10
Grzybno PL 84 D6
Grzybno PL 138 D5
Grzymiszew PL 142 B5
Grzywna PL 138 D5
Gschnitz A 72 B3
Gschwandt A 73 A8
Gschwend D 74 E6
Gstaad CH 31 C11
Gsteig CH 31 C11
Guadahortuna E 53 A10
Guadajoz E 51 D8
Guadalajara E 47 C6
Guadalaviar E 47 D9
Guadalcanal E 51 C8
Guadalcázar E 53 A7
Guadalest E 56 D4
Guadalmez E 54 B3
Guadarrama E 46 C4
Guadassuar E 48 F4
Guadix E 55 E6
Guagno F 37 G9
Guaire IRL 9 C10
Guájar-Faraguit E 53 C9
Gualáv S 88 C6
Gualdo Cattaneo I 62 B3
Gualdo Tadino I 67 F6
Gualtieri I 66 C2
Guarcino I 62 D4
Guarda P 45 C6
Guardamar del Segura E 56 E3
Guardavalle I 59 B9
Guardea I 62 B2
Guardiagrele I 63 C6
Guardia Lombardi I 60 B4
Guardia Perticara I 60 C6
Guardia Piemontese I 60 E6
Guardia Sanframondi I 60 A3
Guardias Viejas E 55 F7
Guardiola de Berguedà E 43 C7
Guardo E 39 C10
Guardramiro E 45 B8
Guareña E 51 B7
Guaro E 53 C7
Guarromán E 54 C5
Guasila I 64 E3
Guastalla I 66 C2
Gubbhögen S 106 C9
Gubbio I 66 F6
Gubbträsk S 107 A13
Guben D 81 C7
Gubin PL 81 C7
Guča SRB 158 F5
Guča Gora BIH 157 D8
Gudar E 48 D3
Gudavac BIH 156 C5
Gudeniki LV 134 C3
Guderup DK 86 F5
Gudhem S 91 C14

Gudhjem DK 89 E7
Gudiena LT 137 D9
Gudinge S 99 A9
Gudme DK 87 E7
Gudmont-Villiers F 26 D3
Gudow D 83 C9
Gudum DK 86 B6
Gudumholm DK 86 B6
Gudvangen N 100 D5
Gudžiūnai LT 134 E7
Guebwiller F 27 E7
Guégon F 22 E6
Güéjar-Sierra E 53 B10
Guémar F 27 D7
Guémené-Penfao F 23 E8
Guémené-sur-Scorff F 22 D5
Guénange F 20 F6
Güeñes E 40 B5
Guenrouet F 23 E8
Guer F 23 E7
Guérande F 22 F7
Guéret F 29 C9
Guérigny F 25 F9
Guerri de la Sal E 33 F8
Güesa E 32 E3
Gueugnon F 30 B5
Gugești RO 161 B10
Güglingen D 27 B10
Guglionesi I 63 D7
Gugutka BG 171 B9
Guia P 44 E3
Guia P 50 E3
Guichen F 23 E8
Guidel F 22 E5
Guide Post GB 5 E13
Guidizzolo I 66 B2
Guidonia-Montecelio I 62 D3
Guiglia I 66 D2
Guignen F 23 E8
Guignes F 25 C8
Guignicourt F 19 F8
Guijo de Coria E 45 D8
Guijo de Galisteo E 45 D8
Guijo de Granadilla E 45 D8
Guijuelo E 45 C9
Guildford GB 15 E7
Guilers F 22 D2
Guilherand F 30 F6
Guilhofrei P 38 E3
Guilhovai P 44 C3
Guillaumes F 36 C5
Guillena E 51 D7
Guillestre F 36 B5
Guilliers F 22 D7
Guillon F 25 E11
Guillos F 32 A4
Guilvinec F 22 E3
Guimarães P 38 F3
Guînes F 15 F12
Guingamp F 22 C5
Guipavas F 22 D3
Guipry F 23 E8
Guisando E 45 D10
Guisborough GB 11 B9
Guiscard F 19 E7
Guise F 19 E8
Guissény F 22 C3
Guissona E 42 D6
Guist GB 15 B10
Guitiriz E 38 B4
Gujan-Mestras F 32 A3
Gulács I 145 G5
Gülbahçe TR 177 C9
Gulbene LV 135 B13
Guldager DK 86 D2
Guldborg DK 84 A1
Gulgamme N 113 B16
Gulianca RO 161 C11
Gülitz D 83 D11
Gullabo S 89 C9
Gullane GB 5 C11
Gullberg S 103 D10
Gullbrandstorp S 87 B11
Gullbranna S 87 B11
Gulleråsen S 103 D9
Gullholmen N 111 C10
Gullön S 109 E15
Gullringen S 92 D7
Gullspång S 91 B15
Gullträsk S 118 B6
Güllübahçe TR 177 D9
Güllüce TR 173 D9
Güllük TR 177 E10
Gullverket N 95 B14
Gulpen NL 183 D7
Gülpınar TR 171 E10
Gulsele S 107 D12
Gulsvik N 95 B11
Gültz D 84 C4
Gülübintsi BG 166 E6
Gülübovo BG 165 E10
Gülübovo BG 166 E6
Gulyantsi BG 160 F5
Gülzow D 83 C12
Gumhöjden S 97 B10
Gumiel de Hizán E 40 E4
Gumiel de Mercado E 40 E4
Gummark S 118 E5
Gummersbach D 21 B9
Gumpelstadt D 79 E7
Gumtow D 83 E12
Gümüşçay TR 173 D7
Gümüşsuyu TR 177 C9
Gümüşyaka TR 173 B9
Gümzovo BG 159 E10
Gunaroš SRB 150 F4
Gundelfingen D 27 D8
Gundelfingen an der Donau D
75 E7
Gundelsheim D 21 F12
Gundershoffen F 27 C8
Gundinci HR 157 B9
Gündoğan TR 173 D8
Gündoğdu TR 173 D10
Güneyli TR 173 C7
Güngörmez TR 173 B8
Gunja HR 157 C10
Gunnarn S 107 A13
Gunnarnes N 113 A14
Gunnarsbyn S 118 B7
Gunnarskog S 97 C8
Gunnarvattnet S 105 C16
Gunnebo S 93 D9
Günstedt D 79 C8
Güntersberge D 79 C8
Guntersblum D 185 E9
Guntersdorf A 77 E10
Günthersleben D 187 B8

Guntramsdorf A 77 F10
Günzburg D 75 F7
Gunzenhausen D 75 D8
Gura-Bicului MD 154 D4
Gura Calitei RO 161 B9
Gura Camencii MD 154 B2
Gura Foii RO 160 D6
Gura Galbenei MD 154 D3
Gurahont RO 151 E9
Gura Humorului RO 153 B7
Gura Ocniței RO 161 D6
Gura Râului RO 152 F3
Gurasada RO 151 F10
Gura Vadului RO 161 C8
Gura Văii RO 153 E9
Gura Vitioarei RO 161 C8
Gurbănești RO 161 E9
Gurghiu RO 152 D5
Guri i Bardhë AL 168 B3
Guri i Zi AL 163 E8
Gurk A 73 C9
Gurkovo BG 166 D5
Gurkovo BG 167 C10
Gürlyano BG 164 E6
Gurrea de Gállego E 41 D10
Gurrë e Madhe AL 168 A3
Gurteen IRL 6 E6
Gușoeni RO 160 D4
Gusow D 80 A6
Guspini I 64 D2
Gussago I 69 B9
Gusselby S 97 C13
Güssing A 149 B6
Gussola I 66 B1
Gußwerk A 148 A4
Gusten D 79 C10
Gusterath D 21 E7
Güstrow D 83 C12
Gusum S 93 C8
Gutach (Schwarzwaldbahn) D
187 E5
Gutau A 77 F7
Gutcher GB 3 D14
Güterfelde D 80 B4
Güterglück D 79 C10
Gütersloh D 17 E10
Guthrie GB 5 B11
Gutorfölde H 149 C7
Gutow D 83 C12
Guttannen CH 70 D6
Guttaring A 73 C10
Gützkow D 84 C4
Guvåg N 110 C8
Güvemalani TR 173 D7
Güvercinlik TR 177 E10
Guxhagen D 78 D5
Güzelbahçe TR 177 C9
Güzelçamli TR 177 D9
Gvardeisk RUS 136 D3
Gvarv N 95 D10
Gvozd HR 148 F5
Gvozdansko HR 156 B5
Gvozd MNE 163 D7
Gwda Wielka PL 85 C11
Gweedore IRL 6 B6
Gwithian GB 12 E4
Gy F 26 F5
Gyál H 150 C3
Gyarmat H 149 B8
Gyékényes H 149 D8
Gyenesdiás H 149 C8
Gyé-sur-Seine F 25 D11
Gyhum D 17 B12
Gyljen S 118 B9
Gylling DK 86 D6
Gymno GR 175 C8
Gyömöre H 149 A9
Gyömrő H 150 C3
Gyöngyös H 150 B4
Gyöngyöspata H 150 B4
Gyönk H 149 C10
Győr H 149 A9
Gyökrőny H 149 C11
Győrság H 149 A9
Győrszemere H 149 A9
Gyõrtelek H 145 H5
Győrújbarát H 149 A9
Győrújfalu H 149 A9
Győrzámoly H 149 A9
Gyrstinge DK 87 E9
Gysinge S 98 B7
Gytheio GR 178 B4
Gyttorp S 97 C12
Gyueshevo BG 164 E5
Gyula H 151 D7
Gyulaháza H 145 G5
Gyulaj H 149 D10
Gyúró H 149 B11
Gzy PL 139 E10

H

Haabneeme EST 131 B9
Haacht B 19 C10
Häädemeeste EST 131 E8
Haaften NL 183 B6
Haag A 77 F9
Haag am Hausruck A 76 F5
Haag in Oberbayern D 75 F11
Haajainen FIN 124 F4
Haaksbergen NL 17 D7
Haaltert B 19 C8
Haanja EST 131 F14
Haapajärvi FIN 123 C14
Haapa-Kimola FIN 127 D15
Haapakoski FIN 115 D3
Haapakoski FIN 124 F8
Haapakumpu FIN 115 D3
Haapalahti FIN 113 E19
Haapamäki FIN 123 C16
Haapamäki FIN 123 D12
Haapamäki FIN 123 F12
Haaparanta FIN 115 E3
Haapavesi FIN 119 F14
Haapsalu EST 130 D7
Haar D 75 F9
Haarajoki FIN 123 F17
Haarajoki FIN 127 E13

Haaraoja FIN 119 F16
Haarasaajo FIN 119 B12
Haarbach D 76 F4
Haarby DK 86 E6
Haaren NL 183 B6
Haarlem NL 16 D3
Haastrecht NL 16 E3
Habaja EST 131 C10
Habartov CZ 75 B12
Habas F 32 C4
Habay-la-Neuve B 19 E12
Häbbersliden S 118 E4
Habiller TR 167 F7
Hablingbo S 93 E12
Habo S 91 D15
Håbol S 91 B10
Habovka SK 147 C9
Habry CZ 77 C8
Habsheim F 27 E7
Hachenburg D 21 C9
Haciaslanlar TR 173 E7
Hacidanişment TR 167 F7
Hacigelen TR 172 D6
Hacıköy TR 172 C6
Hacinas E 40 E5
Hacirahmanli TR 177 B10
Hacivelioba TR 173 D8
Hackås S 102 A8
Hackenheim D 21 E9
Hacketstown IRL 9 C9
Hackleton GB 15 C7
Hacksjö S 107 C11
Hadamar D 21 D10
Hadanberg S 107 D14
Haddebo S 92 B6
Haddington GB 5 D11
Haddiscoe GB 15 B12
Haderslev DK 86 E4
Haderup DK 86 C3
Hadimköy TR 173 B10
Hadleigh GB 15 C10
Hadley GB 10 F7
Hadol F 26 D5
Hadres A 77 E10
Hadsel N 110 C8
Hadsten DK 86 C6
Hadsund DK 86 B6
Hadžići BIH 157 E9
Haelen NL 183 C7
Hafnerbach A 77 F8
Haftersbol S 97 C10
Haga S 98 B8
Hagafoss HR 149 E7
Hagby S 89 B10
Hagebyhöga S 92 C5
Hagen D 17 F8
Hagenbach D 187 C5
Hagenburg D 17 D12
Hagenow D 83 C10
Hagenwerder D 81 D7
Hageri EST 131 C9
Hägerstad S 92 C7
Hagetaubin F 32 C4
I lagctmau F 32 C4
Hagfors S 97 B10
Häggås S 107 C11
Häggdånga S 103 A13
Häggebäcken S 98 B6
Häggenås S 106 E7
Häggnäset S 105 C16
Häggsåsen S 105 E16
Häggsjön S 105 D13
Häggsjövik S 105 D16
Häghig RO 153 F7
Hagley GB 13 A10
Hagondange F 20 F6
Hagsta S 103 E13
Haguenau F 27 C8
Hahausen D 79 C7
Hahnbach D 75 C10
Hahnstätten D 185 D9
Hahót H 149 C7
Haibach D 21 E12
Haibach D 75 D12
Haidmühle D 76 E5
Haiger D 21 C10
Haigerloch D 27 D10
Häijää FIN 127 C9
Hailsham GB 15 F9
Hailuoto FIN 119 D13
Haiming D 76 F3
Haimoo FIN 127 E11
Haina D 75 B8
Haina (Kloster) D 21 B11
Hainburg an der Donau A
77 F11
Hainfeld A 77 F9
Hainichen D 80 E4
Haiterbach D 187 D6
Haitzendorf A 77 F9
Hajala FIN 127 E8
Hajdúböszörmény H 151 B8
Hajdúdorog H 151 B8
Hajdúhadház H 151 B8
Hajdúnánás H 145 H3
Hajdúsámson H 151 B8
Hajdúszoboszló H 151 C7
Hajdúszovát H 151 C7
Hajmáskér H 149 B10
Hajmel AL 163 F8
Hajnáčka SK 147 E9
Hajnoc KS 164 E3
Hajnówka PL 141 E9
Hajós H 150 E3
Hakadal N 95 B13
Håkafot S 105 C16
Hakkenpää FIN 126 D6
Häkkilä FIN 123 E14
Hakokylä FIN 121 E12
Håkøybotn N 111 A16
Hakstabben N 112 C11
Halahora de Sus MD 153 A10
Håland N 94 C4
Halapić BIH 157 D6
Halászi H 146 F4
Halásztelek H 150 C2
Hălăucești RO 153 C9
Halbe D 80 B5
Halbenrain A 148 C5
Hålberg S 109 F14
Halberstadt D 79 C8
Halbjerg DK 90 E7
Halblech D 71 B11
Halbturn A 77 G11
Hălchiu RO 153 F7

Hald DK 86 B4
Hald DK 86 B6
Haldarsvík FO 2 A2
Hald Ege DK 86 C4
Halden N 91 A9
Haldensleben D 79 B9
Hale GB 11 E7
Halen I 183 D6
Halenkov CZ 146 C6
Halenkovice CZ 146 C4
Halesowen GB 13 A10
Halesworth GB 15 C12
Halfing D 72 A5
Halfway IRL 8 E5
Halfweg NL 16 D3
Halhjem N 94 B2
Halič SK 147 E9
Halifax GB 11 D8
Halikko FIN 127 E9
Halimba H 149 B9
Halitpaşa TR 177 C10
Haljala EST 131 C12
Häljarp S 87 D11
Halkia FIN 127 D13
Halkirk GB 3 H10
Halkivaha FIN 127 C9
Halkokumpu FIN 124 F7
Hall S 93 D13
Hälla S 107 D12
Halla-aho FIN 124 C9
Hallabro S 89 C8
Hällabrottet S 92 A6
Halla Heberg S 91 E10
Halland GB 15 F9
Hålland S 105 E14
Hallapuro FIN 123 D12
Hällaryd S 89 C7
Hällbacken S 105 E16
Hällbacken S 109 D12
Hällberga S 98 D7
Hällbo S 103 D11
Hallbodarna S 105 E15
Hällbybrunn S 98 D6
Halle B 19 C9
Halle D 78 C6
Halle NL 183 B8
Halle (Saale) D 79 D10
Halle (Westfalen) D 17 D10
Hällefors S 97 C12
Hälleforsnäs S 93 A9
Hallein A 73 A7
Hällekis S 91 B13
Hällen S 103 E14
Hällen S 105 D16
Hallenberg D 21 B11
Hallencourt F 18 E4
Halle-Neustadt D 79 D10
Hallerndorf D 75 C8
Hällesjö S 103 A11
Hällestad S 92 B7
Hällevadsholm S 91 B10
Hällevik S 88 C7
Hälleviksstrand S 91 C9
Hall-Håxåsen S 106 D8
Hallingby N 95 B12
Hallingeberg S 93 D8
Hällinmäki FIN 124 F9
Hall in Tirol A 72 B3
Hällnäs S 107 C17
Hällnäs S 109 D15
Hällnäs S 109 E13
Hallom S 102 A7
Hallow GB 13 A10
Hällsbäck S 97 B9
Hallsberg S 92 A6
Hällsjö S 107 E13
Hällsta S 98 C9
Hallstahammar S 98 C6
Hallstatt A 73 A8
Hallstavik S 99 B11
Halltorp S 89 C10
Halluin B 19 C7
Hallund DK 86 A6
Hällvik S 109 D14
Hallviken S 106 D8
Hallworthy GB 12 D5
Hälmägel RO 151 E10
Hälmagiu RO 151 E10
Halmeu RO 145 H7
Halmstad S 87 B11
Halna S 92 B4
Halosenniemi FIN 119 D14
Halosenranta FIN 115 E2
Halovo SRB 159 F9
Hals DK 86 B6
Halsa N 104 E4
Halsenbach D 21 D9
Hal'shany BY 137 E13
Hälsingby FIN 122 D7
Hälsjo S 103 C12
Halsøy N 108 E2
Halsskov DK 87 E8
Halstead GB 15 D10
Halsteren NL 16 E2
Halstroff F 20 F6
Halsua FIN 123 D11
Haltern D 17 E8
Halttula FIN 119 C14
Haltwhistle GB 5 F12
Haluna FIN 125 D10
Halvä FIN 129 B11
Halvarsgårdarna S 97 B13
Halver D 17 F9
Halvmämen DK 86 A5
Halwell GB 13 E7
Halže CZ 75 C12
Ham F 19 E7
Hamar N 101 E14
Hamari FIN 119 C14
Hamarøy N 108 C9
Hamarøy N 111 D10
Hambach F 27 B7
Hambergen D 17 B11
Hamble-le-Rice GB 13 D12
Hambrücken D 21 F11
Hambühren D 79 A6
Hamburg D 83 C7
Hamburgsund S 91 B9
Hambye F 23 C9
Hamcearca RO 155 C2
Hämeenkoski FIN 127 C13
Hämeenkyrö FIN 127 B9
Hämeenlinna FIN 127 D11
Hämelhausen D 17 C12
Hameln D 17 D12
Hämerten D 79 A10
Hamica HR 148 E5
Hamidiye TR 167 F9
Hamidiye TR 172 B6
Hamilton GB 5 D8

Hamilton's Bawn GB 7 D9
Hamina FIN 128 D7
Haminalahti FIN 124 E9
Hamit TR 181 C9
Hamitabat TR 173 A7
Hamlagrø N 94 A4
Hamlot N 111 D10
Hamm D 17 E9
Hamm (Sieg) D 185 C8
Hammar S 92 B5
Hammarland FIN 99 B13
Hammarn S 97 C12
Hammarnäs S 105 E16
Hammarsbyn S 102 E5
Hammarstrand S 107 E10
Hammarvika N 104 D5
Hamme B 19 B9
Hammel DK 86 C5
Hammelburg D 74 B6
Hammelev DK 86 E4
Hammelspring D 84 D4
Hamme-Mille B 19 C10
Hammenhög S 88 D6
Hammer N 105 C12
Hammerbrücke D 75 B11
Hammerdal S 106 D8
Hammerfest N 113 B12
Hammershøj DK 86 C5
Hammerum DK 86 C4
Hamminkeln D 17 E7
Hamn N 108 E3
Hamn N 111 B13
Hamna N 114 B8
Hamnavoe GB 3 D14
Hamnavoe GB 3 E14
Hamnbukt N 112 C8
Hamnbukta N 111 B18
Hamneidet N 112 D6
Hamnes N 105 B10
Hamnes N 108 E4
Hamnes N 112 D6
Hamningberg N 114 B9
Hamnøy N 110 E5
Hamnvågnes N 111 B16
Hamoir B 19 D12
Hamois B 19 D11
Hamont B 16 F5
Hampen DK 86 C4
Hampetorp S 92 A7
Håmpjåkk S 116 D4
Hampont F 26 C6
Hampreston GB 13 D11
Hamra S 93 F12
Hamra S 103 C9
Hamrångefjärden S 103 E13
Hamre N 112 C4
Hamry nad Sázavou CZ 77 C9
Ham-sous-Varsberg F 186 C2
Hamstreet GB 15 E10
Hamsund N 111 D10
Ham-sur-Heure B 19 D9
Hamula FIN 123 D16
Hamula FIN 124 D9
Hamzabeyli TR 167 F7
Hanaskog S 88 C6
Hanau D 187 A6
Handbjerg DK 86 C3
Handeloh D 83 D7
Handen S 93 A12
Handest DK 86 B5
Handewitt D 82 A6
Handlová SK 147 D7
Handog S 106 E7
Handöl S 105 E12
Handrabury UA 154 B5
Handrup D 17 C9
Handsjö S 102 B8
Handstein N 108 D4
Handzame B 182 C2
Hanebo S 103 D12
Hanerau-Hademarschen D 82 B6
Hanestad N 101 C13
Hăneşti RO 153 B9
Hangastenmaa FIN 128 B7
Hangelsberg D 80 B5
Hånger S 87 A13
Hangö FIN 127 F8
Hangony H 145 G1
Hangu RO 153 C8
Hangvar S 93 D13
Hanhikoski FIN 115 E2
Hanhimaa FIN 117 C14
Han i Elezit KS 164 E3
Hanikase EST 132 F1
Haniska SK 145 F3
Hankamäki FIN 125 D10
Hankasalem asema FIN 123 F16
Hankasalmi FIN 123 F16
Hankensbüttel D 83 E9
Han Knežica BIH 157 B6
Hanko FIN 127 F8
Hanna PL 141 G9
Hannäs S 93 C8
Hannover D 78 B6
Hannoversch Münden D 78 D6
Hannukainen FIN 117 C11
Hannusperä FIN 119 D15
Hannusranta FIN 121 F10
Hannut B 19 C11
Hanøy N 110 D9
Han-Pijesak BIH 157 D10
Hanshagen D 83 C10
Hańsk Pierwszy PL 141 H8
Hansnes N 112 D4
Hanstedt D 83 D8
Hanstholm DK 86 A3
Han-sur-Nied F 26 C5
Hanušovce nad Topľou SK 145 E4
Hanušovice CZ 77 B11
Hanvec F 22 D3
Haparanda S 119 C12
Hapert NL 183 C6
Häppälä FIN 123 F16
Happburg D 75 D9
Happisburgh GB 15 B12
Haps NL 183 B7
Hapträsk S 118 B4
Hara S 106 E6
Härad S 98 D7
Haradok BY 133 F7
Harads S 118 B5
Häradsbäck S 88 B6
Häradsbygden S 103 E9
Häradshammar S 93 B9
Haradzilavichy Pyershaya BY 133 D4
Haraldseng N 112 B9
Haram N 100 A4
Harang N 104 E6
Harany BY 133 F6
Harasiuki PL 144 C5
Hărău RO 151 F10
Haraudden S 116 E3
Harbachieva BY 133 E6
Harbak N 104 C8
Harbke D 79 B9
Harbo S 98 B8
Harboør DK 86 B2
Harbost GB 2 J4
Harburg (Schwaben) D 75 E8
Harbury GB 13 A12
Hard A 71 C9
Hardbakke N 100 D1
Hardegg A 77 E9
Hardegsen D 78 C6
Hardelot-Plage F 15 F12
Hardenberg NL 17 C7
Harderwijk NL 16 D5
Hardheim D 27 A11
Hardinxveld-Giessendam NL 182 B5
Hardt D 27 D9
Hareid N 100 B4
Harelbeke B 19 C7
Haren NL 17 B7
Haren (Ems) D 17 C8
Hare Street GB 15 D9
Harestua N 95 B13
Harfleur F 23 A12
Harg S 99 B10
Hargesheim D 21 E9
Hargimont B 19 D11
Hargla EST 131 F12
Hargnies F 19 D10
Hargshamn S 99 B10
Harichovce SK 145 F2
Harinkaa FIN 123 E16
Harjakangas FIN 126 B6
Härjäro S 99 D8
Härjåsjön S 102 C7
Harjavalta FIN 126 C7
Harjula FIN 119 C15
Harjumaa FIN 128 B7
Harjunkylä FIN 122 E7
Harjunpää FIN 126 C6
Harju-Risti EST 131 C7
Harka H 149 A7
Härkäjoki FIN 115 D2
Harkakötöny H 150 E4
Harkány H 149 E10
Härkmeri FIN 122 F6
Härkönen FIN 119 C13
Harku EST 131 C9
Hârlău RO 153 C9
Harlech GB 10 F3
Harleston GB 15 C11
Hårlev DK 87 E10
Harlingen NL 16 B4
Harlow GB 15 D9
Harly F 19 E7
Hărman RO 153 F7
Harmånger S 103 C13
Härmänkylä FIN 121 F13
Harmanli TR 173 D9
Härmänmäki FIN 121 F11
Harmannsdorf A 77 F10
Harmelen NL 182 A5
Harmoinen FIN 127 C13
Harmsdorf D 83 C9
Harmston GB 11 E10
Harnes F 18 D6
Härnösand S 103 A14
Haro E 40 C6
Harodz'ki BY 137 E13
Haroldswick GB 3 D15
Haroué F 26 D5
Härpe FIN 127 E14
Harpefoss N 101 C11
Harpenden GB 15 D8
Harplinge S 87 B11
Harpstedt D 17 C11
Harra D 75 B10
Harrachov CZ 81 E8
Harran N 105 B13
Harre DK 86 B3
Harridslev DK 86 C6
Harrietfield GB 5 C9
Harrioja S 119 C11
Harrislee D 82 A6
Harrogate GB 11 D8
Harrsjö S 106 B9
Harrström FIN 122 E6
Harrvik S 107 A10
Harsa S 103 C10
Hårsbäck S 98 C7
Harsefeld D 82 D7
Hârseni RO 152 F6
Hârseşti RO 160 D5
Harsleben D 79 C9
Hårslev DK 86 D6
Hârşova RO 155 D1
Harsprånget S 116 E3
Harstad N 111 C12
Harsum D 78 B6
Harsvik N 104 C8
Harta H 150 D3
Hartberg A 148 B5
Hårte S 103 C13
Hartenholm D 83 C8
Hartha D 80 D3
Harthausen D 21 F10
Hartheim D 27 E8
Hârtieşti RO 160 C6
Hart im Zillertal A 72 B4
Hartkirchen A 76 F5
Hartland GB 12 D6
Hartlepool GB 11 B9
Hartmanice CZ 76 D4
Hartola FIN 127 B15
Harwich GB 15 D11
Harzgerode D 79 C9
Hasanağa TR 173 D10
Hasbuğa TR 173 A8
Haselünne D 17 C8
Hasirciarnavutköy TR 171 B10
Håsjö S 107 F10
Hasköy TR 173 A6
Hasköy TR 177 C9
Haslach an der Mühl A 76 E6
Haslach im Kinzigtal D 27 D9
Hasle CH 70 C5
Hasle DK 88 E7
Haslemere GB 15 E7
Haslev DK 87 E9
Hasloh D 83 C7
Hasløya N 104 E2
Haslund DK 86 C6
Hăşmaş RO 151 D9
Hasparren F 32 D3
Haßbergen D 17 C12
Hassel (Weser) D 17 C12
Hassela S 103 B12
Hassela kyrkby S 103 B12
Hasselfelde D 79 C8
Hasselfors S 92 A5
Hasselt B 19 C11
Hasselt NL 16 C6
Haßfurt D 75 B8
Hassi FIN 127 B13
Hässjö S 103 A14
Haßleben D 79 D9
Haßleben D 84 D5
Hässleholm S 87 C13
Hasslö S 89 C8
Haßloch D 21 F10
Hasslöv S 87 C12
Haßmersheim D 187 C7
Hästbo S 103 E13
Hästholmen S 92 C5
Hastière-Lavaux B 19 D10
Hastings GB 15 F10
Hästnäs S 97 D14
Håstrup DK 86 E6
Hästveda S 87 C13
Hasvåg N 105 C9
Hasvik N 112 C9
Hať CZ 146 B6
Hat' UA 145 G6
Haţeg RO 159 B10
Hatfield GB 11 D10
Hatherleigh GB 12 D6
Hätilä FIN 127 C11
Hatipkışlası TR 181 B7
Hatsola FIN 128 B8
Hattarvík FO 2 A4
Hattem NL 16 D6
Hattersheim am Main D 21 D10
Hattert D 21 C9
Hattfjelldal N 108 E6
Hatting DK 86 D5
Hattingen D 17 F8
Hatton GB 3 L13
Hattstedt D 82 A6
Hattula FIN 127 C11
Hattuvaara FIN 125 E16
Hatulanmäki FIN 124 C8
Hatunkylä FIN 125 D15
Hatvan H 150 B4
Hatzenbühl D 27 B9
Hatzendorf A 148 C6
Hatzfeld (Eder) D 21 C11
Haubourdin F 18 C6
Hauenstein D 186 C4
Haugan N 105 D9
Haugastøl N 94 A7
Hauge N 94 F4
Hauge N 114 E6
Haugen N 110 D7
Haugesund N 94 D2
Haugh of Urr GB 5 F9
Haugland N 108 D5
Haugli N 111 C15
Haugnes N 111 B11
Haugnes N 112 C6
Haugset N 112 D7
Hauho FIN 127 C12
Haukå N 100 C2
Haukela FIN 125 B14
Haukeligrend N 94 C7
Haukijärvi FIN 127 B9
Haukilahti FIN 121 F13
Haukiniemi FIN 121 C13
Haukipudas FIN 119 D14
Haukivaara FIN 125 E15
Haukivuori FIN 124 F8
Haukøy N 111 D11
Haulerwijk NL 16 B6
Haurukylä FIN 119 E15
Haus A 73 B8
Haus N 94 B2
Hausach D 187 E5
Hausen D 75 E11
Hausen bei Würzburg D 187 B9
Häusern D 27 E9
Hausham D 72 A4
Hausjärvi FIN 127 D12
Hauske N 94 D3
Hausleiten A 77 F10
Hausmannstätten A 148 C5
Hautajärvi FIN 115 E6
Hautakylä FIN 121 D10
Hautakylä FIN 123 E12
Haute-Amance F 26 E4
Hautefort F 29 E8
Hauterives F 31 E7
Hauteville-Lompnes F 31 D8
Haut-Fays B 184 D3
Hautmont F 19 D8
Hautomäki FIN 123 E17
Haux F 32 D4
Hauzenberg D 76 E5
Havant GB 14 F7
Havârna RO 153 A9
Havbro DK 86 B4
Havdhem S 93 E12
Hávdna N 113 C15
Havelange B 19 D11
Havelberg D 83 E12
Havelte NL 16 C6
Håven S 103 C9
Haverdal S 87 B11
Haverfordwest GB 12 B5
Haverhill GB 15 C9
Haverlah D 79 B7
Haverö S 103 B9
Haversin B 19 D11
Haverslev DK 86 B5
Håverud S 91 B11
Havířov CZ 146 B6
Havixbeck D 17 E8
Hävla S 92 B7
Havlíčkův Brod CZ 77 C9
Havndal DK 86 B6
Havneby DK 86 E3
Havnebyen DK 87 D8
Havnsø DK 87 D8
Havøysund N 113 A14
Håvra S 103 C10
Havran TR 173 E7
Havrebjerg DK 87 E8
Havsa TR 173 A6
Havsskogen S 99 B11
Havtun N 94 B2
Hawarden GB 10 E5
Hawes GB 11 C7
Hawick GB 5 E11
Hawkhurst GB 15 E10
Hawkinge GB 15 E11
Haxby GB 11 C9
Hayange F 20 F6
Haybes F 184 D2
Haydarli TR 177 D10
Haydere TR 181 A8
Haydon Bridge GB 5 F12
Haydon Wick GB 13 B11
Hayingen D 71 A8
Hayle GB 12 E4
Hay-on-Wye GB 13 A8
Hayrabolu TR 173 B7
Hayton GB 11 D10
Hayvoron UA 154 A5
Haywards Heath GB 15 F8
Hazebrouck F 18 C6
Hazerswoude-Rijndijk NL 182 A5
Haźlach PL 147 B7
Hažlín SK 145 E3
Hazlov CZ 75 B11
Heacham GB 11 F12
Headcorn GB 15 E10
Headford IRL 6 F4
Healeyfield GB 5 F13
Heanor GB 11 E9
Heathfield GB 15 F9
Hebdów PL 143 F9
Hebenhausen (Neu-Eichenberg) D 78 D6
Heberg S 87 B11
Hebertsfelden D 76 F3
Hebnes N 94 D3
Heby S 98 C7
Hèches F 33 D6
Hechingen D 27 D10
Hecho E 32 E4
Hechtel B 19 B11
Hechthausen D 17 A12
Heckelberg D 84 E5
Heckington GB 11 F11
Hedared S 91 D12
Hedberg S 109 F16
Heddesheim D 21 F11
Hédé F 23 D8
Hede S 98 B6
Hede S 102 B6
Hedekas S 91 B10
Hedel NL 16 E4
Hedemora S 97 B14
Heden DK 86 E6
Heden S 102 C4
Heden S 118 C7
Hedenäset S 119 B11
Hedensbyn S 118 B9
Hedensted DK 86 D5
Hedersleben D 79 C9
Hédervár H 146 F4
Hedesunda S 98 B8
Hedeviken S 102 B6
Hedge End GB 13 D12
Hedlunda S 107 B15
Hedmark S 107 B13
Hedsjön S 103 E12
Hee DK 86 C2
Heeg NL 16 C5
Heek D 17 D8
Heel NL 183 C7
Heemsen D 17 C12
Heemskerk NL 16 C3
Heemstede NL 16 D3
Heenvliet NL 182 B4
Heer B 19 D10
Heerde NL 16 D6
Heerenveen NL 16 C5
Heerewaarden NL 183 B6
Heerhugowaard NL 16 C3
Heerlen NL 20 C5
Heers B 19 C11
Heesch NL 16 E5
Heeslingen D 17 B12
Heeßen D 17 D12
Heeswijk NL 16 E4
Heeten NL 183 A8
Heeze NL 16 F5
Heggeli N 111 B13
Heggem N 104 E4
Heggenes N 101 D10
Heggjabygda N 100 C4
Heggland N 90 A5
Heggmoen N 108 B8
Hegra N 105 E10
Hegyeshalom H 146 F4
Hehlen D 78 C5
Heia N 105 C12
Heia N 111 B17
Heide D 82 B6
Heideck D 75 D9
Heidelberg D 21 F11
Heiden D 17 E7
Heidenau D 80 E5
Heidenheim D 75 D8
Heidenheim an der Brenz D 75 E7
Heidenreichstein A 77 E8
Heigenbrücken D 187 A7
Heikendorf D 83 B8
Heikkilä FIN 121 C14
Heikkilä FIN 122 F7
Heiland N 90 B4
Heilbronn D 27 B11
Heilbrunn A 148 B5
Heiligenberg D 27 E11
Heiligenfelde D 83 E10
Heiligenhafen D 83 B9
Heiligenhaus D 17 F7
Heiligenkreuz am Waasen A 148 C5
Heiligenkreuz im Lafnitztal A 148 C6
Heiligenstadt Heilbad D 79 D7
Heiligenstedten D 82 C6
Heiloo NL 16 C3
Heilsbronn D 75 D8
Heiltz-le-Maurupt F 25 C12
Heim N 104 E6
Heimbach D 21 E8
Heimbuchenthal D 187 B7
Heimdal N 100 E3
Heimdal N 104 E8
Heimertingen D 71 A10
Heimseta N 100 C3
Heimsheim D 187 D6
Heinade D 78 C6
Heinämaa FIN 127 D13
Heinämäki FIN 121 F12
Heinämäki FIN 123 D17
Heinävaara FIN 125 E14
Heinävesi FIN 125 F11
Heinebach (Alheim) D 78 D6
Heinersbrück D 81 C7
Heinersdorf D 80 B6
Heinersreuth D 75 C10
Heinijärvi FIN 119 E14
Heinijoki FIN 126 D7
Heiningen D 79 B8
Heinisuo FIN 119 C16
Heinkenszand NL 16 F1
Heinlahti FIN 128 E6
Heino NL 183 A8
Heinola FIN 127 C15
Heinolan kirkonkylä FIN 127 C15
Heinolanperä FIN 119 F14
Heinoniemi FIN 125 F13
Heinsberg D 20 B6
Heinsen D 78 C5
Heinsnes N 105 B12
Heisingen D 183 C10
Heistadmoen N 95 C11
Heist-op-den-Berg B 19 B10
Heitersheim D 27 E8
Heituinlahti FIN 128 C8
Hejls DK 86 E5
Hejnice CZ 81 E8
Hejnsvig DK 86 D4
Hejőpapi H 145 H2
Hejsager DK 86 E5
Hekelgem B 19 C9
Hel PL 138 A6
Helbra D 79 C9
Helchteren B 183 C6
Heldburg D 75 B8
Heldenbergen D 21 D11
Heldrungen D 79 D9
Helechal E 51 B9
Helegiu RO 153 E9
Helensburgh GB 4 C7
Helfenberg A 76 E6
Helgenes N 110 C9
Helgeroa N 90 B6
Helgum S 107 E11
Hell N 105 E9
Hella N 100 D5
Helland N 104 E5
Helland N 111 D11
Hellanmaa FIN 122 D9
Hellarmo N 109 B10
Helle N 90 B5
Hellebæk DK 87 C11
Hellefjord N 113 B11
Hellendoorn NL 183 A8
Hellenthal D 20 D6
Hellenurme EST 131 E12
Hellesøy N 100 E1
Hellested DK 87 E10
Hellesvik N 104 D5
Hellesylt N 100 B5
Hellevad DK 86 E4
Hellevoetsluis NL 16 E2
Helligskogen N 112 E6
Hellín E 55 B9
Hellingly GB 15 F9
Hellnes N 112 C6
Hellsö FIN 126 F4
Hellvi S 93 D13
Hellvik N 94 F3
Helmbrechts D 75 B10
Helme EST 131 E11
Helmond NL 16 F5
Helmsdale GB 3 J9
Helmsley GB 11 C9
Helmstadt D 74 C6
Helmstedt D 79 B9
Heľpa SK 147 D9
Helppi FIN 117 D13
Helpringham GB 11 F11
Helse D 82 C6
Helsingborg S 87 C11
Helsinge DK 87 C10
Helsingfors FIN 127 E12
Helsingør DK 87 C11
Helsinki FIN 127 E12
Helstad N 105 A12
Helston GB 12 E4
Heltermaa EST 130 D6
Heltersberg D 21 F9
Helvaci TR 177 B9
Helvécia H 150 D4
Helvoirt NL 183 B6
Hem DK 86 B3
Hem F 182 D2
Hemau D 75 D10
Hemavan S 108 E9
Hemeiuş RO 153 D9
Hemel Hempstead GB 15 D8
Hemer D 185 B8
Hemfjäll S 109 E12
Hemfjällstangen S 102 D5
Hemhofen D 75 C8
Hemling S 107 D15
Hemme D 82 B6
Hemmet DK 86 D2
Hemmingen D 78 B6
Hemmingen S 107 B17
Hemmingsmark S 118 D6
Hemmoor D 17 A12
Hemnesberget N 108 D6
Hemnestad N 111 C11
Hempnall GB 15 B11
Hempstead GB 15 C9
Hemsbach D 21 E11
Hemsbünde D 82 D6
Hemsby GB 15 B12
Hemse S 93 E12
Hemsedal N 101 E9
Hemsjö S 107 D14
Hemslingen D 82 D7
Hemsloh D 17 C11
Hemsö S 103 A15
Hemyock GB 13 D8
Henån S 91 C10
Hénanbihen F 23 C7
Henarejos E 47 E10
Hencida H 151 C8
Hendaye F 32 D2
Hendon GB 15 D8
Hengelo NL 16 D6
Hengelo NL 17 D7
Hengersberg D 76 E4
Hengevelde NL 183 A9
Henggart CH 27 E10
Hengoed GB 13 B8
Hénin-Beaumont F 18 D6
Henley-on-Thames GB 15 D7
Hennan S 103 B10
Henndorf am Wallersee A 73 A7
Hennebont F 22 E5
Hennef (Sieg) D 21 C8
Hennes N 110 C9
Henne Stationsby DK 86 D2
Hennezel F 26 D5
Hennickendorf D 80 B4
Hennigsdorf Berlin D 80 A4
Henningskälen S 106 D8
Henningsvær N 110 D7
Hennseid N 90 A5
Hennset N 104 E4
Hennstedt D 82 B6
Hennweiler D 21 E8
Henrichemont F 25 F8
Henryków PL 81 E12
Henrykowo PL 139 B9
Henstridge GB 13 D10
Hepola FIN 119 C13
Heppen B 183 C6
Heppenheim (Bergstraße) D 21 E11
Herálec CZ 77 C8
Herálec CZ 77 C9
Herbault F 24 E5
Herbertingen D 27 D11
Herbertstown IRL 8 C6
Herbés E 42 F3
Herbeumont B 184 E3
Herbignac F 23 F7
Herbolzheim D 27 D8
Herborn D 21 C10
Herbrechtingen D 75 E7
Herbstein D 21 C12
Herby PL 142 E6
Herceghalom H 149 A11
Herceg-Novi MNE 162 E6
Hercegovac HR 149 E8
Hercegszántó H 150 F2
Herdecke D 17 F8
Herdorf D 21 C9
Hereclean RO 151 C11
Heréd H 150 B4
Hereford GB 13 A9
Héreg H 149 A11
Herencia E 46 F6
Herend H 149 B9
Herent B 19 C10
Herentals B 19 B10
Herenthout B 182 C5
Hérépian F 34 C5
Herford D 17 D11
Hergatz D 71 B9
Hergiswil CH 70 D6
Herguijuela E 45 F9
Héric F 23 F8
Héricourt F 27 E6
Hérimoncourt F 27 F6
Heringen (Helme) D 79 D8
Heringen (Werra) D 79 E7
Heringsdorf D 83 B10
Heringsdorf, Seebad D 84 C6
Heriot GB 5 D11
Herisau CH 27 F11
Hérisson F 29 B11
Herk-de-Stad B 19 C11
Herkenbosch NL 183 C8
Herkingen NL 182 B4
Herleshausen D 79 D7
Herlev DK 87 D10
Herlufmagle DK 87 E9
Herm F 32 C3
Hermagor A 73 C7
Hermannsburg D 83 E8
Hermanovce SK 145 E3
Hermanowice PL 144 D6
Hermansverk N 100 D5
Heřmanův Městec CZ 77 C9
Herment F 29 D11
Hermersberg D 186 C4
Hermeskeil D 21 E7
Hermisende E 39 E6
Hermsdorf D 79 E10
Hernád H 150 C3
Hernádnémeti H 145 G2
Hernani E 32 D2
Hernansancho E 46 C3
Herne B 19 C9
Herne D 17 E8
Herne Bay GB 15 E11
Herning DK 86 C3
Heroldsbach D 75 C8
Héron B 19 C11
Hérouville-St-Clair F 23 B11
Herøy N 100 B3
Herpf D 79 E7
Herrala FIN 127 D13
Herramélluri E 40 C5
Herräng S 99 B11
Herré F 32 C5
Herre N 90 A6
Herrenberg D 27 C10
Herrera E 53 B7
Herrera del Duque E 45 F10
Herrera de los Navarros E 42 E1
Herrera de Pisuerga E 40 C3
Herrería E 47 C9
Herreruela E 45 F7
Herrestad S 91 C10
Herrieden D 75 D8
Herringbotn N 108 E6
Herrlisheim F 186 D4
Herrljunga S 91 C13
Herrnhut D 81 D7
Herrö S 102 B7
Herrsching am Ammersee D 75 G9
Herrskog S 103 A15
Herrvik S 93 E13
Herry F 25 F8
Hersbruck D 75 C9
Herschbach D 21 C9
Herscheid D 21 B9
Herschweiler-Pettersheim D 186 C3
Herselt B 19 B10
Herslev DK 86 D5
Herstal B 19 C12
Herstmonceux GB 15 F9
Herston GB 3 H11
Herten D 17 E8
Hertford GB 15 D8
Hertník SK 145 E3
Hertsa UA 153 A8
Hertsånger S 118 F6
Hertsjö S 103 D11
Herve B 19 C12
Hervik N 94 D3
Herwijnen NL 183 B6
Herzberg D 80 C4
Herzberg D 83 C11
Herzberg D 84 E3
Herzberg am Harz D 79 C7
Herzebrock-Clarholz D 17 E10
Herzele B 19 C8
Herzfelde D 80 B5
Herzhorn D 17 A12
Herzlake D 17 C9
Herzogenaurach D 75 C8
Herzogenbuchsee CH 27 F8
Herzogenburg A 77 F9
Herzogenrath D 183 D8
Herzsprung D 83 D12
Hesdin F 18 D5
Hesel D 17 B9
Hesjeberg N 111 C13
Hesjestranda N 100 A6
Heskestad N 94 F4
Hespérange L 20 E6
Heßdorf D 75 C8
Hesselager DK 87 E7
Hessen D 79 B8
Hessfjorden N 112 D3
Heßheim D 21 E10
Hessisch Lichtenau D 78 D6
Hessisch Oldendorf D 17 D12
Hest N 100 D3
Hestenesøyri N 100 C4
Hestnes N 104 D5
Hestøy N 108 E3
Hestra S 91 E14
Hestra S 92 D6
Hestvik N 105 B10
Hestvika N 104 D6
Heswall GB 10 E5
Hetekylä FIN 119 D17
Hetés H 149 D9
Hethersett GB 15 B11
Hetlingen D 82 C7
Hettange-Grande F 186 C1
Hettenleidelheim D 186 B5
Hettenshausen D 75 E10
Hettingen D 27 D11
Hetton GB 11 C7
Hettstedt D 79 C10
Hetzerath D 21 E7
Heubach D 187 D8
Heuchelheim D 21 C11
Heuchin F 18 D5
Heudicourt-sous-les-Côtes F 26 C4
Heukelum NL 16 E4
Heusden B 19 B11
Heusden NL 183 B6
Heusenstamm D 21 D11
Heustreu D 75 B7
Heusweiler D 186 C2
Heves H 150 B5
Hévíz H 149 C8
Hevlín CZ 77 E10
Hexham GB 5 F12
Heyrieux F 31 D7
Heysham GB 10 C6
Heythuysen NL 19 B12
Heywood GB 11 D7
Hida RO 151 C11
Hidas H 149 D10
Hidasnémeti H 145 G3
Hiddenhausen D 17 D11
Hiddensee D 84 A4
Hidirköylü TR 177 D10
Hidişelu de Sus RO 151 D9
Hieflau A 73 A10
Hiendelaencina E 47 B7
Hiersac F 28 D5
Hietakangas FIN 115 D3
Hietama FIN 123 E15
Hietanen FIN 117 D11
Hietanen FIN 128 B7
Hietaniemi FIN 115 D6
Hietaniemi FIN 121 B11
Hietaperä FIN 121 F13
Higham Ferrers GB 15 C7
Highampton GB 12 D6
High Bentham GB 10 C6
Highbridge GB 13 C9
Highclere GB 13 C12
High Halden GB 15 E10
High Hawsker GB 11 C10
High Hesket GB 5 F11
High Lorton GB 5 F10
Highnam GB 13 B10
Highworth GB 13 B11
High Wycombe GB 15 D7
Higuera de Arjona E 53 A9
Higuera de la Serena E 51 B8
Higuera de la Sierra E 51 D7
Higuera de Llerena E 51 C8
Higuera de Vargas E 51 C6
Higuera la Real E 51 C6
Higueruela E 55 B10
Higueruelas E 48 E3
Hihnavaara FIN 115 D4
Hiidenkylä FIN 123 C15
Hiidenlahti FIN 125 E10
Hiilikumpu FIN 119 C15
Hiirikylä FIN 125 C10
Hiirola FIN 128 B7
Hiisijärvi FIN 121 F12
Híjar E 42 E3
Hikiä FIN 127 D12
Hilbersdorf D 80 E4
Hilchenbach D 21 C10
Hildburghausen D 75 B8
Hilden D 21 B7
Hilders D 79 E7
Hilderthorpe GB 11 C11
Hildesheim D 78 B6
Hilgertshausen D 75 F9
Hilişeu-Horia RO 153 A8
Hiliuţi MD 153 B10
Hillared S 91 D13
Hille D 17 D11
Hille S 103 E13
Hillebola S 99 B9
Hillegom NL 16 D3
Hillerød DK 87 D10
Hillerse D 79 B7
Hillerslev DK 86 A3
Hillerslev DK 86 E6
Hillerstorp S 88 A5
Hilleshamn N 111 C13
Hillesheim D 21 D7
Hillesøy N 111 A15
Hillevik S 103 E13
Hilli FIN 123 C11
Hillilä FIN 123 B11
Hill of Fearn GB 3 K9
Hillosensalmi FIN 128 C6
Hillsand S 106 C8
Hillsborough GB 7 D10
Hillside GB 5 B12
Hillswick GB 3 E14
Hilltown GB 7 D10
Hilpoltstein D 75 D9
Hilsenheim F 186 E4
Hilton GB 11 F8
Hiltpoltstein D 75 C9
Hiltula FIN 129 B9
Hilvarenbeek NL 183 C6
Hilversum NL 16 D4
Himalansaari FIN 128 C8
Himanka FIN 123 B11
Himarë AL 168 D2
Himberg A 77 F10
Himbergen D 83 D9
Himesháza H 149 D11
Himma EST 131 F14
Himmaste EST 131 E14
Himmelberg A 73 C9
Himmelpforten D 17 A12
Hînceşti MD 154 D3
Hinckley GB 11 F9
Hindås S 91 D11
Hindelang D 71 B10
Hindenburg D 83 E11

Hinderwell GB 11 B10
Hindhead GB 15 E7
Hindley GB 10 D6
Hindon GB 13 C10
Hindrem N 104 D8
Hinganmaa FIN 117 D15
Hingham GB 15 B10
Hinnerjöki FIN 126 C6
Hinnerup DK 86 C6
Hinneryd S 87 B13
Hinojal E 45 E8
Hinojales E 51 C6
Hinojares E 55 D7
Hinojasas de Calatrava E 54 B4
Hinojos E 51 E7
Hinojosa E 47 B9
Hinojosa de Duero E 45 C7
Hinojosa de Jarque E 42 F2
Hinojosa del Duque E 51 B9
Hinojosa del Valle E 51 C7
Hinojosa de San Vicente E 46 D3
Hinova RO 159 D10
Hinte D 17 B8
Hinterhermsdorf D 80 E6
Hinternah D 75 A8
Hinterrhein CH 71 D8
Hintersee A 73 A7
Hintersee D 84 C6
Hinterweidenthal D 186 C4
Hinterzarten D 27 E9
Hinthaara FIN 127 E13
Hinwil CH 27 F10
Hinx F 32 C4
Hippolytushoef NL 16 C3
Hîrbovăț MD 154 C2
Hîrjauca MD 154 C2
Hirka TR 181 B9
Hirnyk UA 144 C9
Hirrlingen D 27 D10
Hirschaid D 75 C9
Hirschau D 75 C10
Hirschberg D 75 B10
Hirschfeld D 80 D5
Hirschhorn (Neckar) D 187 C6
Hirsilä FIN 127 B11
Hirsingue F 27 E7
Hirson F 19 E9
Hîrtop MD 154 D3
Hîrtopul Mare MD 154 C3
Hirtshals DK 90 D6
Hirvas FIN 119 B14
Hirvaskoski FIN 120 D9
Hirvasperä FIN 119 E13
Hirvasvaara FIN 115 E5
Hirvelä FIN 119 D16
Hirvelä FIN 121 F14
Hirvensalmi FIN 128 B6
Hirviäkuru FIN 115 D1
Hirvihaara FIN 127 D13
Hirvijoki FIN 123 E10
Hirvikylä FIN 123 F9
Hirvilahti FIN 124 D8
Hirvineva FIN 119 E14
Hirvivaara FIN 121 E13
Hirvlax FIN 122 D8
Hirwaun GB 13 B7
Hirzenhain D 21 D12
Hisarönü TR 181 C8
Hishult S 87 C12
Hissjön S 122 C4
Histon GB 15 C9
Hita E 47 C6
Hitchin GB 15 D8
Hitis FIN 126 F8
Hittarp S 87 C11
Hittisau A 71 C9
Hitzacker D 83 D10
Hitzendorf A 148 B4
Hitzhusen D 83 C7
Hiukkajoki FIN 129 B12
Hiyche UA 144 C8
Hjäggsjö S 122 C3
Hjallerup DK 86 A6
Hjältevad S 92 D6
Hjärnarp S 87 C11
Hjärsås S 88 C6
Hjärtum S 91 C11
Hjarup DK 86 E4
Hjelle N 100 C6
Hjellestad N 94 B2
Hjellsand N 110 C8
Hjelmeland N 94 D4
Hjelset N 100 A7
Hjerkinn N 101 B11
Hjerm DK 86 C3
Hjo S 92 C4
Hjordkær DK 86 E4
Hjørring DK 90 E7
Hjorted S 93 D8
Hjortkvarn S 92 B6
Hjortsberga S 88 B6
Hjørungavåg N 100 B4
Hjuvik S 91 D10
Hlavani UA 154 F4
Hlebine HR 149 D7
Hligeni MD 154 B3
Hlinaia MD 153 A10
Hlinaia MD 154 C4
Hlinaia MD 154 D5
Hliník nad Hronom SK 147 D7
Hlinné SK 145 F4
Hlinsko CZ 77 C9
Hlohovec SK 146 E5
Hlubočky CZ 146 B4
Hluboká nad Vltavou CZ 77 D6
Hlučín CZ 146 B6
Hlyboka UA 153 A7
Hlybokaye BY 133 F3
Hlyboke UA 155 B5
Hnatkiv UA 154 A2
Hněvotín CZ 77 C12
Hniezdné SK 145 E2
Hnizdychiv UA 145 E9
Hnojník CZ 147 B7
Hnúšťa SK 147 D9
Hobol H 149 D9
Hobøl N 95 C13
Hobro DK 86 B5
Hoburg S 93 F12
Hoçë e Qytetit KS 163 E10
Hoceni RO 153 D12
Hochdonn D 82 B6
Hochdorf CH 27 F9
Hochdorf D 71 A9
Hochfelden F 27 C8
Höchheim D 75 B7
Hochspeyer D 186 C4
Hochstadt (Pfalz) D 187 C5
Höchstadt an der Aisch D 75 C8
Höchstädt an der Donau D 75 E8
Hochstetten-Dhaun D 21 E8
Höchst im Odenwald D 187 B6
Hoçisht AL 168 C4
Hockenheim D 187 C6
Hoczew PL 145 E5
Hodac RO 152 D5
Hodalen N 101 B14
Hoddesdon GB 15 D8
Hodejov SK 147 E10
Hodenhagen D 82 E7
Hodkovice nad Mohelkou CZ 81 E8
Hódmezővásárhely H 150 E5
Hodnet GB 10 F6
Hodod RO 151 C11
Hodonice CZ 77 E10
Hodonín CZ 77 E12
Hodoșa RO 152 D5
Hodruša-Hámre SK 147 E7
Hodsager DK 86 C3
Hodyszewo PL 141 E7
Hoek NL 16 F1
Hoek van Holland NL 16 E2
Hoem N 104 F4
Hoenderloo NL 183 A7
Hœnheim F 186 D4
Hoensbroek NL 19 C12
Hœrdt F 186 D4
Hoeselt B 19 C11
Hoevelaken NL 16 D4
Hoeven NL 16 E3
Hof D 21 C10
Hof D 75 B10
Hof N 95 C12
Hofbieber D 78 E6
Hoffstad N 104 C8
Hofgeismar D 21 B12
Hofheim am Taunus D 21 D10
Hofheim in Unterfranken D 75 B8
Hofles N 105 B11
Hofors S 98 A6
Hofsøy N 111 B13
Hofterup S 87 D11
Höganäs S 87 C11
Högås S 108 E9
Högbacka S 103 D12
Högbo S 103 E12
Högboda S 97 C9
Högbränna S 109 F15
Högen S 103 C13
Högfors S 97 B15
Högfors S 97 C13
Hoghilag RO 152 E5
Hoghiz RO 152 F6
Høgild DK 86 C3
Högland S 107 B9
Höglekardallen S 105 E15
Høgli N 111 B14
Höglunda S 107 E9
Hogosht KS 164 D4
Högrun S 105 D16
Högsåra FIN 126 F7
Högsäter S 91 B11
Högsäter S 96 C6
Högsäter S 97 D8
Högsby S 89 A10
Høgset N 104 F3
Högsjö S 92 A7
Högsjö S 103 A14
Hogstad S 92 C6
Hogstorp S 91 C10
Högträsk S 116 E5
Högvålen S 102 B4
Hőgyész H 149 C10
Hohberg D 186 E4
Hohen-Altheim D 75 E8
Hohenaspe D 82 C7
Hohenau D 76 E5
Hohenau an der March A 77 E11
Hohenberg A 77 G9
Hohenbocka D 80 D6
Hohenbucko D 80 C4
Hohenburg D 75 D10
Hohendorf D 84 B5
Hoheneich A 77 E8
Hohenems A 71 C9
Hohenfels D 75 D10
Hohenfurch D 71 B11
Hohengöhren D 79 A11
Hohenhameln D 79 B7
Hohenkammer D 75 F10
Hohenkirchen D 17 A9
Höhenkirchen-Siegertsbrunn D 75 F10
Hohenleuben D 79 E11
Hohenlockstedt D 82 C7
Hohenmocker D 84 C4
Hohenmölsen D 79 D11
Hohennauen D 83 E12
Hohenpeißenberg D 71 B12
Hohenroth D 75 B7
Hohensaaten D 84 E6
Hohenseeden D 79 B11
Hohenstein-Ernstthal D 79 E12
Hohenthann D 75 E11
Hohenthurm D 79 C11
Hohen Wangelin D 83 C12
Hohenwart D 75 E9
Hohenwarth D 76 D3
Hohenwestedt D 82 B7
Höhn D 21 C9
Hohn D 82 B7
Hohne D 79 A7
Hohnhorst D 17 D12
Hohnstorf (Elbe) D 83 D9
Höhr-Grenzhausen D 21 D9
Hohwacht (Ostsee) D 83 B9
Hoikankylä FIN 124 E7
Hoikka FIN 121 E12
Hoisdorf D 83 C8
Hoisko FIN 123 D11
Højby DK 86 E6
Højby DK 87 D9
Højer DK 86 F3
Højmark DK 86 C2
Højslev DK 86 B4
Højslev Stationsby DK 86 B4
Hok S 92 D4
Hökåsen S 98 C7
Hökerum S 91 D13
Hökhult S 91 A13
Hökhuvud S 99 B10
Hokka FIN 128 B6
Hokkaskylä FIN 123 E12
Hokksund N 95 C11
Hokland N 111 C11
Hökmark S 118 F6
Hökön S 88 C6
Hol N 101 E8
Hol N 111 C11
Holand N 110 D9
Holandsvika N 108 E5
Holasovice CZ 142 G4
Holbæk DK 86 B6
Holbæk DK 87 D9
Holbeach GB 11 F12
Holboca RO 153 C11
Holbøl DK 86 F4
Holbrook GB 15 D11
Holdorf D 17 C10
Holeby DK 83 A10
Hølen N 95 C13
Holešov CZ 146 C5
Holevik N 100 D1
Holguera E 45 E8
Holíč SK 77 E12
Holice CZ 77 B9
Höljes S 102 E4
Holkestad N 110 E8
Holkonkylä FIN 123 E11
Hollabrunn A 77 E10
Hollandscheveld NL 17 C7
Hollange B 19 E12
Hollås N 105 C11
Holle D 79 B7
Høllen N 90 C2
Hollenbach D 75 F9
Hollenbek D 83 C9
Hollenegg A 73 C11
Hollenstedt D 82 D7
Hollenstein an der Ybbs A 73 A10
Hollern-Twielenfleth D 82 C7
Hollfeld D 75 C9
Hollingstedt D 82 B6
Hollington GB 15 F10
Hollingworth GB 11 E8
Hollóháza H 145 F3
Hollola FIN 127 D14
Hollum NL 16 B5
Hollybush GB 4 E7
Hollyford IRL 8 C6
Hollywood IRL 7 F9
Holm D 82 C7
Holm DK 86 E5
Holm N 105 A12
Holm N 110 C9
Holm S 103 A12
Holm S 107 E13
Hol'ma UA 154 B5
Holmajärvi S 111 E18
Holme-Olstrup DK 87 E9
Holme-on-Spalding-Moor GB 11 D10
Holmestrand N 95 D12
Holmfirth GB 11 D8
Holmfors S 118 D4
Holmisperä FIN 123 D14
Holmsjö S 89 C9
Holmsjö S 107 A14
Holmsjö S 107 D12
Holmsund S 122 C4
Holmsvattensel S 118 B6
Holmsveden S 103 D12
Holmträsk S 107 B16
Hölö S 93 A11
Holod RO 151 D9
Hołodowska PL 144 C7
Holoșnița MD 153 A12
Holoubkov CZ 76 C5
Holovets'ko UA 145 E6
Holovne UA 141 H10
Holsbybrunn S 92 E6
Holsljunga S 91 E12
Holsta EST 131 F14
Holstebro DK 86 C3
Holsted DK 86 D3
Hölstein CH 27 F8
Holsworthy GB 12 D6
Holt GB 10 E6
Holt GB 15 B11
Holt N 111 B16
Holt N 111 B17
Holte DK 87 D10
Holten NL 17 D6
Holtet N 102 E3
Holtgast D 17 A9
Holthusen D 83 C10
Holtsee D 83 B7
Holungen D 79 D7
Holwerd NL 16 B5
Holycross IRL 9 C7
Holyhead GB 10 E2
Holywell GB 7 D7
Holywell GB 10 E5
Holywood GB 4 F5
Holzappel D 185 D8
Holzen D 78 C6
Holzgerlingen D 187 D7
Holzhausen an der Haide D 21 D9
Holzheim D 21 D11
Holzheim D 75 E8
Holzheim D 75 E8
Holzheim D 75 F7
Holzkirchen D 72 A4
Holzminden D 21 A12
Holzthaleben D 79 D8
Holzweißig D 79 C11
Holzwickede D 17 E9
Hom DK 87 E9
Homberg (Efze) D 21 B12
Homberg (Ohm) D 21 C11
Hombourg-Budange F 186 C1
Hombourg-Haut F 186 C2
Homburg D 21 F8
Homécourt F 20 F5
Homersfield GB 15 C11
Homesh AL 168 A3
Hommelstø N 108 F4
Hommelvik N 105 E9
Hommersåk N 94 E3
Homna S 103 D10
Homocea RO 153 E10
Homokmégy H 150 E3
Homokszentgyörgy H 149 D9
Homoroade RO 151 B11
Homorod RO 152 E6
Homrogd H 145 G2
Homyel' BY 133 F5
Hondarribia E 32 D2
Hondón de las Nieves E 56 E3
Hondón de los Frailes E 56 E3
Hondschoote F 18 C6
Hône I 68 B4
Hønefoss N 95 B12
Honfleur F 23 B12
Høng DK 87 D8
Honiton GB 13 D8
Honkajoki FIN 122 G8
Honkakoski FIN 126 B7
Honkakylä FIN 122 E9
Honkilahti FIN 126 D7
Honley GB 11 D8
Honningsvåg N 100 B2
Honningsvåg N 113 B16
Hönö S 91 D10
Honoratka PL 142 B5
Honrubia E 47 E8
Honrubia de la Cuesta E 40 F4
Hønseby N 113 B11
Hontacillas E 47 E8
Hontalbilla E 40 F3
Hontanaya E 47 E7
Hontianske Nemce SK 147 E7
Hontoria de la Cantera E 40 D4
Hontoria del Pinar E 40 E5
Hontoria de Valdearados E 40 E4
Hoofddorp NL 16 D3
Hoogerheide NL 16 F2
Hoogersmilde NL 16 C6
Hoogeveen NL 17 C6
Hoogezand-Sappemeer NL 17 B7
Hoogkarspel NL 16 C4
Hoog-Keppel NL 183 B8
Hoogkerk NL 17 B6
Hoogland NL 183 A6
Hoogstede D 17 C7
Hoogstraten B 16 F3
Hoogvliet NL 16 E2
Hook GB 11 D10
Hook GB 14 E7
Hooksiel D 17 A10
Höör S 87 D13
Hoorn NL 16 C4
Hoornaar NL 182 B5
Hopârta RO 152 E3
Hope GB 10 E5
Hope N 100 E3
Hopeman GB 3 K10
Hopen N 111 E10
Hopfgarten im Brixental A 72 B5
Hopfgarten in Defereggen A 72 C6
Hopland N 100 C4
Hoppstädten D 21 E8
Hoppula FIN 115 F2
Hopseidet N 113 B20
Hopsten D 17 D9
Hopton GB 15 B12
Hoptonheath GB 13 A9
Hoptrup DK 86 E4
Horam GB 15 F9
Horažďovice CZ 76 D5
Horb am Neckar D 27 D10
Horbova UA 153 A8
Hörbranz A 71 B9
Hørby DK 90 E7
Hörby S 87 D13
Horcajo de las Torres E 45 B10
Horcajo de los Montes E 46 F3
Horcajo de Santiago E 47 E7
Horcajo Medianero E 45 C10
Horda N 94 C5
Horda S 88 A6
Hörde D 185 B7
Horden GB 11 B9
Hordum DK 86 B3
Horea RO 151 E10
Horeb GB 12 A6
Horești MD 153 C11
Horezu RO 160 C3
Horgen CH 27 F10
Horgenzell D 71 B9
Horgești RO 153 E10
Horgoš SRB 150 E4
Horia RO 153 D9
Horia RO 155 C2
Horia RO 155 D2
Hořice CZ 77 B9
Horinchove UA 145 G7
Horitschon A 149 A7
Horjul SLO 73 D9
Horka D 81 D7
Hôrka SK 145 E1
Hörken S 97 B12
Horley GB 15 E8
Hörlitz D 80 C5
Hormakumpu FIN 117 C14
Hormilla E 40 D6
Horn A 77 E9
Horn N 95 A12
Horn N 108 E3
Horn S 92 D7
Hornachos E 51 B7
Hornachuelos E 51 D9
Horná Kraľová SK 146 E5
Horná Potôň SK 146 E4
Horná Streda SK 146 D5
Horná Štubňa SK 147 D7
Horná Súča SK 146 D5
Horná Ves SK 146 D6
Hornbach D 21 F8
Horn-Bad Meinberg D 17 E11
Hornbæk DK 87 C10
Hornburg D 79 B8
Hornby GB 10 C6
Horncastle GB 11 E11
Horndal N 109 A10
Horndal S 98 B6
Horndean GB 14 F6
Horne DK 86 D3
Horne DK 86 E6
Horne DK 90 D6
Horneburg D 82 C7
Hörnefors S 122 C3
Horné Obdokovce SK 146 E6
Horné Orešany SK 146 E4
Horné Saliby SK 146 E5
Horné Srnie SK 146 C6
Horní Bečva CZ 146 C6
Horní Benešov CZ 146 B5
Horní Beřkovice CZ 76 B6
Horní Cerekev CZ 77 D8
Horní Jelení CZ 77 B10
Horní Jiřetín CZ 80 E5
Horní Lideč CZ 146 C6
Horní Maršov CZ 81 E9
Horní Moštěnice CZ 146 C4
Hornindal N 100 C5
Hørning DK 86 C6
Horní Planá CZ 76 E6
Horní Slavkov CZ 75 B12
Horní Štěpánov CZ 77 C11
Horní Stropnice CZ 77 E7
Horní Suchá CZ 146 B6
Hornmyr S 107 C14
Hornnäs S 97 B9
Hornnes N 90 B2
Hornön S 103 A14
Hornos E 55 C7
Hornow D 81 C7
Hornoy-le-Bourg F 18 E4
Hornsea GB 11 D11
Hörnsjö S 107 D17
Hornslet DK 86 C6
Hornstorf D 83 C11
Hornsyld DK 86 D5
Hörnum D 82 A4
Hornum DK 86 B4
Horný Bar SK 146 F4
Horný Tisovník SK 147 E8
Horný Vadičov SK 147 C7
Horoatu Crasnei RO 151 C10
Horodiște MD 153 A11
Horodiște MD 153 B10
Horodkivka UA 154 A3
Horodło PL 144 B9
Horodniceni RO 153 B8
Horodnye UA 154 F3
Horodok UA 144 D8
Horoměřice CZ 76 B6
Horonda UA 145 G6
Horonkylä FIN 122 E7
Hořovice CZ 76 C5
Horrabridge GB 12 D6
Horreby DK 83 A11
Horred S 91 E11
Hörsching A 76 F6
Horsdal N 108 B7
Horseleap IRL 6 F5
Horsens DK 86 D5
Horsforth GB 11 D8
Horsham GB 15 E8
Hørsholm DK 87 D10
Hörsingen D 79 B9
Horslunde DK 87 F8
Horsmanaho FIN 125 E12
Horsnes N 111 B18
Horšovský Týn CZ 76 C3
Horsskog S 98 B8
Horst NL 16 F6
Horst (Holstein) D 82 C7
Horstedt D 17 B12
Hörstel D 17 D9
Horstmar D 17 D8
Hort H 150 B4
Horten N 95 D12
Hortezuela E 40 F6
Hortigüela E 40 D5
Hortlax S 118 D6
Hortobágy H 151 B7
Horton in Ribblesdale GB 11 C7
Høruphav DK 86 F5
Hørve DK 87 D8
Hörvik S 89 C7
Horw CH 70 C6
Horwich GB 10 D6
Horyniec-Zdrój PL 144 C7
Horyszów PL 144 B8
Hösbach D 21 D12
Hosena D 80 D6
Hosenfeld D 74 A5
Hoset N 108 B8
Hosingen L 20 D6
Hosio FIN 119 C15
Hosjö S 106 E8
Hosjöbottnarna S 105 E15
Hosköy TR 173 C7
Hospital IRL 8 D6
Hossa FIN 121 D14
Hössjö S 122 C3
Hossjön S 107 D9
Hoßkirch D 27 E11
Hosszúhetény H 149 D10
Hosszúpályi H 151 C8
Hosszúpereszteg H 149 B8
Hošťálková CZ 146 C5
Hostalric E 43 D9
Hostens F 32 B4
Hostěradice CZ 77 E10
Hostie SK 146 E6
Hostinné CZ 81 E9
Hošťka CZ 76 B6
Hostomice CZ 76 C6
Hostomice CZ 80 E5
Hoston N 104 E7
Höstoppen S 106 C8
Hostouň CZ 75 C12
Hostrupskov DK 86 E4
Höstsätern S 102 C4
Hot AL 163 E7
Hotarele RO 161 E8
Hoting S 107 C10
Hotinja vas SLO 148 D5
Hotonj BIH 162 D4
Hotton B 19 D11
Hou DK 86 A6
Houbie GB 3 D15
Houdain F 18 D6
Houdan F 24 C6
Houdelaincourt F 26 C3
Houécourt F 26 D4
Houeillès F 32 B6
Houeydets F 33 D6
Houffalize B 19 D12
Houghton le Spring GB 5 F14
Houghton Regis GB 15 D7
Houlbjerg DK 86 C5
Houlgate F 23 B11
Hourtin F 28 E3
Hourtin-Plage F 28 E3
Houten NL 16 D4
Houthalen B 19 B11
Houthulst B 18 C6
Houton GB 3 H10
Houtsala FIN 126 E6
Houtskär FIN 126 E5
Houyet B 184 D3
Hov DK 86 D6
Hov N 101 E12
Hov N 108 D4
Hov N 111 A18
Hova S 92 B4
Hovborg DK 86 D3
Hovda N 94 D4
Hovde N 90 B4
Hovden N 110 C8
Hovdevik N 100 B2
Hove GB 15 F8
Hovedgård DK 86 D5
Hövelhof D 17 E11
Hoven DK 86 D3
Hoveton GB 15 B11
Hověží CZ 146 C6
Hovid S 103 B13
Hovin N 104 E8
Hovingham GB 11 C10
Hovmantorp S 89 B8
Høvringen N 101 C10
Hovslund Stationsby DK 86 E4
Hovsta S 97 D13
Howden GB 11 D10
Howth IRL 7 F10
Höxter D 17 E12
Hoya D 17 C12
Hoya Gonzalo E 55 B9
Høyanger N 100 D4
Høydal N 90 A5
Hoyerswerda D 80 D6
Hoylake GB 10 E5
Høylandet N 105 B12
Hoym D 79 C9
Hoyocasero E 46 D3
Hoyo de Manzanares E 46 C5
Hoyos E 45 D7
Hoyos del Espino E 45 D10
Höytiä FIN 123 F14
Hoyvik FO 2 A3
Hozha BY 137 F8
Hrabove UA 154 A4
Hrabyně CZ 146 B6
Hradec Králové CZ 77 B9
Hradec nad Moravicí CZ 146 B5
Hradec nad Svitavou CZ 77 C10
Hrádek CZ 147 B7
Hrádek nad Nisou CZ 81 E7
Hradenytsi UA 154 D6
Hradešice CZ 76 D5
Hradište SK 146 D6
Hradište pod Vrátnom SK 146 D5
Hradišťko CZ 76 C6
Hraň SK 145 F4
Hranice CZ 75 B11
Hranice CZ 146 B5
Hranovnica SK 145 F1
Hrasnica BIH 157 E9
Hrastnik SLO 73 D11
Hrawzhyshki BY 137 E12
Hrebenyky UA 154 D5
Hreljin HR 67 B10
Hrhov SK 145 F2
Hrimne UA 145 D8
Hriňová SK 147 D9
Hristovaia MD 154 A3
Hrnjadi BIH 156 D5
Hrob CZ 80 E5
Hrochoť SK 147 D8
Hrochův Týnec CZ 77 C9
Hrodna BY 140 C9
Hromnice CZ 76 C4
Hronec SK 147 D9
Hronov CZ 77 B10
Hronovce SK 147 E7
Hronský Beň Beňx SK 147 E7
Hrotovice CZ 77 D10
Hroznová Lhota CZ 146 D4
Hrtkovci SRB 158 D4
Hrubieszów PL 144 B8
Hrușca MD 154 A3
Hrušky CZ 77 E11
Hrușova MD 154 C3
Hrušovany SK 146 E6
Hrušovany nad Jevišovkou CZ 77 E10
Hruštín SK 147 C8
Hruszniew PL 141 F7
Hrvaćani BIH 157 C7
Hrvace HR 156 E6
Hrvatska Dubica HR 157 B6
Hrvatska Kostajnica HR 156 B6
Hrynyava UA 152 B5
Huaröd S 88 D5
Huarte E 32 E2
Hubová SK 147 C8
Hückelhoven D 20 B6
Hückeswagen D 21 B8
Hucknall GB 11 E9
Hucksjöåsen S 103 A10
Hucqueliers F 15 F12
Huddersfield GB 11 D8
Hüde D 17 C10
Hude (Oldenburg) D 17 B10
Hudești RO 153 A9
Hudiksvall S 103 C13
Huécija E 55 F7
Huedin RO 151 D11
Huélago E 55 E6
Huelgoat F 22 D4
Huelma E 53 A10
Huelva E 51 E6
Huelves E 47 D7
Huércal de Almería E 55 F8
Huércal-Overa E 55 E9
Huérguina E 47 D9
Huérmeces E 40 C4
Huerta del Marquesada E 47 D9
Huerta del Rey E 40 E5
Huerta de Valdecarábanos E 46 E5
Huertahernando E 47 C8
Huerto E 42 D3
Huesa E 55 D6
Huesa del Común E 42 E2
Huesca E 41 D11
Huéscar E 55 D7
Huete E 47 D7
Huétor-Tájar E 53 B8
Huétor-Vega E 53 B9
Huévar E 51 E7
Hüfingen D 27 E9
Hufthamar N 94 B2
Hugh Town GB 12 F2
Hugulia N 101 D11
Hugyag H 147 E8
Huhdasjärvi FIN 127 C16
Huhmarkoski FIN 123 D10
Huhtamo FIN 127 C8
Huhti FIN 127 C10
Huhtilampi FIN 125 F14
Huhus FIN 125 E15
Huijbergen NL 182 C4
Huikola FIN 119 E16
Huisheim D 75 E8
Huisinis GB 2 K2
Huissen NL 16 E5
Huissinkylä FIN 122 E8
Huittinen FIN 126 C8
Huizen NL 16 D4
Hujakkala FIN 128 D8
Hukijärvi FIN 121 D10
Hukkajärvi FIN 125 B14
Hulín CZ 146 C4
Hulja EST 131 C12
Huljen S 103 B12
Hulkkola FIN 124 E8
Hull GB 11 D11
Hüllhorst D 17 D11
Hulo EST 130 D6
Hullsjön S 103 A12
Hüls D 183 C8
Hulsberg NL 183 D7
Hulst NL 16 F2
Hult S 91 A15
Hult S 92 D6
Hulterstad S 89 C11
Hultsfred S 92 D7
Hulu S 91 D13
Hulubești RO 160 D6
Hulyanka UA 154 C4
Hum BIH 157 F10
Hum BIH 162 D5
Humalajoki FIN 123 D13
Humanes de Madrid E 46 D5
Humanes de Mohernando E 47 C6
Humberston GB 11 D11
Humbie GB 5 D11
Humble DK 83 A9
Humenné SK 145 F4
Humilladero E 53 B7
Humlebæk DK 87 D11
Humlegårdsstrand S 103 D13
Humlum DK 86 B3
Hummelholm S 107 D17
Hummelo NL 183 A8
Hummelsta S 98 C7
Hummuli EST 131 F12
Hum na Sutli HR 148 D5
Humpolec CZ 77 C8
Humppila FIN 127 D9
Humshaugh GB 5 E12
Huncovce SK 145 E1
Hundåla N 108 E4
Hundberg N 111 B18
Hundberg S 109 F16
Hundborg DK 86 B3
Hundeluft D 79 C11
Hunderdorf D 75 E12
Hundested DK 87 D9
Hundholmen N 111 D11
Hundorp N 101 C11
Hundsangen D 21 D9
Hundshübel D 79 E12
Hundsjön S 118 C7
Hundslund DK 86 D6
Hundvin N 100 E2
Hune DK 86 A5
Hunedoara RO 151 F10
Hünfeld D 78 E6
Hünfelden-Kirberg D 21 D10
Hunge S 103 A9
Hungen D 21 D11
Hungerford GB 13 C11
Hunnebostrand S 91 C9
Hunsel NL 19 B12
Hunspach F 27 C8
Hunstanton GB 11 F12
Huntingdon GB 15 C8
Huntlosen D 17 C10
Huntly GB 3 L11
Hünxe D 183 B9
Hunya H 151 D6
Huopanankoski FIN 123 D15
Hüpstedt D 79 D7
Hurbanovo SK 146 F6
Hurdal N 95 B14
Hurdalsverk N 95 B14
Hurezani RO 160 D3
Huriel F 29 C10
Hurissalo FIN 128 C8
Hurler's Cross IRL 8 C5
Hursley GB 13 C12
Hurst Green GB 15 E9
Hurstpierpoint GB 15 F8
Hurteles E 41 D7
Hürth D 21 C7
Huruiești RO 153 E10
Huruksela FIN 128 D6
Hurup DK 86 B2
Hurva S 87 D12
Huså S 105 E14
Husås S 106 E7
Husasău de Tinca RO 151 D8
Husbands Bosworth GB 13 A12
Husberget S 102 B6
Husbondliden S 107 B15
Husby D 82 A7
Husby S 97 B15
Husby S 99 B9
Hushcha UA 141 H9
Huși RO 153 D12
Husinec CZ 76 D5
Husjorda N 111 D9
Huskvarna S 92 D4
Husnes N 94 C3
Husnicioara RO 159 D10
Husøy N 108 D3
Hussjö S 103 A14
Hustopeče CZ 77 E11
Hustopeče nad Bečvou CZ 146 B5
Husum D 17 C12
Husum D 82 B6
Husum S 107 E16
Husvik N 108 E4
Huta PL 141 H3
Huta Komorowska PL 143 F12
Hutisko-Solanec CZ 146 C6
Hutovo BIH 162 D4
Hütschenhausen D 186 C3
Hüttau A 73 B7
Hüttenberg A 73 C10
Hüttisheim D 74 F6
Hüttlingen D 75 E7
Huttoft GB 11 E12
Hüttschlag A 73 B7
Huttukylä FIN 119 D15
Huttwil CH 27 F8
Huuhilonkylä FIN 121 F13
Huuki S 117 D11
Huutijärvi FIN 127 C11
Huutokoski FIN 124 F9
Huutokoski FIN 125 E12
Huutoniemi FIN 113 E18
Huvåsen S 118 D4
Hüven D 17 C9
Huwniki PL 145 D6
Huy B 19 C11
Hvalpsund DK 86 B4
Hvalsø DK 87 D9
Hvalvik FO 2 A2
Hvam DK 86 B5
Hvannasund FO 2 A3
Hvar HR 156 F5
Hvidbjerg DK 86 B3
Hvide Sande DK 86 C2
Hvidovre DK 87 D10
Hvilsom DK 86 B5
Hvittingfoss N 95 D11
Hvorslev DK 86 C5
Hwlffordd GB 12 B5
Hybe SK 147 C9
Hybo S 103 C11
Hycklinge S 92 D7
Hyères F 36 E4
Hyermanavichy BY 133 F3
Hyervyaty BY 137 D13
Hylen N 94 C5
Hylleråsen N 102 C3
Hyllestad N 100 D2
Hyllinge DK 87 E9
Hyllinge S 87 C11
Hyltebruk S 87 A12

Hymont F 26 D5
Hyönölä FIN 127 E10
Hyrkäs FIN 119 C16
Hyry FIN 119 C14
Hyrynsalmi FIN 121 E11
Hysgjokaj AL 168 C2
Hyssna S 91 D12
Hythe GB 13 D12
Hythe GB 15 E11
Hytti FIN 129 D9
Hyttön S 99 B8
Hyväneula FIN 127 D13
Hyväniemi FIN 121 B11
Hyvärilä FIN 119 F15
Hyvikkälä FIN 127 D12
Hyvinkää FIN 127 D12
Hyvölänranta FIN 119 F16
Hyvönmäki FIN 129 B12
Hyypiö FIN 115 E1
Hyyppä FIN 122 F8
Hyżne PL 144 D5

I

Iablanița RO 159 D9
Iabloana MD 153 B11
Iacobeni RO 152 C6
Iacobeni RO 152 E5
Ialoveni MD 154 D3
Iam RO 159 C7
Ianca RO 160 F4
Ianca RO 161 C10
Iancu Jianu RO 160 E4
Iara RO 152 D3
Iargara MD 154 E2
Iarova MD 153 A12
Iași RO 153 C11
Iasmos GR 171 B8
Ibahernando E 45 F9
Iballë AL 163 E9
Ibănești RO 152 D5
Ibănești RO 153 A8
Ibarra E 32 D1
Ibbenbüren D 17 D9
Ibdes E 47 B9
Ibë AL 168 B2
Ibeas de Juarros E 40 D4
Ibestad N 111 C13
Ibi E 56 D3
Ibos F 32 D5
Ibrány H 145 G4
İbriktepe TR 171 B10
Ibros E 53 A10
Ibstock GB 11 F9
Ichenhausen D 75 F7
Ichenheim D 186 E4
Ichtegem B 18 B7
Icking D 72 A3
Icklesham GB 15 F10
Icklingham GB 15 C10
Iclănzel RO 152 D4
Iclod RO 152 D3
Icoana RO 160 E5
Icușești RO 153 D9
Idanha-a-Nova P 45 E6
Idanha-a-Velha P 45 E6
Idar-Oberstein D 21 E8
Ideciu de Jos RO 152 D5
Iden D 83 E11
Īdeņa LV 133 C1
Idenor S 103 C13
Idestrup DK 83 A11
Idiazabal E 32 D1
Idivuoma S 116 B8
Idkerberget S 97 B13
Idmiston GB 13 C11
Idocin E 32 E3
Idom DK 86 C2
Iđoš SRB 150 F5
Idre S 102 C4
Idrigil GB 2 K4
Idrija SLO 73 D9
Idritsa RUS 133 D5
Idro I 69 B9
Idron-Ousse-Sendets F 32 D5
Idstedt D 82 A7
Idstein D 21 D10
Idvattnet S 107 C12
Iecava LV 135 C8
Iedera RO 161 C7
Ieper B 18 C6
Iepurești RO 161 E7
Ierapetra GR 179 E10
Ieriķi LV 135 B10
Ierissos GR 170 D5
Iernut RO 152 E4
Ieromnini GR 168 E4
Ieropigi GR 168 C5
Ieșelnița RO 159 D9
Ifaistos GR 171 E8
Iffendic F 23 D7
Iffezheim D 187 D5
Ifjord N 113 C19
Ifs F 23 B11
Ifta D 79 D7
Ig SLO 73 E10
Igal H 149 C9
Igalo MNE 162 E6
Igar H 149 C11
Igé F 24 D4
Igea E 41 D7
Igel D 186 B2
Igelfors S 92 B7
Igelstorp S 91 C14
Igensdorf D 75 C9
Igerøy N 108 E3
Igersheim D 74 D6
Iggelheim D 187 C5
Iggensbach D 76 E4
Iggesund S 103 C13
Ighiu RO 152 E3
Igis CH 71 D9
Iglesias I 64 E2
Igliauka LT 137 D8
Igling D 71 A11
Igliškėliai LT 137 D8
Ignalina LT 135 F12
Ignatievo BG 167 C9
İğneada TR 167 F9
Ignești RO 151 E9
Igney F 26 D5
Igornay F 30 A5
Igoumenitsa GR 168 E3
Igralishte BG 169 A9
Igrejinha P 50 B4
Igrici H 145 H2
Igrīve LV 133 B2
Igualada E 43 D7
Igualeja E 53 C6
Igueña E 39 C7
Iguerande F 30 C5
Iharosberény H 149 D8
Ihľany SK 145 E2
Ihlienworth D 17 A11
Ihlowerhörn (Ihlow) D 17 B9
Ihode FIN 126 D6
Iholdy F 32 D3
Ihrhove D 17 B8
Ihrlerstein D 75 E10
İhsaniye TR 173 B10
Ii FIN 119 D14
Iijärvi FIN 113 E20
Iinattijärvi FIN 121 D9
Iironranta FIN 123 E12
Iisalmi FIN 124 C8
Iisvesi FIN 124 E8
Iitti FIN 127 D15
Iitto FIN 116 A6
Iivantiira FIN 121 F13
IJlst NL 16 B5
IJmuiden NL 16 D3
IJsselmuiden NL 16 C5
IJsselstein NL 16 D4
IJzendijke NL 16 F1
Ikaalinen FIN 127 B9
Ikast DK 86 C4
Ikazn' BY 133 E2
Ikervár H 149 B7
Ikhtiman BG 165 E8
İkizdere TR 177 D10
Ikkala FIN 123 F11
Ikkala FIN 127 E11
Ikkeläjärvi FIN 122 F9
Ikla EST 131 F8
Ikornes N 100 B5
Ikosenniemi FIN 119 C17
Ikrény H 149 A9
Ikšķile LV 135 C8
Ilandža SRB 159 C6
Ilanz CH 71 D8
Ilava SK 146 D6
Iława PL 139 C8
Ilbono I 64 D4
Ilchester GB 13 C9
Ildir TR 177 C7
Īle LV 134 C6
Ileana RO 161 D9
Ileanda RO 152 C3
Ilfeld D 79 C8
Ilford GB 15 D9
Ilfracombe GB 12 C6
Ilgižiai LT 134 F6
Ílhavo P 44 C3
Ilia RO 151 F10
Ilica TR 173 E8
Ilidža BIH 157 E9
Ilieni RO 153 F7
Ilijaš BIH 157 E9
Ilindentsi BG 165 F7
Iliokastro GR 175 E7
Ilirska Bistrica SLO 73 E9
Ilk H 145 G5
Ilkeston GB 11 F9
Ilkley GB 11 D8
Illana E 47 D7
Illar E 55 F7
Illats F 32 A5
Illerrieden D 71 A10
Illertissen D 71 A10
Illescas E 46 D5
Ille-sur-Têt F 34 E4
Illiers-Combray F 24 D5
Illingen D 21 F8
Illingen D 187 D6
Illkirch-Graffenstaden F 27 C8
Illmensee D 27 E11
Illmitz A 149 A7
Íllora E 53 B9
Illschwang D 75 D10
Illueca E 41 E8
Illzach F 27 E7
Ilmajoki FIN 122 E9
Ilmatsalu EST 131 E13
Ilmenau D 79 E8
Ilminster GB 13 D9
Ilmmünster D 75 F10
Ilmola FIN 119 C13
Il'nytsya UA 145 G7
Ilok HR 158 C3
Ilola FIN 127 E14
Ilomantsi FIN 125 E15
Ilosjoki FIN 123 D15
Ilovăț RO 159 D10
Ilovica MK 169 B8
Ilovice BIH 157 E9
Ilovița RO 159 D9
Iłów PL 139 F9
Iłowa PL 81 C8
Iłowo Osada PL 139 D9
Ilsbo S 103 C13
Ilsede D 79 B7
Ilsenburg (Harz) D 79 C8
Ilseng N 101 E14
Ilsfeld D 27 B11
Ilskov DK 86 C4
Ilūkste LV 135 E12
Ilva Mare RO 152 C5
Ilva Mică RO 152 C5
Ilvesjoki FIN 122 F9
İlyaslar TR 173 F9
Ilyushino RUS 136 D6
Ilz A 148 B5
Iłża PL 141 H4
Ilze LV 135 D12
Ilzene LV 135 B13
Imari FIN 119 B15
Imatra FIN 129 C10
Imavere EST 131 D11
Imbradas LT 135 E12
Imeľ SK 146 F6
Imèr I 72 D4
Imeros GR 171 C8
Imielnica PL 139 E8
Immeln S 88 C6
Immendingen D 27 E10
Immenhausen D 78 D5
Immenreuth D 75 C10
Immenstaad am Bodensee D 27 E11
Immenstadt im Allgäu D 71 B10
Immingham GB 11 D11
Imnäs S 107 D11
Imola I 66 D4
Imotski HR 157 F7
Imperia I 37 D8
Imphy F 30 B3
Impilakhti RUS 129 B15
Impiö FIN 120 C9
Impruneta I 66 E3
Imrehegy H 150 E3
İmroz TR 171 D9
Imst A 71 C11
Ina FIN 123 D11
Inagh IRL 8 C4
Inancs H 145 G3
Inárcs H 150 C3
Inari FIN 113 F19
Inari FIN 125 D15
Inca E 57 B10
Inch IRL 8 D3
Inch IRL 9 C10
Inchbare GB 5 B11
Incheville F 18 D3
Inchigeelagh IRL 8 E4
Inchnadamph GB 2 J7
Inciems LV 135 B9
Incinillas E 40 C4
İncirliova TR 177 D10
Incisa in Val d'Arno I 66 E3
Incourt B 19 C10
Inčukalns LV 135 B9
Indal S 103 A13
Indalstø N 100 E2
Independenţa RO 155 C1
Independenţa RO 155 F2
Inđija SRB 158 C5
Indra LV 133 E3
Indreabhán IRL 6 F4
Indre Arna N 94 B2
Indre Billefjord N 113 C15
Indre Brenna N 113 B16
Indre Kårvik N 111 A16
Indre Kiberg N 114 C9
Indre Kjæs N 113 B16
Indre Sortvik N 113 B15
Indura BY 140 D9
Indzhe Voyvoda BG 167 E8
İnece TR 167 F8
İnecik TR 173 C7
Ineši LV 135 B11
Ineu RO 151 C9
Ineu RO 151 E8
Infiesto E 39 B9
Ingå FIN 127 E11
Ingared S 91 D11
Ingatestone GB 15 D9
Ingatorp S 92 D6
Ingelfingen D 187 C8
Ingelheim am Rhein D 21 E10
Ingelmunster B 19 C7
Ingelstad S 89 B7
Ingenes N 94 B3
Ingersheim F 27 D7
Ingleton GB 5 F13
Ingleton GB 10 C7
Ingoldmells GB 11 E12
Ingolsbenning S 97 B14
Ingolstadt D 75 E9
Ingrandes F 23 F10
Ingrandes F 29 B7
Ingstrup DK 90 E6
Inguiniel F 22 E5
Ingulsvatn N 105 B14
Ingwiller F 27 C7
Inha FIN 123 E12
Ini GR 178 E9
Iniesta E 47 F9
Inis IRL 8 C5
Inis Córthaidh IRL 9 C9
Inis Díomáin IRL 8 C4
Inistioge IRL 9 D8
Injevo MK 169 A7
Inkberrow GB 13 A11
Inke H 149 D8
Inkee FIN 121 C12
Inkere FIN 127 E9
Inkoo FIN 127 E11
Inndyr N 108 B7
Innerbraz A 71 C9
Innerleithen GB 5 D10
Innernzell D 76 E4
Innertällmo S 107 D13
Innertavle S 122 C4
Innertkirchen CH 70 D6
Innervik S 109 E14
Innervillgraten A 72 C5
Innhavet N 111 E10
Inniscrone IRL 6 D4
Innishannon IRL 8 E5
Innsbruck A 72 B3
Innset N 111 C16
Inntorget N 108 F3
Inowłódz PL 141 G2
Inowrocław PL 138 E5
Ins CH 31 A11
Insch GB 3 L11
Insjön S 103 E9
Ińsko PL 85 D9
Insming F 27 C6
Instefjord N 100 E2
Instinción E 55 F7
Însurăţei RO 161 D11
İntepe TR 171 D10
Interlaken CH 70 D5
Întorsura Buzăului RO 161 B8
Întregalde RO 151 E11
Introbio I 69 B7
Inturkė LT 135 F11
Inver IRL 6 C6
Inverallochy GB 3 K13
Inveran IRL 6 F4
Inveraray GB 4 C6
Inverarity GB 5 B11
Inverarnan GB 4 C7
Inverbervie GB 5 B12
Invercassley GB 2 K7
Invercharnan GB 4 B6
Invergarry GB 4 A7
Invergordon GB 3 K8
Inverkeilor GB 5 B11
Inverkeithing GB 5 C10
Invermoriston GB 2 L7
Inverness GB 3 L8
Inverurie GB 3 L12
Inviken S 106 B8
Inzell D 73 A6
Inzigkofen D 27 D11
Inzing A 72 B3
Inzinzac-Lochrist F 22 E5
Ioannina GR 168 E4
Ion Corvin RO 155 E1
Ion Creangă RO 153 D9
Ionești RO 160 D2
Ionești RO 160 D4
Ion Luca Caragiale RO 161 D7
Ion Roată RO 161 D9
Iordăcheanu RO 161 C8
Ioulis GR 175 D9
Ip RO 151 C10
Ipatele RO 153 D10
Iphofen D 187 B9
Ipiķi LV 131 E10
Ipotești RO 153 B8
Ipotești RO 153 B9
Ippesheim D 75 C7
Ipplepen GB 13 E7
Ipsala TR 171 C10
Ipsheim D 75 C7
Ipstones GB 11 E8
Ipswich GB 15 C11
Iraklela GR 169 B9
Irakleia GR 174 B5
Irakleia GR 176 F5
Irakleio GR 178 E9
Irancy F 25 E10
Iratoșu RO 151 E7
Irdning A 73 A9
Irechekovo BG 167 E7
Iregszemcse H 149 C10
Irgoli I 64 C4
Iria GR 175 E7
Irig SRB 158 C4
Irishtown IRL 6 E5
Irissarry F 32 D3
Irjanne FIN 126 C6
Irlava LV 134 C5
Irlbach D 75 E12
Irninniemi FIN 121 C13
Irodouër F 23 D8
Ironbridge GB 10 F7
Irrel D 20 E6
Irsch D 21 E7
Irsee D 71 B11
Irshava UA 145 G7
Irši LV 135 C11
Irsina I 60 B6
Irsta S 98 C7
Irueste E 47 C7
Irun E 32 D2
Irunea E 32 E2
Irurita E 32 D2
Irurozqui E 32 E3
Irurtzun E 32 E2
Irvine GB 4 D7
Irvinestown GB 7 D7
Irxleben D 79 B9
Isaba E 32 E4
Isaccea RO 155 C2
Isačić BIH 156 C4
Ișalnița RO 160 E3
Isane N 100 C3
Isaris GR 174 E5
Isaszeg H 150 B3
Isätra S 98 C7
Isbergues F 18 C5
Isbister GB 3 D14
Íscar E 40 F2
Isches F 26 D4
Ischgl A 71 C10
Ischia I 60 B1
Ischia di Castro I 62 B1
Ischitella I 63 D9
Isdes F 25 E7
Iselvmoen N 111 C16
Isen D 75 F11
Is-en-Bassigny F 26 D3
Isenbüttel D 79 B8
Isenvad DK 86 C4
Iseo I 69 B9
Iserlohn D 17 F9
Isernhagen D 78 B6
Isernia I 63 D6
Isfjorden N 100 A7
İshakçelebi TR 177 B10
Ishull-Lezhë AL 163 F8
Isigny-sur-Mer F 23 B9
Isili I 64 D3
İskele TR 173 F9
İskender TR 172 A6
Iškoras N 113 E16
Iskra BG 166 F4
Iskrets BG 165 D7
Isla Cristina E 51 E5
İslambeyli TR 167 F9
Isla Plana E 56 F2
Išlaužas LT 137 D8
Islaz RO 160 F5
Isle F 29 D8
Isle of Whithorn GB 5 F8
Isleryd S 92 C4
Isles-sur-Suippe F 19 F9
Īslīce LV 135 D8
İsmailli TR 177 B9
Ismaning D 75 F10
Ismundsundet S 106 E8
Isna P 44 E5
Isnäs FIN 127 E15
Isnello I 58 D5
Isnovăț MD 154 C3
Isny im Allgäu D 71 B10
Iso-Äiniö FIN 127 C13
Iso-Evo FIN 127 C13
Isohalme FIN 115 E3
Isojoki FIN 122 F7
Isokumpu FIN 121 C11
Isokylä FIN 115 E3
Isokylä FIN 119 F14
Isokyrö FIN 122 E8
Isola F 36 C6
Isola 2000 F 37 C6
Isola d'Asti I 37 B8
Isola del Gran Sasso d'Italia I 62 B5
Isola della Scala I 66 B3
Isola delle Femmine I 58 C3
Isola del Liri I 62 D5
Isola di Capo Rizzuto I 61 F8
Isole del Cantone I 37 B9
Isona E 42 C6
Isopalo FIN 115 D2
Isorella I 66 B1
Iso-Vimma FIN 126 C7
Ispagnac F 35 B6
Isperikh BG 161 F9
Ispica I 59 F6
Ispoure F 32 D3
Ispra I 68 B6
Isprigen D 27 C10
Issakka FIN 125 C10
Isselburg D 17 E6
Issigeac F 29 F7
Issime I 68 B4
Isso E 55 C9
Issogne I 68 B4
Issoire F 30 D3
Issoudun F 29 B9
Issum D 17 E6
Is-sur-Tille F 26 E3
Issy-l'Évêque F 30 B4
Istalsna LV 133 D3
Istán E 53 C7
İstanbul TR 173 B10
Istead Rise GB 15 E9
Istebna PL 147 B7
Istebné SK 147 C8
Istenmezeje H 147 E10
Isternia GR 176 D5
Isthmia GR 175 D7
Istiaia GR 175 B7
Istibanja MK 164 F5
Istog KS 163 D9
Istres F 35 C8
Istria RO 155 D3
Istrio GR 181 D7
Istunmäki FIN 123 E16
Isuerre E 32 F3
Iszkaszentgyörgy H 149 B10
Itä-Ähtäri FIN 123 E12
Itä-Aure FIN 123 F10
Itä-Karttula FIN 124 E8
Itäkoski FIN 119 C13
Itäkoski FIN 125 C9
Itäkylä FIN 123 D11
Itäranta FIN 115 F2
Itäranta FIN 120 F9
Itea GR 169 C6
Itea GR 169 D6
Itea GR 169 F7
Itea GR 174 C5
Itero de la Vega E 40 D3
Iteuil F 29 C6
Ithaki GR 174 C2
Itrabo E 53 C9
Itri I 62 E5
Itterbeck D 17 C7
Ittireddu I 64 B2
Ittiri I 64 B2
Ittre B 19 C9
Ituero de Azaba E 45 D7
Itzehoe D 82 C7
Itzstedt D 83 C8
Iurceni MD 154 C2
Ivalo FIN 115 A3
Ivalon Matti FIN 117 B15
Iván H 149 B7
Ivana Franka UA 145 E7
Ivancea MD 154 C3
Ivančice CZ 77 D10
Ivančići BIH 157 D9
Iváncsa H 149 B11
Ivanec HR 148 D6
Ivănești RO 153 D10
Ivangorod RUS 132 C3
Ivanić-Grad HR 149 E6
Ivanivka UA 145 G6
Ivanjica SRB 163 B9
Ivanjska BIH 157 C6
Ivankovo HR 149 F11
Ivano-Frankove UA 144 D8
Ivanovice na Hané CZ 77 D12
Ivanovo BG 161 F7
Ivanovo BG 166 F5
Ivanovo BG 167 C7
Ivanovo SRB 158 D6
Ivanska HR 149 E7
Ivanski BG 167 C8
Ivarrud N 108 F6
Ivarsbjörke S 97 C9
Ivars d'Urgell E 42 D5
Ivaylovgrad BG 171 A10
Iveland N 90 C2
Iver GB 15 D7
Ivești RO 153 E11
Ivești RO 153 F11
Ivrea I 68 C4
İvrindi TR 173 E7
Ivry-la-Bataille F 24 C5
Ivry-sur-Seine F 25 C7
Ivybridge GB 13 E7
Iwaniska PL 143 E11
Iwanowice Włościańskie PL 143 F8
Iwkowa PL 144 D2
Iwye BY 137 F12
Ixelles B 19 C9
Ixworth GB 15 C10
İyaslar TR 177 A10
Iža SK 149 A10
Iza UA 145 G7
Izarra E 40 C6
Izbica PL 144 B7
Izbica Kujawska PL 138 F6
Izbiceni RO 160 F5
Izbicko PL 142 E5
Izbiște MD 154 C4
Izbište SRB 159 C7
Izbižno BIH 157 E10
Izeaux F 31 E7
Izeda P 39 E6
Izegem B 19 C7
Izernore F 31 C8
Izeron F 31 E7
Izgrev BG 161 F9
Izgrev BG 167 E9
Iž Mali HR 67 D11
Izmayil UA 155 C3
İzmir TR 177 C9
Iznájar E 53 B8
Iznalloz E 53 B9
Izola SLO 67 A8
Izsák H 150 D3
Izsófalva H 145 G2
Izvoare RO 160 E2
Izvoarele RO 155 C3
Izvoarele RO 160 E5
Izvoarele RO 160 F6
Izvoarele RO 161 C8
Izvoarele RO 161 E7
Izvoarele Sucevei RO 152 B6
Izvor BG 159 F10
Izvor BG 165 E6
Izvor MK 168 B4
Izvor MK 169 A6
Izvor SRB 159 F8
Izvorovo BG 155 F1
Izvoru RO 160 E6
Izvoru Bârzii RO 159 D10
Izvoru Berheciului RO 153 D10
Izvoru Crișului RO 151 D11

J

Jääjärvi FIN 114 D6
Jaakonvaara FIN 125 D14
Jaala FIN 127 C15
Jaalanka FIN 120 D9
Jaalanka FIN 120 E9
Jääli FIN 119 D15
Jaama EST 132 C2
Jääskänjoki FIN 122 E9
Jääskö FIN 117 D14
Jaatila FIN 119 B14
Jabaga E 47 D8
Jabalanac HR 67 C10
Jabaloyas E 47 D10
Jabalquinto E 53 A9
Jabbeke B 19 B7
Jabel D 83 C13
Jablan Do BIH 162 D5
Jablanica BIH 157 E8
Jabłoń PL 141 G8
Jablonec nad Jizerou CZ 81 E8
Jablonec nad Nisou CZ 81 E8
Jablonica SK 146 D4
Jabłonka PL 147 C9
Jabłonka Kościelna PL 140 E6
Jabłonna PL 139 F10
Jabłonna Lacka PL 141 F6
Jabłonna Pierwsza PL 141 H7
Jablonné nad Orlicí CZ 77 B11
Jablonné v Podještědí CZ 81 E7
Jablonové SK 77 F12
Jabłonowo Pomorskie PL 139 D7
Jablůnka CZ 146 C5
Jablunkov CZ 147 B7
Jabugo E 51 D6
Jabuka BIH 157 E10
Jabuka SRB 158 D6
Jabuka SRB 163 C7
Jabukovac HR 149 F6
Jabukovac SRB 159 E9
Jabukovik SRB 164 D5
Jaca E 32 E4
Jachenau D 72 A3
Jáchymov CZ 76 B3
Jacovce SK 146 D6
Jäderfors S 103 E12
Jadów PL 139 F12
Jädraås S 103 E11
Jadranska Lešnica SRB 158 D3
Jadraque E 47 C7
Jægerspris DK 87 D9
Jægervatnet N 111 A18
Jaén E 53 A9
Jägala EST 131 C10
Jagare BIH 157 C7
Jagerberg A 148 C5
Jagodina SRB 159 F7
Jagodnjak HR 149 E11
Jagodzin PL 81 D8
Jagsthausen D 27 B11
Jagstzell D 75 D7
Jähdyspohja FIN 123 F11
Jahnsfelde D 80 A6
Jahodná SK 146 E5
Jah-Salih AL 163 E9
Jajce BIH 157 D7
Ják H 149 B7
Jakabszállás H 150 D4
Jäkäläväara FIN 121 C10
Jakkukylä FIN 119 D15
Jakkula FIN 122 E8
Jäkkvik S 109 D12
Jaklovce SK 145 F3
Jakobsbakken N 109 B10
Jakobsnes N 114 D8
Jakobstad FIN 122 C9
Jakokoski FIN 125 E13
Jakovlje HR 148 E5
Jakšić HR 149 F9
Jakštaičiai LT 134 D2
Jaktorów PL 141 F3
Jakubany SK 145 E2
Jakubov SK 77 F11
Jakubów PL 141 F5
Jalance E 47 F10
Jalasjärvi FIN 122 F9
Jalhay B 20 C5
Jaligny-sur-Besbre F 30 C4
Jallais F 23 F10
Jalovik SRB 158 D4
Jałówka PL 140 D9
Jalubí CZ 146 C4
Jämaja EST 130 E4
Jämäs FIN 125 B12
Jämejala EST 131 E11
Jameln D 83 D10
Jamena SRB 157 C11
Jamestown IRL 7 F8
Jametz F 19 F11
Jamielnik PL 139 C7
Jämijärvi FIN 126 B8
Jamilena E 53 A9
Jäminkipohja FIN 127 B11
Jämjö S 89 C9
Jammerdal N 96 B7
Jamník SK 145 F2
Jämsä FIN 123 C12
Jämsä FIN 127 B13
Jämsänkoski FIN 127 B13
Jämshög S 88 C7
Jämtön S 118 C8
Jamu Mare RO 159 C7
Janakkala FIN 127 D12
Janapolė LT 134 E4
Jánd H 145 G5
Jandelsbrunn D 76 E5
Janderup DK 86 D2
Jäneda EST 131 C11
Jänickendorf D 80 B4
Janja BIH 158 D3
Janjevë KS 164 D3
Janjići BIH 158 F3
Janjina HR 162 D3
Jänkä FIN 123 D13
Jänkälä FIN 115 D3
Jänkisjärvi S 116 E10
Jánkmajtis H 145 H6
Janków PL 143 B7
Jankowo Dolne PL 138 E4
Jāņmuiža LV 135 B10
Jännevirta FIN 125 E9
Jánoshalma H 150 E3
Jánosháza H 149 B8
Jánoshida H 150 C5
Jánossomorja H 149 A8
Janovice nad Úhlavou CZ 76 D4
Janów PL 140 D8
Janów PL 143 E7
Janowiec Wielkie PL 81 E9
Janowiec PL 141 H5
Janowiec Wielkopolski PL 85 E12
Janów Lubelski PL 144 B5
Janowo PL 139 D10
Janów Podlaski PL 141 F8
Jansjö S 107 D10
Jänsmässholmen S 105 D15
Jaņuciems LV 135 E13
Janville F 24 D6
Janzé F 23 E9
Japca MD 154 B3
Jäppilä FIN 124 F8
Jaraba E 47 B9
Jaraczewo PL 81 C12
Jarafuel E 47 F10
Jaraicejo E 45 E9
Jaraíz de la Vera E 45 D9
Järämä S 116 B6
Jarandilla de la Vera E 45 D9
Järbo S 103 E12
Járdánháza H 145 G1
Jard-sur-Mer F 28 C2
Jaren N 95 B13
Jarfjordbotn N 114 D8
Jargastat N 113 E16
Jargeau F 24 E7
Jarhoinen FIN 117 E11
Jarhois S 117 E11
Jariștea RO 153 F10
Jarkovac SRB 159 C6
Järkvissle S 103 A12
Järlåsa S 98 C8
Järlepa EST 131 C9
Jarmen D 84 C4
Jarménil F 26 D6
Jarmina HR 149 F11
Järna S 93 A11
Järna S 97 A11
Jarnac F 28 D5
Jarnages F 29 C10
Järnäs S 107 E17
Järnäsklubb S 107 E17
Järnforsen S 92 E7
Jarny F 26 B4
Jarocin PL 142 C4
Jarocin PL 144 B5
Jarok SK 146 E5
Jaroměř CZ 77 B9
Jaroměřice CZ 77 C11
Jaroměřice nad Rokytnou CZ 77 D9
Jaroslavice CZ 77 E10
Jarosław PL 144 C6
Jarosławiec PL 85 A11
Jarošov nad Nežárkou CZ 77 D8
Jarovnice SK 145 E3
Järpås S 91 C12
Järpbyn S 105 E14
Järpen S 105 E14
Järpliden S 102 E3
Jarplund-Weding D 82 A6
Jarque E 41 E8
Jarrow GB 5 F14
Järva-Jaani EST 131 C11
Järvakandi EST 131 D9
Järvberget S 107 D13
Järvenpää FIN 117 C12
Järvenpää FIN 122 E7
Järvenpää FIN 124 C8
Järvenpää FIN 125 D10
Järvenpää FIN 127 E13
Järvikylä FIN 119 F17
Järvikylä FIN 123 C13
Järvikylä FIN 123 C13
Jarville-la-Malgrange F 26 C5
Järvirova FIN 117 D12
Järvsand S 107 C9
Järvsjö S 107 B12
Järvsö S 103 C11
Järvsta S 103 E13
Järvtjärn S 118 E5
Järvträsk S 107 A16
Jarzé F 23 E11
Jaša Tomić SRB 159 C6
Jasen BIH 162 D5
Jasenak HR 67 B11
Jasenica BIH 156 C5
Jasenovac HR 157 B6
Jasenovo SRB 159 D7
Jasenovo SRB 163 B8
Jasień PL 81 C8
Jasień PL 85 B13
Jasienica PL 139 F11
Jasienica PL 147 B7
Jasienica Rosielna PL 144 D4
Jasieniec PL 141 G3
Jasika SRB 159 F7
Jasionka PL 144 C5
Jasionna PL 143 E9
Jasionówka PL 140 D8
Jaśliska PL 145 E4
Jasło PL 144 D3
Jašlūnai LT 137 E11
Jasmuiža LV 135 D13
Jasov SK 145 F2
Jásová SK 146 F6
Jassans-Riottier F 30 D6
Jasseron F 31 C7
Jastarnia PL 138 A6
Jastrebarsko HR 148 E5
Jastrowie PL 85 D11
Jastrząb PL 141 H3
Jastrzębia PL 141 H4
Jastrzębia Góra PL 138 A5
Jastrzębie-Zdrój PL 147 B7
Jászapáti H 150 B5
Jászárokszállás H 150 B4
Jászberény H 150 C4
Jászboldogháza H 150 C4
Jászfényszaru H 150 B4
Jászjákóhalma H 150 B5
Jászkarajenő H 150 C5
Jászkisér H 150 C5
Jászladány H 150 C5
Jászszentandrás H 150 B5
Jászszentlászló H 150 D4
Jásztelek H 150 C5
Jatar E 53 C9
Jättendal S 103 C13
Jättensjö S 103 B10
Jatuni FIN 116 B9
Jatzke D 84 C5
Jatznick D 84 C5
Jaulín E 41 F10
Jaun CH 31 B11
Jaunalūksne LV 133 B2
Jaunanna LV 133 B2
Jaunauce LV 134 D5
Jaunay-Clan F 29 B6
Jaunbērze LV 134 C6
Jaunciems LV 134 B5
Jaundundaga LV 130 F4
Jaungulbene LV 135 B13
Jaunjelgava LV 135 C10
Jaunkalsnava LV 135 C11
Jaunklidzis LV 131 F11
Jaunlaicene LV 131 F13
Jaunlutriņi LV 134 C4
Jaunmārupe LV 135 C7
Jaunmuiža LV 135 C11
Jaunmuiža LV 135 C7
Jaunpiebalga LV 135 B12
Jaunpils LV 134 C6
Jaunsāti LV 134 C5
Jaunsēlpis LV 135 C11
Jaunsilava LV 135 D12
Jauntsarats E 32 E2
Jaurakainen FIN 119 D17
Jaurakkajärvi FIN 121 D10
Jaurrieta E 32 E3
Jausiers F 36 C5
Javalí Viejo E 56 F2
Javarus FIN 115 E1
Jávea-Xàbia E 56 D5
Jävenitz D 79 A10
Javerlhac-et-la-Chapelle-St-Robert F 29 D7
Javgur MD 154 D3
Javier E 32 E3
Javorani BIH 157 C7
Javorník CZ 77 B12

Jävre S 118 D6
Javron-les-Chapelles F 23 D11
Jawor PL 81 D10
Jawornik Polski PL 144 D5
Jawor Solecki PL 141 H4
Jaworzno PL 142 D6
Jaworzno PL 143 F7
Jaworzyna Śląska PL 81 E10
Jayena E 53 C9
Jazeneuil F 28 C6
Jebel RO 159 B7
Jebjerg DK 86 B4
Jedburgh GB 5 E11
Jedlanka PL 141 G6
Jedlicze PL 144 D4
Jedlina-Zdrój PL 81 E10
Jedlińsk PL 141 G4
Jedlnia-Letnisko PL 141 H4
Jedlová CZ 77 C10
Jedľové Kostoľany SK 146 E6
Jednorożec PL 139 D11
Jedovnice CZ 77 D11
Jędrzejewo PL 85 E10
Jędrzejów PL 143 E9
Jédula E 52 C5
Jedwabne PL 140 D6
Jedwabno PL 139 C10
Jeesiö FIN 117 D16
Jeesiöjärvi FIN 117 C14
Jegălia RO 161 E11
Jegun F 33 C6
Jegunovce MK 164 E3
Jejsing DK 86 F3
Jēkabpils LV 135 C11
Jektvik N 108 C5
Jelah BIH 157 C8
Jelašca BIH 157 F9
Jelcz-Laskowice PL 81 D12
Jelenia Góra PL 81 E9
Jeleniewo PL 136 E6
Jelenin PL 81 C8
Jelenje HR 67 B9
Jeleśnia PL 147 B8
Jelgava LV 134 C7
Jelka SK 146 E5
Jelling DK 86 D4
Jeloboc MD 154 C3
Jelovica SRB 165 C6
Jełowa PL 142 E5
Jels DK 86 E4
Jelsa HR 157 F6
Jelšane SLO 67 A9
Jelšava SK 145 F1
Jelsi I 63 D7
Jemeppe B 19 D10
Jemgum D 17 B8
Jemielnica PL 142 E5
Jemielno PL 81 C11
Jemnice CZ 77 D9
Jena D 79 E10
Jenbach A 72 B4
Jeneč CZ 76 B6
Jengen D 71 B11
Jenikowo PL 85 C8
Jennersdorf A 148 C6
Jenny S 93 D9
Jenő H 149 B10
Jensvoll N 101 A15
Jeppo FIN 122 D9
Jērcēni LV 131 F11
Jerchel D 79 B9
Jerez de la Frontera E 52 C4
Jerez del Marquesado E 55 E6
Jerez de los Caballeros E 51 C6
Jerfojaur S 109 E16
Jergol N 113 E14
Jergucat AL 168 E3
Jeri LV 131 F10
Jérica E 48 E3
Jerichow D 79 A11
Jerka PL 81 C11
Jernved DK 86 E3
Jerslev DK 87 D8
Jerslev DK 90 E7
Jerstad N 110 C9
Jerte E 45 D9
Jerup DK 90 D7
Jerzens A 71 C11
Jerzmanowa PL 81 C10
Jerzmanowice PL 143 F8
Jerzu I 64 D4
Jesenice CZ 76 B4
Jesenice CZ 77 C7
Jesenice HR 156 D4
Jesenice HR 156 F6
Jesenice SLO 73 D9
Jeseník CZ 77 B12
Jeseník nad Odrou CZ 146 B5
Jesenské SK 147 E10
Jeserig D 79 B11
Jeserig D 79 B12
Jesi I 67 E7
Jesionowo PL 85 D8
Jesolo I 66 A6
Jessen D 80 C3
Jessheim N 95 B14
Jeßnitz D 79 C11
Jesteburg D 83 D7
Jettingen-Scheppach D 75 F7
Jeumont F 19 D9
Jevenstedt D 82 B7
Jever D 17 A9
Jevíčko CZ 77 C11
Jevišovice CZ 77 E10
Jevnaker N 95 B12
Jezera BIH 157 D8
Jezerane HR 67 B11
Jezerc KS 164 E3
Jezero BIH 157 D7
Jezero HR 156 B3
Jeżewo PL 138 C5
Jeżewo PL 140 D7
Jeziorany PL 136 F2
Jeziorzany PL 141 G6
Jeżów PL 141 G1
Jeżowe PL 144 C5
Jeżów Sudecki PL 81 E9
Jiana RO 159 E10
Jibert RO 152 E6
Jibou RO 151 C11
Jichișu de Jos RO 152 C3
Jičín CZ 77 B8
Jidvei RO 152 E4
Jieznas LT 137 D9
Jihlava CZ 77 D9
Jijila RO 155 C2
Jijona-Xixona E 56 D4
Jilava RO 161 E8
Jilavele RO 161 D9
Jilemnice CZ 81 E9
Jílové CZ 80 E6
Jílové u Prahy CZ 77 C7
Jiltjaur S 109 E12
Jimbolia RO 150 F6
Jimena E 53 A10
Jimena de la Frontera E 53 D6
Jimramov CZ 77 C10
Jina RO 152 F3
Jince CZ 76 C5
Jindřichov CZ 77 B12
Jindřichov CZ 142 F4
Jindřichův Hradec CZ 77 D8
Jiříkov CZ 81 E7
Jirkov CZ 76 A4
Jirlău RO 161 C10
Jirnsum NL 16 B5
Jirny CZ 77 B7
Jistebnice CZ 77 D7
Jistebník CZ 146 B6
Jitia RO 161 B9
Jlajkovci SRB 163 C10
Joachimsthal D 84 E5
Joane P 38 F3
Job F 30 D4
Jobbágyi H 147 F9
Jobsbo S 97 B13
Jochberg A 72 B5
Jocketa D 79 E11
Jockfall S 116 E9
Jockgrim D 27 B9
Jódar E 55 D6
Jodłowa PL 144 D3
Jodłownik PL 144 D1
Jodoigne B 19 C10
Joensuu FIN 125 E13
Jõepere EST 131 C12
Joesjö S 108 E8
Joeström S 108 E8
Jõesuu EST 131 E9
Jœuf F 20 F6
Jõgeva EST 131 D12
Jõgua EST 131 C14
Johanngeorgenstadt D 75 B12
Johannisfors S 99 B10
Johannishus S 89 C8
Johanniskirchen D 76 E3
Johansfors S 89 B9
John o'Groats GB 3 H10
Johnston GB 12 B5
Johnstone GB 4 D7
Johnstown IRL 9 C7
Johnstown IRL 9 C10
Johovac BIH 158 D3
Jöhstadt D 76 A4
Jõhvi EST 131 C14
Joigny F 25 E9
Joinville F 26 D3
Joița RO 161 E7
Jokela FIN 119 B16
Jokela FIN 119 E16
Jokela FIN 127 D12
Jokelankylä FIN 123 C14
Jøkelfjordeidet N 112 C9
Jokijärvi FIN 121 C12
Jokijärvi FIN 123 D17
Joki-Kokko FIN 119 D16
Jokikunta FIN 127 E11
Jokikylä FIN 121 E11
Jokikylä FIN 122 E8
Jokikylä FIN 123 C13
Jokikylä FIN 123 C15
Jokilampi FIN 121 C12
Jokimaa FIN 127 D12
Jokioinen FIN 127 D9
Jokiperä FIN 122 E8
Jokipii FIN 122 E9
Jokivarsi FIN 123 E11
Jokivarsi FIN 123 E12
Jokkmokk S 116 E3
Jokūbavas LT 134 E2
Jolanda di Savoia I 66 C4
Jolanki FIN 117 E13
Jolda P 38 E3
Joloskylä FIN 119 D16
Joltai MD 154 E3
Jomala FIN 99 B13
Jømna N 101 E15
Jona CH 27 F10
Jönåker S 93 B9
Jonava LT 137 C9
Joncy F 30 B6
Jondal N 94 B4
Jonesborough GB 7 D10
Joniec PL 139 E10
Joniškėlis LT 135 D8
Joniškis LT 134 D7
Joniškis LT 137 C12
Jonkeri FIN 125 C13
Jönköping S 92 D4
Jonkowo PL 139 C9
Jonku FIN 120 D9
Jonquières F 35 B8
Jonsberg S 93 B9
Jonsered S 91 D11
Jonslund S 91 C12
Jonstorp S 87 C11
Jonzac F 28 E5
Jõõdre EST 130 D7
Joppolo I 59 B8
Jorăști RO 153 F11
Jorba E 43 D7
Jorcas E 42 F2
Jordanów PL 147 B9
Jordanów Śląski PL 81 E11
Jordbro S 99 D10
Jordbru N 108 B9
Jordbrua N 108 D8
Jördenstorf D 83 C13
Jordet N 102 D3
Jork D 82 C7
Jörlanda S 91 D10
Jormvattnet S 105 B16
Jörn S 118 D4
Joroinen FIN 125 F9
Jørpeland N 94 D4
Jørstadmoen N 101 D12
Jošanica BIH 157 E9
Jošanička Banja SRB 163 C10
Jošavka BIH 157 C7
Joseni RO 153 D6
Josenii Bârgăului RO 152 C5
Josifovo MK 169 B7
Josipdol HR 156 B3
Josipovac HR 149 E11
Josnes F 24 E6
Jössefors S 96 C8
Josselin F 22 E6
Jossund N 105 C9
Josvainiai LT 134 F7
Jota N 101 D15
Jou P 38 F5
Jouarre F 25 C9
Joué-lès-Tours F 24 F4
Joué-sur-Erdre F 23 E9
Jougne F 31 B9
Joukokylä FIN 121 D10
Jouques F 35 C10
Joure NL 16 C5
Journiac F 29 F7
Joutenniva FIN 123 B15
Joutsa FIN 127 B15
Joutseno FIN 129 C10
Joutsijärvi FIN 115 E3
Joux-la-Ville F 25 E10
Jouy F 24 C6
Jouy-aux-Arches F 26 B5
Jouy-le-Potier F 24 E6
Jøvik N 111 A18
Jøvik N 111 B13
Joyeuse F 35 B7
Joze F 30 D3
Józefów PL 141 F4
Józefów PL 144 A4
Józefów PL 144 C7
Juankoski FIN 125 D10
Juan-les-Pins F 36 D6
Juban AL 163 E8
Jubë AL 168 B1
Jübek D 82 A6
Jublains F 23 D11
Jubrique E 53 C6
Jüchen D 20 B6
Juchowo PL 85 C10
Jüchsen D 75 B8
Jucu RO 152 D3
Judaberg N 94 D3
Judenbach D 75 B9
Judenburg A 73 B10
Judinsalo FIN 127 B14
Juelsminde DK 86 D6
Jugon-les-Lacs F 23 D7
Jugorje SLO 148 E4
Jugureni RO 161 C8
Juhonpieti S 116 D10
Juhtimäki FIN 127 B9
Juillac F 29 E8
Juillan F 32 D6
Jujurieux F 31 C7
Jukkasjärvi S 116 C5
Juknaičiai LT 134 F3
Juksjaur S 109 E10
Jukua FIN 121 C9
Julåsen S 103 B10
Julbach A 76 E5
Jule N 105 C15
Jülich D 20 C6
Juliénas F 30 C6
Jullouville F 23 C8
Jumaliskylä FIN 121 E13
Jumeaux F 30 E3
Jumilhac-le-Grand F 29 E8
Jumilla E 55 C10
Juminen FIN 125 D9
Jumisko FIN 121 B11
Jumprava LV 135 C9
Jumurda LV 135 C11
Juncal P 44 E3
Juncosa E 42 E5
Juneda E 42 D5
Jung S 91 C13
Jungingen D 27 D11
Junglinster L 20 E6
Jungsund FIN 122 D7
Junik KS 163 E9
Juniskär S 103 B13
Juniville F 19 F9
Jünkerath D 21 D7
Junkerdal N 109 C10
Junnonoja FIN 119 F15
Junosuando S 116 D9
Junqueira P 50 E5
Junsele S 107 D11
Juntinvaara FIN 121 F15
Juntusranta FIN 121 D13
Juodeikiai LT 134 D6
Juodkrantė LT 134 E2
Juodšiliai LT 137 D11
Juodupė LT 135 D11
Juoksengi S 117 E11
Juoksenki FIN 117 E11
Juokslahti FIN 127 B13
Juokuanvaara FIN 119 C13
Juonto FIN 121 F13
Juorkuna FIN 120 E8
Juornaankylä FIN 127 D14
Juostininkai LT 135 E9
Juotasniemi FIN 119 B17
Jupânești RO 160 D3
Jupilles F 24 E3
Juprelle B 19 C12
Jurançon F 32 D5
Jurbarkas LT 136 C6
Jurbise B 19 C8
Jürgenshagen D 83 C11
Jürgenstorf D 84 C3
Jurģi LV 134 C5
Jüri EST 131 C9
Jurignac F 28 D5
Jurilovca RO 155 D3
Jurjevo HR 67 C10
Jūrkalne LV 134 B2
Jurklošter SLO 148 D4
Jurkowice PL 143 E11
Jūrmala LV 134 C7
Jūrmalciems LV 134 D2
Jurmo FIN 126 D5
Jurmo FIN 126 F6
Jurmu FIN 121 D10
Jurovski Brod HR 148 E4
Jursla S 93 B8
Jurva FIN 122 E7
Jussac F 29 F10
Jussey F 26 E4
Juta H 149 D9
Jüterbog D 80 C4
Jutis S 109 D13
Jutrosin PL 81 C12
Jutsajaure S 116 D3
Juujärvi FIN 120 B9
Juuka FIN 125 D12
Juuma FIN 121 B13
Juupajoki FIN 127 B11
Juupakylä FIN 123 F10
Juurikka FIN 125 G14
Juurikkalahti FIN 125 B10
Juurikkamäki FIN 125 E10
Juurikorpi FIN 128 D6
Juuru EST 131 C9
Juustovaara FIN 117 D13
Juutinen FIN 123 B17
Juva FIN 128 B8
Juvanådammet S 107 D12
Juvigné F 23 D9
Juvigny-le-Tertre F 23 C9
Juvigny-sous-Andaine F 23 C10
Juvola FIN 125 F11
Juzennecourt F 26 D2
Juzet-d'Izaut F 33 E7
Jūžintai LT 135 E11
Jyderup DK 87 D8
Jylhä FIN 123 D17
Jylhämä FIN 119 E17
Jyllinge DK 87 D10
Jyllinkoski FIN 122 F8
Jyllintaival FIN 122 E8
Jyrinki FIN 123 C12
Jyrkänkoski FIN 121 B14
Jyrkänkylä FIN 125 B13
Jyrkkä FIN 125 C9
Jystrup DK 87 D9
Jyväskylä FIN 123 F15

K

Kaagjärve EST 131 F12
Kaakamo FIN 119 C12
Kaalepi EST 131 C11
Kaamanen FIN 113 E19
Kaamasjoki FIN 113 E19
Kaamasmukka FIN 113 E18
Kaanaa FIN 127 B11
Kääntöjärvi S 116 D7
Kääpa EST 131 F14
Kääpälä FIN 128 C6
Kaarakkala FIN 124 C8
Kaaraneskoski FIN 117 E12
Käärdi EST 131 E12
Kaarepere EST 131 D13
Kaaresuvanto FIN 116 B9
Kaarina FIN 126 E7
Kaarlela FIN 123 C10
Käärmelehto FIN 117 D15
Kaarnevaara S 117 C10
Kaarnijärvi FIN 115 F1
Kaarßen D 83 D10
Kaarst D 21 B7
Kaasmarkku FIN 126 C7
Kaatsheuvel NL 16 E4
Kaava FIN 113 D18
Kaavi FIN 125 E10
Kaba H 151 C7
Kabakça TR 173 B9
Kabaklar TR 173 E11
Kabakum TR 177 A8
Kabala EST 131 D11
Kåbdalis S 118 B4
Kabelvåg N 110 D7
Kaberneeme EST 131 B10
Kabile LV 134 C4
Kableshkovo BG 167 D9
Kabli EST 131 E8
Kać SRB 158 C4
Kaçanik KS 164 E3
Kačarevo SRB 158 D6
Kachkivka UA 154 A2
Kachurivka UA 154 B5
Kačice CZ 76 B5
Käckelbäcksmon S 103 A13
Kaczory PL 85 D11
Kadaň CZ 76 B4
Kadarkút H 149 D9
Kadiköy TR 173 B9
Kadiköy TR 173 C6
Kadiköy TR 173 C11
Kadiköy TR 177 A9
Kadila EST 131 C12
Kadrifakovo MK 164 F5
Kadrina EST 131 C12
Kadzidło PL 139 D11
Käenkoski FIN 125 E15
Kaerepere EST 131 D9
Kåfjord N 112 D11
Kåfjord N 113 B16
Kåfjorddalen N 112 E6
Kåge S 118 E5
Kågeröd S 87 D12
Kaggebo S 93 D9
Kağıthane TR 173 B10
Kagkadi GR 174 C3
Kahla D 79 E10
Kahl am Main D 187 A7
Kåhög S 91 D11
Kahraman TR 181 A8
Kähtävä FIN 119 F12
Kaïafa GR 174 D4
Käina EST 130 D5
Kainasto FIN 122 F8
Kainourgio GR 174 B3
Kainulasjärvi S 116 D9
Kainuunkylä FIN 119 B11
Kainuunmäki FIN 124 C8
Kaipiainen FIN 128 D7
Kaipola FIN 127 B13
Kairala FIN 115 D2
Kairiai LT 134 E6
Kairiškiai LT 134 D5
Kaisajoki FIN 119 B12
Kaisepakte S 111 D17
Kaisersesch D 21 D8
Kaiserslautern D 21 F9
Kaisheim D 75 E8
Kaišiadorys LT 137 D9
Kaisma EST 131 D9
Kaitainen FIN 124 F9
Kaitainsalmi FIN 121 F11
Kaitajärvi FIN 119 B13
Kaitum S 116 C4
Kaivanto FIN 120 F9
Kaive LV 134 B6
Kaive LV 135 B11
Kajaani FIN 121 F10
Kajal SK 146 E5
Kajanki FIN 117 B11
Kajdacs H 149 C11
Kajew PL 143 B7
Kajoo FIN 125 D12
Kájov CZ 76 E6
Kakanj BIH 157 D9
Kakasd H 149 D11
Kakavi AL 168 E3
Kakenieki LV 134 C6
Kakenstorf D 82 D7
Kakerbeck D 83 E10
Kakhanavichy BY 133 E4
Käkilahti FIN 120 F8
Käkišķe LV 134 D2
Kaklıç TR 177 C8
Kąkolewnica Wschodnia PL 141 G7
Kakolewo PL 81 C11
Kakovatos GR 174 E4
Kakrukë AL 168 C3
Kakskerta FIN 126 E7
Kakslauttanen FIN 115 B2
Kakucs H 150 C3
Kál H 150 B5
Käl S 107 D12
Kälä FIN 127 B15
Kalabakbaşı TR 173 E7
Kålaboda S 118 F5
Kalače MNE 163 D9
Kala Dendra GR 169 B9
Kalaja FIN 123 C14
Kalajärvi FIN 127 E12
Kalajoki FIN 119 F11
Kalak N 113 B19
Kalakangas FIN 123 C14
Kalakoski FIN 123 F10
Kalamaki GR 169 E8
Kalamaki GR 174 D2
Kalamaki GR 175 D8
Kalamaria GR 169 C8
Kalamata GR 174 E5
Kalamos GR 175 C8
Kalamoti GR 177 C7
Kalamoto GR 169 C9
Kalampaka GR 169 E6
Kalampaki GR 171 B6
Kalana EST 130 D4
Kalandra GR 169 E9
Kala Nera GR 169 F9
Kalanistra GR 174 C4
Kalanti FIN 126 D6
Kälarne S 107 F10
Kalathos GR 181 D8
Kalavarda GR 181 D7
Kalavryta GR 174 C5
Kaława PL 81 B9
Kalbe (Milde) D 83 E10
Kalce SLO 73 E9
Kalchevo BG 167 E7
Káld H 149 B8
Kaldabruņa LV 135 D12
Kaldbak FO 2 A3
Kaldfarnes N 111 B12
Kaldfarnes N 111 B13
Kaldfjord N 111 A16
Kaldslett N 111 A16
Kaldvåg N 111 D10
Kaldvik N 111 D11
Kale TR 181 B9
Kalefeld D 79 C7
Kaleköy TR 171 D9
Kälen S 103 A8
Kälen S 103 B11
Kälen S 118 D6
Kalentzi GR 168 F4
Kalesija BIH 157 D10
Kalesmeno GR 174 B4
Kalēti LV 134 D2
Kalety PL 143 E6
Kalevala RUS 121 D17
Kali GR 169 C7
Kali HR 156 D3
Kalianoi GR 175 D5
Kalimanci MK 165 F6
Kalimash AL 163 E9
Kaliningrad RUS 136 D2
Kalinino RUS 136 E6
Kalinovik BIH 157 F9
Kalinovka RUS 136 D4
Kalinowa PL 142 C5
Kalinowo PL 136 F6
Kaliska PL 138 C5
Kalisz PL 142 C5
Kalisz Pomorski PL 85 D9
Kalita EST 131 E9
Kali Vrysi GR 170 B5
Kalix S 119 C10
Kalixforsen S 116 C4
Kalkar D 16 E6
Kalkhorst D 83 C10
Kalki LV 130 F4
Kalkiainen FIN 115 E3
Kalkim TR 173 E7
Kalkkimaa FIN 119 C12
Kalkkinen FIN 127 C14
Kałków PL 77 B12
Kalkūni LV 135 E12
Kall D 21 C7
Kall S 105 E14
Källa S 89 A11
Kallaste EST 131 D14
Kallax S 118 C8
Källberget S 102 A6
Källbomark S 118 D6
Källby FIN 122 C9
Källby S 91 B13
Kalle N 110 D7
Källeboda S 96 D7
Källekärr S 91 C10
Kållered S 91 D11
Kållerud S 91 A12
Kallham A 76 F5
Kallifoni GR 169 F6
Kallifytos GR 171 B6
Kallimasia GR 177 C7
Kallinge S 89 C8
Kalliojoki FIN 121 F15
Kalliopi GR 171 E8
Kalliosalmi FIN 117 E17
Kallirachi GR 171 C7
Kallislahti FIN 129 B10
Kallithea GR 169 D8
Kallithea GR 169 D9
Kallithea GR 169 E7
Kallithea GR 174 D4
Kallithea GR 174 F4
Kallithea GR 175 D8
Kallithea GR 177 D8
Kallithiro GR 169 F6
Kalljord N 110 C9
Kallmet i Madh AL 163 F8
Kallmünz D 75 D10
Kallo FIN 117 D12
Kálló H 150 B3
Kallön S 109 E15
Kalloni GR 171 F10
Kalloni GR 175 D7
Kalloni GR 176 D5
Kállósemjén H 145 H4
Kallsedet S 105 D13
Källsjön S 103 E11
Kallträsk FIN 122 F7
Kallunki FIN 115 E5
Kallunki FIN 121 B13
Kálmánháza H 145 H4
Kalmar S 89 B10
Kalmari FIN 123 E14
Kalmthout B 16 F2
Kalna SRB 164 C5
Kalna SRB 164 D5
Kalná nad Hronom SK 147 E7
Kalnciems LV 134 C7
Kalni LV 134 D4
Kalnieši LV 133 E2
Kalnujai LT 134 F6
Kalocsa H 150 D2
Kalofer BG 165 D10
Kaloi Limenes GR 178 F8
Kaloneri GR 169 D5
Kalo Nero GR 174 E4
Kalos Agros GR 170 B6
Kalotina BG 165 C6
Kalotintsi BG 165 D6
Kaloyanovets BG 166 E5
Kaloyanovo BG 165 E10
Káloz H 149 C10
Kalpaki GR 168 E4
Kalpio FIN 121 E10
Kals am Großglockner A 73 B6
Kaltanėnai LT 135 F11
Kaltbrunn CH 27 F11
Kaltene LV 134 B5
Kaltenkirchen D 83 C7
Kaltennordheim D 79 E7
Kaltensundheim D 79 E7
Kaltinėnai LT 134 E4
Kaluđerica SRB 158 D6
Kalugerovo BG 165 E9
Kalundborg DK 87 D8
Kalupe LV 135 D13
Kałuszyn PL 141 F5
Kaluzhekoye RUS 136 D4
Kalvåg N 100 C1
Kalvarija LT 136 E7
Kalvatn N 100 B4
Kalveliai LT 137 D12
Kalvene LV 134 C3
Kalvi EST 131 C13
Kälviä FIN 123 C10
Kalvik N 109 A10
Kalvitsa FIN 128 B7
Kalvola FIN 127 C11
Kalvträsk S 107 B17
Kalwang A 73 B10
Kalwaria Zebrzydowska PL 147 B9
Kalymnos GR 177 F8
Kalyny UA 145 G8
Kalythies GR 181 D8
Kalyves GR 171 C7
Kalyvia GR 174 B3
Kalyvia GR 174 B3
Kalyvia GR 174 D5
Kalyvia Thorikou GR 175 D8
Kamajai LT 135 E11
Kämäränkylä FIN 121 F14
Kamarde LV 135 D8
Kamares GR 174 C4
Kamares GR 175 F10
Kamariotissa GR 171 D8
Kambja EST 131 E13
Kamburovo BG 166 C6
Kamen BG 166 C5
Kamen D 17 E9
Kamenari BG 166 D6
Kamena Vourla GR 175 B6
Kamen Bryag BG 167 C11
Kamencia SRB 158 F6
Kamenec pod Vtáčnikom SK 147 D7
Kamengrad BIH 156 C6
Kamenica BIH 156 D5
Kamenica BIH 157 D9
Kamenica BIH 158 F3
Kamenica MK 164 E6
Kamenica SK 145 E2
Kamenica SRB 158 E4
Kamenica SRB 164 C5
Kamenica nad Cirochou SK 145 F4
Kamenica nad Hronom SK 147 F7
Kamenicë AL 168 C4
Kamenice CZ 77 C7
Kamenice CZ 77 D9
Kamenicë KS 164 D4
Kamenice nad Lipou CZ 77 D8
Kamenična SK 146 F6
Kamenín SK 147 F7
Kamenka RUS 129 E11
Kamenná Poruba SK 147 C7
Kamennogorsk RUS 129 D11
Kamenný Most SK 147 F7
Kamenný Přívoz CZ 77 C7
Kamenný Újezd CZ 77 E6
Kameno BG 167 D8
Kameno Pole BG 165 C8
Kamenovo BG 161 F8
Kamensko BIH 157 D9
Kamensko HR 149 F8
Kamensko HR 157 E6
Kamenskoye RUS 136 D4
Kamenz D 80 D6
Kamerik NL 182 A5
Kamern D 83 E12
Kames GB 4 D6
Kamëz AL 168 B2
Kamičak BIH 157 C6
Kamicë-Flakë AL 163 E7
Kamień PL 144 C5
Kamieńczyk PL 139 E12
Kamienica PL 145 D1
Kamienica Polska PL 143 E7
Kamieniec PL 81 B10
Kamieniec Ząbkowicki PL 77 A11
Kamienka SK 145 E2
Kamień Krajeński PL 85 C13
Kamienna Gora PL 81 E10
Kamiennik PL 81 E12
Kamień Pomorski PL 85 C7
Kamieńsk PL 143 D8
Kamień Wielkie PL 81 A7
Kamilski Dol BG 171 A10
Kamion PL 139 F9
Kamion PL 141 G2
Kamionka PL 141 H6
Kamiros GR 181 D7
Kamlunge S 119 C9
Kammela FIN 126 D5
Kammen N 112 C4
Kamnik SLO 73 D10
Kamno SLO 73 D8
Kamøyvær N 113 A16
Kamp D 185 D8
Kampanis GR 169 C8
Kampen D 86 F2
Kampen NL 16 C5
Kampenhout B 182 D5
Kämpfelbach D 187 D6
Kampi GR 174 A2
Kampia GR 177 B6
Kampinkylä FIN 122 E8
Kampinos PL 141 F2
Kamp-Lintfort D 17 F7
Kampos GR 174 C5
Kampos GR 174 F5
Kampvoll N 111 B14
Kamsjö S 118 F3
Kamula FIN 123 B16
Kamut H 151 D6
Kam"yane UA 154 A5
Kam"yanka UA 154 D6
Kam"yans'ke UA 154 F4
Kamyanyets BY 141 F9
Kamyanyuki BY 141 E9
Kanaküla EST 131 E10
Kanal SLO 73 D8
Kanala FIN 123 D12
Kanala GR 175 E9
Kanali GR 168 E2
Kanali GR 174 A2
Kanalia GR 169 F8
Kanallaki GR 168 F4
Kanan S 109 F10
Kanatlarci MK 169 B6
Kańczuga PL 144 D5
Kandava LV 134 B5
Kandel D 27 B9
Kandelin D 84 B4
Kandern D 27 E8
Kandersteg CH 70 E5
Kandila GR 174 B2
Kandila GR 174 D5
Kandle EST 131 B12
Kanepi EST 131 F13
Kanestraum N 104 E4
Kanfanar HR 67 B8
Kangas FIN 119 F13
Kangas FIN 122 D9
Kangasaho FIN 123 E13
Kangasala FIN 127 C11
Kangaskylä FIN 119 F16
Kangaskylä FIN 121 E11
Kangaskylä FIN 123 C13
Kangaslahti FIN 125 D10
Kangaslampi FIN 125 F10
Kangasniemi FIN 123 G17
Kangasvieri FIN 123 C13
Kangos S 116 D9
Kangosjärvi FIN 117 C11
Kanianka SK 147 D7
Kaninë AL 168 D2
Kanjiža SRB 150 E5
Kankaanpää FIN 126 B7
Kankaanpää FIN 126 C7
Kankainen FIN 123 F16
Kankari FIN 120 E8
Kånna S 87 B13
Kannas FIN 121 E12
Känne S 103 B9
Kannonjärvi FIN 123 E14
Kannonkoski FIN 123 E14
Kannus FIN 123 C11
Kannusjärvi FIN 128 D7
Kannuskoski FIN 128 D7
Kanpantxua E 41 B6
Kanstad N 111 D10
Kanstadbotn N 111 C10
Kantala FIN 124 F8
Kantanos GR 178 E6
Kantele FIN 127 D14
Kantens NL 17 B7
Kantia GR 175 D6
Kantojärvi FIN 119 C12
Kantojoki FIN 121 B13
Kantokylä FIN 123 B13
Kantola FIN 123 D10
Kantomaanpää FIN 119 B12
Kantorneset N 111 B17
Kantserava BY 133 F4
Kantti FIN 122 F9
Kanturk IRL 8 D5
Kaolinovo BG 161 F10
Kaona SRB 158 F5
Kaonik BIH 157 D8
Kaonik SRB 164 B3
Kapakli TR 173 B8
Kapakli TR 173 D10
Kapanbeleni TR 173 D7
Kapandriti GR 175 C8
Kaparelli GR 175 C7
Kapčiamiestis LT 137 F8
Kapelle NL 16 F1
Kapellen B 16 F2
Kapelle-op-den-Bos B 182 C4
Kapellskär S 99 C12
Kapfenberg A 148 B4
Kapikargin TR 181 C9
Kapitan-Andreevo BG 166 F6
Kapiz TR 181 B9
Kaplava LV 133 E2
Kaplice CZ 77 E7
Kapljuh BIH 156 C5
Kápolna H 150 B5
Kápolnásnyék H 149 B11
Kaposfő H 149 D9
Kaposmérő H 149 D9
Kaposszekcső H 149 D10
Kaposvár H 149 D9
Kapp N 101 E13
Kappel D 21 E8
Kappel-Grafenhausen D 186 E4
Kappeln D 83 A7
Kappelrodeck D 186 D5
Kappl A 71 C10
Kåpponis S 118 B4
Kaprijke B 16 F1
Kaprun A 73 B6
Kapshticë AL 168 C5
Kapsia GR 174 D5
Kaptol HR 149 F9
Kaptsyowka BY 140 C9
Kapušany SK 145 E3
Kapusta FIN 119 B12
Kapuvár H 149 A8
Käpylä FIN 119 F14
Karaağaç TR 173 A7
Karaağaç TR 173 F6
Karaağaçli TR 177 B9
Karabanove UA 154 C5
Karabiga TR 173 D7
Karaböğürtlen TR 181 B9
Karabunar BG 165 E9
Karaburun TR 173 B10
Karaburun TR 177 B7
Karaca TR 181 C8
Karacabey TR 173 D9
Karacadağ TR 167 F9
Karacakılavuz TR 173 B7
Karacaköy TR 173 B9
Karád H 149 C9
Karadzhalovo BG 166 E4
Karahalil TR 173 A7
Karaincirli TR 171 C10
Karainebeyli TR 171 D10
Karaisen BG 166 C4
Karakaja BIH 157 D11
Karakasim TR 172 A6
Karakaya TR 173 F9
Karakoca TR 173 D10
Karaköy TR 173 E6
Karaköy TR 177 B9
Karaköy TR 181 B9
Karakurt TR 177 A10
Karala EST 130 E3
Karaman TR 173 F9
Karamanovo BG 166 B5
Karamehmet TR 173 B8

Karamyshevo RUS 132 F4
Karamyshevo RUS 136 E5
Karancsberény H 147 E9
Karancskeszi H 147 E9
Karancslapujtő H 147 E9
Karancsság H 147 E9
Karankamäki FIN 124 C8
Karaoğlanli TR 177 B10
Karaorman TR 173 E9
Karaova TR 177 E10
Karapchiv UA 152 A6
Karapelit BG 161 F11
Karasjok N 113 E15
Karatoulas GR 174 D4
Karats S 109 C16
Karavas GR 178 C4
Karavelovo BG 165 D10
Karavelovo BG 167 E7
Käravete EST 131 C11
Karavomylos GR 175 B6
Karavukovo SRB 157 B11
Karben D 21 D11
Kårberg S 92 B5
Karbinci MK 164 F5
Kårböle S 103 C9
Kårböleskog S 103 C9
Karbow-Vietlübbe D 83 D12
Karbunarë e Vogël AL 168 C2
Karby D 83 A7
Karby DK 86 B3
Karby S 99 C10
Karcag H 151 C6
Karcsa H 145 G4
Karczew PL 141 F4
Karczmiska Pierwsze PL 141 H6
Kärda S 87 A13
Kardakata GR 174 C1
Kardam BG 155 F2
Kardam BG 166 C6
Kardamaina GR 177 F9
Kardamyli GR 174 F5
Kardašova Řečice CZ 77 D7
Karden D 21 D8
Kardiani GR 176 D5
Kardis S 117 E11
Karditsa GR 169 F6
Karditsomagoula GR 169 F6
Kärdla S 117 D11
Kardon BY 133 F6
Kardos H 150 D6
Kardoskút H 150 E6
Karegasnjarga FIN 113 E16
Kareli LV 134 D4
Karesuando S 116 B8
Kargowa PL 81 B9
Karhi FIN 123 C9
Karhila FIN 123 F13
Karhujärvi FIN 115 F4
Karhukangas FIN 119 F14
Karhula FIN 128 D6
Kariani GR 170 C5
Karigasniemi FIN 113 E16
Karihaugen N 111 D12
Karijoki FIN 122 F7
Karinainen FIN 126 D8
Käringberg S 107 A12
Käringen N 111 D10
Käringsjön S 102 B3
Käringsjövallen S 102 B4
Karinkanta FIN 119 E13
Karis FIN 127 E10
Karise DK 87 E10
Karisjärvi FIN 127 D11
Karitaina GR 174 E5
Karitsa GR 169 D7
Karjalaisenniemi FIN 121 B11
Karjalan kirkonkylä FIN 126 D7
Karjalankylä FIN 119 D15
Karjalankylä FIN 126 D7
Karjalanvaara FIN 120 B9
Karjalanvaara FIN 121 F10
Karjalohja FIN 127 E10
Kärjenkoski FIN 122 F7
Karjulanmäki FIN 123 C13
Karkalou GR 174 D5
Kärki LV 131 F11
Kärkinen FIN 119 F12
Kärkkäälä FIN 123 E16
Kärkkäälä FIN 124 E8
Karkkila FIN 127 D11
Karkku FIN 127 C9
Kärklinieki LV 133 B2
Kärkölä FIN 127 D10
Kärkölä FIN 127 D13
Karksi EST 131 E11
Karksi-Nuia EST 131 E11
Kårkul S 118 B5
Kärla EST 130 E4
Karlå FIN 122 F7
Karlby FIN 126 F4
Karlebotn N 114 C5
Karleby FIN 123 C10
Karlholmsbruk S 99 A9
Karlino PL 85 B9
Kärmuiža LV 134 B4
Karlobag HR 67 C11
Karlovac HR 148 F5
Karlovasi GR 177 D8
Karlovice CZ 142 F3
Karlovo BG 165 D10
Karlovy Vary CZ 76 B3
Karłowice PL 142 E4
Karlsbäck S 107 D15
Karlsbad D 27 C10
Karlsberg S 103 D9
Karlsborg S 92 B5
Karlsburg D 84 C5
Karlsdal S 97 D12
Karlsdorf-Neuthard D 27 B10
Karlsfeld D 75 F9
Karlsfors S 103 C9
Karlshagen D 84 B5
Karlshamn S 89 C7
Karlshöfen D 17 B12
Karlskoga S 97 D12
Karlskrona S 89 C9
Karlsøy N 112 C4
Karlsruhe D 27 B9
Karlstad S 97 D10
Karlstadt D 74 C6
Karlstein an der Thaya A 77 E8
Karlstetten A 77 F9
Karlukovo BG 165 C9
Karmansbo S 97 C14
Karmas S 109 B17
Karmélava LT 137 D9
Kärnä FIN 123 D11
Kärnä FIN 123 D15
Kärna S 91 D10
Karnaliyivka UA 154 E6
Karnice PL 85 B8
Karniewo PL 139 E12
Karnjarga FIN 113 D19

Karnobat BG 167 D7
Karojba HR 67 B8
Karolinka CZ 146 C6
Karonsbo S 107 C13
Karoti GR 171 B10
Karousades GR 168 E2
Karow D 79 B11
Karow D 83 C12
Karpacz PL 81 E9
Kärpänkylä FIN 121 C14
Karpathos GR 181 E6
Karpenisi GR 174 B4
Karperi GR 169 B9
Karpero GR 169 E6
Kärppälä FIN 127 C9
Karpuzlu TR 171 C10
Karpuzlu TR 181 A7
Kärrbackstrand S 102 E4
Karrebæksminde DK 87 E9
Karrenzin D 83 D11
Kärrsjö S 107 D15
Karsakiškis LT 135 E9
Kärsämä FIN 119 E15
Kärsämäki FIN 123 C15
Kärsava LV 133 C3
Karsikas FIN 123 C14
Karsikkoniemi FIN 117 C11
Karsikkovaara FIN 124 B9
Karsimus FIN 115 E12
Karsin PL 138 C4
Karşiyaka TR 173 D9
Karşiyaka TR 177 C9
Karsko PL 85 E8
Kårsta S 99 C10
Karstädt D 83 D10
Karstädt D 83 D11
Kärstna EST 131 E11
Karstula FIN 123 E13
Karszew PL 142 B6
Kartal H 150 B4
Kartavoll N 94 E3
Kartena LT 134 E2
Kartitsch A 72 C6
Kartuzy PL 138 B5
Käru EST 131 D10
Käru EST 131 D12
Karuna FIN 126 E8
Karungi S 119 B11
Karunki FIN 119 B12
Karup DK 86 C4
Kärvåg N 104 E3
Karvala FIN 123 D11
Kärväskylä FIN 123 D15
Karvia FIN 122 F9
Kärvikhamn N 111 B15
Karviná CZ 147 B7
Karvoskylä FIN 123 C14
Karvounari GR 168 F3
Karwica PL 139 C11
Karya GR 169 E7
Karya GR 174 D4
Karya GR 175 D6
Karyes GR 171 D6
Karyes GR 175 E5
Karyotissa GR 169 C7
Karyoupoli GR 178 B3
Karystos GR 175 C9
Kås DK 86 A5
Kašalj SRB 163 C10
Kasejovice CZ 76 D5
Kasendorf D 75 B9
Kasepää EST 131 D14
Kasfjord N 111 C11
Kashirskoye RUS 136 D2
Kaşikçi TR 173 B7
Kašina HR 148 E6
Kaskantyú H 150 D3
Kåskats S 109 C14
Kaskii FIN 129 B9
Kaskinen FIN 122 F6
Kaskö FIN 122 F6
Käsmä FIN 121 C12
Kåsmo N 108 B9
Kåsmolia N 108 B9
Käsmu EST 131 B11
Kaspakas GR 171 E8
Kašperské Hory CZ 76 D5
Kaspichan BG 167 C8
Kassa S 117 D11
Kassandreia GR 169 D9
Kasseedorf D 83 B9
Kassel D 78 D6
Kassiopi GR 168 E2
Kastania GR 168 D4
Kastania GR 168 E5
Kastania GR 169 D7
Kastania GR 169 F8
Kastanies GR 171 A10
Kastanochori GR 169 C10
Kastari FIN 127 C13
Kastellaun D 21 D8
Kastelli GR 174 B4
Kastellia GR 174 B5
Kaštel Stari HR 156 E5
Kaštel Sućurac HR 156 E5
Kaštel Šegarski HR 156 D4
Kasterlee B 16 F3
Kastīre LV 135 D13
Kastl D 75 D10
Kastlösa S 89 C10
Kastneshamn N 111 C13
Kastorf D 83 C9
Kastoria GR 168 C5
Kastorio GR 174 E5
Kastraki GR 174 B3
Kastraki GR 176 E5
Kastrāne LV 135 C10
Kastre EST 131 E14
Kastri GR 169 E8
Kastri GR 175 E6
Kastro GR 175 C7
Kastrosykia GR 174 A2
Kastrova BY 133 E4
Kaszaper H 150 E6
Kaszczor PL 81 C10
Katajamäki FIN 125 D10
Katakolo GR 174 D3
Kåtaliden S 109 F15
Katalin AL 163 E8
Kataloinen FIN 127 C12
Katapola GR 177 F6
Katarraktis GR 177 C7
Kåtaselet S 118 D3
Katastari GR 174 D2
Katerini GR 169 D8
Katerma FIN 125 B12
Kathenoi GR 175 B8
Kathlow D 81 C6
Kätkänjoki FIN 123 E11
Kätkäsuvanto FIN 117 B10
Kätkävaara FIN 119 B13
Kätkesuando S 117 B10
Kédainiai LT 135 F7
Katlenburg-Lindau D 79 C7

Kátlovce SK 146 D5
Kato Achaïa GR 174 C4
Kato Alepochori GR 175 C7
Kato Asites GR 178 E9
Katochi GR 174 C3
Kato Chorio GR 179 E10
Kato Doliana GR 175 E6
Kato Glykovrysi GR 178 B4
Kato Kamila GR 169 B9
Kato Makrinou GR 174 C4
Kato Nevrokopi GR 169 B10
Kato Sounio GR 175 D9
Kato Tithorea GR 175 B6
Katouna GR 174 B3
Kato Vermio GR 169 C7
Kato Vlasia GR 174 C4
Kato Vrontou GR 169 B10
Katowice PL 143 F7
Katranca TR 173 B7
Katrineberg S 103 D11
Katrineberg S 93 B8
Katrineholm S 103 E13
Katsdorf A 76 F6
Katsikas GR 168 E4
Kattavia GR 181 E7
Kattbo S 102 E7
Kattelus FIN 123 F11
Kattilasaari S 119 C11
Kättilstad S 92 C7
Kättilstorp S 91 C14
Kattisavan S 107 B14
Kattisträsk S 118 E3
Katundishtë AL 168 D3
Katunets BG 165 C10
Katunitsa BG 165 D10
Katuntsi BG 169 B9
Katwijk aan Zee NL 16 D2
Katyčiai LT 134 F3
Katymár H 150 E3
Katy Wrocławskie PL 81 D11
Katzenelnbogen D 21 D9
Katzweiler D 21 E9
Kaub D 21 D9
Kaufbeuren D 71 B11
Kaufungen D 78 D6
Kaugurieši LV 135 B11
Kauhajärvi FIN 122 F8
Kauhajärvi FIN 123 D10
Kauhajoki FIN 122 F8
Kauhava FIN 123 D10
Kaukalampi FIN 127 D13
Kaukolikai LT 134 D3
Kaukonen FIN 117 D13
Kauksi EST 131 C14
Kaulille B 183 C7
Kaulinranta FIN 119 B11
Kaulsdorf D 79 E9
Kaunas LT 137 D8
Kaunata LV 133 D3
Kauniainen FIN 127 E12
Kaunisjoensuu S 117 D11
Kaunisvaara S 117 D10
Kaupanger N 100 D6
Kaupiškiai LT 136 D6
Kauppila FIN 123 F11
Kauppilanmäki FIN 124 C8
Kaurajärvi FIN 122 D9
Kaurissalo FIN 126 D5
Kaustinen FIN 123 C11
Kautenbach L 184 E5
Kautokeino N 112 E11
Kautzen A 77 E8
Kauvatsa FIN 126 C7
Kavadarci MK 169 B7
Kavajë AL 168 B2
Kavak TR 173 C6
Kavakdere TR 173 A7
Kavakli TR 173 A7
Kavaklidere TR 181 B8
Kavala GR 171 C6
Kavarna BG 167 C10
Kavarskas LT 135 F9
Kavasila GR 174 C3
Kavastu EST 131 E14
Kavelstorf D 83 C12
Kävlinge S 87 D12
Kavoli GR 171 A11
Kavali TR 167 F8
Kåxås S 105 E14
Käxed S 107 E14
Kaxholmen S 92 D4
Kayabaşi TR 181 B9
Kayalar TR 173 E8
Kayali TR 167 F8
Kayalioğlu TR 177 B10
Kayapa TR 173 F7
Kayatepe TR 181 A8
Käyllä FIN 121 B13
Käymäjärvi S 116 D9
Kayna D 79 E11
Kaynaklar TR 177 C9
Kaynarca TR 173 A7
Kaynardzha BG 161 F10
Kazanka BG 166 E4
Kazanlük BG 166 E4
Kazanów PL 141 H4
Kazár H 147 E9
Kazdanga LV 134 C3
Kazichene BG 165 D7
Kazikli TR 177 E9
Kazimierz Wielka PL 143 F9
Kazimierz Biskupi PL 142 B5
Kazimierz Dolne PL 141 H5
Kazincbarcika H 145 G2
Kazlowshchyna BY 133 E4
Kazly Rūda LT 137 D7
Kažmēirci PL 81 A11
Kaz'yany BY 133 F13
Kaz'yany BY 135 F13
Kçirë AL 163 E8
Kcynia PL 85 E12
Kdyně CZ 76 D4
Keadue IRL 6 D6
Keady GB 7 D9
Kealkill IRL 8 E4
Kebal S 91 B9
Kecerovce SK 145 F3
Kechrokampos GR 171 B7
Kechros GR 171 B9
Kecskéd H 149 A10
Kecskemét H 150 D4
Kédainiai LT 135 F7
Kedros GR 174 A5

Kjdzierzyn-Koźle PL 142 F5
Keele GB 11 E7
Keenagh IRL 7 E7
Keeni EST 131 F11
Kefalos GR 181 C5
Kefalovryso GR 169 E7
Kefenrod D 21 D12
Kefermarkt A 77 F7
Kegums LV 135 C9
Kegworth GB 11 F9
Kehidakustány H 149 C8
Kehl D 27 C8
Kehlen L 20 E6
Kehra EST 131 C10
Kehrig D 21 D8
Kehtna EST 131 D9
Kehvo FIN 125 D9
Keighley GB 11 D8
Keihärinkoski FIN 123 D15
Keikyä FIN 126 C8
Keila EST 131 C8
Keila-Joa EST 131 C8
Keillmore GB 4 D5
Keinäsperä FIN 119 D17
Keipene LV 135 C10
Keiprod N 111 C12
Keiss GB 3 H10
Keitele FIN 123 D16
Keitelepohja FIN 123 D15
Keith GB 3 K11
Kék H 145 G4
Kekava LV 135 C8
Kékcse H 145 G5
Kelankylä FIN 119 C18
Kelberg D 21 D7
Kelbra (Kyffhäuser) D 79 D9
Kelč CZ 146 C5
Kělcyrë AL 168 D3
Kelebia H 150 E4
Kelechyn UA 145 F7
Kelheim D 75 E10
Kelkheim (Taunus) D 187 A5
Kell D 21 E7
Kellas GB 3 K10
Kellas GB 5 B11
Kellenhusen D 83 A9
Kelli GR 169 C6
Kellinghusen D 82 C7
Kellmünz an der Iller D 71 A10
Kello FIN 119 D13
Kellokoski FIN 127 D13
Kelloniemi FIN 115 E3
Kelloniemi FIN 117 D11
Kelloselkä FIN 115 E5
Kells GB 4 F4
Kells GB 7 F9
Kells IRL 8 E2
Kells IRL 9 C8
Kelmė LT 134 E5
Kelmis B 20 C6
Kelontekemä FIN 117 C15
Kelottijärvi FIN 116 A8
Kelso GB 5 D12
Kelujärvi FIN 115 D2
Kelvedon GB 15 D10
Kelvä FIN 125 D14
Kemalpaşa TR 177 C9
Kemberg D 79 C12
Kemecse H 145 G4
Kemence H 147 E7
Kemenesmagasi H 149 B8
Kemenessömjén H 149 B8
Kemerburgaz TR 173 B10
Kémes H 149 E10
Kemeten A 148 B6
Kemi FIN 119 C13
Kemihaara FIN 115 C5
Kemijärvi FIN 115 E3
Kemilä FIN 121 C14
Keminmaa FIN 119 C13
Keminperä FIN 121 D12
Kēmishtaj AL 168 C2
Kemmel B 182 D1
Kemnath D 75 C10
Kemnay GB 3 L12
Kemnitz D 81 D7
Kemnitz D 84 B5
Kempele FIN 119 E15
Kempen D 16 F6
Kempenich D 21 D8
Kempsey GB 13 A10
Kempston GB 15 C8
Kempten (Allgäu) D 71 B10
Kendal GB 10 C6
Kenderes H 150 C5
Kendice SK 145 F3
Kenézlő H 145 G4
Kenfig GB 13 B7
Kengis S 117 D11
Kenilworth GB 13 A11
Kenmare IRL 8 E4
Kenmore GB 5 B9
Kenn D 21 E7
Kennacraig GB 4 D6
Kensaleyre GB 2 L4
Kensworth GB 15 D8
Kentavros GR 171 B7
Kentriko GR 169 B8
Kentro GR 174 D3
Kenyeri H 149 B8
Kenzingen D 27 D8
Kepez TR 173 D10
Kępice PL 85 B11
Kępno PL 142 D6
Kepsut TR 173 E9
Keqekollë KS 164 D3
Keramitsa GR 168 E3
Keramoti GR 171 C7
Kerántojärvi S 116 C9
Kerasia GR 169 D6
Kerasona GR 168 F4
Keräs-Sieppi FIN 117 B11
Keratea GR 175 D8
Kerava FIN 127 E12
Kerecsend H 147 F10
Kerekegyháza H 150 D4
Kerepestarcsa H 150 B3
Keret's ky UA 145 G7
Kerga EST 131 D7
Keri GR 174 D2
Kerimäki FIN 129 B11
Kerisalo FIN 125 E9
Kerkdriel NL 16 E4
Kerkejaure S 118 B3
Kerken D 16 F6
Kerkini GR 169 B8
Kerkonkoski FIN 123 E17
Kerkrade NL 20 C6
Kerkwijk NL 183 B6
Kerkyra GR 168 E2
Kerlouan F 22 C3

Kerma FIN 125 F11
Kermen BG 166 D6
Kernascléden F 22 D5
Kernavė LT 137 D10
Kernhof A 148 A5
Kerns CH 70 D6
Kerpen D 21 C7
Kerrykeel IRL 7 B7
Kershopefoot GB 5 E11
Kersilö FIN 117 C17
Kerspleben D 79 D9
Kerstinbo S 98 B7
Kerteminde DK 86 E7
Kertészsziget H 151 C7
Kertezi GR 174 D4
Kerzers CH 31 B11
Kesälahti FIN 129 B12
Keşan TR 172 C6
Kesäniemenkylä FIN 121 B12
Kesarevo BG 166 C5
Kesasjärv S 118 B8
Kesh IRL 6 D6
Kesh IRL 7 C7
Kesik TR 177 B8
Kesik TR 173 F7
Keskijärvi FIN 125 E14
Keskikylä FIN 119 E13
Keskikylä FIN 119 E15
Keskikylä FIN 119 E13
Keskikylä FIN 122 F9
Keskikylä FIN 119 E13
Keskinen FIN 121 E13
Keskipiiri FIN 119 E14
Keski-Posio FIN 121 C11
Keskusvankila FIN 124 C8
Kjsowo RUS 138 C4
Kessel B 182 C5
Kessel NL 183 C8
Kesselinkylä FIN 125 C14
Kessingland GB 15 C12
Kesten NL 183 B7
Kestilä FIN 119 D14
Kestilä FIN 119 F16
Kestrini GR 168 E3
Keswick GB 10 B5
Keszthely H 149 C8
Kesztölc H 149 A11
Kétegyháza H 151 D7
Kéthely H 149 C8
Ketola FIN 115 E2
Ketomella FIN 117 B12
Ketsch D 21 F11
Kétsoprony H 151 D6
Kettering GB 15 C7
Kettershausen D 71 A10
Kettinge DK 83 A11
Kettletoft GB 3 G11
Kettlewell GB 11 C7
Kettwig D 183 C9
Kéty PL 147 B8
Ketzin D 79 B12
Keula D 79 D8
Keuruu FIN 123 F13
Keutschach am See A 73 C9
Kevägärri FIN 114 F3
Kevelaer D 16 E6
Kevele LV 134 D5
Kevermes H 151 E7
Kevo FIN 113 D19
Keynsham GB 13 C9
Keyritty FIN 125 D10
Kežmarok SK 145 E1
Khadzhidimovo BG 169 A10
Khalamyer"ye BY 133 F6
Kharlu RUS 129 B11
Kharmanli BG 166 F5
Khaskovo BG 166 F5
Khayredin BG 160 F3
Khelyulya RUS 129 B14
Khisarya BG 165 D10
Khiytola RUS 129 C12
Khlivchany UA 144 C8
Kholmets' UA 145 F5
Kholms'ke UA 155 B4
Khorio GR 179 B8
Khrabrovo RUS 136 D2
Khrishteni BG 166 E5
Khust UA 145 G7
Khyriv UA 145 D6
Khvoyna BG 165 F10
Kiannanniemi FIN 121 D14
Kiato GR 175 C6
Kiaunoriai LT 134 E6
Kibæk DK 86 C3
Kibworth Harcourt GB 11 F10
Kiby N 114 C7
Kičevo MK 168 A4
Kichenitsa BG 161 F8
Kichevo BG 167 C8
Kidderminster GB 13 A10
Kidlington GB 13 B12
Kidričevo SLO 148 D5
Kidsgrove GB 11 E7
Kidwelly GB 12 B6
Kiefersfelden D 72 A5
Kiekinkoski FIN 125 B14
Kiekrz PL 81 B11
Kiel D 83 B8
Kielajoki FIN 113 E18
Kielce PL 143 E10
Kiełczygłów PL 143 D6
Kielder GB 5 E11
Kieldrecht B 182 C4
Kiełpino PL 138 B5
Kiemēnai LT 135 D8
Kiemozia PL 141 F1
Kienberg D 75 F11
Kierinki FIN 117 D15
Kierspe D 21 B9
Kieselbach D 79 E7
Kiesilä FIN 128 C7
Kiesimä FIN 123 E17
Kietrz PL 142 F5
Kietz D 81 A7
Kifisia GR 175 C8
Kihelkonna EST 130 E3
Kihlanki FIN 117 C11
Kihlanki S 117 C10
Kihlepa EST 131 E8
Kihlevere EST 131 C12
Kihniö FIN 123 F10
Kiihtelysvaara FIN 125 E14
Kiikala FIN 127 E10
Kiikka FIN 126 C8
Kiikla EST 131 C14
Kiikoinen FIN 126 C8
Kiili EST 131 C9
Kiiminki FIN 119 D15

Kiisa EST 131 C9
Kiiskilä FIN 123 C13
Kiistala FIN 117 C14
Kiiu EST 131 C10
Kiiu-Aabla EST 131 B11
Kije PL 143 E10
Kijevė KS 163 D10
Kijevo HR 156 E5
Kijewo Królewskie PL 138 D5
Kikerino RUS 132 C3
Kikinda SRB 150 F5
Kikół PL 138 E7
Kikorze PL 85 C8
Kikuri LV 134 C3
Kil N 90 B5
Kil S 97 C9
Kilafors S 103 D12
Kilargue IRL 6 D6
Kilba A 77 F8
Kilbeggan IRL 7 F8
Kilbeheny IRL 8 D6
Kilberry GB 4 D5
Kilberry IRL 7 F8
Kilbirnie GB 4 D7
Kilboghamn N 108 D5
Kilbotn N 111 C12
Kilbrittain IRL 8 E5
Kilby S 99 B10
Kilcar IRL 6 C5
Kilchoan GB 4 B4
Kilchrenan GB 4 C6
Kilcock GB 7 F9
Kilcolgan IRL 6 F5
Kilcommon IRL 9 D7
Kilconnell IRL 6 F6
Kilconney IRL 7 D8
Kilcoole IRL 7 F10
Kilcormac IRL 7 F7
Kilcreggan GB 4 C7
Kilcullen IRL 7 F9
Kildare IRL 7 F9
Kildavin IRL 9 C9
Kilden DK 90 E7
Kildimo New IRL 8 C5
Kildonan Lodge GB 3 J9
Kile N 90 A2
Kilen N 95 D9
Kilfenora IRL 6 G4
Kilfinan GB 4 D6
Kilfinnane IRL 8 D6
Kilforsen S 107 D11
Kilgarvan IRL 8 E4
Kilgetty GB 12 B5
Kilglass IRL 6 E5
Kilglass IRL 6 F6
Kilham GB 5 D12
Kilidülbahir TR 171 D10
Kilifarevo BG 166 C5
Kilingi-Nõmme EST 131 E9
Kiliya UA 155 C4
Kilkea IRL 9 C9
Kilkee IRL 8 C3
Kilkeel GB 7 D11
Kilkenny IRL 9 C8
Kilkhampton GB 12 D6
Kilkieran IRL 6 F3
Kilkinlea IRL 8 D4
Kilkis GR 169 C8
Kilkishen IRL 8 C5
Kill IRL 7 F9
Killadysert IRL 8 C4
Killagan Bridge GB 4 E4
Killala IRL 6 D4
Killaloe IRL 8 C6
Killamerry IRL 9 D8
Killann IRL 9 C9
Killarga IRL 6 D6
Killashandra IRL 7 D8
Killavullen IRL 8 D5
Killean GB 4 D5
Killenaule IRL 9 C7
Killimer IRL 8 C4
Killin GB 4 B8
Killinaboy IRL 6 G4
Killinchy GB 7 D11
Killinge S 116 C4
Killingworth GB 5 E13
Killinick IRL 9 D10
Killinkoski FIN 123 F11
Killorglin IRL 8 D3
Killough IRL 7 D11
Killough IRL 7 F10
Killucan IRL 7 E8
Killukin IRL 6 E6
Killundine GB 4 B5
Killurin IRL 9 D9
Killybegs IRL 6 C6
Killyclogher GB 4 F2
Killylea GB 7 D9
Kilmacanogue IRL 7 F10
Kilmacrenan IRL 7 B7
Kilmacthomas IRL 9 D8
Kilmaganny IRL 9 D8
Kilmaine IRL 6 E4
Kilmaley IRL 8 C4
Kilmallock IRL 8 D5
Kilmaluag GB 2 K4
Kilmarnock GB 4 E7
Kilmartin GB 4 C6
Kilmeadan IRL 9 D8
Kilmeedy IRL 8 D5
Kilmelford GB 4 C6
Kilmichael IRL 8 E4
Kilmihill IRL 8 C4
Kilmona IRL 8 E5
Kilmoon IRL 8 C4
Kilmore IRL 8 C5
Kilmore IRL 9 D10
Kilmore Quay IRL 9 D9
Kilmuckridge IRL 9 D10
Kilmurry IRL 8 C5
Kilmurry McMahon IRL 8 C4
Kilnaboy IRL 6 G4
Kilnaleck IRL 7 E8
Kilninian GB 4 B4
Kilninver GB 4 C6
Kilnock IRL 6 E5

Kiloran GB 4 C4
Kilpelä FIN 115 D4
Kilpilahti FIN 127 E14
Kilpisjärvi FIN 112 E6
Kilpua FIN 119 F13
Kilrea GB 4 E3
Kilrean IRL 6 C6
Kilreekill IRL 6 F6
Kilrenny GB 5 C11
Kilronan IRL 6 F3
Kilrush IRL 8 C4
Kilsallagh IRL 6 E5
Kilsaran IRL 7 E9
Kilshanchoe IRL 7 F9
Kilshanny IRL 6 G4
Kilskeer IRL 7 E8
Kilsmo S 92 A7
Kilsund N 90 B4
Kilsyth GB 5 D8
Kiltartan IRL 6 F5
Kiltealy IRL 9 C9
Kiltegan IRL 9 C9
Kiltimagh IRL 6 E5
Kiltogan IRL 9 C9
Kiltoom IRL 6 F6
Kiltsi EST 131 C12
Kiltullagh IRL 6 F5
Kilvakkala FIN 127 B9
Kilvenaapa FIN 119 B16
Kilvo S 116 E6
Kilwaughter GB 4 F5
Kilwinning GB 4 D7
Kilworth IRL 8 D6
Kimasozero RUS 121 F17
Kimberley GB 15 B11
Kimbolton GB 15 C8
Kiminki FIN 123 E13
Kimito FIN 126 E8
Kimle H 146 F4
Kimmeria GR 171 B7
Kimo FIN 122 D8
Kimola FIN 127 C15
Kimonkylä FIN 127 D15
Kimovaara RUS 125 C16
Kimpton GB 15 D8
Kimstad S 92 B7
Kinahmo FIN 125 E13
Kinbrace GB 3 J9
Kincardine GB 5 C9
Kincraig GB 3 L9
Kincses H 149 B10
Kindberg A 148 A4
Kindelbrück D 79 D9
Kinderbeuern D 21 D8
Kinding D 75 E9
Kindsbach D 186 C4
Kindsjön S 102 E4
Kineta GR 175 D7
Kingarrow IRL 6 C6
Kingarth GB 4 D6
Kingisepp RUS 132 C4
Kingsbridge GB 13 E7
Kingsclere GB 13 C12
Kingscourt IRL 7 E9
Kingskerswell GB 13 E7
Kingsland IRL 6 E6
King's Lynn GB 11 F12
Kingsnorth GB 15 E10
Kingsteignton GB 13 D7
Kingsthorne GB 13 B9
Kingston GB 3 K10
Kingston Bagpuize GB 13 B12
Kingston Seymour GB 13 C9
Kingston upon Hull GB 11 D11
Kingswear GB 13 E7
Kingswood GB 13 C9
Kings Worthy GB 13 C12
Kington GB 13 A8
Kingussie GB 5 A8
Kingwilliamstown IRL 8 D4
Kinik TR 173 E7
Kinik TR 177 A9
Kinişärvi FIN 117 D14
Kinloch GB 4 A4
Kinlochard GB 4 C8
Kinlochewe GB 2 K6
Kinlochleven GB 4 B7
Kinloch Rannoch GB 5 B8
Kinloss GB 3 K9
Kinlough IRL 6 D6
Kinn N 111 C10
Kinna S 91 D12
Kinnared S 87 A12
Kinnarp S 91 C14
Kinnarumma S 91 D12
Kinnegad IRL 7 F8
Kinnitty IRL 7 F7
Kinnula FIN 123 D13
Kinnulanlahti FIN 124 C8
Kinrooi B 19 B12
Kinross GB 5 C10
Kinsale IRL 8 E5
Kinsaleberg IRL 9 E7
Kinsarvik N 94 B5
Kintai LT 134 F2
Kintaus FIN 123 F14
Kintbury GB 13 C12
Kintore GB 3 L12
Kinvarra IRL 6 F5
Kioni GR 174 C2
Kipen' RUS 132 B6
Kipfenberg D 75 E9
Kipilovo BG 166 D6
Kipinä FIN 119 D17
Kipoi GR 168 E4
Kipoureio GR 168 E5
Kippel CH 70 E5
Kippen GB 5 C8
Kippenheim D 27 D8
Kir AL 163 E8
Kirakkajärvi FIN 114 D5
Kirakkaköngäs FIN 113 F19
Kirald H 145 G1
Királyegyháza H 149 D9
Királyhegyes H 150 E6
Kiran N 104 C8
Kirazli TR 172 D6
Kirby Muxloe GB 11 F9
Kircasalih TR 173 B6
Kirchanschöring D 73 A6
Kirchardt D 21 F11
Kirchbach D 73 C7
Kirchbach in Steiermark A 148 C5
Kirchberg CH 27 F11
Kirchberg CH 31 A12
Kirchberg D 76 E4
Kirchberg D 79 E12

Kirchberg (Hunsrück) D 185 E7
Kirchberg am Wagram A 77 F9
Kirchberg am Walde A 77 E8
Kirchberg am Wechsel A 148 A5
Kirchberg an der Jagst D 74 D6
Kirchberg an der Pielach A 77 F8
Kirchberg an der Raab A 148 C5
Kirchbichl A 72 A5
Kirchdorf D 17 C11
Kirchdorf D 83 C10
Kirchdorf an der Iller D 71 A10
Kirchdorf an der Krems A 73 A9
Kirchdorf im Wald D 76 A4
Kirchdorf in Tirol A 72 A5
Kirchehrenbach D 75 C9
Kirchellen D 183 B9
Kirchen (Sieg) D 21 C9
Kirchenlamitz D 75 B10
Kirchenthumbach D 75 C10
Kirchgellersen D 83 D8
Kirchhain D 21 C11
Kirchheim D 74 C6
Kirchheim D 78 E6
Kirchheim am Neckar D 187 C7
Kirchheim bei München D
75 F10
Kirchheim-Bolanden D 21 E10
Kirchheim unter Teck D 27 C11
Kirchhundem D 21 B10
Kirchlauter D 75 B8
Kirchlinteln D 17 C12
Kirch Mulsow D 83 C11
Kirchohsen (Emmerthal) D
78 B5
Kirchroth D 75 E12
Kirchschlag in der Buckligen
Welt A 148 A6
Kirchseelte D 17 C11
Kirchtimke D 17 B12
Kirchwalsede D 17 B12
Kirchweidach D 75 F12
Kirchwistedt D 17 B11
Kirchzarten D 27 E8
Kirchzell D 21 E12
Kircubbin GB 7 D11
Kireç TR 173 E9
Kiremitçisalih TR 172 B6
Kirillovskoye RUS 129 E11
Kirjais FIN 126 E6
Kirjavala FIN 129 B12
Kirkağaç TR 177 A10
Kirkbean GB 5 E9
Kirkbride GB 5 F10
Kirkby GB 10 E6
Kirkby in Ashfield GB 11 E9
Kirkby Lonsdale GB 10 C6
Kirkbymoorside GB 11 C10
Kirkby Stephen GB 11 C7
Kirkby Thore GB 5 F11
Kirkcaldy GB 5 C10
Kirkcolm GB 4 F6
Kirkconnel GB 5 E8
Kirkcudbright GB 5 F8
Kirkeby DK 86 E7
Kirkehamn N 94 F5
Kirke Helsinge DK 87 D8
Kirke Hyllinge DK 87 D9
Kirkel-Neuhäusel D 186 C3
Kirkenær N 96 B7
Kirkenes N 114 D8
Kirke Såby DK 87 D9
Kirke Stillinge DK 87 E8
Kirkham GB 10 D6
Kirkinner GB 5 F8
Kirkintilloch GB 5 D8
Kirkjubøur FO 2 B3
Kirkkavak TR 173 B6
Kirkkepenekli TR 173 B8
Kirkkonummi FIN 127 E11
Kirklareli TR 167 F6
Kirkmichael GB 4 E7
Kirkmichael GB 5 B9
Kirk Michael GBM 10 C2
Kirknewton GB 5 D12
Kirkoswald GB 5 F11
Kirkpatrick-Fleming GB 5 E10
Kirkton GB 4 C5
Kirkton of Durris GB 5 A12
Kirkton of Glenisla GB 5 B10
Kirkton of Skene GB 3 L12
Kirktown of Auchterless GB
3 L12
Kirktown of Deskford GB 3 K11
Kirkwall GB 3 H11
Kirn D 21 E8
Kirnujärvi S 116 D10
Kirovsk RUS 129 F14
Kirriemuir GB 5 B10
Kirschweiler D 21 E8
Kirtik S 118 B5
Kirtlington GB 13 B12
Kirton GB 15 C11
Kirton in Lindsey GB 11 E10
Kirtorf D 21 C12
Kiruna S 116 C4
Kisa S 92 D7
Kisač SRB 158 C4
Kisar H 145 G6
Kisbér H 149 A10
Kiselevo PL 185 E7
Kiselevo PL 185 E7
Kiseljak BIH 157 C10
Kiseljak BIH 157 C11
Kiseljak BIH 157 C8
Kisgyőr H 145 G2
Kishkeam IRL 8 D4
Kisielice PL 139 C7
Kisielnica PL 139 D13
Kisko FIN 127 E9
Kiskőre H 150 B5
Kiskőrös H 150 D3
Kiskunfélegyháza H 150 D4
Kiskunhalas H 150 E3
Kiskunlacháza H 150 C3
Kiskunmajsa H 150 E4
Kişlacık TR 167 F9
Kisláng H 149 C10
Kislőd H 149 B9
Kismarja H 151 C9
Kisnána H 147 F10
Kisovec SLO 73 D10
Kissakoski FIN 128 B6
Kissamos GR 178 E6
Kissenbrück D 79 B7
Kißlegg D 71 B9
Kisszállás H 150 E3
Kist D 187 B8
Kistanje HR 156 E4
Kistelek H 150 E4
Kistokaj H 145 G2
Kistrand N 113 C15
Kisújszállás H 150 C6
Kisvárda H 145 G5
Kisvarsány H 145 G5

Kiszkowo PL 81 A12
Kiszombor H 150 E5
Kitee FIN 125 F14
Kiten BG 167 E9
Kitinoja FIN 122 E9
Kitka FIN 121 B12
Kitkiöjärvi S 116 C10
Kitros GR 169 D8
Kitsi FIN 125 D15
Kittajaur S 118 B3
Kittelfjäll S 106 A8
Kittilä FIN 117 C13
Kittsee A 77 F12
Kitula FIN 127 E10
Kitzbühel A 72 B5
Kitzen D 79 D11
Kitzingen D 75 C7
Kitzscher D 79 D12
Kiuce PL 143 F8
Kiukainen FIN 126 C7
Kiurujärvi FIN 115 D2
Kiuruvesi FIN 123 C17
Kivarinjärvi FIN 121 E10
Kivelä FIN 115 F4
Kiveri GR 175 D6
Kivesjärvi FIN 121 F9
Kiveskylä FIN 121 F9
Kiveslahti FIN 120 F9
Kiviapaja FIN 129 B10
Kivijärvi FIN 123 D14
Kivijärvi S 116 E10
Kivik S 88 D6
Kivikangas FIN 123 D12
Kivilahti FIN 125 D14
Kivilompolo FIN 117 A10
Kivilompolo FIN 119 B12
Kivilompolo N 119 B10
Kivioja FIN 119 B14
Kiviperä FIN 121 B14
Kivivaara FIN 121 D11
Kivivaara FIN 125 C16
Kivi-Vigala EST 131 D8
Kivotos GR 168 D5
Kiwity PL 136 E2
Kiyiköy TR 173 A9
Kizilcaova TR 177 C10
Kizilcikdere TR 167 F8
Kizilpinar TR 173 B8
Kizilyaka TR 181 B8
Kjækan N 112 D9
Kjåmes N 111 D11
Kjeldebotn N 111 D12
Kjelkenes N 100 C2
Kjelkvik N 111 D11
Kjellerup DK 86 C4
Kjelling N 108 B7
Kjemmoen N 102 B7
Kjengsnes N 111 C11
Kjerknesvågen N 105 D10
Kjerret N 96 B7
Kjerringdal N 112 C9
Kjerringholmen N 113 B12
Kjerringøy N 108 A8
Kjerringvåg N 104 D5
Kjerringvik N 110 C9
Kjerringvik N 111 D12
Kjerstad N 111 C7
Kjølen N 91 A9
Kjøllefjord N 113 B19
Kjølstad N 101 D10
Kjøpsvik N 111 D11
Kjøra N 104 E7
Kjøsvika N 105 A12
Kjulaås S 98 D7
Klaaswaal NL 16 E2
Klačno SK 147 D7
Kladanj BIH 157 D10
Kladeň D 79 A10
Kladnica SRB 163 C9
Kladnice HR 156 E5
Kladno CZ 76 B6
Kladovo SRB 159 D9
Kladruby CZ 76 C3
Klæbu N 104 E8
Klagenfurt A 73 C9
Klågerup S 87 D12
Klaipėda LT 134 E2
Klaj PL 143 G9
Klakksjorda N 110 C8
Klakksjorda N 110 C8
Klamila FIN 128 D7
Klana HR 67 B9
Klanac HR 156 C3
Klanjec HR 148 D5
Klanxbüll D 86 F3
Klapkalnciems LV 134 B6
Kloštar Ivanić HR 149 E6
Kloštar Podravski HR 149 E8
Kloster DK 86 C2
Klosterfelde D 84 E4
Klosterhäseler D 79 D10
Klösterle A 71 C10
Klostermansfeld D 79 C9
Klosterneuburg A 77 F10
Klosters CH 71 D9
Kloster Zinna D 80 B4
Kloten CH 27 F10
Kloten S 97 C13
Klötze (Altmark) D 79 A9
Klovainiai LT 135 E7
Klovborg DK 86 D4
Klövertråsk S 118 C6
Kløvmoen N 108 E6
Klövsjö S 102 A7
Klubbfors S 118 C5
Klubbvik N 114 C6
Kluczbork PL 142 E6
Kluczewsko PL 143 E8
Kluki PL 143 D7
Kluknava SK 145 F2
Klukowo PL 141 E7
Klumpen S 106 E9
Klundert NL 16 E3
Klungsten S 99 A10
Klupe BIH 157 C8
Kluse D 17 C8
Kľušov SK 145 E3
Klusy PL 139 C13
Klutsjön S 102 B4
Klütz D 83 B13
Klwów PL 141 G3
Klyastsitsy BY 133 E5
Klykoliai LT 134 D5
Klynivka UA 153 A7
Knaben N 94 E6
Knåda S 103 D10
Knaften S 107 C15
Knäred S 87 B11
Knaresborough GB 11 C9
Knarrevik N 94 B2

Kleisoura GR 168 C5
Kleitoria GR 174 D5
Kleiva N 110 C9
Kleive N 100 A7
Klejniki PL 141 E8
Klejtrup DK 86 B5
Klek SRB 158 C5
Klembivka UA 154 A2
Klemenske DK 89 E7
Kneževi Vinogradi HR 149 E11
Kneževo HR 149 E11
Knežha BG 165 C9
Knežice CZ 77 B9
Klenica PL 81 C9
Klenike SRB 164 E4
Klenje SRB 158 D3
Klenovec SK 147 D9
Klepp N 94 E3
Kleppestø N 94 B2
Kleppstad N 110 D7
Kljøsk PL 81 B9
Kleszczele PL 141 E8
Kleszczewo PL 81 B12
Kleszczewo PL 136 F6
Kleszczów PL 143 D7
Klettwitz D 80 C5
Kleve D 16 E6
Klevshult S 92 E4
Kličevac SRB 159 D7
Kličevo MNE 163 D6
Klieken D 79 C11
Klietz D 83 E12
Klikuszowa PL 147 B9
Klim DK 86 A4
Kliment BG 161 F10
Kliment BG 165 D10
Klimentovo BG 167 C9
Klimkovice CZ 146 B6
Klimontów PL 143 E11
Klimontów PL 143 F9
Klimpfjäll S 106 A7
Klin SK 147 C9
Klinča Sela HR 148 E5
Klinë KS 163 D10
Klinë Epërme KS 163 D10
Klingenberg D 80 E5
Klingenberg am Main D 21 E12
Klingenthal D 75 B11
Klingersel S 118 B7
Klingre S 107 E15
Klink D 83 D13
Klinkby DK 86 B2
Klintebjerg DK 86 E6
Klintehamn S 93 E12
Kliplev DK 86 F4
Klippan S 87 C12
Klippen S 107 C13
Klippen S 108 E4
Klippinge DK 87 E10
Klis HR 156 E6
Klisura BG 165 D9
Klisura BG 165 D7
Klisura SRB 164 D5
Klitmøller DK 86 A3
Klitten D 81 D7
Klitten S 102 D7
Klixbüll D 82 A5
Kljajićevo SRB 150 F3
Ključ BIH 157 C6
Kłokot KS 164 E3
Klokkarstua N 95 B13
Klokkerholm DK 86 A6
Klokočevac SRB 159 E9
Klokočevci HR 149 E10
Klokočov SK 147 C7
Klomnice PL 143 E7
Klonowa PL 142 D5
Klooga EST 131 C8
Kloosterhaar NL 17 D7
Kloosterzande NL 16 F2
Klos AL 163 F9
Klos AL 168 B3
Klôse S 107 D16

Knarrlagsund N 104 D6
Knätten S 102 B7
Knebel DK 86 C6
Knesebeck D 83 E9
Knesselare B 19 B7
Knetzgau D 75 C7
Knežak SLO 73 E9
Knežević SLO 73 E9
Knin HR 156 D5
Knislinge S 88 C6
Knittelfeld A 73 B10
Knittlingen D 27 B10
Knīveri LV 134 D3
Knivsta S 99 C9
Knizhovnik BG 166 F5
Knjaževac SRB 164 B5
Knock GB 4 C5
Knock IRL 6 E5
Knock IRL 8 C4
Knockalough IRL 8 C4
Knockanevin IRL 8 D6
Knockban GB 2 K7
Knockbrack IRL 7 C7
Knockbridge IRL 7 E9
Knockcroghery IRL 6 E6
Knocklong IRL 8 D6
Knockmoyle IRL 6 F6
Knocknaboul IRL 8 D4
Knocknacarry GB 4 E4
Knocknacree IRL 9 C9
Knocknagree IRL 8 D5
Knocks IRL 8 E5
Knocktopher IRL 9 D8
Knokke-Heist B 19 B7
Knoppe S 103 B12
Knorrendorf D 84 C4
Knottingley GB 11 D9
Knowle GB 13 A11
Knucklas GB 13 A8
Knud DK 86 B4
Knurów PL 142 F6
Knutby S 99 C10
Knutsbol S 97 D12
Knutsford GB 11 E7
Knyazevo RUS 133 D5
Knyazhe UA 154 A5
Knyazhevo BG 167 E6
Knyazhitsy RUS 132 E4
Knyszyn PL 140 D7
Kobaky UA 152 A6
Kobarid SLO 73 D8
Kobatovci BIH 157 C7
Kobbelveid N 109 A10
Kobbevågnes N 111 B16
Kobbfoss N 114 E7
Kobela EST 131 F12
København DK 87 D11
Kobenz A 73 B10
Koběřice CZ 142 G5
Kobern D 185 D7
Kobersdorf A 149 A6
Kobiele Wielkie PL 143 D8
Kobierzyce PL 81 E11
Kobilyane BG 171 A8
Kobiór PL 143 F6
Koblenz D 21 D9
Kobrow D 83 C11
Kobyla Góra PL 142 D4
Kobylanka PL 85 D7
Kobylany PL 145 D4
Kobylec'ka Polyana UA 145 G9
Kobylin PL 81 C12
Kobyłka PL 139 F11
Kobylnica PL 81 B11
Kobylnica PL 85 B12
Kobylniki PL 139 F9
Kocaavşar TR 173 E8
Kocahidir TR 171 C10
Kočani MK 164 F5
Kocapınar TR 173 E8
Koçarlı TR 177 D10
Kocayazı TR 167 E8
Kocayazı TR 167 F8
Koceljevo SRB 158 E4
Kočani LV 135 A10
Kočerin BIH 157 F8
Kočevje SLO 73 E10
Kočevska Reka SLO 73 E10
Kochanowice PL 142 E6
Kochel am See D 72 A3
Kocherinovo BG 165 E7
Kochmar BG 161 F10
Kochovo BG 167 C7
Kock PL 141 G6
Kočovce SK 146 D5
Kocsér H 150 C4
Kocsola H 149 C10
Kocsord H 145 H5
Koczała PL 85 C12
Kodavere EST 131 D14
Kode S 91 D10
Koděň PL 141 G9
Kodersdorf D 81 D7
Kodesjärvi FIN 122 F7
Kodiksami FIN 126 C6
Kodisjoki FIN 126 C6
Kőditz D 75 B10
Kodrąb PL 143 D8
Kodyma UA 154 A4
Koekelare B 18 B6
Koersel B 183 C6
Koeru EST 131 D12
Koewacht NL 182 C3
Kofçaz TR 167 E8
Köflach A 73 B11
Kofrinar S 103 C10
Koglhof A 148 B5
Kogila N 94 B2
Kohila EST 131 C9
Kohlberg D 75 C11
Köhlen D 17 A11
Kohren-Sahlis D 79 D12
Kohtla-Järve EST 131 C14
Koidula EST 132 F2
Koigi EST 131 D11
Koijärvi FIN 127 D9
Koikkala FIN 128 B8
Koilomeno GR 174 D2
Koilovtsi BG 165 C10
Koimisi GR 169 B9
Koirakoski FIN 124 C9
Koita GR 178 B3
Koitila FIN 121 C11

Koivu FIN 119 B14
Koivujärvi FIN 123 C16
Koivujärvi FIN 123 C16
Koivumäki FIN 123 D12
Koivumäki FIN 123 C9
Koivumäki FIN 125 F11
Koivuniemi FIN 119 C15
Köja S 107 F13
Kojanlanti FIN 125 E11
Kojetín CZ 146 C4
Kóka H 150 C4
Kökar FIN 126 F4
Kokari LV 135 C13
Kokava nad Rimavicou SK
147 D9
Kokelv N 113 B14
Kokemäki FIN 126 C7
Kokini GR 175 E8
Kökkala GR 178 B3
Kokkari GR 177 D8
Kokkinochoma GR 171 C6
Kokkino Nero GR 169 E7
Kokkokylä FIN 119 C17
Kokkola FIN 123 C10
Kokkolahti FIN 125 F12
Kokkosniva FIN 115 D2
Kokkotoi GR 175 A6
Kokkovaara FIN 117 D13
Koklot FIN 122 C7
Kokneze LV 135 C10
Kokonvaara FIN 125 E12
Kokora EST 131 D14
Kokorica SLO 73 D9
Kokory CZ 146 C4
Koksijde B 18 B6
Kokträsk S 109 F18
Kola BIH 157 C7
Kolaçin FIN 161 C6
Kolacze PL 141 H8
Kołaczkowo PL 142 B4
Kołaczyce PL 144 D3
Kolaka GR 175 B7
Koláre SK 147 E8
Kolari FIN 117 D11
Kolari S 117 D11
Kolari SRB 159 D6
Kolárovice SK 147 C7
Kolárovo SK 146 F5
Kolåsen S 105 D13
Kolašin MNE 163 D8
Kolbäck S 98 C6
Kolbacz PL 85 D7
Kolbaskowo PL 84 D6
Kolbermoor D 72 A5
Kolbiel PL 141 F4
Kolbotn N 95 C13
Kolbu N 101 E13
Kolbuddy Górne PL 138 B5
Kolbuszowa PL 144 C4
Kolby DK 86 B4
Koľchyne UA 145 G6
Kolczygłowy PL 85 B12
Kołczyn PL 81 A4
Koldby DK 86 B3
Koldere TR 177 B10
Kolding DK 86 E4
Koler S 118 D5
Kölesd H 149 C11
Kolesjan AL 163 F9
Koleska BIH 157 F9
Kolfosen S 103 E12
Kolga EST 131 C11
Kolga-Aabla EST 131 B11
Kolga-Jaani EST 131 D11
Kolho FIN 123 F13
Koli FIN 125 D13
Kolín CZ 77 C11
Koliñany SK 146 E6
Kolind DK 86 C7
Kolindros GR 169 D8
Kolinec CZ 76 D4
Kolini GR 174 D3
Kolisne UA 154 E5
Kolitzheim D 75 C7
Kolja GR 174 C6
Köljala EST 130 E5
Koljane HR 156 E5
Kolka LV 130 F5
Kolkær DK 86 C4
Kolkanhalti FIN 123 E14
Kolked H 149 E11
Kolkja EST 131 D14
Kolku FIN 123 D16
Kolkonjärvi FIN 121 B10
Kolkwitz D 80 C6
Kollaja FIN 119 D17
Kölleda D 79 D9
Kollines GR 174 E5
Kölln-Reisiek D 82 C7
Kolltveit N 94 B2
Kollund DK 82 A6
Kolmisoppi FIN 124 D9
Köln D 21 C7
Kolnica PL 140 C8
Kolno PL 136 F2
Kolno PL 139 D12
Kolo BIH 157 E7
Koło PL 142 B6
Kołobrzeg PL 85 B9
Kolochau D 80 C4
Kolochava UA 145 G8
Kolonjë AL 168 C2
Kolonowskie PL 142 E5
Kolosjoki FIN 115 C3
Kołosomb BG 171 A8
Kolossi GR 174 E3
Kolosów BY 133 F4
Kolozhytsy RUS 129 E10
Kolpino RUS 129 F14
Kölsätter S 102 B8
Kolsh AL 163 E9
Kolsillre S 103 B11
Kolsko PL 81 C9
Kölsta S 97 C15
Kölsvallen S 102 C9
Kölsvallen S 102 C7
Kolt DK 86 C6
Kolta SK 146 E6
Kolu FIN 123 E12
Koluküla FIN 119 D15
Koluküla FIN 119 D15

Komanos GR 169 D6
Komar BIH 157 D7
Komara GR 171 A10
Komarevo BG 165 B10
Komarica BIH 157 C8
Komárno SK 146 F6
Komárom H 149 A10
Komárov CZ 76 C5
Komarov UA 145 D8
Komarovo RUS 129 E12
Komarówka Podlaska PL 141 G7
Komarów Osada PL 144 B7
Kombuļi LV 133 E2
Komen SLO 73 E8
Komēsi AL 168 A2
Komi GR 176 B5
Komi GR 177 C7
Komin HR 148 D6
Komin HR 157 F8
Komiža HR 63 A10
Komjatice SK 146 E6
Komló H 149 D10
Kömlő H 150 B5
Kömlőd H 149 A10
Kommeno GR 174 A3
Komnina GR 169 C6
Komoran KS 163 D10
Komorniki PL 81 B11
Komorowo PL 139 E12
Komorzno PL 142 D5
Komoshtitsa BG 160 F2
Komossa FIN 122 D9
Komotini GR 171 B8
Kompakka FIN 125 F13
Kompelusvaara S 116 D8
Kömpöc H 150 E4
Kompoti GR 174 A3
Komprachcice PL 142 E4
Kömsi EST 130 D7
Komsomol'sk RUS 136 D2
Komsomol'sk UA 145 G8
Komu FIN 123 C16
Komula FIN 125 C10
Komunari BG 167 C8
Komuniga BG 166 F4
Komylivtsi UA 145 G9
Konak TR 177 C9
Konakpınar TR 173 F8
Konare BG 155 F2
Konare BG 167 C8
Konarzyce PL 139 D13
Konarzyny PL 85 C12
Koncanica HR 149 E8
Konče MK 169 B7
Kondolovo BG 167 E9
Kondratowice PL 81 E12
Kondrať'yevo RUS 129 D9
Koneck PL 138 E6
Kong DK 86 B4
Kong N 113 B14
Konga S 89 B8
Köngäs FIN 115 E1
Köngäs FIN 117 C13
Kongasmäki FIN 121 E10
Kongerslev DK 86 B6
Konginkangas FIN 123 E15
Kongsberg N 95 C11
Kongselva N 110 D9
Kongsfjord N 114 B6
Kongslia N 101 C9
Kongsmoen N 105 B12
Kongsvik N 111 C11
Kongsvinger N 96 B7
Kongsvoll N 104 D6
Konice CZ 77 C11
Koniecpol PL 143 E8
Königheim D 187 B8
Königsberg in Bayern D 75 B8
Königsborn D 79 B10
Königsbronn D 75 E7
Königsbrück D 80 D5
Königsbrunn D 74 F3
Königsdorf D 72 A3
Königsee D 79 E8
Königsfeld im Schwarzwald D
27 D9
Königshofen D 79 D10
Königshütte D 79 C8
Königslutter am Elm D 79 B8
Königsmoos D 75 E9
Königssee D 73 A6
Königstein D 21 D10
Königstein D 80 E6
Königstein im Taunus D 187 A5
Königswartha D 80 D6
Königswiesen A 77 F7
Königswinter D 21 C8
Königs Wusterhausen D 80 B5

Kontiolahti FIN 125 E13
Kontiomäki FIN 121 F11
Kontkala FIN 125 E12
Kontopouli GR 171 E8
Kontovazaina GR 174 D4
Konttajärvi FIN 117 E12
Konttila FIN 119 C15
Konttimäki FIN 125 D9
Konush BG 166 F4
Kóny H 149 A9
Konyár FIN 151 C8
Konyavo BG 165 E6
Konz D 21 E7
Konzell D 75 D12
Koog aan de Zaan NL 16 D3
Koonga EST 131 D8
Koőrtilä FIN 126 B6
Koosa EST 131 D14
Kootstertille NL 16 B6
Kootwijkerbroek NL 183 A7
Kopani GR 168 F4
Kopanica PL 81 B9
Kopanos GR 169 C7
Kopardal N 108 D4
Koparnes N 100 B3
Kopčany SK 77 E12
Koper SLO 67 A8
Kopervik N 94 D2
Kópháza H 149 A7
Kopice PL 142 E3
Kopidlno CZ 77 B8
Kopilovtsi BG 165 C6
Köping S 97 C15
Köpingebro S 88 E5
Köpingsvik S 89 B11
Kopki PL 144 C5
Koplik AL 163 E7
Koplik i Sipërm AL 163 E7
Köpmanholm S 99 C11
Köpmanholmen S 107 E15
Koporiče KS 163 C10
Koporiqë KS 163 C10
Koppang N 101 C14
Koppangen N 111 A19
Kopparberg S 97 C13
Kopparmora S 99 D11
Kopparnäs S 118 C6
Koppelo FIN 114 F3
Koppera N 105 E11
Koppl A 73 A7
Koppom S 96 C7
Koprivets BG 166 C5
Koprivlen BG 169 A10
Koprivnica HR 149 D7
Kopřivnice CZ 146 B6
Koprivshtitsa BG 165 D9
Koprzywnica PL 143 E12
Kopsa FIN 119 E13
Kopstal L 186 B1
Kõpu EST 130 D4
Kõpu EST 131 E10
Koraj BIH 157 C10
Koramoniemi FIN 121 B12
Korbach D 17 F11
Korbevac SRB 164 D5
Korbovo SRB 159 D10
Korčanica BIH 156 C5
Korçë AL 168 C4
Korchiv UA 144 C8
Körchow D 83 D10
Korčula HR 162 D3
Korczew PL 141 F7
Korczyna PL 144 D4
Kordel D 185 E6
Korenita SRB 158 D3
Koŕenov CZ 81 E8
Korenovka FIN 125 E16
Korentovaara FIN 125 E16
Koretin SRB 164 E4
Korfantów PL 142 F4
Korfos GR 175 D7
Korgen N 108 D6
Korgene LV 135 B9
Kórgessaare EST 130 D4
Korholanmäki FIN 121 C12
Korhosenniemi FIN 121 C12
Koria FIN 128 D6
Korinos GR 169 D8
Korinth DK 86 E6
Korinthos GR 175 D6
Korisia GR 175 E9
Korisos GR 168 D5
Korita BIH 156 D5
Korita HR 162 D2
Korita MNE 163 D8
Korithi GR 174 D1
Korkana FIN 121 F15
Korkatti FIN 119 F15
Korkeakangas FIN 125 F14
Korkeakoski FIN 127 B11
Korkee FIN 127 D13
Körkvere EST 130 E6
Korlât D 18 D7
Körmend H 149 B7
Kormista GR 170 C6
Kormu FIN 127 D12
Korňa SK 147 C7
Kornalovychi UA 145 D7
Körner D 79 D8
Korneuburg A 77 F7
Kórnik PL 81 B12
Kornitsa BG 165 F9
Kornofolia GR 171 C9
Kornos GR 171 E8
Kornsjø N 91 B10
Kornwestheim D 27 C11
Környe H 149 A10
Koroleve UA 145 G7
Koromačno HR 67 C9
Koroncó H 149 A9
Koronia GR 175 C6
Koronisia GR 174 A2
Koronouda GR 169 C9
Koronowo PL 138 D4
Koropi GR 175 D8
Koróshegy H 149 C9
Köröslándány H 151 D7
Körösszakál H 151 C9
Körösszegapáti H 151 C9
Koroviya UA 153 A7
Korpela FIN 117 B14
Korpijärvi FIN 119 B13
Korpijoki FIN 123 C16
Korpikå S 119 C10
Korpikylä FIN 119 B11

Korpikylä FIN 121 E12
Korpikylä S 119 B11
Kurpilahti FIN 123 F15
Korpilombolo S 116 E10
Korpilompolo FIN 117 E13
Korpinen FIN 121 C10
Korpinen FIN 125 D10
Korpisel'kya RUS 125 F16
Korpivaara FIN 125 E12
Korpo FIN 126 E6
Korpoström FIN 126 E6
Korsåmon S 103 A12
Korsbäck FIN 122 E6
Korsberga S 89 A8
Korsberga S 91 C15
Korsgården S 103 E10
Korsholm FIN 122 D7
Korskrogen S 103 C10
Korsmyrbränna S 106 E8
Korsnäs FIN 122 E7
Korso FIN 127 E13
Korsør DK 87 E4
Korssjön S 118 F5
Korssund N 100 D1
Korsträsk S 118 C5
Korsvoll N 104 E4
Korsze PL 136 E3
Kortemark B 19 B7
Korten BG 166 D5
Kortenhoef NL 16 D4
Kortesalmi FIN 121 C14
Kortesjärvi FIN 123 D10
Kortessem B 19 C11
Kortevaara FIN 125 B13
Kortgene NL 16 E1
Korthi GR 176 D4
Kortrijk B 19 C7
Kortteenperä FIN 119 B17
Kortteinen FIN 125 D11
Korubaşi TR 171 E10
Korucu TR 173 F7
Koruköy TR 173 C6
Koruköy TR 177 E10
Korva S 119 B11
Korvakumpu FIN 115 D2
Korvala FIN 117 E16
Korvaluoma FIN 126 B8
Korvua FIN 121 D12
Koryčany CZ 77 D12
Korycin PL 140 D8
Koryfasi GR 174 E4
Koryfi GR 169 C8
Korytnica PL 139 F7
Korzenna PL 144 D2
Korzeńsko PL 81 C11
Korzybie PL 85 B11
Kos GR 177 F9
Kosakowo PL 138 A6
Kosanica MNE 163 C7
Košarovce SK 145 E4
Kösching D 75 E10
Kościan PL 81 B11
Kościelec PL 142 B6
Kościelna Wieś PL 142 C5
Kościernica PL 85 B10
Kościerzyna PL 138 B4
Kosd H 150 B3
Kose EST 131 C10
Kose EST 131 F14
Košeca SK 146 C6
Košecké Podhradie SK 146 D6
Kösedere TR 171 E10
Kösedere TR 177 B8
Köseilyas TR 173 B8
Kosel D 82 A7
Koselji BIH 157 E9
Koserow D 84 B6
Košetice CZ 77 C8
Kosharevo BG 165 D6
Koshava BG 159 E11
Košice SK 145 F3
Kosiv UA 152 A6
Kosivs'ka Polyana UA 145 G9
Kosjerić SRB 158 F4
Koška HR 149 E10
Koskama FIN 117 C14
Koskeby FIN 122 D8
Koskela FIN 119 C15
Koskela FIN 123 D11
Koskenkorva FIN 122 E8
Koskenkylä FIN 117 C16
Koskenkylä FIN 121 C14
Koskenkylä FIN 121 F11
Koskenkylä FIN 125 F12
Koskenkylä FIN 126 D7
Koskenmäki FIN 121 C14
Koskenniska FIN 113 F17
Koskenpää FIN 123 F14
Koskenperä FIN 123 C14
Koski FIN 127 E9
Koski FIN 127 E9
Koskimäki FIN 122 E7
Koskinou GR 181 D8
Koskioinen FIN 127 C9
Koškovce SK 145 E4
Koskue FIN 122 F8
Koskullskulle S 116 D5
Koslovets BG 166 C4
Kosmach UA 152 A5
Kosman BIH 157 F10
Kosmas GR 175 E6
Kosmio GR 171 B8
Kosmonosy CZ 77 B7
Kosola FIN 122 D9
Kosova Hora CZ 77 C6
Kosovo HR 156 E5
Kosów Lacki PL 141 E6
Koš́dorf D 80 D4
Kössen A 72 A5
Kosta GR 175 E7
Kosta S 89 B8
Kostakioi GR 174 A2
Košťálov CZ 81 E8
Kostamo FIN 115 E2
Kostandenets BG 166 B6
Kostanjevac HR 148 E4
Kostanjevica SLO 148 E4
Kostel SLO 67 A10
Kostelec nad Černými Lesy CZ 77 C7
Kostelec nad Orlicí CZ 77 B10
Kostelec na Hané CZ 77 C12
Kostenets BG 165 E8
Kostenets BG 165 E8
Kostice CZ 77 E11

Kostinbrod BG 165 D7
Kostolac SRB 159 D7
Kostolné Kračany SK 146 F5
Kostomłoty PL 81 D11
Kostomuksha RUS 121 E16
Kostrzyn PL 81 A7
Kostrzyn PL 81 B12
Kostyzhitsy RUS 132 F6
Kosula FIN 125 E11
Košute HR 157 E6
Kosy UA 154 B5
Kosyny UA 145 G5
Koszalin PL 85 B10
Koszęcin PL 142 E6
Kőszeg H 149 B7
Koszyce PL 143 F10
Kotajärvi FIN 119 D15
Kotala FIN 115 D5
Kotala FIN 123 F12
Kotalanperä FIN 119 D15
Kotas GR 168 C5
Kotë AL 168 D2
Kötegyán H 151 D7
Kotel BG 167 D6
Kőtelek H 150 C5
Kotelow D 84 C5
Kotešová SK 147 C7
Köthen (Anhalt) D 79 C10
Kotikylä FIN 124 D8
Kotila FIN 121 C10
Kotiranta FIN 121 E13
Kotka FIN 128 E6
Kotlin PL 142 C4
Kotly RUS 132 B4
Kotor MNE 163 E6
Kotoriba HR 149 D7
Kotorsko BIH 157 C9
Kotor Varoš BIH 157 C7
Kotovs'k UA 154 B5
Kotraža SRB 158 F5
Kotronas GR 178 B3
Kötschach A 73 C7
Kotsøy N 105 F9
Kottenheim D 185 D7
Kottes A 77 F8
Köttmannsdorf A 73 C9
Köttsjön S 107 E10
Kotuń PL 141 F6
Kötzting D 76 D3
Koudekerke NL 16 F1
Koudum NL 16 C4
Koufalia GR 169 C8
Koufovouno GR 171 B10
Kougsta S 105 E15
Kouklioi GR 168 E4
Koumanis GR 174 D4
Koura FIN 123 E10
Koufim CZ 77 C7
Kourkouloi GR 175 B7
Kournas GR 178 E7
Koutaniemi FIN 121 F10
Koutojärvi S 119 B10
Koutsochero GR 169 E7
Koutsopodi GR 175 D6
Koutsouras GR 179 E10
Koutus FIN 117 E12
Kouva FIN 121 C10
Kouvola FIN 128 D6
Kovachevets BG 166 C6
Kovachevitsa BG 165 F8
Kovachevo BG 166 D6
Kovachevtsi BG 165 D6
Kovachitsa BG 160 F2
Kovači BIH 157 E7
Kovačica SRB 158 C5
Kővágószőlős H 149 D10
Kovallberget S 107 B13
Kovanj BIH 157 E9
Kovarce SK 146 E6
Kovářov CZ 76 C6
Kovdor RUS 115 C8
Kovelahti FIN 126 B8
Kovero FIN 125 E11
Kovilj SRB 158 C5
Kovin SRB 159 D6
Kovjoki FIN 122 C9
Kovland S 103 B13
Kövra S 102 A7
Kovren MNE 163 C8
Kowal PL 139 E7
Kowala-Stjpocina PL 141 H4
Kowale PL 142 D5
Kowale Oleckie PL 136 E5
Kowale-Pańskie PL 142 C6
Kowalewo Pomorskie PL 138 D6
Kowalów PL 81 B7
Kowary PL 81 E9
Kowiesy PL 141 G2
Köyceğiz TR 181 C9
Köyhäjoki FIN 123 C11
Köyliö FIN 126 C7
Koynare BG 165 C9
Koyundere TR 177 B9
Koyunyeri TR 171 C10
Kozani GR 169 D6
Kozarac BIH 157 C6
Kozarac HR 149 E11
Kozar Belene BG 166 C4
Kozármisleny H 149 D10
Kozárovce SK 147 E7
Kozçeşme TR 173 D6
Kozica HR 157 F7
Koziegłowy PL 143 E7
Kozielice PL 85 D7
Kozienice PL 141 G5
Kozina SLO 73 E8
Kožlany CZ 76 C5
Kozloduy BG 160 F3
Kozłów Biskupi PL 141 F2
Kozłowo PL 139 D9
Kozluk BIH 157 C11
Kozły PL 139 F11
Koźminek PL 142 C5
Koźmin Wielkopowski PL 142 C3
Koz'ove UA 145 F7
Kozubszczyzna PL 141 H6
Kożuchów PL 81 C9
Kożuhe BIH 157 C9
Kozy PL 147 B8
Kozyörük TR 173 B6
Krabbendijke NL 16 F1
Krabi EST 131 F13
Kräckelbäcken S 102 C7
Krackow D 84 D6
Kraddsele S 109 E12
Kraftsdorf D 79 E10
Krag PL 85 B11
Kragelund DK 86 C4
Kragerø N 90 B7
Kragi PL 85 C11
Kragujevac SRB 159 E6
Kraj HR 156 E6
Kraj HR 157 F7

Krajenka PL 85 D12
Krajišnik SRB 159 C6
Krajnik Dolny PL 84 D6
Krakača BIH 156 B4
Kråkberget N 110 C8
Kråken S 122 C3
Kråkenes N 100 B2
Kråkerøy N 91 A8
Krakés LT 134 F7
Krakhella N 100 D2
Kråklingbo S 93 E13
Kråklivollen N 105 E9
Kråkmoen N 111 E10
Krakovets' UA 144 D7
Kraków PL 143 F8
Krakow am See D 83 C12
Kråksmåla S 89 A9
Kråkstad N 95 C13
Kralevo BG 167 C7
Králíky CZ 77 B11
Kraljeva BIH 157 D9
Kraljevica HR 67 B10
Kraljevo SRB 158 F6
Kralovice CZ 76 C4
Kráľovský Chlmec SK 145 G4
Kralupy nad Vltavou CZ 76 B6
Králův Dvůr CZ 76 C6
Kramarzyny PL 85 B12
Kramfors S 103 A14
Kramolin BG 166 D4
Krampenes N 114 C8
Kramsach A 72 B4
Kramsk PL 142 B5
Kramvik N 114 C9
Kranenburg D 16 E6
Kranevo BG 167 C10
Krångfors S 118 E4
Krania GR 168 E5
Krania Elassonas GR 169 E6
Kranichfeld D 79 E8
Kranidi GR 175 E7
Kranj SLO 73 D9
Kranjska Gora SLO 73 D8
Krapanj HR 156 E4
Krapets BG 155 F3
Krapiel PL 85 D8
Krapina HR 148 D5
Krapinske Toplice HR 148 D5
Krapkowice PL 142 F4
Krašić HR 148 E4
Krasiczyn PL 144 D6
Krasiv UA 145 D8
Kräslava LV 133 E2
Kraslice CZ 75 B12
Krasnagorka BY 133 E2
Krásná Hora nad Vltavou CZ 76 C6
Krasnapollye BY 133 E6
Krasne PL 139 E10
Krasne PL 144 C5
Krasne UA 154 E4
Kraśniczyn PL 144 B7
Kraśnik PL 144 B5
Krasni Okny UA 154 B4
Krasnobród PL 144 B7
Krasnogorodskoye RUS 133 C4
Krásnohorské Podhradie SK 145 F2
Krasnosielc PL 139 D11
Krasnoselc'koye RUS 129 D11
Krasnosielc PL 139 D11
Krasnoyil's'k UA 153 A7
Krasnoznamensk RUS 136 D5
Krasnystaw PL 144 B7
Krasocin PL 143 E8
Kraste AL 168 B3
Kraszcwice PL 142 C5
Kraszewo PL 139 E9
Kratigos GR 177 A8
Kratišiai LT 135 D9
Kratovo MK 164 E5
Kratte masugn S 98 B6
Krauchenwies D 27 D11
Krauja LV 135 E13
Kraujas LV 135 B11
Krauklį LV 135 B12
Krauschwitz D 81 C7
Krautheim D 74 D6
Kravaře CZ 146 B6
Kravarsko HR 148 E6
Kravoder BG 165 C7
Kraymorie BG 167 E8
Kražiai LT 134 F7
Krčina BIH 157 C11
Krčina BIH 157 C11
Krefeld D 17 F7
Kreiensen D 78 C6
Krekenava LT 135 E8
Krekhovychi UA 145 E9
Krekilä FIN 123 C11
Kremasti GR 181 D8
Kremen BG 165 F8
Kremena BG 155 F2
Kremintsi UA 152 A5
Kremmydia GR 174 F4
Kremna SRB 158 F4
Kremnica SK 147 D7
Krempe D 82 C7
Kremperheide D 17 A12
Krempna PL 145 D4
Krems an der Donau A 77 F9
Kremsbrücke A 73 C8
Kremsmünster A 76 F6
Křepice CZ 77 E11
Krepoljin SRB 159 E8
Kreševo BIH 157 E8
Kreshpan AL 168 C2
Křešice CZ 76 A6
Kresna BG 165 F7
Kresna SLO 73 D10
Kressbronn am Bodensee D 71 B9
Krestena GR 174 D4
Kretinga LT 134 E2
Kretingalė LT 134 E2
Kreuth D 72 A4
Kreuzau D 20 C6
Kreuzlingen CH 27 E11
Kreuztal D 21 C9
Kreuzwertheim D 74 C6
Kreva BY 137 E13
Krezluk BIH 157 D7
Krichim BG 165 E9
Kruft D 185 D7
KriegIach A 148 A5
Kriegstetten CH 27 F8
Krien D 84 C5
Kriens CH 70 C6
Krievciems LV 134 B3
Krieża GR 175 C9
Krikello GR 174 B4

Krikellos GR 174 B3
Krimpen aan de IJssel NL 16 E3
Krimūnas LV 134 C6
Křinec CZ 77 B8
Krinida GR 170 C5
Krinides GR 171 B6
Kriškalni LV 135 C11
Kriškovci BIH 157 C7
Kristberg S 92 B6
Kristdala S 93 E8
Krikhella N 100 D2
Kristiansand N 90 C2
Kristianstad S 88 C6
Kristiansund N 104 E3
Kristiinankaupunki FIN 122 F6
Kristineberg S 107 A15
Kristinefors S 97 C8
Kristinehamn S 97 D11
Kristinestad S 122 F6
Kristoni GR 169 C8
Kristvallabrunn S 89 B10
Kritinia GR 181 D7
Kritsa GR 179 E10
Kritzmow D 83 B12
Krivaja Bara BG 159 F11
Krivača BIH 157 D9
Kriva Feja SRB 164 D5
Krivaja BIH 157 C9
Kriváň SK 147 D8
Krivany SK 145 E2
Kriva Palanka MK 164 E5
Krivi Put HR 67 B10
Krivi Vir SRB 159 F8
Krivodol BG 165 C7
Krivogaštani MK 168 B5
Krivolak MK 169 A7
Križ HR 149 E7
Križanov CZ 77 D10
Križevci HR 149 D7
Křižová CZ 77 D10
Križpolje HR 67 B11
Krk HR 67 B10
Krmčína HR 156 D3
Krnča SK 146 D6
Krnica HR 67 C9
Krnjača SRB 158 D6
Krnja Jela BIH 157 D7
Krnjak HR 148 F5
Krnjeuša BIH 156 C5
Krnjevo SRB 159 E7
Krnov CZ 142 F4
Krobia PL 81 C11
Kroczyce PL 143 E8
Krøderen N 95 B11
Krofdorf Gleiberg D 21 C11
Krog S 103 B9
Krőgis D 80 D4
Krok S 105 E14
Krokees GR 175 F6
Krokeide N 94 B2
Krokek S 93 B8
Kroken N 100 F7
Kroken N 108 F7
Krokfors S 108 F9
Krokfors S 118 B5
Krokio GR 175 A6
Kroknäs S 102 A8
Kroknes N 114 C9
Krokom S 106 E6
Krokos GR 169 D6
Krokowa PL 138 A4
Kroksjö S 107 B13
Kroksjö S 107 D15
Kroksjö S 118 F4
Krokstadelva N 95 C12
Krokstadøra N 104 E7
Krokstranda N 108 D9
Krokströmmen S 102 B8
Kroktjärn S 118 B4
Krokträsk S 118 C8
Królowy Most PL 140 D8
Krölpa D 79 E10
Kroměříž CZ 146 C4
Krommenie NL 16 C3
Krompachy SK 145 F2
Kromsdorf D 79 E9
Kronach D 75 B9
Kronau D 21 F10
Kronauce LV 134 C6
Kronberg im Taunus D 187 A5
Kronlund S 109 E14
Kronoby FIN 123 C10
Kronprinzenkoog D 82 C5
Kronshagen D 83 B8
Kronshtadt RUS 129 F12
Kronstorf A 77 F7
Kropa SLO 73 D9
Kröpelin D 83 B11
Kropp D 82 B7
Kroppenstedt D 79 C9
Kropstädt D 79 C12
Krościenko nad Dunajcem PL 145 E1
Kröslin D 84 B5
Krosna LT 137 E9
Krośnice PL 81 D12
Krośniewice PL 143 B7
Krosno PL 144 D4
Krosno Odrzańskie PL 81 B8
Krossen D 79 E10
Krossen N 90 C2
Krossbø N 95 C8
Krossmoen N 94 E4
Krostitz D 79 D11
Krote LV 134 C3
Krotoszyce PL 81 D10
Krotoszyn PL 142 C3
Krottendorf A 148 B5
Krouna CZ 77 C10
Krousonas GR 178 E8
Kröv D 21 E8
Krovik S 111 E13
Kroyvli GR 171 C9
Krrabë AL 168 B2
Krš HR 156 C3
Kršan HR 67 B9
Krško SLO 148 E4
Krstac MNE 157 F10
Krstinja HR 156 B4
Krtova BIH 157 C9
Kruchowo PL 138 E4
Krujë AL 168 B2
Krumbach A 71 C9

Krumbach A 148 A6
Krumbach (Schwaben) D 71 A10
Krumë AL 163 E9
Krummesse D 83 C9
Krumovgrad BG 171 B9
Krumovo BG 165 E10
Krumovo BG 166 E6
Krumpa (Geiseltal) D 79 D10
Krumvíř CZ 77 E11
Krün D 72 A3
Krunderup DK 86 C3
Kruonis LT 137 D9
Krupac BIH 157 E9
Krupac SRB 165 C6
Krupa na Vrbasu BIH 157 C7
Krupanj SRB 158 E3
Krupe PL 144 A7
Krupina SK 147 E8
Krupište MK 164 F5
Kruså DK 82 A6
Kruševac SRB 164 B3
Kruševica SRB 158 E5
Kruševo MK 168 B5
Kruševo Grdo BIH 157 D8
Krushari BG 155 F1
Kruše e Madhe KS 164 E3
Krushel'nytsya UA 145 E8
Krushevets BG 167 E8
Krushevo BG 166 C4
Krushovitsa BG 160 F3
Krušovce SK 146 D6
Kruszewo PL 85 E11
Kruszwica PL 138 E5
Kruszyna PL 85 D12
Kruszyna PL 143 E7
Krutådal N 108 E7
Krute MNE 163 E7
Kruunupyy FIN 123 C10
Kružlov SK 145 E3
Krya Vrysi GR 169 C7
Kryekuq AL 168 C2
Kryezi AL 163 E9
Kryłów PL 144 B9
Krynica PL 145 E2
Krynica Morska PL 139 B7
Krynice PL 144 B7
Krynki PL 140 D9
Krynychne UA 155 B3
Kryoneri GR 175 C6
Kryoneritis GR 175 B7
Kryopigi GR 169 D9
Krypno Kościelne PL 140 D7
Kryry CZ 76 B4
Krystad N 110 D5
Krystallopigi GR 168 C5
Kryva Balka UA 154 C5
Kryve Ozero UA 154 B6
Kryvorivnya UA 152 A5
Kryzhopil' UA 154 A3
Krzanja MNE 163 C9
Krzanowice PL 146 B6
Krzcin PL 85 D9
Krzelów PL 81 D11
Krzemieniewo PL 81 C11
Krzepice PL 142 E6
Krzepielów PL 81 C10
Krzesk-Królowa Niwa PL 141 F7
Krzeszów PL 81 E10
Krzeszów PL 144 C5
Krzeszowice PL 143 F8
Krzeszyce PL 81 A8
Krzętów PL 143 E8
Krzykosy PL 81 B12
Krzynowłoga Mała PL 139 D10
Krzystkowice PL 81 C8
Krzywcza PL 144 D6
Krzywda PL 141 G6
Krzywiń PL 81 C11
Krzywin PL 84 D6
Krzywowierzba PL 141 G7
Krzyżanowo PL 81 B12
Krzyżanowice PL 146 B6
KrzyżKrzyż PL 85 C9
Ksar Sghir MA 53 E5
Książ Wielki PL 143 F9
Książ Wielkopolski PL 81 B12
Ksiżpol PL 144 C6
Kubanovka RUS 136 D5
Kubbe S 107 D14
Kübekháza H 150 E5
Kübli LV 134 B3
Kublichy BY 133 F4
Kubli LV 133 C11
Kubrat BG 161 F8
Kubuli LV 133 C9
Kuç AL 168 D2
Kučevo SRB 159 E8
Kuchen D 74 E6
Kuchl A 73 A7
Kuchurhan UA 154 D5
Kuchyňa SK 77 F12
Kucice PL 139 E9
Kuciny PL 143 C7
Kučište HR 162 D3
Kuçovë AL 168 C2
Küçükanafarta TR 171 D10
Küçükbahçe TR 177 B7
Küçükçekmece TR 173 B10
Küçükkarıştıran TR 173 B7
Küçükkemerdere TR 177 C10
Küçükköy TR 172 F6
Küçükkumla TR 173 D11
Küçükkuyu TR 172 E6
Küçükyoncali TR 173 B8
Kucura SRB 158 B4
Kuczbork-Osada PL 139 D9
Kudever' RUS 133 C6
Kudirkos Naumiestis LT 136 D6
Kudowa-Zdrój PL 77 B10
Kūdums LV 135 B10
Kufstein A 72 A4
Kuggerud N 96 B6
Kuggören S 103 C14
Kuha FIN 119 C17
Kuhakoski FIN 129 B9
Kühbach D 75 F9
Kuhbier D 83 D12
Kuhfelde D 83 E10
Kühlungsborn, Ostseebad D 83 B11
Kuhmalahti FIN 127 B12
Kuhmo FIN 121 F14
Kuhmoinen FIN 127 B13
Kühndorf D 79 E7
Kühren D 79 D12

Kuhs D 83 C12
Kuhstedt D 17 B11
Kuijõe EST 131 C7
Kuimetsa EST 131 C10
Kuinre NL 16 C5
Kuivajärvi FIN 121 E15
Kuivajõe EST 131 C10
Kuivakangas S 119 B11
Kuivalahti FIN 126 C6
Kuivaniemi FIN 119 C14
Kuivanto FIN 127 D15
Kuivasjärvi FIN 123 F9
Kuivastu EST 130 D6
Kūkas LV 135 C12
Kukės AL 163 E9
Kukkaro FIN 117 D15
Kukasjärvi S 119 B10
Kukës AL 163 E9
Kukko FIN 123 E12
Kukkola FIN 119 C12
Kukkola S 119 C12
Kuklen BG 165 E10
Kuklin PL 139 D9
Kuklinów PL 142 C3
Kukljica HR 156 D3
Kukljin SRB 164 B3
Kukmirn A 148 B6
Kukruse EST 131 C14
Kuktiškės LT 135 F11
Kukulje BIH 157 C7
Kukur AL 168 C3
Kukurečani MK 168 B5
Kula BG 159 F9
Kula HR 149 F9
Kula SRB 158 B4
Kulaši BIH 157 C8
Kulata BG 169 B9
Kulautuva LT 137 D8
Kūļciems LV 134 B6
Kuldiga LV 134 C3
Külefli TR 173 D8
Kuleli TR 173 B6
Kulen Vakuf BIH 156 C5
Kulesze PL 140 D7
Kulho FIN 125 E13
Kulia N 105 D9
Kuliai LT 134 E3
Kulju FIN 127 C10
Kullaa FIN 126 C7
Kullamaa EST 131 C8
Kulleseid N 94 C2
Kulltorp S 88 A5
Kulmain D 75 C10
Kulmbach D 75 B9
Kulpin D 83 C9
Kultima FIN 116 B9
Kuluntalahti FIN 121 F10
Kõlupenai LT 134 E2
Kulva LT 137 C9
Kulvemäki FIN 124 C9
Kulykiv UA 144 D9
Kumachevo RUS 139 A9
Kumane SRB 158 B5
Kumanovo MK 164 E4
Kumbağ TR 173 C7
Kumberg A 148 B5
Kumbri LV 134 C4
Kumbulj LV 135 E13
Kumburun TR 171 E10
Kumhausen D 75 E11
Kumkadi TR 173 D9
Kumla S 97 D13
Kumla kyrkby S 98 C7
Kumlinge FIN 99 B15
Kummer D 83 D10
Kummerow D 83 C13
Kummersdorf D 80 B4
Kummersdorf Gut D 80 B4
Kummunkylä FIN 123 C16
Kumpuranta FIN 125 G12
Kumpuselkä FIN 123 C16
Kumpuvaara FIN 119 C18
Kumrovec HR 148 D5
Kunadacs H 150 D3
Kunágota H 151 E7
Kunbaja H 150 E3
Kunbaracs H 150 D3
Kunčina CZ 77 C11
Kunda EST 131 B13
Kundl A 72 A4
Kunes N 113 C18
Kunfehértó H 150 E3
Kungälv S 91 D10
Kungas FIN 123 C11
Kungsängen S 99 D9
Kungsäter S 88 A3
Kungsbacka S 91 E10
Kungsberg S 103 E12
Kungsfors S 103 E12
Kungsgården S 103 D12
Kungsgården S 103 E12
Kungshamn S 91 C9
Kungshult S 87 D12
Kungsör S 98 D6
Kunhegyes H 150 C6
Kunice PL 81 D10
Kunín CZ 146 B5
Kuningakülä EST 132 C2
Kuniów PL 142 E5
Kunmadaras H 150 C6
Kunovice CZ 146 C4
Kunowice PL 81 B7
Kunowo PL 81 C12
Kunpeszér H 150 D3
Kunrade NL 183 D7
Kunrau D 79 B9
Kunštát CZ 77 C11
Kunszállás H 150 D4
Kunszentmárton H 150 D5
Kunszentmiklós H 150 C3
Kunsziget H 149 A9
Kunvald CZ 77 B11
Kunžak CZ 77 D8
Künzell D 74 A6
Künzelsau D 74 D6
Künzing D 76 E4
Kuohatti FIN 125 C12
Kuohu FIN 123 F14
Kuoksajärvi FIN 117 E15
Kuolayarvi RUS 115 E6
Kuolio FIN 121 C12
Kuomiokoski FIN 128 C7
Kuona FIN 123 C15
Kuopio FIN 124 E9
Kuoppala FIN 122 D9

Kuorevesi FIN 127 B12
Kuortane FIN 123 E11
Kuortti FIN 127 C15
Kuosku FIN 115 D4
Kuossakåbba S 116 D4
Kuouka S 116 E5
Kup PL 142 E4
Kupari HR 162 D5
Küpeler TR 173 E8
Kupferberg D 75 B10
Kupferzell D 74 D6
Kupientyn PL 141 F6
Kupinec HR 148 E5
Kupinovo SRB 158 D5
Kupiškis LT 135 E9
Kupjak HR 67 B10
Küplü TR 171 B10
Kuppenheim D 27 C9
Kuprava LV 133 B3
Kupres BIH 157 D7
Kuprešani BIH 157 D7
Küps D 75 B9
Kurapollye BY 135 F13
Kuratēn AL 168 B2
Kurbnesh AL 163 F9
Kurd H 149 D10
Kürdzhali BG 171 A8
Kurejoki FIN 123 E11
Kuremaa EST 131 D13
Kuremäe EST 132 C2
Kuressaare EST 130 E4
Kurevere EST 130 D4
Kurienkylä FIN 123 F10
Kurikka FIN 122 E8
Kuřim CZ 77 D10
Kurima SK 145 E3
Kurjala FIN 125 E10
Kurjan AL 168 C2
Kurki FIN 121 D10
Kurkiharju FIN 125 D9
Kurkikylä FIN 121 D11
Kurkimäki FIN 124 E9
Kurmene LV 135 D9
Kürnach D 187 B9
Kürnare BG 165 D10
Kürnbach D 27 B10
Kurolanlahti FIN 124 D8
Kuropta RUS 115 D9
Kurort Bad Gottleuba D 80 E5
Kurort Kipsdorf D 80 E5
Kurort Oberwiesenthal D 76 B3
Kurort Schmalkalden D 79 E7
Kurort Steinbach-Hallenberg D 79 E8
Kurów PL 141 H6
Kurowice PL 143 C8
Kurravaara S 116 C4
Kurrokvejk S 109 E14
Kuršėnai LT 134 D5
Kuršiši LV 134 D4
Kursu FIN 115 E4
Kuršumlija SRB 164 C3
Kurtakko FIN 117 D12
Kurtbey TR 172 B6
Kurtna EST 132 C2
Kurtovo Konare BG 165 E9
Kurtti FIN 121 D11
Kurtto FIN 121 E11
Kurtzea E 40 B6
Kuru FIN 127 B12
Kurvinen FIN 121 C14
Kurylówka PL 144 C5
Kurzelów PL 143 E8
Kurzeszyn PL 141 G2
Kurzjtnik PL 139 D8
Kusa LV 135 C12
Kusadak SRB 159 E6
Kuşadasi TR 177 D9
Kuşçayir TR 172 E6
Kusel D 21 E8
Kusey D 79 A9
Kushnytsya UA 145 G7
Kušići SRB 163 C9
Kuside MNE 163 D6
Kuslin PL 81 B10
Kusmark S 118 E5
Küsnacht CH 27 F9
Küssnacht CH 27 F9
Kustavi FIN 126 D5
Küsten D 83 E10
Kusterdingen D 27 C11
Kuštilj SRB 159 C7
Kuta BIH 157 E9
Kutalli AL 168 C2
Kutas H 149 D8
Kutemajärvi FIN 124 F7
Kutenholz D 17 B12
Kuti MNE 163 E7
Kutina HR 149 F7
Kutjevo HR 149 F9
Kutlovo SRB 159 E6
Kutná Hora CZ 77 C8
Kutno PL 143 B7
Kutrikko FIN 115 E5
Kuttanen S 116 B9
Kuttanen FIN 116 B9
Kuttura FIN 117 B16
Kúty SK 77 E12
Kúty UA 152 A6
Kuukasjärvi FIN 119 C17
Kuumu FIN 121 E14
Kuurne B 19 C7
Kuurtola FIN 121 D12
Kuusaa FIN 123 C15
Kuusaa FIN 123 F15
Kuusajärvi FIN 117 C14
Kuusajoki FIN 117 D14
Kuusalu EST 131 C10
Kuusamo FIN 121 C13
Kuusamonkylä FIN 121 F13
Kuusankoski FIN 128 D6
Kuusijärvi FIN 121 D11
Kuusiku EST 131 D9
Kuusiniemi FIN 121 C13
Kuusiranta FIN 120 F9
Kuusirati FIN 119 F14
Kuusivaara FIN 115 E3
Kuusjärvi FIN 125 E11
Kuusjoki FIN 127 D9
Kuuslahti FIN 124 D9
Kuvansi FIN 125 F9
Kuvaskangas FIN 126 B6
Kuyka UA 153 A7
Kuyvozi RUS 129 F13
Kužiai LT 134 E6
Kuzmice SK 145 F4
Kuzmin SRB 158 C3
Kuźmina PL 145 D5
Kuz'molovsky RUS 129 E13
Kuznechnoye RUS 129 C12
Kuźnia Raciborska PL 142 F5

Kuźnica PL 140 C9
Kuźnica Czarnkowska PL 85 E11
Kväcklingen S 103 A12
Kværkeby DK 87 E9
Kværndrup DK 86 E7
Kvalfors N 108 E5
Kvalnes N 110 D6
Kvalnes N 110 E8
Kvalnes N 111 B11
Kvalnes N 114 C8
Kvaløyhamn N 108 E3
Kvaloysletta N 111 A16
Kvaløyvågen N 111 A16
Kvalsaukan N 111 C10
Kvalsund N 113 B12
Kvalsvik N 100 B3
Kvalvåg N 104 E3
Kvalvik N 111 A19
Kvam N 101 C11
Kvannås N 111 B14
Kvanndal N 94 B5
Kvanne N 101 A9
Kvannli N 105 A14
Kvänum S 91 C13
Kvarnberg S 102 D8
Kvarnbyn S 118 F4
Kvarnriset S 118 F5
Kvarnsand S 99 B11
Kvarnsjö S 102 A7
Kvarntäkt S 103 E10
Kvarntorp S 92 A6
Kvarv N 108 B8
Kvarv N 109 B10
Kvasice CZ 146 C4
Kvasy UA 152 A4
Kveaune N 105 C15
Kvėdarna LT 134 E3
Kveinsjøen N 105 A12
Kvelde N 90 A6
Kveli N 105 B15
Kvenvær N 104 D4
Kevlax FIN 122 D7
Kvibille S 87 B11
Kvicksund S 98 D6
Kvidinge S 87 C12
Kvikkjokk S 109 C14
Kvillsfors S 92 E7
Kvinesdal N 94 F5
Kvinlog N 94 E5
Kvissleby S 103 B13
Kvisvik N 104 E3
Kvitblik N 109 B10
Kviteberg N 112 D8
Kviteseid N 95 D8
Kvitnes N 110 C9
Kvitnes N 112 C5
Kvitsøy N 94 D2
Kvívík FO 2 A2
Kvorning DK 86 C5
Kwaadmechelen B 19 B11
Kwidzyn PL 138 C6
Kwieciszewo PL 138 E5
Kwilcz PL 81 A10
Kyan S 103 D10
Kybartai LT 136 D6
Kycklingvattnet S 105 B16
Kydrasivka UA 154 A5
Kyjov CZ 77 D12
Kyläinpää FIN 122 E8
Kylänlahti FIN 125 D13
Kyläsaari FIN 126 B6
Kyleakin GB 2 L5
Kyle of Lochalsh GB 2 L5
Kylerhea GB 2 L5
Kylestrome GB 2 J6
Kylland N 90 B1
Kyllburg D 21 D7
Kyllini GR 174 D3
Kylmäkoski FIN 127 C10
Kylmälä FIN 119 E16
Kymi GR 175 B9
Kymina GR 169 C8
Kyminlinna FIN 128 D6
Kymönkoski FIN 123 D15
Kyndby Huse DK 87 D9
Kyngäs FIN 119 D17
Kynsiperä FIN 121 C11
Kynsivaara FIN 121 C11
Kynšperk nad Ohří CZ 75 B12
Kypärävaara FIN 121 E12
Kyparissia GR 174 E4
Kypasjärv S 119 B10
Kyprinos GR 171 A10
Kypseli GR 175 D7
Kyrgia GR 171 B6
Kyriaki GR 175 C6
Kyritz D 83 E12
Kyrkås S 106 E7
Kyrkhult S 88 C7
Kyrksæterøra N 104 E6
Kyrkslätt FIN 127 E11
Kyrksten S 97 D11
Kyrnychky UA 155 B4
Kyröskoski FIN 127 B9
Kyrsyä FIN 129 B9
Kyslytsya UA 155 C4
Kysucké Nové Mesto SK 147 C7
Kysucký Lieskovec SK 147 C7
Kytäjä FIN 127 D12
Kythira GR 178 C4
Kythnos GR 175 E9
Kytökylä FIN 119 F15
Kytömäki FIN 121 E11
Kyustendil BG 165 E6
Kyyjärvi FIN 123 D13
Kyynämöinen FIN 123 F14
Kyynärö FIN 127 C12

L

Laa an der Thaya A 77 E10
Laaber D 75 D10
La Adrada E 46 D3
Laage D 83 C12
Laagri EST 131 C9
Laaja FIN 121 E12
Laajoki FIN 126 D7
Laakajärvi FIN 125 C10
La Alberca E 45 C8
La Alberca E 56 F2
La Alberca de Záncara E 47 E8
La Alberguería de Argañán E 45 D7
La Albuera E 51 B6
La Aldehuela E 45 D10
La Algaba E 51 E7
La Aliseda de Tormes E 45 D10
La Aljorra E 56 F2
La Almarcha E 47 E8
La Almolda E 42 D3
La Almunia de Doña Godina E 41 F9
Laanila FIN 115 B2
Lääniste EST 131 E14
La Antilla E 51 E5
Laapas FIN 128 D8
Laarkirchen A 76 G5
Laarne B 19 B8
Laasala FIN 123 E12
Laaslich D 83 D11
Laatre EST 131 E10
Laatre EST 131 F12
Laatzen D 78 B6
Laax CH 71 D8
La Azohía E 56 F2
La Baconnière F 23 D10
Labajos E 46 C3
La Balme-de-Sillingy F 31 D9
La Bañeza E 39 D8
Labanoras LT 135 F11
La Barre-de-Monts F 28 B1
La Barre-en-Ouche F 24 C4
La Barthe-de-Neste F 33 D6
Labarthe-Rivière F 33 D7
La Bassée F 18 C6
La Bastide-Clairence F 32 D3
Labastide-d'Anjou F 33 D9
Labastide-d'Armagnac F 32 C5
La Bastide-de-Bousignac F 33 D9
La Bastide-de-Sérou F 33 D8
La Bastide-l'Évêque F 33 B10
Labastide-Murat F 33 A9
La Bastide-Puylaurent F 35 A6
Labastide-Rouairoux F 34 D4
Labastide-St-Pierre F 33 C8
La Bastide-sur-l'Hers F 33 E9
La Bâthie F 31 D9
La Bâtie-Neuve F 36 B4
Lábatlan H 149 A10
Labatut-Rivière F 32 C6
La Baule-Escoublac F 23 F7
La Bazoche-Gouet F 24 D4
La Bazoge F 23 D12
L'Abbaye CH 31 B9
Labégude F 35 A7
La Bégude-de-Mazenc F 35 A8
Labenne F 32 C3
La Bérarde F 31 F9
Labergement-lès-Seurre F 31 A7
Laberget N 111 C13
La Bernerie-en-Retz F 28 A1
Laberweinting D 75 E11
Labin HR 67 B9
Labinot-Mal AL 168 B3
La Bisbal de Falset E 42 E5
La Bisbal del Penedès E 43 E6
La Bisbal d'Empordà E 43 D10
Łabiszyn PL 138 E4
Lablachère F 35 B7
Laboe D 83 B8
La Bonneville-sur-Iton F 24 C5
La Bouëxière F 23 D9
Labouheyre F 32 B4
La Bouilladisse F 35 D10
La Bourboule F 30 D2
Laboutarie F 33 C10
La Bóveda de Toro E 39 F9
Łabowa PL 145 D2
La Brède F 32 A4
La Bréole F 36 C4
La Bresse F 27 D6
La Brillanne F 35 C10
Labrit F 32 B4
La Broque F 27 D7
La Bruffière F 28 A3
Labruguière F 33 C10
L'Absie F 28 B4
La Buisse F 31 E8
Łabunie PL 144 B7
La Bussière F 25 E8
Läby S 99 B9
Laç AL 163 E8
Laç AL 168 A2
La Cabrera E 46 C5
La Caillère-St-Hilaire F 28 B4
Lacalahorra E 55 E6
La Caletta I 64 B4
Lacalm F 30 F2
La Calmette F 35 C7
La Calzada de Oropesa E 45 E10
La Campana E 51 D9
La Cañada de San Urbano E 55 F8
La Cañada de Verich E 42 F3
Lacanau F 28 F3
Lacanau-Océan F 28 E3
Lacanche F 25 F12
La Canourgue F 34 B5
La Capelle F 19 E8
Lacapelle-Barrès F 30 F2
Lacapelle-Marival F 29 F9
Lačarak SRB 158 C4
La Caridad E 39 A6
La Carlota E 53 A7
La Carolina E 54 C5
Lacaune F 34 C4
La Cavada E 40 B4
La Cavalerie F 34 B5
Lacave F 29 F9
Lacco Ameno I 62 F5
Laceby GB 11 D11
Lacedonia I 60 A4
La Cellera de Ter E 43 D9
La Celle-St-Avant F 29 A7
La Cerca E 40 C5
La Cerollera E 42 F3
Laces I 71 D11
La Chaise-Dieu F 30 E4
La Chaize-le-Vicomte F 28 B3
La Chambre F 31 E9
Lachania GR 181 E7
La Chapelaude F 29 C11
La Chapelle F 19 E11
La Chapelle-aux-Bois F 26 D5
La Chapelle-aux-Saints F 29 F9
La Chapelle-d'Abondance F 31 C10
La Chapelle-d'Aligné F 23 E11
La Chapelle-d'Angillon F 25 F7
La Chapelle-de-Guinchay F 30 C6
La Chapelle-des-Fougeretz F 23 D8
La Chapelle-en-Valgaudémar F 31 F9
La Chapelle-en-Vercors F 31 F7
La Chapelle-la-Reine F 25 D8
La Chapelle-Laurent F 30 E3
Lachapelle-sous-Aubenas F 35 A7
La Chapelle-St-André F 25 F9
La Chapelle-St-Laurent F 28 B5
La Chapelle-St-Luc F 25 D11
La Chapelle-St-Quillain F 26 F4
La Chapelle-St-Ursin F 29 A10
La Chapelle-sur-Erdre F 23 F8
Lachar E 53 B9
La Charité-sur-Loire F 25 F9
La Chartre-sur-le-Loir F 24 E4
La Châtaigneraie F 28 B4
La Châtre F 29 B9
La Châtre-Langlin F 29 C8
La Chaume F 25 E12
La Chaussée-St-Victor F 24 E5
La Chaussée-sur-Marne F 25 C12
La Chaux-de-Fonds CH 27 F6
La Chaux-du-Dombief F 31 B8
Lachendorf D 79 A7
Lachen-Speyerdorf D 21 F10
La Cheppe F 25 B12
La Chèze F 22 D6
Lachowo PL 139 D13
Laciċi HR 149 E10
La Cierva E 47 D9
La Ciotat F 35 D10
La Cisterniga E 39 E10
Lack GB 7 C7
Łąck PL 139 F8
Lackamore IRL 8 C6
Läckeby S 89 B10
Łącko PL 145 D1
La Clayette F 30 C5
La Clusaz F 31 D9
La Cluse F 35 A10
La Cluse-et-Mijoux F 31 B9
La Codosera E 45 F6
La Concha E 40 B4
La Condamine-Châtelard F 36 C5
Laconi I 64 D3
La Coquille F 29 D7
La Coronada E 51 B8
La Coronada E 51 C9
La Côte-St-André F 31 E7
La-Couarde-sur-Mer F 28 C3
La Couronne F 28 D6
Lacourt F 33 E8
La Courtine F 29 D10
La Couture-Boussey F 24 C5
Lāčplēsis LV 135 C9
Lacq F 32 D4
La Crau F 36 E4
La Crèche F 28 C5
Lacroix-Barrez F 29 F11
La Croixille F 23 D9
La Croix-Valmer F 36 E5
Lacrouzette F 33 C10
La Cumbre E 45 F9
Łączna PL 143 E10
Łącznik PL 142 F4
Ladánybene H 150 C3
Ladbergen D 17 D9
Ladce SK 146 C6
Lądek PL 142 B4
Lądek-Zdrój PL 77 B11
Ladelund D 82 A6
Ladenburg D 21 F11
Lădeşti RO 160 D4
Ladi GR 171 B10
Ladignac-le-Long F 29 D8
Ladinhac F 29 F11
Ladispoli I 62 D2
Ladoeiro P 45 E6
Ladomirová SK 145 E4
Ladon F 25 D8
Ladozhskoye Ozero RUS 129 E15
Ladushkin RUS 139 A9
Ladybank GB 5 C10
Ladykirk GB 5 D12
Ladysford GB 3 K12
Lādzere LV 134 B5
Ładzice PL 143 D7
Ładzin PL 84 C7
Laekvere EST 131 C13
La Encina E 56 D3
Laer D 17 D8
La Ercina E 39 C9
Lærdalsøyri N 100 D6
Laerma GR 181 D7
Laerru I 64 B2
La Espina E 39 B7
La Estación E 43 D8
La Estrella E 45 E10
Laeva EST 131 E12
La Fare-les-Oliviers F 35 C9
La Farlède F 36 E4
La Fatarrella E 42 E4
La Faurie F 35 A10
La Faute-sur-Mer F 28 C3
La Felipa E 47 F9
La Fère F 19 E7
La Ferrière F 28 B3
La Ferrière-aux-Etangs F 23 C10
La Ferté-Alais F 25 D7
La Ferté-Bernard F 24 D4
La Ferté-Frênel F 24 C4
La Ferté-Gaucher F 25 C9
La Ferté-Imbault F 24 F6
La Ferté-Loupièrre F 25 E9
La Ferté-Macé F 23 C11
La-Ferté-Milon F 25 B9
La Ferté-sous-Jouarre F 25 C9
La Ferté-St-Aubin F 24 E6
La Ferté-St-Cyr F 24 E6
Laferté-sur-Amance F 26 E4
Laferté-sur-Aube F 25 D12
La Férte-Vidame F 24 C4
La Ferté-Villeneuil F 24 E5
Lafitole F 33 D6
Lafkos GR 175 A7
La Flèche F 23 E11
Lafnitz A 148 B6
La Fontaine-St-Martin F 23 E12
La Font de la Figuera E 56 D3
La Force F 29 F6
La Forêt-sur-Sèvre F 28 B4
La Forge F 26 D6
Laforsen S 103 C10
Lafortunada E 33 E6
La Fouillade F 33 B10
La Foux-d'Allos F 36 C5
Lafrançaise F 33 B8
La Fregeneda E 45 C7
La Fresneda E 42 F4
Lafrimbolle F 27 C7
La Frontera E 47 D8
La Fuente de San Esteban E 45 C8
La Fuliola E 42 D6
La Gacilly F 23 E7
La Galera E 42 F4
Lagan S 87 B13
La Garde F 36 E4
La Garde-Adhémar F 35 B8
La Garde-Freinet F 36 E4
Lagardelle-sur-Lèze F 33 D8
Lagarelhos P 38 E5
Lagares da Beira P 44 D5
La Garnache F 28 B2
La Garriga E 43 D8
Lagarrigue F 33 C10
La Garrovilla E 51 B7
La Gaubretière F 28 B3
Lagavara GB 4 E4
Lage D 17 D7
Lage D 17 E11
Lagedi EST 131 C9
Lage Mierde NL 16 F4
Lagerfors S 91 B15
Lagfors S 103 A13
Lagg GB 4 E6
Laggan GB 4 A7
Laggan GB 5 A8
Lagganulva GB 4 C4
Laggarberg S 103 B13
Laghey IRL 6 C6
Laghtgeorge IRL 6 F5
Łagiewniki PL 81 E11
La Gineta E 47 F9
Lagkada GR 177 C7
Lagkadas GR 169 C9
Lagkadia GR 174 D5
La Glacerie F 23 A8
Lagnieu F 31 D7
Lagny-sur-Marne F 25 C8
Lago I 60 E6
Lagoa P 39 F6
Lagoa P 50 E3
Lagoaça P 45 B7
Lago Menor E 57 B11
Lagonegro I 60 C5
Lagor F 32 D4
Lagorce F 28 E5
Lagord F 28 C3
La Gornal E 43 E7
Lagos GR 171 B8
Lagos P 50 E2
Lagosanto I 66 C5
Łagów PL 81 B8
Łagów PL 143 E11
Lagrán E 41 C6
La Granada de Riotinto E 51 D7
La Granadella E 42 E5
La Grand-Croix F 30 D6
La Grande-Combe F 35 B7
La Grande-Motte F 35 C7
La Granja d'Escarp E 42 E4
La Granjuela E 51 C9
Lagrasse F 34 D4
La Grave F 31 E9
Lägsta S 107 D14
La Guarda E 51 B8
Laguardia E 41 C6
La Guardia E 46 E6
La Guardia de Jaén E 53 A9
Laguarta E 32 F5
Laguenne F 29 E9
Laguépie F 33 B9
La Guerche-de-Bretagne F 23 E9
La Guerche-sur-l'Aubois F 30 B2
Laguiole F 30 F2
Laguna Dalga E 39 D8
Laguna de Duero E 39 E10
Laguna de Negrillos E 39 D8
Lagundo I 72 C3
Lagunilla E 45 D9
Lagyna GR 169 C9
Lagyna GR 171 B10
La Haba E 51 B8
Lahana TR 173 B7
La Haye-du-Puits F 23 B8
La Haye-Pesnel F 23 C9
Lähdejänkkä FIN 119 B12
Lähden D 17 C9
Lahenpää S 116 E10
Laheycourt F 26 C3
La Higuera E 55 B10
Lahinch IRL 8 C4
La Hiniesta E 39 E8
La Hinojosa E 47 E8
Lahnajärvi S 116 E8
Lahnalahti FIN 124 F9
Lahnanen FIN 123 C16
Lahnasjärvi FIN 125 C9
Lahnasuando S 116 E9
Lahnstein D 21 D9
Lahntal-Goßfelden D 21 C11
Laholm S 87 C12
Lahonci SLO 148 D6
La Horcajada E 45 D10
La Horra E 40 E4
Lahr (Schwarzwald) D 27 D8
Lähte EST 131 E13
Lahti FIN 126 D6
Lahti FIN 127 D14
Lahtiranta FIN 119 E13
Laichingen D 74 F6
Laide GB 2 K5
Laidi LV 134 C3
Laidze LV 134 B5
Laifour F 184 E2
L'Aigle F 24 C4
La Iglesuela E 46 D3
La Iglesuela del Cid E 42 G3
Laignes F 25 E11
Laigueglia I 37 D8
L'Aiguillon-sur-Mer F 28 C3
Laihia FIN 122 E8
Laikko FIN 129 C11
Laiksjö S 107 C11
Lailly-en-Val F 24 E6
Laimont F 26 C3
Lainate I 69 B7
Lainio S 116 C8
Laino Borgo I 60 D5
Lairg GB 3 J8
La Iruela E 55 D7
Laisbäck S 107 A12
Laisheden S 109 E14
Laissac F 34 B4
Laisvall S 109 D13
Laisvalls by S 109 D13
Laitala FIN 121 E12
Laitikkala FIN 127 C11
Laitila FIN 126 D6
Laiuse EST 131 D13
Laives I 72 D3
Laižuva LT 134 D5
La Jana E 42 F4
La Jarrie F 28 C3
Lajatico I 66 F2
La Javie F 36 C4
Lajeosa P 45 D7
Lajeosa do Mondego P 45 C6
Lajkovac SRB 158 E5
La Jonchère-St-Maurice F 29 C8
La Jonquera E 34 F4
Lajoskomárom H 149 C10
Lajosmizse H 150 C4
La Jumellière F 23 F10
Lakaluoma FIN 123 E10
Lakatnik BG 165 C7
Lakaträsk S 118 B6
Lakavica MK 163 F10
Lakavica MK 169 A7
Lakenheath GB 15 C10
Lakhdenpokh'ya RUS 129 B13
Laki MK 165 F6
Łąkie PL 85 D12
Lakitelek H 150 D4
Lakka GR 168 F3
Lakkoi GR 177 E8
Lakkoi GR 178 E6
Lakkoma GR 169 D9
Lakkoma GR 171 D9
Lakkopetra GR 174 C3
Łąkociny PL 142 C4
Lakomäki FIN 123 E15
Łąkorz PL 139 D7
Lakšárska Nová Ves SK 146 D4
Lakselv N 113 C14
Lakselvsletta N 111 B18
Laksfors N 108 E5
Laktaši BIH 157 C7
Lakuntza E 32 E1
La Lantejuela E 51 E9
La Lapa E 51 C6
Lalapaşa TR 167 F7
Lalas GR 174 D4
L'Albagés E 42 E5
Lalbenque F 33 B9
L'Alcora E 48 D4
L'Alcudia E 48 F3
L'Alcudia de Crespins E 56 D3
Lalevade-d'Ardèche F 35 A7
Lalëz AL 168 A2
L'Alfàs del Pi E 56 D4
Lalín E 38 C3
Lalinac SRB 164 C5
Lalinde F 29 F7
La Línea de la Concepción E 53 D6
Lalioti GR 175 C6
Lallaing F 19 D7
Lalley F 31 F8
Lalm N 101 C10
La Londe-les-Maures F 36 E4
Laloşu RO 160 D4
Laloubère F 33 D6
Lalouvesc F 30 E6
La Louvière B 19 D9
Lalove UA 145 G6
La Loye F 31 A8
L'Alpe-d'Huez F 31 E9
Lalueza E 42 D3
La Luisiana E 51 D9
Laluque F 32 C4
Lam D 76 D4
Lama I 63 C6
La Machine F 30 B3
La Maddalena I 64 A3
La Magdalena E 39 C8
Lamagistère F 33 B7
La Malène F 34 B5
Lamalou-les-Bains F 34 C5
Lama Mocogno I 66 D2
La Manga del Mar Menor E 56 F3
Lamanon F 35 C9
La Marche F 25 F9
Lamarche F 26 D4
Lamarche-sur-Saône F 26 F3
Lamargelle F 25 E12
Lamarque F 28 E4
Lamas P 44 C3
La Massana AND 33 E9
Lamastre F 30 F6
La Mata E 46 E4
La Mata de los Olmos E 42 F3
La Matilla E 46 B5
Lambach A 76 F5
Lamballe F 22 D6
Lambersart F 18 C7
Lambesc F 35 C9
Lambia GR 174 D4
Łambinowice PL 142 E4
Lamborn S 103 E10
Lambourn GB 13 B11
Lambrecht (Pfalz) D 186 C5
Lambsheim D 21 E10
Lamego P 44 B5
La Meilleraye-de-Bretagne F 23 E9
Lameiras P 45 C6
Lamerdingen D 71 A11
L'Ametlla de Mar E 42 F5
Lamezia I 59 B9
Lamia GR 174 B5
Lamiako E 40 B6
La Milesse F 23 D12
Lamlash GB 4 D6
Lammhult S 88 A7
Lammi FIN 123 D11
Lammi FIN 127 C13
Lamminkoski FIN 123 F10
Lamminmaa FIN 122 F8
Lamminperä FIN 119 C16
Lamminvaara FIN 121 B10
La Mojonera E 55 F7
La Môle F 36 E4
Lamon I 72 D4
La Mongie F 33 E6
La Monnerie-le-Montel F 30 D4
La Morera E 51 B6
Lamothe F 30 E3
La Mothe-Achard F 28 B2
Lamothe-Cassel F 33 A8
La Mothe-St-Héray F 28 C5
Lamotte-Beuvron F 24 E7
La Motte-Chalancon F 35 B9
La Motte-du-Caire F 35 B11
Lamovita BIH 157 C6
Lampaanjärvi FIN 124 D7
Lampaul F 22 D1
Lampaul-Guimilau F 22 D3
Lampaul-Plouarzel F 22 D2
Lampeland N 95 C11
Lamperila FIN 124 E8
Lampertheim D 21 E10
Lampertswalde D 80 D5
Lampeter GB 12 A6
Lampinou GR 169 F9
Lampinsaari FIN 119 F14
Lampiselkä FIN 115 D1
Lamprechtshausen A 76 G3
Lampsijärvi FIN 117 E13
Lamsfeld-Groß Liebitz D 80 C6
Lamspringe D 79 C7
Lamstedt D 17 A12
Lamu FIN 119 F16
La Mudarra E 39 E10
La Muela E 41 E9
Lamujoki FIN 119 F16
La Mure F 31 F8
Lamure-sur-Azergues F 30 C5
Lana I 72 C3
Lanabukt N 114 D8
Lanaja E 41 E11
Lanaken B 19 C12
Lanarce F 30 F5
Lanark GB 5 D9
La Nava E 51 D6
La Nava de Ricomalillo E 46 E3
La Nava de Santiago E 45 F8
Lancaster GB 10 C6
Lanchester GB 5 F13
Lanciano I 63 C6
Lanckorona PL 147 B9
Łańcut PL 144 C5
Lancy CH 31 C9
Landau an der Isar D 75 E12
Landau in der Pfalz D 21 F10
Landbobyn S 102 E7
Lande N 105 A13
Landeck A 71 C11
Landeleau F 22 D4
Landen B 183 D6
Landerneau F 22 D3
Landersheim F 27 C7
Landeryd S 87 A12
Landesbergen D 17 C12
Landete E 47 E10
Landévant F 22 E5
Landgraaf NL 20 C6
Landiras F 32 A5
Landivisiau F 22 C3
Landivy F 23 D9
Landkirchen auf Fehmarn D 83 B10
Landön S 105 D16
Landos F 30 F4
Landquart CH 71 D9
Landrecies F 19 D8
Landres F 19 F12
Landsberg am Lech D 71 A11
Landsbro S 92 E5
Landscheid D 185 E6
Landshut D 75 E11
Landskrona S 87 D11
Landsmeer NL 182 A5
Landstuhl D 21 F9
Landudec F 22 D3
Landvetter S 91 D11
Landze LV 134 B3
Lanesborough IRL 7 E7
Lanesøyra N 112 C4
Lanester F 22 E5
La Neuve-Lyre F 24 C4
La Neuveville CH 31 A11
La Neuville-au-Pont F 25 B12
Laneuville-sur-Meuse F 19 F11
Lång S 97 D9
Langå DK 86 C5
Langa E 46 B3
Långå S 102 B5
Langa de Duero E 40 E5
Långalma S 99 B10
Långåminne FIN 122 E7
Långan S 105 D16
Langangen N 90 A6
Långås S 87 B10
Långasjö S 89 B8
Langau A 77 E9
Långbäck S 107 A11
Långbäcken S 107 C14
Langballig D 82 A7
Långban S 97 C11
Långbo S 103 C10
Långbo S 103 D12
Langbunes N 114 C9
Langburkersdorf D 80 D6
Langdorf D 76 D4
Langeac F 30 E3
Langeais F 24 F3
Langebæk DK 87 F10
Långed S 107 D17
Langedijk NL 16 C3
Langeid N 90 B2
Längelmäki FIN 127 B12
Langeln D 79 C8
Langelsheim D 79 C7
Langemark B 18 C6
Langemyr N 90 B3
Langen D 17 A11
Langen D 21 E11
Langenaltheim D 75 E8
Langenau D 75 F7
Langenaubach D 185 C9
Langenberg D 17 E10
Langenberg D 183 C10
Langenburg D 74 D6
Langenenslingen D 27 D11
Langenes N 110 B9
Langenfeld A 71 C11
Langenfeld (Rheinland) D 21 B7
Langenhagen D 78 B6
Langenhahn D 185 C8
Langenhorn D 82 A5
Langenlebarn-Oberhain D 79 E12
Langenlois A 77 F9
Langenlonsheim D 185 E8
Langennaundorf D 80 C4
Langenneufnach D 71 A11
Langenorla D 79 E10
Langenpreising D 75 F10
Langenselbold D 21 D12
Langenthal CH 27 F8
Langenwang A 148 A5
Langenweddingen D 79 B10
Langenzenn D 75 D8
Langenzersdorf A 77 F10
Langeoog D 17 A8
Langeskov DK 86 E7
Langesund N 90 A6
Langevåg N 94 C2
Langevåg N 100 B4
Langewiesen D 79 E8
Langfjordbotn N 112 C9
Länggöns D 21 D11
Langhagen D 83 C12
Langham GB 11 F10
Langhamn N 111 B14
Länghed S 103 D11
Länghem S 91 D13
Langhirano I 66 C1
Langholm GB 5 E11
Langhus N 95 C13
Långlöt S 89 B11
Långnäs S 98 A6
Langnau CH 70 D5
Langnes N 111 B15
Langnes N 114 C4
Langnes N 114 D7
Langø DK 83 A10
Langogne F 30 F4
Langoiran F 28 F5
Langon F 32 A5
Langport GB 13 C9
Langreo E 39 B8
Langres F 26 E3
Langschlag A 77 E7
Långsel S 118 B8
Långsele S 107 C15
Långsele S 107 E12
Langset N 95 B14
Langset N 108 D5
Langset N 109 B9
Långshyttan S 97 B15
Långsjöby S 107 A11
Långskog S 103 B12
Langslett N 112 D6
Langstrand N 112 B11
Langsund S 118 D7
Langsur D 186 B2
Langtoft GB 11 C11
Långträsk S 107 A16
Långträsk S 118 C7
Långträsk S 118 D4
Langueux F 22 D6
Languidic F 22 E5
Languilla E 40 F5
Langula D 79 D7
Långvattnet S 107 D11
Långvattnet S 107 D13
Långvattnet S 118 E4
Långviken S 109 E15
Långviksmon S 107 D15
Långvinds bruk S 103 D13
Langwarden (Butjadingen) D 17 A10
Langwathby GB 5 F11
Langwedel D 17 C12
Langwedel D 83 B7
Langweid am Lech D 75 F8
Łanięta PL 139 F7
Lanivet GB 12 E5
Lanjarón E 53 C10
Lankojärvi FIN 117 E12
Lanloup F 22 C6
Lanmeur F 22 C4
Lanna S 87 A13
Lanna S 92 A5
Länna S 99 C9
Lannach A 148 C4
Lannavaara S 116 B7
Lannemezan F 33 D6
Lannepax F 33 C6
Lannevesi FIN 123 E14
Lannilis F 22 C2
Lannion F 22 C5
Lannoy F 19 C7
Lanobre F 29 E11
La Nocle-Maulaix F 30 B4
Lanouaille F 29 E8
Lánov CZ 81 E9
Lansån S 116 F8
Lansargues F 35 C7
Lansen D 83 C13
Länsikoski FIN 119 C13
Länsikylä FIN 123 E11
Länsipää FIN 119 B12
Länsiranta FIN 117 D16
Länsi-Teisko FIN 127 B10
Lansjärv S 116 E8
Lanškroun CZ 77 C11
Lanslebourg-Mont-Cenis F 31 E10
Lanta F 33 C9
Lantadilla E 40 D3
Lanton F 28 F3
Lantosque F 37 D6
Lantriac F 30 E5
Lanty F 30 B4
La Nucía E 56 D4
Lanuéjouls F 33 B10
Lanurile RO 155 C1
Lanusei I 64 D4
Lanuvio I 62 D3
Lanvollon F 22 C6
Łany PL 142 F5
Lánycsók H 149 D11
Lanz D 83 D11
Lanzahita E 46 D3
Lanžhot CZ 77 E11
Lanzo Torinese I 31 E11
Laon F 19 E8
Laons F 24 C5
La Paca E 55 D9
La Pacaudière F 30 C4
Lapajärvi FIN 115 E4
Lapalisse F 30 C4
La Pallice F 28 C3
La Palma E 56 F3
La Palma del Condado E 51 E6
La Palme F 34 E4
Lapalud F 35 B8
La Palud-sur-Verdon F 36 D4
Lapanj AL 168 D3
Łapanów PL 144 D1
Lapardha AL 168 C2
La Parra E 51 B6
La Parra de Las Vegas E 47 E8
Lapas GR 174 C3
La Pellerine F 23 D9
La Penne F 36 D5
La Peraleja E 47 D7
La Pesga E 45 D8
La Petite-Pierre F 27 C7
La Peza E 55 E6
Lapford GB 13 D7
Lapijoki FIN 126 C6
La Pinilla E 56 F2
Lapinjärvi FIN 127 D15
Lapinkylä FIN 127 E11
Lapinlahti FIN 124 D8
Lapinneva FIN 123 D9
Lapinsalo FIN 123 C17
La Plagne F 31 D10
La Plaza E 39 B7
Laplume F 33 B7
Lapmežciems LV 134 B7
La Pobla de Claramunt E 43 D7
La Pobla del Duc E 56 D4
La Pobla de Lillet E 43 C7
La Pobla de Montornès E 43 E6
La Pobla de Segur E 42 C5
La Pobla de Vallbona E 48 E3
La Pola de Gordón E 39 C8
La Pommeraye F 23 F10
La Porta F 37 G10
La Portellada E 42 F4
La Portera E 47 F10
Lapoș RO 161 C8
La Pouëze F 23 E10
Lapoutroie F 27 D7
Lapovo SRB 159 E7
Lappajärvi FIN 123 D11

Lappe *S* 92 A7
Lappea *FIN* 117 D11
Lappeenranta *FIN* 129 C9
Lappersdorf *D* 75 D11
Lappetelä *FIN* 123 C10
Lappfjärd *FIN* 122 F7
Lappfors *FIN* 123 C10
Lappi *FIN* 119 E14
Lappi *FIN* 121 D13
Lappi *FIN* 126 C6
Lappila *FIN* 127 D13
Lappo *FIN* 126 E5
Lappohja *FIN* 127 F9
Lappträsk *S* 119 B11
Lappuluobbal *N* 113 E13
La Preste *F* 33 F10
La Proveda de Soria *E* 41 D7
Lăpseki *TR* 172 D6
Laptevo *RUS* 133 C5
Lapua *FIN* 123 E10
La Puebla de Almoradiel *E* 47 E6
La Puebla de Arganzón *E* 40 C6
La Puebla de Cazalla *E* 51 E9
La Puebla de los Infantes *E* 51 D9
La Puebla del Río *E* 51 E7
La Puebla de Montalbán *E* 46 E4
La Puebla de Valdavia *E* 39 C10
La Puebla de Valverde *E* 48 D3
La Puerta de Segura *E* 55 C7
La Punt *CH* 71 D9
Lăpuş *RO* 152 C4
Lăpușata *RO* 160 C4
Lăpușnicel *RO* 159 D9
Lăpușnicu Mare *RO* 159 D8
Łapy *PL* 140 E7
L'Aquila *I* 62 C4
Laracha *E* 38 B2
Laracor *IRL* 7 E9
Laragh *IRL* 7 F10
Laragne-Montéglin *F* 35 B10
La Rambla *E* 53 A7
Laranueva *E* 47 C7
La Rasa *E* 40 E5
La Ravoire *F* 31 D8
Larbert *GB* 5 C9
L'Arboç *E* 43 E7
L'Arbresle *F* 30 D6
Lärbro *S* 93 D13
Larceveau-Arros-Cibits *F* 32 D3
Larchamp *F* 23 D9
Larchant *F* 25 D8
Larche *F* 29 E8
Larche *F* 36 C5
Lardaro *I* 69 B10
Larderello *I* 66 F2
Lardero *E* 41 D7
Lardos *GR* 181 D8
Laredo *E* 40 B5
La Redorte *F* 34 D4
Laren *NL* 16 D4
Laren *NL* 183 A8
La Réole *F* 32 A5
Larga *MD* 153 A9
Largan *IRL* 6 D5
L'Argentière-la-Bessée *F* 31 F10
Largoward *GB* 5 C11
Largs *GB* 4 D7
Largu *RO* 161 D10
Lari *I* 66 E2
Lariano *I* 62 D3
La Riba *E* 42 E6
La Riba de Escalote *E* 40 F6
La Ricamarie *F* 30 E5
La Riche *F* 24 F4
La Rinconada *E* 51 E8
Larino *I* 63 D7
Larionovo *RUS* 129 D13
Larisa *GR* 169 E7
Larkhall *GB* 5 D9
Larkollen *N* 95 D13
Larling *GB* 15 C10
L'Armentera *E* 43 C10
Larmor-Plage *F* 22 E5
Larne *GB* 4 F5
La Robla *E* 39 C8
La Roca de la Sierra *E* 45 F7
La Roche *CH* 31 B11
La Roche-Bernard *F* 23 E7
La Roche-Canillac *F* 29 E9
La Roche-Chalais *F* 28 E6
La Roche-de-Rame *F* 31 F10
La Roche-Derrien *F* 22 C5
La Roche-des-Arnauds *F* 35 A10
La Roche-en-Ardenne *F* 19 D12
La Rochefoucauld *F* 29 C6
La Rochelle *F* 28 C3
Larochemillay *F* 30 B5
La Roche-Posay *F* 29 B7
La Rochepot *F* 30 B6
La Roche-sur-Foron *F* 31 C9
La Roche-sur-Yon *F* 28 B3
La Rochette *F* 31 E9
Larochette *L* 20 E6
La Roda *E* 47 F8
La Roda de Andalucía *E* 53 B7
La Roë *F* 23 E9
Laroles *E* 55 F7
La Romana *E* 56 E3
Le Romieu *F* 33 C6
Laroquebrou *F* 29 F10
Laroque-d'Olmes *F* 33 E9
La Roque-Ste-Marguerite *F* 34 B5
Laroque-Timbaut *F* 33 B7
La Rouquette *F* 33 B9
Larraga *E* 32 E2
Larrasoaina *E* 32 E2
Larrau *F* 32 D4
Larrazet *F* 33 C8
Larressore *E* 32 D3
Larrión *E* 32 E1
Larsbo *S* 97 B14
Larseng *N* 111 A16
Larsmo *FIN* 122 C9
Larsnes *N* 100 B3
Laruns *F* 32 E5
Laruscade *F* 28 E5
Larv *S* 91 C13
Larva *E* 55 D6
Larvik *N* 90 A7
Larymna *GR* 175 B7
Lasà *I* 71 D11
La Salle *I* 31 D11
La Salle les Alpes *F* 31 F10
La Salvetat-Peyralès *F* 33 B10
La Salvetat-sur-Agout *F* 34 C4
La Salzadella *E* 48 D5
Läsänkoski *FIN* 128 B6
Las Arenas *E* 39 B10

La Sauvetat-du-Dropt *F* 33 A6
La Savina *E* 57 D7
Lasberg *A* 77 F7
Las Berlanas *E* 46 C3
Lásby *DK* 86 C5
Las Cabezas de San Juan *E* 51 F8
Lascari *I* 58 D4
Las Casas *E* 48 E4
Lascuarre *E* 42 C5
La Seca *E* 39 F10
La Secuita *E* 43 E6
La Séguinière *F* 28 A4
La Selva del Camp *E* 42 E6
La Selve *F* 33 B11
La Sènia *E* 42 F4
La Seyne-sur-Mer *F* 35 D10
Las Herencias *E* 46 E3
Łasin *PL* 138 C7
Lasinja *HR* 148 E5
Łask *PL* 143 C7
Laskarzew *PL* 141 G5
Lasko *SLO* 148 D4
Laskowa *PL* 144 D1
Laskowice *PL* 138 D5
Laskowice *PL* 139 D12
Las Labores *E* 46 F5
Laslea *RO* 152 E5
Las Majadas *E* 47 D8
Las Menas *E* 55 E8
Las Mesas *E* 47 F7
Las Navas de la Concepción *E* 51 D9
Las Navas del Marqués *E* 46 C4
Lasne *B* 182 D4
Las Negras *E* 55 F9
La Solana *E* 55 B6
La Souterraine *F* 29 C8
Lasovo *SRB* 159 F9
Lasowice Małe *PL* 142 E5
Las Palas *E* 56 F2
Las Pedroñeras *E* 47 F7
Las Pedrosas *E* 41 D10
La Spezia *I* 69 E8
Las Plassas *I* 64 D2
Las Rotas *E* 56 D5
Las Rozas de Madrid *E* 46 C5
Lassahn *D* 83 C9
Lassan *D* 84 C5
Lassay-les-Châteaux *F* 23 D11
Lassemoen *N* 105 B13
Lässerud *S* 96 C7
Lasseube *F* 32 D4
Lassigny *F* 18 E6
Lassila *FIN* 126 B7
Lassing *A* 73 A9
Lassing *A* 73 A10
Laßnitzhöhe *A* 148 B5
Lastebasse *I* 69 B11
Las Terreras *E* 55 D9
Las Torres de Cotillas *E* 56 E2
Lastours *F* 33 D10
Lastovo *HR* 162 D2
Lastra a Signa *I* 66 E3
Lastras de Cuéllar *E* 40 F3
Lastrup *D* 17 C9
Lastukoski *FIN* 125 D10
Lastva *BIH* 162 D5
Lašva *BIH* 157 D8
Lasva *EST* 131 F14
Las Veguillas *E* 45 C9
Las Ventas con Peña Aguilera *E* 46 E4
Las Ventas de San Julián *E* 45 D10
Łaszczów *PL* 144 B8
Laszki *PL* 144 C6
Laterza *I* 61 B7
La Teste-de-Buch *F* 32 A3
Lathen *D* 17 C8
Latheron *GB* 3 J10
Latheronwheel *GB* 3 J10
La Thuile *I* 31 D10
Lathus *F* 29 C7
Latiano *I* 61 B9
Latikberg *S* 107 B12
Latille *F* 28 B6
Latina *I* 62 E3
Latisana *I* 73 E7
Latorpsbruk *S* 97 D12
La Torre de Cabdella *E* 33 F7
La Torre de Esteban Hambrán *E* 46 D4
La Torre de l'Espanyol *E* 42 E5
La Tour-Blanche *F* 29 E6
La Tour-d'Auvergne *F* 29 D11
Latour-de-France *F* 34 E4
La Tour-du-Crieu *F* 33 D9
La Tour-du-Pin *F* 31 D7
La Tour-sur-Orb *F* 34 C5
Latowicz *PL* 141 F5
Latva *FIN* 119 F15
Latva *FIN* 120 D7
Latvajärvenperä *FIN* 121 D11
Laubach *D* 21 C11
Laubach *D* 21 D11
Lauben *D* 71 A10
Laubere *LV* 135 C10
Laubusch *D* 80 D6
Lauchhammer *D* 80 D5
Lauchringen *D* 27 E9
Lauciene *LV* 134 B5
Lauda-Königshofen *D* 74 C6
Lauder *GB* 5 D11
Lauderi *LV* 133 D4
Łaudona *LV* 135 C12
Laudun *F* 35 B8
Lauenau *D* 17 D12
Lauenbrück *D* 82 D7
Lauenburg (Elbe) *D* 83 D9
Lauenförde *D* 21 A12
Lauf *D* 186 D5
Laufach *D* 187 A7
Lauf an der Pegnitz *D* 75 C9
Laufen *CH* 27 F8
Laufenburg *CH* 27 E9
Lauffen am Neckar *D* 187 D6
Laugnac *F* 33 B7
Lauingen (Donau) *D* 75 E7

Laujar de Andarax *E* 55 F7
Łaukaa *FIN* 123 F15
Laukeng *N* 112 D9
Lauker *S* 118 C3
Laukka *FIN* 119 E15
Laukkala *FIN* 123 D17
Laukkoski *FIN* 127 E13
Laukna *EST* 131 D8
Lauksargiai *LT* 134 F5
Laukslett *N* 111 A17
Lauksletta *N* 112 C6
Lauksodis *LT* 135 D8
Laukuva *LT* 134 E4
Laukvik *N* 105 C9
Laukvik *N* 110 D7
Laukvik *N* 110 E6
Laukvik *N* 111 A14
Laukvik *N* 111 C13
Laukvik *N* 114 B6
Laukžemė *LT* 134 D2
Laulasmaa *EST* 131 C8
Launac *F* 33 C8
Launceston *GB* 12 D6
La Unión *E* 56 F3
Launkalne *LV* 135 B11
Launonen *FIN* 127 D12
Laupen *CH* 31 B11
Laupheim *D* 71 A9
Laupstad *N* 110 D8
Lauragh *IRL* 8 E3
Lauraguel *F* 33 D10
Laurbjerg *DK* 86 C5
Laureana di Borrello *I* 59 C9
Laurencekirk *GB* 5 B12
Laurencetown *IRL* 6 F6
Laurens *F* 34 C5
Laurenzana *I* 60 C5
Lauria *I* 60 C5
Laurière *F* 29 C8
Laurieston *GB* 5 F8
Laurila *FIN* 119 C13
Laurino *I* 60 C4
Lauris *F* 35 C9
Laurito *I* 60 C4
Lausanne *CH* 31 B10
Lauscha *D* 75 B9
Laußig *D* 79 C12
Laußnitz *D* 80 D5
Laussonne *F* 30 F5
Laussou *F* 33 A7
Lauta *D* 80 D6
Lautamaa *FIN* 119 C12
Lautenbach *F* 27 C9
Lautenbourg *F* 27 C9
Lauterbrunnen *CH* 70 D5
Lautere *LV* 135 C12
Lauterecken *D* 186 B4
Lauterhofen *D* 75 D10
Lautersbach (Hessen) *D* 78 E5
Lauterstein *D* 187 D8
Lautertal *D* 75 B8
Lautiosaari *FIN* 119 C13
Lautrec *F* 33 C10
Lauttavaara *FIN* 121 E10
Lauttijärvi *FIN* 126 B6
Lauve *N* 90 A7
Lauvsnes *N* 105 C9
Lauvstad *N* 100 B3
Lauvuskylä *FIN* 125 C13
Lauvvik *N* 94 E4
Lauzerte *F* 33 B8
Lauzès *F* 33 A9
Lauzun *F* 33 A6
Lavagna *I* 37 C10
Laval *F* 23 D10
Lavala *FIN* 121 D14
Lavalette *F* 33 D10
La Valette-du-Var *F* 35 D10
La Vall d'Uixó *E* 48 E4
La Valle *I* 72 C4
Lavamünd *A* 73 C10
Lavangen *N* 111 C14
Lavangsnes *N* 111 C12
Lavara *GR* 171 B10
Lavardac *F* 33 B6
Lavassaare *EST* 131 D8
Lavaur *F* 33 C9
Lavaveix-les-Mines *F* 29 C10
Lavda *GR* 168 F5
Lavdar i Korçës *AL* 168 C4
La Vecilla *E* 39 C9
La Vega *E* 39 B8
La Vega *E* 39 B9
La Vega *E* 39 B10
Lavelanet *F* 33 E9
Le Vellés *E* 45 B9
Lavello *I* 60 A6
Laven *DK* 86 C5
Lavena Ponte Tresa *I* 69 B6
La Ventosa *E* 47 D8
La Verdière *F* 35 C10
La Vernarède *F* 35 B6
La Verpillière *F* 31 D7
La Verrie *F* 28 B4
La Veuve *F* 25 B11
Lavia *FIN* 126 B8
Laviano *I* 60 B4
La Victoria *E* 53 A7
La Vid *E* 40 E5
Lavik *N* 111 B14
La Villa de Don Fadrique *E* 47 E6
La Ville-aux-Clercs *F* 24 E5
La Villedieu *F* 30 F4
La Villedieu-du-Clain *F* 29 C6
La Villedieu-en-Fontenette *F* 26 E5
Lavinio-Lido di Enea *I* 62 E3
Laviron *F* 26 F6
Lavís *I* 69 A11
Lavit *F* 33 C7
Lavoriškés *LT* 137 D12
La Voulte-sur-Rhône *F* 30 F6
Lavoûte-Chilhac *F* 30 E4
Lavoûte-sur-Loire *F* 30 E4
Lavradio *P* 50 B1
Lavre *P* 50 B3
Lavrio *GR* 175 D9
Lavsjö *S* 107 C11
La Wantzenau *F* 186 D4
Lawers *GB* 5 B8
Lawford *GB* 15 D11
Ławsk *PL* 140 D6
Ławszowa *PL* 81 D8
Ławy *PL* 85 E7
Laxå *S* 92 B5
Laxbäcken *S* 107 B10
Laxe *E* 38 B2

Laxey *GBM* 10 C3
Laxford Bridge *GB* 2 J6
Laxnäs *S* 108 E9
Laxne *S* 93 A10
Laxo *GB* 3 E14
Laxsjö *S* 106 C7
Laxvik *S* 87 B11
Laxviken *S* 106 D7
Layana *E* 32 F3
La Yesa *E* 48 E3
Layos *E* 46 E4
Layrac *F* 33 B7
Laz *HR* 148 E5
Laza *E* 38 D5
Laza *RO* 153 D11
Lazagurría *E* 32 F1
Lazarata *RO* 174 B2
Lăzarea *RO* 153 D7
Lăzăreni *RO* 151 D9
Lazarevac *SRB* 158 E5
Lazarev Krst *MNE* 163 D7
Lazarevo *SRB* 158 C6
Lazdijai *LT* 137 E8
Lazdininkai *LT* 134 E2
Lazdona *LV* 135 C12
Lazdukalns *LV* 133 C2
Lazeshchyna *UA* 152 A4
Lazise *I* 66 B2
Łaziska *PL* 141 H5
Łaziska Górne *PL* 142 F6
Lazkao *E* 32 D1
Lázně Bělohrad *CZ* 77 B9
Lázně Bohdaneč *CZ* 77 B9
Lázně Kynžvart *CZ* 75 B12
Laznica *SRB* 159 E8
Lazonby *GB* 5 F11
Lazuri *RO* 151 B10
Lazuri de Beiuş *RO* 151 D10
Leabgarrow *IRL* 6 C6
Leacht Seoirse *IRL* 6 F5
Leadburn *GB* 5 D10
Leadenham *GB* 11 E10
Leadhills *GB* 5 E9
Leamhcán *IRL* 7 F10
Leamington Spa, Royal *GB* 13 A11
Leányfalu *H* 150 B3
Leap *IRL* 8 E4
Leasingham *GB* 11 E11
Leatherhead *GB* 15 E8
Leavvajohka *N* 113 D17
Łeba *PL* 85 A13
Lebach *D* 21 F7
Lebane *SRB* 164 D4
Le Ban-St-Martin *F* 186 C1
Le Barp *F* 32 A4
Le Bar-sur-Loup *F* 36 D5
Lebbeke *B* 19 B9
Le Béage *F* 30 F5
Le Beausset *F* 35 B6
Lebedivka *UA* 154 F6
Lébénymiklós *H* 149 A8
Lebesby *N* 113 B16
Le Bez *F* 33 C10
Lebiez *F* 18 D4
Le Biot *F* 31 C10
Le Blanc *F* 29 B8
Le Bleymard *F* 35 B6
Lębork *PL* 85 A13
Le Boulou *F* 34 F4
Le Boupère *F* 28 B4
Le Bourg *F* 29 F9
Le Bourg-d'Oisans *F* 31 E9
Le Bourget-du-Lac *F* 31 D8
Le Bousquet-d'Orb *F* 34 C5
Le Breuil *F* 25 C10
Le Breuil *F* 30 B6
Lebrija *E* 51 F7
Le Brouilh-Monbert *F* 33 C6
Le Brusquet *F* 36 C4
Lebução *P* 38 E5
Le Bugue *F* 29 F7
Le Buisson *F* 34 A5
Le Buisson-de-Cadouin *F* 29 F7
Łebunia *PL* 138 B5
Lebus *D* 81 B7
Lebusa *D* 80 C4
Lebyazh'ye *RUS* 129 F11
Leça da Palmeira *P* 44 B3
Leça do Bailio *P* 44 B3
Le Cannet *F* 36 D6
Le Cannet-des-Maures *F* 36 D4
Le Castellet *F* 35 D10
Le Cateau-Cambrésis *F* 19 D8
Le Catelet *F* 19 D7
Le Caylar *F* 34 C5
Le Cayrol *F* 34 A4
Lecce *I* 61 C10
Lecco *I* 69 B7
Lece *SRB* 164 D4
Lécera *E* 42 E2
Lech *A* 71 C10
Lechaina *GR* 174 D3
Lechaio *GR* 175 D6
Lechbruck *D* 71 B11
Le Chambon-Feugerolles *F* 30 E5
Le Chambon-sur-Lignon *F* 30 E5
Lechaschau *A* 71 C11
Le Château-d'Oléron *F* 28 D3
Le Châtelard *F* 31 D8
Le Châtelet *F* 29 B10
Le Chêne *F* 25 C11
Le Chesne *F* 19 E10
Le Cheylard *F* 30 F5
Le Cheylas *F* 31 E8
Lechința *RO* 152 C4
Lechlade *GB* 13 B11
Lechovo *GR* 169 C5
Lechtingen (Wallenhorst) *D* 17 D10
Leciñena *E* 41 E10
Leck *D* 82 A5
Leckaun *IRL* 6 D6
Leckmelm *GB* 2 K6
Le Clapier *F* 34 C5
Le Collet-de-Dèze *F* 35 B6
Le Conquet *F* 22 D2
Le Coteau *F* 30 C5
Le Coudray-St-Germer *F* 18 F4
Lécousse *F* 23 D9
Le Crès *F* 35 C6
Le Creusot *F* 30 B5
Lecrín *E* 53 C9

Le Croisic *F* 22 F6
Le Crotoy *F* 18 D4
Lectoure *F* 33 C7
Łęczna *PL* 141 H7
Łęczyca *PL* 143 B7
Łęczyce *PL* 138 A4
Ledaig *GB* 4 C6
Ledaña *E* 47 E9
Ledanca *E* 47 C7
Lēdas *LV* 134 B5
Ledbury *GB* 13 A9
Lede *B* 19 C8
Ledeč nad Sázavou *CZ* 77 C8
Ledegem *B* 182 D2
Ledenice *BIH* 157 C9
Ledenice *CZ* 77 E7
Lédergues *F* 33 B10
Ledesma *E* 45 B9
Lédignan *F* 35 C7
Ledigos *E* 39 D10
Ledmore *GB* 2 J7
Lednica *SK* 146 C6
Lednice *CZ* 77 E11
Lednické Rovne *SK* 146 C6
Le Donjon *F* 30 C4
Le Dorat *F* 29 C8
Ledrada *E* 45 D9
Lēdurga *LV* 135 B9
Ledusjö *S* 107 D16
Ledvattsfors *S* 109 F16
Łędyczek *PL* 85 C11
Lędzin *PL* 85 B8
Lędziny *PL* 143 F7
Leeds *GB* 11 D8
Leedstown *GB* 12 E4
Leek *GB* 11 E7
Leek *NL* 16 B6
Leeming *GB* 11 C8
Lee Moor *GB* 12 E6
Leende *NL* 16 F5
Leer (Ostfriesland) *D* 17 B8
Leerdam *NL* 16 E4
Leersum *NL* 183 A6
Leese *D* 17 C12
Leeuwarden *NL* 16 B5
Leezdorf *D* 17 B8
Leezen *D* 83 C10
Le Faou *F* 22 D3
Le Faouët *F* 22 D5
Le Fenouiller *F* 28 B2
Leffinge *B* 182 C1
Lefkada *GR* 174 B2
Lefkes *GR* 176 E5
Lefkimmi *GR* 168 F3
Lefkimmi *GR* 171 B10
Lefkonas *GR* 169 B10
Lefkopigi *GR* 169 D6
Lefkothea *GR* 168 B6
Lefktra *GR* 175 C7
Le Fleix *F* 29 F6
Le Folgoët *F* 22 C3
Leforest *F* 182 E2
Le Fossat *F* 33 D8
Le Fousseret *F* 33 D8
Le Fugeret *F* 36 C5
Le Fuilet *F* 23 F9
Leganés *E* 46 D5
Leganiel *E* 47 D7
Legau *D* 71 B10
Łęgbno *PL* 138 B5
Le Gault-Soigny *F* 25 C10
Le Gault-St-Denis *F* 24 D5
Legazpi *E* 32 D1
Legde *D* 83 E11
Legden *D* 17 D8
Legé *F* 28 B2
Lège-Cap-Ferret *F* 28 F3
Le Genest-St-Isle *F* 23 D10
Leggs *GB* 7 C7
Legionowo *PL* 139 F10
Léglise *B* 19 E12
Legnano *I* 69 B6
Legnica *PL* 81 D10
Legnickie Pole *PL* 81 D10
Le Gond-Pontouvre *F* 29 D6
Łęgowo *PL* 138 B6
Legrad *HR* 149 D7
Le Grand-Bornand *F* 31 D9
Le Grand-Bourg *F* 29 C9
Le Grand-Lemps *F* 31 E7
Le Grand-Lucé *F* 24 E3
Le Grand-Pressigny *F* 29 B7
Le Grand-Quevilly *F* 18 F3
Le Grau-du-Roi *F* 35 C7
Le Gros Theil *F* 18 F2
Le Gua *F* 31 E8
Legutiano *E* 41 C6
Legyesbénye *H* 145 G3
Le Havre *F* 23 A12
Lehe *D* 82 B6
Lehliu *RO* 161 E9
Lehliu-Gară *RO* 161 E9
Lehmäjoki *FIN* 122 D8
Lehmen *D* 21 D8
Lehmikumpu *FIN* 119 B14
Lehmivaara *FIN* 117 E11
Lehmo *FIN* 125 E13
Lehndorf *D* 79 E11
Lehnice *SK* 146 E4
Lehnin *D* 79 B12
Le Hohwald *F* 27 D7
Léhon *F* 23 D7
Le Horps *F* 23 D11
Lehota *SK* 146 E5
Le Houga *F* 32 C5
Lehrberg *D* 75 D8
Lehre *D* 79 B8
Lehrte *D* 79 B7
Lehsen *D* 83 D10
Lehtimäki *FIN* 123 E11
Lehtiniemi *FIN* 115 E4
Lehto *FIN* 121 B11
Lehtopää *FIN* 119 F13
Lehtovaara *FIN* 117 C10
Lehtovaara *FIN* 121 C10
Lehtovaara *FIN* 121 E14
Lehtovaara *FIN* 125 D11
Lehtse *EST* 131 C11
Leianokladi *GR* 174 B5
Leibertingen *D* 27 D11
Leiblfing *D* 75 E11
Leibnitz *A* 148 C5
Leicester *GB* 11 F9
Leichlingen (Rheinland) *D* 183 C10
Leiden *NL* 16 D3
Leiderdorp *NL* 16 D3
Leidschendam *NL* 16 D2

Leie *EST* 131 E12
Leifear *IRL* 4 F2
Leiferde *D* 79 B7
Leigh *GB* 10 E6
Leighlinbridge *IRL* 9 C9
Leighton Buzzard *GB* 15 D7
Leikanger *N* 100 B2
Leikanger *N* 100 D5
Léim an Bhradáin *IRL* 7 F10
Leimani *LV* 135 D11
Leimen *D* 21 F11
Leimuiden *NL* 182 A5
Leinburg *D* 75 D9
Leine *N* 101 C9
Leinefelde *D* 79 D7
Leinfelden-Echterdingen *D* 187 D7
Leini *I* 68 C4
Leino *FIN* 121 D12
Leinzell *D* 74 E6
Leioa *E* 40 B6
Leipalingis *LT* 137 E8
Leipheim *D* 75 F7
Leipivaara *FIN* 121 E10
Leipojärvi *S* 116 D6
Leipzig *D* 79 D11
Leira *N* 101 E9
Leira *N* 104 E4
Leira *N* 108 D5
Leirado *E* 38 D3
Leiranger *N* 108 C7
Leirbotn *N* 113 C11
Leiria *P* 44 E3
Leirli *N* 105 B15
Leiro *E* 38 D3
Leirosa *P* 44 D3
Leirvåg *N* 100 E2
Leirvik *FO* 2 A3
Leirvik *N* 94 C2
Leirvik *N* 100 D2
Leirvik *N* 105 B11
Leirvika *N* 108 D6
Leisach *A* 73 C6
Leisi *EST* 130 D5
Leisnig *D* 80 D3
Leißling *D* 79 D10
Leiston *GB* 15 C12
Leitir Ceanainn *IRL* 7 C7
Leitir Mhic an Bhaird *IRL* 6 C6
Leitrim *IRL* 6 D6
Leitza *E* 32 D2
Leitzkau *D* 79 B10
Leivonmäki *FIN* 127 B15
Leivset *N* 108 B9
Leiwen *D* 21 E7
Leixlip *IRL* 7 F10
Lejasciems *LV* 135 B13
Lejasstrazdi *LV* 134 C6
Leka *GR* 177 D8
Lekangen *N* 111 B13
Lekani *GR* 171 B7
Lekárovce *SK* 145 F5
Lekbibaj *AL* 163 E8
Lekečiai *LT* 137 D7
Lekenik *HR* 148 E6
Lekeryd *S* 92 D4
Lekhchevo *BG* 165 B8
Łęki Szlacheckie *PL* 143 D8
Leknes *N* 100 B6
Lekowo *PL* 85 C9
Lekunberri *E* 32 D2
Leland *N* 108 D4
Le Langon *F* 28 C4
Le Lardin-St-Lazare *F* 29 E8
Le Lauzet-Ubaye *F* 36 C4
Le Lavandou *F* 36 E4
Leleasca *RO* 160 D4
Leles *SK* 145 G5
Lelești *RO* 159 C11
Le Leuy *F* 32 C4
Lelice *PL* 139 E8
Le Lion-d'Angers *F* 23 E10
Leliūnai *LT* 135 F10
Lelkowo *PL* 139 B9
Lelle *EST* 131 D9
Le Locle *CH* 31 A10
Lelów *PL* 143 E8
Le Luc *F* 36 E4
Le Lude *F* 23 E12
Lelystad *NL* 16 C4
Lem *DK* 86 C2
Lemberg *D* 27 B8
Lemberg *F* 27 B7
Lembeye *F* 32 D5
Lembras *F* 29 F7
Lembruch *D* 17 D10
Lemele *NL* 16 D6
Lemelerveld *NL* 16 D6
Le Mêle-sur-Sarthe *F* 24 D3
Le Merlerault *F* 23 C12
Le Mesnil-sur-Oger *F* 25 C11
Lemetinvaara *FIN* 121 F12
Lemförde *D* 17 D10
Lemgo *D* 17 D11
Lemi *FIN* 128 D8
Lemierzyce *PL* 81 A7
Lemland *FIN* 99 B14
Lemmenjoki *FIN* 117 A16
Lemmer *NL* 16 C5
Lemnia *RO* 153 E8
Le Molay-Littry *F* 23 B10
Le Monastier *F* 34 A5
Le Monastier-sur-Gazeille *F* 30 F4
Le Monêtier-les-Bains *F* 31 F10
Le Montet *F* 30 C3
Lempäälä *FIN* 127 C10
Lempdes *F* 30 D3
Lempdes *F* 30 E3
Lempyy *FIN* 124 E8
Lemu *FIN* 126 D6
Lemvig *DK* 86 B2

Lemwerder *D* 17 B11
Lemybrien *IRL* 9 D7
Lena *N* 101 E13
Lenart *SLO* 148 C5
Lēnas *LV* 134 C5
Lenauheim *RO* 150 F6
Lencloître *F* 29 B6
Lencouacq *F* 32 B5
Lend *A* 73 B7
Lendak *SK* 145 E1
Lendava *SLO* 149 C6
Lendelede *B* 182 D2
Lendery *RUS* 125 D16
Lendinara *I* 66 B4
Lendum *DK* 90 E7
Lenešice *CZ* 76 B5
Le Neubourg *F* 24 B4
Lengau *A* 72 B6
Lengau *A* 76 F4
Lengdorf *D* 75 F11
Lengede *D* 79 B7
Lengenfeld *D* 79 E11
Lengenwang *D* 71 B11
Lengerich *D* 17 C9
Lengerich *D* 17 D9
Lenggries *D* 72 A4
Lengnau *CH* 27 C11
Lengyeltóti *H* 149 C9
Lenham *GB* 15 E10
Lenhovda *S* 89 B8
Lenine *UA* 154 C5
Léning *F* 27 C6
Le Nizan *F* 32 B5
Lenk *CH* 31 C11
Lenkimai *LT* 134 D2
Lenna *I* 69 B8
Lennartsfors *S* 96 D6
Lennartsnäs *S* 99 D9
Lenne *D* 78 C6
Lennestadt *D* 21 B10
Lenningen *D* 27 C11
Lennsjö *S* 103 C13
Leno *I* 66 B1
Le Noirmont *CH* 27 F6
Lenola *I* 62 E4
Le Nouvion-en-Thiérache *F* 19 D8
Lens *B* 19 C8
Lens *F* 18 D6
Lensahn *D* 83 B9
Lensvik *N* 104 D7
Lent *F* 31 C7
Lent *NL* 183 B7
Lentas *GR* 178 F8
Lenti *H* 149 C7
Lentiai *I* 72 D5
Lentiira *FIN* 121 F14
Lenting *D* 75 E9
Lentini *I* 59 E7
Lentvaris *LT* 137 D11
Lenvik *N* 111 C13
Lenzburg *CH* 27 F9
Lenzen *D* 83 D10
Lenzing *A* 76 G5
Lenzkirch *D* 27 E9
Leoben *A* 77 F10
Leoben *A* 73 C8
Leobendorf *A* 77 F10
Leobersdorf *A* 77 G10
Leogang *A* 73 B6
Léognan *F* 28 F4
Leominster *GB* 13 A9
León *E* 39 C8
Léon *F* 32 C3
Leonberg *D* 27 C11
Léoncel *F* 31 F7
Leonding *A* 76 F6
Leonessa *I* 62 B3
Leonforte *I* 58 D5
Leonidio *GR* 175 E6
Leontari *GR* 174 E5
Leontari *GR* 174 B5
Leopoldov *SK* 146 E5
Leopoldsburg *B* 19 B11
Leopoldsdorf im Marchfelde *A* 77 F11
Leopoldshagen *D* 84 C5
Leopoldshöhe *D* 17 D11
Leorda *RO* 153 B8
Leordeni *RO* 160 D6
Leordina *RO* 152 B4
Leova *MD* 154 E2
Leovo Brdo *MNE* 157 F12
Lepaa *FIN* 127 C11
Le Palais *F* 22 F5
Le Palais-sur-Vienne *F* 29 D8
Le Pallet *F* 23 F9
Le Parcq *F* 18 D5
Lepassaare *EST* 132 F1
Le Passage *F* 33 B7
Le Pavillon-Ste-Julie *F* 25 D10
Lepe *E* 51 E5
Le Péage-de-Roussillon *F* 30 E6
Le Pellerin *F* 23 F8
Le Périer *F* 31 F8
Le Perthus *F* 34 F4
Le Pertre *F* 23 D9
Le Petit-Quevilly *F* 18 F3
Le Pian-Médoc *F* 28 F4
Le Pin-au-Haras *F* 23 C12
L'Épine *F* 25 C11
Le Pin-la-Garenne *F* 24 D4
Lepistönmäki *FIN* 123 D10
Lepitsa *BG* 165 C9
Le Pizou *F* 28 F6
Le Plan *F* 33 D8
Le Plessis-Belleville *F* 25 B8
Le Poët *F* 35 B10
Lepoglava *HR* 148 D6
Le Poinçonnet *F* 29 B9
Le Poiré-sur-Vie *F* 28 B2
Le Pont-de-Beauvoisin *F* 31 D8
Le Pont-de-Claix *F* 31 E8
Le Pont-de-Montvert *F* 35 B6
Le Pontet *F* 35 C8
Leporano *I* 61 C8
Le Porge *F* 28 F3
Le Porge-Océan *F* 28 F3
Le Portel *F* 15 F12
Leposavić *KS* 163 C10
Le Pouldu *F* 22 E4
Le Pouliguen *F* 22 F7
Lepoura *GR* 175 C9
Le Pouzin *F* 30 F6
Leppäjärvi *FIN* 117 B10
Leppäkoski *FIN* 127 D12
Leppälä *FIN* 113 D19
Leppälä *FIN* 126 C6
Leppälänkylä *FIN* 123 E11
Leppälahti *FIN* 124 D8

Leppälahti FIN 125 F12
Leppäselkä FIN 123 D16
Leppävesi FIN 123 F15
Leppävirta FIN 124 F9
Leppiaho FIN 119 C15
Leppikoski FIN 119 D17
Leppiniemi FIN 119 E16
Leppneeme EST 131 B9
Lepsala FIN 127 C15
Lepsäma FIN 127 E12
Lepsény H 149 B10
Leptokarya GR 169 D8
Le Puy-en-Velay F 30 E4
Le Puy-Notre-Dame F 23 F11
Le Quesnoy F 19 D8
Lequile I 61 C10
Ler N 104 E8
Le Raincy F 25 C8
Léran F 33 E9
Lerberget S 87 C11
Lercara Friddi I 58 D4
Lerdala S 91 C14
Léré F 25 F8
Le Relecq-Kerhuon F 22 D3
Lereşti RO 160 C6
Lerici I 69 E8
Lérida F 42 D5
Lerín E 32 F2
Lerkaka S 89 B11
Lerma E 40 D4
Lerm-et Musset F 32 B5
Lermoos A 71 C11
Lerot S 96 C7
Le Rouget F 29 F10
Lérouville F 26 C4
Le Rozier F 34 B5
Lerum S 91 D11
Le Russey F 26 F6
Lervik N 95 D13
Lerwick GB 3 E14
Lesa I 68 B6
Les Abrets F 31 D8
Les Aix-d'Angillon F 25 F8
Lešak KS 163 C10
Lesaka E 32 D2
Les Andelys F 18 F3
Les Angles F 33 E10
Les Angles F 35 C8
Lešani MK 168 B4
Les Arcs F 31 D10
Les Arcs F 36 E4
Les Aubiers F 28 B4
Les Avellanes E 42 D5
Les Avenières F 31 D8
Les Bondons F 35 B6
Les Bordes F 25 E7
Les Borges Blanques E 42 D5
Les Borges del Camp E 42 E6
Les Bouchoux F 31 C8
Les Brenets CH 31 A10
Lesbury GB 5 E13
Les Cabannes F 33 E9
L'Escala E 43 C10
L'Escale F 35 B11
Les Cammazes F 33 D10
Lescar F 32 D5
L'Escarène F 37 D6
Les Cases d'Alcanar E 42 F5
Lesce SLO 73 D9
Lesconil F 22 E2
Les Contamines-Montjoie F 31 D10
Lescun F 32 E4
Lescure-d'Albigeois F 33 C10
Les Deux-Alpes F 31 E9
Les Diablerets CH 31 C11
Les Échelles F 31 E8
Les Églisottes-et-Chalaures F 28 E5
Le Sel-de-Bretagne F 23 E8
Le Sen F 32 B4
Le Sentier CH 31 B9
Les Éparges F 26 C4
Les Epesses F 28 B4
Les Escaldes AND 33 E9
Les Essards-Taignevaux F 31 B7
Les Essarts F 28 B3
Le Seu d'Urgell F 33 F8
Les Eyzies-de-Tayac-Sireuil F 29 F8
Les Fins F 31 A10
Les Forges F 26 D5
Les Fourgs F 31 B9
Les Gets F 31 C10
Leshak KS 163 C10
Leshan KS 163 D9
Les Hautes-Rivières F 184 E2
Les Herbiers F 28 B3
Les Houches F 31 D10
Lesichevo BG 165 E9
Lesično SLO 148 D3
Lesidren BG 165 D9
Lesina I 63 D8
Les Issambres F 36 E5
Lesja N 101 B9
Lesjöfors S 97 C11
Leskava LT 137 D8
Leskelä FIN 119 F15
Lesko PL 145 E5
Leskoec MK 168 B4
Leskova SRB 163 C9
Leskovac SRB 164 D4
Leskovik AL 168 D4
Leskovo BG 161 F11
Les Landes-Genusson F 28 B3
Leslie GB 5 B10
Les Lucs-sur-Boulogne F 28 B3
Lesmahagow GB 5 D9
Les Maillys F 26 F3
Les Marches F 31 E9
Les Martres-de-Veyre F 30 D3
Les Matelles F 35 C6
Les Mazures F 184 E2
Les Mées F 35 B10
Les Menuires F 31 E10
Lesmont F 25 D11
Les Mureaux F 24 C6
Lesna PL 81 D8
Lesneven F 22 C3
Leśnica PL 142 F5
Leśnica SRB 158 D3
Leśniów Wielki PL 81 C8
Lesogorskiy RUS 129 C10
Les Ollières-sur-Eyrieux F 30 F6
Lesovaara FIN 121 D13
Lesovo BG 167 F7
Lesparre-Médoc F 28 E4
Les Peintures F 28 E5
Les Pennes-Mirabeau F 35 D9
Lesperon F 32 B3
Lespezi RO 153 C9

Les Pieux F 23 A8
Lespignan F 34 D5
Lespinassière F 34 D4
Les Planches-en-Montagne F 31 B9
Les Planes d'Hostoles E 43 C9
L'Espluga Calba E 42 E6
L'Espluga de Francolí E 42 E6
Les Ponts-de-Cé F 23 F10
Les Ponts-de-Martel CH 31 A10
Les Preses E 43 C8
Lespugue F 33 D7
Les Rosiers-sur-Loire F 23 F11
Les Rousses F 31 C9
Les Sables-d'Olonne F 28 C2
Lessach A 73 B8
Les Salles-du-Gardon F 35 B7
Lessay F 23 B8
Lessebo S 89 B8
Les Sièges F 25 D10
Lessines B 19 C8
Les Sorinières F 23 F8
Lestene LV 134 C6
Les Ternes F 30 E3
Les Thuiles F 36 C5
Lestijärvi FIN 123 C13
Leština CZ 77 C11
Lestrade F 34 B4
Les Trois-Moutiers F 24 F3
Leşu RO 152 C5
Lesura BG 165 C8
Les Vans F 35 B7
Les Vignes F 34 B5
Leszczyn PL 85 C9
Leszno PL 81 C11
Leszno PL 141 F3
Leszno Górne PL 81 D9
Létavértes H 151 C8
Letca RO 151 C11
Leţcani RO 153 C10
Letca Nouă RO 161 E7
Letchworth Garden City GB 15 D8
Letea Veche RO 153 D9
Le Teich F 32 A3
Le Teil F 35 A8
Le Teilleul F 23 D10
Le Temple F 28 F4
Letenye H 149 D7
Le Theil F 24 D4
Le-Theil-de-Bretagne F 23 E9
Le Thillot F 27 E6
Le Tholy F 27 D6
Le Thor F 35 C8
Letino I 63 E6
Letkés H 147 F7
Letnitsa BG 165 C11
Letoianni I 59 D7
Letonice CZ 77 D11
Le Touquet-Paris-Plage F 15 F12
Le Touvet F 31 E8
Letovice CZ 77 C11
L'Étrat F 30 E5
Le Trayas F 36 E5
Le Tréport F 18 D3
Letsbo S 103 C10
Letschin D 80 A6
Letterfinish IRL 8 E3
Letterkenny IRL 7 C7
Lettermacaward IRL 6 C6
Letterston GB 12 B5
Letur E 55 C8
Le Tuzan F 32 B4
Letzlingen D 79 B9
Leu RO 160 E4
Leuc F 33 D10
Leucate F 34 E5
Leuchars GB 5 C11
Leuchtenberg D 75 C11
Leud RO 152 B4
Leuenberg D 84 E5
Leuglay F 25 E12
Leuk CH 68 A4
Leukerbad CH 70 E5
Leumrabhagh GB 2 J4
Leun D 185 C9
Leuna D 79 D11
Leusden NL 16 D4
Leuşeni MD 154 D2
Leutasch A 71 C11
Leutenberg D 79 E9
Leutershausen D 75 D7
Leutesdorf D 185 D7
Leutkirch im Allgäu D 71 B10
Leuvanjoki FIN 119 D15
Leuven B 19 C10
Leuze-en-Hainaut B 19 C8
Le Val F 36 E4
Le Vallinot-Longeau-Percey F 26 E3
Levan AL 168 C1
Levänen FIN 128 C8
Levang N 108 C9
Levanger N 105 D10
Levanjska Varoš HR 149 F10
Levanto FIN 127 D13
Levanto I 37 C11
Leva Reka BG 165 D9
Levåsjoki FIN 126 B6
Level H 146 F4
Levelek H 145 H4
Leven GB 5 C11
Leven GB 11 D11
Levens F 37 D6
Levens GB 10 C6
L:venwick GB 3 F14
Leverano I 61 C10
Leverburgh GB 2 K2
Le-Verdon-sur-Mer F 28 D3
Leverkusen D 21 B7
Lèves F 24 D5
Levet F 29 B10
Levice SK 147 E7
Levico Terme I 69 A11
Levidi GR 174 D5
Levie F 37 H10
Levier F 31 B9
Le Vigan F 35 B7
Lévignac F 33 C8
Lévignacq F 32 B3
Levijoki FIN 123 E11
Le Ville I 66 F5
Le-Vivier-sur-Mer F 23 C8
Levka BG 166 F6
Levkogeia GR 170 B5
Levoča SK 145 E2
Levonperä FIN 123 C14
Levroux F 29 B9
Levski BG 166 C4
Levunovo BG 169 B9

Lewes GB 15 F9
Lewin Brzeski PL 142 E4
Lewin Kłodzki PL 77 B10
Leyburn GB 11 C8
Leyland GB 10 D6
Leyme F 29 F9
Leysin CH 31 C11
Leytron CH 31 C11
Lézajsk PL 144 C5
Lézan F 35 B7
Lézat-sur-Lèze F 33 D8
Lezay F 28 C5
Lezhë AL 163 F8
Lézignan-Corbières F 34 D4
Lezoux F 30 D3
Lezuza E 55 B8
Lgota Górna PL 143 E7
Lgota Wielka PL 143 D7
Lhenice CZ 76 D6
Lherm F 33 D8
L'Hermenault F 28 B4
L'Honor-de-Cos F 33 B8
L'Hôpital F 186 C2
L'Horme F 30 E6
Lhospitalet F 33 B8
L'Hospitalet de l'Infant E 42 F5
L'Hospitalet de Llobregat E 43 E8
L'Hospitalet-du-Larzac F 34 C5
L'Hospitalet-près-l'Andorre F 33 E9
L'Hostal del Alls E 42 F5
L'Huisserie F 23 D10
Lhuître F 25 C11
Lia N 111 C14
Liabøen N 104 E4
Liancourt F 18 F5
Liapades GR 168 E2
Liart F 19 E9
Liarvåg N 94 D3
Liatorp S 88 B6
Liatroim IRL 6 D6
Libáň CZ 77 B8
Libatse EST 131 D8
Libberton GB 5 D9
Libčany CZ 77 B9
Libčeves CZ 76 B5
Liberadz PL 139 D9
Liberec CZ 81 E8
Libešice CZ 80 E6
Libiąż PL 143 F7
Libice nad Cidlinou CZ 77 B8
Libín B 19 E11
Libina CZ 77 C12
Libochovice CZ 76 B6
Libofshë AL 168 C2
Libohovë AL 168 D3
Libouchec CZ 80 E6
Libourne F 28 F5
Libramont B 19 E11
Librazhd AL 168 B3
Librilla E 55 D10
Libros E 47 D10
Licata I 58 E4
Licciana Nardi I 69 E9
Licenza I 62 C3
Liceras E 40 F5
Lich D 21 C11
Lichfield GB 11 F8
Lichnov CZ 142 F4
Lichnowy PL 138 B6
Lichtaart B 182 C5
Lichte D 75 A9
Lichtenau D 17 E11
Lichtenau D 27 C7
Lichtenstein D 79 E12
Lichtentanne D 79 E11
Lichtenvoorde NL 17 E7
Lichtenwörth A 77 G10
Lichterfelde D 84 E5
Lichtervelde B 19 B7
Liči LV 135 B10
Liči LV 135 C11
Lička Jesenica HR 156 C3
Lički Osik HR 156 D3
Licko Lešće HR 156 C3
Licodia Eubea I 59 E6
Licques F 15 F12
Ličupe LV 135 C10
Licurici RO 160 D3
Lida BY 137 F11
Lidečko CZ 146 C6
Liden S 103 A12
Lidhult S 87 B12
Lidingö S 99 D10
Lidköping S 91 C13
Lido I 66 B5
Lido Adriano I 66 D5
Lido di Classe I 66 D5
Lido di Foce Verde I 62 E3
Lido di Jesolo I 66 A6
Lido di Metaponto I 61 C7
Lido di Ostia I 62 D2
Lido di Siponto I 63 D9
Lido di Spina I 66 C5
Lidoriki GR 174 B5
Lidsdalen S 102 E5
Lidumnieki LV 133 C3
Lidzbark PL 139 D8
Lidzbark Warmiński PL 136 E2
Liebenau D 17 C12
Liebenau D 17 D12
Liebenburg D 79 B7
Liebenfels A 73 C9
Liebenwalde D 84 E4
Lieberose D 80 C6
Liebertwolkwitz D 79 D11
Liebling RO 159 B7
Lieboch A 148 C5
Liebstadt D 80 E5
Liedakkala FIN 119 C13
Liédena E 32 E3
Liedenpohja FIN 123 F11
Liège B 19 C12
Liegi LV 134 C2
Liehittäjä S 119 B10
Liekokylä FIN 119 C16
Lieksa FIN 125 D14
Lielauce LV 134 D4
Lielbērze LV 134 C4
Lielciems LV 130 F4
Lielklapari LV 135 C11
Lielmēmele LV 135 C10
Lielvārde LV 135 C10
Lielvircava LV 134 C7
Liempde NL 183 B6
Lien S 105 D15
Lien S 107 E10
Lienden NL 183 B7

Lienen D 17 D9
Lienz A 73 C6
Liepa LV 135 B10
Liepāja LV 134 C2
Liepāre LV 134 C7
Liepas LV 135 D12
Liepe D 84 E5
Liepen D 84 C4
Liepene LV 134 B3
Liepgarten D 84 C6
Liepiņājärvi FIN 117 B11
Lieplaukalē LV 134 E4
Lieplaukē LT 134 E3
Liepna LV 133 B2
Lieponys LT 137 E10
Liepupe LV 135 B8
Lier N 96 B7
Lierbyen N 95 C12
Liernais F 25 F11
Lierneux B 19 D12
Liesek SK 147 C9
Lieser D 21 E8
Lieshout NL 183 B7
Lieso FIN 127 C12
Liessel NL 16 F5
Liestal CH 27 F9
Liešťany SK 146 D6
Lietavská Lúčka SK 147 C7
Lietekylä FIN 121 E11
Lieto FIN 126 D7
Liétor E 55 B9
Lievestuore FIN 123 F16
Lievoperä FIN 119 F16
Liezen A 73 A9
Liezère LV 135 B12
Liffol-le-Grand F 26 D4
Lifford IRL 4 F2
Liffré F 23 D8
Lifton GB 12 D6
Ligardes F 33 B6
Ligatne LV 135 B10
Ligist A 73 C11
Lignano Pineta I 73 E7
Lignano Sabbiadoro I 73 E7
Lignan-sur-Orb F 34 D5
Ligné F 23 F9
Ligneuville B 20 D6
Lignières F 29 B10
Ligny-en-Barrois F 26 C3
Ligny-le-Châtel F 25 E10
Ligonchio I 66 D1
Ligota PL 142 C4
Ligowo PL 139 E7
Ligueil F 29 A7
Ligugé F 29 B6
Lihme DK 86 B3
Lihula EST 130 D7
Liigvalla EST 131 C12
Liikasenvaara FIN 121 B14
Liikavaara S 116 D6
Liimattala FIN 123 E15
Liimattala FIN 123 E17
Liipantönkkä FIN 122 E9
Liittoperä FIN 123 C16
Liiva EST 130 D6
Lijeŝce BIH 157 B9
Lijeska BIH 158 F3
Lijeva Rijeka MNE 163 D7
Lijevi Dubravčak HR 149 E6
Likavka SK 147 C8
Likenäs S 102 D5
Līksna LV 135 E12
Lilaia GR 175 B6
Liland N 110 D6
Liland N 111 D12
Lilaste LV 135 B8
Liniewo PL 138 B5
L'Île-Bouchard F 24 F3
L'Île-Rousse F 37 F9
Lilienfeld A 77 F9
Lilienthal D 17 B11
Liljendal FIN 127 E15
Liljendal S 97 B11
Lilla S 118 B5
Lilla Edet S 91 C11
Lillåfors S 118 B6
Lilla Tjärby S 87 B12
Lillby FIN 123 D10
Lille F 19 C7
Lille F 19 C7
Lillebo N 102 C3
Lillebonne F 18 E2
Lillehammer N 101 D12
Lillers F 18 C5
Lillesand N 90 C3
Lilleshall GB 11 F7
Lille Skensved DK 87 D10
Lille Værløse DK 87 D10
Lillfjäten S 102 C4
Lillhamra S 102 C8
Lillhärdal S 102 C7
Lillholmsjö S 105 D16
Lillhärad S 105 B16
Lillkågeträsk S 118 E5
Lillkyrka S 98 C8
Lillmörtsjö S 103 B11
Lillo E 47 E6
Lillögda S 107 C13
Lillpite S 118 D6
Lillroten S 103 A14
Lillsaivis S 118 B7
Lillsele S 107 C16
Lillselet S 116 E7
Lillsjöhögen S 106 E8
Lillström S 103 B12
Lillsved S 102 A7
Lillviken S 109 C11
Lilyache BG 165 C8
Lilyak BG 167 C6
Lilyanovo BG 169 A9
Lima S 102 E5
Limana I 72 D5
Limanköy TR 167 F10
Limanowa PL 144 D1
Limatola I 60 A2
Limay F 24 B6
Limbach D 21 F7
Limbach D 186 C2
Limbach-Oberfrohna D 79 E12
Limbadi I 59 B8
Limbaži LV 135 A9
Limbourg B 20 C5
Limburg an der Lahn D 21 D10
Limburgerhof D 187 C5
Lime DK 86 C6

Lienen D 17 D9
Lienz A 73 C6
Limedsforsen S 102 E5
Limenaria GR 171 C7
Limenas GR 171 C7
Limenas Chersonisou GR 178 E9
Limerick IRL 8 C5
Limingen N 105 B15
Limingoān S 116 E4
Liminka FIN 119 E14
Liminpuro FIN 120 F5
Limmared S 91 D13
Limmen NL 16 C3
Limnes GR 175 D6
Limni GR 175 B7
Limnochori GR 169 C6
Limoges F 29 D8
Limogne-en-Quercy F 33 B9
Limone Piemonte I 37 C7
Limone sul Garda I 69 B10
Limonest F 30 D6
Limosano I 63 D7
Limoux F 33 D10
Limpias E 40 B5
Lin AL 168 B4
Linå DK 86 C5
Lina älv S 116 D4
Linakhamari RUS 114 D10
Linards F 29 D9
Linares E 54 C5
Linares de Mora E 48 D3
Linares de Riofrío E 45 C9
Linaria GR 175 B10
Lincent B 19 C11
Lincoln GB 11 E10
Lind DK 86 C3
Lindas N 100 E2
Lindau D 79 B10
Lindau D 82 A7
Lindau (Bodensee) D 71 B9
Lindberg D 76 D4
Linde DK 86 C2
Lindelse DK 87 F7
Linden D 21 C11
Linden D 82 B6
Lindenberg D 80 B6
Lindenberg D 83 D12
Lindenberg im Allgäu D 71 B9
Lindenfels D 21 E11
Lindern (Oldenburg) D 17 C9
Lindesberg S 97 C13
Lindesnäs S 97 B12
Lindewitt D 82 A6
Lindfield GB 15 E8
Lindholmen S 99 C10
Lindi EST 131 E8
Lindknud DK 86 D4
Lindkoski FIN 127 D15
Lindlar D 21 B8
Lindores GB 5 C10
Lindoso P 38 E3
Lindow D 84 E3
Lindsdal S 89 B10
Lindsjö S 103 B12
Lindstedt D 79 B10
Lindved DK 86 D5
Lindwedel D 78 A6
Linge N 100 B6
Lingen (Ems) D 17 C8
Lingenfeld D 21 F10
Lingfield GB 15 E8
Linghed S 103 E10
Linghem S 92 C7
Lingolsheim F 27 C8
Lingrasmo N 111 B18
Linguaglossa I 59 D7
Linguizzetta I 37 G10
Linhares F 44 C6
Linia PL 138 B5
Liniewo PL 138 B5
Linkmenys LT 135 F11
Linköping S 92 C7
Linksness GB 3 H10
Linkuva LT 135 D7
Linlithgow GB 5 D9
Linna EST 131 E11
Linnamäe EST 130 D7
Linnamäe EST 131 F13
Linnankylä FIN 123 F10
Linneryd S 89 B8
Linnich D 20 C6
Linow D 83 D13
Linsell S 102 B6
Linsidemore GB 2 K8
Linthal CH 71 D8
Linthe D 79 B12
Lintig D 17 A11
Lintrup DK 86 E3
Lintula FIN 117 C14
Lintzoain E 32 E3
Linum D 84 E3
Linxe F 32 C3
Linyola E 42 D5
Linz A 76 F6
Linz am Rhein D 21 C8
Liobomlʹ UA 141 H10
Lioliai LT 134 E5
Lioni I 60 B4
Lion-sur-Mer F 23 B11
Liorac-sur-Louyre F 29 F7
Lios Mór IRL 9 D7
Lios Póil IRL 8 D2
Lios Tuathail IRL 8 D4
Lipa BIH 157 C7
Lipa F 139 D10
Lipănești RO 161 C8
Lipany SK 145 E2
Lipar SRB 158 B4
Lipari I 59 C6
Lipawki BY 133 E3
Lipcani MD 153 A9
Lipce Reymontowskie PL 141 G1
Liperi FIN 125 E12
Liphook GB 15 E7
Lipiany PL 85 D7
Lipik HR 149 F8
Lipinki PL 144 D3
Lipinki Łużyckie PL 81 C8
Lipiny PL 81 C9
Lipjan KS 164 D3
Lipka PL 85 D12
Lipkovo MK 164 E4
Lipnica BIH 157 D9
Lipnica PL 85 C12
Lipnica PL 138 D7
Lipnik PL 143 E11
Lipník nad Bečvou CZ 146 B5
Lipniţa RO 161 E11
Lipnitsa BG 165 C8
Lipno PL 81 C10
Lipno PL 139 E7
Lipo DK 86 C6

Lipolist SRB 158 D4
Liposthey F 32 B4
Lipova RO 151 E8
Lipova SK 146 E6
Lipovac HR 157 B11
Lipovac SRB 164 B4
Lipová-Lázně CZ 77 B12
Lipovǎţ RO 153 D11
Lipovec CZ 77 D11
Lipoveni MD 154 D3
Lipovljani HR 149 F7
Lipovo RUS 136 D5
Lipovu RO 160 E3
Lippo RO 160 D11
Lippoldsberg (Wahlsburg) D 78 C6
Lippstadt D 17 E10
Lipsk PL 140 C8
Lipsko PL 141 H5
Liptál CZ 146 C5
Liptovská Kokava SK 147 C9
Liptovská Lúžna SK 147 D8
Liptovská Osada SK 147 D8
Liptovská Teplička SK 147 D10
Liptovské Revúce SK 147 D8
Liptovský Hrádok SK 147 C9
Liptovský Mikuláš SK 147 C9
Lipusz PL 138 B4
Lipůvka CZ 77 D11
Liqenas AL 168 C4
Liré F 23 F9
Lis AL 168 A3
Lisa RO 152 F5
Lisa RO 160 F6
Lisac BIH 157 D8
Lisac HR 162 D4
Lisacul IRL 6 E5
Lisbane GB 7 C11
Lisbellaw GB 7 D7
Lisboa P 50 B1
Lisburn GB 7 D10
Liscannor IRL 8 C4
Liscarney IRL 6 E3
Liscarroll IRL 8 D5
Lisciano Niccone I 66 F5
Liscoteanca RO 161 C11
Lisdoonvarna IRL 6 F4
Liseleje DK 87 C9
Lisets BG 165 C11
Lisewo PL 138 D6
Lisgarode IRL 8 C6
Lisgoold IRL 8 E6
Lisia Góra PL 143 F11
Lisijcice PL 142 F4
Lisieux F 23 B12
Lisiy Nos RUS 129 E13
Lisjö S 97 C15
Liskeard GB 12 E6
Lisková SK 147 C8
Lisków PL 142 C5
Lisky UA 155 C4
Lisle F 29 E7
Lisle GB 4 F3
L'Isle-Adam F 25 B7
L'Isle-de-Noé F 33 C6
L'Isle-d'Espagnac F 29 D6
L'Isle-en-Dodon F 33 D7
L'Isle-Jourdain F 29 C7
L'Isle-Jourdain F 33 C8
L'Isle-sur-la-Sorgue F 35 C9
L'Isle-sur-le-Doubs F 26 F6
L'Isle-sur-Serein F 25 E11
Lisle-sur-Tarn F 33 C9
Lisma FIN 117 B12
Lismakin IRL 9 C7
Lismanaapa FIN 117 D17
Lismarka N 101 D13
Lismore IRL 9 D7
Lisnagry IRL 8 C5
Lisnakill IRL 9 D8
Lisnarrick GB 7 D7
Lisnaskea GB 7 D8
Lisne UA 154 E4
Lišov CZ 77 D7
Lisów PL 142 G5
Lispole IRL 8 D2
Lisronagh IRL 9 D7
Lisryan IRL 7 E8
Liss GB 15 E7
Lisse NL 16 D3
Lissendorf D 185 D6
Lisskogsbränåan S 97 A10
Lissone I 69 B7
Lissycasey IRL 8 C4
List D 86 E2
Listed DK 89 E8
Listerby S 89 C8
Listerlin IRL 9 D8
Listowel IRL 8 D4
Listrac-Médoc F 28 E4
Listry IRL 8 D3
Liszki PL 143 F8
Liszkowo PL 85 D12
Lit S 106 E7
Liţa RO 160 F5
Litakovo BG 165 D8
Litava SK 147 E8
Litene LV 133 B2
Liteni RO 153 B9
Litér H 149 B9
Lit-et-Mixe F 32 B3
Lith NL 183 B6
Lithakia GR 174 D2
Lithi GR 177 C7
Lithines GR 179 E11
Litija SLO 73 D11
Litke H 147 E9
Litlefjord N 113 B14
Litmalahti FIN 125 E10
Litochoro GR 169 D8
Litoměřice CZ 76 A6
Litomyšl CZ 77 C10
Litovel CZ 77 C12
Litschau A 77 E8
Littau CH 70 C6
Littleborough GB 11 D7
Littlehampton GB 15 F7
Littlemill GB 3 K9
Littlemore GB 13 B12
Little Oakley GB 15 D11
Littleport GB 15 C9
Littlestone-on-Sea GB 15 F10
Littleton IRL 9 C7
Littoinen FIN 126 E7
Litva BIH 157 D10
Litvínov CZ 80 E5

Litzendorf D 75 C9
Liudvinavas LT 136 E7
Liukkunen FIN 125 D14
Liuža LV 133 C2
Livada RO 145 H7
Livada RO 151 B9
Livadaki GR 174 D4
Livadeia GR 175 C6
Livadero GR 169 D6
Livadero GR 171 B6
Livadi GR 169 D7
Livadi GR 175 C6
Livadia GR 169 B9
Livaderá SRB 164 C5
Līvāni LV 135 D12
Livari MNE 163 E7
Livarot F 23 B12
Līvbērze LV 134 C6
Livernon F 33 A9
Liverpool GB 10 E6
Livezeni RO 152 D5
Livezi RO 153 E9
Livezi RO 160 D3
Livezile RO 152 C5
Livezile RO 159 D10
Līvi LV 135 B10
Livigno I 71 D10
Livingston GB 5 D9
Livno BIH 157 E7
Livo FIN 119 C17
Livold SLO 73 E10
Livonniska FIN 121 C10
Livorno I 66 E1
Livorno Ferraris I 68 C5
Livron-sur-Drôme F 30 F6
Liw PL 139 F12
Lixing-lès-St-Avold F 186 C2
Lixnaw IRL 8 D3
Lixouri GR 174 C1
Lizard GB 12 F4
Lizarraga E 32 E1
Lizdēni LV 131 F10
Lizums LV 135 B12
Lizy-sur-Ourcq F 25 B9
Lizzanello I 61 C10
Lizzano I 61 C8
Ljaljenča BIH 157 C11
Ljeskode Vode BIH 157 F8
Ljig SRB 158 E5
Ljones N 108 B8
Ljørdal N 102 D4
Ljosland N 90 B1
Ljøsne N 100 D7
Ljuba SRB 164 C4
Ljuberaða SRB 164 C5
Ljubija BIH 156 C6
Ljubinje BIH 162 D5
Ljubiš SRB 158 F4
Ljubljana SLO 73 D10
Ljubogošta BIH 157 E10
Ljuboraja SRB 158 E3
Ljubuški BIH 157 F8
Ljugarn S 93 E13
Ljung S 91 D13
Ljungå S 103 A11
Ljungaverk S 103 B11
Ljungby S 87 B13
Ljungbyhed S 87 C12
Ljungbyholm S 89 B10
Ljungdalen S 102 A4
Ljungsarp S 91 D14
Ljungsbro S 92 B7
Ljungskile S 91 C10
Ljupina H 147 F7
Ljuša BIH 157 D7
Ljuså S 118 C7
Ljusfallshammar S 92 B7
Ljusne S 103 D13
Ljusnedal S 102 A4
Ljustorp S 103 A13
Ljusträsk S 118 C2
Ljusvattnet S 118 E6
Ljuti Dolac BIH 157 F8
Ljutomer SLO 148 C6
Llabjan KS 164 D3
Llagostera E 43 D9
Llamas de la Ribera E 39 C8
Llanaelhaearn GB 10 F3
Llanarth GB 12 A6
Llanarthney GB 12 B6
Llanbadarn Fawr GB 12 A6
Llanbadrig GB 10 E3
Llanbedr GB 10 F3
Llanbedrog GB 10 F3
Llanberis GB 10 E3
Llanbister GB 13 A8
Llanblethian GB 12 B6
Llançà E 34 F5
Llandanwg GB 10 F3
Llanderfel GB 10 F4
Llandeilo GB 12 B7
Llandissilio GB 12 B5
Llandovery GB 13 B7
Llandrillo GB 10 F5
Llandrindod Wells GB 13 A8
Llandudno GB 10 E4
Llandwrog GB 10 E3
Llandysul GB 12 A6
Llanegwad GB 12 B6
Llaneilian GB 10 E3
Llanelli GB 12 B6
Llanelltyd GB 10 F4
Llanelwy GB 10 E5
Llanes E 39 B10
Llanfaelog GB 10 E3
Llangadfan GB 10 F5
Llandagog GB 13 B7
Llangefni GB 10 E3
Llangeler GB 12 A6
Llangelynin GB 10 F3
Llangoed GB 10 E3
Llangollen GB 10 F5
Llangurig GB 13 A7
Llanidloes GB 13 A7
Llanilar GB 12 A6
Llanishen GB 13 B8
Llanllwchaiarn GB 10 F5
Llanllyfni GB 10 E3
Llannerch-y-medd GB 10 E3
Llan-non GB 12 A6
Llannon GB 12 B6

Lissa S 118 B5

Llanrhaeadr-ym-Mochnant GB 10 F5
Llanrhidian GB 12 B6
Llanrhystud GB 12 A6
Llanrug GB 10 E3
Llanrwst GB 10 E4
Llansanffraid Glan Conwy GB 10 E4
Llansannan GB 10 E4
Llansawel GB 12 A6
Llantilio Pertholey GB 13 C8
Llantrisant GB 13 B8
Llantwit Major GB 13 C8
Llanuwchllyn GB 10 F4
Llanwddyn GB 10 F5
Llanwenog GB 12 A6
Llanwnog GB 10 F5
Llanwrtyd Wells GB 13 A7
Llanybydder GB 12 A6
Llapushnik KS 163 D10
Llardecans E 42 E5
Llaurí E 48 F4
Llavorsí E 33 E8
Llay GB 10 E5
Lledrod GB 12 A7
Lleida E 42 E5
Llera E 51 C7
Llerena E 51 C7
Lliria E 48 E3
Llívia E 33 F9
Llodio E 40 B6
Llombai E 48 F3
Lloret de Mar E 43 D9
Lloseta E 49 E10
Llubí E 57 E10
Llucmajor E 57 C10
Lniano PL 138 C5
Lo B 18 C6
Loamneș RO 152 F4
Loano I 37 C8
Loarre E 32 F4
Löbau D 81 D7
Lobbæk DK 89 E7
Lobe LV 135 C10
Löbejün D 79 C10
Lobera de Onsella E 32 F3
Loběřgi LV 131 F12
Łobez PL 85 C9
Lobith NL 183 B8
Löbnitz D 83 B13
Łobodno PL 143 E6
Lobón E 51 B6
Lobonās S 103 C9
Loburg D 79 B11
Łobženica PL 85 D12
Locana I 31 E11
Locarno CH 68 A6
Locate di Triulzi I 69 C7
Loccum (Rehburg-Loccum) D 17 D12
Loceri I 64 D4
Lochaline GB 4 B5
Lochau A 71 B9
Lochawe GB 4 C6
Lochboisdale GB 2 L2
Lochcarron GB 2 L5
Lochdon GB 4 C5
Lochearnhead GB 5 C8
Lochem NL 16 D5
Lochen A 76 F4
Lochend GB 3 L8
Loches F 24 F4
Loch Garman IRL 9 D10
Lochgelly GB 5 C10
Lochgilphead GB 4 C6
Lochgoilhead GB 4 C7
Lochinver GB 2 J6
Lochmaben GB 5 E10
Lochmaddy GB 2 K2
Lochovice CZ 76 B5
Łochów PL 139 E12
Lochranza GB 4 D6
Lochristi B 19 B8
Loch Sgioport GB 2 L2
Lociki LV 135 E13
Lockenhaus A 149 B6
Lockerbie GB 5 E10
Lockne S 106 E7
Löcknitz D 84 D6
Locks Heath GB 13 D12
Lockton GB 11 C10
Locmaria-Plouzané F 22 D2
Locmariaquer F 22 E6
Locminé F 22 E6
Locorotondo I 61 B8
Locquirec F 22 C4
Locri I 59 C9
Locronan F 22 D3
Loctudy F 22 E3
Loculi I 64 C4
Löddeköpinge S 87 D12
Lödderitz D 79 C10
Loddin D 84 B6
Lødding N 105 B10
Loddiswell GB 13 E7
Loddon GB 15 B11
Lodè I 64 B4
Lode LV 135 B10
Loděnice CZ 76 B6
Lodève F 34 C5
Lodi I 69 C8
Løding N 108 B8
Lødingen N 111 D10
Lodi Vecchio I 69 C7
Lodosa E 32 F1
Lödöse S 91 C11
Łodygowice PL 147 B8
Łódź PL 143 C7
Loeches E 46 D6
Loenen NL 183 A8
Löf D 21 D8
Løfallstrand N 94 B4
Lofer A 73 A6
Löffingen D 27 E9
Lofos GR 169 D7
Lofsdalen S 102 B5
Loftahammar S 93 D9
Lofthus N 94 B5
Lofthus N 111 E10
Loftus GB 11 B10
Log SLO 73 D8
Loga N 94 F5
Logatec SLO 73 E9
Lögda S 107 C14
Lögdeå S 107 D16
Loggerheads GB 11 F7
Loghill IRL 8 C4
Logkanikos GR 174 E5
Logofteni MD 153 B11

Logrești RO 160 D3
Logron F 24 D5
Logrono E 41 D7
Logrosán E 45 F10
Løgstør DK 86 B4
Løgstrup DK 86 B4
Løgten DK 86 C6
Løgumkloster DK 86 E3
Lohals DK 87 E7
Lohberg D 76 D4
Lohéac F 23 E8
Lohe-Rickelshof D 82 B6
Lohfelden D 78 D6
Lohijärvi FIN 119 B12
Lohilahti FIN 129 B10
Lohiluoma FIN 122 E8
Lohiniva FIN 117 D13
Lohiranta FIN 121 B12
Lohja FIN 127 E11
Lohjan kunta FIN 127 E11
Lohmar D 21 C10
Lohmen D 83 C12
Löhnberg D 21 C10
Löhne D 17 D11
Lohne (Oldenburg) D 17 C10
Lohne D 84 A5
Lohmen D 80 B6
Lohtaja FIN 123 B11
Lohusuu EST 131 D14
Loiano I 66 D3
Loigny-la-Bataille F 24 D6
Loimaa FIN 127 D9
Loimaan kunta FIN 127 D8
Loiré F 23 E10
Loiri-Porto San Paolo I 64 B3
Loiron F 23 D10
Loisy-sur-Marne F 25 C12
Loitz D 84 C4
Loivos P 38 E5
Loivos do Monte P 44 B5
Loja E 53 B8
Loja LV 135 B9
Løjt Kirkeby DK 86 E4
Loka brunn S 97 C11
Lokakylä FIN 123 D14
Lokalahti FIN 126 D5
Lokavec SLO 73 E8
Lokca SK 147 C8
Loke S 106 F7
Løken N 95 C14
Lokeren B 19 B9
Loket CZ 75 B12
Lokev SLO 73 E8
Lokka FIN 115 C3
Løkken N 104 E7
Løkken N 104 E7
Løksebotn N 111 C14
Lokuta EST 131 D9
Lokuti EST 131 C9
Lokve HR 67 B10
Lokve SLO 73 D8
Lokve SRB 159 C7
Løkvoll N 112 D6
Lolishniy Shepit UA 152 A6
Lollar D 21 C11
L'Ollería E 56 D3
Lom BG 159 F11
Lom N 101 C9
Łomazy PL 141 G8
Lombez F 33 D7
Lombheden S 119 B9
Lomborg DK 86 B2
Lomello I 68 C6
Lomen N 101 D9
Łomianki PL 139 F10
Lomma S 87 D12
Lommatzsch D 80 D4
Lomme F 18 C6
Lommel B 19 B11
Lomnica PL 81 B9
Lomnice CZ 77 D10
Lomnice nad Lužnicí CZ 77 D7
Lomnice nad Popelkou CZ 77 A8
Lomonosov RUS 129 F12
Lompolo FIN 117 B13
Lomsdalen N 101 E12
Lomsjö S 107 C11
Lomsti BG 166 C6
Lomträsk S 109 E18
Lomträsk S 119 B9
Łomża PL 139 D13
Lonato I 66 B1
Lønborg DK 86 D2
Lončari BIH 157 C10
Lončarica HR 149 E8
Londa I 66 E4
Londerzeel B 19 C9
Londinières F 18 E3
London GB 15 D8
Londonderry GB 4 F2
Lone LV 135 D11
Long F 18 D4
Longa GR 174 F4
Longages F 33 D8
Longare I 66 B4
Longares E 41 F9
Longarone I 72 D5
Long Ashton GB 13 C9
Longbenton GB 5 E13
Longbridge Deverill GB 13 C10
Longchaumois F 31 C8
Long Compton GB 13 A11
Long Crendon GB 14 D6
Long Eaton GB 11 F9
Longecourt-en-Plaine F 26 F3
Longerak N 90 B2
Longeville-en-Barrois F 26 C3
Longeville-lès-St-Avold F 186 C2
Longeville-sur-Mer F 28 B2
Longford IRL 7 E8
Longframlington GB 5 E13
Longhope GB 3 H10
Longhope GB 5 E13
Longhorsley GB 5 E13
Long Itchington GB 13 A12
Long Melford GB 15 C10
Longmorn GB 3 K10
Longny-au-Perche F 24 C4
Longobardi I 60 E6
Longobucco I 61 E7
Longomel P 44 F5
Longos GR 168 F3

Longos Vales P 38 D3
Long Preston GB 11 C7
Longré F 28 C5
Longridge GB 10 D6
Long Stratton GB 15 C11
Long Sutton GB 11 F12
Longton GB 10 D6
Longtown GB 5 E11
Longué-Jumelles F 23 F11
Longuenesse F 18 C5
Longueville F 25 C9
Longueville-sur-Scie F 18 E3
Longuyon F 19 F12
Longwood IRL 7 F9
Longwy F 19 F12
Lonigo I 66 B3
Löningen D 17 C9
Łoniów PL 143 E11
Lonja HR 149 F7
Lonjica HR 149 E6
Lonkan N 110 C9
Lonkka FIN 121 D13
Lonny F 184 E2
Lons F 32 D5
Lönsboda S 88 C6
Lonsee D 74 E6
Lons-le-Saunier F 31 B8
Lønstrup DK 90 E6
Lontzen B 183 D8
Lónya H 145 G5
Loon op Zand NL 16 E4
Loos F 182 D2
Loosdorf A 77 F8
Loose GB 15 E10
Lopadea Nouă RO 152 E3
Lopar HR 67 C10
Lopare BIH 157 C10
Lopătari RO 161 C9
Lopate MK 164 E4
Łopatna PL 143 C7
Lopatic MK 168 B5
Lopatovo RUS 132 F5
Lopcombe Corner GB 13 C11
Lope E 53 A8
Lopera E 53 A8
Loppa N 112 C7
Loppersum NL 17 B7
Loppi FIN 127 D11
Lopra FI 2 A3
Lopushna UA 152 A6
Łopuszno PL 143 E9
Lopyan BG 165 D9
Lora N 101 B9
Lora del Río E 51 D8
Loranca de Tajuña E 47 D6
Loràs S 106 E8
Lörby S 88 C7
Lorch D 21 D9
Lorch D 74 E6
Lorcha E 56 D4
Lordelo P 38 F4
Lordosa P 44 C5
Lørenskog N 95 C13
Loreo I 66 B5
Loreto I 67 F8
Loreto Aprutino I 62 C5
Lorgues F 36 D4
Lorient F 22 E5
Lorignac F 28 E4
Loriguilla E 48 E3
Lőrinci H 150 B4
Loriol-sur-Drôme F 30 F6
Lormes F 25 F9
Loro Ciuffenna I 66 E4
Loro Piceno I 67 F7
Lorquin F 186 D1
Lörrach D 27 E8
Lorrez-le-Bocage-Préaux F 25 D8
Lorris F 25 E8
Lorsch D 21 E11
Lørslev DK 90 E7
Lörstrand S 103 C11
Lörudden S 103 B14
Lorup D 17 C9
Lorupe LV 135 B9
Los S 103 C9
Losacino E 39 E7
Losa del Obispo E 48 E3
Los Alcázares E 56 F3
Los Alcàzares E 56 F2
Los Arcos E 32 E1
Losar de la Vera E 45 D9
Los Arenales del Sol E 56 E4
Los Barrios E 53 D6
Los Barrios de Luna E 39 C8
Los Belones E 56 F3
Los Cantareros E 55 D10
Los Corrales E 53 B7
Los Corrales de Buelna E 40 B3
Loscos E 42 E1
Los Dolores E 56 F2
Løset N 101 E14
Los Gallardos E 55 E9
Loschynivka UA 155 C3
Losheim D 21 E7
Los Hinojosos E 47 E7
Łosice PL 141 F7
Łosina PL 141 E5
Łosiów PL 142 E4
Los Maldonados E 56 F2
Los Molinos E 46 C4
Losna N 101 D12
Los Navalmorales E 46 E3
Los Navalucillos E 46 E3
Løsning DK 86 D5
Łosomiaki FIN 125 D11
Losone CH 68 A6
Łososina Dolna PL 144 D2
Losova MD 154 C2
Losovaara FIN 121 E11
Los Palacios y Villafranca E 51 E8
Los Pandos E 40 B4
Los Pedrones E 47 F10
Los Pozuelos de Calatrava E 54 B5
Los Rábanos E 41 E7
Los Royos E 55 D8
Los Santos E 45 C9
Los Santos de Maimona E 51 C7

Loßburg D 27 D9
Losse F 32 B5
Losser NL 17 D7
Lossiemouth GB 3 K10
Lossnitz CH 69 A7
Lostallo CH 69 A7
Lostbridge GB 12 E5
Lostice CZ 77 C11
Los Tojos E 40 B3
Los Villares E 53 A9
Los Yébenes E 46 E5
Löt S 89 B11
Lote N 100 C4
Løten N 101 E14
Lotenhulle B 182 C2
Loth GB 3 J9
Lothmore GB 3 J9
Lotorp S 92 B7
Lotte D 17 D9
Lottefors S 103 D11
Löttorp S 89 A11
Lottum NL 183 C8
Lotyń PL 85 C11
Lotzorai I 64 D4
Louannec F 22 C5
Loučen CZ 77 B8
Loučná nad Desnou CZ 77 B12
Loučovice CZ 76 E6
Loudéac F 22 D6
Loudes F 30 E4
Loudun F 23 F11
Loué F 23 E11
Loue FIN 119 B13
Louejärvi FIN 119 B14
Louejoki FIN 119 B14
Loughborough GB 11 F9
Loughbrickland GB 7 D10
Lougher IRL 8 D3
Loughgall GB 7 D9
Loughglinn IRL 6 E5
Loughton GB 15 D9
Lougratte F 33 A7
Louhans F 31 B7
Louka CZ 146 D4
Loukas GR 174 D5
Loukisia GR 175 C7
Loukkojärvi FIN 119 D15
Loukusa FIN 121 D10
Loulans F 26 F5
Loulay F 28 C4
Loulé P 50 E3
Louny CZ 76 B5
Loupiac F 32 A5
Lourdes F 32 D5
Lourenzá E 38 B5
Loures P 50 B1
Lourgnac F 29 E8
Lourical P 44 D3
Lourinhã P 44 F2
Lourmarin F 35 C9
Louros GR 174 A2
Loury F 24 E7
Lousã P 44 D4
Lousã I 64 D4
Lousada P 38 F3
Louth GB 11 E11
Louth IRL 7 E9
Loutra GR 175 C7
Loutra GR 177 A8
Loutra Aidipsou GR 175 B7
Loutra Eleftheron GR 170 C6
Loutraki GR 169 C6
Loutraki GR 174 B3
Loutraki GR 175 C6
Loutra Kyllinis GR 174 D3
Loutra Smokovou GR 174 A5
Loutra Ypatis GR 174 B5
Loutro GR 169 C7
Loutro GR 169 E6
Loutro GR 174 B3
Loutros GR 171 C9
Louvain B 19 C10
Louvain B 182 D5
Louveigné B 183 D7
Louverné F 23 D10
Louvie-Juzon F 32 D5
Louviers F 18 F3
Louvigné-du-Désert F 23 D9
Louvroil F 19 D8
Louze F 25 D12
Lov DK 87 E9
Lövånger S 118 F6
Lövberg S 107 B13
Lovas HR 157 B11
Lovasberény H 149 B11
Lovászi H 149 D7
Lovászpatona H 149 B9
Lovberg S 106 A7
Lovere I 69 B9
Lovik N 111 C10
Lovikka S 116 D9
Lovinac HR 156 D4
Lovinobaña SK 147 E8
Lovisa FIN 127 E15
Lovište HR 157 F7
Lovliden S 107 B13
Løvlund N 101 D11
Lövnäs S 102 D5
Lövnäs S 102 D5
Lövnäs S 109 D14
Lövnäsvallen S 102 C6
Lovnidol BG 166 D4
Lövö S 103 A15
Lovosice CZ 76 A4
Lovraeid N 94 D4
Lovran HR 67 B9
Lovreć HR 157 F7
Lovreč HR 157 F7
Lovrenc SLO 148 C4
Lovrin RO 150 F6
Løvseie S 118 F6
Lövsjö S 106 B8
Lövsjön S 97 B12
Lövstabruk S 99 B9
Lövstalöt S 99 B9
Lövstrand S 107 C10
Lovund N 108 D3
Lovušte SLO 87 A8
Łowcza PL 141 H8
Löwenberg D 84 D4
Löwenstein D 27 B11

Lower Ballinderry GB 7 C10
Löwer Cam GB 13 B10
Lower Kilchattan GB 4 C4
Lowestoft GB 15 C12
Lowick GB 5 D13
Low Street GB 15 B11
Łowyń PL 81 B9
Loxstedt D 17 B11
Löÿa FIN 123 B11
Loyettes F 31 D7
Loymola RUS 129 B16
Löytö FIN 128 B7
Löytökylä FIN 119 D16
Löytövaara FIN 121 C10
Lozarevo BG 167 D7
Lozen BG 165 E14
Lozen BG 166 C5
Lozen BG 167 E9
Lozenets BG 167 E9
Lozna RO 151 C11
Lozna SRB 158 D3
Loznitsa BG 155 F1
Loznitsa BG 167 C7
Lozorno SK 77 F12
Lozoya E 46 C5
Lozoyuela E 46 C5
Lozuvata UA 154 A4
Lozzo di Cadore I 72 D5
Lú IRL 7 E9
Luanco E 39 A8
Luarca E 39 A6
Lubaczów PL 144 C7
Lubań PL 81 D8
Lubāna LV 135 C13
Lubanowo PL 84 D7
Lübars D 79 B11
Lubartów PL 141 H7
Lubasz PL 85 E11
Lubawa PL 139 D9
Lubawka PL 81 E10
Lübbecke D 17 D11
Lübben D 80 C5
Lübbenau D 80 C5
Lübbow D 83 E10
Lubczyna PL 85 C7
Lube LV 134 B5
Lubеň E 53 B8
Lubeńa SK 147 C8
Lubenec CZ 76 B4
Lubenik SK 145 F1
Lubersac F 29 E8
Lübesse D 83 D10
Lubezere LV 134 B5
Lubiai LT 134 E3
Lubián E 39 D6
Łubianka D 138 D6
Lubichowo PL 138 C5
Lubicz Dolny PL 138 D6
Lubijcin PL 81 B9
Lubień PL 147 B9
Lubień Kujawski PL 139 F7
Lubieszewo PL 85 D9
Lubiń PL 81 C11
Lubin PL 81 D10
Lubina SK 146 D5
Lubiszyn PL 85 E7
Lublin PL 141 H7
Lubliniec PL 142 E6
Lubmin D 84 B5
Lubnia PL 138 C4
Lubnica MK 169 A7
Lubnica SRB 159 F9
Łubnice PL 143 F11
Lubniewice PL 81 A8
Łubno PL 85 B13
Lubno PL 85 D10
Łubno PL 143 B7
Lubochnia PL 141 G2
Lubomierz PL 81 D9
Lubomino PL 139 B9
Luboń PL 81 B11
Luborzyca PL 143 F9
Lubotice SK 145 E3
Łubotin SK 145 E2
Lubowidz PL 139 D8
Łubowo PL 85 C10
Łubowo PL 85 B12
Lubraniec PL 138 E6
Lubrín E 55 E8
Lubrza PL 81 B8
Lubrza PL 142 F4
Lubsko PL 81 C7
Lubstów PL 138 F5
Lubsza PL 142 E4
Lübtheen D 83 D10
Lubuczewo PL 85 A12
Luby CZ 75 B11
Łubycza Królewska PL 144 C8
Lübz D 83 D12
Luc F 33 B11
Luc F 35 A2
Lucainena de las Torres E 55 E8
Lucan IRL 7 F10
Lučani SRB 158 F5
Lúcar E 55 E8
Luçay-le-Mâle F 24 F5
Lucca I 66 E2
Lucca Sicula I 58 D3
Lucé F 24 D5
Luče SLO 73 D11
Lucena E 53 B8
Lucena de Jalón E 41 E9
Lucena del Cid E 48 D4
Lucena del Puerto E 51 E6
Lucenay-lès-Aix F 30 B3
Lucenay-l'Évêque F 25 F11
Luc-en-Diois F 35 A9
Luceni E 41 E9
Lucera I 63 D8
Lucéram F 37 D6
Lucey F 26 C4
Lucfalva H 147 E9
Luchachay BY 133 F3
Lucheux F 18 D5
Lüchow D 83 E10
Luciana E 54 B4
Lucień PL 139 F8
Lucignano I 66 F4
Luciková SLO 87 A8
Lucillo de Somoza E 39 D7
Lucito I 63 D7
Luciu RO 161 D10
Lucka D 79 D11

Luckau D 80 C5
Luckenwalde D 80 B4
Lucksta S 103 B13
Lückstedt D 83 E11
Lúčky SK 147 C8
Luco dei Marsi I 62 D4
Luçon F 28 B3
Lucq-de-Béarn F 32 D4
Luc-sur-Mer F 23 B11
Lucy-le-Bois F 25 E10
Ludag GB 2 L2
Ludanice SK 146 E6
Ludányhalászi H 147 E9
Ludbreg HR 149 D7
Lüdenscheid D 21 B9
Lüdersdorf D 83 C9
Lüdershall GB 13 C11
Ludlow GB 13 A9
Ludogorsi BG 161 F9
Ludoni RUS 132 E5
Ludoș RO 152 F3
Ludres F 186 D1
Luduș RO 152 E4
Ludvigsborg S 87 D13
Ludvika S 97 B13
Ludwigsau-Friedlos D 78 E6
Ludwigsburg D 27 C11
Ludwigsfelde D 80 B4
Ludwigshafen D 27 E11
Ludwigshafen am Rhein D 21 F10
Ludwigslust D 83 D10
Ludwigsstadt D 75 B9
Ludwin PL 141 H7
Ludza LV 133 C3
Lüe F 32 B4
Luelmo E 39 F7
Lüerdissen D 78 C6
Luesia E 32 F3
Lueta RO 153 E6
Lug BIH 162 D5
Lug HR 149 E11
Luga RUS 132 D6
Lugagnano Val d'Arda I 69 C8
Lugano CH 69 A6
Lüganuse EST 131 C14
Lugau D 79 E12
Lugaži LV 131 F11
Lügde D 17 E12
Luglon F 32 B4
Lugnano in Teverina I 62 B2
Lugnås S 91 B14
Lugnvik S 103 A14
Lugnvik S 106 E7
Lugny-lès-Charolles F 30 C5
Lugo E 38 B4
Lugo I 66 D4
Lugo-di-Nazza F 37 G10
Lugones E 39 B8
Lugrin F 31 C10
Lugros E 55 E6
Lugton GB 4 D7
Łuków PL 141 G6
Lugros E 55 E6
Luhačovice CZ 146 C5
Luhalahti FIN 127 B9
Luhamaa EST 132 F1
Luhanka FIN 127 B14
Luhden D 17 D12
Luhe-Wildenau D 75 C11
Lühmannsdorf D 84 B5
Luhtapohja FIN 125 E13
Luhtikylä FIN 127 D13
Luhy UA 154 A4
Luica RO 161 E9
Luica RO 161 E9
Luik B 19 C12
Luik B 183 D7
Luikonlahti FIN 125 E11
Luimneach IRL 8 C5
Luino I 68 B6
Luiro FIN 115 C4
Luiro FIN 115 D3
Luisant F 24 D5
Luizi Călugăra RO 153 D9
Luka BIH 157 F9
Luka SRB 159 E9
Lukácsháza H 149 B7
Luka nad Jihlavou CZ 77 D9
Lukavac BIH 157 C10
Lukavec CZ 77 C7
Lukavica BIH 157 D9
Lukawiec PL 144 C7
Luke MK 164 E5
Lukeswell IRL 9 D8
Łąki BG 165 F10
Lukivtsi UA 152 A6
Lukovë AL 168 E2
Lukovit BG 165 C9
Lukovo HR 67 C10
Lukovo SRB 159 F8
Lukovo SRB 163 C10
Lukovo Šugarje HR 67 D11
Lukovytsya UA 153 A8
Łukowa PL 144 C6
Łukowisko PL 141 G6
Łukminski LT 136 D7
Lukšiai LT 136 D7
Lukštai LT 135 D11
Łuky UA 145 D7
Luleå S 118 C8
Lüleburgaz TR 173 B7
Lüllemäe EST 131 F12
Lullymore IRL 7 F9
Lümanda EST 130 E4
Lumbarda HR 162 D3
Lumbier E 32 E3
Lumbrales E 45 C7
Lumbreras E 41 D6
Lumby DK 86 E6
Lumezzane I 69 B9
Lumijoki FIN 119 E14
Lumimetsä FIN 119 F14
Lumina RO 155 E3
Lumio F 37 F9
Lummelunda S 93 D12
Lumparland FIN 99 B14
Lumphanan GB 3 L11
Lumpiaque E 41 E9
Lumpzig D 79 E11
Lumsden GB 3 L11
Lumsheden S 103 E11
Luna E 41 E10
Luna RO 152 D3
Lunamatrona I 64 D2

Lunano I 66 E5
Lunas F 34 C5
Lunca MD 154 C4
Lunca RO 151 D9
Lunca RO 152 D5
Lunca RO 153 B9
Lunca RO 153 B9
Lunca Banului RO 154 D2
Lunca Bradului RO 152 D6
Lunca Cernii de Jos RO 159 B10
Lunca Corbului RO 160 D5
Lunca de Jos RO 153 D7
Lunca de Sus RO 153 D7
Lunca Ilvei RO 152 C5
Lunca Mureșului RO 152 E3
Luncavița RO 155 C3
Luncavița RO 159 C9
Luncoiu de Jos RO 151 E10
Lund DK 86 D5
Lund N 105 B11
Lund N 110 E8
Lund S 111 C15
Lund S 87 D12
Lundamo N 104 E8
Lundbjörken S 102 E8
Lundby DK 86 F7
Lundby DK 87 E9
Lunde DK 86 D3
Lunde DK 86 A6
Lunde N 95 D10
Lunde N 100 C5
Lunde S 103 A14
Lundeborg DK 87 E7
Lundebyvollen N 102 E3
Lundegård N 94 F6
Lunden D 82 B6
Lundin Links GB 5 C11
Lundsbrunn S 91 C13
Lundsjön S 106 D7
Lünebach D 20 D6
Lüneburg D 83 D8
Lunel F 35 C7
Lünen D 17 E9
Lunery F 29 B10
Lunéville F 26 C5
Lungani RO 153 C10
Lunger S 97 D14
Lungern CH 70 D6
Lungro I 60 D6
Lungsjön S 107 E10
Lungulețu RO 161 D7
Lunino RUS 136 D5
L'Union F 33 C8
Lunkkaus FIN 115 C3
Lunna BY 140 D10
Lunnäset S 102 A5
Lünne D 17 D8
Lunneborg N 111 B16
Lunow D 84 E6
Lunteren NL 183 A7
Luogosanto I 64 A3
Luohua FIN 119 E14
Luokė LT 134 E5
Luokkala FIN 125 E11
Luola-aapa FIN 119 C15
Luoma-aho FIN 123 D11
Luopa FIN 122 E9
Luopajärvi FIN 122 E9
Luopioinen FIN 127 C12
Luostari RUS 114 D1
Luosto FIN 115 D1
Luosu FIN 117 C12
Luotolahti FIN 128 C3
Luovankylä FIN 122 E7
Luovttejohka N 113 C21
Lupac RO 159 C8
Lupandi LV 133 E3
Łupawa PL 85 B12
Lupeni RO 159 C11
Lupiac F 33 C6
Lupiñén E 53 A9
Łupków PL 145 E5
Lupoglav HR 67 B9
Łupowo PL 85 E8
Luppa D 80 D3
Lupoperā FIN 121 D9
Luppy F 26 C5
Lupșa RO 151 E11
Lupșanu RO 161 E9
Luque E 53 A8
Luras I 64 B3
Lurbe-St-Christau F 32 D4
Lurcy-Lévis F 30 B2
Lure F 26 E5
Lurgan GB 7 D10
Lurgan IRL 6 E6
Lurí F 37 F10
Lurøy N 108 D4
Lurury-sur-Arnon F 24 F7
Lusca IRL 7 E9
Lusciano I 60 B2
Luserna San Giovanni I 31 F11
Lushnjë AL 168 C2
Lusi FIN 127 C15
Lusignan F 29 C6
Lusigny-sur-Barse F 25 D11
Lusk IRL 7 E10
Lus-la-Croix-Haute F 35 A10
Lusmini FIN 121 C14
Lusnić BIH 157 E7
Luso P 44 D4
Luspa FIN 116 B8
Luspebryggan S 109 B18
Lussac F 28 F5
Lussac-les-Châteaux F 29 C7
Lussac-les-Églises F 29 C8
Lussan F 35 B7
Lüssow D 83 C12
Lusta GB 2 K3
Lustad N 105 D13
Lustadt D 187 C5
Lustenau A 71 C9
Luster N 100 D6
Lustivere EST 131 D12
Łuszkowo PL 81 B11
Luszyn PL 143 B8
Lutago I 72 C4
Lütau D 83 D9
Lütetsburg D 17 A8
Lutherstadt Wittenberg D 79 C12
Lütjenburg D 83 B9
Lutnes N 102 D4
Lutocin PL 139 E8
Lutomiersk PL 143 C7
Luton GB 15 D8
Lutowiska PL 145 E6
Lutriņi LV 134 C5
Lutry PL 136 E2

Luttenberg NL 183 A8
Lutter am Barenberge D 79 C7
Lutterbach F 27 E7
Lutterworth GB 13 A12
Lututów PL 142 D5
Lützelbach D 21 E12
Lützen D 79 D11
Lutzerath D 21 D8
Lutzingen D 75 E8
Lutzmannsburg A 149 B7
Lützow D 83 C10
Luua EST 131 D13
Luujoki FIN 119 C14
Luukkola FIN 129 C9
Luukkonen FIN 129 B9
Luumäen kk FIN 128 D8
Luumäki FIN 128 D8
Luunja EST 131 E13
Luupujoki FIN 123 C17
Luupuvesi FIN 123 C17
Luusniemi FIN 124 G7
Luusua FIN 115 F2
Luvia FIN 126 C6
Luvos S 109 C16
Lux F 26 E3
Luxembourg L 20 E6
Luxe-Sumberraute F 32 D3
Luxeuil-les-Bains F 26 E5
Luxey F 32 B4
Luyego de Somoza E 39 D7
Luyksgestel NL 183 C6
Luz P 50 E2
Luz P 50 E4
Luz P 51 C5
Luzaga E 47 C8
Lužani HR 157 B8
Luzarches F 25 B7
Luz-Ardiden F 32 E5
Luže CZ 77 C10
Luzech F 33 B8
Lužec nad Vltavou CZ 76 B6
Luzenac F 33 E9
Luzern CH 70 C6
Luzhany UA 153 A7
Luzhki BY 133 F3
Luzianes P 50 D3
Luz i Madh AL 168 B2
Luzino PL 138 A5
Luzmela E 40 B3
Łużna PL 144 D3
Lūžņa LV 130 F3
Lūznava LV 133 D2
Luzón E 47 B8
Luz-St-Sauveur F 32 E6
Luzy F 30 B4
Luzzara I 66 C2
Luzzi I 60 E6
L'viv UA 144 D9
Lwówek PL 81 B10
Lwówek Śląski PL 81 D9
Lyady RUS 132 D4
Lyaskelya RUS 129 B15
Lyaskovets BG 166 C5
Lyavoshki BY 133 E2
Lybokhora UA 145 F6
Lybster GB 3 J10
Lychen D 84 D4
Lycksaberg S 107 A14
Lycksele S 107 B15
Lydd GB 15 F10
Lyderslev DK 87 E10
Lydford GB 12 D6
Lydney GB 13 B9
Lyeninski BY 141 F10
Lyfjord N 111 A16
Lygna N 95 B13
Lykofi GR 171 B10
Lykoporia GR 175 C6
Lyly FIN 127 B11
Lylykylä FIN 121 E11
Lyman UA 155 B6
Lymans'ke UA 154 D5
Lymans'ke UA 155 C2
Lyme Regis GB 13 D9
Lymington GB 13 D11
Lymm GB 10 E7
Lynäs S 103 D12
Lyndhurst GB 13 D11
Lyne DK 86 D3
Lyneham GB 13 B11
Lynemore GB 3 L9
Lyness GB 3 H10
Lyngby DK 87 C7
Lyngdal N 94 F6
Lyngmoen N 112 D5
Lyngså DK 86 A7
Lyngseidet N 111 A19
Lyngsnes N 105 B10
Lynmouth GB 13 C7
Lynton GB 13 C7
Lyntupy BY 137 C13
Lyökki FIN 126 D5
Lyon F 30 E6
Lyons-la-Forêt F 18 F3
Lyrestad S 91 B15
Lyrkeia GR 175 D6
Lysabild DK 86 F6
Lysá pod Makytou SK 146 C6
Łyse PL 139 D12
Lysebotn N 94 D5
Lysekil S 91 C9
Lyshchytsy BY 141 F9
Lysice CZ 77 D11
Lysnes N 111 B14
Łysomice PL 138 D6
Lysøysund N 104 D7
Lysroll N 111 D11
Lyss CH 31 A11
Lysvik N 97 B9
Łyszkowice PL 141 G1
Lytchett Minster GB 13 D10
Lytham St Anne's GB 10 D5
Lytovezh UA 144 B9
Lyubashivka UA 154 B6
Lyuben BG 165 D10
Lyubimets BG 166 F6
Lyubomyrka UA 154 B4
Lyubyntsi UA 145 E8
Lyulyakovo BG 167 D8

M

Maakeski FIN 127 C13
Maalahti FIN 122 E7
Maalismaa FIN 119 D15
Maam IRL 6 E3
Maaninka FIN 124 D8
Maaninkavaara FIN 115 F4
Maanselkä FIN 125 C10
Maaralanpera FIN 123 C16
Maardu EST 131 B10

Maarheeze NL 183 C7
Maaria FIN 126 D7
Maarianvaara FIN 125 E11
Maarn NL 183 A6
Maarssen NL 16 D4
Maarssenbroek NL 183 A6
Maas IRL 6 C6
Maasbracht NL 19 B12
Maasbree NL 16 F6
Maasdam NL 182 B5
Maaseik B 19 B12
Maaselkä FIN 121 F14
Maasen D 17 C11
Maasland NL 16 E2
Maasmechelen B 19 C12
Maassluis NL 16 E2
Maastricht NL 19 C12
Määttälä FIN 123 C12
Määttälänvaara FIN 121 B14
Maavesi FIN 124 F9
Mablethorpe GB 11 E12
Macael E 55 E8
Maçanet de Cabrenys E 34 F4
Maçanet de la Selva E 43 D9
Mação P 44 E5
Măcărești MD 153 C11
Macastre E 48 F3
Maccagno I 68 A6
Macchiagodena I 63 D6
Macclesfield GB 11 E7
Macduff GB 3 K12
Macea RO 151 E7
Maceda E 38 D4
Maceda P 44 C3
Macedo de Cavaleiros P 39 E6
Maceira E 38 D4
Maceira P 44 E3
Macelj HR 148 D5
Macerata I 67 F7
Macerata Feltria I 66 E5
Mâceşu de Jos RO 160 F3
Mâceşu de Sus RO 160 F3
Machados P 50 C5
Machairas GR 174 B3
Machault F 19 F10
Machecoul F 28 B2
Machelen B 182 D4
Machen GB 13 B8
Machern D 79 D12
Machliny PL 85 D10
Machowa PL 143 F11
Machrihanish GB 4 E5
Machynlleth GB 10 F4
Maciejowice PL 141 G5
Macin RO 155 C2
Macinaggio F 37 F10
Măciuca RO 160 D4
Mačkatica SRB 164 D5
Mackenbach D 21 E8
Mackenrode D 79 C8
Mačkovci SLO 148 C6
Macomer I 64 C2
Mâcon F 30 C6
Macosquin GB 4 E3
Macotera E 45 C10
Macroom IRL 8 E5
Macugnaga I 68 B4
Mačvanska Mitrovica SRB 158 D4
Mačvanski Pričinović SRB 158 D4
Mád H 145 G3
Madan BG 165 B10
Madan BG 171 A7
Mädan S 103 A15
Madängsholm S 91 C14
Madara BG 167 C8
Madaras H 150 E3
Mădăraş RO 151 C9
Mădârjac RO 153 C10
Maddalena Spiaggia I 64 E3
Maddaloni I 60 A2
Made NL 16 E3
Madekoski FIN 119 E15
Madeley GB 10 F7
Mäder A 71 C9
Madetkoski FIN 115 C1
Madiran F 32 C5
Madley GB 13 B9
Madliena LV 135 C10
Madocsa H 150 D2
Madona LV 135 C12
Madonna di Campiglio I 69 A10
Madrid E 46 D5
Madridejos E 46 F5
Madrigal de las Altas Torres E 45 B11
Madrigal de la Vera E 45 D10
Madrigal del Monte E 40 D4
Madrigalejo E 45 F9
Madrigueras E 47 F9
Madroñera E 45 E9
Mădulari RO 160 D4
Madzharovo BG 171 A9
Mæl N 95 C9
Maël-Carhaix F 22 D5
Maella E 42 E4
Maello E 46 C3
Maenclochog GB 12 B5
Maenza I 62 D4
Mære N 105 D10
Mäerişte RO 151 C10
Mäetaguse EST 131 C14
Maezlu E 41 C7
Mafra P 50 B1
Magacela E 51 B8
Magallón E 41 E9
Magalluf E 49 E10
Magaña E 41 E7
Magaši BIH 158 E3
Magaz E 40 E3
Magdeburg D 79 B10
Magdeburgerforth D 79 B11
Magenta I 69 C6
Magescq F 32 C3
Mágeşti RO 151 C9
Maggia CH 68 A6
Magherabeg GB 4 F3
Magheralin GB 7 D10
Magherani RO 152 D5
Maghery GB 7 C9
Maghull GB 10 D6
Magione I 66 F5
Măgiotsa EST 132 E1
Mâgireşti RO 153 D9
Maglaj BIH 157 C9
Maglavit RO 159 E11
Magliano de'Marsi I 62 C4

Magliano in Toscana I 65 B4
Magliano Sabina I 62 C2
Maglič SRB 158 F6
Maglie I 61 C10
Maglód H 150 C4
Magnac-Laval F 29 C8
Magné F 28 C4
Magnières F 26 D6
Magnor N 96 C7
Magnuszew PL 141 G4
Magny-Cours F 30 B3
Magny-en-Vexin F 24 B6
Mágocs H 149 D10
Magoula GR 174 E5
Magstrup DK 86 E4
Magueija P 44 B5
Maguilla E 51 C8
Maguiresbridge GB 7 D8
Măgura RO 153 D9
Măgura RO 160 E6
Măgura Ilvei RO 152 C5
Măgurele RO 161 E8
Măgurele RO 161 E8
Măgureni RO 161 C7
Măgureni-Răcătău RO 151 D11
Magy H 145 H4
Magyaralmás H 149 B10
Magyaratád H 149 D9
Magyarbánhegyes H 151 E6
Magyarbóly H 149 E10
Magyaregregy H 149 D10
Magyarhomorog H 151 C8
Magyarkeszi H 149 C10
Magyarnándor H 147 F8
Magyarpolány H 149 B9
Magyarszék H 149 D10
Mahala UA 153 A8
Maheriv UA 144 C8
Mahíde E 39 E7
Mahlberg D 186 E4
Mahlsdorf D 83 E10
Mahlu FIN 123 E14
Mahlwinkel D 79 B9
Mahmudia RO 155 C4
Mahmudiye TR 177 C10
Mahmutköy TR 173 C6
Mahón E 57 B13
Mahora E 47 F9
Mahovo HR 149 E6
Mähring D 75 C12
Mahtra EST 131 C10
Maia P 44 B3
Maials E 42 E5
Măicănești RO 161 C10
Maîche F 27 F6
Maida I 59 B9
Maiden Bradley GB 13 C10
Maidenhead GB 15 D7
Maiden Newton GB 13 D9
Maidens GB 4 E7
Maidstone GB 15 E10
Maienfeld CH 71 C9
Maierato I 59 B9
Maierhöfen D 71 B10
Maieru RO 152 C5
Măieruş RO 153 F7
Maigh Chromtha IRL 8 E5
Maigh Cuilinn IRL 6 F4
Maiglean Rátha IRL 7 E9
Maignelay-Montigny F 18 E6
Maijanen FIN 117 D14
Maillas F 32 B5
Maillebois F 24 C5
Maillezais F 28 C4
Mailly-le-Camp F 25 C11
Mailly-le-Château F 25 E10
Mailly-Maillet F 18 D6
Mailovac SRB 158 D7
Mainaschaff D 187 B7
Mainbernheim D 75 C7
Mainburg D 75 E10
Mainham IRL 7 F9
Mainhardt D 74 D6
Mainiemi FIN 127 B8
Mainistir Eimhín IRL 7 F8
Mainistir Fhear Maí IRL 8 D6
Mainistir Laoise IRL 9 C8
Mainistir na Corann IRL 8 E6
Mainistir na Feile IRL 8 D4
Mainnikkó S 116 D8
Mainvilliers F 24 D5
Mainz D 21 D10
Maiolati Spontini I 67 F7
Maiorca P 44 D3
Maiorga P 44 E3
Mairena del Alcor E 51 E8
Maisach D 75 F9
Maishofen A 73 B6
Maišiagala LT 137 D11
Maissau A 77 E9
Maisse F 25 D7
Maissin B 184 E3
Maivala FIN 125 B14
Maizières-lès-Metz F 186 C1
Majadahonda E 46 D5
Majadas de Tiétar E 45 E9
Majava FIN 121 C12
Majdan BIH 157 D7
Majdan Królewski PL 144 C4
Majdan Nepryski PL 144 C7
Majdanpek SRB 159 E8
Majovakylä FIN 119 C17
Majs H 149 E11
Majšperk SLO 148 D5
Majtum S 109 D18
Makád H 149 B11
Makariv UA 145 A9
Makarska HR 157 F7
Mäkelänranta FIN 121 C13
Mäkikylä FIN 123 C11
Makkola FIN 125 G11
Makkoshotyka H 145 G4
Makkum NL 16 B4
Maklár H 147 F10
Makljenovac BIH 157 C9
Makó H 150 E5
Makoc KS 164 D3
Makonkalns LV 133 D2
Makoszyce PL 142 E4
Makov SK 147 C7
Maków PL 141 G2
Maków PL 141 H1
Maków Mazowiecki PL 139 E11

Maków Podhalański PL 147 B9
Malnes N 110 C8
Makrakomi GR 174 B5
Makresh BG 159 F10
Makri GR 171 C9
Makrisia GR 174 D4
Makrochori GR 169 C7
Makrychori GR 169 E7
Makrygialos GR 169 D8
Makrygialos GR 177 E11
Makrynitsa GR 169 F8
Makryrrachi GR 174 A5
Maksamaa FIN 122 D8
Maksniemi FIN 119 C13
Maksymilianowo PL 138 D5
Malá E 53 B9
Mala IRL 8 D5
Mala S 87 C13
Malå S 107 A15
Mala Bosna SRB 150 E4
Mala Čista HR 156 E4
Malacky SK 77 F12
Málaga E 53 C8
Malagón E 46 F5
Malahide IRL 7 F10
Malahvianvaara FIN 121 E14
Malaia RO 160 C4
Mălăiești MD 154 D5
Málainn Bhig IRL 6 C5
Málainn Mhóir IRL 6 C5
Mala Kladuša BIH 156 B4
Malalbergo I 66 C3
Malá Lehota SK 147 D7
Malamocco I 66 B5
Malancourt F 19 F11
Malandrino GR 174 C5
Malangen N 111 B16
Malangseidet N 111 B16
Malanów PL 142 C5
Malansac F 23 E7
Malaryta BY 141 G10
Mălăşka FIN 119 F16
Mala Subotica HR 149 D7
Malaucène F 35 B9
Malaunay F 18 E3
Malaussane F 32 C5
Mălăvaara FIN 115 E11
Malăvănnäs S 107 A14
Malax FIN 122 E7
Malaya Byerastavitsa BY 140 D9
Malbekkvatn N 114 C7
Malbork PL 138 B7
Malborn D 21 E7
Malbouzon F 30 F3
Malbuisson F 31 B9
Malcesine I 69 B10
Malchin D 83 C13
Malchow D 83 C12
Malcocinado E 51 C8
Malcov SK 145 E3
Malczyce PL 81 D10
Mâldăeni RO 160 E5
Mâldărești RO 160 C4
Maldegem B 19 B7
Malden NL 16 E5
Maldon GB 15 D10
Mafdyty PL 139 C8
Malè I 71 E11
Malechowo PL 85 B11
Maleján E 41 E8
Maleme GR 178 D6
Malemort-du-Comtat F 35 B9
Malemort-sur-Corrèze F 29 E9
Malente D 83 B9
Mălerăs S 89 B9
Males GR 179 B11
Malesco I 68 A6
Malesherbes F 25 D7
Malesina GR 175 B7
Malestroit F 23 E7
Maletto I 59 D6
Malevo BG 166 F5
Malexander S 92 C6
Malfa I 59 B6
Malgersdorf D 75 E12
Malgovik S 107 B10
Malgrat de Mar E 43 D9
Malhadas P 39 E7
Malia GR 178 E9
Malicorne-sur-Sarthe F 23 E11
Maliena LV 133 C2
Mali Idoš SRB 158 B4
Malijai F 36 C4
Malilla S 92 E7
Mali Lošinj HR 67 C9
Mali Mokryany UA 144 D7
Malin IRL 4 E2
Malin Beg IRL 6 C5
Málinec SK 147 D9
Mancha Real E 53 A9
Malines B 182 C4
Mălini RO 153 C8
Malin More IRL 6 C5
Malinovka UA 135 E13
Malinska HR 67 B10
Maliq AL 168 C4
Malishevë KS 163 E10
Maliskylä FIN 123 C14
Malissard F 30 F6
Mali Zvornik SRB 157 D11
Maljaala GR 174 C3
Malkara TR 173 C6
Marķinia Górna PL 139 E13
Malko Gradishte BG 166 F5
Malko Tŭrnovo BG 167 E9
Mallaig GB 4 A5
Mállångsbo S 103 D10
Mallén E 41 E9
Mallentin D 83 C10
Mallersdorf D 75 E11
Malles Venosta I 71 D11
Mallica TR 173 E9
Malling DK 86 C6
Mallniz D 73 C7
Mallow IRL 8 D5
Mallusjoki FIN 127 D14
Mallwyd GB 10 F4
Malm N 105 C10
Malmbäck S 92 D4
Malmberget S 116 D6
Malmby S 98 D8
Malmédy B 20 D6
Malmesbury GB 13 B10
Malmkoping S 93 A9
Malmö S 87 D12
Malmön S 91 C9
Malmslätt S 92 C7
Malnas RO 153 E7
Mălnaş RO 153 E7
Malnate I 69 B6
Malo I 69 B11
Malo Crniće SRB 159 D7
Małogoszcz PL 143 E9
Malo Konare BG 165 E9
Małomice PL 81 C8
Malomir BG 167 E7
Malón E 41 E8
Malona GR 181 D8
Malonno I 69 A8
Malonty CZ 77 E7
Malorad BG 165 C8
Malo Titovo BIH 156 D5
Malovăţ RO 159 D10
Mǎløy N 100 C2
Maloye-Lugovoye RUS 136 D2
Maloye Sitna BY 133 G6
Malpartida de Cáceres E 45 F8
Malpartida de la Serena E 51 B8
Malpartida de Plasencia E 45 E8
Malpas GB 10 E6
Malpica E 53 C8
Malpica de Tajo E 46 E3
Malpica do Tejo P 44 E6
Mālpils LV 135 C9
Malsch D 27 C9
Mâlselv N 111 B16
Malsfeld D 78 D6
Mâlsnes N 111 B16
Mâlsta S 103 A13
Malta I 73 C8
Malta LV 133 D2
Malta P 45 C6
Maltas Trūpi LV 135 D13
Maltby GB 11 E9
Maltby le Marsh GB 11 E12
Maltepe TR 173 D7
Malterdingen D 27 D8
Malters CH 70 C6
Malton GB 11 C10
Malu cu Flori RO 160 C6
Maluenda E 41 F8
Malu Mare RO 160 E3
Malung S 102 E6
Malungsfors S 102 E6
Mǎlupe LV 133 B2
Mălureni RO 160 C5
Mǎluşteni RO 153 E11
Mauszyn PL 143 E8
Malva E 39 E8
Malvaglia CH 71 E7
Malveira P 50 B1
Malvik N 105 D10
Malý Horeš SK 145 G4
Malý H 145 G2
Malý Płock PL 139 D13
Malý Šariš SK 145 E3
Małý Bereznyy UA 145 F5
Mamaia RO 155 E3
Mamarrosa P 44 D3
Mamer L 20 E6
Mamers F 24 D3
Mamici BIH 157 F8
Mamirolle F 26 F5
Mammaste EST 131 E14
Mammendorf D 75 F9
Mammola I 59 C9
Mamone I 64 C3
Mamonovo RUS 139 B8
Mamuras AL 168 A1
Mana MD 154 C3
Manacor E 57 B11
Manage B 19 D9
Manamansalo FIN 120 F9
Mañaria E 41 B6
Mǎnǎs S 97 A9
Manasia RO 161 D9
Manasterz PL 144 C5
Mǎnǎstirea BG 165 F10
Mǎnǎstirea Caşin RO 153 E9
Mǎnǎstirea Humorului RO 153 B7
Manastirica SRB 159 D7
Manastirsko BG 167 D7
Mǎnǎştiur RO 151 F9
Mancera de Abajo E 45 C10
Manchita E 51 B7
Manchester GB 11 E7
Manching D 75 E9
Manchita E 51 B7
Manciano I 65 B5
Mancioux F 33 D7
Mândalo GR 169 C7
Mandal N 90 C1
Mandal N 100 A6
Mandalo GR 169 C7
Mandas I 64 E3
Mandatoriccio I 61 E7
Mandayona E 47 C7
Mandelbachtal-Ormesheim D 186 C3
Mandelieu-la-Napoule F 36 D5
Mandello del Lario I 69 B7
Manderscheid D 21 D7
Mandeure F 27 F6
Mandino Selo BIH 157 E7
Mândok H 145 G5
Mandra GR 175 C7
Mândra RO 152 F6
Mandraki GR 181 C6
Mandres-en-Barrois F 26 D3
Mandriko BG 171 B10
Manduria I 61 C9
Mane F 35 C10
Manea GB 11 G12
Manerbio I 66 B1
Mâneru E 32 E2
Mǎneşti RO 160 D6
Mǎneşti RO 161 D7
Manětín CZ 76 C4
Manfredonia I 63 D9
Mangalia RO 155 F3
Manganeses de la Lampreana E 39 E8
Manganeses de la Polvorosa E 39 D8
Mângbyn S 118 F6

Manger N 100 E2
Mangiennes F 19 F12
Mangotsfield GB 13 C9
Mângbodarna S 102 D6
Mangualde P 44 C5
Manhay B 19 D11
Manhuelles F 26 B4
Mani GR 171 B10
Maniace I 59 D6
Maniago I 73 D6
Maniákoi GR 168 D5
Manieczki PL 81 B11
Manilva E 53 D6
Manisa TR 177 B9
Manises E 48 F4
Manjärvträsk S 118 C4
Mank A 77 F8
Mânkarbo S 99 B8
Mankila FIN 119 E15
Manlay F 25 F11
Manlleu E 43 D8
Manna GR 175 D6
Mannamaa EST 130 D5
Mannersdorf an der Rabnitz A 149 B7
Mannheim D 21 F10
Männikuste EST 131 E8
Manningtree GB 15 D11
Manolada GR 174 C3
Manole BG 165 E10
Manoleasa RO 153 B10
Manoppello I 62 C6
Manorbier GB 12 B5
Manorhamilton IRL 6 D6
Manosque F 35 C10
Manowo PL 85 B10
Manresa E 43 D7
Mǎnsǎsen S 105 E16
Manschnow D 81 A7
Mankila FIN 119 E15
Mansfeld D 79 C9
Mansfield GB 11 E9
Mansfield Woodhouse GB 11 E9
Mansilla E 40 F6
Mansilla de las Mulas E 39 D9
Mansle F 29 D6
Manso F 37 G9
Mansonville F 33 B7
Manston GB 13 D10
Mânstrask S 109 E16
Mantamados GR 177 F10
Mantasia GR 174 A5
Manteigas P 44 C5
Mantel D 75 C11
Manternach L 186 B1
Mantes-la-Jolie F 24 C6
Mantes-la-Ville F 24 C6
Manthelan F 24 F4
Mantila FIN 122 F9
Mantoche F 26 F4
Mantory S 92 C6
Mantoudi GR 175 B7
Mantova I 66 B2
Mäntsälä FIN 127 D13
Mänttä FIN 123 F13
Mäntyharju FIN 128 C6
Mäntyjärvi FIN 117 E14
Mäntyjärvi FIN 121 B10
Mäntylahti FIN 124 D8
Mäntyluoto FIN 126 B5
Mäntyvaara S 116 E6
Manuel E 56 C4
Manulla IRL 6 E4
Mány H 149 A11
Manyas TR 173 D8
Manzac-sur-Vern F 29 E7
Mânzǎleşti RO 161 C9
Manzal de Arriba E 39 E7
Manzanal del Puerto E 39 C7
Manzanares E 55 A6
Manzanares el Real E 46 C5
Manzaneda E 38 D5
Manzanedo E 40 C4
Manzaneque E 46 E5
Manzanera E 48 D3
Manzanilla E 51 E7
Manzano I 73 E7
Manzat F 30 C2
Mar P 38 E2
Mara I 64 C2
Marac F 26 E3
Maracalagonis I 64 E3
Marachkova BY 133 E4
Mǎrǎşǎni RO 160 D5
Maragheh RO 153 F10
Mǎraşu RO 155 D1
Maratea I 60 C5
Marateca P 50 B2
Marathea GR 169 E6
Marathias GR 174 C5
Marathokampos GR 177 D8
Marathonas GR 175 C8
Marathopoli GR 174 E4
Maraussan F 34 D5
Maraye-en-Othe F 25 D10
Marazion GB 12 E4
Marazoleja E 46 C4
Marazovka UA 154 C6
Marbach CH 70 C6
Marbach am Neckar D 27 C11
Marbäck S 91 D13
Marbella E 53 D7
Marboz F 31 C7
Mǎrceni RO 161 C9
Marburg an der Lahn D 21 C11
Marby S 105 E16
Marçà E 42 E5
Marcali H 149 C8
Marcalló H 149 B8
Marcaria I 66 B2
Marcǎuţi MD 153 A10
Marcellina I 62 C3
Marcelová SK 149 A10
Marcenais F 28 E5
Marcenat F 30 E2
March GB 11 F12

Marchamalo E 47 C6
Marchaux F 26 F5
Marche-en-Famenne B 19 D11
Marchegg A 77 F11
Marchena E 51 E9
Marchenoir F 24 E5
Marcheprime F 28 F4
Marchiennes F 19 D7
Marchin B 19 D11
Marchtrenk A 76 F6
Marciac F 33 C6
Marciana I 65 B2
Marciana Marina I 65 B2
Mârcina LV 135 C12
Marcigny F 30 C5
Marcilhac-sur-Célé F 33 A9
Marcilla E 32 F2
Marcillac F 28 E4
Marcillac-la-Croisille F 29 E10
Marcillac-Vallon F 33 B10
Marcillat-en-Combraille F 29 C11
Marcilly-en-Gault F 24 F6
Marcilly-en-Villette F 24 E7
Marcilly-le-Hayer F 25 D10
Marcilly-sur-Eure F 24 C5
Marcinkonys LT 137 E9
Marcinkowice PL 85 D10
Marcinkowice PL 144 D2
Marcinowice PL 81 E10
Marcisző PL 81 E10
Marck F 18 C4
Marckolsheim F 27 D8
Marco de Canaveses P 44 B4
Marcoing F 19 D7
Marcon I 66 A5
Marcoux F 36 C4
Marcq-en-Barœul F 19 C7
Mǎrculeşti MD 153 B12
Mârdaklev S 87 A11
Mardarivka UA 154 B3
Mardeuil F 25 B10
Mârdsele S 107 B16
Mârdsjö S 106 C9
Mârdsjö S 107 C11
Mârdudden S 118 B6
Marebbe I 72 C4
Marennes F 28 D3
Maresfield GB 15 F9
Mareuil F 28 E6
Mareuil-sur-Arnon F 29 B10
Mareuil-sur-Ay F 25 B11
Mareuil-sur-Lay-Dissais F 28 B3
Marey-sur-Tille F 26 E3
Marga RO 159 B9
Margarites GR 178 E7
Mǎrgǎritei RO 161 C9
Margariti GR 168 F3
Margate GB 15 E11
Mǎrgǎu RO 151 D10
Margecany SK 145 F3
Margerie-Hancourt F 25 C12
Margherita di Savoia I 60 A6
Marghita RO 151 C9
Margina RO 151 F9
Marginea RO 153 B7
Mǎrgineni RO 153 D9
Mǎrgineni RO 153 D9
Margionys LT 137 F9
Margone I 31 C11
Margonin PL 85 E12
Margraten NL 19 C12
Margut F 19 F12
Marhaň SK 145 E3
María E 55 D8
Mariac F 30 F5
Mariager DK 86 B5
Maria Lankowitz A 73 B11
Maria Luggau A 73 C6
Marialva P 45 C6
Mariampole LV 133 D2
Mariana E 47 D8
Marianelund S 92 D7
Mariano Comense I 69 B7
Marianopoli I 58 D4
Mariánské Lázně CZ 75 C12
Mariapfarr A 73 B8
Maria Saal A 73 C9
Mariazell A 148 A4
Maribo DK 83 A10
Maribor SLO 148 C5
Marieberg S 92 A6
Marieby S 106 E7
Mariefred S 98 D8
Mariehamn FIN 99 B13
Marieholm S 87 D12
Marieholm S 91 D14
Mariembourg B 19 D10
Marienberg D 80 E4
Marienberg D 80 E4
Marienfliess D 83 D10
Marienhafe D 17 A8
Marienhagen D 78 B6
Marienheide D 21 B9
Mariental D 79 B8
Mariestad S 91 B14
Marifjøra N 100 D6
Marigliano I 60 B2
Marignana F 37 G9
Marignane F 35 D9
Marigné-Laillé F 23 E12
Marigny S 23 B9
Marigny-le-Châtel F 25 D10
Marijampolé LT 136 D7
Marikaj AL 168 B2
Marikostinovo BG 169 B9
Marín E 38 D2
Marina di Alberese I 65 B4
Marina di Amendolara I 61 D7
Marina di Camerota I 60 C4
Marina di Campo I 65 B2
Marina di Carrara I 69 E8
Marina di Castagneto Donoratico I 65 B4
Marina di Cecina I 66 F1
Marina di Chieuti I 63 D8
Marina di Gioiosa Ionica I 59 C9
Marina di Grosseto I 65 B3
Marina di Leuca I 61 D10
Marina di Massa I 69 E8
Marina di Novaglie I 61 D10
Marina di Palma I 58 E4
Marina di Pisa I 66 E1
Marina di Pulsano I 61 C8
Marina di Ragusa I 59 F6
Marina di Ravenna I 66 C5
Marinaleda E 53 B7
Marina Palmense I 67 F8
Marina Romea I 66 C5
Marina Schiavonea I 61 D7
Marinella I 58 D2

Marineo I 58 D3
Marines E 48 E3
Marines F 24 B6
Maringues F 30 D3
Marinha das Ondas P 44 D3
Marinha Grande P 44 E3
Marinhas P 38 E2
Marinići HR 67 B9
Marinka BG 167 E8
Marinkainen FIN 123 C10
Mārinkalns LV 133 B1
Marino I 62 D3
Mar'insko RUS 132 D4
Mariotto I 61 A7
Mārişelu RO 152 C5
Maritsa GR 181 D8
Marizy F 30 B5
Marjaliza E 46 E5
Mårjamaa EST 131 D8
Marjaniemi FIN 119 D13
Marjokylä FIN 127 C14
Marjonieeni FIN 127 C14
Marjovaara FIN 125 E15
Marjusaari FIN 123 D12
Mark GB 13 C9
Mark S 107 B10
Markaryd S 87 C13
Markaz H 147 F10
Markby FIN 122 D9
Markdorf D 27 E11
Markebäck S 92 B5
Markelo NL 17 D7
Market Deeping GB 11 F11
Market Drayton GB 10 F7
Market Harborough GB 15 C7
Markethill GB 7 D9
Market Rasen GB 11 E11
Market Warsop GB 11 E9
Market Weighton GB 11 D10
Markgröningen D 27 C11
Markhus N 94 C4
Marki PL 139 F11
Markina-Xemein E 41 B7
Markinch GB 5 C10
Märkisch Buchholz D 80 B5
Markitta S 116 D7
Markivka UA 154 D5
Markkina FIN 116 B8
Markkleeberg D 79 D11
Markkula FIN 123 C12
Marklohe D 17 C12
Marknesse NL 16 C5
Markneukirchen D 75 B11
Markopoulo GR 175 D8
Markovac SRB 159 E7
Markovac SRB 159 E7
Markovac Našički HR 149 E10
Markovac Trojstveni HR 149 E10
Markowa PL 144 C5
Markranstädt D 79 D11
Marksuhl D 79 E7
Markt Allhau A 148 B6
Marktbergel D 75 D7
Markt Berolzheim D 75 D8
Markt Bibart D 75 C7
Marktbreit D 187 B9
Markt Erlbach D 75 D8
Markt Hartmannsdorf A 148 B5
Marktheidenfeld D 74 C6
Markt Indersdorf D 75 F9
Marktjärn S 103 A11
Marktl D 76 F3
Marktleugast D 75 B10
Marktoberdorf D 71 B11
Marktoffingen D 75 E7
Marktredwitz D 75 B11
Markt Rettenbach D 71 B10
Markt Sankt Martin A 149 A6
Markt Schwaben D 75 F10
Marktseft D 75 C7
Markt Wald D 71 A11
Markusevec HR 148 E6
Markušica HR 149 F11
Markušovce SK 145 F2
Markuszów PL 141 H6
Marl D 17 E10
Marl D 17 E8
Marlborough GB 13 C11
Marldon GB 13 E7
Marle F 19 E8
Marlengo I 72 C3
Marlenheim F 27 C8
Marlhes F 30 E5
Marlishausen D 79 E9
Marlow D 83 B13
Marlow GB 15 D7
Marly F 19 D8
Marly CH 31 B11
Marly F 26 B5
Marma S 99 B8
Marmagne F 25 F7
Marmagne F 30 B5
Marmande F 33 A6
Marmara GR 174 B5
Marmara TR 173 C8
Marmaracik TR 173 B8
Marmaraereğlisi TR 173 C8
Marmari GR 175 C9
Marmaris TR 181 C8
Marmaro GR 177 C7
Marmelar P 50 C4
Marmeleira P 44 F3
Marmelete P 50 E2
Marmirolo I 66 B2
Marmolejo E 53 A8
Marmoutier F 27 C7
Marnardal N 90 C2
Marnäs S 103 E10
Marnay F 26 F4
Marne D 82 C6
Marne-la-Vallée F 25 C8
Marnes N 108 B7
Marnheim D 21 E10
Marnitz D 83 D11
Maroldsweisach D 75 B8
Marolles-les-Braults F 23 D12
Maromme F 18 E3
Maroneia GR 171 C9
Maroslele H 150 E5
Marostica I 72 E4
Maroué F 22 D6
Marousi GR 175 C8
Marpingen D 21 F8
Marpissa GR 176 E5
Marple GB 11 E7
Marpod RO 152 F5
Marquartstein D 72 A5
Marquion F 19 D7
Marquise F 15 F12
Marquixanes F 33 E10
Marradi I 66 D4
Marrasjärvi FIN 117 E14
Marraskoski FIN 117 E14

Marrubiu I 64 D2
Marrum NL 16 B5
Mârşa RO 161 E7
Marsac-en-Livradois F 30 E4
Marsac-sur-Don F 23 E8
Marsaglia I 37 B10
Marsal F 26 C6
Marsala I 58 D1
Mârşani RO 160 E4
Marsannay-la-Côte F 26 F2
Marsanne F 35 A8
Marsberg D 17 F11
Marsciano I 62 B2
Marseillan F 35 D6
Marseille F 35 D9
Marseille-en-Beauvaisis F 18 E4
Marsico Nuovo I 60 C5
Marsico Vetere I 60 C5
Marsillargues F 35 C7
Marsjärv S 118 B8
Mârslet DK 86 C6
Mārsnēni LV 135 B11
Marssac-sur-Tarn F 33 C10
Mårsta S 99 C9
Marstal DK 83 A9
Märstetten CH 27 E11
Marston GB 13 B12
Marstrand S 91 B11
Marstrup DK 86 E4
Mārsylä FIN 123 C11
Marta I 62 B1
Mårtanberg S 103 E9
Martano I 61 C10
Martel F 29 F9
Martelange B 19 E12
Martellago I 66 A5
Martello / 71 D11
Mártély H 150 E5
Marten BG 161 F8
Martfeld D 17 C12
Martfő H 150 C5
Marthon F 29 D6
Martiago E 45 D7
Martignacco I 73 D7
Martigné-Briand F 23 F11
Martigné-Ferchaud F 23 E9
Martigné-sur-Mayenne F 23 D10
Martigny CH 31 C11
Martigny-le-Comte F 30 B5
Martigny-les-Bains F 26 D4
Martigues F 35 D9
Martiherrero E 46 C3
Martim Longo P 50 E4
Martin SK 147 C7
Martina Franca I 61 B8
Martin Brod BIH 156 C5
Martinchel P 44 E4
Martinci SRB 158 C3
Martinci Čepinski HR 149 E10
Martín de la Jara E 53 B7
Martín del Río E 42 F2
Martín de Yeltes E 45 C8
Martinengo I 69 B8
Martineşti RO 151 F11
Martinet E 33 F9
Martinfeld D 79 D7
Martingança P 44 E3
Mārtiniş RO 152 E6
Martín Muñoz de las Posadas E 46 B3
Martinniemi FIN 119 D14
Martino GR 175 B7
Martinporra E 39 B8
Martinsberg A 77 F8
Martinščica HR 67 C9
Martinsicuro I 62 B5
Martis I 64 B2
Martizay F 29 B8
Martley GB 13 A10
Martna EST 130 D7
Martock GB 13 D9
Martonvaara FIN 125 D12
Martorell E 43 E7
Martos E 53 A9
Martres-Tolosane F 33 D8
Mårtsbo S 103 E13
Martti FIN 115 D4
Marttila FIN 127 D8
Marttila FIN 127 D13
Marttisenjärvi FIN 124 C7
Marugán E 46 C4
Maruggio I 61 C9
Marum NL 16 B6
Marum S 99 C12
Mārunţei RO 160 E4
Mărupe LV 135 C8
Maruszów PL 143 D12
Maruszów PL 144 B4
Marvão P 44 F6
Marvejols F 34 A5
Marville F 19 F11
Marxheim D 75 E8
Marxzell D 27 C9
Māry FIN 127 E8
Mar"yanivka UA 154 C4
Marykirk GB 5 B11
Marynychi UA 152 A6
Marypark GB 3 L10
Maryport GB 5 F10
Marywell GB 5 A11
Marzabotto I 66 D3
Marzahna D 79 B12
Marzahne D 79 A12
Marzamemi I 59 F7
Marzan F 23 E7
Mărzăneşti RO 161 F6
Marzling D 75 F10
Masa E 40 C4
Masainas I 64 E2
Masalavés E 48 F3
Masari GR 181 D8
Mas-Cabardès F 33 D10
Mascali I 59 D7
Mascalucia I 59 D7
Mascaraque E 46 E5
Mascarenhas P 38 E5
Maschito I 60 B5
Masclat F 29 F8
Mas de Barberans E 42 F4
Mas de las Matas E 42 F3
Masegosa E 47 C8
Masegoso E 55 B8
Masegoso de Tajuña E 47 C7
Maselheim D 71 A9
Maşera I 68 A5
Maserada sul Piave I 72 E5
Masevaux F 27 E6
Masfjorden N 100 E2
Masham GB 11 C8

Masi N 113 E12
Maside E 38 D3
Masi Torello I 66 C4
Maskalyanyaty BY 133 E7
Maskaur S 109 E14
Masku FIN 126 D7
Maslenika HR 156 D4
Maslinica HR 156 F5
Maşloc RO 151 F7
Maslovare BIH 157 C8
Maśłowice PL 143 D8
Masone I 37 B9
Masquefa E 43 E7
Massa I 69 E9
Massa Fiscaglia I 66 C5
Massa I 61 B8
Massa Lombarda I 66 D4
Massa Lubrense I 60 B2
Massamagrell E 48 E4
Massa Marittimo I 65 A3
Massa Martana I 62 B3
Massarosa I 66 E1
Massat F 33 E8
Massay F 24 F6
Maßbach D 75 B7
Masseret F 29 D9
Masseube F 33 D7
Massford GB 7 D10
Massiac F 30 E3
Massiari EST 131 F9
Massimino I 37 C8
Massing D 75 F12
Mas-St-Chély F 34 B5
Măştăcani RO 155 B2
Mastershausen D 185 D7
Masterud N 96 B7
Mastichari GR 177 F9
Mastrevik N 100 E1
Masua I 64 E1
Masugnsbyn S 116 D8
Masullas I 64 D2
Måsvik N 112 D2
Masyevichy BY 141 G9
Maszewo PL 81 B7
Maszewo PL 85 B13
Maszewo PL 85 D8
Maszewo Duże PL 139 E8
Matabuena E 46 B5
Matadepera E 43 D8
Mataguži MNE 163 E7
Matala FIN 119 C14
Matala N 178 F4
Matalalahti FIN 124 C8
Matalascañas E 51 E6
Matalebreras E 41 E7
Matallana de Valmadrigal E 39 D9
Matamala de Almazán E 41 E6
Matamorosa E 40 C3
Mataporquera E 40 C3
Matapozuelos E 39 F10
Matara FIN 125 D12
Mataragka GR 169 F7
Mataragka GR 174 B3
Mataraselkä FIN 117 C17
Mataró E 43 D8
Mataruge MNE 163 C7
Mataruška Banja SRB 158 F6
Mătăsari RO 160 D6
Mătăsaru RO 161 D6
Mătăsvaara FIN 125 D13
Matca RO 153 F11
Mateeşti RO 160 C3
Matei RO 152 D4
Matelica I 67 F7
Matera I 61 B7
Materija SLO 73 E9
Mateševo MNE 163 D8
Mátészalka H 145 H5
Mateuţi MD 154 B3
Matfors S 103 B13
Matha F 28 D5
Mathay F 27 F6
Mathi I 68 C4
Matignon F 23 C7
Matigny F 18 E7
Matilda FIN 127 E8
Matinlompolo FIN 117 E12
Matino I 61 C10
Matişi LV 131 F10
Matkaniva FIN 119 F14
Matkavaara FIN 121 E12
Matku FIN 127 D10
Matkule LV 134 C5
Matlock GB 11 E8
Matosinhos P 44 B3
Matour F 30 C5
Mátraballa H 147 F10
Mátraderecske H 147 F10
Mátramindszent H 147 F9
Matrand N 96 B7
Mátraszele H 147 E9
Mátraszőlős H 147 F9
Mátraterenye H 147 E9
Mátraverebély H 147 F9
Matre N 94 C3
Matre N 100 E3
Matrei am Brenner A 72 B3
Matrei in Osttirol A 72 B6
Matsdal S 109 E13
Matsouki GR 174 B3
Matt CH 71 E8
Mattaincourt F 26 D5
Mattersburg A 149 A6
Mattighofen A 76 F4
Mattila S 119 C12
Mattilanmäki FIN 115 E4
Mattinata I 63 D10
Mattinen FIN 119 B13
Mattisudden S 116 E3
Mattmar S 105 E15
Mattsmyra S 103 D9
Måttsund S 118 C7
Matuizos LT 137 E10
Matulji HR 67 B9
Matúškovo SK 146 E5
Matyryna BY 133 F5
Maubert-Fontaine F 19 E9
Maubeuge F 19 D8
Maubourguet F 32 C6
Maubuisson F 28 E3
Mauchline GB 5 D8
Maud GB 3 K12
Mauerbach A 77 F10
Mauerkirchen A 76 F4
Mauerstetten D 71 B11
Maughold GBM 10 C3
Mauguio F 35 C7
Maukkula FIN 125 E15
Maula FIN 119 C13
Maulbronn D 27 C10
Mauléon F 28 B4
Mauléon-Barousse F 33 E7

Mauléon-d'Armagnac F 32 C5
Mauléon-Licharre F 32 D4
Maulévrier F 28 A4
Maum IRL 6 E3
Mauna FIN 116 B8
Maunu S 116 B8
Maunujärvi FIN 117 D14
Maunula FIN 119 D15
Maura N 95 B13
Maure-de-Bretagne F 23 E8
Maureillas-las-Illas F 34 F4
Maurens F 29 F6
Mauriac F 28 F5
Mauriac F 29 E10
Mauricemills IRL 8 C4
Maurik NL 183 B6
Maurnes N 110 C9
Mauron F 23 D7
Mauroux F 33 B8
Maurs F 29 F10
Maurset N 94 B6
Maurstad N 100 C2
Mauru FIN 119 B15
Maury F 34 E4
Mautern an der Donau A 77 F9
Mauterndorf A 73 B8
Mautern in Steiermark A 73 B10
Mauth D 76 E5
Mauthausen A 77 F7
Mauthen A 73 C6
Mauves F 30 E6
Mauvezin F 33 C7
Mauvoisin CH 31 C11
Mauzé-sur-le-Mignon F 28 C4
Mavranaioi GR 168 D5
Mavrochori GR 168 C5
Mavrodendri GR 169 D6
Mavrodin RO 160 E6
Mavrokklisi GR 171 B9
Mavromati GR 174 E4
Mavrommati GR 169 F6
Mavrommati GR 175 C7
Mavrorečje SRB 163 B9
Mavrovë AL 168 D2
Mavrovo MK 163 F10
Mavrovouni GR 169 E7
Mavrovouni GR 169 E7
Maxent F 23 E7
Maxéville F 186 D1
Maxial F 44 F2
Maxieira P 44 E5
Mãxineni RO 161 C11
Maxmo FIN 122 D8
Maxsain D 185 C8
Mayakovskoye RUS 136 D5
Maybole GB 4 E7
Maydan UA 145 F7
Mayen D 21 D8
Mayenne F 23 D10
Mayet F 23 E12
Mayfield GB 15 E9
Mayobridge GB 7 D10
Mayorga E 39 D9
Mãyränperä FIN 119 F14
Mayres F 35 A7
Mayrhofen A 72 B4
Mäyry FIN 123 E10
Mayschoss D 21 C8
May's Corner GB 7 D10
Máza H 149 D10
Mazagón E 51 E6
Mazagran F 19 F10
Mažaičiai LT 134 E3
Mazaleón E 42 E4
Mazamet F 33 D10
Mazan F 35 B9
Mazara del Vallo I 58 D2
Mazarakia GR 168 F3
Mazarambroz E 46 E4
Mazarete E 47 C7
Mazarrón E 56 F2
Mazé F 23 F11
Mažeikiai LT 134 D3
Maženiai LT 135 E8
Mazères F 33 D9
Mazerolles F 32 C5
Mazeyrolles F 33 A8
Mazi TR 181 C9
Mazières-en-Gâtine F 28 B5
Mazirbe LV 130 F4
Mažonai LT 134 F4
Mazsalaca LV 131 F10
Mažučište MK 169 B5
Mazzano I 66 A1
Mazzano Romano I 62 C2
Mazzarino I 58 E5
Mazzarrone I 59 E6
Mazzo di Valtellina I 69 A9

Medena-Selišta BIH 157 D6
Medeno Pulje BIH 156 C5
Medenychi UA 145 E8
Medeş BIH 158 D3
Medesano I 66 C1
Medgidia RO 155 E2
Medgyesbodzás H 151 D6
Medgyesegyháza H 151 D6
Medhamn S 91 A14
Mediana E 41 F10
Mediaş RO 152 E4
Medicina I 66 D4
Medieşu Aurit RO 151 B11
Medinaceli E 47 B8
Medina de las Torres E 51 C7
Medina del Campo E 39 F10
Medina de Pomar E 40 C5
Medina de Rioseco E 39 E9
Medina-Sidonia E 52 D5
Medindgénai LT 134 E4
Medinilla E 45 D9
Medininkai LT 137 D12
Mediona E 43 E7
Médis F 28 D4
Medkovets BG 159 F11
Medle S 118 E5
Medlov CZ 77 C12
Medneva LV 133 B3
Medolla I 66 C3
Medousa GR 171 B8
Medovoye RUS 136 D1
Mjdrzechów PL 143 F10
Medşedžiai LT 134 D3
Medskog S 103 E12
Medskogsbygget S 102 B5
Medstugan S 105 D12
Međugorje BIH 157 F8
Medulin HR 67 C8
Međumajdan HR 156 B5
Medumi LV 135 E12
Meduno I 73 D6
Međurečje SRB 163 B9
Međusjö S 103 B10
Međuvođe BIH 157 B6
Medveđa SRB 159 F7
Medveđa SRB 159 F7
Medveđa SRB 164 D4
Medvida HR 156 D4
Medvode SLO 73 D9
Medyka PL 144 D6
Medzibrod SK 147 D8
Medzilaborce SK 145 E4
Meenaclady IRL 6 B6
Meenavean IRL 6 C5
Meer B 182 C5
Meerane D 79 E11
Meerapalu EST 132 E1
Meerbeck D 17 D12
Meerbusch D 17 F7
Meerhout B 183 C6
Meerkerk NL 182 B5
Meerlo NL 183 B8
Meersburg D 27 E11
Meerssen NL 19 C12
Meeuwen B 19 B12
Meaghreb S 105 C13
Megen NL 183 B6
Mega Dereio GR 171 B10
Megala Kalyvia GR 169 F6
Megali Panagia GR 169 D10
Megali Volvi GR 169 C10
Megalochori GR 169 E6
Megalo Chorio GR 174 B4
Megalo Livadi GR 175 E9
Megalopoli GR 174 E5
Megara GR 175 C7
Megardssætra N 105 C13
Megève F 31 D10
Megyaszó H 145 G3
Mehadia RO 159 D9
Mehadica RO 159 C9
Mehamn N 113 A20
Mehedeby S 99 B8
Mehikoorma EST 132 E1
Méhkerék H 151 D7
Mehren D 21 D7
Mehring D 21 E7
Mehrstetten D 74 F6
Mehtäkylä FIN 119 F12
Mehun-sur-Yèvre F 25 F7
Meidrim GB 12 B6
Meigh GB 7 D10
Meigle GB 5 B10
Meijel NL 16 F5
Meikleour GB 5 B10
Meilen CH 27 F10
Meilhan F 32 C5
Meillac F 23 D8
Meillant F 29 B10
Meillerie F 31 C10
Meimoa P 45 D6
Meina I 68 B6
Meine D 79 B8
Meinersen D 79 B7
Meinerzhagen D 185 B8
Meiningen D 79 E7
Meira E 38 B5
Meiringen CH 70 D6
Meisdorf D 79 C9
Meise B 182 D4
Meisenheim D 21 E9
Meißen D 80 D4
Meißenheim D 186 E4
Meitingen D 75 E8
Meix-devant-Virton B 19 E11
Mejlby DK 86 C6
Mejorada E 46 D3
Mejorada del Campo E 46 D6
Mejrup DK 86 C3
Meka Gruda BIH 157 F9
Mekinje SLO 73 D9
Mel I 72 D5
Melalahti FIN 121 F10
Melampes GR 178 F8
Melanthi GR 168 D5
Melay F 25 B10
Melay F 26 E4
Melazzo I 37 B8
Melbã N 111 C11
Melbourn GB 15 C9
Melbu N 110 C8
Melby GB 3 E13
Melchow D 84 E5
Meldal N 104 E7
Meldola I 66 D5
Meldorf D 82 B6
Mele I 37 C9
Melegnano I 69 C7

Melci FIN 121 F10
Melendugno I 61 C10
Melfi I 60 B5
Melfjordbotn N 108 C6
Melgaço P 38 D3
Melgar de Arriba E 39 D9
Melgar de Fernamental E 40 D3
Melgar de Tera E 39 E7
Melhus N 104 E8
Melia GR 169 E8
Meliana E 48 E4
Melick NL 20 B6
Melicucco I 59 C9
Mélida E 32 F2
Melide E 38 C4
Melide P 50 C2
Meligalas GR 174 E4
Meliki GR 169 C7
Melilli I 59 E7
Melineşti RO 160 D3
Meliskerke NL 182 B3
Melissa GR 171 B7
Melissa I 61 E8
Melissano I 61 D10
Melissochori GR 175 C7
Melissopetra GR 168 D4
Melitaia GR 174 A5
Melitopol' UA 154 F6
Melito di Porto Salvo I 59 D8
Melivoia GR 169 E8
Melivoia GR 171 B7
Melk A 77 F8
Melkadalen N 111 D12
Melkefoss N 114 E7
Melksham GB 13 C10
Mellac F 22 E4
Mellajärvi FIN 119 B13
Mellakoski FIN 119 B12
Mellanfjärden S 103 C13
Mellansel S 107 E14
Mellansjö S 103 B10
Mellanström S 109 E15
Mellau A 71 C9
Mellbystrand S 87 B11
Melle B 19 B8
Melle D 17 D10
Melle F 28 C5
Mellen D 83 D11
Mellendorf (Wedemark) D 78 A6
Mellensee D 80 B4
Mellerud S 91 B11
Mellerup DK 86 B6
Mellgård S 103 A9
Mellilä FIN 127 D8
Mellin D 79 A8
Mellingen D 79 E9
Mellrichstadt D 75 B7
Mellösa S 93 A9
Melnica SRB 159 E8
Melnik BG 169 A9
Mělník CZ 77 B6
Mel'nikovo RUS 129 D12
Mellnsils LV 130 F5
Melón E 38 D3
Meloy N 110 C9
Melrand F 22 E5
Melres P 44 B4
Melrose GB 5 D11
Mels CH 71 C8
Melsdorf D 83 B8
Melsungen D 78 D6
Meltaus FIN 117 E14
Meltham GB 11 D8
Melton GB 15 C11
Melton Mowbray GB 11 F10
Meltosjärvi FIN 117 E13
Melun F 25 C8
Melvaig GB 2 K5
Melvich GB 3 H9
Mélykút H 150 E3
Melzo I 69 C7
Memaliaj AL 168 D2
Membrey F 26 E4
Membrilla E 55 B6
Membrío E 45 E6
Memele LV 135 D8
Memleben D 79 D9
Memmelsdorf D 75 C8
Memmingen D 71 B10
Memmingerberg D 71 B10
Memsie GB 3 K12
Menaggio I 69 A7
Menai Bridge GB 10 E3
Menaldum NL 16 B5
Menars F 24 E5
Menasalbas E 46 E4
Menat F 30 C2
Menata I 66 C5
Mendavia E 32 F1
Mende F 34 A6
Menden (Sauerland) D 17 F9
Mendenitsa GR 175 B6
Menderes TR 177 C9
Mendig D 21 D8
Mendiga P 44 E3
Mendigorría E 32 E2
Mendrisio CH 69 B6
Ménéac F 22 D7
Menemen TR 177 B9
Menen B 19 C7
Menesjärvi FIN 117 A16
Ménesplet F 29 E6
Ménessaire F 25 F11
Menet F 29 E11
Menetes GR 181 F6
Menetou-Salon F 25 F7
Menfi I 58 D2
Mengabril E 51 B8
Mengele LV 135 C10
Mengen D 27 E11
Mengeš SLO 73 D9
Mengíbar E 53 A9
Menidi GR 174 A3
Ménil-la-Tour F 26 C4
Ménil-sur-Belvitte F 26 D6
Menin B 19 C7
Menlti B 182 D2
Menkijärvi FIN 123 E11
Menkulas AL 168 C4
Mennecy F 25 D7
Mennetou-sur-Cher F 24 F6
Menou F 25 F9

Mens F 31 F8
Mensignac F 29 E7
Menslage D 17 C9
Mentana I 62 C3
Menteroda D 79 D8
Menteşe TR 181 B8
Menton F 37 D7
Menznau CH 70 C6
Méobecq F 29 B9
Meolo I 72 E5
Méounes-les-Montrieux F 35 D10
Meppel NL 16 C6
Meppen D 17 C8
Mequinenza E 42 E4
Mer F 24 E6
Merag HR 67 C9
Meråker N 105 E11
Meråkervollen N 105 E11
Merano I 72 C3
Méraq F 32 C5
Merasjärvi S 116 C7
Merasjärvi S 117 C10
Merate I 69 B7
Merbes-le-Château B 19 D9
Mercadillo E 40 B5
Mercatale I 66 E5
Mercatello sul Metauro I 66 E5
Mercatino Conca I 66 E6
Mercato San Severino I 60 B3
Mercato Saraceno I 66 E5
Merčez SRB 163 C11
Merching D 71 A11
Merchtem B 19 C9
Mercœur F 29 E9
Mercogliano I 60 B3
Mercuès I 33 B8
Merdignac F 22 D7
Mērdzene LV 133 C3
Mere B 19 C8
Mere GB 13 C10
Méreal S 95 A13
Mereau F 24 F7
Merei RO 161 C9
Merelbeke B 19 C8
Meremäe EST 132 F2
Merenberg D 185 C9
Mereni RO 155 C2
Mereni MD 154 D4
Mérens-les-Vals F 33 F9
Mereşti RO 153 E6
Merәu F 24 D7
Merghindeal RO 152 F5
Mergozzo I 68 B5
Meria F 37 F10
Méribel-les-Allues F 31 E10
Meriç TR 171 B10
Merichas GR 175 E9
Merichleri BG 166 E4
Mérida E 51 B7
Meriden GB 13 A11
Merijärvi FIN 119 F12
Merikarvia FIN 126 B6
Merilläinen FIN 123 C10
Merimasku FIN 126 E6
Měřín CZ 77 D9
Mering D 71 A11
Merişani RO 160 D5
Mérk H 151 B9
Merkendorf A 148 C5
Merkendorf D 75 D8
Merkenes S 109 C11
Merkinė LT 137 E9
Merklín CZ 76 C4
Merklingen D 74 E6
Merksplas B 182 C5
Merlara I 66 B3
Merlevenez F 22 E5
Merlines F 29 D10
Mern DK 87 E10
Mērnieki LV 131 F8
Mernye H 149 C9
Merošina SRB 164 C4
Merrey F 26 D4
Mersch L 20 E6
Merseburg (Saale) D 79 D10
Mersinbeleni TR 177 D10
Mers-les-Bains F 18 D3
Mērsrags LV 134 B6
Mertajärvi S 116 B8
Mertert L 20 E6
Mertesdorf D 186 B2
Merthyr Tydfil GB 13 B8
Mertingen D 75 E8
Mertloch D 185 D7
Mértola P 50 D4
Mertzwiller F 186 D4
Méru F 18 F5
Mervans F 31 B7
Mervent F 28 B4
Merville F 18 C6
Merville F 33 C8
Méry-sur-Seine F 25 C10
Merzen D 17 D9
Merzig D 21 F7
Mesagne I 61 B9
Mesagros GR 175 D8
Mésanger F 23 F9
Mesão Frio P 44 B5
Mesaria GR 177 F6
Meschede D 17 F10
Meschers-sur-Gironde F 28 D4
Mešeišta MK 168 B4
Meselefors S 107 C11
Mesenikolas GR 169 F6
Meşeşenii de Jos RO 151 C10
Mesgrigny F 25 D10
Mesi GR 171 C8
Mesići BIH 157 E11
Mesihovina BIH 157 E7
Mesimeri GR 169 D9
Mesinge DK 86 E7
Meškla GR 178 E6
Meškuičiai LT 134 D6
Meslay-du-Maine F 23 E10
Mesocco CH 71 A8
Mesochora GR 168 E5
Mesochori GR 169 E7
Mesochori GR 181 E6
Mesola I 66 C5
Mesolongi GR 174 C3
Mesopotamia GR 168 C5
Mesopotamos GR 168 F4
Mesoraca I 59 B10
Mesotopos GR 177 A7
Mespelbrunn D 187 B7
Mesquer F 23 F6
Messac F 23 E8
Messanges F 32 C3
Meßdorf D 83 E11

Messei F 23 C10
Messei F 29 D11
Messejana P 50 D3
Messina I 59 C8
Messincourt F 19 E11
Messingen D 17 D8
Messini GR 174 E5
Meßkirch D 27 E11
Messlingen S 102 A4
Meßstetten D 27 D10
Mesta BG 165 F8
Mesta GR 177 C6
Mestanza E 54 B4
Městec Králové CZ 77 B8
Mestervik N 111 B16
Mesti GR 171 C7
Mestlin D 83 C11
Město Albrechtice CZ 142 F4
Město Touškov CZ 76 C4
Mestre I 66 B5
Mesves-sur-Loire F 25 F8
Mesztegnyő H 149 C8
Meta I 60 B2
Métabief F 31 B9
Metagkitsi GR 169 D10
Metajna HR 67 C11
Metallikó GR 169 B8
Metallostroy RUS 129 F14
Metaxades GR 171 B10
Metelen D 17 D8
Meteş RO 151 E11
Metfield GB 15 C11
Methana GR 175 D7
Metheringham GB 11 E11
Methlick GB 3 L12
Methoni GR 178 B2
Methven GB 5 C9
Methwold GB 11 F13
Metković HR 157 F8
Metlika SLO 148 E4
Metnitz A 73 C9
Metochi GR 174 C3
Metochi GR 175 B8
Metovnica SRB 159 F9
Mêtriena UA 175 C12
Metsäkansa FIN 127 C10
Metsäkylä FIN 121 D11
Metsäkylä FIN 128 D7
Metsälä FIN 120 C9
Metsämaa FIN 127 D9
Metschow D 84 C3
Metsküla EST 130 D5
Metslawier NL 16 B6
Metsovo GR 168 E5
Mettäjärvi S 117 E11
Mettendorf D 20 E6
Mettenheim D 75 F11
Mettet B 19 D10
Mettingen D 17 D9
Mettlach D 21 F7
Mettmann D 17 F7
Mettray F 24 F4
Metz F 26 B5
Metzervisse F 20 F6
Metzingen D 27 C11
Meudt D 185 D8
Meulan F 24 B6
Meulebeke B 19 C7
Meung-sur-Loire F 24 E6
Meursault F 30 B6
Meuselwitz D 79 D11
Meuzac F 29 D8
Mevagissey GB 12 E5
Mexborough GB 11 E9
Meximieux F 31 D7
Mey GB 3 H10
Meyenburg D 83 D12
Meylan F 31 E8
Meymac F 29 D10
Meyrargues F 35 C10
Meyreuil F 35 D10
Meyronnes F 36 C5
Meyrueis F 34 B5
Meyssac F 29 E9
Meysse F 35 A8
Meythet F 31 D9
Mezapos GR 178 B3
Mežāre LV 135 C12
Mezdra BG 165 C8
Mèze F 35 D6
Mézel F 36 D4
Mežgale LV 135 D11
Mezhdurech'ye RUS 136 D4
Mezibořl CZ 80 E5
Mežica SLO 73 C10
Mézidon-Canon F 23 B11
Mézières-en-Brenne F 29 B8
Mézières-sur-Issoire F 29 C7
Mézilhac F 30 F5
Mézilles F 25 E9
Mezimĕstí CZ 81 E10
Mézin F 33 B6
Mezio P 44 C5
Mezőberény H 151 D7
Mezőcsát H 147 F11
Mezőcsokonya H 149 D9
Mezőfalva H 149 C11
Mezőgyán H 151 D8
Mezőhegyes H 150 E6
Mezőkeresztes H 145 H2
Mezőkovácsháza H 150 E6
Mezőkövesd H 147 F11
Mezőlak H 149 B8
Mezőnyárád H 145 H2
Mezőörs H 149 A9
Mézos F 32 B3
Mezőszemere H 150 B6
Mezőszentgyörgy H 149 B10
Mezőszilas H 149 C10
Mezőtárkány H 150 B5
Mezőtúr LV 135 D8
Mezőtúr H 150 D6
Mezőzombor H 145 G3
Mezquita de Jarque E 42 F2
Mežvalde LV 134 C6
Mežviki LV 133 C3
Mežvidi LV 134 C4
Mezzana I 69 A10
Mezzanego I 37 C10
Mezzano I 72 D4
Mezzocorona I 69 A11
Mezzojuso I 58 D3
Mezzoldo I 69 A8
Mezzolombardo I 69 A11
Mga RUS 129 F15
Mỉączyn PL 144 B8
Miajadas E 45 F9
Mialet F 29 D7
Miały PL 85 E10
Miasteczko Krajeńskie PL 85 D12
Miastko PL 85 B11

Miastków Kościelny PL 141 G5
Miastkowo PL 139 D12
Miavaig GB 2 J3
Mica RO 152 C3
Mica RO 152 E4
Micăsasa RO 152 E4
Miceşti RO 160 D5
Miceşti de Câmpie RO 152 D4
Michaľany SK 145 F4
Michalová SK 147 D9
Michalovce SK 145 F4
Michałów PL 143 F9
Michałów Górny PL 141 G4
Michałowice PL 142 E3
Michałowice PL 143 F8
Michałowo PL 140 D9
Michelbach an der Bilz D 74 D6
Micheldorf D 73 C9
Micheldorf in Oberösterreich A 73 A9
Michelfeld D 74 D6
Michelstadt D 21 E12
Michendorf D 80 B4
Michorzewo PL 81 B10
Michów PL 141 G6
Mickelspiltom FIN 127 D15
Mickelsträsk S 118 F14
Mickleton GB 5 F12
Mickleton GB 13 A11
Micleşti MD 154 C3
Midbea GB 3 G11
Middagsbukt N 111 B17
Middelbeers NL 183 C6
Middelburg NL 16 E1
Middelfart DK 86 D5
Middelharnis NL 16 E2
Middelkerke B 18 B6
Middelstum NL 17 B7
Middenbeemster NL 16 C4
Middenmeer NL 16 C4
Middeldam GB 5 C14
Middelmarsh GB 13 D10
Middlesbrough GB 11 B9
Middleton GB 11 D7
Middleton Cheney GB 13 A12
Middleton in Teesdale GB 5 F12
Middletown GB 7 D9
Middlewich GB 10 E7
Midhurst GB 15 F7
Midleton IRL 8 E6
Midlum D 17 A11
Midsund N 100 A5
Midtgård N 114 D8
Midtskogberget N 102 D3
Miðvágur FO 2 A2
Midwolda NL 17 B8
Mid Yell GB 3 D14
Miechów N 100 A7
Miechów Charsznica PL 143 F8
Miedes E 41 F9
Miedziana Góra PL 143 E10
Miedzichowo PL 81 B9
Miedzna PL 139 F13
Miedzna PL 141 G4
Miedźno PL 143 E6
Miejdzybórz PL 142 D4
Międzylesie PL 77 B11
Międzyrzec Podlaski PL 141 G4
Międzyrzecz PL 81 B9
Międzyzdroje PL 84 C6
Miehikkälä FIN 128 D8
Miehlen D 185 D8
Miejsce Piastowe PL 145 D4
Miejska Górka PL 81 C11
Mijkinia PL 81 C11
Miekojärvi S 119 B10
Miélan F 33 D6
Mielec PL 143 F11
Mielęcin PL 85 D10
Mieleszyn PL 85 E12
Mielno PL 85 B10
Mieluskylä FIN 119 F14
Miełżyn PL 138 F4
Mieming A 71 C11
Mierasjärvi FIN 113 D19
Mieraslompolo FIN 113 D19
Miercurea-Ciuc RO 153 E7
Miercurea Nirajului RO 152 D5
Miercurea Sibiului RO 152 F3
Mieres E 39 B8
Mieres E 43 C9
Mierlo NL 16 F5
Mierojávri N 113 E11
Mieroszów PL 81 E10
Miers F 29 F9
Mierzęcice PL 143 F7
Mierzyn PL 84 D6
Miesau D 186 C3
Miesbach D 72 A3
Mieścisko PL 85 E12
Miesenbach D 186 C4
Mieślahti FIN 121 E14
Miessaure S 116 E4
Mieste D 79 B9
Mieszków PL 142 B3
Mieszkowice PL 84 E6
Mietingen D 71 A9
Mietków PL 81 E11
Mietoinen FIN 126 D6
Miettilä FIN 129 C10
Mieussy F 31 C10
Mieza E 45 B7
Migennes F 25 E10
Migliarino I 66 C4
Migliarino I 66 C4
Miglianico I 62 C6
Miglionico I 61 B6
Mignaloux-Beauvoir F 29 B6
Mignano Monte Lungo I 60 A1
Migné-Auxances F 29 B6
Mignovillard F 31 B9
Miguel Esteban E 47 E6
Miguelturra E 54 B5
Migushino RUS 133 E7
Mihăeşti RO 160 C4
Mihăeşti RO 160 C5
Mihăeşti RO 160 E5
Mihai Bravu RO 155 D3
Mihai Bravu RO 161 E8
Mihăileni RO 153 B8
Mihăileni RO 153 B8
Mihăileşti RO 161 D9
Mihăileşti RO 161 E8
Mihail Kogălniceanu RO 155 C3
Mihail Kogălniceanu RO 155 D1
Mihail Kogălniceanu RO 155 C2
Mihăileşti MD 154 D3
Mihai Viteazu RO 152 D3
Mihai Viteazu RO 155 D3

Mihajlovac SRB 159 D6
Mihajlovac SRB 159 E9
Mihajlovo SRB 158 C5
Mihălăşeni RO 153 B10
Mihald H 149 C8
Mihalţ RO 152 E3
Mihályi H 149 A8
Miheşu de Câmpie RO 152 D4
Mihla D 79 D7
Miiluranta FIN 123 C16
Mijares E 46 D3
Mijas E 53 C7
Mijdrecht NL 16 D3
Mijoska MNE 163 D7
Mikalayeva BY 133 F6
Mikepércs H 151 C8
Mikhalishki BG 137 D13
Mikhaltsi BG 166 C4
Mikhaylovo BG 165 B8
Mikhaylovo BG 165 C8
Mikitamäe EST 132 E2
Mikitsikha BY 133 F9
Mikkeli FIN 128 B7
Mikkelin mlk FIN 128 B7
Mikkelvik N 112 C3
Mikkola FIN 117 D16
Miklavž SLO 148 C5
Mikleuš HR 149 E8
Mikołajki PL 136 F4
Mikołajki Pomorskie PL 139 C7
Mikołów PL 143 F6
Mikoszewo PL 138 B6
Mikre BG 165 C10
Mikri Volvi GR 169 C10
Mikro Dereio GR 171 B10
Mikrokambos GR 169 C8
Mikromilia GR 170 B6
Mikropoli GR 169 B10
Mikrothives GR 169 F8
Mikrovalto GR 169 D6
Mikstat PL 142 C4
Mikulăš CZ 77 C8
Mikulasovice CZ 80 E6
Mikulčice CZ 77 E12
Mikulov CZ 77 E11
Mikulovice CZ 142 F3
Mikušovce SK 146 C6
Miladinovci MK 164 F4
Milagro E 41 D8
Milagros E 40 E4
Miłakowo PL 139 B8
Milano I 69 C7
Milano Marittima I 66 D5
Milanówek PL 141 F3
Milaş RO 152 D4
Milas TR 181 B7
Milatkoviće SRB 163 C10
Milatos GR 179 E10
Milazzo I 59 C7
Milborne Port GB 13 D10
Milcoiu RO 160 C4
Milcov RO 160 E4
Milcovul RO 161 B10
Mildenhall GB 15 C10
Mildstedt D 82 B6
Mileanca RO 153 A9
Milejczyce PL 141 G7
Milejewo PL 139 B8
Milejów PL 141 H7
Milena I 58 E4
Mileşti RO 153 C12
Milestone IRL 8 C6
Mileto I 59 B9
Milevsko CZ 76 D6
Milfield GB 5 D12
Milfontes P 50 D2
Milford GB 15 F7
Milford IRL 7 B7
Milford IRL 8 D5
Milford Haven GB 12 B4
Milhão P 39 E6
Milhaud F 35 C7
Milići BIH 157 D11
Milicz PL 81 C12
Milies GR 169 F9
Milíkov CZ 147 B7
Milín CZ 76 C6
Milina GR 175 A7
Milis I 64 C2
Militello in Val di Catania I 59 E6
Miliyeve UA 152 A6
Milizac F 22 D2
Miljana HR 148 D5
Miljeno BIH 157 E11
Miljevina BIH 157 E10
Milkel D 81 D6
Milki PL 136 F4
Milkovitsa BG 160 F5
Milk'ovtsi BG 165 D6
Mill NL 16 E5
Millares E 48 F3
Millas F 34 E4
Millau F 34 B5
Millay F 30 B5
Millbrook GB 12 E6
Millbrook IRL 7 E8
Millesimo I 37 C8
Millevaches F 29 D10
Milltown GB 7 D9
Millhouse GB 4 D6
Millières F 26 D3
Millingen aan de Rijn NL 183 B8
Millisle GB 7 C11
Millom GB 10 C5
Millport GB 4 D7
Millstatt A 73 C8
Millstreet IRL 8 D4
Millstreet IRL 9 D7
Milltown GB 11 E6
Milltown IRL 7 F9
Milltown IRL 8 D3
Milltown IRL 8 D3
Milltown Malbay IRL 8 C4
Milly-la-Forêt F 25 D7
Milmarcos E 47 B9
Milmort B 183 D7
Milna HR 156 F5
Milnathort GB 5 C10
Milngavie GB 5 D8
Milnthorpe GB 10 C6
Milo I 59 D7
Milohnić HR 67 B9
Milomłyn PL 139 C8
Milos GR 175 E8
Miloslavov SK 146 E4
Milot AL 163 F8

Milotice CZ 77 E12
Milovaig GB 2 L3
Milovice CZ 77 B7
Milow D 79 A11
Milow D 83 D11
Milówka PL 147 B8
Miltach D 75 D12
Miltenberg D 21 E12
Miltiņi LV 134 C6
Milton GB 2 L8
Milton GB 5 B9
Milton Keynes GB 15 C7
Miltzow D 84 B4
Milutinovac SRB 159 F7
Milverton GB 13 C8
Milz D 75 B8
Mimetiz E 40 B5
Mimizan F 32 B3
Mimizan-Plage F 32 B3
Mimoň CZ 81 E7
Mina de São Domingos P 50 D5
Mín an Chladaigh IRL 6 B6
Minas de Riotinto E 51 D6
Minateda E 55 C9
Minaya E 47 F8
Minde P 44 E3
Mindelheim D 71 A10
Mindelstetten D 75 E10
Minden D 17 D12
Minderhout B 182 C5
Mindnes N 108 E3
Mîndreşti MD 154 B2
Mindszent H 150 D5
Mindszentgodisa H 149 D10
Mindtangen N 108 E3
Mindúnai LT 135 F11
Mindya BG 166 C5
Minehead GB 13 C8
Mineo I 59 E6
Mineralni Bani BG 166 F4
Minerbio I 66 C3
Minervino Murge I 60 A6
Minfeld D 27 B9
Minger MD 154 D2
Minglanilla E 47 E9
Mingorría E 46 C3
Miniac-Morvan F 23 C8
Minićevo SRB 159 F9
Minilov CZ 77 C8
Minne S 103 B9
Minnertsga NL 16 B5
Minnesund N 95 B14
Minnigaff GB 4 F8
Minot F 25 E12
Miñska Mazowiecki PL 141 F5
Minsterley GB 10 F6
Mintilloglio GR 174 C4
Mintiu Gherlii RO 152 C3
Mintlaw GB 3 K13
Mintraching D 75 D11
Minturno I 62 E5
Minucciano I 66 D1
Minusio CH 68 A6
Mioarele RO 160 C6
Mionica SRB 158 E5
Mionnay F 30 D6
Mios F 32 A4
Mira E 47 E10
Mira I 66 B5
Mira P 44 D3
Mirabeau F 35 C10
Mirabel F 45 E8
Mirabel F 33 B8
Mirabel-aux-Baronnies F 35 B9
Mirabella Eclano I 60 A4
Mirabella Imbaccari I 58 E5
Miradoux F 33 C7
Miraflores de la Sierra E 46 C5
Miralcamp E 42 D5
Miramare I 66 D6
Miramas F 35 C9
Mirambeau F 28 E4
Mirambel E 42 F3
Miramont-de-Guyenne F 33 A6
Miranda de Arga E 32 F2
Miranda de Ebro E 40 C6
Miranda do Corvo P 44 D4
Miranda do Douro P 39 E7
Mirande F 33 C6
Mirandela P 45 B9
Mirandilla E 51 A7
Mirandola I 66 C3
Mirandol-Bourgnounac F 33 B10
Miranje HR 156 E4
Mirano I 66 B5
Miras AL 168 C4
Mirash KS 164 E3
Mirăslău RO 152 E3
Miravci MK 169 B7
Miravet E 42 E5
Miravete de la Sierra E 42 F2
Mircea Vodă RO 155 E2
Mircea Vodă RO 161 C10
Mirceşti RO 153 C9
Mircze PL 144 B8
Mirebeau F 26 F3
Mirebeau F 29 B6
Mirecourt F 26 D5
Mirepoix F 33 D9
Mireşu Mare RO 151 C11
Miřetice CZ 77 C9
Mireval F 35 C6
Miričina BIH 157 C9
Mirkovci HR 157 B8
Mirkovo BG 165 D9
Mirlović Zagora HR 156 E5
Mirna SLO 73 E11
Mirna Peč SLO 73 E11
Mirocin RO 144 C6
Mirocin Górny PL 81 C9
Mironeasa RO 153 D10
Miroševce SRB 164 D4
Miroşi RO 160 E5
Miroslava RO 153 C10
Miroslavas LT 137 E8
Mirosławiec PL 85 D9
Mirosloveşti RO 153 C9
Mirošov CZ 76 C5
Mirotice CZ 76 D6
Mirovice CZ 76 C6
Mirow D 83 D13
Mirşid RO 151 C11
Mirsk PL 81 E8
Mirto Crosia I 61 D7
Mirueña de los Infanzones E 45 C10
Mirzec PL 141 H4
Misano Adriatico I 67 E6
Mişca RO 151 D8

Mischii RO 160 E3
Miserey-Salines F 26 F4
Mishnyevichy BY 133 F7
Misi FIN 117 E17
Misilmeri I 58 C3
Miske H 150 E3
Mislina HR 162 D4
Mislinja SLO 73 D11
Mišnjak HR 67 C10
Mison F 35 B10
Missanello I 60 C6
Missenträsk S 107 A17
Missillac F 23 F7
Misso EST 131 F14
Mistelbach A 77 E11
Misterhult S 93 D8
Misterton GB 11 E10
Mistretta I 58 D5
Mistros GR 175 B8
Misurina I 72 C5
Misvær N 108 B9
Mitandersfors S 96 B7
Mitchelstown IRL 8 D6
Mithymna GR 171 F10
Mitoc RO 153 A10
Mitrašinci MK 165 F6
Mitreni RO 161 E9
Mitropoli GR 169 F6
Mitrousi GR 169 B9
Mitrova Reka SRB 163 C9
Mitrovicë KS 163 C10
Mitry-Mory F 25 C8
Mittådalen S 102 A4
Mittelberg A 71 C10
Mittelberg A 71 D11
Mittelbiberach D 71 A9
Mittelkalbach D 74 B6
Mittelsinn D 187 A8
Mittenwald D 72 B3
Mittenwalde D 80 B5
Mittenwalde D 84 D5
Mitterbach am Erlaufsee A 148 A4
Mitterding A 76 F3
Mitterdorf im Mürztal A 148 A5
Mittersheim F 27 C6
Mittersill A 72 B5
Mitterskirchen D 75 F12
Mitterteich D 75 C11
Mittet N 100 A7
Mittlidden S 105 B16
Mittweida D 80 E3
Mitwitz D 75 B9
Mizhhir"ya UA 145 F7
Mizil RO 161 C8
Miziya BG 160 F3
Mjäliby S 88 C7
Mjällom S 107 E14
Mjȅde AL 163 F8
Mjelde N 110 E9
Mjelde N 111 A15
Mjöbäck S 88 A3
Mjöby S 92 C4
Mjøen N 101 E13
Mjøfjell N 100 E5
Mjölby S 92 C6
Mjøndalen N 95 C12
Mjønes N 104 E8
Mjøsjøby S 107 D15
Mjöträsk S 118 B8
Mjøvattnet S 103 A14
Mjøvattnet S 118 E5
Mladá Boleslav CZ 77 B7
Mladá Vožice CZ 77 C7
Mladé Buky CZ 81 E9
Mladenovo SRB 158 C3
Mladenovo SRB 158 C3
Mladikovine BIH 157 D8
Mladinovo BG 166 F6
Mlado Nagoričane MK 164 E4
Mława PL 139 D9
Mlekarevo BG 166 D6
Mlinice BIH 157 D7
Mlinište BIH 157 D6
Młodzieszyn PL 141 F2
Mlynary PL 139 B8
Młynarze PL 139 E11
Mlynys'ka UA 145 E9
Mnichovice CZ 77 C7
Mnichovo Hradiště CZ 77 A7
Mnichów PL 143 E9
Mniów PL 143 E9
Mníšek nad Hnilcom SK 145 F2
Mníšek pod Brdy CZ 76 C6
Mniszew PL 141 G4
Mojzesovo SK 146 E6
Mniszków PL 141 H2
Mo N 100 B3
Mo S 103 D12
Mo S 103 E12
Mo S 107 A14
Mo S 107 D11
Mo S 107 E11
Moacşa RO 153 F7
Moaña E 38 D2
Moara RO 153 B8
Moara Domnească MD 153 B10
Moara Vlăsiei RO 161 D8
Moate IRL 7 F7
Mobberley GB 11 E7
Moby S 103 A12
Mocejón E 46 E5
Močenok SK 146 E5
Mochales E 47 B9
Mochos GR 178 E9
Mochowo PL 139 E8
Mochy PL 81 B10
Mociu RO 152 D4
Möckern D 79 B10
Möckmühl D 27 B11
Mockrehna D 79 C12
Mockträsk S 118 C7
Moclín E 53 B9
Moclinejo E 53 C9
Mocra MD 154 B4
Mocsa H 149 A10
Modane F 31 E10
Modave B 19 D11
Modbury GB 13 E7
Modelu RO 161 E10
Modena I 66 C2
Modi GR 175 B6
Modica I 59 F6
Modigliana I 66 D4
Modliborzyce PL 144 B5
Mödling A 77 F10
Modliszewice PL 141 H2

Modra SK 146 E4
Modran BIH 157 C8
Modrany SK 146 F6
Modreeny IRL 8 C6
Modriach A 73 C11
Modrica BIH 157 C9
Modriš HR 156 B3
Modrý Kameň SK 147 E8
Modugno I 61 A7
Moëlan-sur-Mer F 22 E4
Moelfre GB 10 E3
Moelv N 101 E13
Moen N 111 B16
Moerbeke B 182 C3
Moerkerke B 182 C2
Moers D 17 F7
Moffat GB 5 E10
Mofreita P 39 E6
Mogadouro P 39 F6
Mogata S 93 C8
Mögelin D 79 A11
Møgeltønder DK 86 F3
Mogenstrup DK 87 E9
Moggio Udinese I 73 D7
Mögglingen D 187 D6
Mogielnica PL 141 G3
Mogila MK 168 B5
Mogilany PL 147 B9
Mogilishte BG 167 C10
Mogilno PL 138 E4
Moglia I 66 C2
Mogliano I 67 F7
Mogliano Veneto I 66 A5
Möglingen D 187 D7
Mogón E 55 C6
Mogoşani RO 160 D6
Mogoşeşti RO 153 C10
Mogoşeşti-Siret RO 153 C9
Mogoşoaia RO 161 D7
Moguer E 51 E6
Mogyoród H 150 B3
Mohács H 149 E11
Moharque E 55 C9
Mohed S 103 D12
Mohedas de Granadilla E 45 D8
Mohedas de la Jara E 45 E10
Mohelnice CZ 77 C11
Mohelno CZ 77 D10
Mohernando E 47 C6
Mohill IRL 9 C8
Mohill IRL 7 E7
Möhkö FIN 125 E16
Mohlin CH 27 E8
Möhlau D 79 C11
Moholm S 91 B15
Mohora H 147 F8
Mohorn D 80 E4
Mohyliv Podil's'kyy UA 154 A1
Moi N 94 F5
Moi N 94 F6
Moià E 43 D8
Moiano I 60 A3
Moieciu RO 160 C6
Moimenta da Beira P 44 C5
Moineşti RO 153 E8
Moingt F 30 D5
Móinteach Mílic IRL 7 F8
Moira GB 7 D10
Mo i Rana N 108 D7
Moirans F 31 E8
Moirans-en-Montagne F 31 C8
Moirax F 33 B7
Moires GR 178 E8
Mõisaküla EST 131 E10
Moisburg D 82 D7
Moisdon-la-Rivière F 23 E9
Moisei RO 152 B5
Moisiovaara FIN 121 E13
Moislains F 18 E6
Moissac F 33 B8
Moissac-Bellevue F 36 D4
Moissey F 26 F4
Moita F 37 G10
Moita P 44 D4
Moita P 50 B2
Moixent-Mogente E 56 D3
Mojácar E 55 E9
Mojados E 39 F10
Mojkovac MNE 163 D8
Mojmírovce SK 146 E6
Mojstrana SLO 73 D8
Mojzesovo SK 146 E6
Møkkevik N 110 D9
Möklinta S 98 B7
Mokobody PL 141 F6
Mokrá Hora CZ 77 D11
Mokrance SK 145 F3
Mokre PL 143 F10
Mokren BG 167 D7
Mokresh BG 160 F2
Mokrievo MK 169 B8
Mokrin SRB 150 F5
Mokro BIH 157 E10
Mokronog BIH 156 D5
Mokronoge BIH 157 E7
Móksjy FIN 123 C12
Mol B 16 F4
Mol SRB 150 F5
Mola di Bari I 61 A8
Molaoi GR 178 B4
Molare I 37 B9
Molbergen D 17 C9
Mölbling A 73 C9
Mølby DK 86 E4
Mold GB 10 E5
Moldava nad Bodvou SK 145 F2
Moldjord N 108 C8
Moldoşiṭa RO 153 B7
Moldova Nouă RO 159 D8
Moldova-Suliţa RO 152 B6
Moldoveni RO 153 D9
Moldoviţa RO 153 B7
Møldrup DK 86 B5
Moldvik N 111 C11
Moledo P 38 E2
Moledo P 44 C5
Molelos P 44 C4
Molenbeek-St-Jean B 182 D4
Molenstede B 183 D6
Molescroft GB 11 D11
Molesme F 25 E11
Molety MD 154 D3

Molėtai LT 135 F10
Molfetta I 61 A7
Molfsee D 83 B8
Moliden S 107 E14
Molières F 29 F9
Molières F 33 B8
Molières-sur-Cèze F 35 B7
Moliets-et-Maa F 32 C3
Molina Aterno I 62 C5
Molina de Aragón E 47 C9
Molina de Segura E 56 E2
Molina di Ledro I 69 B10
Molinara I 60 A3
Molinella I 66 C4
Molines-en-Queyras F 31 F10
Molinet F 30 C4
Molinges F 31 C8
Molinicos E 55 C8
Molini di Tures I 72 C4
Molino de Villobas E 32 F5
Molinos E 42 F3
Molins de Rei E 43 E8
Moliterno I 60 C5
Molitg-les-Bains E 34 E4
Molkojärvi FIN 117 D14
Molkom S 97 C10
Mollas AL 168 C3
Mölle S 87 C11
Molledo E 40 B3
Möllenbeck D 84 D4
Möllenhagen D 84 C3
Mollerussa E 42 D5
Molles F 30 C4
Mollet del Vallès E 43 D8
Molliens-Dreuil F 18 E5
Mollis CH 27 F11
Mölln D 83 C9
Mölln D 83 C9
Mollö E 33 F10
Mollösund S 91 C9
Mölltorp S 92 C4
Mölnbo S 93 A10
Mölnlycke S 91 D11
Molnytsya UA 153 A8
Moloha UA 154 E6
Molompize F 30 E3
Molos GR 175 B6
Moloy F 26 E2
Molpe FIN 122 E6
Molschleben D 79 D8
Molsheim F 186 A3
Molunat HR 162 E5
Molve HR 149 D8
Molveno I 69 B10
Molvízar E 53 C9
Mombaldone I 37 B8
Mombeltrán E 45 D10
Mombercelli I 37 B8
Mómbris D 21 D12
Mombuey E 39 D7
Momchilgrad BG 171 A8
Momignies B 19 D9
Momo I 68 B6
Moná BY 137 E11
Monachil E 53 B9
Monacia-d'Aullène F 37 H10
Monaghan IRL 7 D9
Monamolin IRL 9 C10
Monäs FIN 122 C9
Monashi UA 154 E6
Monasterace I 59 C10
Monasterevin IRL 7 F8
Monastir I 64 E3
Monastiraki GR 174 B2
Monbahus F 33 A7
Monbazillac F 29 F6
Moncada E 48 E4
Moncalieri I 37 A7
Moncalvo I 68 C5
Monção P 38 E3
Moncarapacho P 50 E4
Moncaut F 33 B6
Monchio delle Corti I 66 D1
Monchique P 50 E2
Mönchsdeggingen D 75 E8
Mönchhof F 77 G11
Monclar F 33 B7
Moncofa E 48 F4
Moncontour F 22 D6
Moncontour F 28 B5
Moncoutant F 28 B5
Moncrabeau F 33 B6
Monda E 53 C7
Mondariz E 38 D3
Mondariz-Balneario E 38 D3
Mondavezan F 33 D8
Mondavio I 67 E6
Mondéjar E 47 D6
Mondello I 58 C3
Mondeville F 23 B11
Mondolfo I 67 E7
Mondoñedo E 38 B5
Mondorf-les-Bains L 20 E6
Mondoubleau F 24 E4
Mondovì I 37 C7
Mondragon F 35 B8
Mondragone I 62 E5
Mondsee A 73 A7
Monea GB 7 D7
Moneasa RO 151 E9
Moneen IRL 6 F5
Moneglia I 37 C10
Monegrillo E 41 E11
Monein F 32 D4
Monemvasia GR 178 B5
Monesiglio I 37 C8
Monesterio E 51 C7
Monestier-de-Clermont F 31 F8
Monestiés F 33 B10
Monéteau F 25 E10
Moneygall IRL 8 C6
Moneymore GB 4 F3
Moneyreagh GB 7 C11
Monfalcone I 73 E8
Monfero E 38 B3
Monflanquin F 33 A7
Monfort F 33 C7
Monforte da Beira P 45 E6
Monforte d'Alba I 37 B7
Monforte de Lemos E 38 C4
Monforte de Moyuela E 42 E2
Monghidoro I 66 D3
Mongrando I 68 B5
Mongstad N 100 E2
Monguelfo I 72 C5

Monheim D 75 E8
Moniaive GB 5 E9
Monieux F 35 B9
Monifieth GB 5 C11
Monilea IRL 7 E8
Möniste EST 131 F13
Monistrol-d'Allier F 30 F4
Monistrol de Calders E 43 D8
Monistrol de Montserrat E 43 D7
Monistrol-sur-Loire F 30 E5
Monivea IRL 6 F5
Mönkeberg D 83 B8
Mońki PL 140 D7
Monkokehampton GB 12 D6
Monléon-Magnoac F 33 D7
Monmouth GB 13 B9
Monnaie F 24 E4
Mönni FIN 125 E14
Monninkylä FIN 127 E14
Monok H 145 G3
Monolithos GR 181 D7
Monopoli I 61 B8
Monor RO 152 D5
Monor H 150 C3
Monostorapáti H 149 C9
Monostorpályi H 151 C8
Monóvar E 56 E3
Monpazier F 33 A7
Monreal E 32 E3
Monreal del Campo E 47 C10
Monreale I 58 C3
Monreith GB 4 F7
Monroy E 45 E8
Monroyo E 42 F3
Mons B 19 D8
Mons F 34 C4
Mons T 36 B5
Monsampolo del Tronto I 62 B5
Monsaraz P 51 C5
Monschau D 20 C6
Monsec F 29 E7
Monségur F 33 A6
Monselice I 66 B4
Monsempron-Libos F 33 B7
Monserrat E 48 F3
Monsheim D 187 B5
Mönsheim D 187 D6
Mønsted DK 86 C4
Monster NL 16 D2
Mönsterås S 89 A10
Monsummano Terme I 66 E2
Monta I 37 B7
Montabaur D 21 D9
Montaberner E 56 D4
Montady F 34 D5
Montagnac F 34 D5
Montagnana I 66 B3
Montagne F 28 F5
Montagney F 26 F4
Montagnol F 34 C5
Montagrier F 29 E6
Montaigu F 28 B3
Montaigu-de-Quercy F 33 B8
Montaigut F 30 C2
Montaigut-sur-Save F 33 C8
Montaione I 66 E2
Montalbán E 42 F2
Montalbán de Córdoba E 53 A7
Montalbano Elicona I 59 C7
Montalbano Jonico I 61 C7
Montalbo E 47 E7
Montalcino I 65 A4
Montale I 66 E3
Montalegre P 38 E4
Montalieu-Vercieu F 31 D7
Montalivet-les-Bains F 28 E3
Montallegro I 58 E3
Montalto delle Marche I 62 B5
Montalto di Castro I 65 C5
Montalto Marina I 65 C5
Montalto Uffugo I 60 E6
Montalvão P 44 E5
Montamarta E 39 E8
Montana BG 165 C7
Montana CH 31 C11
Montanejos E 48 D3
Montaner F 32 D5
Montano Antilia I 60 C4
Montans F 33 C9
Montaquila I 62 D6
Montargil P 44 F4
Montargis F 25 E8
Montastruc-la-Conseillère F 33 C9
Montataire F 18 F5
Montauban F 33 B8
Montauban-de-Bretagne F 23 D7
Montaudin F 23 D10
Montauriol F 33 A7
Montauroux F 36 D5
Montaut F 32 C4
Montaut F 32 D5
Montaut F 33 D9
Montayral F 33 B7
Montazzoli I 63 D6
Montbard F 25 E11
Montbarrey F 31 A8
Montbazens F 33 B10
Montbazin F 35 C6
Montbazon F 24 F4
Montbéliard F 27 E6
Montbenoît F 31 B9
Montbeton F 33 B8
Montblanc E 42 E6
Montboucher-sur-Jabron F 35 A8
Montbozon F 26 F5
Montbrió del Camp E 42 E6
Montbrison F 30 D5
Montbron F 29 D7
Montbrun F 33 B9
Montbrun-les-Bains F 35 B9
Montcada i Reixac E 43 E8
Montcavrel F 15 F12
Montceau-les-Mines F 30 B5
Montcenis F 30 B5
Montchanin F 30 B5
Montcornet F 19 E9
Montcresson F 25 E8
Montcuq F 33 B8
Montcy-Notre-Dame F 19 E10
Montdardier F 35 C6
Montdidier F 18 E6
Mont-Dore F 30 D2
Monteagudo F 41 F9
Monteagudo de las Salinas E 47 E9
Monteagudo de las Vicarías E 41 F7

Montealegre del Castillo E 55 B10
Montebello Ionico I 59 D8
Montebello Vicentino I 66 B3
Montebelluna I 72 E5
Montebourg F 23 B9
Montebruno I 37 B10
Montecalvo in Foglia I 66 E6
Montecalvo Irpino I 60 A4
Monte-Carlo MC 37 D6
Montecarotto I 67 E7
Montecassiano I 67 F7
Monte Castello di Vibio I 62 B2
Montecastrilli I 62 B2
Montecatini Terme I 66 E2
Montecatini Val di Cecina I 66 F2
Montecchio I 67 E6
Montecchio Emilia I 66 C1
Montecchio Maggiore I 66 A3
Montech F 33 C8
Montechiaro d'Asti I 37 A8
Montechiarugolo I 66 C1
Montecilfone I 63 D7
Montecorice I 60 C3
Montecosaro I 67 F8
Montecreale Valcellina I 73 D6
Montecreto I 66 D1
Monte da Pedra P 44 F5
Monte das Flores P 50 B4
Montederramo E 38 D5
Monte di Procida I 60 B2
Monte do Trigo P 50 C4
Montefalco I 62 B3
Montefalcone di Val Fortore I 60 A4
Montefano I 67 F7
Montefelcino I 67 E6
Montefiascone I 62 B2
Montefiore dell'Aso I 62 A5
Montefiorino I 66 D2
Montefortino I 62 B4
Montefranco I 62 B3
Montefrío E 53 B8
Montegiordano I 61 C7
Montegiorgio I 67 F8
Monte Gordo P 50 E5
Montegranaro I 67 F8
Montegrotto Terme I 66 B4
Montehermoso E 45 D8
Monteiasi I 61 C8
Monteils F 33 B9
Monteiro P 44 A5
Montejaque E 53 C6
Montejícar E 53 A10
Montejo de la Sierra E 46 B5
Montelabbate I 67 E6
Montelanico I 62 D4
Montelavar P 50 B1
Montel-de-Gelat F 29 D11
Monteleone di Puglia I 60 A5
Monteleone d'Orvieto I 62 B2
Monteleone Rocca Doria I 64 C2
Montelepre I 58 C3
Montelibretti I 62 C3
Montélier F 31 F7
Montélimar F 35 A8
Montella I 60 B4
Montellano E 51 E8
Montels F 33 D8
Montelupo Fiorentino I 66 E3
Montelupone I 67 F8
Montemaggiore Belsito I 58 D4
Montemagno I 37 B8
Montemarciano I 67 E7
Montemayor E 53 A7
Montemayor de Pililla E 40 E3
Montembœuf F 29 D7
Montemesola I 61 B8
Montemiletto I 60 A3
Montemilone I 60 A5
Montemolín E 51 C7
Montemonaco I 62 B4
Montemor-o-Novo P 50 B3
Montemurlo I 66 E3
Montemurro I 60 C5
Montenay F 23 D10
Montendre F 28 E5
Montenegro de Cameros E 40 D6
Montenero di Bisaccia I 63 D7
Monteнerodomo I 63 C6
Monte Porzio I 67 E7
Monteprandone I 62 B5
Montepulciano I 62 A1
Monterblanc F 22 E6
Monterchi I 66 F5
Monte Real P 44 E3
Montereale I 62 B4
Montereau-fault-Yonne F 25 D8
Monte Redondo P 44 E3
Monterenzio I 66 D3
Monteriggioni I 66 F3
Monteroduni I 63 D6
Monte Romano I 62 C1
Monteroni d'Arbia I 66 F3
Monteroni di Lecce I 61 C10
Monterosso Almo I 59 E6
Monterosso Calabro I 59 B9
Monterotondo I 62 C3
Monterotondo Marittimo I 66 F2
Monterrei E 38 E5
Monteroso E 38 C4
Monterrubio de la Serena E 51 B9
Monterubbiano I 62 A5
Montesa E 56 D3
Monte San Biagio I 62 E4
Monte San Giovanni Campano I 62 D5
Montesano Salentino I 61 D10
Montesano sulla Marcellana I 60 C5
Monte San Savino I 66 F4
Monte Santa Maria Tiberina I 66 F5
Monte Sant'Angelo I 63 D9
Monte San Vito I 67 E7
Montesarchio I 60 A3
Montescaglioso I 61 B7
Montescudaio I 66 F2
Montese I 66 D2
Montespertoli I 66 E3
Montesquieu-Volvestre F 33 D8
Montesquiou F 33 C6
Montes Velhos P 50 D3
Monteux F 35 B8

Montevago I 58 D2
Montevarchi I 66 E4
Montevecchia I 69 B7
Monteverde I 60 A5
Montevil P 50 C2
Montfaucon F 23 F9
Montfaucon F 29 F9
Montfaucon-d'Argonne F 19 F11
Montfaucon-en-Velay F 30 E5
Montferran-Savès F 33 C7
Montferrat F 36 D4
Montferrier F 33 E9
Montfoort NL 182 A5
Montfort F 23 D8
Montfort F 32 C4
Montfort NL 183 C7
Montfort-en-Chalosse F 32 C4
Montfort-l'Amaury F 24 C6
Montfort-le-Gesnois F 24 D3
Montfort-sur-Risle F 18 F2
Montgai E 42 D5
Montgaillard F 33 D6
Montgaillard F 33 E9
Montgenèvre F 31 F10
Montgeron F 25 C7
Montgiscard F 33 D9
Montguyon F 28 E5
Monthermé F 19 E10
Monthey CH 31 C10
Monthois F 19 F10
Monthureux-sur-Saône F 26 D4
Monti I 64 B3
Monticelli d'Ongina I 69 C8
Monticello F 37 F9
Montichiari I 66 B1
Monticiano I 65 A4
Montiel E 55 B7
Montier-en-Der F 25 D12
Montieri I 65 A4
Montiers-sur-Saulx F 26 C3
Montiglio I 68 C5
Montignac F 29 E8
Montignies-le-Tilleul B 19 D9
Montignoso I 66 D1
Montigny F 27 C4
Montigny-la-Resle F 25 E10
Montigny-le-Roi F 26 D3
Montigny-lès-Metz F 26 B5
Montigny-Mornay-Villeneuve-sur-Vingeanne F 26 E4
Montigny-sur-Aube F 25 E12
Montijo P 51 B6
Montijo P 50 B2
Montilla E 53 A7
Montillana E 53 A9
Montivilliers F 23 A12
Montizón E 55 C6
Montjaux F 34 B4
Montjean F 23 D10
Montjovet I 68 B4
Montlaur F 34 D4
Montlieu-la-Garde F 28 E5
Mont-Louis F 33 F10
Montluçon F 29 C11
Montluel F 31 D7
Montmarault F 30 C2
Montmartin-sur-Mer F 23 C8
Montmédy F 19 E11
Montmélian F 31 D9
Montmelo E 43 D8
Montmeyran F 31 F6
Montmirail F 24 D3
Montmirail F 25 C10
Montmirey-le-Château F 26 F4
Montmoreau-St-Cybard F 29 E6
Montmorillon F 29 C7
Montmorin F 35 B10
Montmorot F 31 B8
Montmort-Lucy F 25 C10
Montoir-de-Bretagne F 23 F7
Montoire-sur-le-Loir F 24 E4
Montoison F 30 F6
Montoito P 50 B4
Montola FIN 124 F8
Montón E 47 B10
Montone I 66 F5
Montopoli di Sabina I 62 C3
Montório al Vomano I 62 B5
Montoro E 53 A8
Montory F 32 D4
Montournais F 28 B4
Montpelier IRL 8 C6
Montpellier F 35 C6
Montpeyroux F 34 A4
Montpezat F 33 D7
Montpezat F 33 D7
Montpezat-de-Quercy F 33 B8
Montpezat-sous-Bauzon F 30 F5
Montpon-Ménesterol F 29 E6
Montpont-en-Bresse F 31 B7
Mont-ras E 43 D10
Montréal F 25 E11
Montréal F 33 C6
Montréal F 33 D10
Montredon-Labessonnié F 33 C10
Montregard F 30 E5
Montréjeau F 33 D7
Montrésor F 24 F5
Montresta I 64 B2
Montret F 31 B7
Montreuil F 15 G12
Montreuil-Bellay F 23 F11
Montreuil-Juigné F 23 E10
Montreux CH 31 C10
Montrevault F 23 F9
Montrevel-en-Bresse F 31 C7
Montrichard F 24 F5
Montricoux F 33 B9
Montrond CH 31 B10
Montrond-les-Bains F 30 D5
Montrose GB 5 B12
Montroy E 48 F3
Monts F 24 F4
Montsalvy F 29 F10
Montsauche-les-Settons F 25 F11
Montségur F 33 E9
Montseny E 43 D8
Montsoué F 32 C4
Mont-sous-Vaudrey F 31 B8
Monts-sur-Guesnes F 29 B6
Montpi P 50 B2
Mont-St-Aignan F 18 F3
Mont-St-Jean F 25 F11
Mont-St-Martin F 19 E12
Mont-St-Vincent F 30 B5
Montsûrs F 23 D10
Montsuzain F 25 D11

Mõntu EST 130 F4
Montuїri E 57 B10
Montvalent F 29 F9
Montville F 18 E3
Montzen B 183 D7
Montzéville F 20 F4
Monza I 69 B7
Monzelfeld D 21 E8
Monzingen D 21 E9
Monzón E 42 D4
Monzón de Campos E 40 D3
Mook NL 183 B7
Moone IRL 7 G9
Moorbad Lobenstein D 75 B10
Moordorf (Südbrookmerland) D 17 B9
Moorends GB 11 D10
Moorenweis D 75 F9
Moorfields GB 4 F5
Moorrege D 82 C7
Moorslede B 19 C7
Moos D 76 E3
Moosbach D 75 C11
Moosburg A 73 C9
Moosburg an der Isar D 75 F10
Moosinning D 75 F10
Mooste EST 131 E14
Mór H 149 B10
Mora E 46 E5
Mora P 50 B3
Mora S 97 B14
Mora S 102 D8
Mora de Rubielos E 48 D3
Moradillo de Roa E 40 E4
Morag PL 139 C8
Mórahalom H 150 E4
Moraice MNE 163 C7
Moraira E 56 D5
Morais P 39 E6
Moraïtika GR 168 E2
Morakovo MNE 163 D7
Móra la Nova E 42 E5
Moral de Calatrava E 54 B5
Moraleda de Zafayona E 53 B9
Moraleja E 45 D7
Moraleja del Vino E 39 F8
Moraleja de Sayago E 45 B9
Morales de Campos E 39 E9
Morales del Vino E 39 F8
Morales de Toro E 39 E9
Morales de Valverde E 39 E8
Moralina E 39 F7
Moräng S 118 D3
Morano Calabro I 60 D6
Morano sul Po I 68 C5
Morar GB 4 B5
Mорареşti RO 160 C5
Morasverdes E 45 C8
Morata de Jalón E 41 F9
Morata de Tajuña E 46 D6
Moratalla E 55 C9
Morava BG 166 C4
Morava SLO 73 E10
Moravany CZ 77 B9
Moravany CZ 77 D11
Moravany SK 145 F4
Moravče SLO 73 E10
Moravice HR 67 B11
Moraviţa RO 159 C7
Morávka CZ 147 B8
Moravská Třebová CZ 77 C11
Moravské Budějovice CZ 77 D9
Moravské Lieskové SK 146 D5
Moravský Beroun CZ 146 B4
Moravský Svätý Ján SK 77 E12
Morawica PL 143 E10
Morawin PL 142 C4
Morbach D 21 E8
Morbegno I 69 A8
Morbier F 31 B9
Mörbisch am See A 149 A7
Mörby S 99 C10
Mörbylånga S 89 B10
Morcenx F 32 B4
Morciano di Leuca I 61 D10
Morciano di Romagna I 66 E6
Morcone I 60 A3
Mordelles F 23 D8
Mordoğan TR 177 B8
Mordy PL 141 F7
More LV 135 B10
Moréac F 22 E6
Moreanes P 50 D4
Morebattle GB 5 D12
Morecambe GB 10 C6
Moreda E 38 B5
Moreda E 55 E6
Morée F 24 E5
Mörel CH 70 E6
Morella E 42 F3
Moreni RO 161 D7
Morenish GB 5 C8
Morentin E 32 E1
Moreruela de Tábara E 39 E8
Mores I 64 B2
Morestel F 31 D7
Moret-sur-Loing F 25 D8
Moretta I 37 B7
Moreuil F 18 E5
Morez F 31 B9
Morfa Nefyn GB 10 F2
Morfasso I 69 D8
Mörfelden D 187 B6
Morfi GR 168 D5
Morfou GR 168 D5
Morfovouni GR 169 F6
Morgat F 22 D2
Morgedal N 95 D8
Morges CH 31 B10
Morgex I 31 D11
Morgongåva S 98 C7
Morhange F 26 C6
Mori I 69 B10
Moria GR 177 A8
Moricone I 62 C3
Morienval F 18 F6
Moriles E 53 B7
Morinë AL 163 E10
Morinë KS 163 E9
Moringen D 78 C6
Morjärv S 118 B9
Mørke DK 86 C6
Mørkøv DK 87 D9
Morkovice CZ 77 D12
Mörkret S 102 C4

Morlaàs F 32 D5
Mouilaix F 22 C4
Morlanne F 32 C4
Morlanwelz B 19 D9
Mörlenbach D 21 E11
Morley F 26 C3
Morley GB 11 D8
Morley's Bridge IRL 8 E4
Mörlunda S 89 A9
Mormanno I 60 D6
Mormant F 25 C8
Mormoiron F 35 C9
Mornant F 30 D6
Mornas F 35 B8
Mornese I 37 B9
Moroeni RO 161 C6
Morolo I 62 D4
Morón de Almazán E 41 F7
Morón de la Frontera E 51 E9
Moros E 41 F8
Morosaglia F 37 G10
Morottaja FIN 115 E4
Morović SRB 158 C3
Morozova RUS 129 F14
Morozovo BG 166 D4
Morozzo I 37 C7
Morpeth GB 5 E13
Mørrevatnet N 104 D8
Morrfjord N 110 D8
Morriston GB 13 B7
Morrovalle I 67 F8
Mörrum S 89 C7
Morsbach D 21 C9
Morschen D 78 D6
Morshyn UA 145 E9
Mörsil S 105 E15
Morsum D 17 C12
Mørsvikbotn N 111 E10
Mortagne-au-Perche F 24 C4
Mortagne-sur-Gironde F 28 E4
Mortagne-sur-Sèvre F 28 A4
Mortágua P 44 D4
Mortain F 23 C10
Mortara I 68 C6
Morteau F 31 A10
Morteaux-Coulibœuf F 23 C11
Mörtebo S 103 E12
Mortegliano I 73 E7
Mortelle I 59 C8
Morteni RO 160 D6
Mortensnes N 112 C11
Mortensnes N 114 C6
Mortimer's Cross GB 13 A9
Morton GB 11 F11
Mortrée F 23 C12
Mörtschach A 73 C6
Mörtsjön S 106 D7
Mörtsjön S 106 E4
Morud DK 86 E6
Morunglav RO 160 E4
Morville GB 10 F6
Mor'ye RUS 129 E15
Morzeszczyn PL 138 C6
Morzine F 31 C10
Mosana MD 153 A11
Mosar BY 133 F2
Mosàs S 92 A6
Mosàtt S 102 B7
Mosbach D 21 F12
Mosbjerg DK 90 D7
Mosborough GB 11 E9
Mosby N 90 C2
Moscavide P 50 B1
Mošćenica HR 148 F6
Mošćenička Draga HR 67 B9
Moschopotamos GR 169 D7
Mosciano Sant'Angelo I 62 B5
Mościcka PL 140 C8
Moscovei MD 154 F2
Moscow GB 5 D8
Moseby DK 86 A5
Mosédis LT 134 D3
Mosel D 79 E11
Möser D 79 B10
Mosina PL 81 B11
Mosjö S 107 E13
Mosjøen N 108 E5
Moskaret N 101 B12
Mosko BIH 162 D5
Moskorzew PL 143 E8
Moskuvaara FIN 115 C1
Moslavna Podravska HR 149 E9
Mosna RO 152 E4
Moşna RO 153 D11
Moşniţa Nouă RO 159 B7
Moso in Passiria I 72 C3
Mosonmagyaróvár H 146 F4
Mosonszolnok H 146 F4
Mošovce SK 147 D7
Moss N 95 D13
Mossala FIN 126 E5
Mossat GB 3 L11
Mossbo S 103 D11
Mössingen D 27 D11
Mossley GB 11 E7
Mossley GB 11 D7
Moss-side GB 4 E3
Mosstakan S 96 C7
Most BG 166 M4
Most CZ 76 A5
Mosteiro E 38 B5
Mosteiro P 44 E5
Mosteiro P 50 D4
Mostek CZ 77 B9
Mošteni RO 161 E7
Mosterhamn N 94 C2
Mostki PL 141 H4
Mostowo PL 139 C9
Most na Soči SLO 73 D8
Móstoles E 46 D5
Mosty PL 141 H4
Mostys'ka UA 144 D7
Mosty u Jablunkova CZ 147 B7
Mosvik N 105 D10
Mosyr UA 144 C9
Moszczenica PL 143 C8
Mota del Cuervo E 47 F7
Mota del Marqués E 39 E9
Moţăieni RO 161 C6
Motala S 92 B6
Motaşсrzyno RO 159 B7
Moţăţei RO 159 E11
Moţca RO 153 C9
Motherwell GB 5 D9
Môtiers CH 31 B10

Motike BIH 156 D6
Motike BIH 157 C7
Motilla del Palancar E 47 E9
Motilleja E 47 F9
Motjärnshyttan S 97 C10
Motovun HR 67 B8
Motril E 55 F6
Motru RO 159 D10
Motta Montecorvino I 63 D8
Motta San Giovanni I 59 C8
Motta Visconti I 69 C6
Motten D 74 B6
Möttingen D 75 E8
Mottola I 61 B8
Möttönen FIN 123 D13
Mötz A 71 C11
Mouchamps F 28 B3
Mouchan F 33 C6
Moudon CH 31 B10
Moudros GR 171 E8
Mougins F 36 D6
Mouhijärvi FIN 127 B9
Moularès F 33 B10
Moulay F 23 D10
Mouleydier F 29 F7
Moulinerne F 23 E11
Moulin-Neuf F 33 D9
Moulins F 30 B3
Moulins-Engilbert F 30 B4
Moulins-la-Marche F 24 C3
Moulis-en-Médoc F 28 E4
Moulismes F 29 C7
Moult F 23 B11
Moulton GB 15 C9
Moulton GB 15 C9
Mountbellew IRL 6 F6
Mountberger GB 5 D10
Mountcharles IRL 6 C6
Mountcollins IRL 8 D4
Mount Hamilton GB 4 F2
Mountjoy GB 4 F2
Mountjoy GB 7 C9
Mountmellick IRL 7 F8
Mount Norris GB 7 D10
Mount Nugent IRL 7 E8
Mountrath IRL 7 F8
Mountshannon IRL 8 C6
Mountsorrel GB 11 F9
Moura P 50 C5
Mourão P 51 C5
Mourenx F 32 D4
Mouriès F 35 C8
Mouries GR 169 B8
Mouriki GR 175 C7
Mourisca do Vouga P 44 C4
Mouriscas P 44 E5
Mournies GR 178 E7
Mourujärvi FIN 121 B11
Mouscron B 19 C7
Moussac F 35 C7
Moussey F 27 D7
Moussoulens F 33 D10
Moussy F 25 F9
Moustéru F 22 C5
Mousteyr F 32 B4
Moustheni GR 170 C6
Moustiers-Ste-Marie F 36 D4
Mouthe F 31 B9
Mouthier-Haute-Pierre F 31 A9
Mouthiers-sur-Boême F 29 D6
Mouthoumet F 34 E4
Moutier CH 27 F7
Moûtiers F 31 E10
Moutiers-les-Mauxfaits F 28 C3
Moutnice CZ 77 E11
Moutsouna GR 177 E6
Moux F 34 D4
Moux-en-Morvan F 25 F11
Mouy F 18 F5
Mouzaki GR 169 F6
Mouzaki GR 174 D4
Mouzay F 19 F11
Mouzon F 19 E11
Moviken S 103 C12
Movila RO 155 D1
Movila Miresii RO 155 C1
Movileni RO 153 C10
Movileni RO 153 F10
Movileni RO 160 E5
Moviliţa RO 153 F10
Moviliţa RO 161 D8
Moville IRL 4 E2
Movollen N 105 F11
Mowtie GB 5 B12
Moy GB 3 L8
Moy GB 7 D9
Moya F 47 E10
Moyasta IRL 8 C3
Moycullen IRL 6 F4
Moy-de-l'Aisne F 19 E7
Moyenmoutier F 27 D6
Moyenneville F 18 D4
Moygashel GB 7 D9
Moyvika UA 154 A2
Moylaw IRL 6 D4
Moylett IRL 7 E8
Moylough IRL 6 F5
Moymore IRL 8 C5
Moyne IRL 7 E7
Moyvalley IRL 7 F9
Moyvore IRL 7 E7
Mozac F 30 D3
Mozăceni RO 160 D6
Mózárbez E 45 C9
Mozelj SLO 73 E10
Mozelos P 44 C5
Mozgovo SRB 159 F8
Mozirje SLO 73 D10
Mozoncillo E 40 F3
Mozsgó H 149 D9
Mozyr' RUS 136 D5
Mračaj BIH 157 E7
Mragowo PL 136 F4
Mrákov CZ 76 D3
Mrakovica BIH 157 B6
Mramor BIH 157 F9
Mratinje MNE 157 F10
Mrežičko MK 169 B6
Mrkalji BIH 157 D10
Mrkonjić-Grad BIH 157 D7
Mrkopalj HR 67 B10
Mrmoš SRB 164 B3
Mrocza PL 85 D13

Mroczeń PL 142 D4
Mroczków PL 141 H3
Mroczno PL 139 D8
Mrozy PL 141 F5
Mścice PL 85 B10
Mściwojów PL 81 D10
Mšené Lázné CZ 76 A6
Mšeno CZ 77 B7
Mshinskaya RUS 132 C6
Mstów PL 143 E7
Mszana PL 147 B7
Mszana Dolna PL 144 D1
Mszczonów PL 141 G3
Muccia I 62 A4
Much D 21 C8
Muchalls GB 5 A12
Mucharz PL 147 B9
Mücheln (Geiseltal) D 79 D10
Muchow D 83 D11
Muchówka PL 144 D1
Much Wenlock GB 10 F6
Mucientes E 39 E9
Mücka D 81 D7
Mücke Große-Eichen D 21 C12
Mücke-Nieder-Ohmen D 21 C12
Muckross IRL 8 D4
Múcsony H 145 G2
Mudanya TR 173 D10
Mudau D 187 B7
Müdelheim D 183 C9
Müden (Aller) D 79 A7
Müden (Örtze) D 83 E8
Mudershach D 185 C8
Mudrets BG 166 E6
Muel E 41 F9
Muelas del Pan E 39 E8
Muff IRL 4 E2
Muga de Sayago E 39 F7
Mugardos E 38 B3
Muge P 44 F3
Mügeln D 80 C4
Mügeln D 80 B10
Mugeni RO 152 E6
Muggensturm D 187 D5
Muggia I 73 E8
Muğla TR 181 B8
Müglen BG 167 D8
Müglizh BG 166 D5
Mugron F 32 C4
Mühlacker D 27 C10
Mühlanger D 79 C12
Mühlbach A 72 B3
Mühlberg D 79 E8
Mühlberg D 80 C5
Mühldorf A 73 C7
Mühldorf am Inn D 75 F12
Mühldorf bei Feldbach A 148 C5
Mühlen A 73 B9
Mühlenbeck D 84 E4
Mühlhausen D 21 F11
Mühlhausen D 75 D9
Mühlhausen (Thüringen) D 79 D7
Mühltroff D 75 A10
Muhola FIN 123 D14
Muhos FIN 119 E15
Muhr am See D 75 D8
Muhur AL 163 F9
Muineachán IRL 7 D9
Muine Bheag IRL 9 C9
Muiños E 38 E4
Muirdrum GB 5 B11
Muirhead GB 5 D8
Muir of Ord GB 2 K8
Muirkirk GB 5 E9
Mujdić BIH 157 D7
Mujejärvi FIN 125 C12
Mukacheve UA 145 G6
Mukařov CZ 77 C7
Mukhavyets BY 141 F9
Mukhovo BG 165 E8
Mukkala FIN 115 D4
Mukkavaara FIN 115 D4
Mula E 55 C10
Mulbarton GB 15 B11
Muleby DK 88 E7
Mulešići BIH 157 C9
Mulfingen D 74 D6
Mülheim an der Ruhr D 17 F7
Mülheim-Kärlich D 185 D7
Mulhouse F 27 E7
Muljava SLO 73 E10
Mullach Íde IRL 7 F10
Mullagh IRL 7 E9
Mullagh IRL 7 F9
Mullaghroe IRL 6 E6
Mullany's Cross IRL 6 D5
Mullartown GB 7 D11
Müllheim D 27 E8
Mullhyttan S 92 A5
Mullingar IRL 7 E8
Mullion GB 12 E4
Müllrose D 80 B6
Mullsjö S 91 D14
Mulrany IRL 6 E3
Mulsanne F 23 E12
Mulseryd S 91 D14
Multia FIN 123 F13
Multperä FIN 121 C15
Mümliswil CH 27 F8
Munakka FIN 122 E9
Muñana E 45 C9
Munapirtti FIN 128 E6
Münchberg D 75 B10
Müncheberg D 80 A6
München D 75 F10
Münchenbernsdorf D 79 E10
Münchenbuchsee CH 31 A11
Münchhausen D 21 C11
Münchsteinach D 75 C8
Münchweiler an der Rodalb D 186 C4
Münchwilen CH 27 F11
Mundaka E 41 B6
Munderkingen D 187 E8
Mundesley GB 15 B11
Mundford GB 15 B10
Mundheim N 94 B3
Mundolsheim F 27 C8
Munebrega E 41 F8
Munera E 55 B8
Mungret IRL 8 C5
Muñico E 45 C10
Muniesa E 42 E2
Munilla E 41 D7
Munka-Ljungby S 87 C11
Munkbyn S 103 B13
Munkebakken N 114 C6
Munkebo DK 86 E7
Munkedal S 91 C10

Munken N 104 D6
Munkflohögen S 106 D7
Munkfors S 97 C10
Munklia N 111 D14
Munksund S 118 D7
Munktorp S 98 C6
Munkzwalm B 19 C8
Munne FIN 128 C7
Münnerstadt D 75 B7
Munningen D 75 E8
Muñogalindo E 46 C3
Munsala FIN 122 D8
Münsingen CH 31 B12
Münsingen D 74 F5
Münster CH 70 E6
Münster D 17 E9
Münster D 21 E11
Münster D 83 E8
Munster F 27 D7
Münsterdorf D 82 C7
Munstergeleen NL 183 D7
Münsterhausen D 75 F7
Münstermaifeld D 185 D7
Muntendam NL 17 B7
Munteni RO 153 F10
Munteni-Buzău RO 161 D9
Muntenii de Jos RO 153 D11
Münzenberg D 21 D11
Münzkirchen A 76 F5
Muodoslompolo S 117 C10
Muonio FIN 117 C11
Muonionalusta S 117 C11
Muotathal CH 71 D7
Muotkajärvi FIN 117 B10
Muotkavaara FIN 117 C12
Mur SRB 163 C9
Muradiye TR 173 D9
Muradiye TR 177 B9
Murakeresztúr H 149 D7
Murań SK 147 D10
Muras E 38 B4
Murasson F 34 C4
Muraste EST 131 C8
Muraszemenye H 149 D7
Murat F 30 E2
Muratlar TR 181 B9
Muratlı TR 173 B7
Murato F 37 F10
Murat-sur-Vèbre F 34 C4
Murau A 73 B9
Murazzano I 37 C8
Murça P 38 F5
Murchante E 41 D8
Mürchevo BG 165 B7
Murcia E 56 F2
Murczyn PL 138 E4
Mur-de-Barrez F 29 F11
Mûr-de-Bretagne F 22 D6
Mur-de-Sologne F 24 F6
Mureck A 148 C5
Mürefte TR 173 C7
Muret F 33 D8
Murgeni RO 153 E12
Murgenthal CH 27 F8
Murgești RO 161 C9
Murgia E 40 C6
Muri CH 27 F9
Muri CH 31 B11
Murias de Paredes E 39 C7
Muriedas E 40 B4
Murighiol RO 155 C4
Murillo de Río Leza E 32 F1
Murillo el Fruto E 32 F3
Murino MNE 163 D8
Murisengo I 68 C5
Murjāni LV 135 B9
Murjek S 116 F5
Murley GB 7 D8
Murlo I 66 F3
Murmastiene LV 135 C13
Murnau am Staffelsee D 72 A3
Muro E 57 B11
Muro F 37 F9
Muro P 38 F2
Muro de Alcoy E 56 D4
Murol F 30 D2
Murole FIN 127 B10
Muron F 28 C4
Murony H 151 D7
Muros E 38 C1
Muros E 39 A7
Muros I 64 B2
Murovane UA 144 C9
Murów PL 142 E4
Murowana Goślina PL 81 A12
Murré AL 168 A3
Murrhardt D 74 E6
Murronkylä FIN 119 E16
Murroogh IRL 6 F4
Mursalli TR 177 D10
Murska Sobota SLO 148 C6
Mursko Središče HR 149 C6
Murtas E 55 F6
Murtede P 44 D4
Murten CH 31 B11
Murter HR 156 E4
Murtino MK 169 B8
Murto FIN 119 E15
Murtolahti FIN 125 D9
Murtomäki FIN 124 B9
Murtomäki FIN 125 D9
Muruamoen N 105 C16
Murvica HR 156 D3
Murviel-lès-Béziers F 34 D5
Mürzsteg A 148 A5
Murzynowo PL 81 A8
Mürzzuschlag A 148 A5
Müsa LV 135 D8
Musbury GB 13 D8
Müschenbach D 185 C8
Musei I 64 E2
Muselievo BG 160 F5
Mushtisht KS 163 E10
Musile di Piave I 72 E6
Muskö S 93 B12
Mussalo FIN 128 E6
Musselburgh GB 5 D10
Musselkanaal NL 17 C8
Mussidan F 29 E6
Mussomeli I 58 D4
Musson B 19 E12
Mussy-sur-Seine F 25 E12
Mustafakemalpaşa TR 173 D9
Mustamaa FIN 119 F17
Mustamaa FIN 123 D10
Mustasaari FIN 122 D7
Mustavaara FIN 121 D12

Mustavaara FIN 121 F12
Mustinlahti FIN 125 E10
Mustjala EST 130 E4
Mustla EST 131 E11
Mustola FIN 114 F4
Mustolanmäki FIN 125 C10
Mustolanmutka FIN 125 B10
Mustvee EST 131 D13
Muszaki PL 139 D10
Muszyna PL 145 E2
Muta SLO 73 C11
Mutala FIN 127 B10
Mutalahti FIN 125 E16
Mütevelli TR 177 B10
Muthill GB 5 C9
Mutilva Baja E 32 E2
Mutné SK 147 C8
Mutriku E 32 D1
Mutterstadt D 21 F10
Mutxamel E 56 E4
Mutzig F 27 C7
Münsterdorf D 82 C7
Mutzschen D 80 D3
Muuga EST 131 C13
Muukajärvi S 116 E10
Muuksi EST 131 B11
Muurame FIN 123 F15
Muurasjärvi FIN 123 C14
Muurikkala FIN 128 D8
Muurla FIN 119 B14
Muurola FIN 119 B14
Muurola FIN 119 B14
Muuruvesi FIN 125 D10
Muxía E 38 B1
Muzillac F 22 E7
Mužla SK 149 A11
Myakishevo RUS 133 C5
Myaretskiya BY 133 F3
Myazhany BY 133 E13
Mybster GB 3 J10
Myckelgensjö S 107 D13
Myckle S 118 E5
Myedna BY 141 G9
Myggenäs S 91 C10
Myggsjö S 102 C8
Myhinpää FIN 124 F7
Myjava SK 146 D5
Mykanów PL 143 E7
Mykhal'cha UA 153 A7
Mykhaylivka UA 154 F5
Myki GR 171 B7
Myklebostad N 110 E9
Mykolaïv UA 145 D8
Mykolaïvka UA 154 E4
Mykolaïvka-Novorosiys'ka UA
  154 E5
Mykonos GR 176 E5
Mykulychyn UA 152 A5
Mykytychi UA 144 B9
Myllykylä FIN 122 E8
Myllykoski FIN 128 D6
Myllykylä FIN 128 D7
Myllylahti FIN 121 D13
Myllymäki FIN 123 E12
Myloi GR 175 E6
Mylopotamos GR 178 C4
Mynämäki FIN 126 D7
Mynttilä FIN 128 C6
Myon F 31 A8
Myory BY 133 E3
Myra GR 169 F4
Myrås S 109 E14
Myre N 110 C9
Myre N 111 B10
Myresjö S 92 E5
Myrhaug N 101 A14
Myrheden S 118 D4
Myrhult S 92 B4
Myrina GR 171 E8
Myriokefala GR 178 E7
Myrkky FIN 122 F7
Myrland N 110 D5
Myrland N 110 D9
Myrland N 111 C10
Myrlandshaugen N 111 C13
Myrmoen N 101 A15
Myrne UA 155 B4
Myrnes N 112 C9
Myrnopillya UA 154 E4
Myrsini GR 174 D3
Myrsini GR 178 B3
Myrskylä FIN 127 D14
Myrties GR 177 F8
Myrviken S 105 E16
Mysen N 95 C14
Myshall IRL 9 C9
Myślachowice PL 143 F7
Myślakowice PL 81 E9
Myślenice PL 147 B9
Myślibórz PL 85 E7
Myślice PL 139 C8
Mysłowice PL 143 F7
Mysovka RUS 134 F2
Mystegna FIN 122 E7
Mystras GR 174 E5
Myszków PL 143 F7
Myszyniec PL 139 D11
Mytikas GR 174 B2
Mytilini GR 177 A8
Mytilinioi GR 177 D8
Mýtna SK 147 E9
Mýto CZ 76 C5

N

Nå N 94 B5
Naaldwijk NL 16 E2
Naamankylä FIN 119 E17
Naamijoki FIN 117 E11
Naantali FIN 126 E7
Naapurinvaara FIN 121 F11
Naarden NL 183 A6
Näärinki FIN 128 B8
Naarn im Machlande A 77 F7
Naartijärvi S 119 C11
Naarva FIN 125 D16
Naas IRL 7 F9
Näätämö FIN 114 D6
Näätänmaa FIN 125 F10
Näätävaara FIN 121 E15
Nabburg D 75 D11
Nábrád H 145 G5
Na Cealla Beaga IRL 6 C6
Náchod CZ 77 B10
Nacina Ves SK 145 F4
Näckådalen S 102 D7
Nackel D 83 E13
Nackenheim D 185 E9

Näcksjö S 103 C12
Na Clocha Liatha IRL 7 F10
Nacpolsk PL 139 E9
Nad IRL 8 D5
Nadalj SRB 158 C4
Nadarzyce PL 85 D11
Nadarzyn PL 141 F3
Naddvik N 100 D6
Nadeş RO 152 E5
Nădlac RO 150 E6
Nădrag RO 159 B9
Nadrichne UA 154 E4
Nádudvar H 151 C7
Năeni RO 161 C8
Nærbø N 94 E3
Nærøset N 101 E13
Nærsnes N 95 C13
Næsbjerg DK 86 D3
Næstved DK 87 E9
Näfels CH 27 F11
Nafferton GB 11 C11
Nafpaktos GR 174 C4
Nafplio GR 175 D6
Nagele NL 16 C5
Naggen S 103 B11
Naglarby S 97 B14
Nagłowice PL 143 E9
Nagold D 27 C10
Nagore E 32 E3
Nago-Torbole I 69 B10
Nagu FIN 126 F6
Nagyatád H 149 D8
Nagybajom H 149 D8
Nagybánhegyes H 151 E6
Nagybaracska H 149 E11
Nagybarca H 145 G2
Nagyberény H 149 C9
Nagyberki H 149 D10
Nagycenk H 149 A7
Nagycsécs H 145 H2
Nagycserkesz H 145 H4
Nagydobos H 145 G5
Nagydorog H 149 C11
Nagyecsed H 145 H5
Nagyfüged H 150 B5
Nagyhalász H 145 G4
Nagyharsány H 149 E10
Nagyhegyes H 151 B7
Nagyigmánd H 149 A10
Nagyiván H 151 C6
Nagykálló H 145 H4
Nagykanizsa H 149 D7
Nagykapornak H 149 C7
Nagykáta H 150 C4
Nagykereki H 151 C8
Nagykőrös H 150 C4
Nagykőrős H 150 C4
Nagykökényes H 150 B4
Nagykovácsi H 149 A11
Nagylak H 150 E6
Nagylóc H 147 E9
Nagylók H 149 C11
Nagylózs H 149 A7
Nagymágocs H 150 D5
Nagymaros H 149 A11
Nagynyárád H 149 F11
Nagyoroszi H 147 F8
Nagyrécse H 149 C8
Nagyrédel H 150 B4
Nagyszénás H 150 D6
Nagyszokoly H 149 C10
Nagytarcsa H 150 B3
Nagytőke H 150 D5
Nagyvarsány H 145 G5
Nagyvázsony H 149 C9
Nagyvisnyó H 145 G1
Naha EST 132 E1
Naharros E 47 D8
Nahe D 83 C8
Nahirne UA 155 C2
Nahrendorf D 83 D9
Naidăş RO 159 D8
Naila D 75 B10
Nailloux F 33 D9
Nailsworth GB 13 B10
Naimakka S 116 A7
Naintré F 29 B6
Naipköy TR 173 C7
Naizin F 22 E6
Najac F 33 B10
Nájera E 40 D6
Nakkälä FIN 117 A11
Nakkerud N 95 B12
Nakkila FIN 126 C7
Náklo CZ 77 C12
Nakło PL 143 E8
Naklo SLO 73 D9
Nakło nad Notecią PL 85 D13
Nakomiady PL 136 E3
Nakotne LV 134 C6
Nakovo SRB 150 F6
Nakskov DK 83 A10
Nalbach D 186 C2
Nalbant RO 155 C3
Nalda E 41 D7
Nálden S 105 E16
Nafjczów PL 141 H6
Nálepkovo SK 145 F2
Näljänkä FIN 121 D11
Nałki FIN 121 E10
Nalliers F 28 C3
Nalžovské Hory CZ 76 D5
Namborn D 21 E8
Nambroca E 46 E5
Namdalseid N 105 C10
Namest RO 160 F6
Náměšť nad Oslavou CZ 77 D10
Náměšť na Hané CZ 77 C12
Námestovo SK 147 C8
Nämpnäs FIN 122 E6
Namsos N 105 C10
Namsskogan N 105 B14
Namsvatn N 105 B15
Namur B 19 D11
Namysłów PL 142 D4
Nana RO 161 E9
Nána SK 147 F7
Nançay F 24 F7
Nanclares de la Oca E 40 C6
Nancy F 26 C5
Nandrin B 183 D6
Nänești RO 161 B10
Nangis F 25 C9
Nannestad N 95 B13
Nanov RO 160 F6
Nant F 34 B5
Nanterre F 25 C7
Nantes F 23 F8
Nanteuil-le-Haudouin F 25 B8

Nantiat F 29 C8
Nantua F 31 C8
Nantwich GB 10 E6
Naousa GR 169 C7
Naousa GR 176 E5
Napajedla CZ 146 C5
Napiwoda PL 139 D9
Napkor H 145 H4
Napola I 58 D2
Napoli I 60 B2
Napp N 110 D5
Năpradea RO 151 C11
Náquera E 48 E4
Năr S 93 E13
Nåra N 100 D1
Nárai H 149 B7
Narberth GB 12 B5
Narbolia I 64 C2
Narbonne F 34 D5
Narbonne-Plage F 34 D5
Narborough GB 15 B10
Narbuvoll N 101 B14
Narcao I 64 E2
Narcy F 25 F9
Nardò I 61 C10
Narechenski Bani BG 165 F10
Narew PL 140 E9
Narewka PL 141 E9
Närhilä FIN 123 E16
Narin IRL 6 C6
Nărînciems LV 134 B4
Narkaus FIN 119 B16
Narken S 116 E9
Narlidere TR 177 C9
Narni I 62 B3
Naro I 58 E4
Narol PL 144 C7
Närpes FIN 122 F6
Narrosse F 32 C3
Narta HR 149 E7
Nartë AL 168 D1
Näruja RO 153 F9
Naruska FIN 115 D6
Naruszewo PL 139 E9
Narva EST 132 C3
Narva FIN 127 C10
Narva-Jõesuu EST 132 C3
Närvijoki FIN 122 E7
Narvik N 111 D13
Narzole I 37 B7
Narzym PL 139 D9
Näs FIN 99 B14
Näs S 93 E12
Näs S 97 B12
Näs S 102 A8
Näsåker S 107 E11
Näsäud RO 152 C4
Nasavrky CZ 77 C9
Näsberg S 103 C10
Nasbinals F 34 A5
Näs bruk S 98 B6
Näsby S 89 C10
Na Sceirí IRL 7 E10
Näset S 103 C9
Nashec KS 163 E10
Našice HR 149 F10
Nasielsk PL 139 E10
Näske S 107 E15
Näsliden S 107 A16
Naso I 59 C6
Nassau D 21 D9
Nassereith A 71 C11
Nässja S 92 C5
Nässjö S 92 D5
Nässjö S 107 B11
Nassogne B 19 D11
Nästätten D 185 D8
Nästeln S 102 A7
Nastola FIN 127 D14
Năsturelu RO 161 F6
Näsum S 88 C7
Nasutów PL 141 H6
Näsviken S 103 C12
Näsviken S 106 D9
Naszály H 149 A10
Natalinci SRB 159 E6
Nateby GB 11 C7
Naters CH 68 A4
Nattavaara S 116 E6
Nattavaara by S 116 E6
Nattheim D 75 E7
Nätraby S 89 C9
Naturno I 71 D11
Naucelle F 33 B10
Naucelles F 29 F10
Naudaskalns LV 133 B2
Nauders A 71 D11
Naudîte LV 134 C6
Nauen D 79 A12
Nauendorf D 79 C10
Nauheim D 21 E10
Naujac-sur-Mer F 28 E3
Naujamiestis LT 135 E8
Naujasis Daugėliškis LT 135 F12
Naujoji Akmenė LT 134 D5
Naujoji Vilnia LT 137 D11
Naukšēni LV 131 F10
Naul IRL 7 E10
Naulaperä FIN 121 E10
Naulavaara FIN 125 C9
Naumburg (Hessen) D 17 F12
Naumburg (Saale) D 79 D10
Naundorf D 80 D4
Naundorf D 80 E4
Naunhof D 79 D12
Nauroth D 21 C9
Naustad N 108 B8
Naustbukta N 105 B11
Naustdal N 100 C3
Nauste N 101 A9
Nautijaur S 109 C17
Nautsi RUS 114 F4
Nautsund N 100 D2
Nava E 39 B9
Navacepeda de Tormes E 45 D10
Navaconcejo E 45 D9
Nava de Arévalo E 46 C3
Nava del Rey E 39 F9
Nava de Sotrobal E 45 C10
Navafría E 46 B5
Navahermosa E 46 E4
Navajas E 48 E4
Naval E 42 C4
Navalagamella E 46 D4
Navalcaballo E 41 E7
Navalcán E 45 D10
Navalcarnero E 46 D4
Navalero E 40 E6
Navalmanzano E 46 B4

Navalmoral E 46 D3
Navalmoral de la Mata E 45 E9
Navalonguilla E 45 D10
Navalosa E 46 D3
Navalperal de Pinares E 46 C4
Navaluenga E 46 D3
Navalvillar de Ibor E 45 E10
Navalvillar de Pela E 45 F9
Navamorcuende E 46 D3
Navan IRL 7 E9
Navapolatsk BY 133 E5
Navarcles E 43 D7
Navardún E 32 E3
Navarredonda de la Rinconada
  E 45 C9
Navarrenx F 32 D4
Navarrés E 48 F3
Navarrete E 41 D6
Navarrevisca E 46 D3
Navàs E 43 D7
Navascués E 32 E3
Navas de Estrena E 46 E3
Navas de Jorquera E 47 F9
Navas del Madroño E 45 E7
Navas del Rey E 46 D4
Navas de Oro E 46 B4
Navas de San Juan E 55 C6
Navasfrías E 45 D7
Navata E 43 C9
Navatalgordo E 46 D3
Nave I 69 B9
Nave P 44 C5
Nave de Haver P 45 C7
Nävekvarn S 93 B9
Navelli I 62 C5
Nåverdal N 101 A12
Näverede S 106 E8
Nave Redonda P 50 E3
Navenga I 68 B4
Näverkärret S 97 C13
Näverrys FIN 119 C15
Naverstad S 91 B10
Navès E 43 D7
Naves F 29 E9
Navezuelas E 45 E10
Navia E 39 A6
Navilly F 31 B7
Navit N 112 D8
Năvodari RO 155 E3
Năvrăgöl S 89 C9
Nawojowa PL 145 D2
Naxos GR 176 E5
Nay-Bourdettes F 32 D5
Nazza D 79 D7
Ndroq AL 168 A2
Nea Agathoupoli GR 169 C8
Nea Alikarnassos GR 178 E9
Nea Anchialos GR 169 F7
Nea Apollonia GR 169 C9
Nea Artaki GR 175 B8
Nea Efesos GR 169 D7
Nea Epidavros GR 175 D7
Nea Figaleia GR 174 E4
Nea Filadelfeia GR 175 C8
Nea Fokaia GR 169 D9
Nea Ionia GR 169 F7
Nea Iraklitsa GR 171 C6
Nea Karvali GR 171 C6
Nea Karya GR 171 C7
Nea Kerdylia GR 169 C10
Nea Kios GR 175 D6
Nea Koroni GR 174 F4
Nea Lampsakos GR 175 C8
Nea Liosia GR 175 C8
Nea Madytos GR 169 C10
Nea Makri GR 175 C8
Nea Malgara GR 169 C8
Nea Mesimvria GR 169 C8
Nea Michaniona GR 169 D8
Nea Moudania GR 169 D9
Nea Olynthos GR 169 D9
Nea Pella GR 169 C8
Nea Peramos GR 171 C6
Nea Peramos GR 175 C7
Nea Plagia GR 169 D9
Neapoli GR 168 D5
Neapoli GR 178 B5
Neapoli GR 178 F9
Nea Poteidaia GR 169 D9
Nea Roda GR 170 D5
Nea Santa GR 169 C8
Nea Santa GR 171 B9
Nea Silata GR 169 D9
Nea Styra GR 175 C9
Neath GB 13 B7
Nea Tiryntha GR 175 D6
Nea Triglia GR 169 D9
Neaua RO 152 E5
Nea Vrasna GR 175 D9
Nea Vyssa GR 171 A11
Nea Zichni GR 169 B10
Nebel D 82 A4
Nébias F 33 E10
Neblje GR 169 B9
Nebljusi HR 156 C4
Nebra (Unstrut) D 79 D10
Nebreda E 40 E5
Nechanice CZ 77 B9
Nerezine HR 67 C9
Neckarbischofsheim D 187 C6
Neckargemünd D 21 F11
Neckarsteinach D 21 F11
Neckarsulm D 21 F12
Neçeşti RO 160 E6
Necton GB 15 B10
Nečujam HR 156 F5
Neda E 38 B3
Nedansjö S 103 B12
Nedašov CZ 146 C6
Neddemin D 84 C4
Nedelino BG 171 B7
Nedelišče HR 149 D6
Nederby DK 86 B4
Nederhogen S 102 B7
Nederhorst den Berg NL 183 A6
Nederlangbroek NL 183 A6
Neder Vindinge DK 87 E9
Nederweert NL 16 F5
Nedlitz D 79 B11
Nedožery-Brezany SK 147 D7
Nedrebø N 94 E4
Nedre Saxnäs S 109 F14
Nedre Soppero S 116 B8
Nedstrand N 94 D3
Nedvědice CZ 77 D10
Nedyalsko BG 167 E7
Njdza PL 142 F5

Neede NL 17 D7
Needham Market GB 15 C11
Neer NL 183 C8
Neermoor D 17 B8
Neerpelt B 19 B11
Neetze D 83 D9
Nefyn GB 10 F2
Negenborn D 78 C6
Negoi RO 160 F2
Negomir RO 159 D11
Negorci MK 169 B7
Negoslavci HR 157 B11
Negotin SRB 159 E10
Negotino MK 169 B7
Negrar I 66 A2
Negrași RO 160 D6
Negredo E 47 B8
Negreira E 38 C2
Nègrepelisse F 33 B9
Negrești RO 153 D10
Negrești-Oaş RO 145 H7
Negri RO 153 D9
Negru Vodă RO 155 F2
Nehoiu RO 161 C8
Neiden IRL 8 E3
Neitaskaite S 116 E8
Neitsuanto S 116 F6
Neittävä FIN 119 E17
Neive I 37 B8
Nejdek CZ 75 B12
Nekézseny H 145 G1
Nekla PL 81 B12
Nekső DK 89 E8
Nelas P 44 C5
Nellim FIN 114 F4
Nellingen D 74 E6
Nelson GB 11 D7
Nemaitonys LT 137 D9
Neman RUS 136 C5
Nemanjica MK 164 F4
Nemanskoye RUS 136 C5
Nembro I 69 B8
Nemea GR 175 D6
Nemčice CZ 146 C4
Němčiněves D 137 D11
Nemesgulács H 149 C8
Nemesnádudvar H 150 E3
Nemesvámos H 149 B9
Nemesvid H 149 C8
Németkér H 149 C11
Nemežis LT 137 D11
Nemours F 25 D7
Nemsdorf-Göhrendorf D 79 D10
Nemšová SK 146 D6
Nemunaitis LT 137 E9
Nemunėlio Radviliškis LT
  135 D9
Nemyriv UA 144 C7
Nenagh IRL 8 C6
Nendaz CH 31 C12
Nenince SK 147 E8
Nenita GR 177 C7
Nennhausen D 79 A12
Nennslingen D 75 D9
Nenonpelto FIN 124 F8
Nentershausen D 21 C9
Nentershausen D 78 D6
Nenthead GB 5 F12
Nenzing A 71 C9
Neo Agioneri GR 169 C8
Neochoraki GR 175 C7
Neochori GR 169 B9
Neochori GR 169 F6
Neochori GR 171 B10
Neochori GR 174 A3
Neo Erasmio GR 171 C7
Neoi Epivates GR 169 C8
Neo Monastiri GR 169 F7
Neoneli I 64 C2
Neo Petritsi GR 169 B9
Neorić HR 156 E6
Neos Kafkasos GR 168 C5
Neos Marmaras GR 169 D10
Neos Mylotopos GR 169 C7
Neos Pagontas GR 175 B8
Neos Pyrgos GR 175 B8
Neos Skopos GR 169 B10
Néoules F 36 E4
Nepi I 62 C2
Nepomuk CZ 76 D5
Nérac F 33 B6
Neratovice CZ 77 B7
Nerău RO 150 F6
Neravai LT 137 E9
Nerchau D 79 D12
Nercillac F 28 D5
Nerdal N 101 A9
Nerde Gårdsjö S 103 E9
Néré F 28 D5
Nereju RO 153 F9
Neresheim D 75 E7
Neresnica SRB 159 E8
Neresnytsya UA 145 G8
Nereta LV 135 D10
Nereto I 62 B5
Nerezine HR 67 C9
Nerežišče HR 156 F6
Néris-les-Bains F 29 C11
Nerja E 53 C9
Nerkoo FIN 124 B8
Nerlia N 108 C7
Nerokouros GR 178 E7
Néronde F 30 D5
Nérondes F 30 B2
Neroth D 21 D7
Nerpio E 55 C8
Nersac F 28 D5
Nersingen D 75 F7
Nerskogen N 101 A11
Nerushay UA 155 B5
Nerva E 51 D6
Nervesa della Battaglia I 72 E5
Nervieux F 30 D5
Nes FO 2 A3
Nes N 95 D9
Nes N 110 D9
Nes N 111 D10
Nes NL 16 B5
Nesbyen N 101 E10
Neschwitz D 80 D6
Nesebŭr BG 167 D9
Neset N 112 C7
Nes Flaten N 94 C5
Nesgrenda N 90 B4
Nesheim N 94 D3
Nesje N 110 D6
Nesjegjerde N 100 A6

Nesland N 110 D5
Neslandsvatn N 90 B5
Nesle F 18 E6
Nesna N 108 D5
Nesovice CZ 77 D12
Nessa F 37 F9
Nesse D 17 B8
Nesseby N 114 C6
Nesselwang D 71 B11
Nesslau D 27 F11
Nessodtangen N 95 C13
Nestani GR 175 D5
Nestby N 108 B9
Nesterov RUS 136 D6
Neston GB 10 E5
Nestorio GR 168 C5
Nestoyita UA 154 B4
Nesttun N 94 B2
Nesvady SK 146 F6
Nesvik N 94 D3
Nethy Bridge GB 3 L9
Netolice CZ 76 D6
Netphen D 21 C10
Netra (Ringgau) D 79 D7
Netretić HR 148 E4
Netstal CH 71 C8
Nettancourt F 25 C12
Nettersheim D 21 D7
Nettetal D 16 F6
Nettuno I 62 E3
Netvořice CZ 77 C7
Neu-Anspach D 21 D11
Neubeckum D 17 E10
Neuberg D 82 A7
Neuberg an der Mürz A 148 A5
Neubeuern D 72 A5
Neubiberg D 75 F10
Neubrandenburg D 84 C4
Neubruchhausen D 17 C11
Neubrunn D 187 B8
Neubukow D 83 B11
Neubulach D 27 C10
Neuburg am Rhein D 187 D5
Neuburg an der Donau D 75 E9
Neuburg-Steinhausen D 83 C11
Neuburxdorf D 80 D4
Neuchâtel CH 31 B10
Neu Darchau D 83 D9
Neudietendorf D 79 E8
Neudorf A 146 F2
Neudrossenfeld D 75 B10
Neuenbürg D 27 C10
Neuendettelsau D 75 D8
Neuenhagen Berlin D 80 A5
Neuenhaus D 17 C8
Neuenhof CH 27 F9
Neuenkirchen D 17 A11
Neuenkirchen D 17 C11
Neuenkirchen D 17 D9
Neuenkirchen D 17 D9
Neuenkirchen D 82 D7
Neuenkirchen D 84 B4
Neuenkirchen (Oldenburg) D
  17 C10
Neuenkirchen-Seelscheid D
  21 C8
Neuenrade D 185 B8
Neuenstadt am Kocher D
  27 C11
Neuenstein D 187 C8
Neuenwalde D 17 A11
Neuerburg D 20 D6
Neufahrn bei Freising D 75 F10
Neufahrn in Niederbayern D
  75 E11
Neufchâteau B 19 E11
Neufchâtel-en-Bray F 18 E3
Neufchâtel-Hardelot F 15 F12
Neufchâtel-sur-Aisne F 19 F9
Neufeld D 17 A12
Neufeld an der Leitha A 77 G10
Neuffen D 27 C11
Neufmanil F 184 E2
Neufra D 27 D11
Neugersdorf D 81 D7
Neuharlingersiel D 17 A9
Neuhaus A 73 A11
Neuhaus A 73 C10
Neuhaus (Oste) D 17 A12
Neuhaus am Inn D 76 F4
Neuhaus am Klausenbach A
  148 C6
Neuhaus am Rennweg D 75 A9
Neuhaus an der Pegnitz D
  75 C10
Neuhausen CH 27 E10
Neuhausen D 80 E4
Neuhausen D 187 D6
Neuhausen ob Eck D 27 E10
Neuhof D 74 B6
Neuhof an der Zenn D 75 D8
Neuhofen D 187 C5
Neuhofen an der Krems A 76 F6
Neuillé-Pont-Pierre F 24 E4
Neuilly F 25 F10
Neuilly-en-Thelle F 18 F5
Neuilly-le-Réal F 30 C3
Neuilly-l'Évêque F 26 E3
Neuilly-St-Front F 25 B9
Neu-Isenburg D 187 A6
Neukalen D 83 C13
Neu Kaliß D 83 D10
Neukirch D 81 D7
Neukirchen D 21 C12
Neukirchen D 80 E3
Neukirchen D 83 B10
Neukirchen am Großvenediger A
  72 B5
Neukirchen an der Enknach A
  76 F4
Neukirchen an der Vöckla A
  76 F4
Neukirchen-Balbini D 75 D11
Neukirchen beim Heiligen Blut
  D 76 D3
Neukirchen vorm Wald D 76 E4
Neukloster D 83 C11
Neulengbach A 77 F9
Neuler D 75 E7
Neulewin D 84 E6
Neulikko FIN 121 E10
Neulise F 30 D5
Neu Lübbenau D 80 B5
Neum BIH 162 D4
Neumagen D 185 E6
Neumarkt am Wallersee A 73 A7
Neumarkt im Mühlkreis A 77 F6

Neumarkt in der Oberpfalz D 75 D9
Neumarkt in Steiermark A 73 B9
Neumarkt-Sankt Veit D 75 F12
Neu Mukran D 84 B5
Neumünster D 83 B7
Neunburg vorm Wald D 75 D11
Neundorf D 75 A11
Neustadt D 79 E10
Neung-sur-Beuvron F 24 E6
Neunkirch CH 27 E10
Neunkirchen A 148 A6
Neunkirchen D 21 C10
Neunkirchen D 21 D8
Neuötting D 75 F12
Neupetershain D 80 C6
Neupölla A 77 E8
Neureichenau D 76 E5
Neuruppin D 83 E13
Neuschönau D 76 E4
Neusiedl am See A 77 G11
Neusorg D 75 C10
Neuss D 21 B7
Neussargues-Moissac F 30 E2
Neustadt D 27 E9
Neustadt D 79 E10
Neustadt D 83 E12
Neustadt (Harz) D 79 C8
Neustadt (Hessen) D 21 C12
Neustadt (Wied) D 21 C8
Neustadt am Kulm D 75 C10
Neustadt am Rübenberge D 78 A5
Neustadt an der Aisch D 75 C8
Neustadt an der Donau D 75 E10
Neustadt an der Waldnaab D 75 C11
Neustadt an der Weinstraße D 21 F10
Neustadt bei Coburg D 75 B9
Neustadt-Glewe D 83 D11
Neustadt in Holstein D 83 B9
Neustadt in Sachsen D 80 D6
Neustift im Stubaital A 72 B3
Neustrelitz D 84 D4
Neutraubling D 75 E11
Neutrebbin D 80 A6
Neu-Ulm D 74 F7
Neuvéglise F 30 F2
Neuves-Maisons F 186 D1
Neuvic F 29 E6
Neuvic F 29 E10
Neuville-aux-Bois F 24 D7
Neuville-de-Poitou F 29 B6
Neuville-les-Dames F 31 C7
Neuville-lès-Dieppe F 18 E3
Neuville-sur-Saône F 30 D6
Neuilly-en-Argonne F 26 B3
Neuvy-le-Roi F 24 E4
Neuvy-Pailloux F 29 B9
Neuvy-St-Sépulchre F 29 B9
Neuvy-sur-Barangeon F 25 F7
Neuweiler D 27 C10
Neuwied D 21 D8
Neuwittenbek D 83 B8
Neu Wulmstorf D 83 D7
Neu Zauche D 80 C6
Neuzelle D 81 B7
Neu Zittau D 80 B5
Névache F 31 E10
Nevarènai LT 134 D4
Neveja LV 130 F4
Neveklov CZ 77 C7
Nevel' RUS 133 D7
Nevele B 19 B8
Neverfjord N 113 C12
Nevernes N 108 F4
Neverness N 110 C9
Neveronys LT 137 D9
Nevers F 30 A3
Nevesinje BIH 157 F9
Nevestino BG 165 E6
Névez F 22 E4
Neviano I 61 C10
Néville F 18 E2
Nevlunghavn N 90 B6
Nevsha BG 167 C8
New Abbey GB 5 E9
New Aberdour GB 3 K12
New Alresford GB 13 C12
Newark-on-Trent GB 11 E10
Newbawn IRL 9 D9
Newbiggin-by-the-Sea GB 5 E13
Newbliss IRL 7 D8
Newborough GB 11 F11
Newbridge GB 13 B8
Newbridge IRL 7 F9
New Buildings GB 4 F2
Newburgh GB 3 L12
Newburgh GB 5 C10
Newbury GB 13 C12
Newby Bridge GB 10 C6
Newcastle GB 9 D11
Newcastle GB 13 A8
Newcastle IRL 7 F10
Newcastle IRL 9 D8
Newcastle Emlyn GB 12 A6
Newcastleton GB 5 E11
Newcastle-under-Lyme GB 11 E7
Newcastle upon Tyne GB 5 F13
Newcastle West IRL 8 D4
New Cumnock GB 5 E8
New Deer GB 3 K12
Newel D 21 E7
Newent GB 13 B10
New Galloway GB 5 E8
New Inn IRL 6 F6
New Inn IRL 7 E8
Newinn IRL 9 C7
New Kildimo IRL 8 C5
Newmarket GB 2 J4
Newmarket GB 15 C9
Newmarket IRL 8 D4
Newmarket IRL 9 D8
Newmarket-on-Fergus IRL 8 C5
Newmill GB 3 K11
New Milton GB 13 D11
Newnham GB 13 B10
New Pitsligo GB 3 K12
Newport GB 3 J10
Newport GB 11 F7
Newport GB 12 A5
Newport GB 13 B9
Newport GB 13 D12
Newport IRL 6 E3
Newport IRL 8 C6
Newport-on-Tay GB 5 C11
Newport Pagnell GB 15 C7

Newport Trench GB 4 F3
New Quay GB 12 A6
Newquay GB 12 E4
New Radnor GB 13 A8
New Romney GB 15 F10
New Ross IRL 9 D9
Newry GB 7 D10
Newton GB 4 C6
Newton GB 10 D7
Newton Abbot GB 13 D7
Newton Aycliffe GB 5 F13
Newton Ferrers GB 12 E6
Newtonhill GB 5 A12
Newton-le-Willows GB 10 E6
Newton Mearns GB 5 D8
Newtonmore GB 5 A8
Newton Stewart GB 4 F8
Newtown GB 10 F5
Newtown GB 13 A9
Newtown IRL 6 F6
Newtown IRL 8 F9
Newtown IRL 9 C8
Newtownabbey GB 4 F5
Newtownbarry IRL 9 C9
Newtownbutler GB 7 D8
Newtown Crommelin GB 4 F4
Newtown Forbes IRL 7 E7
Newtownmountkennedy IRL 7 F10
Newtown Mount Kennedy IRL 7 F10
Newtown St Boswells GB 5 D11
Newtownstewart GB 4 F2
Nexon F 29 D8
Neyland GB 12 B5
Nezamyslice CZ 77 D12
Nezavertailovca MD 154 D5
Nézsa H 147 F8
Nezvěstice CZ 76 C5
Nianfors S 103 C12
Niata GR 175 F6
Nibbiano I 37 B10
Nibe DK 86 B5
Nīca LV 134 D2
Nicastro I 59 B9
Nice F 37 D6
Nīcgale LV 135 D12
Nichelino I 37 A7
Nickelsdorf A 77 G12
Nicolae Bălcescu RO 153 B9
Nicolae Bălcescu RO 153 E9
Nicolae Bălcescu RO 155 D3
Nicolae Bălcescu RO 155 C2
Nicolae Bălcescu RO 160 D4
Nicolae Bălcescu RO 161 E9
Nicolae Titulescu RO 160 E5
Nicolaevca MD 154 B2
Nicolosi I 59 D7
Nicoreni MD 153 B11
Nicoreşti RO 153 E9
Nicosia I 58 D5
Nicotera I 59 B8
Nicşeni RO 153 B9
Niculeşti RO 161 D8
Niculiţel RO 155 C2
Nida LT 134 F1
Nidau CH 27 F7
Nidda D 21 D12
Nidzica PL 139 D9
Niebla E 51 E6
Nieborów PL 141 F2
Niebüll D 82 A5
Niebylec PL 144 D4
Niechanowo PL 138 F4
Niechcice PL 143 D8
Niechonin PL 139 D9
Niechlów PL 81 C10
Niechorze PL 85 B8
Niederaichbach D 75 E11
Niederanven L 20 E6
Niederau D 80 D5
Niederaula D 78 E6
Niederbipp CH 27 F8
Niederbrechen D 21 D10
Niederbreitbach D 185 C2
Niederbronn-les-Bains F 27 C8
Niederfinow D 84 E5
Niederfischbach D 185 C6
Niedergörsdorf D 80 C3
Niederkassel D 21 C8
Niederkirchen D 21 E9
Niederkrüchten D 20 B6
Niederndorf A 72 A5
Niederneisen D 21 D10
Niedernhall D 74 D6
Niederoderwitz D 81 E7
Nieder-Olm D 185 E9
Nieder-Rodenbach D 21 D12
Niederroßla D 79 D9
Niedersachswerfen D 79 C8
Niederstetten D 74 D6
Niederurnen CH 27 F11
Niederviehbach D 75 E11
Niederwerrn D 75 B7
Niederwörresbach D 186 B3
Niederzissen D 21 C10
Niedrzwica Duża PL 141 H6
Niedźwiada PL 141 G7
Niedźwiadna PL 139 C13
Niegosław PL 85 E9
Niegosławice PL 81 C9
Niegowa PL 143 E7
Niegripp D 79 B10
Nieheim D 17 E12
Niekerk NL 16 B6
Niekłań Wielki PL 141 H3
Niekursko PL 85 D10
Niel B 182 C4
Nielisz PL 144 B7
Niemberg D 79 C11
Niemce PL 141 H7
Niemcza PL 81 E11
Niemegk D 79 B12
Niemelä FIN 115 C10
Niemelä FIN 115 E5
Niemelänkylä FIN 119 F12
Niemenkylä FIN 122 E7
Niemenkylä FIN 126 C6
Niemenpää FIN 119 C11
Niemis S 119 C11
Niemisel S 118 B7
Niemisjärvi FIN 123 F16
Niemisjärvi FIN 123 E11
Niemiskylä FIN 123 C17
Niemodlin PL 142 E5
Niemysłów PL 142 C6
Nienadówka PL 144 C5
Nienburg (Saale) D 79 C10

Nienburg (Weser) D 17 C12
Niepars D 84 B3
Niepołomice PL 143 F9
Nieporjt PL 139 F11
Nierstein D 21 E10
Niesa FIN 117 D11
Niesi FIN 117 D15
Niesky D 81 D7
Nieświń PL 141 H2
Nieszawa PL 138 E6
Nietsak S 116 D4
Nietulisko Duże PL 143 E11
Nieul F 29 D8
Nieuw-Amsterdam NL 17 C7
Nieuw-Bergen NL 16 E6
Nieuwegein NL 16 D3
Nieuwe-Niedorp NL 16 C3
Nieuwe Pekela NL 17 B7
Nieuwerkerk NL 16 E2
Nieuwerkerk aan de IJssel NL 16 E3
Nieuwerkerken B 19 C11
Nieuwe-Tonge NL 16 E2
Nieuw-Heeten NL 16 D6
Nieuwkoop NL 16 D3
Nieuw-Loosdrecht NL 183 A6
Nieuw-Milligen NL 183 A7
Nieuw-Namen NL 182 C4
Nieuwolda NL 17 B7
Nieuwpoort B 18 B6
Nieuwveen NL 182 A5
Nieuw-Vennep NL 16 D3
Nieuw-Vossemeer NL 182 B4
Nieuw-Weerdinge NL 17 C7
Nievern D 185 D8
Niewęgłosz PL 141 G7
Niezabyszewo PL 85 B12
Nigrán E 38 D2
Nigrande LV 134 D4
Nigrita GR 169 C10
Nigüelas E 53 C9
Niherne F 29 B9
Niinilahti FIN 123 E15
Niinimaa FIN 123 D11
Niinimäki FIN 125 C10
Niinisalo FIN 126 B8
Niinivaara FIN 125 D11
Niinivesi FIN 123 E14
Niirokumpu FIN 121 B11
Nijar E 55 F8
Nijemci HR 157 B11
Nijkerk NL 16 D5
Nijlen B 19 B10
Nijmegen NL 16 E5
Nijverdal NL 17 D6
Nikaia GR 169 E7
Nikaranperä FIN 123 E14
Nikel' RUS 114 E8
Niki GR 168 C5
Nikisiani GR 170 C6
Nikiti GR 169 D10
Nikkala S 119 C11
Nikkaluokta S 111 E17
Nikkaroinen FIN 127 C14
Nikkeby N 112 C6
Nikodin MK 169 B6
Nikokleia GR 169 C9
Nikolaevo BG 165 C10
Nikolaevo BG 166 D5
Nikola-Kozlevo BG 161 F10
Nikolovo BG 161 F8
Nikolsdorf A 73 C6
Nikopol BG 160 F5
Nikopoli GR 174 A2
Nīkrāce LV 134 C3
Nikšić MNE 163 D6
Nikyup BG 166 C5
Nilivaara FIN 117 C14
Nilivaara S 116 D7
Nilsiä FIN 125 D10
Nilvange F 20 F6
Nim DK 86 D5
Nîmes F 35 C7
Nimigea RO 152 C4
Nimis I 73 D7
Nimisenkangas FIN 125 C11
Nimisjärvi FIN 119 E17
Nimtofte DK 86 C7
Nin HR 67 D11
Nina EST 131 D14
Nindorf D 82 B6
Ninemile Bar GB 5 E9
Ninemilehouse IRL 9 D8
Ninove B 19 C9
Niort F 28 C5
Nirza LV 133 D3
Niš SRB 164 C4
Nisa P 44 E5
Nisbet GB 5 D11
Niscemi I 58 E5
Niška Banja SRB 164 C5
Niskankorpi FIN 123 C13
Niskanpera FIN 119 B15
Nisko PL 144 B5
Niskos FIN 123 E10
Nismes F 19 D10
Nispen NL 16 E2
Nisporeni MD 154 C2
Nissafors FIN 91 E14
Nissan-lez-Enserune F 34 D5
Nissilä FIN 123 C17
Nissinvaara FIN 121 B13
Nissoria I 58 D5
Nissumby DK 86 B2
Nissum Seminarieby DK 86 B2
Nistelrode NL 16 E5
Nistoreşti RO 153 F9
Nītaure LV 135 B10
Nitra SK 146 E6
Nitrianske Hrnčiarovce SK 146 E6
Nitrianske Pravno SK 147 D7
Nitrianske Rudno SK 146 D6
Nitrianske Sučany SK 146 D6
Nitry F 25 E10
Nitta S 91 D13
Nittedal N 95 B13
Nittel D 20 E6
Nittenau D 75 D11
Nittorp S 91 E14
Niukkala FIN 129 B12
Nivå DK 87 D11
Niva FIN 121 F14
Nivala FIN 123 C13
Nivankylä FIN 117 E15
Nivanpää FIN 117 E11
Nivelles B 19 C9
Nivenskoye RUS 136 D2
Nivillac F 23 F7
Nivillers F 18 F5
Nívnice CZ 146 C5
Nivolas-Vermelle F 31 D7

Nivyanin BG 165 C8
Niwiska PL 143 F12
Nižbor CZ 76 C5
Nižná SK 147 C9
Nižná Slaná SK 145 F1
Nižný Hrabovec SK 145 F4
Nižný Hrušov SK 145 F4
Nižný Šipov SK 145 F4
Nizza di Sicilia I 59 D7
Nizza Monferrato I 37 B8
Njavve S 109 C17
Njegoš S 116 D4
Njegovuđa MNE 163 C7
Njé Maj AL 168 C3
Njetjavare S 116 E4
Njivice HR 67 B10
Njurundabommen S 103 B13
Njutånger S 103 C13
No DK 86 C2
Noailhan F 32 C5
Noailles F 18 F5
Noain E 32 E2
Noale I 66 A4
Noalejo E 53 A9
Noasca I 31 E11
Nöbbele S 89 B8
Nobber IRL 7 E9
Nobitz D 79 E11
Noblejas E 46 E6
Noćaj SRB 158 D4
Nocé F 24 D4
Nocera Inferiore I 60 B3
Nocera Terinese I 59 A9
Nocera Umbra I 62 A3
Noceto I 66 C1
Noci I 61 B8
Nociglia I 61 C10
Nociūnai LT 135 F8
Nocrich RO 152 F4
Nødebo DK 87 D10
Nodeland N 90 C2
Nödinge S 91 D11
Nodland N 94 F4
Nods F 26 F5
Noé F 33 D8
Noepoli I 61 C6
Noer D 83 B8
Nœux-les-Mines F 18 D6
Noez F 46 E4
Nofuentes E 40 C5
Nogales E 51 B6
Nogara I 66 B3
Nogaro F 32 C5
Nogent F 26 D3
Nogent-le-Bernard F 24 D3
Nogent-le-Roi F 24 C6
Nogent-le-Rotrou F 24 D4
Nogent-sur-Aube F 25 D11
Nogent-sur-Oise F 18 F5
Nogent-sur-Seine F 25 D10
Nogent-sur-Vernisson F 25 E8
Nogersund S 89 C7
Nógrád H 147 F8
Nógrádmegyer H 147 E9
Nógrádsáp H 147 F8
Nograles E 40 F6
Noguera de Albarracín E 47 D9
Noguères F 32 D4
Nogueruelas E 48 D3
Nohant-Vic F 29 B9
Nohfelden D 21 E8
Nohic F 33 C8
Noia E 38 C2
Noicattaro I 61 A7
Noidans-lès-Vesoul F 26 E5
Noilhan F 33 C7
Noirétable F 30 D4
Noirmoutier-en-l'Île F 28 A1
Noisseville F 26 B5
Noja E 40 B4
Nojorid RO 151 C8
Nokia FIN 127 C10
Nol S 91 D11
Nolay F 30 B6
Noli I 37 C8
Nolimo FIN 121 B11
Nolmyra S 99 B8
Nólsoy FO 2 A3
Nombela E 46 D4
Nomeland N 90 A2
Nomenj SLO 73 D9
Nomeny F 26 C5
Nomexy F 26 D5
Nomia GR 178 B5
Nonancourt F 24 C5
Nonantola I 66 C3
Nonaspe E 42 E4
None I 37 B7
Nonnenweier D 186 E4
Nonnweiler D 21 E8
Nontron F 29 D7
Nonza F 37 F10
Nõo EST 131 E13
Noordwijk aan Zee NL 182 A4
Noordwijk-Binnen NL 16 D2
Noordwijkerhout NL 16 D3
Noordwolde NL 16 C6
Noormarkku FIN 126 B6
Nootdorp NL 182 A4
Nopankylä FIN 122 E8
Noppikoski S 102 D8
Nor S 103 C11
Nora S 97 C13
Nora S 103 A12
Nørager DK 86 B5
Noragugume I 64 C2
Norberg S 97 B14
Norcia I 62 B4
Nordagutu N 95 D10
Nordanås S 103 A13
Nordanås S 107 C14
Nordanås S 109 E11
Nordande S 103 A11
Nordankäl S 107 D10
Nordannälden S 105 E16
Nordannäv S 98 B6
Nordborg DK 86 E4
Nordby DK 86 E2
Nordby DK 86 C7
Norddeich D 17 A8
Norddorf D 82 A4
Nordeide N 100 D3
Norden D 17 A8
Nordenham D 17 B10
Nordendorf D 75 E8
Nordenskov DK 86 D3
Norderåsen S 106 E7
Norderney D 17 A8
Norderö S 105 E16

Norderstedt D 83 C8
Nordfjord N 114 B8
Nordfjordbotn N 111 B17
Nordfjordeid N 100 C3
Nordfold N 110 E9
Nordhalben D 75 B10
Nordhallen S 105 E13
Nordhastedt D 82 B6
Nordhausen D 79 D8
Nordheim D 27 B11
Nordholz D 17 A11
Nordhorn D 17 D8
Nordhuglo N 94 C3
Nordingrå S 103 A15
Nordkil N 111 D10
Nordkirchen D 17 E9
Nordkisa N 95 B14
Nordkjosbotn N 111 B18
Nordland N 110 E4
Nordlenangen N 111 A19
Nordli N 105 C15
Nördlingen D 75 E7
Nordmaling S 107 D17
Nordmannvik N 112 D5
Nordmela N 111 B10
Nordmo N 108 C4
Nordøyvågen N 108 D5
NorŠragota FO 2 A3
Nordråk N 101 E12
Nordsand N 111 C12
Nordsinni N 101 E11
Nordsjö S 103 C12
Nordsjö S 107 D10
Nordsjona N 108 D5
NorŠskáli FO 2 A2
Nordskjør N 104 C3
Nordskot N 110 E8
Nordstemmen D 78 B6
Nord-Værnes N 108 C5
Nordvågen N 113 B17
Nodland N 94 F4
Nordvik N 108 D5
Nordvik S 103 A14
Nordwalde D 17 D8
Noreikiškės LT 137 D8
Norem N 105 D10
Noreña E 39 B8
Noresund N 95 B11
Norg NL 17 B6
Norheimsund N 94 B4
Norinkylä FIN 122 E8
Norje S 88 C7
Norma I 62 D3
Norn S 97 B14
Nornäs S 102 D5
Noroy-le-Bourg F 26 E5
Norppa FIN 123 C11
Norra Åsum S 88 D6
Norra Bredåker S 118 C6
Norra bro S 92 A6
Norra Fjällnäs S 109 D10
Norra Holmnäs S 118 C3
Norråker S 106 C9
Norra Klagshamn S 87 D11
Norra Malånäs S 107 A15
Norra Prästholm S 118 C4
Norra Rödupp S 118 B9
Norra Skärvången S 105 D16
Norra Vallgrund FIN 122 D6
Norra Vi S 92 D6
Norrbäck S 103 B13
Norrbäck S 107 B13
Norrbo S 103 C12
Norrboda S 99 B10
Norrboda S 103 D9
Norrby FIN 122 C9
Norrby S 99 B11
Norrbyberg S 107 B14
Norrbyn S 122 C3
Norrbyskär S 122 C3
Nørre Aaby DK 86 E5
Nørre Alslev DK 84 A1
Nørreballe DK 83 A10
Nørre Bork DK 86 D2
Nørre Broby DK 86 E6
Nørre Felding DK 86 C3
Nørre Halne DK 86 A5
Nørre Kongerslev DK 86 B6
Nørre Nebel DK 86 D2
Norrent-Fontes F 18 C5
Nørre Snede DK 86 D4
Nørresundby DK 86 A5
Nørre Vejrup DK 86 D3
Nørre Vorupør DK 86 B2
Norrfällsviken S 107 F15
Norrfjärden S 103 B13
Norrfjärden S 118 C6
Norrfjärdsen S 122 C3
Norrflärke S 107 D14
Norrfors S 107 D17
Norrfors S 107 D15
Norrgårdssälen S 102 C4
Norr-Greningen S 106 E8
Norrhult-Klavreström S 89 A8
Norrköping S 93 B8
Norrlångträsk S 118 D6
Norr-Moflo S 107 E11
Norrnäs FIN 122 E6
Norrsjön S 106 B8
Norrskedika S 99 B10
Norrstig S 103 A14
Norrstrand S 109 E16
Norrsundet S 103 E13
Norrtälje S 99 C11
Norrträsk S 118 D5
Norrvåge S 107 B13
Norrvik S 107 B13
Nors DK 86 A3
Norsjö S 107 B16
Nörten-Hardenberg D 78 C6
Northallerton GB 11 C9
Northam GB 12 C6
Northampton GB 15 C7
North Berwick GB 5 C11
Northborough GB 11 F11
North Cave GB 11 D10
North Dell GB 2 H3
North Duffield GB 11 D9
Nordheim D 79 C6
North Ferriby GB 11 D10
North Grimston GB 11 C10
North Hykeham GB 11 E10
North Leigh GB 13 B11
North Shields GB 5 E14
North Somercotes GB 11 E12
North Sunderland GB 5 D13
North Tidworth GB 13 C11
Northton GB 2 K2
North Walsham GB 15 B11

Nortwich GB 10 E6
Nortmoor D 17 B9
Norton GB 11 C10
Norton GB 15 C10
Norton Fitzwarren GB 13 C8
Nortorf D 82 B6
Nortrup D 17 C9
Nort-sur-Erdre F 23 F8
Norup DK 86 B6
Norvasalmi FIN 117 E15
Norwich GB 15 B11
Norwick GB 3 D15
Nossa Senhora da Boa Fé P 50 B3
Nossa Senhora da Graça de Póvoa e Meadas P 44 E5
Nossa Senhora da Graça do Divor P 50 B4
Nossa Senhora da Graça dos Degolados P 45 C5
Nossa Senhora das Neves P 50 C4
Nossa Senhora de Machede P 50 B4
Nossebro S 91 C12
Nossen D 80 D4
Nossendorf D 84 C3
Nossentiner Hütte D 83 C12
Noszlop H 149 B8
Notaresco I 62 B5
Notia GR 169 B7
Nõtincs H 147 E9
Noto I 59 F7
Notodden N 95 C10
Notre-Dame-de-Bellecombe F 31 D10
Notre-Dame-de-Gravenchon F 18 F2
Notre-Dame-de-Monts F 28 B1
Notre-Dame-d'Oé F 24 F4
Nötsch im Gailtal A 73 C8
Nottensdorf D 82 D7
Nottingham GB 11 F9
Nottuln D 17 E8
Notviken S 118 C9
Nouan-le-Fuzelier F 24 E7
Nouans-les-Fontaines F 24 E5
Nouart F 19 F11
Nõuni EST 131 E13
Nousiainen FIN 126 D7
Nousionmäki FIN 125 D10
Nousu FIN 115 D5
Nouvion F 18 D4
Nouzilly F 24 E4
Nouzonville F 19 E10
Nõva EST 130 C7
Nova H 149 C7
Nová Baňa SK 147 E7
Nová Bystřice CZ 77 D8
Nová Cerekev CZ 77 D8
Novaci MK 168 B5
Novaci RO 160 C3
Nova Crnja SRB 158 B6
Nová Dedina SK 147 E7
Novadnieki LV 134 C4
Nová Dubnica SK 146 D6
Nova Gorica SLO 73 E8
Nova Gradiška HR 157 B7
Nova Ivanivka UA 154 F3
Novaja Ladoga = Novaya Ladoga RUS
Novaki HR 148 E5
Novakovo BG 166 F4
Nováky SK 147 D7
Novales E 40 B3
Novales E 41 D11
Nova Levante I 72 D4
Novalja HR 67 C10
Novallas E 41 E8
Novalukoml' = Navalukoml'
Nova Makhala BG 165 F9
Nova Nadezhda BG 166 E5
Nova Nekrasivka UA 155 C3
Nová Paka CZ 77 B9
Nova Pazova SRB 158 D5
Nova Pokrovka UA 155 B4
Novara I 68 C6
Novara di Sicilia I 59 C7
Nová Role CZ 75 B12
Nová Sela HR 157 F8
Nova Siri I 61 C7
Novate Mezzola I 69 A7
Nova Topola BIH 157 B7
Nová Varoš SRB 163 C8
Nova Vas SLO 73 E9
Nová Včelnice CZ 77 D8
Nova Zagora BG 166 E5
Nové Hrady CZ 77 E7
Novelda E 56 E3
Novellara I 66 C2
Nové Město nad Metují CZ 77 B10
Nové Mesto nad Váhom SK 146 D5
Nové Město na Moravě CZ 77 C10
Nové Město pod Smrkem CZ 81 E8
Nove Misto UA 145 D6
Noventa di Piave I 72 E6
Noventa Vicentina I 66 B4
Novés E 46 D4
Noves F 35 C8
Nové Veselí CZ 77 C9
Nové Zámky SK 146 F6
Novgorod BG 161 F7
Novi di Modena I 66 C2
Novi Dojran MK 169 B8
Noviergas E 41 E7
Novi Grad BIH 157 B9
Novigrad HR 67 B8
Novigrad HR 156 D4
Novigrad Podravski HR 149 D7
Novi Iskŭr BG 165 D7
Novi Karlovci SRB 158 C5
Novi Kneževac SRB 150 E5

Novi Kozarci SRB 150 F6
Novi Ligure I 37 B9
Novillars F 26 F5
Noville B 182 D5
Novi Marof HR 148 D6
Novion-Porcien F 19 E9
Novi Pazar BG 167 C8
Novi Pazar SRB 163 C10
Novi Sad SRB 158 C4
Novi Šeher BIH 157 C8
Novi Slankamen SRB 158 C5
Novi Travnik BIH 157 D8
Novi Vinodolski HR 67 B10
Novo Beograd SRB 158 D5
Novoborysivka UA 154 C5
Novočići BIH 157 F9
Novo Delchevo BG 169 B9
Novo Korito SRB 159 F9
Novo Miloševo SRB 158 B5
Novomoskovsky RUS 139 A9
Novomykolaivka UA 155 B5
Novo Orahovo SRB 150 F4
Novo Oryakhovo BG 167 D9
Novopetrivka UA 154 B5
Novorzhev RUS 133 B6
Novosamarka UA 154 B5
Novosedly CZ 77 E11
Novoselë AL 168 D1
Novoselë AL 168 C1
Novoselec HR 149 E7
Novoselets BG 166 E6
Novoselija BIH 157 C7
Novoselivka UA 154 B5
Novoselivka UA 154 A6
Novosil's'ke UA 155 C3
Novostroyevo RUS 136 D4
Novot SK 147 C8
Novo Virje HR 149 D8
Novovolyn's'k UA 144 B9
Novoyavorivs'ke UA 144 D8
Novska HR 149 F7
Nový Bor CZ 81 E7
Nový Bydžov CZ 77 B8
Nový-Chevrières F 19 E9
Nový Dvor BY 137 F12
Nový Hrozenkov CZ 146 C6
Nový Jičín CZ 146 B6
Nový Knín CZ 76 C6
Nový Malín CZ 77 C11
Nový Pahost BY 133 F2
Nový Rychnov CZ 77 D8
Novyya Kruki BY 133 E3
Novyy Izborsk RUS 132 F2
Novyy Rozdil UA 145 E9
Nový Život SK 146 E4
Nowa Brzeźnica PL 143 D7
Nowa Cerekwia PL 142 F5
Nowa Chodorówka PL 140 D9
Nowa Dęba PL 143 F12
Nowa Karczma PL 138 B5
Nowa Ruda PL 81 E11
Nowa Sarzyna PL 144 C5
Nowa Słupia PL 143 E11
Nowa Sól PL 81 C9
Nowa Sucha PL 141 F2
Nowa Wieś Ełcka PL 140 C6
Nowa Wieś Lȩborskie PL 85 A13
Nowa Wieś Wielka PL 138 E5
Nowa Wola PL 140 D9
Nowa Wola Gołębiowska PL 141 H4
Nowe PL 138 C6
Nowe Brusno PL 144 C7
Nowe Brzesko PL 143 F9
Nowe Czarnowo PL 84 D6
Nowe Miasteczko PL 81 C9
Nowe Miasto PL 139 E10
Nowe Miasto Lubawskie PL 139 D8
Nowe Miasto nad Pilicą PL 141 G3
Nowe Miasto nad Wartą PL 81 B12
Nowe Ostrowy PL 143 B7
Nowe Piekuty PL 141 E7
Nowe Skalmierzyce PL 142 C4
Nowe Warpno PL 84 C6
Nowinka PL 136 F6
Nowogard PL 85 C9
Nowogród PL 139 D12
Nowogród Bobrzański PL 81 C8
Nowogródek Pomorski PL 85 E8
Nowogrodziec PL 81 D8
Nowosady PL 141 E9
Nowosielec PL 145 D5
Nowosolna PL 143 C8
Nowotaniec PL 145 D5
Nowowola PL 140 D8
Nowy Bartków PL 141 F7
Nowy Duninów PL 139 E7
Nowy Dwór PL 138 C4
Nowy Dwór Gdański PL 138 B6
Nowy Dwór Mazowiecki PL 139 F10
Nowy Kawȩczyn PL 141 G2
Nowy Korczyn PL 143 F10
Nowy Lubliniec PL 144 C7
Nowy Sącz PL 145 D2
Nowy Staw PL 138 B7
Nowy Targ PL 147 C10
Nowy Tomyśl PL 81 B10
Nowy Wiśnicz PL 144 D1
Nowy Żmigród PL 145 D3
Noyal-Muzillac F 22 E7
Noyalo F 22 E6
Noyal-Pontivy F 22 D6
Noyant F 23 E12
Noyarey F 31 E8
Noyen-sur-Sarthe F 23 E11
Noyers F 25 E10
Noyers-sur Cher F 24 F5
Noyers-sur-Jabron F 35 B10
Noyon F 18 E6
Nozay F 23 E8
Nozdrzec PL 144 D5
Nozeroy F 31 B9
Nuaillé-d'Aunis F 28 C4

Nuasjärvi FIN 117 E13
Nubledo E 39 A8
Nucet RO 151 E10
Nuci RO 161 D8
Nucşoara RO 160 C5
Nudersdorf D 79 C12
Nüdlingen D 75 B7
Nudyzhe UA 141 H10
Nueil-sur-Argent F 28 B4
Nuenen NL 16 F5
Nueno E 41 D11
Nueva E 39 B10
Nueva-Carteya E 53 A8
Nueva Jarilla E 52 C4
Nuez de Ebro E 41 E10
Nufăru RO 155 C3
Nughedu di San Nicolò I 64 B3
Nuijamaa FIN 129 D10
Nuillé-sur-Vicoin F 23 E10
Nuits F 25 E11
Nuits-St-Georges F 26 F2
Nukari FIN 127 D12
Ņukši LV 133 D3
Nuland NL 16 E4
Nule I 64 C3
Nules E 48 E4
Nulvi I 64 B2
Numana I 67 E8
Numansdorp NL 16 E2
Nummela FIN 127 E11
Nummi FIN 126 D7
Nummi FIN 127 E10
Nummijärvi FIN 122 F8
Nummikoski FIN 122 F8
Nünchritz D 80 D4
Nuneaton GB 11 F9
Nunkirchen D 186 C2
Nunnanen FIN 117 B12
Nunnanlahti FIN 125 D12
Nuñomoral E 45 D8
Nunsdorf D 80 B4
Nunspeet NL 16 D5
Nuojua FIN 119 E17
Nuoksujärvi S 116 E9
Nuolijärvi FIN 125 C10
Nuoramoinen FIN 127 C14
Nuorgam FIN 113 C20
Nuoritta FIN 119 D16
Nuoro I 64 C3
Nuorunka FIN 120 C9
Nuottavaara FIN 117 D12
Nuottikylä FIN 121 E12
Nur PL 141 E6
Nuragus I 64 D3
Nurallao I 64 D3
Nuraminis I 64 E3
Nureci I 64 D2
Nuriye TR 177 B10
Nurmaa FIN 128 C6
Nurmes FIN 125 C12
Nurmesperä FIN 123 C15
Nurmijärvi FIN 125 C13
Nurmijärvi FIN 127 E12
Nurmo FIN 123 E9
Nürnberg D 75 D9
Nurney IRL 7 F9
Nurri I 64 D3
Nurste EST 130 D4
Nürtingen D 27 C11
Nurzec-Stacja PL 141 F8
Nus I 31 D11
Nusco I 60 B4
Nuşeni RO 152 C4
Nuşfalău RO 151 C10
Nusfjord N 110 D5
Nusnäs S 102 E8
Nusplingen D 27 D10
Nußbach A 76 G6
Nußdorf D 73 A6
Nußdorf am Inn D 72 A3
Nuštar HR 149 F11
Nustrup DK 86 E4
Nuth NL 19 C12
Nutheim N 95 C9
Nuttupperä FIN 123 C15
Nuuksujärvi S 116 C8
Nuupas FIN 119 B16
Nuutajärvi FIN 127 C9
Nuutila FIN 119 F16
Nuutilanmaki FIN 128 B8
Nuvsvåg N 112 C9
Nuvvus FIN 113 D17
Nuxis I 64 E2
Nüziders A 71 C9
Nya Bastuselet S 109 F16
Nyåker S 107 D13
Nyåker S 107 D16
Nyárád H 149 B8
Nyáregyháza H 150 C4
Nyárlőrinc H 150 D4
Nyársapát H 150 C4
Nybble S 91 A15
Nybergsund N 102 D3
Nyborg DK 87 E7
Nyborg N 114 C5
Nyborg S 119 C10
Nybro S 89 B9
Nybrostrand S 88 E5
Nyby FIN 122 E6
Nyby N 113 C15
Nyby S 106 E8
Nybyn S 103 C9
Nybyn S 107 E14
Nybyn S 118 D6
Nýdek CZ 147 B7
Nydri GR 174 B2
Nye S 89 A8
Nyékládháza H 145 H2
Nyelv N 114 C5
Nyergesújfalu H 149 A11
Nyhammar S 97 B12
Nyhem S 103 A10
Nyhem S 109 C14
Ny Højen DK 86 D5
Nyhus N 151 B15
Nyhyttan S 97 C12
Nyírábrány H 151 B9
Nyírcsád H 151 B8
Nyírád H 149 B8
Nyíradony H 151 B8
Nyírbátor H 151 B9
Nyírbéltek H 151 B9
Nyírbogát H 151 B9
Nyírbogdány H 145 G4
Nyíregyháza H 145 H4
Nyírgelse H 151 B8
Nyírgyulaj H 145 H5
Nyíribrony H 145 G4
Nyírkáta H 145 H5
Nyírmada H 145 G5
Nyírmeggyes H 145 H5
Nyírmihálydi H 151 B8
Nyírpazony H 145 H4

Nyírtass H 145 G5
Nyírtelek H 145 G4
Nyírtét H 145 G4
Nyírtura H 145 G4
Nyírvasvári H 151 B9
Nyker DK 89 E7
Nykil S 92 C6
Nykøbing DK 83 A11
Nykøbing Mors DK 86 B3
Nykøbing Sjælland DK 87 D9
Nyköping S 93 B10
Nykrogen S 98 B6
Nykroppa S 97 C11
Nyksund N 110 C7
Nykvåg N 110 C7
Nykvarn S 93 A10
Nykyrke S 92 B5
Nyland S 107 D16
Nyland S 107 E13
Nyland S 122 C2
Nylars DK 89 E7
Nyliden S 107 D15
Nymburk CZ 77 B8
Nymfes GR 168 E2
Nymindegab DK 86 D2
Nymoen N 112 C6
Nynäshamn S 93 B11
Nyneset S 105 C13
Ny Nørup DK 86 D4
Nyoiseau F 23 E10
Nyon CH 31 C9
Nyons F 35 B9
Nyråd DK 87 E9
Nýřany CZ 76 C4
Nýrsko CZ 76 D4
Nyrud N 114 E6
Nysa PL 142 F3
Nysäter S 97 D8
Nysätern S 102 A5
Nysättra S 99 C11
Nysted DK 83 A11
Nysted N 111 C15
Nystrand S 118 E4
Nytrøa N 111 B16
Nyúl H 149 A9
Nyvoll N 113 C11
Nyzhankovychi UA 144 D6
Nyzhni Petrivtsi UA 153 A7
Nyzhni Vorota UA 145 F7
Nyzhniy Bystryy UA 145 G8
Nyzhnya Vysots'ke UA 145 E7
Nyzhnya Yablun'a UA 145 E6

Oadby GB 11 F9
Oakengates GB 10 F7
Oakham GB 11 F10
Oakley GB 13 B12
Oakley GB 13 C12
Oakley GB 15 C7
Oancea RO 154 F2
Oandu EST 131 C13
Oarja RO 160 D6
O Arrabal E 38 D2
Oarța de Sus RO 151 C11
Obal' BY 133 E7
Obal' BY 133 F6
Obalj BIH 157 F9
Oban GB 4 C6
O Barco E 39 D6
Obârșia RO 160 F4
Obârșia-Cloşani RO 159 C10
Obârşia de Câmp RO 159 E11
Obbola S 122 C4
Obdach A 73 B10
Obecnice CZ 76 C5
Obedinenie BG 166 C5
Obejo E 54 C3
O Chao E 38 D2
Oberaich A 73 A7
Oberalm A 73 A7
Ochla NL 16 B5
Ochodnica SK 147 C7
Ochsenfurt D 75 C7
Ochsenhausen D 71 A9
Ochtrup D 17 D8
Ocke S 105 E15
Ockelbo S 103 E12
Ockenheim D 185 E9
Ocna de Fier RO 159 C8
Ocna Mureș RO 152 E3
Ocna Sibiului RO 152 F4
Ocna dugatag RO 152 B3
Ocnele Mari RO 160 C4
Ocnița RO 161 D7
Ocolis RO 151 E11
O Convento E 38 D2
O Corgo E 38 C4
Ocrkavlje BIH 157 E10
Ócsa H 150 C3
Ócsény H 149 D11
Ócsöd H 150 D5
Octeville-sur-Mer F 23 A12
Ocypel PL 138 C5
Odăile RO 161 C9
Ódákra S 87 C11
Odda N 94 B5
Odden N 112 D5
Oddense DK 86 B3
Odder DK 86 D6
Oddsta GB 3 D15
Odeborg S 91 B10
Odeceixe P 50 E2
Odeleite P 50 E4
Odelouca P 50 E3
Odelzhausen D 75 F9
Odemira P 50 D2
Ödena E 43 D7
Odensbacken S 92 A7
Odensberg S 91 C13
Odense DK 86 E6
Odensjö S 93 D4
Odensvi S 93 D8
Oderberg D 84 A6
Oderin D 80 B5
Oderzo I 72 E5
Ödeshog S 92 C5
Odiáxere P 50 E2
Odiham GB 15 E7
Odivelas P 50 B1
Odivelas P 50 C3
Ödkarby FIN 99 B13
Odobeşti RO 153 F10
Odobeşti RO 161 D7

Oberrot D 187 C8
Oberrotweil D 27 D8
Oberschneiding D 75 E12
Oberschützen A 148 B6
Obersiebenbrunn A 77 F11
Obersinn D 74 B6
Obersontheim D 187 C8
Oberspier D 79 D8
Oberstadion D 71 A9
Oberstaufen D 71 B9
Oberstdorf D 71 C10
Oberstenfeld D 27 B11
Oberthal D 21 F8
Oberthulba D 187 A8
Obertilliach A 73 C6
Obertrubach D 75 C9
Obertshausen D 21 D11
Oberursel (Taunus) D 21 D11
Obervellach A 73 C7
Oberviechtach D 75 C11
Oberwald CH 70 D6
Oberwart A 148 B6
Oberwesel D 21 D9
Oberwolfach D 187 E5
Oberwölz A 73 B9
Óbidos P 44 F2
Obiliq KS 164 D3
Obing D 75 F11
Obinitsa EST 132 F1
Obitel BG 167 C7
Objat F 29 E8
Objazda PL 85 A12
Öblarn A 73 B8
Obleševo MK 164 F5
Obliké e Madhe AL 163 E7
Obnova BG 165 C10
Obodivka UA 154 A4
Oboga RO 160 E4
O Bolo E 38 D5
Obón E 42 F2
Obrcri BIH 157 D7
Oborin SK 145 F4
Oboriste BG 165 C10
Oborniki PL 81 A11
Oborniki Śląskie D 81 D11
Obrazów PL 143 E12
Obreja RO 159 C9
Obrenovac SRB 158 D5
Obretenik BG 166 B5
Obrež SRB 158 D4
Obrež SRB 159 F7
Obrigheim D 21 F12
Obrigheim (Pfalz) D 187 B5
Obrnice CZ 76 A5
Obrochishte BG 167 C10
Obrov SLO 67 A9
Obrovac HR 156 D4
Obrovac SRB 158 C3
Obrowo PL 138 E6
Obrtići BIH 157 E10
Obruchishte BG 166 E5
Obryte PL 139 E11
Obrzycko PL 85 E11
Obsza PL 144 C6
Obudovac BIH 157 C10
Obyce SK 146 E6
Obzor BG 167 D9
O Cádavo E 38 B5
Ocaña E 46 E6
Ocana F 37 H9
O Carballiño E 38 D3
O Castelo E 38 D3
O Castro E 38 C2
O Castro de Ferreira E 38 C4
Occhiobello I 66 C4
Occimiano I 68 C6
Očevlja BIH 157 D9
Ochagavía E 32 E3
Ochiltree GB 5 E8
Ocholt D 17 B10

Odolanów PL 142 C4
Odolena Voda CZ 76 B6
Odón E 47 C9
Odoorn NL 17 C7
Odorheiu Secuiesc RO 152 E6
Odry CZ 146 B5
Odrzywół PL 141 G3
Ojos Negros E 47 C10
Ojrzeń PL 139 E10
Ôdsmål S 91 C10
Ødsted DK 86 D4
Odürne BG 165 C10
Odžaci BIH 157 E6
Odžaci SRB 158 B3
Odžak BIH 157 B9
Odžak BIH 157 E6
Odžak BIH 157 F9
Odžak MNE 163 D7
Odzieria LV 135 C11
Oebisfelde D 79 B8
Oedelem B 182 C2
Oederan D 80 E4
Oeffelt NL 16 E5
Oegstgeest NL 16 D3
Oelde D 17 E10
Oelixdorf D 82 C7
Oelsnitz D 75 B11
Oelsnitz D 79 E12
Oene NL 183 A8
Oenkerk NL 16 B5
Oensingen CH 27 F8
Oerel D 17 B12
Oering D 83 C8
Oerlenbach D 75 B7
Oerlinghausen D 17 D11
Oestrich-Winkel D 21 D9
Oettersdorf D 79 E10
Oettingen in Bayern D 75 E8
Oetz A 71 C11
Oetzen D 83 D9
Oeversee D 82 A6
Œyreluy F 32 C3
Ofatinţi MD 154 B4
Ófehértó H 145 H5
Ofena I 62 C5
Offanengo I 69 C8
Offemont F 27 E6
Offenbach am Main D 21 D11
Offenbach an der Queich D 187 C5
Offenberg D 76 E3
Offenburg D 27 C8
Offerdal S 105 E16
Offersøy N 111 D14
Offida I 62 B5
Offingen D 75 F7
Offranville F 18 E3
O Forte E 38 C3
Ofte N 95 D8
Oftering D 76 F6
Oftersheim D 21 F11
Ogenbargen D 17 A9
Oger F 25 C11
Ogeu-les-Bains F 32 D4
Ogéviller F 26 C6
Oggiastro I 60 C4
Ogliastro Cilento I 60 C4
Ogmore GB 13 C7
Ognyanovo BG 169 A10
Ogonelloe IRL 8 C6
Ogoya BG 165 C9
Ogra RO 152 E4
Ogre LV 135 C9
Ogren AL 168 D3
Ogregals LV 135 C9
Ogrezeni RO 161 E7
Ogrodniki PL 139 E12
Ogrodzieniec PL 143 F8
Ogrosen D 80 C6
O Grove E 38 D2
Ogulin HR 67 B11
Oğulpaşa TR 172 A6
Ohaba RO 152 E3
Ohaba Lungă RO 151 F8
Ohanes E 55 E7
Ohey B 19 D11
Ohkola FIN 127 D13
Ohlsbach D 27 D8
Ohlstadt D 72 A3
Ohne D 17 D8
Ohorn D 80 D6
Ohrady SK 146 E5
Ohrdruf D 79 E8
Ohrid MK 168 B4
Öhringen D 27 B11
Ohtaanniemi FIN 125 E11
Ohtanajärvi S 116 D10
Ohukotsu EST 131 C9
Oia P 44 C3
Oiã P 44 C3
Oiartzun E 32 D2
Oichalia GR 169 E6
Øie N 105 B12
Oignies F 18 D6
O Igrexario E 38 D3
Oijärvi FIN 119 C15
Oijen NL 183 B6
Oijusluoma FIN 121 C13
Oikarainen FIN 119 B16
Oileán Ciarraí IRL 8 D4
Oilgate IRL 9 D9
Óímbra E 38 E5
Oinacu RO 161 F8
Oinas FIN 115 E2
Oinasjärvi FIN 124 C9
Oinofyta GR 175 C8
Oinoi GR 175 C7
Oion E 41 C7
O Irixo E 38 C3
Oiron F 28 B5
Oiselay-et-Grachaux F 26 F4
Oisemont F 18 E4
Oisseau F 23 D10
Oissel F 18 F3
Oisterwijk NL 183 B6
Oisu EST 131 D11
Oitti FIN 127 D13
Oituz RO 153 E9
Oitylo GR 178 B3
Oivanki FIN 121 B13
Oizon F 25 F8
Öja FIN 123 C9
Öja S 93 E12
Öjakkala FIN 127 E11
Ojakylä FIN 119 D14
Ojakylä FIN 119 F15
Ojanperä FIN 120 F9
Öjarn S 106 D8

Ojdula RO 153 F8
Öje S 102 E6
Öjebyn S 118 D6
Øjeforsen S 103 B9
Ojén E 53 D7
Øjung S 103 C10
Øjung S 103 C10
Okalewo PL 139 D8
Okány H 151 D7
Okçular TR 181 C9
Økdal N 101 A11
Okehampton GB 12 D6
Okhotnoye RUS 136 D4
Oklaj HR 156 E5
Oknö S 89 A11
Okoč SK 146 F5
Okonek PL 85 C11
Okopy PL 141 H9
Ökoritófülpös H 145 H6
Okorsh BG 161 F10
Okříšky CZ 77 C8
Okrouhlice CZ 77 C8
Okrúhle SK 145 E4
Oksa PL 143 E9
Øksajärvi S 116 C8
Oskakoski FIN 123 D12
Oksava FIN 123 C14
Øksbøl DK 86 D2
Øksbøl DK 86 E5
Øksfjord N 112 C9
Øksnes N 110 D9
Øksneshamn N 110 D9
Oksvoll N 104 D7
Oktonia GR 175 B9
Okučani HR 157 B7
Olague E 32 E2
Olaine LV 135 C8
Olalhas P 44 E4
Oland N 90 B3
Olãneşti MD 154 E5
Olariu RO 160 D4
Olargues F 34 C4
Olari RO 151 E8
Olaszliszka H 145 G3
Olave E 32 E2
Oława PL 81 E11
Olazti E 32 E1
Olba E 48 D3
Olbendorf A 148 B6
Olbernhau D 80 E4
Olbersdorf D 81 E7
Olbersleben D 79 D9
Olbia I 64 B3
Olbijcin PL 144 B5
Olcea RO 151 D8
Oldcastle IRL 7 E8
Old Dailly GB 4 E7
Oldebroek NL 16 D6
Oldedalen N 100 C5
Oldehove NL 16 B6
Oldeide N 100 C2
Oldełø N 100 C5
Olden N 100 C5
Olden S 105 D15
Oldenbrok D 17 B10
Oldenburg D 17 B10
Oldenburg in Holstein D 83 B9
Oldendorf D 17 C8
Oldenswort D 82 B5
Oldenzaal NL 17 D7
Olderdalen N 112 D6
Oldereid N 108 B8
Olderfjord N 113 C15
Oldernes N 113 C13
Oldervik N 111 A18
Oldervik N 113 C13
Oldham GB 11 D7
Old Head IRL 8 E5
Oldisleben D 79 D9
Old Leake GB 11 E12
Oldmeldrum GB 3 L12
Oldsum D 82 A4
Oldtown IRL 7 E10
Oleby S 97 B9
Olecko PL 136 E6
Oleggio I 68 B6
Oleiros P 44 E5
Oleksandrivka UA 154 C6
Oleksiyivka UA 154 B3
Olemps F 33 B11
Olen B 19 B10
Ølen N 94 C3
Olesa de Montserrat E 43 D7
Oleśnica PL 142 D3
Oleśnica PL 143 F11
Oleśnice CZ 77 C10
Olesno PL 142 E6
Olesno PL 143 F10
Oleszyce PL 144 C6
Olevano Romano I 62 D4
Olfen D 17 E8
Olgina EST 132 C3
Olginate I 69 B7
Ølgod DK 86 D3
Olgrinmore GB 3 J9
Olhalvo P 44 F2
Olhão P 50 E4
Olho Marinho P 44 F2
Onancé RO 153 C10
Onchan GBM 10 C3
Onda E 48 E4
Ondara E 56 D5
Ondarroa E 32 D1
Ondřejov CZ 77 C7
Ondres F 32 C3
Oneglia I 37 D8
Onesse-et-Laharie F 32 B3
Oneşti RO 153 E9
Onet-le-Château F 33 B11
Ongles F 35 B10
Oniceni RO 153 D10
Onich GB 4 B6
Onifai I 64 C4
Oniferi I 64 C3
Onițcani MD 154 C4
Onkamaa FIN 128 D7
Onkamo FIN 116 C5
Onkamo FIN 119 D15
Onkamo FIN 125 F11
Onkiniemi FIN 127 C15
Önnestad S 88 C6
Önningby FIN 99 B14
Ónod H 145 G2
Onøya N 108 D4
Onsala S 91 D11
Onsbjerg DK 86 D7
Önsövallen S 102 C7
Ønslev DK 83 A11

Oliveira de Azeméis P 44 C4
Oliveira de Frades P 44 C4
Oliveira do Arda P 44 B4
Oliveira do Bairro P 44 C4
Oliveira do Conde P 44 D5
Oliveira do Douro P 44 B5
Oliveira do Hospital P 44 D5
Olivenza E 51 B5
Oliveri I 59 C7
Olivet F 24 E6
Oliveto Citra I 60 B4
Oliveto Lucano I 60 B6
Olivone CH 71 D7
Ołka SK 145 E4
Olkijoki FIN 119 E13
Olkiluoto FIN 126 C5
Olkkajärvi FIN 117 E16
Olkusz PL 143 F8
Ollaberry GB 3 D14
Ollerton GB 11 E9
Ollerup DK 86 E7
Olliergues F 30 D4
Ollila FIN 123 B13
Ollila FIN 127 D8
Ollilanniemi FIN 121 E12
Ollo E 32 E2
Ollolai I 64 C3
Ollon CH 31 C10
Ollsta S 106 E8
Ölmbrotorp S 97 D13
Ölme S 97 D7
Olmedilla de Roa E 40 E3
Olmedo E 39 F10
Olmedo I 64 B1
Olmeta-di-Tuda F 37 F10
Olmeto F 37 H9
Olmos de Ojeda E 40 C3
Olney GB 15 C7
Olocau E 48 E3
Olocau del Rey E 42 F3
Olofsfors S 107 D16
Olofström S 88 C7
Olombrada E 40 F3
Olomouc CZ 146 B4
Olonne-sur-Mer E 28 B2
Olonzac F 34 D4
Oloron-Ste-Marie F 32 D4
Olost E 43 C8
Olot E 43 C8
Oloví CZ 75 B12
Olovo BIH 157 D9
Olpe D 21 B9
Olřišov CZ 142 G4
Olšany CZ 77 C11
Olšany u Prostějova CZ 77 C12
Olsätter S 97 C10
Olsberg D 17 F10
Olsene B 182 D2
Olsbenning S 97 B15
Ølsemagle DK 87 E10
Olserud S 91 A13
Olszanica PL 145 E5
Olszana PL 142 E3
Olszany PL 144 D6
Olszewo-Borki PL 139 D12
Olsztyn PL 136 F1
Olsztyn PL 143 E7
Olsztynek PL 139 C9
Olszyn PL 141 F8
Olszyna PL 81 D8
Olszyny PL 144 D2
Oltedal N 94 E4
Olten CH 27 F8
Olteneşti RO 153 D11
Olteni RO 160 E6
Oltenița RO 161 E9
Oltina RO 155 E1
Olula del Río E 55 E8
Olustvere EST 131 D11
Olvan E 43 C7
Olvaşjärvi FIN 120 D9
Ólvega E 41 E8
Olvena E 42 C4
Olvera E 51 F9
Olympiada GR 169 C10
Olympiada GR 169 E7
Olympos GR 181 E6
Olzai I 64 C3
Oma N 94 B3
Omagh GB 4 F2
Omalos GR 178 E6
Omarchevo BG 166 E6
Omarska BIH 157 C6
Omaki EST 131 D14
Omegna I 68 B5
Ömerköy TR 173 D9
Ömerli TR 173 B9
O Mesón do Vento E 38 B3
Omessa F 37 G10
Omiš HR 157 F6
Omišalj HR 67 B10
Ommen NL 16 C6
Omne S 107 F14
Omolio GR 169 E7
Omoljica SRB 159 D6
Omont F 19 E10
O Mosteiro E 38 C2
Omurtag BG 167 C6
Omvriaki GR 174 A5
Oña E 40 C5
Ona N 100 A5
Onani I 64 C3
Oñati E 32 D1
Ólvega E 41 E8

Onslunda S 88 D6
Onstmettingen D 27 D10
Onstwedde NL 17 B8
Ontiñena E 42 D4
Ontinyent E 56 D3
Ontojoki FIN 125 B11
Ontonvara RUS 125 E16
Onttola FIN 125 E13
Ontur E 55 B10
Onuškis LT 135 F11
Onuškis LT 137 E10
Onzain F 24 E5
Onzonilla E 39 C8
Ooltgensplaat NL 16 E2
Oonurme EST 131 C13
Oostakker B 19 B8
Oostburg NL 19 B7
Oostende B 18 B6
Oostendorp NL 16 D5
Oosterbeek NL 183 B7
Oosterend NL 16 B4
Oosterhesselen NL 17 C7
Oosterhout NL 16 E3
Oosterwolde NL 16 C6
Oosterzele B 19 C8
Oostham B 183 C6
Oosthuizen NL 16 C3
Oostkamp B 19 B7
Oostkapelle NL 16 E1
Oostmalle B 182 C5
Oost-Souburg NL 16 F1
Oostvleteren B 18 C6
Oost-Vlieland NL 16 B4
Oostvoorne NL 182 B4
Ootmarsum NL 17 D7
Opaka BG 166 C6
Opalenica PL 81 B10
Opalenie PL 138 C6
Ópályi H 145 H5
Opan BG 166 E5
Opařany CZ 77 D6
Opatija HR 67 B9
Opatov CZ 77 C10
Opatovice nad Labem CZ 77 B9
Opatów PL 142 E6
Opatów PL 142 E6
Opatów PL 143 E12
Opatówek PL 142 C5
Opatowiec PL 143 F10
Opava CZ 146 B5
O Pazo E 38 C3
O Pazo de Irixoa E 38 B3
Ope S 106 E7
O Pedrouzo E 38 C3
Opeinde NL 16 B6
Offenbach D 79 F10
Opglabbeek B 183 C7
Opheusden NL 183 B7
Opi I 62 D5
Opitter B 183 C7
Oploo NL 183 B7
Oplotnica SLO 148 D4
Opmeer NL 16 C3
Opochka RUS 133 C5
Opočno CZ 77 B10
Opoczno PL 141 H2
Opoeteren B 183 C7
Opole E 162 B4
Opole Lubelskie PL 141 H5
Oporelu RO 160 D4
Oporets' UA 145 F7
O Porriño E 38 D2
Opoul-Périllos F 34 E4
Opovo SRB 158 C5
Oppach D 81 D7
Oppala S 103 E13
Oppdal N 101 A11
Oppeano I 66 B3
Oppeby S 92 C7
Oppdal N 100 D3
Oppegard N 95 C13
Oppenau D 27 D9
Oppenheim D 21 E10
Oppenweiler D 187 D8
Opphaug N 104 D7
Opphus N 101 D14
Oppido Lucano I 60 B5
Oppido Mamertina I 59 C8
Oppin D 79 C11
Opponitz A 73 A10
Oppurg D 79 E10
Oprisavci HR 157 B9
Oprişor RO 159 E11
Optalj HR 67 B8
Opsa BY 135 E13
Opsaheden S 97 B10
Optași-Măgura RO 160 D5
Ópusztaszer H 150 E5
Opuzen HR 157 F8
Opwijk B 19 C9
Ôr H 145 H5
Ora I 72 D3
Øra N 112 C8
Orada P 50 B5
Oradea RO 151 C8
Oradour-sur-Glane F 29 D8
Oradour-sur-Vayres F 29 D7
Orah BIH 157 D8
Orah BIH 162 D5
Orahovac KS 163 E10
Orahova BIH 157 C7
Orahovica HR 149 E9
Oraio GR 171 B7
Oraiokastro GR 169 C8
Oraison F 35 C10
Orajärvi FIN 117 E12
Orakylä FIN 115 D1
Orange F 35 B8
Orani I 64 C3
Oranienburg D 84 E4
Órán Mór IRL 6 F5
Oranmore IRL 6 F5
Orašac BIH 156 C5
Orašac HR 162 D5
Orašac SRB 164 C5
Orašje BIH 157 B10
Orăștie RO 151 F11
Orăștioara de Sus RO 151 F11
Orașu Nou RO 145 H7
Óratjärn S 103 C10
Orava EST 132 E1
Orava FIN 123 D10
Oravainen FIN 122 D9
Oravais FIN 122 D8
Oravala FIN 128 D6
Öravan S 107 B14
Öravankylä FIN 123 C15
Öravattnet S 106 E9
Oravi FIN 125 F11
Oravikoski FIN 124 E9

Oravisalo FIN 125 F13
Oravița RO 159 C8
Oravivaara FIN 121 E11
Oravská Polhora SK 147 B8
Oravské Veselé SK 147 C8
Oravský Podzámok SK 147 C8
Orba E 56 D4
Orbacém P 38 E2
Örbäck S 97 C15
Orbaden S 103 C11
Ørbæk DK 86 E7
Orbara E 32 E3
Orbassano I 37 A7
Orbe CH 31 B10
Orbeasca RO 160 E6
Orbec F 24 B3
Orbeni RO 153 E10
Orbetello I 65 C4
Örbyhus S 99 B9
Orca P 44 D6
Orce E 55 D8
Orcera E 55 C7
Orchamps-Vennes F 26 F6
Orchies F 19 D7
Orchomenos GR 175 C6
Orchów PL 143 C7
Orchowo PL 138 E5
Orciano di Pesaro I 67 E6
Orcières F 36 B4
Orcival F 30 D2
Ordan-Larroque F 33 C6
Ordes E 38 B3
Ordizia E 32 D1
Ordona I 60 A5
Ordzhonikidze UA 154 C6
Orea E 47 C9
O Real E 38 B3
Örebäcken S 102 C4
Orebić HR 157 G7
Örebro S 97 D13
Ořechov CZ 77 D11
Öregcsertő H 150 D3
Öreglak I 149 C9
Öregrund S 99 B10
Orehoved DK 87 F9
Oreini GR 169 B10
Orekhovitsa BG 165 B9
Orellana de la Sierra E 51 A9
Orellana la Vieja E 51 A8
Ören TR 177 C10
Ören TR 181 B7
Orenhofen D 185 E6
Oreoi GR 175 B7
Orés E 32 F3
Oresh BG 166 B4
Oreshak BG 165 D10
Orestiada GR 171 B11
Öreström S 107 C16
Öretjändalen S 103 A10
Oreye B 19 C11
Orezu RO 161 D9
Orford GB 15 C12
Organi GR 171 B9
Organyà E 43 C6
Orgaz E 46 E5
Orgelet F 31 B8
Ørgenvika N 95 B11
Orgères-en-Beauce F 24 D6
Orgita EST 131 D8
Orgiva E 53 C10
Orgon F 35 C9
Orgosolo I 64 C3
Orhaneli TR 173 E10
Orhaniye TR 171 C10
Orhaniye TR 181 C8
Orhanlar TR 173 E8
Orhei MD 154 C3
Oria E 55 E8
Oria I 61 C9
O Rial E 38 D2
Origny-Ste-Benoîte F 19 E7
Orihuela E 56 E3
Orihuela del Tremedal E 47 C9
Orikhivka UA 154 E5
Orikum AL 168 D1
Orimattila FIN 127 D14
Oriniemi FIN 127 C9
Orio E 32 D1
Oriola P 50 C4
Oriolo I 61 C6
Oriolo Romano I 62 C2
Oripää FIN 126 D8
Orismala FIN 122 E8
Orissaare EST 130 D6
Oristà E 43 D8
Oristano I 64 D2
Oristown IRL 7 E9
Őriszentpéter H 149 C6
Oriv UA 145 E8
Orivedén asema FIN 127 B11
Orivesi FIN 127 B11
Orizare BG 167 D9
Orizari MK 164 F5
Ørjavik N 104 F2
Ørje N 96 D6
Orkanger N 104 E7
Örkelljunga S 87 C12
Örkény H 150 C3
Orla PL 141 E8
Orlamünde D 79 E10
Orlat RO 152 F3
Orlea RO 160 F4
Orléans F 24 E6
Orlești RO 160 D4
Orlivka UA 155 C2
Orlan KS 164 D3
Orlová CZ 146 B6
Orlov Dol BG 166 E6
Orlovets BG 166 C5
Orly PL 144 D6
Orlyak BG 161 F10
Orlyane BG 165 C10
Orma GR 169 C6
Ormanli TR 173 B9
Ormaryd S 92 D5
Ormea I 37 C7
Örményes H 150 C6
Örménykút H 150 D6
Ormos GR 176 D4
Ormos Panormou GR 176 D5
Ormos Prinou GR 171 C7
Ormož SLO 148 D6
Ormskirk GB 10 D6
Ormylia GR 169 D10
Ornaisons F 34 E5
Ornäs S 97 A14
Örnäsudden S 109 E13
Ornavasso I 68 B5
Ørnbau D 75 D8
Ornes N 105 B15
Ørnes N 108 C6

Orneta PL 139 B9
Ørnhøj DK 86 C3
Ornö S 93 A12
Ornontowice PL 142 F6
Örnsköldsvik S 107 E15
Orodel RO 159 E11
Orolik HR 157 B11
Orom SRB 150 F4
Oron-la-Ville CH 31 B10
Oronoz E 32 D2
Orońsko PL 141 H3
Oropa I 68 B4
Oropesa E 45 E10
Oropesa del Mar E 48 D5
Ororbia E 32 E2
Orosei I 64 C4
Orosháza H 150 D6
Oroslavje HR 148 E5
Oroszlány H 149 B10
Orpierre F 35 B10
Orreaga E 32 D3
Orrefors S 89 B9
Orrios E 42 F2
Orrmo S 102 C7
Orroli I 64 D3
Orrviken S 106 E6
Orsa S 102 C8
Orsara di Puglia I 60 A4
Orsay F 24 C7
Örsbäck S 107 D17
Orsennes F 29 C9
Örserum S 92 C5
Orsières CH 31 C11
Örsjö S 89 B9
Ørslev DK 87 E9
Ørsnes N 100 A5
Orsogna I 63 C6
Orsomarso I 60 D5
Orșova RO 159 D9
Ørsta N 94 B2
Ørsted DK 86 C6
Örsundsbro S 99 C8
Ortaca TR 181 C9
Ortacesus I 64 D3
Ortakent TR 177 E9
Ortaklar TR 177 D9
Ortaköy TR 173 B9
Ortala S 99 C11
Orta Nova I 60 A5
Orte I 62 C2
Orten N 100 A5
Ortenberg D 21 D12
Ortenberg D 27 D8
Ortenburg D 76 E4
Orth an der Donau A 77 F11
Orthez F 32 D4
Ortholmen S 102 B4
Orthovouni GR 168 E5
Ortigosa E 41 D6
Ortigueira E 38 A4
Örting DK 86 D6
Ortisei I 72 C4
Ortișoara RO 151 F7
Ortnevik N 100 D4
Orton GB 10 C6
Ortona I 63 C6
Ortovera I 37 C8
Ortrand D 80 D5
Örträsk S 107 C15
Ortueri I 64 C2
Örtülüce TR 173 D7
Ørum DK 86 C5
Ørum DK 86 C7
Orune I 64 C3
Orusco E 47 D6
Orval F 29 B10
Orvalho P 44 D5
Orvault F 23 F8
Orvieto I 62 B2
Örviken S 118 E6
Orvinio I 62 C3
Oryakhovo BG 160 F3
Orzesze PL 142 F6
Orzinuovi I 69 C8
Orzyny PL 139 C11
Orzysz PL 136 F4
Os N 101 B14
Osa N 100 E6
Osa de Vega E 47 E7
Ošani LV 135 D11
Osaonica SRB 163 C9
Osbaldwick GB 11 D9
Os Blancos E 38 D4
Osburg D 186 B2
Øsby DK 86 E5
Osby S 88 C5
Osbyholm S 87 D13
Oščadnica SK 147 C7
Oschatz D 80 D4
Oschersleben (Bode) D 79 B9
Oschiri I 64 B3
Ościsłowo PL 139 E9
Os Dices E 38 C2
Osdorf D 83 B8
Osečina SRB 158 E4
O Seixo E 38 E2
Oseja de Sajambre E 39 B9
Osek CZ 76 C5
Osek CZ 80 E5
Osen N 105 C9
Osen N 108 D6
Osenets BG 166 B6
Ošenieki LV 134 C4
Osera E 41 E10
Oşeşti RO 153 D10
Oset N 101 D10
Ősi H 149 B10
Osica de Sus RO 160 E4
Osidda I 64 B3
Osie PL 138 C5
Osiecino PL 138 E6
Osieck PL 141 G4
Osieczna PL 81 C11
Osieczna PL 138 C5
Osiecznica PL 81 D8
Osiek PL 138 C5
Osiek PL 139 D7
Osiek PL 143 E11
Osiek PL 147 B8
Osiek Jasielski PL 145 D3
Osiek Mały PL 142 B6
Osiek nad Notecią PL 85 D12
Osielsko PL 138 D5
Osiglia I 37 C8
Osijek HR 149 E11
Osikovitsa BG 165 D9
Osilo I 64 B2
Ósimo I 67 F7
Osina DK 85 C8
Osiní I 64 D3
Osiny PL 141 H6
Osio Sotto I 69 C8

Osipaonica SRB 159 D7
Osjaków PL 142 D6
Oskar S 89 B9
Oskar-Fredriksborg S 99 D10
Oskarshamn S 93 E8
Oskarström S 87 B11
Oskava CZ 77 C12
Oskořínek CZ 77 B8
Osľany SK 146 D6
Oslättfors S 103 E12
Osli H 149 A8
Oslo N 95 C13
Osloß D 79 B8
Osma E 40 C5
Osma FIN 117 D15
Osmancali TR 177 B9
Osmancik TR 173 A7
Osmangazi TR 173 D11
Osmaniye TR 173 E10
Osmaniye TR 173 F10
Osmanki FIN 123 C16
Osmanli TR 173 A6
Os'mino RUS 132 C5
Osmo S 93 B11
Osmolin PL 141 F1
Osmoloda UA 145 F9
Osnabrück D 17 D10
Osno Lubuskie PL 81 B7
Osny F 24 B7
Osoblaha CZ 142 H4
Osogna CH 69 A6
Osojnik HR 162 D5
Osoppo I 73 D7
Osor E 43 D9
Osor HR 67 C9
Oşorhei RO 151 C9
Osorno E 40 D3
Osowa PL 136 E6
Osowa Sień PL 81 C10
Osøyri N 94 B2
Ospitaletto I 69 B9
Oss NL 16 E5
Ossa GR 169 C9
Ossa de Montiel E 55 B7
Ossana I 69 A10
Osséja F 33 F9
Ossendrecht NL 182 C4
Ossès F 32 D3
Ossiach A 73 C8
Oßmannstedt D 79 D9
Össa S 98 B7
Östanå S 88 C6
Östanbäck S 118 F4
Östanfjärden S 119 C10
Östansjö S 92 A5
Östansjö S 109 E16
Östanskär S 103 A13
Östanvik S 103 D9
Oštarije HR 156 B3
Ostaszewo PL 138 B6
Östavall S 103 B9
Ostbevern D 17 D9
Østbirk DK 86 D5
Östbjörka S 103 E9
Østby N 91 A9
Østby N 102 D4
Østby S 107 D13
Osted DK 87 D9
Ostellato I 66 C4
Osten D 17 A12
Ostend B 18 B6
Ostend S 182 C1
Ostenfeld (Husum) D 82 B6
Østengård D 86 D4
Østerås S 107 E12
Øster Assels DK 86 B3
Øster Bjerregrav DK 86 C5
Øster Brønderslev DK 86 A5
Osterburg (Altmark) D 83 E11
Osterburken D 27 B11
Østerby D 82 B7
Østerby DK 86 A5
Østerbybruk S 99 B9
Österbymo S 92 D6
Österede S 107 E11
Österfärnebo S 98 B7
Osterfeld D 79 D10
Östergarn S 93 E13
Östergraninge S 107 F12
Österhankmo FIN 122 D7
Osterhever D 82 B5
Osterhofen D 76 E4
Øster Højst DK 86 E4
Osterholz-Scharmbeck D 17 B11
Øster Hornum DK 86 B5
Øster Hurup DK 86 B6
Østerild DK 86 A3
Øster Jølby DK 86 B3
Österjörn S 118 E4
Österlars DK 89 E7
Øster Lindet DK 86 E4
Österlisa S 99 C11
Östermalmsät H 89 E8
Østermarie DK 89 E8
Ostermiething A 76 F3
Östermundigen CH 31 B11
Osternoret S 107 C12
Ostero FIN 122 D8
Osterode am Harz D 79 C7
Osterrönfeld D 82 B7
Österskucku S 102 A8
Östersund S 106 E7
Osterwieck D 79 C7
Øster Tørslev DK 86 B6
Øster Ulslev DK 83 A11
Östervåla S 98 B8
Øster Vedsted DK 86 E3
Østervrå DK 90 E7
Øster Vrøgum DK 86 D2
Osterwieck D 79 C8
Østese N 94 B4
Ostfildern D 187 D7
Östhammar S 99 B10
Ostheim vor der Rhön D 75 B7
Osthofen D 21 E10
Ostia I 62 D2
Ostiano I 66 B1
Ostiglia I 66 B3
Ostiz E 32 E2
Östloning S 103 A13
Östmark S 97 B9
Östmarkum S 107 E14
Östnor S 102 D7
Ostojićevo SRB 150 F5
Ostoros I 145 H1
Ostra I 67 E7
Östra Åliden S 118 E4
Östra RO 152 C2
Östra Ed S 93 C9
Östra Frölunda S 91 E13
Östra Granberg S 118 C4

Östra Grevie S 87 E12
Östra Husby S 93 B9
Östra Ljungby S 87 C12
Östra Löa S 97 C13
Östra Lovsjön S 106 C7
Östra Ormsjö S 107 C10
Östra Ryd S 93 C8
Östra Skrämträsk S 118 E5
Östra Sönnarslöv S 88 D6
Östra Stugusjö S 103 A9
Ostrau D 79 C11
Ostrau D 80 D4
Östra Vemmerlöv S 88 D6
Ostravice CZ 146 B6
Östra Yttermark FIN 122 E6
Ostren AL 168 A3
Ostřetín CZ 77 B10
Ostricourt F 182 E2
Östringen D 21 F11
Ostritsa BG 166 B5
Ostritz D 81 D7
Ostróda PL 139 C8
Stromecko PL 138 D5
Ostroměř CZ 77 B9
Ostroróg PL 81 A10
Ostrov BG 160 F4
Ostrov CZ 76 B3
Ostrov RO 155 D2
Ostrov RO 161 E10
Ostrov RUS 133 D4
Ostrov SK 146 D5
Ostroveni RO 160 F3
Ostrovo BG 161 F9
Ostrov u Macochy CZ 77 D11
Ostrów PL 145 D4
Ostrówek PL 141 G7
Ostrówek PL 142 D6
Ostrowice PL 85 C9
Ostrowiec PL 85 B8
Ostrowiec Świętokrzyski PL 143 E11
Ostrowite PL 138 F5
Ostrowite PL 139 D7
Ostrów Lubelski PL 141 H7
Ostrów Mazowiecka PL 139 E12
Ostrowo PL 138 E5
Ostrów Wielkopolski PL 142 C4
Ostróžac BIH 156 C5
Ostróžac BIH 157 E8
Ostrožeň PL 141 G5
Østrup DK 86 B4
Ostrzeszów PL 142 D4
Ostuni I 61 B9
Ostvik S 118 E6
Ostwald F 186 D4
Osula EST 131 F13
Osuna E 53 B6
Ošupe LV 135 C12
Osvallen S 102 A4
Osvanmo S 107 D10
Ovar P 44 C3
Ovaro I 73 D6
Ovča SRB 158 D6
Ovcha Mogila BG 166 C4
Ovcharovo BG 166 B6
Ovcheполtsi BG 165 E9
Ove DK 86 B5
Ovelgönne D 17 B10
Överammer S 107 E10
Överäng S 105 D14
Overås N 100 A8
Overath D 21 C8
Överberg S 102 B8
Øverbygd N 111 C17
Överbyn S 103 C12
Overdinkel NL 183 A10
Øvergård N 111 B16
Overhalla N 105 B11
Överhogdal S 102 B7
Överhörnäs S 107 E15
Over Hornbæk DK 86 C5
Overijse B 19 C10
Överissjö S 107 C13
Păcureți RO 161 C8
Pacyna PL 143 B8
Pacy-sur-Eure F 24 B5
Paczków PL 77 B12
Padalsjoki FIN 127 C13
Padborg DK 82 A6
Padbury GB 14 D7
Padej SRB 150 F5
Padene HR 156 D5
Paderne P 50 E3
Paderne de Allariz E 38 D4
Padeș RO 159 C10
Padesh BG 165 F7
Padew Narodowa PL 143 F12
Padežine BIH 157 F8
Padiham GB 11 D7
Pădina RO 159 E11
Padina RO 161 D10
Padina SRB 159 C7
Padinska Skela SRB 158 D5
Padirac F 29 F9
Padise EST 131 C8
Padoby BY 133 F2
Padoux F 26 D6
Padova I 66 B4
Padria I 64 C2
Padrón E 38 C2
Padru I 64 B4
Padstow GB 12 D5
Padsvillye BY 133 F3
Padul E 53 B9
Padula I 60 C5
Paduli I 60 A3
Padure LV 134 C3
Pădureni RO 153 D12
Paesana I 37 B6
Paese I 72 E5
Pag HR 67 D11
Pagani I 60 B3
Paganica I 62 C4
Paganico I 65 B4
Pagėgiai LT 134 F3
Pagiriai LT 135 F8
Pagiriai LT 137 D11
Paglieta I 63 C6
Pagnes I 64 D2
Pabradė LT 137 D12
Pabu F 22 C5
Pacanów PL 143 F11
Paceco I 58 D2
Pacheia Ammos GR 179 E10
Pachino I 59 F7
Pachni GR 171 B7
Paciano I 62 C4
Pácin H 145 G4
Pačir SRB 150 F3
Pack A 73 C10
Pačlavice CZ 77 D12
Pacos de Ferreira P 38 F3
Pacov CZ 77 D8
Pacsa H 149 C8
Ottweiler D 21 F8
Otwock PL 141 F4
Otxandio E 41 B6
Otyń PL 81 C9
Otzing D 76 E3
Ouanne F 25 E9
Ouarville F 24 D6
Ouca P 44 C3
Oucques F 24 E5
Oud-Beijerland NL 16 E2
Ouddorp NL 182 B3
Oudehaske NL 16 C5
Oudemirdum NL 16 C5
Oudenaarde B 19 C8
Oudenbosch NL 16 E3
Oudenburg B 18 B7
Oudeschild NL 16 B3
Oude-Tonge NL 16 E2
Oud-Gastel NL 16 E2
Oudon F 23 F9
Oud-Turnhout B 16 F3
Oud-Vossemeer NL 16 E2
Oudzele B 182 C2
Oued Laou MA 53 F6
Ouffet B 19 D11
Oughterard IRL 6 C4
Ougney F 26 F4
Ouguela P 45 F6
Ouistreham F 23 B11
Oulainen FIN 119 F13
Oulanka FIN 115 F5
Oulchy-le-Château F 25 B9
Oulder B 20 D6
Oullins F 30 D6
Oulton GB 15 C12
Oundle GB 15 C8
Oupeye B 19 C12
Ouranoupoli GR 170 D5
Oure DK 87 E7
Ourense E 38 D4
Ourique P 50 D3
Ourol E 38 A4
Ouroux-en-Morvan F 25 F10
Ouroux-sur-Saône F 31 B8
Ourville-en-Caux F 18 E2
Oust F 33 E8
Outakoski FIN 113 D16
Outarville F 24 D7
Outeiro P 38 E2
Outeiro P 39 E6
Outeiro de Rei E 38 B4
Outeiro Seco P 38 E5
Outokumpu FIN 125 E12
Outomuro E 38 D4
Outreau F 15 F12
Outwell GB 11 F12
Ouveillan F 34 D4
Ouzouer-le-Marché F 24 E6
Ouzouer-sur-Loire F 25 E7
Ovada I 37 B9
Ovanåker S 103 D10
Ovanmo S 107 D10
Ovar P 44 C3
Ovaro I 73 D6
Ovča SRB 158 D6

Oxelösund S 93 B10
Oxenhope GB 11 D8
Oxentea MD 154 C4
Oxford GB 13 B12
Oxhalsö S 99 C11
Oxie S 87 D12
Oxkangar FIN 122 D8
Oxshott GB 15 E8
Oxted GB 15 E9
Oxton GB 5 D11
Oxylithos GR 175 B9
Øyangen N 104 E7
Øydegarden N 104 E4
Øyenkilen N 91 A8
Øyer N 101 D12
Øyeren N 96 B7
Øyjord N 108 B9
Oy-Mittelberg D 71 B10
Øynes N 108 B9
Øynes N 111 C11
Oyonnax F 31 C9
Øyslebø N 90 C2
Oyten D 17 B12
Øyvatnet N 111 C12
Oza E 38 B3
Ozaeta E 41 C7
Ozalj HR 148 E4
Ožárow PL 143 E12
Ożarów Mazowiecki PL 141 F3
Ožbalt SLO 148 C4
Özbaşı TR 177 D9
Özbek TR 177 C9
Ózd H 145 G1
Oždany SK 147 E9
Özdere TR 177 D9
Ożenna PL 145 E4
Ozerki RUS 136 D5
Ozery RUS 136 E4
Ozieri I 64 B3
Ozimek PL 142 E5
Ozimica BIH 157 D9
Özlüce TR 181 B9
Ozoir-la-Ferrière F 25 C8
Ozolaine LV 133 D2
Ozoli LV 131 F9
Ozoli LV 134 B4
Ozoli LV 135 C12
Ozolmuiža LV 133 D2
Ozolnieki LV 134 C7
Ozora H 149 C10
Ozorków PL 143 C7
Ozun RO 153 F7
Ozzano dell'Emilia I 66 D3
Ozzano Monferrato I 68 C5

P

Pääaho FIN 121 D10
Pääjärvi FIN 123 E13
Paakinmäki FIN 121 F11
Paakkila FIN 125 E11
Paakkola FIN 119 C13
Paal B 183 C6
Paalasmaa FIN 125 D12
Paaso FIN 127 C15
Paasvere EST 131 C13
Paatela FIN 129 B9
Paattinen FIN 126 D7
Paatus FIN 113 D17
Paavola FIN 119 E14
Pabaiskas LT 135 F9
Paberžė LT 137 D11
Pabianice PL 143 C7
Pabillonis I 64 D2
Pabiržė LT 135 D9
Pabneukirchen A 77 F7
Pabrade LT 137 D12

Pähl D 72 A3
Pahlen D 82 B6
Pahranichny BY 140 D9
Pahtaoja FIN 119 C14
Paião P 44 D3
Paide EST 131 D11
Paignton GB 13 E7
Paihola FIN 125 E13
Päijälä FIN 127 B12
Paikuse EST 131 E9
Pailhès F 33 D8
Paillet F 32 A5
Paimbœuf F 23 F7
Paimela FIN 127 C14
Paimio FIN 126 E8
Paimpol F 22 C5
Paimpont F 23 D7
Painswick GB 13 B10
Painten D 75 E10
Paipis FIN 127 E13
Paisley GB 5 D8
Paistu EST 131 E11
Paisua FIN 124 C7
Päivähäjoki FIN 115 F2
Päiväjoki FIN 115 F2
Pajala S 117 D10
Pajares de la Lampreana E 39 E8
Pajarón E 47 E9
Pajjczno PL 143 D6
Pajukoski FIN 125 C11
Pajukoste FIN 113 C20
Pajūris LT 134 F4
Pajuskylä FIN 124 D7
Pajuvaara FIN 121 D14
Páka H 149 C7
Pakaa FIN 127 D14
Pakalnė LT 134 F2
Pakalniai LT 135 F10
Pakapė LT 134 E6
Pakarila FIN 123 C11
Pakisjärvi FIN 117 C12
Pakkala FIN 127 C11
Pakod H 149 C8
Pakość PL 138 E5
Pakosław PL 81 C12
Pakoštane HR 156 E4
Pákozd H 149 B11
Pakrac HR 149 F8
Pakruojis LT 134 E7
Paks H 149 C11
Paksuniemi S 116 C5
Pala EST 131 D13
Palacios del Sil E 39 C7
Palacios de Sanabria E 39 D6
Palaciosrubios E 45 B10
Palade EST 130 D5
Palafrugell E 43 D10
Palagianello I 61 B7
Palagiano I 61 B8
Palagonia I 59 E6
Palaia I 66 E2
Palaia Fokaia GR 175 D8
Palaikastro GR 179 E11
Palaiochora GR 178 F6
Palaiochori GR 169 D6
Palaiochora GR 169 D10
Palaiochori GR 175 C7
Palaiokastritsa GR 168 E2
Palaiokastro GR 177 D9
Palaiokipos GR 177 A7
Palaiokomi GR 170 C5
Palaiomonastiro GR 169 F6
Palaiopoli GR 176 D4
Palaiopyrgos GR 169 E8
Palaiopyrgos GR 169 E8
Palaiopyrgos GR 174 C4
Palaiovracha GR 174 B5
Palairos GR 174 B2
Palaiseau F 25 C7
Palamas GR 169 F7
Palamós E 43 D10
Palamuse EST 131 D13
Palanca RO 153 D8
Palanga LT 134 E2
Pålänge S 119 C9
Palanzano I 66 D1
Palárikovo SK 146 E6
Palas de Rei E 38 C4
Palata I 63 D7
Palata BY 133 E7
Pālatca RO 152 D4
Palau I 64 A3
Palavas-les-Flots F 35 C6
Palazzo Adriano I 58 D3
Palazzolo sull'Oglio I 69 B8
Palazzolo Acreide I 59 E6
Palazzo San Gervasio I 60 B6
Paldiski EST 131 C8
Pale BIH 157 E10
Pāle LV 131 F9
Paleičiai LT 134 F2
Palena I 63 D6
Palencia E 40 D2
Palenciana E 53 B7
Palenzuela E 40 D3
Palermo AL 168 D2
Palermo I 58 C3
Palešnica PL 144 D2
Palestrina I 62 D3
Pälevenelė LT 135 E10
Palež BIH 158 E3
Palhaça P 44 C3
Pálháza H 145 G4
Palia Kavala GR 171 C6
Paliano I 62 D4
Palić SRB 150 E4
Palinges F 30 B5
Palinuro I 60 C4
Paliouri GR 169 E9
Paliouria GR 169 E6
Palis F 25 D10
Paliseul B 19 E11
Palivere EST 131 D7
Palizzi I 59 D9
Paljakka FIN 121 B14
Paljakka FIN 121 C11
Pälkäne FIN 127 C11
Pälkem S 118 B7
Palkino RUS 132 F3
Palkisoja FIN 115 A2
Palkovice CZ 146 B6
Palladio GR 171 B8
Pallagorio I 61 E7
Pallarés E 51 C7
Pallas Grean New IRL 8 C6
Pallas Green IRL 8 C6
Pälli FIN 119 E16
Palling D 75 F12

Palluau F 28 B2
Palluau-sur-Indre F 29 B8
Palma P 50 C2
Palma Campania I 60 B3
Palma del Río E 51 D9
Palma de Mallorca E 49 E10
Palma di Montechiaro I 58 E4
Palmadula I 64 B1
Palmanova E 49 E10
Palmanova I 73 E7
Palmaz P 44 C4
Palmeira P 38 E3
Palmela P 50 B2
Palmi I 59 C8
Pálmonostora H 150 D4
Palmse EST 131 B11
Palnackie GB 5 F9
Palneca F 37 H10
Palo del Colle I 61 A7
Palohuornas S 116 E6
Palojärvi FIN 115 E2
Palojärvi FIN 117 A10
Palojärvi FIN 117 E14
Palojoensuu FIN 116 B10
Palokki FIN 125 E11
Palomaa FIN 113 E19
Palomäki FIN 125 D11
Palomar de Arroyos E 42 F2
Palomares del Río E 51 E7
Palomas E 51 B7
Palombara Sabina I 62 C3
Palombaro I 63 C6
Palomenė LT 137 D9
Palomera E 47 D8
Palomeras del Campo E 47 E7
Palomonte I 60 B4
Palonoja FIN 115 B2
Palonselkä FIN 117 D13
Palonurmi FIN 125 D10
Paloperä FIN 115 F4
Palos de la Frontera E 51 E6
Palosenjärvi FIN 124 C8
Palotabozsok H 149 D11
Palotáshalom H 150 B4
Palovaara FIN 119 B12
Palovaara FIN 119 B16
Palovaara FIN 121 E13
Palovaara FIN 125 E14
Pals E 43 D10
Pålsboda S 92 A6
Palsmane LV 135 B12
Palsselkä FIN 117 D16
Pålsträsk S 118 C6
Paltamo FIN 121 F10
Paltanen FIN 124 F7
Paltaniemi FIN 121 F10
Paltin RO 153 F9
Păltiniş RO 153 A9
Păltiniş RO 159 C9
Păltinoasa RO 153 B7
Pal'tsevo RUS 129 D10
Paludi I 61 D7
Paluel F 18 E2
Paluknys LT 137 E10
Paluzza I 73 C7
Palyatskishki BY 137 E11
Palyessye BY 135 F12
Palzem D 20 E6
Pambukovica SRB 158 E4
Pameče SLO 73 C11
Pamfylla GR 177 A8
Pamhagen A 149 A7
Pamiers F 33 D9
Pampāļi LV 134 C4
Pamparato I 37 C7
Pampelonne F 33 B10
Pampilhosa P 44 D4
Pampilhosa da Serra P 44 D5
Pampliega E 40 D4
Pamplona E 32 E2
Pampow D 83 C10
Pamproux F 28 C5
Pamukçu TR 173 E8
Panaci RO 152 C6
Panagia GR 171 C7
Panagia GR 171 E8
Panagia GR 178 E9
Panagyurishte BG 165 D9
Panagyurski Kolonii BG 165 D9
Panahor AL 168 C2
Panaitolio GR 174 B3
Panaja AL 168 C1
Pănăşeşti MD 154 C3
Panassac F 33 D7
Pănătău RO 161 C8
Panazol F 29 D8
Pancalieri I 37 B7
Pancar TR 177 C9
Pancarköy TR 173 B7
Pănceşti RO 153 E10
Pančevo SRB 158 D6
Pancharevo BG 165 D7
Panciu RO 153 F10
Pancorbo E 40 C5
Pâncota RO 151 E8
Pancrudo E 42 F1
Pánd H 150 C4
Pandėlys LT 135 D10
Pandino I 69 C8
Pandrup DK 86 A5
Pandy GB 13 B9
Panelia FIN 126 C6
Panemunė LT 136 C4
Panemunėlis LT 135 E10
Panes E 39 B10
Pănet RO 152 D4
Panevėžys LT 135 E8
Panga EST 130 D4
Pângărați RO 153 D8
Pange F 186 C1
Panicale I 62 A2
Panichkovo BG 166 F4
Panissières F 30 D5
Paniza E 41 F9
Panjas F 32 C5
Panjevac SRB 159 E8
Panjik BIH 157 C9
Panka FIN 124 D7
Pankajärvi FIN 125 D14
Pankakoski FIN 125 D14
Panker D 83 B9
Panki PL 142 E6
Pannarano I 60 A3
Pannes F 25 D8
Panni I 60 A4
Panningen NL 16 F5
Pannonhalma H 149 A9
Panóias P 50 D3
Panorama GR 169 C9
Panormos GR 178 E8
Panschwitz-Kuckau D 80 D6
Pantanassa GR 178 B4
Päntäne FIN 122 F8
Pantelimon RO 155 D2
Pantelimon RO 161 E8
Panticeu RO 152 C3
Panticosa E 32 E5
Pantoja E 46 D5
Panttikylä FIN 122 F8
Panttila FIN 122 E8
Pant-y-dwr GB 13 A8
Paola I 60 E6
Pap H 145 G5
Pápa H 149 B8
Papadianika GR 178 B4
Papasidero I 60 D5
Pápateszér H 149 B9
Papenburg D 17 B8
Papendorf D 83 B12
Papendrecht NL 16 E3
Papilė LT 134 D5
Papilys LT 135 D10
Papín SK 145 E5
Papkeszi H 149 B10
Paplaka LV 134 D2
Papowo Biskupie PL 138 D6
Pappades GR 175 B7
Pappados GR 177 A7
Pappenheim D 75 E8
Papradno SK 146 C6
Paprotnia PL 141 F6
Par GB 12 E5
Parabita I 61 C10
Paraćin SRB 159 F7
Paracuellos E 47 E9
Paracuellos de Jarama E 46 C5
Parád H 147 F10
Parada P 45 C6
Parada de Ester P 44 C4
Parada de Pinhão P 38 F4
Parada de Rubiales E 45 B10
Parada de Sil E 38 D4
Paradas E 51 E9
Paradeisi GR 181 D8
Paradeisia GR 174 E5
Paradeisos GR 171 B7
Paradela E 38 C5
Paradela P 38 E4
Paradela P 44 B5
Paradyż PL 141 H2
Parainen FIN 126 E7
Parakalamos GR 168 E4
Parakka S 116 D7
Parakoila GR 177 A7
Paralepa EST 130 D7
Paralia GR 174 C4
Paralia GR 175 F6
Paralia Avdiron GR 171 C7
Paralia Saranti GR 175 C6
Paralia Tyrou GR 175 E6
Paralio Astros GR 175 E6
Paramé F 23 C8
Parâmio P 39 E6
Páramo del Sil E 39 C7
Paramythia GR 168 F4
Paranesti GR 171 B6
Paranhos P 44 D5
Parantala FIN 123 E15
Parapotamos GR 168 E3
Paras N 111 B19
Părău RO 152 F6
Parava RO 153 E9
Paravola GR 174 B4
Paray-le-Monial F 30 C5
Parcani MD 154 B3
Parcent E 56 D4
Parcé-sur-Sarthe F 23 E11
Parchen D 79 B11
Parchim D 83 D11
Parchovany SK 145 F4
Parchów PL 81 D9
Parchowo PL 85 B13
Parciaki PL 139 D11
Parcoul F 28 E6
Parczew PL 141 G7
Pardais P 50 B5
Pardies F 32 D4
Pardilhó P 44 C3
Pardoși RO 161 C9
Pardubice CZ 77 B9
Parechcha BY 137 F9
Paredes de Coura P 38 E2
Paredes de Nava E 39 D10
Pareja E 47 C7
Parempuyre F 28 F4
Parenti I 61 E6
Parentis-en-Born F 32 B3
Parets del Vallès E 43 D8
Parey D 79 B10
Parga GR 168 F3
Pârgăreşti RO 153 E9
Pargas FIN 126 E7
Parghelia I 59 B8
Pargny-sur-Saulx F 25 C12
Pargolovo RUS 129 E13
Parhalahti FIN 119 F12
Päri EST 131 E11
Parigné-l'Évêque F 24 E3
Parikkala FIN 129 B12
Parincea RO 153 E10
Paris F 25 C7
Parisot F 33 B9
Parisot F 33 C9
Parissavaara FIN 125 E16
Pärjänsuo FIN 120 C9
Părjol RO 153 D9
Park GB 4 F2
Parkajoki S 117 C10
Parkalompolo S 116 C9
Parkano FIN 123 F10
Parkkila FIN 121 D11
Parkkila FIN 123 C14
Parkkila FIN 128 B7
Parkkima FIN 123 C15
Parkkuu FIN 127 B10
Parksepa EST 131 F13
Parkstein D 75 C11
Parkua FIN 125 B9
Parkumäki FIN 129 B10
Parla E 46 D5
Parlan F 29 F10
Parma I 66 C1
Parndorf A 77 G11
Pärnu EST 131 E8
Pärnu-Jaagupi EST 131 D9
Paroikia GR 176 E5
Parola FIN 127 C11
Paron F 25 D9
Parowa PL 81 D8
Parrillas E 45 D10
Pärsama EST 130 D5
Parsau D 79 A8
Parsberg D 75 D10
Pârscov RO 161 C9
Pârşcoveni RO 160 E4
Parsęcko PL 85 C11
Parstein D 84 E6
Partakko FIN 113 E20
Partaloa E 55 E8
Partanna I 58 D2
Parteboda S 103 A10
Partenen A 71 D10
Partenstein D 74 B6
Pârteştii de Jos RO 153 B7
Parthenay F 28 B5
Partheni GR 177 E8
Partinello F 37 G9
Partinico I 58 C3
Partizani BG 167 C8
Partizani SRB 158 E5
Partizánska Ľupča SK 147 C8
Partizánske SK 146 D6
Partney GB 11 E12
Parton GB 10 B4
Partry IRL 6 E4
Partsi EST 131 E14
Parudaminys LT 137 D11
Pårup DK 86 C4
Parva RO 152 C5
Parvialnen S 119 C11
Påryd S 89 B9
Parysów PL 141 G5
Parzęczew PL 143 C7
Pasai Donibane E 32 D2
Paşaköy TR 171 C10
Paşaköy TR 171 E10
Paşaköy TR 173 E8
Pasaköy TR 177 B10
Pasalankylä FIN 125 D10
Paşayiğit TR 172 C6
Paşcani RO 153 C9
Pasching A 76 F6
Paseka CZ 77 C12
Pas-en-Artois F 18 D5
Pasewalk D 84 C6
Pasi FIN 128 D7
Pasiàn di Prato I 73 D7
Pasiano di Pordenone I 73 E6
Pasieki PL 139 E12
Pasiene LV 133 D4
Pasikovci HR 149 F9
Paskalevets BG 166 C4
Paskalevo BG 155 F1
Påskallavik S 89 A10
Pasłęk PL 139 B8
Pasmajärvi FIN 117 D12
Pašman HR 156 E3
Passage East IRL 9 D9
Passail A 148 B5
Passais F 23 C10
Passau D 76 E4
Passignano sul Trasimeno I 66 F5
Passow D 84 D6
Passy F 31 D10
Pastavy BY 135 F13
Pastende LV 134 B5
Pasto FIN 123 E10
Pastoriza E 38 B5
Pastrana E 47 D7
Păstrăveni RO 153 C9
Pašuliene LV 135 E12
Pasvalys LT 135 D8
Pašvitinys LT 134 D7
Pasym PL 139 C10
Pasytsely UA 154 B5
Pászab H 145 G4
Paszowice PL 81 D10
Pásztó H 147 F9
Pasztowa Wola PL 141 H4
Pata SK 146 E5
Pataias P 44 E3
Patak H 147 E8
Patana FIN 123 D11
Pătârlagele RO 161 C8
Patay F 24 D6
Patchway GB 13 B9
Pateley Bridge GB 11 C8
Pateniemi FIN 119 D14
Patergassen A 73 C8
Paterna E 48 E4
Paterna del Campo E 51 E7
Paterna del Madera E 55 B8
Paterna del Río E 55 E7
Paterna de Rivera E 52 C5
Paternion A 73 C8
Paternò I 59 D6
Paterno I 60 C5
Paternopoli I 60 B4
Patersdorf D 76 D3
Paterud S 96 C7
Patiška Reka MK 164 F3
Pátka H 149 B11
Patmos GR 177 E8
Patna GB 4 E7
Pątnów PL 142 D6
Patokoski FIN 117 E14
Patoniemi FIN 121 B12
Patoniva FIN 113 D19
Patos AL 168 C2
Patra GR 174 C4
Pătrăuţi RO 153 B8
Patrica I 62 D4
Patrick GBM 10 C2
Patrimonio F 37 F10
Patrington GB 11 D11
Pátroha H 145 G4
Pattada I 64 B3
Pattensen D 78 B6
Patterdale GB 10 B6
Patti I 59 C6
Pattijoki FIN 119 E13
Pättikkä FIN 116 A7
Pătulele RO 159 E10
Patumšiai LT 134 E5
Pâturages B 182 E3
Páty H 149 A11
Pau F 32 D5
Păuca RO 152 E3
Paudorf A 77 F9
Pauilhac F 33 C7
Pauillac F 28 E4
Paukarlahti FIN 124 E9
Paukkaja FIN 125 E14
Paukkeri FIN 120 D9
Paul P 44 D5
Paularo I 73 C7
Păuleni-Ciuc RO 153 E7
Pauleşti MD 154 C2
Păuleşti RO 151 B10
Paulhac-en-Margeride F 30 F3
Paulhan F 34 C5
Paulilatino I 64 C2
Paulinenaue D 83 E13
Păuliş RO 151 E8
Paulistrom S 92 E7
Paüls E 42 F4
Paulx F 28 B2
Păunești RO 153 E10
Pausa D 79 E11
Păuşeşti RO 160 C4
Păuşeşti-Măglaşi RO 160 C4
Pauträsk S 107 B13
Pauvres F 19 F10
Pavel BG 166 C5
Pavel Banya BG 166 D4
Pavia I 69 C7
Pavia P 50 B3
Pavia di Udine I 73 E7
Pavías E 48 E4
Pavie F 33 C7
Pavilly F 18 E2
Pāvilosta LV 134 C2
Pavleševci MK 164 F4
Pavliani GR 174 B5
Pavlikeni BG 166 C4
Pavliš SRB 159 C7
Pavlivka UA 154 C5
Pavlivka UA 154 F4
Pavlos GR 175 B7
Pavlovac HR 149 E8
Pavlovce nad Uhom SK 145 F5
Pavullo nel Frignano I 66 D2
Pavy RUS 132 E6
Päwesin D 79 A12
Pawłosiów PL 144 D6
Pawłówek PL 138 D4
Pawłowice PL 81 C11
Pawłowiczki PL 142 F5
Pawonków PL 142 E6
Paxton GB 5 D12
Payerne CH 31 B10
Paymogo E 51 D5
Payrac F 29 F8
Payrin-Augmontel F 33 C10
Payzac F 29 E8
Pazardzhik BG 165 E9
Pazarič BIH 157 E9
Pazarköy TR 173 E7
Pazin HR 67 B8
Paziols F 34 E4
Pázmánd H 149 B11
Pazos E 38 D2
Pchelarovo BG 166 F4
Pchelin BG 165 E8
Pcim PL 147 B9
Pčinja MK 164 E4
Peacehaven GB 15 F8
Peal de Becerro E 55 D6
Péaule F 23 E7
Pébrac F 30 E4
Peccia CH 71 E7
Peccioli I 66 E2
Pécel H 150 C3
Peceneaga RO 155 C2
Pečenjevce SRB 164 C4
Pechea RO 155 B1
Pechenga RUS 114 D10
Pechina E 55 F8
Pechory RUS 132 F2
Peći BIH 156 D5
Pecica RO 151 E7
Pećigrad BIH 156 B4
Pećinci SRB 158 D4
Peceneaga RO 155 F2
Peciu Nou RO 159 B7
Pecka CZ 77 B9
Pecka SRB 158 E4
Pečky CZ 77 B8
Pięcław PL 81 C10
Pečovská Nová Ves SK 145 E3
Pecq B 19 C7
Pécs H 149 D10
Pécsvárad H 149 D10
Pečurice MNE 163 E7
Pięczniew PL 142 C6
Pedaso I 62 A5
Pededze LV 133 B2
Pederobba I 72 E4
Pedersker DK 89 E7
Pedersöre FIN 122 C9
Pedino GR 169 C8
Pedrafita do Cebreiro E 38 C5
Pedrajas de San Esteban E 40 F2
Pedralba E 48 E3
Pedralba de la Pradería E 39 D6
Pedraza de Campos E 39 E10
Pedrera E 53 B7
Pedro Abad E 53 A8
Pedro Bernardo E 46 D3
Pedroche E 54 C3
Pedrógão P 44 E3
Pedrógão P 45 D6
Pedrógão P 50 C4
Pedrógão Grande P 44 E4
Pedrógão Pequeno P 44 E4
Pedro-Martínez E 55 D6
Pedro Muñoz E 47 F7
Pedrosa E 40 B4
Pedrosa del Príncipe E 40 D3
Pedrosillo de los Aires E 45 C9
Pedroso E 41 D6
Pedroso P 44 B3
Pedrouzos E 38 C2
Peebles GB 5 D10
Peel GBM 10 C2
Peenemünde D 84 B5
Peer B 19 B11
Peera FIN 112 F7
Peetri EST 131 D11
Pefki GR 175 A7
Pefkofyto GR 168 D4
Pefkoi GR 179 E10
Pefkos GR 178 E9
Pega P 45 D6
Pegalajar E 53 A9
Pegau D 79 D11
Peggau A 148 B4
Pegli I 37 C9
Pegnitz D 75 C10
Pego E 56 D4
Pego P 44 F4
Pegões P 50 B2
Pięgów PL 81 D11
Peguera E 49 E9
Pehčevo MK 165 F6
Pehkolanlahti FIN 120 F9
Pehlivanköy TR 173 B6
Peillac F 23 E7
Peille F 37 D6
Peine D 79 B7
Peio I 71 E11
Peipin F 35 B10
Peipohja FIN 126 C7
Peïra-Cava F 37 D6
Peiraias GR 175 D8
Peißen D 79 C10
Peißen D 79 C11
Peißenberg D 72 A3
Peiting D 71 B11
Peitz D 80 C6
Peize NL 17 B7
Pejë KS 163 D9
Pekankylä FIN 121 E13
Pekanpää FIN 119 B11
Pekkala FIN 119 B17
Pelagićevo BIH 157 C10
Pelago I 66 E4
Pelahustán E 46 D3
Pelarrodríguez E 45 C8
Pelasgia GR 175 B6
Pelči LV 134 C3
Pełczyce PL 85 D8
Peleagonzalo E 39 F9
Pelēči LV 135 D13
Pelekas GR 168 E2
Peleta GR 175 E6
Pelhřimov CZ 77 D8
Pelinei MD 154 F2
Pelinia MD 153 B11
Pelishat BG 165 C10
Pélissanne F 35 C9
Pelitköy TR 173 F6
Pelkoperä FIN 119 F15
Pelkosenniemi FIN 115 D2
Pella GR 169 C8
Pellaro I 59 C8
Pellegrino Parmense I 69 D8
Pellegrue F 28 F6
Pellérd H 149 D10
Pellesmäki FIN 124 E9
Pellestrina I 66 B5
Pellevoisin F 29 B8
Pellinki FIN 127 E14
Pellizzano I 69 A10
Pello FIN 117 E11
Pello S 117 E11
Pellosniemi FIN 128 C7
Pelm D 21 D7
Peloche E 45 F10
Pelovo BG 165 C9
Pelplin PL 138 C6
Pelsin D 84 C5
Pelso FIN 119 E16
Peltokangas FIN 123 D12
Peltosalmi FIN 124 C8
Peltovuoma FIN 117 B12
Pélussin F 30 E6
Pelvoux F 31 F9
Pély H 150 C5
Pelynt GB 12 E5
Pembrey GB 12 B6
Pembridge GB 13 A9
Pembroke GB 12 B5
Pembroke Dock GB 12 B5
Pembury GB 15 E9
Pemfling D 75 D12
Pempelijärvi S 116 E8
Peñacerrada E 41 C6
Penacova P 44 D4
Peñafiel E 40 E3
Penafiel P 44 B4
Peñaflor E 51 D9
Peñaflor de Hornija E 39 E10
Penagos E 40 B4
Peñalba E 42 E3
Peñalén E 47 C8
Peñalsordo E 51 B9
Penalva do Castelo P 44 C5
Penamacor P 45 D6
Peñaranda de Bracamonte E 45 C10
Peñaranda de Duero E 40 E5
Peñarroya de Tastavins E 42 F4
Peñarroya-Pueblonuevo E 51 C9
Peñarrubia E 55 C8
Penarth GB 13 C8
Peñascosa E 55 B8
Peñas de San Pedro E 55 B9
Peñausende E 39 F8
Penc H 150 B3
Pencader GB 12 A6
Pěnčín CZ 81 E8
Pendeen GB 12 E3
Pendilhe P 44 C5
Pendine GB 12 B5
Pendlebury GB 11 D7
Penedo Gordo P 50 D4
Penedono P 44 C6
Penela P 44 D4
Pénestin F 22 F7
Penészlek H 151 B9
Pengfors S 107 D17
Pengsjö S 107 D13
Pengsjö S 107 D17
Penha Garcia P 45 D6
Peniche P 44 F2
Penicuik GB 5 D10
Penikkajärvi FIN 121 C14
Peninki FIN 123 D15
Peninver GB 4 E5
Peñíscola E 48 D5
Penistone GB 11 D8
Penkridge GB 11 F7
Penkule LV 134 D6
Penkun D 84 D6
Penly F 18 E3
Penmarch F 22 E3
Pennabilli I 66 E5
Penna in Teverina I 62 C2
Pennapiedimonte I 63 C6
Pennautier F 33 D10
Penne F 33 B9
Penne I 62 C5
Penne-d'Agenais F 33 B7
Pennyghael GB 4 C4
Penrhiw-pâl GB 12 A6
Penrhyn Bay GB 10 E4
Penrith GB 5 F11
Penryn GB 12 E4
Pensala FIN 122 D9
Pentalofo GR 174 C3
Pentalofos GR 168 D5
Pentalofos GR 171 A10
Pentapoli GR 169 B10
Penteoria GR 174 C5
Pentinniemi FIN 119 C16
Pentir GB 10 E3
Pentone I 59 B10
Pentraeth GB 10 E3
Pentre GB 13 B8
Pentrefoelas GB 10 E4
Penttäjä S 117 E11
Penttilänvaara FIN 121 C12
Penvénan F 22 C5
Penybont GB 13 A8
Penybontfawr GB 10 F5
Pen-y-fai GB 13 B7
Penzance GB 12 E3
Penzberg D 72 A3
Penzlin D 84 D4
Péone F 36 C5
Pepelow D 83 B11
Pepeni MD 154 B2
Pepingen B 19 C9
Pepinster B 19 C12
Peplos GR 171 C10
Pipowo PL 81 C12
Përqin AL 168 B2
Peque E 39 D7
Pér H 149 A9
Pêra P 50 E3
Perabroddzye BY 133 E2
Perachora GR 175 C6
Perafita E 43 C8
Perä-Hyyppä FIN 122 F8
Peraia GR 169 C6
Peraia GR 169 C8
Perais P 44 E5
Perälä FIN 122 F7
Peralada E 43 C10
Peraleda de la Mata E 45 E10
Peraleda del Zaucejo E 51 C8
Peralejos E 42 G1
Peralejos de las Truchas E 47 C9
Perales del Alfambra E 42 F2
Perales del Puerto E 45 D7
Peralta E 32 F2
Peralta de Alcofea E 42 D3
Peralta de la Sal E 42 D4
Peraltilla E 42 C3
Peralva P 50 E4
Peralveche E 47 C8
Perama GR 168 E4
Perama GR 175 D8
Perama GR 178 E8
Perämäki FIN 122 D9
Peramola E 42 C6
Peranka FIN 121 D13
Peränne FIN 123 F11
Perä-Posio FIN 121 B10
Perarolo di Cadore I 72 D5
Peräseinäjoki FIN 123 E10
Perast MNE 163 E6
Perävaara FIN 115 E2
Perbál H 149 A11
Perchtoldsdorf A 77 F10
Percy F 23 C9
Perdasdefogu I 64 D3
Perdaxius I 64 E2
Perdifumo I 60 C4
Perdiguera E 41 E10
Perdika GR 168 F3
Perdika GR 175 D7
Perdiki GR 177 D7
Perdikkas GR 169 C6
Perduhovo Selo BIH 157 D6
Perechyn UA 145 F5
Peredo P 39 F6
Peregu Mare RO 151 E6
Perehins'ke UA 145 F9
Pereiras P 50 E3
Pereiro E 38 A4
Pereiro P 50 E4
Pereiro de Aguiar E 38 D4
Perekhrestove UA 154 C5
Pereíta MD 153 A9
Pereruela E 39 F8
Peresecina MD 154 C3
Peressaare EST 131 C13
Peretu RO 160 E6
Pereyma UA 154 A5
Perfugas I 64 B2
Perg A 77 F7
Pergine Valdarno I 66 F4
Pergine Valsugana I 69 A11
Pergola I 67 E6
Perho FIN 123 D12
Periam RO 151 E6
Periana E 53 C8
Pericei RO 151 C10
Périers F 23 B9
Perieți RO 160 E5
Perieți RO 161 D10
Périgueux F 29 E7
Perikleia GR 169 B7
Perila EST 131 C10
Perilla de Castro E 39 E8
Perín-Chym SK 145 F3
Peripravа RO 155 C5
Periș RO 161 D7
Perișani RO 160 C4
Perișor RO 160 E2
Perișoru RO 161 E11
Perissa GR 179 C9
Peristasi GR 169 D8
Peristera GR 169 C9
Peristeri GR 175 C8
Perithori GR 169 B10
Perivoli GR 168 E5
Perivoli GR 168 F3
Perivoli GR 174 A5
Perivoli GR 174 B5
Perivolia GR 178 E7
Perjasica HR 156 B3
Perkáta H 149 B11
Perkiömäki FIN 123 D9
Perl D 20 F6
Perlat AL 163 F8
Perleberg D 83 D11
Perlejewo PL 141 E7
Perlez SRB 158 C5
Perloja LT 137 E9
Perły PL 136 E4
Permani HR 67 B9
Permantokoski FIN 117 F16
Përmet AL 168 D3
Pernå FIN 127 E15
Pernarava LT 134 F7
Pernarec CZ 76 C4
Pernegg an der Mur A 148 B4
Pernersdorf A 77 E10
Pernes P 44 F3
Pernes-les-Fontaines F 35 C9
Perni GR 171 B7
Pernik BG 165 D7
Perniö FIN 127 E9
Perniön asema FIN 127 E9
Pernitz A 77 G9
Pernu FIN 121 B10
Pero I 69 B7
Peroguarda P 50 C3
Pérols F 35 C6
Péron F 31 C8
Perondi AL 168 C2
Péronnas F 31 C7
Péronne F 18 E6
Perosa Argentina I 31 F11
Pero Viseu P 44 D6
Perpignan F 34 E4
Perranporth GB 12 E4
Perrecy-les-Forges F 30 B5
Perreux F 30 C5
Perrigny F 31 B8
Perrogney-les-Fontaines F 26 E3
Perros-Guirec F 22 C5
Perrum-Åbmir FIN 113 E19
Persan F 25 B7
Persåsen S 102 A7
Persberg S 97 C11
Persbo S 97 B13
Persenbeug A 77 F8
Pershagen S 93 A11
Pershamawskaya BY 133 E4
Pershore GB 13 A10
Pershotravneve UA 155 C4
Pershyttan S 97 D13
Persnäs S 89 A11
Persön S 118 C8
Perstorp S 87 C12
Perth GB 5 C10
Perthes F 25 D8
Pertouli GR 168 E5
Perttaus FIN 117 D15
Pertteli FIN 127 E9
Perttula FIN 127 E12
Pertuis F 35 C10
Pertunmaa FIN 127 C15
Pertusa E 42 C3
Peruc CZ 76 B5
Perućac SRB 158 F3
Perućica BIH 157 F10
Perugia I 66 F5
Perukka FIN 119 F17
Perunkajärvi FIN 117 E15
Perushtitsa BG 165 E10
Perušić HR 156 C3
Péruwelz B 19 C8
Pervalka LT 134 F2
Pervenchères F 24 D3
Pervomaisc MD 154 D5
Pervomayskoye RUS 129 E12
Perwez B 19 C10
Pesadas de Burgos E 40 C4
Pesaro I 67 E6
Pescaglia I 66 E1
Pescantina I 66 B2
Pescara I 63 C6
Pescari RO 159 D8
Pescasseroli I 62 D5
Pesceana RO 160 D4
Peschadoires F 30 D3
Peschici I 63 D10
Peschiera del Garda I 66 B2
Pescia I 66 E2
Pescina I 62 C5
Pescocostanzo I 62 D6
Pescolanciano I 63 D6
Pescopennataro I 63 D6
Pescorocchiano I 62 C4
Pesco Sannita I 60 A3
Peseux CH 31 B10
Peshkopi AL 163 F9
Peshtera BG 165 E9
Pesiökylä FIN 121 E12
Pesiönranta FIN 121 E12
Pesmes F 26 F4
Pesnica SLO 148 C5
Pesochnyy RUS 129 E13
Peso da Régua P 44 B5
Pesquera de Duero E 40 E3
Pessac F 28 F4
Pessalompolo FIN 117 F12
Pessan F 33 C7
Pesse NL 17 C6
Pessin D 80 A3
Peštani MK 168 B4
Peştera RO 155 E2
Peştişani RO 159 C11
Pestișu Mic RO 151 F10
Pesués E 40 B3
Pešurići BIH 157 E11
Petacciato I 63 C7
Petäikkö FIN 119 E16
Petäiskylä FIN 125 C12
Petäjäjärvi FIN 119 C17
Petäjäkangas FIN 119 D17
Petäjäskoski FIN 119 B14
Petäjäskoski FIN 119 F13
Petäjävesi FIN 123 F14
Petalax FIN 122 E6
Petalidi GR 174 F4
Pétange L 20 E5
Petas GR 174 A3
Petelea RO 152 D5
Peteranec HR 149 D7
Peterborough GB 11 F11
Peterculter GB 3 L12
Peterhead GB 3 K13
Péteri H 150 C3
Peterlee GB 5 F14
Petersberg D 74 A6
Petersdorf D 75 E9
Petersdorf auf Fehmarn D 83 B10
Petersfield GB 15 E7
Petershagen D 17 D11
Petershagen D 80 B6
Peterswell IRL 6 F5
Pétervására H 147 E10
Pethelinos GR 169 C10
Petilia Policastro I 59 A10
Petín E 38 D5
Petisträsk S 107 B17
Petite-Rosselle F 186 C2
Petit-Mars F 23 F9
Petitmont F 186 D2
Petit-Noir F 31 B7
Petko Karavelovo BG 166 C5
Petko Slaveykov BG 165 C10
Petkula FIN 115 C1
Petkus D 80 C4
Petlovača SRB 158 D3
Pet Mogili BG 166 E6
Petneháza H 145 G5
Petőfibánya H 150 B4
Petra E 57 B11
Petra GR 171 F10
Petrăchioaia RO 161 D8
Petrades GR 172 B6
Petralia-Soprana I 58 D5
Petran AL 168 D3
Petrana GR 169 D6
Petrella Salto I 62 C4
Petrella Tifernina I 63 D7
Petrer E 56 E3
Petreşti RO 151 B9
Petreşti RO 160 D6
Petreştii de Jos RO 152 D3
Petreto-Bicchisano F 37 H9
Petriano I 67 E6
Petricani RO 153 C8
Petrich BG 169 B9
Petrijevci HR 149 E11
Petrila RO 160 C2
Petrinja HR 148 F6
Petriș RO 151 E9
Petritoli I 62 A5
Petrivka UA 154 D4
Petrivs'k UA 154 E3
Petrochori GR 174 B4

Petrodvorets *RUS* 129 F12
Pétrola *E* 55 B9
Petromaki *FIN* 125 E9
Petronà *I* 59 A10
Petroşani *RO* 160 C2
Petrota *GR* 166 F6
Petroussa *GR* 170 B6
Petrov *CZ* 146 D4
Petrova *RO* 152 B4
Petrovac *MNE* 163 E6
Petrovac *SRB* 159 E7
Petrovany *SK* 145 F3
Petrovaradin *SRB* 158 C4
Petrovec *MK* 164 F4
Petrovice *CZ* 76 C6
Petrovice u Karvine *CZ* 147 B7
Petroviči *BIH* 157 D10
Petroviči *MNE* 162 D6
Petrovo *BG* 169 B9
Petrovo *RUS* 136 D1
Petrovo Selo *SRB* 159 D9
Petruma *FIN* 125 F11
Petru Rareş *RO* 152 C4
Petruşeni *MD* 153 B10
Petřvald *CZ* 146 B6
Petřvald *CZ* 146 B6
Petsakoi *GR* 174 C5
Petsmo *FIN* 122 D7
Petten *NL* 16 C3
Pettigo *GB* 7 C7
Pettineo *I* 58 D5
Petting *D* 73 A6
Pettneu am Arlberg *A* 71 C10
Pettorano sul Gizio *I* 62 D5
Petworth *GB* 15 F7
Peujard *F* 28 E5
Peura *FIN* 119 B14
Peurajärvi *FIN* 119 B16
Pevensey *GB* 15 F9
Peveragno *I* 37 C7
Pewsey *GB* 13 C11
Pewsum (Krummhörn) *D* 17 B8
Pexonne *F* 27 D6
Peymeinade *F* 36 D5
Peynier *F* 35 D10
Peypin *F* 35 D10
Peyrat-le-Château *F* 29 D9
Peyrehorade *F* 32 C3
Peyriac-Minervois *F* 34 D4
Peyrieu *F* 31 D8
Peyrins *F* 31 E7
Peyrolles-en-Provence *F* 35 C10
Peyruis *F* 35 B10
Pézenas *F* 34 D5
Pjzino *RO* 151 E9
Pezinok *SK* 146 E4
Pezuls *F* 29 F7
Pfaffenberg *D* 75 E11
Pfaffendorf *D* 80 B6
Pfaffenhausen *D* 71 A10
Pfaffenhofen an der Ilm *D* 75 E10
Pfaffenhofen an der Roth *D* 187 E9
Pfaffenhoffen *F* 27 C8
Pfäffikon *CH* 27 F10
Pfaffing *D* 75 F11
Pfalzfeld *D* 185 D8
Pfalzgrafenweiler *D* 27 C10
Pfarrkirchen *D* 76 F3
Pfarrweisach *D* 75 B8
Pfarrwerfen *A* 73 B7
Pfedelbach *D* 27 B11
Pflach *A* 71 B11
Pfons *A* 72 B3
Pförring *D* 75 E10
Pforzen *D* 71 B11
Pforzheim *D* 27 C10
Pfreimd *D* 75 D11
Pfronstetten *D* 27 D11
Pfronten *D* 71 B11
Pfullendorf *D* 27 E11
Pfullingen *D* 27 D11
Pfunds *A* 71 D11
Pfungstadt *D* 21 E11
Pfyn *CH* 27 E10
Phalsbourg *F* 27 C7
Philippeville *B* 19 D10
Philippine *NL* 182 S3
Philippsburg *D* 187 C5
Philippsreut *D* 76 E5
Piacenza *I* 69 C8
Piadena *I* 66 B1
Piana *F* 37 G9
Piana *GR* 174 D5
Piana Crixia *I* 37 C8
Piana degli Albanesi *I* 58 D3
Piancastagnaio *I* 62 B1
Piandimeleto *I* 66 E5
Pîàn di Scò *I* 66 E4
Pianella *I* 62 C6
Pianello Val Tidone *I* 37 B10
Piano del Voglio *I* 66 D3
Pianoro *I* 66 D3
Pianosa *I* 65 B2
Pianotolli-Caldarello *F* 37 J10
Pians *A* 71 C11
Piansano *I* 62 B1
Pianu *RO* 152 F2
Piaseczno *PL* 85 D7
Piaseczno *PL* 141 F4
Piasek *PL* 84 E6
Piaski *PL* 81 C12
Piaski *PL* 141 H7
Piastów *PL* 141 F3
Piątek *PL* 143 B7
Piątnica Poduchowna *PL* 139 D13
Piatra *RO* 160 F6
Piatra Neamţ *RO* 153 D8
Piatra Olt *RO* 160 E4
Piatra ḑoimului *RO* 153 D8
Piau-Engaly *F* 33 E6
Piazza al Serchio *I* 66 D1
Piazza Armerina *I* 58 E5
Piazza Brembana *I* 69 B8
Piazzatorre *I* 69 B8
Piazzola sul Brenta *I* 66 A4
Pibrac *F* 33 C8
Pičan *HR* 67 B9
Picar *AL* 168 D3
Picassent *E* 48 F4
Picauville *F* 23 B9
Picerno *I* 60 B5
Nichei *D* 83 D10
Pichl bei Wels *A* 76 F5
Pickering *GB* 11 C10
Pico *I* 62 E5
Picón *E* 54 A4

Picoto *P* 44 B3
Picquigny *F* 18 E5
Pidbuzh *UA* 145 E7
Pidhorodtsi *UA* 145 E7
Pidlisne *UA* 153 A7
Piebalgas *LV* 135 C8
Piechcin *PL* 138 E5
Piechowice *PL* 81 E9
Piecki *PL* 139 C11
Piecnik *PL* 85 D10
Piedicorte-di-Gaggio *F* 37 G10
Piedicroce *F* 37 G10
Piedimonte Etneo *I* 59 D7
Piedimonte Matese *I* 60 A2
Piedimulera *I* 68 A5
Piedrabuena *E* 54 A4
Piedrafita de Babia *E* 39 C7
Piedrahita *E* 45 D10
Piedralaves *E* 46 D3
Piedras Albas *E* 45 E7
Piedras Blancas *E* 39 A8
Piedruja *LV* 133 E2
Piegaro *I* 62 B2
Piégut-Pluviers *F* 29 D7
Piehinki *FIN* 119 E12
Piekary Śląskie *PL* 143 F6
Piekielnik *PL* 147 C9
Piekoszów *PL* 143 E9
Pieksämäen mlk *FIN* 124 F8
Pieksämäki *FIN* 124 F8
Pielavesi *FIN* 123 D17
Pieleşti *RO* 160 E3
Pielgrzymka *PL* 81 D9
Pienava *LV* 134 C6
Pieniążnica *PL* 85 C11
Pieniężno *PL* 139 B9
Pieńkowo *PL* 85 B11
Piennes *F* 19 F12
Pieńsk *PL* 81 D8
Pienza *I* 62 A1
Piera *E* 43 D7
Pierowall *GB* 3 G11
Pierre-Buffière *F* 29 D8
Pierre-Châtel *F* 31 F8
Pierre-de-Bresse *F* 31 B9
Pierrefeu-du-Var *F* 36 E4
Pierrefitte-Nestalas *F* 32 E5
Pierrefitte-sur-Aire *F* 26 C3
Pierrefonds *F* 18 F6
Pierrefontaine-les-Varans *F* 26 F4
Pierrefort *F* 30 F2
Pierrelatte *F* 35 B8
Pierrepont *F* 19 F12
Pierres *F* 24 C6
Pierrevert *F* 35 C10
Piershill *NL* 182 B4
Piertinjaure *S* 109 C17
Pierzchnica *PL* 143 E10
Piesau *D* 75 A9
Pieścirogi *PL* 139 E10
Piesendorf *A* 73 B6
Pieski *PL* 81 B8
Piesport *D* 185 E6
Pieštany *SK* 146 D5
Pieszkowo *PL* 136 D7
Pieszyce *PL* 81 E11
Pietrabbondante *I* 63 D8
Pietracatella *I* 63 D7
Pietracorbara *F* 37 F10
Pietra-di-Verde *F* 37 G10
Pietragalla *I* 60 B5
Pietralba *F* 37 F9
Pietra Ligure *I* 37 C8
Pietralunga *I* 66 F5
Pietramelara *I* 60 A2
Pietramontecorvino *I* 63 D8
Pietraperzia *I* 58 E5
Pietraporzio *I* 36 C6
Pietrari *RO* 160 C4
Pietrasanta *I* 66 E1
Pietravairano *I* 60 A2
Pietroasa *RO* 151 D9
Pietroasele *RO* 161 C9
Pietroşani *RO* 161 F7
Pietrosella *I* 37 H9
Pietroşiţa *RO* 161 C6
Pietrowice Wielkie *PL* 142 F5
Pieve d'Alpago *I* 72 D5
Pieve del Cairo *I* 68 C6
Pieve di Bono *I* 69 B10
Pieve di Cadore *I* 72 D5
Pieve di Cento *I* 66 C3
Pieve di Soligo *I* 72 E5
Pieve di Teco *I* 37 C7
Pieve Fosciana *I* 66 D1
Pievepelago *I* 66 D2
Pieve Santo Stefano *I* 66 E5
Pieve Torina *I* 62 A4
Pieve Vergonte *I* 68 A5
Piffonds *F* 25 D9
Piges *GR* 174 B5
Pigi *GR* 169 C6
Pigi *GR* 177 A7
Piglio *I* 62 D4
Pigna *I* 37 D7
Pignans *F* 36 E4
Pignataro Interamna *I* 62 E5
Pignataro Maggiore *I* 60 A2
Pignola *I* 60 B5
Pihlajakoski *FIN* 127 B13
Pihlajalahti *FIN* 127 B10
Pihlajalahti *FIN* 129 B9
Pihlajavaara *FIN* 125 D16
Pihlajavesi *FIN* 123 F12
Pihlava *FIN* 126 B6
Pihtipudas *FIN* 123 D15
Piikkiö *FIN* 126 E8
Piilijärvi *S* 116 C6
Piiloperä *FIN* 121 B12
Piippola *FIN* 119 F15
Piispajärvi *FIN* 119 F13
Piirsalu *EST* 131 C8
Piispa *FIN* 125 D9
Piispajärvi *FIN* 121 B13
Piittisjärvi *FIN* 119 B17
Pijnacker *NL* 16 D2
Pikkarala *FIN* 119 E15
Pikkula *FIN* 119 D17
Piktupenai *LT* 134 F3
Pila *I* 66 C5
Piła *PL* 85 D11
Pilar de la Mola *E* 57 D8
Pilise *S* 51 E7
Pilawa *PL* 141 G5
Piława Górna *PL* 81 E11
Pilchowice *PL* 142 F6
Pilda *LV* 133 D3
Piles *I* 56 D4
Pilgrimstad *S* 103 A9
Pili *GR* 175 B8
Pilica *PL* 143 F8
Pilis *H* 150 C4

Piliscsaba *H* 149 A11
Pilisszántó *H* 149 A11
Pilisszentiván *H* 149 A11
Pilisvörösvár *H* 149 A11
Pill *A* 72 B4
Pilling *GB* 10 D6
Pilníkov *CZ* 77 A9
Pilpala *FIN* 127 D11
Pilsach *P* 39 C11
Pilsting *D* 75 E12
Pilskalns *LV* 135 B13
Pilträsk *S* 118 C4
Pilu *RO* 151 D7
Pilviškiai *LT* 136 D7
Pilzno *PL* 143 G11
Pimentel *I* 64 E3
Pimperne *GB* 13 D10
Pimpiö *S* 117 E10
Piña de Campos *E* 40 D3
Piña de Esgueva *E* 40 E3
Piñar *E* 53 B10
Pinarbaşı *TR* 171 E10
Pinarca *TR* 173 B9
Pinarejo *E* 47 E8
Pinarhisar *TR* 173 A8
Pinarköy *TR* 181 B7
Pinasca *I* 31 F11
Pincehely *H* 149 C10
Pinchbeck *GB* 11 F11
Pinczów *PL* 143 E10
Pindstrup *DK* 86 C6
Pineda de Cigüela *E* 47 D7
Pineda de la Sierra *E* 40 D5
Pineda de Mar *E* 43 D9
Pinela *P* 39 E6
Piñel de Abajo *E* 40 E3
Pinerolo *I* 31 F11
Pineto *I* 62 B6
Piney *F* 25 D11
Pinggau *A* 148 B6
Pinhal Novo *P* 50 B2
Pinhanços *P* 44 D5
Pinhão *P* 44 B5
Pinheiro *P* 50 C2
Pinheiro Grande *P* 44 F4
Pinhel *P* 45 C6
Pinhoe *GB* 13 D8
Pinilla de Molina *E* 47 C9
Pinilla de Toro *E* 39 E9
Pinkafeld *A* 148 B6
Pinneberg *D* 82 C7
Pinnow *D* 81 C7
Pino *F* 37 F10
Pino *E* 39 E7
Pino del Río *E* 39 C10
Pinofranqueado *E* 45 D8
Pinols *F* 30 E3
Piñor *E* 38 D3
Pinoso *E* 56 E2
Pinos-Puente *E* 53 B9
Pinsac *F* 29 F9
Pinsió *FIN* 127 B9
Pintamo *FIN* 121 D10
Pintano *E* 32 E3
Pinto *E* 46 D5
Pinwherry *GB* 4 E7
Pinzano al Tagliamento *I* 73 D6
Pinzio *P* 45 C6
Pinzolo *I* 69 A10
Piobbico *I* 66 E6
Piolenc *F* 35 B8
Pioltello *I* 69 C7
Piombino *I* 65 B3
Piombino Dese *I* 72 E4
Pionerskiy *RUS* 139 A9
Pionki *PL* 141 H4
Pionsat *F* 29 C11
Pioraco *I* 67 F6
Piornal *E* 45 D9
Piossasco *I* 31 F11
Piotrkowice *PL* 81 D11
Piotrków Kujawski *PL* 138 E5
Piotrków Trybunalski *PL* 143 D8
Piove di Sacco *I* 66 B4
Piovene Rocchette *I* 69 B11
Piperskärr *S* 93 D8
Pipirig *RO* 153 C8
Pipriac *F* 23 E8
Piqeras *AL* 168 D2
Pir *RO* 151 C9
Piraino *I* 59 C6
Piran *SLO* 67 A8
Pirčiupiai *LT* 137 E10
Pirdop *BG* 165 D9
Pirg *AL* 168 C4
Pirgovo *BG* 161 F7
Piriac-sur-Mer *F* 22 F6
Piricse *H* 151 B9
Pirin *BG* 169 A10
Pirinçci *TR* 173 D10
Pîrjolteni *MD* 154 C2
Pirkkala *FIN* 127 C11
Pîrlița *MD* 153 C11
Pîrlița *MD* 154 A2
Pirmasens *D* 21 F9
Pirna *D* 80 E5
Pirmmill *GB* 4 D6
Pirot *SRB* 164 C6
Pirovac *HR* 156 E4
Pirtó *H* 150 E3
Pirttijoki *FIN* 121 E9
Pirttikoski *FIN* 119 B18
Pirttikoski *FIN* 119 F12
Pirttikoski *FIN* 127 C10
Pirttimäki *FIN* 123 C17
Pirttimäki *FIN* 124 E7
Pirttimäki *FIN* 125 C10
Pirttinen *FIN* 122 D10
Pirttivaara *FIN* 121 D14
Pirttivuopio *S* 111 E17
Pisa *FIN* 119 B14
Pisa *H* 66 E1
Pisanets *BG* 161 F8
Pisarovina *H* 148 E4
Pisarovo *BG* 165 C9
Pischeldorf in der Steiermark *A* 148 B5
Pişchia *RO* 151 F7
Pisciotta *I* 60 C4
Pişcolt *RO* 151 B9
Piscu *RO* 155 B1
Piscu Vechi *RO* 159 F11
Píšece *SLO* 148 D5
Písečná *CZ* 77 B12
Písek *CZ* 76 D6
Písek *CZ* 147 B7
Pishcha *UA* 141 G9
Pishchana *UA* 154 A5
Pishchanka *UA* 154 A3
Pisisaare *EST* 131 D11

Piskokefalo *GR* 179 E11
Piškorevci *HR* 157 B9
Pisoderi *GR* 168 C5
Pisogne *I* 69 B9
Pissonas *GR* 175 B8
Pissos *F* 32 B4
Pistiana *GR* 168 F5
Pisticci *I* 61 C7
Pisto *FIN* 121 D13
Pistoia *I* 66 E2
Pisz *PL* 139 C12
Piszczac *PL* 141 G8
Pitagowan *GB* 5 B9
Pitäjänmäki *FIN* 123 C15
Pitarque *E* 42 F2
Piteå *S* 118 D6
Piteşti *RO* 160 D5
Pithiviers *F* 25 D7
Pitigliano *I* 65 B5
Pitkäjärvi *FIN* 127 D9
Pitkälä *FIN* 129 B11
Pitkälahti *FIN* 124 E9
Pitkäsenkylä *FIN* 119 F12
Pitkyaranta *RUS* 129 B15
Pitlochry *GB* 5 B9
Pitomača *HR* 149 E8
Pitrags *LV* 130 F4
Pîtres *F* 55 F6
Pîtres *F* 18 F3
Pitscottie *GB* 5 C11
Pitsinaiika *GR* 174 C4
Pitstone *GB* 15 D7
Pitsund *S* 118 D7
Pitt *GB* 13 C12
Pittem *B* 19 C7
Pitten *A* 148 A6
Pittentrail *GB* 3 K8
Pittenweem *GB* 5 C11
Pitvaros *H* 150 E6
Pivašiūnai *LT* 137 E9
Pivka *SLO* 73 E9
Pivnice *SRB* 158 B4
Piwniczna-Zdrój *PL* 145 E2
Pizarra *E* 53 C7
Pizzighettone *I* 69 C8
Pizzo *I* 59 B9
Pizzoferrato *I* 63 D6
Pizzoli *I* 62 C4
Pjedsted *DK* 86 D4
Pjelax *FIN* 122 F6
Pjenovac *BIH* 157 D10
Pjesker *S* 118 C3
Plaaz *D* 83 C12
Plabennec *F* 22 C3
Placencia de las Armas *E* 32 D1
Plachkovtsi *BG* 166 D4
Plācis *LV* 135 B10
Plaffeien *CH* 31 B11
Plagia *GR* 169 B8
Plaidt *D* 21 D8
Plăieşii de Jos *RO* 153 E8
Plaintel *F* 22 D6
Plaisance *F* 33 C6
Plaisance-du-Touch *F* 33 C8
Plaisir *F* 24 C6
Plaka *GR* 174 A5
Plaka *GR* 171 D8
Plaka *GR* 175 C6
Plaka *GR* 179 B7
Plakias *GR* 178 E7
Plakovo *BG* 166 D4
Plana *BIH* 157 G9
Planá *CZ* 75 C12
Plana *I* 69 D10
Planá nad Lužnicí *CZ* 77 D7
Plaňany *CZ* 77 B8
Plancher-Bas *F* 27 E6
Plancoët *F* 23 C7
Plancy-l'Abbaye *F* 25 C10
Plan-de-Baux *F* 31 F7
Plan-de-la-Tour *F* 36 E5
Plandište *SRB* 159 C7
Plan-d'Orgon *F* 35 C8
Planegg *D* 75 F9
Planès *F* 33 F10
Plãni *LV* 131 F11
Plánice *CZ* 76 D4
Planina *SLO* 73 D8
Planina *SLO* 148 D4
Planina *SRB* 158 F3
Planinica *SRB* 159 F9
Planjane *HR* 156 E5
Plankenfels *D* 75 C9
Planos *GR* 174 D2
Plasencia *E* 45 D8
Plasencia del Monte *E* 41 D10
Plaški *HR* 156 B3
Plassen *N* 102 D4
Pláštovce *SK* 147 E7
Plasy *CZ* 76 C4
Plataies *GR* 175 C7
Platamona Lido *I* 64 B1
Platamonas *GR* 169 E8
Platamonas *GR* 171 B7
Platania *I* 59 A9
Platanias *GR* 175 A7
Platanistos *GR* 175 C10
Platanorrevma *GR* 169 D7
Platanos *GR* 174 C4
Platanos *GR* 175 A6
Platanos *GR* 178 C5
Platanos *GR* 178 B4
Platanovrysi *GR* 174 C4
Plătăreşti *RO* 161 E8
Plataria *GR* 168 F3
Plate *D* 83 C11
Plateliai *LT* 134 D3
Platerów *PL* 141 F7
Plati *GR* 171 A10
Platì *I* 59 C9
Platiana *GR* 174 D4
Platičevo *SRB* 158 D4
Platja d'Aro *E* 43 D10
Platja de Nules *E* 48 F4
Platone *LV* 134 C7
Platta *GR* 169 C8
Plattling *D* 76 E3
Platy *GR* 169 C8

Plavy *CZ* 81 E8
Pławno *PL* 85 C10
Plaza *E* 40 B6
Plazac *F* 29 E8
Plażów *PL* 144 C7
Pleaux *F* 29 E10
Plech *D* 75 C9
Plecka Dąbrowa *PL* 143 B8
Pleine-Fougères *F* 23 C8
Pleikšių *LV* 133 D2
Pleinfeld *D* 75 D8
Plélan-le-Grand *F* 23 D7
Plélo *F* 22 C6
Plémet *F* 22 D6
Plénée-Jugon *F* 23 C7
Pléneuf-Val-André *F* 22 C6
Pleniţa *RO* 159 E11
Plentzia *E* 40 B6
Plérin *F* 22 C6
Plescop *F* 22 E5
Pleşcuţa *RO* 151 E9
Pleşeni *MD* 153 C12
Plešivec *SK* 145 F1
Plesná *CZ* 75 B11
Plesná *D* 144 D2
Pleşoiu *RO* 160 E4
Plessa *D* 80 D5
Plessé *F* 23 E8
Plestin-les-Grèves *F* 22 C4
Pleszew *PL* 142 C4
Pleternica *HR* 157 B8
Plettenberg *D* 21 B9
Pleubian *F* 22 C5
Pleudihen-sur-Rance *F* 23 C8
Pleumartin *F* 29 B7
Pleumeur-Bodou *F* 22 C4
Pleurs *F* 25 C10
Pleuven *F* 22 E3
Pleven *BG* 165 C10
Plevnik-Drienové *SK* 147 C7
Pleyben *F* 22 D4
Pleyber-Christ *F* 22 C4
Pliego *E* 56 E2
Plienciems *LV* 134 B5
Pliešovce *SK* 147 E8
Pliezhausen *D* 187 D6
Plikati *GR* 168 D4
Plisa *BY* 133 F3
Pliska *BG* 167 C8
Plitvica *HR* 156 C4
Pljevlja *MNE* 163 C7
Pljenovac *BIH* 157 D10
Pljesker *S* 118 C3
Plobannalec *F* 22 E3
Plobsheim *F* 186 E4
Ploče *HR* 157 F7
Ploče *LV* 134 C2
Plochingen *D* 187 D6
Pločica *SRB* 159 D7
Płociczno *PL* 136 E6
Płock *PL* 139 E8
Plodovoye *RUS* 129 D13
Ploegsteert *B* 182 D1
Ploemeur *F* 22 E5
Ploeren *F* 22 E6
Ploërmel *F* 23 E7
Plœuc-sur-Lié *F* 22 D6
Plogonnec *F* 22 D3
Plogshagen *D* 84 A4
Ploieşti *RO* 161 D8
Plomari *BG* 177 B7
Plombières-les-Bains *F* 26 E5
Plomeur *F* 22 E3
Plomin *HR* 67 B9
Plomodiern *F* 22 D3
Plön *D* 83 B8
Plonéour-Lanvern *F* 22 E3
Plonévez-du-Faou *F* 22 D4
Plonévez-Porzay *F* 22 D3
Płońsk *PL* 139 E9
Plop *MD* 153 A11
Plopana *RO* 153 D10
Plopeni *RO* 161 C7
Plopi *MD* 154 B4
Plopii-Slăviteşti *RO* 160 F5
Plopşoru *RO* 160 D2
Plopu *RO* 161 C8
Plosca *RO* 160 E6
Ploscoş *RO* 152 D3
Ploska *UA* 152 B6
Płoskinia *PL* 139 B8
Płośnica *PL* 139 D9
Plößberg *D* 75 C11
Płoty *PL* 85 C8
Plötzin *D* 79 B12
Plötzky *D* 79 B10
Plou *E* 42 F2
Plouagat *F* 22 C5
Plouaret *F* 22 C5
Plouarzel *F* 22 D2
Plouay *F* 22 E5
Ploubalay *F* 23 C7
Ploubazlanec *F* 22 C5
Ploubezre *F* 22 C5
Ploudalmézeau *F* 22 C2
Ploudiry *F* 22 D3
Plouéscat *F* 22 C3
Plouézec *F* 22 C6
Ploufragan *F* 22 D6
Plougasnou *F* 22 C4
Plougastel-Daoulas *F* 22 D3
Plougonven *F* 22 C4
Plougonver *F* 22 C5
Plougrescant *F* 22 C5
Plouguenast *F* 22 D6
Plouguerneau *F* 22 C2
Plouguernével *F* 22 D5
Plouguiel *F* 22 C5
Plouguin *F* 22 C2
Plouha *F* 22 C6
Plouharnel *F* 22 F5
Plouhinec *F* 22 D3
Plouhinec *F* 22 E5
Plouigneau *F* 22 C4
Ploumagoar *F* 22 C5
Ploumilliau *F* 22 C4
Plounévez-Moëdec *F* 22 C5
Plounévez-Quintin *F* 22 D5
Plouray *F* 22 D5
Plouvorn *F* 22 C3
Plouyé *F* 22 D4
Plouzané *F* 22 D2
Plouzévédé *F* 22 C3
Pluck *IRL* 7 C7
Plüderhausen *D* 187 D8
Plugari *RO* 153 C10
Plumbridge *GB* 4 F2
Plumelec *F* 22 E6
Pluméliau *F* 22 E6
Plumergat *F* 22 E6
Plumlov *CZ* 77 D12
Plunéret *F* 22 E6

Plungė *LT* 134 E3
Pluszkiejmy *PL* 136 E5
Pluvigner *F* 22 E5
Plužine *BIH* 157 F9
Plužine *MNE* 157 F10
Płużnica *PL* 138 D6
Pluzunet *F* 22 C5
Plwmp *GB* 12 A6
Plymouth *GB* 12 E6
Plympton *GB* 12 E6
Plymstock *GB* 12 E6
Plytra *GR* 178 B4
Plyussa *RUS* 132 E5
Plyusy *BY* 133 E2
Plzeň *CZ* 76 C4
Pniewo *PL* 85 D11
Pniewo *PL* 139 E11
Pniewo *PL* 139 B8
Pniewy *PL* 81 A10
Pniewy *PL* 141 G3
Poarta Albă *RO* 155 E2
Pobedím *SK* 146 D5
Pobedino *RUS* 136 D6
Poběžovice *CZ* 75 C12
Pobiedno *PL* 145 D5
Pobiedziska *PL* 81 B12
Pobierowo *PL* 85 B7
Pobikry *PL* 141 E7
Pobladura del Valle *E* 39 D8
Poblete *E* 54 B5
Pobłocie *PL* 85 A13
Poboleda *E* 42 E5
Poboru *RO* 160 D5
Pobožje *MK* 164 E3
Počátky *CZ* 77 D8
Poceirão *P* 50 B2
Pöchlarn *A* 77 F8
Pociems *LV* 131 F9
Počítelj *BIH* 157 F8
Pociumbeni *MD* 153 B10
Pöcking *D* 75 G9
Pocking *D* 76 F4
Pocklington *GB* 11 D10
Pocola *RO* 151 D9
Pocrnje *BIH* 157 F9
Pocsaj *H* 151 C8
Pócspetri *H* 145 H4
Poczesna *PL* 143 E7
Podareš *MK* 169 A8
Podari *RO* 160 E3
Podayva *BG* 161 F9
Podbiel *SK* 147 C8
Podbořany *CZ* 76 B4
Podborov'ye *RUS* 132 F4
Podbožur *MNE* 163 D6
Podbrdo *BIH* 157 B7
Podbrdo *SLO* 73 D8
Podbrezová *SK* 147 D9
Podčetrtek *SLO* 148 D5
Poddębice *PL* 143 C6
Poděbrady *CZ* 77 B8
Podedwórze *PL* 141 G8
Podegrodzie *PL* 145 D2
Podelzig *D* 81 B7
Podem *BG* 165 C10
Podeni *RO* 159 D10
Podenii Noi *RO* 161 C8
Podensac *F* 32 A5
Podenzana *I* 69 E8
Podenzano *I* 37 B11
Podersdorf am See *A* 77 G11
Podgajci Posavski *HR* 157 C10
Podgaje *PL* 85 D11
Podgora *HR* 157 F7
Podgorač *SRB* 159 B7
Podgorač *HR* 149 E9
Podgorci *RO* 161 C10
Podgorica *MNE* 163 D7
Podgorica *SLO* 73 D9
Podgorie *AL* 168 C4
Podgoritsa *BG* 167 C6
Podgórze *PL* 139 D13
Podgrab *BIH* 157 E10
Podgrade *BIH* 157 E8
Podhorod *SK* 145 F5
Podhum *BIH* 157 E8
Podivín *CZ* 77 E11
Podkova *BG* 171 B8
Podkowa Leśna *PL* 141 F3
Podkrajewo *PL* 139 D9
Podkrepa *BG* 166 E5
Podkum *SLO* 73 D11
Podlapača *HR* 156 C3
Podlehnik *SLO* 148 D5
Podles *MK* 169 A6
Podligoglav *SLO* 73 D10
Podmilačje *BIH* 157 D7
Podnanos *SLO* 73 E8
Podnovlje *BIH* 157 C9
Podochori *GR* 170 C6
Podogora *GR* 174 B3
Podoima *MD* 154 B3
Podoleni *RO* 153 D9
Podoli *CZ* 77 D11
Podolie *SK* 146 D5
Podolínec *SK* 145 E2
Podorozhnye *UA* 145 E9
Podosoje *BIH* 162 D5
Podrašnica *BIH* 157 D7
Podravske Sesvete *HR* 149 D8
Podsreda *SLO* 148 D5
Podturen *HR* 149 D7
Podu Iloaiei *RO* 153 C10
Podujevë *KS* 164 D3
Podu Turcului *RO* 153 E10
Podvelež *BIH* 157 F8
Podvrška *SRB* 159 D9
Podvysoká *SK* 147 C7
Podwilk *PL* 147 B9
Poederlee *B* 182 C5
Poeni *RO* 160 E6
Poeniţa *MD* 153 A11
Pofi *I* 62 D4
Pogăceaua *RO* 152 D4
Pogar *BIH* 157 D9
Poggendorf *D* 84 B4
Poggiardo *I* 61 C10
Poggibonsi *I* 66 F3
Poggio Berni *I* 66 E5
Poggio Bustone *I* 62 B3
Poggio Catino *I* 62 C3
Poggiodomo *I* 62 B4
Poggio Imperiale *I* 63 D8
Poggio-Mezzana *F* 37 G10
Poggio Mirteto *I* 62 C3
Poggio Moiano *I* 62 C3
Poggio Picenze *I* 62 C5

Puggio Renatico *I* 66 C4
Poggiorsini *I* 60 B6
Poggio Rusco *I* 66 C3
Pöggstall *A* 77 F7
Pogny *F* 25 C11
Pogoanele *RO* 161 D9
Pogoniani *GR* 168 E3
Pogorzela *PL* 81 C12
Pogorzelice *PL* 85 B13
Pogradec *AL* 168 C4
Pogrodzie *PL* 139 B8
Pohja *FIN* 127 C12
Pohja *FIN* 127 D12
Pohja-Lankila *FIN* 129 C11
Pohjasenvaara *FIN* 117 D11
Pohjaslahti *FIN* 119 B17
Pohjaslahti *FIN* 123 F12
Pohjavaara *FIN* 121 F11
Pohjois-Ii *FIN* 119 D14
Pohjoisjärvi *FIN* 123 F13
Pohorelá *SK* 147 D10
Pohořelice *CZ* 77 E11
Pohronská Polhora *SK* 147 D9
Pohronský Ruskov *SK* 147 F7
Poian *RO* 153 E8
Poiana *RO* 161 D7
Poiana Blenchii *RO* 152 C3
Poiana Câmpina *RO* 161 C7
Poiana Cristei *RO* 161 B9
Poiana Lacului *RO* 160 D5
Poiana Mare *RO* 159 F11
Poiana Mărului *RO* 160 B6
Poiana Sibiului *RO* 152 F3
Poiana Stampei *RO* 152 C6
Poiana Teiului *RO* 153 C7
Poiana Vadului *RO* 151 D10
Poibrene *BG* 165 E8
Pöide *EST* 130 D6
Poienari *RO* 153 D10
Poienarii Burchii *RO* 161 D8
Poienarii de Argeş *RO* 160 C5
Poieneşti *RO* 153 D11
Poieni *RO* 151 D10
Poienile de Sub Munte *RO* 152 B4
Poijula *FIN* 121 D10
Poikajärvi *FIN* 117 E15
Pöikva *EST* 131 D10
Poinçon-lès-Larrey *F* 25 E11
Poing *D* 75 F10
Pointis-Inard *F* 33 D7
Poirino *I* 37 B7
Poiseux *F* 25 F9
Poissons *F* 26 D3
Poissy *F* 24 C7
Poitiers *F* 29 B6
Poix-de-Picardie *F* 18 E4
Poix-Terron *F* 19 E10
Pojan *AL* 168 C4
Pojanluoma *FIN* 122 E9
Pojatno *HR* 148 E5
Pojejena *RO* 159 D8
Pojo *FIN* 127 E10
Pojorâta *RO* 152 B6
Pókaszepetk *H* 149 C7
Poki *LV* 134 C7
Pokka *FIN* 117 B15
Poklečani *BIH* 157 E7
Pokoj *BIH* 156 C4
Pokój *PL* 142 E4
Pokrówka *PL* 141 H8
Pokupsko *HR* 148 F5
Polac *KS* 163 D10
Polača *HR* 156 D5
Polače *HR* 162 D3
Pola de Allande *E* 39 B6
Pola de Laviana *E* 39 B8
Pola de Lena *E* 39 B8
Pola de Siero *E* 39 B8
Pola de Somiedo *E* 39 B7
Polaincourt-et-Clairefontaine *F* 26 E5
Połajewo *PL* 85 E11
Polán *E* 46 E4
Polanica-Zdrój *PL* 77 B10
Połaniec *PL* 143 F11
Polanów *PL* 85 B11
Polatsk *BY* 133 F5
Polch *D* 21 D8
Polcirkeln *S* 116 C6
Polczyno *PL* 138 A5
Połczyn Zdrój *PL* 85 C10
Polegate *GB* 15 F9
Polena *BG* 165 F7
Poleñino *E* 41 E11
Polepy *CZ* 76 A6
Polesella *I* 66 C4
Polessk *RUS* 136 D3
Polgár *H* 145 H3
Polgárdi *H* 149 B10
Polgaste *EST* 131 F13
Polia *I* 59 B9
Poliçan *AL* 168 C3
Poliçan *AL* 168 D3
Police *PL* 84 C7
Police nad Metují *CZ* 81 E10
Polichni *GR* 169 C8
Polička *CZ* 77 C10
Policoro *I* 61 C7
Policzna *PL* 141 H5
Polignano a Mare *I* 61 B8
Poligny *F* 31 B8
Polikrayshte *BG* 166 C5
Polisot *F* 25 D11
Polistena *I* 59 C9
Politika *GR* 175 B8
Pölitz *D* 83 C11
Polizzi Generosa *I* 58 D5
Põlja *FIN* 124 D7
Poljana *SRB* 159 D7
Poljanak *HR* 156 C4
Poljana Pakračka *HR* 149 F7
Poljane *SLO* 73 D9
Poljčane *SLO* 148 D5
Polje *BIH* 157 C8
Poljica *HR* 156 D3
Poljice *BIH* 157 D10
Poljice-Popovo *BIH* 162 D5
Polkowice *PL* 81 D10
Polla *I* 60 B4
Põllakka *FIN* 125 F11
Pöllau *A* 148 B5
Pöllauberg *A* 148 B5
Polle *D* 78 C5
Pollença *E* 57 B11
Pollenfeld *D* 75 E9
Pollenza *I* 67 F7
Pollfoss *N* 100 C7
Polliat *F* 31 C7
Pollica *I* 60 C4
Pollina *I* 58 D5

Pollitz D 83 E11
Pollos E 39 F9
Polmak N 113 C20
Polminhac F 29 F11
Polmont GB 5 D9
Polo FIN 121 C12
Polomka SK 147 D9
Polop E 56 D4
Pölöske H 149 C7
Połoski PL 141 G8
Polovragi RO 160 C3
Polperro GB 12 E5
Pöls A 73 B10
Polsbroek NL 182 B5
Polsingen D 75 E8
Polska Cerekiew PL 142 F5
Polski Gradets BG 166 E6
Polski Trümbesh BG 166 C5
Polsko Kosovo BG 166 C5
Polso FIN 123 D12
Poltár SK 147 E9
Põltsamaa EST 131 D11
Põlula EST 131 C13
Polumir SRB 163 B10
Pofupin PL 81 B8
Põlva EST 131 E14
Polvela FIN 125 D12
Polvenkylä FIN 122 E8
Polverigi I 67 E7
Polvijärvi FIN 125 E12
Polyana UA 145 F6
Polyanets'ke UA 154 A6
Polyantho GR 171 B8
Polyany RUS 129 E11
Polyatsite BG 167 D8
Polydendro GR 169 C7
Polydrosos GR 175 B6
Polygyros GR 169 D9
Polykarpi GR 169 C7
Polykastano GR 168 D5
Polykastro GR 169 C8
Polymylos GR 169 D7
Polyneri GR 168 D5
Polypotamo GR 168 C5
Polzela SLO 73 D11
Pölzig D 79 E11
Pomaluengo E 40 B4
Pomarance I 66 F2
Pomarão P 50 D4
Pomarez F 32 C4
Pomarico I 61 B7
Pomarkku FIN 126 B7
Pomârla RO 153 A8
Pomáz H 150 B3
Pombal P 38 F5
Pombal P 44 E3
Pomer E 41 E8
Pomeroy GB 7 C9
Pomezeu RO 151 D9
Pomezí CZ 77 C10
Pomezia I 62 D3
Pomi RO 151 B11
Pomiechówek PL 139 F10
Pömiö FIN 119 C17
Pommard F 30 A6
Pommelsbrunn D 75 C10
Pommersfelden D 75 C8
Pomol BIH 157 D10
Pomorie BG 167 D9
Pomorsko PL 81 B8
Pompaire F 28 B5
Pompei I 60 B3
Pompey F 26 C5
Pompía GR 178 E8
Pompignan F 35 C6
Pomysk Mały PL 85 B13
Poncin F 31 C7
Ponferrada E 39 C7
Poniatowa PL 141 H6
Poniatowo PL 139 D8
Poniec PL 81 C11
Poniklá CZ 81 E8
Poniky SK 147 D8
Ponoarele RO 159 D10
Ponor RO 151 E11
Ponoshec KS 163 E9
Pons F 28 D4
Ponsa FIN 127 B11
Ponsacco I 66 E2
Pont-à-Celles B 19 C9
Pontacq F 32 D5
Pontailler-sur-Saône F 26 F3
Pontaix F 31 F7
Pont-à-Marcq F 19 C7
Pont-à-Mousson F 26 C5
Pontardawe GB 13 B7
Pontarion F 29 D9
Pontarlier F 31 B9
Pontassieve I 66 E3
Pontaubault F 23 C9
Pont-Audemer F 18 F2
Pontault-Combault F 25 C8
Pontaumur F 29 D11
Pont-Aven F 22 E4
Pont-Canavese I 68 C4
Pontcharra F 31 E9
Pontchâteau F 23 F7
Pont-Croix F 22 D3
Pont-d'Ain F 31 C7
Pont-de-Buis-lès-Quimerch F 22 D3
Pont-de-Chéruy F 31 D7
Pont-de-Larn F 33 C10
Pont-de-l'Isère F 30 E6
Pont-de-Loup B 182 E5
Pont-de-Poitte F 31 B8
Pont-de-Roide F 27 A7
Pont-de-Salars F 34 B4
Pont de Suert E 33 E7
Pont-de-Vaux F 31 C6
Pont-de-Veyle F 30 D6
Pont-d'Hérault F 35 B6
Pont-d'Ouilly F 23 C11
Pont-du-Casse F 33 B7
Pont-du-Château F 30 D3
Pont-du-Navoy F 31 B8
Ponte I 60 A3
Ponte Aranga E 38 B4
Ponteareas E 38 D3
Pontebba I 73 C7
Pontecagnano Faiano I 60 B3
Ponte Caldelas E 38 D3
Ponteceso E 38 B2
Pontechianale I 36 B6
Pontecorvo I 62 E5
Pontecurone I 37 B9
Ponte da Barca P 38 E3
Pontedassio I 37 D8
Pontedecimo I 37 B9
Ponte de Lima P 38 E2
Ponte dell'Olio I 37 B11
Pontedera I 66 E2
Ponte de Sor P 44 F4

Pontedeume E 38 B3
Ponte di Legno I 69 A10
Ponte di Piave I 72 E5
Ponte do Rol P 44 F2
Pontefract GB 11 D9
Ponte Gardena I 72 C4
Pontelagoscuro I 66 C4
Ponteland GB 5 E13
Pontelandolfo I 60 A3
Ponte-Leccia F 37 G10
Pontelongo I 66 B5
Ponte nelle Alpi I 72 D5
Ponte Nizza I 37 B9
Ponte Nossa I 69 B8
Ponte Nova I 72 D3
Ponte-en-Royans F 31 E7
Pontenure I 69 C8
Pontenx-les-Forges F 32 B3
Ponte San Nicolò I 66 B4
Ponte San Pietro I 69 B8
Ponte Valga E 38 C2
Pontevedra E 38 D2
Pontével P 44 F3
Pont-Évêque F 30 D6
Pontevico I 66 B1
Pont-Farcy F 23 C9
Pontfaverger-Moronvilliers F 19 F9
Pontgibaud F 30 D2
Pont-Hébert F 23 B9
Pontinha P 50 B1
Pontinia I 62 E4
Pöntiö FIN 120 F7
Pontivy F 22 D6
Pont-l'Abbé F 22 E3
Pont-la-Ville F 25 D12
Pont-les-Moulins F 26 F5
Pont-l'Évêque F 23 B12
Pontlevoy F 24 F5
Pontoise F 24 B7
Pontokomi GR 169 D6
Pontones E 55 C7
Pontonnyy RUS 129 F14
Pontonx-sur-l'Adour F 32 C4
Pontoon IRL 6 E4
Pontorson F 23 C8
Pontpoint F 18 F6
Pontremoli I 69 E8
Pontrhydfendigaid GB 13 A7
Pontrieux F 22 C5
Pontrilas GB 13 B9
Ponts E 42 D6
Pöntsö FIN 117 C12
Pont-Ste-Marie F 25 D11
Pont-Ste-Maxence F 18 F6
Pont-St-Esprit F 35 B8
Pont-St-Martin I 68 B4
Pont-sur-Yonne F 25 D9
Pontvallain F 23 E12
Pontyberem GB 12 B6
Pontycymer GB 13 B7
Pontypool GB 13 B8
Pontypridd GB 13 B8
Ponyativka UA 154 D6
Ponza I 62 F3
Ponzone I 37 B8
Poola FIN 122 E7
Poole GB 13 D11
Poolewe GB 2 K5
Pooley Bridge GB 5 F11
Pool of Muckhart GB 5 C9
Pootsi EST 131 E8
Pope LV 134 B3
Popeasca MD 154 D5
Poperinge B 18 C6
Popești RO 151 C9
Popești RO 153 C10
Popești RO 160 C4
Popești RO 160 E6
Popești-Leordeni RO 161 E8
Popielów PL 142 E4
Popina BG 161 E9
Popintsi BG 165 E9
Popitsa BG 165 C8
Poplaca RO 152 F4
Popoli I 62 C5
Popovača HR 149 E7
Popovica SRB 159 E9
Popovitsa BG 166 E4
Popovo BG 166 C5
Popów PL 141 F1
Popów PL 143 D6
Poppenhausen D 75 B7
Poppenricht D 75 D10
Poppi I 66 E4
Poprad SK 145 E1
Popricani RO 153 C11
Poproč SK 145 F2
Popsko BG 171 A9
Poráč HR 149 C6
Porażba PL 143 E7
Porcari I 66 E2
Porcia I 73 E6
Porcsalma H 145 H6
Porcuna E 53 A8
Pordenone I 73 E6
Pordim BG 165 C10
Porjba PL 143 F7
Porjba-Kocjby PL 139 E12
Poreč HR 67 B8
Pori FIN 126 C6
Porice BIH 157 D8
Porjus S 116 E3
Porkhov RUS 132 F6
Porkkala FIN 127 F11
Porkuni EST 131 C11
Porlammi FIN 127 D15
Porlezza I 69 A7
Porlock GB 13 C7
Pornainen FIN 127 E13
Pornassio I 37 C7
Pornic F 23 F7
Pornichet F 23 F7
Poroina Mare RO 159 E10
Poros GR 174 C2
Poros GR 175 D7
Porozina HR 67 B9
Porpi GR 171 B8
Porquerolles I 35 D10
Porras FIN 127 D10
Porraskoski FIN 127 D13
Porrentruy CH 27 F7
Porretta Terme I 66 D2
Porsangmoen N 113 D14
Pörsänmäki FIN 124 D8
Porsåsen N 102 E3

Porsgrunn N 90 A6
Porsi S 118 B5
Porspoder F 22 C2
Port N 113 D17
Porta T 33 E9
Portadown GB 7 D10
Portaferry GB 7 D11
Portaje E 45 E7
Portakallik TR 181 B8
Portalegre P 44 F6
Portals Vells E 49 F10
Portaria GR 169 D9
Portaria GR 175 B8
Portarlington IRL 7 F8
Port Askaig GB 4 D4
Portavogie GB 7 D12
Portbail F 23 B8
Port-Barcarès F 34 E5
Portbou F 34 F5
Port Brillet F 23 D10
Portchester GB 13 D12
Port d'Andratx E 49 E9
Port-de-Bouc F 35 D8
Port-de-Piles F 29 A7
Port de Pollença E 57 B11
Port-des-Barques F 28 D3
Port de Sóller E 49 E10
Portel P 50 C4
Portel-des-Corbières F 34 D4
Portell de Morella E 42 F3
Port Ellen GB 4 D4
Port-en-Bessin-Huppain F 23 B10
Portencross GB 4 D7
Port Erin GBM 10 C2
Portes-lès-Valence F 30 F6
Portets F 28 F5
Portet-sur-Garonne F 33 C8
Port Eynon GB 12 B6
Port Glasgow GB 4 D7
Porth GB 13 B8
Porthcawl GB 13 C7
Port Henderson GB 2 K5
Porthleven GB 12 E4
Porthmadog GB 10 F3
Porticcio F 37 H9
Portici I 60 B2
Portieux F 26 D5
Portilla E 47 D8
Portilla de la Reina E 39 B10
Portillo E 40 F2
Portillo de Toledo E 46 D4
Portimão P 50 E2
Portimo FIN 119 B16
Portimojärvi FIN 119 B11
Portishead GB 13 C9
Port-Joinville F 28 B1
Portknockie GB 3 K11
Port Láirge IRL 9 D8
Portland IRL 6 F6
Port-la-Nouvelle F 34 D5
Port Laoise IRL 7 F8
Portlaoise IRL 7 F8
Portlethen GB 5 A12
Port-Leucate F 34 E5
Port Logan GB 4 F7
Port-Louis F 22 E5
Portmage IRL 8 E2
Portmahomack GB 3 K9
Portman E 56 F3
Portmarnock IRL 7 F10
Port Mearnóg IRL 7 F10
Portmuck GB 4 F5
Port-na-Con GB 2 H7
Portnaguran GB 2 J4
Portnahaven GB 4 D3
Portnalong GB 2 L4
Port-Navalo F 22 E6
Porto E 39 D6
Porto I 62 A2
Porto P 44 B3
Porto Alto E 39 D6
Porto Azzurro I 65 B2
Porto Botte I 64 E2
Portobravo E 38 C2
Porto Cervo I 64 A4
Porto Cesareo I 61 C9
Portocheli GR 175 E7
Portocolom E 57 C11
Porto Covo da Bandeira P 50 D2
Porto Cristo E 57 B11
Porto d'Ascoli I 62 B5
Porto de Lagos P 50 E2
Porto de Mós P 44 E3
Porto do Son E 38 C1
Porto Empedocle I 58 E4
Porto Ercole I 65 C4
Portoferraio I 65 B2
Portofino I 37 C10
Port of Ness GB 2 J4
Porto Garibaldi I 66 C5
Porto Germeno GR 175 C7
Portogruaro I 73 E6
Porto Koufo GR 170 E5
Porto Levante I 59 C6
Porto Levante I 66 B5
Pórtom FIN 122 E7
Portomaggiore I 66 C4
Portomarín E 38 C4
Port Omna IRL 6 F6
Portopalo di Capo Passero I 59 F7
Porto Petro E 57 C11
Portør N 90 B5
Porto Rafti GR 175 D9
Porto Recanati I 67 E8
Porto Rotondo I 64 A4
Portorož SLO 67 B8
Porto San Giorgio I 67 F8
Porto San Paolo I 64 B4
Porto Sant'Elpidio I 67 E8
Porto Santo Stefano I 65 C4
Portoscuso I 64 E1
Porto Tolle I 66 C5
Porto Torres I 64 B1
Porto-Vecchio F 37 H10
Portovenere I 69 E8
Portoviro I 66 B5
Portpatrick GB 4 F6
Portrane IRL 7 F10
Port Reachrann IRL 7 F10
Portreath GB 12 E4
Portree GB 2 L4
Portroe IRL 8 C6
Portrush GB 4 E3
Portsalon IRL 4 E1
Portsmouth GB 13 D12
Portsoy GB 3 K11
Port-Ste-Marie F 33 B6
Portstewart GB 4 E3
Port-St-Louis-du-Rhône F 35 D8
Port St Mary GBM 10 C2

Port-St-Père F 23 F8
Port-sur-Saône F 26 E5
Port Talbot GB 13 B7
Portugalete E 40 B5
Portumna IRL 6 F6
Port-Vendres F 34 E5
Port William GB 4 F7
Poruba SK 147 D7
Porubne UA 153 A8
Porumbacu de Jos RO 152 F4
Porvoo FIN 127 E14
Porządzie PL 139 E11
Porzuna E 46 F4
Posada E 39 B8
Posada I 64 B4
Posada de Valdeón E 39 B10
Posadas E 53 A6
Poşaga RO 151 E11
Poschiavo CH 69 A9
Posedarje HR 156 D3
Poseidonia GR 176 E5
Poseritz D 84 B4
Poseşti RO 161 C8
Pösing D 75 D12
Posio FIN 121 B11
Positano I 60 B3
Possagno I 72 E4
Posseberg S 97 D13
Possendorf D 80 E5
Possesse F 25 C12
Pößneck D 79 E10
Posta I 62 B4
Poşta Câlnău RO 161 C9
Postal I 72 C3
Posta Piana I 60 A5
Postau D 75 E11
Posterholt NL 20 B6
Postiglione I 60 B4
Postojna SLO 73 E9
Postolika PL 139 F11
Postoloprty CZ 76 B5
Postomino PL 85 B11
Postřelmov CZ 77 C11
Postupice CZ 77 C7
Posušje BIH 157 F7
Poświętne PL 140 E7
Poświętne PL 141 G2
Potamia GR 171 B8
Potamia GR 174 F5
Potamochori GR 171 B8
Potamoi GR 170 B6
Potamos GR 168 E4
Potamos GR 178 C4
Potashnya UA 154 A5
Potcoava RO 160 E5
Potigowo PL 85 A11
Potenza I 60 B5
Potenza Picena I 67 F8
Potes E 39 B10
Potidania GR 174 C5
Potigny F 23 C11
Potkraj BIH 157 E7
Potku FIN 119 E17
Potlogi RO 161 D7
Potočac SRB 159 F7
Potočani BIH 157 E7
Potoci BIH 156 D6
Potoci BIH 157 F8
Potok Złoty PL 143 E7
Potsdam D 80 B4
Pötsõnvaara FIN 125 D16
Potštát CZ 146 B5
Pottenstein A 77 G10
Pottenstein D 75 C9
Potterne GB 13 C10
Potters Bar GB 15 D8
Pöttmes D 75 E9
Potton GB 15 C8
Pöttsching A 146 F2
Potworów PL 141 G3
Pouancé F 23 E9
Pougny F 25 F9
Pougues-les-Eaux F 30 A3
Pougy F 25 D11
Pouillon F 32 C4
Pouilly-en-Auxois F 25 F12
Pouilly-sous-Charlieu F 30 C5
Pouilly-sur-Loire F 25 F8
Pouilly-sur-Saône F 31 A7
Poulaines F 24 F6
Pouldreuzic F 22 E3
Poulgorm Bridge IRL 8 E4
Pouligny-St-Pierre F 29 B8
Poulithra GR 175 E6
Poullaouen F 22 D4
Poulnamucky IRL 9 D7
Poulstrup DK 90 E7
Poulton-le-Fylde GB 10 D6
Pounta GR 176 E5
Poupas F 33 C7
Pourcieux F 35 D10
Pouri GR 169 F9
Pourrain F 25 E9
Pourrières F 35 C10
Pousada P 45 C6
Pousos P 44 E3
Poussan F 35 D6
Poussay F 26 D5
Poussu FIN 121 C13
Pouxeux F 26 D6
Pouyastruc F 33 D6
Pouydesseaux F 32 C5
Pouzac F 33 E6
Pouzay F 24 F4
Pouzauges F 28 B4
Pré-en-Pail F 23 D11
Prees GB 10 F6
Preetz D 83 B8
Préfailles F 23 F7
Preganziol I 72 E5
Pregarten A 77 F7
Pregrada HR 148 D5
Preignan F 33 C7
Preili LV 135 D13
Premià de Mar E 43 E8
Premilcuore I 66 E4
Prémilhat F 29 C11
Premnitz D 79 A11

Pozezdrze PL 136 E4
Pozharan KS 164 E3
Pozherevitsy RUS 133 B7
Poznań PL 81 B11
Pozo Alcón E 55 D7
Pozoamargo E 47 F9
Pozoantiguo E 39 E9
Pozoblanco E 54 C3
Pozo Cañada E 55 B9
Pozo de Guadalajara E 47 D6
Pozohondo E 55 B9
Pozo-Lorente E 47 F10
Pozondón E 47 C10
Pozořice CZ 77 D11
Pozorrubio E 47 E7
Pózrzadło Wielkie PL 85 D9
Pozuel del Campo E 47 C10
Pozuelo E 55 B8
Pozuelo de Alarcón E 46 D5
Pozuelo de Aragón E 41 E9
Pozuelo del Páramo E 39 D8
Pozuelo del Rey E 46 D6
Pozuelo de Zarzón E 45 D8
Pozuelos de Calatrava E 54 B4
Pozza di Fassa I 72 D4
Pozzallo I 59 F6
Pozzolo Formigaro I 37 B9
Pozzomaggiore I 64 C2
Pozzuoli I 60 B2
Pozzuolo del Friuli I 73 E7
Prača BIH 157 E10
Prachatice CZ 76 D6
Pracht D 21 C9
Prackenbach D 76 D3
Prádanos de Ojeda E 40 C3
Pradejón E 32 F1
Pradelles F 30 F4
Prádena E 46 B5
Prades F 33 S9
Prades F 33 E10
Prades-d'Aubrac F 34 A4
Pradillo E 41 D6
Pradines F 33 B8
Prado P 38 E3
Prado de la Guzpeña E 39 C9
Prado del Rey E 53 C5
Pradoluengo E 40 D5
Praestbro DK 86 A6
Praestø DK 87 E10
Pragelato I 31 E10
Pragersko SLO 148 D5
Prägraten A 72 B5
Praha CZ 77 B6
Prahecq F 28 C5
Prahovo SRB 159 E10
Praia a Mare I 60 D6
Praia da Barra P 44 C3
Praia da Rocha P 50 E2
Praia da Tocha P 44 D3
Praia de Esmoriz P 44 C3
Praia de Mira P 44 D3
Praiano I 60 B3
Praid RO 152 E6
Prăjeni RO 153 B10
Prakovce SK 145 F2
Pralognan-la-Vanoise F 31 E10
Pralyetarsk BY 133 F2
Pramanda GR 168 E5
Prambachkirchen A 76 F5
Pranjani SRB 158 E5
Prapatnica HR 156 E5
Prašice SK 146 D6
Praszka PL 142 D5
Prata di Pordenone I 73 E6
Pratau D 79 C12
Prat de Comte E 42 F4
Pratdip E 42 F5
Pratella I 60 A2
Prato I 66 E3
Prato allo Stelvio I 71 D11
Pratola Peligna I 62 C5
Pratovecchio I 66 E4
Prats de Lluçanès E 43 C8
Prats-de-Mollo-la-Preste F 33 F10
Pratteln CH 27 E8
Prauliena LV 135 C12
Prauthoy F 26 E3
Pravda BG 161 F10
Pravdinsk RUS 136 D3
Pravets BG 165 D8
Pravia E 39 B7
Pravisdomini I 73 E6
Praz-sur-Arly F 31 D10
Prebold SLO 73 D11
Prečac F 32 B5
Preci I 62 B4
Précigné F 23 E11
Prečín SK 147 C7
Précy-sous-Thil F 25 F11
Predappio F 66 D4
Predazzo I 72 D4
Predeal RO 161 B7
Predeal-Sărari RO 161 C8
Predejane SRB 164 D5
Predeşti RO 160 E3
Preding A 148 C5
Predlitz A 73 B8
Predmeja SLO 73 E8
Předměřice nad Labem CZ 77 B9
Predosa I 37 B9
Pré-en-Pail F 23 D11
Prees GB 10 F6
Preetz D 83 B8
Préfailles F 23 F7
Preganziol I 72 E5
Pregarten A 77 F7
Pregrada HR 148 D5
Preignan F 33 C7
Preili LV 135 D13
Premià de Mar E 43 E8
Premilcuore I 66 E4
Prémilhat F 29 C11
Premnitz D 79 A11
Premosello Chiovenda I 68 A5

Prenzlau D 84 D5
Préporché F 30 B4
Přerov CZ 146 C4
Prerow am Darß, Ostseebad D 83 B13
Preselentsi BG 155 F2
Prešovo SRB 164 E4
Presicce I 61 D10
Přeštice CZ 76 C4
Prestatyn GB 10 E5
Prestbakken N 111 C15
Prestbury GB 13 B10
Pre-St-Didier I 31 D10
Prestebakke N 91 B10
Presteigne GB 13 A8
Prestfoss N 95 B12
Preston GB 5 D12
Preston GB 10 D6
Prestwick GB 4 E7
Prettin D 80 C3
Pretushë AL 168 C4
Pretzfeld D 75 C9
Pretzier D 83 E10
Pretzsch D 79 C12
Pretzschendorf D 80 E5
Preuilly-sur-Claise F 29 B7
Preuteşti RO 153 C8
Prevalje SLO 73 C10
Prévenchères F 35 A6
Préveranges F 29 C10
Prevešt SRB 159 F7
Preveza GR 174 B2
Prevršac HR 156 B5
Prezid HR 73 D10
Prez-sous-Lafauche F 26 D3
Priaranza del Bierzo E 39 C6
Pribelja BIH 157 D6
Pribeta SK 146 F6
Pribinić BIH 157 D8
Pribislavec HR 149 D6
Priboieni RO 160 D6
Priboj BIH 157 C10
Priboj SRB 163 D8
Příbor CZ 146 B6
Priborn D 83 D13
Příboy BG 165 D6
Příbram CZ 76 C6
Pribrezhnoye RUS 136 D1
Pribude HR 156 E5
Pribylina SK 147 C9
Přibyslav CZ 77 C9
Prichaly RUS 134 F2
Prichsenstadt D 75 C7
Pridvorci BIH 157 F9
Pridvorci BIH 157 F9
Priedaine LV 134 C3
Priedes LV 131 F9
Priego E 47 D7
Priego de Córdoba E 53 B8
Priekule LT 134 D3
Priekule LV 134 D3
Priekuli LV 135 B10
Prienai LT 137 D8
Prienai LT 137 D12
Prien am Chiemsee D 72 A5
Prieros D 80 B5
Prieß SK 146 D6
Priešnitz D 79 D11
Priešnitz D 79 D11
Priestewitz D 80 D5
Prievidza SK 147 D7
Priežmale A 148 F2
Prignac-et-Marcamps F 28 E5
Prigor RO 159 D9
Prigoria RO 160 C3
Prigradica HR 162 D2
Prigrevica SRB 158 B3
Prijeboj HR 156 C4
Prijedor BIH 157 C6
Prijepolje SRB 163 C8
Prikuli LV 135 D13
Priladozhskiy RUS 129 F15
Prilep MK 169 B6
Prilike SRB 158 F5
Prillimäe EST 131 C9
Primel-Trégastel F 22 C4
Primolano I 72 E4
Primorsk RUS 129 C13
Primorsk RUS 139 A9
Primorsko BG 167 E9
Primor'ye RUS 139 A9
Primošten HR 156 E4
Princes Risborough GB 15 D7
Princetown GB 12 D7
Prinos GR 171 C7
Prinsenbeek NL 16 E3
Prinzhöfte D 17 C11
Priolithos GR 174 D5
Priolo Gargallo I 59 E7
Prioro E 39 C10
Priozersk RUS 129 C13
Priponeşti RO 153 E10
Prirechnyy RUS 114 E8
Prisăcani RO 153 C11
Priseaca RO 160 D4
Priseltsi BG 167 C9
Prishtinë KS 164 D3
Prisjan SRB 164 C6
Prisoja MNE 163 D8
Prisoje BIH 157 E7
Prissac F 29 B8
Prissé F 30 C6
Priština KS 164 D3
Pristol RO 159 E10
Pritzerbe D 79 B11
Pritzwalk D 83 D12
Privas F 30 F6
Priverno I 62 E4
Privlaka HR 67 D11
Privlaka HR 157 B10
Prizna HR 67 C10
Prizren KS 163 E10
Prizzi I 58 D3
Prkosi BIH 156 C5
Prnjavor BIH 157 C8
Prnjavor SRB 158 D3
Proaza E 39 B7
Probištip MK 164 E5
Probota RO 153 C10
Probstzella D 75 B9
Probus GB 12 E5

Prochoma GR 169 C8
Prochowice PL 81 D10
Procida I 60 B2
Prodromos GR 175 C6
Produleşti RO 161 D7
Proença-a-Nova P 44 E5
Proença-a-Velha P 45 D6
Profen D 79 D11
Profesor-Ishirkovo BG 161 F10
Profilia GR 181 D7
Profitis GR 169 C7
Profitis Ilias GR 178 E8
Profondeville B 19 D10
Progonat AL 168 D2
Prohn D 84 B4
Prokhladnoye RUS 134 F2
Prokopi GR 175 B7
Prokuplje SRB 164 C4
Prolaz BG 167 D6
Prolog BIH 157 E6
Promachoi GR 169 C7
Promna PL 141 G3
Promyri GR 175 A7
Pronsfeld D 20 D6
Propriano F 37 H9
Prosek CZ 77 C10
Prosek AL 163 F8
Prosenik BG 167 D8
Prosenjakovci SLO 149 C6
Prosetín CZ 77 C9
Proshkava BY 133 F4
Prosknytes GR 171 C8
Prosotsani GR 170 B5
Prosperous IRL 7 F9
Prossedi I 62 D4
Prostějov CZ 77 D12
Prostki PL 140 C6
Prostřední Bečva CZ 146 C6
Prószków PL 142 E4
Proszowice PL 143 F9
Proszówki PL 143 F9
Proti GR 170 C3
Protići BIH 157 D6
Protivanov CZ 77 D11
Protivín CZ 76 D6
Protokklisi GR 171 B10
Protoria GR 178 E9
Prötzel D 80 A5
Provadiya BG 167 C8
Provatas GR 169 B9
Provenchères-sur-Fave F 27 D7
Provins F 25 C9
Provo SRB 158 D4
Prozor SRB 159 E8
Prozor HR 156 C3
Prrenjas AL 168 B4
Pruchnik PL 144 D6
Prudhoe GB 5 F13
Prudnik PL 142 F4
Prudzinki BY 133 E4
Prugoc KS 164 D3
Prügy H 145 G3
Prüm D 20 D6
Pruna E 51 F9
Prundeni RO 160 D4
Prundu RO 161 E8
Prundu Bârgăului RO 152 C5
Prunières F 36 B4
Pruniers-en-Sologne F 24 F6
Prunişor RO 159 D10
Prusac BIH 157 D7
Prušánky CZ 77 E11
Prusice PL 81 D11
Prusinovice CZ 146 C5
Prüšiši LV 135 B13
Pruszcz PL 138 D4
Pruszcz PL 138 D5
Pruszcz Gdański PL 138 B6
Pruszków PL 141 F3
Prutz A 71 C11
Pružina SK 146 C6
Prvačina SLO 73 E8
Pryamobalka UA 154 F4
Prymors'ke UA 155 B6
Prymors'ke UA 155 B6
Pryozerne UA 155 B6
Prypruttya UA 153 A8
Przasnysz PL 139 D10
Przechlewo PL 85 C12
Przecław PL 143 F11
Przecław PL 143 F11
Przedbórz PL 141 H3
Przedecz PL 138 F6
Przejazdowo PL 138 B6
Przelewice PL 85 D8
Przemęt PL 81 B10
Przemków PL 81 D9
Przemyśl PL 144 D6
Przerośl PL 136 E6
Przewale PL 144 B8
Przewłoka PL 141 G8
Przeworno PL 81 E12
Przeworsk PL 144 C5
Przewóz PL 81 D7
Przeździatka PL 141 F6
Przezdzijk Wielki PL 139 C7
Przezmark PL 139 C7
Przine-Zdralovac BIH 156 D6
Przodkowo PL 138 B5
Przybiernów PL 85 C7
Przyborów PL 81 C9
Przyborowice PL 139 F9
Przybranowo PL 138 E6
Przygodzice PL 142 C4
Przykona PL 142 C5
Przyłęk PL 141 G1
Przylep PL 81 C8
Przylesie PL 142 E3
Przyrów PL 143 E8
Przysieki PL 144 D3
Przystajń PL 142 E6
Przystawowice Duże PL 141 H3
Przysucha PL 141 H3
Przysów PL 144 C4
Przytoczna PL 81 A9
Przytoczno PL 141 G6
Przytuły PL 140 D6
Przytyk PL 141 H3
Przywidz PL 138 B5
Psača MK 164 E5
Psachna GR 175 B8
Psara GR 177 B6
Psarades GR 168 C5
Psari GR 174 C4
Psari GR 175 D6
Psathopyrgos GR 174 C4
Psinthos GR 181 D8
Pskov RUS 132 F3
Psychiko GR 169 B10
Psychro GR 178 E9
Pszczew PL 81 B9
Pszczółki PL 138 B6

Pszczonów PL 141 G1
Pszczyna PL 147 B7
Pteleos GR 175 A6
Pteri GR 174 C5
Ptolemaïda GR 169 C6
Ptuj SLO 148 D5
Publier F 31 C10
Puchberg am Schneeberg A 146 F1
Pucheni RO 160 C6
Puchenii Mari RO 161 D8
Puchheim D 75 F9
Púchov SK 146 C6
Pucioasa RO 161 C6
Pučišće HR 157 F6
Puck PL 138 A5
Puckaun IRL 8 C6
Puçol E 48 E4
Pudasjärven kirkko FIN 119 D17
Pudasjärvi FIN 119 D17
Puddletown GB 13 D10
Puderbach D 185 C8
Pudinava LV 133 C3
Pudsey GB 11 D8
Puebla de Albortón E 41 F10
Puebla de Alcocer E 51 B9
Puebla de Alfindén E 41 E10
Puebla de Almenara E 47 E7
Puebla de Beleña E 47 C6
Puebla de Don Fadrique E 55 D8
Puebla de Don Rodrigo E 46 F3
Puebla de Guzmán E 51 D5
Puebla de la Calzada E 51 B6
Puebla de la Reina E 51 B7
Puebla de Lillo E 39 B9
Puebla del Maestre E 51 C7
Puebla del Príncipe E 55 B7
Puebla del Prior E 51 B7
Puebla del Salvador E 47 E9
Puebla de Obando E 45 F7
Puebla de Sanabria E 39 D6
Puebla de Sancho Pérez E 51 C7
Puebla de San Miguel E 47 D10
Puebla de Yeltes E 45 C8
Puente de Domingo Flórez E 39 D6
Puente de Génave E 55 C7
Puente del Congosto E 45 D9
Puente de Montañana E 42 C5
Puente de San Miguel E 40 B3
Puente-Genil E 53 B7
Puente la Reina E 32 E2
Puentenansa E 40 B3
Puente Viesgo E 40 B4
Puerto de Béjar E 45 D9
Puerto de Mazarrón E 56 F2
Puerto de San Vicente E 45 E10
Puerto Lápice E 46 F6
Puertollano E 54 B4
Puerto Lumbreras E 55 D9
Puerto Real E 52 C4
Puerto Seguro E 45 C7
Puerto Serrano E 51 F8
Pueyo E 32 E2
Pueyo de Santa Cruz E 42 D4
Pufeşti RO 153 E10
Puget-Théniers F 36 D5
Puget-Ville F 36 E4
Pugnochiuso I 63 D10
Puhja EST 131 E12
Puhos FIN 121 D10
Puhos FIN 125 F13
Puhovac BIH 157 D9
Pui RO 159 B11
Puiatu EST 131 E10
Puieşti RO 153 E11
Puieşti RO 161 C10
Puig E 48 E4
Puigcerdà E 33 F9
Puigpunyent E 49 E10
Puig-reig E 43 D7
Puikkola FIN 115 E3
Puikule LV 131 F9
Puimoisson F 36 D4
Puiseaux F 25 D7
Puisieux F 18 D6
Puisseguin F 28 F5
Puisserguier F 34 D5
Puivert F 33 E10
Pujaut F 35 B8
Pujols F 28 F5
Pujols F 33 B7
Puka EST 131 E12
Pukaro FIN 127 D15
Pukavik S 88 C7
Pukë AL 163 E8
Pukiš BIH 157 C10
Pukkila FIN 127 D14
Pulkonkoski FIN 124 D8
Pulpí E 55 E9
Pulsa FIN 128 D8
Pulsano I 61 C8
Pulsen D 80 D4
Pulskala FIN 115 D4
Pulsnitz D 80 D6
Pulsujärvi S 116 B6
Pułtusk PL 139 E11
Pulversheim F 27 E7
Pumpėnai LT 135 E8
Pumpuri LV 134 C4
Pumsaint GB 13 A7
Pūņas LV 134 B4
Puņat HR 67 B10
Pundsvik N 111 D12
Punduri LV 133 D3
Pungeşti RO 153 D10
Punghina RO 159 E10
Punia LT 137 D9
Punkka FIN 128 C7
Punta Ala I 65 B3
Punta Križa HR 67 C9
Punta Sabbioni I 66 B5
Punta Umbría E 51 E6
Puokio FIN 120 F3
Puolakkavaara FIN 115 D1

Puolanka FIN 121 E10
Puoliväli FIN 124 D9
Puoltikasvaara S 116 D6
Puottaure S 118 B4
Pūpoli LV 133 D2
Puraci BIH 157 C8
Puračić BIH 157 C10
Purani RO 161 F6
Puras FIN 121 E14
Purbach am Neusiedler See A 77 G11
Purcari MD 154 D5
Purchena E 55 E8
Pūre LV 134 B5
Purfleet GB 15 E9
Purgstall an der Erlauf A 77 F8
Purila EST 131 C9
Purkersdorf A 77 F10
Purkijaur S 109 C18
Pürksi EST 130 C7
Purley GB 15 E8
Purmerend NL 16 C3
Purmo FIN 123 C9
Purmojärvi FIN 123 D10
Purmsāti LV 134 D3
Purnu S 116 E6
Purnumukka FIN 115 B2
Purnuvaara FIN 121 C12
Purnuvaara S 116 D6
Purola FIN 128 L6
Purontaka FIN 123 C12
Purujärvi FIN 129 B12
Purujosa E 41 E8
Purullena E 55 E6
Pūrvenets BG 165 E10
Purviniškė LT 137 D7
Pürvomay BG 166 E4
Pürvomay BG 169 B9
Puša LV 133 D2
Pušalotas LT 135 E8
Puschendorf D 75 C8
Pushkinskiye Gory RUS 133 B5
Pušmucova LV 133 C3
Püspökladány H 151 C7
Püssi EST 131 C14
Pusterwald A 73 B9
Pusté Úľany SK 146 E5
Pustków PL 143 F11
Pustomyty UA 144 D8
Pustoshka RUS 133 D6
Pŭstrovo BG 166 E4
Pusula FIN 127 E11
Puszcza Mariańska PL 141 G2
Puszczykowo PL 81 B11
Pusztaföldvár H 150 D6
Pusztakovácsi H 149 C9
Pusztamérges H 150 E4
Pusztamonostor H 150 B4
Pusztaszabolcs H 149 B11
Pusztaszer H 150 D4
Pusztavacs H 150 C4
Pusztavám H 149 B10
Putaja FIN 126 C8
Putanges-Pont-Écrepin F 23 C11
Putbus D 84 A4
Putifigari I 64 B1
Putignano I 61 B8
Putikko FIN 129 B11
Putinci SRB 158 D4
Putineiu RO 160 F5
Putineiu RO 161 F7
Putkivaara FIN 119 B17
Putlitz D 83 D12
Putna RO 153 B7
Putnok H 145 G1
Putte B 19 B10
Putte NL 16 D5
Puttgarden D 83 A10
Püttlingen D 21 F7
Putula FIN 127 C13
Putyla UA 152 B6
Putzar D 84 C5
Putzkau D 80 D6
Puukari FIN 125 C11
Puukkokumpu FIN 119 C14
Puumala FIN 129 B9
Puurmani EST 131 D12
Puurs B 19 B9
Puurtila FIN 129 B9
Puutossalmi FIN 124 E9
Puutturinjärvi FIN 119 E17
Puybrun F 29 F9
Puycasquier F 33 C7
Puygouzon F 33 C10
Puylaroque F 33 B9
Puylaurens F 33 C10
Puy-l'Évêque F 33 A8
Puymirol F 33 B7
Puymoyen F 29 D6
Puyôo F 32 C4
Pwllheli GB 10 F3
Pyaozerskiy RUS 121 C17
Pyatidorozhnoye RUS 139 B9
Pyatirech'ye RUS 137 F11
Pyershamayski BY 137 F11
Pyhäjärvi FIN 113 F16
Pyhäjärvi FIN 115 D2
Pyhäjoki FIN 119 F12
Pyhäjoki FIN 126 C7
Pyhäkylä FIN 121 D12
Pyhältö FIN 128 D7
Pyhämaa FIN 126 D5
Pyhänkoski FIN 119 F12
Pyhäntä FIN 119 F16
Pyhäntä FIN 121 F11
Pyhäntaka FIN 127 C14
Pyhäranta FIN 126 D5
Pyhäsalmi FIN 123 C15
Pyhäselkä FIN 125 F13
Pyhe FIN 126 D6
Pyhra A 77 F9
Pyhtää FIN 128 E6
Pyle GB 13 B7
Pyles GR 181 E6
Pyli GR 169 F6
Pyli GR 175 C8
Pyli GR 177 E9
Pylkönmäki FIN 123 E13
Pylos GR 174 F4
Pylypets' UA 145 F7
Pyntäinen FIN 126 B6
Pyrbaum D 75 D9
Pyrgetos GR 169 E8
Pyrgi GR 177 C6
Pyrgiotika GR 175 D6
Pyrgoi GR 169 C6
Pyrgoi GR 170 R4
Pyrgos GR 174 D3
Pyrgos GR 176 E6
Pyrgos GR 177 D8
Pyrgos GR 178 E9

Pyrgos Dirou GR 178 B3
Pyrrönperä FIN 123 B15
Pyrsogianni GR 168 D4
Pyrzyce PL 85 D7
Pyšely CZ 77 C7
Pyskowice PL 142 F6
Pyssyperä FIN 121 D10
Pystan' UA 152 A6
Pysznica PL 144 B5
Pythagoreio GR 177 D8
Pythio GR 169 D7
Pythio GR 171 C7
Pyli FIN 125 F11

Q

Qafzez AL 168 D4
Qelëz AL 163 E8
Qeparo AL 168 D2
Qerret AL 168 B2
Quadrazais P 45 D7
Quadri I 63 D7
Quakenbrück D 17 C9
Qualiano I 60 B2
Quaregnon B 182 E3
Quargnento I 37 B9
Quarona I 68 B5
Quarrata I 66 E3
Quarré-les-Tombes F 25 F10
Quarteira P 50 E3
Quartell E 48 E4
Quarten CH 27 F11
Quartu Sant'Elena I 64 E3
Quatre-Champs F 19 F10
Quatretonda E 56 D4
Quattro Castella I 66 C1
Quedlinburg D 79 C9
Queenborough GB 15 E10
Queensbury GB 11 D8
Queenstown IRL 8 E6
Queidersbach D 21 F9
Queige F 31 D9
Queiriga P 44 C5
Quel E 41 D7
Quelaines-St-Gault F 23 E10
Quellendorf D 79 C11
Queluz P 50 B1
Quemada E 40 E4
Quend F 18 D3
Quendorf D 17 D8
Queralbs E 33 F10
Querenhorst D 79 B8
Querfurt D 79 D10
Quérigut F 33 E10
Quern D 82 A7
Quernheim D 17 D10
Quero E 47 E6
Quero I 72 E4
Querrieu F 18 E5
Quesa E 48 E3
Quesada E 55 D6
Quesnoy-sur-Deûle F 18 C7
Quessoy F 22 D6
Questembert F 22 E6
Quettehou F 23 A9
Quettreville-sur-Sienne F 23 C9
Quevauvillers F 18 E4
Queyrac F 28 E4
Quézac F 29 F10
Quiaios P 44 D3
Quiberon F 22 F5
Quickborn D 83 C7
Quierschied D 21 F8
Quiévrain B 19 D8
Quiévrechain F 182 E3
Quiliano I 37 C8
Quillan F 33 E10
Quillebeuf-sur-Seine F 18 F2
Quimper F 22 E3
Quimperlé F 22 E4
Quin IRL 8 C5
Quincinetto I 68 C4
Quincy-Voisins F 25 C8
Quingey F 26 F4
Quinson F 36 D4
Quinssaines F 29 C11
Quinta de la Serena E 51 B8
Quintana del Castillo E 39 C7
Quintana del Pino E 40 C4
Quintana del Puente E 40 D3
Quintana de Rueda E 39 C9
Quintana-Martín Galíndez E 40 C5
Quintanapalla E 40 D4
Quintanar de la Orden E 47 E6
Quintanar de la Sierra E 40 E5
Quintanar del Rey E 47 F9
Quintana Redonda E 41 E6
Quintanilla de Onésimo E 40 E3
Quintenas F 30 E6
Quintin F 22 D6
Quinto CH 71 D7
Quinto E 41 F11
Quintos P 50 D4
Quinzano d'Oglio I 69 C9
Quiroga E 38 D5
Quiruelas de Vidriales E 39 D8
Quismondo E 46 D4
Quissac F 35 C7
Quittebeuf F 24 B4
Qukës AL 168 B3

R

Raab A 76 F5
Raabs an der Thaya A 77 E8
Raahe FIN 119 E12
Raajärvi FIN 115 E1
Rääkkylä FIN 125 F13
Raalte NL 16 D6
Raamsdonksveer NL 16 E3
Raanujärvi FIN 117 E13
Raappananmäki FIN 121 E10
Raasiku EST 131 C10
Raate FIN 121 E14
Raattama FIN 117 B13
Rab HR 67 C10
Rabac HR 67 B9
Rabaçal P 44 D4
Rabaçal P 45 C6
Rábade E 38 B4
Rábaganţ RO 151 D9
Rábahídvég H 149 B7
Rábakecöl H 149 B8
Rábapatak H 149 B8
Rabastens F 33 C9
Rabastens-de-Bigorre F 33 C6
Rábatamási H 149 A8

Raba Wyżna PL 147 B9
Rabbalshede S 91 B9
Rabča SK 147 C8
Rabčice SK 147 B9
Rabe SRB 150 E5
Rabenstein an der Pielach A 77 F8
Raben Steinfeld D 83 C11
Råberg S 107 B13
Rabino PL 85 C9
Rabisha BG 159 E10
Rabivere EST 131 C9
Rabka PL 147 B9
Råbke D 79 B8
Rabrovo BG 159 E10
Rabrovo SRB 159 D8
Rača SRB 158 E6
Rača SRB 164 D3
Răcăciuni RO 153 E9
Racale I 61 D10
Rácalmás H 149 B11
Racalmuto I 58 E4
Răcari RO 161 D7
Răcăşdia RO 159 D8
Racconigi I 37 B7
Rače SLO 148 D5
Rachanie I 144 B8
Rachecourt-sur-Marne F 26 C3
Raches GR 175 B6
Raches GR 177 D7
Răchiţi RO 153 B9
Răchitoasa RO 153 E10
Răchitova RO 159 B10
Rachoni GR 171 C7
Raciąż PL 138 C4
Raciąż PL 139 E9
Racibórz PL 142 F5
Raciechowice PL 144 D1
Racimierz PL 85 D7
Račinovci HR 157 C10
Račišće HR 162 D3
Rāciu RO 152 D4
Răciula MD 154 C2
Ráckeve H 149 B11
Racksätter S 97 D14
Racksund S 109 E16
Racławice PL 143 F9
Răcoasa RO 153 E9
Racova RO 153 D10
Racoviţa RO 159 B8
Racoviţa RO 160 B4
Racoviţa RO 161 C10
Racoviţeni RO 161 C9
Raczki PL 136 E6
Rączki PL 139 D9
Rád H 150 B3
Råda S 91 C13
Råda S 97 B9
Råda S 97 B10
Rada de Haro E 47 E7
Radalj SRB 158 E3
Radanovo BG 166 C5
Rădăşeni RO 153 C8
Rădăuţi RO 153 B7
Rădăuţi-Prut RO 153 A9
Raddestorf D 17 D11
Raddi in Chianti I 66 F3
Raddusa I 59 E6
Radė AL 168 B2
Radeberg D 80 D5
Radebeul D 80 D5
Radeburg D 80 D5
Radeče SLO 73 D11
Radcin PL 85 B9
Radefeld D 79 D11
Radegast D 79 C11
Rädelsbräten S 102 A3
Radenci SLO 148 C6
Rădeni MD 153 C12
Rădeşti RO 152 E3
Radevormwald D 21 B8
Radibor D 80 D6
Radičić BIH 157 C7
Radicofani I 65 B6
Radicondoli I 66 F3
Radilovo BG 165 E9
Radis D 79 C12
Radizelj SLO 148 D5
Radko Dimitrievo BG 167 C8
Radków PL 77 B10
Radlje ob Dravi SLO 73 C11
Radljevo SRB 158 D5
Radnevo BG 166 E5
Radnica CZ 76 C5
Radoaia MD 153 B12
Radočelo BIH 157 D7
Radohova BIH 157 D7
Rădoieşti RO 160 E6
Radojevo SRB 159 C7
Radolfzell am Bodensee D 27 E10
Radom PL 141 H4
Rådom S 107 E11
Radomin PL 139 D7
Radomireşti RO 160 E5
Radomirsti BG 165 D7
Radomsko PL 143 D7
Radomyšl nad Sanem PL 144 B4
Radomyśl Wielki PL 143 F11
Radonice CZ 76 B5
Radopole LV 133 C1
Radošina SK 146 D5
Radošovce SK 146 D4
Radoszyce PL 141 H2
Radovan RO 160 E3
Radovanu RO 161 E9
Radovets BG 167 E7
Radoviš MK 169 A7
Radovljica SLO 73 D9
Radovnica SRB 164 D5
Radowo Małe PL 85 C8
Radožda MK 168 B4
Radslavice CZ 146 C5
Radstadt A 73 B7
Răducăneni RO 153 D11
Radučić HR 156 D5
Raduil BG 165 E8
Radujevac SRB 159 E10
Radun' BY 137 E10

Radvanice CZ 81 E10
Radvaň nad Laborcom SK 145 E4
Radwanice PL 81 C9
Radymno PL 144 D6
Radzanów PL 139 E9
Radzanów PL 141 G3
Radzanowo PL 139 E8
Radzice Duże PL 141 H2
Radzicz PL 85 D12
Radzieje PL 136 E4
Radziejów PL 138 E5
Radziejowice PL 141 F3
Radziemice PL 143 F9
Radziłów PL 140 D6
Radzików PL 81 B7
Radzyń Chełmiński PL 138 D6
Radzyń Podlaski PL 141 G7
Ræhr DK 86 A3
Raeren B 20 C6
Raesfeld D 17 E7
Rafelbunyol E 48 E4
Raffadali I 58 E4
Rafford GB 3 K9
Rafina GR 175 C9
Raforsen S 107 E10
Råfov RO 161 D8
Rafsbotn N 113 C12
Raften N 110 D9
Raftsjöhöjden S 106 D8
Ragaciems LV 134 B6
Rágama E 45 C10
Ragana LV 135 B9
Rageliai LT 135 E11
Rägelin D 83 D13
Raglan GB 13 B9
Rågланда S 91 A13
Ragösen D 79 B12
Raguhn D 79 C11
Ragunda S 107 E10
Ragusa I 59 F6
Raguva LT 135 E9
Rahden D 17 D11
Råne N 111 E11
Rånea S 118 C8
Rånes F 23 C11
Rahkio FIN 127 D8
Rahkonen FIN 123 C12
Rahman RO 155 D2
Råholt N 95 B14
Rahula FIN 128 B7
Rahumäe EST 132 E1
Raiano I 62 C5
Raikku FIN 125 F12
Räimä FIN 124 D9
Rain D 75 E8
Rainbach im Mühlkreis A 77 E6
Raippo FIN 129 D9
Räisälä FIN 115 E3
Raisdorf D 83 B8
Raisio FIN 126 E7
Raiskio FIN 119 C16
Raiskio FIN 125 B12
Raismes F 19 D7
Raistakka FIN 121 B11
Rait GB 5 C10
Raitajärvi S 119 B10
Raitoo FIN 127 C11
Raja-Jooseppi FIN 115 B4
Rajala FIN 117 C16
Rajamäki FIN 127 E12
Rajastrand S 106 B8
Rajcza PL 147 B8
Rájec CZ 77 D11
Rajec SK 147 C7
Rajecká Lesná SK 147 C7
Rajgród PL 140 C7
Rajhrad CZ 77 D11
Rajince SRB 164 E4
Rajka H 146 F4
Raka SLO 148 E4
Rakamaz H 145 G3
Rakek SLO 73 E9
Rakevo BG 165 C7
Rakhiv UA 152 A4
Rakh'ya RUS 129 E14
Rakita BG 165 C9
Rakita BG 165 D6
Rakitna SLO 73 E9
Rakitovec SLO 67 B8
Rakitovo BG 165 F9
Rakke EST 131 D12
Rakkeby DK 90 B6
Rakkestad N 95 D14
Raklitsa BG 167 D7
Rákóczifalva H 150 C5
Rákócziújfalu H 150 C5
Rakoniewice PL 81 B10
Rakoshyn UA 145 G6
Rakova Bara SRB 159 D8
Rakovica HR 156 C4
Rakovník KS 163 E10
Rakovitsa BG 159 F9
Rakovník CZ 76 B5
Rakovo BG 165 C6
Rakovski BG 165 E10
Rakow D 84 B4
Raków PL 143 E11
Rakvere EST 131 C12
Ralingen D 21 E7
Ralja SRB 158 D6
Rälla S 89 B11
Råsäla FIN 125 E9
Ram SRB 159 D7
Ramacca I 59 E6
Rämälä FIN 123 E12
Ramales de la Victoria E 40 B5
Ramalhal P 44 F2
Ramatuelle F 36 E5
Ramberg N 110 D5
Rambervillers F 26 D6
Rambin D 84 B4
Rambouillet F 24 C6
Rambrouch L 19 E12
Rambucourt F 26 C4
Ramelton IRL 7 B7
Râmeţ RO 152 E3
Ramillies B 182 D5
Ramingstein A 73 B8
Ramirás E 38 D4
Ramløse DK 87 C10
Ramma S 102 D6
Ramme DK 86 C2
Rammelsbach D 186 B3
Rammingen D 75 E7
Râmna RO 159 C8
Ramnäs S 98 C6
Ramnes N 95 D11
Râmnicelu RO 161 C10
Râmnicelu RO 161 C11
Râmnicu Sărat RO 161 C10
Râmnicu Vâlcea RO 160 C4

Rasova BG 155 E1
Rasovo BG 159 F11
Raspenava CZ 81 E8
Rasquera E 42 E5
Rast RO 160 F2
Rastatt D 27 C9
Rastdorf D 17 C9
Rasteby N 111 A19
Råsted DK 86 B5
Rastede D 17 B10
Rastenfeld A 77 E8
Raštević HR 156 D4
Rasti HR 117 C14
Rasti FIN 125 C13
Rastinkylä FIN 125 C13
Råstolita RO 152 D5
Rastošnica BIH 157 C10
Rastovac MNE 163 D6
Rastow D 83 D10
Råstrand S 107 A14
Răsuceni RO 161 E7
Rasueros E 45 B10
Rasvåg N 94 F5
Raszków PL 142 C4
Raszyn PL 141 F3
Rataje SRB 164 C3
Rätan S 102 B8
Ratan S 122 C5
Rätansbyn S 102 B8
Ratasjärvi FIN 117 E11
Ratasvuoma FIN 119 B13
Rateče SLO 73 C8
Ratekau D 83 C9
Răteşti RO 160 D6
Rathangan IRL 7 F9
Råth Bhoth IRL 4 F1
Råth Caola IRL 8 C5
Rathconrath IRL 7 E7
Rathcoole IRL 7 F10
Råth Cúil IRL 7 F10
Råth Domhnaigh IRL 9 C7
Rathdowney IRL 9 C8
Råth Droma IRL 9 C10
Rathdrum IRL 9 C10
Rathenow D 79 A11
Rathfriland GB 7 D10
Rathgormuck IRL 9 D8
Råth Iomgháin IRL 7 F9
Rathkeale IRL 8 C5
Rathkeevin IRL 9 D7
Rathlee IRL 6 D4
Rathluirc IRL 8 D5
Råth Mealtáin IRL 7 B7
Rathmolyon IRL 7 F9
Rathmore IRL 8 D4
Rathmullan IRL 4 E1
Råth Naoi IRL 9 C10
Rathnew IRL 7 G10
Rathnure IRL 9 D9
Ratho GB 5 D10
Rathowen IRL 7 E7
Rathstock D 81 A7
Rathumney IRL 9 D9
Rathvilly IRL 9 C9
Ratiboř CZ 146 C5
Ratić BIH 158 D3
Ratingen D 21 B7
Ratíškovice CZ 77 E12
Rátka H 145 G3
Ratkovo KS 163 E10
Ratkovo SRB 158 C3
Ratnieki LV 133 D2
Ratoath IRL 7 E10
Rattelsdorf D 75 B8
Ratten A 148 B5
Rattenberg A 72 B4
Rattosjärvi FIN 117 E13
Rattray GB 5 B10
Rättsel S 118 C3
Rättvik S 103 E9
Ratvika N 104 D8
Ratzeburg D 83 C9
Rätzlingen D 79 B9
Raubach D 185 C8
Rauda LV 135 C12
Raudâna N 90 B4
Raudanjoki FIN 117 D16
Raudaskylä FIN 123 B13
Raudasmäki FIN 123 B13
Raudeberg N 100 C2
Râu de Mori RO 159 C10
Raudėnai LT 134 D5
Raudondvaris LT 137 D8
Raudonė LT 134 F6
Rauen D 80 B6
Raufoss N 101 E13
Rauha FIN 129 C10
Rauhala FIN 117 C12
Raulhac F 29 F11
Rauma FIN 126 C6
Rauna LV 135 B11
Raunds GB 15 C7
Rauris A 73 B6
Râu Sadului RO 160 B4
Rauschenberg D 21 C11
Raussila FIN 128 D6
Rautajärvi FIN 127 C12
Rautalampi FIN 124 E7
Rautaperä FIN 114 E4
Rautas S 111 D18
Rautavaara FIN 125 C10
Rautenkranz D 75 B11
Rautila FIN 119 F11
Rautila FIN 126 D6
Rautio FIN 120 F3
Rautionmäki FIN 123 E16
Rautjärven kk FIN 129 C11
Rautjärvi FIN 129 C11
Rautuskylä FIN 117 C13
Rauvanniemi FIN 129 B11
Rauzan F 28 F5
Ravadinovo BG 167 E9
Ravanusa I 58 E4
Rava-Rus'ka UA 144 C8
Ravasd H 149 A9
Ravča HR 157 F7
Ravda BG 167 D9
Ravels B 16 F3
Ravelsbach A 77 E9
Rävemåla S 89 B9
Ravenglass GB 10 C5
Ravenna I 66 D5
Ravensburg D 71 B9
Ravenstein NL 16 E5
Ravières F 25 E11
Ravijoki FIN 128 D8
Ravik N 108 B7
Rävlanda N 91 D12
Ravna Dubrava SRB 164 C5
Ravna Gora HR 67 B10
Ravna Reka SRB 159 E8
Ravne SLO 73 D11

Ravne na Koroškem SLO 73 C10
Ravnets BG 167 D8
Ravni BIH 157 F8
Ravnište SRB 164 C3
Ravnje SRB 158 D3
Ravno BIH 157 E7
Ravno BIH 162 D4
Ravnogor BG 165 F9
Ravno Selo SRB 158 C4
Ravnshøj DK 90 E7
Ravnstrup DK 86 C4
Rävsön S 103 A15
Ravsted DK 86 E4
Rawa Mazowiecka PL 141 G2
Rawicz PL 81 C11
Rawmarsh GB 11 E9
Rawtenstall GB 11 D7
Raykovo BG 171 A7
Rayleigh GB 15 D10
Rayol-Canadel-sur-Mer F 36 E4
Räyrinki FIN 123 D11
Ražana SRB 158 E4
Ražanac HR 156 D3
Ražanj SRB 159 F8
Războieni RO 153 C9
Razboj BIH 157 C7
Razbojna SRB 164 C3
Razdelna BG 167 C9
Razdol BG 165 F6
Razdrto SLO 73 E9
Razès F 29 C8
Razgrad BG 160 F2
Razgrad BG 167 D6
Rážljevo BIH 157 C10
Razlog BG 165 F7
Razlovci MK 165 F6
Ražňany SK 145 E3
Ráztočno SK 147 D7
Răzvad RO 161 D6
Reading GB 14 E7
Reaghstown IRL 7 E9
Real P 38 F3
Réalmont F 33 C10
Realmonte I 58 E3
Réalville F 33 B8
Rear Cross IRL 8 C6
Réaup F 33 B6
Reay GB 3 H9
Rebais F 25 C9
Rebbenesbotn N 112 C2
Rebecq B 19 C9
Rébénacq F 32 D5
Rebild DK 86 B5
Rebollosa de Jadraque E 47 B7
Reboly RUS 125 C15
Rebordelo E 38 B3
Rebordelo P 38 E5
Rebra RO 152 C4
Rebricea RO 153 D11
Rebrişoara RO 152 C4
Rebrovo BG 165 D7
Rebůrkovo BG 165 D8
Reca SK 146 E4
Reçan KS 163 E10
Recanati I 67 F7
Recaş RO 151 F8
Recco I 37 C10
Recea MD 153 B11
Recea MD 154 C3
Recea RO 151 B12
Recea RO 152 F5
Recea RO 160 D6
Recea-Cristur RO 152 C3
Recess IRL 6 F3
Recey-sur-Ource F 25 E12
Réchicourt-le-Château F 27 C6
Rechlin D 83 D13
Rechnitz A 149 B6
Recht B 20 D6
Rechtenbach D 74 C6
Reci RO 153 F7
Recke D 17 D8
Recklingen CH 70 E6
Recklinghausen D 17 E8
Recoaro Terme I 69 B11
Recoubeau-Jansac F 35 A9
Recsk H 147 F10
Recuerda E 40 F6
Recz PL 85 D9
Rjeczno PL 141 H1
Reda PL 138 A5
Redalen N 101 E13
Redange L 20 E5
Redcar GB 11 B9
Redcross IRL 9 C10
Reddelich D 83 B11
Redditch GB 13 A11
Réde H 149 B9
Redea RO 160 E4
Redefin D 83 D10
Redhill GB 15 E8
Rédics H 149 C6
Rediu RO 153 C11
Rediu RO 153 D9
Rediu RO 153 F11
Rediul Mare MD 153 A11
Rednitzhembach D 75 D9
Redon F 23 E7
Redondela E 38 D2
Redondelo P 38 E4
Redondo P 50 B4
Redován E 56 E3
Red Point GB 2 K5
Redruth GB 12 E4
Redsted DK 86 B3
Reduzum NL 16 B5
Rjdzikowo PL 85 B12
Rjdziny PL 143 E7
Reen IRL 8 E3
Reens IRL 8 C5
Reepham GB 15 B11
Rees D 16 E6
Reßum D 17 B11
Reetz D 79 B11
Reetz D 83 D11
Reftele S 87 A13
Regalbuto I 59 D6
Regen D 76 E4
Regensburg D 75 D11
Regensdorf CH 27 F9
Regenstauf D 75 D11
Reggello I 66 E4
Reggio di Calabria I 59 C8
Reggiolo I 66 C2
Reggio nell'Emilia I 66 C2
Reghin RO 152 D5
Reghiu RO 153 F9

Regna S 92 B7
Regnitzlosau D 75 B11
Régny F 30 C5
Regöly H 149 C10
Regozero RUS 121 D17
Regrstrup DK 87 D9
Reguengo E 38 D2
Reguengos de Monsaraz P 50 C4
Rehau D 75 B11
Rehburg (Rehburg-Loccum) D 17 D12
Rehden D 17 C10
Rehling D 75 F8
Rehlingen-Siersburg D 21 F7
Řehlovice CZ 80 E5
Rehmsdorf D 79 D11
Rehna D 83 C10
Rehula FIN 129 C9
Reibitz D 79 C11
Reichelsheim (Odenwald) D 187 B6
Reichenau an der Rax A 148 A5
Reichenbach CH 70 D5
Reichenbach D 79 E11
Reichenbach D 187 B6
Reichenberg D 74 C6
Reichenfels A 73 B10
Reichertsheim D 75 F11
Reichia GR 178 B5
Reichling D 71 B11
Reichmannsdorf D 75 A9
Reicholzheim D 74 C6
Reichraming A 73 A9
Reichshoffen F 27 C8
Reiden CH 27 F8
Reigada P 45 C7
Reigate GB 15 E8
Reignac F 28 E4
Reignier F 31 C9
Reil D 21 D8
Reilingen D 187 C6
Reillanne F 35 C10
Reillo E 47 E9
Reims F 19 F9
Reina E 51 C8
Reinach CH 27 F8
Reinach CH 27 F9
Reinbek D 83 C8
Reinberg D 84 B4
Reine N 110 E5
Reinfeld (Holstein) D 83 C8
Reinheim D 21 E11
Reinosa E 40 C3
Reinøysund N 114 D8
Reinsfeld D 21 E7
Reinskard N 112 D4
Reinskloster N 104 D7
Reinstad N 111 C10
Reinsvik N 104 E3
Reinsvoll N 101 E13
Reipa N 108 C6
Reisbach D 75 E12
Reischach D 75 F12
Reisjärvi FIN 123 C13
Reiskirchen D 21 C11
Reiss GB 3 J10
Reitan N 100 B8
Reitan N 101 A14
Reitano I 58 D5
Reith bei Seefeld A 72 B3
Reit im Winkl D 72 A5
Reittiö FIN 125 D9
Reivyčiai LT 134 D4
Rejmyre S 92 B7
Rejowiec PL 141 H8
Rejsby DK 86 E3
Reka HR 149 F7
Rekava LV 133 B3
Rekavice BIH 157 C7
Reken D 17 E8
Rekijoki FIN 127 E9
Rekken NL 17 D7
Reklynets' UA 144 C9
Rekovac SRB 159 F7
Rekowo PL 85 B12
Relíquias P 50 D3
Relleu E 56 D4
Rellingen D 83 C7
Rém H 150 E3
Remagen D 21 C8
Rémalard F 24 D4
Rembercourt-Sommaisne F 26 C3
Remda D 79 E9
Remels (Uplengen) D 17 B9
Remennikovo RUS 133 C5
Remeskylä FIN 123 C16
Remetea RO 151 D9
Remetea RO 152 D6
Remetea Chioarului RO 152 B3
Remetea Mare RO 151 F7
Remeţi RO 145 H8
Remetine HR 149 D6
Remetské Hámre SK 145 F5
Remich L 20 E6
Remicourt F 183 D6
Remiremont F 26 D6
Remmam S 107 D14
Remmen S 103 B12
Remmet S 102 B7
Remnes N 108 D6
Remolinos E 41 E9
Remouchamps B 183 E7
Remoulins F 35 C8
Remplin D 83 C13
Remscheid D 21 B8
Remte LV 134 C5
Remungol F 22 E6
Rémuzat F 35 B9
Rena N 101 D14
Renaison F 30 C4
Renålandet S 106 D8
Renazé F 23 E9
Rencēni LV 131 F10
Renchen D 27 C9
Renda LV 134 B4
Rendsburg D 82 B7
Renedo E 39 E10
Renedo E 40 B4
Renedo de la Vega E 39 D10
Renedo de Valdavia E 40 C3
Renens CH 31 B10
Renesse NL 16 E1
Renfrew GB 5 D8
Rengerslausen D
Renginio GR 175 B6

Rengsdorf D 21 C8
Rengsjö S 103 D12
Renholmen S 118 D6
Reni UA 155 C2
Renko FIN 127 D11
Renkomäki FIN 127 D14
Renkum NL 183 B7
Renndal N 104 E6
Rennerod D 21 C10
Rennertshofen D 75 E9
Rennes F 23 D8
Rennes-les-Bains F 33 E10
Renningen D 27 C10
Rennweg A 73 B8
Renon I 72 C3
Rens DK 86 F4
Rensjön S 111 D18
Renström S 118 E4
Renswoude NL 183 A7
Rentina GR 174 A4
Rentjärn S 107 A15
Rentweinsdorf D 75 B8
Renwez F 19 E10
Renzow D 83 C10
Repbäcken S 97 A13
Répcelak H 149 B8
Repedea RO 152 B4
Repino RUS 129 E12
Repki PL 141 F6
Replot FIN 122 D6
Repojoki FIN 117 B15
Repolka RUS 132 C6
Reposaari FIN 126 B5
Repparfjord N 113 C13
Reppen D 81 B12
Reppenstedt D 83 D8
Reps AL 163 F8
Repton GB 11 F8
Repvåg N 113 B16
Requejo E 39 D6
Requena E 47 F10
Réquista F 33 B10
Rerik, Ostseebad D 83 B11
Resana I 72 E4
Resarö S 99 D10
Resavica SRB 159 E8
Resele S 107 E12
Resen BG 166 C5
Resen MK 168 B5
Resenbro DK 86 C5
Resende P 44 B5
Reşetari HR 157 B7
Resko PL 85 C8
Reşita RO 159 C8
Resna MNE 163 E6
Resolven GB 13 B7
Respenda de la Peña E 39 C10
Resse (Wedemark) D 78 A6
Ressons-sur-Matz F 18 E6
Restelice KS 163 F10
Restinga MA 53 E6
Reston GB 5 D12
Resuttano I 58 D5
Retamal E 51 B8
Retford GB 11 E10
Rethel F 19 E9
Rethem (Aller) D 17 C12
Rethymno GR 178 E7
Retie B 16 F4
Retiers F 23 E9
Retje SLO 73 E10
Retortillo E 45 C8
Retortillo de Soria E 40 F6
Retournac F 30 E5
Rétság H 147 F8
Retuerta del Bullaque E 46 F4
Retunen FIN 125 E11
Retz A 77 E9
Reuden D 79 B11
Reuilly F 24 F7
Reurieth D 75 B8
Reus E 42 E6
Reusel NL 16 F4
Reut D 76 F3
Reute D 27 D8
Reutel MD 153 B11
Reuterstadt Stavenhagen D 84 C3
Reutlingen D 27 D11
Reutte A 71 C11
Reutuaapa FIN 119 B15
Reuver NL 16 F6
Revel F 33 D10
Revello I 37 B6
Revest-du-Bion F 35 B10
Révfülöp H 149 C9
Revholmen N 91 B9
Reviga RO 161 D10
Revigny-sur-Ornain F 26 C2
Revilla de Collazos E 40 C3
Revilla del Campo E 40 D4
Revin F 19 E10
Revine-Lago I 72 E5
Řevnice CZ 76 C6
Řevničov CZ 76 B5
Revø I 72 D3
Revonlahti FIN 119 E13
Revsnes N 100 D6
Revsnes N 111 C11
Revúca SK 147 D10
Rewal PL 85 B8
Rexbo S 103 E9
Reyrieux F 30 D6
Rezé F 23 F8
Rēzekne LV 133 C2
Rezi H 149 C8
Rezina MD 154 B3
Rēžna LV 133 D2
Rezovo BG 167 E10
Rezzato I 66 A1
Rezzoaglio I 37 B10
Rgotina SRB 159 E9
Rhade D 17 B12
Rhauen D 21 E8
Rhayader GB 13 A7
Rheda-Wiedenbrück D 17 E10
Rhede D 17 E7
Rhede (Ems) D 17 B8
Rheden NL 183 A8
Rheinau D 27 C8
Rheinbach D 21 C7
Rheinberg D 17 E7
Rheinböllen D 185 E8
Rheinbreitbach D 21 C8
Rheinbrohl D 185 D7
Rheine D 17 D8
Rheinfelden (Baden) D 27 E8
Rheinsberg D 84 D3
Rheinstetten D 27 C9

Rheinzabern D 187 C5
Rhêmes-Notre-Dame I 31 D11
Rhêmes-St-Georges I 31 D11
Rhenen NL 16 E5
Rhens D 185 D8
Rhiconich GB 2 J7
Rhinau F 27 D8
Rhinow D 83 E12
Rhisnes B 182 D5
Rho I 69 B7
Rhode IRL 7 F8
Rhoden (Diemelstadt) D 17 F12
Rhoon NL 182 B4
Rhoose GB 13 C8
Rhosllanerchrugog GB 10 E5
Rhôs-on-Sea GB 10 E4
Rhossili GB 12 B6
Rhuddlan GB 10 E5
Rhydaman GB 12 B7
Rhyl GB 10 E5
Rhymney GB 13 B8
Riace I 59 C9
Riachos P 44 F3
Riaillé F 23 E9
Rialp E 33 F8
Riaño E 39 C10
Riano I 62 C3
Rians F 35 C10
Riantec F 22 E5
Rianxo E 38 C2
Riaz CH 31 B11
Riba E 40 B4
Ribadavia E 38 D3
Ribadelago E 39 D6
Riba de Mouro P 38 D3
Ribadeo E 38 A5
Riba de Saelices E 47 C8
Ribadesella E 39 B9
Ribaforada E 41 D8
Ribafrecha E 32 F1
Ribarci SRB 164 C4
Ribare SRB 164 C4
Ribari SRB 158 D3
Ribaritsa BG 165 D9
Riba-roja d'Ebre E 42 E4
Riba-roja de Turia E 48 E3
Ribbåsen S 102 D7
Ribchester GB 10 D6
Ribe DK 86 E3
Ribeauvillé F 27 D7
Ribécourt-Dreslincourt F 18 E6
Ribeira E 38 C3
Ribeira de Pena P 38 E4
Ribemont F 19 E7
Ribera I 58 E3
Ribérac F 29 E6
Ribera del Fresno E 51 B7
Ribesalbes E 48 D4
Ribes de Freser E 33 F10
Ribiţa RO 151 E10
Ribnica BIH 157 D9
Ribnica BIH 157 D9
Ribnica SLO 148 C4
Ribnica SRB 158 F4
Ribnik HR 148 E4
Řibřany MD 154 B4
Ribnitz-Damgarten D 83 B12
Ribnovo BG 165 F8
Ribota E 40 F5
Ricadi I 59 B8
Riccall GB 11 D9
Ricchia GB 13 C8
Riccia I 63 E7
Riccio I 66 F5
Riccò del Golfo di Spezia I 69 E8
Richardménil F 26 C5
Richelieu F 29 A6
Richhill GB 7 D9
Richka UA 152 A5
Richmond GB 11 C8
Richvald SK 145 E3
Rickebo S 103 D11
Rickenbach D 27 E8
Rickinghall GB 15 C10
Rickling D 83 B8
Rickmansworth GB 15 D8
Ricla E 41 E9
Ricse H 145 G4
Ridasjärvi FIN 127 D13
Riddarhyttan S 97 C14
Ridderkerk NL 16 E3
Riddes CH 31 C11
Ridica SRB 150 F3
Ridzene LV 135 B9
Riebniņš LV 135 D13
Riebiņi LV 135 D13
Riec-sur-Belon F 22 E4
Ried CH 68 A3
Riede D 17 C11
Riedenburg D 75 E10
Rieder D 79 C9
Ried im Innkreis A 76 F4
Ried im Oberinntal A 71 C11
Ried im Zillertal A 72 B4
Ried in der Riedmark A 77 F7
Riedlingen D 71 A8
Riegelsberg D 21 F7
Riegersburg A 148 B5
Riego de la Vega E 39 D8
Riehe (Suthfeld) D 78 B5
Riehen CH 27 E8
Rielasingen-Worblingen D 27 E10
Riello E 39 C8
Rielves E 46 E4
Riemst B 19 C12
Rieneck D 187 A8
Rieni RO 151 D9
Rieponlahti FIN 124 E7
Riepsdorf D 83 B10
Riesa D 80 D4
Rieseby D 83 A7
Riestedt D 79 D9
Rietavas LT 134 E3
Rietberg D 17 E10
Rieth D 84 C6
Riethoven NL 183 C6
Rieti I 62 C3
Rietschen D 81 D7
Rieumes F 33 D8
Rieupeyroux F 33 B10
Rieutort-de-Randon F 34 A5
Rieux F 33 D8
Rieux F 33 D8
Rifiano I 72 C3
Riffenmatt CH 31 B11
Rīga LV 135 C8
Rigaio GR 169 F8
Rigaud F 36 D5
Riggisberg CH 31 B11
Rignac F 33 B10

Rignano Flaminio I 62 C2
Rignano Garganico I 63 D9
Rignano sull'Arno I 66 E3
Rigny-le-Ferron F 25 D10
Rigny-sur-Arroux F 30 B5
Rigny-Ussé F 24 F3
Rigside GB 5 D9
Rihtniemi FIN 126 C5
Riihimäki FIN 127 D12
Riihivaara FIN 125 C14
Riikonkumpu FIN 117 C14
Riipi FIN 117 C13
Riippi FIN 122 F7
Riisipere EST 131 C9
Riistavesi FIN 125 E10
Riitiala FIN 127 B8
Riječa BIH 157 D8
Riječa BIH 157 F11
Rijeka HR 67 B9
Rijeka Crnojevića MNE 163 E7
Rijen NL 16 E3
Rijkevorsel B 16 F3
Rijnsburg NL 16 D2
Rijsbergen NL 16 E3
Rijsel F 19 C7
Rijssen NL 17 D7
Rijswijk NL 16 D2
Rikava LV 133 C2
Riksgränsen S 111 D16
Rila BG 165 E7
Rilhac-Rancon F 29 D8
Rilland NL 182 C4
Rillé F 23 F12
Rillo de Gallo E 47 C9
Rimavská Baňa SK 147 D9
Rimavská Seč SK 145 G1
Rimavská Sobota SK 147 E10
Rimavské Janovce SK 147 E10
Rimbach D 76 D3
Rimbach D 187 B6
Rimbo S 99 C10
Rimetea RO 152 E3
Rimforsa S 92 C7
Rimicāni LV 135 D12
Rimini I 66 D6
Rimjokk S 118 B5
Rimmilä FIN 127 D11
Rimóc H 147 E9
Rimogne F 184 E2
Rimont F 33 E8
Rimpar D 74 C6
Rimsbo S 103 D11
Rimšė LT 135 E12
Rimšėnai LT 135 F12
Rimske Toplice SLO 73 D11
Rimsting D 72 A5
Rinchnach D 76 E4
Rincón de la Victoria E 53 C8
Rincón de Soto E 41 D8
Rinda LV 134 A3
Rindal N 104 E6
Rindsholm DK 86 C4
Rineia GR 176 E5
Rinella I 59 B6
Ringamon S 93 C8
Ringaudai LT 137 D8
Ringe D 17 C7
Ringe DK 86 E6
Ringebu N 101 C12
Ringelia N 101 E12
Ringen N 95 B12
Ringford GB 5 F8
Ringhals S 87 A10
Ringleben D 79 D9
Ringsend GB 4 E3
Ringsta S 106 E7
Ringvattnet S 106 C8
Ringwood GB 13 D11
Rinkaby S 88 D6
Rinkabyholm S 89 B10
Rinkenæs DK 86 F5
Rinkilä FIN 129 B10
Rinloan GB 5 A10
Rinn S 87 A10
Rinnen IRL 8 C4
Rinøyvåg N 111 D10
Rintala FIN 123 D10
Rinteln D 17 D12
Rio GR 174 C4
Rio Caldo P 38 E3
Rio de Mel P 44 D5
Rio de Moinhos P 50 B4
Rio de Moinhos P 50 D3
Rio de Onor P 39 E6
Rio di Pusteria I 72 C4
Riofrío E 45 C10
Riofrío de Aliste E 39 E7
Riógordo E 53 C8
Rioja E 55 F8
Riola Sardo I 64 D2
Riolobos E 45 E8
Riolo Terme I 66 D4
Riols F 34 C4
Riom F 30 D3
Riomaggiore I 69 E8
Rio Maior P 44 F3
Riom-ès-Montagnes F 29 C11
Rion-des-Landes F 32 C4
Rionegro del Puente E 39 D7
Rio nell'Elba I 65 B2
Rionero in Vulture I 60 B5
Rionero Sannitico I 63 D6
Rions F 32 A5
Riorges F 30 C5
Ríos E 38 E5
Rioseco de Tapia E 39 C8
Rio Tinto P 44 B3
Rio Torto P 38 E5
Rioz F 26 F5
Ripač BIH 156 C4
Ripacandida I 60 B5
Ripalimosano I 63 D7
Ripanj SRB 158 D5
Riparbella I 66 F2
Ripatransone I 62 B5
Ripe I 67 E7
Ripi I 62 D4
Ripiceni RO 153 B10
Ripley GB 11 D8
Ripley GB 11 E9
Ripoll E 43 C8
Ripon GB 11 C8
Riposto I 59 D7
Rips NL 183 B7
Riquewihr F 27 D7

Risan MNE 163 D6
Risarven S 103 C10
Risbäck S 106 B9
Risberg S 102 D6
Risca GB 13 B8
Rişca RO 151 D11
Rîşcani MD 153 B11
Riscle F 32 C5
Risdal N 90 B3
Risede S 106 C8
Rish BG 167 D7
Risinge S 92 B7
Risliden S 107 B16
Risnabben S 118 D3
Risnes N 94 E5
Risør N 90 B5
Risøyhamn N 111 C10
Rissa N 104 D7
Rissnaben S 118 D4
Riste FIN 125 B12
Risteli FIN 125 B12
Risti EST 131 D8
Ristiina FIN 128 B7
Ristijärvi FIN 121 F11
Ristilä FIN 121 B11
Ristilampi FIN 117 E17
Ristinen FIN 124 D7
Ristinkylä FIN 125 E12
Ristioja FIN 117 E13
Ristonmännikkö FIN 117 D16
Risträsk S 107 B12
Risudden S 119 B11
Risum-Lindholm D 82 A5
Rītausmas LV 135 D8
Rite LV 135 D10
Rīteri LV 135 C11
Ritini GR 169 D7
Ritola FIN 123 E14
Ritterhude D 17 B11
Rittersdorf D 185 D5
Rittersgrün D 75 B12
Riudarenes E 43 D9
Riudecols E 42 E5
Riudoms E 42 E6
Riutta FIN 123 C13
Riutula FIN 113 F18
Rīva LV 134 B3
Riva del Garda I 69 B10
Riva di Solto I 69 B9
Riva di Tures I 72 C5
Rivanazzano I 37 B10
Rivardo Ligure I 37 C9
Rivarolo Canavese I 68 C4
Rivarolo Mantovano I 66 B1
Rivas-Vaciamadrid E 46 D6
Rive-de-Gier F 30 D6
Rivedoux-Plage F 28 C3
Rivello I 60 C5
Riverchapel IRL 9 C10
Rivergaro I 37 B10
Rivero E 40 B3
Riverstown IRL 7 F7
Riverstown IRL 8 E6
Rivery F 18 E5
Rives F 31 E8
Rivesaltes F 34 E4
Rivière-sur-Tarn F 34 B5
Rivignano I 73 E7
Rivinperä FIN 119 F16
Rivodutri I 62 B3
Rivoli I 68 C3
Rivolta d'Adda I 69 C8
Rixensart B 19 C10
Rixheim F 27 E7
Rixö S 91 C9
Riza GR 175 C6
Rizes GR 174 E4
Rizomata GR 169 D7
Rizomylos GR 169 F7
Rizziconi I 59 C8
Rjånes N 100 B3
Rjukan N 95 C9
Rø DK 89 E7
Ro I 66 C4
Roa S 103 A14
Roa E 40 E4
Roade GB 15 C7
Roadside GB 3 H10
Roadside of Kinneff GB 5 B12
Roager DK 86 E3
Roald N 100 A4
Roan N 104 C3
Roanne F 30 C5
Roata de Jos RO 161 E7
Roath GB 13 C8
Röbäck S 122 C4
Robănești RO 160 E4
Robbio I 68 C6
Robeasca RO 161 C10
Robecco d'Oglio I 69 C9
Röbel D 83 D13
Robella I 68 C5
Robert-Espagne F 26 C3
Roberton GB 5 D9
Roberton GB 5 E11
Robertsfors S 118 F5
Robežnieki LV 133 E3
Robiac-Rochessadoule F 35 B7
Robilante I 37 C7
Robin Hood's Bay GB 11 C10
Robion F 35 C9
Robledo E 55 B8
Robledo de Chavela E 46 C4
Robledo del Mazo E 46 E3
Robledollano E 45 E10
Robles de la Valcueva E 39 C9
Robliza de Cojos E 45 C9
Robøle N 101 E11
Robredo E 41 E11
Robres E 41 E11
Robres del Castillo E 32 F1
Roč HR 67 B9
Rocamadour F 29 F9
Roca Vecchia I 61 C10
Roccabianca I 66 B1
Roccadaspide I 60 C4
Rocca d'Evandro I 60 A1
Rocca di Cambio I 62 C5
Rocca di Mezzo I 62 C5
Rocca di Neto I 61 E7
Rocca di Papa I 62 D3
Roccafranca I 69 C9
Roccagloriosa I 60 C4
Roccagorga I 62 D4
Rocca Grimalda I 37 B9
Rocca Imperiale I 61 C7
Roccalbegna I 65 B5
Roccalumera I 59 D7

Roccamandolfi I 63 D6
Rocca Massima I 62 D3
Roccamena I 58 D3
Roccamonfina I 60 A1
Roccamontepiano I 62 C6
Roccanova I 60 C6
Roccapalumba I 58 D4
Rocca Pia I 62 D5
Roccaraso I 62 D6
Rocca San Casciano I 66 D4
Rocca San Giovanni I 63 C6
Roccasecca I 62 D5
Roccasecca dei Volsci I 62 E4
Rocca Sinibalda I 62 C3
Roccastrada I 65 A4
Roccavione I 37 C6
Roccella Ionica I 59 C9
Rocchetta Sant'Antonio I 60 A4
Rochdale GB 11 D7
Roche GB 12 E5
Rochechouart F 29 D7
Rochefort B 19 D11
Rochefort F 28 D4
Rochefort-en-Terre F 23 E7
Rochefort-Montagne F 30 D2
Rochefort-sur-Nenon F 26 F4
Rochehaut B 184 E3
Roche-la-Molière F 30 E5
Rochemaure F 35 A8
Roches-Bettaincourt F 26 D3
Rocheservière F 28 B2
Rochester GB 5 E12
Rochester GB 15 E10
Rochetaillée F 26 E3
Rochford GB 15 D10
Rochfortbridge IRL 7 F8
Rochin F
Rochlitz D 79 D12
Rociana del Condado E 51 E6
Ročinj SLO 73 D8
Rociu RO 160 D6
Rockanje NL 182 B4
Rockchapel IRL 8 D4
Rockcliffe GB 5 F9
Rockcorry IRL 7 D8
Rockenhausen D 21 E9
Rockesholm S 97 C12
Rockhammar S 97 C13
Rockhill IRL 8 D5
Rockingham GB 11 F10
Rockmills IRL 8 D6
Rocknebyy S 89 B10
Röcknitz D 79 D12
Rocourt-St-Martin F 25 B9
Rocroi F
Rodach bei Coburg D 75 B8
Roda de Bara E 43 E6
Roda de Ter E 43 D8
Rodalben D 21 F9
Rodaljice HR 156 D3
Rõdášel S 118 F3
Rodberg N 95 B9
Rödbergshamn N 111 B15
Rødby DK 83 A10
Rødbyhavn DK 83 A10
Rødding DK 86 B3
Rødding DK 86 E4
Rödeby S 89 C9
Rodeiro E 38 C4
Rødekro DK 86 E4
Rodel GB 2 K3
Rodellar E 32 F5
Rodelle F 34 A4
Roden NL 17 B6
Ródenas E 47 C10
Rodenkirchen (Stadland) D 17 B10
Rödental D 75 B9
Rodewald D 17 D12
Rodewisch D 75 A11
Rodez F 33 B11
Rodi Garganico I 63 D9
Roding D 75 D12
Rodingträsk S 107 C14
Rödjebro S 99 B8
Rødkærsbro DK 86 C4
Rodleben D 79 C11
Rødlia N 108 E2
Rødmyra S 103 C11
Rodna RO 152 C5
Rododafni GR 174 C5
Rodolivos GR 170 C5
Rödön S 105 E16
Rodopoli GR 169 B9
Rodopos GR 178 D6
Rodos GR 181 D8
Rødovre DK 87 D10
Rødsand N 111 B13
Rødsand N 114 D8
Rødseidet N 105 B11
Rödvattnet S 107 D13
Rødvig DK 87 F10
Roela EST 131 C13
Roermond NL 20 B5
Roeselare B 19 C7
Roeşti RO 160 D4
Roetgen D 20 C6
Rofors S 92 C5
Rofrano I 60 C4
Rogač HR 156 F4
Rogačica SRB 158 E4
Rogaška Slatina SLO 148 D5
Rogaszyce PL 142 D4
Rogate GB 15 E7
Rogatec SLO 148 D5
Rogatica BIH 157 E11
Rogätz D 79 B10
Roggel NL 16 F5
Roggenburg D 75 F7
Roggendorf D 83 C10
Roggentin D 84 D3
Roggiano Gravina I 60 D6
Roghudi I 59 C8
Rogienice Wielkie PL 139 D13
Rogil P 50 E2
Rogliano F 37 F10
Rognac F 35 D9
Rognan N 108 B9
Rognes F 35 C9
Rognes N 104 E8
Rogovë KS 163 E9
Rogovka LV 133 C2
Rogów PL 141 G1
Rogowo PL 139 D7
Rogozen BG 165 B8
Rogoznica HR 156 E4
Rogoźnica PL 81 D10
Rogoźniczka PL 141 F7

Rogoźno PL 85 E12
Rogslösa S 92 C5
Rogsta S 102 A8
Kogsta S 103 C13
Roguszyn PL 139 F12
Rohan F 22 D6
Röhlingen D 75 E7
Rohlsdorf D 83 D11
Rohlsdorf D 83 D12
Rohod H 145 G5
Rohovce SK 146 E4
Rohožník SK 77 F12
Rohr D 79 E8
Rohrau A 77 F11
Rohrbach D 75 E10
Rohrbach in Oberösterreich A 76 E5
Rohrbach-lès-Bitche F 27 B7
Rohrberg D 83 E10
Rohr in Niederbayern D 75 E10
Röhrmoos D 75 F9
Röhrnbach D 76 E5
Rohrsen D 17 C12
Rohuküla EST 130 D6
Roiffieux F 30 E6
Roisel F 19 E7
Roismala FIN 127 C8
Roivainen FIN 115 B2
Roiz E 40 B3
Roja LV 134 A5
Rojales E 56 E3
Röjan S 102 B7
Röjdåfors S 97 B8
Rojewo PL 138 E5
Rökå S 107 A15
Rokai LT 137 D8
Rokiciny PL 143 C8
Rokietnica PL 81 A11
Rokietnica PL 144 D6
Rokiškis LT 135 E11
Rokitno PL 141 F8
Rokksøy N 111 C10
Røkkum N 101 A8
Røkland N 108 C9
Roklum D 79 B8
Roknäs S 118 D6
Rokycany CZ 76 C5
Rokytnice CZ 146 C4
Rokytnice v Orlických Horách CZ 77 B10
Rolampont F 26 E3
Rold DK 86 B5
Røldal N 94 C5
Rolde NL 17 C7
Rolfs S 119 C10
Rolfstorp S 87 A10
Rollag N 95 B10
Rollán E 45 C9
Rolle CH 31 C9
Rolsted DK 86 E7
Rolvåg N 108 D3
Rolvsnes N 94 C2
Rolvsøy N 95 D14
Rom D 83 D11
Rom F 29 C6
Roma I 62 D3
Roma RO 153 B9
Roma S 93 D12
Romagnano Sesia I 68 B5
Romagné F 23 D9
Romainmôtier CH 31 B9
Romakkajärvi FIN 117 E13
Roman BG 165 C9
Roman RO 153 D9
Romana I 64 C2
Românaşi RO 151 C11
Româneşti RO 153 B10
Romāni RO 153 D9
Romanija BIH 157 E10
Romano d'Ezzelino I 72 E4
Romano di Lombardia I 69 B8
Romanones E 47 C7
Romanovce MK 164 E4
Romanovo RUS 136 D1
Romanowo PL 85 E11
Romanshorn CH 27 F11
Romans-sur-Isère F 31 E7
Romanu RO 155 C1
Romazy F 23 D9
Rombas F 20 F6
Rombiolo I 59 B9
Romeira P 44 F3
Rometta I 59 C7
Romeu P 38 E5
Romford GB 15 D9
Romhány H 147 F8
Römhild D 75 B8
Romillé F 23 D8
Romilly-sur-Seine F 25 C10
Rommerskirchen D 21 B7
Rømønsæter N 102 C3
Romorantin-Lanthenay F 24 F6
Romos RO 151 F11
Romppala FIN 125 E13
Romrod D 21 C12
Romsey GB 13 D12
Rømskog N 96 C6
Romsley GB 13 A10
Romstad N 105 C11
Romuli RO 152 B4
Rönäs S 108 C8
Rønbjerg DK 86 B3
Roncade I 72 E6
Roncadelle I 66 A1
Roncal E 32 E4
Roncegno I 69 A11
Ronce-les-Bains F 28 D3
Ronchamp F 26 E6
Ronchi dei Legionari I 73 E7
Ronciglione I 62 C2
Ronco Canavese I 68 C4
Roncone I 69 B10
Ronco Scrivia I 37 B9
Ronda E 53 C6
Rønde DK 86 C6
Rondissone I 68 C4
Rone S 93 E12
Ronehamn S 93 E12
Rong N 94 A1
Rõngu EST 131 E12
Rönnäng S 91 D10
Rönnäs S 107 B10
Rönnbacken S 103 E11
Rönnberg S 109 E17
Rönnberget S 118 C8
Rønne DK 88 E7
Rønnebæk DK 87 E9
Ronneburg D 79 E11
Ronneby S 89 C8
Ronnebyhamn S 89 C8

Rønnede DK 87 E10
Ronnenberg D 78 B6
Rönneshytta S 92 B6
Rönnholm S 107 D16
Rønningen N 111 C15
Rönnliden S 109 F17
Rönnöfors S 105 D15
Rönö S 93 C9
Ronov nad Doubravou CZ 77 C9
Ronsberg D 71 B10
Ronse B 19 C8
Ronshausen D 78 E6
Ronvik N 108 B5
Rooaun IRL 6 F6
Roodeschool NL 17 B7
Roosendaal NL 16 E2
Roosinpohja FIN 123 F13
Roosky IRL 7 E7
Roosna-Alliku EST 131 C11
Ropa PL 145 D3
Ropaži LV 135 C9
Ropcha UA 153 A7
Ropczyce PL 143 F12
Ropeid N 94 D4
Roperuelos del Páramo E 39 D8
Ropienka PL 145 D5
Ropinsalmi FIN 116 A7
Ropotovo MK 168 B5
Roquebillière F 37 C6
Roquebrun F 34 C5
Roquebrune-Cap-Martin F 37 D6
Roquebrune-sur-Argens F 36 E5
Roquecor F 33 B7
Roquecourbe F 33 C10
Roquefort F 32 B5
Roquemaure F 35 B8
Roquesteron F 36 D6
Roquetas E 42 F5
Roquetas de Mar E 55 F7
Roquevaire F 35 D10
Rørbakken N 111 C14
Rørberg S 103 E12
Rørby DK 87 D8
Rore BIH 157 D6
Røros N 101 A14
Rørvattnet S 105 D16
Rørvig DK 87 D9
Rørvik N 94 F5
Rørvik N 105 B10
Rørvik N 110 D7
Rörvik S 88 A7
Rosà I 72 E4
Rosala FIN 126 F7
Rosal de la Frontera E 51 D5
Rosans F 35 B9
Rosapenna IRL 7 B7
Rosário P 50 D3
Rosarno I 59 C8
Rosavci BIH 157 C6
Rosbach vor der Höhe D 21 D11
Roscanvel F 22 D2
Ros Cathail IRL 6 F4
Rosche D 83 E9
Roscigno I 60 C4
Rościszewo PL 139 E8
Roscoff F 22 C4
Ros Comáin IRL 6 E6
Roscommon IRL 6 E6
Ros Cré IRL 9 C7
Roscrea IRL 9 C7
Rosdorf D 78 D6
Rose I 60 E6
Rose MNE 162 E6
Rosée B 19 D10
Rosehearty GB 3 K12
Rosemarkie GB 3 K8
Rosen BG 167 E9
Rosenallis IRL 7 F8
Rosendal N 94 C4
Rosenfeld D 27 D10
Rosenfors S 92 E7
Rosengarten D 83 D7
Rosenheim D 72 A5
Rosenlund S 91 D13
Rosenow D 84 C4
Rosenthal D 21 C11
Roserberg S 99 C9
Roses E 43 C10
Roseţi RO 161 E10
Roseto Capo Spulico I 61 D7
Roseto degli Abruzzi I 62 B6
Roseto Valfortore I 60 A4
Roshchino RUS 129 E12
Rosheim F 27 C7
Roshven GB 4 B5
Roşia RO 151 D9
Roşia RO 152 F4
Roşia de Amaradia RO 160 C3
Roşia de Secaş RO 152 E3
Roşia Montană RO 151 E11
Rosica LV 133 D3
Rosice CZ 77 D9
Rosice CZ 77 D10
Rosières F 30 E4
Rosières-en-Santerre F 18 E6
Roşieşti RO 153 E11
Rosignano Marittimo I 66 F1
Roşile RO 160 D3
Roşiori RO 153 D10
Roşiori RO 161 D10
Roşiori de Vede RO 160 E6
Rositsa BG 155 F1
Rositsa BY 133 E3
Rositz D 79 D11
Rosiyanivka UA 154 C3
Roskhill GB 2 L3
Roskilde DK 87 D10
Rosko PL 85 E10
Roskovec AL 168 C2
Roskow D 79 B12
Röslau D 75 B10
Roslev DK 86 B3
Rosmalen NL 16 E4
Rosmaninhal P 45 E6
Ros Mhic Thriúin IRL 9 D9
Rosnowo PL 85 B9
Rosolina I 66 B5
Rosolina Mare I 66 B5
Rosolini I 59 F6
Rosoman MK 169 A6
Rosoy F 25 D9
Rösrath D 21 C8
Rossano I 61 D7
Rossano Veneto I 72 E4
Roßbach D 76 E3
Rossbol S 106 E7
Ross Carbery IRL 8 E4
Rosscahill IRL 6 F4
Rosscor GB 6 D6

Roßdorf D 21 E11
Rossell E 42 F4
Russelló E 42 D5
Rosses Point IRL 6 D5
Rossett GB 10 E6
Rossfjord N 111 B15
Roßhaupten D 71 B11
Rossiglione I 37 B9
Rossignol B 19 E11
Rössing (Nordstemmen) D 78 B6
Rossington GB 11 E9
Rossio ao Sul do Tejo P 44 F4
Roßla D 79 D9
Rosslare IRL 9 D10
Rosslare Harbour IRL 9 D10
Roßlau D 79 C11
Rosslea GB 7 D8
Roßleithen A 73 A9
Rossnowlagh IRL 6 C6
Rossön S 107 D10
Ross-on-Wye GB 13 B9
Rossosz PL 141 G6
Rossoszyca PL 142 C6
Rossow D 83 D13
Roßtal D 75 D8
Rossum NL 183 B6
Rössvassbukta N 108 E7
Rossvik N 105 A11
Rossvoll N 104 E4
Rossvoll N 108 B5
Roßwein D 80 D4
Røst N 108 A3
Røstbo S 103 D11
Röstånga S 87 C12
Rostarzewo PL 81 B10
Röste S 103 D11
Rostellan IRL 8 E6
Rostock D 83 B12
Rostrenen F 22 D5
Rostrevor GB 7 D10
Röström S 107 C10
Rostrup DK 86 B5
Rostundelva N 112 D6
Rosturk IRL 6 E3
Rostuša MK 168 A4
Røstvollen N 102 B3
Røsvik N 109 B9
Rosvik S 118 D7
Röszke H 150 E5
Rot S 102 D7
Rota E 52 C4
Rota N 111 E10
Rota Greca I 60 E6
Rot am See D 74 D7
Rot an der Rot D 71 A10
Rotava CZ 75 B12
Rotberget N 97 A8
Roteberg S 103 D10
Rotello I 63 D7
Rotenburg (Wümme) D 17 B12
Rotenburg an der Fulda D 78 D6
Rötgesbüttel D 79 B8
Rotgülden A 73 B7
Roth D 75 D9
Rothbury GB 5 E13
Röthenbach an der Pegnitz D 75 D9
Rothenberg D 21 E11
Rothenbuch D 74 C5
Rothenburg (Oberlausitz) D 81 D7
Rothenburg ob der Tauber D 75 D7
Rothéneuf F 23 C8
Rothenfels D 74 C6
Rothenschirmbach D 79 D10
Rothenstein D 79 E10
Rotherham GB 11 E9
Rothes GB 3 K10
Rothesay GB 4 D6
Rotheux-Rimière B 19 C11
Rothiesholm GB 3 G11
Rothley GB 11 F9
Kothrist CH 27 F8
Rothwell GB 11 D9
Rothwell GB 15 C7
Rothwesten (Fuldatal) D 78 D6
Rotimlja BIH 157 F8
Rotimjoki FIN 123 C17
Rotnäset S 106 C9
Rotonda I 60 C6
Rotondella I 61 C7
Rotselaar B 19 C10
Rotsjö S 103 A13
Rotsjön S 118 F4
Rotsund N 112 D4
Rott D 71 B11
Rottach-Egern D 72 A4
Rott am Inn D 75 G11
Røttangen N 111 C10
Rottenacker D 71 A9
Röttenbach D 75 D9
Rottenbach D 79 E9
Rottenbuch D 71 B11
Rottenburg am Neckar D 27 D10
Rottenburg an der Laaber D 75 E11
Rottendorf D 74 C7
Rottenmann A 73 A9
Rotterdam NL 16 E3
Rotthalmünster D 76 F4
Röttingham D 74 C6
Rottleberode D 79 D8
Rottne S 89 B8
Rottneros S 97 C9
Rottofreno I 69 C8
Rottweil D 27 D10
Rötviken S 105 D16
Rötz D 75 D12
Rouans F 23 F8
Roubaix F 19 C7
Rouchovany CZ 77 D10
Rõuge EST 131 F13
Rouen F 18 F3
Rouffach F 27 E7
Rouffignac F 29 E7
Rougé F 23 E9
Rougemont F 26 F5
Rougemont-le-Château F 27 E6
Roughton GB 15 B11
Rougnac F 29 E7
Rouillac F 29 D6
Rouillé F 28 C6
Roujan F 34 C5
Roukala FIN 119 F11
Roukalahti FIN 125 F13

Roulans F 26 F5
Roulers B 19 C7
Roulers B 182 D2
Roumazières-Loubert F 29 D7
Roumoules F 36 D4
Roundstone IRL 6 F3
Roundway GB 13 C11
Roundwood IRL 7 F10
Rouravaara FIN 117 C14
Roure I 31 E11
Rousínov CZ 77 D11
Rousky GB 4 F2
Rousset F 35 D10
Roussillon F 30 E6
Roussillon F 35 B7
Rousson F 35 B7
Routot F 18 F2
Rouvroy F 182 E1
Rouvroy-sur-Audry F 19 E10
Rouy F 30 A4
Rovala FIN 115 C8
Rovala FIN 115 E1
Rovaniemi FIN 117 F15
Rovanpää FIN 117 C15
Rovanpää FIN 115 D2
Rovapää FIN 115 D2
Rovato I 69 B9
Rovegno I 37 B10
Roverbella I 66 B2
Roveredo CH 69 A7
Rovereto I 69 B11
Rövershagen D 83 B12
Roverud N 96 B7
Roviano I 62 C3
Rovies GR 175 B7
Rovigo I 66 B4
Rovinari RO 159 D11
Rovine RO 157 B7
Rovinj HR 67 B8
Rovinka SK 146 E4
Rovišće HR 149 E7
Rovisuvanto FIN 113 E16
Rovsättra S 99 B10
Rów PL 85 E7
Rowde GB 13 C10
Równa PL 142 C6
Rownaye BY 133 F6
Roxmo S 93 A8
Roxton GB 15 C8
Royal Wootton Bassett GB 13 B11
Royan F 28 D3
Royat F 30 D3
Roybon F 31 E8
Roybridge GB 4 B7
Roydon GB 15 C11
Roye F 18 E6
Royère-de-Vassivière F 29 D9
Røykenes N 111 C10
Røykkä FIN 127 E11
Roylyanka UA 154 B3
Røyrvik N 105 B15
Røyse N 95 B12
Royston GB 15 C8
Royton GB 11 D7
Röyttä FIN 119 C12
Roytvollen N 105 A12
Royuela E 47 D10
Roza BG 166 E6
Rožaje MNE 163 D9
Rozalén del Monte E 47 E7
Rozalimas LT 134 E7
Rózan PL 139 E11
Rózanki PL 85 E8
Rozavlea RO 152 B4
Rozay-en-Brie F 25 C8
Roždalovice CZ 77 B8
Rozdil UA 145 E9
Rozdil'na UA 154 D6
Rozdražew PL 142 C4
Rozenburg NL 182 B4
Rozendaal NL 183 A7
Roženica HR 148 E5
Rozes IV 135 B11
Rozhniv UA 152 A6
Rozhnyativ UA 145 F9
Rozino BG 165 D10
Rožmitál pod Třemšínem CZ 76 C5
Rožňava SK 145 F2
Rožniatów PL 142 B6
Roznov RO 153 D9
Rožnov pod Radhoštěm CZ 146 C6
Roznowo PL 85 E11
Rozogi PL 139 C11
Rozovets BG 166 E4
Rozoy-sur-Serre F 19 E9
Rozprza PL 143 D8
Roztoka Wielka PL 145 E2
Roztoky CZ 76 B5
Roztoky UA 152 A6
Rozula LV 135 B9
Rožupe LV 135 D12
Rozvadov CZ 75 C12
Rozzano I 69 C7
Rrëshen AL 163 F8
Rrogozhinë AL 168 B2
Rromanat AL 168 B2
Rtkovo SRB 159 D10
Rtyně v Podkrkonoší CZ 77 B10
Ru E 38 B3
Rua P 44 C5
Ruabon GB 10 F5
Ruaudin F 23 E12
Ruba LV 134 D5
Rúbañ SK 146 F6
Rubano I 66 B4
Rubashki BY 133 F3
Rubayo E 40 B4
Rubbestadneset N 94 C2
Rubena E 40 D4
Rubene LV 135 B10
Rubeņi LV 135 D11
Rubí E 43 E8
Rubiá E 39 D6
Rubí de Bracamonte E 40 F2
Rubielos de la Cérida E 47 C10
Rubielos de Mora E 48 D3
Rubiera I 66 C2
Rubik AL 163 F8
Rublacedo de Abajo E 40 C5
Rucăr RO 160 C6
Rucava LV 134 D2
Ruciane-Nida PL 139 C12
Rückersdorf D 80 C5
Ruda PL 142 D6
Ruda S 89 A10
Rudabánya H 145 G2
Ruda Maleniecka PL 141 H2
Rudamina LT 137 D11

Rudamina LT 137 E7
Ruda Różaniecka PL 144 C7
Rudartsi BG 165 D7
Ruda Śląska PL 142 F6
Rudbārži LV 134 C3
Ruddervoorde B 182 C2
Rude LV 134 B5
Rude LV 134 D2
Rudelzhausen D 75 E10
Rudersberg D 74 E6
Rudersdorf A 148 B6
Rüdersdorf Berlin D 80 B5
Rüdesheim D 185 E8
Rudice BIH 156 C5
Rudina SK 147 C7
Rūdiškės LT 137 D10
Rudka BIH 157 B7
Rudky UA 145 D7
Rudná CZ 76 B6
Rudna PL 81 C10
Rudna Glava SRB 159 E9
Rudňany SK 145 F2
Rudna Wielka PL 81 C11
Rudne UA 144 D8
Rudnica PL 81 A8
Rudnica SRB 163 C10
Rudnik BG 167 D9
Rudnik PL 142 F5
Rudnik SRB 158 E5
Rudniki PL 142 D6
Rudnik nad Sadem PL 144 C5
Rüdnitz D 84 E5
Rudno PL 141 G6
Rudno SRB 163 C10
Rudnya UA 145 E8
Rudnytsya UA 154 A3
Rudo BIH 158 F3
Rudolfov CZ 77 E7
Rudolstadt D 79 E9
Rudozem BG 171 B7
Rudsgrendi N 95 C9
Rudsjön S 107 D12
Rudston GB 11 C11
Ruds Vedby DK 87 D8
Rudzāti LV 135 D12
Rudziczka PL 142 F4
Rudziniec PL 142 F5
Rue F 18 D4
Ruelle E 39 E10
Rugāji LV 133 B2
Rugby GB 13 A12
Rugeley GB 11 F8
Rugge N 110 C8
Rugince MK 164 E4
Ruginești RO 153 E10
Ruginoasa RO 153 C9
Rügland D 75 D8
Rugles F 24 C4
Rugvica HR 148 E6
Ruha FIN 123 E9
Ruhala FIN 124 C2
Ruhla D 79 E7
Ruhland D 80 D5
Ruhmannsfelden D 76 E3
Rühn D 83 C11
Ruhpolding D 73 A6
Ruhstorf an der Rott D 76 F4
Ruidera E 55 B7
Ruikka FIN 119 B14
Ruinas I 64 D2
Ruinen NL 16 C6
Ruinerwold NL 16 C6
Ruiselede B 19 B7
Ruismäki FIN 123 C10
Ruivães P 38 E3
Ruja PL 81 D10
Rüjiena LV 131 F10
Rujišta BIH 157 F8
Ruka FIN 121 B13
Rukajärvi FIN 121 B13
Rukkisperä FIN 119 E14
Ruma SRB 158 C4
Rumboci BIH 157 E7
Rumburk CZ 81 E7
Rumelange L 20 F6
Rumelifeneri TR 173 B11
Rumenka SRB 158 C4
Rumes B 19 C7
Rumia PL 138 A5
Rumigny F 19 E9
Rumilly F 31 D8
Rummu EST 131 C8
Rummukkala FIN 125 F12
Rumo FIN 125 C11
Rumont F 26 C3
Rumšiškės LT 137 D9
Rumskulla S 92 D7
Rumst B 19 B9
Rumyantsevo BG 165 C9
Runabergs S 102 B11
Runcorn GB 10 E6
Runcu RO 160 C3
Runcu RO 160 C4
Runcu RO 160 C6
Rundēni LV 133 D3
Rundfloen N 102 D4
Rundhaug N 111 B16
Rundmoen N 108 D8
Rundvik S 107 D16
Rungsted DK 87 D11
Runhällen S 98 B7
Runik KS 163 D10
Runkel D 185 D9
Runni FIN 124 C7
Runović HR 157 F7
Runsten S 89 B11
Runtuna S 93 B10
Ruohokangas FIN 115 A3
Ruohola FIN 119 C15
Ruokojärvi FIN 117 D12

Ruokojärvi FIN 129 R11
Ruokojärvi S 117 E10
Ruokolahti FIN 129 D7
Ruokoniemi FIN 129 B10
Ruokotaipale FIN 128 C8
Ruolahti FIN 127 B13
Ruoms F 35 B7
Ruona FIN 119 B17
Ruona FIN 123 E11
Ruonajärvi FIN 117 D13
Ruopsa FIN 115 E2
Ruorasmäki FIN 127 B15
Ruotaanmäki FIN 124 D7
Ruoti I 60 B5
Ruotsalo FIN 123 C10
Ruotsinkylä FIN 127 D15
Ruotsinpyhtää FIN 127 E15
Ruottisenharju FIN 120 D9
Ruovesi FIN 123 G12
Rupa HR 67 B9
Rupea RO 152 E6
Ruppovaara FIN 125 F14
Rupt-sur-Moselle F 26 E6
Rus E 55 C6
Rus RO 152 C3
Rusånes N 108 C9
Rusănesti RO 160 F5
Rusca Montană RO 159 B9
Ruscova RO 152 B4
Rusdal N 94 E4
Ruse BG 161 F7
Ruše SLO 148 C5
Rusele S 107 B14
Ruseni MD 153 A10
Ruşeţu RO 161 D10
Ruševo HR 149 F9
Rush IRL 7 E10
Rushden GB 15 C7
Rusiec PL 143 D6
Rusii-Munţi RO 152 D5
Rusinovo MK 165 F6
Rusinów PL 141 H3
Rusinowo PL 85 D10
Ruskeala RUS 129 B14
Ruskele S 107 B15
Ruski Krstur SRB 158 B3
Rusko FIN 126 D7
Rusko Selo SRB 150 F6
Ruskov SK 145 F3
Rusksträsk S 107 B15
Rusnė LT 134 F2
Rusokastro BG 167 E8
Rüsselsheim D 21 D10
Russelv N 112 D5
Russhaugen N 111 D11
Russi I 66 D5
Rust A 77 G11
Rustad N 95 B13
Rustad N 101 D14
Rustrel F 35 C9
Ruswil CH 27 F9
Ruszów PL 81 D8
Rutalahti FIN 123 G15
Rute E 53 B8
Rute S 93 D13
Rutesheim D 187 D6
Rüthen D 17 F10
Ruthin GB 10 E5
Rüti CH 27 F10
Rutigliano I 61 A8
Rutino I 60 C4
Rutka-Tartak PL 136 E6
Rutki-Kossaki PL 140 D6
Rutledal N 100 D2
Rutoš SRB 163 B8
Rutten NL 16 C5
Rütten-Scheid D 183 C9
Rutvik S 118 C8
Ruukki FIN 119 E14
Ruunaa FIN 125 D14
Ruurlo NL 17 D6
Ruusa EST 131 E14
Ruusmäe EST 131 F14
Ruutana FIN 123 C17
Ruutana FIN 127 B12
Ruuvaoja FIN 115 C5
Ruvanaho FIN 115 F6
Ruvaslahti FIN 125 E12
Ruvo del Monte I 60 B5
Ruvo di Puglia I 61 A6
Ruy F 31 D7
Ruynes-en-Margeride F 30 E3
Růzhovo Konare BG 165 E10
Ruzhintsi BG 159 F10
Ružina UA 133 D2
Ružindol SK 146 E5
Ružomberok SK 147 C8
Ruzsa H 150 E4
Ry DK 86 C5
Ryabovo RUS 129 E10
Ryakhovo BG 161 F8
Ryakhovtsite BG 165 C11
Ryabachiy RUS 134 F1
Rybany SK 146 D6
Rybczewice Drugie PL 144 A6
Rybitví CZ 77 B9
Rybnik PL 142 F6
Rybno PL 139 C8
Rybno PL 141 F2
Ryboły PL 140 E8
Rychliki PL 139 C8
Rychnov nad Kněžnou CZ 77 B10
Rychnowo PL 139 C9
Rychtal PL 142 D4
Rychvald CZ 146 B6
Rychwał PL 142 B6
Ryczów PL 141 G4
Ryczywół PL 85 E11
Ryd S 88 B6
Rydaholm S 88 B6
Rydal S 91 D12
Rydboholm S 91 D12
Ryde DK 86 C3
Ryde GB 13 D12
Rydet S 91 E11
Rydöbruk S 87 B12
Rydsgård S 87 E13
Rydsnäs S 92 D6
Rydułtowy PL 142 F5
Rydzyna PL 81 C11
Rye GB 15 F10
Ryen N 90 C3
Ryeng N 114 D9
Ryes F 23 B10
Rygge N 95 D13
Ryggesbro S 103 D10

Ryglice PL 144 D3
Rygnestad N 94 D6
Ryhälä FIN 129 B9
Ryhall GB 11 F11
Ryjewo PL 138 C6
Rykene N 90 C4
Ryki PL 141 G5
Rymań PL 85 C9
Rymanów PL 145 D4
Rýmařov CZ 81 G12
Rýmattylä FIN 126 E6
Rymnio GR 169 D6
Ryn PL 136 F4
Rynarzewo PL 138 D4
Rynkeby DK 86 C7
Ryńsk PL 138 D6
Ryomgård DK 86 C7
Rypefjord N 113 B12
Rypin PL 139 D7
Rysjedal N 100 D2
Ryslinge DK 86 E7
Ryssby S 88 B6
Rysum (Krummhörn) D 17 B8
Rytel PL 138 C4
Rytilahti FIN 115 E3
Rytinki FIN 120 C9
Rytky FIN 123 C17
Rytkynkylä FIN 119 F14
Ryttylä FIN 127 D12
Rytwiany PL 143 E11
Ržanovo MK 168 B4
Rząśnik PL 139 E11
Rzeczenica PL 85 C11
Rzeczyca PL 141 G2
Rzeczyca PL 142 C6
Rzigonowo PL 139 D10
Rzejowice PL 143 D8
Rzekuń PL 139 D12
Rzepiennik Strzyżewski PL 144 D3
Rzepin PL 81 B7
Rzerzyczyce PL 143 E7
Rzesznikowo PL 85 C8
Rzeszów PL 144 C5
Rzgów PL 143 C8
Rzgów Pierwszy PL 142 B5
Rzuców PL 141 H3

S

Sääksjärvi FIN 123 D11
Sääksjärvi FIN 127 C10
Sääksjärvi FIN 127 D13
Sääksmäki FIN 127 C11
Saal D 83 B12
Saal an der Donau D 75 E10
Saalbach-Hinterglemm A 73 B6
Saalburg D 75 B10
Saales F 27 D7
Saalfeld D 79 E9
Saalfelden am Steinernen Meer A 73 B6
Saanen CH 31 C11
Saarbrücken D 21 F7
Saarburg D 21 E7
Sääre EST 130 F4
Saarela FIN 125 C13
Saaren kk FIN 128 B9
Saarenkylä FIN 117 E15
Saaresmäki FIN 124 B7
Saari FIN 129 B12
Saariharju FIN 120 C9
Saarijärvi FIN 123 E14
Saari-Kämä FIN 119 B16
Saarikoski FIN 112 F7
Saarikoski FIN 119 C15
Saarikoski FIN 119 E14
Saarikylä FIN 121 D13
Saario FIN 125 F14
Saaripudas FIN 117 D11
Saariselkä FIN 115 B2
Saarivaara FIN 121 E14
Saarivaara FIN 125 F15
Saarlouis D 21 F7
Saarwellingen D 21 F7
Saas EST 131 C10
Sääse EST 131 C12
Saas Fee CH 68 A4
Saas Grund CH 68 A4
Sääksjärvi FIN 127 D15
Säävälä FIN 119 D16
Šabac SRB 158 D4
Sabadell E 43 D8
Sãbãoani RO 153 C9
Sabarat F 33 D8
Sabatynivka UA 154 A6
Sabaudia I 62 E4
Sabbioneta I 66 C1
Sabero E 39 C9
Sabile LV 134 B5
Sabiñánigo E 32 E5
Sabinov SK 145 E3
Sabiote E 55 C6
Sables-d'Or-les-Pins F 23 C7
Sablé-sur-Sarthe F 23 E11
Sablet F 35 B9
Sabnie PL 141 F6
Sabres F 32 B4
Sabro DK 86 C6
Sabrosa P 38 F4
Sabugal P 45 D6
Sabugueiro P 44 D5
Sabugueiro P 50 B3
Sãcãdat RO 151 C9
Săcãlãşeni RO 152 B3
Săcãlaz RO 151 F7
Sacañet E 48 E3
Săcãşeni RO 151 C10
Sacavém P 50 B1
Sacecorbo E 47 C8
Sacedón E 47 C7
Sãcel RO 152 B4
Sãcel RO 152 E5
Sãcele RO 155 E3
Sãcele RO 161 B7
Sãcelu RO 160 C3
Săceni RO 160 E6
Saceruela E 54 B3
Sachseln CH 70 D6
Sachsenberg (Lichtenfels) D 21 B11
Sachsenburg A 73 C7
Sachsenhagen D 17 D12
Sachsenhausen (Waldeck) D 17 F12
Sachsenheim D 27 C11
Sacile I 72 E5
Sacoşu Turcesc RO 159 B7
Sacović BIH 156 E6
Sacquenay F 26 E3
Sacramenia E 40 E4
Sacu RO 159 B9

Săcueni *RO* 151 C9
Săcuieu *RO* 151 D10
Sačurov *SK* 145 F4
Sada *E* 38 B3
Sádaba *E* 32 F3
Sadala *EST* 131 D13
Sadali *I* 64 D3
Sadina *BG* 166 C6
Sadki *PL* 85 D12
Sadkowice *PL* 141 G3
Sadkowo *PL* 85 C10
Sadlinki *PL* 138 C6
Sadova *MD* 154 C2
Sadova *RO* 152 B6
Sadova *RO* 160 F3
Sadove *UA* 154 F4
Sadovets *BG* 165 C9
Sadovo *BG* 165 E10
Sadowne *PL* 139 E12
Sadská *CZ* 77 B7
Sadu *RO* 160 B4
Sädvaluspen *S* 109 D12
Sæbo *N* 94 B6
Sæbo *N* 100 B4
Sæbøvik *N* 94 C3
Sæby *DK* 87 D8
Sæby *DK* 90 E8
Sæd *DK* 86 F3
Saelices *E* 47 E7
Saelices de la Sal *E* 47 C8
Saelices del Rio *E* 39 D9
Saelices de Mayorga *E* 39 D9
Saerbeck *D* 17 D9
Særslev *DK* 86 D6
Sæter *N* 104 E6
Sætra *N* 104 E6
Sætre *N* 95 C13
Saeul *L* 20 E5
Savareid *N* 94 B3
Safaalan *TR* 173 B9
Safara *P* 51 C5
Säffle *S* 91 A12
Saffré *F* 23 E8
Saffron Walden *GB* 15 C9
Sâg *RO* 151 C10
Sâg *RO* 159 B7
Sagama *I* 64 C2
Sagard *D* 84 A5
Sage *D* 17 C10
Săgeata *RO* 161 C9
Sågen *S* 97 B11
Sagiada *GR* 168 E3
Sağirlar *TR* 173 F9
Sağlamtaş *TR* 173 C7
Sâgmyra *S* 103 E9
Sagna *RO* 153 D10
Sagone *F* 37 G9
Sagres *P* 50 E2
Sagstua *N* 95 B15
Sâgu *RO* 151 E7
Sagunto *E* 48 E4
Sagvåg *N* 94 C2
Ságvár *H* 149 C10
Sagy *F* 31 B7
Sahagún *E* 39 D9
Sahaidac *MD* 154 D3
Sahalahti *FIN* 127 C11
Sahankylä *FIN* 122 F8
Saharna Nouă *MD* 154 B3
Săhăteni *RO* 161 C8
Şahin *TR* 173 B6
Şahinli *TR* 173 D6
Sahl *DK* 86 C5
Sahrajärvi *FIN* 123 F14
Sahun *E* 33 E6
Sahune *F* 35 B9
Šahy *SK* 147 E7
Saiakopli *EST* 131 C12
Saighdinis *GB* 2 K2
Saija *FIN* 115 D5
Säijä *FIN* 127 C10
Saikari *FIN* 124 E7
Saillagouse-Llo *F* 33 F10
Saillans *F* 35 A9
Sail-sous-Couzan *F* 30 D4
Saimaanharju *FIN* 129 C9
Säimen *FIN* 125 F12
Sains-Richaumont *F* 19 E8
St Abbs *GB* 5 D12
St-Affrique *F* 34 C4
St-Agnan *F* 30 B4
St-Agnan-en-Vercors *F* 31 F7
St-Agnant *F* 28 D4
St-Agnant-de-Versillat *F* 29 C9
St Agnes *GB* 12 E4
St-Agrève *F* 30 E5
St-Aignan *F* 24 F5
St-Aignan-sur-Roë *F* 23 E9
St-Aigulin *F* 28 E5
St-Albain *F* 30 C6
St-Alban *F* 22 C6
St-Alban-Leysse *F* 31 D8
St Albans *GB* 15 D8
St-Alban-sur-Limagnole *F* 30 F3
St-Amand-en-Puisaye *F* 25 E9
St-Amand-les-Eaux *F* 19 D7
St-Amand-Longpré *F* 24 E5
St-Amand-Montrond *F* 29 B11
St-Amand-sur-Fion *F* 25 C12
St-Amans *F* 34 A5
St-Amans-des-Cots *F* 30 F2
St-Amans-Soult *F* 33 D10
St-Amant-de-Boixe *F* 29 D6
St-Amant-Roche-Savine *F* 30 D4
St-Amant-Tallende *F* 30 D3
St-Amarin *F* 27 E7
St-Ambroix *F* 35 B7
St-Amour *F* 31 C7
St-Andiol *F* 35 C8
St-André *F* 34 E4
St-André-de-Corcy *F* 31 D6
St-André-de-Cruzières *F* 35 B7
St-André-de-Cubzac *F* 28 F5
St-André-de-l'Eure *F* 24 C5
St-André-de-Sangonis *F* 34 C5
St-André-de-Valborgne *F* 35 B6
St-André-le-Gaz *F* 31 D8
St-André-les-Vergers *F* 25 D11
St Andrews *GB* 5 C11
St-Angel *F* 29 D10
St Anne *GBG* 23 A7
St-Anthème *F* 30 D4
St-Antonin-Noble-Val *F* 33 B9
St-Août *F* 29 B9
St-Apollinaire *F* 26 F3
St-Arcons-d'Allier *F* 30 E4
St-Arnoult-en-Yvelines *F* 24 C6
St Asaph *GB* 10 E5
St-Astier *F* 29 E7
St-Astier *F* 29 F6

St Athan *GB* 13 C8
St-Auban *F* 36 D5
St-Auban-sur-l'Ouvèze *F* 35 B9
St-Aubin *F* 31 A7
St-Aubin-Château-Neuf *F* 25 E9
St-Aubin-d'Aubigné *F* 23 D8
St-Aubin-de-Blaye *F* 28 E4
St-Aubin-du-Cormier *F* 23 D9
St-Aubin-lès-Elbeuf *F* 18 F3
St-Aubin-sur-Mer *F* 23 B11
St-Aulaye *F* 29 E6
St Austell *GB* 12 E5
St-Avé *F* 22 E6
St-Avertin *F* 24 F4
St-Avold *F* 26 B6
St-Ay *F* 24 E6
St-Ayguilf *F* 36 E5
St-Barthélemy-d'Agenais *F* 33 A6
St-Barthélemy-de-Vals *F* 30 E6
St-Bauzille-de-Putois *F* 35 C6
St-Béat *F* 33 E7
St-Beauzély *F* 34 B4
St Bees *GB* 10 C4
St-Benin-d'Azy *F* 30 A3
St-Benoît *F* 29 B6
St-Benoît *F* 33 D10
St-Benoît-du-Sault *F* 29 C8
St-Benoît-sur-Loire *F* 25 E7
St-Béron *F* 31 D8
St-Berthevin *F* 23 D10
St-Bertrand-de-Comminges *F* 33 D7
St-Blaise *CH* 31 A10
St-Blaise-la-Roche *F* 27 D7
St-Blin-Semilly *F* 26 D3
St-Boil *F* 30 B6
St-Bonnet-de-Bellac *F* 29 C7
St-Bonnet-de-Joux *F* 30 B5
St-Bonnet-en-Bresse *F* 31 B7
St-Bonnet-en-Champsaur *F* 36 B4
St-Bonnet-le-Château *F* 30 E5
St-Bonnet-le-Froid *F* 30 E5
St-Bonnet-sur-Gironde *F* 28 E4
St-Branchs *F* 24 F4
St Brelade *GBJ* 23 B7
St-Brevin-les-Pins *F* 23 F7
St-Briac-sur-Mer *F* 23 C7
St-Brice-en-Coglès *F* 23 D9
St-Brieuc *F* 22 D6
St-Bris-le-Vineux *F* 25 E10
St-Brisson *F* 25 F11
St-Broing-les-Moines *F* 25 E12
St Buryan *GB* 12 E3
St-Calais *F* 24 E4
St-Cannat *F* 35 C9
St-Céré *F* 29 F9
St-Cergue *CH* 31 C9
St-Cergues *F* 31 C9
St-Cernin *F* 29 E10
St-Chaffrey *F* 31 F10
St-Chamand *F* 33 A8
St-Chamas *F* 35 C9
St-Chamond *F* 30 E6
St-Chaptes *F* 35 C7
St-Chef *F* 31 D7
St-Chély-d'Apcher *F* 30 F3
St-Chély-d'Aubrac *F* 34 A4
St-Chinian *F* 34 C4
St-Christol *F* 35 B9
St-Christol-lès-Alès *F* 35 B7
St-Christoly-Médoc *F* 28 E4
St-Christophe *I* 31 D11
St-Christophe-en-Bazelle *F* 24 F6
St-Christophe-en-Brionnais *F* 30 C5
St-Ciers-sur-Gironde *F* 28 E4
St-Cirq-Lapopie *F* 33 B9
St-Clair-du-Rhône *F* 30 E6
St-Clar *F* 33 C7
St-Claud *F* 29 D6
St-Claude *F* 31 C8
St Clears *GB* 12 B5
St-Clément *F* 25 D9
St-Clément *F* 26 C6
St-Clément *F* 29 E9
St-Clément *GBJ* 23 B7
St-Clément-de-Rivière *F* 35 C6
St Columb Major *GB* 12 E5
St Combs *GB* 3 K13
St-Constant *F* 29 F10
St-Cosme-en-Vairais *F* 24 D3
St-Cricq-Chalosse *F* 32 C4
St-Cyprien *F* 29 F8
St-Cyprien *F* 33 E10
St-Cyprien *F* 34 E5
St-Cyr-sur-Loire *F* 24 F4
St-Cyr-sur-Mer *F* 35 D10
St Cyrus *GB* 5 B12
St David's *GB* 9 E12
St Day *GB* 12 E4
St-Denis *F* 25 C7
St-Denis-d'Anjou *F* 23 E11
St-Denis-de-Gastines *F* 23 D10
St-Denis-de-Jouhet *F* 29 B9
St-Denis-de-Pile *F* 28 F5
St-Denis-d'Oléron *F* 28 C3
St-Denis-en-Bugey *F* 31 D7
St-Denis-lès-Bourg *F* 31 C7
St Denis *GB* 12 E5
St-Désert *F* 30 B6
St-Didier-en-Velay *F* 30 E5
St-Didier-sur-Chalaronne *F* 30 C6
St-Dié *F* 27 D6
St-Dier-d'Auvergne *F* 30 D3
St-Dizier *F* 25 C12
St-Dizier-Leyrenne *F* 29 C9
St-Dolay *F* 23 F8
St-Donat-sur-l'Herbasse *F* 31 E7
St-Doulchard *F* 25 F7
Ste-Adresse *F* 23 A12
Ste-Bazeille *F* 33 A6
Ste-Cécile-les-Vignes *F* 35 B8
Ste-Croix *CH* 31 B10
Ste-Croix *F* 31 F7
Ste-Croix-Volvestre *F* 33 D8
Ste-Engrâce *F* 32 D4
Ste-Enimie *F* 34 B5
Ste-Eulalie d'Olt *F* 34 B4
Ste-Eulalie-en-Born *F* 32 B3
Ste-Feyre *F* 29 C9
Ste-Foy-de-Peyrolières *F* 33 D8
Ste-Foy-la-Grande *F* 29 F6
Ste-Foy-l'Argentière *F* 30 D5
Ste-Foy-lès-Lyon *F* 30 D6
Ste-Foy-Tarentaise *F* 31 D10

Ste-Geneviève *F* 18 F5
Ste-Geneviève-sur-Argence *F* 30 F2
St-Égrève *F* 31 E8
Ste-Hélène *F* 28 F4
Ste-Hermine *F* 28 B3
St-Élix-le-Château *F* 33 D8
St-Élix-Theux *F* 33 D6
Ste-Lizaigne *F* 29 A10
St-Éloy-les-Mines *F* 30 C2
Ste-Lucie-de-Tallano *F* 37 H10
Ste-Marguerite *F* 186 E2
Ste-Marie *F* 34 E5
Ste-Marie-aux-Mines *F* 27 D7
Ste-Maure-de-Peyriac *F* 33 B6
Ste-Maure-de-Touraine *F* 24 F4
Ste-Maxime *F* 36 E5
Ste-Menehould *F* 25 B12
Ste-Mère-Église *F* 23 B9
St-Émiland *F* 30 B5
St Endellion *GB* 12 D5
St Enoder *GB* 12 E5
Ste-Orse *F* 29 E8
Ste-Pazanne *F* 23 F8
Ste-Radegonde *F* 28 B5
St-Erme-Outre-et-Ramecourt *F* 19 E8
St Erth *GB* 12 E4
Saintes *F* 28 D4
Ste-Sabine *F* 25 F12
Ste-Savine *F* 25 D11
Ste-Sévère-sur-Indre *F* 29 C10
St-Esteben *F* 32 D3
St-Estèphe *F* 28 E4
St-Estève *F* 34 E4
Ste-Suzanne *F* 23 D11
St-Étienne *F* 30 E5
St-Étienne-de-Baïgorry *F* 32 D3
St-Étienne-de-Fontbellon *F* 35 A7
St-Étienne-de-Fursac *F* 29 C9
St-Étienne-de-Montluc *F* 23 F8
St-Étienne-de-St-Geoirs *F* 31 E7
St-Étienne-de-Tinée *F* 36 C5
St-Étienne-du-Bois *F* 31 C7
St-Étienne-du-Rouvray *F* 18 F3
St-Étienne-les-Orgues *F* 35 B10
St-Étienne-lès-Remiremont *F* 26 D6
St-Étienne-Vallée-Française *F* 35 B6
Ste-Tulle *F* 35 C10
Ste-Vertu *F* 25 E10
St-Fargeau *F* 25 E9
St-Félicien *F* 30 E6
St-Félix-Lauragais *F* 33 D9
St Fergus *GB* 3 K13
St Fillans *GB* 5 B8
St-Firmin *F* 26 D5
St-Firmin *F* 31 F9
St-Flavy *F* 25 D10
St-Florent *F* 37 F9
St-Florent-des-Bois *F* 28 B3
St-Florentin *F* 25 D10
St-Florent-le-Vieil *F* 23 F9
St-Florent-sur-Cher *F* 29 B10
St-Flour *F* 30 E3
St-Flovier *F* 29 B8
St-Fons *F* 30 D6
St-Fort-sur-Gironde *F* 28 E4
St-Frajou *F* 33 D7
St-François-Longchamp *F* 31 E9
St-Front-de-Pradoux *F* 29 E6
St-Fulgent *F* 28 B3
St-Galmier *F* 30 D5
St-Gaudens *F* 33 D7
St-Gaultier *F* 29 B8
St-Gein *F* 32 C5
St-Gély-du-Fesc *F* 35 C6
St-Genest-Malifaux *F* 30 E5
St-Geniez *F* 35 B10
St-Geniez-d'Olt *F* 34 B4
St-Genis-de-Saintonge *F* 28 E4
St-Genis-Laval *F* 30 D6
St-Genis-Pouilly *F* 31 C9
St-Genix-sur-Guiers *F* 31 D8
St-Genou *F* 29 B8
St-Geoire-en-Valdaine *F* 31 E8
St-Georges-Buttavent *F* 23 D10
St-Georges-d'Aurac *F* 30 E4
St-Georges-de-Commiers *F* 31 E8
St-Georges-de-Didonne *F* 28 D4
St-Georges-de-Luzençon *F* 34 B4
St-Georges-de-Mons *F* 30 D2
St-Georges-de-Reneins *F* 30 C6
St-Georges-des-Groseillers *F* 23 C10
St-Georges-d'Oléron *F* 28 D3
St-Georges-du-Vièvre *F* 18 F2
St-Georges-en-Couzan *F* 30 D4
St-Georges-les-Baillargeaux *F* 29 B6
St-Georges-sur-Baulche *F* 25 E10
St-Georges-sur-Cher *F* 24 F5
St-Georges-sur-Loire *F* 23 F10
St-Geours-de-Maremne *F* 32 C3
St-Gérand-le-Puy *F* 30 C4
St-Germain-Chassenay *F* 30 B3
St-Germain-de-Calberte *F* 35 B6
St-Germain-de-la-Coudre *F* 24 D4
St-Germain-des-Fossés *F* 30 C3
St-Germain-d'Esteuil *F* 28 E4
St-Germain-du-Bel-Air *F* 33 A8
St-Germain-du-Bois *F* 31 B7
St-Germain-du-Corbéis *F* 23 D12
St-Germain-du-Plain *F* 31 B6
St-Germain-du-Puy *F* 25 F7
St-Germain-du-Teil *F* 34 B5
St-Germain-en-Laye *F* 24 C7
St-Germain-Laval *F* 30 D5
St-Germain-les-Belles *F* 29 D8
St-Germain-les-Vergnes *F* 29 E9
St-Germain-l'Herm *F* 30 E4
St Germans *GB* 12 E6
St-Germé *F* 32 C5
St-Gervais *F* 28 B1
St-Gervais-d'Auvergne *F* 30 C2
St-Gervais-la-Forêt *F* 24 E5
St-Gervais-les-Bains *F* 31 D10
St-Gervais-les-Trois-Clochers *F* 29 B6
St-Gervais-sur-Mare *F* 34 C5

St-Géry *F* 33 B9
St-Ghislain *B* 19 D8
St-Gildas-de-Rhuys *F* 22 E6
St-Gildas-des-Bois *F* 23 E7
St-Gilles *F* 35 C7
St-Gilles-Croix-de-Vie *F* 28 B2
St-Gingolph *F* 31 C10
St-Girons *F* 33 E8
St-Girons-Plage *F* 32 C3
St-Gobain *F* 19 E7
St-Guénolé *F* 22 E3
St-Guilhem-le-Désert *F* 35 C6
St-Haon-le-Châtel *F* 30 C4
St-Héand *F* 30 D5
St Helens *GB* 10 E6
St Helier *GBJ* 23 B7
St-Herblain *F* 23 F8
St-Hilaire *F* 33 D10
St-Hilaire-de-Brethmas *F* 35 B7
St-Hilaire-de-Riez *F* 28 B2
St-Hilaire-des-Loges *F* 28 C4
St-Hilaire-de-Villefranche *F* 28 D4
St-Hilaire-du-Harcouët *F* 23 C9
St-Hilaire-du-Rosier *F* 31 E7
St-Hilaire-Fontaine *F* 30 B4
St-Hilaire-St-Florent *F* 23 F11
St-Hippolyte *F* 27 F6
St-Hippolyte *F* 27 F6
St-Hippolyte-du-Fort *F* 35 C6
St-Honoré-les-Bains *F* 30 B4
St-Hostien *F* 30 E5
St-Hubert *B* 19 D11
St-Imier *CH* 31 A9
St-Ismier *F* 31 E8
St Ive *GB* 12 E6
St Ives *GB* 12 E4
St-Izaire *F* 34 C4
St-Jacques-de-la-Lande *F* 23 D8
St-James *F* 23 C9
St-Jean *F* 33 C8
St-Jean-Bonnefonds *F* 30 E5
St-Jean-Brévelay *F* 22 E6
St-Jean-d'Angély *F* 28 D4
St-Jean-de-Bournay *F* 31 D7
St-Jean-de-Daye *F* 23 B9
St-Jean-de-la-Ruelle *F* 24 E6
St-Jean-de-Losne *F* 26 F3
St-Jean-de-Luz *F* 32 D2
St-Jean-de-Maurienne *F* 31 E9
St-Jean-de-Mauréjols-et-Avéjan *F* 35 B7
St-Jean-de-Monts *F* 28 B1
St-Jean-de-Sixt *F* 31 D9
St-Jean-de-Védas *F* 35 C6
St-Jean-d'Illac *F* 28 F4
St-Jean-du-Bruel *F* 34 B5
St-Jean-du-Falga *F* 33 D9
St-Jean-du-Gard *F* 35 B6
St-Jean-le-Centenier *F* 35 A8
St-Jean-le-Pied-de-Port *F* 32 D3
St-Jean-Poutge *F* 33 C6
St-Jean-sur-Erve *F* 23 D11
St-Joachim *F* 23 F7
St John *GBJ* 23 B7
St John's Chapel *GB* 5 F12
St John's Town of Dalry *GB* 5 E10
St-Jores *F* 23 B9
St-Jorioz *F* 31 D9
St-Jory *F* 33 C8
St-Jouan-des-Guérets *F* 23 C8
St-Jouin-Bruneval *F* 23 A12
St-Jouin-de-Marnes *F* 28 B5
St-Julien *F* 31 C7
St-Julien *F* 31 C9
St-Julien-Beychevelle *F* 28 E4
St-Julien-Boutières *F* 30 F5
St-Julien-Chapteuil *F* 30 E5
St-Julien-de-Concelles *F* 23 F9
St-Julien-de-Vouvantes *F* 23 E9
St-Julien-du-Sault *F* 25 D9
St-Julien-du-Verdon *F* 36 D5
St-Julien-en-Beauchêne *F* 35 A10
St-Julien-en-Born *F* 32 B3
St-Julien-en-Genevois *F* 31 C9
St-Julien-l'Ars *F* 29 B7
St-Julien *F* 29 D7
St-Just *F* 35 B8
St Just *GB* 12 E3
St-Just-en-Chaussée *F* 18 E5
St-Just-en-Chevalet *F* 30 D4
St-Just-Ibarre *F* 32 D3
St-Justin *F* 32 C5
St Just in Roseland *GB* 12 E4
St-Just-la-Pendue *F* 30 D5
St-Just-Luzac *F* 28 D3
St-Just-Sauvage *F* 25 C10
St-Just-St-Rambert *F* 30 E5
St Keverne *GB* 12 E4
St-Lambert-des-Levées *F* 23 F11
St-Lary-Soulan *F* 33 E6
St-Laurent *F* 34 C5
St-Laurent-Bretagne *F* 32 D5
St-Laurent-d'Aigouze *F* 35 C7
St-Laurent-de-Carnols *F* 35 B8
St-Laurent-de-Cerdans *F* 34 F4
St-Laurent-de-Chamousset *F* 30 D5
St-Laurent-de-la-Cabrerisse *F* 34 D4
St-Laurent-de-la-Salanque *F* 34 E4
St-Laurent-de-Neste *F* 33 D6
St-Laurent-des-Autels *F* 23 F9
St-Laurent-du-Pont *F* 31 E8
St-Laurent-du-Var *F* 37 D6
St-Laurent-en-Caux *F* 18 E2
St-Laurent-en-Grandvaux *F* 31 B8
St-Laurent-les-Bains *F* 35 A7
St-Laurent-Médoc *F* 28 E4
St-Laurent-Nouan *F* 24 E6
St-Laurent-sur-Gorre *F* 29 D7
St-Laurent-sur-Sèvre *F* 28 B4
St-Léger *B* 19 E12
St-Léger-des-Vignes *F* 30 B4
St-Léger-en-Yvelines *F* 24 C5
St-Léger-sous-Beuvray *F* 30 B5
St-Léonard *F* 27 D6
St-Léonard-de-Noblat *F* 29 D8
St Leonards *GB* 13 D11
St-Lizier *F* 33 D8
St-Lô *F* 23 B9
St-Lon-les-Mines *F* 32 C3

St-Loubès *F* 28 F5
St-Louis-lès-Bitche *F* 186 D3
St-Loup-de-la-Salle *F* 30 B6
St-Loup-Lamairé *F* 28 B5
St-Loup-sur-Semouse *F* 26 E5
St-Lubin-des-Joncherets *F* 24 C5
St-Lunaire *F* 23 C7
St-Lupicin *F* 31 C8
St-Lyé *F* 25 D10
St-Lys *F* 33 D8
St-Macaire *F* 32 A5
St-Macaire-en-Mauges *F* 23 F10
St-Magne *F* 32 A4
St-Magne-de-Castillon *F* 28 F5
St-Maime *F* 35 C10
St-Maixent-l'École *F* 28 C5
St-Malo *F* 23 C7
St-Malo-de-la-Lande *F* 23 B8
St-Mamert-du-Gard *F* 35 C7
St-Marcel *F* 24 B5
St-Marcel *F* 29 B9
St-Marcel *F* 30 B6
St-Marcel-d'Ardèche *F* 35 B8
St-Marcel-lès-Annonay *F* 30 E6
St-Marcel-lès-Sauzet *F* 35 A8
St-Marcel-lès-Valence *F* 31 F6
St-Marcellin *F* 31 E7
St-Marc-sur-Seine *F* 25 E12
St-Mards-en-Othe *F* 25 D10
St Margaret's Hope *GB* 3 H11
St-Marsal *F* 34 F4
St-Mars-d'Outillé *F* 24 E3
St-Mars-du-Désert *F* 23 F9
St-Mars-la-Brière *F* 24 D3
St-Mars-la-Jaille *F* 23 E9
St-Martial *F* 35 B6
St-Martial-de-Nabirat *F* 29 F8
St-Martial-de-Valette *F* 29 D7
St-Martin *F* 35 D10
St Martin *GBG* 22 B6
St Martin *GBJ* 23 B7
St-Martin-Boulogne *F* 15 F12
St-Martin-d'Ablois *F* 25 B10
St-Martin-d'Arrossa *F* 32 D3
St-Martin-d'Auxigny *F* 25 F7
St-Martin-de-Belleville *F* 31 E10
St-Martin-de-Castillon *F* 35 C10
St-Martin-de-Crau *F* 35 C8
St-Martin-de-Landelles *F* 23 D9
St-Martin-de-Londres *F* 35 C6
St-Martin-d'Entraunes *F* 36 C5
St-Martin-de-Ré *F* 28 C3
St-Martin-des-Besaces *F* 23 B10
St-Martin-des-Champs *F* 32 C4
St-Martin-de-Seignanx *F* 32 C3
St-Martin-de-Valamas *F* 30 F5
St-Martin-de-Valgalgues *F* 35 B7
St-Martin-d'Hères *F* 31 E8
St-Martin-d'Oney *F* 32 C4
St-Martin-du-Mont *F* 31 C7
St-Martin-du-Var *F* 37 D6
St-Martin-le-Beau *F* 24 F4
St-Martin-l'Ouanne *F* 25 E9
St-Martin-Valmeroux *F* 29 E10
St-Martin-Vésubie *F* 37 C6
St-Martory *F* 33 D7
St Mary's *GB* 3 H11
St-Mathieu *F* 29 D7
St-Mathurin *F* 28 B2
St-Maur *F* 29 B9
St-Maurice *CH* 31 C10
St-Maurice-de-Lignon *F* 30 E5
St-Maurice-des-Lions *F* 29 D7
St-Maurice-la-Souterraine *F* 29 C8
St-Maurice-l'Exil *F* 30 E6
St-Maurice-Navacelles *F* 35 C6
St-Maurin *F* 33 B7
St-Max *F* 26 C5
St-Maximin-la-Ste-Baume *F* 35 D10
St-Médard-en-Jalles *F* 28 F4
St-Méen-le-Grand *F* 23 D7
St-Méloir-des-Ondes *F* 23 C8
St-Memmie *F* 25 C11
St-Menoux *F* 30 B3
St Merryn *GB* 12 D5
St-Mesmin *F* 25 D10
St-Mesmin *F* 29 E8
St-Michel *F* 19 E7
St-Michel *F* 28 D6
St-Michel *F* 33 D6
St-Michel-Chef-Chef *F* 23 F7
St-Michel-de-Castelnau *F* 32 B5
St-Michel-de-Maurienne *F* 31 E9
St-Michel-en-l'Herm *F* 28 C3
St-Michel-Mont-Mercure *F* 28 B4
St-Michel-sur-Meurthe *F* 27 D6
St-Mihiel *F* 26 C4
St Monans *GB* 5 C11
St-Montant *F* 35 B8
St-Nabord *F* 26 D6
St-Nauphary *F* 33 C8
St-Nazaire *B* 37 F9
St-Nazaire-le-Désert *F* 35 A9
St-Nectaire *F* 30 D2
St Neots *GB* 15 C9
St-Nicolas *B* 183 D7
St-Nicolas *F* 18 D6
St-Nicolas-d'Aliermont *F* 18 E3
St-Nicolas-de-la-Grave *F* 33 B8
St-Nicolas-de-Port *F* 26 C5
St-Nicolas-de-Redon *F* 23 E7
St-Nicolas-du-Pélem *F* 22 D5
St-Oedenrode *NL* 16 E4
St-Omer *F* 15 D10
St-Orens-de-Gameville *F* 33 C9
St Osyth *GB* 15 D11
St-Ost *F* 33 D6
St-Ouen *F* 18 D5
St-Ouen *F* 24 B5
St-Ouen *GBJ* 23 B7
St-Ouen-des-Toits *F* 23 D10
St-Pair-sur-Mer *F* 23 C8
St-Palais *F* 32 D3
St-Palais-sur-Mer *F* 28 D3
St-Pal-de-Chalancon *F* 30 E5
St-Pal-de-Mons *F* 30 E5
St-Pantaléon *F* 33 B8
St-Pantaléon *F* 33 B8
St-Papoul *F* 33 D10
St-Pardoux-Isaac *F* 33 A6
St-Pardoux-la-Rivière *F* 29 D7
St-Parize-le-Châtel *F* 30 B3
St-Parres-lès-Vaudes *F* 25 D11
St-Paterne *F* 23 D12
St-Paterne-Racan *F* 24 E4
St-Paul *F* 36 B5
St-Paul-Cap-de-Joux *F* 33 D9
St-Paul-de-Fenouillet *F* 33 E11
St-Paul-de-Jarrat *F* 33 E9

St-Paul-en-Born *F* 32 B3
St-Paul-en-Forêt *F* 36 D5
St-Paul-et-Valmalle *F* 35 C6
St-Paulien *F* 30 E4
St-Paul-le-Jeune *F* 35 B7
St-Paul-lès-Dax *F* 32 C3
St-Paul-lès-Durance *F* 35 C10
St-Paul-Trois-Châteaux *F* 35 B8
St-Pé-de-Bigorre *F* 32 D5
St-Pée-sur-Nivelle *F* 32 D2
St-Péray *F* 30 F6
St-Père *F* 25 F10
St-Père-en-Retz *F* 23 F7
St Peter in the Wood *GBG* 22 B6
St Peter Port *GBG* 22 B6
St-Phal *F* 25 D10
St-Philbert-de-Bouaine *F* 28 B2
St-Philbert-de-Grand-Lieu *F* 28 A2
St-Pierre *I* 31 D11
St-Pierre-d'Albigny *F* 31 D9
St-Pierre-de-Chignac *F* 29 E7
St-Pierre-de-Côle *F* 29 E7
St-Pierre-de-la-Fage *F* 34 C5
St-Pierre-de-Maillé *F* 29 B7
St-Pierre-de-Plesguen *F* 23 D8
St-Pierre-des-Champs *F* 34 D4
St-Pierre-des-Corps *F* 24 F4
St-Pierre-des-Échaubrognes *F* 28 A4
St-Pierre-des-Landes *F* 23 D9
St-Pierre-des-Nids *F* 23 D11
St-Pierre-de-Trivisy *F* 33 C10
St-Pierre-d'Irube *F* 32 D3
St-Pierre-d'Oléron *F* 28 D3
St-Pierre-du-Chemin *F* 28 B4
St-Pierre-du-Mont *F* 32 C4
St-Pierre-Église *F* 23 A9
St-Pierre-en-Faucigny *F* 31 C9
St-Pierre-en-Port *F* 18 E1
St-Pierre-le-Moûtier *F* 30 B3
St-Pierre-lès-Elbeuf *F* 18 F3
St-Pierre-lès-Nemours *F* 25 D8
St-Pierre-Montlimart *F* 23 F9
St-Pierre-Quiberon *F* 22 E5
St-Pierre-sur-Dives *F* 23 B11
St-Plancard *F* 33 D7
St-Pois *F* 23 C9
St-Poix *F* 23 E9
St-Pol-de-Léon *F* 22 C4
St-Pol-sur-Mer *F* 18 B5
St-Pol-sur-Ternoise *F* 18 D5
St-Pompont *F* 29 F8
St-Pons *F* 36 C5
St-Pons-de-Thomières *F* 34 D4
St-Porchaire *F* 28 D4
St-Pourçain-sur-Sioule *F* 30 C3
St-Prex *CH* 31 C9
St-Priest *F* 30 D6
St-Priest-de-Champs *F* 30 D2
St-Priest-Laprugne *F* 30 D4
St-Priest-Taurion *F* 29 D8
St-Privat *F* 29 E10
St-Privat-d'Allier *F* 30 F4
St-Prix *F* 30 C4
St-Projet *F* 33 B9
St-Puy *F* 33 C6
St-Quentin *F* 19 E7
St-Quentin-la-Poterie *F* 35 B7
St-Quirin *F* 27 C7
St-Rambert-d'Albon *F* 30 E6
St-Rambert-en-Bugey *F* 31 D7
St-Raphaël *F* 36 E5
St-Remèze *F* 35 B7
St-Rémy *F* 31 B6
St-Rémy-de-Provence *F* 35 C8
St-Remy-en-Bouzemont-St-Genest-et-Isson *F* 25 C12
St-Rémy-sur-Avre *F* 24 C5
St-Rémy-sur-Durolle *F* 30 D4
St-Renan *F* 22 D2
St-Révérien *F* 25 F10
St-Rhemy *I* 31 D11
St-Riquier *F* 18 D4
St-Romain-en-Gal *F* 30 D6
St-Romain-sur-Cher *F* 24 F5
St-Romans *F* 31 E7
St-Rome-de-Cernon *F* 34 B4
St-Rome-de-Tarn *F* 34 B4
St-Saëns *F* 18 E3
St Sampson *GBG* 22 B6
St-Saturnin-lès-Apt *F* 35 C9
St-Saud-Lacoussière *F* 29 D7
St-Saulge *F* 25 F9
St-Sauves-d'Auvergne *F* 29 D11
St-Sauveur *F* 22 D5
St-Sauveur-Gouvernet *F* 35 B9
St-Sauveur-Lendelin *F* 23 B9
St-Sauveur-le-Vicomte *F* 23 B8
St-Sauveur-sur-Tinée *F* 36 C5
St-Sauvy *F* 33 C7
St-Savin *F* 28 E5
St-Savin *F* 29 B7
St Saviour *GBJ* 23 B7
St-Sébastien-de-Morsent *F* 24 B5
St-Sébastien-sur-Loire *F* 23 F8
St-Seine-l'Abbaye *F* 25 F12
St-Sernin *F* 35 A7
St-Sernin-sur-Rance *F* 34 C4
St-Seurin-sur-l'Isle *F* 28 E5
St-Sever *F* 32 C4
St-Sever-Calvados *F* 23 C9
St-Siméon-de-Bressieux *F* 31 E7
St-Simon *F* 19 E7
St-Simon *F* 29 F11
St-Sorlin-d'Arves *F* 31 E9
St-Soupplets *F* 25 B8
St-Sulpice *F* 33 C8
St-Sulpice-Laurière *F* 29 C8
St-Sulpice-les-Champs *F* 29 D10
St-Sulpice-les-Feuilles *F* 29 C8
St-Sulpice-sur-Lèze *F* 33 D8
St-Sulpice-sur-Risle *F* 24 C4
St-Sylvain *F* 33 B11
St-Symphorien *F* 30 F4
St-Symphorien-de-Lay *F* 30 D5
St-Symphorien-sur-Coise *F* 30 D5
St Teath *GB* 12 D5
St-Thégonnec *F* 22 C4
St-Thibéry *F* 34 D5
St-Thiébault *F* 26 D4
St-Thurien *F* 22 E4
St-Trivier-de-Courtes *F* 31 C7
St-Trivier-sur-Moignans *F* 30 C6
St-Trojan-les-Bains *F* 28 D3

St-Tropez *F* 36 E5
St-Uze *F* 30 E6
St-Valérien *F* 25 D9
St-Valery-en-Caux *F* 18 E2
St-Valery-sur-Somme *F* 18 D4
St-Vallier *F* 30 E6
St-Vallier *F* 36 D5
St-Vallier-de-Thiey *F* 36 D5
St-Varent *F* 28 B5
St-Vaury *F* 29 C9
St-Victor *F* 30 A6
St-Victor-de-Cessieu *F* 31 D7
St-Victoret *F* 35 D9
St-Victor-la-Coste *F* 35 B8
St Vigeans *GB* 5 B11
St-Vigor-le-Grand *F* 23 B10
St-Vincent *I* 68 B4
St-Vincent-de-Connezac *F* 29 E6
St-Vincent-de-Paul *F* 32 C4
St-Vincent-les-Forts *F* 36 C4
St-Vit *F* 26 F4
St-Vite *F* 33 B7
St-Vith *B* 20 D6
St-Vivien-de-Médoc *F* 28 E3
St-Xandre *F* 28 C3
St-Yan *F* 30 C5
St-Ybars *F* 33 D9
St-Yorre *F* 30 C3
St-Yrieix-la-Perche *F* 29 D8
St-Yrieix-sur-Charente *F* 29 D6
St-Yvy *F* 22 E4
St-Zacharie *F* 35 D10
Sainville *F* 24 D6
Saissac *F* 33 D10
Saittarova *S* 116 C8
Saivomuotka *S* 116 B10
Saïx *F* 33 D10
Sajaniemi *FIN* 127 D11
Šahyajince *SRB* 164 E5
Šajkaš *SRB* 158 C5
Sajóbábony *H* 145 G2
Sajókaza *H* 145 G2
Sajókereszúr *H* 145 G2
Sajólád *H* 145 G2
Sajószentpéter *H* 145 G2
Sajószöged *H* 145 H3
Sajóvámos *H* 145 G2
Sájvis *S* 119 C11
Saka *LV* 134 C2
Sakajärvi *S* 116 D5
Sakalishcha *BY* 133 E5
Sakaravaara *FIN* 121 E12
Šakiai *LT* 136 D7
Säkinmäki *FIN* 123 F16
Sakızköy *TR* 173 B7
Säkkilä *FIN* 121 B12
Sakshaug *N* 105 D10
Saksild *DK* 86 D6
Sakskøbing *DK* 83 A11
Saksun *FO* 2 A2
Sakule *SRB* 158 C6
Säkylä *FIN* 126 C7
Šakyna *LT* 134 D6
Sala *LV* 134 C5
Sala *LV* 135 C11
Sala *S* 98 C2
Šaľa *SK* 146 E5
Salaca *LV* 131 F10
Sălacea *RO* 151 C9
Salacgrīva *LV* 131 F8
Sala Consilina *I* 60 C5
Salagnac *F* 29 E8
Salahmi *FIN* 124 C7
Salaise-sur-Sanne *F* 30 E6
Salakas *LT* 135 E12
Salakos *GR* 181 D7
Salakovac *BIH* 157 F8
Salamajärvi *FIN* 123 D13
Salamanca *E* 45 C9
Salamina *GR* 175 D7
Salandra *I* 61 B6
Salanki *FIN* 117 B13
Salantai *LT* 134 E3
Salar *E* 53 B8
Sălard *RO* 151 C9
Salardu *E* 33 E7
Salarli *TR* 172 B6
Salas *E* 39 B7
Salaš *SRB* 159 E8
Salas de los Infantes *E* 40 D5
Salash *BG* 164 B6
Salaspils *LV* 135 C9
Sălaşu de Sus *RO* 159 C10
Sălățig *RO* 151 C11
Sălătrucel *RO* 160 C4
Sălătrucu *RO* 160 C5
Salaunes *F* 28 F4
Salberg *S* 107 D16
Salbertrand *I* 31 E10
Sälboda *S* 97 C8
Salbohed *S* 98 C6
Salbris *F* 24 F7
Salbu *N* 100 D2
Salcea *RO* 153 B8
Salching *D* 75 E12
Salcia *RO* 160 F5
Salcia *RO* 160 F5
Salcia *RO* 161 C8
Salcia Tudor *RO* 161 C10
Sălcile *RO* 161 D8
Šalčininkai *LT* 137 E11
Šalčininkėliai *LT* 137 E11
Sălciua *RO* 151 E11
Salcombe *GB* 13 E7
Sălcuţa *MD* 154 D4
Sălcuţa *RO* 160 E2
Saldaña *E* 39 C10
Saldenburg *D* 76 E4
Saldón *E* 47 D10
Salduero *E* 40 E6
Saldus *LV* 134 C4
Sale *GB* 11 E7
Saleby *S* 91 C13
Salem *D* 71 B11
Salem *D* 83 C9
Salemi *I* 58 D2
Salen *GB* 4 B5
Sälen *S* 102 D5
Salernes *F* 36 D4
Salerno *I* 60 B3
Salers *F* 29 E10
Salettes *F* 30 F4
Saleux *F* 18 E5
Salford *GB* 11 E7
Salgamli *TR* 173 B6
Salgótarján *H* 147 E9
Salgueiro *P* 44 E5
Salhus *N* 94 A2
Sali *HR* 156 E3
Salice Salentino *I* 61 C9

Saliceto I 37 C8
Saliena LV 135 C7
Saliena LV 135 E13
Salles-de-Béarn F 32 D4
Salies-du-Salat F 33 D7
Salignac-Eyvignes F 29 F8
Salillas de Jalón E 41 E9
Salinas E 39 A8
Salinas E 56 D3
Salinas del Manzano E 47 D9
Salinas de Pamplona E 32 E2
Salinas de Pisuerga E 40 C3
Salin-de-Giraud F 35 D8
Saline di Volterra I 66 F2
Sälinkää FIN 127 D13
Salins F 29 E10
Salins-les-Bains F 31 B8
Salir P 50 E3
Salisbury GB 13 C11
Sălişte RO 152 F3
Săliştea RO 151 F11
Sălişte de Sus RO 152 B4
Salka SK 147 F7
Sall DK 86 C5
Sal'kove UA 154 A5
Salla FIN 131 D12
Salla FIN 115 E5
Sallanches F 31 D10
Sallent E 43 D7
Sallent de Gállego E 32 E5
Salles F 32 A4
Salles-Curan F 34 B4
Salles-d'Angles F 28 D5
Salles-la-Source F 33 B11
Salles-sur-l'Hers F 33 D9
Sallgast D 80 C5
Sälliku EST 131 C14
Sallingberg A 77 F8
Sallins IRL 7 F9
Sällsjö S 105 E15
Sallypark IRL 8 C6
Salme EST 130 E4
Salmerón E 47 C8
Salmeroncillos de Abajo E 47 C7
Salmi FIN 123 E10
Salmi S 119 B10
Salmijärvi FIN 121 D10
Salminen FIN 121 D12
Salminen FIN 124 E8
Salmivaara FIN 115 E4
Salmiyarvi RUS 114 E8
Salmoral E 45 C10
Salmtal D 21 E7
Salnava LV 133 C3
Salnö S 99 C11
Salo FIN 127 E9
Salò I 69 B10
Salobre E 55 B7
Salobreña E 53 C9
Saločiai LT 135 D8
Saloinen FIN 119 E12
Salon F 25 C11
Salon-de-Provence F 35 C9
Salonkylä FIN 123 C11
Salonpää FIN 119 E14
Salonta RO 151 D8
Salorino E 45 F6
Salornay-sur-Guye F 30 B6
Salorno I 69 A11
Salou E 42 E6
Salouël F 18 E5
Šalovci SLO 148 C6
Salsäker S 107 F14
Salsbruket N 105 B11
Salsburgh GB 5 D9
Salses-le-Château F 34 E4
Sălsig RO 151 B11
Salsomaggiore Terme I 69 D8
Salt E 43 D9
Saltara I 67 E6
Saltash GB 12 E6
Saltburn-by-the-Sea GB 11 B10
Saltcoats GB 4 D7
Salteras E 51 E7
Salthill IRL 6 F4
Salto P 38 E4
Saltoníškės LT 137 D11
Saltrød N 90 C4
Saltsjöbaden S 99 D10
Saltum DK 90 E6
Saltvik FIN 99 B14
Saltvik S 103 C13
Saludecio I 67 E6
Saluggia I 68 C5
Salur TR 173 D8
Salussola I 68 C5
Salutaguse EST 131 C9
Saluzzo I 37 B6
Salva RO 152 C4
Salvacañete E 47 D10
Salvagnac F 33 C9
Salvaleón E 51 B6
Salvaterra de Magos P 50 A2
Salvaterra do Extremo P 45 E7
Salvatierra E 32 E1
Salvatierra de los Barros E 51 C6
Salvatierra de Santiago E 45 F8
Salve I 61 D10
Salviac F 33 A8
Sály H 145 H2
Salzburg A 73 A7
Salzgitter D 79 B7
Salzhausen D 83 D8
Salzhemmendorf D 78 B6
Salzkotten D 17 E11
Salzmünde D 79 C10
Salzwedel D 83 E10
Salzweg D 76 E4
Samadet F 32 C5
Samaila SRB 158 F6
Samarate I 68 B6
Samarica HR 149 E7
Samarina GR 168 D5
Samarineşti RO 159 D11
Samassi I 64 E2
Samatan F 33 D7
Sambade P 39 F6
Sâmbăta RO 151 D9
Sambiase S 59 B9
Samboal E 40 F3
Samborzec PL 143 E12
Sambuca di Sicilia I 58 D3
Sambuca Pistoiese I 66 D3
Sambuco I 36 C6
Sâmbureşti RO 160 D4
Samedan CH 71 D9
Sameiro P 44 D6
Samer F 15 F12
Šameş L 39 B9
Sami GR 174 C2
Samil P 39 E6
Samir de los Caños E 39 E7

Şamli TR 173 E8
Sammakko S 116 E7
Sammakkola FIN 125 C10
Sammaljoki FIN 127 C9
Sammatti FIN 127 E10
Samnaun CH 71 D10
Samobor HR 148 E5
Samões P 38 F5
Samokov BG 165 E8
Samokov MK 164 F3
Samolaco I 69 A7
Samora Correia P 50 B2
Šamorín SK 146 E4
Samos E 38 C5
Samos GR 177 D8
Samoš SRB 159 C6
Samothraki GR 171 D9
Samovodene BG 166 C5
Samper de Calanda E 42 E3
Sampeyre I 37 B6
Sampierdarena I 37 C9
Sampieri I 59 F6
Sampigny F 26 C4
amşud RO 151 C10
Samswegen D 79 B10
Samtens D 84 B4
Samuelsberg N 112 D6
Samugheo I 64 D2
Samuil BG 167 C7
Samuilovo BG 166 C5
San Adrián E 32 F2
San Agustín de Guadalix E 46 C5
Sanaigmore GB 4 D4
San Amaro E 38 D3
Sânandrei RO 151 F7
San Andrés del Rabanedo E 39 C8
San Antolín E 39 B6
San Antonio E 47 E10
Sanary-sur-Mer F 35 D10
San Asensio E 40 C6
San Bartolomé de las Abiertas E 46 E3
San Bartolomé de la Torre E 51 E5
San Bartolomé de Pinares E 46 C3
San Bartolomeo al Mare I 37 D8
San Bartolomeo in Galdo I 60 A4
San Basilio I 64 D3
San Benedetto dei Marsi I 62 D5
San Benedetto del Tronto I 62 B5
San Benedetto Po I 66 B2
San Benito E 54 B3
San Benito de la Contienda E 51 B5
San Biagio di Callalta I 72 E5
San Biagio Platani I 58 D4
San Bonifacio I 66 B3
San Buono I 63 D7
San Candido I 72 C5
San Carlos del Valle E 55 B6
San Casciano dei Bagni I 62 B1
San Casciano in Val di Pesa I 66 E3
San Cataldo I 58 E4
San Cataldo I 61 C10
San Cebrián de Castro E 39 E8
Sâncel RO 152 E3
Sancergues F 25 F8
Sancerre F 25 F8
San Cesario sul Panaro I 66 C3
Sancey-le-Grand F 26 F6
Sancheville F 24 D6
Sanchidrián E 46 C3
San Chirico Nuovo I 60 B6
San Chirico Raparo I 60 C6
San Cibrão das Viñas E 38 D4
San Cipirello I 58 D3
San Cipriano d'Aversa I 60 B2
San Clemente E 47 F8
San Clemente I 67 F8
San Clodio E 38 E3
Sancoins F 30 B2
San Colombano al Lambro I 69 C7
San Cosme E 38 A5
San Costantino Albanese I 61 C6
San Costanzo I 67 E7
Sâncrăieni RO 153 E7
Sâncraiu RO 151 D10
Sâncraiu de Mureş RO 152 D5
San Cristóbal de Entreviñas E 39 D8
San Cristóbal de la Vega E 46 B3
Sancti-Spíritus E 45 C7
Sancti-Spíritus E 51 B9
Sand N 94 D4
Sand N 95 B15
Sand (Bad Emstal) D 17 F12
Sanda S 93 E12
Sandager DK 86 E5
Sandamendi E 40 B5
San Damiano d'Asti I 37 B8
San Damiano Macra I 37 C6
Sandane N 100 C4
San Daniele del Friuli I 73 D7
San Daniele Po I 66 B1
Sandanski BG 169 A9
Sandared S 91 D12
Sandarne S 103 D13
Sandau D 83 E12
Sandbach GB 11 E7
Sandberg D 74 B7
Sandby DK 87 F8
Sande D 17 B10
Sande N 95 C12
Sande N 100 D3
Sande N 94 D4
Sandefjord N 90 A7
Sandeggen N 111 A17
Sandeid N 94 D3
Sandelva N 112 D7
San Demetrio Corone I 61 D6
San Demetrio ne Vestini I 62 C5
Sander N 96 B6
Sandersdorf D 79 C11
Sandershausen (Niestetal) D 78 D6
Sandersleben D 79 C10
Sandes N 110 C3
Sandes N 110 C9
Sandfjord N 114 B9
Sandfors S 118 E5
Sandgarth GB 3 G11
Sandhausen D 21 F11
Sandhead GB 4 F7
Sandhem S 91 D14

Sandhult S 91 D12
Sandhurst GB 15 E7
Sandiás E 38 D3
Sandillon F 24 E7
Sandkrug D 84 E5
Sandl A 77 E7
Sandland N 112 C8
Sandnäset S 102 A8
Sandnes N 90 A5
Sandnes N 94 E3
Sandnes N 105 C10
Sandnes N 111 C11
Sandneshamn N 111 A15
Sandnessjøen N 108 D4
Sando E 45 C8
Sandomierz PL 143 E12
Sândominic RO 153 D7
San Donaci I 61 C9
San Donà di Piave I 72 E6
San Donato di Lecce I 61 C10
San Donato di Ninea I 60 D6
San Donato Milanese I 69 C7
San Donato Val di Comino I 62 D5
Sándorfalva H 150 E5
Sandown GB 13 D12
Sandøy N 100 A5
Sandplace GB 12 E6
Šandrovac HR 149 E8
Sandsele N 107 A13
Sandsend GB 11 C11
Sandsjö S 102 C8
Sandsjöfors S 92 E5
Sandsjönäs S 107 A13
Sandslån S 107 E13
Sandstad N 104 D6
Sandstedt D 17 B11
Sandstrak N 108 D3
Sandstrand N 111 C12
Sandtangen N 114 D7
Sandtorg N 111 C12
Sandträsk S 118 B6
Sänduleni RO 153 E8
Sănduleşti RO 152 D3
Sandur FO 2 B3
Sandvatn N 94 F5
Sandved DK 87 E9
Sandvik N 101 D15
Sandvik N 108 B7
Sandvik N 111 A16
Sandvik N 111 B14
Sandvik N 113 B16
Sandvika N 95 C13
Sandvika N 105 D12
Sandviken S 103 E12
Sandviken S 107 E15
Sandviken S 107 F13
Sandviksjön S 106 D7
Sandvikvåg N 94 C2
Sandwich GB 15 E11
Sandwick GB 3 F14
Sandy GB 15 C8
Sanem L 20 E5
San Emiliano E 39 C8
San Esteban de Gormaz E 40 E5
San Esteban de la Sierra E 45 C9
San Esteban de Litera E 42 D4
San Esteban del Molar E 39 D8
San Esteban del Valle E 46 D3
San Fele I 60 B5
San Felice a Cancello I 60 A2
San Felice Circeo I 62 E4
San Felices de los Gallegos E 45 C7
San Felice sul Panaro I 66 C3
San Ferdinando I 59 C8
San Ferdinando di Puglia I 60 A6
San Fernando E 52 D4
San Fernando de Henares E 46 D5
San Fili I 60 E6
San Filippo del Mela I 59 C7
San Francisco Javier E 57 D8
San Fratello I 59 C6
Sanfront I 37 B6
Sånga S 107 E13
Sangarcía E 46 C4
Sangaste EST 131 F12
Sangatte F 15 F12
San Gavino Monreale I 64 D2
Sångbäcken S 102 B6
San Gemini I 62 B3
Sângeorgiu de Mureş RO 152 D5
Sângeorgiu de Pădure RO 152 E5
Sângeorz-Băi RO 152 C5
Sânger RO 152 D4
Sangerhausen D 79 D9
San Germano Chisone I 31 F11
Sângeru RO 161 C8
Sangijän S 119 C11
San Gimignano I 66 F3
San Ginesio I 62 A4
Sanginjoki FIN 119 E16
Sanginkylä FIN 119 E17
San Giorgio a Liri I 62 E5
San Giorgio della Richinvelda I 73 D6
San Giorgio del Sannio I 60 A3
San Giorgio di Lomellina I 68 C6
San Giorgio di Nogaro I 73 E7
San Giorgio di Piano I 66 C3
San Giorgio Ionico I 61 C8
San Giorgio la Molara I 60 A4
San Giovanni a Piro I 60 C4
San Giovanni Bianco I 69 B8
San Giovanni d'Asso I 66 F4
San Giovanni Gemini I 58 D4
San Giovanni Incarico I 62 D4
San Giovanni in Croce I 66 B1
San Giovanni in Fiore I 61 E7
San Giovanni in Persiceto I 66 C3
San Giovanni Lupatoto I 66 B3
San Giovanni Rotondo I 63 D9
San Giovanni Suergiu I 64 E1
San Giovanni Teatino I 63 C6
San Giovanni Valdarno I 66 E4
San Giuliano Terme I 66 E1
San Giuseppe Jato I 58 D3
San Giuseppe Vesuviano I 60 B3
San Leo I 66 E5
San Leonardo de Yagüe E 40 E5
San Leonardo in Passiria I 72 C3
San Lorenzo I 59 D7

San Gregorio Matese I 60 A2
Sangüesa E 32 E3
San Guiliano Milanese I 69 C7
San Guim de Freixenet E 43 D6
Sanguinet F 32 B3
Sanguinetto I 66 B3
Sani GR 169 D7
San Ildefonso E 46 C5
Sanislău RO 151 B9
Sanitz D 83 B12
San Javier E 56 F3
San Jordi E 42 F4
San Jorge de Alor E 51 B5
San José E 55 F8
San José del Valle E 52 C5
San José de Malcocinado E 52 D5
San Juan E 41 B6
San Juan de Alicante E 56 E4
San Juan de Aznalfarache E 51 E7
San Juan de la Nava E 46 D3
San Juan del Puerto E 51 E6
San Justo de la Vega E 39 D7
Sankt Aegyd am Neuwalde A 77 G9
Sankt Andrä A 73 C11
Sankt Andrä am Zicksee A 149 A7
Sankt Andreasberg D 79 C8
Sankt Anna S 93 C9
Sankt Anna am Aigen A 148 C5
Sankt Anton an der Jeßnitz A 77 G8
Sankt Augustin D 21 C8
Sankt Gallen A 73 A10
Sankt Gallen CH 27 F11
Sankt Gallenkirch A 71 C9
Sankt Gangloff D 79 E10
Sankt Georgen am Walde A 77 F7
Sankt Georgen im Schwarzwald D 27 D9
Sankt Gilgen A 73 A7
Sankt Goar D 21 D9
Sankt Goarshausen D 21 D9
Sankt Ingbert D 21 F8
Sankt Jakob im Rosental A 73 C9
Sankt Jakob im Walde A 148 B5
Sankt Jakob in Defereggen I 72 C5
Sankt Johann am Tauern A 73 B9
Sankt Johann im Pongau A 73 B7
Sankt Johann im Walde A 73 C6
Sankt Johann in Tirol A 72 A5
Sankt Julian D 21 E9
Sankt Katharinen D 185 C7
Sankt Lambrecht A 73 B9
Sankt Leonhard am Forst A 77 F8
Sankt Leonhard am Hornerwald A 77 E9
Sankt Leonhard im Pitztal A 71 C11
Sankt Lorenz A 73 A7
Sankt Lorenzen im Gitschtal A 73 C7
Sankt Lorenzen im Lesachtal A 73 C6
Sankt Lorenzen im Mürztal A 148 B4
Sankt Lorenzen ob Murau A 73 B9
Sankt Marein im Mürztal A 148 B4
Sankt Margarethen D 17 A12
Sankt Margarethen an der Raab A 148 B5
Sankt Margarethen bei Knittelfeld A 73 B10
Sankt Margarethen im Burgenland A 77 G11
Sankt Mårgen D 27 D9
Sankt Martin A 73 B7
Sankt Martin A 77 E7
Sankt Martin im Mühlkreis A 76 F6
Sankt Michael im Burgenland A 148 B6
Sankt Michael im Lungau A 73 B8
Sankt Michael in Obersteiermark A 73 B11
Sankt Michaelisdonn D 82 C6
Sankt Moritz CH 71 D9
Sankt Nikolai im Saustal A 148 C4
Sankt Nikolai im Sölktal A 73 B9
Sankt Olof S 88 D6
Sankt Oswald bei Freistadt A 77 E7
Sankt Oswald ob Eibiswald A 73 C11
Sankt Pankraz A 73 B7
Sankt Paul im Lavanttal A 73 C10
Sankt Peter am Kammersberg A 73 B9
Sankt Peter an Ottersbach A 148 C5
Sankt-Peterburg RUS 129 F13
Sankt Peter-Freinstein A 73 B11
Sankt Peter in der Au A 77 F7
Sankt Peter-Ording D 82 B5
Sankt Pölten A 77 F9
Sankt Radegund A 76 F5
Sankt Ruprecht an der Raab A 148 B5
Sankt Stefan im Gailtal A 73 C8
Sankt Stefan ob Leoben A 73 B10
Sankt Stefan ob Stainz A 148 C4
Sankt Ulrich bei Steyr A 76 F6
Sankt Valentin A 77 F7
Sankt Veit an Vogau A 148 C5
Sankt Veit an der Glan A 73 C9
Sankt Veit an der Gölsen A 77 F9
Sankt Veit im Pongau A 73 B7
Sankt Veit in Defereggen A 72 C5
Sankt Wendel D 21 F8
Sankt Wolfgang D 75 F11
Sankt Wolfgang im Salzkammergut A 73 A7
San Lazzaro di Savena I 66 D3
San Leo I 66 E5
San Leonardo de Yagüe E 40 E5
San Leonardo in Passiria I 72 C3
San Lorenzo I 59 D7
San Lorenzo al Mare I 37 D7

San Lorenzo Bellizzi I 61 D6
San Lorenzo de Calatrava E 54 C5
San Lorenzo de El Escorial E 46 C4
San Lorenzo de la Parrilla E 47 E8
San Lorenzo di Sebato I 72 C4
San Lorenzo in Campo I 67 E6
San Lorenzo Nuovo I 62 B1
San Luca I 59 D9
Sanlúcar de Barrameda E 52 C4
Sanlúcar de Guadiana E 50 E5
Sanlúcar la Mayor E 51 E7
San Lucido I 60 E6
Sanluri I 64 D2
San Maddalena Vallalta I 72 C5
San Mamés de Campos E 40 D2
San Marcello I 67 E7
San Marcello Pistoiese I 66 D2
San Marco Argentano I 60 D6
San Marco dei Cavoti I 60 A3
San Marco in Lamis I 63 D9
San Marcos E 38 B3
San Marino RSM 66 E5
San Martín E 32 D1
San Martín E 40 B4
Sânmartin RO 151 C8
Sânmartin RO 152 C4
Sânmartin RO 153 E7
San Martín de la Vega E 46 D5
San Martín de la Vega del Alberche E 45 D10
San Martín de Montalbán E 46 E4
San Martín de Pusa E 46 E3
San Martín de Unx E 32 E2
San Martín de Valdeiglesias E 46 D4
San Martino Buon Albergo I 66 B3
San Martino di Castrozza I 72 D4
San Martino di Lupari I 72 E4
San Martino di Venezze I 66 B4
San Martino in Badia I 72 C4
San Martino in Passiria I 72 C3
San Martino in Pensilis I 63 D8
San Mateo de Gállego E 41 E10
San Mauro Castelverde I 58 D5
San Mauro Forte I 61 C6
San Mauro Marchesato I 61 E7
San Mauro Pascoli I 66 D5
San Mauro Torinese I 68 C4
San Menaio I 63 D9
San Michele al Tagliamento I 73 E6
San Michele Mondovì I 37 C7
San Michele Salentino I 61 B9
San Miguel de Arroyo E 40 F3
San Miguel de Bernuy E 40 F4
San Miguel de Salinas E 56 F3
Sânmihaiu Almaşului RO 151 C11
Sânmihaiu de Câmpie RO 152 D4
Sânmihaiu Român RO 159 B7
San Millán de la Cogolla E 40 D6
San Miniato I 66 E2
Sänna S 92 B5
Sannahed S 92 A6
Sannazzaro de'Burgondi I 69 C6
Sannicandro di Bari I 61 B7
Sannicandro Garganico I 63 D9
Sannicola I 61 C10
San-Nicolao F 37 G10
San Nicolás del Puerto E 51 C8
Sânnicolau Mare RO 150 E6
San Nicolò I 66 C3
San Nicolò d'Arcidano I 64 D2
San Nicolò Gerrei I 64 E3
Sanniki PL 139 F8
San Pablo de los Montes E 46 E4
San Pancrazio I 72 C3
San Pancrazio Salentino I 61 C9
San Paolo di Civitate I 63 D8
San Pedro E 55 B8
San Pedro de Alcántara E 53 D7
San Pedro de Ceque E 39 D7
San Pedro del Arroyo E 46 C3
San Pedro de Latarce E 39 E9
San Pedro del Pinatar E 56 F3
San Pedro del Romeral E 40 B4
San Pedro de Rozados E 45 C9
San Pedro Manrique E 41 D7
San Pedro Palmiches E 47 D8
San Pellegrino Terme I 69 B8
Sânpetru RO 153 F7
Sânpetru de Câmpie RO 152 D4
Sânpetru Mare RO 150 E6
San Piero a Sieve I 66 E3
San Piero Patti I 59 C6
San Pietro I 59 B7
San Pietro di Cadore I 73 C6
San Pietro in Cariano I 66 A2
San Pietro in Casale I 66 C3
San Pietro in Guarano I 61 E6
San Pietro Vernotico I 61 C10
San Polo d'Enza I 66 B1
San Prospero I 66 C3
Sanquhar GB 5 E9
San Quirico d'Orcia I 65 A5
San Rafael del Río E 42 F4
San Remo I 37 D7
San Román E 38 C5
San Román de Cameros E 41 D7
San Román de la Cuba E 39 D10
San Román de los Montes E 46 D3
San Roque E 38 B2
San Roque E 38 D3
San Roque E 53 D8
San Rufo I 60 C4
Sansac-de-Marmiesse F 29 F10
San Salvador de Cantamunda E 40 C3
San Salvatore I 64 D1
San Salvatore Monferrato I 37 B9
San Salvo I 63 C7
San Sebastián de los Ballesteros E 53 A7
San Sebastián de los Reyes E 46 C5

San Secondo Parmense I 66 C1
Sansepolcro I 66 E5
San Severa I 62 C1
San Severino Lucano I 60 C6
San Severino Marche I 67 F7
San Severo I 63 D8
San Silvestre de Guzmán E 51 E5
Sânsimion RO 153 E7
Sanski Most BIH 157 C6
Sansol E 32 E1
San Sosti I 60 D6
San Sperate I 64 E3
San Spirito I 61 A7
Sant RO 152 C5
Santa Amalia E 51 A7
Santa Ana E 55 B9
Santa Ana de Pusa E 46 E3
Santa Ana la Real E 51 D6
Santa Bárbara E 42 F5
Santa Bárbara de Casa E 51 D5
Santacara E 32 F2
Santa Catalina de Armada E 38 B2
Santa Catarina P 50 C3
Santa Catarina da Fonte do Bispo P 50 E4
Santa Caterina dello Ionio I 59 B10
Santa Caterina di Pittinuri I 64 C2
Santa Caterina Villarmosa I 58 D5
Santa Cesarea Terme I 61 C10
Santa Cilia de Jaca I 32 E4
Santa Clara-a-Nova P 50 E3
Santa Clara-a-Velha P 50 D3
Santa Clara de Louredo P 50 D4
Santa Coloma de Farners E 43 D9
Santa Coloma de Queralt E 43 D6
Santa Colomba de Somoza E 39 D7
Santa Columba de Curueño E 39 C9
Santa Comba Dão P 44 D4
Santa Comba de Rossas P 39 E6
Santa Cristina d'Aro E 43 D9
Santa Cristina de la Polvorosa E 39 D8
Santa Croce Camerina I 59 F6
Santa Croce del Sannio I 60 A3
Santa Croce di Magliano I 63 D8
Santa Croce sull'Arno I 66 E2
Santa Cruz E 38 B2
Santa Cruz da Tapa P 44 C4
Santa Cruz de Bezana E 40 B4
Santa Cruz de Campézo E 32 E1
Santa Cruz de la Serós E 32 E4
Santa Cruz de la Sierra E 45 F9
Santa Cruz de la Zarza E 47 E6
Santa Cruz de los Cáñamos E 55 B7
Santa Cruz del Retamar E 46 D4
Santa Cruz de Moya E 47 E10
Santa Cruz de Mudela E 55 B6
Santadi I 64 E2
Santa Domenica Talao I 60 D5
Santa Domenica Vittoria I 59 D6
Santa Elena S 92 B5
Santa Elena de Jamuz E 39 D8
Santa Elisabetta I 58 E4
Santaella S A3
Santa Engracia E 32 F1
Santa Eufemia E 54 B3
Santa Eugèni I 49 E10
Santa Eulalia E 39 B8
Santa Eulalia E 47 C10
Santa Eulalia E 39 C9
Santa Eulàlia E 51 A5
Santa Eulalia del Río E 57 D8
Santa Eulàlia de Oscos E 38 B5
Santa Eulàlia de Riuprimer E 43 D8
Santa Fé E 53 B9
Santa Fiora I 65 B5
Santa Giusta I 64 D2
Santa Giustina I 72 D5
Sant'Agata de'Goti I 60 A3
Sant'Agata del Bianco I 59 D8
Sant'Agata di Esaro I 60 D5
Sant'Agata di Militello I 59 C6
Sant'Agata di Puglia I 60 A5
Sant'Agata Feltria I 66 E5
Santa Giusta I 64 D2
Sant'Agostino I 66 C3
Santa Iria P 50 D4
Santa Justa P 50 A3
Sant'Alberto I 66 C5
Santa Liestra y San Quílez E 33 F6
Santa Luce I 66 F2
Santa Lucia I 64 B4
Santa Lucia del Mela I 59 C7
Santa Lucía de Moraña E 38 C2
Santa Luzia P 50 D3
Santa Magdalena de Pulpís E 48 D5
Santa Mare RO 153 B10
Santa Margalida E 57 B11
Santa Margarida da Serra P 50 C2
Santa Margarida de Montbui E 43 D7
Santa Margarida do Sádao P 50 C3
Santa Margherita di Belice I 58 D3
Santa Margherita Ligure I 37 C10
Santa Maria CH 71 D10
Santa María E 32 F4
Santa María de Cayón E 40 B4
Santa María de Corcó E 43 C8
Santa María de Huertas E 41 F7
Santa María del Berrocal E 45 C10
Santa María del Camí E 49 E10
Santa María del Campo E 40 D4
Santa María del Campo Rus E 47 E8
Santa Maria della Versa I 37 B10
Santa Maria del Cedro I 60 D5
Santa María de los Llanos E 47 F7
Santa María del Páramo E 39 D8

Santa María del Val E 47 C8
Santa María de Nieva E 55 E9
Santa Maria di Castellabate I 60 C3
Santa Maria di Sala I 66 A5
Santa María la Real de Nieva E 46 B4
Santa Maria Maggiore I 68 A5
Santa Maria Navarrese I 64 D4
Santa Maria Nuova I 67 F7
Sântămăria-Orlea RO 159 B10
Santa Maria Rezzonico I 69 A7
Santa-Maria-Siché F 37 H9
Santa Marina E 60 C5
Santa Marina del Rey E 39 C8
Santa Marina Salina I 59 B6
Santa Marinella I 62 C1
Santa Marta E 51 B6
Santa Marta de Penaguião P 44 B5
Santa Marta de Tormes E 45 C9
Sant'Ambroggio F 37 F9
Santana P 44 D3
Santana P 50 C1
Sântana RO 151 E8
Santana da Serra P 50 D3
Santana de Cambas P 50 D4
Santana do Mato P 50 B3
Sant'Anastasia I 60 B2
Sant'Anatolia di Narco I 62 B3
Santander E 40 B4
Sant'Andrea Apostolo dello Ionio I 59 B10
Sant'Andrea Frius I 64 E3
Sântandrei RO 151 C8
Sant'Angelo P 50 D3
Sant'Angelo a Fasanella I 60 C4
Sant'Angelo dei Lombardi I 60 B4
Sant'Angelo di Brolo I 59 C6
Sant'Angelo in Lizzola I 67 E6
Sant'Angelo in Vado I 66 E5
Sant'Angelo Lodigiano I 69 C7
Sant'Angelo Muxaro I 58 E4
Santa Ninfa I 58 D3
Sant'Anna Arresi I 64 E2
Sant'Antimo I 60 B2
Sant'Antioco I 64 E1
Sant Antoni de Portmany E 57 D7
Sant'Antonio Abate I 60 B3
Sant'Antonio di Gallura I 64 B3
Sant'Antonio di Santadi I 64 D1
Santanyí E 57 C11
Santa Olalla E 46 D4
Santa Olalla del Cala E 51 D7
Santa Pau E 43 C9
Santa Pola E 56 E3
Santar P 44 C5
Sant'Arcangelo I 60 C6
Santarcangelo di Romagna I 66 E5
Santarém P 44 F3
Sant'Arsenio I 60 C4
Santas Martas E 39 D9
Santa Severina I 61 E7
Santa Sofia I 66 E4
Santa Sofia d'Epiro I 61 D6
Santa Susana P 50 B3
Santa Susana P 50 C3
Santa Teresa di Gallura I 64 A3
Santa Teresa di Riva I 59 D7
Santău RO 151 C10
Santa Uxía de Ribeira E 38 C2
Santa Venerina I 59 D7
Santa Vitória P 50 D3
Santa Vitória do Ameixial P 50 B4
Sant Boi de Llobregat E 43 E8
Sant Carles de la Ràpita E 42 F5
Sant Celoni E 43 E8
Sant Cugat del Vallès E 43 D8
Sant'Egidio alla Vibrata I 62 B5
Sant'Elia a Pianisi I 63 D7
Sant Elia Fiumerapido I 62 D5
Sant Elm E 49 E9
Sant Telmo E 51 D6
Sant'Elpidio a Mare I 67 F8
San Teodoro I 64 B4
Santeramo in Colle I 61 B7
Santervás de la Vega E 39 C10
Santes Creus E 43 E6
Sant Feliu de Guíxols E 43 D10
Sant Feliu de Pallerols E 43 C8
Sant Feliu Sasserra E 43 D8
Santhià I 68 C5
Sant Hilari Sacalm E 43 D9
Sant Hipòlit de Voltregà E 43 C8
Santiago de Alcántara E 45 E6
Santiago de Calatrava E 53 A8
Santiago de Compostela E 38 C2
Santiago de Covelo E 38 D3
Santiago de la Espada E 55 C7
Santiago de la Ribera E 56 F3
Santiago del Campo E 45 E8
Santiago do Cacém P 50 C2
Santiago do Escoural P 50 B3
Santiagomillas E 39 D7
Santibáñez de Béjar E 45 D9
Santibáñez de la Peña E 39 C10
Santibáñez de la Sierra E 45 D9
Santibáñez de Tera E 39 E8
Santibáñez de Vidriales E 39 D7
Santibáñez el Bajo E 45 D8
Santibáñez Zarzaguda E 40 C4
Sant'Ilario d'Enza I 66 C1
Santillana E 40 B3
Sântimbru RO 152 E3
Santiponce E 51 E7
Santisteban del Puerto E 55 C6
Santiuste de San Juan Bautista E 46 B3
Santiz E 45 B9
Sant Jaime Mediterráneo E 57 B13
Sant Jaume d'Enveja E 42 F5
Sant Joan de Labritja E 49 F8
Sant Joan de les Abadesses E 43 C8
Sant Joan de Vilatorrada E 43 D7
Sant Joan les Fonts E 43 C9
Sant Josep de sa Talaia E 57 D7
Sant Julià de Lòria AND 33 F9
Sant Llorenç de Morunys E 43 C7
Sant Llorenç des Cardassar E 57 B11

Sant Lluís E 57 B13
Sant Martí de Tous E 43 D7
Sant Martí Sarroca E 43 E7
Sant Mateu E 42 G4
Sant Miquel de Balansat E 57 C7
Santo Aleixo P 50 B5
Santo Aleixo da Restauração P 51 C5
Santo Amador P 51 C5
Santo André P 50 C2
Santo Antoniño E 38 C2
Santo António dos Cavaleiros P 50 B1
Santo Domingo de la Calzada E 40 D6
Santo Domingo de Silos E 40 E5
Santo Estêvão P 50 B2
Santo Estêvão P 50 B4
Santo Isidro de Pegões P 50 B2
Santok PL 85 E8
Santomera E 56 E2
Sant Omero I 62 B2
Santoña E 40 B5
Santo Pietro I 58 E6
Santo-Pietro-di-Tenda F 37 F10
Santo-Pietro-di-Venaco F 37 G10
Santo Stefano al Mare I 37 D7
Santo Stefano Belbo I 37 B8
Santo Stefano d'Aveto I 37 B10
Santo Stefano di Cadore I 72 C6
Santo Stefano di Camastra I 58 C5
Santo Stefano di Magra I 69 E8
Santo Stefano Quisquina I 58 D3
Santo Stino di Livenza I 73 E6
Santo Tomé E 55 C6
Santovenia E 39 E8
Santpedor E 43 D7
Sant Pere de Ribes E 43 E7
Sant Pere de Torelló E 43 C8
Sant Pere Pescador E 43 C10
Sant Pol de Mar E 43 D9
Santpoort NL 182 A5
Sant Privat d'en Bas E 43 C8
Sant Quintí de Mediona E 43 E7
Sant Quirze de Besora E 43 C8
Sant Sadurní d'Anoia E 43 E7
Santullano E 39 B8
Santu Lussurgiu I 64 C2
Santurtzi E 40 B5
Sant Vicenç dels Horts E 43 E8
Sant Vicenç de Castellet E 43 D7
San Venanzo I 62 B2
San Vendemiano I 72 E5
San Vero Milis I 64 C2
San Vicente de Alcántara E 45 F6
San Vicente de Arana E 32 C1
San Vicente de la Barquera E 40 B3
San Vicente de la Sonsierra E 40 C6
San Vicente del Raspeig E 56 E3
San Vicente de Palacio E 46 B3
San Vicente de Toranzo E 40 B4
San Vicenzo E 38 C2
San Vincenzo I 59 B7
San Vincenzo I 65 A3
San Vincenzo Valle Roveto I 62 D5
San Vitero E 39 E7
San Vito I 64 E4
San Vito al Tagliamento I 73 E6
San Vito Chietino I 63 C6
San Vito dei Normanni I 61 B9
San Vito di Cadore I 72 D5
San Vito lo Capo I 58 C2
San Vito Romano I 62 D3
San Vito sullo Ionio I 59 B9
San Vittoria in Matenano I 62 A4
Sanxenxo E 38 D2
Sanxhax AL 168 A2
Sanza I 60 C5
Sânzieni RO 153 E8
Sanzoles E 39 F8
São Barnabé P 50 E4
São Bartolomeu P 44 F5
São Bartolomeu da Serra P 50 C2
São Bartolomeu de Messines P 50 E3
São Bento do Cortiço P 50 B4
São Brás P 50 D4
São Brás de Alportel P 50 E4
São Brás do Regedouro P 50 C3
São Brissos P 50 C4
São Cosmado P 44 B5
São Domingos P 50 D2
São Facundo P 44 F4
São Francisco da Serra P 50 C2
São Geraldo P 50 B3
São Gregório P 50 B4
São Jacinto P 44 C3
São João da Madeira P 44 C4
São João da Pesqueira P 44 B6
São João da Venda P 50 E4
São João do Campo P 44 D4
São João dos Caldeireiros P 50 D4
São José da Lamarosa P 44 F5
São Lourenço de Mamporcão P 50 B4
São Luís P 50 D2
São Manços P 50 C4
São Marcos da Ataboeira P 50 D4
São Marcos da Serra P 50 E3
São Marcos do Campo P 50 C4
São Martinho da Cortiça P 44 D4
São Martinho das Amoreiras P 50 D3
São Martinho de Angueira P 39 E7
São Martinho do Porto P 44 E2
São Matias P 50 C4
São Miguel de Acha P 45 D6
São Miguel de Machede P 50 B4
São Miguel do Outeiro P 44 C4
São Miguel de Rio Torto P 44 F4
São Miguel do Pinheiro P 50 D4
Saône F 36 F5
São Pedro da Cadeira P 44 F2
São Pedro de Muel P 44 E2
São Pedro de Solis P 50 E4
São Pedro do Sul P 44 C4
Saorge F 37 D7
São Romão P 51 B5

São Romão do Sado P 50 C3
São Sebastião dos Carros P 50 D4
São Teotónio P 50 D2
Saou F 35 A9
São Vicente P 38 E5
São Vicente da Beira P 44 D5
Sáp H 151 C7
Sapanca TR 171 E10
Săpânţa RO 145 H8
Sapareva Banya BG 165 E7
Saparevo BG 165 E7
Săpata RO 160 D5
Sapes GR 171 B9
Sapna BIH 157 C11
Sa Pobla E 57 B11
Săpoca RO 161 C9
Sapotskin BY 137 F8
Sappada I 73 C6
Sappee FIN 127 C11
Sappen N 112 D7
Sappisaasi S 116 E7
Sapri I 60 C5
Sapsalampi FIN 123 F11
Sapsoperä FIN 125 B11
Sara FIN 122 F9
Saraby N 113 C12
Saracena I 60 D6
Saračinec HR 148 D6
Sărafovo BG 167 D9
Saraiki LV 134 C2
Sărăisniemi FIN 119 F17
Saraiu RO 155 D2
Sarajärvi FIN 120 C9
Sarajärvi FIN 129 B11
Sarajevo BIH 157 E9
Saramo FIN 125 C12
Saramon F 33 C7
Saran F 24 E6
Sáránd H 151 C8
Sarandë AL 168 E3
Sarantaporo GR 169 D7
Sarantsi BG 165 D8
Sa Ràpita E 57 C10
Sarasău RO 145 H8
Sarata UA 154 E5
Sărata Galbenă MD 154 D2
Sărata-Monteoru RO 161 C9
Sărata Nouă MD 154 E2
Sărăteni MD 154 D2
Sărătenii Vechi MD 154 D3
Saray TR 173 B8
Sarayakpınar TR 167 F7
Saraylar TR 173 C8
Šarbanovac SRB 159 F9
Sărbeni RO 161 E6
Sárbogárd H 149 C11
Sarcelles F 25 C7
Sarconi I 60 C5
Sardara I 64 D2
Šardice CZ 77 E12
Sardinia GR 174 B3
Sardoal P 44 E4
Sare F 32 D2
S'Arenal E 49 E10
Šarengrad HR 158 C3
Sarentino I 72 C3
Sárevere EST 131 D10
Sarezzo I 69 B9
Sargans CH 71 C8
Sariai LT 137 C13
Saribeyler TR 173 F8
Saricaali TR 171 C10
Sarıçam TR 177 B9
Sarichioi RO 155 D3
Saridanişment TR 167 F7
Sariegos E 39 C8
Sarikemer TR 177 D9
Sarıköy TR 173 D8
Sariñena E 42 D3
Šariške Michaľany SK 145 E3
Sariyer TR 173 B11
Sarjankylä FIN 123 B14
Sarkad H 151 D7
Sarkadkeresztúr H 151 D7
Särkelä FIN 121 C12
Särkijärvi FIN 117 C11
Särkijärvi FIN 119 C15
Särkijärvi FIN 120 E9
Sárkikorpi FIN 125 D12
Särkikylä FIN 123 D11
Särkilahti FIN 127 B14
Särkilahti FIN 129 B11
Särkiluoma FIN 121 B14
Särkimo FIN 122 D8
Särkisalmi FIN 129 B11
Särkisalo FIN 123 E16
Särkisalo FIN 114 F4
Sarköy TR 173 C7
Sarlat-la-Canéda F 29 F8
Sarliac-sur-l'Isle F 29 E7
Sârmaş RO 152 D6
Sârmaşag RO 151 C10
Sármellék H 149 C8
Sarmijärvi FIN 114 F4
Sarmizegetusa RO 159 B10
Sârna S 102 C1
Sarnadas do Ródão P 44 E5
Sarnaki PL 141 F7
Sarnano I 62 A4
Sárnate LV 134 B3
Sarniç TR 177 C9
Sarnico I 69 B8
Sarno I 60 B3
Sarnowa PL 81 C11
Särnstugan S 102 C5
Särö S 91 D10
Sarochyna BY 133 F5
Saronno I 69 B7
Sárosd H 149 B11
Šarospatak H 145 G4
Šarovce SK 147 E7
Sarow D 84 C4
Sarpsborg N 95 D14
Sarracín E 40 D4
Sarral E 42 E6
Sarralbe F 27 C7
Sârrance F 32 C4
Sarrancolin F 33 E6
Sàrraquinhos P 38 E4
Sarràs F 39 E6
Sarre GB 15 E11
Sarre I 31 D11
Sârreaus E 38 D4
Sarrebourg F 27 C7
Sarreguemines F 27 B7
Sárrétudvari H 151 C12

Sarre-Union F 27 C7
Sarria E 38 C5
Sarrià de Ter E 43 C9
Sarrians F 35 B8
Sarrión E 48 D3
Sarroca de Lleida E 42 E5
Sarroch I 64 E3
Sarròd H 149 A7
Sarrola-Carcopino F 37 G9
Sarron F 32 C5
Sarry F 25 C11
Sarsina I 66 E5
Sarstedt D 78 B6
Sárszentágota H 149 C11
Sárszentlőrinc H 149 C11
Sart B 183 D7
Sartaguda E 32 F1
Sarteano I 62 B1
Sartène F 37 H9
Sarti GR 170 D5
Sartilly F 23 C9
Sartininkai LT 134 F3
Sarud H 150 B6
Saru Dornei RO 152 C6
Şaruhanli TR 177 B10
Sarule I 64 C3
Sărulești RO 161 C9
Sărulești RO 161 E9
Sárvár H 149 B7
Sarvela FIN 122 F9
Sarvijoki FIN 122 E7
Sarvikumpu FIN 125 F12
Sárviz E 32 E5
Sarvisvaara S 116 E6
Särvsjön S 102 A5
Sar''ya BY 133 E3
Sarzana I 69 E8
Sarzeau F 22 E6
Sarzedas P 44 E5
Sarzedo P 44 B5
Sasa MK 164 E6
Sasalli TR 177 C8
Sasamón E 40 D3
Sasbach D 27 C9
Sasbachwalden D 186 D5
Sasca Montană RO 159 D8
Saschiz RO 152 E5
Sásd H 149 D10
Sasina BIH 157 C6
Sasnava LT 137 D7
Sassali FIN 117 D15
Sassano I 60 C5
Sassari I 64 B2
Sassello I 37 C8
Sassen D 84 B4
Sassenage F 31 E8
Sassenberg D 17 D10
Sassenheim NL 16 D3
Sassetta I 65 A3
Sassnitz D 84 A5
Sassocorvaro I 66 E5
Sassoferrato I 67 F6
Sasso Marconi I 66 D3
Sassuolo I 66 C2
Sástago E 41 F11
Šaštín-Stráže SK 77 E12
Sas Van Gent NL 16 F1
Sáta H 145 G2
Satão P 44 C5
Satchinez RO 151 F7
Šateikiai LT 134 E3
Šatenās villastad S 91 C12
Säter S 97 B14
Sätervallen S 102 A5
Säti LV 134 C5
Satiķi LV 134 C5
Satillieu F 30 E6
Satkūnai LT 134 E5
Satnica Đakovačka HR 149 F10
Sätofta S 87 D13
Sátorajáújhely H 145 G4
Satovcha BG 170 A5
Satow D 83 C11
Satriano di Lucania I 60 B5
Satrup D 82 A7
Sattajärvi FIN 119 B12
Sattajärvi S 117 D10
Sattanen FIN 117 D17
Satteins A 71 C9
Satteldorf D 75 D7
Satter S 116 E7
Sattledt A 76 F6
Satulung RO 151 B11
Satu Mare RO 151 B10
Saubusse F 32 C3
Saúca E 47 B7
Sauca MD 154 A1
Săuca RO 151 C9
Saucats F 32 A4
Săucești RO 153 D9
Sauclières F 34 C5
Sauda N 94 C4
Saue EST 131 C9
Sauerlach D 75 G10
Sauga EST 131 E8
Saugnacq-et-Muret F 32 B4
Saugos LT 134 F2
Saugues F 30 F4
Saujon F 28 D4
Sauk AL 168 B2
Sauka LV 135 D10
Šaukėnai LT 134 E5
Saukko FIN 125 C11
Saukkoaapa FIN 115 D2
Saukkojärvi FIN 119 B16
Saukkola FIN 127 E10
Saukkoriipi FIN 117 E12
Saukonkylä FIN 123 E11
Sauland N 95 C9
Saulce-sur-Rhône F 35 A8
Sauldorf D 27 E11
Saulepi EST 130 E7
Săulești RO 160 D2
Saulgau F 71 A9
Saulgrub D 71 B12
Saulheim D 21 E10
Šaulia RO 152 D4
Saulieu F 25 F11
Saulkalne LV 135 C8
Saulkrasti LV 135 B8
Sault F 35 B9
Sault-de-Navailles F 32 C4
Sault-lès-Rethel F 19 C9
Saulx F 26 E5
Saulxures-sur-Moselotte F 27 E6
Saulzais-le-Potier F 29 B11
Saumos F 28 F3

Saumur F 23 F11
Şaunajärvi FIN 125 C13
Saunakylä FIN 123 D13
Saunavaara FIN 115 D3
Saundersfoot GB 12 B5
Săurat F 33 E9
SaurieŝI LV 135 C8
Sauris I 73 D6
Saursfjord N 110 E9
Sausnēja LV 135 C11
Sausset-les-Pins F 35 D9
Saussy F 26 F2
Sautens A 71 C11
Sautinl LV 135 B8
Sautron F 23 F8
Sauto Kraftverk N 113 D12
Sauvagnon F 32 D4
Sauve F 35 C6
Sauveterre-de-Béarn F 32 D4
Sauveterre-de-Guyenne F 28 E5
Sauveterre-la-Lémance F 33 A8
Sauviat-sur-Vige F 29 C9
Sauvo FIN 126 E8
Sauxillanges F 30 D3
Sauzon F 22 F5
Sauzé-Vaussais F 29 C6
Sava I 61 C9
Sava SLO 73 D10
Săvădisla RO 151 D11
Savalia GR 174 D3
Savaloja FIN 119 E15
Săvar S 122 C5
Săvârşin RO 151 E10
Săve S 91 D10
Savelli I 61 E7
Savenay F 23 F8
Săveni RO 153 B9
Săveni RO 161 D11
Saverdun F 33 D9
Saverna EST 131 E13
Saverne F 27 C7
Sävi FIN 126 B8
Săviă FIN 123 D17
Saviaho FIN 125 C10
Savières F 25 D10
Savigliano I 37 B7
Savignac-les-Églises F 29 E7
Savignano Irpino F 60 A5
Savignano sul Rubicone I 66 D5
Savigné-l'Évêque F 23 D12
Savigneux F 30 D5
Savigny-en-Sancerre F 25 F8
Savigny-sur-Braye F 24 E4
Savijärvi FIN 125 D11
Savikylä FIN 125 C11
Savilahti FIN 129 C10
Savines-le-Lac F 36 B4
Săvinești RO 153 D8
Savino Selo SRB 158 B4
Saviranta FIN 121 F10
Saviselkä FIN 123 B16
Savitaipale FIN 128 C8
Sävja S 99 C9
Šavnik MNE 157 G11
Savognin CH 71 D9
Savoisy F 25 E11
Savona I 37 C8
Savonlinna FIN 129 B10
Savonranta FIN 125 F12
Savran' UA 154 A6
Sävsjön S 97 C11
Savsjön S 97 C12
Savudrija HR 67 B7
Savukoski FIN 115 D4
Sawin PL 141 H8
Sawston GB 15 C9
Sax E 56 D3
Saxdalen S 97 B12
Saxen A 77 F7
Saxhyttan S 97 C11
Saxilby GB 11 E10
Saxmundham GB 15 C11
Saxnäs S 106 B8
Saxon CH 31 C11
Saxthorpe GB 15 B11
Saxvallen S 105 C3
Sayalonga E 53 C8
Sayatón E 47 D7
Sayda D 80 E4
Săynäjä FIN 121 B13
Säynätsalo FIN 123 F15
Säyneinen FIN 125 D10
Sázava CZ 77 C7
Sazlı TR 171 E10
Sazlı TR 177 D9
Sazoba TR 173 D7
Sazoba TR 177 B10
Scaër F 22 D4
Scăeşti RO 160 E3
Scafa I 62 C5
Scalasaig GB 4 C3
Scalby GB 11 C11
Scalea I 60 D5
Scaletta Zanclea I 59 C7
Scandale I 61 E7
Scandiano I 66 C2
Scandicci I 66 E3
Scandriglia I 62 C3
Scano di Montiferro I 64 C2
Scansano I 65 B4
Scânteia RO 153 D11
Scânteia RO 161 D10
Scânteieşti RO 153 F12
Scanzano Jonico I 61 C7
Scapa GB 3 H11
Scarborough GB 11 C11
Scardovari I 66 C5
Scarinish GB 4 B3
Scario I 60 C4
Scărişoara RO 160 F5
Scarlino I 65 B3
Scarperia I 66 E3
Scartaglen IRL 8 D4
Scartaglin IRL 8 D4
Šćenica-Bobani BIH 162 D5
Scerni I 63 C7
Scey-sur-Saône-et-St-Albin F 26 E4
Schaafheim D 187 B7
Schaan FL 71 C9
Schaarsbergen NL 183 A7
Schacht-Audorf D 82 B6
Schaerbeek B 19 C9
Schaesberg NL 20 C6
Schafflund D 82 A6
Schaffhausen CH 27 E10
Schafstädt D 79 D10

Schafstedt D 82 B6
Schäftlarn D 75 G9
Schagen NL 16 C3
Schaijk NL 183 B7
Schalchen A 76 F4
Schalkau D 75 B9
Schalkhaar NL 183 A8
Schalksmühle D 17 F9
Schänis CH 27 F11
Schapen D 17 D9
Schaprode D 84 A4
Scharbeutz D 83 B9
Schardenberg A 76 E4
Schärding A 76 E4
Scharendijke NL 16 E1
Scharnebeck D 83 D9
Scharnhofen D 71 A9
Scharnstein A 73 A8
Scharrel (Oldenburg) D 17 B9
Schashagen D 83 B9
Schattendorf A 149 A7
Schebheim D 75 C7
Scheemda NL 17 B7
Scheer D 27 D11
Scheeßel D 82 D6
Schefflenz D 21 F12
Scheggia e Pascelupo I 67 F6
Scheggino I 62 B3
Scheia RO 153 B8
Scheia RO 153 C11
Scheibbs A 77 F8
Scheiblingkirchen A 148 A6
Scheidegg D 71 B9
Scheifling A 73 B9
Scheinfeld D 75 C7
Schela RO 155 B1
Schela RO 160 C2
Schelklingen D 74 F6
Schellerten D 79 B7
Schenefeld D 17 A9
Schenefeld D 83 C7
Schenkenfelden A 76 E6
Schenkenzell D 187 E5
Schenklengsfeld D 78 E6
Schermbeck D 17 E7
Schermen D 79 B10
Schermerhorn NL 16 C3
Scherpenheuvel B 19 C10
Scherpenzeel NL 16 D4
Scherwiller F 27 D7
Scherzingen CH 27 E11
Schiavi di Abruzzo I 63 D6
Schiedam NL 182 B4
Schieder-Schwalenberg D 17 E12
Schieren L 20 E6
Schierling D 75 E11
Schiermonnikoog NL 16 B6
Schiers CH 71 D9
Schiffdorf D 17 A11
Schifferstadt D 21 F10
Schifflange L 20 F6
Schiffweiler D 186 C3
Schijndel NL 16 E4
Schilde B 16 F3
Schillingen D 186 B2
Schillingsfürst D 75 D7
Schilpario I 69 A9
Schiltach D 27 D9
Schiltigheim F 27 C8
Schimatari GR 175 C8
Schinnen NL 183 D7
Schinos GR 174 B3
Schinveld NL 20 C5
Schio I 69 B11
Schipkau D 80 C5
Schipluiden NL 182 B4
Schkeuditz D 79 D11
Schkölen D 79 D10
Schköna D 79 C12
Schkopau D 79 D10
Schladen D 79 B8
Schladming A 73 B8
Schlangen D 17 E11
Schlangenbad D 21 D10
Schleching D 72 A5
Schleiden D 20 C6
Schleife D 81 C7
Schleinbach A 77 F10
Schleitheim CH 27 E10
Schleiz D 79 E10
Schlema D 79 E12
Schlepzig D 80 B5
Schleswig D 82 A7
Schleusingen D 75 A8
Schleswig D 82 A7
Schleusingen D 75 A8
Schleußingen D 75 A8
Schlier D 71 B9
Schlierbach A 73 A9
Schlieren CH 27 F9
Schliersee D 72 A4
Schlitters A 72 B4
Schlitz D 78 E6
Schlossberg A 148 C4
Schloss Holte-Stukenbrock D 17 E11
Schlossvippach D 79 D9
Schlosswil CH 70 D5
Schlotheim D 79 D8
Schluchsee D 27 E9
Schlüchtern D 74 B6
Schlüsselfeld D 75 C8
Schmallenberg D 21 B10
Schmelz D 21 F7
Schmidgaden D 75 D10
Schmiedmühlen D 75 D11
Schmiedeberg D 80 E5
Schmölln D 79 E11
Schmölln D 84 C6
Schnackenburg D 83 D11
Schnaittach D 75 C9
Schneeberg D 79 E12
Schneidlingen D 79 C9
Schneizlreuth D 73 A6
Schnelldorf D 187 C9
Schneverdingen D 82 D7
Schnürpflingen D 187 E8
Schobüll D 82 B6
Schodnia PL 142 E5
Schoenberg B 20 D6
Scholen D 17 C11
Schollene D 83 E12

Schöllkrippen D 187 A7
Schöllnach D 76 E4
Schömberg D 27 D10
Schömberg D 187 D6
Schönaich D 187 D7
Schönau D 76 F3
Schönau im Schwarzwald D 27 E8
Schönbach D 187 A9
Schönberg D 83 C9
Schönberg D 84 B3
Schönberg (Holstein) D 83 B8
Schönberg am Kamp A 77 E9
Schönberg im Stubaital A 72 B3
Schönborn D 80 C5
Schondra D 74 B6
Schönebeck D 83 B10
Schönebeck (Elbe) D 79 B10
Schöneck D 79 A8
Schönecken D 20 D6
Schönenberg-Kübelberg D 186 C3
Schönermark D 84 D4
Schönewalde D 80 C4
Schönewörde D 79 A8
Schongau D 71 B11
Schönhausen D 79 B8
Schönkirchen D 83 B8
Schönow D 84 E5
Schönsee D 75 C12
Schöntal D 74 D6
Schönthal D 75 D12
Schönwalde D 80 C5
Schönwalde am Bungsberg D 83 B9
Schönwies A 71 C11
Schoondijke NL 16 F1
Schoonebeek NL 17 C7
Schoonhoven NL 16 E3
Schoorl NL 16 C3
Schopfheim D 27 E8
Schopfloch D 75 D7
Schöppenstedt D 79 B8
Schoppernau A 71 C10
Schöppingen D 17 D8
Schörfling am Attersee A 73 A8
Schorndorf D 74 E6
Schorndorf D 75 D12
Schortens D 17 A9
Schoten B 16 F2
Schotten D 21 D12
Schramberg D 27 D9
Schrecksbach D 21 C12
Schrems A 77 E8
Schrepkow D 83 E12
Schrieseheim D 21 F11
Schröder A 73 B9
Schrobenhausen D 75 E9
Schrozberg D 74 D6
Schruns A 71 C9
Schübelbach CH 27 F10
Schuby D 82 A6
Schulenberg im Oberharz D 79 C7
Schull IRL 8 E3
Schulzendorf D 84 E6
Schüpfheim CH 70 D6
Schuttertal D 186 E4
Schutterwald D 186 E4
Schüttorf D 17 D8
Schwaan D 83 C12
Schwabach D 75 D9
Schwäbisch Gmünd D 74 E6
Schwäbisch Hall D 74 D6
Schwabmünchen D 71 A11
Schwabstedt D 82 B6
Schwaförden D 17 C11
Schwaigern D 27 B11
Schwalbach D 21 D7
Schwalmstadt-Treysa D 21 C12
Schwalmstadt-Ziegenhain D 21 C12
Schwanberg A 73 C11
Schwanden CH 71 C8
Schwandorf D 75 D11
Schwanebeck D 79 C9
Schwanenstadt A 76 F5
Schwanewede D 17 B11
Schwangau D 71 B11
Schwanstetten D 75 D9
Schwarme D 17 C12
Schwarmstedt D 82 E7
Schwarz D 83 D13
Schwarza D 79 B8
Schwarzach D 79 E9
Schwarzau am Steinfeld A 148 A5
Schwarzenau A 77 E8
Schwarzenbach A 149 A6
Schwarzenbach am Wald D 75 B10
Schwarzenbek D 83 C8
Schwarzenberg D 79 E11
Schwarzenborn D 78 E5
Schwarzenfeld D 75 D11
Schwarzheide D 80 D5
Schwaz A 72 B4
Schwedeneck D 83 B8
Schwedt an der Oder D 84 D6
Schwegenheim D 187 C5
Schwei (Stadland) D 17 B10
Schweiburg D 17 B10
Schweich D 21 E7
Schweigen-Rechtenbach D 27 B8
Schweighouse-sur-Moder F 186 D4
Schweinfurt D 75 B7
Schweinitz D 80 C4
Schweinrich D 83 D13
Schwelm D 17 F8
Schwendau D 72 B4
Schwendi D 71 A9
Schwenningen D 27 D10
Schwepnitz D 80 D5
Schwerin D 83 C10
Schweringen D 17 C12
Schwerte D 17 F9
Schwichtenberg D 84 C5
Schwieberdingen D 27 C11
Schwiesau D 79 A9
Schwindegg D 75 F11
Schwinkendorf D 83 C13
Schwoich A 72 A5
Schwyz CH 71 C7
Sciacca I 58 D3
Sciara I 58 D4
Scicli I 59 F6
Scigliano I 61 E6
Scilla I 59 C8

Ścinawa PL 81 D10
Scionzier F 31 C10
Scoarţa RO 160 C2
Scobinţi RO 153 C9
Scoglitti I 58 F5
Scolaticci I 59 C6
Scole GB 15 C11
Sconser GB 2 L4
Scopello I 68 B5
Scoppito I 62 C4
Scorbé-Clairvaux F 29 B6
Scordia I 59 E6
Scornicești RO 160 D5
Scorrano I 61 C10
Scorţaru Nou E 161 C11
Scorţeni MD 154 C3
Scorţeni RO 153 D9
Scorţeni RO 161 C7
Scortoasa RO 161 C9
Scorton GB 11 C8
Scorzè I 66 A5
Scotch Corner GB 11 C8
Scotch Corner IRL 7 D9
Scotshouse IRL 7 D7
Scourie GB 2 J6
Scousburgh GB 3 F14
Scrabster GB 3 H9
Screeb IRL 6 F3
Screggan IRL 7 F7
Scremerston GB 5 D13
Scribbagh IRL 6 D6
Scrioaştea RO 160 E5
Scriob IRL 6 F3
Sculeni MD 153 C11
Scundu RO 160 D4
Scunthorpe GB 11 D10
Scurcola Marsicana I 62 C4
Scurtu Mare RO 160 E6
Scutelnici RO 161 D9
Seaca RO 160 C5
Seaca RO 160 F6
Seaca de Pădure RO 160 E3
Seaford GB 15 F9
Seaham GB 5 F14
Seahouses GB 5 D13
Seamer GB 11 C11
Seapatrick GB 7 D10
Seara P 38 E2
Seascale GB 10 C5
Seaton GB 13 D8
Seaton GB 13 B8
Seaton Delaval GB 5 E13
Seaton Sluice GB 5 E14
Seaview GB 13 D12
Sebal P 44 D3
Sébazac-Concourès F 34 B4
Sebbersund DK 86 B5
Sebecleby SK 147 E9
Sebedražie SK 147 D7
Sebeș RO 152 F3
Sebersdorf A 148 B5
Sebezh RUS 133 D4
Sebiş RO 151 E9
Sebnitz D 80 E6
Seč CZ 77 C9
Sečanj SRB 159 C6
Seča Reka SRB 158 E4
Secãria RO 161 C7
Secaş RO 151 F9
Sece LV 135 C10
Secemin PL 143 E8
Seckach D 27 B11
Seckau A 73 B10
Seclin F 19 C7
Secondigny F 28 B5
Sečovce SK 145 F4
Sečovská Polianka SK 145 F4
Secu RO 160 E2
Secueni RO 152 E5
Secuieni RO 153 D9
Secuieni RO 153 D10
Secusigiu RO 151 E6
Seda LT 134 D4
Seda LV 131 F11
Sedan F 19 E10
Sedano E 40 C4
Seddülbahir TR 171 D10
Seden DK 86 E6
Sedere LV 135 E12
Séderon F 35 B10
Sedgefield GB 5 F14
Sedico I 72 D5
Sedilo I 64 C2
Sedini I 64 B2
Sedlarica HR 149 E8
Sedlčany CZ 77 C6
Sedlec Prčice CZ 77 C7
Sedlice CZ 76 D5
Sedlice SK 145 F3
Sedliská SK 145 F4
Sedlnice CZ 146 B6
Sedrina I 69 B8
Šeduva LT 134 E7
Sędziejowice PL 143 D7
Sędzin PL 138 E6
Sędziszów PL 143 E9
Sędziszów Małopolski PL 143 F12
See A 71 C10
See A 73 B7
Seeach D 79 D8
Seebach D 187 D5
Seebergen D 79 E8
Seeboden A 73 C8
Seebruck D 72 A5
Seeburg D 79 C7
Seedorf D 83 C9
Seefeld D 75 F9
Seefeld D 80 A5
Seefeld (Stadland) D 17 B10
Seefeld in Tirol A 72 B3
Seeg D 71 B11
Seehausen D 79 B9
Seehausen D 84 D5
Seehausen (Altmark) D 83 E11
Seeheim-Jugenheim D 21 E11
Seekirchen am Wallersee A 73 A7
Seelow D 80 A6
Seelze D 78 B6
Seend GB 13 C10
Seeon D 72 A5
Sées F 23 C12
Seesen D 79 C7
Seeshaupt D 72 A3
Seethal A 73 B8
Seevetal D 83 D8
Seewalchen A 148 A4
Seewiesen A 148 A4
Séez F 31 D10
Seferihisar TR 177 C8
Sefkerin SRB 158 C6

Sefrivatn N 105 A14
Seftigen CH 31 B12
Segalstad N 101 D12
Şegarcea RO 160 E3
Segarcea-Vale RO 160 F5
Segeletz D 83 E13
Segersäng S 93 A11
Segersta S 103 D11
Segerstad S 89 C11
Segesd H 149 D8
Seggiano I 65 B5
Séglien F 22 D5
Seglinge FIN 99 B15
Seglingsberg S 98 C6
Seglodden N 114 C9
Seglvik N 112 C7
Segmon S 97 D9
Segni I 62 D4
Segonzac F 28 D5
Segorbe E 48 E4
Segovia E 46 C4
Segré F 23 E10
Ségrie F 23 D12
Ségur F 34 B4
Segura P 45 E7
Segura de la Sierra E 55 C7
Segura de León E 51 C6
Segura de los Baños E 42 F2
Segurilla E 46 D3
Sehlde D 79 B7
Sehma D 76 A3
Sehnde D 79 B6
Seia P 44 D5
Şeica Mare RO 152 E4
Şeica Mică RO 152 E3
Seiches-sur-le-Loir F 23 E11
Seiersberg A 148 B4
Seierstad N 105 B10
Seifhennersdorf D 81 E7
Seignelay F 25 E10
Seignelégier CH 27 F6
Seilhac F 29 E9
Seillans F 36 D5
Seilles B 183 E6
Seimeni RO 155 E2
Seinäjoki FIN 122 E9
Seini RO 151 B11
Seinsheim D 75 C7
Seipäjärvi FIN 117 D16
Seirijai LT 137 E8
Seissan F 33 D7
Seitajärvi FIN 115 C3
Şeitin RO 150 E6
Seix F 33 E8
Seixal P 50 B1
Sejerby DK 87 D8
Sejerslev DK 86 B3
Sejet DK 86 D5
Sejny PL 136 E7
Sekkemo N 112 D8
Sękowa PL 145 D3
Sękowo PL 81 A10
Sel S 107 E10
Sel S 107 E13
Seła HR 149 E6
Selånger S 103 B13
Selanovtsi BG 160 F3
Selänpää FIN 128 C6
Selargius I 64 E3
Şelaru RO 160 E6
Selattyn GB 10 F5
Selaya E 40 B4
Selb D 75 B11
Selbekken N 104 E7
Selbitz D 75 B10
Selbu N 105 E10
Selbustrand N 105 E9
Selby GB 11 D9
Selcë AL 163 D8
Selce HR 67 B10
Selce SK 147 D8
Selci Đakovački HR 149 F10
Selçuk TR 177 D10
Selde DK 86 B4
Selegas I 64 D3
Šelenice AL 168 C2
Selent D 83 B8
Selero GR 171 B7
Sélestat F 27 D7
Selet S 118 C7
Selet S 122 B3
Seleuş RO 151 E8
Seleuş RO 151 C6
Selevac SRB 159 E6
Seleznevo RUS 129 D10
Selfjord N 110 D5
Šelji LV 131 F10
Selice SK 146 E5
Seligenstadt D 187 A6
Şelimbăr RO 152 F4
Şelimiye TR 177 E10
Selimpaşa TR 173 B9
Selimşahlar TR 177 B9
Selishtë AL 168 A3
Selishte BG 165 E7
Selişte SRB 159 F9
Selitë AL 168 C2
Selja S 102 D7
Selje N 100 B2
Seljeli N 108 D6
Seljelynes N 111 B17
Seljenes N 113 B15
Seljord N 95 D9
Selkälä S 116 E8
Selkälä FIN 115 E6
Selkirk GB 5 D11
Selkopp N 113 B14
Selkoskylä FIN 121 D13
Sella E 56 D4
Sellano I 62 B3
Sellasia GR 174 E5
Selles-St-Denis F 24 F6
Selles-sur-Cher F 24 F6
Sellia GR 178 E7
Sellia Marina I 59 B10
Sellières F 31 B8
Sellin, Ostseebad D 84 B5
Sellindge GB 15 E10
Selling DK 86 C6
Sellingen N 17 C8
Sellrain A 72 B3
Sellye H 149 E9
Selm D 17 E8
Selmes P 50 C4
Selmsdorf D 83 C9
Selnes N 104 D7
Selnes N 111 B17
Selnes N 111 C13
Selo DII 137 D10
Selommes F 24 E5
Selongey F 26 E3
Selonnet F 36 C4

Selow D 83 C11
Seløy N 108 D3
Selsey GB 15 F7
Selsingen D 17 B12
Selsjön S 107 E12
Selsøyvika N 108 C4
Selters (Westerwald) D 21 C9
Seltjärn S 107 D13
Seltz F 27 C9
Selva E 57 B10
Selva I 61 B8
Selva N 104 D7
Selva dei Molini I 72 C4
Selva di Progno I 69 B11
Selva di Val Gardena I 72 C4
Selvær N 108 C3
Selvåg N 97 D9
Selvino I 69 B8
Selvazzano Dentro I 66 B4
Selyatyn UA 152 B6
Selzthal A 73 A9
Sem N 95 D12
Seman AL 168 C1
Sembadel F 30 E4
Sembrancher CH 31 C11
Sēme LV 134 B6
Séméac F 33 D6
Sémelay F 30 B4
Semeliškės LT 137 D10
Semeljci HR 149 F11
Semeni MD 153 C11
Semenivka UA 154 E6
Semerovo SK 146 E6
Semič SLO 73 E11
Semide P 44 D4
Semily CZ 81 E8
Seminara I 59 C8
Semizovac BIH 157 E9
Semlac RO 151 E6
Semlow D 83 B13
Semmenstedt D 79 B8
Semoutiers-Montsaon F 26 D3
Sempach CH 27 F9
Semproniano I 65 B5
Semriach A 148 B5
Šemša SK 145 F3
Šemševo MK 164 E3
Semur-en-Auxois F 25 E11
Semur-en-Brionnais F 30 C5
Semussac F 28 D4
Sena E 42 D3
Seña SK 145 F3
Senales I 71 D11
Senarpont F 18 E4
Sénas F 35 C9
Sencelles E 57 B10
Senčur SLO 73 D9
Send GB 15 E7
Senden D 75 F7
Sendenhorst D 17 E9
Sendim P 38 F7
Sendim P 39 F7
Şendreni RO 155 C1
Şendriceni RO 153 B8
Senec SK 146 E4
Seneffe B 19 C9
Seneghe I 64 C2
Senes E 55 E8
Senez F 36 D4
Senftenberg A 77 E9
Senftenberg D 80 C6
Sengouagnet F 33 E7
Senhora do Rosário P 45 F6
Senica SK 146 D4
Senice na Hané CZ 77 C12
Senigallia I 67 E7
Senis I 64 D2
Senise I 60 C6
Senj HR 67 C10
Senje SRB 159 F7
Senjehesten N 111 B12
Senjehopen N 111 B13
Senjski Rudnik SRB 159 F8
Sen'kava BY 133 D3
Šenkvice SK 146 E4
Senlis F 25 B8
Sennan S 87 B11
Sennariolo I 64 C2
Sennecey-le-Grand F 30 B6
Sennels DK 86 B3
Sennen GB 12 E3
Sennik BG 165 D11
Sennori I 64 B2
Sennwald CH 71 C8
Sennybridge GB 13 B7
Senohrad SK 147 E8
Senokos BG 167 B10
Senonches F 24 C5
Senones F 27 D6
Senorbì I 64 D3
Senouillac F 33 C9
Senovo BG 161 F9
Senožeče SLO 73 E9
Sens F 25 D9
Sens-de-Bretagne F 23 D8
Senta SRB 150 F5
Sentein F 33 E7
Senterada E 33 F7
Šentilj SLO 148 C5
Šentjernej SLO 148 E4
Šentjur pri Celju SLO 148 D4
Senuc F 19 F11
Seon CH 27 F9
Šepak BIH 157 C10
Sepekov CZ 77 D6
Sepino I 60 A3
Sępólno Krajeńskie PL 85 D13
Sępólno Wielkie PL 85 C11
Seppois-le-Bas F 27 E7
Şepreuş RO 151 D8
Septèmes-les-Vallons F 35 D9
Septemvri BG 165 E9
Septemvriytsi BG 160 F2
Septeuil F 24 C6
Septfonds F 33 B9
Septmoncel F 31 C8
Sepulcro-Hilario E 45 C8
Sepúlveda E 40 F4
Sequals I 73 D6
Sequeros E 45 D8
Seraincourt F 19 E9
Seraing B 19 C12
Séranon F 36 D5
Seravezza I 66 E1
Şerbăneşti RO 160 E5
Şerbettar TR 173 B6
Šerboc KS 163 D10
Şercaia RO 152 F6
Serdiana I 64 E3
Sereď SK 146 E5
Seredka RUS 132 E3
Seredyne UA 145 F6

Seredžius LT 137 C7
Seregélyes H 149 B11
Seregno I 69 B7
Séreilhac F 29 D8
Šērene LV 135 C10
Sérent F 22 E6
Serényfalva H 145 G1
Sergen TR 167 F9
Sergines F 25 D9
Sergnano I 69 C8
Serhat TR 172 E6
Serhiyivka UA 154 B6
Seriate I 69 B8
Sérifontaine F 18 F4
Serifos GR 175 E10
Sérignan F 34 D5
Sérignan-du-Comtat F 35 B8
Serina I 69 B8
Serino I 60 B3
Serinyà E 43 C9
Sermano F 37 G10
Sermenin MK 169 B7
Sermide I 66 C3
Sermoneta I 62 D3
Sermoyer F 31 B6
Serno D 79 C11
Serock PL 138 D5
Serock PL 139 E11
Serón E 55 E8
Serón de Nájima E 41 F7
Serooskerke NL 182 B3
Seròs E 42 E4
Serpa P 50 D4
Serpins P 44 D4
Serpneve UA 154 E5
Serqueux F 26 E4
Serquigny F 24 B4
Serra E 48 E4
Serracapriola I 63 D8
Serrada E 39 E10
Serra de'Conti I 67 E7
Serra-di-Ferro F 37 H9
Serradilla E 45 E8
Serradilla del Arroyo E 45 C8
Serra-di-Scopamène F 37 H10
Serramanna I 64 E2
Serramazzoni I 66 D2
Serranillos E 46 D3
Serra Riccò I 37 B9
Serra San Bruno I 59 B9
Serrastretta I 59 A10
Serravalle RSM 66 E5
Serravalle di Chienti I 62 A3
Serravalle Scrivia I 37 B9
Serre I 60 B4
Serrejón E 45 E9
Serrenti I 64 E2
Serres F 35 B10
Serres GR 169 B10
Serres-Castet F 32 D5
Serri I 64 D3
Serriera F 37 G9
Serrières-de-Briord F 31 D7
Serrières F 30 E6
Serrig D 21 E7
Serritslev DK 90 E6
Serrungarina I 67 E6
Sers F 29 D6
Sersale I 59 A10
Sertã P 44 E4
Sertolovo RUS 129 E13
Servance F 26 E6
Serverette F 30 F3
Servia GR 169 D7
Servian F 34 D5
Serviana GR 168 E4
Servigliano I 62 A4
Servon-sur-Vilaine F 23 D9
Šervoż I 69 C11
Sery F 19 E9
Serzedo P 44 B3
Sesa E 42 D3
Sesava LV 134 D7
Seseña E 46 D5
Seskarö S 119 C11
Seskinore GB 7 C8
Sesma E 32 F1
Sessa Aurunca I 60 A1
Sessa Cilento I 60 C4
Ses Salines E 57 C11
Sesta Godano I 69 E8
Šestanovac HR 157 F6
S'Estanyol de Migjorn E 57 C10
Sestao E 40 B6
Sestino I 66 E5
Sesto I 72 C5
Sesto al Reghena I 73 D6
Sesto Calende I 68 B6
Sesto Campano I 60 A2
Sesto Fiorentino I 66 E3
Šeštokai LT 137 E7
Sestola I 66 D2
Sesto San Giovanni I 69 B7
Sestriere I 31 F10
Sestri Levante I 37 C10
Sestrimo BG 165 E8
Sestroretsk RUS 129 E12
Sestu I 64 E3
Šešuoliai LT 135 F9
Sesvete HR 148 E6
Šeta LT 135 F8
Sète F 35 D6
Setenil E 51 F9
Setermoen N 111 C15
Seternes N 100 A6
Setiles E 47 C9
Šetivoho BIH 158 F3
Šetonje SRB 159 E7
Setter GB 3 E14
Settimo San Pietro I 64 E3
Settimo Torinese I 68 C4
Settimo Vittone I 68 B4
Settle GB 11 C7
Setúbal P 50 B2
Seubersdorf in der Oberpfalz D 75 D10
Seui I 64 D3
Seuil-d'Argonne F 26 C3
Seulo I 64 D3
Seurre F 21 A7
Seva E 43 D8
Sevar BG 161 F9
Sevaster AL 168 C2
Sevel DK 86 C3

Sevenoaks GB 15 E9
Sevenum NL 16 F6
Sévérac-le-Château F 34 B5
Sever do Vouga P 44 C4
Severin HR 149 E7
Severinovca MD 154 A3
Severnyak BG 155 F1
Seveso I 69 B7
Ševětín CZ 77 D7
Sevettijärvi FIN 114 E5
Sevid HR 156 E5
Sévignacq F 32 D5
Sevilla E 51 E8
Sevilla la Nueva E 46 D4
Sevilleja de la Jara E 46 E3
Sevnica SLO 148 D4
Sevojno SRB 158 F4
Sévrier F 31 D9
Sexdrega S 91 D13
Seyches F 33 A6
Seyda D 79 C12
Seymen TR 173 B9
Seymen TR 173 B9
Seyne F 36 C4
Seynes F 35 B7
Seynod F 31 D9
Seyrek TR 177 B8
Seyssel F 31 D8
Seysses F 33 C8
Sežana SLO 73 E8
Sézanne F 25 C10
Sezemice CZ 77 B9
Sezimovo Ústí CZ 77 D7
Sezze I 62 E4
Sfaka GR 179 E10
Sfântu Gheorghe RO 153 F7
Sfântu Gheorghe RO 161 D9
Sfendami GR 169 D8
Sfinteşti RO 160 E6
Sgiogarstaigh GB 2 J4
's-Gravendeel NL 16 E3
's-Gravenhage NL 16 D2
's-Gravenmoer NL 182 B5
's-Gravenpolder NL 16 F1
's-Gravenvoeren B 183 D7
's-Gravenzande NL 16 E2
Sgurgola I 62 D4
Shabla BG 155 F3
Shaftesbury GB 13 C10
Shalfleet GB 13 D12
Shalwy IRL 6 C5
Shanacrane IRL 8 E4
Shanagolden IRL 8 C4
Shanavogh IRL 8 C4
Shankill IRL 7 F10
Shanklin GB 13 D12
Shanlaragh IRL 8 E4
Shantonagh IRL 7 D9
Shanvus IRL 6 D6
Shap GB 10 B6
Sharashova BY 141 E10
Sharavogue IRL 7 F7
Sharkawshchyna BY 133 F2
Sharkovo BG 167 E7
Shatilava BY 133 F6
Shats'k UA 141 H9
Shaverki RUS 125 D17
Shawbost GB 2 J3
Shchyrets' UA 145 D8
's-Heerenberg NL 16 E6
's-Heerenhoek NL 182 C3
Sheerness GB 15 E10
Sheffield GB 11 E9
Shefford GB 15 D8
Shelekhove UA 154 B6
Shëmri AL 163 E9
Shëngjergj AL 168 B3
Shëngjin AL 163 F8
Shepit UA 152 B6
Shepshed GB 11 F9
Shepton Mallet GB 13 C9
Sherborne GB 13 D10
Sherborne St John GB 13 C12
Sherburn in Elmet GB 11 D9
Shercock IRL 7 E9
Sheringham GB 15 B11
Sherston GB 13 B10
's-Hertogenbosch NL 16 E4
Shetaj AL 168 A2
Shevchenkove UA 155 B4
Shieldaig GB 2 K5
Shifnal GB 11 F7
Shijak AL 168 B2
Shildon GB 5 F13
Shillelagh IRL 9 C9
Shinfield GB 15 E7
Shinness Lodge GB 2 J8
Shinrone IRL 7 G7
Shipka BG 166 D4
Shipkovo BG 165 D10
Shipley GB 11 D8
Shipston on Stour GB 13 A11
Shipton GB 10 F6
Shiroka Lŭka BG 165 F10
Shirokë AL 163 E7
Shivachevo BG 166 D6
Shkodër AL 163 E8
Shkorpilovtsi BG 167 D9
Shlissel'burg RUS 129 F15
Shmoylovo RUS 132 F4
Sho BY 133 F4
Shoreham-by-Sea GB 15 F8
Shotts GB 5 D9
Shrewsbury GB 10 F6
Shrewton GB 13 C11
Shrivenham GB 13 B11
Shrule IRL 6 E4
Shtëpaj AL 168 C3
Shtërmen AL 168 C3
Shtërpcë KS 164 E3
Shtime KS 164 E3
Shtiqën AL 163 E9
Shtit BG 166 F6
Shtrŭklevo BG 161 F8
Shumen BG 167 C7
Shumilina BY 133 F7
Shushicë AL 168 B3
Shymkove UA 145 G7
Shyroke UA 154 C4
Shyryayeve UA 154 C6
Siamanna I 64 D2
Sianów PL 85 B10
Siatista GR 169 D6
Šiaulėnai LT 134 E6
Šiauliai LT 134 E6
Sibari I 61 D6
Sibbhult S 88 C6
Sibbo FIN 127 E13
Šibenik HR 156 E4

Sibinj HR 157 B8
Sible Hedingham GB 15 D10
Sibnica SRB 158 E5
Sibo S 103 D12
Sibot RO 151 F11
Sibsey GB 11 E12
Sic RO 152 D3
Síćevo SRB 164 C5
Sichevița RO 159 D8
Sicienko PL 138 D4
Siciny PL 81 C11
Sickte D 79 B8
Sicula RO 151 E8
Şiculeni RO 153 E7
Siculiana I 58 E3
Sidari GR 168 E2
Sidbury GB 13 D8
Sidcup GB 15 E9
Siddeburen NL 17 B7
Siddi I 64 D2
Sideby FIN 122 F6
Sidensjö S 107 E14
Siderno I 59 C9
Sidgunda LV 135 B10
Sidirokastro GR 169 B9
Sidirokastro GR 174 E4
Sidironero GR 171 B6
Sidmouth GB 13 D8
Sidrabiņi LV 135 C11
Sidsjö S 103 A9
Sidskogen S 103 C10
Siebe N 112 F11
Siebengewald NL 183 B8
Siebenlehn D 80 D4
Siecieborzyce PL 81 C9
Sieciechów PL 141 G5
Siedlanka PL 143 F12
Siedlce PL 141 F6
Siedlec PL 81 B10
Siedlice PL 85 C8
Siedliska PL 144 D7
Siedlisko PL 81 C9
Siedlisko PL 85 E10
Siedliszcze PL 141 H8
Siedliszcze PL 144 A8
Siegburg D 21 C8
Siegen D 21 C10
Siegenburg D 75 E10
Sieggraben A 149 A6
Sieghartskirchen A 77 F10
Siegsdorf D 73 A6
Siekasjärvi S 117 E10
Siekkinen FIN 121 C11
Sielec PL 144 A8
Sielnica SK 147 D8
Siemianowice Śląskie PL 143 F7
Siemianówka PL 141 E9
Siemiatycze PL 141 E7
Siemień PL 141 G7
Siemkowice PL 143 D6
Siemyśl PL 85 B9
Siena I 66 F3
Sieniawa PL 144 C6
Sieniec PL 142 D6
Siennica PL 141 F5
Siennica Różana PL 144 A7
Sienno PL 143 D11
Sieppijärvi FIN 117 D11
Siepraw PL 147 B9
Sieradz PL 142 C6
Sieradza PL 143 F10
Sieraków PL 81 A10
Sieraków PL 143 F7
Sierakówek PL 139 F7
Sierakowice PL 138 B5
Sierck-les-Bains F 20 F6
Sierentz F 27 E7
Sierksdorf D 83 B9
Sierningzwenzy PL 85 C10
Sierpc PL 139 E8
Sierczyno PL 85 C10
Sieroszewice PL 142 C4
Sierosław PL 81 A10
Sierpc PL 139 E8
Sierra de Fuentes E 45 F8
Sierra de Luna E 41 D10
Sierra de Yeguas E 53 B7
Sierra Engarcerán E 48 D5
Sierre CH 31 C12
Sierro E 55 E8
Siershahn D 185 D8
Siersleben D 79 C10
Siete Iglesias de Trabancos E 39 F9
Sietow D 83 D13
Şieu RO 152 C5
Şieu-Măgheruş RO 152 C4
Şieu-Odorhei RO 152 C4
Şieuţ RO 152 D5
Sieversdorf D 83 E13
Sieverstedt D 82 A6
Sievi FIN 123 C13
Sievin asema eli Korhoskylä FIN 123 C12
Siewierz PL 143 F7
Sifferbo S 97 A13
Sifjord N 111 B13
Sig DK 86 D3
Sigean F 34 D4
Sigerfjord N 111 C10
Siggelkow D 83 D11
Siggerud N 95 C13
Sighetu Marmaţiei RO 145 H8
Sighişoara RO 152 E5
Sigillo I 67 E6
Sigmaringen D 27 D11
Sigmaringendorf D 27 D11
Sigmen BG 167 D7
Sigmundsherberg A 77 E9
Signa I 66 E3
Signau CH 70 D5
Signes F 35 D10
Signy-l'Abbaye F 19 E9
Signy-le-Petit F 19 E9
Sigogne F 28 D5
Sigoulès F 29 F6
Sigri GR 177 A6
Sigtuna S 99 C9
Sigüeiro E 38 C3
Sigüenza E 47 B7
Sigües E 32 E3
Sigulda LV 135 B10
Sihlea RO 161 C9
Sihelné SK 147 C8
Sihtuuna FIN 119 B13
Sihva EST 131 E12
Siikainen FIN 126 B6
Siikajoki FIN 119 E13
Siika-Kämä FIN 119 B16

Siikakoski FIN 128 B8
Siilinjarvi FIN 124 D9
Siimusti EST 131 D12
Siironen FIN 119 F11
Siivikko FIN 121 D10
Sijarinska Banja SRB 164 D3
Sijekovac BIH 157 B8
Sijsele B 182 C2
Sikås S 106 D8
Sikeå S 118 F5
Sikfors S 118 D4
Sikirevci HR 157 B9
Siklós H 149 E10
Siknäs S 118 C9
Sikole SRB 159 E9
Sikórz PL 139 E8
Sikovuono FIN 113 F18
Sïkrags LV 130 F4
Siksele S 107 B16
Siksjö S 107 C13
Siksjön S 102 C8
Siksjönäs S 107 B10
Sikšņi LV 134 D2
Sil S 107 D10
Silajāni LV 133 D1
Šilalė LT 134 F4
Silandro I 71 D11
Silanus I 64 C2
Silavēveri LV 135 D10
Šilavotas LT 137 D8
Silba HR 67 D10
Silbaš SRB 158 C3
Silene LV 135 E13
Silenen CH 71 D7
Silenrieux B 19 D9
Siles E 55 C7
Silfiac F 22 D5
Siligo I 64 B2
Šilindia RO 151 E8
Siliqua I 64 E2
Siliştea RO 155 C1
Siliştea RO 155 D3
Siliştea RO 160 E6
Siliştea Crucii RO 160 E2
Siliştea Nouă RO 160 E5
Silistra BG 161 E10
Silivaşu de Câmpie RO 152 D4
Silivri TR 173 B9
Siljan N 95 D11
Siljansnäs S 102 E8
Siljeåsen S 106 C9
Silkeborg DK 86 C5
Silla E 48 F4
Sillamäe EST 132 C2
Sillano I 66 D1
Sillanpää FIN 123 D11
Sillankylä FIN 128 E6
Sillans-la-Cascade F 36 D4
Sillebotten S 96 D7
Sillé-le-Guillaume F 23 D11
Sillerö S 97 A10
Sillian A 73 C6
Silloth GB 5 F10
Sillre S 103 A12
Silnowo PL 85 C10
Silo HR 67 B10
Sils CH 71 E9
Sils E 43 D9
Silsjönäs S 107 D10
Siltaharju FIN 115 C1
Siltakylä FIN 128 E6
Silte S 93 E12
Sïlukalns LV 133 C13
Šilutė LT 134 F2
Šiluva LT 134 E6
Silva LV 135 B11
Silvalen N 108 D3
Silvaplana CH 71 E9
Silvares P 44 D5
Silveiras P 50 B3
Silverdalen S 92 D7
Silvermines IRL 8 C6
Silverstone GB 13 A12
Silverton GB 13 D8
Silvi I 62 B6
Silz A 71 C11

Sindal DK 90 E7
Sindel BG 167 C9
Sindelfingen D 27 C10
Sindi EST 131 E9
Sindia I 64 C2
Sindos GR 169 C8
Sinekçi TR 173 D7
Sinekli TR 173 B9
Sinemorets BG 167 E9
Sines P 50 D2
Sineşti RO 153 C10
Sineşti RO 160 D3
Sineşti RO 161 D8
Sinetänsalmi FIN 117 E14
Sinettä FIN 117 E14
Sineu E 57 B11
Singen (Hohentwiel) D 27 E10
Sïngera MD 154 D3
Sïngerei MD 153 B12
Singhofen D 21 D9
Singsjön S 106 E8
Singureni RO 161 E7
Singusdal N 90 A4
Sinimäe EST 132 C2
Siniscola I 64 B4
Sinj HR 157 E6
Sinlabajos E 46 B3
Sin-le-Noble F 19 D7
Sinn D 21 C10
Sinnai I 64 E3
Sinnes N 94 E5
Sinoie RO 155 D3
Sinole LV 135 B12
Sinopoli I 59 C8
Sins CH 27 F9
Sinsheim D 21 F11
Sint Annaland NL 16 E2
Sint Annaparochie NL 16 B5
Sint Anthonis NL 16 E5
Sintautai LT 136 D7
Šintava SK 146 E5
Sintea Mare RO 151 D8
Sintereag RO 152 C4
Sinteu RO 151 C10
Sint-Genesius-Rode B 182 D4
Sint-Gillis-Waas B 16 F2
Sint-Huibrechts-Lille B 183 C6
Sint Jansteen NL 182 C4
Sint-Katelijne-Waver B 19 B10
Sint-Laureins B 182 C3
Sint-Lenaarts B 182 C5
Sint Maartensdijk NL 16 E2
Sint-Margriete B 182 C3
Sint-Maria-Lierde B 19 C8
Sint-Martens-Latem B 19 B8
Sint Michielsgestel NL 183 B6
Sint Nicolaasga NL 16 C5
Sint-Niklaas B 19 B9
Sint Odilienberg NL 183 C8
Sint-Pauwels B 182 C4
Sint Philipsland NL 16 E2
Sint-Pieters-Leeuw B 19 C9
Sintra P 50 B1
Sint-Truiden B 19 C11
Sint Willebrord NL 16 E3
Sinzheim D 27 C9
Sinzig D 21 C8
Sióagárd H 149 C10
Siófok H 149 C10
Sion CH 31 C12
Sion RO 161 C8
Sion Mills GB 4 F2
Šipca MD 154 C3
Šipinen FIN 121 F12
Šipkovica MK 163 E10
Sipola FIN 119 F15
Şipote RO 153 C10
Şipotina MD 154 C2
Šipovo BIH 157 D7
Sipplingen D 27 E11
Sippola FIN 128 D7
Sira N 94 F5
Sirač HR 149 E8
Siracusa I 59 C7
Siran F 29 F10
Sirbmá N 113 C19
Siret RO 153 B8
Siretel RO 153 C9
Sirevåg N 94 F3
Sirgala EST 132 C2
Şiria RO 151 E8
Širig SRB 158 C4
Sirineasa RO 160 D4
Širitovci HR 156 E5
Siriu RO 161 C9
Sirkka FIN 117 C13
Sirkkakoski FIN 117 E12
Sirkkamäki FIN 123 E16
Sirmione I 66 B2
Şirna RO 161 D7
Sirnach CH 27 F11
Sirniö FIN 121 C12
Sirnitz A 73 C9
Sirod F 31 B8
Sirogojno SRB 158 F4
Sirok H 145 H1
Široki Brijeg BIH 157 F8
Sirolo I 67 E8
Siròr I 72 D4
Sirotsina BY 133 F5
Siruela E 54 B2
Sirutiškis LT 135 F8
Širvintos LT 137 C10
Sisak HR 149 F6
Sisante E 47 F8
Sişcani MD 154 D2
Sisco F 37 F10
Şişeşti RO 152 B3
Şişeşti RO 159 D10
Şişli TR 173 B10
Sissa I 66 C1
Sissach CH 27 F8
Sisses GR 178 E8
Sissonne F 19 E8
Sistarovăţ RO 151 F8
Sisteron F 35 B10
Sistranda N 104 D5
Sistrans A 72 B3
Sita Buzăului RO 161 B8
Sitaniec PL 144 B7
Siteia GR 179 E11
Sitges E 43 E7
Sitkówka-Nowiny PL 143 D10
Sitnica BIH 157 C7
Sitochori GR 169 C10
Sitovo BG 161 E10
Sitsyenyets BY 133 E6
Sittard NL 16 F5
Sittensen D 82 D7
Sittingbourne GB 15 E10
Sitzendorf an der Schmida A 77 E9

Sitzenroda D 80 D3
Siulaisiadar GB 2 J4
Siuntio FIN 127 E11
Siuro FIN 127 C9
Siurua FIN 119 D16
Siurunmaa FIN 115 D1
Sivac SRB 158 B3
Sivakka FIN 125 C13
Sivakkajoki FIN 119 B13
Sivakkavaara FIN 125 E11
Siverić HR 156 E5
Siverskiy RUS 132 C7
Sivertgården N 108 E7
Sivry B 19 D9
Sivry-sur-Meuse F 19 F11
Sixarby S 99 B9
Six-Fours-les-Plages F 35 D10
Sixmilebridge IRL 8 C5
Sixmilecross GB 7 C8
Six Road Ends GB 4 F5
Sixt-Fer-à-Cheval F 31 C10
Sizun F 22 D3
Sjemeć BIH 158 F3
Sjenica SRB 163 C9
Sjetlina BIH 157 E10
Sjoa N 101 C11
Sjøåsen N 105 C10
Sjöbo S 87 D13
Sjöbotten S 118 E6
Sjöbränet S 107 C17
Sjøholt N 100 B5
Sjølund DK 86 E5
Sjömarken S 91 D12
Sjonbotn N 108 D6
Sjørring DK 86 B3
Sjørslev DK 86 C4
Sjørup DK 86 C4
Sjösa S 93 B10
Sjösäter S 99 B11
Sjötofta S 91 E13
Sjötorp S 91 B14
Sjoutnäset S 106 B7
Sjøvassbotn N 111 B17
Sjøvegan N 111 C14
Sjövik S 91 D11
Sjulsåsen S 106 C7
Sjulsmark S 118 C7
Sjunnen S 92 E6
Sjuntorp S 91 C11
Sjursvik N 111 B12
Skademark S 107 E16
Skælsør DK 87 E8
Skærbæk DK 86 E3
Skævinge DK 87 D10
Skaftung FIN 122 F6
Skagen DK 90 D8
Skagersvik S 91 B15
Skäggebyn S 91 A12
Skagshamn S 107 E16
Skaidi N 113 C13
Skaidiškės LT 137 D11
Skaill GB 3 H11
Skaista LV 133 E2
Skaistgiriai LT 135 E8
Skaistgirys LT 134 D6
Skaistkalne LV 135 D9
Skala GR 174 C2
Skala GR 175 B7
Skala GR 175 F6
Skala GR 177 E8
Skała PL 143 F8
Skala Eresou GR 177 A6
Skala Kallonis GR 177 A7
Skala Marion GR 171 C7
Skålan S 102 A7
Skaland N 111 B13
Skala Oropou GR 175 C8
Skálavík FO 2 B3
Skalbmierz PL 143 F9
Skåle N 105 C15
Skålevik N 90 C3
Skälgården S 103 A12
Skáli FO 2 A3
Skalica SK 146 D4
Skalice CZ 81 E7
Skalité SK 147 C7
Skalitsa BG 166 E6
Skallelv N 114 C8
Skällinge S 87 A10
Skallvik S 93 C9
Skalmodal S 108 F8
Skalmsjö S 107 D13
Skalná CZ 75 B11
Skålö S 97 A11
Skaloti GR 171 B6
Skals DK 86 B4
Skålsjön S 103 D10
Skalstugan S 105 D12
Skålsvik N 108 B7
Skålvallen S 103 C10
Skån S 103 B11
Skanderåsen S 102 A7
Skanderborg DK 86 C5
Skånes-Fagerhult S 87 C12
Skåne-Tranås S 88 D5
Skånevik N 94 C3
Skåningen N 112 C4
Skaņkalne LV 131 F10
Skänninge S 92 C6
Skanör med Falsterbo S 87 E11
Skansbacken S 97 B11
Skansen N 105 D9
Skansholm S 107 B10
Skansnäs S 107 A10
Skansnäs S 109 E13
Skansnäset S 106 C9
Skåpafors S 91 A11
Skąpe PL 81 B8
Skapiškis LT 135 E10
Skår N 94 D4
Skara S 91 C13
Skäran S 118 F6
Skarberget N 111 D11
Skärblacka S 92 B7
Skarda S 107 C15
Skardmodalen N 108 F7
Skardmunken N 111 A18
Skardstein N 111 B11
Skardsvåg N 113 A16
Skare N 94 C5
Skåre S 97 D9
Skärhamn S 91 D10
Skarkdalen S 102 A4
Skärkind S 92 C7
Skarnes N 96 B6
Skärplinge S 99 B9
Skarp Salling DK 86 B4
Skarrild DK 86 D3
Skärså S 103 D13
Skarsfjord N 112 D2
Skärsjövålen S 102 B5
Skarstad N 111 D11
Skärstad S 92 D4
Skarsvåg N 111 B15
Skarszewy PL 138 B5
Skårup DK 86 E7
Skarv N 112 C11
Skärvången S 105 D16
Skarvfjordhamn N 112 B11
Skarvsjöby S 107 B12
Skaryszew PL 141 H4
Skarżysko-Kamienna PL 141 H3
Skasenden N 96 B7
Skästra S 103 C11
Skatamark S 118 C7
Skatan S 103 B13
Skattkärr S 97 D10
Skattungbyn S 102 D8
Skatvik N 111 B14
Skaudvilė LT 134 F5
Skaugvoll N 108 C7
Skaulo S 116 D6
Šķaune LV 133 D3
Skavdal N 111 B10
Skave DK 86 C3
Skavnakk N 112 C7
Skawina PL 143 G8
Skebobruk S 99 C11
Skebokvarn S 93 A9
Skeda udde S 92 C7
Šķēde LV 134 C4
Skede S 92 E6
Skedevi S 92 B7
Skedsmokorset N 95 B14
Skee S 91 B9
Skegness GB 11 E12
Skegrie S 87 E12
Skei N 100 C4
Skei N 105 A11
Skela SRB 158 D5
Skelby DK 87 E9
Skelde DK 82 A7
Skelhøje DK 86 C4
Skellefteå S 118 E5
Skelleftehamn S 118 E6
Skelmersdale GB 10 D6
Skelton GB 11 B10
Šķeltova LV 133 D2
Skelund DK 86 B6
Skelwick GB 3 G11
Skėmiai LT 134 E7
Skenderaj KS 163 D10
Skender Vakuf BIH 157 D7
Skenfrith GB 13 B9
Skepasto GR 174 C5
Skępe PL 139 E7
Skepplanda S 91 D11
Skeppshamn S 103 B14
Skeppshult S 87 A12
Skeppsmalen S 107 E16
Skerries IRL 7 E10
Skhidnytsya UA 145 E7
Ski N 95 C13
Skiathos GR 175 A7
Skibbereen IRL 8 E4
Skibbild DK 86 C3
Skibby DK 87 D9
Šķibe LV 134 C6
Skibinge DK 87 E10
Skibotn N 111 B19
Skidal' BY 140 C10
Skiemonys LT 135 F10
Skien N 90 A6
Šķieneri LV 135 B13
Skierbieszów PL 144 B7
Skierniewice PL 141 G2
Skiippagurra N 114 C4
Šķilbēni LV 133 B3
Skillebotn N 108 F3
Skillefjordnes N 113 C11
Skillingaryd S 92 E4
Skillinge S 88 E6
Skillvassbakk N 111 D10
Skinias GR 178 E9
Skinnarud N 101 E12
Skinnskatteberg S 97 C14
Skipmannvik N 109 B9
Skipness GB 4 D6
Skipsea GB 11 D11
Skipton GB 11 D7
Skiptvet N 95 D14
Skirlaugh GB 11 D11
Skitenelv N 111 A17
Skiti GR 169 E8
Skivarp S 87 E13
Skive DK 86 B4
Skivjan KS 163 E9
Skivsjön S 107 C16
Skiwy Duże PL 141 F7
Skjærhalden N 91 A9
Skjåholmen N 113 B12
Skjånes N 113 B18
Skjånes N 113 B21
Skjåvika N 108 E6
Skjeberg N 91 A9
Skjeggedal N 90 B3
Skjelelv N 111 C13
Skjellbreid N 105 C14
Skjelman N 111 A17
Skjelnes N 111 A18
Skjelstad N 105 D10
Skjelvik N 108 B7
Skjern DK 86 D3
Skjern N 105 C9
Skjerstad N 108 B9
Skjervøy N 112 C6
Skjød DK 86 C5
Skjold N 111 B17
Skjoldastraumen N 94 D3
Skjolden N 100 D7
Skjombotn N 111 D13
Skjøtningberg N 113 A19
Sklithro GR 169 E8
Skobelevo BG 166 D4
Skoby S 99 B10
Skočivir MK 169 C6
Škocjan SLO 148 E4
Skoczów PL 147 B7
Skodborg DK 86 E4
Skodje N 100 A5
Skøelv N 111 B15
Škofja Loka SLO 73 D9
Škofljica SLO 73 E10
Skog S 103 D12
Skogaholm S 92 A6
Skoganvarri N 113 D15
Skoger N 95 C12
Skogfoss N 114 E7
Skoghall S 97 D9
Skogly N 114 E6
Skogmo N 105 B12
Skogn N 105 D10
Skogså S 118 C7
Skogsby S 89 B11
Skogsfjord N 112 C3
Skogshöjden S 91 C11
Skogstorp S 87 B10
Skogstorp S 98 D6
Skogstue N 112 D11
Skogum N 114 E6
Skoki PL 85 E12
Sköldinge S 93 A8
Skole UA 145 E8
Skollenborg N 95 C11
Sköllersta S 92 A6
Skoltenes N 110 C8
Skoltevatn N 114 E7
Skołyszyn PL 144 D3
Skomlin PL 142 D5
Skonseng N 108 D7
Skönvik S 103 E12
Skopelos GR 175 A8
Skopelos GR 177 A7
Skopi GR 179 E11
Skopje MK 164 F3
Skopos GR 169 C6
Skopos GR 171 B7
Skopun FO 2 B3
Skórcz PL 138 C6
Skorica SRB 159 F8
Skorild N 104 E6
Skorogoszcz PL 142 E4
Skoroszyce PL 142 E3
Skorovatn N 105 B14
Skorped S 107 E13
Skorpetorp S 89 A10
Skørping DK 86 B5
Skorstad N 105 B10
Skórzec PL 141 F6
Skoteini GR 174 D5
Skotfoss N 90 A6
Skotina GR 169 D8
Skotoussa GR 169 B9
Skotselv N 95 C11
Skotterud N 96 C7
Skottsund S 103 B13
Skoura GR 175 E5
Skourta GR 175 C8
Skoutari GR 169 B10
Skoutari GR 178 B4
Skoutaros GR 171 F10
Skovby DK 86 C5
Skövde S 91 C14
Skoved S 107 E14
Skovlund DK 86 D3
Skovsgård DK 86 A4
Skra GR 169 B7
Skräddrabo S 103 D10
Skradin HR 156 E4
Skråmestø N 100 E1
Skranstad N 110 E9
Skravena BG 165 D8
Skrea S 87 B11
Skreia N 101 E13
Skriaudžiai LT 137 D8
Skrinyano BG 165 E6
Skřipov CZ 146 B5
Skrīveri LV 135 C10
Skröven S 116 E7
Skrøytnes N 114 E7
Skrudaliena LV 135 E13
Skrunda LV 134 C4
Skruv S 89 B8
Skrwilno PL 139 D8
Skrzatusz PL 85 D11
Skrzyńsko PL 141 H3
Skrzyszów PL 143 G11
Skucani BIH 157 E6
Skudeneshavn N 94 D2
Skuhrov nad Bělou CZ 77 B10
Skujene LV 135 B10
Skujetnieki LV 133 C2
Skuķi LV 133 E3
Skuldelev DK 87 D10
Skule S 107 E14
Skulerud N 95 C15
Skulgammen N 111 A17
Skulsfjord N 111 A16
Skulsk PL 138 F5
Skulte LV 135 B8
Skulte LV 135 C7
Skultorp S 91 C14
Skultuna S 98 C6
Skuodas LT 134 D3
Skurträsk S 107 C16
Skurup S 87 E13
Skuteč CZ 77 C9
Skutskär S 103 E13
Skutvik N 110 D9
Skutvik N 111 B16
Skwierzyna PL 81 A9
Skýcov SK 146 D6
Skydra GR 169 C7
Skyllberg S 92 B6
Skylnäs S 103 A9
Skyros GR 175 B10
Skyttmon S 106 E9
Skyttorp S 99 B9
Slabodka BY 133 E2
Słaboszów PL 143 F9
Sládkovičovo SK 146 E5
Slagavallen S 102 B5
Slagelse DK 87 E8
Slagnäs S 109 E15
Slaidburn GB 10 D7
Slaka S 92 C7
Slampe LV 134 C6
Slane IRL 7 E9
Slanec SK 145 F3
Slangerup DK 87 D10
Slănic RO 161 C7
Slănic Moldova RO 153 E8
Slano HR 162 D4
Slantsy RUS 132 C3
Slaný CZ 76 B6
Slap BIH 158 F3
Slap MNE 163 D7
Slap SLO 73 D8
Šlapaberžė LT 135 F7
Šlapanice CZ 77 D11
Slåpträsk S 107 A15
Slate LV 135 D12
Slatina BIH 157 C7
Slatina BIH 157 C8
Slatina BIH 157 E8
Slatina BIH 157 E10
Slatina HR 149 E9
Slatina RO 153 C8
Slatina RO 160 E4
Slatina SRB 158 E4
Slatiňany CZ 77 C9
Slatina-Timiş RO 159 C9
Slatino MK 168 B4
Slatinski Drenovac HR 149 E9
Slătioara RO 160 C3
Slătioara RO 160 E4
Slato BIH 157 F9
Slättberg S 102 D8
Slättholmen N 110 D8
Slättmon S 103 A13
Slattum N 95 C13
Slava Cercheză RO 155 D3
Slava Rusă RO 155 D3
Slaveino BG 165 F10
Slavičín CZ 146 C5
Slavinja SRB 165 C6
Slavkov CZ 146 B5
Slavkovichi RUS 132 F5
Slavkov u Brna CZ 77 D11
Slavonice CZ 77 E8
Slavonski Brod HR 157 B9
Slavošovce SK 145 F1
Slavotin BG 165 B7
Slavovitsa BG 160 F4
Slavovitsa BG 165 E9
Slavsk RUS 136 C4
Slavs'ke UA 145 F7
Slavsko Polje HR 148 F5
Slavyani BG 165 C10
Slavyanovo BG 165 C10
Slavyanovo BG 166 C6
Slavyanovo BG 166 F5
Sława PL 81 C10
Sławatycze PL 141 G9
Sławięcin PL 85 C13
Sławków PL 143 F7
Sławno PL 85 B11
Sławoborze PL 85 C9
Sławsko PL 85 B11
Sleaford GB 11 F11
Sledmere GB 11 C10
Sleen NL 17 C7
Sleidinge B 182 C3
Sleights GB 11 C10
Slemmestad N 95 C12
Ślesin PL 138 D4
Ślesin PL 138 F5
Sletta N 112 C9
Slevik N 91 A8
Sliač SK 147 D8
Slidre N 101 D9
Sliedrecht NL 16 E3
Šlienava LT 137 D9
Sligachan GB 2 L4
Sligeach IRL 6 D6
Sligo IRL 6 D6
Slimminge DK 87 E9
Slimnic RO 152 F4
Slinfold GB 15 E8
Slipra N 105 D9
Slišane SRB 164 D4
Slite S 93 D13
Sliven BG 166 D6
Slivileşti RO 159 D11
Slivnitsa BG 165 D7
Slivo Pole BG 161 F8
Śliwice PL 138 C5
Sllatinë e Madhe KS 164 D3
Slobidka UA 154 B4
Slobozia MD 154 D5
Slobozia RO 160 D6
Slobozia RO 161 D10
Slobozia RO 161 F7
Slobozia Bradului RO 161 C10
Slobozia Ciorăşti RO 161 B10
Slobozia Conachi RO 155 B1
Slobozia Mândra RO 160 F5
Slobozia Mare MD 155 B2
Slobozia Moară RO 161 D7
Slochteren NL 17 B7
Slöinge S 87 B11
Słomniki PL 143 F9
Słonowice PL 85 C9
Słońsk PL 81 A7
Slootdorp NL 16 C3
Slottsskogen S 99 C9
Slough GB 15 D7
Sloupnice CZ 77 C10
Sløvåg N 100 E2
Slovenj Gradec SLO 73 C11
Slovenska Bistrica SLO 148 D5
Slovenská Ľupča SK 147 D8
Slovenská Ves SK 145 E1
Slovenske Konjice SLO 148 D4
Slovenské Nové Mesto SK 145 G4
Slovenský Grob SK 146 E4
Slovinci HR 157 B6
Slovinky SK 145 F2
Sløvra N 110 D8
Slov"yanoserbka UA 154 D5
Słowik PL 143 C7
Słubice PL 81 B7
Słubice PL 139 F8
Sluderno I 71 D11
Sluis NL 19 B7
Sluiskil NL 16 F1
Šluknov CZ 81 D6
Slunj HR 156 B4
Słupca PL 142 B4
Słupcza PL 144 B4
Słupia PL 141 G1
Słupia PL 143 D9
Słupia PL 143 E8
Słupno PL 139 E8
Słupsk PL 85 B12
Slušovice CZ 146 C5
Slussfors S 109 F11
Słuszków PL 142 C5
Slyuda RUS 115 D8
Smailholm GB 5 D11
Smålandsstenar S 87 A12
Smalåsen N 105 A14
Smalfjord N 113 C21
Smalininkai LT 136 C6
Smalvos LT 135 E12
Smârdan RO 155 C1
Smârdan RO 155 C2
Smārde LV 134 C6
Smârdioasa RO 161 F6
Smardzewice PL 141 H2
Smardzewo PL 81 B9
Smardzko PL 85 C9
Smarhon' BY 137 E13
Šmarje pri Jelšah SLO 148 D5
Šmarjeta SLO 148 E4
Šmartno SLO 73 D10
Šmartno SLO 73 D11
Smarves F 29 B6
Smedby S 89 B10
Smederevo SRB 159 D6
Smederevska Palanka SRB 159 E6
Smedjebacken S 97 B13
Smedsbyn S 118 C8
Smedvik N 110 D6
Smeeni RO 161 C9
Smęgorzów PL 143 F11
Smelror N 114 C10
Smelteri LV 135 D13
Smętowo Graniczne PL 138 C6
Smidary CZ 77 B8
Smidstrup DK 86 D5
Smidstrup DK 87 C10
Śmigiel PL 81 B11
Smilčić HR 156 D4
Smilde NL 17 C6
Smilets BG 165 E9
Smilevo MK 168 B5
Smilgiai LT 135 D9
Smilgiai LT 135 E8
Smilgiai LT 137 D8
Smilgynai LT 134 E2
Smilovci SRB 165 C6
Śmiłowice PL 138 E7
Śmiłowo PL 85 D11
Smiltene LV 135 B11
Smiltynė LT 134 E2
Smilyan BG 171 A7
Smines N 110 C8
Smiřice CZ 77 B9
Smirnenski BG 159 F11
Smirnenski BG 161 F8
Smiugard N 101 D11
Smižany SK 145 F2
Smögen S 91 C9
Smokvica HR 162 D2
Smokvica MK 169 B7
Smołdzino PL 85 A12
Smolenice SK 146 D4
Smolice PL 81 C12
Smolmark S 96 C7
Smolnica PL 84 E7
Smolník SK 145 F2
Smolyan BG 171 A7
Smolyanovtsi BG 165 C6
Smørfjord N 113 B15
Smulți RO 153 F11
Smyadovo BG 167 C8
Smygehamn S 87 E12
Smyków PL 143 D9
Snagov RO 161 D8
Snainton GB 11 C10
Snaith GB 11 D9
Snålroa N 102 E2
Snappertuna FIN 127 E10
Snaptun DK 86 D6
Snarby N 111 A18
Snåre FIN 123 C10
Snartemo N 94 F6
Snåsa N 105 C12
Snave Bridge IRL 8 E4
Snedsted DK 86 B3
Sneek NL 16 B5
Sneem IRL 8 E3
Snejbjerg DK 86 C3
Snēpele LV 134 C3
Snerta N 101 C15
Snertinge DK 87 D8
Snesslinge S 99 B10
Snesudden S 118 B4
Snettisham GB 11 F13
Śniadowo PL 139 D12
Sniķere LV 134 D6
Snina SK 145 F5
Šnjegotina Velika BIH 157 C8
Snøde DK 87 E7
Snøfjord N 113 B14
Snogebæk DK 89 E8
Snoghøj DK 86 D5
Snoldelev DK 87 D10
Soajo P 38 E3
Soarş RO 152 F5
Soave I 66 B3
Søberg N 110 C7
Soběslav CZ 77 D7
Sobienie-Jeziory PL 141 G4
Sobolew PL 141 G5
Sobota PL 143 B8
Soboth A 73 C11
Sobotín CZ 77 B12
Sobotište SK 146 D4
Sobotka CZ 77 B8
Sobótka PL 81 E11
Sobótka PL 142 C4
Sobótka PL 143 E12
Sobowidz PL 138 B6
Sobra HR 162 D4
Sobradelo E 39 D6
Sobradiel E 41 E9
Sobrado E 38 B3
Sobrado E 38 D3
Sobral da Adiça P 51 C5
Sobral de Monte Agraço P 50 A1
Sobrance SK 145 F5
Sobreira Formosa P 44 E5
Søby DK 86 F6
Soča SLO 73 D8
Sočanica KS 163 C10
Soçanicë KS 163 C10
Socchieve I 73 D6
Sočerga SLO 67 B8
Sochaczew PL 141 F2
Sochaux F 27 E6
Sochocin PL 139 E9
Sochos GR 169 C9
Socodor RO 151 D7
Socol RO 159 D7
Socond RO 151 B10
Socovos E 55 C9
Socuéllamos E 47 F7
Sodankylä FIN 117 D17
Söderåkra S 89 C10
Söderala S 103 D12
Söderås S 103 E9
Söderbärke S 97 B14
Söderboda S 99 B10
Söderby-Karl S 99 C11
Söderfors S 98 B8
Söderhamn S 103 D13
Söderköping S 93 C8
Söderkulla FIN 127 E13
Södersvik S 99 C11
Södertälje S 93 A11
Södra Åbyn S 118 E5
Södra Brännträsk S 118 C4
Södra Drängsmark S 118 E5
Södra Harads S 118 B5
Södra Johannisberg S 109 F15
Södra Löten S 102 E4
Södra Sandby S 87 D12
Södra Sandträsk S 107 A16
Södra Sunderbyn S 118 C7
Södra Tresund S 107 A10
Södra Vallgrund FIN 122 D6
Södra Vi S 92 D7
Sodražica SLO 73 E10
Soerendonk NL 16 F5
Soest D 17 E10
Soest NL 16 D4
Soesterberg NL 183 A6
Sofades GR 169 F7
Sofia MD 153 B11
Sofiko GR 171 B11
Sofiko GR 175 D7
Sofiya BG 165 D7
Sofporog RUS 121 C17
Şofrîncani MD 153 A10
Şofronea RO 151 E7
Sofronievo BG 160 F3
Søften DK 86 C6
Søftestad N 90 A4
Sofular TR 181 A9
Sögel D 17 C9
Sogndalsfjøra N 100 D6
Søgne N 90 C2
Soğucak TR 173 A8
Soğucak TR 173 F8
Soğucak TR 177 D9
Soğukoluk TR 181 A7
Söğüt TR 181 C8
Söğütalan TR 173 D10
Soham GB 15 C9
Sohatu RO 161 E9
Soheit-Tinlot B 19 D11
Sohland D 80 D6
Sohodol RO 151 E11
Sohren D 21 E8
Soidinkumpu FIN 121 B12
Soidinvaara FIN 121 F12
Soignies B 19 C9
Soikko FIN 119 C14
Şoimari RO 161 C8
Şoimi RO 151 D9
Şoimuş RO 151 F10
Soing F 26 E4
Soings-en-Sologne F 24 F6
Soini FIN 123 E12
Soinilansalmi FIN 125 F10
Soinlahti FIN 124 C8
Soissons F 19 F7
Soivio FIN 121 C13
Soizy-aux-Bois F 25 C10
Sójkowa PL 144 C5
Söjtör H 149 C7
Sokal' UA 144 C9
Söke TR 177 D9
Soklot FIN 122 C9
Sokna N 95 B11
Soknedal N 104 F8
Sokobanja SRB 159 F8
Sokojärvi FIN 125 D14
Sokolac BIH 157 E10
Sokolany PL 140 D8
Sokolce SK 146 F5
Sokolivka UA 154 A3
Sokółka PL 140 D9
Sokółki PL 136 E5
Sokolnice CZ 77 D11
Sokolniki PL 142 D5
Sokolov CZ 75 B12
Sokolovac HR 149 D7
Sokolovce SK 146 D5
Sokolovići BIH 157 E10
Sokolovo BG 166 C5
Sokolovo BG 167 C10
Sokolovo BIH 157 C6
Sokołów Małopolski PL 144 C5
Sokołów Podlaski PL 141 F6
Sokoły PL 140 E7
Sokorópátka H 149 B9
Sokyrnytsya UA 145 G7
Sól PL 144 B6
Soľ SK 145 F4
Sola N 94 E3
Solacolu RO 161 E9
Solana de los Barros E 51 B6
Solana del Pino E 54 C4
Solana de Rioalmar E 45 C11
Søland N 95 B10
Solarino I 59 E7
Solaro F 37 H10
Solberg N 101 E15
Solberg N 111 B14
Solberg S 107 D11
Solberg S 107 D13
Solberga S 92 D5
Solbjerg DK 86 C6
Solca RO 153 B7
Solčava SLO 73 D10
Solda I 71 D11
Şoldăneşti MD 154 B3
Şoldanu RO 161 E9
Soldatnes N 113 D14
Sölden A 71 D12
Soldeu AND 33 E9
Solec Kujawski PL 138 D5
Solec-Zdrój PL 143 F10
Solenzara F 37 H10
Solesino I 66 B4
Solesmes F 19 D7
Solesmes F 23 E11
Soleşti RO 153 D11
Soleto I 61 C10
Solf FIN 122 D7
Solférino F 32 B4
Solferino I 66 B2
Solfjellsjøen N 108 D4
Soliera I 66 C2
Solignano I 69 D8
Solihull GB 13 A11
Solin HR 156 E5
Solina PL 145 E5
Solingen D 21 B8
Solivella E 42 E6
Soljani HR 157 C10
Sölje S 97 D8
Solkei FIN 128 C8
Söll A 72 A5
Sollas GB 2 K2
Sollebrunn S 91 C12
Sollefteå S 107 E12
Sollenau A 77 G10
Sollenkroka S 99 D11
Sollentuna S 99 D9
Sóller E 49 E10
Sollerön S 102 E8
Søllested DK 83 A10
Sollichau D 79 C12
Solliès-Pont F 36 E4
Solliès-Toucas F 36 E4
Sollihøgda N 95 C12
Söllingen D 79 B8
Sollstedt D 79 D8
Solmaz TR 181 B9
Solms D 21 C10
Solnice CZ 77 B10
Solnik BG 167 D9
Solofra I 60 B3
Solojärvi FIN 113 F18
Solomiac F 33 C7
Solomos GR 175 D6
Solopaca I 60 A3
Solórzano E 40 B4
Solosancho E 46 C3
Sološnica SK 146 E4
Solothurn CH 27 F8
Solotvyna UA 145 H8
Soløy N 111 C14
Solre-le-Château F 19 D9
Solrød Strand DK 87 D10
Solsem N 105 A11
Solskjela N 104 E4
Sølsnes N 100 A6
Solsona E 43 D7
Solsvik N 94 B1
Solt H 150 D3
Soltau D 83 E7
Soltendieck D 83 E9
Sol'tsy RUS 132 E7
Soltszentimre H 150 D3
Soltvadkert H 150 D3
Solumshamn S 103 A14
Solva GB 9 E12
Solvalla S 99 C10
Solvarbo S 97 B14
Sölvesborg S 88 C7
Solvorn N 100 D6
Solymár H 149 A11
Soma TR 177 A10
Somain F 19 D7
Somberek H 149 D11
Sombernon F 25 F12
Sombor SRB 150 F3
Sombreffe B 19 C10
omcuța Mare RO 151 B11
Somercotes GB 11 E9
Someren NL 16 F5
Somerniemi FIN 127 D10
Somero FIN 127 D10
Someronkylä FIN 119 F12
Somerovaara FIN 119 D16
Sõmerpalu EST 131 F13
Somerton GB 13 C9
Sõmeru EST 131 C12
Someş=-Odorhei RO 151 C11
Somianka PL 139 E11
Sominy PL 85 B13
Somlóvásárhely H 149 B8
Sommacampagna I 66 B2
Somma Lombardo I 68 B6
Sommariva del Bosco I 37 B7
Sommarøy N 110 C9
Sommarøy N 111 A15
Sommarset N 109 A10
Sommatino I 58 E4
Somme-Leuze B 19 D11
Sommen S 92 C5
Sommepy-Tahure F 19 F10
Sömmerda D 79 D9
Sommerfeld D 84 E4
Sommersted DK 86 E4
Sommesous F 25 C11
Somme-Suippe F 25 B12
Sommevoire F 25 D12
Sommières F 35 C7
Sommières-du-Clain F 29 C6
Somogyapáti H 149 D9
Somogyjád H 149 D9
Somogyszob H 149 D8
Somogyudvarhely H 149 D8
Somogyvár H 149 C9
Somonino PL 138 B5
Somontín E 55 E8
Somotor SK 145 G4
Somova RO 155 C3
Somovit BG 160 F5
Sompa EST 131 C14
Sompolno PL 138 F6
Sompujärvi FIN 119 C14
Somzée B 19 D9
Son N 95 C13
Son NL 16 E4
Sona I 66 B2
Sona N 105 E10
Şona RO 152 E4
Sonceboz CH 27 F7
Soncillo E 40 C4
Soncino I 69 C8
Sonda EST 131 C13
Sondalo I 69 A9
Sondeled N 90 B5
Sønder Balling DK 86 B3
Sønder Bjerre DK 86 D5
Sønder Bjert DK 86 E5
Sønderborg DK 86 F5
Sønderby DK 87 D10
Sønder Dråby DK 86 B3
Sønder Felding DK 86 D3
Sønderho DK 86 E2
Sønderholm DK 86 A5
Sønder Hygum DK 86 E3
Sønder Nissum DK 86 C2
Sønder Omme DK 86 D3
Sønder Onsild DK 86 B5
Sønder Rubjerg DK 90 E6
Sondershausen D 79 D8
Søndersø DK 86 E6
Sønder Stenderup DK 86 E5
Sønder Vilstrup DK 86 E5
Sønder Vissing DK 86 C5
Sønder Vium DK 86 D2
Sondori LV 133 C2
Sondrio I 69 A8
Soneja E 48 E4
Songe N 90 B5
Songeons F 18 E4
Sonim P 38 E5
Sonka FIN 117 E14
Sonkajärvi FIN 124 C9
Sonkakoski FIN 124 C9
Sonkamuotka FIN 117 B10
Sonneberg D 75 B9
Sonneborn D 79 E8
Sonnefeld D 75 B9
Sonnewalde D 80 C5
Sonnino I 62 E4
Sonntag A 71 C9
Sonntagberg A 77 G7
Sonseca E 46 E5
Son Servera E 57 B11
Sońsk PL 139 E10
Sonstorp S 92 B7
Sonta SRB 157 A11
Sontheim an der Brenz D 75 E7
Sonthofen D 71 B10
Sontra D 78 D6
Soodla EST 131 C10
Söörmarkku FIN 126 B6
Soorts-Hossegor F 32 C3
Sopeira E 33 F7
Sopelana E 40 B6
Sopilja BIH 157 F9
Sopište MK 164 F3
Soponya H 149 B10
Šoporňa SK 146 E5
Sopot BG 165 C9
Sopot BG 165 D10
Sopot PL 138 B6
Sopot RO 160 E3

Sopot SRB 158 D6
Sopotnica MK 168 B5
Şopotu Nou RO 159 D8
Soppela FIN 115 E3
Sopron H 149 A7
Sopronkövesd H 149 A7
Sora I 62 D5
Soraga I 72 D4
Soragna I 66 C1
Söråker S 103 A14
Sörång S 103 D11
Sorano I 62 B1
Sørarnøy N 108 B6
Sør-Audnedal N 90 C1
Sorbas E 55 E8
Sorbie GB 5 F8
Sorbiers F 30 E5
Sörbo S 103 D11
Sörböle S 103 B13
Sorbolo I 66 C1
Sörby S 97 C9
Sörbygden S 103 A11
Sørbymagle DK 87 E8
Sörbyn S 118 B7
Sörbyn S 118 E4
Sorcy-St-Martin F 26 C4
Sord IRL 7 F10
Sørdal N 109 C10
Sorde-l'Abbaye F 32 C3
Sore F 32 B4
Sørebo N 100 D3
Sören S 118 C9
Søreng N 111 B19
Soresina I 69 C8
Sorèze F 33 D10
Sörfjärden S 103 B13
Sørfjord N 108 D5
Sørfjord N 111 C14
Sørfjorden N 111 C10
Sørfjordmoen N 109 A10
Sörflärke S 107 E13
Sörfors S 103 B13
Sörfors S 122 C4
Sörforsa S 103 C12
Sorge D 79 C8
Sorges F 29 E7
Sorgono I 64 C3
Sorgues F 35 B8
Sørheim N 100 D6
Soria E 41 E7
Soriano Calabro I 59 B9
Soriano nel Cimino I 62 C2
Sorihuela E 45 D9
Sorihuela del Gaudalimar E 55 C6
Sorisdale GB 4 B4
Sørkjosen N 112 D6
Sørkjosen N 112 D6
Sorkwity PL 136 F3
Sørland N 110 E4
Sørlenangen N 111 A19
Sørli N 105 C15
Sørli N 111 B14
Sörmark S 97 B8
Sörmjöle S 122 C4
Sørmo N 111 C16
Sorn GB 5 D8
Sornac F 29 D10
Sörnoret S 107 C12
Sorø DK 87 E9
Soroca MD 154 A2
Sorokino RUS 133 B7
Soroni GR 181 D7
Sorradile I 64 C2
Sørreisa N 111 B15
Sorrento I 60 B2
Sorring DK 86 C5
Sørrollnes N 111 C12
Sorsakoski FIN 124 F9
Sorsele S 109 E14
Sörsjön S 102 D5
Sorso I 64 B2
Sörstafors S 98 C6
Sørstraumen N 112 D8
Sort E 33 F8
Sortavala RUS 129 B14
Sortelha P 45 D6
Sortino I 59 E7
Sörtjärn S 102 B8
Sortland N 110 C9
Sør-Tverrfjord N 112 C8
Sõru EST 130 D5
Sørum N 101 E11
Sorumsand N 95 C14
Sorunda S 93 A11
Sörup D 82 A7
Sørvad DK 86 C3
Sørvær N 112 B8
Sörvåge S 107 E15
Sørvågen N 110 E5
Sørvágur FO 2 A2
Sörvattnet S 102 B4
Sørvik N 111 C13
Sörvik S 97 B13
Sørvika N 101 B15
Sörviken S 107 D9
Sorvilán E 55 F6
Sos F 33 B6
Sosandra GR 169 C7
Sösdala S 87 C13
Sos del Rey Católico E 32 E3
Sosedno RUS 132 E4
Soses E 42 D4
Soshe-Ostrivs'ke UA 154 C5
Sösjö S 103 A9
Sóskút H 149 B11
Sośnica PL 85 D10
Sośnie PL 142 D4
Sośno PL 138 D4
Sosnovka RUS 136 D3
Sosnovo RUS 129 D13
Sosnovyy Bor RUS 129 F11
Sosnowica PL 141 G8
Sosnowiec PL 143 F7
Sosnówka PL 141 G8
Soso FIN 119 E15
Sospel F 37 D6
Sossonniemi FIN 121 C14
Sost F 33 E7
Šoštanj SLO 73 D11
Sostis GR 171 B8
Sot N 96 C6
Şotânga RO 160 D6
Sotés E 41 D6
Sotiel Coronada E 51 D6
Sotillo de la Adrada E 46 D3
Sotillo del Rincón E 41 E6
Sotin HR 157 B11
Sotkajärvi FIN 119 E16
Sotkamo FIN 121 F11
Soto E 39 A7
Soto de la Vega E 39 D8
Soto del Real E 46 C5
Soto de Ribera E 39 B8
Soto en Cameros E 41 D7
Sotopalacios E 40 D4
Sotos E 47 D8
Sotoserrano E 45 D8
Soto y Amio E 39 C8
Sotres E 39 B10
Sotresgudo E 40 C3
Şotrile RO 161 C7
Sotrondio E 39 B8
Sotta F 37 H10
Sotteville-lès-Rouen F 18 F3
Sottomarina I 66 B5
Sottrum D 17 B12
Sottunga FIN 99 B15
Sotuélamos E 55 A7
Soual F 33 C10
Soubès F 34 C5
Soucy F 25 D9
Souda GR 178 E7
Soudan F 23 E9
Soueix F 33 E8
Souesmes F 24 F7
Soufflenheim F 27 C8
Soufli GR 171 B10
Sougia GR 178 E6
Souillac F 29 F8
Souilly F 26 B3
Souk el Had el Rharbia MA 52 E5
Souk-Khémis-des-Anjra MA 53 E5
Soukolojärvi S 119 B11
Souk Tleta Taghramet MA 53 E6
Soulac-sur-Mer F 28 D3
Soulaines-Dhuys F 25 D12
Soulatgé F 33 E11
Souli GR 175 D6
Soullans F 28 B2
Soulom F 32 E5
Soultz-Haut-Rhin F 27 E7
Soultz-sous-Forêts F 27 C8
Soumagne B 19 C12
Soumoulou F 32 D5
Souppes-sur-Loing F 25 D8
Souprosse F 32 C4
Sourdeval F 23 C10
Soure P 44 D3
Sournia F 33 E10
Souro Pires P 45 C6
Sourpi GR 175 A6
Sours F 24 D6
Sourzac F 29 E6
Sousceyrac F 29 F10
Sousel P 50 B4
Soustons F 32 C3
Southam GB 13 A12
Southampton GB 13 D12
South Anston GB 11 E9
South Bank GB 11 B9
Southborough GB 15 E9
South Cave GB 11 D10
South Chard GB 13 D9
Southend GB 4 E5
Southend-on-Sea GB 15 D10
Southery GB 11 F12
Southgate GB 15 D8
South Harting GB 15 F7
South Kelsey GB 11 E11
South Kirkby GB 11 D9
Southminster GB 15 D10
South Molton GB 13 C7
South Ockendon GB 15 D9
Southport GB 10 D5
South Queensferry GB 5 D10
South Shields GB 5 F14
Southwell GB 11 E10
Southwold GB 15 C12
South Woodham Ferrers GB 15 D10
Souto E 38 C4
Souto P 38 E2
Souto P 44 E4
Souto P 45 D7
Souto da Casa P 44 D5
Soutuperä FIN 123 B14
Souvala GR 175 D8
Souvigny F 30 B3
Şovarna RO 159 D10
Søvassli N 104 E6
Sovata RO 152 D6
Soveja RO 153 E9
Soverato I 59 B10
Soveria F 37 G10
Soveria Mannelli I 59 A9
Sovetsk RUS 136 C4
Sovetskiy RUS 129 D10
Sovići BIH 157 F7
Sovicille I 66 F3
Søvik N 100 A4
Søvind DK 86 D5
Sowno PL 85 B11
Sowno PL 85 D7
Soyaux F 29 D6
Soye F 26 F5
Soylu TR 173 B7
Soymy UA 145 F7
Soyons F 30 F6
Sozopol BG 167 E9
Spa B 19 D12
Spa IRL 8 D3
Spabrücken D 21 E9
Špačince SK 146 E5
Spačva HR 157 B10
Spadafora I 59 C7
Spaichingen D 27 D10
Spalding GB 11 F11
Spálené Poříčí CZ 76 C5
Spalt D 75 D8
Spangenberg D 78 D6
Spanish Point IRL 8 C4
Spantekow D 84 C5
Spanţov RO 161 E9
Sparanise I 60 A2
Sparbu N 105 D10
Spāre LV 134 B4
Sparreholm S 93 A9
Spartà I 59 C8
Sparti GR 174 E5
Sparto GR 174 B3
Spartylas GR 168 E2
Spasovo BG 155 F2
Spata GR 175 D8
Spay D 185 D8
Spean Bridge GB 4 B7
Specchia I 61 D10
Speen GB 13 C12
Speia MD 154 D4
Speicher D 21 E7
Speichersdorf D 75 C10
Spello I 62 B3
Spenge D 17 D10
Spennymoor GB 5 F13
Spentrup DK 86 B6
Spercheiada GR 174 B5
Sperlinga I 58 D5
Sperlonga I 62 E4
Spermezeu RO 152 C4
Spersboda S 99 C11
Spetalen N 95 D13
Spetses GR 175 E7
Spey Bay GB 3 K10
Speyer D 21 F10
Spezzano Albanese I 61 D6
Spiczyn PL 141 H7
Spiddal IRL 6 F4
Spielberg bei Knittelfeld A 73 B10
Spiere B 182 D2
Spiesen-Elversberg D 21 F8
Spiez CH 70 D5
Spigno Monferrato I 37 B8
Spigno Saturnia I 62 E5
Spiinigied'di N 113 E15
Spijk NL 17 B7
Spijkenisse NL 16 E2
Spikberg S 118 B5
Spilamberto I 66 C3
Spili GR 178 E8
Spilimbergo I 73 D6
Spilinga I 59 B8
Spillersboda S 99 C11
Spillum N 105 C11
Spilsby GB 11 E12
Spinazzola I 60 B6
Spincourt F 19 F12
Špindlerův Mlýn CZ 81 E9
Spinea I 66 B5
Spineni RO 160 D5
Spinetoli I 62 B5
Spink IRL 9 C8
Spinuş RO 151 C9
Špionica BIH 157 C10
Špišić-Bukovica HR 149 E8
Spiss A 71 D10
Spišská Belá SK 145 E1
Spišská Nová Ves SK 145 F2
Spišská Stará Ves SK 145 E1
Spišská Teplica SK 145 E1
Spišské Bystré SK 145 F1
Spišské Podhradie SK 145 F2
Spišské Vlachy SK 145 F2
Spišský Hrušov SK 145 F2
Spital am Pyhrn A 73 A9
Spital am Semmering A 148 A5
Spitsyno RUS 132 D2
Spittal GB 3 J10
Spittal an der Drau A 73 C7
Spittal of Glenshee GB 5 B10
Spitz A 77 F8
Spjald DK 86 C3
Spjelkavik N 100 B4
Spjutsbygd S 89 C9
Spjutsund FIN 127 E14
Split HR 156 E5
Splügen CH 71 D8
Spodnja Idrija SLO 73 D9
Spodnje Hoče SLO 148 C5
Spodsbjerg DK 87 F7
Spofforth GB 11 D9
Spoleto I 62 B3
Spoltore I 63 C6
Spondigna I 71 D11
Spontin B 19 D11
Spornitz D 83 D11
Spotorno I 37 C8
Spraitbach D 74 E6
Sprakensehl D 83 E9
Sprâncenata RO 160 E5
Sprängsviken S 103 A14
Spreenhagen D 80 B5
Spremberg D 80 C6
Sprendlingen D 185 E8
Spresiano I 72 E5
Spriana I 69 A8
Sprimont B 19 C12
Spring RO 152 F3
Springe D 78 B6
Springholm GB 5 E9
Springliden S 107 A16
Sproatley GB 11 D11
Sprockhövel D 17 F8
Sproge S 93 E12
Sprogi LV 135 D10
Sprova N 105 C10
Sprowston GB 15 B11
Sproxton GB 11 C9
Spunģēni LV 135 C11
Spuž MNE 163 D7
Spychowo PL 139 C11
Spydeberg N 95 C14
Spytihněv CZ 146 C5
Spytkowice PL 143 G7
Spytkowice PL 147 B9
Squillace I 59 B10
Squinzano I 61 C10
Sráid an Mhuilinn IRL 8 D4
Sraith Salach IRL 6 F3
Sranea IRL 6 D6
Srath an Urláir IRL 7 C7
Srbac BIH 157 B8
Srbobran SRB 158 B4
Srbovac KS 163 D10
Srđevići BIH 157 E6
Srebrenica BIH 158 E3
Srebrenik BIH 157 C10
Srebŭrna BG 161 E10
Sredets BG 166 E5
Sredets BG 167 E8
Središče SLO 148 D6
Sredishte BG 161 F10
Srednje BIH 157 D9
Srednjevo SRB 159 D8
Sredno Gradište BG 166 E4
Śrem PL 81 B12
Sremčica SRB 158 D5
Sremska Kamenica SRB 158 C4
Sremska Mitrovica SRB 158 D4
Sremski Karlovci SRB 158 C4
Srenica BIH 156 D6
Srnice BIH 157 C9
Śrockowo PL 136 E4
Środa Śląska PL 81 D11
Środa Wielkopolska PL 81 B12
Srpska Crnja SRB 158 B6
Srpski Itebej SRB 159 B6
Srpski Miletić SRB 157 A11
Sta S 105 E13
Staatz A 77 E10
Stabbfors S 108 E8
Stabbursnes N 113 C14
Stabroek B 16 F2
Stabulnieki LV 135 D13
Staburags LV 135 C11
Staburnaäs S 107 B11
Staby DK 86 C2
Stachy CZ 76 D5
Stade D 17 A12
Staden B 18 C7
Stadl-Paura A 76 F5
Stadra S 97 C12
Stadsbygd N 104 E7
Stadskanaal NL 17 C7
Stadtallendorf D 21 C12
Stadtbergen D 75 F8
Stadthagen D 17 D12
Stadtilm D 79 E9
Stadtkyll D 21 D7
Stadtlauringen D 75 B7
Stadtlohn D 17 E7
Stadtroda D 79 E10
Stadtschlaining A 148 B6
Stadum D 82 A6
Stäfa CH 27 F10
Staffanstorp S 87 D12
Staffelstein D 75 B8
Staffin GB 2 K4
Staffolo I 67 F7
Stafford GB 11 F7
Stahovica SLO 73 D10
Stai N 101 D14
Staicele LV 131 F9
Staig D 74 F6
Stainach A 73 A9
Staindrop GB 11 B8
Staines-upon-Thames GB 15 E7
Stainforth GB 11 C7
Stainforth GB 11 D9
Staintondale GB 11 C11
Stainville F 26 C3
Stainz A 148 C4
Staiti I 59 D9
Stakčín SK 145 F5
Stakevtsi BG 164 B6
Stākļi LV 135 B13
Stakiai LT 134 F6
Stakkvik N 112 D4
Stakliškės LT 137 D9
Stakroge DK 86 D3
Stalać SRB 159 F7
Stalbe LV 135 B10
Stålbo S 98 B7
Stalbridge GB 13 D10
Stalden CH 68 A4
Staldzene LV 134 B3
Stalgėnai LT 134 E3
Stalģene LV 135 C7
Stalham GB 15 B12
Stalheim N 100 E5
Stalidzāni LV 135 C13
Staliogargo N 113 B12
Stall A 73 C7
Stallarholmen S 98 D8
Ställberg S 97 C12
Ställdalen S 97 C12
Stallwang D 75 D12
Stalon S 107 B9
Stalowa Wola PL 144 B5
Stâlpeni RO 160 C5
Stâlpu RO 161 C9
Stamboliyski BG 165 E10
Stambulčić BIH 157 E10
Stamford GB 11 F11
Stamford Bridge GB 11 D10
Stamfordham GB 5 E13
Stammham D 75 E9
Stamna GR 174 B3
Stamovo BG 166 E5
Stams A 71 C11
Stamstik N 110 E9
Stamsund N 110 D6
Stânceni RO 152 D6
Stăncuţa RO 155 D1
Standdaarbuiten NL 182 B5
Standish GB 10 D6
Stăneşti RO 159 C11
Stăneşti RO 161 F7
Stånga S 93 E12
Stângăceaua RO 160 D2
Stangnes N 111 B13
Stångviken S 105 D16
Stanhoe GB 15 B10
Stanhope GB 5 F12
Stănileşti RO 154 D2
Stanin PL 141 G6
Stănişeşti RO 153 E10
Stanišić SRB 150 F3
Stanišinci SRB 163 B10
Stanisławów PL 141 F5
Stăniţa RO 153 C10
Štanjel SLO 73 E8
Staňkov CZ 76 C4
Stankovany SK 147 C8
Stanley GB 5 C10
Stanley GB 5 F13
Stanley GB 11 D9
Stannington GB 5 E13
Stanomino PL 85 C9
Stanos GR 169 C10
Stanos GR 174 B3
Stan'ovsti BG 165 D6
Stans CH 71 D6
Stansted Mountfitchet GB 15 D9
Stantër KS 163 D10
Stanton GB 15 C10
Stanzach A 71 C11
Stanz im Mürztal A 148 B5
Stapar SRB 158 B3
Stapel D 83 D9
Stapelburg D 79 C8
Stapelfeld D 83 C8
Staphorst NL 16 C6
Staplehurst GB 15 E10
Stąporków PL 141 H3
Stara Błotnica PL 141 G3
Stará Bystrica SK 147 C7
Starachowice PL 143 D11
Stara Gradina HR 149 E9
Stará Huť CZ 76 C6
Stara Kamienica PL 81 E9
Stara Kamionka PL 140 D9
Stara Kiszewa PL 138 C5
Stara Kornica PL 141 F7
Stara Kul'na UA 154 B4
Stara Łubianka PL 85 D11
Stará Ľubovňa SK 145 E2
Stara Moravica SRB 150 F3
Stara Novalja HR 67 C10
Stara Pazova SRB 158 D5
Stara Ploščica HR 149 E7
Stara Reka BG 166 D6
Stara Rudnica PL 84 E6
Stara Sil' UA 145 E6
Stara Ţsarychanka UA 154 E5
Stará Turá SK 146 D5
Stara vas-Bizeljsko SLO 148 E5
Stará Ves nad Ondřejnicí CZ 146 B6
Staravina MK 169 B6
Stara Wieś PL 144 B6
Stara Zagora BG 166 E5
Stara Zhadova UA 153 A7
Starčevo SRB 158 D6
Starchiojd RO 161 C8
Starcross GB 13 D8
Stare Babice PL 141 F3
Stare-Bogaczowice PL 81 E10
Stare Budkowice PL 142 E5
Stařeč CZ 77 D9
Stare Czarnowo PL 85 D7
Stare Dąbrowa PL 85 D8
Stare Dolistowo PL 140 C7
Stare Hołowczyce PL 141 F7
Stare Kurowo PL 85 E9
Staré Město CZ 77 B11
Staré Město u Uherského Hradiště CZ 146 C4
Stare Miasto PL 142 B5
Stare Pole PL 139 B7
Stare Puchały PL 141 E7
Stare Selo UA 144 D9
Stare Strącze PL 81 C10
Stargard Szczeciński PL 85 D8
Star Huta SK 147 E8
Stari LV 135 B13
Stari Banovci SRB 158 D5
Staříč CZ 146 B6
Stari Dulići BIH 157 F10
Starigrad HR 67 C10
Starigrad HR 156 D3
Starigrad HR 156 F6
Stari Gradac HR 149 E8
Stari Kuty UA 152 A6
Stari Log SLO 73 E10
Stari Majdan BIH 156 C6
Stari Mikanovci HR 157 B10
Stari Trg SLO 67 B11
Stari Trg SLO 73 E9
Stari Troyany UA 155 B4
Starkenberg D 79 E11
Stärkesmark S 122 B3
Starnberg D 75 G9
Starogard PL 85 C9
Starogard Gdański PL 138 C6
Staroglavice BIH 158 E3
Starokozache UA 154 E5
Staro Oryakhovo BG 167 D9
Staropatitsa BG 159 F9
Staro Petrovo Selo HR 157 B8
Starosel BG 165 E10
Staro Selo BG 161 F9
Staro Selo BIH 157 D7
Staro Selo SRB 159 E7
Staroseltsi BG 165 B9
Starosiedle PL 81 C7
Starowa Góra PL 143 C7
Staroye Syalo BY 133 F7
Staro Zhelezare BG 165 E10
Starożreby PL 139 E8
Startforth GB 11 B8
Starup DK 86 E5
Stary Brus PL 141 H8
Stary Cykarzew PL 143 E7
Stary Dzierzgoń PL 139 C7
Stary Dzikowiec PL 144 C4
Stary Kisielin PL 81 C9
Stary Kobrzyniec PL 139 E7
Starý Kolín CZ 77 B8
Stary Majdan PL 144 C6
Starynovichy BY 133 F6
Stary Pahost BY 133 F3
Starý Plzenec CZ 76 C4
Stary Sącz PL 145 D2
StarýStarý SK 145 E1
Stary Szelków PL 139 E11
Stary Targ PL 139 C7
Stary Uścimów PL 141 H7
Staryy Sambir UA 145 E6
Stary Zamość PL 144 B7
Starzyno PL 138 A5
Staškov SK 147 C7
Staßfurt D 79 C10
Staszów PL 143 E11
Stathelle N 90 A6
Statland N 105 C10
Statsås S 107 B11
Statzendorf A 77 F9
Stăuceni MD 154 C3
Stăuceni RO 153 B9
Stauchitz D 80 D4
Staufenberg D 21 C11
Staupitz D 80 C5
Stavalj SRB 163 C9
Stavang N 100 C2
Stavanger N 94 E3
Stavaträsk S 118 D4
Stavchany UA 153 A8
Stave N 111 B10
Staveley GB 11 E9
Stavelot B 20 D5
Stavenisse NL 16 E2
Stavern N 90 B7
Stavertsi BG 165 B9
Stavky UA 144 A9
Stave UA 145 F6
Stavning DK 86 D2
Stavoren NL 16 C4
Stavre S 103 A9
Stavre S 105 E16
Stavreviken S 103 A13
Stavrodromi GR 174 D4
Stavros GR 169 C7
Stavros GR 169 C10
Stavros GR 169 F7
Stavros GR 174 C2
Stavroupoli GR 171 B7
Stavrove UA 154 B5
Stavsätra S 103 C10
Stavsnäs S 99 D11
Stavtrup DK 86 C6
Staw PL 85 E7
Stawiguda PL 139 C9
Stawiski PL 139 D13
Stawiszyn PL 142 C5
Steane N 95 D9
Stjbark PL 139 C9
Steblevë AL 168 B3
Stebnyk UA 145 E8
Steccato I 61 E7
Štěchovice CZ 76 C6
Stechow D 79 A11
Steckborn CH 27 E10
Stedesdorf D 17 A9
Stedten D 79 D10
Steeg A 71 C10
Steenbergen NL 16 E2
Steenderen NL 183 A8
Steenvoorde F 18 C6
Steenwijk NL 16 C6
Steeton GB 11 D8
Stefanaconi I 59 B9
Ştefan cel Mare RO 153 D9
Ştefan cel Mare RO 153 D11
Ştefan cel Mare RO 153 E9
Ştefan cel Mare RO 155 E1
Ştefan cel Mare RO 160 E3
Ştefan cel Mare RO 160 F4
Ştefăneşti MD 154 E5
Ştefăneşti RO 153 B10
Ştefăneşti RO 160 D5
Ştefăneşti RO 161 D9
Ştefăneştii de Jos RO 161 D8
Stefani GR 175 C8
Štefanje HR 149 E7
Stefan Karadzha BG 167 C8
Stefan-Karadzhovo BG 167 E7
Štefanov SK 146 D4
Stefanovikeio GR 169 F8
Stefanovo BG 167 C9
Stefanovouno GR 169 E7
Ştefan Vodă MD 154 D5
Ştefan Vodă RO 161 E10
Ştefeşti RO 161 C7
Steffisburg CH 70 D5
Stegaurath D 75 C8
Stege DK 87 F10
Stegelitz D 79 B10
Stegersbach A 148 B6
Stegna PL 138 B7
Stegny PL 139 B8
Stehag S 87 D12
Ştei RO 151 D9
Steigen N 110 E8
Steigra D 79 D10
Steimbke D 17 C12
Stein D 75 D9
Stein NL 19 C12
Steinach D 75 B8
Steinach D 75 E12
Steinach D 186 E5
Steinach am Brenner A 72 B3
Stein am Rhein CH 27 E10
Steinau D 17 A11
Steinau an der Straße D 74 B5
Steinbach D 21 C11
Steinbach D 80 E4
Steinbach am Attersee A 73 A8
Steinbach am Wald D 75 B9
Steinbakk N 114 E7
Steinberg D 75 D11
Steinberg D 82 A7
Steine N 105 D11
Steine N 110 C7
Steinen D 27 E8
Steinfeld A 73 C7
Steinfeld D 186 C5
Steinfeld D 187 B8
Steinfeld (Oldenburg) D 17 C10
Steinfjord N 111 B13
Steinfort L 20 E5
Steinfurt D 17 D8
Steingaden D 71 B11
Steinhagen D 17 D10
Steinhagen D 84 B3
Steinheim D 17 E12
Steinheim N 111 B15
Steinheim am Albuch D 187 D9
Steinheim an der Murr D 187 D7
Steinhöring D 75 F11
Steinhorst D 83 E8
Steinigtwolmsdorf D 80 D6
Steinkirchen D 82 C7
Steinkjer N 105 C11
Steinland N 110 C9
Steinløysa N 100 A7
Steinsdorf D 81 B7
Steinsfeld D 75 D7
Steinshamn N 100 A5
Steinsholt N 95 D11
Steinskjærnes N 114 D7
Steinsland N 94 B2
Steinsvik N 100 C3
Steinwenden D 186 C4
Steinwiesen D 75 B9
Stejaru RO 155 D3
Stejaru RO 160 E5
Stekene B 19 B9
Stelle D 83 D8
Stellendam NL 16 E2
Stelnica RO 155 E1
Stelpe LV 135 C9
Stemland N 108 B9
Stemmen D 82 D7
Stemnes N 111 D13
Stemnitsa GR 174 D5
Stemshorn D 17 D10
Stenåsa S 89 B11
Stenay F 19 F11
Stenbacken S 111 D17
Stenbjerg DK 86 B2
Stenbo S 93 E8
Stendal D 79 A10
Stende LV 134 B5
Stenderup DK 86 D3
Steneset N 108 D4
Stengelse N 113 D11
Stenhammar S 91 B13
Stenhamra S 99 D9
Stenhousemuir GB 5 C9
Stenico I 69 A10
Steninge S 87 B11
Stenis S 102 E7
Stenkumla S 93 D12
Stenkyrka S 93 D13
Stenlille DK 87 D9
Stenløse DK 87 D10
Stennäs S 107 D14
Stenness GB 3 E13
Steno GR 174 D5
Steno GR 175 E5
Stensån S 103 B9
Stensele S 107 A12
Stensjö S 107 E10
Stensjön S 92 D5
Stenskär S 99 B10
Stenstorp S 91 C14
Stensträsk S 107 A17
Stenstrup DK 86 E6
Stensund S 109 D15
Stensund S 109 F13
Stensved DK 87 F10
Stenton GB 5 D11
Stenträsk S 118 B3
Stenudden S 109 C14
Stenum DK 90 E6
Stenungsund S 91 C10
Stenvad DK 86 C7
Stenzharychi UA 144 B9
Stepanci MK 169 B6
Stepanivka UA 154 D5
Štěpánov CZ 77 C12
Stepen BIH 157 F10
Stepnica PL 84 C7
Stepojevac SRB 158 D5
Stepping DK 86 E4
Sterdyń-Osada PL 141 E6
Sterławki-Wielkie PL 136 E4
Sterna GR 171 A10
Sterna GR 175 D6
Sterna HR 67 B8
Sternberg D 83 C11
Šternberk CZ 146 B4
Sternes GR 178 D7
Stes-Maries-de-la-Mer F 35 D7
Stęszew PL 81 B11
Štětí CZ 76 B6
Stetten am kalten Markt D 27 D11
Steuerberg A 73 C9
Steutz D 79 C11
Stevenage GB 15 D8
Stevenston GB 4 D7
Stevensweert NL 183 C7
Stevnstrup DK 86 C5
Stewarton GB 4 D7
Stewartstown GB 7 C9
Steyerberg D 17 C12
Steyning GB 15 F8
Steyr A 76 F6
Steyregg A 76 F6
Stěžery CZ 77 B9
Stezherovo BG 166 C4
Stężyca PL 138 B4
Stężyca PL 141 G5
Stia I 66 E4
Stibb Cross GB 12 D6
Stickney GB 11 E12
Stidsvig S 87 C12
Stiege D 79 C8
Stiens NL 16 B5
Stienta I 66 C4
Stigen S 91 B11
Stigliano I 60 C6
Stignano I 59 C9
Stigsjö S 103 A14
Stigtomta S 93 B9
Stijena BIH 156 C5
Stikli LV 134 B4
Stilligarry GB 2 L2
Stilling DK 86 C5
Stillington GB 11 C9
Stillorgan IRL 7 F10
Stilo I 59 C9
Stilton GB 11 G11
Stimpfach D 75 D7
Stintino I 64 B1
Stio I 60 C4
Štip MK 164 F5
Stirfaka GR 174 B5
Stiring-Wendel F 21 F7
Stirling GB 5 C9
Štitar HR 157 B10
Štitar SRB 158 D4
Štítina CZ 146 B6
Štítnik SK 145 F1
Štíty CZ 77 C11
Ştiubieni RO 153 B9
Ştiuca RO 159 B8
Ştivan HR 67 C9
Stjær DK 86 C5
Stjärnfors S 97 C13
Stjärnhov S 93 A9
Stjärnorp S 92 B7
Stjørdalshalsen N 105 E9
Støa N 101 E14
Støa N 102 D4
Stobiecko Miejskie PL 143 D7
Stobreć HR 156 E6
Stoby S 87 C13
Stochov CZ 76 B5
Stocka S 103 C13
Stockach D 27 E11
Stockamöllan S 87 D12
Stockaryd S 88 A7
Stöcke S 122 C4
Stockelsdorf D 83 C9
Stockenboi A 73 C8
Stockerau A 77 F10
Stockheim D 75 B9
Stockholm S 99 D10
Stocking A 148 C5
Stockport GB 11 E7
Stocksfield GB 5 F13
Stockstadt am Rhein D 21 E10
Stockton-on-Tees GB 11 B9
Stockvik S 103 B13
Stoczek PL 139 E12
Stoczek Łukowski PL 141 G5
Stod CZ 76 C4
Stöde S 103 B12
Stoeneşti RO 160 C4
Stoeneşti RO 160 C6
Stoeneşti RO 160 E5
Stoeneşti RO 161 E7
Stoer GB 2 J6
Stoholm DK 86 C4
Stoianovca MD 154 E2
Stoicăneşti RO 160 E5
Stoileşti RO 160 D4
Stoina RO 160 D3
Stojakovo MK 169 B8
Stojdraga HR 148 E5
Stojnci SLO 148 D5
Stoke Ash GB 15 C11
Stoke-on-Trent GB 11 E7
Stokesay GB 13 A9
Stokesley GB 11 C9
Stokite BG 166 D4
Stokka N 108 E3
Stokkasjøen N 108 E4
Stokkdal N 111 D12
Stokke N 90 A7
Stokkemarke DK 83 A10
Stokkvågen N 108 D5
Stokmarknes N 110 C8
Štoky CZ 77 D9
Stolac BIH 157 F8
Stolberg (Harz) Kurort D 79 C8
Stolberg (Rheinland) D 20 C6
Stołczno PL 85 C12
Stolerova LV 133 D3
Stollberg D 79 E12
Stöllet S 97 B9
Stolmen N 94 B2
Stolniceni MD 154 D3
Stolniceni-Prăjescu RO 153 C9
Stolnici RO 160 D5
Stolnik BG 165 D8
Stolno PL 138 D6
Stolpe D 83 B9
Stolpe D 84 E6
Stolpen D 80 D6
Stolzenau D 17 C12
Stomio GR 169 E8
Stömne S 97 D8
Ston HR 162 D4
Stone GB 11 F7

Stone GB 13 B10
Stonehaven GB 5 B12
Stonehouse GB 5 D9
Stong N 94 D3
Stongfjorden N 100 D2
Stonglandseidet N 111 B13
Stonybreck GB 3 F13
Stoob A 149 A7
Stöpen S 91 C14
Stopiče SLO 148 E4
Stopki PL 136 E3
Stopnica PL 143 F10
Storå N 111 D11
Storå S 97 C13
Stora Åby S 92 C5
Storåbränna S 106 D7
Stora Höga S 91 C10
Stora Levene S 91 C12
Stora Melby S 91 C12
Stora Mellösa S 92 A6
Storarmsjö S 107 C16
Storås N 104 E7
Storåsen S 103 A10
Störåsen S 106 D7
Stora Skedvi S 97 B14
Stora Tallberg S 109 E17
Stora Vika S 93 B11
Storbäck S 106 B9
Storbacka FIN 123 D10
Storbäcken S 102 C4
Storberg S 109 E16
Stor-Blåsjön S 105 B16
Storbo S 102 C3
Storbogaren S 107 D14
Storbränna S 106 D7
Storbräntan S 118 E4
Storbukt N 113 B12
Storby FIN 99 B13
Stordal N 100 B6
Štore SLO 148 D4
Storebø N 94 B2
Storebro S 92 D7
Storebru N 100 C3
Store Damme DK 84 A2
Store Darum DK 86 E3
Store Heddinge DK 87 E10
Storeidet N 111 E10
Storekorsnes N 112 C11
Storelv N 112 B10
Store Merløse DK 87 D9
Støren N 104 E8
Storenga N 112 D7
Store Rise DK 83 A8
Store Rørbæk DK 86 E3
Storfjäten S 102 C5
Storfjord N 111 B18
Storfjordbotn N 113 C18
Storfors S 97 C11
Storforshei N 108 D8
Storhågna S 102 A7
Storhallaren N 104 D5
Stor-Hallen S 102 A7
Storhogen S 106 E8
Stor-Hullsjön S 103 A12
Štorje SLO 73 E8
Storjola S 106 B7
Storjord N 109 C9
Storjorda N 108 C6
Storjorda N 111 C11
Storkow D 80 B5
Storli N 101 A10
Storlien S 105 E12
Stormi FIN 127 C9
Stornara I 60 A5
Stornarella I 60 A5
Stornäs S 106 A8
Stornäs S 107 A11
Stornäset S 107 C10
Stornes N 111 C11
Storneshamn N 112 D7
Stornoway GB 2 J4
Storo I 69 B10
Storobăneasa RO 161 F6
Storodden N 104 E6
Storöhamn S 119 C10
Storozhynets' UA 153 A7
Storrington GB 15 F8
Storrøsta N 101 B13
Storsand S 103 C13
Storsand S 118 B5
Storsandsjö S 107 C17
Störsätern S 102 B3
Storsävarträsk S 118 F3
Storsele S 107 D14
Storseleby S 107 B11
Storseløy N 108 C4
Storsjö S 102 A5
Storskog S 109 E10
Storslett N 112 D7
Storsletta N 112 D6
Storsteinnes N 111 A18
Storsteinnes N 111 B17
Storsund S 118 C5
Storuman S 107 A12
Storvik N 108 C6
Storvik N 110 C9
Storvik N 112 C9
Storvik N 112 D7
Storvik S 103 E12
Storvorde DK 86 A6
Storvreta S 99 C9
Štós S 145 F2
Stößen D 79 D10
Stössing A 77 F9
Stoszowice PL 81 E11
Støtt N 108 C5
Stötten am Auerberg D 71 B11
Stotternheim D 79 D9
Stouby DK 86 D5
Stoumont B 19 D12
Stourbridge GB 13 A10
Stourport-on-Severn GB 13 A10
Støvran N 108 B7
Støvring DK 86 B5
Støvset N 108 B8
Stow GB 5 D11
Stowięcino PL 85 A12
Stowmarket GB 15 C10
Stow-on-the-Wold GB 13 B11
Stoyan Mikhaylovski BG 167 C8
Stoyanovo BG 165 C10
Stoykite BG 165 F10
Stozher BG 167 C9
Stożne PL 136 E5
Stra I 66 B3
Strabane GB 4 F2
Strabla PL 141 E8
Strachan GB 5 B11
Strachówka PL 139 F12
Strachur GB 4 C6
Stracin MK 164 E5

Stračiūnai LT 137 E9
Strackholt (Großefehn) D 17 B9
Strączno PL 85 D10
Stradalovo BG 165 E6
Stradbally IRL 7 F8
Stradbroke GB 15 C11
Stradella I 69 C7
Stradi LV 135 B13
Stradishall GB 15 C10
Stradone IRL 7 E8
Stradsett GB 11 F12
Straelen D 16 F6
Stragari SRB 158 E6
Strai N 90 C2
Straimont B 19 E11
Straja RO 153 B7
Strakhilovo BG 166 C5
Strakonice CZ 76 D5
Stralki BY 133 E4
Straloch GB 5 B9
Strålsnäs S 92 C6
Stralsund D 84 B4
Strambino I 68 C4
Stramproy NL 19 B12
Strâmtura RO 152 B4
Stráňavy SK 147 C7
Strančice CZ 77 C7
Strand N 101 D15
Strand N 110 C9
Strand S 106 D9
Stranda N 100 B5
Strandå N 108 A8
Strandby DK 86 B4
Strandby DK 90 E8
Strande D 83 B8
Strandnorum S 91 C10
Strandval N 105 B10
Strangford GB 7 D11
Stranghele N 100 E6
Strängnäs S 98 D8
Strangolagalli I 62 D4
Strångsjö S 93 B8
Stráni CZ 146 D5
Stranocum GB 4 E4
Stranorlar IRL 7 C7
Stranraer GB 4 F6
Stråoane RO 153 F10
Strasatti I 58 D2
Strasbourg F 27 C8
Strasburg D 84 D5
Strășeni MD 154 C3
Stražice CZ 76 C5
Strass D 75 E12
Strasskirchen D 75 E12
Straßwalchen A 76 G4
Stratford IRL 7 G9
Stratford-upon-Avon GB 13 A11
Strathaven GB 5 D8
Strathblane GB 5 D8
Strathpeffer GB 2 K7
Strathy GB 3 H9
Strathyre GB 5 C8
Stratinska BIH 157 C6
Stratiyivka UA 154 A4
Stratoni GR 169 C10
Stratoniki GR 169 C10
Stratos GR 174 B3
Straubing D 75 E12
Straum N 104 D5
Straum N 108 E5
Straume N 90 A2
Straume N 110 C4
Straumen N 104 E4
Straumen N 105 D10
Straumen N 108 B8
Straumen N 109 B10
Straumen N 111 A19
Straumen N 111 C11
Straumen N 114 B7
Straumfjord N 110 C9
Straumfjorden N 100 B5
Straumnes N 108 B9
Straumsnes N 108 B9
Straumsnes N 110 C8
Straumsnes N 111 B13
Straumstad N 111 B17
Straunen N 111 B15
Straupe LV 135 B9
Straupitz D 80 C6
Strausberg D 80 A5
Straußfurt D 79 D8
Stravaj AL 168 B3
Strawczyn PL 143 E9
Straža SRB 159 D7
Strazhitsa BG 166 C5
Stráž nad Nežárkou CZ 77 D7
Stráž nad Nisou CZ 81 E8
Strážnice CZ 146 D4
Stráž pod Ralskem CZ 81 D7
Strážské SK 145 F4
Štrba SK 147 C7
Streatley GB 13 B12
Strečno SK 147 C7
Streda nad Bodrogom SK 145 G4
Streek D 17 B10
Street GB 13 C9
Strehaia RO 159 D11
Strehla D 80 D4
Strejeşti RO 160 D4
Strekov SK 146 F6
Strelac AL 168 C4
Strelcě AL 168 C4
Strelcha BG 165 D9
Strellc i Epërm KS 163 D9
Strēlnieki LV 135 C8
Strem A 149 B6
Strembo I 69 A10
Stremţ RO 152 E3
Strenči LV 131 F11
Strendur FO 2 A3
Strengberg A 77 F7
Strengelvåg N 110 C10
Strengen A 71 C10
Strengen N 90 A6
Stresa I 68 B6
Stretford GB 11 E7
Stretham GB 15 C9
Streufdorf D 75 B7
Strezimirovtsi BG 164 D5
Strib DK 86 D5
Striberg S 97 C12

Stříbro CZ 76 C3
Strichen GB 3 K12
Strigno I 72 D4
Štrigova HR 148 C6
Strijen NL 16 E3
Strimasund S 108 D8
Strimoniko GR 169 B9
Strinda N 111 E10
Strittjomvare S 109 E16
Strizivojna HR 157 B9
Strmec HR 148 E5
Strmen HR 149 F7
Strmica BIH 156 D5
Strmica HR 156 D5
Ströbeck D 79 C8
Strobl A 73 A7
Strøby DK 87 E10
Strøby Egede DK 87 E10
Stroești RO 160 C3
Stroevo BG 165 E10
Strofylia GR 175 B7
Ströhen D 17 C11
Stroiești RO 153 B8
Strokestown IRL 6 E6
Ström S 108 E8
Strömbäck S 122 C4
Strömbacka S 103 C12
Stromberg D 185 E8
Stromeferry GB 2 L5
Strömfors S 118 C4
Strömholm S 109 E15
Stromiec PL 141 G4
Strommen N 95 C13
Strömmer S 96 C6
Strömnäs S 107 B10
Strömnäs S 118 B5
Stromness GB 3 H10
Strömsberg S 99 B9
Strömsbro S 103 E13
Strömsbruk S 103 C13
Strömsholm S 98 C6
Strømsmoen N 111 C16
Strömsnäs S 107 E9
Strömsnäsbruk S 87 B13
Strömstad S 91 B9
Strömsund S 106 D9
Strömsund S 107 A11
Stronachlachar GB 4 C7
Stroncone I 62 C3
Strongoli I 61 E8
Stronie Śląskie PL 77 B11
Stronsdorf A 77 E10
Strontian GB 4 B5
Stropi LV 135 E13
Stropkov SK 145 E4
Stroppiana I 68 C5
Stroppo I 36 B6
Stroud GB 13 B10
Strövelstorp S 87 C11
Strovija MK 168 A5
Stróża PL 147 B9
Štrpce KS 164 E3
Struer DK 86 C3
Strugari RO 153 D9
Strugi-Krasnyye RUS 132 E5
Strullendorf D 75 C8
Strumë AL 168 C2
Strumica MK 169 B8
Strumień PL 147 B7
Strumkivka UA 145 G5
Strumok UA 155 B4
Strumyani BG 165 F7
Strunga RO 153 C10
Strunkovice nad Blanicí CZ 76 D6
Strupl I LT 133 C1
Struth D 79 D7
Strūžāni LV 133 C2
Stružec HR 149 E7
Stryama BG 165 E10
Stryków PL 143 C8
Stryksele S 107 C16
Stryn N 100 C5
Stryy UA 145 E8
Strzałą PL 141 F6
Strzałkowo PL 142 B4
Strzebień PL 143 E6
Strzegocin PL 139 E10
Strzegom PL 81 E10
Strzegowo PL 139 E9
Strzelce PL 143 B7
Strzelce Krajeńskie PL 85 E9
Strzelce Opolskie PL 142 E5
Strzelce Wielkie PL 143 D7
Strzeleczki PL 142 F4
Strzelin PL 81 E12
Strzelno PL 138 E5
Strzepcz PL 138 B5
Strzyżewice PL 144 A5
Strzyżów PL 144 D4

Sturefors S 92 C7
Stüri LV 134 C5
Sturkö S 89 C9
Šturlić BIH 156 B4
Sturminster Newton GB 13 D10
Šturovo MK 164 F5
Štúrovo SK 149 A11
Sturry GB 15 E11
Sturzelbronn F 27 B8
Stuttgart D 27 C11
Stützerbach D 79 E8
Styggedalen N 111 B19
Stylida GR 175 B6
Styra GR 175 C9
Styrnäs S 107 E13
Styrsö S 91 D10
Styrrmanstø N 111 A18
Suances E 40 B3
Suatu RO 152 D3
Subačius LT 135 E9
Subaşı TR 171 B10
Subaşı TR 173 B9
Subaşı TR 177 C9
Subate LV 135 D11
Subbiano I 66 E4
Subiaco I 62 D4
Subkowy PL 138 B6
Subotica SRB 150 E4
Subotište SRB 158 D4
Subotniki BY 137 E12
Sučany SK 147 C7
Suceava RO 153 B8
Suceveni RO 153 E12
Sučevići HR 156 D5
Suceviţa RO 153 B7
Sucha PL 139 B7
Suchá Hora SK 147 C9
Suchá Loz CZ 146 D5
Suchań PL 85 D8
Suchá nad Parnou SK 146 E4
Suchdol CZ 77 C8
Suchdol nad Lužnicí CZ 77 E7
Suchdol nad Odrou CZ 146 B5
Suchedniów PL 143 D10
Suchowola PL 140 C8
Suchożebry PL 141 F6
Suchy Dąb PL 138 B6
Suchy Las PL 81 B11
Sucina I 56 F3
Suciu de Sus RO 152 C4
Suckow D 83 D11
Sucleia MD 154 D5
Sučuraj HR 157 F7
Sudanell E 42 D5
Sudargas LT 136 D6
Sudbury GB 15 C10
Suddenfoord D 183 A10
Suddesjaur S 109 E17
Süden D 82 B5
Süderbrarup D 82 A7
Süderhastedt D 82 B6
Süderlügum D 82 A5
Süderstapel D 82 B6
Sudervė LT 137 D11
Sudiţi RO 161 D11
Sudkov CZ 77 C11
Südlohn D 17 E7
Sudok S 118 B4
Sudoměřice CZ 146 D4
Sudova Vyshnya UA 144 D7
Sudovec HR 149 D6
Sudrabkalns LV 135 D12
Suđurađ HR 162 D4
Sudwalde D 17 C11
Sueca E 48 F4
Süedinenie BG 165 E10
Suelli I 64 D3
Suèvres F 24 E5
Şugag RO 152 F3
Suha BIH 157 D9
Suha BIH 157 F10
Suhaia RO 160 F6
Suharău RO 153 A8
Suharekë KS 163 E10
Suhl D 79 E8
Suhlendorf D 83 E9
Suhmura FIN 125 F13
Suho Polje BIH 157 C11
Suhopolje HR 149 E8
Šuica BIH 157 E7
Suici RO 160 C5
Şuiavaara S 116 B9
Suilly-la-Tour F 25 F9
Suinula FIN 123 F11
Suinula FIN 127 B12
Suippes F 25 B11
Sukeva FIN 124 C8
Sukhindol BG 166 C4
Sukhodil UA 145 E10
Sukošan HR 156 D3
Sükösd H 150 E2
Sukovo BG 165 C6
Sukow D 83 C11
Sul N 105 D12
Suldrup DK 86 B5
Sulechów PL 81 B9
Sulęcin PL 81 B8
Sulęczyno PL 138 B4
Sulejów PL 141 H1
Sulejówek PL 141 F4
Suleskar N 94 D5
Sulesund N 100 B4
Şuletea RO 153 E11
Sulina RO 155 D4
Sulingen D 17 C11
Suliszewo PL 85 D9
Sulița RO 153 B9
Sulitjelma N 109 B11
Sulkava FIN 123 D17
Sulkavanjärvi FIN 123 D16
Sulkavankylä FIN 123 F11
Sułkowice PL 147 B9
Sullington GB 15 F8
Sully F 30 A5
Sully GB 13 C8
Sully-sur-Loire F 25 E7
Sulmierzyce PL 142 C4
Sulmierzyce PL 143 D7
Sulmona I 62 C5
Sulniac F 22 E6
Sułoğlu TR 167 F7

Sułoszowa PL 143 F8
Sułów PL 81 D12
Sułów PL 144 B6
Suldal DK 86 A5
Sultaniça TR 171 C10
Sultaniye TR 173 C10
Sultanköy TR 171 B10
Sultanköy TR 173 B8
Suluca TR 171 C10
Suluca TR 172 D6
Sulvik S 96 C7
Sulviken S 105 D14
Sulz A 71 C9
Sulz am Neckar D 27 D10
Sulzbach an der Murr D 27 B11
Sulzbach-Laufen D 74 E6
Sulzbach-Rosenberg D 75 C10
Sulzbach/Saar D 186 C2
Sulzdorf an der Lederhecke D 75 B8
Sulzemoos D 75 F9
Sulzfeld D 187 C6
Sulzfeld D 187 C6
Sulzheim D 75 C7
Sulzthal D 75 B7
Sumartin HR 157 F6
Sumba FO 2 C3
Şumeçani HR 149 C8
Sümeg H 149 C8
Sumène F 35 B6
Šumiac SK 145 F1
Sumiainen FIN 123 E16
Šumice CZ 146 C5
Sumiswald CH 70 C5
Summer Bridge GB 11 C8
Summerhill IRL 7 F9
Šumperk CZ 77 C11
Sumsa FIN 121 F14
Šumvald CZ 77 C12
Sumvitg CH 71 D7
Sunäkste LV 135 D11
Sunbury GB 15 E8
Sund N 110 D5
Sund N 110 D5
Sund S 92 D6
Sund S 103 B10
Sund S 107 E14
Sundborn S 103 E10
Sundby DK 86 B3
Sundby DK 86 B3
Sundby FIN 122 C9
Sunde N 94 C3
Sunde N 108 B9
Sunde N 104 C8
Sunderland GB 5 F14
Sundern (Sauerland) D 17 F10
Sundet S 105 D10
Sundklakk N 110 D7
Sundnäs S 109 D14
Sundom FIN 122 D7
Sundom S 118 C8
Sundre S 93 F12
Sundsbruk S 103 B13
Sundsjö S 103 A10
Sundsli N 90 A3
Sundsvall S 103 B13
Sundvollen N 95 B12
Sungurlare BG 167 D7
Sunhultsbrunn S 92 D5
Suni I 64 C2
Sunja HR 149 F7
Sünna D 79 E7
Sunnan N 105 C11
Sunnanå S 97 C14
Sunnansjö S 97 B12
Sunnansjö S 107 E14
Sunnäs S 103 A13
Sunndal N 94 C3
Sunndalsøra N 101 A9
Sunne S 97 C10
Sunne S 103 A14
Sunne S 106 E6
Sunnemo S 97 C10
Sunnersta S 107 D12
Sunningdale GB 15 E8
Suntaži LV 135 C10
Suodenniemi FIN 126 B8
Suojanperä FIN 114 E4
Suojoki FIN 122 F7
Suolahti FIN 123 E15
Suolijoki FIN 119 B14
Suolijoki FIN 119 B14
Suolela FIN 119 C15
Suomenniemi FIN 128 C7
Suomijärvi FIN 122 F9
Suommu FIN 115 E4
Suomusjärvi FIN 127 E10
Suomussalmi FIN 121 E12
Suonenjoki FIN 124 E8
Suoniemi FIN 127 C9
Suonnankylä FIN 121 B11
Suontee FIN 124 E8
Suopajärvi FIN 117 E15
Suorajärvi FIN 121 E11
Suovaara FIN 121 F11
Suovanlahti FIN 123 D16
Superdévoluy F 35 A10
Supersano I 61 C10
Supertarska Draga HR 67 C10
Supetar HR 156 F6
Supino I 62 D4
Suplac de Barcău RO 151 C10
Suplacu RO 152 C4
Supraśl PL 140 D8
Supur RO 151 C10
Súr H 149 B10

Surfleet GB 11 F11
Surgères F 28 C4
Súria E 43 D7
Surier I 31 D11
Surnadalsøra N 104 F5
Sürnevo BG 166 E5
Sürnitsa BG 165 F9
Šúrovce SK 146 E5
Surte S 91 D11
Survilišķis LT 135 F8
Surju EST 131 E10
Surwold D 17 C9
Sury-le-Comtal F 30 D5
Surzur F 22 E6
Susa I 31 E11
Suşani RO 160 D4
Šušara SRB 159 D7
Susch CH 71 D10
Susegana I 72 E5
Susek SRB 158 C4
Süsel D 83 B9
Suseni RO 152 D5
Suseni RO 153 D7
Suseni RO 160 D5
Sushitsa BG 166 C5
Sušice CZ 76 D5
Susiec PL 144 C7
Šuškova UA 133 D4
Susleni MD 154 C3
Susurluk TR 173 D9
Susuzmüsellim TR 173 B7
Susz PL 139 C7
Sutera I 58 D4
Suteşti RO 160 D4
Suţeşti RO 161 C10
Sutina BIH 157 E7
Sutivan HR 156 F5
Sutjeska SRB 158 C6
Sütlüce TR 173 B7
Sutomore MNE 163 E7
Sutri LV 135 D12
Sutri I 62 C2
Sutterton GB 11 F11
Süttő H 149 A10
Sutton GB 15 C9
Sutton Bridge GB 11 F12
Sutton Coldfield GB 11 F8
Sutton in Ashfield GB 11 E9
Sutton-on-the-Forest GB 11 C9
Suure-Jaani EST 131 D10
Suurejõe EST 131 D10
Suuremõisa EST 130 D5
Suurimäki FIN 124 D8
Suurmaki FIN 125 E11
Suur-Miehikkälä FIN 128 D8
Suurpea EST 131 B11
Suutarinkylä FIN 119 E15
Suutarinkylä FIN 119 F17
Suvainiškis LT 135 D10
Suvanto FIN 115 D2
Suvantokumpu FIN 117 C15
Suvereto I 65 A3
Suviekas LT 135 E11
Suvodol MK 169 B6
Suvorovo MD 155 B2
Suvorove UA 155 B3
Suwałki PL 136 E6
Suystamo RUS 129 B15
Suze-la-Rousse F 35 B8
Suzzara I 66 C2
Svabensverk S 103 D10
Svalboviken S 93 A8
Svalenik BG 166 C5
Svalläng DK 87 D8
Svaløv S 87 D12
Svalsta S 93 B9
Svalyava UA 145 G5
Svanå S 98 C6
Svanabyn S 107 C11
Svanberga S 99 C11
Svaneke DK 89 E8
Svanesund S 91 C10
Svängsta S 89 C7
Svaningen S 106 D8
Svannäs S 109 D15
Svännäs S 107 B11
Svansele S 107 B10
Svansele S 106 B8
Svanskog S 91 A12
Svanström S 118 E5
Svantjärnåsen S 102 D7
Svanträsk S 118 C3
Svanvik N 114 E8
Svanvik S 91 C10
Svappavaara S 116 C6
Svardal N 101 A12
Svärdsjö S 103 E10
Svarinci LV 133 D3
Svarstad N 95 D11
Svartå FIN 127 E11
Svartå S 92 A5
Svartbäck S 103 A11
Svartbyn S 119 B10
Svarte S 87 E13
Svartemyr N 100 D3
Svärtinge S 92 B8
Svartlå S 118 B6
Svartnäs S 103 D10
Svartnäs S 111 B17
Svartöstaden S 118 C8
Svartträsk S 107 A12
Svartvik S 103 B13
Svartvik S 103 D13
Svartvik S 103 A13
Svatava CZ 75 B12
Svätuše S 145 G4
Svätý Jur SK 146 E4
Svätý Peter SK 146 F6
Svebølle DK 87 D8
Svedala S 87 D12
Svėdasai LT 135 E10
Svedja S 103 C12
Svedje S 106 C9
Svedje S 107 D15
Svédlar SK 145 F2
Sveg S 102 B7
Sveggesundet N 104 E3
Šveicarija LT 137 C9
Sveindal N 90 C1
Sveio N 94 C2
Svejbæk DK 86 C5
Svekļi LV 135 D13

Švėkšna LT 134 E3
Svelgen N 100 C2
Svellingen N 104 D5
Svelvik N 95 C12
Svenčionėliai LT 135 F11
Svenčionys LT 135 F12
Svendborg DK 86 E7
Svene N 95 C11
Svenljunga S 91 E13
Svenningdal N 108 F5
Svensbu N 111 A18
Svensbyn S 118 D6
Svenshögen S 91 C10
Svenstavik S 102 A7
Svenstrup DK 86 B5
Svenstrup DK 86 E5
Svenstrup DK 87 E8
Svente LV 135 E12
Šventežeris LT 137 E8
Šventoji LT 134 D2
Sverepec SK 146 C6
Sveta Marija HR 149 D7
Světciems LV 131 F8
Svēte LV 134 C7
Sveti Nikola BG 167 C10
Sveti Nikola MNE 163 E7
Sveti Nikole MK 164 F4
Sveti Rok HR 156 D4
Sveti Stefan MNE 163 E6
Světlá Hora CZ 142 F3
Světlá nad Sázavou CZ 77 C8
Svetlen BG 166 C6
Svetlogorsk RUS 139 A9
Svetly RUS 139 A9
Svetogorsk RUS 129 C10
Svetozar Miletić SRB 150 F3
Svetvinčenat HR 67 B8
Svezhen BG 165 D11
Švica HR 67 C11
Svidník SK 145 E4
Svihov CZ 76 D4
Sviibi EST 130 D6
Svilajnac SRB 159 E7
Svilengrad BG 166 F6
Svindinge DK 86 E7
Svinesund S 91 A9
Svingen N 111 A18
Svingvoll N 101 D12
Svinhult S 92 D6
Svinia SK 145 E3
Sviniţa RO 159 D9
Svinná SK 146 D6
Svinnersta S 92 B5
Svinninge DK 87 D8
Svinninge S 99 D11
Svínoy FO 2 A4
Svinvika N 104 E3
Svir' BY 137 D13
Svirkos LT 135 F12
Svishtov BG 166 B5
Svislach BY 140 D10
Svit SK 145 E1
Svitávka CZ 77 C11
Svitavy CZ 77 C10
Svitene LV 135 D7
Svitlodolyns'ke UA 154 E5
Svityaz' UA 141 H9
Svoboda BG 165 F1
Svoboda BG 166 E4
Svoboda BG 166 E4
Svoboda nad Úpou CZ 81 E9
Svobodinovo BG 166 F4
Svođe SRB 164 D5
Svodín SK 146 F6
Svodna BIH 156 B6
Svoge BG 165 D7
Svogerslev DK 87 D10
Svolvær N 110 D8
Svorkmo N 104 E7
Svratka CZ 77 C10
Svrčinovec SK 147 C7
Svrljig SRB 164 C5
Svullrya N 96 B7
Swadlincote GB 11 F8
Swaffham GB 15 B10
Swalmen NL 20 B6
Swan IRL 9 D8
Swanage GB 13 D11
Swanley GB 15 E9
Swanlinbar IRL 7 D7
Swansea GB 13 B7
Swanton Morley GB 15 B10
Swarożyn PL 138 B6
Swarzędz PL 81 B12
Swatragh GB 4 F3
Sway GB 13 D11
Świątki PL 139 C9
Świbno PL 138 B6
Świderki PL 141 G6
Świdnica PL 81 E10
Świdnica PL 81 B9
Świdnik PL 141 H7
Świdwin PL 85 C10
Świebodzice PL 81 E10
Świebodzin PL 81 B9
Świecie PL 138 D5
Świeciechowa PL 81 C11
Świeciechów-Duży PL 144 B4
Świedziebnia PL 139 D8
Świekatowo PL 138 B6
Świeradów-Zdrój PL 81 E8
Świercze PL 139 E10
Świerczów PL 142 E4
Świerklaniec PL 143 F6
Świerklany Górne PL 142 F6
Świerzawa PL 81 D10
Świerże PL 141 H9
Świerzenko PL 85 B11
Świerzno PL 85 C7
Świeszyno PL 85 B10
Świętajno PL 139 C11
Świętajno PL 139 C11
Świętochłowice PL 143 F6
Świętoszów PL 81 D9
Świfterbant NL 16 C5
Świlcza PL 144 C4
Swindon GB 13 B11
Swineshead GB 11 F11
Swinford IRL 6 E5
Świnna PL 147 B8
Świnoujście PL 84 C6
Swinton GB 5 D12
Swinton GB 11 C9
Swords IRL 7 F10
Swornegacie PL 85 C13
Syalyawshchyna BY 133 E5
Sycewice PL 85 B11
Syców PL 142 D4
Sydalen N 110 D7

Sydänmaa FIN 123 E10
Sydänmaankylä FIN 123 C16
Sydnes N 94 C3
Syelischa BY 133 F4
Syfteland N 94 B2
Sykaminia GR 171 F10
Sykäräinen FIN 123 C12
Syke D 17 C11
Sykea GR 178 B4
Syki GR 169 F9
Sykia GR 169 E7
Sykia GR 170 D5
Sykies GR 169 F7
Sykkylven N 100 B5
Sykorrachi GR 171 C9
Sykourio GR 169 E8
Sylling N 95 C12
Sylte N 100 B6
Symbister GB 3 E14
Symi GR 181 C7
Synej AL 168 B2
Synevyr UA 145 G8
Synevyrs'ka Polyana UA 145 F8
Synod Inn GB 12 A6
Synsiö FIN 123 F17
Synyak UA 145 F6
Syötekylä FIN 121 C10
Sypniewo PL 85 D11
Sypniewo PL 139 D11
Syrau D 75 A11
Syre GB 3 J8
Syrgenstein D 75 E7
Syri FIN 123 C13
Syrjä FIN 125 F10
Sysmä FIN 127 B14
Sysslebäck S 102 E4
Syston GB 11 F9
Syväjärvi FIN 117 D15
Syvänniemi FIN 124 E8
Syvärinpää FIN 125 D9
Syvde N 100 B3
Sydsnes N 100 B3
Syvota GR 168 F3
Syvros GR 174 B2
Systen DK 90 E7
Syyspohja FIN 129 C10
Szabadegyháza H 149 B11
Szabadhidvég H 149 C10
Szabadkígyós H 151 D7
Szabadszállás H 150 E4
Szabolcsbáka H 145 G5
Szada H 150 B3
Szadek PL 143 C6
Szaflary PL 147 C10
Szajol H 150 C5
Szakály H 149 C10
Szakcs H 149 C10
Szakmár H 150 D3
Szakoly H 151 B8
Szákszend H 149 A10
Szalánta H 149 E10
Szalaszend H 145 G3
Szalkszentmárton H 150 D3
Szalonna H 145 G2
Szamosszeg H 145 G5
Szamotuły PL 81 A11
Szank H 150 D4
Szany H 149 B8
Szár H 149 B11
Szarvas H 150 D6
Szászberek H 150 C5
Szatmárcseke H 145 G6
Szatymaz H 150 E5
Százhalombatta H 149 B11
Szczaniec H 81 B9
Szczawin Kościelny PL 139 F8
Szczawne PL 145 E5
Szczawnica PL 145 E2
Szczawno-Zdrój PL 81 E10
Szczebrzeszyn PL 144 B6
Szczecin PL 84 D7
Szczecinek PL 85 C11
Szczekociny PL 143 E8
Szczepankowo PL 139 D12
Szczepanowo PL 138 E4
Szczerców PL 143 D7
Szczucin PL 143 F11
Szczuczyn PL 140 C6
Szczurkowo PL 136 E2
Szczurowa PL 143 F10
Szczutowo PL 139 E8
Szczyrk PL 147 B8
Szczytna PL 77 B10
Szczytniki PL 142 C5
Szczytno PL 139 C10
Szécsény H 147 E9
Szederkény H 149 E10
Szedres H 149 D11
Szeged H 150 E5
Szeghalom H 151 C7
Szegi H 145 G3
Szegvár H 150 D5
Székely H 145 G4
Székesfehérvár H 149 B10
Székkutas H 150 D6
Szekszárd H 149 C11
Szemud PL 138 B5
Szendehely H 147 F8
Szendrő H 145 G2
Szendrőlád H 145 G2
Szentendre H 150 B3
Szentes H 150 D5
Szentgál H 149 B9
Szentgotthárd H 148 C6
Szentistván H 150 B6
Szentkirály H 150 D4
Szentlászló H 149 D9
Szentőrinc H 149 D9
Szentpéterfa H 149 B6
Szepetnek H 149 D7
Szepietowo PL 141 E7
Szerecseny H 149 B9
Szeremle H 149 D11
Szerencs H 145 G3
Szerep H 151 C7
Szerzyny PL 144 D3
Szestno PL 136 F3
Szigetbecse H 149 B11
Szigethalom H 150 C2
Szigetszentmiklós H 150 C3
Szigetvár H 149 D8
Szihalom H 150 B5
Szikszó H 145 G2
Szil H 149 A8
Szilvásvárad H 145 G1
Szirák H 147 F9
Szirmabesenyő H 145 G2
Szkaradowo PL 81 C12
Szklarska Poręba PL 81 E9
Szklary Górne PL 81 D10

Szlichtyngowa PL 81 C10
Szob H 147 F7
Sződ II 150 B3
Szőgliget H 145 F2
Szokolya H 147 F8
Szolnok H 150 C5
Szőlősgyörök H 149 C9
Szombathely H 149 B7
Szomód H 149 A10
Szomolya H 145 H1
Szówsko PL 144 C6
Szpetal Górny PL 138 E7
Szprotawa PL 81 C9
Szreńsk PL 139 D9
Szropy PL 139 C7
Sztabin PL 140 C8
Sztum PL 138 C7
Sztutowo PL 139 B7
Szubin PL 138 D4
Szőcsi H 150 B4
Szudziałowo PL 140 D9
Szügy H 147 E8
Szuhogy H 145 G2
Szulborze Wielkie PL 141 E6
Szumowo PL 139 E13
Szurdokpüspöki H 147 F9
Szydłów PL 143 E11
Szydłowiec PL 141 H3
Szydłowo PL 85 D11
Szydłowo PL 139 D9
Szymanów PL 141 F2
Szymonka PL 136 F4
Szynkielów PL 142 D6
Szypliszki PL 136 E7

T

Taagepera EST 131 F11
Taalintehdas FIN 126 E8
Taapajärvi FIN 117 D13
Taastrup DK 87 D10
Tab H 149 C10
Tabajd H 149 B11
Tabaky UA 155 B3
Tabanera de Cerrato E 40 D3
Tábara E 38 E8
Tabarz D 79 E8
Tabasalu EST 131 C9
Tabdi H 150 D3
Taberg S 91 D15
Tabernas E 55 E8
Taberno E 55 E8
Tabivere EST 131 D13
Taboada E 38 C4
Taboadela E 38 D4
Tábor CZ 77 D7
Táborfalva H 150 C3
Tábua P 44 D4
Tabuaço P 44 B5
Tabuenca E 41 E8
Täby S 99 C10
Tác H 149 B10
Tacen SLO 73 D9
Tacherting D 75 F12
Tachov CZ 75 C12
Tackåsen S 103 D9
Tăcuta RO 153 D11
Tadasuni I 64 C2
Tadcaster GB 11 D9
Tadley GB 13 C12
Taebla EST 130 D7
Tælavåg N 94 B1
Taevaskoja EST 131 E14
Tafalla E 32 E2
Tafers CH 31 B11
Taff's Well GB 13 B8
Tafjord N 100 B6
Täfteå S 107 E15
Täfteå S 122 C4
Taga RO 152 C4
Tagaranna EST 130 D4
Taggia I 37 D7
Taghmon IRL 9 D9
Tagliacozzo I 62 C4
Taglio di Po I 66 B5
Tagllu-Isolaccio I 37 G10
Tagnon F 19 F9
Tägsjöberg S 107 D11
Tahal E 55 E8
Tähemaa EST 131 E14
Tahilla IRL 8 E3
Tahitótfalu H 150 B3
Tähtelä FIN 115 D3
Taibón Agordino I 72 D5
Taïde P 38 E3
Tain GB 3 K8
Tainiemi FIN 119 C15
Tainijoki FIN 119 C15
Tain-l'Hermitage F 30 E6
Taintrux F 27 D6
Taio I 72 D3
Taipale FIN 119 B15
Taipale FIN 119 C16
Taipale FIN 123 D17
Taipale FIN 124 B8
Taipale FIN 126 B8
Taipaleenharju FIN 119 D17
Taipalsaari FIN 129 C9
Taipalus FIN 123 E11
Taivalkoski FIN 121 C11
Taivassalo FIN 126 D6
Taizé F 30 B6
Tajmište MK 168 A4
Tajno Łanowe PL 140 C7
Takácsi H 149 B8
Takamaa FIN 127 B10
Takeley GB 15 D9
Takene S 97 C9
Takene S 97 D10
Taklax FIN 122 E6
Taksony H 150 C3
Taktakenéz H 145 G3
Taktaszada H 145 G3
Talais F 28 E3
Talamantes E 41 E8
Talamona I 69 A8
Talamone I 65 B4
Talange F 186 C1
Talant F 26 F3
Talarrubias E 51 A9
Talaván E 45 E8
Talavera de la Reina E 46 E3
Talavera la Real E 51 B6
Talayuela E 45 E9
Talayuelas E 47 E10
Talea RO 161 C7
Talence F 28 F4
Talensac F 23 D8
Tales F 48 E4
Taleža BIH 162 D5
Talgarreg GB 12 A6
Talgarth GB 13 B8
Talhadas P 44 C4

Tali EST 131 E9
Taliard F 36 C4
Ialiesin GB 10 F4
Táliga E 51 B5
Tälje S 103 A10
Talla I 66 E4
Tallås S 103 E11
Tallås S 109 E14
Tallåsen S 103 C11
Tällberg S 103 E10
Tallberg S 118 B8
Taller F 32 C3
Tallinn EST 131 C9
Talljärv S 118 B8
Talloires F 31 D9
Tallone F 37 G11
Tallós E 38 C2
Tallow IRL 8 D6
Tallsjö S 107 C14
Tallvik S 109 E9
Talmaciu RO 160 B4
Talmay F 26 F3
Talmaz MD 154 D5
Talmont F 28 D4
Talmont-St-Hilaire F 28 C2
Talpa RO 160 E6
Talsano I 61 C8
Talsi LV 134 B5
Taluskylä FIN 119 F12
Talviainen FIN 127 B12
Talvik N 112 C10
Tama E 39 B10
Tămădău Mare RO 161 E9
Tamajón E 47 B6
Tamames E 45 C8
Tamarë AL 163 E8
Tamarino BG 167 E7
Tamarite de Litera E 42 D4
Tamashowka BY 141 G9
Tamási H 149 C10
Tamaşl RO 153 D10
Tâmboeşti RO 161 B10
Tâme S 118 E6
Tamis TR 177 C11
Tamm D 27 C11
Tammela FIN 121 C15
Tammela FIN 127 D15
Tammensiel D 82 A5
Tammijärvi FIN 127 B14
Tammiku EST 131 C12
Tammisaari FIN 127 F9
Tammispää EST 131 D14
Tâmna RO 159 D11
Tamnay-en-Bazois F 30 A4
Tamnes N 101 A15
Tamnič SRB 159 E9
Tampere FIN 127 C10
Tamsalu EST 131 C12
Tamsweg A 73 B8
Tamurejo E 54 B3
Tamsweg A 73 B8
Tana Bru N 113 C21
Tanacu RO 153 D11
Tanaji LV 135 C12
Tananes N 114 B4
Tananger N 94 E3
Tănăsoaia RO 153 E10
Tananella I 64 B4
Tancarville F 18 F1
Tandådalen S 102 D4
Ţăndărei RO 161 D11
Țândő S 102 E5
Tandragee GB 7 D10
Tandsbyn S 106 E7
Tandsjöborg S 102 C8
Tang IRL 7 E7
Tångaberg S 87 A10
Tångavaene IRL 6 C6
Tångböle S 105 E14
Tange DK 86 C5
Tangen N 95 A12
Tangen N 101 E14
Tangen N 111 B14
Tanger MA 52 E5
Tångeråsen S 105 D15
Tangerhütte D 79 B10
Tangermünde D 79 A10
Tångstamon S 107 E11
Tangstedt D 83 C8
Tängvattnet S 108 E8
Tanhua FIN 115 D3
Taninges F 31 C10
Tankapirtti FIN 115 B3
Tankavaara FIN 115 B2
Tanlay F 25 E11
Tann D 76 F3
Tann (Rhön) D 79 E7
Tanna D 75 B10
Tännäs S 102 A3
Tannay F 19 E10
Tannay F 25 F10
Tänndalen S 102 A3
Tanne D 79 C8
Tannenbergsthal D 75 B11
Tännesberg D 75 C11
Tannhausen D 79 A10
Tännheim A 71 C11
Tannila FIN 119 D15
Tännö S 88 A4
Tannroda D 79 E9
Tannsjön S 106 D9
Tanowo PL 84 C6
Tansa RO 153 D10
Țânțăreni RO 160 D3
Tantonville F 26 D5
Tanumshede S 91 B9
Tanvald CZ 81 E8
Taormina I 59 D7
Tapa EST 131 C11
Tapanikylä FIN 121 F13
Tapfheim D 75 E8
Tapia de Casariego E 39 A6
Tápióbicske H 150 C4
Tápiógyörgye H 150 C4
Tapionkylä FIN 117 E14
Tapionniemi FIN 115 E2
Tápióság H 150 C4
Tápiószecső H 150 C4
Tápiószele H 150 C4
Tápiószentmárton H 150 C4
Tápiószőlős H 150 C4
Táplánszentkereszt H 149 B7
Tapojärvi FIN 117 C11
Tápolca H 149 C8
Tappeluft N 112 C9
Tappenbeck D 79 B8
Tappernøje DK 87 E9
Taps DK 86 E4

Tapsony H 149 D8
Tar H 147 F9
Taracena E 47 C6
Taraclia MD 154 E4
Taraclia RO 160 D6
Taradeau F 36 E4
Taradell E 43 D8
Taramundi E 38 B5
Tarancón E 47 E6
Tarano I 62 C3
Taranto I 61 C8
Tarany H 149 D8
Tarare F 30 D5
Tarascon F 35 C8
Tarascon-sur-Ariège F 33 E9
Tarashany UA 153 A8
Tarazona E 41 E8
Tarazona de la Mancha E 47 F9
Tárbena E 56 D4
Tarbert GB 2 K3
Tarbert GB 4 D5
Tarbert GB 4 D6
Tarbert IRL 8 C4
Tarbes F 33 D6
Tarbja EST 131 D11
Tarbolton GB 4 D11
Tárcaia RO 151 D9
Tarcal H 145 G3
Tarcău RO 153 D8
Tarcea RO 151 C9
Tarcento I 73 D7
Tarčin BIH 157 E9
Tarczyn PL 141 G3
Tard H 145 H2
Tardajos E 40 D4
Tardelcuende E 41 E6
Tardets-Sorholus F 32 D4
Tardienta E 41 D10
Tardona H 145 G2
Țăreuca MD 154 B3
Târgale LV 134 B3
Targon F 28 F5
Târgoviște RO 161 D6
Targowa Górka PL 85 F12
Târgu Bujor RO 153 F11
Târgu Cărbuneşti RO 160 D3
Târgu Frumos RO 153 C9
Târgu Jiu RO 159 C11
Târgu Lăpuș RO 152 C3
Târgu Mureş RO 152 D5
Târgu Neamţ RO 153 C8
Târgu Ocna RO 153 E9
Târgu Secuiesc RO 153 E8
Târguşor RO 155 E2
Târgu Trotuş RO 153 E9
Tarhos RO 151 D7
Tarifa E 53 D5
Țarigrad MD 153 A9
Tarján H 149 A11
Tárkány H 149 A9
Tarleton GB 10 D6
Târlișua RO 152 C4
Tarłów PL 143 E11
Târlungeni RO 161 B7
Tarm DK 86 D3
Tarmstedt D 17 B12
Târnaby S 108 E9
Tărnes N 104 E4
Târnet N 114 D8
Tarnobrzeg PL 143 E12
Tarnogród PL 144 C6
Tárnok H 149 B11
Tarnos F 32 C3
Tarnoszyn PL 144 C8
Târnova RO 151 E8
Tarnow D 83 C12
Tarnów PL 85 E7
Tarnów PL 143 F10
Tarnowiec PL 144 D4
Tarnówka PL 85 D11
Tarnówko PL 85 E11
Tarnowo Podgórne PL 81 B11
Tarnów Opolski PL 142 E5
Tarnowskie Góry PL 142 F6
Tärnsjö S 98 B7
Tärnvik N 108 A9
Tärnvik N 113 C18
Taron-Sadirac-Viellenave F 32 C5
Tarouca P 44 B5
Tarp D 82 A6
Tarp DK 86 D2
Tarpa H 145 G6
Tarprubežiai LT 136 E7
Tarquinia I 62 C1
Tarquinia Lido I 62 C1
Tarragona E 42 E6
Tàrrajaur S 109 D18
Tàrrega E 42 D6
Tarrel GB 3 K9
Tarrenz A 71 C11
Tarrio E 38 B3
Tarroja de Segarra E 42 D6
Tärs DK 87 E8
Tärs DK 90 E7
Tarsele S 107 C13
Tarsia I 60 D6
Târşolţ RO 145 H7
Târstad N 111 D12
Tartas F 32 C4
Tărtăşeşti RO 161 D7
Tartu EST 131 E13
Tårup DK 87 E7
Tarutyne UA 154 E4
Tarvaala FIN 123 E16
Tarvasjoki FIN 126 D8
Tarves GB 3 L12
Tarvisio I 73 C8
Tarvola FIN 123 D11
Taşağıl TR 173 A4
Taşca RO 153 D8
Tåsjö S 107 C9
Taşlıc MD 154 C5
Tekija BIH 157 D11
Tășnad RO 151 C10
Tass H 150 C3
Tassagh GB 7 D9
Tassin-la-Demi-Lune F 30 D6
Taszár H 149 D9
Tát H 149 A11

Tata H 149 A10
Tatabánya H 149 A10
Tataháza H 150 E3
Tătărani RO 153 D11
Tătărani RO 160 D6
Tătărăşti RO 153 E11
Tătărăşti de Jos RO 160 E6
Tătărăştii de Sus RO 160 E6
Tătărăuca MD 153 A12
Tatarbunary UA 154 F5
Tatarevo BG 166 E4
Tatarköy TR 173 B7
Tatarlar TR 167 F7
Tátárszentgyörgy H 150 C3
Tating D 82 B5
Tatlısu TR 173 B8
Tatranská Javorina SK 145 E1
Tattershall GB 11 E11
Tătuleşti RO 160 D5
Tau N 94 D3
Tauberbischofsheim D 74 C6
Taucha D 79 D11
Tauche D 80 B6
Tauer D 81 C6
Taufkirchen D 75 F10
Taufkirchen D 75 F11
Taufkirchen (Vils) D 75 F11
Taujénai LT 135 F9
Taul MD 153 A11
Taulé F 22 C4
Taulignan F 35 B8
Taunton GB 13 C8
Taunusstein D 21 D10
Tauplitz A 73 A9
Taurage LT 134 F4
Tauragnai LT 135 F11
Tauralaukis LT 134 E2
Taurasi I 60 A3
Taurene LV 135 B11
Täureni RO 152 D4
Taurianova I 59 C8
Taurisano I 61 D10
Taurupe LV 135 C10
Tauste E 41 E9
Täuţ RO 151 D9
Tăuteu RO 151 C9
Tăuţii-Măgherăuş RO 151 B12
Tauves F 29 D11
Tauvo RO 119 D14
Tauxe UA 154 A6
Tavaco F 37 G10
Tavagnacco I 73 D7
Tavankut SRB 150 E4
Tavannes CH 27 F7
Tavant F 24 F3
Tavarnelle Val di Pesa I 66 E3
Tavastila FIN 128 D6
Tavastkenkä FIN 119 F16
Tavaux F 31 A7
Taveiro P 44 D3
Tavel F 35 B8
Tavelsjö S 122 C4
Tavera F 37 G9
Taverham GB 15 B11
Taverna I 59 A10
Tavernay F 30 A5
Tavernelle I 62 A2
Tavernes F 36 D4
Tavernes de la Valldigna E 56 C4
Taverny F 25 B7
Tavernspite GB 12 B5
Tavertet E 43 D8
Taviano I 61 D10
Tavira P 50 E4
Tavistock GB 12 D6
Tavullia I 67 E6
Tawern D 186 B2
Taxenbach A 73 B6
Taxiarchis GR 169 D10
Taxobeni MD 153 C11
Tayfur TR 171 D10
Tayinloan GB 4 D5
Iaylor's Cross IRL 7 F7
Taynuilt GB 4 C6
Tayport GB 5 C11
Tayvallich GB 4 C5
Tázlár H 150 D4
Tazones E 39 A8
Tczew PL 138 B6
Tczów PL 141 H4
Teaca RO 152 D5
Teano I 60 A2
Tearce MK 164 E3
Teasc RO 160 E3
Teba E 53 C7
Tebar E 47 E8
Tebay GB 10 C6
Tebstrup DK 86 D5
Techendorf A 73 C7
Techirghiol RO 155 E3
Tecuci RO 153 F10
Tedavnet IRL 7 D8
Teeriranta FIN 121 C14
Teerivaara FIN 120 D9
Tefeli GR 178 E9
Tegelen NL 16 F6
Tegeltråsk S 107 D13
Teggiano I 60 C5
Téglás H 151 B8
Teglio I 69 A8
Tegnéset S 107 C16
Teichwolframsdorf D 79 E11
Teignmouth GB 13 D8
Teijo FIN 127 E8
Teikosuvanto FIN 117 E11
Teillay F 23 E8
Teillet F 33 C10
Teişani RO 161 C8
Teisendorf D 73 A6
Teisko FIN 127 B11
Teisnach D 76 D4
Teistungen D 79 D7
Teiu RO 160 D6
Teiuş RO 152 E3
Teixeiro E 38 B3
Teixoso P 44 D6
Tejadillos E 47 D9
Tejado E 41 E7
Tejeda de Tiétar E 45 D9
Tejn DK 89 E7
Tekeler TR 181 A7
Tekeli TR 177 C9
Tekeriš SRB 158 D4
Tekirdağ TR 173 C7
Tekovské Lužany SK 147 E7
Teksdal N 104 D7
Telaki PL 141 E6

Telč CZ 77 D8
Telciu RO 152 C4
Teldau D 83 D9
Telečka SRB 150 F3
Telega RO 161 C7
Telekgerendás H 151 D6
Teleneşti MD 154 B2
Telerig BG 161 F11
Telese I 60 A3
Teleşti RO 159 C11
Telford GB 10 F7
Telgate P 17 E9
Telgte D 17 E9
Telhado P 44 D6
Telish BG 165 C9
Teliu RO 153 F7
Teliucu Inferior RO 159 B10
Teljo FIN 125 C13
Telkkälä FIN 119 C17
Tellancourt F 19 E12
Tellejåkk S 118 B3
Tellin B 19 E11
Tellingstedt D 82 B6
Telneset N 101 B13
Telnice CZ 77 D11
Telões P 38 F4
Telšiai LT 134 E4
Telti I 64 B3
Teltow D 80 B4
Tembleque E 46 E6
Temelin CZ 77 D7
Temeleuţl MD 153 C12
Temenni GR 174 C5
Temerin SRB 158 C4
Temmes FIN 119 E15
Tempi GR 169 E8
Tempio Pausania I 64 B3
Temple Bar GB 12 A6
Temple Ewell GB 15 E11
Templemore IRL 9 C7
Templepatrick GB 4 F4
Temple Sowerby GB 5 F11
Templeton GB 12 B5
Templeuohy IRL 9 C7
Templeuve F 182 D2
Templin D 84 D5
Temse B 19 B9
Temska SRB 164 C6
Temù I 69 A9
Tenala FIN 127 E9
Tenay F 31 D8
Ten Boer NL 17 B7
Tenbury Wells GB 13 A9
Tenby GB 12 B5
Tence F 30 E5
Tende F 37 C7
Tendilla E 47 C7
Tendu F 29 B9
Teneniai LT 134 F3
Tenevo BG 167 E7
Tengelic H 149 C11
Tengen D 27 E10
Tengesdal N 94 C3
Tenhult S 92 D4
Teningen D 27 D8
Tenja HR 149 F11
Tenk H 150 B5
Tennänget S 102 C6
Tennenbronn D 27 D9
Tenneville B 19 D12
Tennevoll N 111 C12
Tennilä FIN 119 B16
Tennilä FIN 127 D13
Tennskjer N 111 B15
Tennstrand N 110 D9
Tenterden GB 15 E10
Tentúgal P 44 D3
Teora I 60 B4
Teovo MK 169 B8
Tepasto FIN 117 C13
Tépe H 151 C8
Tepeboz TR 177 B7
Tepecik TR 173 B10
Tepecik TR 173 E10
Tepelenë AL 168 D3
Teplá CZ 76 C3
Teplice CZ 80 E5
Teplice nad Metují CZ 81 E10
Teplička SK 145 F2
Teplička nad Váhom SK 147 C7
Tepsa FIN 117 C15
Ţepu RO 153 F10
Ter Aar NL 182 A5
Teramo I 62 B5
Tērande LV 134 B3
Ter Apel NL 17 C8
Teratyn PL 144 B8
Tērbạặ AL 168 C2
Terborg-Silvolde NL 16 E6
Terchová SK 147 C8
Tereblya UA 145 G8
Teregova RO 159 C9
Teremia Mare RO 150 F6
Terena P 50 B5
Teresa E 48 E3
Teresa de Cofrentes E 47 F10
Teresin PL 141 F2
Terespol PL 141 F9
Teresva UA 145 G8
Terezín CZ 76 A6
Terezino Polje HR 149 E8
Tergnier F 19 E7
Tergu I 64 B2
Terheijden NL 182 B5
Terikeste EST 131 E14
Terjärv FIN 123 C11
Terka PL 145 E5
Tērliczko CZ 146 B6
Terlizzi I 61 A7
Terme Luigiane I 60 E5
Térmens E 42 D5
Termignon F 31 E10
Terminiers F 24 D6
Termini Imerese I 58 D4
Termoli I 63 D7
Termon IRL 7 B7
Termonfeckin IRL 7 E10
Ternaard NL 16 B5
Ternberg A 76 G6
Terndrup DK 86 B6
Terneuzen NL 16 F1
Ierni I 62 B3
Ternitz A 148 A6
Ternove UA 145 G8
Ternovka UA 153 A8
Terpezita RO 160 E3
Terpni GR 169 C9

Tcrpsithea GR 169 E7
Terpyllos GR 169 B8
Terracina I 62 E4
Terrades E 34 F4
Terrak N 105 A12
Terralba I 64 D2
Terranova da Sibari I 61 D6
Terranova di Pollino I 60 D6
Terranuova Bracciolini I 66 E4
Terrassini I 58 C3
Terrassa E 43 D8
Terrasson-Lavilledieu F 29 E8
Terraube F 33 C7
Terravecchia I 61 E7
Terricciola I 66 E2
Terriente E 47 D10
Terrin IRL 7 E8
Terrinches E 55 B7
Terrou F 29 F9
Terrugem P 50 B1
Terrugem P 51 B5
Terryglass IRL 6 F6
Terslev DK 87 E9
Tērstenik KS 164 D2
Tertenia I 64 D4
Teruel E 47 D10
Tervajoki FIN 122 D8
Tervakoski FIN 127 D12
Tervavaara FIN 121 D11
Tervel BG 161 F11
Terves F 28 B4
Tērvete LV 134 D6
Tervo FIN 123 E17
Tervola FIN 119 B13
Tervolan asema FIN 119 B13
Tervuren B 19 C10
Tés H 149 B10
Tešanj BIH 157 C8
Těšany CZ 77 D11
Těšedíkovo SK 146 E5
Tesero I 72 D4
Tešica SRB 164 C4
Tesimo I 72 C3
Tesjoki FIN 127 E15
Teslić BIH 157 C8
Teslui RO 160 D4
Teslui RO 160 E4
Tespe D 83 D8
Tessenderlo B 19 B11
Tessin D 83 B12
Tesson F 28 D4
Tessy-sur-Vire F 23 C9
Testa del Gargano I 63 D10
Testa dell'Acqua I 59 F6
Testelt B 182 C5
Teşvikiye TR 173 C11
Tét H 149 A9
Tetbury GB 13 B10
Teţcani MD 153 A9
Teţchea RO 151 C9
Teteringen NL 182 B5
Teterow D 83 C13
Tetětlen H 151 C7
Teteven BG 165 D9
Teti I 64 C3
Tetney GB 11 E11
Tetoiu RO 160 D3
Tétouan MA 53 E6
Tettens D 17 A9
Tettnang D 71 B9
Tetyń PL 85 D7
Teublitz D 75 D11
Teuchern D 79 D11
Teufen CH 27 F11
Teufenbach A 73 B9
Teulada I 56 F2
Teulada I 64 F2
Teunz D 75 D11
Teupitz D 80 B5
Teurajärvi FIN 117 D11
Teurajärvi S 116 E9
Teuro FIN 127 D10
Teuschnitz D 75 B9
Teutschenthal D 79 D10
Teuva FIN 122 F7
Tevaniemi FIN 127 B9
Tevansjö S 103 B9
Tevel H 149 D10
Tēvenäni LV 133 C1
Tevfikiye TR 171 E10
Teviothead GB 5 E11
Tewkesbury GB 13 A10
Teyssieu F 29 F9
Thal D 79 E7
Thale (Harz) D 79 C9
Thaleischweiler-Fröschen D 186 C4
Thalfang D 21 E7
Thalheim D 79 C11
Thalheim bei Wels A 76 F6
Thaljina BIH 157 F7
Thalmässing D 75 D9
Thalwil CH 27 F10
Thame GB 14 D7
Thann F 27 E7
Thannhausen D 75 F7
Thaon-les-Vosges F 26 D5
Tharandt D 80 E5
't Harde NL 16 D5
Tharsis E 51 D5
Thasos GR 171 C7
Thatcham GB 13 C12
Thaumiers F 29 B11
Thaxted GB 15 D9
Thaya A 77 E8
Thayngen CH 27 E10
Theale GB 13 C12
Thedinghausen D 17 C12
Theillay F 24 F7
Theißen D 79 D11
Theix F 22 E6
Them DK 86 C5
Themar D 75 B8
The Mumbles GB 12 B6
Thenay F 29 B8
Thénezay F 28 B5
Thenon F 29 E8
Theologos GR 171 C7
Théoule-sur-Mer F 36 D5
The Pike IRL 9 D7
Therma GR 171 B7
Therma GR 169 C9
Thermi GR 169 C9
Thermisia GR 175 E7
Thermo GR 174 B4
Thermopyles GR 175 B6
Thérouanne F 18 C5
The Sheddings GB 4 F4
Thespies GR 175 C7
Thesprotiko GR 168 F4
Thessaloniki GR 169 C8
The Stocks GB 15 E10

Thetford GB 15 C10
Theth AL 163 E8
Theux B 19 C12
Thèze F 32 D5
Thèze F 35 B10
Thiaucourt-Regniéville F 26 C4
Thiberville F 24 B3
Thibie F 25 C11
Thiéblemont-Farémont F 25 C12
Thiendorf D 80 D5
Thiene I 72 E3
Thierhaupten D 75 E8
Thierrens CH 31 B10
Thiers F 30 D4
Thiersee A 72 A5
Thiersheim D 75 B11
Thiesi I 64 B2
Thießow D 84 B5
Thiézac F 29 E11
Thimert-Gâtelles F 24 C5
Thin-le-Moutier F 19 E10
Thionville F 20 F6
Thiron Gardais F 24 D4
Thirsk GB 11 C9
Thisted DK 86 B3
Thisvi GR 175 C6
Thiva GR 175 C7
Thivars F 24 D5
Thiviers F 29 E7
Thizy F 30 C5
Thoirette F 31 C8
Thoiry F 24 C6
Thoissey F 30 C6
Tholen NL 16 E2
Tholey D 21 F8
Thomastown IRL 9 C8
Thommen B 20 D6
Thônes F 31 D9
Thonnance-lès-Joinville F 26 D3
Thonon-les-Bains F 31 C9
Thorame-Haute F 36 C5
Thoras F 30 F4
Thoré-la-Rochette F 24 E4
Thorenc F 36 D5
Thorigny-sur-Oreuse F 25 D9
Thörl A 73 A11
Thorn NL 19 B12
Thornaby-on-Tees GB 11 B9
Thornbury GB 13 B9
Thorne GB 11 D10
Thorney GB 11 F11
Thornhill GB 5 E9
Thorning DK 86 C4
Thornton GB 10 D5
Thorpe-le-Soken GB 15 D11
Thorpe Market GB 15 B11
Thorpeness GB 15 C12
Thorsager DK 86 C6
Thorshøj DK 90 E7
Thorsø DK 86 C5
Thouarcé F 23 F11
Thouaré-sur-Loire F 23 F9
Thouars F 28 B5
Thouria GR 174 E5
Thourotte F 18 F6
Thrapston GB 15 C7
Threshfield GB 11 C7
Thropton GB 5 E13
Thrumster GB 3 J10
Thuès-entre-Valls F 33 E10
Thueyts F 35 A7
Thuin B 19 D9
Thuine D 17 D9
Thuir F 34 E4
Thum D 80 E3
Thun CH 70 D5
Thundersley GB 15 D10
Thüngen D 74 C6
Thüngersheim D 74 C6
Thuré F 29 B6
Thuret F 30 D3
Thurey F 31 B7
Thüringen A 71 C9
Thurins F 30 D6
Thürkow D 83 C12
Thurlby GB 11 F11
Thurles IRL 9 C7
Thurnau D 75 B9
Thursby GB 5 F10
Thurso GB 3 H9
Thury-Harcourt F 23 C11
Thusis CH 71 D8
Thwaite GB 11 C7
Thyborøn DK 86 B2
Thyez F 31 C10
Thymiana GR 177 C7
Thyregod DK 86 D4
Thyrnau D 76 E5
Tia Mare RO 160 F5
Tiana I 64 C3
Țibana RO 153 D10
Țibănești RO 153 D10
Tibble S 99 D9
Tiberget S 102 D6
Tibi I 56 D3
Tibolddaróc H 145 H2
Tibro S 92 C4
Tibucani RO 153 C9
Țice BIH 156 D6
Ticehurst GB 15 E9
Ticha BG 167 D6
Tichá CZ 146 B6
Tichilești RO 155 C1
Tičići BIH 157 D9
Ticknall GB 11 F9
Ticleni RO 160 D2
Țicușu RO 152 F6
Ticvaniu Mare RO 159 C8
Tidaholm S 91 C14
Tidan S 91 B15
Tiddische D 79 A8
Tidenham GB 13 B9
Tidersrum S 92 D7
Tiebas E 32 E2
Tiedra E 39 E9
Tiefenbach D 75 D12
Tiefenbach D 76 E4
Tiefenbronn D 27 C10
Tiefencastel CH 71 D9
Tiefensee D 84 E5
Tiel NL 16 E4
Tielen B 182 C5
Tielt B 19 C7
Tiemassaari FIN 125 F10
Tienen B 19 C10
Tiengen D 27 E9
Tiercé F 23 E11
Tierga E 41 E8
Tierp S 99 B9
Tierzo E 47 C9
Tifești RO 153 F10
Țigănași RO 153 C10
Țigănești RO 160 F6

Tigare BIH 158 E3
Tighina MD 154 D4
Tighira MD 153 C11
Tignale I 69 B10
Tignes F 31 E10
Tigveni RO 160 C5
Tigy F 25 E7
Tiha Bârgăului RO 152 C5
Tihany H 149 C9
Tihemetsa EST 131 E10
Tihilä FIN 123 C16
Tihusniemi FIN 124 F9
Tiistenjoki FIN 123 E17
Tijesno HR 156 E4
Tijola E 55 E8
Tíjola S 91 A8
Tikkakoski FIN 123 F15
Tikkala FIN 123 E14
Tikkala FIN 125 F14
Tikkurila FIN 127 E13
Tikob DK 87 C10
Tilburg NL 16 E4
Tilbury GB 15 E9
Til-Châtel F 26 E3
Tildarg GB 4 F4
Tileagd RO 151 C9
Tilehurst GB 13 C12
Tilh F 32 C4
Tilişca RO 152 F3
Tillac F 33 D6
Tillberga S 98 C7
Tillicoultry GB 5 C9
Tillières-sur-Avre F 24 C5
Tilloy-et-Bellay F 25 B12
Tillyfourie GB 3 L11
Tilly-sur-Seulles F 23 B10
Tilvikai LT 134 E3
Tilža LV 133 C2
Tim DK 86 C2
Timahoe IRL 7 G8
Timár H 145 G3
Timelkam A 76 F5
Timiryazevo RUS 136 C4
Timişeşti RO 153 C9
Timişoara RO 151 F7
Timmele S 91 D13
Timmendorfer Strand D 83 C9
Timmernabben S 89 B10
Timmersdala S 91 B14
Timola FIN 125 F9
Timoleague IRL 8 E5
Timolin IRL 7 G9
Timoniemi FIN 121 F13
Timovaara FIN 125 D12
Timrå S 103 A13
Timring DK 86 C3
Timsgearraidh GB 2 J2
Tinahely IRL 9 C10
Tinajas E 47 D7
Tinalhas P 44 E5
Tinca RO 151 D8
Tinchebray F 23 C10
Tineo E 39 B7
Tingere LV 134 B5
Tinglev DK 86 F4
Tingsryd S 89 B7
Tingstad S 93 B8
Tingstäde S 93 D13
Tingvatn N 94 F6
Tingvoll N 100 A8
Tingwall GB 3 G10
Tinja BIH 157 C10
Tinjan HR 67 B8
Tinn N 95 C9
Tinnoset N 95 C10
Tinos GR 176 D5
Tinosu RO 161 D8
Tinqueux F 19 F8
Tintagel GB 12 D5
Tinténiac F 23 D8
Tintern Parva GB 13 B9
Tințești RO 161 C9
Țințigny B 19 E12
TinūžI LV 135 C9
Tiobraid Árann IRL 8 D6
Tione di Trento I 69 A10
Tipasoja FIN 125 C10
Tipperary IRL 8 D6
Tiptree GB 15 D10
Tipu EST 131 E10
Tîra MD 154 B2
Tiranë AL 168 B2
Tiranges F 30 E4
Tirano I 69 A9
Tiraspol MD 154 D5
Tiraspolul Nnu MD 154 D5
Tire TR 177 C10
Tiream RO 151 B9
Țirețl LV 134 C7
Tirgo E 40 C6
Tiriez E 55 B8
Tîrg E 48 D5
Tiriolo I 59 B10
Tirkšliai LT 134 D4
Tîrnova MD 153 A11
Tirro FIN 113 F14
Tirschenreuth D 75 C11
Tirstrup DK 86 C7
Tirteafuera E 54 B4
Tirza LV 135 B12
Tisău RO 161 C9
Tišča BIH 157 D10
Tishevitsa BG 165 C8
Tishono RUS 136 D3
Tišice CZ 77 B7
Tismana RO 159 D10
Tišnov CZ 77 D10
Tisovec SK 147 D9
Tistrup Stationsby DK 86 D3
Tisvilde DK 87 C10
Tiszaalpár H 150 D4
Tiszabezdéd H 145 G6
Tiszabő H 150 C5
Tiszabura H 150 C5
Tiszacsege H 151 B8
Tiszadada H 145 G3
Tiszaderzs H 150 B6
Tiszadob H 145 G3
Tiszaeszlár H 145 G3
Tiszaföldvár H 150 D5
Tiszafüred H 150 B6
Tiszagyenda H 150 C6
Tiszaigar H 150 B6
Tiszajenő H 150 C5
Tiszakanyár H 145 G4
Tiszakarád H 145 G4
Tiszakécske H 150 D5

Tiszakerecseny H 145 G5
Tiszakeszi H 151 B6
Tiszakürt H 150 D5
Tiszalök H 145 G3
Tiszalúc H 145 G3
Tiszanagyfalu H 145 G3
Tiszanána H 150 B6
Tiszaörs H 150 B6
Tiszapalkonya H 145 H3
Tiszapüspöki H 150 C5
Tiszaroff H 150 C5
Tiszasas H 150 D5
Tiszasüly H 150 C5
Tiszaszalka H 145 G5
Tiszaszentimre H 150 C6
Tiszasziget H 150 E5
Tiszatarján H 147 F12
Tiszatelek H 145 G4
Tiszatenyő H 150 C5
Tiszaug H 150 D5
Tiszaújváros H 145 H3
Tiszavárkony H 150 C5
Tiszavasvári H 145 H3
Titaguas E 47 E10
Titel SRB 158 C5
Țiteşti RO 160 C6
Tithorea GR 175 B6
Tito I 60 B5
Titova Korenica HR 156 C4
Titov Drvar BIH 156 D5
Titran N 104 D4
Tittelsnes N 94 C3
Titting D 75 E9
Tittmoning D 76 F3
Titu RO 161 D7
Titulcia E 46 D5
Tiukuvaara FIN 117 C13
Tiurajärvi FIN 117 C12
Tivat MNE 163 E6
Tivenys E 42 F5
Tiverton GB 13 D8
Tivissa E 42 E5
Tivoli I 62 D3
Tizzano F 37 H9
Tjæreborg DK 86 E3
Tjäkkjokk S 109 E15
Tjällmo S 92 B6
Tjamotis S 109 C16
Tjappsåive S 109 E17
Tjärmyrberget S 106 C9
Tjärn S 107 D13
Tjärnäs S 98 A6
Tjärnberg S 107 C13
Tjärstad S 92 C7
Tjäruträsk S 118 B8
Tjautas S 116 D5
Tjeldnes N 111 D11
Tjeldstø N 100 A1
Tjelle N 100 A7
Tjentište BIH 157 F10
Tjöck FIN 122 F6
Tjøme N 90 A7
Tjønnefoss N 90 B4
Tjorhom N 94 E4
Tjörnarp S 87 D13
Tjøtta N 108 E3
Tjuda FIN 126 E8
Tjuvskjær N 111 C13
Tkon HR 156 E3
Tleñ PL 138 C5
Tlmače SK 147 E7
Tłuchowo PL 139 E7
Tlumačov CZ 146 C5
Tłuszcz PL 139 F11
Toab GB 3 F14
Toaca RO 152 D5
Tóalmás H 150 C5
Toano I 66 D2
Tobar an Choire IRL 6 D5
Tobarra E 55 B9
Tobercurry IRL 6 D5
Tobermore GB 4 F3
Tobermory GB 4 B4
Tobo S 99 B9
Tobyn S 97 C8
Tocane-St-Apre F 29 E6
Tocco da Casauria I 62 C5
Tocha P 44 D3
Töcksfors S 96 C6
Tocón E 53 B9
Todal N 104 F6
Toddington GB 13 B11
Todi I 62 B2
Todireni RO 153 B10
Todirești RO 153 C9
Todirești RO 153 C9
Todirești RO 153 B10
Todmorden GB 11 D7
Todolella E 42 F3
Todorič BIH 157 D7
Todor-Ikonomovo BG 161 F10
Todorovo BG 161 F9
Todtmoos D 27 E8
Todtnau D 27 E8
Toén E 38 D4
Toft GB 3 E14
Toft N 108 F3
Tofta S 87 A10
Tofta S 93 D12
Tofte N 95 C13
Töftedal S 91 B10
Tofterup DK 86 D3
Toftir FO 2 A3
Toftlund DK 86 E4
Tofyeli BY 133 F3
Togher IRL 7 E10
Togher IRL 7 F7
Togher IRL 8 E4
Togston GB 5 E13
Tohmajärvi FIN 125 F14
Tohmo FIN 115 E2
Toholampi FIN 123 C12
Toija FIN 127 E10
Toijala FIN 127 C10
Toila EST 132 C2
Toirano I 37 C8
Toivakka FIN 123 F16
Toivakka FIN 123 F16
Toivala FIN 124 E9
Toivola FIN 128 C6
Tojaci MK 169 B6
Tójby FIN 122 F6
Tök H 149 A11
Tokachika BG 171 B9
Tokaj H 145 G3
Tokarnia PL 143 E9
Tokarnia PL 147 B9
Tokod H 149 A11
Tököl H 149 B11
Tokrajärvi FIN 125 E15
Toksovo RUS 129 E14
Tolastadh Úr GB 2 J4
Tolbaños E 46 C3

Tolbert NL 16 B6
Tolcsva H 145 G3
Toledo E 46 E4
Tolentino I 67 F7
Tolfa I 62 C1
Tolga N 101 B14
Toliejai LT 135 F10
Tolja FIN 119 B17
Tolk D 82 A7
Tolkmicko PL 139 B8
Tollarp S 88 D5
Tollered S 91 D11
Tollesbury GB 15 D10
Tollo I 63 C6
Tølløse DK 87 D9
Töllsjö S 91 D12
Tolmachevo RUS 132 D6
Tolmezzo I 73 D7
Tolmin SLO 73 D8
Tolna H 149 D11
Tolnanémedi H 149 C10
Tolne DK 90 E7
Tolo GR 175 D6
Tolochănești MD 153 A11
Tolonen FIN 117 E14
Tolosa E 32 D1
Tolosa P 44 F5
Tolosenmäki FIN 125 F14
Tolox E 53 C7
Tolšići BIH 157 D10
Tolva E 42 C5
Tolva FIN 115 E3
Tolvyarvi RUS 125 F16
Tolve I 60 B6
Tomai MD 154 D2
Tomai MD 154 E3
Tomar P 44 E4
Tomares E 51 E7
Tomašec I 62 C3
Tomaševac SRB 158 C6
Tomaševo MNE 163 D8
Tomašica BIH 157 C6
Tomášikovo SK 146 E5
Tomášovce SK 147 E9
Tomaszów Lubelski PL 144 C7
Tomaszów Mazowiecki PL 141 G2
Tomatin GB 3 L9
Tombebœuf F 33 A6
Tomelilla S 88 D5
Tomelloso E 47 F6
Tomeşti RO 151 E10
Tomeşti RO 151 F9
Tomeşti RO 153 C11
Tomice PL 147 B8
Tomintoul GB 3 L10
Tomislavgrad BIH 157 E7
Tømmerneset N 111 E10
Tommerup DK 86 E6
Tomnavoulin GB 3 L10
Tömörkény H 150 D5
Tompa H 150 E4
Tomra N 100 A5
Tomşani RO 161 D8
Tona I 64 C3
Tonara I 64 C3
Tonbridge GB 15 E9
Torpo N 101 E9
Tønder DK 86 F3
Tonezza del Cimone I 69 B11
Tongeren B 19 C11
Tongland GB 5 F9
Tongue GB 2 J8
Tönisvorst D 183 C8
Tonkopuro FIN 115 E4
Tonna GB 13 B7
Tonnay-Boutonne F 28 D4
Tonnay-Charente F 28 D4
Tonnerre F 25 E10
Tonnes N 108 C5
Tönning D 82 B6
Tønsberg N 95 D12
Tönsen S 103 D12
Tonstad N 94 F5
Tonsvik N 111 A17
Toombeola IRL 6 F3
Toomebridge GB 4 F4
Tootsi EST 131 D9
Topalu RO 155 D2
Topares E 55 D8
Toparlar TR 181 C9
Topchii BG 161 F9
Töpchin D 80 B5
Topeno FIN 127 D11
Tophisar TR 173 B9
Topleţ RO 159 D9
Topliceni RO 161 C10
Topli Do SRB 165 C6
Topliţa RO 152 D6
Topliţa RO 159 B10
Töplitz D 79 B12
Topojë AL 168 C1
Topola SRB 158 E6
Topolčani MK 168 B5
Topoľčany SK 146 D6
Topoľčianky SK 146 E6
Topolia GR 178 E6
Topólka PL 138 E6
Topolnica RO 159 D9
Topoľníky SK 146 F5
Topolog RO 155 D2
Topolovac HR 149 F6
Topolovăţu Mare RO 151 F8
Topoloveni RO 160 D6
Topolovgrad BG 166 E6
Topolovnik SRB 159 D7
Topolovo BG 166 F4
Topoľšica SLO 73 D11
Toponica SRB 158 E5
Toporec SK 145 E1
Toporivtsi UA 153 A8
Toporów PL 81 B8
Toporu RO 161 E7
Toporzyk PL 85 C10
Toppenstedt D 83 D8
Topraisar RO 155 E2
Topsham GB 13 D8
Topusko HR 156 B4
Torá E 43 D6
Toral de los Guzmanes E 39 D8
Toral de los Vados E 39 C6
Torano Castello I 60 E6
Torasalo FIN 125 F10
Toras-Sieppi FIN 117 C11
Torballi TR 177 C9
Torbjörntorp S 91 C14
Torbole I 69 B10

Torcy F 30 B5
Torda SRB 158 B5
Tordas H 149 B11
Tordehumos E 39 E9
Tordera E 43 D9
Tordesillas E 39 E10
Tordesilos E 47 C9
Töre S 118 C9
Töreboda S 91 B15
Toreby DK 83 A11
Torekov S 87 C11
Torella del Sannio I 63 D7
Torella dei Lombardi I 60 B4
Torelló E 43 C8
Toreno E 39 C6
Torestorp S 91 E12
Torgau D 80 C3
Torgelow D 84 C6
Torgiano I 62 A2
Torhamn S 89 C9
Torhout B 19 B7
Tori EST 131 E9
Torigni-sur-Vire F 23 B10
Torija E 47 C6
Torino I 68 C4
Toritto I 61 B7
Torkanivka UA 154 A4
Torkovichi RUS 132 D7
Torla E 32 E5
Torma EST 131 D13
Tormac RO 159 F8
Törmänen FIN 113 E19
Törmänki FIN 117 E13
Törmänmäki FIN 121 E10
Törmäsenvaara FIN 121 C13
Törmäsjärvi FIN 119 B12
Tormestorp S 87 C13
Tormón E 47 D10
Tormore GB 4 D6
Tornadizos de Ávila E 46 C3
Tornala SK 145 G1
Tornavacas E 45 D9
Tornby DK 90 D6
Tornemark DK 87 D9
Tornes N 100 A6
Tørnes N 111 D11
Tornesch D 82 C7
Tornimäe EST 130 D6
Tornio FIN 119 C12
Tornjoš SRB 150 F4
Torno I 69 B7
Tornos E 47 C10
Tornow D 84 D4
Toro E 39 E9
Torö S 93 B11
Törökbálint H 149 B11
Törökszentmiklós H 150 C5
Torony H 149 B7
Toros BG 165 D9
Toroshino RUS 132 F4
Torsø S 91 B14
Torp FIN 99 B13
Torpa S 92 D6
Torphins GB 3 L11
Torpo N 101 E9
Torpoint GB 12 E6
Torpsbruk S 88 A7
Torquay GB 13 E7
Torquemada E 40 D3
Torraiba de Calatrava E 54 A5
Torralba I 64 B2
Torralba I 64 B2
Torralba de Aragón E 41 E10
Torralba de El Burgo E 40 E6
Torralba de los Sisones E 47 C10
Torralba de Oropesa E 45 E10
Torrão P 50 C3
Torre das Vargens P 44 F5
Torre de Coelheiros P 50 B4
Torre de Dona Chama P 38 E5
Torre de Embesora E 48 D4
Torredeita P 44 C4
Torre de Juan Abad E 55 B6
Torre del Bierzo E 39 C7
Torre del Burgo E 47 C6
Torre del Campo E 53 A9
Torre del Greco I 60 B2
Torre del Mar E 53 C8
Torredembarra E 43 E6
Torre de Miguel Sesmero E 51 B6
Torre de Moncorvo P 45 B6
Torre de'Passeri I 62 C5
Torre de Santa María E 45 F8
Torredonjimeno E 53 A9
Torre do Terrenho P 44 C6
Torrefarrera E 42 D5
Torregamones E 39 F7
Torregrossa E 42 D5
Torreiglesias E 46 B4
Torreira P 44 C3
Torrejoncillo E 45 E8
Torrejoncillo del Rey E 47 D7
Torrejón de Ardoz E 46 D6
Torrejón del Rey E 46 C6
Torrelacárcel E 47 C10
Torrelaguna E 46 C5
Torrelapaja E 41 E8
Torrelas E 41 E8
Torrelles de Foix E 43 E7
Torrelobatón E 39 E9
Torrelodones E 46 C5
Torremaggiore I 63 D8
Torremanzanas-La Torre de les Macanes E 56 D4
Torremayor E 51 B6
Torremegía E 51 B7
Torre Mileto I 63 D9
Torremocha E 45 F8
Torremocha de Jiloca E 47 C10
Torremolinos E 53 D7

Torrenostra E 48 D5
Torrent E 48 F4
Torrente del Cinca E 42 E4
Torrenueva E 55 B6
Torreorgaz E 45 E8
Torre Orsaia I 60 C4
Torre-Pacheco E 56 F3
Torre Pellice I 31 F11
Torreperogil E 53 C6
Torres S 103 A9
Torresandino E 40 E4
Torre San Giovanni I 61 D10
Torre Santa Susanna I 61 C10
Torres de Albánchez E 55 C7
Torres de Berrellén E 41 E9
Torres de la Alameda E 46 D6
Torres del Carrizal E 39 E8
Torresmenudas E 45 B9
Torres Novas P 44 F3
Torres Vedras P 44 F2
Torrevelilla E 42 F3
Torrevieja E 56 F3
Torrice I 62 D4
Torricella I 61 C9
Torricella in Sabina I 62 C3
Torricella Peligna I 63 C6
Torricella Sicura I 62 B5
Torricella Taverne CH 69 A6
Torrico E 45 E10
Torri del Benaco I 69 B10
Torridon GB 2 K5
Torriglia I 37 B10
Torrijas E 48 D3
Torrijo E 41 E8
Torrijo del Campo E 47 C10
Torrijos E 46 E4
Torrin GB 2 L4
Tørring DK 86 D4
Tørring N 105 C10
Torrita di Siena I 66 F4
Torroal P 50 C2
Torroella de Montgrí E 43 C10
Torrox E 53 C9
Torrubia del Campo E 47 E7
Torrubia de Soria E 41 E7
Tørrvika N 104 C7
Torsåker S 98 A6
Torsång S 97 B14
Torsås S 89 C10
Torsby S 97 B9
Torsby S 97 C9
Torsebro S 88 C6
Torshälla S 98 D6
Tórshavn FO 2 A3
Torsholma FIN 126 E5
Torsken N 111 B13
Torslanda S 91 D10
Torsminde DK 86 C2
Torsö S 91 B14
Torsvåg N 112 C4
Törtel H 150 C4
Tortella I 43 C9
Torteval GBG 22 B6
Torthorwald GB 5 E9
Tortinmäki FIN 126 D7
Tórtola de Henares E 47 C6
Tórtoles de Esgueva E 40 E3
Tortoli I 64 D4
Tortomanu RO 155 E2
Tortona I 37 B9
Tortora I 60 D5
Tortoreto I 62 B5
Tortorici I 59 C6
Tortosa E 42 F5
Tortozendo P 44 D5
Tortuera E 47 C9
Tortuna S 98 C7
Toruń PL 138 D6
Torun' UA 145 F8
Torup S 87 B12
Tõrva EST 131 E11
Tor Vaianica I 62 D2
Torvenkylä FIN 119 F11
Torvik N 104 B3
Torvik N 104 F4
Torvikbukt N 104 F3
Tørvikbygd N 94 B4
Torvinen FIN 117 D17
Torviccón E 55 F6
Torvsjö S 107 C12
Torysa SK 145 E2
Torzym PL 81 B8
Tosca P 45 B6
Tošćani SK 146 B6
Tosno RUS 132 D6
Tossa de Mar E 43 D9
Tossåsen S 102 A5
Tossåsen S 102 A7
Tossavanlahti FIN 123 D16
Tosse F 32 C3
Tössse S 91 B12
Tossicia I 62 B5
Tosside GB 11 C7
Tõstamaa EST 131 E7
Tostedt D 82 D7
Tószeg H 150 C5
Toszek PL 142 F6
Totana E 55 D10
Totebo S 93 D8
Tôtes F 18 E3
Tótkomlós H 150 E6
Totland GB 13 D11
Totra S 103 E13
Tótszerdahely H 149 D7
Tõttdal N 105 C10
Tottijärvi FIN 127 C9
Totton GB 13 D12
Tótvázsony H 149 B9
Touça P 45 B6
Toucy F 25 E9
Touffailles F 33 B8
Touget F 33 C7
Toul F 26 C4
Toulon-sur-Allier F 30 B3
Toulon-sur-Arroux F 30 B5
Toulouges F 34 E4
Toulouse F 33 C8
Tounj HR 156 B3
Touques F 23 B12
Tourch F 22 D4
Tourcoing F 19 C7
Tourlaville F 23 A8
Tournai B 19 C7
Tournan-en-Brie F 25 C8
Tournay F 33 D6
Tournecoupe F 33 C7
Tournefeuille F 33 C8

Tournon-d'Agenais F 33 B7
Tournon-St-Martin F 29 B7
Tournon-sur-Rhône F 30 E6
Tournus F 30 B6
Tourny F 24 B6
Tourouvre F 24 C4
Tours F 24 F4
Tourteron F 19 C10
Tourtoirac F 29 E8
Toury F 24 D6
Tous E 48 F3
Tõusi EST 131 D7
Touvois F 28 B2
Toužim CZ 76 B3
Tovačov CZ 146 C4
Tovarlševo SRB 158 C3
Tovarné SK 145 F4
Tovarnik HR 157 B11
Toven N 108 D7
Tovrljane SRB 164 C3
Towcester GB 14 C7
Tower IRL 8 E5
Toymskardlia N 106 A5
Töysä FIN 123 E11
Traar D 183 C9
Trabada E 38 B5
Trabanca E 45 B8
Trabazos E 39 F7
Traben D 21 E8
Trąbki PL 144 C7
Trąbki Wielkie PL 138 B6
Traboch A 73 B10
Trabotivište MK 165 F6
Traby BY 137 E12
Trachili GR 175 R9
Tradate I 69 B6
Trädet S 91 D14
Trædal N 111 D10
Trafrask IRL 8 E3
Tragacete E 47 D9
Tragana GR 175 B6
Tragano GR 174 D3
Tragjas AL 168 D2
Tragwein A 77 F7
Traian RO 153 D10
Traian RO 155 C1
Traian RO 160 E4
Traian RO 160 F6
Traian Vuia RO 151 F9
Traid E 47 C9
Traiguera E 42 F4
Train D 75 E9
Traînel F 25 D9
Traïnou F 24 E7
Traisen A 77 F9
Traiskirchen A 77 F10
Traismauer A 77 F9
Traitsching D 75 D12
Trakai LT 137 E11
Trakovice SK 146 E5
Traksèdžiai LT 134 F2
Tralee IRL 8 D3
Trá Lí IRL 8 D3
Tramacastilla E 47 D9
Tramagal P 44 F4
Tramariglio I 64 B1
Tramatza I 64 C2
Tramayes F 30 C6
Tramelan CH 27 F7
Trá Mhór IRL 9 D8
Tramonti di Sopra I 73 D6
Tramonti di Sotto I 73 D6
Tramore IRL 9 D8
Tramutola I 60 C5
Tranäs S 92 D5
Tranbjerg DK 86 C6
Trancoso P 44 C5
Tranebjerg DK 86 D7
Tranemo S 91 E13
Trängen S 105 D15
Trânghalla S 92 D4
Trängslet S 102 D6
Trångsviken S 105 E16
Trani I 61 A6
Trannes F 25 D12
Tranovalto GR 169 D6
Tranøy N 111 D10
Trans F 23 D8
Trans-en-Provence F 36 D4
Transtrand S 102 D5
Transtrand S 102 C5
Tranum DK 86 A4
Tranvik S 99 D11
Trapani I 58 C2
Trapene LV 135 B13
Traplice CZ 146 C4
Trappes F 24 C7
Trarbach D 185 C12
Traryd S 87 B13
Trasacco I 62 D5
Träskvik FIN 122 F7
Trasmiras E 38 D4
Trasobares E 41 E8
Tratalias I 64 E2
Traun A 76 F6
Traunreut D 73 A6
Traunstein D 73 A6
Traupis LT 135 E9
Trava SLO 73 E9
Tråvad S 91 C13
Travagliato I 66 A1
Travanca do Mondego P 44 D4
Travassó P 44 C4
Travemünde D 83 C9
Travenbrück D 83 C8
Travers CH 31 B10
Traversetolo I 66 C1
Trávnica SK 146 E6
Travnik BIH 157 D8
Travo I 37 B11
Trawniki PL 141 H8
Trawsfynydd GB 10 F4
Trbovlje SLO 73 D11
Trbuk BIH 157 C9
Trebaseleghe I 72 E5
Trebatice SK 146 D5
Trebatsch D 80 B6
Třebechovice pod Orebem CZ 77 B9
Trebel D 83 D9
Treben D 79 D11
Třebenice CZ 76 B5
Trebenow D 84 C5
Trèbes F 33 D10
Trébeurden F 22 C4
Třebíč CZ 77 D9
Trebinje BIH 162 D5
Trebisacce I 61 D7
Trebišov SK 145 F4
Trebnje SLO 73 E11

Trebolle E 38 C4
Třeboň CZ 77 D7
Trebsen D 79 D12
Trebujena E 51 F7
Trebur D 21 E10
Trecastagni I 59 D7
Trecate I 68 C6
Trecchina I 60 C5
Trecenta I 66 B3
Tredegar GB 13 B8
Tredington GB 13 A11
Tredozio I 66 D4
Treehoo IRL 7 D8
Trefaldwyn GB 10 F5
Trefeglwys GB 10 F4
Treffen A 73 C8
Treffort-Cuisiat F 31 C7
Treffurt D 79 D7
Trefriw GB 10 E4
Trefynwy GB 13 B9
Tregaron GB 13 A7
Trégastel F 22 C4
Tregde N 90 C2
Tregnago I 66 A3
Tregony GB 12 E5
Trégueux F 22 D6
Tréguier F 22 C5
Trégunc F 22 E4
Tregynon GB 10 F5
Trehörna S 92 C5
Trehörningsjö S 107 D15
Treia D 82 A6
Treia I 67 F7
Treignac F 29 D9
Treigny F 25 E9
Treimani EST 131 F8
Treis D 185 D7
Trekanten S 89 B10
Treklyano BG 165 D6
Trélazé F 23 F11
Trelech GB 12 B6
Trélissac F 29 E7
Trelleborg S 87 E12
Trelleck GB 13 B9
Trélon F 19 D9
Tremadog GB 10 F3
Tremblay-les-Villages F 24 C5
Tremedal de Tormes E 45 B8
Tremelo B 19 C10
Trémentines F 23 F10
Tremês P 44 F3
Tréméven F 22 E4
Tremezzo I 69 B7
Trémolat F 29 F7
Třemošná CZ 76 C4
Trémouilles F 34 B4
Tremp E 42 C5
Trenance GB 12 E4
Trenčianska Turná SK 146 D6
Trenčianske Jastrabie SK 146 D6
Trenčianske Stankovce SK 146 D5
Trenčianske Teplice SK 146 D6
Trenčín SK 146 D6
Trendelburg D 21 A12
Trengereid N 94 B3
Trensacq F 32 B4
Trent D 84 A4
Trenta SLO 73 D8
Trentels F 33 B7
Trento I 69 A11
Tréon F 24 C5
Treorchy GB 13 B7
Trepča HR 148 F5
Treppeln D 81 B7
Trept F 31 D7
Trepuzzi I 61 C10
Trequanda I 66 F4
Tres Cantos E 46 C5
Trescléoux F 35 B10
Trescore Balneario I 69 B8
Tresenda I 69 A9
Tresfjord N 100 A6
Tresigallo I 66 C4
Tresjuncos E 47 E7
Treski EST 132 F2
Treskog S 97 C8
Trešnjevica SRB 158 F5
Tresnuraghes I 64 C2
Trespaderne E 40 C5
Tressait GB 5 B9
Třešť CZ 77 D8
Tretower GB 13 B8
Trets F 35 D10
Tretten N 101 D12
Treuchtlingen D 75 E8
Treuenbrietzen D 79 B12
Treungen N 90 A4
Trévé F 22 D6
Trevélez E 55 F6
Tréveray F 26 C3
Trèves F 34 B5
Trevi I 62 B3
Treviana E 40 C5
Trévières F 23 B10
Treviglio I 69 B8
Trevignano Romano I 62 C2
Trévillers F 27 F6
Treviño E 40 C6
Treviso I 72 E5
Trevllazër AL 168 C2
Trevões P 44 B6
Trévoux F 30 D6
Trézelles F 30 C4
Trezzo sull'Adda I 69 B8
Trgovište SRB 164 E5
Trhová Hradská SK 146 F5
Trhové Sviny CZ 77 E7
Trhovište SK 145 F4
Trhový Štěpánov CZ 77 C8
Triacastela E 38 C5
Triaize F 28 C3
Trianta GR 181 D8
Triantaros GR 176 D5
Tribalj HR 67 B10
Tribanj-Krušćica HR 156 D3
Tribehou F 23 B9
Tribsees D 83 B13
Tribunj HR 156 E4
Tricarico I 60 B6
Tricase I 61 D10
Tricesimo I 73 D7
Trichiana I 72 D5
Tricot F 18 E6
Trieben A 73 A9
Triebes D 79 E11
Trie-Château F 18 F4
Trier D 21 E7
Trierweiler D 186 B7
Trieste I 73 E8
Trie-sur-Baïse F 33 D6
Trieux F 20 F5
Trifeşti RO 153 C11
Trifeşti RO 153 D9
Triftern D 76 F4
Trigaches P 50 C4
Trigance F 36 D4
Triggiano I 61 A7
Triglitz D 83 D12
Trignac F 23 F7
Trigrad BG 165 F9
Triguères F 25 E8
Trigueros E 51 E6
Trigueros del Valle E 39 E10
Triigi EST 130 D5
Trikala GR 169 E6
Trikāta LV 131 F11
Trikeri GR 175 A7
Trilj HR 157 E6
Trillevallen S 105 E14
Trillick GB 7 D8
Trillo E 47 C7
Trilofo GR 174 E5
Trilofos GR 169 D8
Trilport F 25 C8
Trim IRL 7 E9
Trimdon GB 5 F14
Trimley St Mary GB 15 D11
Trimmis CH 71 D9
Trimsaran GB 12 B6
Trindade P 38 F5
Trindade P 50 D4
Třinec CZ 147 B7
Tring GB 15 D7
Trinità d'Agultu I 64 B2
Trinitapoli I 60 A6
Trino I 68 C5
Trins A 72 B3
Trinta P 45 C6
Trinwillershagen D 83 B13
Triollo E 39 C10
Triora I 37 D7
Tripkau D 83 D10
Tripoli GR 174 D5
Tripotama GR 174 D4
Tripotamos GR 169 C7
Trippstadt D 21 F9
Triptis D 79 E10
Tritenii de Jos RO 152 D4
Trittau D 83 C8
Trittenheim D 21 E7
Trivalea-Moşteni RO 160 E6
Trivento I 63 D7
Trivero I 68 B5
Trivigno I 60 B5
Trizac F 29 E11
Trnakovac HR 157 B7
Trnava CZ 146 C5
Trnava SK 146 E5
Trnava SRB 158 F5
Trnavá Hora SK 147 D7
Trnjani BIH 157 C6
Trnovci MK 168 B5
Trnovec Bartolovečki HR 149 D6
Trnovec nad Váhom SK 146 E5
Trnovica BIH 157 F9
Trnovo BIH 157 E9
Tro N 108 E4
Troarn F 23 B11
Tröbitz D 80 C4
Trochtelfingen D 27 D11
Trödje S 103 E13
Troense DK 86 E7
Trofa P 38 F2
Trofaiach A 73 B11
Trofors N 108 E5
Trogir HR 156 E5
Trøgstad N 95 C14
Troia I 60 A4
Tróia P 50 C2
Troianul RO 160 F6
Troina I 59 D6
Troisdorf D 21 C8
Troisfontaines F 186 D3
Trois-Ponts B 19 D12
Troissereux F 18 F5
Trois-Vèvres F 30 B3
Troisvierges L 20 D6
Troitsoe MD 154 D4
Trojane SLO 73 D10
Trojanów PL 141 G5
Troldhede DK 86 D3
Trollbukta N 113 C19
Trollhättan S 91 C11
Trollvik N 112 D6
Tromello I 69 C6
Tromsdalen N 111 A16
Tromsø N 111 A16
Tromvik N 111 A15
Tronco P 38 E5
Trondenes N 111 C12
Trondheim N 104 E8
Trones N 105 B13
Trongisvágur FO 2 B3
Tronnes N 108 C8
Trönninge S 87 B11
Trönningeby S 87 A10
Trönö S 103 D12
Trontano I 68 A5
Tronvik N 105 D9
Tronville-en-Barrois F 26 C3
Tronzano Vercellese I 68 C5
Troo F 24 E4
Troon GB 4 D7
Trooz B 183 D7
Tropaia GR 174 D4
Tropea I 59 B8
Trory GB 7 D7
Trosa S 93 B11
Troshan AL 163 F8
Trösken S 98 B7
Troškūnai LT 135 E9
Trošmarija HR 148 F4
Trossin D 79 C12
Trossingen D 27 D10
Tröstau D 75 B10
Trostberg D 75 F12
Trostyanets' UA 145 E9
Trostyanets' UA 153 A12
Troszyn PL 139 D12
Troubky CZ 146 C4
Troubsko CZ 77 D10
Troutbeck GB 10 C6
Trouville-sur-Mer F 23 B12
Trouy F 29 A10
Troviscal P 44 E4
Trowbridge GB 13 C10
Troyan BG 165 D10
Troyanovo BG 167 D8
Troyes F 25 D11
Troyits'ke UA 154 B6
Troyits'ke UA 154 D6
Troyon F 26 B3
Trpanj HR 157 F7
Trpejca MK 168 C4
Trpezi MNE 163 D9
Trpinja HR 157 B10
Trsa MNE 157 F10
Trstená SK 147 C9
Trstené pri Hornáde SK 145 F3
Trstenik HR 162 D3
Trstenik SRB 163 B11
Trstice SK 146 E5
Trstín SK 146 D4
Trubar BIH 156 D5
Trubia E 39 B8
Truchas E 39 D7
Truchtersheim F 27 C8
Trud BG 165 E10
Trudovets BG 165 D8
Trudy BY 133 E6
Trujillanos E 51 B7
Trujillo E 45 F9
Trulben D 27 B8
Trŭn BG 165 D6
Trun CH 71 D7
Trun F 23 C12
Trŭnchovitsa BG 165 C11
Truro GB 12 E4
Truşeşti RO 153 B10
Trusetal D 79 E7
Trush AL 163 F7
Truskava LT 135 F8
Truskavets' UA 145 E8
Trŭstenik BG 161 F7
Trŭstenik BG 165 C9
Trustrup DK 87 C7
Trutnov CZ 81 E9
Try N 90 C2
Tryavna BG 166 D4
Trybusivka UA 154 A3
Tryfos GR 174 B3
Tryggelev DK 83 A9
Trygona GR 168 E5
Tryńcza PL 144 C6
Tryserum S 93 C9
Trysil N 102 D3
Trysunda S 107 E15
Tryškiai LT 134 D5
Tržac BIH 156 C4
Trzcianka PL 85 D10
Trzcianka PL 139 E12
Trzcianne PL 140 D7
Trzciel PL 81 B9
Trzebiatów PL 85 B8
Trzebiechów PL 81 B9
Trzebiel PL 81 C7
Trzebielino PL 85 B12
Trzebień PL 81 D9
Trzebieszów PL 141 G7
Trzebieszowice PL 77 B11
Trzebież PL 84 C7
Trzebinia PL 143 F7
Trzebiszewo PL 81 A8
Trzebnica PL 81 D12
Trzebnice PL 81 D10
Trzebownisko PL 144 C5
Trzeciewiec PL 138 D5
Trzemeszno PL 138 E4
Trzemeszno Lubuskie PL 81 B8
Trześcianka PL 140 E8
Trześniów PL 145 D4
Trzeszczany Pierwsze PL 144 B8
Tržič SLO 73 D9
Trzcińsko-Zdrój PL 84 E7
Trzyciąż PL 143 F8
Trzydnik Duży PL 144 B5
Tsagkarada GR 169 F9
Tsakarisianos GR 174 C2
Tsalapitsa BG 165 E10
Tsamantas GR 168 E3
Tsaparevo BG 169 A9
Tsareva Livada BG 166 D4
Tsarev Brod BG 167 C8
Tsarevo BG 167 E9
Tsarimir BG 165 E10
Tsaritsani GR 169 E7
Tsar Kaloyan BG 161 F8
Tsar-Petrovo BG 159 F10
Tschagguns A 71 C9
Tschernitz D 81 C7
Tsebrykove UA 154 C6
Tselina BG 166 E4
Tsenovo BG 166 B5
Tserovo BG 165 C7
Tserovo BG 165 E9
Tsiistre EST 131 F14
Tsirguliina EST 131 F12
Tsivaras GR 178 E7
Tsooru EST 131 F13
Tsotili GR 168 D5
Tsoukalades GR 174 B2
Tsŭrvaritsa BG 165 E6
Tsvetino BG 165 F8
Tsyatsyerki BY 133 E2
Tua N 105 D9
Tuaim IRL 6 E5
Tuaim Beola IRL 6 F3
Tuam IRL 6 E5
Tuamgraney IRL 8 C5
Tubbercurry IRL 6 D5
Tubbergen NL 17 D7
Tubilla del Agua E 40 C4
Tübingen D 27 C11
Tubize B 19 C9
Tubre I 71 D10
Tučepi HR 157 F7
Tuchan F 34 E4
Tüchen D 83 D12
Tuchheim D 79 B11
Tuchola PL 138 C4
Tuchomie PL 85 B12
Tuchów PL 144 D3
Tuchowicz PL 141 G6
Tuckur FIN 122 D8
Tuczna PL 141 G8
Tuczno PL 85 D10
Tudela E 41 D8
Tudela de Duero E 40 E2
Tudora RO 153 B9
Tudor Vladimirescu RO 155 B1
Tudu EST 131 C13
Tudulinna EST 131 C14
Tudweiliog GB 10 F2
Tuejar E 47 E10
Tuenno I 72 D3
Tufeni RO 160 E5
Tufeşti RO 155 D1
Tuffé F 24 D4
Tufjord N 113 A12
Tuhkakylä FIN 125 B10
Tui E 38 D2
Tuili I 64 D2
Tuin MK 168 A5
Tuiskula FIN 122 E8
Tūja LV 135 B8
Tukhkala RUS 121 C16
Tukhol'ka UA 145 F7
Tukums LV 134 C6
Tula I 64 B2
Tulach Mhór IRL 7 F8
Tulare SRB 164 D3
Tuławki PL 136 F2
Tulbing A 77 F10
Tulca RO 151 D8
Tulce PL 81 B12
Tulcea RO 155 C3
Tulčík SK 145 E3
Tulette F 35 B8
Tulgheş RO 153 D7
Tuli BIH 162 D5
Tuliszków PL 142 B5
Tulje BIH 162 D5
Tulka S 99 B11
Tulla IRL 8 C5
Tullaghan IRL 6 D6
Tullamore IRL 7 F8
Tulle F 29 E9
Tullebølle DK 87 F7
Tulleng N 111 A15
Tulleråsen S 105 E16
Tullingsås S 106 D9
Tullins F 31 E7
Tulln A 77 F10
Tullow IRL 9 C9
Tully GB 7 D7
Tully GB 7 D8
Tullyallen IRL 7 E10
Tullyvin IRL 7 D8
Tulnici RO 153 F9
Tulos RUS 125 C14
Tulovo BG 166 D5
Tułowice PL 139 F9
Tułowice PL 142 E4
Tulppio FIN 115 C6
Tulsk IRL 6 E6
Tulstrup DK 87 D10
Tulucești RO 155 B2
Tumba S 93 A11
Tumbo S 98 D6
Tume LV 134 C6
Tummel Bridge GB 5 B8
Tumšupe LV 135 B9
Tun S 91 C12
Tunadal S 103 B13
Tuna-Hästberg S 97 B13
Tunari RO 161 D8
Tunbridge Wells, Royal GB 15 E9
Tunga GB 2 J4
Tungozero RUS 121 C17
Tunnerstad S 92 C4
Tunnhovd N 95 B9
Tunnsjø-Røyrvika N 105 B14
Tunsjön S 107 E12
Tunstall GB 15 C11
Tuntenhausen D 72 A5
Tunvågen S 102 A8
Tuohikotti FIN 128 C7
Tuohikylä FIN 115 E5
Tuolluvaara S 116 C4
Tuomikylä FIN 122 E9
Tuomioja FIN 119 E14
Tuorila FIN 126 B6
Tuoro sul Trasimeno I 66 F5
Tuovilanlahti FIN 124 D8
Tupilați RO 153 C9
Tuplice PL 81 C7
Tuppurinmäki FIN 125 E10
Tura H 150 B4
Turanlar TR 177 D10
Turany SK 147 C8
Turawa PL 142 E5
Turba EST 131 C8
Turbe BIH 157 D8
Turbenthal CH 27 F10
Turburea RO 160 D3
Turceni RO 160 D2
Turcia E 39 C8
Turčianske Teplice SK 147 D7
Turcifal P 44 F2
Turcinești RO 160 C2
Turcoaia RO 155 C2
Turda RO 152 D3
Turdaş RO 151 F11
Turégano E 46 B4
Turek PL 142 B6
Tureni RO 152 D3
Turenki FIN 127 D12
Turew PL 81 B11
Turgeliai LT 137 E12
Tŭrgovishte BG 167 C7
Turgut TR 181 B8
Turgutalp TR 177 A10
Turgutbey TR 173 B7
Turgutlu TR 177 C10
Turgutreis TR 177 F9
Türi EST 131 D10
Turi I 61 B8
Turia RO 153 E8
Turić BIH 157 C10
Turie SK 147 C7
Turija BIH 157 C9
Turija SRB 158 B4
Turija SRB 159 D8
Turís E 48 F3
Turiya BG 166 D4
Türje H 149 C8
Turka UA 145 E7
Túrkeve H 150 C6
Türkgücü TR 173 B8
Türkheim D 71 A11
Turki LV 135 D12
Türkmenli TR 171 E10
Turkova BY 133 E4
Turkovići BIH 162 D4
Turku FIN 126 E7
Turlava LV 134 C3
Turleque E 46 E5
Turmantas LT 135 E12
Turmenti BIH 162 D5
Turna LV 131 F11
Tŭrnak BG 165 C9
Turňa nad Bodvou SK 145 F2
Turnau A 148 A4
Tŭrnava BG 165 B8
Turnberry GB 4 E7
Turners Hill GB 15 E8
Turnhout B 16 F3
Turnišče SLO 149 C6
Türnitz A 77 G9
Turnov CZ 81 E8
Turnu Măgurele RO 160 F5
Turnu Roşu RO 160 B4
Turnu Ruieni RO 159 C9
Turobin PL 144 B6
Turośl PL 139 C12
Turośl PL 139 D17
Turów PL 141 G7
Turowo PL 85 C11
Turquel P 44 F3
Turrach A 73 C8
Turre E 55 E9
Turri I 64 D2
Turriff GB 3 K12
Tursi I 61 C6
Turt RO 145 H7
Turtel MK 164 F5
Turtola FIN 117 E11
Turulung RO 145 H7
Turup DK 86 E5
Tur"ya-Bystra UA 145 F6
Tur"ya-Polyana UA 145 F6
Turyatka UA 153 A8
Tur"ye UA 145 E7
Tur"yi Remety UA 145 F6
Turynka UA 144 C9
Turza Wielka PL 139 D9
Turzovka SK 147 C7
Tusa I 58 D5
Tuscania I 62 C1
Tuse DK 87 D9
Tuset N 105 E10
Tušilović HR 148 F5
Tuşnad RO 153 E7
Tussenhausen D 71 A11
Tüßling D 75 F12
Tuszów Narodowy PL 143 F11
Tuszyma PL 143 F12
Tuszyn PL 143 C8
Tutbury GB 11 F8
Tutjunniemi FIN 125 F13
Tutora RO 153 C11
Tutova RO 153 E11
Tutow D 84 C4
Tutrakan BG 161 E9
Tuttlingen D 27 E10
Tütüncü TR 173 D8
Tutzing D 72 A3
Tützpatz D 84 C4
Tuudi EST 130 D7
Tuukkala FIN 127 B16
Tuuliharju FIN 117 D13
Tuulimäki FIN 121 F11
Tuulos FIN 127 C12
Tuupovaara FIN 125 F15
Tuuri FIN 123 E11
Tuusjärvi FIN 125 E10
Tuusniemi FIN 125 E10
Tuusula FIN 127 E12
Tuv N 101 E8
Tuv N 108 B8
Tuvattnett S 106 D7
Tuve S 91 D10
Tuvnes N 104 D5
Tuvträsk S 107 B15
Tuxford GB 11 E10
Tuzburgazi TR 177 D9
Tuzculu TR 177 B8
Tŭzha BG 166 D4
Tuzi MNE 163 E7
Tužina SK 147 D7
Tuzla BIH 157 C10
Tuzla RO 155 E3
Tuzla TR 171 E10
Tužno HR 148 D6
Tuzora MD 154 C2
Tuzsér H 145 G5
Tvååker S 87 A10
Tvärålund S 107 C17
Tvärån S 118 C6
Tväråträsk S 107 A13
Tvardița MD 154 E3
Tvärsele S 106 B8
Tvärskog S 89 B10
Tvede DK 86 B6
Tvedestrand N 90 B4
Tveit N 90 C3
Tveit N 94 D4
Tverai LT 134 E4
Tverečius LT 135 F13
Tverråga N 108 D7
Tverråmo N 109 B10
Tverrelmo N 111 C18
Tversted DK 90 D7
Tving S 89 C8
Tvis DK 86 C3
Tvøroyri FO 2 B3
Tvorozhkovo RUS 132 E4
Tvrdošín SK 147 C9
Tvrdošovce SK 146 E6
Tvŭrditsa BG 166 D5
Twardogóra PL 142 D3
Twatt GB 3 G10
Tweedmouth GB 5 D12
Tweedsmuir GB 5 D10
Twello NL 16 D6
Twist D 17 C8
Twiste (Twistetal) D 17 F11
Twistringen D 17 C11
Two Mile Borris IRL 9 C7
Twomileborris IRL 9 C7
Two Mile Bridge IRL 7 F8
Tworóg PL 142 E6
Twyford GB 13 C12
Twyford GB 15 E7
Twyning GB 13 A10
Tyachiv UA 145 G8
Tychero GR 171 B10
Tychówko PL 85 C10
Tychowo PL 85 C10
Tychy PL 143 F6
Tyczyn PL 144 D5
Tydal N 105 E11
Tydavnet IRL 7 D8
Tyfors S 97 B11
Tygelsjö S 87 D11
Tyinkrysset N 101 D8
Tykocin PL 140 D7
Tylawa PL 145 E4
Tylissos GR 178 E9
Tyllinge S 93 C8
Tymianowa PL 145 D1
Tylösand S 87 B11
Tylstrup DK 86 A5
Tymbark PL 144 D1
Tymień PL 85 B9
Tymowa PL 81 D10
Tympaki GR 178 E8
Tynderö S 103 B14
Tyndrum GB 4 C7
Týnec nad Labem CZ 77 B8
Týnec nad Sázavou CZ 77 C7
Tynemouth GB 5 E14
Tyngsjö S 97 B10
Tyniewicze Małe PL 141 E8
Týniště nad Orlicí CZ 77 B10
Tynkä FIN 119 F12
Týn nad Vltavou CZ 77 D6
Tynset N 101 B13
Typpö FIN 119 F12
Typpyrä FIN 117 E14
Tyrämäki FIN 121 D12
Tyrävaara FIN 121 D12
Tyrawa Wołoska PL 145 D5
Tyresö S 99 D10
Tyringe S 87 C13
Tyristrand N 95 B12
Tyrjänsaari FIN 125 E15
Tyrnävä FIN 119 E15
Tyrnavos GR 169 E7
Tyrrellspass IRL 7 F8
Tyrväntö FIN 127 C11
Tysnes N 111 D10
Tysse N 94 B3
Tysse N 100 D2
Tyssebotnen N 100 E3
Tyssedal N 94 B5
Tystberga S 93 B10
Tyszowce PL 144 B8
Tytuvėnai LT 134 E6
Tyukod H 145 H6
Tyulenovo BG 167 B11
Tywyn GB 10 F3
Tyykiluoto FIN 119 D14
Tzermiado GR 178 E9
Tzummarum NL 16 B5

U

Uachdar GB 2 L2
Uachtar Ard IRL 6 F4
Ub SRB 158 E5
Übach-Palenberg D 183 D8
Ubby DK 87 D8
Úbeda E 53 A10
Überherrn D 21 F7
Überlingen D 27 E11
Übersee D 72 A5
Ubli HR 162 D2
Ubli MNE 163 D6
Ubli MNE 163 D7
Ubrique E 53 C6
Ubstadt-Weiher D 21 F11
Ucciani F 37 G9
Uccle B 19 C9
Ucea RO 152 F5
Uceda E 46 C6
Ucel F 35 A7
Ucero E 40 E5
Ucha P 38 E2
Uchanie PL 144 B8
Uchaux F 35 B8
Uchizy F 30 B6
Uchte D 17 D11
Üchtelhausen D 75 B7
Uchtspringe D 79 A10
Uckange F 186 C1
Uckfield GB 15 F9
Uckro D 80 C5
Uclés E 47 E7
Üçpinar TR 177 B9
Uda RO 160 D5
Udanin PL 81 D10
Udavské SK 145 F4
Udbina HR 156 C4
Udby DK 87 D9
Uddebo S 91 E13
Uddeholm S 97 B10
Uddel NL 183 A7
Uddevalla S 91 C10
Uddheden S 97 C8
Uddington GB 5 D9
Uden NL 16 E5
Udenhout NL 16 E4
Udenisht AL 168 C4
Uderns A 72 B4
Üdersdorf D 21 D7
Udeşti RO 153 B8
Udiča SK 146 C6
Udine I 73 D7
Udorpie PL 85 B13
Üdruma EST 131 D8
Udrycze PL 144 B7
Uebigau D 80 C4
Ueckermünde D 84 C6
Uehlfeld D 75 C8
Uelsen D 17 D7
Uelzen D 83 E9
Uetendorf CH 31 B12
Uetersen D 82 C7
Uettingen D 74 C6
Uetze D 79 B7
Uffculme GB 13 D8
Uffenheim D 75 C7
Uffing am Staffelsee D 72 A3
Uftrungen D 79 C8
Ugāle LV 134 B4
Ugao SRB 163 C9
Ugarana E 40 B6
Uge DK 86 F4
Ugelbølle DK 86 C6
Ugento I 61 D10
Ugerløse DK 87 D9
Uggdal N 94 B2
Uggelheden S 102 E3
Uggelhuse DK 86 C6
Uggerby DK 90 D7
Uggerslev DK 86 D6
Uggiano la Chiesa I 61 C10
Ugijar E 55 F6
Ugine F 31 D9
Uglen BG 165 C9
Uglev DK 86 B3
Ugljan HR 67 D11
Ugljane HR 157 E6
Ugljevik BIH 157 C11
Ugod H 149 B9
Uğurchin BG 165 C9
Uğurlu TR 171 D9
Uharte-Arakil E 32 E2
Uherské Hradiště CZ 146 C4
Uherský Brod CZ 146 C5
Uhingen D 74 E6
Uhldingen D 27 E11
Uhlířské Janovice CZ 77 C8
Uhlstädt D 79 E9
Uhniv UA 144 C8
Uhtna EST 131 C13
Uhyst D 81 D7
Uig GB 2 K4
Uimaharju FIN 125 E14
Uimila FIN 127 C15
Uitgeest NL 16 C3
Uithoorn NL 16 D3
Uithuizen NL 17 B7
Uivar RO 159 B6
Ujazd PL 141 G1
Ujazd PL 142 F5
Újezd CZ 77 C12
Újezd CZ 146 C5
Újfehértó H 151 B8
Újhartyán H 150 C3
Újkér H 149 B7
Újkígyós H 151 D7
Újléta H 151 C8
Újpetre H 149 E10
Ujście PL 85 D11
Ujsoły PL 147 C8
Újszalonta H 151 D7
Újszász H 150 C5
Újszentiván H 150 E5
Újszentmargita H 151 B7
Újszilvás H 150 C4
Újtikos H 145 H3
Újudvar H 149 C7
Ukhozhany UA 154 A5
Ukkola FIN 125 E14
Ukmergė LT 135 F9
Ukri LV 134 D6
Ula BY 133 F6
Ula TR 181 B8
Ulamiş TR 177 C8
Uland S 103 A14
Ulan-Majorat PL 141 G6
Ulanów PL 144 C5
Ulaş TR 173 B8
Ulassai I 64 D4
Ula Tirso I 64 C2
Ulbjerg DK 86 B4
Ulbroka LV 135 C8
Ulbster GB 3 J10
Ulcinj MNE 163 F7
Uldum DK 86 D5
Ulefoss N 95 D10
Uleila del Campo E 55 E8
Ülenurme EST 131 E13
Ulëz AL 163 F8
Ulfborg DK 86 C2
Ulft NL 16 E6
Ulhówek PL 144 C8
Ulič SK 145 F5
Ulicoten NL 182 C5
Ulieş RO 152 E6
Ulieşti RO 161 D6
Ulila EST 131 E12
Uljanik HR 149 E8
Uljma SRB 159 C7
Ullånger S 107 E14
Ullapool GB 2 K6
Ullared S 87 A11
Ullatti S 116 D7
Ullava FIN 123 C11
Ullbergsträsk S 107 A17
Ulldecona E 42 F4
Ulldemolins E 42 E5
Ullerslev DK 86 E7
Ullervad S 91 B14
Üllés H 150 E4
Ulleskelf GB 11 D9
Ullisjaur S 107 A10
Ullits DK 86 B4
Üllő H 150 C3
Ullsfjord N 111 A18
Ulm D 74 F6
Ulma RO 152 B6
Ulmbach D 74 B5
Ulme P 44 F4
Ulmen D 21 D7
Ulmeni RO 151 C11
Ulmeni RO 161 C9
Ulmeni RO 161 E9
Ulmi RO 161 D6
Ulmu RO 161 D10
Ulmu RO 161 E9
Ulog BIH 157 E9
Uløybukta N 112 D6
Ulricehamn S 91 D13
Ulrichsberg A 76 E5
Ulrichstein D 21 C12
Ulrika S 92 C6
Ulriksberg S 97 B12
Ulriksfors S 106 D9
Ulrum NL 16 B6
Ulsberg N 101 A11
Ulsta GB 3 D14
Ulsted DK 86 A6
Ulsteinvik N 100 B3
Ulstrup DK 86 C5
Ulstrup DK 87 D7
Ulsvåg N 111 D10
Ultrå S 107 E16
Uluabat TR 173 D9
Ulucak TR 177 B9
Ulucak TR 177 C9
Ulukonak TR 181 A7
Ulvåker S 91 C14
Ulvenhout NL 16 E3
Ulverston GB 10 C5
Ulvik N 100 E5
Ulvila FIN 126 C6
Ulvöhamn S 107 E15
Ulvsjön S 102 C7
Ulvsjön S 103 B11
Ulvvik S 103 A14
Ul'yanovka UA 154 A6
Ul'yanovo RUS 136 D5
Umag HR 67 B8
Umberleigh GB 12 D7
Umbertide I 66 F5
Umbrăreşti RO 153 F10
Umbriatico I 61 E7
Umbukta N 108 D8
Umčari SRB 158 D6
Umeå S 122 C4
Umfors S 108 E9
Umgransele S 107 B14
Umhausen A 71 C11
Umin Dol MK 164 E4
Umka SRB 158 D5
Umkirch D 27 D8
Umljanović HR 156 E5
Ummeljoki FIN 128 D6
Ummern D 79 A7
Umnäs S 109 F11
Ümraniye TR 173 B11
Umurbey TR 172 D6
Umurga LV 135 A9
Uña E 47 D9
Uña de Quintana E 39 D7
Unaja FIN 126 C6
Únanov CZ 77 E10
Unapool GB 2 J6
Unari FIN 117 D15
Unbyn S 118 C7
Uncastillo E 32 F3
Undenäs S 92 B4
Undereidet N 112 D9
Underfossen N 113 C18
Undersåker S 105 E14
Undingen D 27 D11
Undløse DK 87 D9
Undva EST 130 D3
Undy GB 13 B9
Unelanperä FIN 120 F9
Ungerhausen D 71 A10
Ungheni MD 153 C11
Ungheni RO 152 D5
Ungheni RO 160 E5
Ungra RO 152 F6
Unguraşi RO 152 C4
Ungureni RO 153 B9

Ungureni RO 153 D10
Ungurpils LV 131 F9
Unhais da Serra P 44 D5
Unhais-o-Velho P 44 D5
Unhošt CZ 76 B6
Uničov CZ 77 C12
Uniejów PL 142 C6
Unieux F 30 E5
Unín SK 146 D4
Unirea RO 152 E3
Unirea RO 155 C1
Unirea RO 155 F3
Unirea RO 159 B10
Unirea RO 159 E11
Unirea RO 161 C9
Unisław PL 138 D5
Unkel D 21 C8
Unken A 73 A6
Unlingen D 71 A9
Unna D 17 E9
Unnaryd S 87 B13
Unnau D 185 C8
Unnstorp S 102 D7
Unset N 101 C14
Unsholtet N 101 A14
Unstad N 110 D6
Untamala FIN 122 D9
Untamala FIN 126 D6
Unțeni RO 153 B9
Unterägeri CH 27 F10
Unterammergau D 71 B12
Unterdießen D 71 B11
Untergriesbach D 76 E5
Unterhaching D 75 F10
Unterkulm CH 27 F9
Unterlüß D 83 E8
Untermaßfeld D 75 A7
Untermerzbach D 75 B8
Untermünkheim D 74 D6
Unterneukirchen D 75 F12
Unterpleichfeld D 75 C7
Unterreit D 75 F11
Unterschächen CH 71 D7
Unterschleißheim D 75 F10
Untersiemau D 75 B8
Untersteinach D 75 B10
Unterweißenbach A 77 F7
Unterwössen D 72 A5
Unverre F 24 D5
Upavon GB 13 C11
Upenieki LV 134 C5
Upenieki LV 135 D12
Upesgrīva LV 134 B6
Upgant-Schott D 17 A8
Úpice CZ 77 A10
Upinniemi FIN 127 E11
Uplyme GB 13 D9
Upninkai LT 137 D10
Upper Knockando GB 3 L10
Upperlands GB 4 F3
Upphärad S 91 C11
Uppingham GB 11 F10
Upplanda S 99 B9
Upplands-Väsby S 99 C9
Uppsala S 99 C9
Uppsälje S 97 A11
Uppsete N 100 E5
Uppsjö S 103 C12
Upton upon Severn GB 13 A10
Upyna LT 134 E5
Upyna LT 134 F4
Upytė LT 135 E8
Urafirth GB 3 E14
Urago d'Oglio I 69 B8
Uraiújfalu H 149 B7
Uras I 64 D2
Ura Vajgurore AL 168 C2
Uraz PL 81 D11
Urbach D 21 C9
Urbania I 66 E6
Urbar D 185 D8
Urbe I 37 C9
Urberach D 187 B6
Urbino I 66 E6
Urbisaglia I 67 F7
Urbise F 30 C4
Určice CZ 77 D12
Urda E 46 F5
Urdari RO 160 D2
Urdax-Urdazuli E 32 D2
Urdorf CH 27 F9
Urdos F 32 E4
Urduña E 40 C6
Ure N 110 D6
Urecheni RO 153 C9
Urechești RO 153 E10
Urechești RO 161 B10
Urë e Shtrenjtë AL 163 E8
Urepel F 32 D3
Ureterp NL 16 B6
Urga LV 131 F9
Úrhida H 149 B10
Úri H 150 C4
Uri I 64 B2
Uricani RO 159 C11
Uriménil F 26 D5
Uringe S 93 A11
Uriu RO 152 C4
Urjala FIN 127 C10
Urk NL 16 C5
Ürkmez TR 177 C8
Úrkút H 149 B9
Urla TR 177 C8
Urlați RO 161 D8
Urlingford IRL 9 C7
Urmeniș RO 152 D4
Urmince SK 146 D6
Urnäsch CH 27 F11
Urnieta E 32 D2
Üröm H 150 B3
Urovica SRB 159 E9
Urrea de Gaén E 42 E3
Urrea de Jalón E 41 E9
Urretxu E 32 D1
Urriés E 32 E3
Urros P 45 B6
Urroz E 32 E2
Urrugne F 32 D2
Ursberg D 71 A10
Ursensollen D 75 D10
Urshult S 89 B7
Ursviken S 118 E6
Urszulin PL 141 H8
Urt F 32 D3
Urtenen CH 31 A11
Urtimjaur S 116 E5
Urueña E 39 E9
Ururi I 63 D8

Urzicuța RO 160 E3
Urzulei I 64 C4
Urzy F 30 A3
Usagre E 51 C7
Ušari BIH 157 C7
Ušče SRB 163 C10
Uschlag (Staufenberg) D 78 D6
Uście Gorlickie PL 145 D3
Uście Solne PL 143 F10
Uscio I 37 C10
Usedom D 84 C5
Usellus I 64 D2
Useras E 48 D4
Ushachy BY 133 F5
Uši LV 130 F5
Usingen D 21 D11
Usini I 64 B2
Usk GB 13 B9
Uskali FIN 125 F14
Uskedal N 94 C3
Üsküdar TR 173 B11
Üsküp TR 167 F8
Uslar D 78 C6
Usma LV 134 B4
Úsov CZ 77 C11
Uspenivka UA 154 E5
Usquert NL 17 B7
Ussana I 64 E3
Ussassai I 64 D3
Usseglio I 31 E11
Ussel F 29 D10
Ussel F 30 E2
Usson-du-Poitou F 29 C7
Usson-en-Forez F 30 E4
Ustaoset N 95 B8
Ustaritz F 32 D3
Ust'-Chorna UA 145 G8
Ust'-Dolyssy RUS 133 D7
Uštěk CZ 80 E6
Uster CH 27 F10
Ustibar BIH 158 B3
Ustica I 58 B3
Ustikolina BIH 157 E10
Ústí nad Labem CZ 80 E6
Ústí nad Orlicí CZ 77 C10
Ustiprača BIH 157 E8
Ustirama BIH 157 E8
Ustka PL 85 A11
Ustou F 33 E8
Ustovo BG 171 A7
Ustroń PL 147 B7
Ustronie Morskie PL 85 B9
Ustrzyki Dolne PL 145 E6
Ustya UA 154 E1
Ustyluh UA 144 B9
Uszód H 149 C11
Uszew PL 144 D2
Utajärvi FIN 119 E16
Utåker N 94 C3
Utakleiv N 110 D6
Utanede S 103 A12
Utanen FIN 119 E16
Utansjö S 103 A14
Utanskog S 107 C12
Utarp D 17 A8
Utbjoa N 94 C3
Utebo E 41 E10
Utelle F 37 D6
Utena LT 135 F11
Utersum D 82 A4
Uthaug N 104 D7
Uthleben D 79 D8
Uthlede D 17 B11
Utiel E 47 E10
Utne N 94 B5
Utö S 93 B12
Utoropy UA 152 A6
Utrecht NL 16 D4
Utrera E 51 E8
Utrillas E 42 F2
Utrine SRB 150 F4
Utro N 104 C8
Utsjoki FIN 113 D18
Utskor N 110 C8
Uttendorf A 72 B6
Uttendorf A 76 F4
Uttenweiler D 71 A9
Utterbyn S 97 B9
Utterliden S 109 F17
Uttersberg S 97 C14
Uttersjö S 107 D14
Utterslev DK 87 F8
Utti FIN 128 D6
Utting am Ammersee D 71 A12
Utula FIN 129 C9
Utvalnäs S 103 E13
Utvik N 100 C5
Utvorda N 105 B9
Utzedel D 84 C4
Uuemõisa EST 130 D7
Uukuniemi FIN 129 B13
Uulu EST 131 E9
Uura FIN 121 F10
Uurainen FIN 123 E14
Uuro FIN 122 F8
Uusikaarlepyy FIN 122 C9
Uusikartano FIN 126 D7
Uusikaupunki FIN 126 D5
Uusikylä FIN 123 D12
Uusikylä FIN 127 D15
Uusi-Värtsilä FIN 125 F14
Uva FIN 121 E11
Uvac BIH 158 F4
Uvåg N 110 C8
Úvaly CZ 77 B7
Uvanå S 97 B10
Uvdal N 95 B9
Üvecik TR 171 E10
Uzašali LT 135 E11
Uzbetchcha BY 133 F7
Uzdin SRB 158 C6
Uzel F 22 D6
Uzer F 35 A7
Uzerche F 29 E9
Uzès F 35 B7
Uzhhorod UA 145 F5
Uzhok UA 145 F6
Užice SRB 158 F4
Uzlovoye RUS 136 D5
Uznach CH 27 F10
Uznové AL 168 C2
Użpaliai LT 135 E11
Uzrechcha BY 133 F3
Uzundzhovo BG 166 F5

Uzunköprü TR 172 B6
Uzunkuyu TR 177 C8
Užentis LT 134 E5

V

Vaadinselkä FIN 115 C5
Vaajakoski FIN 123 F15
Vaajasalmi FIN 124 E7
Vääkiö FIN 121 D12
Vaala FIN 119 E17
Vaalajärvi FIN 117 D16
Vaale D 82 C6
Vaalimaa FIN 128 D8
Vaals NL 20 C6
Vaarakylä FIN 121 C11
Vaarankylä FIN 121 D11
Vaaranniva FIN 121 D11
Vaaraperä FIN 121 C13
Vaaraslahti FIN 123 D17
Väärinmaja FIN 124 G2
Vaas F 24 E3
Vaasa FIN 122 D7
Vaassen NL 16 D5
Väätäiskylä FIN 123 E13
Väätsa EST 131 D10
Vaattojärvi FIN 117 D12
Vabole LV 135 D12
Vabre F 33 C10
Vabres-l'Abbaye F 34 C4
Vác H 150 B3
Văcărești RO 161 D6
Vaccarizzo Albanese I 61 D6
Váchartyán H 150 B3
Vacheresse F 31 C10
Vachov CZ 76 D5
Vacov CZ 76 D5
Vacqueyras F 35 B8
Vácrátót H 150 B3
Văculești RO 153 B8
Vad RO 152 C3
Vad S 97 B14
Vadakste LV 134 D5
Vadaktai LT 135 E8
Vădastra RO 160 F4
Vădăstrița RO 160 F4
Vădeni RO 153 F7
Väderstad S 92 C5
Vad Foss N 90 B5
Vadheim N 100 D3
Vadla N 94 D4
Vadocondes E 40 E4
Vadokliai LT 135 E8
Vado Ligure I 37 C8
Vadskinn N 111 C11
Vadsø N 114 C7
Vadstena S 92 C5
Vadu Crișului RO 151 D10
Vadu lui Isac MD 155 B2
Vadu Izei RO 145 H8
Vadul lui Vodă MD 154 C4
Vadul Turcului MD 154 B3
Vadum DK 86 A5
Vadu Moldovei RO 153 C8
Vadu Moților RO 151 E10
Vadu Pașii RO 161 C9
Vaduz FL 71 C9
Vadžgirys LT 134 F5
Væggerløse DK 83 A11
Vafaiika GR 171 B7
Vafiochori GR 169 B8
Våg N 94 D2
Vågaholmen N 108 C5
Vågåmo N 101 C10
Vagan BIH 157 D6
Vågan N 111 B14
Vägdalen S 106 D9
Våge N 94 B3
Våge N 94 D4
Vaggatem N 114 E6
Vaggeryd S 92 E4
Vägholmane N 100 A4
Vagia GR 175 C7
Văgiulești RO 159 D10
Vaglia I 66 E3
Vaglio Basilicata I 60 B5
Vagli Sotto I 66 D1
Vagney F 26 D6
Vagnhärad S 93 B11
Vagnsunda S 99 C11
Vagos P 44 C3
Vägsele S 107 B14
Vägsodden N 108 E3
Vágur FO 2 C3
Vähäjoki FIN 119 B14
Vähäkangas FIN 123 B13
Vähäkyrö FIN 122 D8
Vähäniva FIN 116 B9
Vahanka FIN 123 E13
Vahastu EST 131 D10
Vahenurme EST 131 D8
Vähikkälä FIN 127 D12
Vahojärvi FIN 127 B10
Váhovce SK 146 E5
Vahterpää FIN 127 E15
Vahto FIN 126 D7
Vaiamonte P 44 F6
Vaiano I 66 E3
Vaičkūniškės LT 137 D10
Vaida EST 131 C9
Vaidava LV 135 B10
Vaideeni RO 160 C3
Vaidotai LT 137 D11
Vaiges F 23 D11
Vaiguva LT 134 E5
Vaikko FIN 125 D11
Vailly-sur-Aisne F 19 F9
Vailly-sur-Sauldre F 25 F8
Vaimastvere EST 131 D12
Vaimela EST 131 F14
Vaimõisa EST 131 D8
Vainikkala FIN 129 D9
Vainiūnai LT 137 E9
Vainode LV 134 D3
Vainotiškiai LT 134 F7
Vairano Patenora I 60 A2
Vairano Scalo I 60 A2
Väisälä FIN 121 E11
Vaison-la-Romaine F 35 B9
Vaïssac F 33 B9
Vaivio FIN 125 E12
Vaivre-et-Montoille F 26 E5
Vaja H 145 H5
Vajangu EST 131 C12
Vajdácska H 145 G4
Vaje N 90 B4

Våje N 110 D5
Vajkal AL 168 A3
Vajmat S 109 C18
Vajska SRB 157 B11
Vajszló H 149 E9
Vajta H 149 C11
Vakarel BG 165 D8
Vakern S 97 B11
Vakiflar TR 173 B8
Vaklino BG 155 F3
Vaksdal N 94 B3
Vaksevo BG 165 E6
Vaksince MK 164 E4
Vál H 149 B11
Valada P 44 F3
Vålådalen S 105 E13
Valadares P 38 F3
Valajanaapa FIN 119 C15
Valajaskoski FIN 119 B14
Valaliky SK 145 F3
Valand N 90 C2
Valandovo MK 169 B8
Vålånger S 103 A14
Valanida GR 169 E7
Valanjou F 23 F11
Valareña E 41 D9
Valaská SK 147 D9
Valaská Belá SK 146 D6
Valašská Bystřice CZ 146 C6
Valašská Polanka CZ 146 C6
Valašské Klobouky CZ 146 C5
Valašské Meziříčí CZ 146 C5
Vålax FIN 127 E14
Valberg F 36 C5
Valberg N 110 D6
Vålberg S 97 D9
Valbiska HR 67 B9
Valbo S 103 E13
Valbom P 44 B3
Valbona I 48 E3
Valbondione I 69 A9
Valbonnais F 31 F8
Valbonne F 36 D6
Valbuena de Duero E 40 E3
Valča SK 147 C7
Valcabrère F 33 D7
Vălcani RO 150 E6
Vălcele RO 153 F7
Vălcele RO 160 E5
Vălcelele RO 161 D10
Vălcelele RO 161 E10
Valdagno I 69 B11
Valdahon F 26 F5
Valdaora I 72 C5
Valddak N 113 C14
Valdealgorfa E 42 E3
Valdeblore F 37 C6
Valdecaballeros E 45 F10
Valdecañas de Tajo E 45 E9
Valdecarros E 45 C10
Valdecilla E 40 B4
Valdecuenca E 47 D10
Valdefuentes E 45 F8
Valdeganga E 47 F9
Valdek LV 134 C5
Valdelacasa E 45 C9
Valdelacasa de Tajo E 45 E10
Valdelamusa E 51 D6
Valdelinares E 48 D3
Valdemanco del Esteras E 54 B3
Valdemārpils LV 134 B5
Valdemarsvik S 93 C9
Valdemeca E 47 D9
Valdemorillo E 46 C4
Valdemoro E 46 D5
Valdemoro-Sierra E 47 D9
Valdenoches E 47 C6
Valdeobispo E 45 D8
Valdeolivas E 47 C8
Valdepeñas E 55 B6
Valdepeñas de Jaén E 53 A9
Valderas E 39 D8
Val-de-Reuil F 18 F3
Valderice I 58 C2
Valderiès F 33 C10
Valderøy N 100 A4
Valderrobres E 42 F4
Val de Santo Domingo E 46 D4
Valdestillas E 39 F9
Valdetorma E 42 F4
Valdetorres E 51 B7
Valdeverdeja E 45 E10
Valdevimbre E 39 D8
Valdgale LV 134 B5
Valdice CZ 77 B8
Valdidentro I 71 E10
Valdilecha E 47 D6
Val-d'Isère F 31 E10
Valdisotto I 71 E10
Val-d'Izé F 23 D9
Valdobbiadene I 72 E4
Valdoie F 27 E6
Valdunquillo E 39 D9
Vale GBG 22 B5
Våle N 95 D12
Våle S 103 A8
Valea Adîncă MD 154 A3
Valea Argovei RO 161 E9
Valea Călugărească RO 161 D8
Valea Chioarului RO 151 C11
Valea Ciorii RO 161 D11
Valea Crișului RO 153 F7
Valea Danului RO 160 C5
Valea Doftanei RO 161 C7
Valea Dragului RO 161 E8
Valea Ierii RO 151 D11
Valea Largă RO 152 D4
Valea lui Mihai RO 151 B9
Valea Lungă RO 152 E4
Valea Lungă RO 160 D4
Valea Măcrișului RO 161 D9
Valea Mare MD 153 C11
Valea Mare RO 160 D3
Valea Mare RO 160 D4
Valea Mare RO 160 E4
Valea Mare-Pravăț RO 160 C6
Valea Mărului RO 153 F11
Valea Moldovei RO 153 C8
Valea Nucarilor RO 155 C3
Valea Râmnicului RO 161 C10
Valea Salciei RO 161 C9
Valea Sării RO 153 F9
Valea Seacă RO 153 C9
Valea Seacă RO 153 D10
Valea Stanciului RO 160 F3
Valea Teilor RO 155 C3
Valea Ursului RO 153 D10
Valea Viilor RO 152 E4
Valea Vinului RO 151 B11
Vale da Rosa P 50 E4

Vale das Mós P 44 F4
Vale de Açor P 44 F5
Vale de Açor P 50 D4
Vale de Cambra P 44 C4
Vale de Cavalos P 44 F4
Vale de Espinho P 45 D7
Vale de Estrela P 45 C6
Vale de Figueira P 44 F4
Vale de Lobo P 50 E3
Vale de Prazeres P 44 D6
Vale de Reis P 50 C3
Vale de Salgueiro P 38 E5
Vale de Santarém P 44 F3
Vale do Peso P 44 F5
Válega P 44 C3
Valen N 105 B9
Valença P 38 D2
Valença do Douro P 44 B5
Valençay F 24 F6
Valence F 30 E6
Valence F 33 B7
Valence-d'Albigeois F 33 B10
Valence-sur-Baïse F 33 C6
Valencia E 48 F4
Valencia de Alcántara E 45 F6
Valencia de Don Juan E 39 D8
Valencia de las Torres E 51 C7
Valencia del Mombuey E 51 C5
Valencia del Ventoso E 51 C7
Valenciennes F 19 D8
Våleni RO 153 D11
Văleni RO 160 E5
Vălenii de Munte RO 161 C8
Valensole F 35 C10
Valentano I 62 B1
Valentigney F 27 F6
Valenza I 37 A9
Valenzano I 61 A7
Valenzuela E 53 A8
Valenzuela de Calatrava E 54 B5
Våler N 95 D13
Våler N 101 E15
Valera de Arriba E 47 E8
Valernes F 35 B10
Vales Mortos P 50 D5
Valestrand N 94 A2
Valevåg N 94 C2
Valfabbrica I 66 F6
Valfarta E 42 D3
Valfroicourt F 26 D5
Valfurva I 71 E10
Valga EST 131 F12
Valgalciems LV 134 B5
Valgale LV 134 B4
Valgrisenche I 31 D11
Valgu EST 131 D9
Valguarnera Caropepe I 58 E5
Valgunde LV 134 C7
Valhelhas P 44 D6
Valhermoso E 47 C9
Vålhovd N 101 E12
Välijoki FIN 119 B15
Välikangas FIN 119 B16
Väli-Kannus FIN 123 C11
Valikardhë AL 168 A3
Välikylä FIN 123 C11
Valimi GR 174 D5
Văliug RO 159 C9
Valjevo SRB 158 E4
Valjok N 113 D16
Valjunquera E 42 F4
Valka LV 131 F11
Valkeajärvi FIN 123 F12
Valkeakoski FIN 127 C11
Valkeala FIN 128 D6
Valkeiskylä FIN 124 C8
Valkeiskylä FIN 125 D10
Valkenburg NL 19 C12
Valkenswaard NL 16 F4
Valkininkai LT 137 E10
Valkla EST 131 C11
Valko FIN 127 E15
Valkó H 150 B4
Valla S 93 A8
Valla S 107 E16
Vall d'Alba E 48 D4
Valldemossa E 49 E10
Valle E 40 B3
Valle LV 135 C9
Valle N 90 B6
Valle N 94 D5
Valle Castellana I 62 B5
Vallecorsa I 62 E4
Valle de Abdalajís E 53 C7
Valle de la Serena E 51 B9
Valle de Matamoros E 51 C6
Valle de Santa Ana E 51 C6
Valle di Cadore I 72 C5
Valledoria I 64 B2
Vallelunga Pratameno I 58 D4
Valle Mosso I 68 B5
Vallen S 107 D15
Vallen S 118 F6
Vallenca E 47 D10
Vallendar D 185 D8
Vallentuna S 99 C10
Vallerås S 102 E6
Valleraugue F 35 B6
Vallermosa I 64 E2
Vallerotonda I 62 D5
Vallersund N 104 C7
Vallervatnet N 105 B15
Vallet F 23 F9
Valley D 72 A4
Valley GB 10 E2
Vallfogona de Riucorb E 42 D6
Vallières F 29 D10
Vallioniemi FIN 121 B12
Vallo della Lucania I 60 C4
Vallo di Nera I 62 B3
Valloire F 31 E9

Vallombrosa I 66 E4
Vallon-en-Sully F 29 B11
Vallon-Pont-d'Arc F 35 B7
Vallorbe CH 31 B9
Vallorcine F 31 C10
Vallouise F 31 F9
Vallrun S 105 D16
Valls E 42 E6
Vallsbo S 103 E12
Vallsjön S 103 A11
Vallsta S 103 C11
Vallstena S 93 D13
Vallvik S 103 C12
Valmadrera I 69 B7
Valmadrid E 41 F10
Valmen N 101 D15
Valmiera LV 131 F10
Valmiermuiža LV 131 F10
Valmojado E 46 D4
Valmont F 18 E2
Valmontone I 62 D3
Valmorel F 31 E9
Valmy F 25 B12
Valnes N 108 B7
Valognes F 23 A9
Valongo P 38 F4
Valongo P 44 F5
Válor E 55 F6
Valoria la Buena E 40 E2
Valøy N 105 B9
Valøy N 105 C11
Valpaços P 38 E5
Valpalmas E 41 D10
Valpelline I 31 D11
Valperga I 68 C4
Valpovo HR 149 E10
Valpperi FIN 126 D7
Valras-Plage F 34 D5
Valréas F 35 B8
Valros F 34 D5
Vals CH 71 D8
Valsavarenche I 31 D11
Vålse DK 87 F9
Valseca E 46 B4
Valsequillo E 51 C9
Valsgård DK 86 B5
Valsgarth GB 3 D15
Valshed S 103 A8
Valsinni I 61 C6
Valsjöbyn S 105 C16
Valsjön S 103 B13
Valška SRB 158 E6
Valskog S 97 C14
Vals-les-Bains F 35 A7
Valstagna I 72 E4
Val-Suzon F 26 E2
Valtablado del Río E 47 C8
Valtero GR 169 B9
Valtice CZ 77 E11
Valtiendas E 40 F4
Valtierra E 41 D8
Valtimo FIN 125 C11
Valtola FIN 128 C7
Valtopina I 62 A3
Valtos GR 171 A10
Valtournenche I 68 B4
Valu lui Traian RO 155 E2
Valun HR 67 C9
Valuste EST 131 E11
Valverde E 47 D10
Valverde de Burguillos E 51 C6
Valverde de Júcar E 47 E8
Valverde de la Virgen E 39 C8
Valverde del Camino E 51 D6
Valverde del Fresno E 45 D7
Valverde de Leganés E 51 B6
Valverde de Llerena E 51 C8
Valverde del Majano E 46 C4
Valverde de Mérida E 51 B7
Valvika S 118 B7
Valvträsk S 118 B7
Valyra GR 174 E4
Vama RO 145 H7
Vama RO 153 B7
Vama Buzăului RO 161 B7
Vamberk CZ 77 B10
Vamdrup DK 86 E4
Vamhus S 102 D7
Vamlingbo S 93 F12
Vammala FIN 127 C9
Vammen DK 86 B5
Vamos GR 178 E7
Vámosmikola H 147 F7
Vámospércs H 151 B8
Vámosújfalu H 145 G3
Vámpula FIN 126 C8
Vamvakofyto GR 169 B9
Vana-Koiola EST 131 F14
Vânători RO 152 C5
Vânători RO 153 C9
Vânători RO 153 D9
Vânători RO 155 B2
Vânători RO 153 B7
Vânătorii Mici RO 161 E7
Vânători-Neamţ RO 153 C8
Vanault-les-Dames F 25 C12
Vana-Vigala EST 131 D8
Vana-Võidu EST 131 E11
Váncsod H 151 C8
Vânda FIN 127 E12
Vandel DK 86 D4
Vandellós E 42 E5
Vandenesse F 30 B4
Vandenesse-en-Auxois F 25 F12
Vandœvre-lès-Nancy F 186 D1
Vandoies I 72 C4
Vändra EST 131 D9
Vändträsk S 118 C6
Vandžiogala LT 135 F7
Väne LV 134 C5
Väne-Åsaka S 91 C11
Vänersborg S 91 C11
Vañes E 40 C3
Vang N 101 D9
Vang S 92 B7
Vangaži LV 135 B9
Vänge S 93 E13
Vänge S 99 C9
Vangshamn N 111 B15
Vangshylla N 105 D10
Vangsnes N 100 D5
Vanha-Kihlanki FIN 117 C10
Vanhakylä FIN 122 F7
Vanhakylä FIN 129 B9
Vänjaurbäck S 107 C15
Vänjaurträsk S 107 C15

Vânjuleţ RO 159 E10
Vânju Mare RO 159 E10
Vannareid N 112 C4
Vännäs S 122 C3
Vännäsberget S 118 B9
Vännäsby S 122 C3
Vannavalen N 112 C4
Vänne N 90 B2
Vannes F 22 E6
Vannvåg N 112 C4
Vannvikan N 104 D8
Vänö FIN 126 F7
Vansbro S 97 A11
Vanse N 94 F5
Vansjö S 103 C9
Vantaa FIN 127 E12
Vanttausjärvi FIN 119 B17
Vanttauskoski FIN 119 B17
Vanvey F 25 E12
Vanyarc H 147 F8
Vanzone I 68 B5
Vaour F 33 B9
Vápenná CZ 77 B12
Vaplan S 105 E16
Vaqueiros P 50 E4
Vara EST 131 D13
Vara S 91 C12
Vara del Rey E 47 F8
Varades F 23 F9
Vărădia RO 159 C8
Vărădia de Mureş RO 151 E9
Varages F 35 C10
Varaire F 33 B9
Varajärvi FIN 119 B13
Varajoki FIN 121 F14
Varakļāni LV 135 C13
Varallo I 68 B5
Varangerbotn N 114 C5
Varano de'Melegari I 69 D8
Varapodio I 59 C8
Vărăşti RO 161 E8
Văratec RO 153 C8
Varaždin HR 149 D6
Varaždinske Toplice HR 149 D6
Varazze I 37 C9
Varberg S 87 A10
Vârbilău RO 161 C7
Varbla EST 130 E7
Varbó H 145 G2
Varbola EST 131 C8
Varces-Allières-et-Risset F 31 E8
Vârciorog RO 151 D9
Varda GR 174 C3
Vardali GR 174 A5
Varde DK 86 D2
Vardim BG 161 F6
Vardište BIH 158 F3
Vårdö FIN 99 B14
Vardø N 114 C10
Vårdomb H 149 D11
Varejoki FIN 119 B13
Varekil S 91 C10
Varel D 17 B10
Varéna LT 137 E9
Varengeville-sur-Mer F 18 E2
Varenna I 69 A7
Varennes-en-Argonne F 19 F11
Varennes-St-Sauveur F 31 C7
Varennes-sur-Allier F 30 C4
Varennes-Vauzelles F 30 A3
Vareš BIH 157 D9
Varese I 69 B6
Varese Ligure I 37 C11
Varetz F 29 E8
Vârfu Câmpului RO 153 B8
Vârfuri RO 161 C7
Vârfurile RO 151 E10
Vårgårda S 91 C12
Vârghiş RO 153 E7
Vargön S 91 C11
Vargträsk S 107 C15
Varhaug N 94 E3
Vari GR 175 D8
Vari GR 176 E4
Variaş RO 151 E6
Varik NL 183 B6
Variku EST 130 C7
Varilhes F 33 D9
Varimbombi GR 175 C8
Varín SK 147 C7
Väring S 91 B14
Variņi LV 135 B12
Variskylä FIN 121 F13
Varislahti FIN 125 E11
Varistaipale FIN 125 E11
Varjakka FIN 119 E14
Varjisträsk S 109 D18
Varkaliai LT 134 E3
Varkaus FIN 125 F9
Vârkava LV 135 D13
Varkhi BY 133 E7
Vârlezi RO 153 F11
Varlosen (Niemetal) D 78 D6
Värme LV 134 C4
Värmlandsbro S 91 A13
Varna BG 167 C9
Varna I 72 C4
Varna SRB 158 D4
Várnamo S 88 A4
Värnäs S 97 B10
Varnavas GR 175 C8
Varnhem S 91 C14
Varniai LT 134 E4
Varnja EST 131 E14
Varnsdorf CZ 81 E7
Varntresken N 108 E7
Varnyany BY 137 D13
Vārobacka S 87 A10
Varonichy BY 133 F5
Varonka BY 133 F2
Városföld H 150 D4
Városlőd H 149 B9
Varoška Rijeka BIH 156 B5
Varpaisjärvi FIN 124 D9
Vårpalota H 149 B10
Varparanta FIN 125 G11
Varparanta FIN 125 F12
Varpsjö S 107 C11
Varpuselkä FIN 115 C5
Varpuvaara FIN 115 E4
Värriö FIN 115 D3
Varrio FIN 115 E2
Vars F 29 D6
Vars F 36 B5
Vârşand RO 151 D7
Vârşani H 147 E8
Värsås S 91 C15
Varsi I 69 D8
Värska EST 132 F2
Vârşolţ RO 151 C10

Varsseveld NL 17 E6
Vårst DK 86 B6
Vårsta S 93 A11
Varstu EST 131 F13
Varteig N 95 D14
Vartemyagi RUS 129 E13
Vârteşcoiu RO 153 F10
Vartholomio GR 174 D3
Vartius FIN 121 E14
Vârtoape RO 160 E6
Vartofta S 91 C14
Vârtop RO 160 E2
Värtsilä FIN 125 F15
Varuträsk S 118 E5
Varvara BG 165 E9
Varvara BG 167 E9
Varvara GR 169 C10
Varvarin SRB 159 F7
Varvasaina GR 174 D4
Värve LV 134 B3
Varvikko FIN 115 E4
Várvölgy H 149 C8
Vârvoru de Jos RO 160 E3
Varyazh UA 144 B9
Vârzăreşti MD 154 C2
Varzi I 37 B10
Varzo I 68 A5
Varzy F 25 F9
Vasa FIN 122 D7
Vasalemma EST 131 C8
Vasanello I 62 C2
Vasaniemi FIN 115 D2
Vasankari FIN 119 F11
Vasaraperä FIN 121 B12
Vásárosdombó H 149 D10
Vásárosnamény H 145 G5
Vaşcău RO 151 E10
Väse S 97 D10
Vashkivtsi UA 153 A7
Vashtëmi AL 168 C4
Vasilaţi RO 161 E8
Vasilika GR 169 D9
Vasilika GR 177 A7
Vasiliki GR 174 B2
Vasiliko GR 175 C8
Vasilikos GR 174 D2
Vasilis GR 169 F7
Vasilitsi GR 178 B2
Vasil Kolarov BG 165 F10
Vasil Levski BG 166 E5
Vasilopoulo GR 174 B3
Vasilovtsi BG 159 F11
Vasil'yevo RUS 132 F2
Vaškai LT 135 D8
Vaski LV 134 C6
Vaškiai LT 134 E2
Väskinde S 93 D12
Vaskio FIN 127 E9
Vaskivesi FIN 123 F11
Vasknarva EST 132 C2
Vaskút H 150 E2
Vaskuu FIN 123 F11
Vasles F 28 B5
Vaslui RO 153 D11
Vasmegyer H 145 G4
Vassaras GR 175 E6
Vassbo S 102 C4
Vassbotn N 111 C13
Vassbygdi N 100 E6
Vassdalen N 111 C14
Vassdalsvik N 108 C6
Vassenden N 100 D4
Vassieux-en-Vercors F 31 F7
Vassmolösa S 89 B10
Vassnäs S 105 D14
Vassor FIN 122 D8
Vasstrand N 111 A15
Vassy F 23 C10
Vasszécsény H 149 B7
Västana S 103 A12
Västanå S 103 B13
Västanå S 107 E16
Västanbäck S 107 D12
Västanfjärd FIN 126 E8
Västannäs S 118 B9
Västansjö S 103 A17
Västansjö S 103 C12
Västansjö S 107 A9
Västansjö S 107 C13
Västansjö S 107 E12
Västansjö S 108 E9
Västansjön S 103 B12
Västanvik S 103 E8
Vastemõisa EST 131 E10
Västerås S 98 C7
Västeråsen S 107 F11
Västerberg S 103 E12
Västerby S 97 B14
Västerbyn S 99 B10
Västerfärnebo S 98 C6
Västerhejde S 93 D12
Västerhus S 107 E15
Västerlandsjö S 107 E15
Västerljung S 93 B10
Västermyckeläng S 102 D7
Västerottna S 97 C8
Västerträsjö S 103 C11
Västervik S 93 D9
Västilä FIN 127 B12
Vastinki FIN 123 E13
Västinniemi FIN 125 E10
Vasto I 63 C7
Vastorf D 83 D9
Västra Åmtervik S 97 C9
Västra Bodarna S 91 D11
Västra Eneby S 92 C7
Västra Fagelberget S 105 C17
Västra Harg S 92 C6
Västra Hjåggböle S 118 E5
Västra Husby S 93 C8
Västra Karup S 87 C11
Västra Kiilisjärvi S 119 B10
Västra Lainejaure S 107 A15
Västra Ormsjö S 107 C10
Västra Sjulsmark S 118 F5
Västra Stugusjö S 103 A9
Västra Tåsjö S 106 C9
Västra Torup S 87 C13
Västra Yttermark FIN 122 E6
Vastse-Kuuste EST 131 E13
Vastseliina EST 132 F1
Vasvár H 149 B7
Vasylivka UA 155 B3
Vasylivka UA 155 B4
Vaszar H 149 B9
Vatan F 29 A9
Vătava RO 152 D5
Văte S 93 E12
Vatera GR 177 A7
Vaterholmsbru N 105 D11
Vatero GR 169 D6

Vaterstetten D 75 F10
Vatheia GR 178 C3
Vathy GR 175 C8
Vathy GR 177 E8
Vathylakkos GR 169 C8
Vathylakkos GR 169 D6
Vathys GR 177 F9
Vati GR 181 D7
Vatican City E 62 D2
Vatici MD 154 C3
Vatjusjärvi FIN 123 B14
Vatla EST 130 D7
Vatland N 94 F6
Vatnås S 103 C13
Vatne N 94 E3
Vatne N 100 A5
Vatolakkos GR 169 D5
Vatoussa GR 177 A7
Vatra Dornei RO 152 C6
Vatra Moldoviţei RO 153 B7
Vats N 101 E8
Vatta H 145 H2
Vattholma S 99 B9
Vattjom S 103 B13
Vattlång S 103 C13
Vattrång S 103 C13
Vattukylä FIN 119 F14
Vatula FIN 127 B8
Våtvoll N 111 C10
Vaubadon F 23 B10
Vaubecourt F 26 C3
Vauchassis F 25 D10
Vauclaix F 25 F10
Vauconcourt-Nervezain F 26 E4
Vaucouleurs F 26 C4
Vaudémont F 26 D5
Vaugneray F 30 D6
Vauldalen N 101 A16
Vaulx-en-Velin F 30 D6
Vaulx-Milieu F 31 D7
Vauvenargues F 35 C10
Vauvert F 35 C7
Vauvillers F 26 E5
Vaux-le-Pénil F 25 C8
Vaux-sur-Mer F 28 D3
Vaux-sur-Sûre B 19 E12
Vavdos GR 169 D9
Vaxbo S 103 D12
Vaxholm S 99 D10
Växjö S 89 B7
Våxtorp S 87 C12
Väylä FIN 113 E20
Väylänpää FIN 117 D11
Vayrac F 29 F9
Vayres F 28 B5
Väyrylä FIN 121 E10
Vaysal TR 167 F7
Väystäjä FIN 119 B12
Včelná CZ 77 E6
Veašhkoonjarga FIN 113 F20
Veauche F 30 D5
Veavågen N 94 D2
Vebbestrup DK 86 B5
Veberöd S 87 D13
Veblungsnes N 100 A7
Vebron F 35 B6
Vecate LV 131 F10
Vecauce LV 134 D6
Vecbebri LV 135 C10
Vecchiano I 66 E1
Vechelde D 79 B7
Vechta D 17 C10
Vecinos E 45 C9
Veckerhagen (Reinhardshagen)
   D 78 D4
Veckrape LV 135 C10
Veclaicene LV 131 F14
Vecmikeļi LV 134 D6
Vecpiebalga LV 135 B11
Vecpils LV 134 C2
Vecsaikava LV 135 C12
Vecsalaca LV 131 F8
Vecsaule LV 135 D8
Vecsés H 150 C3
Vecses H 150 C3
Veckulte LV 135 B8
Vecslabada LV 133 D3
Vecumnieki LV 135 C9
Veda S 103 A14
Vedde DK 87 D9
Veddelev DK 87 D10
Veddige S 88 A2
Veddum DK 86 B6
Vēde LV 134 B3
Vedea RO 160 D5
Vedea RO 161 F7
Vedevåg S 97 C13
Vedjeön S 106 C8
Vedum S 91 C13
Veendam NL 17 B7
Veenendaal NL 16 D5
Veenhusen D 17 B8
Veensgarth GB 3 E14
Veere NL 182 B3
Veerle B 182 C5
Vefling DK 86 E6
Vegacervera E 39 C8
Vega de Espinareda E 39 C6
Vegadeo E 38 B5
Vega de Pas E 40 B4
Vega de Tirados E 45 B9
Vega de Valcarce E 39 C6
Vega de Valdetronco E 39 E9
Veganzones E 46 B5
Vegaquemada E 39 C9
Vegarienza E 39 C7
Vegarshei N 90 B4
Vegas del Condado E 39 C9
Vegas de Matute E 46 C4
Végby S 91 D13
Végegyháza H 151 E6
Veggen N 111 D13
Vegger DK 86 B5
Veghel NL 16 E5
Veglie I 61 C9
Vegset N 105 C12
Vehkajärvi FIN 127 B12
Vehkalahti FIN 127 B15
Vehkalahti FIN 128 D7
Vehkataipale FIN 129 C9
Vehlow D 83 D12
Vehmaa FIN 126 D6
Vehmaa FIN 128 B8
Vehmasjärvi FIN 125 C10
Vehmersalmi FIN 125 E10
Vehniä FIN 123 F15

Vehu FIN 123 E12
Vehvilä FIN 124 E8
Veidholmen N 104 D3
Veidneset N 113 B18
Veigy-Foncenex F 31 C9
Veihtivaara FIN 121 E14
Veikkola FIN 127 E11
Veimo N 105 D11
Veinge S 87 B12
Veiros P 50 B4
Veisiejai LT 137 E8
Veitastrond N 100 D6
Veitsbronn D 75 C8
Veitsch A 148 A5
Veitservasa FIN 117 C13
Velosnes F 19 E11
Velp NL 183 B7
Velpke D 79 B8
Velten D 84 E4
Veltruby CZ 77 B8
Veltrusy CZ 76 B6
Velturno I 72 C4
Velušina MK 168 C5
Velvary CZ 76 B6
Velventos GR 169 D7
Velyatyn UA 145 G7
Velyka Horozhanna UA 145 D8
Velyka Kisnytsya UA 154 A2
Velyka Kopanya UA 145 G7
Velyka Mykhaylivka UA 154 C5
Velyka Tur"ya UA 145 E9
Velyki Kom"yaty UA 145 G6
Velyki Luchky UA 145 G6
Velyki Mosty UA 144 C9
Velykokomarivka UA 154 C5
Velykoploske UA 154 C6
Velykokozymenove UA 154 C6
Velykyy Berezny UA 145 F5
Velykyy Bychkiv UA 145 H9
Velykyy Rakovets' UA 145 G7
Velžys LT 135 E8
Vemb DK 86 C2
Vemdalen S 102 B6
Vemdalsskalet S 102 B6
Véménd H 149 D11
Vemhån S 102 B7
Vemundvik N 105 B11
Vena S 92 D7
Venaco CH 31 C11
Venafro I 62 E6
Venansault F 28 B2
Venarey-les-Laumes F 25 E11
Venaria I 68 C4
Venarotta I 62 B4
Venås S 103 C11
Venasca I 37 B6
Venčane SRB 158 E5
Vence F 36 D6
Venciūnai LT 137 E9
Venda Nova P 38 E4
Vendargues F 35 C6
Vendas Novas P 50 B3
Vendays-Montalivet F 28 E3
Vendenheim F 186 D4
Vendeuvre-du-Poitou F 29 B6
Vendeuvre-sur-Barse F 25 D11
Vendinha P 50 C4
Vendœuvres F 29 B8
Vendôme F 24 E5
Veneheitto FIN 119 F17
Venejärvi FIN 117 D12
Venelles F 35 C9
Vénès F 33 C10
Venesjärvi FIN 126 B7
Veneskoski FIN 123 E10
Venetmäki FIN 124 D7
Venetmäki FIN 124 F7
Venetpalo FIN 123 C15
Venets BG 161 F7
Venets BG 167 D7
Venevere EST 131 C13
Venezia I 66 B5
Vengasaho FIN 119 D16
Vengsoy N 111 A16
Venialbo E 39 F8
Vénissieux F 30 D6
Venizel F 19 F7
Venjan S 102 D6
Venlo NL 16 F6
Venna GR 171 B9
Vennesla N 90 C2
Vennesund N 105 A12
Venosa I 60 B5
Venoy F 25 E10
Venray NL 16 E5
Vensac F 28 E3
Venta LT 134 D5
Venta LV 134 C4
Venta de Baños E 40 E3
Venta del Charco E 54 C4
Venta del Moro E 47 E10
Venta de los Santos E 55 C6
Venta las Ranas E 39 A8
Venta Nueva E 39 B6
Ventas de Huelma E 53 B9
Ventas de Zafarraya E 53 C8
Ventava LV 134 B3
Ventavon F 35 B10
Venteuges F 30 F4
Ventimiglia I 37 D7
Ventiseri F 37 H10
Ventnor GB 13 D12
Ventry IRL 8 D2
Ventschow D 83 C11
Ventspils LV 134 B3
Venzone I 73 D7
Vép H 149 B7
Vepriai LT 135 F9
Vepsä FIN 119 E16
Vepsä FIN 125 C12
Vepsä FIN 125 F14
Vera E 55 E9
Vera Cruz P 50 C3
Verbania I 68 B6
Verberie F 18 F6
Verbicaro I 60 D5
Verbier CH 31 C11
Verbiţa RO 159 E11
Verbka UA 154 A6
Vercelli I 68 C5
Vercel-Villedieu-le-Camp F
   26 F5
Verchen D 84 C3
Verd SLO 73 E10
Verdaches F 36 C4
Verdalen N 94 E3
Verdalsøra N 105 D10
Verden (Aller) D 17 C12
Verdikoussa GR 169 E6
Verdohý AL 168 D4
Verdun F 26 B3
Verdun-sur-Garonne F 33 C8

Velký Osek CZ 77 B8
Veľký Šenov CZ 80 D6
Veľky Slavkov SK 145 E1
Veľký Týnec CZ 146 B4
Veľký Újezd CZ 146 B4
Vellahn D 83 D9
Vellberg D 74 D6
Velletri I 62 D3
Vellevans F 26 F6
Velling DK 86 C2
Vellinge S 87 E12
Vellisca E 47 D7
Vellmar D 78 D6
Velo GR 175 D6
Velosnes F 19 E11
Veluwe GR 175 D6
Velp NL 183 B7
Velpke D 79 B8
Velten D 84 E4
Veltruby CZ 77 B8
Veltrusy CZ 76 B6
Velturno I 72 C4
Velušina MK 168 C5
Velvary CZ 76 B6
Velventos GR 169 D7
Verbania I 68 B6
Verl D 17 E11
Verla FIN 128 C6
Verlaine B 19 C11
Vermand F 19 E7
Vermenton F 25 E10
Vermeş RO 159 B8
Vermiglio I 69 A10
Vermiosa P 45 C7
Vermosh AL 163 D8
Vernante I 37 C7
Vernantes F 23 F12
Vernayaz CH 31 C11
Vern-d'Anjou F 23 E10
Vernèrice CZ 80 E6
Verneşti RO 161 C9
Vernet F 33 D8
Vernet-les-Bains F 33 E10
Verneuil-sur-Avre F 24 C4
Verneuil-sur-Vienne F 29 D8
Vernier CH 31 C9
Vernio I 66 D3
Verniolle F 33 D9
Vernole I 61 C10
Vernon F 24 B5
Vernouillet F 24 C5
Vernoux-en-Vivarais F 30 F6
Vern-sur-Seiche F 23 D8
Verny F 26 B5
Veróčemaros H 147 F8
Veroia GR 169 D7
Verolanuova I 69 C9
Veroli I 62 D4
Verona I 66 B2
Verosvres F 30 C5
Verpelét H 145 H1
Verrabotn N 105 D9
Verran N 105 D9
Verres I 68 B4
Verrières F 29 C7
Versailles F 24 C7
Vers-en-Montage F 31 B8
Versmold D 17 D10
Versoix CH 31 C9
Verson F 23 B11
Vers-Pont-du-Gard F 35 C8
Vert F 32 B4
Vertaillac F 29 E6
Vértesacsa H 149 B11
Vértesboglár H 149 B11
Vértessomló H 149 A10
Vértesszőlős H 149 A10
Vertheuil F 28 E4
Verton F 18 D4
Vertou F 23 F9
Vertus F 25 C11
Verucchio I 66 E5
Verviers B 19 C12
Vervins F 19 E8
Verwood GB 13 D11
Verzino I 61 E7
Verzy F 25 B11
Vesanto FIN 124 D8
Vesala FIN 119 D16
Vesamäki FIN 123 F15
Vesanka FIN 123 F15
Vesanto FIN 123 E16
Vescovato I 66 B1
Vese H 149 D8
Vesela Dolyna UA 154 E4
Veselava LV 135 B10
Veselé SK 146 D5
Veselets BG 161 F9
Veselie BG 167 E9
Veselinovo BG 167 D8
Vesijako FIN 127 C12
Vesijärvi FIN 122 F7
Vesilahti FIN 127 C10
Vesime I 37 B8
Vesivehmaa FIN 127 C14
Vesløs DK 86 A3
Vesnovo RUS 136 D5
Vesoul F 26 E5
Vespolate I 68 C6
Vessa GR 177 C7
Vessem NL 16 F4
Vessigebro S 87 B11
Vestad N 101 C13
Vestby N 95 C13
Vestby N 102 D2
Vestbygd N 111 D10
Vestbø N 94 D3
Vestebæk DK 86 A5
Vestenås N 100 B5
Vester Åby DK 86 E6
Vesterås N 105 C12
Vesterby DK 87 F8
Vester Hæsinge DK 86 E6
Vester Hassing DK 86 A6
Vester Herborg DK 86 C3
Vester Hjermitslev DK 90 E6
Vester Hornum DK 86 B4

Verdun-sur-le-Doubs F 31 B7
Verebiesa LT 137 E8
Veresegyház H 150 B3
Vereşti RO 153 B8
Verfeil F 33 C8
Verfeil F 33 C9
Vergale LV 134 C2
Vergaville F 27 C6
Verges E 43 C10
Vergèze F 35 C7
Verghereto I 66 E5
Vergi EST 131 B12
Vergigny F 25 D10
Vergina GR 169 D7
Vergongheon F 30 E3
Vergt F 29 E7
Vergulessa RO 160 D4
Vericl BIH 157 C6
Verín E 38 E5
Verl D 17 E11
Verla FIN 128 C6
Verlaine B 19 C11
Verma N 100 B8
Vermand F 19 E7
Vermenton F 25 E10
Vermeş RO 159 B8
Vermiglio I 69 A10
Vermiosa P 45 C7
Vermosh AL 163 D8
Vernante I 37 C7
Vestermarie DK 89 E7
Vester Nebel DK 86 D4
Vesterø Havn DK 87 A7
Vestertana N 113 C20
Vesterup DK 86 B2
Vestervig DK 86 B2
Vestiena LV 135 C11
Vestmanna FO 2 A2
Vestnes N 100 A6
Vestone I 69 B9
Vestpollen N 110 D8
Vestre Gausdal N 101 D12
Vestre Jakobselv N 114 C6
Vestvågen N 108 E4
Veszkény H 149 A8
Veszprém H 149 B9
Veszprémvarsány H 149 B9
Vésztő H 151 D7
Veţca RO 152 E5
Veţel RO 151 F10
Veteli FIN 123 D11
Veternik SRB 158 C4
Vetersko MK 164 F4
Vétheuil F 24 B6
Vetiş RO 151 B10
Vetlefjorden N 100 D5
Vetovo BG 161 F8
Vetovo HR 157 B7
Vetralla I 62 C2
Vetren BG 165 E9
Vetren BG 166 E5
Vetren BG 167 D8
Vetrino BG 167 C9
Vetrişoaia RO 154 E2
Větřní CZ 76 E6
Vetschau D 80 C6
Vetsikko FIN 113 D19
Vettasjärvi S 116 D3
Vettelschoss D 185 C7
Vetterslev DK 87 E9
Vetto I 66 D1
Veulettes-sur-Mer F 18 E2
Veurne B 18 B6
Vevang N 104 E3
Vevčani MK 168 B4
Vevey CH 31 C10
Vevi GR 169 C6
Vex CH 31 C11
Vexala FIN 122 D8
Veynes F 35 A10
Veyre-Monton F 30 D3
Vèzach FIN 117 F8
Vézac F 29 F8
Vézelay F 25 F10
Vézelise F 26 D5
Vézénobres F 35 B7
Vezins F 23 F10
Vézins-de-Lévézou F 34 B4
Vezza d'Oglio I 69 A9
Vezzani F 37 G10
Vezzano I 69 A11
Vezzano I 66 C2
Viadana I 66 C2
Viala du Tarn F 34 B4
Vialas F 35 B6
Viana E 32 E1
Viana de Cega E 39 E10
Viana do Alentejo P 50 C4
Viana do Bolo E 38 D5
Viana do Castelo P 38 E2
Vianden L 20 E6
Viane F 34 C4
Vianen NL 16 E4
Viannos GR 178 E9
Viaño Pequeno E 38 B3
Vianos E 55 B8
Viantie FIN 119 C12
Viareggio I 66 E1
Viarmes F 25 B7
Vias F 34 D5
Viaşvesi FIN 126 C6
Viatodos P 38 F2
Viator E 55 F8
Viazac F 33 A10
Vibble S 93 D12
Vibbyn S 118 C7
Vibonati I 60 C5
Viborg DK 86 C4
Vibo Valentia I 59 B9
Vibraye F 24 D4
Viby DK 87 D10
Viby S 92 A6
Vic E 43 D8
Vícar E 55 F7
Vicari I 58 D4
Vicarstown IRL 7 F8
Vicchio I 66 E3
Vicdessos F 33 E9
Vic-en-Bigorre F 33 D6
Vicenza I 66 A4
Vic-Fezensac F 33 C6
Vichy F 30 C3
Vickan S 91 E11
Vic-le-Comte F 30 D3
Vico F 37 G9
Vico del Gargano I 63 D9
Vico Equense I 60 B2
Vicoforte I 37 C7
Vico nel Lazio I 62 D4
Vicovaro I 62 D3
Vicovu de Jos RO 153 B7
Vicovu de Sus RO 153 B7
Vicq-Exemplet F 29 B10
Vic-sur-Cère F 29 F11
Vic-sur-Seille F 26 C6
Victoria RO 153 C11
Victoria RO 160 D3
Victoria RO 161 C10
Victor Vlad Delamarina RO
   159 B8
Vidaga LV 135 B12
Vidago P 38 E4
Vidais P 44 F2
Vidāle LV 130 F4
Vidamlya BY 141 F9
Vidângoz E 32 E3
Višareiši FO 2 A3
Vidauban F 36 D4
Vidče CZ 146 C6
Viddal N 100 B5
Viddalba I 64 A2
Videbæk DK 86 C3
Videle RO 161 E7
Videm SLO 73 E10
Videm SLO 148 D5
Videmonte P 44 C6
Videniškiai LT 135 F10
Vidhas AL 168 B3
Vidigueira P 50 C4
Vidin BG 159 F10
Vidiškiai LT 135 F9
Vidlin GB 3 E14
Vidnava CZ 77 B12
Vidovec HR 148 D5
Vidovice BIH 157 C10
Vidra RO 151 E9
Vidra RO 153 F9
Vidrare N 111 D13
Vidrenjak HR 149 E7
Vidrieres E 43 D9
Vidriži LV 135 B9
Vidsala LV 135 D11
Vidsel S 118 D5
Vidstrup DK 90 D6
Viduklė LT 134 F5
Vidzy BY 135 F13
Viechtach D 76 D3
Vieille-Brioude F 30 E3
Vieira de Leiria P 44 E2
Vieira do Minho P 38 E3
Vieki FIN 125 D12
Viekšniai LT 134 D5
Vielank D 83 D10
Vielha E 33 E7
Vielle-Aure F 33 E6
Vielle-St-Girons F 32 C3
Vielmur-sur-Agout F 33 C10
Vielsalm B 20 D5
Vielverge F 26 F3
Vienenburg D 79 C8
Vieniba LV 134 C6
Vienne F 30 D6
Vieques F 37 C6
Vieremä FIN 124 C8
Viereth-Trunstadt D 75 C8
Vierlingsbeek NL 16 E5
Viernau D 79 E8
Viernheim D 21 E11
Vierraden D 84 D6
Viersen D 16 F6
Vierumäki FIN 127 C14
Vierville-sur-Mer F 23 B10
Vierzon F 24 F7
Viesecke D 83 D12
Viesīte LV 135 D11
Vieste I 63 D10
Viešvėnai LT 134 E4
Viešvilė LT 136 C5
Vietas S 109 A15
Vietri di Potenza I 60 B5
Vietri sul Mare I 60 B3
Vieux-Boucau-les-Bains F 32 C3
Vieux-Condé F 182 D5
Vievis LT 137 D10
Vif F 31 E8
Vig DK 87 D9
Víganti LV 135 D13
Vigarano Mainarda I 66 C3
Vigasio I 66 B2
Vigaun A 73 A7
Vigdenes N 105 D9
Vigeland N 94 F6
Vigeois F 29 E9
Vigevano I 69 C6
Vigge S 102 A7
Vigge S 103 B2
Viggianello F 37 H9
Viggianello I 60 D6
Viggiano I 60 C5
Vigfaš SN 147 D8
Vigliano Biellese I 68 B5
Vignacourt F 18 D5
Vignale Monferrato I 37 A8
Vignanello I 62 C2
Vigneulles-les-Hattonchâtel F
   26 C4
Vignola I 66 D3
Vignola Mare l'Agnata I 64 A3
Vignory F 26 D3
Vigny F 24 B6
Vigo E 38 D2
Vigodarzere I 66 B4
Vigo di Cadore I 72 D5
Vigo di Fassa I 72 D4
Vigone I 31 F11
Vigonza I 66 B4
Vigo Rendena I 69 A10
Vigrestad N 94 E3
Viguzzolo I 37 B9
Vigy F 20 F6
Vihalsen N 104 E5
Vihanti FIN 119 F13
Vihiers F 23 F10
Vihtari FIN 125 F11
Vihtasuo FIN 125 C12
Vihtavuori FIN 123 F15
Vihteljärvi FIN 126 B8
Vihti FIN 127 E11
Vihtijärvi FIN 127 D12
Vihula EST 131 B12
Viiala FIN 127 C10
Viiksimo FIN 121 F15
Viile Satu Mare RO 151 B10
Viimsi EST 131 C9
Viinamäki FIN 125 B10
Viinijärvi FIN 125 E12
Viinikka FIN 123 D16
Viinikoski FIN 119 D17
Viiratsi EST 131 E11
Viirinkylä FIN 119 B17
Viirre FIN 119 F12
Viisarimäki FIN 123 F16
Viişoara MD 153 B10
Viişoara RO 151 C11
Viişoara RO 152 D3
Viişoara RO 152 E3
Viişoara RO 153 A9
Viişoara RO 153 A11
Viişoara RO 153 E11
Viişoara RO 160 F6
Viitaila FIN 127 C13
Viitala FIN 123 C16
Viitamäki FIN 125 B10
Viitaniemi FIN 125 D11
Viitapohja FIN 127 B10
Viitaranta FIN 115 E3
Viitasaari FIN 123 D15
Viitavaara FIN 121 E13
Viitavaara FIN 121 E13
Viitka EST 132 F1
Viitna EST 131 C12
Viivikonna EST 132 C2
Vijciems LV 131 F11
Vik N 90 C4
Vik N 94 B2
Vik N 108 B9
Vik N 108 F3
Vik N 108 F3
Vik S 88 D6

Vika FIN 117 E16
Vika N 101 A15
Vika S 97 A14
Vikajärvi FIN 117 E16
Vikan N 104 E5
Vikan N 105 B10
Vikarbyn S 97 B15
Vikarbyn S 103 E9
Vikartovce SK 145 F1
Vikbyn S 97 B15
Vike N 100 E3
Vike S 103 A12
Vikebukt N 100 A6
Vikedal N 94 D3
Viken S 87 C11
Viken S 103 B9
Viken S 103 B11
Vikersund N 95 C11
Vikeså N 94 E4
Vikevåg N 94 D3
Vikholmen N 108 D4
Viķi LV 131 F9
Vikingstad S 92 C6
Vikmanshyttan S 97 B14
Vikna N 105 B9
Vikoč BIH 157 F10
Vikøyri N 100 D5
Vikran N 111 A16
Vikran N 111 C12
Viksberg S 97 B14
Viksjö S 103 A13
Viksjöfors S 103 D10
Viksmon S 107 E12
Vīksna LV 133 B2
Viktarinas LT 137 E8
Vikten N 110 C6
Viktorivka UA 154 C6
Vikýřovice CZ 77 C11
Vila E 38 E3
Vila Boa P 45 D7
Vila Boa do Bispo P 44 B4
Vila Caiz P 38 F3
Chã de Sá P 44 C5
Vila Cova da Lixa P 38 F3
Vilada E 43 C7
Viladamat E 43 C10
Vila da Ponte P 38 E4
Viladecans E 43 E8
Vila de Cruces E 38 C3
Vila de Rei P 44 E4
Vila do Bispo P 50 E2
Vila do Conde P 38 F2
Viladrau E 43 D8
Vilafamés E 48 D4
Vilafant E 43 C9
Vila Fernando P 51 B5
Vila Flor P 38 F5
Vila Franca das Naves P 45 C6
Vilafranca de Bonany E 57 B11
Vilafranca del Penedès E 43 E7
Vila Franca de Xira P 50 B2
Vilagarcía de Arousa E 38 C2
Vilajuïga E 34 F5
Vilaka LV 133 B3
Vilalba E 38 B4
Vilallonga E 33 F10
Vilamarxant E 48 E3
Vilamoura P 50 E3
Vilāni LV 133 C1
Vila Nogueira de Azeitão P 50 B1
Vilanova E 38 B5
Vila Nova da Baronia P 50 C3
Vilanova d'Alcolea E 48 D5
Vilanova de Arousa E 38 C2
Vila Nova de Cacela P 50 E5
Vila Nova de Famalicão P 38 F2
Vila Nova de Foz Côa P 45 B6
Vila Nova de Gaia P 44 B3
Vilanova de la Barca E 42 D5
Vilanova de L'Aguda E 42 D6
Vilanova de Meià E 42 D6
Vila Nova de Ourém P 44 E3
Vila Nova de Paiva P 44 C5
Vila Nova de Poiares P 44 D4
Vilanova de Prades E 42 E5
Vila Nova de São Bento P 50 D5
Vilanova de Sau E 43 D8
Vilanova i la Geltrú E 43 E7
Vila Pouca da Beira P 44 D5
Vila Pouca de Aguiar P 38 E4
Vila Praia de Âncora P 38 E2
Vilar P 38 E3
Vilar P 44 C2
Vilarandelo P 38 E5
Vilarchao E 38 D4
Vilar da Veiga P 38 E3
Vilar de Andorinho P 44 B3
Vilar de Barrio E 38 D4
Vilar de Santos E 38 D4
Vilardevós E 38 E5
Vila Real P 38 F4
Vila Real de Santo António P 50 E5
Vilarelho da Raia P 38 E5
Vilar Formoso P 45 C7
Vilarinho da Castanheira P 45 B6
Vilarinho do Bairro P 44 D3
Vilariño de Conso E 38 D5
Vila-rodona E 43 E6
Vila Ruiva P 50 C4
Vila Seca P 38 E2
Vilaseca de Solcina E 42 E6
Vilassar de Mar E 43 D8
Vilasund S 108 D3
Vila Velha de Ródão P 44 E5
Vila Verde P 38 F3
Vila Verde P 38 F4
Vila Verde P 44 E4
Vila Verde da Raia P 38 E5
Vila Verde de Ficalho P 51 D5
Vila Viçosa P 50 B5
Vilce LV 134 D7
Vilches E 55 C6
Vildbjerg DK 86 C3
Vilémov CZ 77 C9
Vilgåle LV 134 C3
Vilhelmina S 107 B11
Vilia GR 175 C7
Viljakkala FIN 127 B9
Viljandi EST 131 E11
Viljevo HR 149 E10
Viljolahti FIN 125 F10
Vikavičkis LT 136 D7
Vilķene LV 131 F9
Vilkija LT 137 C8
Vilkýškiai LT 134 F4
Villa Bartolomea I 66 B3

Villabate I 58 C3
Villablanca E 51 E5
Villablino E 39 C7
Villabona E 32 D1
Villabrágima E 39 E9
Villabuena del Puente E 39 F9
Villac F 29 E8
Villacañas E 46 E6
Villa Carcina I 69 B9
Villacarriedo E 40 B4
Villacarrillo E 55 C6
Villa Castelli I 61 B8
Villacastín E 46 C4
Villach A 73 C8
Villacidro I 64 E2
Villaciervos E 41 E7
Villaconejos E 46 D6
Villaconejos de Trabaque E 47 D8
Villada E 39 D10
Villa d'Almè I 69 B8
Villa del Prado E 46 D4
Villa del Río E 53 A8
Villadepera S 39 F7
Villa de Ves E 47 F10
Villadiego E 40 C2
Villadose I 66 B4
Villadossola I 68 A5
Villaeles de Valdavia E 39 C10
Villaescusa de Haro E 47 E7
Villaescusa la Sombría E 40 D5
Villafáfila E 39 E8
Villafeliche E 47 B10
Villaflores E 45 C9
Villafranca d'Asti I 37 B8
Villafranca de Córdoba E 53 A7
Villafranca de Ebro E 41 E10
Villafranca del Bierzo E 39 C6
Villafranca del Campo E 47 C10
Villafranca del Cid E 48 D4
Villafranca de los Barros E 51 B7
Villafranca de los Caballeros E 46 F6
Villafranca di Verona I 66 B2
Villafranca in Lunigiana I 69 E8
Villafranca-Montes de Oca E 40 D5
Villafranca Tirrena I 59 C7
Villafranco del Guadalquivir E 51 E7
Villafrati I 58 D3
Villafrechos E 39 E9
Villafruela E 40 E4
Villafuerte E 40 E3
Villagarcía de Campos E 39 E9
Villagarcía de la Torre E 51 C7
Villagarcía del Llano E 47 F9
Villagio Mancuso I 59 A10
Villagonzalo E 51 B7
Villagrande Strisaili I 64 D4
Villaharta E 54 C3
Villåhde FIN 127 D14
Villahermosa E 55 B7
Villahermosa del Río E 48 D4
Villaherreros E 40 D3
Villahizán E 40 D4
Villahoz E 40 D4
Villaines-en-Duesmois F 25 E12
Villaines-la-Juhel F 23 D11
Villajoyosa-la Vila Joiosa E 56 D4
Villala FIN 125 F13
Villala FIN 129 D9
Villa Lagarina I 69 B11
Villalago I 62 D5
Villalar de los Comuneros E 39 E9
Villa Latina I 62 D5
Villalba de Duero E 40 E4
Villalba de Guardo E 39 C10
Villalba de la Sierra E 47 D8
Villalba de los Alcores E 39 E10
Villalba de los Barros E 51 B6
Villalba del Rey E 47 D7
Villalba dels Arcs E 42 E4
Villalba de Rioja E 40 C6
Villalcampo E 39 E7
Villalcázar de Sirga E 40 D2
Villalengua E 41 F8
Villalgordo del Júcar E 47 F8
Villa Literno I 60 A2
Villalobos E 39 E9
Villalón de Campos E 39 D9
Villalonga E 56 D4
Villalpando E 39 E9
Villalpardo E 47 F9
Villaluenga de la Sagra E 46 D5
Villalumbroso E 39 D10
Villamalea E 47 F9
Villamañán E 39 D8
Villamanrique E 55 B7
Villamanrique de la Condesa E 51 E7
Villamartín de Campos E 39 D10
Villamassargia I 64 E2
Villamayor E 45 C9
Villamayor de Calatrava E 54 B4
Villamayor de Campos E 39 E9
Villamayor de Santiago E 47 E7
Villamayor de Treviño E 40 D3
Villamediana E 40 D3
Villamediana de Iregua E 32 F1
Villamejil E 39 C7
Villameriel E 45 F9
Villamiel S 45 D7
Villa Minozzo I 66 D1
Villamor de los Escuderos E 39 F8
Villamuelas E 46 E5
Villamuriel de Cerrato E 40 E3
Villandraut F 32 B5
Villanova I 61 B9
Villanova d'Albenga I 37 C8
Villanova d'Asti I 37 B7
Villanova del Battista I 60 A4
Villanovafranca I 64 D3
Villanova Monferrato I 68 C5
Villanova Monteleone I 64 B1
Villanova Truschedu I 64 D2
Villanova Tulo I 64 D3
Villanterio I 69 C7
Villanúa E 32 E4
Villanubla E 39 E10

Villanueva de Alcardete E 47 E6
Villanueva de Alcorón E 47 C8
Villanueva de Algaidas E 53 B8
Villanueva de Argaño E 40 D4
Villanueva de Bogas E 46 E5
Villanueva de Cameros E 41 D6
Villanueva de Castellón E 56 C4
Villanueva de Córdoba E 54 C3
Villanueva de Gállego E 41 E10
Villanueva de Gómez E 46 C3
Villanueva de la Cañada E 46 D5
Villanueva de la Concepción E 53 C7
Villanueva de la Fuente E 55 B7
Villanueva de la Jara E 47 F9
Villanueva de la Reina E 53 A9
Villanueva del Arzobispo E 55 C6
Villanueva de las Cruces E 51 D5
Villanueva de la Serena E 51 B8
Villanueva de las Torres E 55 D6
Villanueva de la Vera E 45 D10
Villanueva del Campo E 39 E9
Villanueva del Duque E 54 C3
Villanueva del Fresno E 51 C5
Villanueva de los Castillejos E 51 D5
Villanueva de los Infantes E 55 B7
Villanueva del Rey E 51 C9
Villanueva del Río Segura E 55 C10
Villanueva del Río y Minas E 51 D8
Villanueva del Rosario E 53 C8
Villanueva del Trabuco E 53 B8
Villanueva de Mesía E 53 B8
Villanueva de San Carlos E 54 B5
Villanueva de San Juan E 51 E9
Villanueva de Tapia E 53 B8
Villanueva de Valdegovia E 40 C5
Villanuño de Valdavia E 40 C2
Villány H 149 E10
Villa Opicina I 73 E8
Villapalacios E 55 B7
Villaperuccio I 64 E2
Villapiana I 61 D6
Villapiana Lido I 61 D6
Villa Poma I 66 C3
Villapourçon F 25 F10
Villaputzu I 64 E4
Villaquejida E 39 D8
Villaquilambre E 39 C8
Villaralbo E 39 F8
Villaralto E 54 C3
Villarcayo E 40 C4
Villard-Bonnot F 31 E8
Villard-de-Lans F 31 E8
Villar de Cañas E 47 E7
Villar de Ciervo E 45 C7
Villardeciervos E 39 E7
Villardefrades E 39 E9
Villar del Arzobispo E 48 E3
Villar de la Yegua E 45 C7
Villar del Buey E 39 F7
Villar del Cobo E 47 D9
Villar del Humo E 47 E9
Villar de los Barrios E 39 C6
Villar de los Navarros E 42 E1
Villar del Pedroso E 45 E10
Villar del Rey E 45 F7
Villar del Salz E 47 C10
Villar de Olalla E 47 D8
Villar de Peralonso E 45 B8
Villar de Rena E 45 F9
Villar de Torre E 40 D6
Villardompardo E 53 A8
Villareal E 48 E4
Villarejo de Fuentes E 47 E7
Villarejo de Montalbán E 46 E3
Villarejo de Orbigo E 39 C8
Villarejo de Salvanés E 47 D6
Villa Rendena I 69 A10
Villarente E 39 C8
Villares de la Reina E 45 B9
Villargordo E 53 A9
Villargordo del Cabriel E 47 E10
Villarino de los Aires E 39 F7
Villarluengo E 42 F3
Villarosa I 58 D5
Villarquemado E 47 C10
Villarramiel E 39 D10
Villarrasa E 51 E6
Villarreal de Huerva E 47 B10
Villarrín de Campos E 39 E8
Villarrobledo E 47 F7
Villarrodrigo E 55 C7
Villarroya de la Sierra E 41 F8
Villarroya de los Pinares E 42 F2
Villarrubia de los Ojos E 46 F5
Villarrubia de Santiago E 46 E6
Villarrubio E 47 E7
Villars F 29 E7
Villars F 30 D5
Villars-Colmars F 36 C5
Villars-les-Dombes F 31 D7
Villars-sur-Var F 36 D6
Villarta de la Sierra E 41 F8
Villarta de los Montes E 46 F3
Villarta de San Juan E 46 F6
Villasalto I 64 E3
Villasana de Mena E 40 B5
Villasandino E 40 D3
Villa San Giovanni I 59 C8
Villa San Pietro I 64 E3
Villa Santa Maria I 63 D6
Villasante de Montija E 40 B5
Villa Santina I 73 D6
Villasarracino E 40 D3
Villasavary F 33 D10
Villasayas E 41 F6
Villaseco de Laciana E 39 C7
Villaseca de la Sagra E 46 D5
Villaseco de los Gamitos E 45 B8
Villaseco de los Reyes E 45 B8
Villaseco del Pan E 39 E8
Villasequilla de Yepes E 46 E5
Villasimius I 64 E4
Villasmundo I 59 E7
Villasor I 64 E3
Villaspeciosa I 64 E2
Villasrubias E 45 D7
Villastar E 47 D10

Villasur de Herreros E 40 D5
Villatobas E 46 E6
Villatoro E 45 C10
Villatoya E 47 F10
Villatuerta E 32 E2
Villaumbrales E 39 D10
Villaurbana I 64 D2
Villava E 32 E2
Villavallelonga I 62 D5
Villavelayo E 40 E6
Villaverde de Guadalimar E 55 C7
Villaverde del Río E 51 D8
Villaverde y Pasaconsol E 47 E8
Villavernia I 37 B9
Villaviciosa E 39 B9
Villaviciosa de Córdoba E 54 C2
Villaviciosa de Odón E 46 D5
Villavieja E 48 E4
Villavieja de Yeltes E 45 C8
Villaviudas E 40 E3
Villayón E 39 B6
Villazanzo de Valderaduey E 39 C10
Villé F 27 D7
Villebois-Lavalette F 29 E6
Villebrumier F 33 C8
Villecomtal F 33 A11
Villecomte F 25 E11
Villecroze F 36 D4
Villedaigne F 34 D4
Villedieu-la-Blouère F 23 F9
Villedieu-les-Poêles F 23 C9
Villedieu-sur-Indre F 29 B9
Ville-en-Tardenois F 20 F1
Villefagnan F 28 C6
Villefontaine F 31 D6
Villefort F 35 B6
Villefranche-d'Albigeois F 33 C10
Villefranche-d'Allier F 30 C2
Villefranche-de-Lauragais F 33 D9
Villefranche-de-Lonchat F 28 F6
Villefranche-de-Panat F 34 B4
Villefranche-de-Rouergue F 33 B10
Villefranche-du-Périgord F 33 A8
Villefranche-sur-Cher F 24 F6
Villefranche-sur-Mer F 37 D6
Villefranche-sur-Saône F 30 D6
Villefranque F 32 D3
Villegas E 40 D3
Villel E 47 D10
Villelaure F 35 C9
Villemandeur F 25 E8
Villemomble F 25 C8
Villemorien F 25 D11
Villemoustaussou F 33 D10
Villemur-sur-Tarn F 33 C9
Villena E 56 D3
Villenauxe-la-Grande F 25 C10
Villeneuve CH 31 C10
Villeneuve F 33 B10
Villeneuve F 35 C10
Villeneuve-au-Chemin F 25 D10
Villeneuve-d'Allier F 30 D4
Villeneuve-d'Ascq F 19 C7
Villeneuve-de-Berg F 35 A2
Villeneuve-de-Marsan F 32 C5
Villeneuve-de-Rivière F 33 D7
Villeneuve-la-Guyard F 25 D9
Villeneuve-l'Archevêque F 25 D10
Villeneuve-lès-Avignon F 35 C8
Villeneuve-lès-Béziers F 34 D5
Villeneuve-Loubet F 36 D6
Villeneuve-sur-Allier F 30 B3
Villeneuve-sur-Lot F 33 B7
Villeneuve-sur-Yonne F 25 D9
Villeneuve-Tolosane F 33 C8
Villepinte F 33 D10
Villercomtal F 33 A11
Villeréal F 33 A7
Villerest F 30 D5
Villerías E 39 E9
Villerouge-Termenès F 34 D4
Villers-Bocage F 18 C5
Villers-Bocage F 23 B10
Villers-Bretonneux F 18 E6
Villers-Carbonnel F 18 E6
Villers-Cotterêts F 19 F7
Villers-Écalles F 18 E2
Villers-en-Argonne F 25 B12
Villersexel F 26 E5
Villers-Farlay F 31 A8
Villers-le-Bouillet B 183 D6
Villers-le-lac F 31 A10
Villers-lès-Nancy F 26 C5
Villers-Outréaux F 19 D7
Villers-sur-Glâne CH 31 B11
Villers-sur-Mer F 23 B11
Villerville F 23 B12
Villeseneux F 25 C11
Ville-sur-Tourbe F 20 F3
Villetta Barrea I 62 D5
Villeurbanne F 30 D6
Villeveyrac F 35 C6
Villevocance F 30 E6
Villié-Morgon F 30 C6
Villiers-Charlemagne F 23 E10
Villiers-en-Lieu F 25 C12
Villiers-le-Sec F 26 D3
Villiers-St-Benoît F 25 E9
Villiers-St-Georges F 25 C9
Villieu-Loyes-Mollon F 31 D7
Villikkala FIN 128 D6
Villingen D 27 D9
Villingsberg S 97 D12
Villmar D 185 D9
Villoldo E 39 D10
Villora E 47 E9
Villoria E 45 C10
Villoruela E 45 B9
Villotte-sur-Aire F 26 C3
Villshärad S 87 B11
Villvattnet S 118 E4
Vilnius LT 137 D11
Vilovi d'Onyar E 43 D9
Vilppula FIN 123 F12
Vilpulka LV 131 F10
Vils A 71 B11
Vils DK 86 B3
Vilsbiburg D 75 F11
Vilseck D 75 C10
Vil'shanka UA 154 A3
Vilshofen D 76 E4

Vilshult S 88 C7
Vilslev DK 86 E3
Vilsted DK 86 B4
Vilsund Vest DK 86 B3
Vilusi BIH 157 C7
Vilusi MNE 162 D6
Viluste EST 132 F1
Vilvestre E 45 B7
Vilvoorde B 19 C9
Vilzēni EST 131 F10
Vima Mică RO 152 C3
Vimbodí E 42 E6
Vimeiro P 44 F2
Vimercate I 69 B7
Vimeiro P 50 B4
Vimioso P 39 E6
Vimmarvattnet S 107 D9
Vimmerby S 92 D7
Vimory F 25 E8
Vinac BIH 157 D7
Vinadio I 37 C6
Vinaixa E 42 E5
Vinařice CZ 76 B6
Vinaròs E 42 G4
Vinarsko BG 167 D8
Vinäs S 102 E8
Vinassan F 34 D5
Vinay F 31 E7
Vinberg S 87 B11
Vinça F 34 E4
Vinča SRB 158 D6
Vincey F 26 D5
Vinchiaturo I 63 E7
Vinci I 66 E2
Vind DK 86 C3
Vindblæs DK 86 B4
Vindeballe DK 86 F6
Vindeby DK 86 F7
Vindel-Ånäset S 118 F3
Vindelgransele S 107 A14
Vindeln S 107 C17
Vinderei RO 153 E11
Vinderslev DK 86 C4
Vinderup DK 86 C3
Vindhella N 100 D7
Vindinge DK 87 D10
Vindinge DK 87 E7
Vindsvik N 94 D4
Vinebre E 42 E5
Vineuil F 29 E8
Vineuil F 24 E6
Vinga RO 151 E7
Vingåker S 92 A7
Vingång S 102 E4
Vingrau F 34 E4
Vingrom N 101 D12
Vinhais P 39 E6
Vinhas P 39 E6
Vinica HR 148 D6
Vinica MK 164 F5
Vinica SLO 67 B11
Viničné SK 146 E4
Viniegra de Arriba E 40 D6
Vinine BIH 157 G8
Vinišče HR 156 F5
Vinje N 94 C7
Vinje N 100 E4
Vinjeøra N 104 E6
Vinkovci HR 149 F11
Vinkt B 182 C2
Vinliden S 107 B13
Vinné SK 145 F4
Vinnersjö S 98 B7
Vinnes N 94 B2
Vinnesvåg N 94 B2
Vinni EST 131 C12
Vinninga S 91 C13
Vinningen D 27 B8
Vinodol SK 146 E6
Vinograd BG 166 C5
Vinogradets BG 165 E9
Vinon-sur-Verdon F 35 C10
Vinsa S 116 E9
Vinslöv S 87 C13
Vinsobres F 35 B9
Vinstra N 101 C11
Vinstra N 101 D12
Vintervollen N 114 D8
Vintilă Vodă RO 161 C9
Vintjärn S 103 E13
Vintrosa S 97 D12
Vintturi FIN 123 C11
Vințu de Jos RO 152 E2
Viñuelas E 46 C6
Vinuesa E 40 E6
Vinzelberg D 79 A10
Viöl D 82 A6
Violay F 30 D5
Violès F 35 B8
Vipava SLO 73 E8
Vipe LT 135 D12
Viperești RO 161 C8
Vipiteno I 72 C3
Vipperød DK 87 D9
Vipperow D 83 D13
Vir BIH 157 E7
Vir SLO 73 D10
Vira S 93 B8
Virawla BY 133 E7
Virazeil F 33 A6
Virbalis LT 136 D6
Virbi LV 134 B5
Virçe RO 161 D11
Vīre F 23 C10
Vireşti LV 135 B12
Vireux-Molhain F 184 D2
Vireux-Wallerand F 19 D10
Virey-sous-Bar F 25 D11
Virgen A 72 B5
Virginia IRL 7 E8
Viriat F 31 C7
Virieu-le-Grand F 31 D8
Virigneux F 30 D5
Viriginin F 31 D8
Viriville F 31 E7
Virķēni LV 131 F10
Virkkala FIN 127 E10
Virkkula FIN 121 B13
Virkkunen FIN 121 C10
Virklund DK 86 C5
Virmaanpää FIN 124 E8
Virmaila FIN 127 C13
Virmutjoki FIN 129 C10
Virolahden kk FIN 128 D8
Virolahti FIN 128 D8
Virovitica HR 149 E8

Vilshult S 88 C7
Virpe LV 134 B4
Virrat FIN 123 F11
Virsbo S 97 C15
Virserum S 89 A9
Virtaniemi FIN 114 F4
Virtasalmi FIN 124 F8
Virton B 19 E12
Virtsu EST 130 D7
Virttaa FIN 126 D8
Viru-Jaagupi EST 131 C12
Viru-Nigula EST 131 C13
Viry F 31 C9
Vis HR 63 A10
Visaginas LT 135 E12
Viškaio Rūda LT 137 D7
Visan F 35 B8
Vişani RO 161 C10
Višåsen S 103 A13
Visbek D 17 C10
Visborg DK 86 B6
Visby DK 86 E3
Visby S 93 D12
Visé B 19 C12
Višegrad BIH 158 F3
Visegrád H 149 A11
Viserba I 66 D6
Viseu P 44 C5
Vişeu de Jos RO 152 B4
Vişeu de Sus RO 152 B4
Vishnyeva BY 137 E13
Vishvograd BG 166 C4
Visiedo E 42 F1
Visikums LV 133 B2
Vişina RO 160 D6
Vişina RO 160 F4
Vişinesti RO 160 D6
Vişinesti RO 161 C7
Visingsö S 92 C5
Visjövalen S 105 E12
Viskafors S 91 D13
Viskan S 103 B11
Viškļ LV 135 D13
Visланda S 88 B7
Visnes N 94 D2
Višnja Gora SLO 73 E10
Višnjićevo SRB 158 D3
Višňová CZ 81 E8
Višňové CZ 77 E10
Višňové SK 147 C7
Visoca MD 153 A11
Viso del Marqués E 55 B5
Visoki BIH 157 D9
Visoko BIH 157 D9
Visone I 37 B9
Visonta I 150 B5
Visp CH 68 A4
Vissac-Auteyrac F 30 E4
Vissani GR 168 E4
Visselfjärda S 89 B9
Visselhövede D 82 E7
Vissenbjerg DK 86 E6
Visso I 62 B4
Vissoie CH 68 A4
Vist N 105 D10
Vistabella del Maestrazgo E 48 D4
Vistbäcken S 118 C5
Vişţea RO 152 F5
Vistheden S 118 C5
Visthus N 108 E4
Visytyтis LT 136 E6
Visuvesi FIN 123 F11
Visznek H 150 B5
Vita I 58 D2
Vità S 118 C4
Vitaby S 88 D6
Vitåfors S 118 C5
Vitanova SK 147 C9
Vitanovac SRB 159 F6
Vitanovac SRB 164 C5
Vīťaz SK 145 F2
Vitberget S 118 C4
Viterbo I 62 C2
Viterne F 26 C5
Vitez BIH 157 D8
Vítézná CZ 77 B9
Viti KS 164 E3
Vitigudino E 45 B8
Vitina BIH 157 F8
Vitina GR 174 D5
Viting S 94 B3
Vitinja BY 133 F7
Viti S 116 E9
Vitivoren N 114 D8
Vitolište MK 169 B6
Vitomireşti RO 160 D4
Vitomiricë KS 163 D9
Vitorchiano I 62 C2
Vitoria-Gasteiz E 41 C6
Vitoševac SRB 159 F7
Vitovlje BIH 157 D8
Vitré F 23 D9
Vitrey-sur-Mance F 26 E4
Vitrolles F 35 D9
Vitry-en-Artois F 18 D6
Vitry-en-Perthois F 25 C12
Vitry-le-François F 25 C12
Vitry-sur-Loire F 30 B4
Vittangi S 116 C7
Vittaryd S 87 B13
Vitteaux F 25 F12
Vittel F 26 D4
Vittinge S 98 C8
Vittjärv S 118 C7
Vittoria I 58 F5
Vittorio Veneto I 72 E5
Vittsjö S 87 C13
Vitulano I 60 A3
Vitulazio I 60 A2
Vitvattnet S 102 B8
Vitvattnet S 107 D16
Vitvattnet S 119 B13
Vitzenburg D 79 D10
Viuruniemi FIN 125 E11
Vivario F 37 G10
Vivastbo S 98 B7
Viveiro E 38 A4
Vivel del Río Martín E 42 F2
Viver E 48 E3
Viverols F 30 E4
Viveros E 55 B7
Vivier-au-Court F 19 E10
Viviers F 35 A8
Viviez F 33 A10
Vivild DK 86 C6
Viv-le-Fesq F 35 C7
Vivonne F 29 C6
Vix F 25 E12
Vix F 28 C4

Vizantea-Livezi RO 153 F9
Vize TR 173 A8
Vizille F 31 E8
Vižinada HR 67 B8
Vizitsa BG 167 E9
Vizovice CZ 146 C5
Vizslás H 147 E9
Vizzini I 59 E6
Vlaardingen NL 16 E2
Vlachata GR 174 C2
Vlacherna GR 174 D5
Vlachia GR 175 B7
Vlachiotis GR 175 F6
Vlachokerasia GR 174 D5
Vlachovice CZ 146 C5
Vladaia RO 159 E11
Vladaya BG 165 D7
Vlădeni RO 153 A9
Vlădeni RO 153 C10
Vlădeni RO 155 D1
Vlădeşti RO 154 F2
Vlădeşti RO 160 C3
Vlădeşti RO 160 C5
Vladičin Han SRB 164 D5
Vlădila RO 160 E4
Vladimir MNE 163 E7
Vladimir RO 160 D3
Vladimirci SRB 158 D4
Vladimirescu RO 151 E7
Vladimirovac SRB 159 C6
Vladimirovo BG 161 F11
Vladimirovo BG 165 B7
Vladinya BG 165 C9
Vladislav CZ 77 D9
Vlad Țepeş RO 161 E10
Vladychen UA 155 B3
Vlăhiţa RO 153 D6
Vlahovici BIH 157 F9
Vlanduk BIH 157 D8
Vlaole SRB 159 E8
Vlase SRB 164 D5
Vlasenica BIH 157 D11
Vlašići HR 156 D3
Vlašim CZ 77 C7
Vlasina Okruglica SRB 164 D5
Vlăsineşti RO 153 A9
Vlasotince SRB 164 D5
Vlatkovići BIH 157 D7
Vlčany SK 146 E5
Vlčnov CZ 146 D5
Vledder NL 16 C6
Vleuten NL 16 E4
Vlijmen NL 16 E4
Vlissingen NL 16 F1
Vlochos GR 169 E7
Vlorë AL 168 D1
Vlotho D 17 D11
Vlycho GR 174 B2
Vnanje Gorice SLO 73 D9
Vnorovy CZ 146 D4
Voćin HR 149 E9
Vöcklabruck A 76 F5
Vöcklamarkt A 76 F5
Voden BG 161 F9
Voden BG 167 E7
Voderady SK 146 E5
Vodica BIH 157 C8
Vodice HR 67 B9
Vodice HR 156 E4
Vodňany CZ 76 D6
Voditsa BG 166 C6
Vodjenica BIH 156 C6
Vodňany CZ 76 D6
Vodnjan HR 67 C8
Vodskov DK 86 A6
Vodstrup DK 86 B3
Voe GB 3 E14
Voel DK 86 C5
Voerde (Niederrhein) D 17 E7
Voerendaal NL 183 D7
Voerladegård DK 86 C5
Voerså DK 86 A6
Vogatsiko GR 168 D5
Vogelenzang NL 182 A5
Vogelgrun F 27 D8
Vogelsang D 84 D4
Vogelsdorf D 80 B5
Vogelweh D 21 F9
Voghera I 37 B10
Voghiera I 66 C4
Vognill N 101 A11
Vognsild DK 86 B4
Vogošća BIH 157 E9
Vogt D 71 B9
Vogtareuth D 72 A6
Vogüé F 35 A7
Vohburg an der Donau D 75 E10
Vohenstrauß D 75 C11
Vöhl D 21 B11
Võhma EST 131 D11
Vohonjoki FIN 120 B9
Vöhringen D 27 D10
Vöhringen D 75 F7
Voicesti RO 160 D4
Void-Vacon F 26 C4
Voikkaa FIN 128 C6
Voikoski FIN 128 C6
Voila RO 152 F5
Voilleconte F 25 C12
Voineasa RO 160 C3
Voineasa RO 160 C5
Voineşti RO 153 C10
Voineşti RO 160 C6
Voiron F 31 E8
Vöistre EST 131 E8
Voiteg RO 159 C7
Voiteur F 31 B8
Voitsberg A 73 B11
Voivodeni RO 152 D5
Vojakkala FIN 119 C12
Vojakkala FIN 127 D11
Vojčice SK 145 F4
Vojens DK 86 E4
Vojka SRB 158 D5
Vojkovic BIH 157 E9
Vojnić HR 148 F5
Vojnik MK 164 E4
Vojnik SLO 148 D4
Vojtjajaure S 108 E4
Voka EST 132 C2
Vokány H 149 E10
Vokil BG 161 F10
Voknavolok RUS 121 E16
Voksa N 100 B2
Volakas GR 170 B5
Volary CZ 76 E5
Volda N 100 B4
Voldby DK 86 C6
Voldby DK 87 C7
Voldum DK 86 C6

Volendam NL 16 D4
Volgsele S 107 B11
Volimes GR 174 D2
Volintiri MD 154 E5
Volissos GR 177 C6
Voljevac BIH 157 E8
Voljice BIH 157 E8
Volkach D 75 C7
Volkel NL 183 B7
Völkermarkt A 73 C10
Volketswil CH 27 F10
Völklingen D 21 F7
Volkmarsen D 17 F12
Volkovija MK 163 F10
Voll N 101 E13
Völlen D 17 B8
Vollenhove NL 16 C5
Vollersode D 17 B11
Vollsjö S 87 D13
Volmunster F 27 B7
Voloiac RO 159 D11
Voloka UA 153 A7
Volonne F 35 B11
Volos GR 169 F8
Volosovo RUS 132 C5
Volosyanka UA 145 F6
Volovăt RO 153 B7
Volovets' UA 145 F7
Volovo BG 166 B6
Volpago del Montello I 72 E5
Volpedo I 37 B9
Volpiano I 68 C4
Völs A 72 B3
Völschow D 84 C4
Voltaggio I 37 B9
Volta Mantovana I 66 B2
Volterra I 66 F2
Voltlage D 17 D9
Voltri I 37 C9
Voltti FIN 122 D9
Volturara Appula I 63 E8
Volturara Irpina I 60 B3
Volturino I 63 E8
Voluntari RO 161 E8
Volvic F 30 D3
Volx F 35 C10
Volya Arlamiws'ka UA 144 D7
Volynė CZ 76 D5
Vomp A 72 B4
Voneshta Voda BG 166 D5
Vonge DK 86 D4
Vonges F 26 F3
Voni GR 178 E9
Vonitsa GR 174 B2
Võnnu EST 131 E14
Võõpste EST 131 E14
Võõpsu EST 132 E2
Voorburg NL 16 D2
Voore EST 131 D13
Voorhout NL 182 A4
Voorschoten NL 16 D2
Voorst NL 16 D6
Voorthuizen NL 183 A7
Voose EST 131 C10
Võra FIN 122 D8
Voranava BY 137 E11
Vorbasse DK 86 D4
Vorchdorf A 76 F5
Vorden NL 16 D6
Vordernberg A 73 A10
Vordingborg DK 87 E9
Vordorf D 79 B8
Vorë AL 168 B2
Voreppe F 31 E8
Vorey F 30 E4
Vorgod DK 86 C3
Vormsele S 107 B15
Vormstad N 104 E7
Vormsund N 95 B14
Vormträsk S 107 B15
Vorna FIN 119 F15
Vorniceni RO 153 B9
Voroi GR 178 E8
Vorokhta UA 152 A5
Vorona RO 153 B9
Vorra D 75 C9
Vorsau A 148 B5
Vorst B 19 B11
Vorţa RO 151 E10
Võru EST 131 F14
Vorwerk D 17 B12
Voskopojë AL 168 C4
Voslăbeni RO 153 D7
Voss N 100 E4
Vosselaar B 16 F3
Voštane HR 157 E6
Võsu EST 131 B11
Votice CZ 77 C7
Votonosi GR 168 F5
Voudia GR 179 B8
Vougeot F 26 F2
Vouillé F 28 C5
Vouillé F 29 B6
Voukolies GR 178 E6
Voula GR 175 D8
Voulaines-les-Templiers F 25 E12
Vouliagmeni GR 175 D8
Voulpi GR 174 A4
Voulx F 25 D8
Vouneuil-sous-Biard F 29 B6
Vouneuil-sur-Vienne F 29 B7
Vourgareli GR 168 F5
Vourvourou GR 169 D10
Voutenay-sur-Cure F 25 E10
Voutezac F 29 E8
Voutianoi GR 174 E5
Vouvant F 28 B4
Vouvray F 24 F4
Vouvry CH 31 C10
Vouzela P 44 C4
Vouzi GR 174 A5
Vouziers F 19 F10
Vouzon F 24 E7
Voves F 24 D6
Vowchyn BY 141 F8
Vowkawshchyna BY 133 G2
Voxna S 103 D10
Voynika BG 167 E7
Voynitsa RUS 121 D15
Voynovo BG 161 F10
Voynyagovo BG 165 D10
Vozmediano E 41 E8
Voznesenka-Persha UA 154 E4
Vrå DK 90 E6
Vrabevo BG 165 D10
Vráble SK 146 E6
Vračev Gaj SRB 159 D7
Vraćevšnica SRB 158 E6
Vrachasi GR 179 E10
Vrachati GR 175 D6
Vrachesh BG 165 D8

Vrachnaiika GR 174 C4
Vrachos GR 168 D5
Vracov CZ 146 D4
Vrådal N 95 D8
Vrakúň SK 146 F5
Vrané nad Vltavou CZ 76 C6
Vrani RO 159 C8
Vranino BG 167 B10
Vranisht AL 163 E9
Vranisht AL 168 D2
Vranjak BIH 157 C7
Vranje SRB 164 D4
Vranjska Banja SRB 164 D5
Vranovice CZ 77 E11
Vranov nad Topľou SK 145 F4
Vransko SLO 73 D10
Vrapčište MK 163 F10
Vrapčići BIH 157 F8
Vrasene B 182 C4
Vrasna GR 169 C10
Vratarnica SRB 159 F9
Vratimov CZ 146 B6
Vratnica MK 164 E3
Vratsa BG 165 C8
Vrattsa BG 165 E6
Vražogrnac SRB 159 F9
Vrbanja BIH 157 C7
Vrbanja HR 157 C10
Vrbanjci BIH 157 C7
Vrbas SRB 158 B4
Vrbaška BIH 157 B7
Vrbica SRB 158 D5
Vrbica CZ 77 E11
Vrbnik HR 67 B10
Vrbnik HR 156 D5
Vrbno pod Pradědem CZ 142 F3
Vrbovac SRB 159 F9
Vrbovce SK 146 D4
Vrbové SK 146 D5
Vrbovec HR 149 E6
Vrbovsko HR 67 B11
Vrchlabí CZ 81 E9
Vrčin SRB 158 D6
Vrdy CZ 77 C8
Vrebac HR 156 C4
Vrécourt F 26 D4
Vreden D 17 D7
Vreeland NL 183 A6
Vrees D 17 C9
Vrellë KS 163 D9
Vrelo SRB 164 C4
Vrena S 93 B9
Vrensted DK 90 E6
Vřesina CZ 146 B6
Vresse B 19 E10
Vresthena GR 175 E6
Vretstorp S 92 A5
Vrgorac HR 157 F7
Vrhnika SLO 73 E9
Vrhopolje BIH 157 C6
Vrhovine HR 156 C3
Vridsted DK 86 C4
Vries NL 17 B7
Vriezenveen NL 17 D7
Vrigstad S 92 E4
Vrinners DK 86 C6
Vrisa GR 177 A7
Vrizy F 19 F10
Vrlika HR 156 E5
Vrnjačka Banja SRB 163 B10
Vrnograč BIH 156 B4
Vron F 18 D4
Vrontados GR 177 C7
Vrontero GR 168 C5
Vrontou GR 169 D7
Vroomshoop NL 17 D7
Vrosina GR 168 E4
Vrouchas GR 179 E10
Vroutek CZ 76 B4
Vrouwenpolder NL 16 E1
Vrpolje HR 156 E5
Vrpolje HR 157 B9
Vrrin AL 168 B1
Vršac SRB 159 C7
Vršani BIH 157 C11
Vrsar HR 67 B8
Vrsi HR 156 D3
Vrtoče BIH 156 C5
Vrtojba SLO 73 E8
Vrulja MNE 163 C7
Vrútky SK 147 C7
Vrutok MK 163 F10
Vrův BG 159 E10
Vrysia GR 169 F7
Vrysoula GR 168 F4
Všemina CZ 146 C5
Všeruby CZ 76 C4
Všetaty CZ 77 B7
Vsetín CZ 146 C5
Vsevolozhsk RUS 129 E14
Vübel BG 160 F5
Vučijak BIH 157 C8
Vučja Lokva SRB 163 C10
Vučje SRB 164 D4
Vught NL 16 E4
Vüglevtsi BG 166 D5
Vuka HR 149 F10
Vukova Gorica HR 148 F4
Vukovar HR 157 B11
Vuku N 105 D11
Vulcan RO 159 C11
Vulcan RO 160 B6
Vulcana-Băl RO 160 C6
Vülchedrum BG 160 F2
Vülchidol BG 167 C9
Vulpeni RO 160 D3
Vultureni RO 152 D3
Vultureni RO 153 C8
Vultureşti RO 153 D11
Vultureşti RO 160 C4
Vulturu RO 155 D2
Vulturu RO 161 B10
Vuobmaved FIN 113 E16
Vuohijärvi FIN 128 C6
Vuohtomäki FIN 123 C16
Vuojärvi FIN 117 E12
Vuokatti FIN 121 F11
Vuokko FIN 125 D12
Vuolijoki FIN 120 F9
Vuolle FIN 123 C11
Vuollerim S 118 B5
Vuonisjärvi FIN 125 D14
Vuonislahti FIN 125 D13
Vuonos FIN 125 E12
Vuontisjärvi FIN 117 B12
Vuorenmaa FIN 124 G9
Vuorenmaa FIN 126 C8
Vuoreslahti FIN 121 F9
Vuorimäki FIN 123 E11
Vuorimäki FIN 124 C9

Vuoriniemi FIN 129 B11
Vuosaari FIN 177 F13
Vuosanka FIN 121 F13
Vuostimo FIN 115 E2
Vuostimojärvi FIN 115 E2
Vuotner S 118 C3
Vuotso FIN 115 B2
Vuottas S 118 B7
Vuottolahti FIN 120 F9
Vuotunki FIN 121 B14
Vürbitsa BG 166 E4
Vürbitsa BG 167 D7
Vurpăr RO 152 F4
Vürshets BG 165 C8
Vushtrri KS 164 D2
Vustsye BY 133 E3
Vutcani RO 153 E11
Vuzenica SLO 73 C11
Vuzlove UA 145 G5
Vvedenka UA 154 E4
Vyalets BY 133 F3
Vyalikaya Byerastavitsa BY 140 D10
Vyalikaya Stayki BY 133 F5
Vyalikaye Syalo BY 133 F3
Vyarkhovichy BY 141 F8
Vyartsilya RUS 125 F15
Vyaz RUS 132 C7
Vyčapy-Opatovce SK 146 E6
Východná SK 147 C9
Vydeniai LT 137 E9
Vydrany SK 146 E5
Vyerkhnyadzvinsk BY 133 E3
Vyetryna BY 133 F4
Vyhne SK 147 D7
Vyhoda UA 145 F8
Vy-lès-Lure F 26 E5
Vylkove UA 155 C5
Vylok UA 145 G6
Vynnyky UA 144 D9
Vynohradiv UA 145 G7
Vynohradivka UA 154 F4
Vyritsa RUS 132 C7
Vyronas GR 175 D8
Vyroneia GR 169 B9
Vyshgorodok RUS 133 B3
Vyshka UA 145 F6
Vyshkiv UA 145 F8
Vyshkove UA 145 G7
Vyshneve UA 154 F5
Vyshniv UA 141 H10
Vyskod' RUS 132 F7
Vyškov CZ 77 D12
Vyšné Ružbachy SK 145 E2
Vyšný Mirošov SK 145 E3
Vyšný Orlík SK 145 E4
Vyšný Šipov SK 145 E3
Vysoká nad Kysucou SK 147 C7
Vysokaye BY 141 F8
Vysoké Mýto CZ 77 C10
Vysokoye RUS 136 D4
Vysotsk RUS 129 D10
Vyšší Brod CZ 76 E6
Vyssinia GR 168 C5
Vytina GR 174 D5
Vyzhnytsya UA 152 A6
Vyžuonos LT 135 E11
Vzmor'ye RUS 139 A9

W

Waabs D 83 A7
Waal D 71 B11
Waalre NL 16 F4
Waalwijk NL 16 E4
Waarschoot B 19 B8
Wabern D 21 B12
Wąbrzeźno PL 138 D6
Wachenheim an der Weinstraße D 187 C5
Wachock PL 143 D11
Wachow D 79 A12
Wachtebeke B 19 B8
Wächtersbach D 21 D12
Wacken D 82 B6
Wackersdorf D 75 D11
Waddewitz D 83 D9
Waddington GB 11 E11
Waddinxveen NL 16 D3
Wadebridge GB 12 D5
Wädenswil CH 27 F10
Wadern D 21 E7
Wadersloh D 17 E10
Wadgassen D 21 F7
Wadhurst GB 15 E9
Wadlew PL 143 D8
Wadowice PL 147 B9
Wadowice Górne PL 143 F11
Wądroże Wielkie PL 81 D10
Waganiec PL 138 E6
Wagenfeld D 17 C11
Wagenhoff D 79 A8
Wageningen NL 16 E5
Waghäusel D 21 F11
Waging am See D 73 A6
Wagna A 148 C5
Wagrain A 73 B7
Wągrowiec PL 85 E12
Wahlhausen D 79 D6
Wahlsdorf D 80 C4
Wahlstedt D 83 C8
Wahrenholz D 79 A8
Waiblingen D 27 C11
Waibstadt D 187 C6
Waidhaus D 75 C11
Waidhofen an der Thaya A 77 E8
Waidhofen an der Ybbs A 77 G7
Waigolshausen D 75 C7
Waimes B 20 D6
Wain D 71 A10
Wainfleet All Saints GB 11 E12
Wainhouse Corner GB 12 D5
Waischenfeld D 75 C9
Waizenkirchen A 76 F5
Wakefield GB 11 D8
Wakendorf II D 83 C8
Walberswick GB 15 C12
Wałbrzych PL 81 E10
Walburg D 78 D6
Walchum D 17 C8
Wałcz PL 85 D10
Wald CH 27 F10
Wald D 27 E11
Wald D 75 D11
Waldachtal D 27 C10
Waldböckelheim D 185 E8
Waldbreitbach D 185 C7
Waldbröl D 21 C9
Waldbrunn-Lahr D 21 C11
Waldburg D 71 B9
Waldbüttelbrunn D 74 C6
Walddrehna D 80 C5

Waldegg A 77 G10
Waldenbuch D 27 C11
Waldenburg CH 27 F8
Waldenburg D 74 D6
Waldenburg D 79 E11
Walderbach D 75 D11
Waldershof D 75 C11
Waldesch D 185 D8
Waldfischbach-Burgalben D 21 F9
Waldhausen A 77 F8
Waldhausen im Strudengau A 77 F7
Waldheim D 80 D4
Walding A 76 F6
Waldkappel D 78 D6
Waldkirch D 27 D8
Waldkirchen D 76 E5
Waldkraiburg D 75 F11
Wald-Michelbach D 187 B6
Waldmohr D 21 F8
Waldmünchen D 75 D12
Waldrach D 21 E7
Waldsassen D 75 B11
Waldsee D 187 C5
Waldshut D 27 E9
Waldstatt CH 27 F11
Waldstetten D 75 E7
Waldstetten D 187 D7
Walenstadt CH 71 C9
Walferdange L 20 E6
Walim PL 81 E10
Walkendorf D 83 C13
Wallasey GB 10 E5
Walldorf D 21 D11
Walldorf D 21 F11
Walldorf D 79 E7
Walldürn D 21 E11
Wallenfels D 75 B9
Wallerfing D 76 E4
Wallern im Burgenland A 149 A7
Wallersdorf D 75 E12
Wallerstein D 75 E7
Wallgau D 72 A3
Wallhausen D 75 D7
Wallhausen D 185 E8
Wallisellen CH 27 F10
Walls GB 3 E14
Wallsbüll D 82 A6
Wallstawe D 83 D9
Walmer GB 15 E11
Walsall GB 11 F8
Walschleben D 79 D8
Walsoken GB 11 F12
Walsrode D 82 E7
Waltenhofen D 71 B10
Waltershausen D 79 E8
Waltham on the Wolds GB 11 F10
Walton-on-Thames GB 15 E8
Walton on the Naze GB 15 D11
Wamba E 39 E10
Wamel NL 183 B6
Wanderup D 82 A6
Wandlitz D 84 E4
Wandre B 183 D7
Wang A 77 F8
Wangen CH 27 F8
Wangen im Allgäu D 71 B9
Wängi CH 27 E10
Wankendorf D 83 B8
Wanna D 17 A11
Wanne-Eikel D 183 B10
Wanroij NL 183 B7
Wanssum NL 183 B8
Wantage GB 13 B12
Wanze B 19 C11
Wanzleben D 79 B9
Wapenveld NL 16 D6
Wąpiersk PL 139 D8
Waplewo PL 139 C9
Wąpnica PL 85 D8
Wąpno PL 85 E12
Warberg D 79 B8
Warboys GB 15 C9
Warburg D 17 F12
Warcop GB 11 B7
Warcq F 20 F5
Wardenburg D 17 B10
Wardington GB 13 A12
Ware GB 15 D8
Waregem B 19 C8
Wareham GB 13 D10
Waremme B 19 C11
Waren D 83 C13
Warendorf D 17 E9
Warffum NL 17 B7
Warin D 83 C11
Waringstown GB 7 D10
Wark GB 5 E12
Warka PL 141 G4
Warlingham GB 15 E8
Warloy-Baillon F 18 D6
Warlubie PL 138 C6
Warmeriville F 19 F9
Warmington GB 13 A12
Warminster GB 13 C10
Warmond NL 182 A5
Warmsen D 17 D11
Warnemünde D 83 B12
Warngau D 72 A4
Warnice PL 85 D7
Warnice PL 85 E7
Warnino PL 85 B10
Warnow D 83 C12
Warnsveld NL 16 D6
Warrenpoint GB 7 D10
Warrington GB 10 E6
Warsingsfehn D 17 B8
Warslow GB 11 E8
Warstein D 17 F10
Warszawa PL 141 F4
Warszkowo PL 85 B11
Warta PL 142 C6
Warta Bolesławiecka PL 81 D9
Wartburg an der Krems A 76 G6
Wartenberg D 75 F10
Wartenberg-Angersbach D 78 E5
Warth A 71 C10
Wartin D 84 D6
Wartkowice PL 143 C7
Warwick GB 13 A11
Warwick Bridge GB 5 F11
Warzyce PL 144 D4
Wasbek D 83 B7
Wasbister GB 3 G10
Wäschenbeuren D 74 E6

Wąsewo PL 139 E12
Washington GB 5 F13
Wasigny F 19 E9
Wasilków PL 140 D8
Waśniów PL 143 E11
Wąsosz PL 81 C11
Wąsosz PL 140 C6
Wąsowo PL 81 B10
Waspik NL 16 E3
Wasselonne F 27 C7
Wassenaar NL 16 D2
Wassenberg D 20 B6
Wasseralfingen D 75 E7
Wasserbillig B 185 B2
Wasserburg am Inn D 75 F11
Wasserliesch D 186 B2
Wasserlosen D 74 B7
Wassertrüdingen D 75 D8
Wassigny F 19 D8
Wassy F 26 C2
Wasungen D 79 E7
Watchet GB 13 C8
Watchgate GB 10 C6
Waterbeck GB 5 E10
Waterford IRL 9 D8
Watergrasshill IRL 8 D6
Wateringen NL 182 A4
Waterland-Oudeman B 182 C3
Waterloo B 19 C9
Waterlooville GB 14 F6
Waterville IRL 8 E2
Watford GB 15 D8
Wathlingen D 79 A7
Watlington GB 14 D6
Watten F 18 C5
Watten GB 3 J10
Wattenbek D 83 B8
Wattens A 72 B4
Watten-Scheid D 183 C10
Wattenwil CH 31 B12
Wattlebridge GB 7 D8
Watton GB 15 B10
Wattwil CH 27 F11
Wavre B 19 C10
Wavrin F 18 C6
Wąwelno PL 85 D13
Wąwelno PL 142 E4
Wąwolnica PL 141 H6
Wawrów PL 85 E8
Wawrzeńczyce PL 143 F9
Waxweiler D 20 D6
Waziers F 182 E2
Weaverham GB 10 E6
Wechmar D 79 E8
Wechselburg D 79 D12
Wedde NL 17 B8
Weddingstedt D 82 B6
Wedel (Holstein) D 82 C7
Wedmore D 13 C8
Wednesbury GB 11 F7
Weede D 83 C8
Weedon Bec GB 13 A12
Weelde B 182 C5
Weem GB 5 B9
Weener D 17 B8
Weerberg A 72 B4
Weerselo NL 17 D7
Weert NL 16 F5
Weesen CH 27 F11
Weesp NL 16 D4
Weeze D 16 E6
Weferlingen D 79 B9
Wegberg D 20 B6
Wegenstedt D 79 B9
Weggis CH 71 C6
Wegscheid A 148 A4
Wegscheid D 76 E5
Wehdel D 17 A11
Wehl NL 16 E6
Wehr D 27 E8
Wehrbleck D 17 C11
Wehringen D 71 A11
Weibern D 183 E10
Weibersbrunn D 74 C5
Weichering D 75 E9
Weichs D 75 F9
Weida D 79 E11
Weidenberg D 75 C10
Weiden in der Oberpfalz D 75 C11
Weidenstetten D 187 D8
Weidenthal D 21 F9
Weiding D 75 D12
Weiersbach D 186 B3
Weigersdorf D 81 D7
Weihmichl D 75 E11
Weikersheim D 74 D6
Weil D 71 A11
Weil am Rhein D 27 E8
Weilbach D 21 E12
Weilburg D 21 D10
Weil der Stadt D 27 C10
Weilerbach D 186 C4
Weilerswist D 21 C7
Weilheim an der Teck D 74 E6
Weilheim in Oberbayern D 72 A3
Weilmünster D 21 D10
Weimar D 79 E9
Weinbach D 185 D9
Weinböhla D 80 D5
Weinfelden CH 27 E11
Weingarten D 71 B9
Weingarten (Baden) D 187 C6
Weinheim D 21 E11
Weinsberg D 21 E12
Weinsheim D 20 D6
Weinstadt D 27 C11
Weischlitz D 75 B11
Weisen D 83 D11
Weisendorf D 75 C9
Weismain D 75 B9
Weißach D 27 C10
Weißbriach A 73 C7
Weißenbach am Lech A 71 C11
Weißenberg D 81 D7
Weißenbrunn D 75 B9
Weißenburg in Bayern D 75 D8
Weißenfels D 79 D10
Weißenhorn D 75 F7
Weißensee D 79 D9
Weißenstadt D 75 B10
Weißenstein A 73 C8
Weißenthurm D 185 D7
Weißig D 80 D6
Weißkeißel D 81 D7
Weißkirchen in Steiermark A 73 B10
Weißkollm D 80 D6
Weißwasser D 81 D7

Weistrach A 77 F7
Weiswampach L 20 D6
Weisweil D 27 D8
Weitbruch F 186 D4
Weitefeld D 185 C8
Weiten A 77 F8
Weitensfeld A 73 C9
Weiterstadt D 187 B6
Weitra A 77 E7
Weixdorf D 80 D5
Weiz A 148 B5
Wejherowo PL 138 A5
Wekerom NL 16 D5
Welkenraedt B 20 C5
Well NL 16 E6
Wellaune D 79 C12
Welle D 82 D7
Wellen B 183 D6
Wellesbourne GB 13 A11
Wellheim D 75 E9
Wellin B 19 D11
Welling D 21 D8
Wellingborough GB 15 C7
Wellington GB 10 F6
Wellington GB 13 C8
Wellingtonbridge IRL 9 D9
Wellington Bridge IRL 9 D9
Wells GB 13 C9
Wells-next-the-Sea GB 15 B10
Welney GB 11 F12
Wels A 76 F6
Welschbillig D 21 E7
Welshpool GB 10 F5
Welsickendorf D 80 C4
Welsleben D 79 C10
Welver D 17 E9
Welwyn GB 15 D8
Welwyn Garden City GB 15 D8
Welzheim D 74 E6
Welzow D 80 C6
Wem GB 10 F6
Wembdon GB 13 C8
Wemding D 75 E8
Wemeldinge NL 182 B4
Wemyss Bay GB 4 D7
Wendeburg D 79 B7
Wendelsheim D 21 E10
Wendelstein D 75 D9
Wenden D 21 C9
Wendens Ambo GB 15 C9
Wendisch Priborn D 83 D12
Wendisch Rietz D 80 B6
Wendlingen am Neckar D 27 C11
Wendover GB 15 D7
Wenduine B 182 C2
Wengen CH 70 D5
Wengsel (Isterberg) D 17 D8
Wenningsen (Deister) D 78 B6
Wenningstedt D 86 F2
Wenns A 71 C11
Wentorf D 83 C8
Wentorf bei Hamburg D 83 D8
Wenzenbach D 75 D11
Wenzlow D 79 B11
Wépion B 182 E5
Werbach D 74 C6
Werben D 80 C6
Werben (Elbe) D 83 E11
Werbig D 80 C4
Werbkowice PL 144 B8
Werbomont B 19 D12
Werdau D 79 E11
Werder D 79 B12
Werder D 84 C4
Werdohl D 17 F9
Werfen A 73 B7
Werkendam NL 182 B5
Werl D 17 F10
Werlte D 17 C9
Wermelskirchen D 185 B7
Wermsdorf D 80 D3
Wernau D 27 C11
Wernberg-Köblitz D 75 C11
Werndorf A 148 C5
Werne D 17 E9
Werneck D 75 C7
Werneuchen D 80 A5
Wernigerode D 79 C8
Wernshausen D 79 E7
Werpeloh D 17 C9
Wertach D 71 B10
Wertheim D 74 C6
Werthenstein CH 70 C6
Werther D 79 D8
Werther (Westfalen) D 17 D10
Wertingen D 75 E8
Wervershoof NL 16 C4
Wervik B 19 C7
Wesel D 17 E7
Wesenberg D 84 D3
Wesendorf D 79 A8
Wesepe NL 183 A8
Wesoła PL 141 F4
Wesselburen D 82 B5
Wesseling D 21 C7
Wesseln D 82 B6
Wessem NL 183 C7
Weßling D 75 F9
Wessobrunn D 71 B12
West Auckland GB 5 F13
West Bridgford GB 11 F9
West Bromwich GB 11 F8
Westbury GB 13 C10
Westendorf A 72 B5
Westensee D 83 B7
Westerbeck (Sassenburg) D 79 A8
Westerbork NL 17 C7
Westerburg D 21 C9
Westerdale GB 3 J10
Westeregeln D 79 C9
Westerende-Kirchloog (Ihlow) D 17 B8
Westergate GB 15 F7
Westergellersen D 83 D8
Westerhaar NL 17 D7
Westerheim D 187 D8
Westerholt D 17 A8
Westerhorn D 82 C7
Westerhoven NL 183 C6
Westerland D 86 F2
Westerlo B 19 B10
Westerrönfeld D 82 B7
Westerstede D 17 B9
Westerstetten D 74 E6
Westervoort NL 16 E5
Westerwalsede D 17 B7

Westhill GB 3 L12
Westhofen D 187 B5
Westhoffen F 186 D3
Westkapelle NL 19 A7
West Kilbride GB 4 D7
West Kirby GB 10 E5
West Knapton GB 11 C10
West Lavington GB 13 C11
Westleton GB 15 C12
West Linton GB 5 D10
Wooe Looe GB 12 E6
West Lulworth GB 13 D10
Westmalle B 16 F3
West Malling GB 15 E9
Meon Hout GB 13 C12
West Mersea GB 15 D9
West Moors GB 13 D11
Westness GB 3 G10
Westnewton GB 5 F10
Weston GB 11 F7
Weston GB 13 B9
Weston-super-Mare GB 13 C9
Westonzoyland GB 13 C9
Westport IRL 6 E3
Westport Quay IRL 6 E3
West Somerton GB 15 B12
West Tarbert GB 4 D6
West-Terschelling NL 16 B4
Westward Ho! GB 12 C6
West Wellow GB 13 C11
West Winch GB 11 F12
Wethau D 79 D10
Wetheral GB 5 F11
Wetherby GB 11 C10
Wetlina PL 145 E5
Wetter (Hessen) D 21 C11
Wetter (Ruhr) D 185 B7
Wetteren B 19 B8
Wetterzeube D 79 D11
Wettin D 79 C10
Wettingen CH 27 F9
Wettrup D 17 C9
Wetzikon CH 27 F10
Wetzlar D 21 C11
Wevelgem B 19 C7
Wewelsfleth D 17 A12
Wexford IRL 9 D10
Weyarn D 72 A4
Weybridge GB 15 E8
Weyerbusch D 21 C9
Weyer Markt A 73 A10
Weyersheim F 27 C8
Weyhausen D 79 B8
Weyhe D 17 C11
Weymouth GB 13 D10
Whalton GB 5 E13
Whauphill GB 4 F8
Wheddon Cross GB 13 C7
Wherwell GB 13 C12
Whiddon Down GB 13 D7
Whitburn GB 5 D9
Whitby GB 11 C10
Whitchurch GB 10 F6
Whitchurch GB 13 B8
Whitchurch GB 15 D7
Whitecross GB 7 D9
Whitegate IRL 8 C6
Whitegate IRL 8 E6
Whitehall GB 3 G11
Whitehall GB 9 C8
Whitehaven GB 10 B4
Whitehead GB 4 F5
Whitehill GB 15 E7
Whitehills GB 3 K11
Whitfield GB 15 E11
Whithorn GB 5 F8
Whiting Bay GB 4 E6
Whitland GB 12 B5
Whitley Bay GB 5 E14
Whitstable GB 15 E11
Whittington GB 10 F5
Whittlesey GB 11 F11
Wiartel PL 139 C12
Wiatrowo PL 85 E12
Wiązów PL 81 E12
Wiązowna PL 141 F4
Wiązownica PL 144 C6
Wichelen B 19 B8
Wick GB 3 J10
Wicke GB 13 C7
Wick GB 15 F7
Wickede (Ruhr) D 185 B8
Wickenrode (Helsa) D 78 D6
Wickford GB 15 D10
Wickham GB 13 C12
Wickham Market GB 15 C11
Wicklow IRL 7 G10
Wicko PL 85 A13
Widawa PL 143 D6
Widecombe in the Moor GB 13 D7
Widnau CH 71 C9
Widnes GB 10 E6
Widuchowa PL 84 D6
Wijcborg PL 85 D12
Wieck am Darß D 83 B13
Wieczfnia Kościelna PL 139 D9
Wieda D 79 C8
Wiedensahl D 17 D12
Wiederau D 80 E3
Wiednitz D 80 D6
Wiefelstede D 17 B10
Wiehe D 79 D9
Wiehl D 21 C9
Wiek D 84 A4
Wijkszyce PL 142 F5
Wielbark PL 139 D10
Wieleń PL 85 E10
Wielenbach D 72 A3
Wielgie PL 139 E7
Wielgomłyny PL 143 D8
Wielichowo PL 81 B10
Wieliczka PL 143 G9
Wieliczki PL 136 F6
Wielka Wieś PL 143 F8
Wielkie Oczy PL 144 C7
Wielki Klincz PL 138 B5
Wielopole Skrzyńskie PL 143 G12
Wielowieś PL 142 E6
Wielsbeke B 182 D2
Wieluń PL 142 D6
Wiemersdorf D 83 C7
Wien A 77 F10
Wienerbruck A 77 G8
Wiener Neustadt A 77 G10
Wieniawa PL 141 H4
Wieniec PL 138 E6
Wienrode D 79 C8
Wiepke D 79 B9
Wieprz PL 147 B8
Wieprz PL 147 B8
Wiercień Duży PL 141 F7

Wierden NL 17 D7
Wieren D 83 E9
Wieringerwerf NL 16 C4
Wiernsheim D 187 D6
Wieruszów PL 144 C5
Wierzbica PL 141 H4
Wierzbica PL 141 H8
Wierzbica Górna PL 142 D4
Wierzbicin PL 85 C8
Wierzbinek PL 138 F6
Wierzbno PL 139 F12
Wierzbowa PL 81 D9
Wierzchlas PL 142 D6
Wierzchosławice PL 138 E5
Wierzchosławice PL 143 F10
Wierzchowo PL 85 C11
Wierzchowo PL 85 D10
Wierzchucino PL 138 A5
Wies A 148 C4
Wiesa D 80 E3
Wiesau D 75 C11
Wiesbaden D 21 D10
Wieselburg A 77 F8
Wiesen A 149 A6
Wiesen CH 71 D9
Wiesen D 74 B5
Wiesenau D 81 B7
Wiesenburg D 79 B11
Wiesenfelden D 75 D12
Wiesensteig D 187 D8
Wiesent D 75 D11
Wiesenthau D 75 C9
Wiesentheid D 75 C7
Wiesloch D 21 F11
Wiesmath A 148 A6
Wiesmoor D 17 B9
Wieszowa PL 142 F6
Wietmarschen D 17 C8
Wietze D 78 A6
Wietzen D 17 C12
Wietzendorf D 83 E7
Wiewiórczyn PL 143 C7
Wigan GB 10 D6
Wiggensbach D 71 B10
Wigierska Górka PL 147 B8
Wigliniec PL 81 D8
Wigmore GB 13 A9
Wigorzewo PL 136 E4
Wigoryzno PL 85 C9
Wigrów PL 139 F13
Wigrzynice PL 81 B8
Wigrzynowo PL 139 F9
Wigston GB 11 F9
Wigton GB 5 F10
Wigtown GB 5 F8
Wijchen NL 16 E5
Wijewo PL 81 C10
Wijhe NL 183 A8
Wijk aan Zee NL 16 D3
Wijk bij Duurstede NL 16 E4
Wijk en Aalburg NL 183 B6
Wil CH 27 F11
Wilamowice PL 147 B8
Wilczyta PL 138 F5
Wilczogóra PL 138 F5
Wilczyn PL 138 F5
Wildalpen A 73 A10
Wildau D 80 B5
Wildberg D 27 C10
Wildberg D 83 E13
Wildberg D 84 C4
Wildeck-Richelsdorf D 79 E7
Wildendürnbach A 77 E10
Wildenfels D 79 E12
Wildeshausen D 17 C10
Wildflecken D 74 B6
Wildon A 148 C5
Wildpoldsried D 71 B10
Wildshut A 76 F3
Wilga PL 141 G4
Wilhelminadorp NL 183 C6
Wilhelmsburg A 77 F9
Wilhelmsburg D 84 C5
Wilhelmsdorf D 27 E11
Wilhelmshaven D 17 A10
Wilkau-Haßlau D 79 E12
Wilkinstown IRL 7 E9
Wilkołaz Pierwszy PL 144 A5
Wilków PL 141 H5
Wilków PL 142 E3
Wilkowice PL 147 B8
Wilkowo PL 81 B8
Willand GB 13 D8
Willebadessen D 17 E12
Willebroek B 19 B9
Willemstad NL 16 E2
Willich D 17 F7
Willingdon GB 15 F9
Willingen (Upland) D 17 F11
Willingshausen D 21 C12
Willisau CH 27 F9
Williton GB 13 C8
Willstätt D 27 C8
Wilmslow GB 11 E7
Wilnis NL 182 A5
Wilnsdorf D 21 C10
Wilp NL 183 A8
Wilsdruff D 80 D5
Wilsickow D 84 D5
Wilster D 82 C6
Wilsum D 17 C7
Wiltersdorf A 77 E11
Wiltingen D 21 E7
Wilton GB 13 C11
Wiltz L 20 E5
Wimblington GB 11 F12
Wimborne Minster GB 13 D11
Wimereux F 15 F12
Wimmelburg D 79 C10
Wimmis CH 70 D5
Wimpassing A 148 A6
Wincanton GB 13 C10
Winchburgh GB 5 D10
Winchelsea GB 15 F10
Wincheringen D 186 B1
Winchester GB 13 C12
Wincrange L 20 D5
Winda PL 136 E3
Windach D 71 A12
Windeby D 83 B7
Windermere GB 10 C6
Windesheim D 21 E9
Windhagen D 21 C8
Windigsteig A 77 E8
Windischeschenbach D 75 C11
Windischgarsten A 73 A9
Windorf D 76 E4
Windsbach D 75 D8
Windsor GB 15 E7
Wingate GB 5 F14

Wingene B 19 B7
Wingen-sur-Moder F 27 C7
Winklarn D 75 D11
Winkleigh GB 13 D7
Winklern A 73 C6
Winklern bei Oberwölz A 73 B9
Winnenden D 27 C11
Winnert D 82 B6
Winnica PL 139 E10
Winningen D 185 D8
Winnweiler D 186 B4
Winschoten NL 17 B8
Winsen (Aller) D 83 E7
Winsen (Luhe) D 83 D8
Winsford GB 10 E6
Wińsko PL 81 D11
Winslow GB 15 D7
Winssen NL 183 B7
Winston GB 81 D8
Winsum NL 16 B5
Winterberg D 21 B11
Winterbourne Abbas GB 13 D9
Winterfeld D 83 E10
Winterswijk NL 17 E7
Winterthur CH 27 F10
Winterton GB 11 D10
Winton GB 11 C7
Wintrich D 185 E6
Wintzenheim F 27 D7
Winwick GB 15 C8
Winzenburg D 78 C6
Winzer D 76 E4
Wipperdorf D 79 D8
Wipperfürth D 21 C8
Wippra Kurort D 79 C9
Wirdumer (Wirdum) D 17 B8
Wirges D 185 D8
Wirksworth GB 11 E8
Wirsberg D 75 B10
Wisbech GB 11 F12
Wischhafen D 17 A12
Wishaw GB 5 D9
Wiskitki PL 141 F2
Wisła PL 147 B7
Wiślica PL 143 F10
Wismar D 83 C10
Wiśniew D 141 F6
Wiśniewo PL 139 D9
Wiśniowa PL 144 D1
Wiśniowa PL 144 D4
Wissant F 15 F12
Wissembourg F 27 B8
Wissen D 21 C9
Wissenkerke NL 16 E1
Wistedt D 82 D7
Wisznia Mała PL 81 D12
Wisznice PL 141 G6
Witaszyce PL 142 C4
Witham GB 15 D10
Witheridge GB 13 D7
Withernsea GB 11 D12
Witkowo PL 85 D10
Witkowo PL 138 F4
Witley GB 15 E7
Witmarsum NL 16 B4
Witney GB 13 B12
Witnica PL 84 E6
Witnica PL 85 E7
Witonia PL 143 B8
Witosław PL 85 D12
Witry-lès-Reims F 19 F9
Wittdün D 82 A4
Witten D 17 F8
Wittenbach CH 27 F11
Wittenberge D 83 E11
Wittenburg D 83 D10
Wittenförden D 83 C10
Wittenhagen D 84 B4
Wittenheim F 27 E7
Wittibreut D 76 F3
Wittichenau D 80 D6
Wittighausen D 74 C6
Wittingen D 83 E9
Wittlich D 21 E7
Wittmar D 79 B8
Wittmund D 17 A9
Wittstock D 83 D12
Witzenhausen D 78 D6
Witzin D 83 C11
Witzwort D 82 B5
Wiveliscombe GB 13 C8
Wivenhoe GB 15 D10
Wizajny PL 136 E6
Wizernes F 18 C5
Wizna PL 140 D6
Władysławów PL 142 B5
Władysławowo PL 138 A5
Wleń PL 81 D9
Włocławek PL 138 E7
Włodawa PL 141 G9
Włodzienin PL 142 F4
Włodzimierzów PL 143 D8
Włostów PL 143 E11
Włoszakowice PL 81 C10
Włoszczowa PL 143 E8
Wöbbelin D 83 D11
Woburn GB 15 D7
Wodynie PL 141 F5
Wodzierady PL 143 C7
Wodzisław PL 143 E9
Wodzisław Śląski PL 142 F5
Woensdrecht NL 182 C4
Woerden NL 16 D3
Wœrth D 27 C8
Wohlen CH 27 F9
Wohlen CH 31 B11
Wohlmirstedt D 79 D9
Wohltorf D 83 C8
Wöhrden D 82 B6
Wohyń PL 141 G6
Woippy F 26 B5
Wojaszówka PL 144 D4
Wojcieszków PL 141 G6
Wojcieszów PL 81 E9
Wójcin PL 138 E5
Wojkowice PL 143 F7
Wojnicz PL 143 G10
Wojnowo PL 138 D4
Wojsławice PL 144 B5
Woking GB 15 E7
Wokingham GB 15 E7
Wola PL 138 E7
Wola Mołodiatycka PL 144 C6
Wolanów PL 141 H7
Wola-Rębkowska PL 141 H9
Wola Uhruska PL 141 H9
Wola Wierzbowska PL 141 G5
Wolbórz PL 141 H1
Wolbrom PL 143 F8
Wolczyn PL 142 D5
Woldegk D 84 D5

Woldendorp NL 17 B8
Wolfach D 27 D9
Wolfegg D 71 B9
Wolfen D 79 C11
Wolfenbüttel D 79 B8
Wolfersheim D 21 D11
Wolfersheim D 17 F12
Wolfis D 79 E7
Wolfpassing A 77 F8
Wolfratshausen D 72 A3
Wolfsberg A 73 C10
Wolfsburg D 79 B8
Wolfstein D 21 E9
Wolgast D 84 B5
Wolhusen CH 70 C6
Wolin PL 84 C7
Wólka PL 139 E7
Wólka PL 141 H7
Wólka Dobryńska PL 141 F8
Wolkersdorf A 77 F11
Wollaston D 75 B7
Wollerau CH 27 F10
Wolmirstedt D 79 B10
Wolnzach D 75 E11
Wołomin PL 139 F11
Woloskowola PL 141 H8
Wołów PL 81 D11
Wolpertshausen D 74 D6
Wolpertswende D 71 B9
Wolphaartsdijk NL 182 B3
Wölpinghausen D 17 D12
Wolsingham GB 5 F13
Wolsztyn PL 81 B10
Woltersdorf D 80 A5
Woltersdorf D 83 E10
Wolvega NL 16 C6
Wolverhampton GB 11 F7
Wombwell GB 11 D9
Wommelgem B 19 B10
Wommels NL 16 B5
Wonfurt D 75 B7
Wonsees D 75 C9
Woodbridge GB 15 C11
Woodcote GB 13 B12
Woodford IRL 6 F6
Woodhall Spa GB 11 E11
Woodland GB 5 F13
Woodley GB 15 E7
Woodstock GB 13 B12
Woodton GB 15 C11
Woodtown IRL 7 E9
Wool GB 13 D10
Wooler GB 5 D12
Wootton Bassett GB 13 B11
Worb CH 31 B12
Worbis D 79 D7
Worcester GB 13 A10
Wördern A 77 F10
Worfield GB 11 F7
Wörgl A 72 B5
Workington GB 5 F9
Worksop GB 11 E9
Workum NL 16 C4
Wörlitz D 79 C11
Wormeldange L 20 E6
Wormerveer NL 16 D3
Wormhout F 18 C5
Worms D 21 E10
Worpswede D 17 B11
Wörrstadt D 21 E10
Wörschach A 73 A9
Wortel B 182 C5
Wörth A 73 B6
Wörth GB 15 E8
Wörth am Main D 187 B7
Wörth am Rhein D 27 B9
Worthing GB 15 F8
Woudenberg NL 183 A6
Woudrichem NL 16 E3
Woudsend NL 16 C5
Woustviller F 27 B7
Wouw NL 16 E3
Woźniki PL 143 E7
Wragby GB 11 E11
Wrangle GB 11 E12
Wrecsam GB 10 E6
Wrejcyca Wielka PL 143 E6
Wredenhagen D 83 D13
Wrelton GB 11 C10
Wremen D 17 A11
Wrestedt D 83 E9
Wrexham GB 10 E6
Wriedel D 83 D8
Wriezen D 84 E6
Wrist D 82 C7
Wróblew PL 142 C6
Wrocław PL 81 D12
Wrohm D 82 B6
Wronki PL 85 E10
Wronki PL 136 E5
Wrotnów PL 139 E8
Wrząjelka PL 142 B6
Wrzelowiec PL 144 A4
Wrzeście PL 85 A12
Września PL 85 F13
Wrzosowo PL 85 B9
Wschowa PL 81 C10
Wulfen D 79 C10
Wulfersdorf A 83 D12
Wülfershausen an der Saale D 75 B7
Wulfsen D 83 D8
Wulften D 79 C7
Wulkau D 83 E12
Wullersdorf A 77 E10
Wundschuh A 148 C4
Wünnenberg D 17 E11
Wünsdorf D 80 B4
Wunsiedel D 75 B11
Wunstorf D 78 B5
Wuppertal D 17 F8
Wurmlingen D 27 D10
Würselen D 20 C6
Wurzbach D 75 B10
Würzburg D 74 C6
Wurzen D 79 D12
Wüstenrot D 27 B11
Wusterhausen D 83 E12
Wusterhausen D 84 B5
Wusterhusen D 84 B5
Wustermark D 79 A12
Wusterwitz D 79 B11
Wustrau-Altfriesack D 84 E3
Wustrow D 83 E10
Wustrow D 84 D3
Wustrow, Ostseebad D 83 B12
Wutöschingen D 27 E9
Wuustwezel B 19 B9
Wyczechy PL 85 C12
Wydminy PL 136 F5
Wye GB 15 E10

Wygoda PL 143 E7
Wygon PL 85 D9
Wyhl D 27 D8
Wyk auf Föhr D 82 A5
Wylatowo PL 138 E4
Wylye GB 13 C11
Wymondham GB 15 B11
Wyre Piddle GB 13 A10
Wyrozjby-Konaty PL 141 F6
Wyry PL 143 F6
Wyryki-Połód PL 141 G8
Wyrzysk PL 85 D12
Wyśmierzyce PL 141 G3
Wysoka PL 85 D11
Wysoka PL 85 E8
Wysoka Kamieńska PL 85 C7
Wysokie PL 136 F6
Wysokie PL 85 D12
Wysokie Mazowieckie PL 141 E7
Wysowa PL 145 E3
Wyszanów PL 142 D5
Wyszki PL 141 E7
Wyszogród PL 139 F9
Wyszyny PL 85 E11
Wythall GB 13 A11
Wytczno PL 141 H8

X

Xanceda E 38 B3
Xanten D 17 E6
Xanthi GR 171 B7
Xarrë AL 168 E3
Xàtiva E 56 D3
Xeraco E 56 C4
Xeresa E 56 C4
Xermade E 38 B4
Xerta E 42 F5
Xertigny F 26 D5
Xifiani GR 169 C7
Xino Nero GR 169 C6
Xinzo de Limia E 38 D4
Xirivella E 48 F4
Xirochori GR 174 D4
Xirokampi GR 174 F5
Xirokampo GR 177 E8
Xiropotamos GR 170 B6
Xonrupt-Longemer F 27 D6
Xove E 38 A4
Xunqueira de Ambía E 38 D4
Xylagani GR 171 C8
Xylokastro GR 175 C6
Xyloupoli GR 169 C9

Y

Yablanitsa BG 165 C9
Yablanovo BG 167 D7
Yabluniv UA 152 A5
Yabŭlchevo BG 167 D8
Yabŭlkovo BG 166 E4
Yağci TR 173 C7
Yağcilar TR 173 F8
Yağcili TR 173 F8
Yagoda BG 166 D5
Yakimovo BG 160 F2
Yakoruda BG 165 E8
Yakovo BG 169 A9
Yaliçiflik TR 173 D10
Yalikavak TR 177 E9
Yalikoy TR 173 B9
Yalova TR 171 D10
Yambol BG 167 E7
Yamkino RUS 132 E3
Yamm RUS 132 E3
Yampil' UA 154 A2
Yangi TR 181 C9
Yanguas E 41 D7
Yanikağil TR 173 B8
Yaniskoski RUS 114 F3
Yankavichy BY 133 E5
Yankovo BG 167 C8
Yantarnyy RUS 139 A8
Yapildak TR 172 D6
Yaraş TR 181 B8
Yareva BG 135 F13
Yarlovo BG 165 E7
Yarm GB 11 C9
Yarmouth GB 13 D12
Yarnton GB 13 B12
Yarove UA 154 E4
Yarrow GB 5 D11
Yasen BG 165 C10
Yasen' UA 145 F9
Yasenkovo BG 167 B7
Yasenovets BG 161 F9
Yasinia UA 152 A4
Yasna Polyana BG 167 E9
Yasnoye RUS 134 F3
Yassiören TR 173 B10
Yasski RUS 132 F7
Yatağan TR 181 B8
Yate GB 13 B10
Yatova E 48 F3
Yavoriv UA 145 E7
Yavoriv UA 152 A5
Yaxley GB 11 F11
Yaylagöne TR 172 C6
Yazıbaşı TR 177 C7
Yazıköy TR 181 C6
Yazna BG 133 F4
Yazvina BY 133 F7
Ybbs an der Donau A 77 F8
Ybbsitz A 77 G7
Ychoux F 32 B4
Ydby DK 86 B2
Ydes F 29 E10
Ydra GR 175 E7
Ydrefors S 92 D7
Y Drenewydd GB 10 F5
Yeadon GB 11 D8
Yealmpton GB 12 E7
Yebra E 47 D7
Yebra de Basa E 32 F5
Yecla E 56 D2
Yecla de Yeltes E 45 C8
Yedy BY 133 F2
Yémeda E 47 E9
Yemişendere TR 181 B9
Yenice TR 171 C10
Yenice TR 173 D7
Yenice TR 173 D7
Yenice TR 181 B8
Yeniçiftlik TR 173 B8
Yeniçiftlik TR 173 D7
Yeniçiftlik TR 177 B8
Yenifoça TR 177 B8
Yenihisar TR 177 E9
Yeniköy TR 172 D6

Yeniköy TR 173 B6
Yeniköy TR 173 E8
Yeniköy TR 177 B9
Yeniköy TR 177 B10
Yeniköy TR 177 C9
Yeniköy TR 177 D10
Yeniköy TR 177 E10
Yeniköy TR 181 B8
Yenimuhacirköy TR 172 C6
Yenişakran TR 177 B9
Yenne F 31 D8
Yeovil GB 13 D9
Yepes E 46 E5
Yerkesik TR 181 B8
Yerseke NL 16 F2
Yershovo RUS 132 F3
Yerville F 18 E2
Yesa E 32 E3
Yeşilsırt TR 173 B7
Yeşilyurt TR 181 B8
Yeste E 55 C8
Yevtodiya UA 154 B4
Y Fenni GB 13 B8
Ygos-St-Saturnin F 32 C4
Ygrande F 30 B2
Ykspihlaja FIN 123 C10
Ylakiai LT 134 D3
Yläköngäs FIN 113 D17
Ylä-Luosta FIN 125 D11
Ylämaa FIN 129 D9
Ylämylly FIN 125 E13
Yläne FIN 126 D7
Ylä-Valtimo FIN 125 C11
Ylihärmä FIN 122 D9
Yli-Ii FIN 119 D15
Ylijärvi FIN 128 D3
Yli-Kärppä FIN 119 C15
Ylikiiminki FIN 119 D16
Yli-Körkkö FIN 119 B16
Ylikulma FIN 127 E8
Yli-Kurki FIN 121 D10
Ylikylä FIN 115 C4
Ylikylä FIN 117 E15
Ylikylä FIN 123 D12
Ylikylä FIN 125 C12
Yli-Kyrö FIN 117 B12
Yli-Lesti FIN 123 D13
Yli-Liakka FIN 119 C12
Yli-Livo FIN 120 C9
Yli-Muonio FIN 117 B10
Yli-Nampa FIN 117 E16
Ylinenjärvi S 117 E10
Yli-Olhava FIN 119 C15
Ylipää FIN 119 E12
Ylipää FIN 119 E13
Ylipää FIN 119 E13
Ylipää FIN 119 E14
Ylipää FIN 119 E15
Ylipää FIN 123 C11
Ylipää FIN 123 D11
Yli-Paakkola FIN 119 B13
Yli-Siurua FIN 119 C17
Ylistaro FIN 122 E8
Yli-Tannila FIN 119 D16
Ylitornio FIN 119 B11
Yli-Utos FIN 120 E8
Yli-Valli FIN 123 F9
Ylivieska FIN 123 B13
Yli-Vuotto FIN 119 E17
Ylläsjärvi FIN 117 C12
Ylöjärvi FIN 127 B10
Ylönkylä FIN 127 E9
Ylvingen N 108 E3
Ymonville F 24 D6
Ynysddu GB 13 B8
Yoğuntaş TR 167 F8
Yolageldi TR 173 A6
Yonkovo BG 161 F9
York GB 11 D9
Youghal IRL 9 E7
Yovkovo BG 155 F2
Yoxford GB 15 C11
Ypäjä FIN 127 D9
Ypäjänkylä FIN 127 D9
Ypati GR 174 B5
Yport F 18 E1
Yppäri FIN 119 E12
Ypsonas CY 177 D6
Ypyä FIN 123 C13
Yrittäperä FIN 121 D10
Yrttivaara S 116 E7
Ysane S 88 C3
Ysbyty Ystwyth GB 13 A7
Yset N 101 A12
Ysselsteyn NL 183 C7
Yssingeaux F 30 E5
Ystad S 87 E13
Ystalyfera GB 13 B7
Ystebrød N 94 F3
Ystradgynlais GB 13 B7
Ytre Arna N 94 B2
Ytre Billefjord N 113 C15
Ytre Kjæs N 113 B16
Ytre Sandvik N 113 C15
Ytterån S 105 E16
Ytterås S 105 D14
Ytterberg S 102 B8
Ytter-Busjö S 107 B15
Ytteresse FIN 123 C10
Yttergran S 99 C9
Ytterhogdal S 102 B8
Yttermalung S 102 E7
Ytterturningen S 103 B9
Yttervik S 109 E18
Yttre Lansjärv S 116 E8
Yukaribey TR 177 A9
Yukarikizilca TR 177 C10
Yukhavichy BY 133 D5
Yuncler E 46 D5
Yuncos E 46 D5
Yundola BG 165 E8
Yunquera E 53 C7
Yunquera de Henares E 47 C6
Yuper BG 161 F8
Yuratsishki BY 137 E12
Yurachky BY 133 F5
Yürücekler TR 173 E10
Yürük TR 173 C7
Yutz F 20 F6
Yuzhnyy RUS 136 D2
Yvignac F 23 D7
Yvoir B 19 D10
Yvoire F 31 C9
Yvonand CH 31 B10
Yxnerum S 93 C8
Yxsjö S 107 C13
Yxsjöberg S 97 B12

Yxskaftkälen S 106 D8
Yzeure D 30 B3
Yzeures-sur-Creuse F 29 B7

Z

Zaamslag NL 182 C3
Zaandam NL 16 D3
Zaazver"ye BY 133 F5
Žabala RO 153 F8
Žabalj SRB 158 C4
Žabari SRB 159 E7
Zabeltitz-Treugeböhla D 80 D5
Žabia Wola PL 141 F3
Žabica BIH 162 D5
Žabice SLO 67 A9
Žabiele D 139 D12
Zabierzów PL 143 F8
Ząbki PL 141 F4
Ząbkowice Śląskie PL 81 E11
Žabljak MNE 163 C7
Zabłudów PL 140 D8
Žabno HR 149 E7
Żabno PL 143 F10
Žabno PL 144 B6
Zabok HR 148 D5
Žabokreky SK 147 C7
Žabokreky nad Nitrou SK 146 D6
Zabolova LV 133 A2
Zabór PL 81 C9
Zabor"ye BY 133 E6
Žabów PL 85 D8
Zabowo PL 85 D8
Zăbrani RO 151 E8
Zábřeh CZ 77 C11
Zabrze PL 142 F6
Zabūrdo BG 165 F10
Zabuzhzhya UA 141 H9
Zacharo GR 174 E4
Zaclău RO 155 C2
Žaclér CZ 81 E9
Zaczopki PL 141 F6
Zadar HR 156 D3
Zadunayivka UA 154 F4
Zádveřice CZ 146 C5
Zadzim PL 142 C6
Zadzyezhzha BY 133 E3
Zafarraya E 53 C8
Zafírovo BG 161 F9
Zafra E 51 C7
Zafra de Záncara E 47 E7
Zafrilla E 47 D9
Žaga SLO 73 D8
Zagań D 81 C8
Žagarė LT 134 D6
Žagare RO 153 F8
Zagarise I 59 A10
Zagkliveri GR 169 C9
Žaglav HR 67 E11
Zagnańsk PL 143 E10
Zagon RO 153 F8
Zagora GR 169 F9
Zagorë AL 168 D2
Zagorje SLO 73 E9
Zagorje ob Savi SLO 73 D10
Zagórów PL 142 B4
Zagortsi BG 167 E8
Zagórz PL 145 D5
Zagra E 53 B9
Zagra RO 152 C4
Zagrazhden BG 160 F5
Zagrazhden BG 166 F3
Zagrodno PL 81 D9
Zagrović HR 156 E5
Žagubica SRB 159 E8
Zagvozd HR 157 F7
Zagwiździe PL 142 D4
Zagyvarékas H 150 C5
Zahara E 51 F9
Zahara de los Atunes E 52 D5
Zahinos E 51 C6
Zahna D 79 C12
Zahnitkiv UA 154 A3
Záhony H 145 G5
Zahor"ye BY 133 E5
Záhorská Ves SK 77 F11
Zăicani MD 153 B10
Zaiceva LV 133 B2
Zaidín E 42 D4
Žaiginys LT 134 F6
Zaim MD 154 D4
Zajas MK 168 A4
Zaječar SRB 159 F9
Zaječí CZ 77 E11
Zaječov CZ 76 C5
Zajezierze PL 141 H4
Zákamenné SK 147 C8
Zákány H 149 D7
Zákányszek H 150 E4
Zakharnichy BY 133 E5
Zakliczyn PL 144 D2
Zaklików PL 144 B4
Zakłopača BIH 157 D11
Zakoma BIH 157 E10
Zakopane PL 147 C9
Zakros GR 179 E11
Zakrzew PL 141 H4
Zakrzewo PL 85 D12
Zakrzewo PL 138 E6
Zakrzówek-Wieś PL 144 B5
Zákupy CZ 81 E7
Zala E 53 C8
Zalaapáti H 149 C8
Zalabér H 149 C8
Zalaegerszeg H 149 C8
Zalakaros H 149 C8
Zalakomár H 149 C8
Zalalövő H 149 C7
Zalamea de la Serena E 51 B8
Zalamea la Real E 51 D6
Zalaszántó H 149 C8
Zalaszentbalázs H 149 C7
Zalaszentgrót H 149 C8
Zalaszentiván H 149 C7
Zalău RO 151 C11
Zalavár H 149 C8
Zalavár RO 153 D9
Zalavas LT 137 D13
Zaldibar E 41 B6
Zaḷenieki LV 134 C7
Zalesie PL 85 E13
Zalesie PL 141 F6
Zalesie Śląskie PL 142 F5
Zaleśje LV 133 E3
Zales'ye RUS 136 D3
Zaleszany PL 144 B4

Zalewo PL 139 C8
Zalha RO 152 C3
Zălitie LT 135 C8
Zalivnoye RUS 136 D2
Zaltbommel NL 16 E4
Zańuski PL 139 E10
Žalužje BIH 158 E3
Zalve LV 135 D10
Zalyessye BY 133 F3
Zalyessye BY 137 E13
Zam RO 151 E9
Zamárdi H 149 C9
Zamarte PL 85 C12
Żamberk CZ 77 B10
Zambrana E 40 C6
Zămbreasca RO 160 E6
Zambrów PL 140 E6
Zambujal de Cima P 50 C1
Zambujeira do Mar P 50 D2
Zamcjin PL 85 D9
Zamfirovo BG 165 C7
Zamogil'ye RUS 132 E3
Zámoly H 149 B10
Zamora E 39 E8
Zamość PL 139 D8
Zamość PL 144 B7
Zamoshsha BY 133 F4
Zamostea RO 153 B8
Zams A 71 C11
Zámutov SK 145 F4
Zandhoven B 19 B10
Zandov CZ 80 E6
Zandvliet B 16 F2
Zandvoort NL 16 D3
Zănești RO 153 D9
Zaniemyśl PL 81 B12
Zante LV 134 C5
Zaorejas E 47 C8
Zaovine SRB 158 F3
Zapałów PL 144 C6
Zaplanik BIH 162 D5
Zaplyus'ye RUS 132 E6
Zăpodeni RO 153 D11
Zapolice PL 142 C6
Zapolyarnyy RUS 114 E9
Zapol'ye RUS 132 E6
Zaporozhskoye RUS 129 D14
Zappeio GR 169 F7
Zapponeta I 60 A5
Zaprešić HR 148 E5
Zapruddzye BY 133 F3
Zaptviv UA 145 E9
Zaragoza E 41 E10
Zărand RO 151 E8
Zaraisk RUS 85 C9
Zarasai LT 135 E12
Zaratamo E 40 B6
Zaratán E 39 E10
Zarautz E 32 D1
Zarcilla de Ramos E 55 D9
Zarjby PL 143 E7
Zarjby-Kościelne PL 139 E13
Zarechcha BY 133 F5
Žarėnai LT 134 E4
Zaręby PL 143 E7
Żarki PL 143 E7
Żarki Wielkie PL 81 C7
Zărnești RO 160 B6
Zărnești RO 161 C7
Žarnovica SK 147 D7
Żarnów PL 141 H2
Żarnowiec PL 143 F8
Zaronava BY 133 F4
Zaros GR 178 E8
Žarošice CZ 77 D11
Żarów PL 81 E10
Zarpen D 83 C9
Zarren B 182 C2
Zarrentin D 83 C9
Zarszyn PL 145 D5
Żary PL 81 C8
Zarza Capilla E 51 B9
Zarza de Alange E 51 B7
Zarza de Granadilla E 45 D8
Zarza de Tajo E 47 D6
Zarzadilla de Totana E 55 D9
Zarza la Mayor E 45 D6
Zarzecze PL 144 D6
Zarzuela del Monte E 46 C4
Zarzuela del Pinar E 40 F3
Zas E 38 B2
Zasa LV 135 D11
Zaskarki BY 133 F5
Žaškov SK 147 C8
Žasliai LT 137 D10
Zásmuky CZ 77 C8
Zasów PL 143 F11
Zastražišće HR 157 F6
Zaton HR 162 D5
Zaton HR 162 D5
Zátor CZ 142 F4
Zator PL 143 G7
Zatory PL 139 E11
Zătreni RO 160 D3
Zatyshshya UA 154 C5
Zau de Câmpie RO 152 D4
Zavadka UA 145 E7
Závadka nad Hronom SK 147 D9
Zavala BIH 162 D4
Zavalje BIH 156 C4
Zavallya UA 153 A7
Zavattarello I 37 B10
Zăvăznă Poruba SK 147 C9
Zaventem B 19 C9
Zavet BG 161 F8
Zavidovići BIH 157 D9
Zavlaka SRB 158 E3
Zavoia HR 157 D12
Závod SK 77 E12
Zavoj SRB 165 C6
Zavrč SLO 148 D6
Zavyachellye BY 133 F4
Zavydovychi UA 144 D9
Zawada PL 81 C8
Zawada PL 142 E4
Zawada PL 144 B7
Zawada PL 144 D7
Zawadzkie PL 142 E6
Zawichost PL 143 E12
Zawidów PL 81 D8

Zawidz Kościelny PL 139 E8
Zawiercie PL 143 F7
Zawoja PL 147 B9
Zawonia PL 81 D12
Zaytsevo RUS 132 F4
Žažina HR 148 E6
Zázrivá SK 147 C8
Žažvic HR 156 E4
Zbąszyn PL 81 B9
Zbąszynek PL 81 B9
Zbehy SK 146 E6
Zberoaia MD 153 D12
Zbiczno PL 139 D7
Zbiersk PL 142 C5
Zbiroh CZ 76 C5
Zblewo PL 138 C5
Zbludowice PL 143 F10
Zbójna PL 139 D12
Zbójno PL 139 D7
Zborov SK 145 E3
Zborovice CZ 146 C4
Zborov nad Bystricou SK 147 C7
Zbraslav CZ 77 D10
Zbraslavice CZ 77 D8
Zbrzeźnica PL 140 D6
Zbuczyn Poduchowny PL 141 F6
Ždala HR 149 D8
Ždánice CZ 77 D12
Žďár CZ 77 A8
Žďár nad Sázavou CZ 77 C9
Zdenci HR 149 E9
Ždiar SK 145 E1
Zdice CZ 76 C5
Zdihovo HR 67 B11
Zdíkov CZ 76 D5
Ždírec nad Doubravou CZ 77 C9
Zdounky CZ 146 C4
Zdralovac BIH 157 E6
Zdravets BG 167 C8
Zdravinje SRB 164 C3
Ždrelo SRB 159 E8
Zdunje MK 164 F3
Zduńska Wola PL 143 C6
Zduny PL 81 C12
Zduny PL 141 F1
Zdynia PL 145 E3
Zdziarzec PL 143 F11
Zdziechowa PL 85 E13
Zdzieszowice PL 142 F5
Zdziłowice PL 144 B6
Zjbowice PL 142 E5
Žebrák CZ 76 C5
Zebreira P 45 E6
Zebrene LV 134 C5
Zebrzydowa PL 81 D8
Zechlin Dorf D 83 D13
Zechlinerhütte D 84 D3
Zeddam NL 183 B8
Zeddiani I 64 D2
Zedelgem B 19 B7
Zederhaus A 73 B8
Žednik SRB 150 F4
Žjdowice PL 142 E6
Zeebrugge B 19 B7
Zeeland NL 16 E5
Zeewolde NL 183 A7
Zegama E 32 E1
Żegiestów PL 145 E2
Żegljane MK 164 E4
Żegocina PL 144 D1
Zehdenick D 84 E4
Zehna D 83 C12
Žehra SK 145 F2
Zehren D 80 D4

Zeilarn D 76 F3
Zeimelis LT 135 D8
Żeimiai LT 135 F8
Zeiselmauer A 77 F10
Zeiskam D 187 C5
Zeist NL 16 D4
Zeithain D 80 D4
Zeitlofs D 74 B6
Zeitz D 79 D11
Zejmen AL 163 F8
Želazków PL 142 C5
Zele B 19 B9
Żelechlinek PL 141 G2
Żelechów PL 141 G5
Zelena UA 152 A5
Zelena UA 152 B5
Zelena UA 153 A9
Železné SK 146 E5
Zeleni Jadar BIH 158 E3
Zelenikovo BG 166 E4
Zelenikovo MK 164 F4
Zelenogorsk RUS 129 E12
Zelenogradsk RUS 136 D1
Zelenohirs'ke UA 154 B6
Železná Ruda CZ 76 D4
Železné SK 147 D8
Železnice CZ 77 B8
Železniki SLO 73 D9
Železný Brod CZ 81 E8
Zelhem NL 16 D6
Želiezovce SK 147 F7
Zelina HR 148 E6
Zelinja BIH 157 C9
Želino MK 164 F3
Żeliv CZ 77 D7
Željuša BIH 157 F8
Żelków-Kolonia PL 141 F6
Zell D 75 B10
Zell (Mosel) D 21 D8
Zella-Mehlis D 79 E8
Zell am Harmersbach D 27 D9
Zell am Main D 187 B8
Zell am See A 73 B6
Zell am Ziller A 72 B4
Zell im Wiesental D 27 E8
Zellingen D 74 C6
Zell-Pfarre A 73 C9
Zelmenļ LV 134 D6
Želovce SK 147 E8
Zelów PL 143 D7
Zeltingen-Rachtig D 21 E8
Zeltiņi LV 135 B13
Zeltweg A 73 B10
Želva LT 135 F10
Zelzate B 19 B8
Žemaičiu Naumiestis LT 134 F3
Żemberovce SK 147 E7
Zemblak AL 168 C4
Zembrów PL 141 E6
Zembrzyce PL 147 B9
Zemen BG 165 E6
Zemeno GR 175 C6
Zemeş RO 153 D8
Zemianska Olča SK 146 F5
Zemīte LV 134 C5
Zemitz D 84 C5
Zemné SK 146 F6
Zemplénagárd H 145 G5
Zemplínske Hámre SK 145 F5
Zemst B 19 C9
Zemun SRB 158 D5
Zenica BIH 157 D8
Zennor GB 12 E3

Zentene LV 134 B5
Žepa BIH 157 E11
Žepče BIH 157 D9
Žeravice CZ 146 C4
Zerbst D 79 C11
Zerf D 21 E7
Zerind RO 151 D8
Žerków PL 142 B4
Zernez CH 71 D10
Zernien D 83 D9
Zernitz D 83 E12
Zero Branco I 72 E5
Zerpenschleuse D 84 E5
Zerrenthin D 84 D6
Zestoa E 32 D1
Žetale SLO 148 D5
Zetea RO 152 E6
Zetel D 17 B9
Zet'ovo BG 166 E4
Zeulenroda D 79 E10
Zeven D 17 B12
Zevenaar NL 16 E6
Zevenbergen NL 16 E3
Zevgolatio GR 175 D6
Zevio I 66 B3
Zeytinalani TR 181 C9
ZeytinbağI TR 173 D10
Zeytindağ TR 177 B9
Zeytinli TR 177 C8
Zeytinli TR 173 E6
Zeytinliova TR 177 B10
Zgierz PL 143 C7
Zgłobice PL 143 G10
Zgornje Bitnje SLO 73 D9
Zgornje Jezersko SLO 73 D9
Zgornji Duplek SLO 148 C5
Zgorzelec PL 81 D7
Zgropolci MK 169 A6
Zgurita MD 153 A11
Zhabinka BY 141 F10
Zhdenyovo UA 145 F7
Žheger KS 164 E3
Zheleznodorozhnyy RUS 136 E3
Zhelyazkovo BG 167 E8
Zhelyu Voyvoda BG 167 D6
Zheravna BG 167 D6
Zhilino RUS 136 D4
Zhitkovo RUS 129 D11
Zhitnitsa BG 167 E8
Zhitom AL 168 C2
Zhodzishki BY 137 D13
Zhorany UA 141 H9
Zhovkva UA 144 C9
Zhovtantsi UA 144 D9
Zhovtneve UA 144 D9
Zhovtneve UA 155 B3
Zhovtyy Yar UA 154 F5
Zhupranny BY 137 E13
Zhur KS 164 E2
Zhyvyrka UA 144 C9
Zhydachiv UA 145 E9
Zhyrmuny BY 137 E11
Žiar nad Hronom SK 147 D7
Zibalai LT 137 C10
Zibello I 66 B1
Zibreira P 44 F3
Zicavo F 37 H10
Žichovice CZ 76 D5
Zickhusen D 83 C10
Zidani Most SLO 73 D11
Zidarovo BG 167 E8
Žídikai LT 134 D4
Ziduri RO 161 C10

Zijbice PL 81 E12
Zieułkalne LV 134 D6
Ziegelroda D 79 D9
Ziegendorf D 83 D11
Ziegenrück D 79 E10
Ziegra D 80 D4
Zieleniewo PL 85 B9
Zieleniewo PL 85 D9
Zielitz D 79 B10
Zielkowice PL 141 F2
Zielona PL 139 D8
Zielona Chocina PL 85 C12
Zielona Góra PL 81 C9
Zielona Góra PL 85 E11
Zielona PL 139 F11
Zielonki PL 143 F8
Zieluń PL 139 D8
Ziemeri LV 131 F14
Ziemnice Wielkie PL 142 E4
Ziemupe LV 134 C2
Zierenberg D 17 F12
Zierikzee NL 16 E1
Ziersdorf A 77 E9
Zierzow D 83 D11
Ziesar D 79 B11
Žiežmariai LT 137 D9
Žigljen HR 67 C10
Žiguri LV 133 B3
Žihárec SK 146 E5
Žihle CZ 76 B4
Zilaiskalns LV 131 F10
Žilina SK 147 C7
Žilinai LT 137 E10
Žilinai LT 137 E10
Zillis CH 71 D8
Ziltendorf D 81 B7
Zilupe LV 133 D4
Zimandu Nou RO 151 E7
Zimbor RO 151 C11
Zimmersrode (Neuental) D 21 B12
Zimnicea RO 160 F6
Zimnitsa BG 167 D7
Zindaičiai LT 134 F5
Žinin PL 138 E4
Znojmo CZ 77 E10
Zinkgruvan S 92 B6
Zinnowitz D 84 B5
Ziras LV 134 B3
Zirc H 149 B9
Zirchow D 84 C6
Žiri SLO 73 D9
Zirndorf D 75 D8
Zîrneşti MD 154 E2
Zirnl LV 134 C4
Ziros GR 179 E11
Žirovnice CZ 77 D8
Zistersdorf A 77 E11
Žitište SRB 158 C5
Žitkovac SRB 164 B4
Žitni Potok SRB 164 C4
Žitomislić BIH 157 F8
Žitorsđa SRB 164 C4
Žitoše MK 168 B5
Zitsa GR 168 E4
Zitz D 79 B11
Živaja HR 157 B6
Živinice BIH 157 D10
Živogošće HR 157 F7
Žiželice CZ 77 B8
Zizers CH 71 D9
Zizurkil E 32 D1
Zlarin HR 156 E4
Zlata SRB 164 C4
Zlatar BG 167 C7

Zlatar HR 148 D6
Zlatar-Bistrica HR 148 D6
Zlataritsa BG 166 C5
Zlaté Hory CZ 142 F3
Zlaté Klasy SK 146 E5
Zlaté Moravce SK 146 E6
Zlaten Rog BG 159 E10
Zlatna RO 151 E11
Zlatna Panega BG 165 C9
Zlatograd BG 171 B8
Zlatokop SRB 164 D4
Žľawieš Wielka PL 138 D5
Žľebič SLO 73 E10
Žľeby CZ 77 C8
Zletovo MK 164 F5
Žľibinai LT 134 E4
Zliv CZ 76 D6
Žľjebovi BIH 157 D10
Žľlakugan KS 164 D2
Žľoczniec PL 85 C10
Žľoczew PL 142 D6
Zlokuchene BG 165 E8
Zlonice CZ 76 B5
Žľota PL 141 G2
Žľota PL 143 F10
Žľotniki Kujawskie PL 138 E5
Žľotoryja PL 81 D9
Žľotów PL 85 D12
Žľoty Stak PL 77 B11
Žľozela BIH 157 D7
Žľutice CZ 76 B4
Zmajevac BIH 156 C5
Zmajevac HR 149 E11
Zmajevo SRB 158 C4
Zmeyovo BG 166 E5
Žmigród PL 81 D11
Žmijavci HR 157 F7
Žminj HR 67 B8
Žmudź PL 144 A8
Znamensk RUS 136 D3
Žnin PL 138 E4
Znojmo CZ 77 E10
Zoagli I 37 C10
Zóblitz D 80 E4
Zoelen NL 183 B6
Zoersel B 16 F3
Zoetermeer NL 16 D2
Zofingen CH 27 F8
Zogno I 69 B8
Zografou GR 175 D8
Zola Predosa I 66 C3
Zolder B 19 B11
Zoldo Alto I 72 D5
Żółkiewka-Osada PL 144 B6
Żółkow D 83 C11
Zollikon CH 27 F10
Zolotkovychi UA 144 D6
Žóftnica PL 85 C11
Żofynia PL 144 C5
Zomba H 149 D11
Zomergem B 19 B8
Zonhoven B 19 C11
Zoni GR 171 A10
Zoniana GR 178 E8
Zonnebeke B 18 C6
Zonza F 37 H10
Żórawina PL 81 E12
Zörbig D 79 C11
Zorita E 45 F9
Zorita del Maestrazgo E 42 F3
Zorleni RO 153 E11

Zorlenţu Marc RO 159 C8
Zorneding D 75 F10
Zornheim D 21 E10
Zörnigal D 79 C12
Zornitsa BG 167 E7
Zornitsa BG 167 E7
Žory FR 142 F6
Zossen D 80 B4
Zottegem B 19 C8
Zoutkamp NL 16 B6
Zoutleeuw B 183 D6
Zovi Do BIH 157 F9
Zovka RUS 132 E4
Zreče SLO 148 D4
Zrenjanin SRB 158 C5
Zrin HR 156 B5
Zrinski Topolovac HR 149 D7
Zrmanja Vrelo HR 156 D5
Zrnovci MK 164 F5
Zruč CZ 76 C4
Zruč nad Sázavou CZ 77 C8
Zsadány H 151 D7
Zsáka H 151 C7
Zsámbék H 149 B11
Zsámbok H 150 B4
Zsana H 150 E4
Zscherben D 79 D10
Zschopau D 80 E4
Zschortau D 79 D11
Zsombó H 150 E4
Zuberec SK 147 C9
Zubia E 53 B9
Zubiaur E 40 B6
Zubičl BIH 157 D8
Zubiena I 68 C4
Zubieta E 32 D1
Zubieta E 32 D2
Zubin Potok KS 164 D2
Zubiri E 32 E2
Zubff CZ 146 C6
Zubrohlava SK 147 C9
Žubrów PL 81 B8
Žuć SRB 164 C3
Zucaina E 48 D4
Zuchwil CH 27 F8
Zudaire E 32 E1
Zudar D 84 B4
Zuera E 41 E10
Zufre E 51 D7
Zug CH 27 F10
Zuhatzu-Kuartango E 40 C6
Zuheros E 53 A8
Zuid-Beijerland NL 182 B4
Zuidhorn NL 16 B6
Zuidland NL 182 B4
Zuidlaren NL 17 B7
Zuidwolde NL 17 C6
Zuienkerke B 182 C2
Zújar E 55 D7
Žuków PL 141 F2
Žuków PL 141 G8
Žukowice PL 81 C9
Žukowo PL 138 B5
Žuljana HR 162 D3
Žulová CZ 77 B12
Zülpich D 21 C7
Zulte B 19 C7
Zumaia E 32 D1
Zumarraga E 32 D1
Zundert NL 16 F3
Zungri I 59 B8
Zunzarren E 32 E3

Zúras LV 134 B3
Zúrgena E 55 E8
Zürich CH 27 F10
Zurndorf A 77 G12
Zürnevo BG 161 F10
Zuromin PL 139 D8
Zurow D 83 C11
Zurzach CH 27 E9
Zusmarshausen D 75 F8
Züssow D 83 C11
Züssow D 84 C5
Žuta Lokva HR 67 C11
Žutautai LT 134 E2
Zutendaal B 19 C12
Zutphen NL 16 D6
Žužemberk SLO 73 E10
Zvečan KS 164 D2
Zvejniekciems LV 135 B8
Zverino BG 165 C8
Zvezdel AL 168 C4
Zvezdel BG 171 B8
Zvezdets BG 167 E8
Zvolen SK 147 D8
Zvolenská Slatina SK 147 D8
Zvonce SRB 164 D6
Zvorištea RO 153 B8
Zvornik BIH 157 D11
Zwartemeer NL 17 C8
Zwartsluis NL 16 C6
Zweeloo NL 17 C7
Zweibrücken D 21 F8
Zweisimmen CH 31 B11
Zwenkau D 79 D11
Zwethau D 80 C4
Zwettl A 77 E8
Zwevegem B 19 C7
Zwevezele B 182 C2
Zwickau D 79 E12
Zwiefalten D 27 D11
Zwierzyn PL 85 E9
Zwierzyniec PL 144 B6
Zwiesel D 76 D4
Zwijndrecht B 19 B9
Zwijndrecht NL 16 E3
Zwinge D 79 C7
Zwingen CH 27 F8
Zwingenberg D 21 E11
Zwochau D 79 D11
Zwoleń PL 141 H5
Zwolle NL 16 C6
Zwönitz D 79 E12
Zwota D 79 B12
Zyabki BY 133 F4
Zyal'ki BY 133 E4
Zyalyonka BY 133 E5
Zychlin PL 143 B8
Żydowo PL 85 B11
Żydowo PL 85 F13
Žygaičiai LT 134 F4
Zygos GR 171 B6
Zygry PL 143 C6
Żyniai LT 134 F2
Żyraków PL 143 F11
Žyrardów PL 141 G3
Żyrzyn PL 141 H6
Żytkiejmy PL 136 E5
Żytniów PL 142 D6
Zytno PL 143 E8
Żywiec PL 147 B8
Żywocice PL 142 F4

Æ
Ærøskøbing DK 86 F6

Ø
Ødis DK 86 E4
Ødsted DK 86 D4
Øie N 105 B12
Økdal N 101 A12
Øksfjord N 112 C9
Øksnes N 110 C8
Øksneshamn N 110 D9
Ølen N 94 C3
Ølgod DK 86 D3
Ølholm DK 86 D5
Ølsted DK 86 E5
Ølsted DK 87 D10
Ølstykke DK 87 D10
Ønslev DK 83 A11
Øra N 112 C8
Ørbæk DK 86 E7
Ørgenvika N 95 B11
Ørjavik N 104 F2
Ørje N 96 D6
Ørnes N 108 C6
Ørnhøj DK 86 C3
Ørslev DK 87 E9
Ørsnes N 100 A5
Ørsta N 100 B4
Ørsted DK 86 C6
Ørting DK 86 D6
Ørum DK 86 C5
Ørum DK 86 C7
Øsby DK 86 F5
Østbirk DK 86 D5
Østby N 91 A9
Østby N 102 D4
Østengård DK 86 D4
Øster Assels DK 86 B3
Øster Bjerregrav DK 86 C5
Øster Brønderslev DK 86 A5
Østerby DK 86 A5
Øster Hornum DK 86 B5
Øster Hurup DK 86 B6
Øster Højst DK 86 E4
Østerild DK 86 A3
Øster Jølby DK 86 B3
Østerlars DK 89 E7
Øster Lindet DK 86 E4
Østermarie DK 89 E8
Øster Tørslev DK 86 C6
Øster Ulslev DK 83 A11
Øster Vedsted DK 86 E3
Østervrå DK 90 E7
Øster Vrøgum DK 86 D2
Østesø N 94 B1
Østrup DK 86 B4
Øverbygd N 111 C17
Øvergard N 111 B18
Øvre Alta N 113 D11

Øvre Kildal N 112 D7
Øvrella N 95 C10
Øvre Rendal N 101 C14
Øvre Årdal N 100 D7
Øvre Åstbru N 101 D13
Øyangen N 104 E7
Øydegarden N 104 D8
Øyenkilen N 91 A8
Øyer N 101 D12
Øyeren N 96 B7
Øyjord N 108 B9
Øynes N 108 B9
Øynes N 101 A10
Øyslebø N 90 C2
Øyvatnet N 111 C12

Å
Å N 104 F7
Å N 110 E4
Å N 111 B12
Å N 111 C13
Åberget S 109 E18
Åbo S 103 C10
Åbodarna S 107 E14
Åbogen N 96 B7
Åbosjö S 107 D13
Åby S 89 A7
Åby S 93 B8
Åbyen DK 90 D7
Åbyggeby S 103 E13
Åbyn S 118 D6
Åbytorp S 92 A6
Ådalsliden S 107 E11
Ådum DK 86 D3
Åfarnes N 100 A7
Åfjord N 104 D8
Åfoss N 90 A6
Ågerup DK 87 D10
Ågotnes N 94 B2
Ågskaret N 108 C5
Åheim N 100 B3
Åhus S 88 D6
Åkarp S 87 D12
Åkerbränna S 107 C11
Åkerby S 99 B9
Åkerholmen S 118 C6
Åkersberga S 99 D10
Åkers styckebruk S 98 D8
Åkerstrømmen N 101 C14
Åknes N 110 C9
Åkran N 105 D12
Åkrehamn N 94 D2
Åkullsjön S 118 C7
Åkvisslan S 107 E13
Ål N 101 E9
Ålberga S 93 B9
Ålbo S 98 B7
Ålbæk DK 90 D7
Åle DK 86 D5
Åled S 87 B11

Ålem S 89 B10
Ålen N 101 A14
Ålesund N 100 B4
Ålgnäs S 103 D12
Ålgård N 94 E3
Ålhult S 92 D7
Ålloluokta S 109 B17
Ålmo N 104 E4
Ålsrode DK 87 C7
Ålstad N 110 E9
Ålund S 118 D6
Ålvik N 94 B4
Ålvund N 101 A9
Ålvundeid N 101 A9
Ålåsen S 106 D7
Åmdals Verk N 95 D8
Åminne FIN 122 E7
Åminne S 87 A14
Åmland N 94 F5
Åmli N 90 A3
Åmli N 90 B3
Åmmeberg S 92 B6
Åmot N 94 C7
Åmot N 95 B11
Åmot N 95 C11
Åmot S 103 D4
Åmotfors S 96 C7
Åmsele S 107 B16
Åmsosen N 94 D3
Åmynnet S 107 E15
Åmål S 91 A12
Åmål S 91 B12
Åmøyhamn N 108 C5
Åna-Sira N 94 F4
Åndalsnes N 100 A7
Åneby N 95 B13
Ånes N 104 E4
Ånge S 103 A10
Ånge S 109 E14
Ångelsberg S 97 C15
Ångersjö S 102 C8
Ånn S 105 E13
Ånstad N 110 C8
Ånsvik N 109 B9
Ånäset S 118 F6
Årbostad N 111 C13
Årby DK 87 D8
Årbyn S 118 C8
Årdal N 100 C4
Årdalstangen N 100 D7
Åre S 105 E14
Årfor N 105 B11
Årgård N 105 C10
Århult N 89 A10
Århus DK 86 C6
Årnes N 92 A4
Årnes N 95 B14
Årnes N 104 F5
Årnes N 111 B15
Årnäs S 91 B14

Åros N 95 C12
Årosjåkk S 111 E17
Årre DK 86 D3
Årrenjarka S 109 C15
Årsandøy N 105 B11
Årsdale DK 89 E8
Årset N 105 A11
Årslev DK 86 E6
Årstein N 111 C14
Årsunda S 98 A7
Årvik N 100 B3
Årviksand N 112 C6
Årvågen N 104 E5
Åryd S 89 B7
Åryd S 89 C8
Årøybukta N 111 A19
Årøysund N 90 A7
Ås N 95 C13
Ås N 105 E11
Ås S 96 C7
Ås S 106 E7
Ås S 107 E11
Åsa N 95 B12
Åsa S 91 E11
Åsan N 105 B12
Åsarna S 102 A7
Åsby S 87 A10
Åse N 110 C8
Åsebyn S 96 D7
Åseda S 89 A8
Åsegg N 105 C9
Åsele S 107 C12
Åselet S 118 D4
Åsen N 105 D10
Åsen S 102 C7
Åsen S 102 E7
Åsen S 106 E7
Åsen S 107 E11
Åsenbruk S 91 B11
Åseral N 90 B1
Åshammar S 103 E12
Åskilje S 107 B13
Åskloster S 91 E11
Åsli N 101 E11
Åsljunga S 87 C12
Åsmansbo S 97 B13
Åsmarka N 101 D13
Åsnäs S 92 A8
Åsköping S 92 A8
Åssjö S 103 B12
Åstan N 104 E7
Åsteby S 97 C11
Åstorp S 87 C11
Åstrand N 97 B9
Återvänningen S 103 A13
Åtorp S 92 A4
Åträsk S 118 B7
Åträsk S 118 D5
Åttonträsk S 107 C14
Åtvidaberg S 92 C7
Åva FIN 126 E5

Åvestbo S 97 C14
Åvist FIN 122 D9

Ä
Äetsä FIN 126 C8
Ähtäri FIN 123 E12
Ähtärinranta FIN 123 E12
Äijäjoki FIN 116 B10
Äijälä FIN 123 E16
Äkäsjokisuu FIN 117 C11
Äkäslompolo FIN 117 C12
Älandsbro S 103 A14
Älgarås S 92 B4
Älgered S 103 B12
Älghult S 89 A9
Älmestad S 91 D13
Älmhult S 88 B6
Älmsta S 99 C11
Älta S 99 D10
Älvdalen S 102 D8
Älvho S 102 D8
Älvkarleby S 103 E13
Älvkarleö S 99 A8
Älvros S 102 B4
Älvsbyn S 118 C6
Älvsered S 87 A11
Älvängen S 91 D11
Ämmälänkylä FIN 123 E9
Ämmänsaari FIN 121 E12
Åmådalen S 102 D8
Ång S 92 C3
Ånge S 105 E16
Ångebo S 103 C11
Ångelholm S 87 C12
Ångersjö S 122 C3
Ångeslevä FIN 119 E15
Ångeträsk S 118 B8
Ångesån S 116 E8
Ångom S 103 B13
Äppelbo S 97 B11
Ärla S 98 D7
Ärnäs S 102 D5
Ärnäs S 102 E5
Ärtled S 103 E11
Ärtrik S 107 E11
Äsarp S 91 C13
Äsbacka S 103 D11
Äsbjörnås S 103 E13
Äsby S 107 D13
Äsperöd S 87 D13
Ässjö S 103 B13
Ätran S 87 A11
Äystö FIN 122 F7

Ö
Öckerö S 91 D10
Ödeborg S 91 B10
Ödeshog S 92 C5
Ödkarby FIN 99 B13

Ödsmål S 91 C10
Ödåkra S 87 C11
Öja FIN 123 C10
Öja S 93 E12
Öjarn S 106 D6
Öjebyn S 118 D6
Öje S 102 E6
Öjeforsen S 103 B9
Öjingsvallen S 103 C8
Öksajärvi S 116 C6
Öksajärvi S 116 C6
Öllölä FIN 125 F15
Ölmbrotorp S 97 D13
Ölme S 97 D11
Ölsboda S 92 A4
Ömossa FIN 122 F7
Önnestad S 88 C6
Önningeby Å 99 B14
Öratjärn S 103 C10
Öravan S 107 B14
Öravattnet S 106 E9
Örbyhus S 99 B9
Örbäck S 97 C15
Örebro S 97 D13
Örebäcken S 102 C4
Öregrund S 99 B10
Öreström S 107 C16
Öretjändalen S 103 A10
Örkelljunga S 87 C12
Örnsköldsvik S 107 E15
Örnhörnäs S 107 E13
Örsbäck S 107 D17
Örserum S 92 C5
Örsjö S 89 B9
Örsundsbro S 99 C9
Örträsk S 107 C15
Örviken S 118 E6
Ösmo S 93 B11
Östa S 98 B7
Östanfjärden S 119 C10
Östansjö S 92 A5
Östansjö S 109 E16
Östanskär S 103 A13
Östanvik S 103 D9
Östavall S 103 B9
Östbjörka S 103 E10
Östby S 107 D13
Österbybruk S 99 B9
Österbymo S 92 D6
Österede S 107 E11
Österforse S 107 E12
Österfärnebo S 98 B7
Östergarn S 93 E13
Östergraninge S 107 F12

Österskucku S 102 A8
Östersund S 106 E7
Östersundom FIN 127 E13
Östervåla S 98 B8
Österås S 107 E12
Östhammar S 99 B10
Östloning S 103 A13
Östmark S 97 B8
Östmarkum S 107 E14
Östnor S 102 D7
Östra Ed S 93 C9
Östra Frölunda S 91 E13
Östra Granberg S 118 C4
Östra Grevie S 87 E11
Östra Husby S 93 B9
Östra Ljungby S 87 C12
Östra Lovsjön S 106 D7
Östra Löa S 97 C13
Östra Ormsjö S 107 D16
Östra Ryd S 93 C8
Östra Skråmträsk S 118 E5
Östra Stugusjö S 103 B9
Östra Sönnarslöv S 88 D6
Östra Yttermark FIN 122 E6
Östra Åliden S 118 D4
Överammer S 107 E9
Överberg S 102 B7
Överbyn S 103 C12
Överhogdal S 102 B8
Överhörnäs S 107 E15
Överisssjö S 107 C13
Överkalix S 119 B9
Överlanda S 91 E12
Överlännäs S 107 E13
Övermalax FIN 122 E7
Övermark FIN 122 E6
Övermorjärv S 118 B9
Övernäs S 109 D14
Överstbyn S 118 B7
Övertorneå S 119 B11
Överturingen S 102 B9
Övertänger S 103 E10
Överum S 93 D8
Överäng S 105 D14
Överö FIN 99 B15
Öv Långträsk S 109 E16
Övra S 107 D11
Övre Bredåker S 118 C6
Övre Flåsjön S 118 B7
Övre Soppero S 116 B7
Övre Tväråsel S 118 C5
Övsjöbyn S 107 E9
Oxabäck S 91 E12

TRAVELLERS' CHOICE™ 2013
Top 25 European Destinations

PARIS, FRANCE

Everyone who visits Paris for the first time probably has the same punchlist of major attractions to hit: The Louvre, Notre Dame, The Eiffel Tower, etc. Just make sure you leave some time to wander the city's grand boulevards and eat in as many cafes, bistros and brasseries as possible. And don't forget the shopping—whether your tastes run to Louis Vuitton or Les Puces (the flea market), you can find it here.

DON'T MISS

Musee de l'Orangerie
Jardin des Tuileries, 75001 Paris

Luxembourg Gardens
Rue de Vaugirard, Boulevard St. Michel, Rue Auguste-Comte, and Rue Guynemer, 75006 Paris

Notre Dame Cathedral
6 place du Parvis Notre-Dame | Ile de la Cité, 75004 Paris

LONDON, UNITED KINGDOM

There's so much to see and do in London, it's easy to be overwhelmed. Major sights like the Tower of London and Buckingham Palace are on most visitors' itineraries, but no matter what your interests, you'll probably find something here. Art lovers should make a beeline for the National Gallery and the Tate Modern. If military history's your thing, don't miss the Cabinet War Rooms.

DON'T MISS
Victoria and Albert Museum
Cromwell Road | South Kensington, London SW7 2RL
Churchill War Rooms
Clive Steps | King Charles Street, London SW1A 2AQ
Olympic Stadium
Loop Road | Stratford, London E20 2ST

ROME, ITALY

It's nicknamed the Eternal City for a reason. In Rome, you can drink from a street fountain fed by an ancient aqueduct. Or see the same profile on a statue in the Capitoline Museum and the guy making your cappuccino (which, of course, you know never to order after 11am). Rome is also a city of contrasts—what other place on earth could be home to both the Vatican and La Dolce Vita?

DON'T MISS
Trevi Fountain (Fontana di Trevi)
Piazza di Trevi, 00187 Rome
The Vatican Museum
Viale Vaticano, 00165 Rome
Pantheon
Piazza della Rotonda, 00186 Rome

BARCELONA, SPAIN

Stroll Las Ramblas and enjoy Barcelona's unique blend of Catalan culture, distinctive architecture, lively nightlife and trendy, stylish hotels. You'll find Europe's best-preserved Gothic Quarter here, as well as amazing architectural works by Gaudi. La Sagrada Familia, considered Gaudi's masterpiece, is still under construction (your entrance fee helps to fund the project). Check out La Boqueria market for fantastic local delicacies.

DON'T MISS
Guell Palace
Carrer Nou de la Rambla 3-5, Barcelona
St. Mary of the Sea Cathedral (Eglesia de Santa Maria del Mar) Placa Santa Maria 1, La Ribera, Ciutat Vella | Placa Santa Maria, 08003 Barcelona
Camp Nou
Avinguda Aristides Maillol, 08028 Barcelona

VENICE, ITALY

Stunning architecture. Mysterious passageways. And of course, the canals. Venice is one of the most alluring cities in the world—the type of place where, as a visitor, you'll welcome getting lost (as you inevitably will). Relax in Piazza San Marco, take a moonlit gondola ride or taste the original Bellini at Harry's Bar. Or just wander. No matter where you go, you'll find history, beauty and romance.

DON'T MISS
Grand Canal
Ponte della Guerra, 31024 Venice
Palazzo Ducale
Piazza San Marco, 31024 Venice
Saint Mark's Basilica (Basilica di San Marco)
San Marco 328, 30124 Venice

FLORENCE, ITALY

Everyone's heard that the Doors of Paradise, the Duomo, and Michelangelo's David are captivating, but in Florence, beauty can sneak up on a traveller unexpectedly. You'll duck into a random church to escape the heat only to spend two hours staring at an impossibly pure blue in a fresco. It's just that kind of place. Don't miss the sunset over the Arno and the famous wines of the Chianti region just south of town.

DON'T MISS
Statue of David Galleria dell'Accademia | Via Ricasoli 58-60, 50122 Florence
Piazza del Duomo
Florence
Palazzo Vecchio
Piazza della Signoria, Florence

PRAGUE, CZECH REPUBLIC

We hear the question, "What's the next Prague?" a lot. But while we're all for discovering great new destinations, we hardly think Prague is over. Sure, everyone's heard of it, but it's still a grand city with extraordinary historic and cultural sights, and it's definitely worth a visit. Prague Castle and the synagogues and cemetery of the Jewish quarter are must-sees. Nightlife here is diverse and plentiful.

DON'T MISS
Old Town Square (Staromestske namesti)
Prague
Charles Bridge (Karluv Most) Between Mala Strana and the Old Town, Prague 11000
Prague Castle (Prazsky hrad)
Prague 11908

World's largest travel site®

www.tripadvisor.co.uk

8 BERLIN, GERMANY

Berlin is an edgy city, from its fashion to its architecture to its charged political history. The Berlin Wall is a sobering reminder of the hyper-charged post-war atmosphere, and yet the graffiti art that now covers its remnants has become symbolic of social progress. Check out the Weltzeituhr (world time) Clock, topped by a model of the solar system.

DON'T MISS
Brandenburg Gate (Brandenburger Tor)
Unter den Linden | Pariser Platz, 10117 Berlin
Memorial of the Berlin Wall
Bernauer Strasse 111/119, 13355 Berlin
Museumsinsel (Museum Island)
Bodestrasse 1-3, 10117 Berlin

9 ISTANBUL, TURKEY

Europe and Asia meet in Istanbul, and throughout this vibrant city, you'll find centuries-old mosques, churches and markets happily co-existing with modern restaurants, galleries and nightclubs. And plan on visiting a hamman (traditional Turkish bath)—for about $20 your skin will be scrubbed clean. And we mean scrubbed. Your wimpy loofah has nothing on this.

DON'T MISS
Sultanahmet District
Sultanahmet, Istanbul
Bosphorus Strait
Istanbul Bosphorus, Istanbul
Suleymaniye Mosque
Mimar Sinan Cd, Suleymaniye Mh, Istanbul

10 ST. PETERSBURG, RUSSIA

The second largest city in Russia, St. Petersburg is the country's cultural heart. View splendid architectural gems like the Winter Palace and the Kazan Cathedral, and give yourself plenty of time to browse the world-renowned art collection of the Hermitage. Sprawling across the Neva River delta, St. Petersburg offers enough art, nightlife, fine dining and cultural destinations for many repeat visits.

DON'T MISS
Church of Our Savior on Spilled Blood
2b Naberezhnaya Kanala Gribboyedova, St. Petersburg
Catherine Palace and Park 7, Sadovaya Str. | Pushkin, St. Petersburg
State Hermitage Museum and Winter Palace
34 Dvortsovaya Naberezhnaya, St. Petersburg 190000

11 AMSTERDAM, THE NETHERLANDS

Amsterdam is truly a biker's city, although pedaling along the labyrinthine streets can get a little chaotic. Stick to walking and you won't be disappointed. The gentle canals make a perfect backdrop for exploring the Jordaan and Rembrandtplein square. The Anne Frank House is one of the most moving experiences a traveler can have, and the Van Gogh Museum boasts a sensational collection of works.

DON'T MISS
Anne Frank House (Anne Frankhuis)
Prinsengracht 267, Amsterdam 1016 GV
Prinsengracht
Dam Square, Amsterdam
Van Gogh Museum
Paulus Potterstraat 7

12 MADRID, SPAIN

Madrid is the financial and cultural hub for Spain, and much of Southern Europe. There is a huge amount to see and do there, as well as excellent nightlife in terms of bars, restaurants, clubs and entertainment. As the area has been inhabited since Roman times, there are also plenty of historical sites to explore and enjoy. You can also visit the Bernabéu stadium, home of football giant Real Madrid.

DON'T MISS
Prado Museum
Calle Ruiz de Alarcon 23, 28014 Madrid
Thyssen-Bornemisza Museum (Museo Thyssen-Bornemisza) Paseo del Prado, 8, 28014 Madrid
Royal Palace of Madrid
Calle Bailen, 28071 Madrid

13 VIENNA, AUSTRIA

If you currently think your neighbourhood coffee shop is nice, you might want to stay out of Vienna's coffeehouses. After you've gotten used to these palatial, yet welcoming cafes—and their delicious coffee and Sacher torte—your local café will pale in comparison. Between coffee breaks, visitors can explore Vienna's Schonbrunn Palace and Imperial Palace.

DON'T MISS
Historic Center of Vienna
Vienna, Austria (Innere Stadt)
Schonbrunn Palace (Schloss Schonbrunn)
Vienna 1130, Austria
Imperial Palace (Hofburg)
Michaelerkuppel | Hofburg, Vienna 1010, Austria

14 DUBLIN, IRELAND

You've probably heard that Guinness tastes better in Dublin (fresh from the factory), but what you may not know is that Dublin is a perfect destination for the whole family. No, we're not suggesting you let the kiddies drink a pint. Instead, take them to the Dublin Zoo, to feed the ducks in Stephen's Green or on a picnic in Phoenix Park. Scholars can walk in the literary footsteps of such writers as Yeats and Joyce.

DON'T MISS
National Museum of Ireland - Archaeology
Kildare Street, Dublin
St. Stephen's Green
at the top end of Grafton St, Dublin 2
The Merry Ploughboy Irish Music Pub
Edmondstown Road | Rockbrook, Dublin Dublin 16

15 MUNICH, GERMANY

Munich was almost completely destroyed in two world wars, yet it's managed to recreate much of its folkloric, Bavarian past. Oktoberfest is legendary, but you can visit the Hofbrauhaus any time of year for an immense beer. Olympiapark, the site of the 1972 games, is not to be missed. Also take time to visit the concentration camp at Dachau—an intense, yet unforgettable, glimpse into the not-too-distant horrors of the Holocaust.

DON'T MISS
English Garden
Englischer Garten 3, 80538 Munich, Bavaria
Marienplatz Marienplatz, Munich, Bavaria
Deutsches Museum
Museumsinsel 1, 80538 Munich, Bavaria

16 LISBON, PORTUGAL

Lisbon, the capital city of Portugal, has become an increasingly popular place to visit in recent years, with a warm Mediterranean climate in spite of its place facing the Atlantic Ocean. Full of bleached white limestone buildings and intimate alleyways, Lisbon's mix of traditional architecture and contemporary culture makes it the perfect place for a family holiday.

DON'T MISS
Oceanario de Lisboa Esplanada D. Carlos I - Doca dos Olivais, Lisbon 1990-005
Gulbenkian Museum (Museu Calouste Gulbenkian) Avenida de Berna 45a, Lisbon
Belem
Avenida Brasilia, Lisbon 1400-038

World's largest travel site®

www.tripadvisor.co.uk

17
BUDAPEST, HUNGARY

Over 15 million gallons of water bubble daily into Budapest's 118 springs and boreholes. The city of spas offers an astounding array of baths, from the sparkling Gellert Baths to the vast 1913 neo-baroque Szechenyi Spa to Rudas Spa, a dramatic 16th-century Turkish pool with original Ottoman architecture. The "Queen of the Danube" is also steeped in history, culture and natural beauty.

DON'T MISS
Szimpla Kert
Kazinczy utca 14, Budapest 1075
Shoes on the Danube Promenade
On the bank of the Danube, Budapest
Fisherman's Bastion (Halaszbastya)
Tarnork Utca 28, Budapest

18
ATHENS, GREECE

Once known for smog, traffic and tacky architecture, Athens is a city reformed thanks to the 2004 Summer Olympics. Spotless parks and streets, an ultra-modern metro, new motorways, an accessible airport and all signs in perfect English make the city easily negotiable. Key sites of Western history, from the Acropolis to the Temple of Olympian Zeus, are also here.

DON'T MISS
Parthenon (Parthenonas) Acropolis | Top of Dionyssiou Areopagitou, Athens 10558
Acropolis (Akropolis)
Dionysiou Areopagitou Street, Athens 10558
The Acropolis Museum Dionysiou Areopagitou 15 | Makrigianni District, Athens 11742

19
MILAN, ITALY

History lovers should know that Milan is not all about trendy shops and designer clothes. Among the city's many historical attractions are La Scala Opera, the Milan Cathedral, the National Museum of Science and Technology and Santa Maria della Grazie, the church that preserves da Vinci's "Last Supper".

DON'T MISS
Cathedral (Duomo)
Piazza del Duomo, 20122 Milan
L'Ultima Cena
Piazza Santa Maria delle Grazie 2, 20123 Milan
Galleria Vittorio Emanuele II
Piazza del Duomo, Milan

20
DUBROVNIK, CROATIA

Dubrovnik, in the extreme south of Croatia, is known as the Pearl of the Adriatic. A rich and powerful city state until 1806, the proud city once known as Ragusa has a population of over 120,000. Structural damage suffered during the siege of 1991 and 1992, at the hands of the Yugoslav People's Army, has been repaired and visitors once again flock to this tranquil city, nestled between the Adriatic and Dinaric Alps.

DON'T MISS
Ancient City Walls Placa ulica 32 | just inside Pile Gate, to the left., Dubrovnik 20000
Old Town
Dubrovnik
Dubrovnik Cable Car
Frana Supila 35a, Dubrovnik

21
KRAKOW, POLAND

Retaining its old-world ambiance and charm, Krakow is the prettiest of Poland's main cities, having escaped the worst of WWII bombing. The former Polish capital's atmospheric Old Town and Kazimierz's streets in the Jewish district are crammed with exciting galleries, cafes, pubs and restaurants.

DON'T MISS
Krakow's Historic Centre
Krakow
Main Market Square (Rynek Glowny)
Center of Old Town, Krakow
Wawel Cathedral
Wawel Hill, Krakow 31-001

22
MOSCOW, RUSSIA

The political, scientific, historical, architectural and business centre of Russia, Moscow displays the country's contrasts at their most extreme. The ancient and modern exist side by side in this city of 10 million. Catch a metro from one of the ornate stations to see Red Square, the Kremlin, the nine domes of St Basil's Cathedral, Lenin's Mausoleum, the KGB Museum and other symbols of Moscow's great and terrible past.

DON'T MISS
St. Basil's Cathedral (Pokrovsky Sobor)
2 Krasnaya Ploshchad, Moscow
Red Square (Krasnaya ploshchad)
Krasnaya ploshchad, Moscow
Moscow Kremlin (Moskovsky Kreml)
Red Square, Moscow

23
OIA, GREECE

Oia is carved out of the cliffs, and visitors can see houses built for Venetian sea captains as well as the more typical "cave houses" of the villagers. You'll find the pure white buildings with colourful roofs that are typical of Greek architecture, and you'll probably enjoy poking around the town. But don't breeze through in an hour—you must stay for the sunset. It's legendary.

DON'T MISS
SAFOWI Santorini Food and Wine Connection
P.O. Box 23020, Oia TK 84702
Sunset Oia Sailing Day Tour
Oia 84702
Amoudi Bay
Oia

24
ZERMATT, SWITZERLAND

When most people think of Zermatt, they think of one thing: The Matterhorn. This ultimate Swiss icon looms over Zermatt, first drawing visitors here in the 1860s. The village of Zermatt itself is lovely and car-free, with old-fashioned brown chalets and winding alleys. (Don't worry, you don't have to walk everywhere—there are electric vehicles and horse-drawn cabs).

DON'T MISS
The Matterhorn
Zermatt
Gornergrat Bahn
Zermatt 3920
Matterhorn Glacier Paradise
Zermatt 3920

25
NAPLES, ITALY

Romantic Naples, two hours south of Rome, is the largest city in southern Italy. It has some of the world's best opera houses and theatres, and is often called an open-air museum, because of its many historic statues and monuments. Join families on promenade as the sun sets on the Bay of Naples. View finds from Pompeii and Herculaneum, at the Museo Archeologico Nazionale.

DON'T MISS
Museo Cappella Sansevero
Via F. De Sanctis 19 / 21, 80134 Naples
San Gregorio Armeno Piazzetta San Gregorio Armeno 1 | Spaccanapoli, Naples
National Archaeological Museum (Museo Archeologico Nazionale)
Piazza Museo 19, 80135 Naples

TRAVELLERS' CHOICE™ 2013
Top 25 Hotels in Europe

1

1
Onyria Marinha Edition Hotel & Thalasso
Quinta da Marinha, Rua do Clube, 2750-002 Cascais, Portugal
ESTREMADURA
Tel: +351 21 486 01 50
onyriamarinha.com
339 reviews

2
Rudding Park Hotel
Follifoot, Harrogate HG3 1JH, England
YORKSHIRE
Tel: +44 1423 871350
ruddingpark.co.uk
1879 reviews

3
Four Seasons Hotel Istanbul at Sultanahmet
Tevkifhane Sokak No. 1, Sultanahmet-Eminönü, 34110, Istanbul, Turkey
ISTANBUL
Tel: +90 212 402 3000
fourseasons.com/istanbul
564 reviews

4
Aria Hotel
Tržiště 9, 118 00, Prague 1, Czech Republic
BOHEMIA
Tel: +420 225 334 111
ariahotel.net
817 reviews

5
Hotel Belvedere
V.le Gramsci 95, 47838 Riccione, Italy
EMILIA-ROMAGNA
Tel: +39 0541 601506
belvederericcione.com
709 reviews

6
Hotel Alpenhof Hintertux
Hintertux 750, A-6293 Tux
AUSTRIAN ALPS
Tel: +43 5287 85 50
alpenhof.at
230 reviews

7
Neorion Hotel
Orhaniye Street No 14, Sirkeci, 34110, Istanbul, Turkey
ISTANBUL
Tel: +90 212 527 90 90
neorionhotel.com
1036 reviews

8
Four Seasons Hotel Gresham Palace
Széchenyi István tér 5-6., 1051 Budapest, Hungary
BUDAPEST
Tel: +36 1 268 6000
fourseasons.com/budapest
629 reviews

9
The Milestone Hotel
1 Kensington Court, London, W8 5DL, United Kingdom
LONDON
Tel: +44 20 7917 1000
milestonehotel.com
749 reviews

10
Gamirasu Cave Hotel
Ayvali Koyu 50400 Urgup, Cappadocia, Turkey
NEVSEHIR PROVINCE
Tel: +90 384 354 5815
gamirasu.com
535 reviews

11
Harvey's Point
Lough Eske, Donegal Town, County Donegal, Ireland
COUNTY DONEGAL
Tel: +353 74 9722208
harveyspoint.com
1248 reviews

12
Quinta Jardins do Lago
Rua Dr. João Lemos Gomes 29, São Pedro,Funchal, Madeira 9000-208, Portugal
MADEIRA ISLANDS
Tel: +351 291 750 100
jardinsdolago.com
409 reviews

13
Grand Hotel Kronenhof
Via Maistra 130, Pontresina 7504, Switzerland
SWISS ALPS
Tel: +41 81 830 30 30
kronenhof.com
314 reviews

14
Alchymist Grand Hotel and Spa
Tržiště 19, 110 00, Prague 1, Czech Republic
BOHEMIA
Tel: +420 257 286 011
alchymisthotel.com
988 reviews

15
Ellenborough Park
Southam Road, Cheltenham Spa, Gloucestershire, GL52 3NJ, England
COTSWOLDS
Tel: +44 1242 808 917
ellenboroughpark.com
304 reviews

16
Lindos Blu
85107 Vlicha Lindos, Rhodes, Greece
DODECANESE
Tel: +30 22440 32110
lindosblu.gr
401 reviews

17
Sirkeci Konak Hotel
Taya Hatun Sokak No 5, Sirkeci, 34120, Istanbul, Turkey
ISTANBUL
Tel: +90 212 528 43 44
sirkecikonak.com
1827 reviews

18
Hotel Sultania
Ebusuud Cad. Mehmet Murat Sok. No 4, Sirkeci, 34110, Istanbul, Turkey
ISTANBUL
Tel: +90 212 528 0806
hotelsultania.com
1063 reviews

19
Hotel Amira Istanbul
Kucuk Ayasofya Mah. Mustafapasa Sok. No 43, Sultanahmet, 34122, Istanbul, Turkey
ISTANBUL
Tel: +90 212 516 16 40
hotelamira.com
1239 reviews

20
Four Seasons Hotel Firenze
Borgo Pinti, 99, 50121 Firenze, Italy
TUSCANY
Tel: +39 055 2626 1
fourseasons.com/florence
462 reviews

21
Casa Hotel
Lockoford Lane, Chesterfield, S41 7JB, England
DERBYSHIRE
Tel: +44 1246 245 999
casahotels.co.uk
413 reviews

22
Hotel Borgo Pantano
Traversa Fontana Mortella, 13 int. 4, 96100 Syracuse, Italy
SICILY
Tel: +39 0931 721 993
borgopantano.it
347 reviews

23
Marrol's Boutique Hotel Bratislava
Tobrucka 4, 811 02 Bratislava, Slovakia
BRATISLAVA
Tel: +421 2 577 84 600
hotelmarrols.sk
491 reviews

24
The St. Regis Florence
Piazza Ognissanti 1, Firenze 50123, Italy
TUSCANY
Tel: +39 055 27161
stregisflorence.com
425 reviews

25
The Residence Porto Mare (Porto Bay)
Rua de Leichlingen 7, Funchal, Madeira 9004-566, Portugal
MADEIRA ISLANDS
Tel: +351 291 708 700
portobay.com
270 reviews